HEADS UP, ENTERTAINMENT HOUNDS!
There's more fun where this came from ...

MUSICHOUND ROCK
The Essential Album Guide

Everything you need to know about buying the best rock albums is right here. Look up any of 2,000 pivotal artists who perform classic, alternative and modern rock and you'll find not only reviews of all their albums, but also suggestions for what to buy, what to avoid and what's worth searching for. Includes a free rock CD sampler and a huge resources section with web page information and more.

Gary Graff • 1996 • paperback with music CD • **ISBN** 0-7876-1037-2 • **$24.95**

VIDEOHOUND'S PREMIERES
The Only Guide to Video Originals and Limited Releases

More than 500 movies released every year are never shown in theaters, but go directly to video. There's a lot of interesting stuff among them, from kiddie movies to sleazy action flicks. And now, this one-of-a-kind guide reviews and rates 1,000 of the best and worst for hours of great alternative entertainment.

Mike Mayo • 1997 • paperback • **ISBN** 0-7876-0825-4 • **$17.95**

MUSIC FESTIVALS
from Bach to Blues

Music loving travel hound Tom Clynes takes you on a cross-country tour of more than 1,000 great festivals celebrating all kinds of music, from bluegrass to Chicago blues and from alternative to opera. You'll read all about where to go and what to expect when you get there.

Tom Clynes • 1996 • paperback • **ISRN** 0-7876-00

D1569599

AND, COMING THIS WINTER ...

THE ULTIMATE FAN BOOK

The first affordable guide to one of Americaís favorite spectator sports:

NASCAR: THE ULTIMATE FAN BOOK
(Covering every race since the beginning of NASCAR history!)

VISIBLE INK PRESS

Also from Visible Ink Press®

MusicHound™ Rock: The Essential Album Guide

*"This is a thoughtful
and opinionated
guide for newcomers.
For longtime fans,
this tome will spark
some fun arguments."*
—Minneapolis Star Tribune

MusicHound Rock profiles and reviews the work of nearly 2,000 pivotal artists and groups who perform classic, alternative and modern rock. Provides a complete list of albums, with suggestions for "What to Buy," "What to Buy Next" and "What to Avoid," as well as details on the performer's career, influences and impact on other musicians. Plus, a Producer Index, Record Label Directory, Web Site Guide and Resources Section. Also includes a free music CD sampler from RCA®.

Gary Graff
ISBN 0-7876-1037-2
911 pages

Music Festivals from Bach to Blues:
A Traveler's Guide

*"A unique listener's
guide to all genres
of tuneful revelry
across North America"*
—Time International

Music lovers, vacationers and students alike will welcome this comprehensive travel guide. Seasoned traveler Tom Clynes takes you to a wide variety of music festivals in the U.S. and Canada. More than 1,001 entries provide full descriptions of the artistic focus, who's performing and what festival-goers can expect from headliners. Also includes a guide to music workshops.

Tom Clynes
ISBN 0-7876-0823-8
582 pages

More than 1,000 COUNTRY ARTISTS, including

Alabama	Joe Diffie	Bill Monroe
Harley Allen	The Eagles	Mark O'Connor
Pete Anderson	Steve Earle	Buck Owens
Gene Autry	Vince Gill	Elvis Presley
Bad Livers	Faith Hill	Kim Richey
The Blasters	Waylon Jennings	LeAnn Rimes
Blue Rodeo	George Jones	Marty Robbins
Suzy Bogguss	Alison Krauss	George Strait
BR5-49	k.d. lang	Travis Tritt
Garth Brooks	Jim Lauderdale	Shania Twain
Junior Brown	Brenda Lee	Hank Williams
Glen Campbell	Patty Loveless	Hank Williams Jr.
The Carter Family	Lyle Lovett	Tammy Wynette
Deana Carter	Barbara Mandrell	Wynonna
Patsy Cline	Kathy Mattea	Trisha Yearwood
The Derailers	Reba McEntire	Dwight Yoakam

and many more!

musicHound

COUNTRY
The
Essential
Album
Guide

Edited by Brian Mansfield and Gary Graff

VISIBLE
INK
PRESS

Detroit • New York • Toronto • London

musicHound™ COUNTRY
The Essential Album Guide

Published by Visible Ink Press ®
a division of Gale Research
835 Penobscot Building
Detroit, MI 48226-4094

Visible Ink Press, MusicHound, the MusicHound logo, and A Cunning Canine Production are trademarks of Gale Research.

Most Visible Ink Press books are available at special quantity discounts when purchased in bulk by corporations, organizations, or groups. Customized printings, special imprints, messages, and excerpts can be produced to meet your needs. For more information, contact Special Markets Manager, Gale Research, 835 Penobscot Bldg., Detroit, MI 48226. Or call 1-800-776-6265.

Guitar image © 1997, PhotoDisc, Inc.

Library of Congress Cataloging-in-Publication Data

MusicHound country : the essential album guide / edited by Brian
    Mansfield and Gary Graff.
        p.   cm.
    Includes bibliographical references and index.
    ISBN 1-57859-006-X (alk. paper)
    1. Country music—Discography.   I. Mansfield, Brian, 1963-   .
II. Graff, Gary.
ML156.4.C7M87 1997
016.781642'0266—dc21
                                   97-5277
                                    CIP
                                    MN

ISBN 1-57859-006-X
Printed in the United States of America
All rights reserved
10 9 8 7 6 5 4 3 2 1

musicHound CONTENTS

COUNTRY MUSIC: THE ROAD GOES ON FOREVER

by jim lauderdale xi

Music is magic. Its ability to transform and move the listener is amazing.

Country music is vast in its collection of great singers, writers, producers and pickers. It is indeed an art form; though, for the most part, its creators, movers and shakers were unaware of the impact and historical contribution they were making at the time. It lives and breathes in the recordings and continues to change and grow. It has progressed dramatically from its humble rural origins to be heard and played worldwide.

The roots of the country music's family tree are in fiddle tunes and folk ballads brought over from Ireland, Scotland and England, across the water, passed on and embellished in the mountains, hills and farms of the Carolinas, Tennessee and the Virginias. Songs of struggle, life and death, lost love and celebration. In the late 1920s, primitive early recordings in Bristol, Virginia, began to take off in a big way with the Carter Family and Jimmie Rodgers, whose 78 rpm records sold like hotcakes across the nation and influenced an upcoming generation of country singers. Hank Williams hit the world like a fireball in the late 1940s. His influence is still heard today after his early death at age 29 in 1953. In the late 1950s through the 1960s, a kind of golden era of country music was ushered in, with the likes of Lefty Frizzell, George Jones, Buck Owens, Johnny Cash, Merle Haggard, Kitty Wells, Patsy Cline, Loretta Lynn, Tammy Wynette and Dolly Parton—to name a few of the greats to emerge when country music blossomed.

While most aspiring hopefuls came to Nashville with hopes of breaking into the industry, different states and regions spawned their own greats, and still do.

Bakersfield, California, had the "Bakersfield Sound"—its two most famous residents being Buck and Merle. Not to be overlooked from the West Coast are Wynn Stewart, Joe Maphis, Merle Travis and Rose Maddox, to name just a few. Texas has a huge list of country giants—Willie Nelson, Waylon Jennings, Johnny Bush, Roy Orbison and Buddy Holly (these two rockers left a huge impact on country music), Jerry Jeff Walker, Joe Ely and many others.

Country music is broad. There are distinct styles with their own lineages. Bluegrass, for instance, began with Bill Monroe in 1949. Early members Flatt & Scruggs went out on their own, making vital new music along with the Stanley Brothers and others, and developed a rich heritage. I remember hearing Scruggs' banjo instrumental "Foggy Mountain Breakdown" for the first time; I was mesmerized and inspired to take up the banjo. Ralph Stanley's voice inspired me to sing. Ricky Skaggs, Keith Whitley, Marty Stuart and Vince Gill were teenage bluegrass prodigies before their country success. Alison Krauss continues to bring a new audience to this form, to which she has added her own touch.

There is Western swing, whose king was Bob Wills; he added fiddles and steel guitar to big band dance music in the 1940s, making his own hybrid. That torch is carried today by Asleep at the Wheel.

It has been said that rock and roll was born from a mixture of country, gospel and blues. In the early days of rock 'n' roll Elvis Presley, Carl Perkins, Johnny Cash and Jerry Lee Lewis created music where the lines blurred between country and something brand new. Later on they would all have important country chart success. Ironically, country music was almost eclipsed by its offspring as the world rocked out. But there were enough faithful fans and great music to keep it going through a lean period. And country crept into rock, touching the Rolling Stones, the Grateful Dead, Bob Dylan, Leon Russell and Elvis Costello, among others, who were treating their listeners to their own take on country. The late Gram Parsons was a former member of the Byrds and co-founder of the country-rock group the Flying Burrito Brothers. He became pals with the Stones' Keith Richards, who developed a passion for Gram's country musings. His singing partner Emmylou Harris went on to record achingly beautiful albums on her own and remains one of the most distinctive voices in any musical genre.

The sound of rock is in a lot of newer country music because many of country's present generation grew up listening to whatever pop, rock or R&B was on the radio, along with country.

There are certain periods or years that stand out. One such recent landmark year was the "Class of '87," which gave us releases by Steve Earle, Dwight Yoakam, Lyle Lovett, k.d. lang and Nanci Griffith—each with a different style to be reckoned with. There are writers behind the hits such as the great Harlan Howard ("I Fall to Pieces," "Tiger by the Tail," "Streets of Baltimore"), who influenced Rodney Crowell ("Ain't Living Long Like This," "Til I Gain Control Again"), who was a big influence on many others.

There are musicians and producers integral to bringing the country sound to life. Like acoustic bass virtuoso Roy Huskey Jr., who inherited the job from his dad; guitar legends Chet Atkins and James Burton; and fiddle wizards like Kenny Baker, Johnny Gimbel and Mark O'Connor. And then there are the great pedal steel guitar players: Buddy Emmons, Al Perkins, Dan Dugmore, Bucky Baxter, Tommy Spurlock, Robby Turner . . . pedal steel is one of my favorite instruments. On the producer side we go from Owen Bradley to Billy Sherrill to a new generation that includes Pete Anderson, Richard Bennett, Emory Gordy Jr. and Blake Chancey, who are shaping today's sounds.

Independent record labels with acts who may not fall into the current mainstream may offer some of the best music you will ever hear. Singer/songwriters such as Buddy Miller, Lucinda Williams, Rosie Flores, Guy Clark, Chris Gaffney and many other greats are all on indie labels.

Whether you are already a fan or a new convert, it's good to have a guide to country music—I guess this book is a kind of encyclopedia since it also contains discographies and reviews. All I can say is I haven't read any of mine; if they are glowing, I'd say they are "tasteful and insightfully written," and if they are less than glowing, I'd say, "remember that reviews are just that writer's opinion and you should judge for yourself."

After all, there is a lot to discover and hear in country music. For instance, how influences interconnect and intertwine: George Jones and Merle Haggard influenced so many male country singers (such as George Strait, who influenced Garth Brooks). Patty Loveless replaced Loretta Lynn on the Wilburn Brothers' television show. Have you ever seen a clip or do you remember Porter Wagoner's show on TV? It's great. It started in the early 1960s and brought the cream of country's crop to America's living room, inspiring many a kid who dreamed of being on the show someday—me included. I also enjoyed Glen Campbell's summer television show, with his frequent guest banjo player—writer John Hartford, whose "Gentle on My Mind" is one of the most recorded songs of all time.

Today Nashville is bursting at the seams with music in the mainstream and on the fringes. A new crop of upstarts from Austin to Boston, New York City to Los Angeles are creating their own brand of country. The family tree is growing. It won't be long before they'll have to put out a larger version of this book. By the way, to our good fortune, many of the veteran giants, geniuses, visionaries and angels are still with us. Still performing and, at times, still recording. We can honor them by supporting their current work, seeing them live and discovering past recordings. You owe it to yourself.

Last night I spent a blissful evening at the Ryman Auditorium (the old home of the Grand Ole Opry, which has re-opened for concert use and is full of memories of days gone by). The program I listened to was in honor of the late Bill Monroe. Among those in the lineup of the country and bluegrass who's who on stage were Jimmy Martin, Connie Smith, Del McCoury and Ralph Stanley (who, though still sick with pneumonia, discharged himself from the hospital at 6:45 that morning so he could make the trip from his home in the hills of Virginia to make the event). His voice, as in past recordings and performances, gave me chills as always. It has lost none of its awesome power. We all stood up, cheering wildly, as this 70-year-old force of nature walked triumphantly across that hallowed stage, adding one more night of magic to music history.

In this thumbnail sketch, I'm bound to have accidently left out many names, important facts and events. But read on—they're in these pages. This is just a beginning . . . happy reading.

Jim Lauderdale

Jim Lauderdale is one of Nashville's most successful songwriters. Recently named Breakthrough Songwriter of the Year by Music Row, his songs have been recorded by the likes of George Strait, Vince Gill, Mark Chesnutt and Patty Loveless. His latest album, Persimmons, *is available on Upstart Records.*

COUNTRY MUSIC CONNECTION

by suzy bogguss **xiii**

Byron Berline played on my first record in Peoria, Illinois. How would I get one of the greatest fiddlers in bluegrass to play on my record? Well, I had dated Mitch Corbin, who played in a Chicago bluegrass band called Special Consensus. Byron, who had known Mitch since Mitch was a kid, was about to travel home from Washington, DC, to Los Angeles, so we called him to ask if he'd make a pit stop in Burlington, Iowa, and meet us in Peoria. From the airport he drove an hour and a half to the studio, which was in some guy's basement, played on three songs, and I payed him a six-pack of Michelob. Byron Berline flew on to Los Angeles, and I got his name on my album.

I love stories like that. I'm a geek about that kind of stuff. I love to hear the way people got turned on to music and who their heroes are. The book you're holding emphasizes one of the things that somehow has gotten lost in the commercialization of the country music field: a lot of musicians, including major artists, have deep roots that go to obscure places. *MusicHound Country* explores those roots in depth. In these pages, you'll read not only about the songs that you hear every day on the radio but about all sorts of country music—honky-tonk and Western swing, bluegrass and country-rock, folk, Cajun and Tejano. And if you follow the arrows in the Influences section for each artist, you'll find connections you never dreamed existed.

When I came to Nashville for the first time, I drove around town with that first album I'd made in 1981. I had two days, because I had a six-night-a-week singing job. I got to Nashville at five o'-clock in the morning, watched Ralph Emery and got fired up. Inspired, I bought a map of the stars' homes, and then I took my album around to all the people on that map.

Years later, I took a gig with a group called the Ozone Ramblers. We were on our way to play in Mexico City and stopped in Dallas to see Ricky Skaggs play the Dallas Palace. I put one of my 1981 albums on the stage, and Ricky said, "I already have that." It blew my mind that he had that record and that he knew that he had it! And I'll bet you anything the reason he looked at that record in the first place was that he saw that Byron Berline had played on it. Otherwise, why would he even have picked it up?

Connections again. Ricky had married Sharon White of the Whites, and I had left a copy of the album at the Whites' house during that 48-hour trip to Nashville. So obviously she took the record with her when she got married. Now, this is exciting stuff for a kid who's trying to get started. All of the connections between artists were so important to me at the time, because that's how I networked my way into knowing some people.

The connections exist between types of music too. I am the ultimate eclectic person; I love many different styles of music. There's a thread that ties swing and bluegrass and folk together. It all fits. When I was younger and eager to learn, every time I got turned onto a new artist, I was frenzied to find out the players on the records. Then I'd go out and buy the records those players had done.

I lived in a tiny town called Kewanee, Illinois, but I had a friend named Randy Lane who worked in Chicago three days a week. Randy would visit all the great record stores up there, like Rose's, and bring me back gift packages. We had our own little society that would get together and listen to four or five albums a week. Of course, I would pick whichever ones I was crazy about and learn the songs for my six-set shows. I'd be doing 120 songs a night, so I was always looking for new stuff to learn.

I dated a guy who was into folk acts like the Chad Mitchell Trio. He exposed me to a lot of cool stuff—some very obscure artists like Dave Van Ronk and others who are virtually unknown in Nashville. I used to go see Shel Silverstein, John Prine, Steve Goodman, Bob Gibson and Tom Paxton. That was part of the stuff that was creeping into me; that's why I have such a folky side. At the same time, I was also getting exposed to straight country like Lefty Frizzell and contemporary bluegrass acts like Tony Rice, the Seldom Scene and the Red Clay Ramblers. I even got Mike Auldridge, who played for the Seldom Scene, to play on one of my albums a while back. After a while, I could hear the same wonderful thing happening in all these types of music.

When I got to Nashville and landed a record deal, I couldn't believe that I could get some of those people to play on my record. Wendy Waldman produced my first record, and I had been a huge Wendy Waldman fan. It was quite a trip when I said, "I want Mark O'Connor and Mac McAnally," and she said, "Oh, yeah, they're friends of mine!" Eventually they became friends of mine, too. That was such an amazing thing to me, coming from this little town, reading *Frets* magazine, and studying the backs of record jackets, to suddenly be meeting and playing with my heroes.

When my album *Give Me Some Wheels* came out, I went on the road and did a lot of schmoozing with people in the radio and music retail industries. One night, I had dinner with the executives of a national music-store chain, and most of them had been musicians. It was so fun talking to them, and we were getting down to it—after a couple of bottles of wine, people really loosen up. We got to talking about the loss of the mom-and-pop record stores. We'd all grown up with that feeling of going into a record store and having somebody actually say, "You've got to hear this." It was a wonderful resource. Music just falling into your lap.

Today, where do you go for those kind of connections? Some of the chains are trying hard, with the listening booths and things like that, to get people excited about albums before taking them out the door—and a lot of the people working in those places are really into the music. But still, when you go into some of the category-killer-type super-stores, they've almost destroyed that feeling of intimacy. Some of the best of them have great staff and a nice ambience, where you can get a cup of cappucino and look at and listen to the books or the discs. But a lot of the stores have grown too big and impersonal, and when you talk to the clerks there they don't have a clue about anything. Their sections are so small you can't find anything that's not current and selling a zillion copies. That's a shame, because that was one of the things I loved about those years of going to the Strawberries and the Peaches, where you could just buy out of the cut-out bins for $1.88 and find something that was a real gem. Making that surprise connection with a wonderful record is harder to do, though there's a lot of great music out there.

I don't always get that feeling in record stores anymore, but reading *MusicHound Country* helps bring it back. The people who wrote it are obviously music lovers, and they've worked hard to make it an entertaining and reliable guide for all types of country music lovers. It's a necessity for album-jacket readers like me. Like the folks at Rose's, *MusicHound Country* makes great recommendations about what to listen to, from the obscure to the legends. It'll help you make those vital connections.

Suzy Bogguss

Suzy Bogguss is a respected singer/songwriter who won the Academy of Country Music's Top New Female Vocalist award for 1988 and the Country Music Association's Horizon Award in 1992. She has collaborated with such songwriters as Chet Atkins, Steve Dorff and Matraca Berg. Her latest album, Give Me Some Wheels, *is available on Capitol Nashville Records.*

WHAT DO YOU CALL COUNTRY?

by brian mansfield

"Country," Tom T. Hall said back in 1974, "is what you make it." These days, a lot of people try to make a lot of different things country. For some people, country began with Garth Brooks. For others, it ended with Hank Williams. Depending on the vantage point, country is Western music, it's not Western music, it's only music with fiddles and pedal steel, it's sung with a Southern accent but isn't bluegrass, and it's any kind of rural-bred Anglo-American music. If you believe certain people, some rock is country, or at least it is if it sticks around 20 years until a guy in a cowboy hat starts singing it. Folks have been arguing about the definition of country music since long before any of the people who worked on this book were born. We say let 'em.

After all, half the fun of loving music is debating its merits with other people who love it. *MusicHound Country* is not only an authoritative guide to the best country recordings available today but also a catalyst for good conversations—even arguments. No matter what your definition of country may be—does it encompass Lynyrd Skynyrd? Bela Fleck & the Flecktones? John Prine? Bryan White? Pat Boone? The Jayhawks?—we think you'll find *MusicHound* a useful and entertaining resource.

We haven't stuck close to any traditional definition of country music, mainly because we know too many country fans who also don't, and because country, like any vital musical genre, is continuously evolving and finding influences from outside its immediate scope. Within these pages, you'll find evaluations of music by cowboy singers of the 1920s, bluegrass musicians of the 1930s, pop singers of the 1940s, teen idols of the 1950s, folk activists of the 1960s, countrypolitan crooners of the

1970s, hat acts of the 1980s and alternative-country types of the 1990s. We're not about to tell 'em they're not country, even if they'd say they weren't themselves; we've seen too many other people who've believed otherwise. Yes, we've got George Jones, Kitty Wells, Merle Haggard, Dolly Parton, Charley Pride and Shania Twain. We've also got Johnny Tillotson, Claire Lynch, Carson Robison, James Talley, Sandy Posey, Jason & the Scorchers and Alvin & the Chipmunks. You won't find a more wide-ranging group of country or sort-of country or almost-country artists anywhere.

That said, *MusicHound Country* doesn't purport to be an obsessively comprehensive, musicological reference. We've tried to limit our reviews to albums currently in print in the United States. In some cases, we have also written about important albums available in other countries—particularly Canada, which has had an increasing presence in the worldwide country market in the past few years, and Germany, whose Bear Family label continues to produce quality reissues at a staggering rate. Also, where we had writers who were familiar with a particular artist's catalog, we've made recommendations for albums worth searching for. In practical terms, this means that some artists who had significant recording careers—Hank Locklin, for instance—don't get the kind of space their place in history might suggest, primarily because the record companies for which they did their best work haven't seen fit to keep their recordings in print.

We're also not an encyclopedia, though we try to give plenty of good biographical information. The discussions within these pages try to place an artist within a larger musical framework. To that end, almost every entry will have a list of artists in similar musical veins who either preceded or followed that act. In some cases, these are direct historical connections—Bill Monroe naturally influenced Lester Flatt and Earl Scruggs, since they played in his band—and they may just reflect a musical similarity; in other cases, it's because of something they've got in common—Brenda Lee, Tanya Tucker and LeAnn Rimes all being teenage singers with tremendous voices, for example. And if you get tired of our perspective, we give you others. We asked more than 40 artists to provide lists of five albums they think fans of theirs would also enjoy. Some of them are obvious—David Lee Murphy thinks his fans would like Waylon Jennings, no big surprise there. Others are more far-fetched: if Shania Twain says a lot of her fans buy Smashing Pumpkins albums, who are we not to believe her? Ultimately, whether you take your purchasing cues from us or Alan Jackson isn't so im-

portant as your simply enjoying this book. We've worked hard to make *MusicHound Country* fun and worthwhile, and we've probably discovered just as much music as you will (there's nothing like putting a book together to teach you the extent of your own ignorance).

So sit back and make your list of albums to buy, or go to your local music store with MusicHound on the leash—either way, *MusicHound Country* will sniff out the best of what you love and may even lead you to areas of country music you never knew existed. Buy it all or focus on your favorite styles, it doesn't matter. After all, country is what you make it. We're just here to point out the possibilities.

Brian Mansfield

So how do you use *MusicHound Country*? Here's what you'll find in the entries, and what we intend to accomplish with each point:

- An introductory paragraph, which will give you not only biographical information but also a sense of the artist's or group's sound and its stature in the country—and overall music—pantheon.

- **What to Buy:** The album or albums that we feel are essential purchases for consuming this act. It may be a greatest hits set, or it may be a particular album that captures the essence of the artist in question. In any event, this is where you should start—and don't think it wasn't hard to make these choices when eyeballing the catalogs of Johnny Cash, Willie Nelson, Dolly Parton and some of the other country titans.

- **What to Buy Next:** In other words, once you're hooked, these will be the most rewarding next purchases.

- **What to Avoid:** Seems clear enough. This is Hound poop.

- **The Rest:** Everything else that's available for this act, rated with the Hound's trusty bone scale (see below for more on this).

- **Worth Searching For:** An out-of-print gem. A bootleg. A guest appearance on another artist's album or a film soundtrack song. Something that may require some looking but will reward you for the effort.

- ◀◀: The crucial influences on this act's music.

- ▶▶: The acts that have been influenced by this artist or group. Used only where applicable; it's a little early for LeAnn Rimes or Anita Cochran to have influenced anybody.

Now, you ask, what's with those bones? (Down, boy! Sheesh. . . .) It's not hard to figure out—🦴🦴🦴🦴🦴 is nirvana (not Nirvana), a **WOOF** is dog food. Keep in mind that the bone ratings don't pertain just to the act's own catalog but to its worth in the whole music realm. Therefore a lesser act's **What to Buy** choice might rate no more than 🦴🦴🦴; some even rate 🦴🦴, a not-so-subtle sign that you might want to think twice about that act.

As with any opinions, all of what you're about to read is subjective and personal. MusicHound has a bit of junkyard dog in it, too; it likes to start fights. We hope it does, too. Ultimately, we think the Hound will point you in the right direction, and if you buy the 🦴🦴🦴🦴🦴 and 🦴🦴🦴🦴 choices, you'll have an album collection to howl about. But if you've got a bone to pick, the Hound wants to hear about it—and promises not to bite (but maybe bark a little bit). If you think we're wagging our tails in the wrong direction or lifting our leg at something that doesn't deserve it, let us know. If you think an act has been capriciously excluded—or charitably included—tell us. After all, there will be more *MusicHound*s coming your way in the future—and we want those jazz, blues, classical and other music fans to get the benefit of the country and rock Hounds' experience. And MusicHound will revisit the country world in the not-too-distant future.

EDITORS

Brian Mansfield grew up in Nashville where country music was an inevitability, though he didn't actually start buying country albums until he was in college. He began writing professionally in 1985 and has covered the Nashville music scene for the *Nashville Scene* and *The Tennessean*. He is currently the Nashville editor of *New Country* magazine, and has written about country music for *Country America, Music Row, Country Song Roundup, Daily Variety* and *Request*. His work has also appeared in *Spin, CD Review* and the *Nashville Banner*. He is a member of the board of advisors for the National Music Critics Association. A graduate of Boston's Berklee College of Music, he currently lives in Nashville with his wife and two sons, in a house that seriously needs more shelves.

Gary Graff is an award-winning music journalist and supervising editor of the *MusicHound* series. His work appears regularly in *Replay, Guitar World, ICE,* the *San Francisco Chronicle,* the *Detroit Sunday Journal/Detroit Journal,* Michigan's *Oakland Press,* the *Detroit Jewish News, New Country, Country Song Roundup* and other publications. A regular contributor to Mr. Showbiz/Wall of Sound and the SW Radio Networks, his "Rock 'n' Roll Insider" show airs weekly on WRIF-FM in Detroit. He is also a board member of the National Music Critics Association and co-producer of the Motor City/Detroit Music Awards. He lives in the Detroit suburbs with his wife, twin stepsons, daughter and the ghost of the world's oldest (and hungriest) goldfish.

MANAGING EDITOR
Dean Dauphinais

COPY EDITOR
Pam Shelton is a freelance writer and copy editor living in suburban Detroit. She used to write a bluegrass column for *Country in the City News*.

MUSICHOUND STAFF
Michelle Banks, Christa Brelin, Jim Craddock, Judy Galens, Jeff Hermann, Brad Morgan, Leslie Norback, Christopher Scanlon, Terri Schell, Carol Schwartz, Devra Sladics, Christine Tomassini

TECHNOLOGY WIZARD
Jeffrey Muhr

RESEARCH (DETROIT)
Carrie Bissey, Julia Daniel, Andy Malonis, Tamara Nott, Gary Oudersluys, Maureen Richards, Tracie Richardson, Cheryl Warnock

RESEARCH (NASHVILLE)
Craig Shelburne, Nikki Nenno

DATA ENTRY
Kathy Dauphinais

ART DIRECTION
Tracey Rowens

GRAPHIC SERVICES
Randy Bassett, Pam Reed, Barbara Yarrow

PERMISSIONS
Maria Franklin

PRODUCTION
Mary Beth Trimper, Dorothy Maki, Evi Seoud, Shanna Heilveil

TYPESETTING
Marco Di Vita of The Graphix Group

MARKETING & PROMOTION
Kim Intindola, Betsy Rovegno, Susan Stefani, Jenny Sweetland, Lauri Taylor

MUSICHOUND DEVELOPMENT
Martin Connors, Julia Furtaw, Rebecca Nelson

CONTRIBUTORS
Grant Alden has been writing about music since the first B-52s album came out. He lives in Nashville and is co-editor of *No Depression* magazine. He is a contributor to *MusicHound Rock.*

Linda Andres has a master's degree in creative writing from Wayne State University and is an editor at Gale Research.

Gil Asakawa is the content editor for America Online's Digital City Denver, co-author of *The Toy Book* (Knopf, 1992) and has written for *Rolling Stone, Pulse, Creem, No Depression, New Country, MusicHound Rock* and other publications.

Robert Baird is music editor of *Stereophile Magazine* in Santa Fe, New Mexico.

Deborah Barnes is the entertainment editor for *New Country* magazine and a contributing editor to *Disney Adventures,* an entertainment magazine for children.

Stephen L. Betts is a Nashville-based columnist for *Country Song Roundup* magazine and researcher for the TNN shows *Today's Country* and *This Week In Country Music.*

Peter Blackstock is co-editor of the alternative country bi-monthly *No Depression,* a senior editor at the northwestern music biweekly *The Rocket,* a weekly columnist for the daily *Seattle Post-Intelligencer* and a contributor to *MusicHound Rock.*

Denise Burgess is a staff member of *New Country* magazine and an aspiring songwriter who has worked for Willie Nelson Enterprises.

Ken Burke is a singer/songwriter/comedian whose column, "The Continuing Saga Of Dr. Iguana," has been running in small press publications since 1985.

Dick Byington is a radio personality for 98 WSIX-FM in Nashville, Tennessee, and a staff member at *New Country* magazine.

Bob Cannon is a songwriter and journalist who has written for magazines such as *Entertainment Weekly, New Country, TuTTi* and *Parenting,* and for the *New York Daily News.*

Randall T. Cook is a certified air force brat, part-time urban miner, former country and rock disc jockey and staff member at *New Country* magazine.

Chris Dickinson is the pop music critic for the *St. Louis Post-Dispatch.* Her work has also appeared in the *Journal of Country Music, New Country,* the *Chicago Tribune* and *Request.*

Daniel Durchholz is the editor of *Replay* magazine, a contributing editor at *Request* and a contributor to *MusicHound Rock.* He lives in Eden Prairie, Minnesota, with his wife Mary, son Wolfgang, and a basement full of CDs and LPs he's been saving for just this occasion.

Bill Friskics-Warren is a Nashville-based freelance writer whose work has appeared in *New Country, No Depression, The Oxford American,* the *Nashville Scene* and the *Washington Post.*

Jon Hartley Fox is an award-winning writer and record producer who lives in Sacramento, California. He is a 20-year veteran of the bluegrass wars.

Douglas Fulmer is a Cleveland-based freelance writer who writes extensively for the *Cleveland Plain Dealer* and has contributed to *Bluegrass Unlimited, New Country, Country Weekly, Bluegrass Now* and other publications.

Gary Pig Gold is a native of Toronto, Canada, and has been publishing his very own music fanzine, *The Pig Paper,* since 1975. Although he has since escaped to Hoboken, New Jersey, he remains active as a writer, songwriter, arranger, producer and performer of quasi-legendary status.

Bill Hobbs is a Nashville freelance writer and former music magazine writer and editor.

Cyndi Hoelzle is a Nashville freelance journalist who covers music and the music industry for publications such as *Radio &*

Records, Music Business International and Gavin, where she spent 12 years as country editor and Nashville bureau chief.

Steve Holtje is a freelance writer and editor in New York whose work has appeared in Creem, New Power Generation, the New Review, MusicHound Rock and other publications.

Steve Knopper is a Chicago-based freelance writer who has contributed to Rolling Stone, Newsday, Request, George, Billboard, the Chicago Tribune, the Chicago Reader, MusicHound Rock, the Rocky Mountain News and SW Radio Networks.

Beth Lockamy is on staff at New Country magazine.

Liz Lynch is an Evanston, Illinois, writer and novelist who has written for the Chicago Sun-Times, the Miami Herald, the Fort Lauderdale Sun-Sentinel, Replay magazine and MusicHound Rock.

Ronnie McDowell is the nationwide telemarketing sales director for New Country magazine and is no kin to the singer of the same name (though it helps him get good dinner reservations).

David Menconi is the music critic at the Raleigh (North Carolina) News & Observer and has written for Spin, Billboard, Request and MusicHound Rock. He is also a contributing editor for No Depression magazine.

David Okamoto is the music editor for the Dallas Morning News and a contributing editor to ICE. His work has also appeared in Jazziz, Rolling Stone, CD Review and MusicHound Rock.

Allan Orski is an associate editor at the New Review in New York City and has written for Rolling Stone Online, SW Radio Networks and MusicHound Rock.

Alan Paul is a senior editor of Guitar World magazine and the executive editor of Guitar World Online. His writing has appeared in many publications, including the New Yorker, Mojo, People and MusicHound Rock.

Rick Petreycik lives in Black Rock, Connecticut, and has written for Guitar Player, Country Guitar, Musician, Fender Frontline and the Hartford Courant.

Randy Pitts has labored in the vineyards of traditional music in various circumstances for nearly 20 years, most recently as artistic director of The Freight and Salvage in Berkeley, California, where he worked from 1989 until 1996; he saw Onie Wheeler in Vietnam as part of Roy Acuff's U.S.O. show on Easter Sunday, 1967.

Doug Pullen is the music and media writer for the Flint (Michigan) Journal and Booth Newspapers. He is a contributor to MusicHound Rock.

Leland Rucker has been writing about popular music since 1975 and is the managing editor of Blues Access, a quarterly journal of blues music published in Boulder, Colorado. He is the co-author of The Toy Book (Knopf, 1992) and is editor of the upcoming MusicHound Blues (Visible Ink Press, 1997).

Judy R. Rabinovitz is an aspiring singer/songwriter and freelance music writer based in Nashville. She is currently on staff at New Country magazine.

Christopher Scapelliti is an associate editor of Guitar magazine and a contributor to MusicHound Rock.

Joel Selvin has covered pop music for the San Francisco Chronicle since 1970 and is the author of six books on the subject. He co-produced the Dick Dale album Tribal Thunder and is a contributor to MusicHound Rock.

Craig Shelburne lives in Nashville and has written for the Nashville Scene, Gospel Voice, Music City News and New Country.

David Simons is a freelance writer who fronts a rock band, the Raymies, in New England.

David Sokol is a longtime resident of western Massachusetts and has been New Country magazine's editor in chief since the magazine began publishing in March, 1994.

Mario Tarradell is the country music critic for the Dallas Morning News. His work has also appears in Replay and New Country magazines.

David Yonke writes about popular music for the Toledo Blade and is a contributor to MusicHound Rock.

musicHound ACKNOWLEDGMENTS

My wife Nancy and my sons Nick and Zach basically watched their husband and father disappear from the day after Christmas until Valentine's Day. These three wonderful people endured the flu, e. coli and a trip to the emergency room while I locked myself in my office and they could not have been nicer about it. Nick asked that this book be dedicated to him in exchange for his patience—in the absence of a dedication page, this will have to do. I love you guys.

My parents, John and Betty Mansfield, and in-laws, Glen and Marian McDoniel, provided general support and baby-sitting without which *MusicHound Country* could not have been completed on time.

Many writers whose names do not appear in this book have provided encouragement and assistance. Without people like Robert K. Oerrman, Jay Orr and David Ross, I would never have been in a position to work on this book. Thanks also to my bosses at *New Country* magazine—Jim Connell, Ellen Holmes and David Sokol—for their understanding as *MusicHound Country* neared deadline and ate up more and more of my time.

A number of Nashville companies provided invaluable services in the research and compilation of this book. The staff at the Country Music Foundation gave tremendous assistance in checking facts and unearthing obscure information. The Ernest Tubb Record Shop offered many suggestions and insights, even while happily emptying our pockets. The International Marketing Group sold us hundreds of albums at wholesale prices. Both IMG and Ernest Tubb are excellent resources for locating hard-to-find recordings.

Many organizations supplied information for the appendices, including the Country Music Association, the Academy of Country Music, the National Academy of Recordings Arts and Sciences, the International Fan Club Organization, the Nashville Music Awards, the Canadian Country Music Association, and others.

The good folks at the Datawatch Corporation will never know how much they contributed to *MusicHound Country,* but their Virex program cured the two infected computers that for a long time held the only two versions of this book.

Brian Mansfield

When we put out word that the next MusicHound project, following *MusicHound Rock,* would be a country book, the response was lots of raised eyebrows and skeptical side-glances. "You like that stuff?" many of my friends and colleagues asked. Well, yes, I do—proudly, by the way. As *MusicHound Country* shows, country is an important American art form with a rich history that's influenced all aspects of our popular culture, including rock 'n' roll. Country is, ultimately, a field of storytellers, and their tales are of universal themes—broken hearts, triumph over adversity, the God-given right to let out a good "Yee-hah!!" when you feel like it. To me, this was the logical next bone for MusicHound to bite on.

That said, I hardly consider myself on expert on country, which made me appreciate my co-editor, Brian Mansfield, all the more. Half the fun was getting to tap his country knowledge and enrich myself on the cheap. The other half, of course, was getting to know Brian better, as a journalist and as a person. We had a blast doing the book, and I think it shows in the following pages.

The folks at Visible Ink Press were again a pleasure to work with, unbridled in their enthusiasm about the project. Martin Connors, Terri Schell and Rebecca Nelson helped us hone the book's vision and explore its possibilities. Jennifer Sweetland was understanding in balancing the publicity needs for *MusicHound Rock* with the development of *MusicHound Country*. And in Kim Intindola, we have fresh energy that will help take the *MusicHound* series another step or two—or more.

I'd particularly like to thank Dean Dauphinais, who became the *MusicHound* managing editor with the *Country* book. Dean brings plenty of fresh energy to the project, too, and was particularly committed to helping take the lessons we learned with the *Rock* book and making sure they were applied to *Country*. Job finished, we can now return his children, Sam and Josh, to him.

The *MusicHound Rock* acknowledgments was a list Cecille B. DeMille would be proud of, so all those people can consider themselves thanked again. That said, I'd like to thank all of the contributors—those who came on board for *Country* and those who also contributed to *Rock*. Dan Durchholz, a close friend in "real life" anyway, remained a solid source of support, as did Stephen Scapelliti, my tireless, will-work-for-food attorney and contract negotiator. Thanks also to Chris Richards of Repeat the Beat, who helped in compiling the list. And besides the music industry folks who helped with the *Rock* book, additional thanks go to a country contingent that includes Lisa Shively, Paula Batson, Glen Dicker and Susan Niles. My friend and occasional conspirator Michael Watts, who produces some of the best country events in the Detroit area, has my gratitude for pounding the virtues of country into my head all these years.

I had hoped a second book would not have to be published with this acknowledgment, but my thanks, support and solidarity go to the people of the Metropolitan Detroit Council of Newspaper Unions, most of whom—as of this writing (and hopefully not much longer)—remain on the streets fighting for justice and good faith bargaining. We've learned a lot during this struggle, and we've taught a lot as well. I hope people are listening, and I pray our efforts are rewarded over time.

My family's interest in country music is modest (the Chipmunks' version of "Achy Breaky Heart" gets more play in our house than Billy Ray Cyrus'), but they were nonetheless supportive and enthusiastic about this project. Thanks go to the assorted Galantys and Brysks, as well as to my brother Harvey and his wife Vicki. My parents, Milt and Ruthe Graff, have another title for the mantle. My stepsons, Josh and Ben, and my daughter, Hannah, maintained a careful balance between "hanging out" in the office and getting underfoot, but they know (I hope) that they're always welcome. Ditto my wife, Judy, who I know was pleased to see that the process was a little easier—and that the computer didn't crash—this time. Thanks again, and I love you all.

Gary Graff

musicHound

COUNTRY

ROY ACUFF

Born September 15, 1903, in Maynardville, TN. Died November 23, 1992, in Nashville, TN.

An institution. The King of Country Music, elected to the Country Music Hall of Fame in 1962 (the first living artist to be so honored), was a starring member of the Grand Ole Opry from 1938 until his death. Violinist, singer, bandleader, publisher (Acuff–Rose), Acuff was the first star developed by the Opry primarily as a vocalist; he was enormously popular through the 1940s, with such classic hits as "The Wabash Cannonball," "The Great Speckled Bird," "Wreck on the Highway" and "Fireball Mail." His impassioned, powerful (and loud) vocal style owed much to the Baptist hymns he sang as a youth. He also featured first-rate string bands, in which his great dobroists always figured prominently: first Clell Summey ("Cousin Jody") and later Beecher Kirby ("Bashful Brother Oswald"). Acuff was among many traditional country music artists whose stature received an unexpected boost as a result of participation in the Nitty Gritty Dirt Band's *Will the Circle Be Unbroken.*

what to buy: *The Essential Roy Acuff 1936–1949* (Columbia/Legacy, 1992, prod. various) 🎻🎻🎻🎻 contains 20 of Acuff's most familiar hits from 1936 to 1949; the "Wabash Cannonball" here is a 1947 remake with Acuff as featured vocalist. *Roy Acuff Columbia Historic Edition* (Columbia, 1985, prod. various) 🎻🎻🎻🎻 is an outstanding reissue featuring the initial recording of "The Wabash Cannonball" featuring vocalist "Dynamite" Hatcher,

along with 15 other vintage recordings from Acuff's earliest days. *The King of Country Music* (Bear Family, 1993, prod. various) 🎻🎻🎻 is an interesting two-CD set of Acuff's post-Columbia 1950s recordings for MGM, Decca and Capitol.

the rest:
Best of Roy Acuff (Curb, 1991) 🎻🎻

worth searching for: Two reissues on Rounder, *Roy Acuff: 1936–1939 "Steamboat Whistle Blues"* (Rounder, 1985, prod. Lou Curtiss) 🎻🎻🎻🎻, and *Roy Acuff & the Smoky Mountain Boys 1939–41* (Rounder, 1988, prod. Lou Curtiss) 🎻🎻🎻🎻, contain more outstanding recordings of vintage Acuff and his bands.

influences:
▶▶ Hank Williams, George Jones

Randy Pitts

EDDIE ADCOCK
See: Country Gentlemen

TRACE ADKINS

Born Tracey Darrell Adkins, January 13, 1962, in Springhill, LA.

At 6'6", Trace Adkins is an imposing man. But it's his commanding baritone that immediately makes people pay attention, like they know he has something important to say. Adkins grew up in a musical family; his mom and all his aunts sang in the choir at church, and one of his uncles recorded gospel albums. When Adkins was in high school, he joined the New Commitment Quartet, a gospel group that released two independent albums (now out of print). He played football at Louisiana Tech, where he earned a degree in petroleum technology. However, Adkins always knew exactly what he wanted to do, and it wasn't drilling oil wells. Though he put his degree to work as a derrick man, Adkins' commitment to music never wavered. You want proof? While working on the rigs, Trace seriously injured his little finger. When the doctor told him he would never again be able to move his finger, Trace asked him to just make sure it could fit around the neck of the guitar. (Check out the evidence on the inside of the CD cover.)

what's available: In his solo debut *Dreamin' Out Loud* (Capitol, 1996, prod. Scott Hendricks) ♪♪♪, which contains his hits "There's a Girl in Texas" and "Every Light in the House," Trace differentiates himself from the pack.

influences:
◀◀ Tracy Lawrence

Cyndi Hoelzle

DAVID "STRINGBEAN" AKEMAN

See: Stringbean

RHETT AKINS

Born October 13, 1969, in Valdosta, GA.

A Georgia native who worked for his father's oil and gas distributorship and once harbored dreams of being an NFL quarterback, Rhett Akins didn't seriously consider singing as a career until he was in his 20s. In 1992, at age 22, he moved to Nashville and within a year had offers from three different record companies. His biggest singles have included "That Ain't My Truck" (1995) and "Don't Get Me Started" (1996).

what's available: While Akins has a good grounding in traditional country—he does great Porter Wagoner and Bill Monroe impressions—his music possesses a distinctively youth-oriented slant. His debut single from *A Thousand Memories* (Decca, 1995, prod. Mark Wright) ♪♪♪ was a first-love rocker called "What They're Talkin' About." Other singles like "I Brake for Brunettes" and "That Ain't My Truck" weren't as good, but some of the album cuts showed promise. The best songs on *Somebody New* (Decca, 1996, prod. Mark Wright) ♪♪♪, like "Don't Get Me Started," celebrate young love and pack the immediate wallop of a good crush. Elsewhere, the pleasures often pass as quickly.

Influences.
◀◀ Hank Williams Jr., George Strait, Garth Brooks
▶▶ David Kersh, Gary Allan

Brian Mansfield

ALABAMA

Formed as Wildcountry, 1969, in Fort Payne, AL. Became Alabama in 1977.

Randy Owen, guitar, vocals; Jeff Cook, keyboards, fiddle; Teddy Gentry, bass; Bennett Vartanian, drums (1969–76); Jackie Owen, drums (1976–77); Rick Scott, drums (1977–79); Mark Herndon, drums (1979–present).

Back in 1979, when Alabama was signed to RCA Records, no seasoned label executive could have predicted that this watered-down Southern rock band would become the most successful country group of all time. But 17 years after its major-label debut album hit the charts, Alabama remains a commercially viable entity, with regular Top 10 hits and gold albums. While these boys no longer pull the multiplatinum numbers of their early 1980s heyday, their record is quite impressive at a time when the country music industry spits out hit songs, not long-lasting careers. Alas, there has been a hefty creative price to pay for mainstream success. In the beginning, Alabama was basically the small-town man's Lynyrd Skynyrd, playing pop-laced Southern rock with touches of bluegrass and country. Early efforts weren't spectacular, but they were consistently enjoyable—at least as guilty pleasures. There were moments of near genius, though: the down-home feel of "Tennessee River," "Mountain Music" and "Dixieland Delight" sounded like something your grandpa would play on the banjo. Alabama had crossover dreams, too. "Feels So Right," "Love in the First Degree" and "Take Me Down" were big, catchy pop hits tailored for driving with the windows rolled down.

But by the late 1980s, the formula grew stale. After peaking with its best album to date, 1985's *40 Hour Week*, Alabama sank into country-pop pablum. Too many ballads and too many songs about family and the ecology gave way to the abominable 1990s material. With the exception of 1990's splendid "Jukebox in My Mind," the quartet cranked out one pathetic song after another. The titles alone indicate the level of banality: "I'm in a Hurry (And Don't Know Why)," "Take a Little Trip," "T.L.C. A.S.A.P." and the absolute worst, "The Maker Said Take Her." These days, an Alabama album is distinctive for how bad it can actually turn out. Surprisingly, its recent *Christmas Volume II* set proved better and fresher than anything the band had recorded during the last six years. Maybe there's something inspiring in the cool air that blows during the holiday season.

what to buy: *40 Hour Week* (RCA, 1985, prod. Harold Shedd and Alabama) 𝄞𝄞𝄞 is the group's most cohesive record. The hits—particularly "40 Hour Week (For a Livin')" and the lovely ballad "There's No Way"—are especially strong. Also, such album cuts as "Louisiana Moon" and "Down on Longboat Key" bring out a bit of sensuality in Randy Owen's otherwise stiff voice.

what to buy next: *Greatest Hits* (RCA, 1986, prod. Alabama and Harold Shedd) 𝄞𝄞𝄞 is a good companion to *40 Hour Week*. "She and I," one of the new songs on this set, has a playful, John Mellencamp-ish flavor, and the group's best singles, including "Mountain Music" and "Tennessee River," are here. If you want another CD, pick up *My Home's in Alabama* (RCA, 1980, prod. Harold Shedd, Larry McBride, Alabama and Sonny Limbo) 𝄞𝄞𝄞. The record's sound is slicked-up Southern rock but it has a lived-in feel that's contagious.

what to avoid: In a nutshell, stay away from the 1990s studio albums: *Pass It On Down* (RCA, 1990, prod. Josh Leo, Larry Michael Lee and Alabama) 𝄞𝄞, *American Pride* (RCA, 1992, prod. Josh Leo, Larry Michael Lee and Alabama) 𝄞𝄞 and *Cheap Seats* (RCA, 1993, prod. Josh Leo, Larry Michael Lee and Alabama) 𝄞𝄞 are interchangeably weak. *In Pictures* (RCA, 1995, prod. Emory Gordy Jr. and Alabama) 𝄞 is notably atrocious. Hearing any of the hits from these albums on the radio is enough; don't waste your money.

the rest:
Feels So Right (RCA, 1981) 𝄞𝄞𝄞
Mountain Music (RCA, 1982) 𝄞𝄞𝄞
The Closer You Get (RCA, 1983) 𝄞𝄞𝄞
Roll On (RCA, 1984) 𝄞𝄞𝄞
Christmas (RCA, 1985) 𝄞𝄞𝄞
The Touch (RCA, 1986) 𝄞𝄞
Just Us (RCA, 1987) 𝄞𝄞
Alabama Live (RCA, 1988) 𝄞𝄞
Southern Star (RCA, 1989) 𝄞𝄞
Greatest Hits II (RCA, 1991) 𝄞𝄞𝄞
Greatest Hits Vol. III (RCA, 1994) 𝄞𝄞
Christmas Volume II (RCA, 1996) 𝄞𝄞𝄞𝄞
Dancin' on the Boulevard (RCA, 1997) 𝄞𝄞

worth searching for: Alabama turns in a reverential rendition of Merle Haggard's "Sing Me Back Home" on *Mama's Hungry Eyes: A Tribute to Merle Haggard* (Arista, 1994, prod. various) 𝄞𝄞𝄞𝄞, an outstanding homage to the legendary Hag that features stellar performances by such folks as Brooks & Dunn, Clint Black, Pam Tillis, Radney Foster, Alan Jackson and Emmylou Harris. Although an undeserved commercial flop, this album definitely merits a listen.

influences:
◄◄ Lynyrd Skynyrd, Eagles, Atlanta Rhythm Section
►► Restless Heart, Little Texas, Ricochet

Mario Tarradell

PAT ALGER
Born September 23, 1947, in Long Island City, NY.

A singer/songwriter with considerable performing experience, Pat Alger became one of the most successful songwriters in country music during the late 1980s and continuing into the 1990s, penning hits for Garth Brooks, Hal Ketchum, Kathy Mattea, Don Williams, Trisha Yearwood, Nanci Griffith and others. His own performing style is understatezd and intimate, as one might expect from a veteran of coffeehouses and listening rooms.

what's available: *True Love & Other Short Stories* (Sugar Hill, 1991, prod. Pat Alger, Jim Rooney) 𝄞𝄞𝄞 is a chance to hear the man who wrote them sing "Once in a Very Blue Moon," "Lone Star State of Mind," "True Love," "Small Town Saturday Night," "Going Gone," and "She Came from Fort Worth." *Seeds* (Sugar Hill, 1993, prod. Jim Rooney) 𝄞𝄞𝄞 contains more originals from this highly successful writer of hits for others, including Alger's version of the huge Garth Brooks hit "The Thunder Rolls."

influences:
◄◄ Don Williams, Kris Kristofferson
►► Fred Koller, Steve Seskin

Randy Pitts

GARY ALLAN
Born Gary Herzberg, December 5, 1967, near Whittier, CA.

Gary Allan may turn out to be one of the more legitimate heirs of the California country sound of Buck Owens and Wynn Stewart. A southern California native who grew up surfing, Allan avoided both the Nashville record-by-numbers and roots-rock Los Angeles scenes. Instead, he has developed a sound that has both its own edge and commercial sensibility.

what's available: *Used Heart for Sale* (Decca, 1996, prod. Mark Wright) 𝄞𝄞𝄞 is a promising debut that manages to combine songs by Faron Young, Garth Brooks and Jim Lauderdale into a cohesive, honky-tonk whole. Allan's first hit from the album came from a ballad, "Her Man," but he's at his best when tearing through songs like "Living in a House Full of Love" or George Ducas' "Send Back My Heart."

influences:

◀◀ Mark Chesnutt, George Strait, Dwight Yoakam

Brian Mansfield

HARLEY ALLEN

Born January 23, 1956, in Dayton, OH.

One of the most talked-about Nashville singer-songwriters in recent years, Harley Allen's major label debut came in 1997 on Mercury Records. But as a performer and songwriter, he'd already gained a sterling reputation. The son of bluegrass great Red Allen (whose real name is Harley), the young Harley Allen was 14 when he joined his three brothers in a bluegrass group with their dad, working mainly out of Dayton, although Harley Allen Sr. and most of his family were originally from Hazard, Kentucky. After more than two decades of playing bluegrass, Allen moved to Nashville in 1989, where he quickly became a staff writer for a major publishing firm and recorded the demos that eventually earned him his record deal. His touring days behind him (until recently, anyway), Allen's songs were recorded by artists such as Linda Ronstadt, Garth Brooks, Alison Krauss and Alan Jackson. Jackson, in fact, chose two of Allen's songs as title tracks of his albums *Everything I Love* and *Who I Am*. Allen's debut earned raves for the recondite lyrics and fresh approach, sorely missed in so much of the country music of the 1990s.

what to buy: *Another River* (Mercury, 1997, prod. Carson Chamberlain and Dirk Johnson) ♫♫♫♫ is a magnificent and simple record that gives one pause to wonder how close this must be to what Keith Whitley could have achieved had he lived. He surely would have mined Allen's vast catalog for material. Any number of the tracks featured here could easily become hits for other artists. It's a gripping "debut."

the rest:

Across the Blueridge Mountains (Folkways) ♫♫♫

influences:

◀◀ Keith Whitley, Red Allen

▶▶ Vince Gill, Tim McGraw

Stephen L. Betts

RED ALLEN

Born Harley Allen, February 12, 1930, in Pigeon Roost, KY. Died April 3, 1993, in Dayton, OH.

One of the truly underrated singers in the history of bluegrass, Harley "Red" Allen was a master of the "high lonesome" style and a major influence on subsequent generations of bluegrass vocalists. Allen first rose to prominence during the mid-1950s, joining forces with the Osborne Brothers for a string of memorable MGM recordings (especially "Once More"). After parting with the Osbornes in 1958, Allen spent most of the rest of his career leading his own band (usually called the Kentuckians), working in Washington, DC, and Dayton, Ohio, and recording for such labels as Folkways, Melodeon, Rebel and County. An intense and powerful singer, Allen worked from the late 1960s on with his four sons (Neal, Greg, Ronnie and Harley), who also performed separately as the Allen Brothers. Red Allen's last recording was the Grammy-nominated *Bluegrass Reunion* in 1992.

Some of Red Allen's most inspired music was made with mandolinist Frank Wakefield, the player David Grisman says "split the mandolin atom." Allen and Wakefield first worked together in Dayton, recording for the Kentucky label in 1954; they reunited in Washington, DC, during the early 1960s, recording an influential album for Folkways, *Red Allen, Frank Wakefield and the Kentuckians*. The partnership ended when Wakefield joined the Greenbriar Boys in 1964, though Allen and Wakefield would occasionally play together during the years before Allen's death.

what's available: In an age when the complete works of many lesser artists are available, virtually nothing by Red Allen is in print. Recorded within the last year of Allen's life, *Bluegrass Reunion* (Acoustic Disc, 1992, prod. David Grisman) ♫♫♫ puts the legendary singer together with David Grisman, Herb Pedersen, Jim Buchanan, Lance Kerwin and special guest Jerry Garcia. The Allen-Pedersen duet on "Letter from My Darlin'" is the highlight, but some older songs associated with Allen ("She's No Angel," "Is This My Destiny") are also pretty satisfying. Not prime Red Allen by any stretch, but until promised reissues of the County, Rebel and Folkways recordings materialize, this will have to do. *The Kitchen Tapes* (Acoustic Disc, 1994, prod. David Grisman, Peter K. Siegel) ♫♫♫♫, which captures Allen and Frank Wakefield sitting around the kitchen table one day in 1963, is an unexpected treat, featuring the two on a collection of 25 songs and tunes. It's raw, loose and rough as a cob, but the music is transcendent. In addition to the off-hand intensity of songs like "I'm Just Here to Get My Baby out of Jail" and "I'm Blue, I'm Lonesome," the highlights include several original instrumentals by Wakefield ("New Camptown Races," "Catnip," "Hey Mr. Mando").

influences:

◄◄ Bill Monroe, Jimmy Martin

►► Harley Allen, James King

Jon Hartley Fox

RED ALLEN & FRANK WAKEFIELD

See: Red Allen

REX ALLEN

Born December 31, 1920, in Wilcox, AZ.

One could almost think of Rex Allen as Walt Disney's singing cowboy, since the one-time professional rodeo rider narrated more than 80 films for Disney. Allen also made 32 Westerns, beginning in 1950 with *The Arizona Cowboy* for Republic Pictures. Allen began performing on radio during the 1940s, first with a show in Trenton, New Jersey, then with Chicago's National Barn Dance and finally the CBS radio network. He briefly had his own TV show, *Frontier Doctor,* during the 1950s. Allen had only a few hit singles, but spread them out over three decades. They included "Afraid" (#14, 1949), "Crying in the Chapel" (#4, 1953) and "Don't Go Near the Indians" (#4, 1962). Allen was elected to the Cowboy Hall of Fame in 1968.

what's available: Rex Allen's many records are out of print in the United States, though he has two albums available through European labels: *Voice of the West* (Bear Family) and *Lonesome Letter Blues* (Collectables). *The Singing Cowboys* (Warner Western, 1995, prod. various) ♬♬♬ is an album Allen and his son, Rex Allen Jr., made together in 1995. It features recordings originally made for either Allen or Allen Jr.'s albums with new vocal tracks added to create the duets. The three tracks that come from Allen's original recordings are all public domain cowboy songs: "Tyin' Knots in the Devil's Tail," "Little Joe the Wrangler" and "When the Work's All Done This Fall."

influences:

◄◄ Gene Autry, Tex Ritter, Roy Rogers

►► Rex Allen Jr., Riders in the Sky

Brian Mansfield

REX ALLEN JR.

Born August 23, 1947, in Chicago, IL.

Rex Allen's namesake was the only one of his four children to follow him into recording. Rex Allen Jr. began touring with his father when he was just 6. While on the road, he began to learn how to play guitar and how to be a rodeo clown. His recording career didn't do much until he signed with Warner Bros. during the early 1970s. He has had more than 30 charting singles, but only a handful of those have reached the Top 10. He has stayed in front of his audience by regular appearances on *The Statler Brothers Show* on TNN, which led to his own series, *Yesteryear.*

what to buy: Released when Allen got his own TNN series, *The Very Best of Rex Allen Jr.* (Warner Bros., 1994, prod. various) ♬♬♬ shows why Allen was picked to host a nostalgia show. These recordings, which include most of Allen's biggest hits, feature songs like "Lonely Street" and "I'm Getting Good at Missing You (Solitaire)." Hits range from mid-tempo to slow, and Allen's modest baritone is easy on the ears.

what to buy next: Though Rex Allen Jr. had recorded a concept album about his father (*Cat's in the Cradle,* currently out of print), he'd never recorded with him until *The Singing Cowboys* (Warner Western, 1995, prod. various) ♬♬♬, which takes original tracks from earlier albums by the Allens and revamps them with the other's voice.

what to avoid: *Today's Generation* (SSS International) **WOOF!** Made sometime during the late 1960s or early 1970s, this is a mildly psychedelic folk-pop album that should be avoided by all but the strangely curious.

influences:

◄◄ Rex Allen, Glen Campbell, Bobby Goldsboro

Brian Mansfield

TERRY ALLEN

Born Terrence Lain Allen, May 7, 1943, in Wichita, KS.

Terry Allen was making Americana music about 20 years before it was cool. That makes his survival in the fickle world of country music, even fringe country music, all the more amazing. A visual artist and songwriter, Allen cut his teeth on rock, country blues and folk as a kid growing up in West Texas. He moved to San Francisco at age 19, a true multimedia artist who dabbled in music, art, theater and film. He moved to Lubbock during the late 1970s, at a time when the Texas Panhandle city had become a hotbed of rootsy, rockified country blues with local artists such as Joe Ely and Butch Hancock, and a lively club scene that was visited by the Fabulous Thunderbirds, Delbert McClinton and Stevie Ray Vaughan in his pre-Double Trouble days. Allen's songs lean on sparse, often acoustic or bare instrumentation as his wizened rasp of a voice veers from the profoundly poignant to hysterically cynical. After all these years—most of Allen's early albums were sold through his mail-order label, Fate, now run by his daughter-in-law in Austin—he's begun to find an audience outside of the cultish, chic Texas fringe art crowd thanks to a deal with North Carolina's Sugar Hill Records, which released his last two albums and plans to reissue earlier work. Allen told William D. Kerns of the *Lubbock Avalanche–Journal:* "People tell me it's country music, and I ask, 'Which country?'"

what to buy: Allen met drifters like Ely after he left sunny California for the dingy, flat Bible Belt town of Lubbock during the late 1970s. But their artistic sensibilities were a good fit, and Ely's brazen, devil-may-care approach to country, rock and folk rubbed off impressively on his new friend on *Lubbock (on Everything)* (Sugar Hill, 1979, prod. Terry Allen) ♫♫♫, a wide-ranging work as sprawling and colorful as the hard Southern plains folk who inspired it.

what to buy next: *Human Remains* (Sugar Hill, 1996, prod. Terry Allen, Lloyd Maines) ♫♫♫ rocks a little harder than some of his more folk- and country-influenced work. David Byrne, Joe Ely and the Sexton Brothers, Charlie and Will, make appearances. *The Silent Majority: Terry Allen's Greatest Missed Hits* (Fate, 1993, prod. various) ♫♫♫ compiles a sampling of Allen's music for films, including contributions to Byrne's *True Stories* soundtrack along with songs for theatrical and dance productions.

what to avoid: Allen's music has always been an acquired taste, but the uneven *Bloodlines* (Fate, 1983, prod. Lloyd Maines, Terry Allen) ♫♫ is a little hard to swallow. Allen's current label, Sugar Hill, planned to reissue it as a two-for-one package with *Smokin' the Dummy* in 1997.

the rest:
Juarez (Fate, 1981) ♫♫
Smokin' the Dummy (Fate, 1982) ♫♫♫
Pedal Steel/Rollback (Fate, 1985) ♫♫
Bloodlines/Smokin' the Dummy (Sugar Hill, 1997) ♫♫♫

worth searching for: Allen's involvement in theater is almost as significant as his musical output, with two records worth finding. *Amerasia* (Fate, 1984, prod. Terry Allen) ♫♫♫ is an out-of-print album that followed a play about Amerasian children in South Vietnam, while *Songs from Chippy* (Hollywood, 1994, prod. Joe Ely, Terry Allen) ♫♫♫ features two originals and two

songs he helped write for the musical theater piece based on the diaries of a 1930s Texas madame that Allen conceived with wife and actress Jo Harvey Allen and fellow Texans Ely, Hancock and Jo Carol Pierce.

influences:
◀◀ Hank Williams, Buddy Holly
▶▶ Joe Ely, Butch Hancock, Jimmie Dale Gilmore

Doug Pullen

AMY ALLISON /PARLOR JAMES

Born June 24, 1958, in New York, NY.

The daughter of jazz great Mose Allison, Amy Allison puts contemporary twists on the lyin'/cheatin'/drinkin' themes made popular during the 1960s, often by playing the remorseful antagonist rather than the victim: she's the one pouring a shot and pouring her heart into an apology letter in the waltzing "Cheater's World" and sorting through the foggy details of a one-night stand in the hangover-nursing "The Whiskey Makes You Sweeter." Her quavering, nasal alto and humorous viewpoints—marked by daring, deliberately awkward rhymes ("If you cared just a smidgen/you'd walk through that kitchen")—sometimes paint her as a satirist rather than a backhanded traditionalist. But, like Junior Brown, Allison's pure-hearted intentions shine through via her deeply rooted affection for country music's heritage—in this case, Loretta Lynn's late 1960s declarations of independence. In between East Coast club shows with her band, the Maudlins, Allison collaborates with former Lone Justice guitarist Ryan Hedgecock in a promising gothic-country duo called Parlor James.

what to buy: Allison's *The Maudlin Years* (Koch, 1996, prod. Brian Dewan, Jordan Chassan, others) ♫♫♫♫ is drawn from demo sessions recorded between 1987–93, but the twangy, low-fi performances hold together remarkably well. In between such trademark ballads as "Cheater's World" and "The Whiskey Makes You Sweeter," Allison tackles society's bias against interracial dating in the deceptively catchy "Hate at First Sight" and drowns her sorrows in "Garden State Mall" by replacing an alcoholic bender with a shopping binge ("I bought some perfume at Saks/Blue jeans at the Gap/And a whole album for just one song").

what to buy next: Parlor James' debut, *Dreadful Sorry* (Discovery, 1996, prod. Malcolm Burn, Parlor James) ♫♫♫, is a six-song collection of fleshed-out four-track recordings that echo the

Dave Alvin (© **Ken Settle**)

gothic blues of Gillian Welch and the spooky soundscapes of Lisa Germano.

worth searching for: A country-rock compilation of 7" truck-stop jukebox singles called *Rig Rock Truck Stop* (Diesel Only, 1993, prod. various) 🎵🎵🎵 includes a different recording of "Cheater's World," discernable mainly by a clearer, more forceful Allison vocal.

influences:
⏪ Loretta Lynn, Syd Straw

David Okamoto

DAVE ALVIN

Born November 11, 1955, in Los Angeles, CA.

As a member of the Blasters, Dave Alvin coined the term "American Music," and he has spent the rest of his career defining it by crafting a distinctive brand of music commonly called roots—a genre that draws on such solidly domestic forms as country, vintage R&B, rockabilly and blues. After a split with his brother Phil ended the Blasters' too-brief run, Alvin joined X for one album, then began a solo career that has been defined by songs with a gift for narrative and a fine poetic sense that cuts through Alvin's brusk delivery. He also plays a mean lead guitar. Of late, Alvin has gained a reputation as producer of West Coast roots music, and he put together the excellent Merle Haggard tribute *Tulare Dust* in 1994.

what to buy: *Blue Blvd* (HighTone, 1991, prod. Chris Silagyi, Dave Alvin, Bruce Bromberg) 🎵🎵🎵🎵 reads like a book of short stories and rocks like nobody's business. "Haley's Comet," co-written with Tom Russell, recounts the dubious end of rock 'n' roll legend Bill Haley, while "Andersonville" is the most vivid song about the Civil War since "The Night They Drove Old Dixie Down." *King of California* (HighTone, 1994, prod. Greg Leisz) 🎵🎵🎵🎵 is an acoustic-based album on which Alvin finally grew into his voice, allowing quieter arrangements to show off its distinctiveness rather than its limitations. You could carp about Alvin taking yet another run at "Fourth of July," but such songs as "Barn Burning," which rolls like a freight train, and the lush title track, Alvin's best ballad ever, more than make up for the repetition.

what to buy next: *Romeo's Escape* (Epic, 1987, prod. Steve Berlin, Mark Linett) ♫♫♫ contains some of Alvin's finest songs, including several reprised from the Blasters' albums. And while some of the arrangements—notably "Border Radio"—cast the songs in new light, Alvin's limited vocal abilities hold him back. *Museum of Heart* (HighTone, 1993, prod. Chris Silagyi, Bruce Bromberg, Dave Alvin) ♫♫♫ is a wrenching album of heartbreak, as most of its 13 tracks sift through the shards of a shattered relationship. The best of the lot, "Don't Talk about Her" and "A Woman's Got a Right," could be seen as the laments of a man smart enough to see both sides of the story.

the rest:

Dave Alvin & the Guilty Men—*Interstate City* (HighTone, 1996) ♫♫♫♫

worth searching for: *The Pleasure Barons Live in Las Vegas* (HighTone, 1993, prod. Mark Linett, Country Dick Montana) ♫♫♫ is of more interest to serious fans of any one of the principals—Alvin, Mojo Nixon, and the late, lamented Country Dick Montana—than it is to the general populace. Alvin's cover versions of "Closing Time" and "Gangster of Love" stand out, but Country Dick's Tom Jones medley has to be heard to be believed.

influences:

◀◀ Big Joe Turner, Sonny Burgess, Chuck Berry, Hank Williams, Merle Haggard

▶▶ Big Sandy & His Fly-Rite Boys, Reverend Horton Heat, Jason & the Scorchers

see also: *Blasters*

Daniel Durchholz

PHIL ALVIN

Born March 6, 1953, in Los Angeles, CA.

Alvin served as mouthpiece for brother Dave's songs in the 1980's rockabilly punk outfit the Blasters, but he's taken more of a Ry Cooder-ish ethnomusicological tack on his own. He can seem pedantic, but Alvin knows his stuff—and, man oh man, what a voice.

what to buy: If a confident smile had a sound, it would be Alvin singing "Someone Stole Gabriel's Horn." That's one of the songs on Alvin's wonderful solo debut, *Un "Sung Stories"* (Slash, 1986, prod. Phil Alvin, Pat Burnett) ♫♫♫, which hits the perfect balance between scholarly authenticity and goofball fun. Never one to shy away from a challenge, Alvin sets his swaggering country-blues bullroar against the astral polyrhythms of the Sun Ra Arkestra and Dirty Dozen Brass Band, and more than holds his own.

the rest:

County Fair 2000 (HighTone, 1994) ♫♫♫

influences:

◀◀ Big Joe Turner, Hank Williams, Cab Calloway

see also: *Blasters*

David Menconi

THE AMAZING RHYTHM ACES

Formed 1972, in Memphis, TN. Disbanded 1980. Reunited 1994.

Russell Smith, guitar, vocals; Butch McDade, drums, percussion; Barry "Byrd" Burton, guitar, dobro (1972–77); Billy Earhart III, keyboards; Jeff Davis, bass; Duncan Cameron, guitar (1977–80, 1994); Danny Parks, guitar (1996–present).

Formed by Russell Smith and Butch McDade, the Amazing Rhythm Aces were essentially a country band that blended elements of old-time music, bluegrass, R&B and Western swing into its repertoire. The band is probably most well known for the hit single "Third Rate Romance," which appeared on its debut album, *Stacked Deck*. Subsequent albums lacked *Stacked Deck*'s verve and drive, although in 1976 Russell's "The End Is Not in Sight" garnered the band a Grammy award. After the group formally disbanded in 1980, Billy Earhart joined the Bama Band, Duncan Cameron joined Sawyer Brown and Russell Smith, after releasing a solo album, joined Run C&W, a country/bluegrass group that parodied the rap phenomenon.

what's available: The group reunited in 1994 and released *Ride Again* (ARA, 1994, prod. Russell Smith) ♫♫♫, for which they hand-picked their favorite Aces tunes from the past and re-recorded them.

worth searching for: *Stacked Deck* (MCA, 1975, prod. Barry "Byrd" Burton) ♫♫♫ contains "Third Rate Romance," which showcases some hot guitar playing by Barry Burton, and the bluesy, gospel-tinged "Life's Railway to Heaven."

influences:

◀◀ Boxtops

▶▶ Sammy Kershaw, Sawyer Brown

see also: *Sawyer Brown*

Rick Petreycik

AL ANDERSON

Born July 26, 1947, in Windsor, CT.

Singer/songwriter/guitarist Al Anderson charted his first single in 1967 when his band the Wildweeds hit #88 on *Billboard* with "No Good to Cry," a song later recorded by early Allman Brothers incarnation the Hour Glass. He recorded one album with the Wildweeds (Vanguard, 1970) and released his self-titled solo debut in 1972 (also on Vanguard). Anderson spent most of the 1970s and all of the 1980s with visionary musical boundary-stretchers NRBQ and saw his songs covered by a host of acts, including Dave Edmunds, the Long Ryders and the Fabulous Thunderbirds. *Musician* magazine named Anderson one of the top 100 guitar players of the century in 1993. He left NRBQ in the early 1990s to devote more time to songwriting and has become one of country music's most in-demand songwriters. He has collaborated with the Mavericks' Raul Malo, Hal Ketchum, Carlene Carter and Lari White and written songs recorded by all of the above, as well as by Deana Carter, Tanya Tucker, Jerry Lee Lewis, Sammy Kershaw and Aaron Tippin, to name a few.

what to buy: *Pay Before You Pump* (Imprint, 1996, prod. Scott Baggett) ♫♫♫♫ is a sinewy gumbo of the musical styles that have always been at the heart of Anderson's songs: Memphis soul, New Orleans funk, Western swing, country, rockabilly and rock. It includes the songwriter's versions of tunes recorded by Tippin and Shenandoah as well as co-writes with John Hiatt, Bill Lloyd, Sharon Rice and Nashville songwriting aces Craig Wiseman and Bob DiPiero.

what to buy next: *Peek-a-Boo: The Best of NRBQ 1969–1989* (Rhino, 1990, prod. various; prod. for CD by Bill Inglot) ♫♫♫♫ is the essential introduction to this savvy journeyman band, with Anderson's signature as a songwriter and player etched throughout. The collection contains "Get Rhythm," the Johnny Cash song that Big Al delivered convincingly enough to pass for its author.

worth searching for: *Wildweeds* (Vanguard, 1970, prod. Maynard Solomon) ♫♫♫, the first album to bear an Anderson songwriting credit (he wrote 11 of the 12 cuts; the other is Arthur

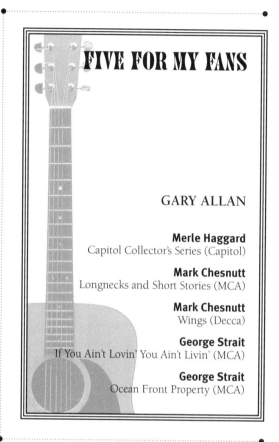

FIVE FOR MY FANS

GARY ALLAN

Merle Haggard
Capitol Collector's Series (Capitol)

Mark Chesnutt
Longnecks and Short Stories (MCA)

Mark Chesnutt
Wings (Decca)

George Strait
If You Ain't Lovin' You Ain't Livin' (MCA)

George Strait
Ocean Front Property (MCA)

Crudup's "My Baby Left Me"), is a long-out-of-print folk- and country-rock gem that, even with its undisciplined sound, points to Anderson's burgeoning songwriting gifts. Two of the songs here were covered by Matthews' Southern Comfort, Ian Matthews' popular turn-of-the-1970s folk-rock band.

influences:

◀◀ Chuck Berry, Johnny Cash

▶▶ Carlene Carter, John Hiatt

David Sokol

BILL ANDERSON

Born November 1, 1937, in Columbia, SC.

Born in South Carolina, Bill Anderson grew up in Georgia, then considered the heartland of country music. He began working on his guitar chording at an early age. While in high school, he formed his own country band and won a talent contest for one of his original songs. After high school, Anderson attended the University of Georgia, where he earned his B.A. in journalism. During his college years Anderson played shows in Atlanta and surrounding suburbs while hosting his own radio program. Meanwhile, he kept writing country songs, getting his first break in 1958 when Ray Price turned his "City Lights" into a hit. Shortly after that, Anderson signed with Decca and began touring and recording on his own. By the 1960s, his credits snowballed with such chart-toppers as "Tips of My Fingers" and the Jim Reeves hit "I Missed Me." Other Anderson #1 songs included "Happy Birthday to Me," "Walk Out Backwards," "Po' Folks" and "8 x 10." Anderson's hit parade lasted into the 1970s, with hits such as "I Still Feel the Same Way about You," "Country D.J.," "I Can't Wait Any Longer" and "Double S." He also enjoyed duet success with Mary Lou Turner and Jan Howard. The 1980s began a new phase of Anderson's career as he turned his sights toward television, particularly emceeing game shows. He has enjoyed a revival of late, co-hosting the Grand Ole Opry's television interview show on TNN and writing with newer artists such as Steve Wariner.

what to buy: *Whispering Bill: Bill Anderson's Greatest Hits* (Varese Sarabande, 1996, prod. various) covers the different stages of Anderson's career. It contains his ballads (the ones that earned him the nickname) as well as his honky-tonk numbers and country disco songs.

what to buy next: *Greatest Songs* (Curb, 1996, prod. various) overlaps a bit with *Whispering Bill*, but it's the next best compilation.

what to avoid: *Country Music Heaven* (Curb, 1992, prod. various) is the weakest of Curb's Anderson packages.

the rest:
The Best of Bill Anderson (Curb, 1991)

influences:
◀◀ Red Foley, Roy Acuff
▶▶ Steve Wariner, Vince Gill

Ronnie McDowell

JOHN ANDERSON
Born December 13, 1954, in Orlando, FL.

They don't call John Anderson the "Comeback Kid" for nothing. Anderson's curving, pained vocals made "I'm Just an Old Chunk of Coal (But I'm Gonna' Be a Diamond Someday)" a huge hit during the late 1970s. The chunky singer from Florida reeled off more than a dozen hits before he seemingly disappeared in the

late 1980s. Actually, Anderson kept plugging away, changing record companies before settling with upstart BNA and reviving his career during the 1990s with "Seminole Wind." Drawing on pop, rock and folk as well as traditional country influences, Anderson wraps his slow, nasal twang around breezy melodies in a way that hasn't changed all that much over the years, but manages to stay fashionable most of the time.

what to buy: *Seminole Wind* (BNA, 1992, prod. James Stroud and John Anderson) brought back Anderson's winsome sound convincingly. Anderson brings a timeless quality to songs like "Tequila Night" and the title track, to name a few. There's nary a weak link on this inspired return to form, and new friends like Dire Straits' Mark Knopfler chip in.

what to buy next: Unfortunately, most of Anderson's early albums on Warner Bros. are no longer in print, but the label had the foresight—and profit motive—to keep most of those hits alive on a pair of greatest hits collections. The first, *Greatest Hits* (Warner Bros., 1984, prod. various), includes some of Anderson's most impressive work, including the breezy "Swingin'," the wistful "1959" and "I'm Just An Old Chunk of Coal."

what to avoid: *Greatest Hits Vol. 2* (Warner Bros., 1984, prod. various) is not as consistent nor as interesting as its predecessor, since it documents Anderson's more sporadic output during his final years with the label.

the rest:
Too Tough to Tame (Liberty, 1990)
Solid Ground (BNA, 1993)
Country 'til I Die (BNA, 1994)
Christmas Time (BNA, 1994)
Swingin' (BNA, 1995)
Paradise (BNA, 1996)
Greatest Hits (BNA, 1996)

worth searching for: The classy, refined production on Anderson's first digitally recorded album, *Blue Skies Again* (MCA, 1987, prod. Jimmy Bowen, John Anderson), enhances a good mix of originals and covers, including a duet with Waylon Jennings on Jennings' "Somewhere between Ragged and Right."

influences:
◀◀ George Jones, Merle Haggard
▶▶ Randy Travis, Ricky Van Shelton

Doug Pullen

Pete Anderson (© Ken Settle)

LYNN ANDERSON

Born September 26, 1947, in Grand Forks, ND.

Lynn Anderson came to country music through her mother, singer-songwriter Liz Anderson, who wrote "(My Friends Are Gonna Be) Strangers" and "The Fugitive" for Merle Haggard and had her own Top Five hit in 1967 with "Mama Spank." Anderson's first love, though, was horses; she was a frequent ribbon winner at equestrian shows during her teens. As her mother began to place songs, young Lynn began to sing and make records: she had her first Top Five hit in 1967 with "If I Kiss You (Will You Go Away)" on Chart Records. She joined the cast of *The Lawrence Welk Show* in 1968, but left when she married Glenn Sutton and the couple moved to Hendersonville, Tennessee. Sutton, who had country ambitions himself, wrote Jerry Lee Lewis' "What Made Milwaukee Famous" as well as Anderson's hit "You're My Man." He also produced many of Anderson's records. Anderson's hits spanned more than 20 years and included a handful of #1 hits, none more successful than 1970's "Rose Garden," which also reached #3 on the pop chart. "Rose Garden" became Anderson's signature song, winning her a Grammy award, the 1971 Country Music Association Female Vocalist of the Year honor, plus a gold single and album. Anderson and Sutton divorced in 1977, and she also had an unsuccessful second marriage that ended in a bitter divorce battle in 1981. The problems and publicity surrounding her second divorce effectively ended Anderson's singing career, though she occasionally continued to make fine albums into the 1990s.

what to buy: Even with its early 1970s production mindset, the music on Anderson's *Greatest Hits* (Columbia, 1972, prod. Glenn Sutton) 🎵🎵🎵 holds up well almost three decades later. It includes "Rose Garden," of course, as well as follow-up chart-toppers "How Can I Unlove You" and "You're My Man." Anderson tends to get lumped in with the many female singers who fell in behind Dolly Parton, Tammy Wynette and Loretta Lynn, but this is an album well worth hearing. The songs on *Country Spotlight* (Dominion, 1991) 🎵🎵🎵 are faithful rerecordings of her hits.

what to buy next: Smarting from the effects of a divorce on her career, the one-time California Horse Show Queen returned to her first love—horses—and made an album reflecting just that. *Cowboy's Sweetheart* (LaserLight, 1992, prod. Ralph Jungheim) 🎵🎵🎵 contains the obvious Western numbers ("I Want to Be a Cowboy's Sweetheart," "The Wayward Wind"), but also her own versions of songs associated with Dan Fogelberg ("Run for the Roses"), Rodney Crowell ("Even Cowgirls Get the Blues") and Michael Johnson ("Ponies"). That Anderson would come up with an album this good so many years after her commercial peak suggests that her career could have become even bigger than it did.

influences:
◄◄ Liz Anderson, Dolly Parton
►► Barbara Mandrell, Trisha Yearwood

Brian Mansfield

PETE ANDERSON

Born July 23, 1948, in Detroit, MI.

Pete Anderson silently shares in the success of fellow Midwesterner Dwight Yoakam as his producer and guitarist. Save the occasional solo, Anderson—raised amidst the rock and Motown influences of Detroit, but with lots of country played at home by his parents—has rarely ventured into the spotlight. But in the early 1990s he set up his own label, Little Dog, originally to release his solo work. The label has begun to take on new acts that catch the adroit producer's ear, with plans to branch out beyond country.

what's available: Anderson's solo album, *Working Class* (Little Dog, 1994, prod. Anthony Crawford, Pete Anderson) 🎵🎵🎵, emphasizes his blues and rock roots more than anything he's done with Yoakam, but his retro sensibilities aren't too hard to find.

influences:
◄◄ Buck Owens, Elvis Presley
►► Dwight Yoakam, Sara Evans

Doug Pullen

ARCHER/PARK

Vocal duo formed 1993, in Nashville, TN. Disbanded 1996.

Randy Archer (born in Swainsboro, GA), vocals; Johnny Park (born in Arlington, TX), vocals.

Randy Archer and Johnny Park each moved to Nashville, searching (unsuccessfully) for record deals. The pair got separate songwriting deals at the same publishing company, where they hooked up and decided to go it as a duo.

what's available: *We Got a Lot in Common* (Atlantic, 1994, prod. Randy Scruggs) 🎵🎵 proves that Archer & Park have a lot in common with Brooks & Dunn, Orrall & Wright, Baker & Myers, and not much that distinguishes them from any of those duos. Featured songs include "Where There's Smoke" ("you'll find my old flame"—their hit) and "Your Ol' Rock" ("is just a stone's throw away").

influences:
◄◄ Brooks & Dunn
►► Thrasher Shiver

Brian Mansfield

influences:
◄◄ Pete Cassell, Bing Crosby
►► Jim Reeves, Ricky Van Shelton

Stephen L. Betts

EDDY ARNOLD

Born May 15, 1918, in Henderson, TN.

A sharecropper's son whose mother taught him guitar, Eddy Arnold went from playing on a local radio station in nearby Jackson, Tennessee, to earning a spot as vocalist with Pee Wee King's popular outfit, the Golden West Cowboys, from 1940 to 1943. Signing to RCA in 1944, the "Tennessee Plowboy," as he had become known, was soon managed by Colonel Tom Parker, who later handled Elvis' career. While his crooning led to both wide acceptance from pop audiences and numerous television appearances, Eddy Arnold became, and remains today, the #1 recording artist in country music, with nearly 150 charted singles over four decades. During the mid-1960s, Arnold's career hit its zenith: he was elected to the Country Music Hall of Fame in 1966, a year *before* he was named the first Country Music Association Entertainer of the Year. From his Western-influenced hits like "Cattle Call," (#1, 1955), to the enormous success of pop ballads like "I'll Hold You in My Heart (till I Can Hold You in My Arms)" (#1 for 21 weeks in 1947), Arnold's influence on country artists who successfully crossed over to pop throughout the 1950s and 1960s (not mention the last three decades) has probably been underestimated—and certainly not as well documented by his longtime record label as it should be.

what to buy: *The Essential Eddy Arnold* (RCA, 1996, prod. various) 🎵🎵🎵🎵🎵 is the best of the best, although it includes only 20 tracks.

what to buy next: *The Best of Eddy Arnold* (RCA, 1988, prod. various) 🎵🎵🎵 is an older, shorter (and cheaper) variation of *Essential,* but the biggest hits are here, and in their original versions, unlike many of the reissues.

what to avoid: With the *Essential* CD now available, both *Greatest Hits* (Curb, 1991) 🎵🎵 and *Greatest Songs* (Curb, 1995) 🎵are obsolete.

the rest:
Pure Gold (RCA, 1992) 🎵🎵🎵
Last of the Love Song Singers: Now and Then (RCA, 1993) 🎵🎵
Memories Are Made of This (Mercury, 1995) 🎵🎵🎵

ERNEST ASHWORTH

Born December 15, 1928, in Huntsville, AL.

Ernest Ashworth came to country music through radio, performing on Alabama stations before joining WSIX in Nashville. He first recorded as Billy Worth for MGM in 1955, but had his hits as Ernest (and later "Ernie") Ashworth, beginning in 1960 with "Each Moment (Spent with You)" on Decca. His only #1 came in 1963 with "Talk Back Trembling Lips"; it became such a signature song for him that he wore spangled suits embroidered with big red lips. He joined the Grand Ole Opry the next year and continued having hits through 1970. Ashworth is still in radio: he's built a second career on buying, reviving and re-selling small AM radio stations in the South.

what's available: *Greatest Hits* (Curb, 1991, prod. various) 🎵🎵, a 12-song collection, culls the most popular tunes from Ashworth's heyday with Hickory Records (1962–68). It's mostly flimsy honky-tonk, and Ashworth's nasal voice makes him hard to listen to for long stretches, but his most maudlin songs (i.e., "Talk Back Trembling Lips," "The DJ Cried") are entertaining.

Brian Mansfield

ASLEEP AT THE WHEEL

Formed 1970, in Paw Paw, WV.

Ray Benson, guitar, vocals; Lucky Oceans, pedal steel; Leroy Preston, drums, guitar, vocals; and a cast of nearly thousands.

The brainchild and passion of its towering frontman and sole surviving founding member, Ray Benson, Asleep at the Wheel got its start in West Virginia as an attempt to keep the spirit of traditional country and Western music, particularly Western swing, alive. Benson moved the band to Austin, Texas, during the early 1970s and managed to weather myriad personnel changes while keeping his artistic vision intact. Musically the group pays tribute to and updates Texas swing, blues, rock and even pop—along with jazz, Cajun, blues, rock and hardcore country. Its various lineups have included double fiddle, accordion, pedal steel, sax, guitar, mandolin, keyboards and harmonica, with each new face bringing something fresh to the mix. Recognition has come slowly to this eclectic, elastic band of Texas transplants. But it has come. Among the group's recent accolades are two Grammys for its loving Bob Wills tribute album.

what to buy: For lots of pure Wheel fun, check out the boxed set *Still Swingin'* (Liberty, 1994, prod. various) 𝄞𝄞𝄞𝄞, which features a wide range of material, from previously unreleased obscurities to remakes of AATW staples featuring such high profile guests as Garth Brooks and Dolly Parton. This exhaustive collection features 51 tracks, including Wheel spokes like "Take Me Back to Tulsa," "Route 66," "The Letter That Johnny Walker Read" and some of its best lesser-known stuff, like the torchy "Ruler of My Heart" (featuring former AATW vocalist Chris O'Connell).

what to buy next: *Asleep at the Wheel: Tribute to the Music of Bob Wills and the Texas Playboys* (Liberty, 1993, prod. Ray Benson and Allen Reynolds) 𝄞𝄞𝄞 is the most ambitious album this little ol' swing band from Texas ever attempted. Wills is the band's sturdiest musical root, so with surviving Playboys Johnny Gimble and Eldon Shamblin in tow, the Wheels and guests (Lyle Lovett, Chet Atkins, Vince Gill, George Strait, Garth Brooks) eloquently and faithfully recreated Wills' signatures, including "Red Wine" and "Corine, Corina." The album won two Grammys and spawned a line dance remix album (Liberty, 1994, prod. Ray Benson and Allen Reynolds) 𝄞𝄞.

what to avoid: Benson has spent most of the 1990s looking back on the band's career, with hits albums, live albums and a box set. A misguided attempt to combine all of those formats, *Greatest Hits (Live & Kickin')* (Arista, 1992, prod. Ray Benson) 𝄞𝄞, doesn't do the band's live show, or its legacy, any justice.

the rest:
Asleep at the Wheel (MCA, 1985) 𝄞𝄞
10 (Epic, 1987) 𝄞𝄞𝄞
Western Standard Time (Epic, 1988) 𝄞𝄞𝄞
Keepin' Me Up Nights (Arista, 1990) 𝄞𝄞
The Swingin' Best of (Epic, 1992) 𝄞𝄞𝄞
The Wheel Keeps on Rollin' (Capitol, 1995) 𝄞𝄞

worth searching for: The Wheel's earliest, edgier efforts are long out of print. One vinyl album worth tracking down is *Collison Course* (Capitol, 1978, prod. Ray Benson) 𝄞𝄞𝄞𝄞, which captured the band in all its stylistic diversity, with two fiddlers, velvet-voiced singer Chris O'Connell and pedal steel guitarist extraordinaire Lucky Oceans.

influences:
◄◄ Bob Wills, Phil Harris, Count Basie, Merle Haggard
►► Lyle Lovett and His Large Band, Marty Stuart, Mark O'Connor, Alison Krauss

Doug Pullen

ASYLUM STREET SPANKERS
Formed 1995, in Austin, TX.

Josh Arnson, guitar, vocals; Pops Bayless, banjo, mandolin, ukelele, vocals; Jimmie Dean, brush snare, vocals; Guy Forsyth, guitar, vocals, harmonica; Olivier Giraud, guitar, vocals; Mysterious John, vocals, kazoo; Christina Marrs, vocals, ukelele; Kevin Smith, upright bass; Stanley Smith, clarinet, vocals; Wammo, washboard, vocals.

These 10 musicians have Austin branded on their performances, and they make no apologies for it. After all, they're some of the city's best musicians. As veterans of a handful of separate electric bands, the players found a magical sound one drunken night at the Llano Hotel: when all got there, nobody had brought the PA. Thus, the Spankers' debut is a largely engaging example of Texas musical purity.

what's available: The Spankers recorded *Spanks for the Memories* (Watermelon, 1996, prod. Mark Rubin) 𝄞𝄞𝄞 with one microphone in the living room of an historic Austin house. The resulting sound quality is a love letter to the days of vinyl. A nod to Lee Harvey Oswald suggests a twisted nostalgia as well; there's also a healthy chunk of nudge-nudge humor in general here, initially evidenced by the band's name.

influences:
◄◄ Homer & Jethro, Skillet Lickers, everyone else named in "Starting to Hate Country"

Craig Shelburne

CHET ATKINS
Born June 20, 1924, in Lutrell, TN.

An internationally known guitar wizard who guided many artists' careers (from Elvis to Dottie West to Steve Wariner) as label executive/producer for RCA, Chet Atkins, for better or worse, was an important contributor to what became known as the "Nashville Sound"—also referred to as "countrypolitan" music, mixing pop rhythms and instrumentation with country elements, and incorporating classical, jazz and other music as well. Atkins' first instrument was a fiddle, which he learned as a child before switching to guitar at age nine. His first professional job was as part of the Bill Carlisle Show on WNOX radio in Knoxville. Other artists he worked with early in his career included Homer and Jethro, Mother Maybelle and the Carter Sisters and Red Foley. Hired as assistant to RCA label executive Steve Sholes in 1952, Atkins played on numerous sessions for other artists, recorded many solo albums featuring his Merle Travis-influenced finger-picking style, and began producing countless records for RCA artists. He also helped guide the careers of artists on other labels, most notably the Everly Brothers. By 1957 Atkins was in charge of recording operations for RCA's Nashville office, and became a label vice-president in 1968. After winning a number of Grammys and Country Music Association awards throughout the 1970s, Atkins left RCA in 1982 to sign with Columbia Records, for whom he continues to record. Highlights of the last decade include his tasteful collaborations with artists like Dire Straits' leader Mark Knopfler, Suzy Bogguss and Steve Wariner. Atkins was elected to the Country Music Hall of Fame in 1973.

what to buy: In spite of limited chart success, *The Essential Chet Atkins* (RCA, 1996, prod. various) ♪♪♪♪ is a collection of 20 tracks that are a good indication of Atkins' influence as instrumentalist and producer.

what to buy next: Chet Atkins and Mark Knopfler's *Neck and Neck* (CBS, 1990, prod. Mark Knopfler) ♪♪♪♪ is a collaborative effort that, while sticking pretty close to the pattern established by most of Atkin's recent records, is distinguished by the sheer joy the two obviously have in working together. *The RCA Years* (RCA, 1992, prod. various) ♪♪♪♪, a two-CD set, isn't quite the value of *The Essential,* but it's still worthwhile.

the rest:
Chet Atkins Picks on the Beatles (RCA, 1966/1996) ♪♪♪♪
East Tennessee Christmas (Columbia, 1983) ♪♪♪
Street Dreams (Columbia, 1986) ♪♪♪
Sails (Columbia, 1987) ♪♪♪
Chet Atkins, C.G.P. (Columbia, 1989) ♪♪♪♪
Read My Licks (Sony, 1994) ♪♪♪
Almost Alone (Sony, 1996) ♪♪♪

influences:
◄◄ Merle Travis, Les Paul
►► Mark Knopfler, Lenny Breau

Stephen L. Betts

MIKE AULDRIDGE
See: Seldom Scene, Chesapeake

REID & COLEMAN AULDRIDGE
See: Seldom Scene, Chesapeake

AUSTIN LOUNGE LIZARDS
Formed 1980, in Austin, TX.

Hank Card, vocals, guitar; Conrad Deisler, vocals, guitar; Tom

Chet Atkins **(AP/Wide World Photos)**

Pittman, vocals, banjo, pedal steel; Michael Stevens bass, vocals (1980–84); Tim Wilson, mandolin, fiddle, vocals (1980–84); Kirk Williams, bass, vocals (1984–95); Paul Sweeney, mandolin, vocals (1984–93); Richard Bowden, fiddle, mandolin, vocals (1993–present); Boo Resnick, bass, vocals (1995–present).

It's telling that in the *Austin Chronicle*'s annual readers poll, the award the Austin Lounge Lizards have walked away with more than once is Best None of the Above Band, for this ensemble does indeed resist categorization. Offering the instrumentation and harmonies of a progressive bluegrass outfit, the group quotes liberally from rock 'n' roll songs (a mandolin-driven cover of Pink Floyd's "Brain Damage" is a notable example), and comes with a wry sense of humor to boot. It may be a stretch, but imagine the cast of *Hee Haw* if it was mildly dosed with LSD and had an Ivy League education (founders Card and Diesler met while both were history majors at Princeton). Detractors could probably tag the group a novelty, but the Lizards offer ample chops to go along with the yuks. And because the Lizards hail from the American music capital of Austin, their records are laced with guest appearances by such notables as

Junior Brown, Ray Benson, Katy Moffatt, Marcia Ball, Charlie Sexton and Jerry Jeff Walker.

what to buy: *The Highway Cafe of the Damned* (self-released, 1988/Watermelon, 1993, prod. Conrad Deisler) 🎝🎝🎝 offers the Lizards' most potent brew of bluegrass and hilarity. The titles— "Industrial Strength Tranquilizer," "When Drunks Go Bad" and "The Chester Nimitz Oriental Garden Waltz"—give some indication of the level of hijinks going on here. Meanwhile, "The Ballad of Ronald Reagan" indulges the group's political streak, and "Cornhusker Refugee" stands as perhaps the first (and only) gay-themed country song.

what to buy next: "Small Minds" (Watermelon, 1995, prod. Conrad Deisler) 🎝🎝🎝 fires satirical salvos at a number of targets: know-it-alls ("Old Blevins," "Gingrich the Newt") and know-nothings ("Life Is Hard, but Life Is Hardest When You're Dumb") take it in the neck all the same. And the New York downtown hipster scene gets a long-distance wake-up call with a version of Terry Allen's "Truckload of Art." Funny stuff. The six-song EP *Live Bait* (Watermelon, 1996, prod. Conrad Deisler) 🎝🎝🎝 contains a quick tour of Lizard history, from the witty 1981 tune "The Car Hank Died In" to the relatively recent political track "Teenage Immigrant Welfare Mother on Drugs."

the rest:

Creatures from the Black Saloon (self-released, 1984/Watermelon, 1993) 🎝🎝🎝

Lizard Vision (Flying Fish, 1991) 🎝🎝🎝

Paint Me on Velvet (Flying Fish, 1993) 🎝🎝🎝

influences:

◀◀ Homer & Jethro, John Hartford, Frank Zappa

▶▶ Junior Brown

Dan Durchholz

GENE AUTRY

Born Orvon Gene Autry, September 29, 1907, in Tioga Springs, TX.

In his younger days in Sepulpa, Oklahoma, Gene Autry passed the night working as a railroad telegraph operator. He picked his guitar to break the monotony and made up the occasional tune. One customer who heard his voice told him to quit the dead-end job and try the exciting, relatively new realm of radio. The customer was Will Rogers. Autry heeded his advice, headed to New York and never looked back.

Like Roy Rogers and Tex Ritter, Autry is also widely regarded for his endearing Western films, in which his heroic singing cowboy characters saved the day more than 100 times. Any American who was a youngster during the days of the 10-cent, double-feature matinee remembers the silver screen Autry. Kids today, however, are usually more familiar with the Christmas carols Autry introduced: "Frosty the Snow Man," "Rudolph, the Red-Nosed Reindeer" and the self-penned "Here Comes Santa Claus." Autry's mainstream hits include "Back in the Saddle Again," "Deep in the Heart of Texas" and "Don't Fence Me In"; a song written with Fred Rose during World War II, "At Mail Call Today," sold more than a million copies. An astute businessman as well, Autry also co-founded an American League professional baseball team, the Los Angeles Angels, now located in Anaheim.

what to buy: *The Essential Gene Autry (1933–1946)* (Columbia/Legacy, 1992, prod. various) 🎝🎝🎝 collects 18 songs from Autry's years with the Oriole, Vocalion, Okeh and Columbia labels. It includes not only such signature Western songs as 1939's "Back in the Saddle Again," but examples of the pop-oriented fare that Autry favored ("Blueberry Hill," "Maria Elena") as well.

what to buy next: The three-disc compilation *Sing, Cowboy, Sing: The Gene Autry Collection* (Rhino, 1997) 🎝🎝🎝 features much of the music from *Essential* but extends the scope to his later Columbia years, when Autry built a new career singing the original versions of holiday tunes like "Here Comes Santa Claus" and "Rudolph, the Red-Nosed Reindeer." This collection also includes previously unreleased transcriptions from *The Melody Ranch Radio Show*.

the rest:

Columbia Historic Edition (Columbia, 1982) 🎝🎝🎝

Country Music Hall of Fame Album (Columbia, 1987) 🎝🎝🎝

A Gene Autry Christmas (Columbia/Legacy, 1994) 🎝🎝🎝

Back in the Saddle Again (ASV, 1996) 🎝🎝🎝

worth searching for: In his early recording days, Autry seems to have been influenced almost equally by Jimmie Rodgers and Robert Johnson. *Blues Singer 1929–1931: "Booger Rooger Saturday Night"* (Legacy, 1996, prod. Lawrence Cohn) 🎝🎝🎝 shows a side of the singer that is otherwise largely hidden.

influences:

◀◀ Sons of the Pioneers, Jimmie Rodgers

▶▶ Rex Allen, Riders in the Sky

Craig Shelburne and Brian Mansfield

HOYT AXTON

Born May 25, 1938, in Duncan, OK.

From a songwriting family (his mother, Mae Axton, co-wrote

"Heartbreak Hotel"), the bearish, gruffy-voiced Axton has been a prolific songwriter and actor (*Heart Like a Wheel, Gremlins*) and sometime performer/recording artist. His songs have been covered by the Kingston Trio, Waylon Jennings, Glen Campbell, Tanya Tucker, John Denver and Commander Cody, although his biggest hits came from Three Dog Night ("Joy to the World," "Never Been to Spain") and Steppenwolf ("Snowblind Friend," "The Pusher"). Axton's albums were more modest, but he had a minor country hit with 1974's "When the Morning Comes."

what's available: *American Originals* (Capitol, 1992, prod. Todd Everett) 🎵🎵🎵 includes down-home sessions with the cream of L.A. folk/country musicians, the best of Axton's early 1970s Capitol work.

worth searching for: They're long out of print, but two of his A&M albums—*Life Machine* (A&M, 1974) 🎵🎵🎵, which includes "When the Morning Comes," and *Road Songs* (A&M, 1977) 🎵🎵🎵, a best-of—include some of his best writing and typically professional musicianship.

influences:
◀◀ Elvis Presley, Waylon Jennings
▶▶ Three Dog Night, Bobby Bare

Leland Rucker

STEVE AZAR

Born Stephen Thomas Azar, April 11, 1964, in Greenville, MS.

Although he grew up in the blues-soaked Mississippi Delta and claims to be very influenced by the music of that region, Steve Azar's debut has been produced so slicky that any resemblance to roots music is gone. It seems that in his effort to wed country and the blues, he's betrayed both. Azar's been at this a long time—he was writing songs and leading the church choir by the time he was in eighth grade, and when he was 15 he convinced his father to drive him from Mississippi to Nashville to record a demo. You have to believe that he could make a better record than his first one if given the chance.

what's available: Azar co-wrote 11 of the 12 songs on his debut, *Heartbreak Town* (River North, 1996, prod. Joe Thomas) 🎵🎵.

influences:
◀◀ Billy Dean, David Gates, Neil Diamond

Cyndi Hoelzle

THE BACKSLIDERS

Formed 1991, in Raleigh, NC.

Chip Robinson, vocals, guitar; Steve Howell, guitar, vocals; Brad Rice, guitar (1994–present); Danny Kurtz, bass; Jeff Dennis, drums.

The Backsliders were always a great band, but didn't become a special one until Brad Rice signed on as lead guitarist in 1994, adding a punkier fire to their hardcore honky-tonk. With Rice playing Johnny Thunders to Steve Howell's Buck Owens and Chip Robinson's . . . well, Chip Robinson, the Backsliders stepped to the forefront of 1990s alternative country.

what to buy: The group's full-length debut, *Throwin' Rocks at the Moon* (Mammoth/Atlantic, 1997, prod. Pete Anderson) 🎵🎵🎵, is full of tremendous songs you'd swear you've heard before—not because they're derivative, but because they're damn good, especially when Robinson sings 'em.

the rest:
From Raleigh, North Carolina (Mammoth EP, 1996) 🎵🎵🎵

influences:
◀◀ Beat Farmers, Flying Burrito Brothers, Neil Young, Buck Owens, True Believers

David Menconi

BAD LIVERS

Formed 1990, in Austin, TX.

Danny Barnes, banjo, guitar, mandolin, vocals; Ralph White, fiddle, accordion; Mark Rubin, bass, tuba, vocals; Bob Grant, mandolin, guitar.

Call it thrash-grass or bluegrass-punk, call it pickin'-and-grimacin', but don't call the Bad Livers late to dinner. This genre-busting trio plays a postmodern form of bluegrass that is informed as much by the Butthole Surfers and Motörhead as it is by Bill Monroe and Ralph Stanley. *Delusions of Banjer*, after all, was produced by Butthole Surfer Paul Leary, and the group has been known to reel off a high-stepping version of rock icon Iggy Pop's "Lust for Life" that inspires fits of furious tater-diggin'. It would be easy to dismiss the group as a novelty—Rubin's occasional tuba playing sticks out like a sore thumb—but they've got the chops to back up their non-traditional take on a traditional music.

Joan Baez (© Ken Settle)

what to buy: *Horses in the Mines* (Quarterstick, 1994, prod. Danny Barnes) ♬♬♬♬ contains plenty of attitude, but for the most part de-emphasizes the novelty elements that occasionally dominate *Delusions of Banjer*. Anyone doubting the Livers' ability to play pure bluegrass should check out their lightning-fast take on the old-time breakdown "Blue Ridge Express." White's "Chainsaw Therapy" is a fine fiddle tune, and the group's punk influences get a nod on "Puke Grub."

the rest:

Dust on the Bible (self-released, 1991/Quarterstick, 1994) ♬♬♬
Delusions of Banjer (Quarterstick, 1992) ♬♬♬♭
Hogs on the Highway (Sugar Hill, 1997) ♬♬♬♭

worth searching for: Seek out *The Golden Years* (Southern Studios, 1992, prod. Bad Livers) ♬♬♬♬, an import-only gold-vinyl EP that collects early radio transcriptions of covers and a medley of fiddle tunes.

influences:

◀◀ Bill Monroe, Ralph Stanley, Killbilly, Motörhead

Daniel Durchholz

JOAN BAEZ

Born January 9, 1941, in Staten Island, NY.

The acknowledged diva of the folk-music world, Joan Baez has recorded albums in five different decades and remains an influence to a whole new generation of female song interpreters today. Baez peaked commercially some 35 years ago with an array of studio and live albums that celebrated the protest movement and helped give credentials to the writings of Bob Dylan and Phil Ochs. Though that movement faded, Baez nonetheless remained a "committed" artist, and at the same time delved into a variety of new music forms, including Celtic, Latin and country. During the early 1970s Baez brought Robbie Robertson's "The Night They Drove Old Dixie Down" within a whisker of the top of the charts, and a few years later went gold again with her collection *Diamonds and Rust* before reuniting with Dylan in the Rolling Thunder Review. Recently, Baez has toured and recorded with such folk and country voices as Mary Chapin Carpenter, Tish Hinojosa and Dar Williams.

what to buy: Baez's most influential work comes from her early 1960s period, a good chunk of which is included on *The First Ten Years* (Vanguard, 1970/1987, prod. Maynard Solomon) ♬♬♬♬, also a sampler of Baez's later-1960s folk, Dylan and country soundings.

what to buy next: More than 20 years since its release, *Diamonds and Rust* (A&M, 1975, prod. David Kershenbaum) ♬♬♬♬ remains a remarkable "comeback" album, in which Baez demonstrated to the world that she wasn't about to be retired as an old-fogie folkie. Besides the memorable title track (her own), she covers Jackson Browne, John Prine and the Allman Brothers with real flair.

the rest:

Joan Baez in Concert, Volume 1 (Vanguard, 1962/1990) ♬♬♬♬
Joan Baez in Concert, Volume 2 (Vanguard, 1963/1990) ♬♬♬♬
Farewell Angelina (Vanguard, 1965) ♬♬♬♬
Noel (Vanguard, 1966) ♬♬♬
Joan (Vanguard, 1967) ♬♬♬
Any Day Now (Vanguard, 1968) ♬♬♬
Baptism (Vanguard, 1968) ♬♬♬
One Day at a Time (Vanguard, 1969) ♬♬
David's Album (Vanguard, 1969) ♬♬
Carry It On (Vanguard, 1972) ♬♬♬
Ballad Book (Vanguard, 1972) ♬♬♬♭
Hits/Greatest and Others (Vanguard, 1973) ♬♬♬♭
Lovesong Album (Vanguard, 1975) ♬♬♬

From Every Stage (A&M, 1976) ♪♪♪

Best Of (A&M, 1977) ♪♪♪

Blowin' Away (Epic Legacy, 1977/1990)

Honest Lullaby (Vanguard 1979/1990) ♪♪♪

The Night They Drove Old Dixie Down (Vanguard, 1979) ♪♪♪♪

Country Music (Vanguard, 1979) ♪♪♪

Very Early Joan (Vanguard, 1983) ♪♪♪♪

The Contemporary Ballad Book (Vanguard, 1987) ♪♪♪

Ballad Book, Volume 2 (Vanguard, 1990) ♪♪♪

Play Me Backwards (Virgin, 1992) ♪♪♪

Rare Live and Classic (Vanguard, 1993) ♪♪♪

Joan Baez Ballad Book (Vanguard, 1994) ♪♪♪♪

Ring Them Bells (Guardian, 1995) ♪♪♪

influences:

◀◀ Mother Maybelle Carter, Bob Dylan

▶▶ Nitty Gritty Dirt Band, Mary Chapin Carpenter

David Simons

BAILLIE & THE BOYS

Formed c. 1977, in NJ.

Kathie Baillie, vocals, guitar; Michael Bonagura, vocals, guitar; Allan LeBouef, vocals (1986–88); Roger McVay, vocals, bass (1995–present).

Kathie Baillie and Michael Bonagura were husband-and-wife backup singers when they moved to Nashville in 1983. With Allan LeBouef, they had toured as Baillie & the Boys, but Baillie and Bonagura had also sung studio harmonies for the Ramones and the Talking Heads. In Nashville, their credits ran toward Randy Travis and Dan Seals, and the trio eventually signed with RCA. With their unique vocal combination of female lead and two male harmonies, Baillie & the Boys had 10 Top 40 singles between 1987 and 1991, including "Long Shot" and "(I Wish I Had A) Heart of Stone." LeBouef left in 1988, and the group performed as a duo until 1995.

what's available: Though it contains none of the group's hits, *Lovin' Every Minute* (Intersound, 1996, prod. Michael Bonagura) ♪♪♪ may be Baille & the Boys' most musically satisfying album. Produced by Bonagura and mixed by long-time friend (and one-time Ramones producer) Ed Stasium, the album has a lean, tough sound that makes the most of the act's power-pop influences. Vince Gill is featured on "You're My Weakness," which he wrote with Kathie Baillie.

worth searching for: Baillie & the Boys released three albums and a greatest hits compilation for RCA, though all have gone out of print. The CD version of *The Best of Baillie & the Boys*

(RCA, 1991, prod. Kyle Lehning, John Boylan) ♪♪♪♪ contains all 10 of Baillie & the Boys' charting hits for RCA. (The cassette leaves off "Perfect.")

influences:

◀◀ Dan Seals

▶▶ Foster & Lloyd

Brian Mansfield

BAKER & MYERS

Formed 1994, in Nashville, TN.

Gary Baker (born Niagara Falls, NY), lead vocals; Frank Myers (born Dayton, OH), harmony vocals.

Gary Baker and Frank Myers were just another pair of frequent writing partners until John Michael Montgomery and then All-4-One had huge hits with a song of theirs called "I Swear." (The song and its recordings ended up winning country and R&B Grammys, a Country Music Association award, plus honors from the Nashville Songwriters Association and *Billboard*.) Suddenly, like seemingly every other pair of successful writers in Nashville, they were a duo as well. And, like most of those others duos, Baker & Myers have had a harder time finding their voice as artists than they did as writers.

Before recording together, Baker had performed with the pop act LeBlanc & Carr and country group the Shooters. Myers had appeared on Porter Wagoner's television show at age 14 and later played guitar for Eddy Raven. They have numerous individual songwriting credits, but they also wrote Alabama's "Once Upon a Lifetime" and "T.L.C. A.S.A.P." (with producer Josh Leo).

what's available: When the guys who created "I Swear" decide to sing the songs instead of just write them, you expect material at least as good as what they gave away. No such luck: *Baker & Myers* (MCG/Curb, 1994, prod. Nelson Larkin, Michael Hollandsworth) ♪♪ is strictly run-of-the-songmill country, with Everlys-like harmonies at the best moments.

influences:

◀◀ John Michael Montgomery, Orrall & Wright

▶▶ Archer/Park

Brian Mansfield

KENNY BAKER
/KENNY BAKER & JOSH GRAVES

Born June 26, 1926, in Jenkins, KY.

The man Bill Monroe called "the greatest bluegrass fiddler in the world" served three tours of duty with Monroe's Blue Grass Boys between 1957–84 after starting with Don Gibson in 1953. Baker worked extensively with dobroist John Graves (formerly with Flatt & Scruggs) during the 1990s.

what to buy: *Master Fiddler* (County, 1993, prod. Gary B. Reid) ♪♪♪♪ is one of the very best bluegrass fiddle albums to showcase Baker's work between 1968 and 1983. The 20 cuts include traditional numbers, songs learned as a child and six Baker originals, including "Grassy Fiddle Blues."

what to buy next: *The Puritan* (Rebel, 1972, prod. Dave Samuelson) ♪♪♪ Baker's earliest collaborations with Josh Graves, finds the noted fiddler playing guitar. *The Puritan* collects 24 songs the pair recorded in 1972 and 1973.

the rest:

Kenny Baker & Josh Graves—*The Puritan Sessions* (Rebel, 1972/1989) ♪♪♪

worth searching for: On *Darkness on the Delta* (County, 1980), Baker and another former Blue Grass Boy, fiddler Bobby Hicks, join together for an all-instrumental album of 11 originals, traditional numbers and bluegrass standards, including four from their original boss, Bill Monroe.

influences:

◄◄ Bill Monroe, Don Gibson

►► Bobby Hicks, Blaine Sprouse

Douglas Fulmer

BUTCH BALDASSARI

See: Lonesome Standard Time

DEWEY BALFA /THE BALFA BROTHERS

Born March 20, 1927, in Big Mamou, LA. Died June 17, 1992.

Master Cajun fiddler Dewey Balfa, along with his brothers Will, Harry and Rodney, was an early ambassador for traditional Cajun music around the world, first appearing at the Newport Folk Festival in 1964, playing guitar accompaniment with Gladius Thibodeaux and Louis Lejeune. Their wildly well-received performance led to Dewey's triumphant return three years later with a band that included brothers Rodney and Will, daughter Nelda and Hadley Fontenot. Dewey also had a long performing and recording career with the great accordionist Nathan Abshire, accompanying him on records from the 1950s onward. After the deaths of Rodney and Will in an auto accident in 1979,

Dewey continued to be a frequent, much loved and highly respected performer in traditional music venues of all types throughout the world.

what to buy: *The Balfa Brothers Play Traditional Cajun Music* (Swallow, 1967/1974, prod. Floyd Soileau) ♪♪♪♪ contains two classic albums the Balfas recorded for Swallow.

what to buy next: On *Under a Green Oak Tree* (Arhoolie, 1976) ♪♪♪♪, a Cajun supergroup composed of Dewey Balfa, Marc Savoy, and D.L. Menard plays a classic repertoire of traditional Cajun music. Also check out the Balfa Brothers' *J'ai Vu Le Loup, Le Renard et La Belette* (Rounder, 1975, prod. Gerard Dole) ♪♪♪.

the rest:

(With others) *Fait a La Main—Cajun Legend* (Swallow, 1991)

worth searching for: *Balfa Brothers—New York Concerts Plus* (1991, Ace) ♪♪♪ is a reissue of a Swallow album with many additional, previously unissued tracks. *The Good Times Are Killing Me* (Swallow, 1975, prod. Floyd Soileau) ♪♪♪ contains inspired recordings with Nathan Abshire.

influences:

◄◄ Leo Soileau, Harry Choates

►► Balfa Toujours, Steve Riley & the Mamou Playboys

Randy Pitts

DAVID BALL

Born July 9, 1953, in Rock Hill, SC.

Because he is the son of a Baptist preacher and a member of a musical family, there is an orthodoxy to David Ball's work, albeit in the musical, not the religious sense. A strict honky-tonker, Ball worships at the house of Hank, Lefty and Ol' Possum, and his offerings are songs of heartbreak amply embellished with fiddle and pedal steel guitar. Ball grew up on the South Carolina folk and country circuits, then moved to Austin, Texas, after signing on with Uncle Walt's Band. There he was exposed to hardcore Texas honky-tonk and Western swing, the elements that now dominate his sound. Ball is a fine singer and a songwriter with a sharp and often witty edge to his turns of phrase.

what to buy: The title track of *Thinkin' Problem* (Warner Bros., 1994, prod. Blake Chancey) ♪♪♪ is a pun so obvious that it's amazing no one thought of it until Ball took the charts by storm with what became one of the biggest singles of 1994. Ball's wit extends to "Blowin' Smoke" ("I say I've burned her memory/But I'm just blowin' smoke"), and "Honky-Tonk Healin'" ("It took some neon nurses around the clock to pull me through"). Ball also knows his way around a sensitive ballad, as he shows on "12/12/84" and "When the Thought of You Catches Up with Me." Altogether, it's a fine, well-rounded album. Ball's follow-up, *Starlite Lounge* (Warner Bros., 1995, prod. Ed Seay, Steve Buckingham) 𝄞𝄞𝄞𝄞 is just as good, led by the hard-charging "Hangin' In and Hangin' On" and the clever "Circle of Friends."

the rest:

David Ball (RCA, 1994) 𝄞𝄞𝄞

influences:

◀◀ George Jones, Webb Pierce, Hank Williams, Gary Stewart

▶▶ Royal Wade Kimes

Daniel Durchholz

MOE BANDY

Born February 12, 1944, in Meridian, MS.

Mississippi-born, Texas-raised Moe Bandy was a real throwback at the height of his success, making some of the finest roadhouse honky-tonk records at a time when the commercial drift of country music was toward the countrypolitan sound. In the best tradition of his honky-tonk forebears, Bandy sang about drinking and (especially) cheating with a doleful, wryly remorseful delivery that, while lacking the true grit of honky-tonk greats Hank Williams and George Jones, emphasized the sorry state to which his hell raising and philandering had brought him . Such classic titles as "Honky Tonk Amnesia," "It Was Always So Easy (To Find an Unhappy Woman)," "Hank Williams, You Wrote My Life," "That's What Makes the Jukebox Play," "Barstool Mountain" and "She's Not Really Cheatin' (She's Gettin' Even)" tell the story. His early hits were for GRC; when that label folded, Bandy signed with Columbia, who also bought his GRC masters. In 1986 he moved to MCA/Curb, and his honky-tonk sound on his solo albums all but disappeared amidst a sea of crossover-inspired arrangements, though he continued to cut good honky-tonk duets with buddy Joe Stampley, including 1979's #1, "Just Good Ol' Boys" and "Where's the Dress," their Boy George-inspired crossdressing spoof, also a Top 10 hit.

what to buy: *Honky Tonk Amnesia — The Hard Country Sound of Moe Bandy* (Razor & Tie, 1996, prod. Ray Baker) 𝄞𝄞𝄞𝄞𝄞 reissues the best of Moe's GRC and Columbia hits. *Greatest Hits* (Columbia, 1982, prod. Ray Baker) 𝄞𝄞𝄞𝄞 is a smaller sampling from the same period.

what to avoid: On *Greatest Hits* (Curb, 1990, prod. Ray Kennedy) 𝄞𝄞 Moe succumbs to the Nashville Sound, including

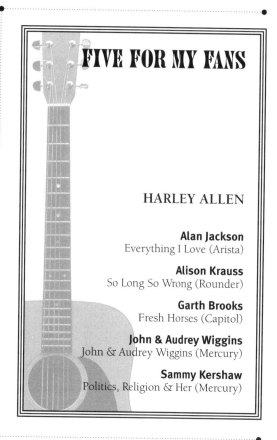

FIVE FOR MY FANS

HARLEY ALLEN

Alan Jackson
Everything I Love (Arista)

Alison Krauss
So Long So Wrong (Rounder)

Garth Brooks
Fresh Horses (Capitol)

John & Audrey Wiggins
John & Audrey Wiggins (Mercury)

Sammy Kershaw
Politics, Religion & Her (Mercury)

George Bush's fave, "Americana"; the pain is alleviated somewhat by a nice reading of Kevin Welch's "Too Old to Die Young."

the rest:

No Regrets (Curb, 1988) 𝄞𝄞
Many Mansions (Curb, 1989) 𝄞𝄞
Sings Great American Cowboy Songs (K-Tel, 1991) 𝄞𝄞
Live in Branson, MO, USA (Laserlight, 1993) 𝄞
You Haven't Heard the Last of Me (MCA, 1995) 𝄞𝄞

worth searching for: Moe Bandy & Joe Stampley's *Greatest Hits* (Columbia, 1982, prod. Ray Baker) 𝄞𝄞𝄞𝄞 is the best of Joe and Moe.

influences:

◀◀ Hank Williams, Lefty Frizzell

▶▶ Aaron Tippin, David Frizzell

Randy Pitts

BOBBY BARE

Born Robert Joseph Bare, April 7, 1935, in Ironton, OH.

With a career spanning 40 years, Bobby Bare has earned a much deserved reputation as a talented songwriter, singer, producer and sometime actor. Signed to RCA by Chet Atkins, Bare charted songs such as "Detroit City," "500 Miles Away from Home" and "The Streets of Baltimore" early in his career, and later collaborations with author, poet and songwriter Shel Silverstein resulted in several hit singles and the albums *Bobby Bare Sings Lullabies, Legends and Lies, Sleeper Whenever I Fall* and *Down and Dirty.*

what's available: There's a tremendous amount of overlap between *The Best of Bobby Bare* (Razor & Tie, 1994, prod. various) ♪♪♪♪ and *The Essential Bobby Bare* (RCA, 1997, prod. various) ♪♪♪♪. The Razor & Tie collection, however, focuses on Bare's 1960s records, such as "Detroit City," "500 Miles Away from Home" and "The Streets of Baltimore." *Essential* has those songs, but it also contains music from Bare's second stint at RCA (1973–77), during which he became something of an old-guard proponent of the Outlaw movement and made records with Silverstein like "Daddy What If" and the chart-topping "Marie Laveau."

worth searching for: Bare's career has been well chronicled overseas with three German collections. *The Mercury Years: Volumes I, II and III* (Bear Family) collects his early 1970s recordings between runs at RCA. Then there's the four-disc set *All American Boy* (Bear Family) and *Lullabies, Legends and Lies* (Bear Family), which covers his later years with RCA.

influences:
◀◀ Waylon Jennings
▶▶ Tom T. Hall, Jerry Reed

Randall T. Cook and Brian Mansfield

RUSS BARENBERG

Russ Barenberg is a virtuoso acoustic guitarist with a background in bluegrass. His albums under his own name exhibit a myriad of influences, from calypso to traditional Appalachian and Celtic fiddle tunes to inventive original compositions. He has also toured extensively and recorded with fellow virtuosos dobroist Jerry Douglas and bassist Edgar Meyer.

what's available: *Hollywood Rehearsal* (Rounder, 1987, prod. various) ♪♪♪ is a compilation of tracks from Barenberg's Rounder albums up to that point. Atmospheric, beautifully played, and at times captivating, *Moving Pictures* (Rounder, 1988, prod. Russ Barenberg) ♪♪♪ contains seven Barenberg original compositions and two traditional numbers. Accompanists include Stuart Duncan, Bela Fleck, Jerry Douglas, Mark O'Connor, Mark Schatz and Edgar Meyer. *Skip, Hop, & Wobble* (Sugar Hill, 1993, prod. Russ Barenberg, Jerry Douglas, Edgar Meyer) ♪♪♪♪ is one of the most enjoyable instrumental albums from the acoustic music scene in years, a breath of acoustic fresh air, showcasing the many talents of Douglas, Barenberg and Meyer—three outstanding pickers.

influences:
◀◀ Chet Atkins, Doc Watson
▶▶ David Grier, Scott Nygaard

Randy Pitts

MANDY BARNETT

Born September 28, 1975, in Crossville, TN.

A torch-country singer in the Patsy Cline mold, Mandy Barnett's career got a big boost from playing Cline in the Ryman Auditorium production of *Always . . . Patsy Cline*, a musical about the singer's life, while still a teen. She was originally signed to a record deal at age 13, but none of those tracks were released. Tapped to play Cline at age 18, Barnett appeared in the musical for two seasons (more than 200 shows) before signing with a new record label.

what's available: Barnett sings 18 of Cline's songs on the live cast recording of *Always . . . Patsy Cline* (MCA, 1995, prod. Steve Tillisch) ♪♪♪. It's hard to surpass a legend. *Mandy Barnett* (Asylum, 1996, prod. Bill Schnee, Kyle Lehning) ♪♪♪♪, Barnett's solo debut, is an album Cline might have made herself, if she were just getting started today and had access to songs by hip country writers Jim Lauderdale, who contributed "Planet of Love" and "Maybe," and Kostas, who co-wrote "Now That's All Right with Me." Barnett also tackles Willie Nelson's "Three Days," though not as effectively as k.d. lang.

influences:
◀◀ Patsy Cline, k.d. lang, Jim Lauderdale, Mavericks
▶▶ LeAnn Rimes

Bill Hobbs

BASHFUL BROTHER OSWALD

Born Beecher "Pete" Kirby, December 26, 1911, in Sevierville, TN.

As part of Roy Acuff's Crazy Tennesseans, the early incarnation of the Smoky Mountain Boys, Bashful Brother Oswald provided the distinctive and perhaps most essential ingredient in their mountain-influenced sound: the dobro. Bib overalls, big shoes and an exaggerated laugh all became part of Oswald's act, perhaps obscuring the fact that he was a skilled musician, not only on dobro, but banjo and guitar as well. In 1971 "Os" appeared on the landmark Nitty Gritty Dirt Band album, *Will the Circle Be Unbroken*. He continued to work with Roy Acuff until Acuff 's death in 1992. Today he remains a fairly active performer and a member of the Grand Ole Opry, where he performs frequently with fellow Smoky Mountain Boy Charlie Collins.

what to buy: *Brother Oswald* (Rounder, 1995, prod. Tut Taylor) ♫♫♫♫ is a CD reissue of Oswald's solo debut, originally released in 1972. Guests include Norman Blake, Tut Taylor and, of course, Charlie Collins.

what to buy next: Although the remainder of Oswald's Rounder LP's have yet to be released on CD, they're worthy of reissue. *That's Country* (Rounder, 1974) ♫♫♫ features vocals by Collins and Oswald, and assistance from Sam Bush.

the rest:
Oz and Charlie (Rounder, 1976) ♫♫♫
Don't Say Aloha (Rounder, 1978) ♫♫♫

influences:
◀◀ Cliff Carlisle, Cousin Jody
▶▶ Josh Graves, Jerry Douglas

Stephen L. Betts

THE BASS MOUNTAIN BOYS

Formed 1974, in Burlington, NC. Disbanded 1995.

Original members: **Mike Wilson, guitar, vocals (1974–95); John Maness, bass; Jeff Maness, banjo; Joel Maness, mandolin; Jeff Miller, guitar. Additional members: Mike Auldridge, mandolin, vocals; Mike Street, bass, vocals; Johnny Ridge, fiddle, guitar, vocals; Jim Mills, banjo, guitar, vocals; others.**

The Bass Mountain Boys were a mostly traditional-style bluegrass band mainly noted for their energetic, almost frantic live performances. The band was organized in 1974 around the three Maness brothers, all of whom eventually left the band.

what to buy: *My God Made It All* (Pinecastle, 1995, prod. Butch Baldassari) ♫♫♫ is the best of the band's all-gospel recordings, with each member getting a chance to take the lead vocals on one or more of the 12 songs.

what to buy next: *Love of a Woman* (Pinecastle, 1994, prod. Butch Baldassari) ♫♫♫ is a mix of traditional and contemporary bluegrass. The 12 songs on this album include covers of Merle Haggard's "You Don't Have Far to Go" and Porter Wagoner's "Big Wind."

the rest:
18 Wheels (CMH, 1989) ♫♫♫
Carolina Calling Me (Pinecastle, 1992) ♫♫♫

influences:
◀◀ Johnson Mountain Boys, Doyle Lawson & Quicksilver
▶▶ Traditional Grass, Warrior River Boys

Douglas Fulmer

THE BEAT FARMERS

Formed 1983, in San Diego, CA. Disbanded 1995.

Jerry Raney, vocals, guitar; Rolle Dexter, bass; Country Dick Montana (born Dan McClain; died 1995), drums, vocals; Buddy Blue, guitar, vocals (1983–86); Joey Harris, vocals, guitar (1986–95).

Pre-Dwight Yoakam country music spent the first half of the 1980s choking on its own schlock. The only place you heard honest twang back then was from such underground rock bands as X, Jason and the Scorchers and this crack country-rock crew from Mojo Nixon's hometown. The Beat Farmers were the last word in beer-soaked good times, especially drummer/ringleader Country Dick Montana's basso profundo tales of debauchery. Unfortunately, their live appeal never quite translated to records. And as time wore on, their onstage alcoholic excesses began to approach George Jones-ian proportions. Years of self-abuse finally caught up with Montana in 1995, when he died onstage in Canada of heart failure at age 40. He left behind a partially finished solo album that his bandmates helped complete for posthumous release.

what to buy: For pure unpretentious charm, it would be tough to top the Beat Farmers' debut, *Tales of the New West* (Rhino, 1985, prod. Steve Berlin, Mark Linett) ♫♫♫♫. Montana's two vocal cameos set the tone, especially the epochal "California Kid" (imagine Johnny Cash covering "Big Bad John"). Elsewhere, every note rings perfectly true, on ace originals as well as covers of everybody from John Stewart to the Velvet Underground.

what to buy next: Although one hesitates to encourage the Beat Farmers' boozy mythology, *Loud and Plowed and . . . LIVE!!* (Curb, 1990, prod. Denny Bruce) ♫♫♫ does make for a representative sampler. Recorded before a well-oiled New

Year's Eve hometown crowd, it captures the band in prime form on a career-spanning selection of material. The group's swan song, *Manifold* (Sector 2, 1995, prod. Beat Farmers) ♪♪♪, contains "Texas Heat," a fare-thee-well song written by Harris and sung by Montana that qualifies as both eerie and sad.

what to avoid: By any standard, *Best of the Beat Farmers* (Curb, 1995, prod. various) ♪ is appallingly shoddy. Ten tracks (none from their best album) and just 35 minutes. Awful. If you want a compilation, stick with the live album.

the rest:
Glad 'n' Greasy (Demon EP, 1986/Rhino, 1991) ♪♪♪
Van Go (Curb/MCA, 1986) ♪♪♥
The Pursuit of Happiness (Curb/MCA, 1987) ♪♪♪
Poor & Famous (Curb/MCA, 1989) ♪♪
Viking Lullabies (Sector 2, 1994) ♪♪♥

worth searching for: *The Pleasure Barons Live in Las Vegas* (HighTone, 1993, prod. Mark Linett, Country Dick Montana) ♪♪♥ is a relaxed and friendly outing by the Pleasure Barons— an ad hoc 13-piece outfit featuring Montana and Harris with Mojo Nixon, Rosie Flores, Katy Moffatt, Dave Alvin, John Doe and others.

solo outings:
Joey Harris:
Joey Harris and the Speedsters (MCA, 1983) ♪♪
(With Buddy Blue/The Jacks)*Jacks Are Wild* (Rounder, 1988) ♪♪♪
Guttersnipes 'n' Zealots (Rhino, 1991) ♪♪♥

Country Dick Montana:
The Devil Lied to Me (Bar None, 1996) ♪♪♪

influences:
◄◄ Johnny Cash, Flying Burrito Brothers, Rolling Stones, Neil Young

►► Backsliders, Go to Blazes, Old 97's, Uncle Tupelo

David Menconi

BEAUSOLEIL
Formed 1975, in Lafayette, LA.

Michael Doucet, fiddle, vocals; David Doucet; Billy Ware, percussion; Tommy Alesi, drums (1977–present); Jimmy Breaux, accordion (1988–present); Al Tharp, bass, banjo, fiddle, backing vocals (1990–present); Errol Verret, accordion (1975–87); Tommy Comeaux, bass, mandolin (1975–90); Robert Vignaud, bass (1982–84).

Led by fiddler, singer and Acadian/Cajun zealot Michael Doucet, Beausoleil is not only Louisiana's premier Cajun band, but dur-

ing the past 10 years it has also become the best-known regional or "world music" band from North America. When Europeans, for example, think of Cajun music, they inevitably think of Beausoleil. Based in acoustic Cajun music—a fiddle and accordion-led genre that generally follows two forms: the waltz and the two-step—Beausoleil (most of whose lyrics are sung in French) has consistently had the vision and instrumental skill to add elements of New Orleans R&B, blues, folk, jazz and country to its very vital take on traditional french music from Louisiana.

A Cajun music, culture and history enthusiast since teenagehood, Doucet made a trip to France in 1973 that convinced him of the value of his native culture. He returned to Louisiana determined to play the string music that had come to Louisiana from France via the Acadian people of eastern Canada. Combining musical history and infectious dance music, Beausoleil (named for Acadian resistance leader Joseph Broussard, who's nickname was "Beausoleil") was initially the alter ego of a regionally famous cosmic Cajun band called Coteau. Fronted by Michael Doucet and known locally as "the Cajun Grateful Dead," Coteau lasted until 1977 when it broke up and Beausoleil continued on. The fledgling group recorded its first album for Pate Marconi/EMI in France in 1976. The second disc, *The Spirit of Cajun Music,* was made in the U.S. for Louisiana-based Swallow Records in 1977. The band signed with Arhoolie Records during the early 1980s and in the fashion of that label released a number of traditional music records, one of which, the soundtrack to the film *Belizaire the Cajun,* won a Grammy nomination. Constant touring and a revival of interest in all things Cajun (thanks in large part to New Orleans chef Paul Prudhomme) aided and abetted the band's growing popularity.

In 1986 the bandmembers quit their day jobs and committed to music full time. In that same year they released four albums: the *Belizaire the Cajun* soundtrack, *Allons a Lafayette, Christmas Bayou* and *Bayou Boogie,* the last of which was the band's first disc for Rounder Records. *Bayou Boogie* was also the first time the band recorded with electric instruments. At the same time the band was featured several times on *Prairie Home Companion* and was invited to play Carnegie Hall. In 1990 Beausoleil signed with Rhino Records' RNA imprint (which was later changed to Forward Records). Three consecutive Beausoleil albums won Grammy nomination in the Best Contemporary Folk category: 1989's *Bayou Cadillac,* 1991's *Cajun Conja* and 1993's *La Dan e de la Vie.* In 1991 Mary Chapin Carpenter won a Grammy for "Down at the Twist and Shout," a song she'd written about Beausoleil. When she performed the song during the Grammys telecast, the band joined her onstage, a feat they repeated at the 1997 Super Bowl. The band has even come to the attention of the rock community; *Rolling Stone* referred to them as "the best damned dance you'll ever hear." Having performed at two presidential inaugurations—Jimmy Carter (1977) and Bill Clinton (1993)—Beausoleil continues to tour over 200 nights a year.

what to buy: *Bayou Deluxe: The Best of Michael Doucet & Beausoleil* (Rhino, 1993, prod. various) 🎵🎵🎵 is probably the best place to jump into Beausoleil's ever-expanding catalog. Upbeat tunes like "Vieux Crowley" mix with slower, more introspective numbers like "Je M'Endors." Drawn from eight different albums and two compilation discs, this collection is a generous slice of the many sides to this traditional music powerhouse.

what to buy next: Choosing one album by a band that has yet to make even a mediocre disc is nearly impossible. *Bayou Cadillac* (Rounder, 1989, prod. Michael Doucet, Ken Gorz, Ken Irwin) 🎵🎵🎵 gets the nod on the strength of classic Louisiana tunes like "Bon Temps Rouler" and great Doucet originals like "Valse Bebe." Add to that the fact that the band stretches here into a successful "Bo Diddley" and "Iko Iko" and you have one of their best. Again, though, this is strictly a matter of taste: *Cajun Conja* (Rhino, 1991, prod. Al Tharp, Michael Doucet) 🎵🎵🎵 and *La Danse de la Vie* (Rhino, 1993, prod. John Jennings, Michael Doucet, Beausoleil) 🎵🎵🎵 are very close seconds.

the rest:
Spirit of Cajun Music aka *Louisiana Cajun Music* (Swallow, 1977) 🎵🎵🎵
Michael Doucet dit Beausoleil (Arhoolie, 1981, LP, 1994) 🎵🎵🎵
Zydeco Gris Gris (Swallow, 1985) 🎵🎵🎵
Allons a Lafayette & More with Canray Fontenot (Arhoolie, 1986) 🎵🎵🎵
Christmas Bayou (Swallow, 1986)
Bayou Boogie (Rounder, 1986) 🎵🎵🎵
Belizaire the Cajun (Arhoolie, 1986) 🎵🎵🎵
Hot Chili Mama (Arhoolie, 1988) 🎵🎵🎵
Live! From the Left Coast (Rounder, 1989) 🎵🎵🎵
Deja Vu (Swallow, 1990) 🎵🎵🎵
Parlez-Nous a Boire (Arhoolie, 1991) 🎵🎵🎵
L'Echo (Forward, 1994) 🎵🎵🎵
L'Amour ou la Folie (Rhino, 1997) 🎵🎵🎵

worth searching for: *Vintage Beausoleil* (Music of the World, 1995, prod. Bob Haddad) 🎵🎵🎵 collects live performances from 1986–87 in New York City. Several are from a rain-delayed Central Park concert where the band is responding to the enthusiasm of the muddy, dedicated crowd. Another disc worth hunting down is *Le Hoogie Boogie*, a charming children's record of

Cajun music featuring Michael Doucet, his wife Sharon Arms Doucet and the members of Beausoleil (Rounder, 1992) 🎵🎵🎵.

solo outings:
Michael Doucet:
Beau Solo (Arhoolie, 1990) 🎵🎵🎵
Michael Doucet & Cajun Brew (Rounder, 1988) 🎵🎵🎵

influences:
◄◄ Amedé Ardoin, Dewey Balfa, Canray Fontenot
►► Filé, Balfa Toujours

Robert Baird

BEKKA & BILLY /BILLY BURNETTE
Formed in 1996.

Billy Burnette (born May 8, 1953, in Memphis, TN), vocals, guitar; Bekka Bramlett (born April 19, 1968, in Westwood, CA), vocals.

The son of Dorsey ("Tall Oak Tree") and nephew of rockabilly pioneer Johnny ("You're Sixteen"), Billy Burnette started out as a songwriter during the early 1970s. Among the artists who covered his tunes were Charlie Rich, Eddy Raven, Ray Charles, Conway Twitty, Loretta Lynn, Glen Campbell, the Everly Brothers and Jerry Lee Lewis. Between 1979–81 he made a stab at roots music, and in 1987 Fleetwood Mac asked him to join the band when Lindsey Buckingham left. One of the tunes he wrote for the band, "When the Sun Goes Down," received a smattering of country airplay and was almost released as a single off the group's *Behind the Mask* album. In 1993 Burnette recorded the country-tinged *Coming Home* for the Capricorn label. Two years later he rejoined Fleetwood Mac, which had replaced the sultry Stevie Nicks with Bekka Bramlett, daughter of Delaney and Bonnie Bramlett. Burnett and Bramlett eventually spun off as a duo, recording their first album for ALMO Sounds in 1996.

what to buy: *Bekka & Billy* (ALMO Sounds, 1997, prod. Garth Fundis) 🎵🎵🎵 turned out to be a successful collaboration, at least artistically. Bekka Bramlett has the potential to become one of Nashville's most impassioned singers, and she lends a perfect soul foil to Burnett's rockabilly-influenced songs. The duo wrote or co-wrote nearly every song on the album, which features Vince Gill playing guitar on two cuts.

worth searching for: *Billy Burnette* (Columbia, 1980, prod. Barry Seidel) 🎵🎵🎵 features a decent cover of his dad's "Honey Hush" as well as the muscular, guitar-driven "Don't Say No." *Coming Home* (Capricorn, 1993, prod. Mark Wright) 🎵🎵🎵 is country with an edge. "Tangled Up in Texas" really kicks, while "I Still Remember How to Miss You" and "Let Your Heart Make Up Your Mind" display a cool mix of twang, rhythm and emotion.

influences:
◀◀ Johnny & Dorsey Burnette, Delaney & Bonnie, Fleetwood Mac, Buckingham-Nicks

Rick Petreycik and Brian Mansfield

RICO BELL

Born Eric Bellis.

Rico Bell is a sometime member of the Mekons, British cult favorites known for their radical politics, alcoholic consumption and insurgent punk blare. Bell's accordion playing helped give the band's 1986 LP, *Edge of the World*, its sprawling, boozy charm.

what's available: *The Return of Rico Bell* (Bloodshot, 1996, prod. Jon Langford) ♫♫, Bell's solo U.S. debut, features country-flavored pub rock that's too laid back for its own good.

influences:
◀◀ Ronnie Lane, Brinsley Schwarz

Bill Friskics-Warren

VINCE BELL

Born in Dallas, TX.

That Vince Bell has a career in music, or that he ever recorded an album, is almost beside the point. That he is alive is miracle enough. A promising singer/songwriter who toured Texas one roadhouse at a time, Bell's life was rudely interrupted in 1982 when, on the way home from the studio, he was struck down by a drunk driver. His injuries were so serious that an obituary mistakenly ran in the Austin *American-Statesman*. After learning to walk and talk again, and then learning to play and sing, Bell set about reclaiming his career.

what's available: *Phoenix* (Watermelon, 1994, prod. Bob Neuwirth) ♫♫♫♫ is an album of small vignettes, full of rough edges and hard truths—not particularly easy to take, especially given Bell's gruff voice. But, as is the case with the songs of John Prine and Randy Newman, Bell's work deserves a close listen. Plus, it's hard to go wrong with a supporting cast that includes Lyle Lovett, Victoria Williams, John Cale, Stephen Bruton, Mickey Raphael, David Mansfield and Geoff Muldaur. The highlight is "Woman of the Phoenix," which is perhaps best known in Nanci Griffith's version.

influences:
◀◀ John Prine, Townes Van Zandt, Randy Newman

Daniel Durchholz

THE BELLAMY BROTHERS
Formed in Darby, FL.

Howard Bellamy (born February 2, 1946), vocals, guitar; David Bellamy (born September 16, 1950), vocals, guitar, keyboards.

David and Howard Bellamy grew up in the same Florida music scene that produced the Allman Brothers, though the Bellamys' music eventually leaned to a pop/country sound. The brothers have never played exactly by Nashville's rules, which probably both attracted their initial success and shortened their radio careers. Though they've spent their recording careers as a country act, their first single for Warner Bros., "Let Your Love Flow," was a folk-rock number that topped the pop chart while reaching only #21 on the country side. The Bellamys' next #1 came at country three years later with "If I Said You Have a Beautiful Body Would You Hold It Against Me" (also a Top 40 pop hit). The duo would have another nine chart-toppers and many other hits over the next decade, including "Dancin' Cowboys," "Do You Love as Good as You Look" and "Too Much Is Not Enough," a duet with the Forester Sisters. Though their days as hitmakers seem to be over, the duo has maintained an audience with humor, a do-it-yourself work ethic and an eclectic approach to country that incorporates Caribbean rhythms (a la Jimmy Buffett) and dance-floor beats; their 1996 album *Dancin'* features dance remixes of many of their biggest records.

what to buy: *Greatest Hits, Volume 1* (Curb, 1982/1995) ♫♫♫♫ contains the Bellamys' two crossover hits ("Let Your Love Flow," "Beautiful Body") and eight other early hits. You've got to appreciate an act that can hit the Top 20 with a song like "Get Into Reggae Cowboy."

what to buy next: *Greatest Hits, Volume 2* (Curb, 1986/1995, prod. various) ♫♫♫♫ shows the Bellamys' transition from cosmic cowboys to easygoing Baby Boomers, signalled by the duo's 1985 hit "Old Hippie." The songs on this album may not be as familiar, but they're quite good. And the Bellamys' humor is mellowing with age, as evidenced by the touchingly funny "Lie to You for Your Love."

what to avoid: *Latest & Greatest* (Intersound, 1992, prod. various) ♫♫ packages some hits with inferior newer material.

the rest:
One Way Love (Branson, 1991) ♫♫

Howard (l) and David Bellamy: The Bellamy Brothers **(Archive Photos)**

Best of the Bellamy Brothers (Curb, 1992) 🎵🎵🎵
Rip Off the Knob (Intersound, 1993) 🎵🎵🎶
Take Me Home (Branson, 1993) 🎵🎵
Let Your Love Flow: 20 Years of Hits (Intersound, 1994) 🎵🎵🎵🎶
Sons of Beaches (Intersound, 1995) 🎵🎵🎵
Dancin' (Intersound, 1996) 🎵🎵🎵

worth searching for: *Greatest Hits, Volume Three* (MCA/Curb, 1989, prod. various) 🎵🎶 has 1987's "Kids of the Baby Boom," the only #1 not covered by the two earlier collections. The rest follows the duo's chart decline during the late 1980s.

influences:
⏪ Loggins & Messina, Brewer & Shipley, Jimmy Buffett
⏩ Brooks & Dunn

Brian Mansfield

MAC BENFORD &
THE WOODSHED ALL-STARS

Formed in NY.

Mac Benford, banjo, vocals; Marie Burns, mandolin, vocals; John Kirk, fiddle, vocals; John Rossbach, guitar, vocals; Pete Sutherland, fiddle, vocals; Doug Henrie, bass.

Formed in upstate New York, Mac Benford and the Woodshed All-Stars are an old-time string band with a refreshing difference. The lovely Celtic-influenced voice of Marie Burns enhances the band sound, which otherwise relies heavily on clawhammer banjo and North Georgia twin fiddles. Most of the members are involved in other bands and recording projects, notably Marie, who records with sisters Jeannie and Annie in a folky/bluegrass trio.

what's available: *Willow* (Rounder, 1995) 🎵🎵🎵 is enjoyable listening.

solo outings:

Marie Burns:

(With the Burns Sisters) *Close to Home* (Philo, 1995) ♪♪♪

John Rossbach:

Never Was Plugged (Alcazar, 1996) ♪♪♪

influences:

◀◀ Carter Family, Skillet Lickers

▶▶ Freight Hoppers, Dry Branch Fire Squad

Stephen L. Betts

STEPHANIE BENTLEY

Born April 29, 1963, in Thomasville, GA.

Stephanie Bentley's first two singles, "Who's That Girl," and "Heart Half Empty," gave her success at radio, but didn't really define her as an artist. It wasn't until her record label began revealing the cooler songs on her debut album that her personality came through. Credit for finding those great songs has to go to Bentley (she obviously was taking notes on her favorite songwriters during her years as a demo singer) and her producer Paul Worley, who became a fan after hearing her demo of "Shake the Sugar Tree." (Trivia alert: Worley later cut "Sugar Tree" with Pam Tillis, but couldn't get Stephanie's voice out of his mind–so he kept Stephanie's demo vocal, and used it as a background part on the finished record.)

what's available: Bentley's debut, *Hopechest* (Epic, 1995, prod. Todd Wilkes, Paul Worley) ♪♪♪, contains hidden jewels, including songs by Matraca Berg, John Hiatt, Kevin Welch and Hugh Prestwood.

influences:

◀◀ Trisha Yearwood

▶▶ Mindy McCready

Cyndi Hoelzle

MATRACA BERG

Born February 3, 1964, in Nashville, TN.

Born and bred into the business of her hometown—her mother was session singer and songwriter Icee Berg, her step-father songwriter/guitarist Dave Kirby and her third cousin none other than Patsy Cline—Matraca Berg has made her mark as a songwriter but has yet to taste success as a singer of her own material. "Faking Love," a song Berg co-wrote with Bobby Braddock, scored a #1 hit for T.G. Sheppard and Karen Brooks during 1983, and many chart successes

have followed, including Tanya Tucker's "Girls Like Me," Trisha Yearwood's "Wrong Side of Memphis," Patty Loveless' "That Kind of Girl" and Deana Carter's "Strawberry Wine." Berg's songs reflect the complicated circumstances that have often marked her own life, but they are sharply rendered, never descending to bathos. Both of her titles are inexplicably out of print, and both are worth seeking out; she is currently signed to Rising Tide.

what to buy: The feel of Berg's sophomore effort, *The Speed of Grace* (RCA, 1993, prod. Stewart Levine) ♪♪♪, is less Music Row than bluesy Southern roadhouse. Such songs as "Slow Poison" and "Tall Drink of Water" cop pretty boldly from the Bonnie Raitt school, but Berg's strong songwriting stands up to the comparison. There's also an edgy cover of Dolly Parton's "Jolene." Overall, Berg's confidence as a performer seems to have taken a quantum leap from her debut.

the rest:

Lying to the Moon (RCA, 1990) ♪♪♪

influences:

◀◀ Bobbie Gentry, Dolly Parton, Bonnie Raitt

▶▶ Gretchen Peters, Deana Carter

Dan Durchholz

BYRON BERLINE

Born July 6, 1944, in CA.

Fiddler Byron Berline mixes bluegrass, Western swing and old-time and Texas-style fiddling into his style. He's worked as a regular member of Bill Monroe's Blue Grass Boys, Country Gazette, Sundance, Berline-Crary-Hickman and its successor, California. One of the most in-demand fiddlers in the world, Berline has recorded with Monroe, the Dillards, Vince Gill, Bob Dylan, the Rolling Stones, the Eagles and others.

what to buy: Bluegrass, Western swing, country, rock and a little Cajun mix on *Fiddle & a Song* (Sugar Hill, 1995, prod. Byron Berline) ♪♪♪, an album worth buying just for "Sally Goodin," on which Bill Monroe and Earl Scruggs play together for the first time since 1948. Old Sundance bandmate Vince Gill sings Monroe's "Rose of Old Kentucky."

what to buy next: *Jumpin' the Strings* (Sugar Hill, 1990, prod. Byron Berline) ♪♪♪, a collection of an amazing 21 original fiddle tunes, is a showcase for Berline's writing skills and his mastery of a wide range of fiddle styles.

the rest:

(With Dan Crary and John Hickman) *Night Run* (Sugar Hill, 1984) 𝄢𝄢𝄢𝄢

(With Hickman) *Double Trouble* (Sugar Hill, 1986, 1995) 𝄢𝄢𝄢𝄢

(With Crary and Hickman) *B-C-H* (Sugar Hill, 1987) 𝄢𝄢𝄢𝄢

(With Crary and Hickman) *Now They Are Four* (Sugar Hill, 1989) 𝄢𝄢𝄢

(With California) *Traveler* (Sugar Hill, 1992) 𝄢𝄢𝄢

influences:

◀◀ Country Gazette, Bill Monroe

▶▶ Laurel Canyon Ramblers, Jason Carter, Stuart Duncan

Douglas Fulmer

BERLINE-CRARY-HICKMAN

See: Byron Berline

CRYSTAL BERNARD

Born September 30, in TX.

An actress best known for her roles on *Wings, It's a Living* and *Happy Days*, Crystal Bernard began a second career in 1996 as a country singer. Unlike many other actresses, she entered Nashville the right way: she approached the town at the peak of her career and worked within the industry—writing songs, singing backup and producing videos—before setting out on her own. She also recorded a duet with Peter Cetera called "(I Wanna Take) Forever Tonight" and had songs cut by Paula Abdul, Lisa Stansfield and Debbie and Angie Winans. It didn't hurt that she had a legitimate country credit from early in her career, having joined Bobbie Gentry's Las Vegas show at age 14.

what's available: As actress-turned-singer albums go, *The Girl Next Door* (River North, 1996, prod. Biff Watson, David Rhyne) 𝄢𝄢𝄢 is fairly successful. Bernard has a fine if somewhat wispy voice, and she co-wrote the album's most distinctive songs, including "Have We Forgotten What Love Is," a duet with Billy Dean that was a low-charting hit.

influences:

◀◀ Bobbie Gentry, Billy Dean

Brian Mansfield

JOHN BERRY

Born September 14, 1959, in Aiken, SC.

John Berry cut six independent albums before his mix of 1970s rock, Southern boogie and country—and his huge, gritty, go-for-broke voice—caught the ear of Capitol Records. More bluesy rock than country, Berry's records fit perfectly during the early 1990s country boom, offering familiar themes wrapped in a contemporary pop-country sound. His "Kiss Me in the Car" was one of the best song titles of 1993, and the record was, deservedly, a hit. Berry underwent brain surgery in 1994 to drain a cyst.

what to buy: *John Berry* (Capitol, 1993, prod. Jimmy Bowen, Chuck Howard) 𝄢𝄢𝄢 captures Berry at his best, with the hits "Kiss Me in the Car," "What's in It for Me," "You and Only You" and "Your Love Amazes Me." The latter became Berry's first #1 hit while he was hospitalized for brain surgery.

what to buy next: *Standing on the Edge* (Capitol, 1995, prod. Jimmy Bowen, Chuck Howard) 𝄢𝄢𝄢 is a good second helping of Berry, though the song selection is a little more uneven and the production is a bit more anthemic. It features the hits "Every Time My Heart Calls Your Name," "Standing on the Edge of Goodbye," "If I Had Any Pride Left at All," and "I Think about It All the Time." *O Holy Night* (Capitol, 1995, prod. Chuck Howard, John Berry) 𝄢𝄢𝄢𝄢, Berry's Christmas album, is less commercial and more personal than most country Christmas albums. A fervent spiritual mood and a clear statement of personal faith showcases Berry's vocal talent.

the rest:

Things Are Not the Same (Capitol, 1986/1994) 𝄢𝄢

Saddle the Wind (Capitol, 1990/1994) 𝄢𝄢

Faces (Capitol, 1996) 𝄢𝄢𝄢

influences:

◀◀ Gary Morris

▶▶ Ty Herndon

Bill Hobbs

BIG HOUSE

Formed 1995, in Bakersfield, CA.

Monty Byrom, guitar, lead vocals; David Neuhauser, guitar; Chuck Seaton, guitar; Sonny California, harmonica, percussion; Ron Mitchell, bass; Tanner Byrom, drums.

This California sextet keeps alive the Bakersfield tradition, not so much in sound as in attitude. Big House plays bar-band country, with Sonny California's harmonica replacing the traditional melodic role of fiddle.

what's available: On *Big House* (MCA, 1997, prod. Peter Bunetta, Monty Byrom, David Neuhauser) 𝄢𝄢𝄢 lead singer Monty Byrom's rasp recalls Paul Rodgers, so at its best ("You

Ain't Lonely Yet," "Cold Outside"), Big House sounds like coun-trified Bad Company. That's arguably a radical change for the country market, but it's not necessarily an improvement.

influences:

◀◀ Bad Company, Confederate Railroad

Brian Mansfield

BIG SANDY & HIS FLY-RITE BOYS

Formed as Big Sandy & the Fly-Rite Trio, 1988, in Orange County, CA. Became Big Sandy & His Fly-Rite Boys in February 1993.

Big Sandy (born Robert Williams), vocals, acoustic guitar; Wally Her-som, upright bass; Will Brokenbourgh, drums (1988–89); Bobby Trim-ble, drums (1989–present); T.K. Smith, guitar (1988–93); Ashley King-man, guitar (1993–present); Lee Jeffriess, steel guitar (1991–present).

Exactly why hefty frontman Robert Williams transformed him-self into Big Sandy isn't clear. Maybe it's because Robert Williams & His Fly-Rite Boys doesn't ring right. Whatever the name, this ensemble shuffled its way into the "alternative country" movement during 1994, with a melting pot sound that tapped into the traditions of rockabilly, Western swing and hill-billy music. Hailing from the West Coast environment that spawned legends Merle Haggard and Buck Owens, Big Sandy & His Fly-Rite Boys concentrate on the "Western" half of coun-try & Western. Dressed in duds your grandfather might have worn back in his heyday—complete with colorful scarf ties—this quintet brings the past to the present with unabashed au-thenticity and verve. Both live and on record Big Sandy & His Fly-Rite Boys revel in a no-frills musical philosophy that clashes with every over-produced note of Nashville's mainstream coun-try repertoire. Both of the group's albums brim with the spirit that launched the genre decades ago; 1994's *Jumpin' from 6 to 6* offers a hodge-podge mix of traditional country styles, while its follow-up, 1995's *Swingin' West*, sticks closer to Western swing. It's obvious, though, that Big Sandy's vision is appreci-ated by a varied audience. The group has opened shows for acts as diverse as country upstarts the Mavericks, psycho-trashbilly kingpin Reverend Horton Heat and mopey alternative rocker Morrissey.

what to buy: *Swingin' West* (HighTone, 1995, prod. Dave Alvin) ♫♫♫♫ offers a swinging, more streamlined approach than the band's versatile debut. Whether it be the sly pleasures of "My Sinful Days Are Over" and "Blackberry Wine" or the blues-tinged wonder of "Let Me in There, Baby" and "If I Wrote a

Song (about Our Love Affair)," this effort cuts to the heart of Big Sandy & His Fly-Rite Boys.

the rest:

Jumpin' from 6 to 6 (HighTone, 1994) ♫♫♫
Feelin' Kind of Lucky (HighTone, 1997)

worth searching for: Big Sandy & the Fly-Rite Trio recorded one album that was released in the United States, *Fly Right* (Diony-sis, 1990, prod. Robert Williams). Another album as the Fly-Rite Trio, *On the Go* (No Hit Records, 1991, prod. Robert Williams) was released only in England.

influences:

◀◀ Tex Williams, Bob Wills, Hank Williams, Asleep at the Wheel

▶▶ Derailers, Dale Watson, Cowboys & Indians

Mario Tarradell

CLINT BLACK

Born February 4, 1962, in Long Branch, NJ.

With respect for the past but a flair for innovation, Clint Black may be the perfect contemporary country artist. He draws heavily on the honky-tonk and Western swing traditions of Merle Haggard and Bob Wills, respectively, but he is, after all, a child of the 1960s and 1970s, which means he grew up on the Beatles, FM rock and, significantly, the "sensitive" singer/song-writer era spawned by James Taylor. Black, who co-writes nearly all of his material with his guitarist, Hayden Nicholas, is a gifted lyricist able to address topics relevant to contemporary times, particularly on *Killin' Time*, where ennui in the wake of the tumultuous 1980s is the guiding emotion. A terrific singer and capable harmonica player, Black is the real deal, and he's kept his career on track despite a celebrity marriage (to former *Knot's Landing* star Lisa Hartman) and an occasional hankering after an acting career of his own.

what to buy: *Killin' Time* (RCA, 1989, prod. James Stroud, Mark Wright) ♫♫♫♫ is a pure country classic, balanced perfectly be-tween the honky-tonk and Western swing traditions, yet it's ut-terly contemporary in attitude and subject matter. And the hits just keep on comin': "A Better Man," "Nobody's Home," "Walkin' Away," "Nothing's News" and the title track. Likely the most impressive debut album since Randy Travis' *Storms of Life*. *Greatest Hits* (RCA, 1996, prod. James Stroud, Clint Black, Mark Wright) ♫♫♫♫ is a heapin' helpin' of Black's best, plus a

Clint Black (© Ken Settle)

handful of previously unreleased tracks. There's too little of *Killin' Time*, perhaps, but you should own that one as well. The new material—three originals and a live cover of the Eagles' "Desperado"—is of a piece with the rest, but the set is docked half a bone for Black's insistence on letting his wife, whose singing career flopped long ago, sing backup. One Linda Mc-Cartney is enough.

what to buy next: After a noble but failed effort at using his studio band for his sophomore effort, Black was back with *The Hard Way* (RCA, 1992, prod. James Stroud, Clint Black) *ZZZ*, which covers all the bases, from the nimble rocker "We Tell Ourselves" and the breezy "When My Ship Comes In" to the classic weeper "Burn One Down."

what to avoid: If you're looking for a holiday turkey, go to the Piggly Wiggly. Or give *Looking for Christmas* (RCA, 1995, prod. James Stroud, Clint Black) *ZZ*, an overreaching effort, a spin.

the rest:
Put Yourself in My Shoes (RCA, 1990) *ZZZ*
No Time to Kill (RCA, 1993) *ZZZ*
One Emotion (RCA, 1994) *ZZZ*

worth searching for: Among the compilations Black has participated in are the *Roy Rogers Tribute* (RCA, 1991) *ZZZ*, on which he duets with the famed cowboy on "Hold On, Partner," and *Rhythm, Country and Blues* (MCA, 1994) *ZZZ*, on which he sings Aretha Franklin's "Chain of Fools" with the Pointer Sisters.

influences:
◀◀ Merle Haggard, Bob Wills, James Taylor, Eagles
▶▶ Tracy Byrd, Mark Chesnutt

Daniel Durchholz

BLACKHAWK

Formed c. 1991, in Nashville, TN.

Henry Paul, vocals, guitar, mandolin; Dave Robbins, vocals, keyboards; Van Stephenson, vocals, guitar.

Maybe it's the rock background the band's members have or maybe it's the relative absence of fiddles and steel guitars in the music, but BlackHawk has never gotten the respect to match its success. Henry Paul was an early rhythm guitarist for the Outlaws and also fronted the Henry Paul band. Van Stephenson and Dave Robbins had co-written a number of songs for Restless Heart and others. (Stephenson also had a small pop hit, "Modern Day Delilah," in 1984.) Like many other Nashville acts, they came together to write songs and only later

entertained the notion of performing together. BlackHawk built their sound around three-part harmonies and (for country) complex chord progressions; the songs leaned toward down-home metaphysics. The combination worked: each of the trio's first two albums produced numerous hit singles and sold more than a million copies.

what's available: BlackHawk has shown signs of becoming one of the most consistent hitmakers of the 1990s. Four of the five singles from *BlackHawk* (Arista, 1994, prod. Mark Bright, Tim DuBois) *ZZZ* hit the Top 10, including "Every Once in a While," "I Sure Can Smell the Rain" and "That's Just about Right." The follow-up, *Strong Enough* (Arista, 1995, prod. Mark Bright) *ZZZ*, featured "I'm Not Strong Enough to Say No," a killer single written by Def Leppard/Shania Twain producer R.J. "Mutt" Lange.

influences:
◀◀ Outlaws, Restless Heart
▶▶ Jeff Black, Sky Kings

Brian Mansfield

NORMAN BLAKE /NORMAN & NANCY BLAKE /NORMAN BLAKE & TONY RICE

Born March 10, 1938, in Chattanooga, TN.

A disciple of Doc Watson, Norman Blake is a breathtaking acoustic guitar player. His flair for lightning-fast picking coupled with syncopated rhythms adorn his best recordings, which were made for the Rounder label. In addition to his solo work, Blake is a much sought-after session musician. His superb picking has graced the recordings of artists such as John Hartford, Joan Baez, Kris Kristofferson and, recently, Steve Earle.

what to buy: *Whiskey before Breakfast* (Rounder, 1976, prod. Norman Blake) *ZZZ* is really a duo album that features guitarist Charlie Collins.

what to buy next: *The Norman and Nancy Blake Compact Disc* (Rounder, 1986, prod. Norman Blake) *ZZZ* teams the super picker with his wife, Nancy, on cello and mandolin. Blake and Tony Rice's *Blake & Rice* (Rounder, 1987, prod. Norman Blake) *ZZZ* is a guitar player's delight, as Blake exchanges runs, fills and riffs with Rice, another super picker from the Doc Watson/Clarence White school.

Phil Alvin of the Blasters (© Ken Settle)

the rest:

Back Home in Sulphur Springs (Rounder, 1974/1995) 🎵🎵

Full Moon on the Farm (Rounder, 1981) 🎵🎵🎵

Original Underground Music from the Mysterious South (Rounder, 1983) 🎵🎵🎵

Nashville Blues (Rounder, 1984) 🎵🎵🎵

Lighthouse on the Shore (Rounder, 1985) 🎵🎵🎵

Slow Train through Georgia (Rounder, 1987) 🎵🎵🎵

(With Nancy Blake) *Natasha's Waltz* (Rounder, 1987) 🎵🎵🎵

(With N. Blake) *Blind Dog* (Rounder, 1988) 🎵🎵

(With Tony Rice) *Norman Blake and Tony Rice 2* (Rounder, 1990) 🎵🎵🎵

(With N. Blake) *While Passing along This Way* (Shanachie, 1994) 🎵🎵🎵

influences:

◀◀ Doc Watson

▶▶ Vince Gill, Steve Wariner

Rick Petreycik

THE BLASTERS

Formed 1979, in Los Angeles, CA. Disbanded 1986.

Phil Alvin, vocals, guitar; Dave Alvin, guitar; John Bazz, bass; Bill Bateman, drums; Gene Taylor, piano.

The Blasters may have been at the forefront of the late-1970s/early-1980s rockabilly revival, but that's not the whole story. It's instructive to remember that the band members were contemporaries with X and Dwight Yoakam, and were equally conversant with both. The group combined the energy of the burgeoning L.A. punk scene with a solid base in rock 'n' roll history, plus a taste for R&B and country. This was not a simple revivalism, but a genuine expression of a shared musical sensibility that drew on, but didn't ape, Jerry Lee Lewis, Big Joe Turner, Hank Williams and many others. Unfortunately, only two of the group's titles remain in print.

what to buy: *The Blasters Collection* (Slash/Warner Bros., 1990, prod. Blasters, Jeff Eyrich) 🎵🎵🎵🎵 is the place to start, for it contains the lion's share of the group's A-level material, including "Marie Marie," "So Long Baby Goodbye" and the genre-defining "American Music."

the rest:

The Blasters (Slash/Warner Bros., 1981) 🎵🎵🎵

worth searching for: Several of the group's out-of-print titles are worth a look: *Over There: Live at the Venue, London* (Slash/Warner Bros., 1982, prod. Blasters) 🎵🎵🎵, a jumping live recording; *Non Fiction* (Slash/Warner Bros., 1983, prod. Jeff Eyrich) 🎵🎵🎵, a somewhat overwrought stab at socially conscious topics; and *Hard Line* (Slash/Warner Bros., 1985, prod. Jeff Eyrich) 🎵🎵🎵, a slight return to form. The group's independently released debut, *American Music* (Rollin' Rock, 1980, prod. Blasters) 🎵🎵🎵🎵, is a highly sought collector's item.

influences:

◀◀ Big Joe Turner, Jerry Lee Lewis, Chuck Berry, Hank Williams

▶▶ Reverend Horton Heat, Jason & the Scorchers, Dwight Yoakam

see also: *Dave Alvin, Phil Alvin*

Daniel Durchholz

RALPH BLIZARD & THE NEW SOUTHERN RAMBLERS

Current band formed 1982.

Ralph Blizard (born December 5, 1918, in Kingsport, TN), fiddle, vocals; Phil Jamison, guitar, bass; John Herrman, banjo, bass; Gordy Hinners, banjo; John Lilly, bass, guitar, mandolin.

Ralph Blizard formed his current band in 1982, fiddling in a style he refers to as "Appalachian Mountain Longbow." While in high school Blizard played with his band, the Southern Ramblers, on radio stations throughout Tennessee, Kentucky and Virginia, then left the music business for 25 years to work at the Eastman/Kodak Company. Upon retirement he re-formed the Ramblers and toured the country, participating in numerous festivals and workshops and promoting the group's distinct brand of traditional Appalachian music.

what's available: *Southern Ramble* (Rounder, 1995, prod. Phil Jamison, Gordy Hinners) 🎵🎵🎵🎵 is a delightful mix of traditional tunes and a few originals by Blizard and other band members.

influences:

◀◀ Carter Family, Doc Addington

▶▶ Freight Hoppers, Mac Benford & the Woodshed All-Stars

Stephen L. Betts

BLOOD ORANGES /WOODEN LEG /BEACON HILLBILLIES

Formed 1987, in Boston, MA.

Cheri Knight, guitar, vocals; Jimmy Ryan, vocals, mandolin; Mark Spencer, guitar.

Combining the efforts of three significantly talented musicians, the Blood Oranges were somewhat like the Buffalo Springfield of alternative country music, releasing only a couple of albums that were a few years ahead of their time but serving as a proving ground for its members' future projects. Alternative country became more of a buzz word during the mid-1990s, but the Blood Oranges had created an intriguing, inventive and eminently listenable hybrid of rock, bluegrass, country, punk and pop from the decade's outset. By 1995, however, side projects began to pull bandmembers in different directions; though they've never formally called it quits and indeed have hinted at the possibility of future Blood Oranges records, all three have kept themselves plenty busy during the last couple years. Jimmy Ryan continued working with a more specifically bluegrass-oriented act called the Beacon Hillbillies and recorded an album of his own (with considerable help from Mark Spencer) under the name Wooden Leg. Cheri Knight's solo debut attracted major-label interest, and Spencer became a guitarist-for-hire of considerable note with the likes of Freedy Johnston, Lisa Loeb and Kelly Willis, as well as furthering his career as a producer out of his own home studio.

what to buy: *The Crying Tree* (East Side Digital, 1994, prod. Eric "Roscoe" Ambel) 🎵🎵🎵🎵 is the apex of the Blood Oranges' output, a confident, inspired collection of instantly catchy rockers, darkly haunting ballads and bluegrassy stompers. Knight's solo debut, *The Knitter* (ESD, 1996, prod. Eric "Roscoe" Ambel) 🎵🎵🎵🎵, proved she was more than capable of carrying the load on her own, focusing on the more song-oriented side of the Oranges' material and including should-be hits and classics such as "Light in the Road" and "Last Barn Dance."

what to buy next: *Corn River* (ESD, 1990, prod. Paul Kolderie, Blood Oranges) 🎵🎵🎵, the band's debut, is a bit more tentative than *The Crying Tree* but proves the Oranges were onto something quite early in their career; the disc also introduced songwriter Jim McGinniss' classic balled "Thief." *Wooden Leg* (ESD, 1996, prod. Spencer) 🎵🎵🎵, in effect a Ryan solo disc, is less immediately catchy than Knight's debut but has its own allure in more of a quirky string band vein.

the rest:

Lone Green Valley (EP) (ESD, 1992) 🎵🎵🎵

solo outings:

Jimmy Ryan:

(With the Beacon Hillbillies) *Duffield Station* (ESD, 1992) 🎵🎵🎵

(With the Beacon Hillbillies) *More Songs of Love and Murder* (ESD, 1994) 🎵🎵🎵

(With the Beacon Hillbillies) *A Better Place* (ESD, 1996) 🎵🎵🎵

influences:

◀◀ Jason & the Scorchers, Rank & File, Clash, Patsy Cline

▶▶ Marty Stuart, Buckets, Angry Johnny & the Killbillies

Peter Blackstock

BLUE HIGHWAY

Formed 1994, in Johnson City, TN.

Shawn Lane, fiddle, mandolin, vocals; Wayne Taylor, bass, vocals; Tim Stafford, guitar, vocals; Rob Ickes, dobro, vocals; Jason Burleson, banjo, mandolin.

Arguably the most impressive new bluegrass band of the 1990s, Blue Highway had a breakthrough year in 1996, winning awards from the International Bluegrass Music Association for Best Emerging Artist and Album of the Year. (Rob Ickes also won solo honors for Dobro Player of the Year.) Organized by five youthful musicians (with experience in the bands of Alison Krauss, Doyle Lawson and Ricky Skaggs) who wanted to perform mostly original material in a democratic setting, Blue Highway is blessed with three outstanding lead singers (Taylor, Lane and Stafford), several good songwriters, an approach that's modern yet rooted in traditional bluegrass and a captivating sound that's unlike any other band in bluegrass.

what's available: *It's a Long, Long Road* (Rebel, 1995, prod. Blue Highway) 🎵🎵🎵🎵, the band's award-winning debut, spent several months at the top of the national bluegrass charts, spawning three Top 10 singles, "In the Gravel Yard, " "Lonesome Pine" and the title song. Other highlights include Wayne Taylor's historical saga "Before the Cold Wind Blows" and Tim Stafford's "Farmer's Blues." *Wind to the West* (1996, Rebel, prod. Blue Highway) 🎵🎵🎵 builds on the band's strong debut with seven good new songs, a Merle Haggard cover and a foray into a more country sound on "I Can Stand the Truth." Exceptional performances on a pair of old gospel songs, "Two Coats" and "God Moves in a Windstorm, " demonstrate the band's feel for traditional material.

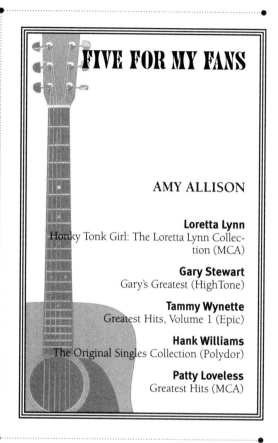

FIVE FOR MY FANS

AMY ALLISON

Loretta Lynn
Honky Tonk Girl: The Loretta Lynn Collection (MCA)

Gary Stewart
Gary's Greatest (HighTone)

Tammy Wynette
Greatest Hits, Volume 1 (Epic)

Hank Williams
The Original Singles Collection (Polydor)

Patty Loveless
Greatest Hits (MCA)

influences:

◀◀ Nashville Bluegrass Band, Alison Krauss, Doyle Lawson

▶▶ Rarely Herd

Jon Hartley Fox

BLUE MOUNTAIN

Formed 1991, in Los Angeles, CA.

Cary Hudson, guitar, vocals, mandolin; Laurie Stirratt, bass, vocals; Frank Coutch, drums.

After the breakup of the Hilltops, a slightly punkier alt.country band that included Hudson, Stirratt, and Stirratt's brother John, currently of Wilco, the members of Blue Mountain repaired to their former Mississippi home, and to their musical roots as well. Drawing on country, Southern rock, and Neil Young-style acoustic-guitar-and-harmonica balladry, the husband-and-wife team of Hudson and Stirratt went through a succession of drummers before settling on Coutch. For a trio, Blue Mountain is extraordinarily versatile, turning in raging rockers that, even at their edgiest, are shot through with an appealing melodicism, and folkish country tunes, many of which recount the simple, bucolic pleasures of the South.

what's available: *Dog Days* (Roadrunner, 1995, prod. Eric "Roscoe" Ambel) 🎵🎵🎵 is a memorable effort from start to finish. The band's ensemble playing is tight, and Ambel's production is nearly perfect. More important, though, these songs are actually about something: "Mountain Girl" is a gorgeous mandolin-driven remembrance of good times past; "A Band Called Bud" reports the hapless history of Memphis' Grifters, a band that never really made it but refuses to quit; "ZZQ" celebrates a now-defunct Mississippi radio station whose playlist was laced with punk rock; and "Jimmy Carter" is a surprising two-stepper that posits the oft-denounced ex-president as a great man, if not a great politician. Hudson's vocals are soulful, if unspectacular, but that's in keeping with the band's m.o. It's never flashy, but it's as easy to get into as a favorite old pair of shoes.

worth searching for: The group's self-released debut, *Blue Mountain* (4 Barrel, 1993, prod. Blue Mountain) 🎵🎵🎵, contains a handful of songs that eventually wound up on *Dog Days*, but it sounds like the $1,000 it cost to make it. Also, *The Hilltops* (Fishtone, 1992/Black Dog 1996, prod. Hilltops) 🎵🎵🎵, which saw its initial release only after that band split, was recently reissued.

influences:
◀◀ Creedence Clearwater Revival, Uncle Tupelo, Blue Rodeo

Daniel Durchholz

BLUE RODEO

Formed 1981, in Toronto, Canada.

Jim Cuddy, vocals, guitar; Greg Keelor, vocals, guitar; Bazil Donovan, bass; Cleave Anderson, drums (1981–89); Mark French, drums (1989–92); Glenn Milchem, drums (1992–present); Bob Wiseman, keyboards and harmonica (1981–92); James Gray, keyboards (1992–present); Kim Deschamps, various instruments (1992–present).

A bizarre eclectic streak notwithstanding, Blue Rodeo has always played straightforward and exceptionally well-written country/folk songs that recall the Byrds, the Band and the Everly Brothers. The band's songwriting team, high school pals Keelor and Cuddy, have a knack for catchy tunes (notably, "What Am I Doing Here") and methodically layer them with organs and chiming electric guitars. Wiseman's presence on keyboards has always given Blue Rodeo an edge—judging from his solo albums, he's a lovable spaz who has trouble keeping his weird and interesting ideas in check. Oddly, after he left, Blue Rodeo released its most unexpectedly offbeat album, the spacey funk experiment *Nowhere to Here*. Fiercely popular in Canada, the band has yet to fully conquer U.S. radio stations and pop charts.

what to buy: Though Keelor and Cuddy never come up with anything as revolutionary as their pop forebears (Beatles John Lennon and Paul McCartney or even Squeeze's Chris Difford and Glenn Tilbrook), *Casino* (Atlantic, 1990, prod. Pete Anderson) 🎵🎵🎵 is enjoyable and consistent.

what to buy next: *Diamond Mine* (Discovery, 1989, prod. Malcolm Burn, Blue Rodeo) 🎵🎵🎵 and *Outskirts* (Atlantic, 1987, prod. Terry Brown) 🎵🎵🎵 have a hungry enthusiasm, as if the band is willing to write its way to superstardom; and the songs are excellent.

what to avoid: Give them credit for experimenting, but *Nowhere to Here* (Discovery, 1995, prod. Blue Rodeo) 🎵🎵 is just too spacey and its attempts at funk aren't exactly Parliament or Sly Stone.

the rest:
Lost Together (Discovery, 1992) 🎵🎵🎵
Five Days in July (Discovery, 1993) 🎵🎵🎵

worth searching for: Bob Wiseman's solo albums, especially *In By Of* (Bar/None, 1994, prod. Bob Wiseman) 🎵🎵🎵🎵, a raucous carnival that rips on Ice Cube's anti-semitism and wraps bizarre sounds around Wiseman's friendly high-pitched whine.

influences:
◀◀ The Band, Byrds, Beatles, Squeeze, Everly Brothers, Elvis Costello
▶▶ Counting Crows, Hootie & the Blowfish, Toad the Wet Sprocket, Gin Blossoms

Steve Knopper

BLUE SHADOWS

Formed 1990, in Vancouver, British Columbia, Canada. Disbanded 1995.

Billy Cowsill, vocals, rhythm guitar; Jeffrey Hatcher, vocals, lead guitar; Barry Muir, vocals, bass; J.B. Johnson, drums.

After a decade spent recovering from his stint as leader of America's self-proclaimed "First Family of Song," the Cowsills, big brother Bill found himself in Vancouver where, during 1979, he formed Canada's legendary Blue Northern band. Unfortunately, Blue Northern was so ahead of its time in what had not yet become the "new country" genre that its only record slipped through the cracks without a trace. The experience dispirited Cowsill so deeply that he was about to seek refuge in Nashville's Songwriters Row. What stopped him was Manitoba-native Jeffrey Hatcher, veteran of several renowned Canadian bands (Fuse, Jeffrey Hatcher & the Big Beat) and a highly re-garded "walking pop and country songbook." Providing the perfect foil to Cowsill's somewhat gruffer world-weariness, the duo immediately began writing and performing together, forming Blue Shadows soon afterward. As raucous and exuberant on stage as they were defiantly radio-ready on record, the band was poised to tackle the U.S. market head-on when, falling victim to the deadly Canadian Curse (too much roadwork/too little industry support), the group disbanded on Christmas Day 1995. Cowsill, however, continues to be active with behind the scenes work in his adopted country, most recently recording with Canadian folk hero Murray McLaughlin.

what's available: Their Juno (Canadian Grammy equivalent)-nominated debut, *On the Floor of Heaven* (Sony Music Canada, 1993, prod. Jeffrey Hatcher, Billy Cowsill) ♫♫♫, has been per-fectly described as "Hank Williams goes to the Cavern Club," and the follow-up, *Lucky to Me* (Sony Music Canada, 1995, prod. Jeffrey Hatcher, Billy Cowsill) ♫♫♫, soundly expands on this in-novative yet hummable Beatles-invade-Bradley's-Barn ethos.

influences:
◀◀ Beatles, Foster & Lloyd
▶▶ Waltons, Ghost Rockets

Gary Pig Gold

THE BLUE SKY BOYS

Brother vocal duo from Hickory, NC.

Bill Bolick (born October 28, 1917); Earl Bolick (born November 16, 1919).

Bill and Earl Bolick's singing style—close harmony coupled with simple guitar accompaniment—influenced dozens of duet acts through the years, including the Louvins, the Delmores, and even the Everly Brothers. In 1936 Bill and Earl (who chose a name—the Blue Sky Boys—that didn't include "Brothers" to set themselves apart from other brother duets) were working on radio station WGST in Atlanta, when they first recorded for Victor. After World War II they resumed their career, continuing to record for RCA, until they disbanded in 1951. By 1963, how-ever, the Blue Sky Boys were back together, propelled by the old-time/folk revival then sweeping the country. Their last recordings were made for the Starday label in 1975.

what to buy: *The Blue Sky Boys* (Rounder, 1996, prod. Ken Irwin) ♫♫♫♫, taken from the Bolick's 1975 Starday sessions, is a great place to start. Forty years into their career the Blue Sky Boys' harmony is still awe-inspiring.

what to buy next: *In Concert, 1964* (Rounder, 1989, prod. Bill Bolick, Ken Irwin) ♫♫♫♫ includes several of the duo's best-known songs, as well as a few they'd never recorded before. Another feature is Earl's portrayal of hayseed comic character Uncle Josh, a regular part of their early radio shows.

the rest:
On Radio, Volume One (Copper Creek, 1993) ♫♫♫
On Radio, Volume Two (Copper Creek, 1993) ♫♫♫
Farm and Fun Time Favorites, Volume One (Copper Creek, 1994) ♫♫♫
Farm and Fun Time Favorites, Volume Two (Copper Creek, 1994) ♫♫♫
The Sunny Side of Life (Rounder, 1993) ♫♫♫

influences:
◀◀ Bradley Kincaid, Mac & Bob
▶▶ Louvin Brothers, Whitstein Brothers

Stephen L. Betts

THE BLUEGRASS CARDINALS

Formed 1974, in Los Angeles, CA. Disbanded 1997.

Don Parmley, banjo (1974–96); David Parmley, guitar (1974–93); Bill Bryson, bass; Randy Graham, mandolin; Herschel Sizemore, man-dolin; John Davis, bass; Warren Blair, fiddle; Norman Wright, man-dolin; Larry Stephenson, mandolin; Ernie Sykes, bass; Tim Smith, fid-dle; Ronnie Bowman, bass; Greg Luck, guitar; Keith Pyrtle, guitar; Lester Deaton, bass; others.

Banjo player Don Parmley performed with several Los Angeles-area bluegrass bands including the Hillmen (with Vern Gosdin and Chris Hillman) before forming the traditional-style Blue-grass Cardinals with son David in 1974. David left the band in 1993 to unsuccessfully pursue a career in country music and eventually formed the bluegrass band David Parmley, Scott Vestal and Continental Divide. The Cardinals disbanded in Janu-ary 1997 with Don Parmley's retirement.

what to buy: *The Bluegrass Cardinals* (Copper Creek, 1997) ♫♫♫, the group's debut, originally released on Sierra, is the only Bluegrass Cardinals album currently available on CD.

the rest:

Welcome to Virginia (Rounder, 1977)
Livin' in the Good Old Days (CMH, 1978)
Sunday Mornin' Singin' (CMH, 1980)

influences:

◄◄ Hillmen

►► David Parmley, Scott Vestal & Continental Divide

Douglas Fulmer

SUZY BOGGUSS

Born Susan Kay Bogguss, December 30, 1956, in Aledo, IL.

Suzy Bogguss has been one of the primary beneficiaries of the broad definition of country music during the 1990s, but she's also one of the artists whose work helped broaden it in the first place. Bogguss came up on the coffeehouse scene, then toured the country in a camper, busking and playing whatever gigs she could scare up. Eventually she moved to Nashville, then played for tourists at Dolly Parton's Tennessee theme park. Along the way Bogguss picked up a wide array of influences, from folk and country to pop and rock. Looking back now, her initial foray into recording seems more free-spirited than the country-pop that marked her later work with famed producer Jimmy Bowen, but even more recent years included some innovative and eclectic work. Bogguss isn't in the upper echelon of Nashville stars, though she deserves to be, and her most recent release offers indications of a new, energetic direction. Can't wait to see what happens next.

what to buy: Recorded after her years travelling alone and before Nashville got its hooks into her, *Somewhere in Between* (Liberty, 1989, prod. Wendy Waldman) ♫♫♫♫ is an utterly charming debut, ranging from the Merle Haggard-penned title tune and Hank Williams' "My Sweet Love Ain't Around" to material that's more Western than country, typified by a terrific reading of Patsy Montana's "I Want to Be a Cowboy's Sweetheart." *Greatest Hits* (Liberty, 1994, prod. various) ♫♫♫ contains Bogguss' most essential chart material, but it's docked a bone for hewing to Nashville's stingy unspoken 10-cuts-per-album rule. As a result, there's nothing from her largely self-penned album *Something Up My Sleeve*. A duet with Lee Greenwood ("Hopelessly Yours") is a relatively poor substitute.

what to buy next: *Give Me Some Wheels* (Capitol, 1996, prod. Trey Bruce, Scott Hendricks) ♫♫♫♫ is as energetic and supercharged as its title would suggest. Bogguss rocks like never before on the title tune, and the album contains some of the most sharply rendered material about relationships she's ever done, including "Let's Get Real" and "She Said, He Heard." It's her best since *Aces*. Speaking of which, *Aces* (Liberty, 1991, prod. Jimmy Bowen, Suzy Bogguss) ♫♫♫♫ is Bogguss' best Bowen-produced album, and it's the one that brought her fully into the Nashville fold with a raft of hit singles, notably Nanci Griffith's "Outbound Plane" and Cheryl Wheeler's "Aces." The album earned her a belated nod from the Country Music Association, which gave her its Horizon Award. Where were they in 1989?

the rest:

Moment of Truth (Liberty, 1990) ♫♫♫
Voices in the Wind (Liberty, 1992) ♫♫♫
Something up My Sleeve (Liberty, 1993) ♫♫♫
(With Chet Atkins) *Simpatico* (Liberty, 1994) ♫♫♫

influences:

◄◄ Nanci Griffith, Patsy Montana, Linda Ronstadt

►► Faith Hill, Terri Clark

Daniel Durchholz

JAMES BONAMY

Born April 29, 1972 in Daytona Beach, FL.

A high school jock who preferred Bon Jovi to Moe Bandy, James Bonamy didn't embrace the music his father loved until he was a student at the University of Alabama, where he won a shot on "The Country Boy Eddie Show" in Birmingham—the same break that helped break Tammy Wynette a generation before. Bonamy is blessed with contemporary country's prerequisite good looks, aw-shucks demeanor and a pleasant voice, but it's too early to tell if he has the talent, the drive and the desire to go the long haul, despite the name of his first album.

what's available: Bonamy's debut album *What I Live to Do* (Epic, 1995, prod. Doug Johnson) ♫♫ sounds like it came off the Music City assembly line. Same goes for "Dog on a Toolbox," the cheeky 1996 novelty hit that gained Bonamy a toehold on country radio.

influences:

►► Bon Jovi, Garth Brooks, Clint Black

Doug Pullen

Suzy Bogguss (© Ken Settle)

EDDIE BOND

Born July 1, 1933, in Memphis, TN.

Eddie Bond was a solid fixture on the Memphis country music scene in 1954, when the young Elvis Presley auditioned for his band. Bond, put off by both Presley's music and his lack of personal hygiene, turned him down, telling him to "stick with driving a truck. You'll never make it as a singer." Bond has been in Presley's shadow ever since. A professional singer since age 15, Bond cut his first sides for the Ekko label in 1955—fast hillbilly tunes that were given plenty of exposure through Bond's appearances on the *Louisiana Hayride* but suffered through poor distribution. In 1956 Mercury/Starday hired Bond to be its version of Elvis Presley. Bond, always honest about his motives ("The more I shake this leg, the more it's gonna cost you"), put aside his distaste for the new music long enough to cut some first-rate rockabilly sides. His cover of Sonny Fisher's "Rockin' Daddy" is definitive, and it sold quite well in the mid-South. At his peak Bond toured on package shows with Carl Perkins and Roy Orbison and taught them both a thing or two about showmanship.

Bond spent much of his time in the commercial doldrums, however. His gospel and Carl Smith tribute albums were career highlights, but for the most part his work as a straight country singer is bland and undistinguished. Bond simply sounded better doing Presley than he did doing Bond. Eventually he recognized this; during the late 1970s he could be seen doing public appearances in an Elvis-style jumpsuit and capitalizing on Memphis' storied rockabilly past. Today the bulk of Bond's U.S. fame is due to his work in Memphis radio and TV, where he has hosted several popular programs. He currently owns a radio station in Hernando, Mississippi, and is a big star in Holland, where he drives crowds wild with his Presleyesque performances.

what to buy: *Rockin' Daddy* (Bear Family, 1993, prod. various) ♫♫♫ is a two-CD set of Bond's rockabilly, country and gospel recordings from his tenures at Ekko, Mercury, Sun and Phillips International between 1955–62.

what to buy next: On *Rockin' Daddy from Memphis, Tennessee* (Rockhouse, 1982, prod. Dave Travis) ♫♫♫, producer Travis' band makes Bond rock hotter than usual.

what to avoid: *Walking Tall—The Legend of Buford Pusser* (Enterprise, 1973, prod. Jack Clement) **WOOF!** is Bond's original, unused score and narration for the movie *Walking Tall*, a lachrymose glorification of a martyred sheriff.

the rest:
Eddie Bond Sings Carl Smith (Tab, 1983) ♫♫♫

Early Original Recordings (White Label, 1985) ♫♫♫
Rockin' Daddy (Stomper Time, 1993) ♫♫

worth searching for: *Mercury Rockabillies* (Mercury/Phillips, 1975, comp. Bill Millar) ♫♫♫ contains four of Bond's best rockabilly sides for Starday, including one track by Conway Twitty, one by J.P. Richardson (the Big Bopper) and various tracks by Curtis Gordon and others. A good place to start.

influences:
◄◄ Elvis Presley, Carl Smith
►► Dave Travis, Crazy Cavan & the Rhythm Rockers, Chris Isaak

Ken Burke

JOHNNY BOND

Born Cyrus Whitfield Bond, June 1, 1915, in Enville, OK. Died June 12, 1978.

One of the most diverse talents of the early West Coast country scene, Johnny Bond started out singing Western music but quickly expanded his scope. He and Jimmy Wakley formed the Jimmy Wakely Trio with Dick Reinhart during the 1930s; they joined Gene Autry's *Melody Ranch Show* in 1940, and Bond remained with the show as a comic sidekick through the end of its run. Through that role, he gained notoriety with his novelty numbers about drunkenness (both spoken and sung). He had early hits with covers of the Merle Travis numbers "Divorce Me C.O.D." and "So Round, So Firm, So Fully Packed"; in 1963, his version of "Hot Rod Lincoln" reached #26 on the pop chart. Bond's recordings (mostly for Columbia and Starday) ranged from cowboy music to Western swing to honky tonk to comedy, but he's best known for the comedy. He was also successful in other areas. He had roles in a number of films. He wrote oft-recorded songs like "Tomorrow Never Comes," "I Wonder Where You Are Tonight" and the Western standard "Cimarron." He was the first person to publish Harlan Howard's songs, and he served as director of the Country Music Association during the 1970s. He died of a heart attack in 1978.

what to buy: Nearly all of Bond's available recordings come from his years with Starday during the 1960s. That company continuously repackages the same tracks under different titles, so they're practically interchangeable. However, if you can find *Sick, Sober & Sorry* (Country Road, 1976) ♫♫♫, it provides a glimpse into Bond's broad talents with his hit "Sick, Sober and Sorry," the hot rod tune "Fireball," a live version of Cowboy Copas' big hit "Alabam" with Copas plus a couple of swing instrumentals. Released in 1976 on cassette, it's not easy to find, but it is available.

what to buy next: *Three Sheets in the Wind* (Country Road, 1976) *♫♫* is another budget cassette focusing on Bond's musical side. The title track was a Top 30 hit in 1963. Only one cut, "That Dang Hangover," appears on *Sick, Sober & Sorry*.

what to avoid: Bond's lone stateside CD issue, *The Wild, Wicked but Wonderful West* (Starday, 1987) *♫*, is a Western album that shows a side of the performer not often seen in the novelty numbers and comedy bits that comprise the cassette packages. That is, it would show that different side if it didn't sound so horrible that it's almost impossible to listen to.

the rest:

Best of Country (Richmond, 1985) *♫♫*
Best of Comedy (Richmond, 1985) *♫♫*
Ten Little Bottles (Richmond, 1985) *♫♫*
Truckstop Comedy (King, 1995) *♫♫*

influences:

◀◀ Gene Autry, Merle Travis

▶▶ Jimmy Wakely, Commander Cody & His Lost Planet Airmen

Brian Mansfield

SIMON BONNEY

Born June 3, 1961, in Sydney, Australia.

A friend of the members of Australia's legendary Birthday Party, Bonney's band Crime and the City Solution incorporated some of that group's members upon its dissolution. And, like Birthday Party leader Nick Cave, Bonney has a romantic attraction to American mythology, which on his solo albums he complements with mostly original music heavily influenced by country. His instrumentally versatile wife, Bronwyn Adams, features heavily in their sound, as does Dwight Yoakam's bassist J.D. Foster.

what to buy: The concept album *Everyman* (Mute, 1995, prod. Gareth Jones) *♫♫♫* includes covers of a couple famous country standards, "Goodtime Charlie's Got the Blues" and "Blue Eyes Crying in the Rain," but sometimes moves away from the debut's slightly stronger stylistic focus with prominent horns, psychedelic keyboards and, on some cuts, cello. Still, Bonney's vocals and touches of banjo and dobro keep the country spirit alive. "A White Suit in Memphis," an oddball semi-tribute to Johnny Cash and Elvis Presley, is one of several tracks more memorable than anything on the previous record.

what to buy next: Sonically luscious, *Forever* (Mute, 1992, prod. Gareth Jones) *♫♫♫* lays vast shimmering heaps of reverb on everything (except for a few tracks where, for contrast, Bon-

ney's voice is very close and dry), with lots of slide and dobro. It sustains its mood very effectively, but none of the songs stick in the memory afterwards.

worth searching for: Not released in the U.S., *Don't Walk Away from Love* (Mute EP, 1996) *♫♫* offers remixes of familiar tracks. Bonney also has songs in the Wim Wenders films *Faraway, So Close* and *Wings of Desire*.

influences:

◀◀ Nick Cave, Cowboy Junkies

▶▶ U2

Steve Holtje

KARLA BONOFF /BRYNDLE

Born December 27, 1951, in Los Angeles, CA.

A singer/songwriter who came to prominence when Linda Ronstadt chose three of her songs to perform on her *Hasten Down the Wind* album, Karla Bonoff has had a solo career marked by consistently good material but precious little public acclaim. As a performer, Bonoff—who first hit the stage with the singer-songwriter collective Bryndle (which also included Kenny Edwards, Andrew Gold, and Wendy Waldman)—displays considerable charm and intellect, if not overpowering expressiveness. In other words, it's clear why her chief success has been as a songwriter. Still, her albums have their moments, and looking back on them now—particularly the first three—they recall a time during the late 1970s when an "El-Lay" singer/songwriter was something to be. Songs from Bonoff's first trio of albums were covered by Nicolette Larson, Bonnie Raitt, Maria Muldaur, Kim Carnes and Judy Collins, among others.

In recent years, Bonoff has turned her eye toward Nashville. Wynonna Judd scored a country smash with "Tell Me Why," and Bonoff has written for and performed on albums by Reba McEntire, Kathy Mattea and Judd, among others. That makes perfect sense, since Bonoff's brand of West Coast pop now passes for Nashville country. What goes around comes around.

what to buy: *Karla Bonoff* (Columbia, 1977, prod. Kenny Edwards) *♫♫♫♫* reprises versions of "Someone to Lay Down beside Me," "Lose Again" and "If He's Ever Near" from Ronstadt's *Hasten Down the Wind*. But the surprise here is that, in taking those three, Ronstadt didn't exhaust Bonoff's supply of good songs. The album also features the lovely waltz "Home," the lightly rocking "I Can't Hold On" and "Isn't It Always Love," and the yearning "Falling Star."

what to buy next: *New World* (Gold Castle, 1988/MusicMasters, 1995, prod. Mark Goldenberg) ♫♫♫, in its initial release, predated the adult contemporary format by enough time to keep it from getting the attention it deserves. Goldenberg's too-rich production aside, the album contains Bonoff's best batch of songs since her debut—including "All My Life," which Linda Ronstadt and Aaron Neville turned into a Grammy-winning hit. Bryndle, which re-formed during 1993, finally put out an album two years later: *Bryndle* (MusicMasters, 1995, prod. Josh Leo, Bryndle) ♫♫♫ was mostly written collaboratively, and the album sounds like an old-fashioned guitar pull. All four members trade lead vocals and contribute honeyed harmonies.

what to avoid: *Restless Nights* (Columbia, 1979, prod. Kenny Edwards) ♫♫ is pleasant, but carried mostly by its two covers—the Searchers' "When You Walk in the Room" (the inspiration for Pam Tillis' 1994 cover of the song) and the traditional "The Water Is Wide"—than by Bonoff originals.

the rest:
Wild Heart of the Young (Columbia, 1982) ♫♫♫

worth searching for: *Soundtrack from Thirtysomething* (Geffen, 1991, prod. various) ♫♫ is a compilation from the television drama on which Bonoff performs "The Water Is Wide."

influences:

◀◀ Stone Poneys, Laura Nyro, Wendy Waldman

▶▶ Kathy Mattea, Wynonna Judd, Trisha Yearwood, Mary Chapin Carpenter

Daniel Durchholz

BOONE CREEK

Formed 1977, in KY.

Ricky Skaggs, mandolin, fiddle, guitar, lead vocals; Jerry Douglas, dobro, vocals; Terry Baucom, banjo, fiddle, vocals; Wes Golding, guitar, lead and harmony vocals; Steve Bryant, bass, bass vocals.

Ricky Skaggs' last bluegrass band before he went into country music was together only briefly but had an influence that reached beyond its limited recorded output, as Skaggs, Douglas and Baucom went on to success individually and with other bands. Boone Creek mixed modern treatment of bluegrass standards with Golding's originals.

what's available: Sugar Hill rereleased the formerly out-of-print *One Way Track* (Sugar Hill, 1977/1991) ♫♫♫♫ with three bonus live tracks added to the 10 original songs. Skaggs'

bluesy lead vocals are strong and the four-part harmony on "Daniel Prayed" and "Little Community Church" is devastating. The fine vocal work is supported by intricate and imaginative picking, including Skaggs' fiery fiddling on "Sally Goodin."

worth searching for: *Boone Creek* (Sugar Hill, 1977, prod. Boone Creek) ♫♫♫♫ is the band's fine debut effort.

influences:

◀◀ J.D. Crowe & the New South, Country Gentlemen

▶▶ Doyle Lawson & Quicksilver, IIIrd Tyme Out, Ricky Skaggs & Kentucky Thunder

see also: *Ricky Skaggs, Jerry Douglas*

Douglas Fulmer

PAT BOONE

Born Charles Eugene Boone, June 1, 1934, in Jacksonville, FL.

Though he's now known best for his gospel albums and support of Republican politicians, Boone was once nearly crowned the king of rock 'n' roll—with more pop hits during the late 1950s and early 1960s than any artist, save Elvis Presley. Raised in rural Tennessee, Boone parlayed an appearance on the *Ted Mack Amateur Hour* television show into a year-long stint on Arthur Godfrey's amateur show and a recording contract. Boone enjoyed a few pop hits with such songs as "Two Hearts, Two Kisses" in 1955, but it wasn't until he began recording sanitized, de-ethnicized versions of R&B and rock hits—including Little Richard's "Tutti Frutti" and "Long Tall Sally"—that Boone's place in history was assured. With his crewcut and white buckskin shoes, Boone was the perfect bridge between early rock 'n' roll "race records" and the white pop mainstream, covering tunes by Fats Domino, Ivory Joe Hunter and others. Beatlemania eventually made his efforts irrelevant, but not before Boone had moved on to his own television show and movie soundtrack work. In all, Boone enjoyed 38 chart-topping pop hits. In 1996, however, he began preparing an album of heavy metal covers while also working the infomercial circuit, proving himself an opportunist of the highest caliber.

what to buy: Most of what's available are retrospectives, holiday collections and Christian recordings. Many—though not all—of the hits are on *Pat Boone's Greatest Hits* (MCA, 1993, prod. various) ♫♫.

what to buy next: There's also a video anthology of his chart successes, *40 Years of Hits* (Rhino, 1995) ♫♫♫, or you can dig for the hard-to-find *Jivin' Pat* (Bear Family, 1986) ♫♫♫, a sardonic collection of his rock covers.

the rest:

Best Of (MCA, 1982) 🎵🎵🎵

Greatest Hits (Curb, 1990) 🎵🎵🎵

A Date with Pat Boone (Pair, 1992) 🎵🎵

Pat's Greatest Hits (Curb, 1994) 🎵🎵

worth searching for: Boone actually has quite a wit, which he displays on *In a Metal Mood: No More Mr. Nice Guy* (MCA, 1997, prod. Michael Lloyd, Jeffrey Weber) 🎵🎵🎵, a collection of covers of heavy metal tunes by the likes of Ozzy Osbourne, Metallica and, of course, Alice Cooper. On the one hand, Boone thinks it's a tremendous joke (which it is); on the other, he plays it straight with some complex, if kinda goofy, big-band charts.

influences:

◀◀ Elvis Presley

▶▶ Johnny Tillotson, Debby Boone, Chris Isaak

Eric Deggans and Brian Mansfield

LIBBI BOSWORTH

Born in Galveston, TX.

It's hard to believe Libbi Bosworth went through phases as a punk rocker and a jazz student at the Berklee School of Music. From the genuine spirit of her debut album, *Outskirts of You*, it sounds like she was born to sing and write country music. Before those stylistic excursions, Bosworth grew up on the jukebox songs of Loretta Lynn, Tammy Wynette, George Jones and Merle Haggard. Her late father, a truck driver by profession and a country music aficionado by heart, introduced the impressionable child to the diehard tunes that became the sound track of truckers' lives. On her own at 16, Bosworth roamed the country before settling back in Texas to satisfy the craving that would never leave her until she fed it. She kicked around Austin for a while, got an original song recorded by fellow Austinite Kelly Willis ("Up All Night") and eventually recorded her debut CD in the Texas capitol and the famed Music City. Along the way she's garnered kudos from influential Texas country-folkie Jimmie Dale Gilmore and Lucinda Williams' former guitarist, Gurf Morlix.

what's available: *Outskirts of You* (Freedom, 1996, prod. Earl B. Freedom, Bill Dwyer, Mike Poole) 🎵🎵🎵🎵 is an auspicious debut. With a voice that's a mixture of Patsy Cline, Emmylou Harris and Kelly Willis, as well as a keen sense for the purity of country, Bosworth turned out a record brimming with integrity. From the waltzy title cut to the rocking "Up All Night" and the autobiographical "My Old Man," this album offers a new Texas artist with national potential.

Pat Boone **(Agency for the Performing Arts)**

worth searching for: Like many of her Texas-based contemporaries—Don Walser, Dale Watson, the Derailers—Bosworth is a featured artist on *Austin Country Nights* (Watermelon, 1995, prod. Rob Patterson, Mike Stewart) 🎵🎵🎵🎵, a compilation of the Texas capitol's best acts. Bosworth's cut, the harmonica-driven country blues scorcher "Baby, Maybe Then I'll Love You," is one of 13 gems on this fine set.

influences:

◀◀ Patsy Cline, Loretta Lynn, Kelly Willis

Mario Tarradell

THE BOTTLE ROCKETS

Formed 1993, in Festus, MO.

Brian Henneman, guitar, vocals; Tom Parr, guitar; Mark Ortmann, drums; Tom Ray, bass.

Like Ronnie Van Zandt and Lynyrd Skynyrd before them, Brian Henneman and the Bottle Rockets are not the unreconstructed hawbucks they seem at first glance. Their songs, which are populated with hot-to-trot trailer mamas and Confederate-flag-waving idiots, are deceptively simple, conveying a deeply conflicted sense of small-town values as they alternately celebrate redneck culture and mercilessly lampoon it.

what to buy: *The Brooklyn Side* (East Side Digital, 1994/Tag Atlantic 1995, prod. Eric "Roscoe" Ambel) 𝄢𝄢𝄢𝄢 is the group's second album and contains a more refined version of the country-grunge groove introduced on its debut. "Welfare Music" may place the band on the fightin' side of Merle Haggard, or, at the very least, Rush Limbaugh, but it deftly humanizes America's lower social strata. "1,000 Dollar Car" shows off Henneman's sense of humor, yet the hilarity offered by "Sunday Sports" is merely a disguise for the protagonist's genuine sense of desperation. But the album's most harrowing number is Parr's "What More Can I Do?," a sharply told tale of domestic abuse that would have been a great theme song for the O.J. Simpson trial.

the rest:
Bottle Rockets (East Side Digital, 1993) 𝄢𝄢𝄢𝄢

worth searching for: Prior to forming the band, Henneman—a former Uncle Tupelo roadie—released the single "Indianapolis" (Rockville, 1993, prod. Coffee Creek, Jack Petracek) 𝄢𝄢𝄢𝄢, on which he is backed by Tupelo partners Jay Farrar and Jeff Tweedy.

influences:
◀◀ Lynyrd Skynyrd, Neil Young, ZZ Top, Buck Owens
▶▶ V-Roys

Daniel Durchholz

JIMMY BOWEN
Born James Albert Bowen, November 30, 1937, in Santa Rita, NM.

Along with Buddy Knox, Jimmy Bowen formed the Rhythm Orchids at West Texas College in 1955. The group came to Norman Petty Studios in late 1956 to record some masters, which they then sold to Roulette Records. Roulette released two million-selling singles under the names of the group's vocalists, Buddy Knox's "Party Doll" and Bowen's "I'm Stickin' with You." Bowen also scored a pop hit in 1957 with "Warm Up to Me Baby," but by 1959 he had quit performing to write and produce. He worked with Glen Campbell, Dean Martin and Frank Sinatra in the 1960s, and from the 1970s to the 1990s was responsible for establishing several Nashville record labels, including MCA, Warner Bros. and Liberty, as major commercial forces.

what's available: *The Best of Jimmy Bowen* (Collectibles, 1991) 𝄢𝄢, a reissue of Bowen's first album, is a good example of the kind of soft rockabilly that bubbled in the wake of Elvis' explosion. It sounds pretty tame nowadays, though.

worth searching for: From the Rhythm Orchids: *The Complete Roulette Recordings* (Sequel) 𝄢𝄢𝄢; from Buddy Knox: *The Best of Buddy Knox* (Rhino, 1990) 𝄢𝄢𝄢, more gentle rockabilly from the Rhythm Orchids' other (better) singer.

influences:
◀◀ Buddy Knox, Elvis Presley
▶▶ Crickets, Rick Nelson, Eddie Cochran

Bob Cannon

RONNIE BOWMAN
See: Lonesome River Band

BOXCAR WILLIE
Born Lecil Travis Martin, September 1, 1931, in Sterratt, TX.

A tremendous country entertainer, Boxcar Willie did not achieve international fame with his trademark hobo persona until middle age. Following a career in the U.S. Air Force as a flight engineer, Boxcar Willie returned to his first love, country music. While performing at a Nashville club in 1977, he was booked by promoter Drew Taylor for a European tour. His platinum album *King of the Road* and several appearances at the Wembley Music Festival attest to his overseas popularity. Closer to home, he has been a member of the Grand Ole Opry since 1981 and a mainstay in Branson, Missouri, with his style of "pure" country music. Sadly, the Boxcar has recently entered semi-retirement due to poor health.

what to buy: *Rocky Box* (K-Tel, 1993, prod. Boxcar Willie, Lou Whitney & the Skeletons) 𝄢𝄢𝄢𝄢, recorded with Missouri rock band the Skeletons, brought Boxcar renewed critical acclaim during the 1990s, well after his hitmaking days were over. *Rocky Box* is a tremendously fun roots rock/country album, with spirited versions of Johnny Cash's "Train of Love," Moon Mulican's "Pipeliner Blues" and even "Achy Breaky Heart."

the rest:
Grassy Box (Gem) 𝄢𝄢𝄢
Hey, Man! (Gem) 𝄢𝄢𝄢
King of the Road (Gem) 𝄢𝄢𝄢
Winds of Yesterday (Gem) 𝄢𝄢𝄢
Boxcar Blues (Madacy) 𝄢𝄢𝄢
The Spirit of America (Madacy, 1991) 𝄢𝄢𝄢
(With others) *Stars Sing Songs for Kids! Volume 2* (Little Morganville, 1994) 𝄢𝄢
Boxcar Willie & Friends—Live at Wembley (Pickwick, 1995) 𝄢𝄢

influences:
◀◀ Roy Acuff, Grandpa Jones, Slim Whitman
▶▶ Vernon Oxford

Randall T. Cook

BOY HOWDY

Formed 1990, in CA.

Cary Park, guitar, mandolin, vocals; Larry Park, guitar, fiddle, vocals; Jeffrey Steele, lead vocals, bass; Hugh Wright, drums, vocals.

California country group Boy Howdy, formed around the dual-guitar sound of brothers Larry and Cary Park, rose to brief fame during the mid-1990s with a series of power-country ballads. The group had played the Los Angeles club scene before signing with Curb Records. Shortly after the release of the group's debut, drummer Hugh Wright was struck by a car while trying to help another accident victim. He spent five months in a coma but eventually recovered to rejoin the band.

what's available: *Welcome to Howdywood* (Curb, 1992, prod. Chris Farren) ♪♪ is just about everything that Nashvillians mistrust about Californians singing country and precious little of the things they value (i.e., Buck, Merle and Dwight). The Park brothers display some impressive chops, but they use them on stuff like a double-time breakdown of the Kinks' "You Really Got Me." *She'd Give Anything* (Curb EP, 1994, prod. Chris Farren) ♪♪♪ contains three of the group's hits, including "They Don't Make 'Em Like That Anymore" and "She'd Give Anything" (also a pop hit for Gerald LeVert as "I'd Give Anything"), in a scant six songs. How much more cost effective can you get? *Born That Way* (Curb, 1995, prod. Chris Farren) ♪♪ contains Boy Howdy's one other Top 40 hit, "True to His Word." Their choice of covers improved, too: this time they did Stephen Stills' "Love the One You're With."

influences:
◀◀ Little Texas, Restless Heart
▶▶ Smokin' Armadillos, Burnin' Daylight

Brian Mansfield

THE BOYS FROM INDIANA

Formed 1973, in Sunman, IN. Disbanded 1994.

Aubrey Holt, guitar, vocals; Tom Holt, mandolin, bass, guitar, vocals; Jerry Holt, bass vocals; Paul Mullins, fiddle (1973–79); Noah Crase, banjo (1973–79); Harley Gabbard, dobro; Sam Jeffries, fiddle; Tony Holt, bass; Jamie Johnson, mandolin; Cabe Conley, banjo; others.

FIVE FOR MY FANS

KATHY BAILLIE
(of Baillie & the Boys)

Linda Ronstadt
Hasten Down the Wind (Elektra)

Joni Mitchell
Blue (Reprise)

Joni Mitchell
Court and Spark (Elektra)

Joni Mitchell
Turbulent Indigo (Reprise)

Beatles
Beatles '65 (Capitol)

Formed around the nucleus of brothers Aubrey, Tom and Jerry Holt, the Boys from Indiana were a fixture on the bluegrass festival circuit for two decades. The band came together after Aubrey Holt failed to establish himself as a songwriter in Nashville. They were known for structuring their shows around a theme, such as "The Pioneers of Bluegrass." They disbanded in 1994 after brothers Tom and Jerry left the group.

what's available: *Touchin Home'* (Rebel, 1992, prod. Aubrey Holt, Buddy Spicher) ♪♪♪ contains 12 songs, including eight originals and the buck Owens/Don Rich instrumental "Cajun Fiddle." It's a relaxed album, with the instrumental work usually backing up the vocals rather than being in the forefront.

influences:
◀◀ Bill Monroe, Flatt & Scruggs
▶▶ Traditional Grass

Douglas Fulmer

$\frac{4}{6}$ br5-49

BR5-49

Formed 1993, in Nashville, TN.

Gary Bennett, vocals, guitar; Don Herron, steel guitar, mandolin, fiddle; Smilin' Jay McDowell, upright bass; Chuck Mead, vocals, guitars; "Hawk" Shaw Wilson, drums.

Revisionist visionaries or a hillbilly Sha-Na-Na? That's the challenge facing BR5-49 as the quirky quintet attempts to prove there's some staying power behind the endearing shtick that made it 1996's twangiest buzz band. Adopting its moniker from the phone number for Junior Samples' used car lot on *Hee Haw*, the group set up shop in the window of Robert's Western World, a boot store/nightclub on Nashville's Lower Broadway, and was soon luring everyone from Faron Young and Willie Nelson to the Mavericks and Trisha Yearwood to its much-touted five-hour, request-driven shows. Their smirking but heartfelt take on tradition includes vintage wardrobes, an awesome arsenal of Hank Williams, Buck Owens, Mel Tillis, Carl Smith and Billy Joe Shaver covers, and the band-penned novelties "Me 'n' Opie (Down by the Duck Pond)" and the pinup-worshipping "Bettie Bettie." Now signed to Arista and touring beyond the comfy confines of Robert's, BR5-49 must find a way to maintain its reputation as an unstumpable human jukebox without lapsing into kitschy predictability, and to use country music's past as a foundation, not a crutch.

what to buy: BR5-49's spirited, spit-polished, self-titled studio debut (Arista, 1996, prod. Jozef Nuyens, Mike Janas) 𝄢𝄢𝄢 boasts faithful but unspectacular covers of such Robert's-era favorites as "Crazy Arms," Gram Parsons' "Hickory Wind" and Webb Pierce's "I Ain't Never." The contemporary perspective of such Chuck Mead-penned numbers as "Lifetime to Prove" and the swinging "Little Ramona (Gone Hillbilly Nuts)" updates the group's sound without diluting its roots-conscious purity.

the rest: *Live from Robert's* (Arista EP, 1996) 𝄢𝄢𝄢

influences:
◀◀ Hank Williams, Asleep at the Wheel, Ray Price, Junior Brown
▶▶ Dave & Deke Combo, Derailers

David Okamoto

THE BRADY BUNCH

See: Maureen McCormick

PAUL BRANDT

Born in Calgary, Alberta, Canada

Paul Brandt worked as a pediatric nurse north of the border before becoming a full-time country singer. He's one of the few country singers (Wade Hayes is another) in recent memory who has a legitimate bass range, which he can use to dramatic effect.

what's available: Brandt looked like a skinny kid in an oversized black hat when *Calm before the Storm* (Warner Bros., 1996, prod. Josh Leo) 𝄢𝄢𝄢 came out, but that turned out to be a total package. Not only does he have a phenomenal range (at one point he makes a run of more than two octaves in a matter of measures), but he also writes most of the album's best songs, including the smash ballad "I Do," which he penned for a friend's wedding. Brandt brings pop elements into his country in a way that's thrilling, and he's definitely got a way with a love song. In a year that often ignored young hat acts, Brandt established himself as a promising star.

influences:
◀◀ Wade Hayes
▶▶ David Kersh, Gary Allan

Brian Mansfield

BREAD

See: David Gates

GARY BREWER

Born April 19, 1965, in KY.

A bluegrass guitar player with a traditional-based style, Gary Brewer formed his band the Kentucky Ramblers at age 15. He began making has mark on the national bluegrass scene during 1994, when he was picked to tour with Bill and James Monroe's "Father and Son" tour. Monroe became one of Brewer's biggest boosters, giving him an original song for one album and playing on the recording.

what to buy: *Guitar* (Copper Creek, 1995, prod. Gary Brewer, Stretchgrass Productions) 𝄢𝄢𝄢 is an all-instrumental effort including a generous 18 songs mixing traditional numbers, originals and covers. Included are three Bill Monroe songs, including the previously unrecorded "The Old Kentucky Blues."

what to buy next: Brewer got some attention by getting Bill Monroe to appear with him on the cover of *Money to Ride the Train* (Copper Creek, 1994, prod. Gary Brewer & the Kentucky Ramblers) 𝄢𝄢𝄢, although Monroe doesn't appear on the album. It includes an unusual choice in Creedence Clearwater Revival's "Looking out My Back Door" and three originals, including the title cut.

the rest:

Down Home Memories (Copper Creek, 1990) 🎵🎵🎵

Going Back to Kentucky (Copper Creek, 1992) 🎵🎵🎵

Nearing Jordan's Crossing (Copper Creek, 1993) 🎵🎵🎵

Live in Europe (Copper Creek, 1996) 🎵🎵🎵

influences:

◀◀ Bill Monroe, Doc Watson, Larry Sparks

▶▶ Norman Blake, Traditional Grass

Douglas Fulmer

LISA BROKOP

Born June 6, 1973, in Surrey, British Columbia, Canada.

Lisa Brokop was already an accomplished singer and actress in Canada by age 20 when she came to Nashville. A series of independent singles recorded at age 16 helped her win newcomer and female vocalist awards from the British Columbia Country Music Association during the early 1990s. She also starred in the film *Harmony Cats.*

what's available: *Every Little Girl's Dream* (Capitol, 1994, prod. Jerry Crutchfield) 🎵🎵🎵 is an uneven though occasionally promising debut. In *Lisa Brokop* (Capitol, 1996, prod. Jerry Crutchfield, Josh Leo) 🎵🎵🎵, Brokop sounds more self-assured and the song selection is better. Though it still didn't yield her a breakthrough hit, the album features fine, up-tempo pop country numbers like "West of Crazy," "Language of Love" and "Before He Kissed Me" and a fine remake of Jennifer Warnes' 1979 hit "I Know a Heartache When I See One." Brokop's powerful voice, though, is most effective on two ballads, the anti-alcohol anthem "She Can't Save Him" and Steve Wariner's unconditional love song "At the End of the Day."

influences:

◀◀ Michelle Wright, Trisha Yearwood

Bill Hobbs

DAVID BROMBERG

Born September 19, 1945, in Philadelphia, PA.

A New York session musician who first came to prominence playing on Bob Dylan's *Self Portrait* and *New Morning* albums, stringed instrument virtuoso David Bromberg cut a wholly unconventional series of 10 albums for the Columbia and Fantasy

Lisa Brokop (© Ken Settle)

labels through the 1970s that matched his refined acoustic musicianship with a wacky sense of humor. Linda Ronstadt, Emmylou Harris, Dr. John, Bonnie Raitt, Ricky Skaggs and members of the Grateful Dead have all made guest appearances on his recordings, underlining Bromberg's reputation as a musician's musician. He abruptly quit recording and touring to concentrate on making and repairing instruments, and has released records and performed rarely since 1981.

what to buy: *How Late'll Ya Play 'Til* (Fantasy, 1976, prod. Steve Burgh, David Bromberg) 🎵🎵🎵🎵 is a two-disc set—one live, one studio—that's available either individually or together and finds Bromberg at the height of his powers, supported by a remarkable band.

what to buy next: His debut, *David Bromberg* (Columbia, 1971, prod. David Bromberg) 🎵🎵🎵, blends the bluesey with the blowzy, the wry with the wistful, and showcases his considerable skills.

the rest:

Demons in Disguise (Columbia, 1972) 🎵🎵🎵

Wanted Dead or Alive (Columbia, 1974) 🎵🎵🎵
Midnight on the Water (Columbia, 1975) 🎵🎵🎵🎵
Reckless Abandon (Fantasy, 1977) 🎵🎵🎵
My Own House (Fantasy, 1978) 🎵🎵🎵
You Should See the Rest of the Band (Fantasy, 1980) 🎵🎵🎵
Long Way from Here (Fantasy, 1986) 🎵🎵🎵
Sideman Serenade (Rounder, 1989) 🎵🎵🎵

worth searching for: Bromberg plays in a relaxed Western swing vein on the Vassar Clements album *Hillbilly Jazz* (Flying Fish, 1977) 🎵🎵🎵🎵.

influences:

◀◀ Bob Dylan, Bill Monroe, Rev. Gary Davis
▶▶ David Grisman, Loudon Wainwright

Joel Selvin

BROOKS & DUNN

Formed c. 1990, in Nashville, TN.

Kix Brooks (born Leon Eric Brooks III, May 21, 1955, in Shreveport, LA), vocals, guitar; Ronnie Dunn (born June 1, 1953, in Coleman, TX), vocals, guitar.

Kix Brooks and Ronnie Dunn were two sons of oil workers who found limited success on their own. Brooks had moved to Music City in 1979 and had songs cut by Highway 101, Crystal Gayle and the Nitty Gritty Dirt Band. Dunn had two charting singles for Churchill Records during the early 1980s and won the Marlboro National Talent Search in 1989. When they came together at the suggestion of Arista-Nashville label-head Tim DuBois, the course of their careers changed drastically. With both singers easily topping six feet, Brooks & Dunn cut an impressive figure of cowboy machismo, and success followed immediately: each of the duo's first four singles topped the chart, and their first four albums have each gone multi-platinum. The duo's 1992 hit "Boot Scootin' Boogie," previously cut by Asleep at the Wheel, became the first country single to have a separate dance version. After winning the Country Music Association's Vocal Duo of the Year a record five consecutive times (they took over when the Judds broke up), the act became CMA's Entertainer of the Year in 1996.

what to buy: *Brand New Man* (Arista, 1991, prod. Scott Hendricks, Don Cook) 🎵🎵🎵🎵 is a fine commercial debut packed with five hit singles. The title track uses Pentecostal imagery to depict the redeeming power of love, and "Boot Scootin' Boogie" kicked off the line dance craze.

what to avoid: *Hard Workin' Man* (Arista, 1993, prod. Scott Hendricks, Don Cook) 🎵🎵 offers plenty of hits ("We'll Burn That Bridge," "She Used to Be Mine," "Rock My World (Little Country Girl)," but a year's worth of touring took its effect on the duo's songwriting.

the rest:
Waitin' on Sundown (Arista, 1994) 🎵🎵🎵
Borderline (Arista, 1996) 🎵🎵🎵

solo outings:
Kix Brooks:
Kix Brooks (Capitol, 1989) 🎵🎵🎵

influences:

◀◀ Asleep at the Wheel,
▶▶ Gibson/Miller Band, Archer/Park

Brian Mansfield

GARTH BROOKS

Born February 7, 1962, in Tulsa, OK.

Garth Brooks did nothing less than change the face of music—country and popular—during the early 1990s. The son of singer Colleen Carroll, Brooks took traditional sounds and blended them with the arena rock of his youth (the guy's a stone Kiss, Boston and Styx fan) and his affinity for singer/songwriters such as James Taylor, Dan Fogelberg and Bob Seger. That's Garth: The Music, hailing from an apprenticeship in clubs and as a demo singer in Nashville. Then there's Garth: The Package, a flashy, stomping spectacle that the Oklahoma State University advertising major (and jock) used to drag country music—which was just starting to get used to videos—into the modern world. His pyrotechnic-laden shows were something this audience had never seen from its performers, even the ones who did put a little bit of rock into their sound. And when the pop mainstream dubbed Brooks the "safe" country star to like, it was all over. Declaring a wish to be "the artist of the decade for the '90s," Brooks started the decade with two albums—*No Fences* and *Ropin' the Wind*—that sold more than 10 million copies each, *Ropin' the Wind* being the first album in history to debut at #1 on both *Billboard*'s pop and country charts. The ratings for his NBC-TV specials were huge, and his retrospective *The Hits* remains the best-selling country best-of set, with

Garth Brooks (© Ken Settle)

seven million copies sold. And it was Brooks' boot that kicked open the door for Alan Jackson, Shania Twain, Trisha Yearwood, Brooks & Dunn and all the other country stars who found the early 1990s to be their music's biggest boom time since the days of *Urban Cowboy*.

Brooks has suffered some backlash, although minimal; some found Brooks' talk of retirement in 1992—in order to spend more time with his wife, Sandy, and their then-newborn daughter Taylor—to be calculated and disingenuous. Brooks was even sued that same year by an Oklahoma doctor who claimed his wife died because she could not reach 911 on the same day lines were jammed by Brooks fans trying to buy tickets for a hometown show. But Brooks has countered any adversity by maintaining his integrity: he's held ticket prices to $18 (how many rock superstars do that?); and he forced conservative radio programmers to embrace a more tolerant viewpoint with his 1992 hit "We Shall Be Free." The greatest challenge facing Brooks isn't his fault; in the wake of his success, every record company in Nashville—and beyond—worked overtime to find Garth soundalikes. If imitation is the sincerest form of flattery, then Brooks should be one immensely flattered dude.

what to buy: *No Fences* (Liberty, 1990, prod. Allen Reynolds) ♪♪♪♪ and *Ropin' the Wind* (Liberty, 1991, prod. Allen Reynolds) ♪♪♪♪ show that in addition to strong singles, Brooks could fill entire albums with quality material. *No Fences*' "Mr. Blue," for instance, packs as much power as "The Thunder Rolls" or "Unanswered Prayers"—although "Friends in Low Places" is a hard anthem to compete with. *Ropin'* has the hymn-like "The River" as well as the evocative "Rodeo" and his cover of Billy Joel's "Shameless."

what to buy next: *The Hits* (Liberty, 1994, prod. Allen Reynolds) ♪♪♪♪♪ is a generous sampling of the singles Brooks regularly shot to the top of the country charts. And don't overlooks his debut, *Garth Brooks* (Liberty, 1989, prod. Allen Reynolds) ♪♪♪♪, whose aces—"Much Too Young (to Feel This Damn Old)" and "The Dance"—remain among the best songs in his canon.

what to avoid: Brooks takes some chances on *Fresh Horses* (Capitol, 1995, prod. Allen Reynolds) ♪♪♪—notably the Celtic flavor of "Ireland"—but it doesn't have the same fresh crackle of its predecessors.

the rest:
Beyond the Season (Liberty, 1992) ♪♪♪
The Chase (Liberty, 1992) ♪♪♪♪
In Pieces (Liberty, 1993) ♪♪♪♪

worth searching for: *The Hits* was accompanied by *Garth Brooks CD Zooming* (Liberty, 1994) ♪♪♪, an inventive—if slightly bizarre—run through snippets of every song Brooks had recorded to that point. Also, *The Garth Brooks Collection* (1994, prod. Allen Reynolds) ♪♪♪♪—given away as a promotion with McDonald's—picks some of Brooks' lesser album tracks to highlight his prowess as a songwriter.

influences:

◄◄ Eddy Arnold, Willie Nelson, Porter Wagoner, Randy Travis, George Strait, Kiss, Boston, Styx, Bob Seger, James Taylor, Dan Fogelberg, Glen Campbell

►► John Michael Montgomery, Tim McGraw, Clay Walker, Chris Ward, David Kersh

see also: *Ty England*

Gary Graff

KIX BROOKS
See: Brooks & Dunn

THE BROTHER BOYS

Eugene Wolf, vocals; Ed Snodderly, vocals, guitar, dobro, fiddle, harmonica.

Though not brothers, Eugene Wolf and Ed Snodderly owe much to the classic country brother duets. They are no mere "retro act," however, instead playing what they call "New Hillbilly Music." Backed on their recordings by a variety of instrumentation, the Brother Boys deftly back their harmony vocals with a mix of bluegrass, country and country/blues with a discernable rock influence.

what's available: On *Plow* (Sugar Hill, 1992, prod. Jerry Douglas) ♪♪♪, six originals are mixed with covers of songs from the Wilburn Brothers, Loretta Lynn and Bill Anderson. *Presley's Grocery* (Sugar Hill, 1996, prod. Ed Snodderly) ♪♪♪♪ is a refreshing mix of bluegrass songs like Bill Monroe's "Can't You Hear Me Calling," traditional country ("Those Two Blue Eyes") and rockabilly-flavored originals ("Let's Shake Loose").

influences:
◄◄ Wilburn Brothers, Louvin Brothers, Everly Brothers
►► Tony Rice, Jerry Douglas

Douglas Fulmer

BROTHER OSWALD

See: Bashful Brother Oswald

BROTHER PHELPS

See: Kentucky HeadHunters

ALISON BROWN

Born August 7, 1962, in Hartford, CT.

Besides being one of the few women to make her reputation on the banjo, Brown is a progressive instrumentalist who's equally at home in traditional bluegrass and in more experimental settings. After moving to San Diego at age 12, she went to Harvard, where she studied pre-med, history and literature. She then received her M.B.A. from UCLA and worked as an investment banker before devoting herself fully to music. Brown played with Alison Krauss & Union Station from 1989–91 and in 1993 founded Small World Music, which evolved into the singer-songwriters' label Compass Records in 1995.

what to buy: *Quartet* (Vanguard, 1996, prod. Garry West) ♫♫♫♫, Brown's fourth album, is a delight featuring John Burr on piano, Garry West on bass and Rick Reed on drums. With its heavy jazz and Latin overtones, it won't remind anyone of Earl Scruggs, but Brown's use of the five-string is consistently clever, exciting and melodic.

what to buy next: *Look Left* (Vanguard, 1994, prod. Garry West) ♫♫♫♫, Brown's third album, contains more elements of pure bluegrass but expands her sound into Cajun ("Étouffee Brutus?"), jazz ("Look Left") and world beat ("Deep North"). A smorgasbord of styles that holds together and makes a pretty grand statement.

the rest:
Simple Pleasures (Vanguard, 1990) ♫♫♫
Twilight Motel (Vanguard, 1992) ♫♫♫♫

worth searching for: Alison Krauss & Union Station's *I've Got That Old Feeling* (Rounder, 1990, prod. Bil VornDick, Jerry Douglas) ♫♫♫♫, Michelle Shocked's *Arkansas Traveler* (Mercury, 1992, prod. Michelle Shocked) ♫♫♫ and Clive Gregson's *I Love This Town* (Compass, 1996, prod. Clive Gregson, Garry West) ♫♫♫♫ all feature Brown's playing.

influences:
◀◀ Alison Krauss, Bela Fleck, David Grisman, Tony Trischka
▶▶ Kate Campbell, Clive Gregson

Bob Cannon and Douglas Fulmer

GREG BROWN

Born in IA.

Iowa singer/songwriter Greg Brown possesses a quirky sensibility and gift of wordplay, a wry, ironic stage presence and a rumbling, phlegmatic baritone voice that has found much favor with festivalgoers and folk club fans over the past 15 years. Probably the Brown song most familiar to traditional country music fans is "The Train Carrying Jimmie Rodgers Home," which was recorded by the Nashville Bluegrass Band. It also appears on his first Red House album.

what to buy: *Down in There* (Red House, 1990, prod. Bo Ramsey) ♫♫♫♫ contains 10 of Brown's most endearing, quirky originals. *The Live One* (Red House, 1995) ♫♫♫♫ captures Brown in the venue best suited for full appreciation of his sense of humor and wordplay.

what to buy next: On *Songs of Innocence and Experience* (Red House, 1986, prod. Bob Feldman, Greg Brown) ♫♫♫♫, Brown sets to music and sings the poems of William Blake, while Michael Doucet accompanies on fiddle. Greg Brown and Bill Morrissey team up on *Friend of Mine* (Philo, 1993, prod. Ellen Karas) ♫♫♫♫, a batch of songs they've sung together at parties, backstage and in green rooms. The album has a loose, amiable feel to it, and the repertoire is eclectic enough—everything from "Little Red Rooster" and "You Can't Always Get What You Want" to Hank Williams' "I'll Never Get Out of This World Alive."

the rest:
44 & 66 (Red House, 1980) ♫♫♫
In the Dark with You (Red House, 1986) ♫♫♫
One More Goodnight Kiss (Red House, 1987) ♫♫♫
One Big Town (Red House, 1989) ♫♫♫
Dream Cafe (Red House, 1992) ♫♫♫♫
Bathtub Blues (Red House, 1993) ♫♫♫
The Poet Game (Red House, 1994) ♫♫♫
Further In (Red House, 1996) ♫♫♫

influences:
◀◀ John Prine, Tom Waits
▶▶ Bill Morrissey, John Gorka

Randy Pitts

HYLO BROWN

Born Frank Brown, April 20, 1922, in River, KY.

A bluegrass lead singer much lauded for his legendary range (thus the nickname), Hylo Brown is among the few fortunates from the early days of bluegrass to record extensively for a major label. Born in eastern Kentucky, he first recorded four sides for Capitol in 1954 before becoming a featured vocalist with Flatt & Scruggs. He split from the legendary bluegrass duo to form the Timberliners, who recorded a classic bluegrass album for Capitol in 1958 and shared Flatt & Scruggs' television work for Martha White Mills as sort of a second unit until videotape and syndication doomed that enterprise. Brown later returned to work for Flatt & Scruggs and recorded four bluegrass albums for Starday during the 1960s. Since then he's worked mostly as a soloist, recording with decreasing frequency for such small labels as Rural Rhythm, K-Ark, Jessup, and Atteiram.

what's available: *Hylo Brown & the Timberliners* (Bear Family, 1992, prod. Ken Nelson) ♫♫♫ contains the complete session work done by Brown for Capitol, including many tracks previously reissued. It contains 46 tracks in all, with extensive notes and discography. Along with the classic bluegrass here, an unissued session attempting to update Hylo's sound with the Jordanaires' overdubbed vocals and "modern" instrumentation is included. On *In Concert* (Copper Creek, 1995) ♫♫♫, a 1959 concert recording from Brown's heyday, he shows off his natural high lead tenor voice to great effect, sometimes shifting into falsetto, on a program of mostly traditional bluegrass material featuring a great band.

influences:

◀◀ Flatt & Scruggs, Bradley Kincaid

▶▶ Vern Williams

Randy Pitts

JIM ED BROWN

See: The Browns

JUNIOR BROWN

Born June 12, 1952, in Cottonwood, AZ.

There's something decidedly but delightfully off-center about Junior Brown, and it's not just the angle of his cowboy hat. Maybe it's his instrument of choice, a self-invented combination six-string and steel guitar that he calls a "guit-steel." Maybe it's songs with such titles as "My Wife Thinks You're Dead," "Venom Wearin' Denim" and "What's Left Just Won't Go Right." Or maybe it's his unflappable allegiance to a brave vision that melds the hardcore honky tonk of Ernest Tubb with the string-bending, mind-blowing fury of Jimi Hendrix, with everything from Ray Price to Don Ho thrown in. Such a hip hybrid immediately made him a hero in his home base of Austin,

Texas, but most of America—whose exposure to Brown has come chiefly from goofy CMT videos for "My Wife Thinks You're Dead" and truckstop songsmith Red Simpson's "Highway Patrol"—still thinks of him as a poker-faced novelty act. Listen carefully and you'll realize that beneath the tailored two-piece suits and the clever wordplay is a soft-spoken preservationist for the roots of country music and a hard-nosed champion for the brave struggles of working-class America who just happens to have a great sense of humor.

what to buy: "My Wife Thinks You're Dead" and "Highway Patrol" are the hilarious CMT hits that drew listeners to *Guit with It* (Curb, 1993, prod. Junior Brown) ♫♫♫, but the hidden treats are the pun-filled "Still Life with Rose," in which the singer tells an ex-flame that she can't hold a candle to a painting of his new love ("Still life with Rose is better/Than life with you could ever be"), and the 11-minute instrumental "Guit-Steel Blues."

what to buy next: On *Semi Crazy* (MCG/Curb, 1996, prod. Junior Brown) ♫♫♫, Brown seamlessly works his stunning fretwork into his songs without turning them into jams and showcases his narrative flair with his ode to blue collar pride, "Joe the Singing Janitor," and "Parole Board," a hope-deprived prisoner's suicide lament that would even bring tears to Merle Haggard's eyes. However, the out-of-place, disc-capping medley of surf classics like "Pipeline" and "Walk Don't Run" is a conceptual wipeout.

what to avoid: *Junior High* (MCG/Curb, 1995, prod. Junior Brown) ♫♫ is a five-song EP boasting barely discernible remakes of "Highway Patrol" and "My Wife Thinks You're Dead," designed chiefly to give radio the illusion that the label was working songs from a "new" album instead of the two-year-old *Guit with It*. It also fooled Grammy voters, who nominated it for Country Album of the Year, and consumers, who bought it without knowing that its much-superior predecessor existed.

the rest:

12 Shades of Brown (Curb, 1993) ♫♫♫

worth searching for: Brown and Red Simpson duet on "Nitro Express" from *Rig Rock Deluxe* (Upstart, 1996, prod. various) ♫♫♫, a collection of truck driving anthems sung by the likes of Don Walser, Buck Owens, Kelly Willis and others.

influences:

◀◀ Ernest Tubb, Jimi Hendrix, Red Simpson, Buck Owens

▶▶ Cornell Hurd Band, BR5-49

David Okamoto

Junior Brown (Curb Records)

MARTY BROWN

Born July 25, 1965, in Maceo, KY.

Waylon Jennings once asked the musical question, "Are you sure Hank done it this way?" In the case of Marty Brown, the answer is, "Pretty damn near." Busting out of his tobacco-farming hometown and heading to Nashville with little more than a guitar, a pillowcase full of songs and a head full of dreams, Brown slept on the streets of Music City until his music finally got a fair hearing. What connects Brown to honky-tonk heroes like Williams, though, is not merely the tales of hardship or the dramatic catch in his voice, but the plainspokenness of his lyrics. But unlike Hank, who threw his fame away, the dream has not entirely come true for Brown. He recorded three fine albums for MCA, but they failed to catch on with the record-buying public, so he retreated to the independent label HighTone in 1996. There may be no justice in the world, but if there were, there'd be no country music.

what to buy: One of the finest pure honky-tonk albums of the last decade, *Wild Kentucky Skies* (MCA, 1993, prod. Richard Bennett, Tony Brown) 𝄞𝄞𝄞𝄞 contains a startling array of emotions, from the cocksure "Let's Begin Again"—in which Brown tells an estranged lover, "Break his heart and let's begin again"—to the grievous lament "She's Gone," in which Brown bays at the moon from a graveyard over a lover's demise. In between is a humorous attempt at relationship counseling ("I'd Rather Fish than Fight"), a fine train song ("Freight Train") and a pair of gorgeous ballads ("God Knows," "Wild Kentucky Skies"). It's a nearly perfect effort.

what to avoid: How's this for irony? On *Here's to the Honky Tonks* (HighTone, 1996, prod. Marty Brown, Bruce Bromberg) 𝄞𝄞, Brown moves to just the sort of independent label that has long supported renegade country music. But instead of delivering just that, Brown turns in his most conventional effort ever. It's far from a disaster, but it's definitely a step in the wrong direction.

the rest:

High and Dry (MCA, 1991) ♫♫♫♫
Cryin', Lovin', Leavin' (MCA, 1994) ♫♫♫♫

influences:

◀◀ Hank Williams, Lefty Frizzell, Jimmie Rodgers
▶▶ Wayne Hancock, Greg Garing

Daniel Durchholz

ROGER BROWN & SWING CITY

Born March 16, 1962, in TX.

As a songwriter, western Texas native Roger Brown has had cuts by Randy Travis, George Strait, Clay Walker, John Michael Montgomery and others. As a performer, he fronts a full-fledged Western swing band, complete with twin fiddles and horn section.

what's available: *Roger Brown & Swing City* (Decca, 1996, prod. Brian Tankersley, Roger Brown) ♫♫♫♡, Brown's five-song debut EP, updates the Western swing notion to modern-day Nashville. Unlike Asleep at the Wheel, Brown doesn't play off the renegade Texan image—this is straight-down-the-middle line dance country that plays off the musical notions of Bob Wills instead of Merle Haggard.

influences:

◀◀ Bob Wills, Milton Brown, Asleep at the Wheel

Brian Mansfield

T. GRAHAM BROWN

Born Anthony Graham Brown, October 30, 1954, in Atlanta, GA.

T. Graham Brown approached country music with one foot firmly planted in R&B and straight-ahead blues territory. He fronted a soul band, Rack of Spam, in 1979, also formed his own country group and worked local clubs near his University of Georgia base. Brown even sang a few jingles for Taco Bell, McDonald's, Miller and Budweiser. He made his way into the Nashville country conglomerate after becoming a staff songwriter for CBS. Signing with Capitol proved fruitful: from 1985–91 he charted 16 hits, including a trio of #1 singles—"Hell and High Water," "Don't Go to Strangers" and "Darlene." His voice, a big instrument prone to showiness but powerful nonetheless, fits nicely around classics such as "I Tell It Like It Used to Be" and the aforementioned "Don't Go to Strangers." But as the new traditionalist movement gave way to the 1990s country boom, Brown's simmering country-blues style fell out of favor. He lost his Capitol recording contract in 1992, and in-

terest from Warner Bros. and Columbia never materialized. Today, Brown tours the club circuit as an oldies act.

what to buy: When Columbia came calling in late 1994, Brown rerecorded his career songs for *Super Hits* (Columbia, 1995, prod. Joe Casey) ♫♫♫♡. These newer renditions don't sound much different than the originals and Brown's voice is still a robust tool. Plus, the CD carries a $10 retail price, making it a good buy for a recent recording.

the rest:

I Tell It Like It Used to Be (Green Line, 1986) ♫♫♫
All-Time Greatest Hits (Curb, 1993) ♫♫♫
Don't Go to Strangers (Kingfisher, 1996) ♫♫♫
Best of T. Graham Brown (Curb, 1997) ♫♫

worth searching for: *Bumper to Bumper* (Capitol, 1990, prod. Barry Beckett, T. Graham Brown) ♫♫♫♡ remains Brown's most satisfying Capitol effort. From the smooth ode to adolescence "Moonshadow Road" to the scorching "Blues of the Month Club" and the seamless country-blues anthem "If You Could Only See Me Now," this album showcases vocal growth and thoughtful songwriting.

influences:

◀◀ Otis Redding, Ronnie Milsap
▶▶ Neal McCoy, John Berry

Mario Tarradell

JANN BROWNE

Born March 14, 1954, in Anderson, IN.

Jann Browne is a singer with a bit of an edge to her voice, as well as a talented songwriter whose style proved a bit too challenging for mass acceptance, even as the neo-traditionalist movement of the late 1980s–early 1990s emerged. Although born in Indiana, Browne made her way to southern California during the mid-1970s, singing in clubs before touring with the Western swing outfit Asleep at the Wheel for two years beginning in 1981. Her devotion to pure country music and the West Coast influence on her sound are obvious (she duets on the Davis Sisters' "I Forgot More Than You'll Ever Know" and with Wanda Jackson on her debut), and her original tunes are generally refreshing and unique. A major attraction overseas, Browne is currently working on a live album in France.

what to buy: *Tell Me Why* (Curb, 1990, prod. Steve Fishell) ♫♫♫♫♡ is her first and best, featuring moderate hits such as "Tell Me Why," penned by Gail Davies, and the snappy Jamie O'Hara tune, "You Ain't Down Home."

what to buy next: *It Only Hurts When I Laugh* (Curb, 1991, prod. Steve Fishell) 🎵🎵🎵 leans a little heavier on pop-rock, with still satisfying results.

the rest:

Count Me In (Cross Three, 1995) 🎵🎵🎵

influences:

◄◄ Wanda Jackson, Emmylou Harris

►► Joy Lynn White, Rosie Flores

Stephen L. Betts

THE BROWNS /JIM ED BROWN

Jim Ed Brown (born April 1, 1934, in Sparkman, AR), vocals; Maxine Brown (born April 27, 1932, in Samti, LA), vocals; Bonnie Brown (born July 31, 1937), vocals.

Family harmony, enhanced by pristine production, were trademarks of the Brown siblings' many hits throughout the 1950s and 1960s. Starting out as a duo in 1952, Jim Ed and Maxine appeared on Little Rock radio's *Barnyard Frolics,* with sister Bonnie joining the act in 1955. By that time Jim Ed and Maxine had been recording for the Fabor label, scoring their first Top 10 hit, "Looking Back to See," in 1954. Subsequent hits featured the trio, signed to RCA in 1956. Jim Ed, Maxine and Bonnie placed four more hits in the country Top 10 during the next three years, including their best-known hit, the country/pop smash "The Three Bells." In 1963 the Browns joined the Grand Ole Opry, but they disbanded four years later, with Jim Ed pursuing a successful solo career; he also dueted with Helen Cornelius on a handful of hits during the late 1970s. Maxine and Bonnie retired from the music business to raise families, performing sporadically. The trio reunited in 1996 for an album of gospel music and appeared on the Grand Ole Opry, where Jim Ed continues to perform on a regular basis. The Browns' chart success may have been short-lived, but their easygoing manner and flawless harmonies assure them a place in country music history.

what to buy: *The Essential Jim Ed Brown and the Browns* (RCA, 1996, prod. various) 🎵🎵🎵🎵 is fairly comprehensive. Spanning 20 years, it combines the trio's biggest hits with Jim Ed's solo work, including some of his more honky-tonk-oriented material such as "Pop a Top." A minor complaint: the Top 10 "I Heard the Bluebirds Sing" is missing, and material such as "Broad Minded Man" is decidedly un-PC for the 1990s.

what to buy next: *Family Bible* (Step One, 1996) 🎵🎵🎵🎵 is fascinating for several reasons. The album cover features only vintage photographs of the trio, but this is newly recorded music, proving that even at this stage in their careers their harmonies are still unmatched. The gospel-oriented material is well-chosen and lovingly rendered, leaving one wishing the Browns were recording and performing on a regular basis.

influences:

◄◄ Jim Reeves

►► Kendalls, Dave & Sugar

Stephen L. Betts

ED BRUCE

Born William Edwin Bruce Jr. December 29, 1940, in Keiser, AR.

Never an outlaw on his own, Ed Bruce nevertheless penned one of the movement's anthems in "Mammas Don't Let Your Babies Grow Up to Be Cowboys." Raised in Memphis, Bruce made his first records as "Edwin Bruce" for Sun during the late 1950s. He moved to Nashville in 1964, where he joined the Marijohn Wilkins Singers (Wilkins was the writer of "Waterloo," "The Long Black Veil" and other songs); made commercials, including tourism spots for the state of Tennessee; and had a local TV show from 1969–74. Bruce had a role on the TV series *Maverick* and wrote the show's theme song; he also had songs cut by Tanya Tucker ("The Man That Turned My Mama On") and Charlie Louvin ("See the Big Man Cry"). His "Save Your Kisses" was the b-side of Tommy Roe's pop smash "Sheila." As a singer, Bruce had hits for United Artists, MCA and RCA. "Mammas" was his first big hit in 1975, though Waylon & Willie would take it to the top of the chart three years later. Bruce's baritone was a perfect vehicle for his cowboy-themed songs, but he also had hits with softer, more romantic numbers like "You're the Best Break This Old Heart Ever Had" and the semi-disco "You Turn Me On (Like a Radio)."

what's available: *The Best of Ed Bruce* (Varese Sarabande, 1995, prod. various) 🎵🎵🎵🎵 compiles the best of Bruce's recordings for United Artists, MCA and RCA and shows him to be an artist capable of a wide variety of music, not to mention a top-notch songwriter (he co-wrote 10 of the collection's 18 tracks). The album includes nearly all of Bruce's significant hits, plus "Theme from 'Bret Maverick.'"

influences:

◄◄ Waylon Jennings

►► Don Williams, Royal Wade Kimes

Brian Mansfield

BRUSH ARBOR

Formed 1972, in San Diego, CA.

Jim Rice, vocals, guitar; Joe Rice, vocals, mandolin; Wayne Rice, vocals (1972); Kevin Watkins, drums; Brad Carr, guitar; Steve Wilkinson, bass; Gordon Jenewein, keyboards; James Harrah, guitar (1972–76); Mike Holtzer, drums; Dave Rose, bass, vocals; Dale Cooper, guitar (mid-1970s); others.

Formed originally as a bluegrass act by the Rice brothers, Brush Arbor took its name from the shelters that protected revival meetings from the elements. The group took its mix of bluegrass and country to Capitol Records during the early 1970s, where the band recorded two albums (both now out of print). Brush Arbor had a number of charting singles, though none made the Top 40 (1973's "Brush Arbor Meeting" came closest, at 41). Still, so few bands were recording during that time that the group won the Academy of Country Music's vocal group award in 1973. The group left Capitol and cut an album for Monument during 1976 that included a tribute to Emmylou Harris called "Emmylou." The group turned more and more to its religious background and by the 1990s had become a popular act in the "positive country" field.

what's available: Brush Arbor has always harbored some pop influences (the group once cut Gilbert O'Sullivan's "Alone Again (Naturally)"). Couple that to Christian music's tendency to head for the middle of the road, and *Brush Arbor* (Benson, 1994, prod. Mark Craig, Michael Sykes) 🎵🎵 and *The Way the River Runs* (Benson, 1996, Mark Craig) 🎵🎵 become bland despite their good intentions. *The Way the River Runs* has the benefit of a more acoustic instrumentation and two bluegrass cuts tagged on the end.

influences:
◀◀ Dillards, Hillmen
▶▶ Ken Holloway, Diamond Rio

Brian Mansfield

STEPHEN BRUTON

Born in Ft. Worth, TX.

Like many Texans, Stephen Bruton crosses musical boundaries easily and with little trepidation. The son of a jazz drummer, he used to play house guitar for Texas fiddle conventions during the day, then hit black blues bars at night. Kris Kristofferson chose him as his guitarist in 1971, and Bruton later played for Bob Dylan, Bonnie Raitt and others. He has crossed paths with fellow Texans T-Bone Burnett and Delbert McClinton; his songs have been sung by Willie Nelson and the Highwaymen. Releasing his first album in 1994, Bruton has also become a popular producer of Texas music, having worked with Jimmie Dale Gilmore, Chris Smither, Alejandro Escovedo and others.

what's available: *What It Is* (dos, 1993, prod. Tom Canning) 🎵🎵🎵🎵, Bruton's debut as a frontman, starts in the Texas roadhouse and just keeps going. It's by turns bluesy, raucous and sentimental and showcases Bruton's varied talents as a writer and player; *Right on Time* (dos, 1995, prod. Tom Canning) 🎵🎵🎵🎵 is in the same musical vein, but with a brighter (and at times downright spiritual) outlook.

influences:
◀◀ Bonnie Raitt, Kris Kristofferson, Delbert McClinton
▶▶ Lee Roy Parnell

Brian Mansfield

BRYNDLE

See: Karla Bonoff

RICHARD BUCKNER

Born in Chico, CA.

Though this San Francisco singer-songwriter's twang resembles Dwight Yoakam's, it carries a soft, emotional intensity instead of a honky-tonking joy. Critics compared him to the comparatively upbeat Gram Parsons when his debut, *Bloomed*, came out during 1995, but a heavy sense of dread hangs over Buckner's best songs. "22," for example, is a classic country tearjerker about suicide, only much darker and scarier, like the script for a good horror movie. On *Devotion + Doubt,* producer J.D. Foster contributes droning pump organs, rumbling drums and whining dobros—and the overall sound complements Buckner's observations about tightening throats, deadly highways and lying awake at 4 a.m. By the time he opens "On Travelling" with the words "I love you, darling," you just know something terrible is going to happen.

what to buy: *Bloomed* (Dejadisc, 1995, prod. Lloyd Maines) 🎵🎵🎵🎵 would be a great album if it were just "22" and 11 lemons. Although the songs of lost love, misery, tears and snuffed fires inside occasionally get heavy-handed, Buckner establishes himself as an important new voice in country music.

the rest:
Devotion + Doubt (MCA, 1996) 🎵🎵🎵

influences:
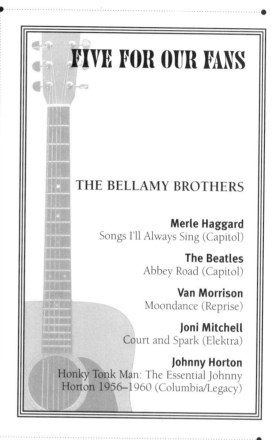

◀◀ Dwight Yoakam, Gram Parsons, Violent Femmes, Johnny Cash, Cowboy Junkies

▶▶ Gillian Welch

Steve Knopper

JIMMY BUFFETT

Born December 25, 1946, in Pascagoula, MS.

Jimmy Buffett came to Nashville with hopes of becoming a country and folk singer, and even though he eventually made his mark as a tropical troubadour, his country roots still show. Buffett's songs about beaches, boats, booze and women offer a temporary escape for every office-bound baby boomer with a mortgage, three-car garage and a surly boss. Few can resist the singer/songwriter's balmy fantasyland filled with palm trees, fast boats, cold beer, cheeseburgers, margaritas and romance. Sure, there are sharks to reckon with and volcanoes to flee and broken hearts to mend, but Buffett's songs assure us they can be dealt with. Buffett majored in journalism at Auburn University and the University of Southern Mississippi, then worked briefly at *Billboard* magazine before heading to Nashville to write songs. A failed marriage and a move to Key West, Florida, triggered a new appreciation for the healing powers of the tropical sun. Buffett started out writing earnest, positive songs with humor and wit, and his audiences grew slowly but steadily. He scored his first big hit in 1974 with the wonderfully wistful ballad "Come Monday," but it was the booze-in-the-blender philosophical shrug of "Margaritaville" that put the wind in Buffett's sails. With little radio play and a glaring shortage of hit singles—but a large and loyal group of fans known as Parrotheads—Buffett has become one of the wealthiest beach bums in history.

what to buy: *Songs You Know by Heart: Jimmy Buffett's Greatest Hit(s)* (MCA, 1985, prod. Jimmy Buffett) ♪♪♪♪ is an essential first step for anyone curious about the Parrothead phenomenon. The album includes the hit(s) ("Margaritaville," "Cheeseburger in Paradise") and concert favorites ("Fins," "Volcano," "Pencil Thin Mustache"). Buffett's breakthrough album, *Changes in Latitudes, Changes in Attitudes* (MCA, 1977, prod. Norbert Putnam) ♪♪♪♪ is a perfect sampler of feel-good folk-rockers (the title track, "Margaritaville") and pensive ballads ("Biloxi," "Wonder Why We Ever Go Home"). Another good overview is offered on *Feeding Frenzy* (MCA, 1990, prod. Michael Utley, Elliot Scheiner) ♪♪♪♪, a live recording featuring 72 minutes worth of classic concert craziness.

FIVE FOR OUR FANS

THE BELLAMY BROTHERS

Merle Haggard
Songs I'll Always Sing (Capitol)

The Beatles
Abbey Road (Capitol)

Van Morrison
Moondance (Reprise)

Joni Mitchell
Court and Spark (Elektra)

Johnny Horton
Honky Tonk Man: The Essential Johnny Horton 1956–1960 (Columbia/Legacy)

what to buy next: If Buffett has cast his spell on you, you won't mind indulging in the four-disc box set *Boats Beaches Bars & Ballads* (Margaritaville/MCA, 1992, prod. various) ♪♪♪♪, an extensive retrospective dividing the 72 songs included by the categories listed in the title. *Living and Dying in 3/4 Time* (MCA, 1974, prod. Don Gant) ♪♪♪ captures the lyrical charm of early Buffett ("Come Monday," "The Wino and I Know"), while *Banana Wind* (Margaritaville/MCA, 1996, prod. Russ Kunkel) ♪♪♪ shows some justifiable crankiness ("Jamaica Mistaica," "Cultural Infidel") along with Buffett's first instrumental tune, the steel-drum calypso title track.

what to avoid: Keep out of the way of *Last Mango in Paris* (MCA, 1985, prod. Jimmy Bowen) **WOOF!** and *Off to See the Lizard* (MCA, 1989, prod. Elliot Scheiner) ♪, which, after their one-trick titles, wander around in a sea of overly slick production, losing sight of Buffett's laid-back charm.

Jimmy Buffett (Jean Pagliuso)

the rest:

A White Sport Coat and a Pink Crustacean (MCA, 1973) 𝄞𝄞𝄞

A-1-A (MCA, 1974) 𝄞𝄞𝄞𝄞

Havana Daydreamin' (MCA, 1976) 𝄞𝄞𝄞

Son of a Son of a Sailor (MCA, 1978) 𝄞𝄞𝄞

You Had to Be There (MCA, 1978) 𝄞𝄞𝄞

Volcano (MCA, 1979) 𝄞𝄞𝄞

Coconut Telegraph (MCA, 1981) 𝄞𝄞𝄞

Somewhere over China (MCA, 1981) 𝄞𝄞

One Particular Harbor (MCA, 1983) 𝄞𝄞

Riddles in the Sand (MCA, 1985) 𝄞𝄞

Floridays (MCA, 1986) 𝄞𝄞

Hot Water (MCA, 1988) 𝄞𝄞

Before the Beach (Margaritaville/MCA, 1993) 𝄞𝄞𝄞

Fruitcakes (Margaritaville/MCA, 1994) 𝄞𝄞𝄞

Barometer Soup (Margaritaville/MCA, 1995) 𝄞𝄞𝄞

Christmas Island (Margaritaville/MCA, 1996) 𝄞𝄞𝄞

worth searching for: *All the Greatest Hits* (Prism Leisure, 1994, prod. various) 𝄞𝄞𝄞𝄞, a British hits collection, is a bit more generous than *Songs You Know by Heart*.

Influences.

◀◀ Gamble Rogers, Irma Thomas, Benny Spellman, Jerry Jeff Walker

▶▶ Iguanas, Subdudes, Blues Traveler

David Yonke

LUKE & JENNY ANNE BULLA

Formed in Grant's Pass, OR.

Luke Bulla (born 1981), fiddle; Jenny Anne Bulla (born 1982), fiddle.

Siblings Luke and Jenny Anne Bulla entered their first fiddle contest in 1987 at ages six and five, respectively. By 1990 they'd become so proficient in bluegrass and Texas fiddling styles—Luke placed in the Top 10 at the Grand Masters Fiddling Championships—that the pair became something of a sensation in the fiddling-contest world.

what's available: *Luke and Jenny Anne Bulla* (Rounder, 1992, prod. Bil VornDick) 𝄞𝄞𝄞, recorded when Luke was 11 and Jenny Anne 10, shows two musicians with unlimited promise. They're accompanied on these largely traditional tunes by a band that includes their father on guitar, Mark Schatz on bass and Butch Baldassari on mandolin.

influences:

◀◀ Mark O'Connor, Alison Krauss

▶▶ Chris Thile

Brian Mansfield

THE BUM STEERS

Formed in southern CA.

Mark Fosson, vocals, guitar, mandolin, harmonica; Edward Tree, guitars, vocals; Taras Prodaniuk, bass, vocals; Billy Block, drums, vocals.

The Bum Steers are products of Los Angeles' Palomino Club scene, and its members have individual credits that include stints with Jim Lauderdale, Billy Joe Shaver, Juice Newton and Dwight Yoakam. Drummer Billy Block founded the Western Beat Barndance, a weekly jam session at the Palomino; later, he moved to Nashville and started hosting a second show, renamed the Western Beat Roots Revival.

what's available: The country-rock of *The Bum Steers* (Western Beat, 1996, prod. Edward Tree, Bum Steers) 𝄞𝄞𝄞 is just barely outside the contemporary country mainstream, but more rock-oriented fans will appreciate the twangy guitars on songs like "Dancin' on the Levee" and "Hitchhikin' Heart." The band uses its well-learned lessons in Nashville songcraft to hilarious effect in "NatKingColePorterWagonerSortOfThing."

influences:

◀◀ Dwight Yoakam, Desert Rose Band

Brian Mansfield

SONNY BURGESS

Born Albert Burgess, May 28, 1931, in Newport, AR.

With his flaming red suit, red shoes, red guitar and dyed red hair, Sonny Burgess probably looked like the devil incarnate to audiences in Arkansas and Tennessee circa 1956. And he pretty much sounded like him, too, on the discs he recorded for Sun between 1956–58. Such songs as "We Wanna Boogie," "Red Headed Woman" and "Ain't Got a Thing" featured shouted, nearly unintelligible vocals, slapback bass, thundering drums, pounding piano, machine gun bursts of guitar and a blurting, out-of-context trumpet. They were wild even by Sun standards—perhaps too wild, for his intense mix of rockabilly boogie and white-boy R&B never earned Burgess more than a regional hit. He retreated to playing in Conway Twitty's band and eventually took a day job, but was coaxed out of rock 'n' roll retirement in 1986 to play with the Sun Rhythm Section. During the 1990s Burgess began recording and touring again on his own; while there's less danger than nostalgia in his performances, Burgess is still something special.

what to buy: The best of his Sun sides can be found on *Hittin' That Jug! The Best of Sonny Burgess* (AVI, 1995, prod. Sam Phillips, Jack Clement) 🎵🎵🎵🎵; more than a hour's worth of glorious chaos, in two-and-a-half minute bursts.

the rest:

We Wanna Boogie (Rounder, 1990) 🎵🎵🎵🎵
Tennessee Border (HighTone, 1992) 🎵🎵🎵
Sonny Burgess (Rounder, 1996) 🎵🎵🎵🎵

worth searching for: Any of Burgess's original Sun singles would make fine souvenirs of a memorable era.

influences:

◀◀ The same natural (or supernatural) forces that created Jerry Lee Lewis

▶▶ Dave Alvin, Bruce Springsteen

Daniel Durchholz

T-BONE BURNETT

Born John Henry Burnett January 14, 1948, in St. Louis, MO.

One of popular music's true men out of time, T-Bone Burnett is

an old-school moralist in the mold of his one-time employer Bob Dylan—which is to say that Burnett's God is one of wrath. He can be pretentious and overbearing, but Burnett's saving grace is that he tends to be at least as hard on himself as he is on his writerly creations. He initially gained notice as part of Dylan's Rolling Thunder Revue during the mid-1970s, and as one-third of Rolling Thunder-spinoff, the Alpha Band. Burnett was the one who wrote the "weird" songs on the Alpha Band's three albums, the surreal narratives that namechecked obscure artists and faded starlettes. He has continued on a similar course of wiseacre existentialism on his solo albums, insuring his following will remain cult-sized. Providing partial compensation is Burnett's acclaim as a producer for Counting Crows, Los Lobos, Sam Phillips (his wife), Peter Case, Gillian Welch, Jimmie Dale Gilmore, the Wallflowers and Marshall Crenshaw, among many others.

what to buy: *T-Bone Burnett* (Dot, 1986, prod. David Miner) 🎵🎵🎵🎵 is the purest and most unadorned country music he's ever made, a folksy effort knocked out in four days just like they used to do way back when. In stark contrast is the lush bombast of *Proof through the Night* (Warner Bros., 1983, prod. Jeff Eyrich) 🎵🎵🎵🎵, a guest-laden supersession that was Burnett's big shot at stardom. *Proof* may be the definitive Burnett album, encapsulating his bad as well as good tendencies. It's his preachiest work, certainly (especially the narcissist character sketch "The 1960s"), but also his most accessible.

what to buy next: Burnett's first post-Alpha Band album, *Truth Decay* (Takoma, 1980, prod. Reggie Fisher) 🎵🎵🎵🎵, is Christian cosmic cowboy music that picks up where his former band left off. The follow-up EP *Trap Door* (Warner Bros., 1982, prod. Reggie Fisher, T-Bone Burnett) 🎵🎵🎵🎵 is slicker but also hookier. It also has, in the deadpan rockabilly reading of "Diamonds Are a Girl's Best Friend," Burnett's single finest on-record moment.

the rest:

J. Henry Burnett, the B-52 Band & the Fabulous Skylarks (Uni, 1972) 🎵🎵🎵
Behind the Trap Door (Demon EP, 1984) 🎵🎵🎵
The Talking Animals (Columbia, 1988) 🎵🎵🎵🎵
The Criminal under My Own Hat (Columbia, 1992) 🎵🎵🎵🎵
Sahib: Tooth of Crime (Bar/None, 1997)

worth searching for: *When the Night Falls* (Bench, 1990, prod. Reggie Fisher) 🎵🎵🎵, a quasi-Rolling Thunder reunion featuring Burnett and Black Tie, a group composed of many longtime cronies, including Billy Swan and his old Alpha Bandmates Steven Soles and David Mansfield. There's also the reissue of

T-Bone Burnett **(AP/Wide World Photos)**

Elvis Costello's 1986 Burnett-produced masterpiece *King of America* (Rykodisc, 1995) 𝄞𝄞𝄞𝄞; among the reissue's bonus tracks are two songs Costello recorded with Burnett under the name the Coward Brothers—Leon Payne's "They'll Never Take Her Love From Me," and the brilliant proto-twangcore "The People's Limousine."

influences:

◀◀ Bob Dylan, Kris Kristofferson, Roger McGuinn, Buddy Holly, Randy Newman, Van Dyke Parks, John Prine

▶▶ Peter Case, Tonio K., Joe Henry, Alejandro Escovedo

David Menconi

DORSEY BURNETTE

Born December 28, 1932, in Memphis, TN. Died August 19, 1979.

Like a number of faded rock 'n' roll mavericks, Dorsey Burnette slid securely into the country field after his career in pop came to a close when "Tall Oak Tree" and "Hey Little One" faded off the charts in 1960. Recording for more than a dozen labels up to his death, and even notching a few mid-chart country hits,

he never left any lasting work in the field behind him, and his career in country is largely a forgotten footnote to his earlier work. Burnette will more likely be best remembered for his service with his brother, Johnny Burnette, in the Rock and Roll Trio, a pioneer Memphis rockabilly band that cut a searing album during the band's brief career. He and his brother then moved to Hollywood and wrote hits for Ricky Nelson ("Waitin' in School," "It's Late") before brother Johnny hit the Top 40 on his own, followed shortly thereafter by brother Dorsey. Sadly, his many recordings have been out of print for years.

worth searching for: Copies of the Rock and Roll Trio album *Johnny Burnette and the Rock and Roll Trio* (Coral, 1956) 𝄞𝄞𝄞𝄞 routinely fetch four-figure prices among collectors, although the music has been reissued and bootlegged over the years in less collectible editions.

influences:

◀◀ Elvis Presley, Roy Hamilton

▶▶ Glen Campbell, Rocky Burnette

Joel Selvin

JOHNNY BURNETTE

Born March 24, 1934, in Memphis, TN. Died August 1, 1964, in Clear Lake, CA.

Johnny Burnette went to the same high school in Memphis as Elvis Presley. He and brother Dorsey Burnette were troubled boys, sent to Catholic schools for discipline, not religion. But these two hardscrabble sometimes prize fighters—with guitarist Paul Burlison—led the Rock and Roll Trio, one of the first rockabilly outfits to emerge from local Memphis hillbilly roadhouses. Although the trio cut one of the great rock 'n' roll albums of the 1950s, the Burnettes would be left with very little to show for it; after the band broke up during an onstage fistfight between the two brothers, the Burnettes and their families moved to Los Angeles, where they showed up on Ricky Nelson's door one day, offering to write songs for the burgeoning teen idol. Such Burnette compositions as "Waitin' in School," "It's Late" and "Believe What You Say" became landmarks in the Nelson repertoire. But Johnny Burnette was destined to become best known for the sappy teen pop he himself recorded—but did not write—under the supervision of producer Snuff Garrett, especially two Top 10 hits, "You're Sixteen" and "Dreamin'." When he died in a boating accident in 1964, his career was in decline.

what to buy: Germany's Bear Family's compilation of all the 1956–57 sessions by the Johnny Burnette Trio, *Rockabilly Boogie* (Bear Family, 1989, prod. Bob Thiele, Paul Cohen) ♪♪♪♪ leaves little doubt how masterful Burnette's early recordings were.

what to buy next: His years at Liberty Records have been scrupulously covered with *You're Sixteen: The Best of Johnny Burnette* (EMI, 1992, prod. various) ♪♪♪, 25 songs and a 13-minute interview (huh?), although his best-known material is not necessarily his best.

influences:
◀◀ Elvis Presley, Howlin' Wolf, Hank Williams
▶▶ Eddie Cochran, Yardbirds, Stray Cats

                                                Joel Selvin

BURNS SISTERS

Sister group from Binghamton, NY.

Marie Burns, Jeannie Burns, Annie Burns.

The seventh, eighth and ninth of 12 children, Marie, Jeannie and Annie Burns are now based in Ithaca, New York. The sisters began singing together in 1980, cut two albums of pop-rock material for Columbia during the 1980s as a fivesome (along with sisters Terry and Sheila), then split up for several years. Terry became a Nashville songwriter and Sheila taught art in Ithaca. In 1991 solo projects by Marie, Jeannie and Annie were combined to make the self-distributed *Songs of the Heart*, and in 1993 the three reunited and were signed to Philo Records. Their sound is country-based folk, with shimmering harmonies that are a consistent highlight.

what to buy: Produced by the former E Street Band bassist, *In This World* (Philo, 1997, prod. Garry Tallent) ♪♪♪♪ is the Burns' most exhilarating and focused work, adding a dash of rock to their sound and featuring adventurous vocal interplay and strong songwriting on tracks like "Dance upon This Earth" and "Johnny Got a Gun."

what to buy next: *Close to Home* (Philo, 1995, prod. Rich De-Paolo) ♪♪♪♪, the Burns Sisters' first official trio album, is a more rustic affair, stressing their folk and gospel roots on tunes like "I Am a Patriot" and "Into the Wind."

the rest:
Tradition: Holiday Songs Old and New (Philo, 1997) ♪♪♪♪

worth searching for: The *Atlantic City* soundtrack, on which they sing briefly. Also *The Burns Sisters* (Columbia, 1986); *En-*dangered Species* (Columbia, 1989); and *Songs of the Heart* (self-released, 1991, available through P.O. Box 845, Ithaca, NY 14851). Mac Benford & the Woodshed All-Stars' *Willow* (Rounder, 1996) features Marie Burns.

solo outings:
Annie Burns:
(With the Rain) *Annie Burns and the Rain* (Art for Art's Sake, 1992)

influences:
◀◀ Sweethearts of the Rodeo, Kate & Anna McGarrigle, Whites
▶▶ Cox Family, Beth & April Stevens, McCarters

                                                Bob Cannon

GEORGE BURNS

Born Nathan Birnbaum, January 20, 1896, in New York City. Died March 9, 1996.

One of the great entertainers of the 20th century, George Burns' career covered almost everything—vaudeville, radio, television, films and recordings. And, of course, it took him to Nashville, where he had a #15 hit with "I Wish I Was 18 Again" in 1980 at age 84. He died in early 1996, just weeks after reaching his 100th birthday.

what's available: *Young at Heart* (Mercury, 1996, compilation prod. Kira Florita) ♪♪ collects Burns' country recordings. The arrangements are strictly easy listening, but Burns fans will find plenty to wax nostalgic over, including "I Wish I Was 18 Again." The rest of the album leans towards the standards that comprised Burns' repertoire, but there is a cute version of the Statler Brothers' "Whatever Happened to Randolph Scott." Burns is joined by Bobby Vinton on *As Time Goes By* (Curb, 1992, prod. Michael Lloyd) ♪, a seriously cheesy duet album that plays off the age difference between the two singers.

influences:
◀◀ Statler Brothers
▶▶ Statler Brothers

                                                Brian Mansfield

JAMES BURTON & RALPH MOONEY

Formed briefly c. 1967.

James Burton (born August 21, 1939, in Shreveport, LA), guitar; Ralph Mooney (born September 16, 1928, in Duncan, OK), pedal steel.

One of the half-dozen or so most influential guitarists in country music, James Burton began playing guitar at age 12 and by age 14 was a house guitarist for the *Louisiana Hayride* radio show. Coming to prominence backing Ricky Nelson, Burton also did notable work for Gram Parsons, Elvis Presley, Emmylou Harris and Jerry Lee Lewis, and also played on countless rock and country sessions. Ralph Mooney is a steel player who wrote Ray Price's hit "Crazy Arms" and played numerous sessions, many of them on classic Buck Owens and Merle Haggard recordings. Burton and Mooney can be heard together on Haggard's "Tonight the Bottle Let Me Down," among other things.

what's available: Burton and Mooney recorded one album together, *Corn Pickin' and Slick Slidin'* (See for Miles, 1968/1993, prod. Ken Nelson) ✧✧✧, in 1967. Producer Ken Nelson, who also worked with Owen and Haggard at the time, had heard the two play together and asked them to record an instrumental album, a la Jimmy Bryant and Speedy West. Instead of heading off into swing territory, the two pickers stuck to their country roots with covers of songs like "I'm a Lonesome Fugitive," "Your Cheatin' Heart" and "There Goes My Everything." As with most instrumentalists who make their reputations with brilliant, brief solos and licks, Burton and Mooney don't sustain the kind of magic they do when backing singers, but this is an entertaining and instructive album for blossoming country pickers.

influences:

◀◀ Speedy West & Jimmy Bryant, Chet Atkins

▶▶ Junior Brown

Brian Mansfield

JOHNNY BUSH

Born John Bush Shin III, February 17, 1935, in Houston, TX.

Born in the heart of country-and-western territory, Johnny Bush learned to play guitar from his father at age nine. He played at school events as a teen and knew he wanted to make music his life. Bush received his first paying gig at San Antonio's Texas Star Inn during 1952, accompanying himself on guitar. After several years he changed his approach, taking up drums and joining a band with a young sideman named Willie Nelson. When Nelson's recording career took off during the early 1960s, he asked Bush to come along as drummer. That tour lasted only a year, but Bush then hooked up with Ray Price, who eventually recorded one of Bush's songs, "Eye for an Eye." When Bush began recording demos during the mid-1960s with little interest from labels, Nelson financed a recording session that produced his first single and album, both called "Sound of a Heartache." Bush leased the recordings to Stop, which would also release such hits as "You Gave Me a Mountain," the Ray

Price-penned "Each Time" and "Undo the Right," later covered by Wade Hayes. Bush signed to RCA in 1972 and spent three years there; his most significant record of that time was 1972's "Whiskey River," which would later become Nelson's signature concert song. He has since recorded for a number of smaller labels. Bush also owns the master versions of his recordings and has released them himself, which means they can be hard to find. Still, that's better treatment than he would have gotten from, say, RCA. He continues to play and record as a honky-tonk cult figure in Texas.

what to buy: *Greatest Hits 1968–1972* (self-released, 1993, prod. Tommy Hill) ✧✧✧✧ contains the best of Bush's recordings for Stop, including his two Top 10 hits "Undo the Right" and "You Gave Me a Mountain."

what to buy next: *Greatest Hits Volume One* (BMG, 1994) ✧✧✧✧ compiles his RCA recordings.

the rest:

Sound of a Heartache (self-released) ✧✧✧✧

Whiskey River/There Stands the Glass (self-released, 1993) ✧✧✧

Johnny Bush Is Back (Collectibles, 1996) ✧✧✧✧

worth searching for: Just about everything of Bush's is going to involve some serious searching, unless you live in the Houston area. *Time Changes Everything* (self-released, 1994) ✧✧✧ is particularly interesting; these are his 1990 recordings with the Bandoleros Band, the release of which was delayed for years because they happened to be in Willie Nelson's studio when the Internal Revenue Service descended and confiscated all the tapes.

influences:

◀◀ Bob Wills, Ray Price, Willie Nelson

▶▶ Tracy Byrd, Mark Chesnutt

Ronnie McDowell

SAM BUSH

Born April 13, 1952, in Bowling Green, KY.

Bush was a founding member of the innovative New Grass Revival and a regular part of Emmylou Harris' Nash Ramblers before making his debut as a solo recording artist in 1996. The three-time International Bluegrass Music Association Mandolin Player of the Year is one of the most in-demand session players

Tracy Byrd (© Ken Settle)

in Nashville, with credits on albums by Trisha Yearwood, Pam Tillis and others.

what's available: In *Glamour & Grits* (Sugar Hill, 1996, prod. Sam Bush) 🎵🎵🎵 Bush mixes traditional bluegrass sounds with a little rock 'n' roll. Former New Grass Revival mates John Cowan and Bela Fleck are among an impressive group of guests. Includes high-powered originals and even a cover of Bob Marley's "Is This Love."

influences:

◀◀ New Grass Revival, Bill Monroe

▶▶ Butch Baldassari, John Reischman

Douglas Fulmer

CARL & PEARL BUTLER

Husband-and-wife vocal duo.

Carl Butler (born June 2, 1927, in Knoxville, TN; died September 4, 1992); Pearl Butler (born September 30, 1927, in Nashville, TN; died March 3, 1989).

Carl and Pearl Butler enjoyed considerable chart success during the late 1950s and through the 1960s with a hard-country duet style that combined Carl's love of old-time country gospel singing and wife Pearl's heartfelt, emotional harmonies. Their biggest hit, 1962's "Don't Let Me Cross Over," was their first; in fact, it was the first time Pearl had ever been inside a recording studio, but her plaintive harmony vocal added just the right touch to Carl's unabashedly country lead vocal. The duo continued to record and perform, making some exemplary hard country duets in a time when Nashville was moving away from that sound, but they never topped the success of their first duet effort.

what's available: Unfortunately, none of the duo's hits are available in their original form save on scattered compilations, but *Crying My Heart Out for You* (Bear Family, 1993, prod. Richard Weize) 🎵🎵🎵 is a nice package of good remakes of their hits in the style of the originals, along with other traditional country fare.

influences:

◀◀ Wilma Lee & Stoney Cooper, Bailes Brothers

▶▶ Stonewall Jackson, Gram Parsons and Emmylou Harris

Randy Pitts

TRACY BYRD

Born December 18, 1966, in Vidor, TX.

Maybe there's something in the water down there in Beaumont, Texas. Of course, it's where George Jones grew up, but in recent times the town and its neighbor, Vidor, have given the world three new stars in Mark Chesnutt, Clay Walker and Tracy Byrd. Byrd is a traditionalist through and through, following in the footsteps of Jones and George Strait in keeping country pure and ignoring pop influences, no matter the sales potential. The level of performance is consistently high on Byrd's four albums, though his choice of material is less so. For every proven winner such as "Holdin' Heaven" or "Lifestyles of the Not So Rich and Famous," there's a boneheaded throwaway like "4 to 1 in Atlanta" or a bathetic ballad. Still, Byrd is young, and his career is promising—provided his selection of future material is sound.

what to buy: *No Ordinary Man* (MCA, 1994, prod. Jerry Crutchfield) 🎵🎵🎵 is the album on which Byrd fully hit his stride, checking in with "Lifestyles of the Not So Rich and Famous," a song displaying a wry sense of humor that has become a trademark. It crops up again on "Redneck Roses" and "Pink Flamingos." There's also the devout love song "Keeper of the Stars" and the pure honky-tonk rocker "Watermelon Crawl." Byrd's most recent effort, *Big Love* (MCA, 1996, prod. Tony Brown) 🎵🎵🎵, is equally good, especially the sprightly "Don't Love Make a Diamond Shine," the witty "Cowgirl" and a choice cover of Johnny Paycheck's 1971 hit "Don't Take Her She's All I Got."

the rest:

Tracy Byrd (MCA, 1993) 🎵🎵🎵

Love Lessons (MCA, 1995) 🎵🎵🎵

influences:

◀◀ George Strait, George Jones, Mark Chesnutt

▶▶ Clay Walker

Daniel Durchholz

THE BYRDS

Formed 1964, in Los Angeles, CA. Disbanded 1973.

Roger McGuinn (born James Joseph McGuinn III), guitar, vocals; Chris Hillman, bass, vocals (1964–68); Gene Clark, vocals, tambourine (1964–66; died May 24, 1991); David Crosby, guitar, vocals (1964–67); Michael Clarke, drums, vocals (1964–67; died December 19, 1993); Kevin Kelley, drums, vocals (1967–68); Gram Parsons (born Cecil Ingram Connor III), guitar, vocals (1967–68; died September 19, 1973); Gene Parsons, drums, vocals (1968–72); Skip Battin, bass, vocals (1968–73); John York, bass (1968); Clarence White, guitar, vocals (1968–73); John Guerin, drums (1972–73).

When the Byrds signed up Gram Parsons as a pianist in 1967, the group had already helped changed the course of popular music on the strength of five studio albums dominated by Roger McGuinn's 12-string guitar and the band's choirboy harmonies and folk/rock instrumentation. Country-boy trust funder Parsons turned the band inside out; with the release of *Sweetheart of the Rodeo* the next year, for better or worse, the Byrds kick-started the country/rock movement. Though there are hints in the Byrds' previous albums (see Chris Hillman's "Time Between" on *Younger Than Yesterday* or "Wasn't Born to Follow" on *Notorious Byrd Brothers*), nobody was ready for *Sweetheart*'s stone country pretensions, wide enough to encompass Parsons' "Hickory Wind" and "One Hundred Years from Now," the Louvin Brothers' "The Christian Life," Woody Guthrie's "Pretty Boy Floyd" and Bob Dylan's "Nothing Was Delivered" and "You Ain't Going Nowhere." Parsons would leave with Hillman to form the even more countrified Flying Burrito Brothers soon after *Sweetheart*'s release, and all subsequent Byrds releases, many with former bluegrass picker Clarence White on guitar, include country elements.

what to buy: *Sweetheart of the Rodeo* (Columbia, 1968/Columbia Legacy, 1997, prod. Gary Usher) ♫♫♫♫ is the album that pointed rock back in the direction of country. The 1997 digital update includes tracks not included on the original, including rehearsal recordings of Parsons teaching songs to the others.

what to buy next: *Sweetheart*'s follow-up, *Dr. Byrds and Mr. Hyde* (Columbia, 1969/Columbia Legacy, 1997, prod. Bob Johnston) ♫♫♫, adds heavier rock settings back into the mix, with generally pleasing results like "This Wheel's on Fire," "Drug Store Truck Driving Man" and "Bad Night at the Whiskey."

what to avoid: Like the pictures of the individual members on the front cover, *The Byrds* (Asylum, 1973, prod. David Crosby) ♫ was stitched together, with no group identity remaining.

the rest:
Mr. Tambourine Man (Columbia, 1965/Columbia Legacy, 1996) ♫♫♫♫♫
Turn! Turn! Turn! (Columbia, 1966/Columbia Legacy, 1996) ♫♫♫♫
Fifth Dimension (Columbia, 1966/Columbia Legacy, 1996) ♫♫♫
Greatest Hits (Columbia, 1967) ♫♫♫♫
Younger than Yesterday (Columbia, 1967/Columbia Legacy, 1996) ♫♫♫♫
The Notorious Byrd Brothers (Columbia, 1968/Columbia Legacy, 1997) ♫♫♫♫
Pre-Flyte (Together, 1969/Columbia, 1973) ♫♫♫
The Ballad of Easy Rider (Columbia, 1970/Columbia Legacy, 1997) ♫♫♫
Byrdmaniax (Columbia, 1971) ♫♫

Roger McGuinn of the Byrds. (© Ken Settle)

Farther Along (Columbia, 1971) ♫♫
The Best of the Byrds (Greatest Hits, Volume 2) (Columbia, 1972) ♫♫♫
The Byrds Play Dylan (Columbia, 1980) ♫♫♫
The Original Singles 1965–1967 (Columbia, 1981) ♫♫♫
The Very Best of the Byrds (Pair, 1986) ♫♫♫
20 Essential Tracks from the Boxed Set: 1965–1990 (Columbia, 1992) ♫♫♫♫

worth searching for: *The Byrds* (Columbia, 1990, prod. various) ♫♫♫♫ is a boxed set actually worth its price, with four discs that pretty much cover the band's entire output, including several *Sweetheart of the Rodeo* outtakes (some of which pop up on the Legacy reissue).

solo outings:
Roger McGuinn:
Roger McGuinn (Columbia, 1973) ♫♫♫♫
Peace on You (Columbia, 1974) ♫♫
Roger McGuinn and Band (Columbia, 1975) ♫♫
Cardiff Rose (Columbia, 1976) ♫♫
Thunderbyrd (Columbia, 1977) ♫♫
Back from Rio (Arista, 1991) ♫♫

Born to Rock and Roll (Columbia Legacy, 1991) 🎵🎵🎵🎵
Live from Mars (Hollywood, 1996) 🎵🎵

McGuinn, Clark & Hillman:
McGuinn, Clark and Hillman (Capitol, 1979) 🎵🎵🎵

Gene Clark:
Two Sides to Every Story (Polydor, 1977) 🎵🎵🎵
Echoes (Legacy, 1991) 🎵🎵🎵🎵
Looking for a Connection (Dos, 1994) 🎵🎵
This Byrd Has Flown: The Essential Gene Clark (Monster Music, 1996) 🎵🎵🎵🎵

influences:

⏪ Merle Haggard, Bob Dylan, Flatt & Scruggs, Pete Seeger, Weavers, Limelighters

⏩ Flying Burrito Brothers, Dillard & Clark, Country Gazette, Poco, Neil Young & Crazy Horse, Manassas, Stephen Stills Band, Crosby, Stills & Nash, James Gang, Barnstorm, Linda Ronstadt, Eagles, Rick Nelson & the Stone Canyon Band, Desert Rose Band

see also: *Gram Parsons, Flying Burrito Brothers, Chris Hillman*

Leland Rucker

THE CACTUS BROTHERS
Formed as Walk the West, in Nashville, TN.

Paul Kirby, lead vocals, guitar; Will Golemon, guitar, banjo; John Golemon, bass; Johnny Tulucci, drums; Jim Fungaroli, steel guitar, dobro (1994–present); Tramp, fiddle, mandolin, guitar, vocals; David Schnaufer, dulcimer (left 1994).

In Nashville during the 1980s acts like Steve Earle and Jason and the Scorchers blurred the lines between the city's rock and country scenes. One of the popular regional groups then was Walk the West, which later evolved into the Cactus Brothers. The Cactus Brothers were more acoustic-oriented, with dulcimer, dobro and banjo featured, but just as eclectic. Even though they never found national success, they were tremendously popular among the locals. Lead singer Paul Kirby's fa-

ther, Dave Kirby, co-wrote the Charley Pride and Texas Tornados hit "Is Anybody Goin' to San Antone."

what's available: *24 Hrs., 7 Days a Week* (Capitol, 1995, prod. Randy Scruggs) 🎵🎵🎵🎵, the Cactus Brothers' second album, went nowhere in the United States (though the group has become popular in sections of Europe), but it's an entertaining album for people with diverse tastes. At the time, the group was one of the only major-label country acts to use banjo on their records, and the songs include renditions of Lucinda Williams' "He Never Got Enough Love," Creedence Clearwater Revival's "Lodi" and Red Simpson's "Highway Patrol"—which pretty much sets the parameters of the band's musical tastes.

worth searching for: Walk the West is the Cactus Brothers' rock alter ego. On *Walk the West* (Capitol) 🎵🎵🎵 you can still hear the country influence among the crash of guitars. *The Cactus Brothers* (Liberty, 1993, prod. Allen Reynolds, Mark Miller, John Lomax III, Melanie Wells) 🎵🎵🎵🎵 is a mixed bag of material, ranging from string band instrumentals to rocked-out covers of country standards like "Sixteen Tons."

solo outings:
David Schnaufer:
Dulcimer Player Deluxe (SFL, 1989) 🎵🎵🎵🎵
Dulcimer Sessions (SFL, 1992) 🎵🎵🎵🎵

influences:
⏪ Jason & the Scorchers, Kentucky HeadHunters
⏩ BR5-49, Keith Urban

Brian Mansfield

CALIFORNIA
See: Byron Berline

SHAWN CAMP
Born August 29, in Little Rock, AR.

Raised in rural Perryville, Arkansas, Shawn Camp began playing guitar at age eight and fiddle at 15. He joined Oklahoma's Signal Mountain Boys as a teen, then moved to Nashville and was hired to play fiddle for the Osborne brothers. Later he worked as a songwriter and also as a sideman for Jerry Reed, Alan Jackson, Trisha Yearwood and Shelby Lynne before signing with Reprise Records for one album.

what's available: In addition to his bluegrass background, Camp has a winning way with a song hook. He wrote or co-wrote all but one song on *Shawn Camp* (Reprise, 1993, prod. Mark Wright) ♫♫♫, which features appearances by Lynne, Alison Krauss, Jim Lauderdale and guitarist James Burton. It combines elements of bluegrass, rockabilly, honky tonk and pop, all sung in Camp's charming tenor. It yielded only two small hits, "Fallin' Never Felt So Good" and "Confessin' My Love," but "K-I-S-S-I-N-G" was covered later by Rhett Akins.

influences:

◀◀ Roger Miller, Elvis Presley

▶▶ Rhett Akins, Dean Miller

Brian Mansfield

GLEN CAMPBELL

Born April 22, 1936, just outside Billstown, AR.

Although unjustly remembered as a somewhat ingratiating, over-the-top cornball (his hugely successful CBS-TV series *The Glen Campbell Goodtime Hour* can still strike terror into the faint-of-heart), Campbell's long and successful career as an entertainer is testament to the obvious drive and abundant talent behind the rhinestones. First leaving home as a teen to tour with his Uncle Dick Bills' Western swing combo, Campbell landed in Los Angeles in 1960 at the perfect time to make use of his growing prowess on the guitar. During the next five years he was one of the city's most sought-after studio musicians, performing behind everyone from Phil Spector to Frank Sinatra. He was even a bona fide Beach Boy for a while! Campbell also worked with his friend Jimmy Bowen for an L.A. music publisher and performed in an early incarnation of Merle Haggard's Strangers alongside James Burton and Glen D. Hardin. Signing himself to Capitol Records in 1962, Campbell quickly scored a Top 20 country hit with "Kentucky Means Paradise." He first appeared on the pop charts three years later with a version of Donovan's "Universal Soldier," and in 1967 his signature tune, John Hartford's "Gentle on My Mind," placed respectably on both the country *and* pop charts. But it wasn't until he began recording the brilliant songs of Jimmy Webb that he became a regular visitor to the Top 10 ("By the Time I Get to Phoenix," "Wichita Lineman" and "Galveston" remain classics of their genre). After several years spent entertaining on both the small and big screens (joking that his role in *True Grit* helped co-star John Wayne win an Academy Award), he returned to the top of the charts in 1975 ("Rhinestone Cowboy") and again in 1977 ("Southern Nights") before hitting the scandal sheets with Tanya Tucker and letting years of pharmaceutical

FIVE FOR MY FANS

BEKKA BRAMLETT
(of Bekka & Billy)

Delaney & Bonnie & Friends
D & B Together (Columbia)

Vince Gill
High Lonesome Sound (MCA)

Etta James
At Last! (Chess)

Journey
Escape (Columbia)

Randy Travis
Forever and Ever, Amen (Warner Bros.)

dabbling get the better of him. The following decade was spent bouncing somewhat aimlessly from label to label and from style to style (including successful reunions on MCA with Jimmys Bowen and Webb), culminating with a self-confessed "workhorse" stint in the lounges of Branson's country-chic. The 1990s, however, found Campbell both physically and spiritually cleansed and refreshed, and he remains a popular performer—and red-hot guitarist—to this day. And he can still sing Jimmy Webb like nobody else can.

what to buy: The *Essential Glen Campbell* series (Liberty/ Capitol Nashville, 1995, prod. various) ♫♫♫ gathers, in three volumes, all the hits in gorgeous sound as well as just enough rarities, instrumentals and live recordings to demonstrate both the depth and scope of this decidedly all-around entertainer.

what to buy next: Capitol has just begun a long-overdue reissue of Campbell's earliest albums, starting with his very first

Glen Campbell **(AP/Wide World Photos)**

from 1962, *Big Bluegrass Special* (Capitol Nashville, 1996, prod. Nick Venet) ♪♪♪, originally released under the Green River Boys moniker. Also newly available are his three fine breakthrough albums from 1967 and 1968: *Gentle on My Mind* (Capitol Nashville, 1996, prod. Al DeLory) ♪♪♪; *By the Time I Get to Phoenix* (Capitol Nashville, 1996, prod. Al DeLory) ♪♪♪♪; and *Wichita Lineman* (Capitol Nashville, 1996, prod. Al DeLory) ♪♪♪♪.

what to avoid: Sidestep the tepid *Christmas with Glen Campbell* (Laserlight, 1995) ♪♪. Also note: an absolute myriad of greatest hits and concert recordings has been rendered superfluous by the *Essential* series.

the rest:
Old Town Home (Atlantic, 1982) ♪♪♡
Letter to Home (Atlantic, 1983) ♪♪♡
Favorite Hymns (Word/Epic, 1992) ♪♪♪
Wings of Victory (Intersound International, 1996) ♪♪♡
The Glen Campbell Collection (1962–1989) (Razor & Tie, 1997) ♪♪♪♪
Jesus and Me: The Collection (New Haven, 1997) ♪♪

worth searching for: Campbell's oft-overlooked gift as an instrumentalist is readily apparent on any of the budget reissues of his early Folkswingers recordings, particularly the *12-String Guitar* albums on World Pacific and also his just-before-fame work with the baroque Beach Boy band Sagittarius alongside Gary Usher, Terry Melcher, Bruce Johnston and Curt Boetcher.

influences:
◀◀ Roger Miller, Django Reinhardt, Jimmy Dickens
▶▶ Jim Stafford, Ricky Skaggs, Garth Brooks

Gary Pig Gold

KATE CAMPBELL

Born October 31, 1961, in New Orleans, LA.

Born in New Orleans, Campbell grew up in Sledge, Mississippi, where her father was a Baptist pastor. She picked up the ukelele at age four and the piano at age six. She eventually moved to Nashville, though she went to college in Alabama. A clear-voiced singer/songwriter whose vivid, literarily-driven lyrics paint powerful images of Southern life in the style of Eudora Welty and Flannery O'Connor, Campbell creates refreshingly intelligent country-folk that's energizing as well as evocative.

what's available: *Songs from the Levee* (Large River, 1994/Compass, 1995, prod. Johnny Pierce, Jim Emrich) ♪♪♪♪, Campbell's debut album, is a rich collection of story songs that reaches a peak with the nostalgic "Wild Iris" and "A Cotton Field Away," a reflective tale about prejudice. It's smart stuff that never slips into pretentiousness. *Moonpie Dreams* (Compass, 1997, prod. Johnny Pierce) ♪♪♪♪ begins with a funky, horn-driven song about pop culture and prehistory called "When Panthers Roamed in Arkansas." Campbell's second outing is more musically varied than *Levee*, and packs just as much lyrical punch. Other highlights include the folky "Delmus Jackson" (a tribute to an old janitor) and her ode to a vintage family car ("Galaxie 500"). With songs like "Moonpie Dreams" and "See Rock City," *Moonpie Dreams* shows signs of becoming a minor Southern classic.

influences:
◀◀ Bobbie Gentry, Iris DeMent, Mary Chapin Carpenter, Nanci Griffith, Emmylou Harris
▶▶ Carrie Newcomer, Lucy Kaplansky, Lynn Miles

Bob Cannon and Brian Mansfield

STACY DEAN CAMPBELL

Born July 27, 1967, in Carlsbad, NM.

Stacy Dean Campbell passed up a chance to become an Oklahoma County sheriff's deputy to move to Nashville and become a country singer. With his matinee idol looks and captivating voice, Campbell seemed a sure bet for stardom

what's available: *Hurt City* (Columbia, 1995, prod. Blake Chancey, Wally Wilson) 🎵🎵🎵 is more "up" musically, but the lyrics are unrelentingly down on love. In contrast, Campbell's debut, *Lonesome Wins Again* (Columbia, 1992, prod. Brent Maher) 🎵🎵🎵, while occasionally somber and much more sparse musically, contains songs that offer more hope. The first album features more of Campbell's own songwriting, and there are gems like "Poor Man's Rose" and the haunting "Would You Run"; for *Hurt City*, Campbell turned to several of Music City's top tunesmiths, past and present. On *Hurt City*, you get wall-of-sound production and songs like a cover of Jim Ed Brown's honky-tonker "Pop a Top," the Ricky Nelson-ish "Why You Been Gone So Long," the Roy Orbisonesque "I Can Dream" and a version of Steve Earle's "Sometimes She Forgets" that cuts much closer to the core of the song than Travis Tritt's calypso-beat version. On the other hand, *Lonesome Wins Again* offers a leaner production that puts Campbell's dramatic voice front and center, whether on the gorgeous, lean love song "Poor Man's Rose" or the muscular rockabilly-influenced "Rosalee."

influences:

◄◄ Gene Pitney, Roy Orbison, Johnny Cash, Marty Robbins, Everly Brothers

►► Steve Kolander, Dean Miller

Bill Hobbs

RAY CAMPI

Born April 20, 1934, in New York, NY.

Ray Campi has been playing his blend of folk, country and rockabilly for more than 40 years. Campi's family moved to Austin, Texas, during 1944, and the area's mix of blues, country and Western swing inspired him to take up the guitar. In 1949 he and his band, Ramblin' Ray & the Ramblers, started heating up their Western swing with a little boogie on radio shows for KTAE and KNOW. So when rock 'n' roll hit during the mid-1950s, Campi had already mastered its root forms. Campi's first single for TNT Records ("Caterpillar" b/w "Play It Cool") is considered a genre classic today, but in 1956 it sold well only in Texas. Follow-up releases fared no better; a 1960 single on Dot earned

him national exposure on *American Bandstand,* but the rockabilly rage had cooled by then. Campi then moved to California and recorded on small labels there without success (he once actually received a royalty check for three cents).

In 1964 Campi dropped out of the music business and began a teaching career in Los Angeles, but during 1971 extreme rockabilly enthusiast Ron Weiser coaxed him into recording for his label, Rollin' Rock. Campi's Rollin' Rock LPs were poorly distributed, handmade affairs, but they sounded genuine and are cherished by collectors and fans worldwide. Touring during occasional leaves from teaching, Campi has developed a solid fan base in Switzerland, Finland, Germany and Spain (where his rare early records are sold for astronomical prices). On stage, Campi is a rare rockabilly who plays a stand-up bass while he sings, and he incites audiences by slapping it, standing on it and gesturing with it as if the bulky instrument were a guitar. Opening for neo-rockabilly Robert Gordon during the late 1970s, Campi went over so much better than the show's star that his remaining appearances were canceled. In 1979 Campi gave a standout performance in the British documentary *Blue Suede Shows,* but the film was scarcely seen in America. After Rollin' Rock folded during the early 1980s, Campi recorded well-received country LPs for Rounder and Flying Fish, as well as more rockabilly material for the European Rockhouse label. Reissues on Bear Family and Eagle have kept his name alive with fans, and 1997 saw the release of three new CDs by this persistent foot soldier of American roots music.

what to buy: Rosie Flores & Ray Campi's *A Little Bit of Heartache* (Watermelon, 1997, prod. Billy Troy, Ray Campi) 🎵🎵🎵 is a mostly acoustic tribute to Jimmy Heap and His Melodymakers recorded in 1990.

what to buy next: *Hollywood Cats* (Part Records, 1994, prod. Ron Weiser, Ray Campi) 🎵🎵🎵 is a reissue of Campi's last wild LP for Rollin' Rock. *Rockabilly Rocket* (Magnum, 1994, prod. Ray Campi, Ron Weiser) 🎵🎵🎵 is a repackaging of more Rollin' Rock material from the 1970s.

what to avoid: On *Rockin' around the House* (Rockhouse, 1994) 🎵, the spirit is there but the sound is weak, and the Dutch band can't keep up.

the rest:

Gone Gone Gone (Rounder, 1980) 🎵🎵🎵
The Original Rockabilly Album (Magnum Force, 1990) 🎵🎵🎵
Ray Campi with Friends in Texas (Flying Fish, 1991) 🎵🎵🎵
The History of D Records (Starday, 1996) 🎵🎵🎵

Perpetual Stomp (Dionysus, 1997) 𝄞𝄞𝄞
Train Whistle Blue (Sci-Fi Western/Lost Episode, 1997) 𝄞𝄞
Ray Campi 1954–1968 (Eagle) 𝄞𝄞

worth searching for: *Eager Beaver Boy/Rockabilly* (Bear Family) 𝄞𝄞𝄞 has the best of Campi's work for Ron Weiser's legendary Rollin' Rock label. On *Taylor, Texas 1988* (Bear Family, 1988, prod. Ray Campi) 𝄞𝄞𝄞 Campi returns to his roots in folk and Western swing.

influences:
◄◄ Mac Curtis, Jackie Lee Cochran, Johnny Carroll
►► Rosie Flores, Dave Alvin

Ken Burke

BOB CARLIN
Born March 17, 1953, in New York, NY.

Bob Carlin is one of the most knowledgeable of the younger generation of old-timey musicians; in addition to recording several albums of his own, he has produced several anthologies of archival banjo recordings. He's considered one of the leading modern proponents of the clawhammer banjo style on the traditional music scene today.

what to buy: *Banging and Sawing* (Rounder, 1996, prod. Bob Carlin) 𝄞𝄞𝄞𝄞 is devoted to traditional fiddle and banjo tunes; first recorded 1982–84, this CD reissue contains nine previously unissued tracks.

what to buy next: Carlin and John Hartford join forces for *The Fun of Open Discussion* (Rounder, 1995, prod. Bob Carlin, John Hartford) 𝄞𝄞𝄞, a whimsical musical dialogue between Carlin and Hartford, who brings his considerable knowledge of old-time banjo and fiddle tunes to bear here.

worth searching for: *Melodic Clawhammer Banjo* (Kicking Mule, 1977, prod. Bob Carlin) 𝄞𝄞𝄞𝄞 was Carlin's first album and still counts among his most enjoyable.

influences:
◄◄ Tommy Jarrell, Fred Cockerham
►► Dirk Powell, Walt Koken

Randy Pitts

BILL CARLISLE /THE CARLISLES
Born December 19, 1908, in Wakefield, KY.

Bill Carlisle is one of the best-known singers of country novel-ties, if for no other reason than he's sung them longer than just about anybody else. He and his brother Cliff performed as the Carlisle Brothers beginning in 1930. After Cliff retired in 1947, Bill formed his own group, the Carlisles, in 1951. The Carlisle Brothers had but one Top 10 hit, a humorous reworking of "Rainbow at Midnight," but the Carlisles had many, "No Help Wanted," a #1 hit in 1953, among them. The Carlisles joined the Grand Ole Opry in 1954, and Bill Carlisle continues to keep Opry audiences in stitches well into the 1990s, though he now has to use a walker as a prop.

what's available: Bill Carlisle's *No Help Wanted* (King, 1994, prod. Tommy Hill) 𝄞𝄞𝄞 is a five-song collection of tunes that the Carlisles have performed on the Opry for more than 40 years. The most famous of these—"Iz Zat You, Myrtle," "No Help Wanted" and "Too Old to Cut the Mustard"—were at one time considered mildly bawdy.

influences:
◄◄ Uncle Dave Macon
►► Grandpa Jones

Brian Mansfield

THE CARLISLES
See: Bill Carlisle

CAROLINA
See: Lou Reid

MARY CHAPIN CARPENTER
Born February 21, 1958, in Princeton, NJ.

Mary Chapin Carpenter's country sounds a lot like Nick Lowe's high-powered late-1970s rock 'n' roll. Though her voice has a hint of a Southern twang and her lyrics occasionally focus on honky-tonks and highways, she studies the Beatles and Joni Mitchell much more than Merle Haggard or Johnny Cash. Either way, she has managed to build a big audience of mainstream country fans and neo-folkies clinging to albums by Carpenter's friends, Shawn Colvin and Rosanne Cash. Her best songs, including "I Feel Lucky" and a slicker version of Lucinda Williams' "Passionate Kisses," have hit the top of the country charts, and she consistently racks up Grammys and Country Music Association awards.

what to buy: *Come On Come On* (Columbia, 1992, prod. John Jennings, Mary Chapin Carpenter) 𝄞𝄞𝄞 contains a whopping

Mary Chapin Carpenter (AP/**Wide World Photos**)

seven hit singles, including "I Feel Lucky," which uses Lyle Lovett and Dwight Yoakam as hunks, and "Passionate Kisses."

what to buy next: *Shootin' Straight in the Dark* (Columbia, 1990, prod. John Jennings, Mary Chapin Carpenter) ♪♪♪, the beginning of Carpenter's breakthrough, contains the romp "Down at the Twist and Shout." *Stones in the Road* (Columbia, 1994, prod. John Jennings, Mary Chapin Carpenter) ♪♪♪♪ has generally quieter and more introspective songs.

the rest:
Hometown Girl (Columbia, 1988) ♪♪♪
State of the Heart (Columbia, 1989) ♪♪♪
A Place in the World (Columbia, 1996) ♪♪♪

worth searching for: *On Location: Conversation and Music by Mary Chapin Carpenter*, a one-hour radio special on CD from 1992 that features Carpenter talking about the songs from her first four albums.

influences:
◀◀ Carlene Carter, Beatles, Joni Mitchell, Bob Dylan, Rosanne Cash

▶▶ Shawn Colvin, Trisha Yearwood, Patty Loveless, Suzy Bogguss, Dar Williams

Steve Knopper

THE CARPETBAGGERS

Formed 1990, in Minneapolis, MN.

Rich Copley, bass, vocals; John Magnuson, guitar, vocals; Mike Crabtree, lead guitar, vocals.

This rockabilly trio recalls the no-frills sound of Johnny Cash, with a canny mix of cleverly written originals and the occasional cover of a country classic.

what to buy: The 'Baggers' debut, *Country Miles Apart* (Clean/Twin/Tone, 1992, prod. Carpetbaggers, Tom Herbers)

♬♬ establishes the group's bare-bones approach to rockabilly with tight, catchy tunes such as "Empties at My Feet" and "Always a Pallbearer," as well as a cover of Bill Anderson's "The Cold Hard Facts of Life."

what to buy next: The nearly as good *Sin Now . . . Pray Later* (Hightone, 1996, prod. Ed Ackerson) ♬♬ keeps things simple, but in addition to the galloping "My Jeannie's in a Bottle" and "Absent without Leaving," the 'Baggers delve into dark sounds on "The Way You Left Me" and add fiddle and stacked harmonies on "Don't Ask and I Won't Tell."

the rest:
Nowhere to Go but Down (Clean/ Twin/Tone, 1993) ♬♬

influences:
◄◄ Johnny Cash, Johnny Burnette
►► BR5-49, Big Sandy & His Fly-Rite Boys, Son Volt

Bob Cannon

BRUCE CARROLL

Born December 5, 1953, in Smyrna, GA.

One of contemporary Christian music's most popular country-influenced artists, Bruce Carroll shies from the country tag, preferring a sound like 1970's singer/songwriter folk-pop. Raised in Texas, Carroll overcame an alcohol addiction and found his faith with the help of his older brother, Milton, who married singer Barbara Fairchild. Carroll won country-gospel Grammys for his albums *The Great Exchange* and *Sometimes Miracles Hide*, though subsequent recordings have sounded less and less country.

what to buy: Carrol and his label briefly entertained notions of crossing him into the mainstream country market, so *Sometimes Miracles Hide* (Word, 1991, prod. Brown Bannister, Tom Hemby) ♬♬ features appearances by Vince Gill, Ricky Skaggs, Paul Overstreet and Mark O'Connor. It also contains some wonderful story songs in the title track, "If We Only Had the Heart" and "I'd Rather See a Sermon." The album won Carroll his second Grammy.

what to buy next: Carroll's first Grammy winner, *The Great Exchange* (Word, 1990, prod. Bubba Smith) ♬♬, features a top-notch band consisting of players from the country and Christian session world. The members of New Grass Revival appear on the song "Wake the Dead."

the rest:
Something Good Is Bound to Happen (Word/New Canaan, 1987) ♬♬
Richest Man in Town (Word/New Canaan, 1988) ♬♬
Walk On (Word, 1993) ♬♬
One Summer Evening . . . Live (Word, 1994) ♬♬♬
Speed of Light (Benson, 1996) ♬♬♬

influences:
◄◄ James Taylor, Dan Fogelberg
►► Skip Ewing

Brian Mansfield

JEFF CARSON

Born December 16, 1963, in Tulsa, OK.

Jeff Carson made his mark in 1996 with the tear-jerking ballads "Not on Your Love," and "The Car," both #1 records. His vocal style is very similar to Garth Brooks, and he took the same route to success—singing demos in Nashville during the early 1990s.

what's available: Carson included seven songs on his debut that he originally heard when he sang demos. Consequently, *Jeff Carson* (MCG/Curb, 1996, prod. Chuck Howard) ♬♬♬ is full of "hit songs," but not much personality.

influences:
◄◄ Garth Brooks, James Taylor

Cyndi Hoelzle

THE CARTER FAMILY /THE CARTER SISTERS & MOTHER MAYBELLE

Formed 1927, in VA.

A.P. Carter (born Alvine Pleasant Carter, April 15, 1891, in Maces Spring, VA; died November 7, 1960), vocals (1927–43); Sara Carter (born Sara Dougherty, July 21, 1898; died January 8, 1979), autoharp, vocals (1927–43); Maybelle Carter (born Maybelle Addington, May 10, 1909; died October 3, 1978), guitar, vocals (1927–78). Original group disbanded in 1943, reformed as the Carter Sisters & Mother Maybelle: Maybelle Carter, Anita Carter, Helen Carter and June Carter.

died 5/15/2003

The history of modern country music began in 1927 with the Carter Family. New York record executive Ralph Peer discovered the band when it performed at a portable recording studio he had set up in rural Bristol, Tennessee. To the sparse accompaniment of Sara's autoharp and Maybelle's guitar, the group poured out songs of sadness, hard work and an unwavering commitment to Biblical tenets. Peer was particularly impressed with the Carters' rhythmically sophisticated vocal delivery, punctuated by subtle harmonies, as well as Maybelle's uncanny ability to pick the melody of a tune on the bass strings of her guitar while simultaneously strumming the rhythm on the treble strings. Between 1927–41, the group recorded more than 270 songs, including chestnuts such as "Keep on the Sunny Side," "Wildwood Flower," "My Clinch Mountain Home," "Wabash Cannonball" and "I Never Will Marry." The Carter Family tradition is being carried on today by Maybelle's daughters, Helen, Anita and June, and June's daughter, Carlene. That foursome released a wonderful album in 1988 titled *Wildwood Flower*, which features Carter Family material such as "Worried Man Blues," "Dixie Darlin'" and "Church in the Wildwood."

what to buy: *Anchored in Love: Their Complete Victor Recordings 1927–1928* (Rounder, 1993) 𝄞𝄞𝄞𝄞 covers the first historical recording session the Carters did for Ralph Peer. Among the classics are "Wildwood Flower," "Single Girl" and "Keep on the Sunny Side." *When the Roses Bloom in Dixieland: Their Complete Victor Recordings 1929–1930* (Rounder, 1995) 𝄞𝄞𝄞𝄞 consists of 10 songs recorded in sessions from the end of 1929 and six songs from May 1930. Among the gems included are "When the Roses Bloom in Dixieland," "Carter's Blues," "Jimmy Brown the Newsboy" (which would become a Flatt & Scruggs mainstay), and "Wabash Cannonball," which the Carters taught Roy Acuff, who would subsequently popularize the tune as the Grand Ole Opry's theme.

what to buy next: *My Clinch Mountain Home: Their Complete Victor Recordings 1928–1929* (Rounder, 1993) 𝄞𝄞𝄞𝄞 consists of material recorded at the second Peer recording session, including "I'm Thinking Tonight of My Blue Eyes" and "Foggy Mountain Top." *Sunshine in the Shadows: Their Complete Victor Recordings 1931–1932* (Rounder, 1996) 𝄞𝄞𝄞𝄞 includes "Lonesome for You" and features A.P. and Sara alternating verses, buoyed by Maybelle's new flattop Gibson guitar. Also included are two comedy skits featuring Jimmie Rodgers.

the rest:
20 of the Best of the Carter Family (RCA International, 1984) 𝄞𝄞𝄞𝄞𝄞
Wildwood Flower (Mercury, 1988) 𝄞𝄞𝄞𝄞
Diamonds in the Rough (Copper Creek, 1989) 𝄞𝄞𝄞
Country Music Hall of Fame Series (MCA, 1991) 𝄞𝄞𝄞𝄞𝄞
Clinch Mountain Treasures (County, 1991) 𝄞𝄞𝄞𝄞
Worried Man Blues: Their Complete Victor Recordings 1930 (Rounder, 1995) 𝄞𝄞𝄞𝄞𝄞

worth searching for: The Carter Sisters' *Wildwood Flower* (Mercury, 1988, prod. Jack Clement) 𝄞𝄞𝄞 features Helen, Anita, June and Carlene performing Carter Family classics such as "Worried Man Blues," "Dixie Darlin'," and "Church in the Wildwood."

influences:
▶▶ Johnny Cash, June Carter, Carlene Carter, Rosanne Cash

Rick Petreycik

CARLENE CARTER

Born Rebecca Carlene Smith, September 26, 1955, in Madison, TN.

When she broke away from stepfather Johnny Cash's touring band and started her solo career in 1978, Carlene Carter clearly was more intent on being the black sheep of the legendary Carter Family than being the Woman in Black. Blessed with a sassy, resonant voice that was all spitfire and polish, the brash, blue-eyed daughter of June Carter and Carl Smith had more in common with the energetic British new wave scene than pre-*Urban Cowboy* Nashville. On her early albums, she rebelled against her family tree by covering Elvis Costello and Graham Parker songs, collaborating with Parker's backing band, the Rumour, and eventually marrying singer/producer Nick Lowe. Before their divorce, they would create two rowdy triumphs—1980's *Musical Shapes* (featuring a cheesy duet with Dave Edmunds on Richard Dobson's "Baby Ride Easy" that actually grazed the charts) and 1981's raucous, R&B-flavored *Blue Nun*, which Warner Bros. refused to release in the U.S. Returning to the family fold and touring with the Carter Family helped Carlene reconnect with her country roots, and in 1990 she reemerged with the twangy, heir-triggered *I Fell in Love*. Carter reached the pinnacle of closure on 1995's *Little Acts of Treason* by dueting with her father on "Loose Talk" and inviting Cash and the Carter Family to join her on A.P. Carter's 1928 composition, "The Winding Stream."

what to buy: Her comeback, *I Fell in Love* (Reprise, 1990, prod. Howie Epstein) 𝄞𝄞𝄞𝄞, is the album she always had in her—smart, spunky country music with a rock 'n' roll edge and a pop sensibility. Highlights include the rollicking title track, "Come On Back" and "Me and the Wildwood Rose," a touching tribute to grandma Maybelle Carter. *Little Love Letters* (Giant, 1993, prod. Howie Epstein) 𝄞𝄞𝄞𝄞 is equally heartfelt but more playful, employing the sounds of empty dishwasher detergent bottles as percussion and bouncier rhythms on "Every Little Thing" and "I Love You 'Cause I Want To" (written with Radney Foster). The real jawdropper, however, is Benmont Tench's "Unbreakable Heart," a lullaby-like lament ("From an angel's wings to a fallen star/God makes everything but unbreakable hearts") that Carter coos with amazing grace.

what to buy next: In between such strutting Carter originals as "Too Bad about Sandy" and "I'm So Cool," *Musical Shapes* (Warner Bros., 1980, prod. Nick Lowe) &&&& boasts feverish romps through "Ring of Fire" and "Foggy Mountain Top" that should appeal to fans who discovered her via *I Fell in Love* and alternative country fanatics alike. The catch: for the moment, it's available on CD only as a British import on Demon Records, paired with the fine but decidedly un-country *Blue Nun* (Warner Bros. import, 1981, prod. Nick Lowe, Roger Bechirian) &&&&.

what to avoid: Cold, synthesizer-drenched *C'est C Bon* (Epic, 1983, prod. Roger Bechirian) **WOOF!** is utterly charmless and virtually guitar-less. If you need further warning, the highlight is Jerry Lee Lewis' "Breathless"—which is turned into a ballad. Unlike *Musical Shapes*, however, this album is available on CD in the U.S. via Razor & Tie. Go figure.

the rest:
Carlene Carter (Warner Bros., 1978) &&&
Two Sides to Every Woman (Warner Bros., 1979) &&
Little Acts of Treason (Giant, 1995) &&&
Hindsight 20/20 (Giant, 1996) &&&&

worth searching for: Back when they both harbored pop-star dreams, Carter and Robert Ellis Orrall teamed up on the catchy "I Couldn't Say No," a Top 40 hit that can be excavated on a vinyl Orrall EP titled *Special Pain* (RCA, 1983, prod. Roger Bechirian) &&&.

influences:
◀◀ Carter Family, Nick Lowe, Emmylou Harris
▶▶ Kelly Willis, Trisha Yearwood

David Okamoto

DEANA CARTER

Born January 4, 1966, in Nashville, TN.

Making an impression in a year that introduced teen queen LeAnn Rimes and made Shania Twain's *The Woman in Me* the biggest-selling album by a female artist in country music history was no easy task. But Deana Carter, the outspoken daughter of renowned session guitarist Fred Carter Jr. (Marty Robbins' "El Paso," Simon & Garfunkel's "The Boxer"), broke out in 1996 with some quirky calling cards: a sandpaper-scruffed voice limited in range but abundant in down-home spunk; a wardrobe that favored bell bottoms over bare midriffs; and a

debut album boasting the attention-grabbing title of *Did I Shave My Legs for This?* However, Carter's most endearing quality was her frankness, a straight-from-the-heart, shoot-from-the-hip honesty that came across defiant without being militant and added a refreshing edge to an otherwise typical-sounding Nashville debut.

what's available: "Strawberry Wine," a Matraca Berg-Gary Harrison homage to lost innocence, set the stage, but *Did I Shave My Legs for This?* (Capitol, 1996, prod. Chris Farren, Jimmy Bowen, John Guess) &&& succeeds on the strength of Carter's own compositions, including the feisty "I've Loved Enough to Know" and the wicked title track, which skewers the insensitivity of the male ego with pride and precision.

worth searching for: A 1995 version of *Did I Shave My Legs for This?* (EMI, prod. Jimmy Bowen) &&&, released only in Europe, boasts nine different Carter-penned tracks, including "Angel without a Prayer," "Rita Valentine" and the moving "We Share a Wall."

influences:
◀◀ Tanya Tucker, Lorrie Morgan
▶▶ Mila Mason, Anita Cochran

David Okamoto

WILF CARTER /MONTANA SLIM

Born December 18, 1904, in Gaysboro, Nova Scotia. Died Dec. 5, 1996.

Wilf Carter was Canada's first country star and a cowboy singer who was a legitimate cowboy. He was raised on a ranch in Alberta and took the stage name Montana Slim for his first U.S. recordings in 1937. He continued to record until his retirement in 1980, and he took Jimmie Rodgers' country yodeling style and expanded it in the Swiss style. Carter wrote more than 500 songs and recorded primarily for RCA Canada, Decca and Starday.

what's available: *Montana Slim—Wilf Carter* (Starday, 1967) && was recorded well after Carter's heyday, but it's a good example of his prodigious yodeling capabilities on songs like "Frankie & Johnny" and "On Top of Old Smokey" as well as the then-topical "A Mother's Son in Vietnam." If you want Carter's yodeling, don't look for it in *Montana Slim* (Hollywood/IMG, 1988) &&. There's only a couple of good examples. Instead, Carter leans more toward melodramatic story songs like "Two Little Girls in Blue" and "The Little Shirt My Mother Made for

Me." It does, however, contain "Hey Hey Mr. D.J.," a clever plea for airplay that originally appeared as a B-side.

influences:

◄◄ Jimmie Rodgers

►► Patsy Montana, Hank Snow

Brian Mansfield

LIONEL CARTWRIGHT

Born February 10, 1960, in Gallipolis, OH.

In retrospect, Lionel Cartwright seems one of the first Nashville casualties of the 1990s country boom. A talented songwriter with a knack for crafting pristine melodies and thoughtful lyrics, Cartwright emerged in 1989, the year Garth Brooks' debut album hit the streets. *Lionel Cartwright* melded equal parts California pop, Appalachian traditionalism and radio-ready Nashville country. His voice is in the same fluid, country-pop style that has established Steve Wariner as an influential artist. "Give Me His Last Chance," with its Bruce Hornsby-ish piano intro and breezy feel, broke Cartwright big at radio. But the rest of that first album has a less urban personality; fiddles and steel guitars colored the project a warm, earthy brown. It was indeed a promising start. His sophomore effort, 1990's *I Watched It on the Radio*, lost some of the debut's back-porch charm; the production was a tad slicker just as the songs got better. Again, working as chief songwriter, Cartwright created a solid batch of tunes, including the picturesque title track and the gorgeous heartbreaker, "Say It's Not True." Yet while radio was mostly on his side, sales were not, and MCA executives figured Cartwright needed an album filled with country-lite pop that would garner incessant radio attention. Enter 1991's *Chasin' the Sun*, a collection of mostly banal love songs that cut Cartwright's songwriting duties in half while stripping away much of his artistic integrity. He got his #1 hit, the mediocre "Leap of Faith," but the rest of the singles stiffed. After the first two releases from a proposed fourth album bombed, the set was scrapped from MCA's schedule and Cartwright was dropped from the label. He's since been writing more songs in a fruitless effort to nab another recording contract, though he has managed one lucrative break: Kathy Mattea recorded his lovely "If That's What You Call Love" for her album *Love Travels*.

worth searching for: All three of Cartwright's CDs are out-of-print. Focus your search on the first two only, though. *Lionel Cartwright* (MCA, 1989, prod. Tony Brown, Steuart Smith) �⚇⚇⚇ is his countriest collection, while *I Watched It on the Radio*

(MCA, 1990, prod. Steuart Smith, Tony Brown) ⚇⚇⚇ is more polished but still engaging. Both showcase Cartwright's songwriting strengths.

influences:

◄◄ Glen Campbell, Steve Wariner

►► Bryan White, Jeff Wood

Mario Tarradell

JOHNNY CASH

Born February 26, 1932, in Kingsland, AR.

A larger-than-life figure that looms over the history of country music and rock 'n' roll as well, Johnny Cash scarcely needs an introduction to anyone whose ears have been open during the past 40 years. Yet for someone who is as recognizable as Mount Rushmore, Cash has always been a surprisingly mercurial artist; he was the most country-leaning of the Sun rockabilly crowd, yet his pill-popping, hell-raising lifestyle would likely make any of today's alternarockers blanch. Soon after he embraced country he threw over Nashville, moving instead to California, where he remained, for better and worse, his own man. Amid the politically conservative world of country music, Cash has always been a firebrand, championing minority rights, especially for Native Americans, and condemning the Vietnam war. And he traded songs with the rock world, notably with Bob Dylan, and in later years, with Bruce Springsteen and U2. Yet for all that, he is a passionately evangelical Christian whose best friends are the Rev. Billy Graham on the one hand, and fellow hellraiser Waylon Jennings on the other. Not for nothing did Kris Kristofferson celebrate him as "a walking contradiction." A member of the Country Music Hall of Fame, the Rock and Roll Hall of Fame and Nashville's Songwriter's Hall of Fame—the only artist who has been thrice honored—Cash casts as long a shadow as anyone over almost the whole of American popular music.

what to buy: Might as well begin at the beginning. Cash started out with the rest of the rockabillies at Sun Records, where he developed his trademark boom-chicka-boom sound on such classics as "Folsom Prison Blues," "Hey Porter," "Get Rhythm" and "I Walk the Line." *The Sun Years* (Sun/Rhino, 1990, prod. Jack Clement) ⚇⚇⚇⚇ collects all of those tunes plus many more. The fruits of Cash's labors at his second label are amply covered on *The Essential Johnny Cash, 1955–1983* (Columbia/Legacy, 1992, prod. various) ⚇⚇⚇⚇, a three-disc set that belongs in every serious collection of country music. For the budget-minded, there's *Columbia Records, 1958–1986* (Columbia,

1987, prod. various) *♫♫♫♫*, a single-disc collection that will suffice but also whet your appetite for the larger set. Cash's roots are in folk music as much as in country, and *American Recordings* (American, 1994, prod. Rick Rubin) *♫♫♫♫* returns him to the form he had not explored extensively since the early part of his Columbia era. Featuring songs by younger rockers, the album and its attendant hoopla introduced Cash to a new generation of fans who likely had never heard him before.

what to buy next: *At Folsom Prison/At San Quentin* (Columbia, 1975, prod. Bob Johnston) *♫♫♫♫♫* compiles Cash's two legendary prison recordings from the late 1960s on one disc, and it constitutes some of the bravest recordings ever made. Before the very definition of a captive audience, Cash's "Folsom Prison Blues," "Wanted Man," "Cocaine Blues" and "San Quentin" tell it like it is to the degree that you expect a riot to bust out any minute. *Classic Cash* (Mercury, 1988, prod. Johnny Cash) *♫♫♫♫* is one of those rare occasions when an album featuring re-recordings doesn't merely avert disaster; it actually offers a few new insights into such well-known favorites as "Get Rhythm" and "Sunday Morning Coming Down." Another exception to the rule, *Water from the Wells of Home* (Mercury, 1988, prod. Jack Clement) *♫♫♫♫* transcends the usual empty hype that attends most duet albums—this one with vocalists Emmylou Harris, Tom T. Hall, Hank Williams Jr., the Everly Brothers and Paul McCartney, among others.

what to avoid: Most of Cash's unworthy albums have fallen out of print. In assessing those that remain, take as a general rule of thumb the old saw that you get what you pay for. Steer clear of the many budget releases of Cash's work that exist, such as *Super Hits* (Columbia Special Products, 1994) *♫♫♫*, *The Ultimate Johnny Cash* (Bransounds, 1994) *♫♫♫* and *The Many Sides of Johnny Cash* (Columbia Special Products, 1993) *♫♫♫*. They may contain several hits apiece, but for the most part, have too few tracks to make them truly worthwhile.

the rest:
Now There Was a Song! Memories from the Past (Columbia, 1960) *♫♫♫*
Ring of Fire: The Best of Johnny Cash (Columbia, 1963) *♫♫♫*
Blood, Sweat and Tears (Columbia, 1963) *♫♫♫*
Bitter Tears: Ballads of the American Indian (Columbia, 1964) *♫♫♫*
Greatest Hits Volume 1 (Columbia, 1967) *♫♫♫♫*
Greatest Hits Volume 2 (Columbia, 1971) *♫♫♫♫*
(With Jerry Lee Lewis and Carl Perkins) *The Survivors* (Columbia, 1982/Razor & Tie, 1995) *♫♫♫*
Biggest Hits (Columbia, 1982) *♫♫♫*

(With Waylon Jennings) *Heroes* (Columbia, 1986/Razor & Tie, 1995) *♫♫♫*
(With Elvis Presley, Lewis and Perkins) *Complete Million Dollar Session* (Charly, 1987) *♫♫♫♫*
Boom Chicka Boom (Mercury, 1990) *♫♫♫*
Patriot (Columbia, 1990) *♫♫*
The Mystery of Life (Mercury, 1991) *♫♫♫*
Man in Black (1959–1962) (Bear Family, 1991)
The Gospel Collection (Columbia/Legacy, 1992) *♫♫♫*
Wanted Man (Mercury, 1994) *♫♫♫*
Unchained (American Recordings, 1996) *♫♫♫♫*

worth searching for: Hardcore Cash fans with truly deep pockets will want the comprehensive multi-disc sets released in Europe by the Bear Family label. They include *The Man in Black (1951–58)* (Bear Family, 1990) *♫♫♫♫*; *The Man in Black (1959–62)* (Bear Family) *♫♫♫♫*; and *The Man in Black (1963–69)* (Bear Family, 1995) *♫♫♫♫*. They're great, but be prepared to mortgage the house.

influences:
◀◀ Louvin Brothers, Carter Family, Jimmie Rodgers
▶▶ Bob Dylan, Waylon Jennings, Kris Kristofferson, Marty Stuart, Bruce Springsteen, Rosanne Cash, Carlene Carter, Nick Lowe, Mekons

see also: *Highwaymen*

Daniel Durchholz

ROSANNE CASH

Born May 24, 1956, in Memphis, TN.

Rosanne Cash survived her Nashville Royalty pedigree (her dad is Johnny Cash) to carve out an identity during the 1980s as an innovative and remarkably successful country artist. On a string of records starting in 1979, Cash and producer/husband Rodney Crowell progressively expanded the boundaries of what a female performer could accomplish in Nashville, and her emphatic fusion of hard-hitting rock and classic country scored big on the hidebound Nashville radio charts. Cash's sound on those records can be considered maverick for its time, and for originality and gutsiness compares favorably even now to such latter-day country queens as Shania Twain.

Johnny Cash (© Ken Settle)

But Cash's critically acclaimed balancing act crashed in 1990. With her marriage to Crowell dissolving and her affinity for the country establishment plummeting, Cash released the somber, commercially disastrous *Interiors* and packed it in for life in a Greenwich Village brownstone. She has concentrated since on raising her three daughters, writing fiction (her first collection, *Bodies of Water,* appeared in 1996) and recording spare, ironic songs with a lyric confessionalism that's about as far from conventional Nashville tunesmithing as you can get. It's also awfully good.

what to buy: *King's Record Shop* (Columbia, 1988, prod. Rodney Crowell) &&&& is unquestionably the summation of Cash's Nashville work. It arcs smoothly from wistful pop ("If You Change Your Mind") to playful nostalgia ("Tennessee Flat Top Box") to edgy social balladry ("Rosie Strike Back," a call to arms for battered wives). Cash authoritatively demonstrates that she could take everything Nashville threw at her and throw it right back. Her first major effort, *Right or Wrong* (Columbia, 1979, prod. Rodney Crowell) &&& still sounds surprisingly fresh, with the title tune's ironic exploration of adultery and the first of Cash's sassy take-that-guys anthems, "Man Smart, Woman Smarter." Cash's current incarnation is best represented by *Ten Song Demo* (Capitol, 1996, prod. John Leventhal, Rosanne Cash) &&&&, a stripped-down collection redolent of her frank, biting wit. After listening to "Take This Body," just try looking at a cosmetic surgery ad without wincing.

what to buy next: *Seven Year Ache* (Columbia, 1981, prod. Rodney Crowell) &&&& features some of the trenchant songwriting (the title track and "Blue Moon with Heartache") that would blossom more fully for Cash once she began to leave the country-heartbreak constraints behind. She also has gender-bending fun with "My Baby Thinks He's a Train" and "What Kinda Girl?"

what to avoid: On *Interiors* (Columbia, 1990, prod. Rosanne Cash) &, as the analysts say, Cash had some issues to work through and, by God, she did—with a frankness that teeters into the maudlin. Significant in that it marks Cash's definitive break with Nashville power pop, but not a pretty sight. Or sound.

the rest:
Somewhere in the Stars (Columbia, 1982) &&&
Rhythm and Romance (Columbia, 1985) &&&
The Wheel (Columbia, 1993) &&&&

worth searching for: *Live at the Bottom Line* (RSM) is a clean-sounding bootleg of a hot 1988 performance in New York.

influences:
◄◄ Roy Orbison, Everly Brothers, Emmylou Harris, Joni Mitchell, Johnny Cash, Rodney Crowell
►► Mary Chapin Carpenter, Shawn Colvin

Elizabeth Lynch

GARY CHAPMAN

Born August 19, 1957, in Waurika, OK.

Gary Chapman, Gospel Music Songwriter of the Year in 1982, toiled in obscurity for years, known to Nashville insiders as a gifted singer and songwriter whose work has been covered by artists as diverse as Alabama and Vanessa Williams. To the public, he's Mr. Amy Grant, the Christian-turned-pop singer's husband, sometimes producer, writer and band member. A contemporary gospel singer whose music blends pop, country and rock, Chapman came into his own with 1993's critically acclaimed *The Light Inside*, a surprisingly subtle Christian pop record with a strong country feel. Chapman's identity, especially in country music, is now firmly established since he became the host of TNN's "Prime Time Country" talk show in 1996.

what to buy: *The Light Inside* (Reunion, 1993, prod. Michael Omartian) &&& was nearly seven years in the making, time Chapman took to kick a drug habit, raise three kids and save his marriage to the fast-rising Grant. All of those life experiences, plus a renewed sense of faith, imbue this personal yet accessible record.

the rest:
Shelter (Reunion, 1996) &&&
The Early Years (Lamb & Lion Records, 1996) &&

worth searching for: A 1987 foray into country, *Everyday Man*, is out of print.

influences:
◄◄ Chet Atkins, Bill Monroe
►► Amy Grant

Doug Pullen

MARSHALL CHAPMAN

Born January 7, 1949, in Spartanburg, SC.

If Mary Chapin Carpenter had been born a decade earlier and in the South—and wanted to be a scruffy rock 'n' roller instead of a smooth country popster—she'd have been Marshall Chapman. Chapman went to Vanderbilt, not Brown like Carpenter, but the upper-crust education put some depth into her songs, just like knocking around Europe and waiting tables in Nashville lent them a strong dose of reality. Chapman's best songs put both facets of her life to work, although many of them merely give the what-for to a seemingly endless string of men that were bad for/to her. But that's just Chapman's luck; her songs of female liberation pre-dated the Nashville trend by years, and her records have never sold well. But that hasn't stopped artists like Emmylou Harris, Jimmy Buffett, Conway Twitty and others from covering her songs, earning her enough cash to keep her where she belongs—still in the music business and fronting her own band, coyly tagged the Love Slaves.

what to buy: In lieu of a comprehensive best-of album, the live release *It's about Time . . .* (Margaritaville, 1995, prod. Marshall Chapman, Michael Utley) *♪♪♪* finds Chapman performing before a literally captive audience—in this case, the inmates of the Tennessee State Prison for Women. It's strangely appropriate, for so many of her songs are about women who are driven over the edge by a bad relationship—the very reason many of the women find themselves before her. Chapman's performance is in its own way as liberating as Johnny Cash's was at Folsom Prison in 1969.

what to buy next: Having slipped between the cracks of the record industry, Chapman recorded and released a pair of albums on her own Tall Girl label, an act of self-determination that proves she listens to the advice she dispenses in her own songs. *Dirty Linen* (Tall Girl, 1987, prod. Marshall Chapman) *♪♪♪* and *Inside Job* (Tall Girl, 1991, prod. Marshall Chapman, James Hollihan Jr.) are by far her best studio efforts, containing "Bad Debt" and "Betty's Bein' Bad" from *Linen* and "Real Smart Man" and "It's Never Too Late to Have a Happy Childhood" from *Inside*.

the rest:

Take It on Home (Rounder, 1982) *♪♪♪*
Love Slave (Margaritaville, 1996) *♪♪♪*

worth searching for: Chapman's first three albums are more rock-oriented, and all three were ahead of their time in how she comes on like a punk/country rebel. All three—*Me, I'm Feelin' Free* (Epic, 1977) *♪♪♪*, *Jaded Virgin* (Epic, 1978) *♪♪♪* and *Marshall* (Epic, 1978) *♪♪♪*—are worth searching for in used-LP bins. Listen up for "Don't Make Me Pregnant" on *Jaded* and "Rode Hard and Put Up Wet" from *Feelin' Free*.

influences:

◀◀ Wanda Jackson, Bonnie Raitt

▶▶ k.d. lang, Michelle Shocked, Ashley Cleveland

Dan Durchholz

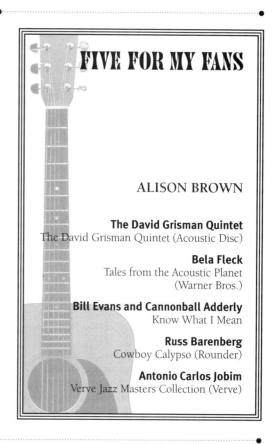

FIVE FOR MY FANS

ALISON BROWN

The David Grisman Quintet
The David Grisman Quintet (Acoustic Disc)

Bela Fleck
Tales from the Acoustic Planet
(Warner Bros.)

Bill Evans and Cannonball Adderly
Know What I Mean

Russ Barenberg
Cowboy Calypso (Rounder)

Antonio Carlos Jobim
Verve Jazz Masters Collection (Verve)

RAY CHARLES

Born Ray Charles Robinson, September 23, 1930, in Albany, GA.

By the time he decided to try his hand at recording an album of country & western favorites in 1962, Ray Charles was already a genre-busting superstar who, in such songs as "What'd I Say" and "I Got a Woman," mated gospel music with R&B, giving rise to what would come to be known as soul music. Charles was an adept jazz player as well, and also had begun to venture into what would eventually be called concept albums. So why not try a country album?

Actually, there was more to it than that. After all, Charles had grown up in Georgia and Florida, where hillbilly and country music was in the air and the Grand Ole Opry was on the radio. Charles couldn't have foreseen the tremendous impact the two-volume *Modern Sounds in Country and Western Music* would have, earning him a string of hit singles, but more importantly, crossing him over to a pop audience and making him an international star. The greater significance of the recordings, though, is perhaps more subtle. Up to that point, country music was as prohibitively white as the front of the bus. Charles has often been chided for his apolitical stance, particularly during the upheaval of the 1960s. But to record a pair of country albums just as the civil rights movement was reaching its height was an act of bravery that seems absolutely astonishing today.

After *Modern Sounds*, Charles recorded other country material, but it is scattered throughout his catalog. He returned to the form full-time for a few years during the 1980s, when he recorded a string of rather uneven albums for Columbia—some of which remain in print, but all of which hold something of value, if only for Charles' knowing, pain-drenched voice, which is, after all, perfect for country music.

what to buy: *Modern Sounds in Country and Western Music* (ABC, 1962/Rhino, 1988, prod. Sid Feller, Joe Adams) 𝄢𝄢𝄢𝄢 contains the original classic album, plus three bonus tracks. Listening to the album now—and it still sounds great, not like an artifact at all—it's amazing how much of himself Charles brings to written and/or made popular by Hank Williams, Eddy Arnold, the Everly Brothers and others. The arrangements are not unlike what he had been doing with his own band at that time, and they are not compromised at all to fit a new format. The deep-seated connection between country music and rhythm & blues has been much commented on in recent times, but never has it been stated so clearly, or so boldly, as on this album.

what to buy next: *Greatest Country & Western Hits* (DCC Compact Classics, 1988, prod. Sid Feller) 𝄢𝄢𝄢𝄢 collects 20 tracks from 1962–65, and while it lacks the historical authenticity of the Rhino reissue, it offers a better overview of the period.

the rest:
Wish You Were Here Tonight (Columbia, 1983) 𝄢𝄢𝄢
Do I Ever Cross Your Mind? (Columbia, 1984) 𝄢𝄢𝄢
Friendship (Columbia, 1984) 𝄢𝄢𝄢
The Spirit of Christmas (Columbia, 1985) 𝄢𝄢
From the Pages of My Mind (Columbia, 1986) 𝄢𝄢
Just between Us (Columbia, 1988) 𝄢𝄢𝄢
Seven Spanish Angels and Other Hits (Columbia, 1989) 𝄢𝄢𝄢𝄢

influences:
◄◄ Hank Williams, Eddy Arnold, Gene Autry, Grand Ole Opry

►► Lyle Lovett, Charlie Pride, Crystal Gayle, Bobbie Gentry, Shelby Lynne

Daniel Durchholz

THE CHARLES RIVER VALLEY BOYS

Formed late 1950s, in Cambridge, MA. Disbanded 1970.

Jim Field, guitar, vocals; Bob Siggins, banjo, vocals; Joe Val, mandolin, vocals; Everett A. Lilly, bass. Earlier members include John Cooke, guitar; Fritz Richmond, tenor, bass kazoo; Ethan Signer, mandolin, fiddle.

The Charles River Valley Boys had a profound influence on the burgeoning bluegrass scene around Boston during the early 1960s. Playing a mixture of old-time and bluegrass music at a number of clubs and coffeehouses in the area, they came to the attention of producer Paul Rothchild, whose later credits as producer included the Doors, Janis Joplin and Bonnie Raitt. Rothchild, working at Elektra Records, heard a tape of the group doing bluegrass versions of Beatles songs and pitched the idea of an entire album to the label. Although the marketing of the record proved disastrous and it was a commercial failure, the music today remains a fitting tribute to the impact and versatility of the Fab Four and is, sadly, the only recorded work on CD by the CRVB. A major turning point for the group had been the addition of staunch traditionalist Joe Val on vocals and mandolin, who remained with the group from 1963 to 1967. In 1970, with the group disbanded, Val formed the New England Blue Grass Boys and recorded several successful (and easier to find) albums.

what's available: If the marketing department at Elektra hadn't gotten scared it would have titled *Beatle Country* (Rounder, 1966/1995, prod. Paul Rothchild, Peter K. Siegel) 𝄢𝄢𝄢𝄢 the more accurately descriptive *Beatle Bluegrass*. Perhaps it works because it was done at the height of Beatlemania, and not as a revisionist afterthought. These songs lend themselves well to bluegrass arrangements. The Homer & Jethro-type send up of "Yellow Submarine" is a real hoot, but this is hardly a novelty record.

worth searching for: *Charles River Valley Boys* (Prestige/Folklore, 1962, prod. Paul Rothchild) 𝄢𝄢𝄢𝄢, a long out-of-print LP, features brilliant bluegrass music and hilarious liner notes.

influences:
◄◄ Charlie Poole & the North Carolina Ramblers, Flatt & Scruggs

►► Joe Val & the New England Bluegrass Boys, Del McCoury Band

Stephen L. Betts

CHESAPEAKE

Formed 1992, in Silver Spring, MD.

Mike Auldridge, pedal steel, dobro, lap steel, vocals; Jimmy Gaudreau, mandolin, vocals; T. Michael Coleman, bass, vocals; Moondi Klein, vocals, guitar, piano.

If there were such a thing as a bluegrass supergroup, Chesapeake would be the first. Consisting of three former members of the influential Seldom Scene ensemble and one ex-player of the Tony Rice Unit, the group has forged a respectable reputation in the acoustic music world. But some bluegrass purists might call what this quartet does blasphemy. While maintaining its high-lonesome bluegrass foundation, Chesapeake experiments with country instrumentation, bluesy arrangements and pop harmonies to create a sound less rural than traditional bluegrass. Call it urban grass. Essentially, this fresh approach makes Chesapeake more diverse than, say, a band that steadfastly follows Bill Monroe's muse. Group members can easily put their own stamp on a familiar English ballad like "Blackjack Davey" or such modern-day rock cuts as Van Morrison's "Moondance" and Little Feat's "Let It Roll." Chesapeake's adventurous spirit has not gone unnoticed. Bluegrass and rockabilly great Doc Watson has said that "Chesapeake is one of the best bands I've listened to in a long time. They can take a tune like 'Shady Grove' and make it sound thoroughly contemporary without losing all the original flavor." You can't buy that kind of endorsement.

what to buy: Chesapeake's second album, *Full Sail* (Sugar Hill, 1995, prod. Chesapeake, Bill Wolf) *♫♫♫♫*, best represents the band's philosophy. The care and innovation that goes into each song makes it a cinch to accept the Carter Family's classic "Are You Tired of Me My Darling" in the same disc with second-generation bluegrass (Ricky Skaggs' "One Way Track") and a bluesy rock tune like Little Feat's "Let It Roll."

the rest:
Rising Tide (Sugar Hill, 1994) *♫♫♫*

worth searching for: Three out of four Chesapeakes guest on Doc Watson's jubilant *Docabilly* (Sugar Hill, 1995, prod. T. Michael Coleman) *♫♫♫♫*, an album that finds the veteran covering a slew of 1950s songs, from "Walking after Midnight" to "Heartbreak Hotel" to "Train of Love." The record also features supporting performances by Marty Stuart, Junior Brown and Duane Eddy.

influences:
◀◀ Seldom Scene, Tony Rice Unit, Ricky Skaggs

▶▶ Front Range, Bad Livers

Mario Tarradell

KENNY CHESNEY

Born March 26, 1968, in Knoxville, TN.

Raised in the same eastern Tennessee town as Chet Atkins and blessed with a classic hard-country voice that sounds as old as the hills and far older than his years, Chesney may have been destined to become a country performer. Even the closing of his first record label couldn't stop him.

what's available: *All I Need to Know* (BNA, 1995, prod. Barry Beckett) *♫♫♫* is Chesney at his most country—this is the real stuff, all fiddles and steel and twang. Chesney is equally at home on rousing country love songs like the title track, "Fall in Love" and "Honey Would You Stand by Me" as he is on tender ballads like "The Tin Man" and "Grandpa Told Me So." A real gem is "Between Midnight and Daylight," an unvarnished picture of a honky-tonk's last call for alcohol. *Me and You* (BNA, 1996, prod. Barry Beckett) *♫♫♫* is more polished, but still solid country.

worth searching for: *In My Wildest Dreams* (Capricorn, 1994, prod. Barry Beckett) *♫♫♫♫*, out of print since Capricorn closed its country division, is as solid as its successors and features Chesney's first recording of "The Tin Man."

influences:
◀◀ Aaron Tippin, Keith Whitley
▶▶ Ken Mellons

Bill Hobbs

MARK CHESNUTT

Born September 6, 1963, in Beaumont, TX.

Aside from his 1993 Horizon Award from the Country Music Association, Mark Chesnutt's not much of an award winner. He's not very talkative or flashy; he's a honky-tonker in the mold of George Strait, a guy who just goes about his business and gets an audience because he does it so well. He began doing it in 1981, when he issued his first independent-label single. Chesnutt released one single a year until he got his MCA record deal in 1990, and he also played a brief stint at Jones Country, George Jones' Texas theme park. Starting with the 1990 single "Too Cold at Home," he has spun some of the best Texas honky-tonk of the decade, recording tunes by such cutting-edge singer/songwriters as Jim Lauderdale, Steve Earle and Todd Snider. Chesnutt hasn't achieved the widespread fame of

Mark Chesnutt **(AP/Wide World Photos)**

fellow traditionalists Alan Jackson and George Strait, but promising young honky-tonkers like Gary Allan have already begun to name him as a role model.

what to buy: *Longnecks & Short Stories* (MCA, 1992, prod. Mark Wright) ♪♪♪♪ is just a flat-out phenomenal country record. "Old Flames Have New Names" places him squarely in George Strait swing territory; "I'll Think of Something" revives an almost-forgotten 1974 Hank Williams hit; and "Who Will the Next Fool Be" shows the bluesy influence of Charlie Rich. Plus, Chesnutt has a wicked sense of humor that occasionally comes to play. He's maybe the only guy who could sing Dennis Linde's "Bubba Shot the Jukebox" without sounding like a total dipstick. The humor's there in "Old Country," too; it's just a lot more subtle.

what to buy next: Though few people noticed it, *Wings* (Decca, 1995, prod. Mark Wright) ♪♪♪♪ was a honky-tonk concept album—or, perhaps, soap opera, since the first song is "As the Honky Tonk Turns." In a time when most country singers had forsaken the topics, Chesnutt sang not only about drinking and

cheating but also about the desperation that often drives the activities. *Greatest Hits* (Decca, 1996, prod. various) ♪♪♪♪ contains 10 hits and two new songs. As good as it is—with songs like "Bubba Shot the Jukebox," "Goin' through the Big D" and "Brother Jukebox"—it's hardly the be-all and end-all of Chesnutt's career. Chesnutt's music has too much depth to be captured in a dozen tracks.

what to avoid: Ironically, *Almost Goodbye* (MCA, 1993, prod. Mark Wright) ♪♪♪ is Chesnutt's most successful album in terms of generating hits. It produced three consecutive #1s: "It Sure Is Monday," "Almost Goodbye" and "I Just Wanted You to Know." Unfortunately, the rest of the album doesn't measure up to that standard. "It Sure Is Monday" and "Almost Goodbye" are available on Chesnutt's *Greatest Hits*.

the rest:
Too Cold at Home (MCA, 1990) ♪♪♪♪
What a Way to Live (Decca, 1994) ♪♪♪

influences:

◀◀ George Strait, George Jones

▶▶ Tracy Byrd, Gary Allan

Brian Mansfield

VIC CHESNUTT

Born November 12, 1964, in Jacksonville, FL.

Championed early on by R.E.M.'s Michael Stipe, Vic Chesnutt rose from wholly inauspicious beginnings during the late-1980s Athens, Georgia, scene to gradually become one of the most respected and admired songwriters of his generation. Confined to a wheelchair since an early-1980s car accident, Chesnutt was quite content to play the occasional local gig until Stipe goaded him into the studio in 1988 to record his debut album, *Little*. Chesnutt's minimalist musical tendencies, acute singing drawl and highly personalized lyrical portraits invited comparisons to such Southern Gothic literary figures as William Faulkner and Flannery O'Connor. Subsequent albums found him working in more intricate backing instrumentation and crafting music that ranged from folk to country to feedback-buzzed rock 'n' roll.

In 1996, Chesnutt made the move from tiny Texas Hotel to Capitol, which issued his major-label debut, *About to Choke*, at the same time Columbia Records released a tribute album, *Sweet Relief II: Gravity of the Situation*. *Sweet Relief II* featured artists from Smashing Pumpkins to Hootie & the Blowfish to Joe Henry and sister-in-law Madonna covering Chesnutt's songs.

what to buy: Like a classic Polaroid snapshot capturing a special moment in time, *Little* (Texas Hotel, 1990) ⅋⅋⅋⅋⅋ remains Chesnutt's most endearing album, recorded almost entirely solo acoustic and full of such singularly engaging character sketches as "Isadora Duncan" and "Danny Carlisle." For those who prefer a bit more musical accompaniment, *Is the Actor Happy?* (Texas Hotel 1995, prod. John Keane) ⅋⅋⅋⅋ is the best of the rest, balancing such beautifully lilting ballads as "Sad Peter Pan" and "Guilty by Association" against a few more upbeat yet quirky pop numbers.

what to buy next: *West of Rome* (Texas Hotel 1992, prod. Michael Stipe) ⅋⅋⅋⅋ is slightly less consistent but includes some of Chesnutt's finest songs, including "Sponge" and "Stupid Preoccupations." *About to Choke* (Capitol 1996, prod. various) ⅋⅋⅋⅋ showed the move to a major label didn't mean a refining of Chesnutt's approach; it's just as gloriously skewed as his other records. *Drunk* (Texas Hotel 1993) ⅋⅋⅋ is a scattered but occasionally brilliant effort, with Syd Straw guesting on one track.

what to avoid: Chesnutt teamed up with fellow Georgians Widespread Panic for an album under the band name Brute titled *Nine High a Pallet* (Capricorn, 1995) ⅋⅋⅋; though the full-band backing is a nice change of pace, the material isn't up to Chesnutt's usual standards.

worth searching for: *Sweet Relief II: Gravity of the Situation* (Columbia, 1996) ⅋⅋⅋⅋ showed Chesnutt's songs to be remarkably adaptable to mainstream acts; among the highlights are Garbage's instantly catchy take on "Kick My Ass" and Soul Asylum's emotionally draining rendition of "When I Ran Off And Left Her."

influences:

◀◀ Jack Logan, R.E.M., Nick Drake, Jimmy Webb

▶▶ Live, Mark Eitzel

Peter Blackstock

CHARLIE CHESTERMAN

Born February 8, 1960, in Des Moines, IA.

After establishing his reputation with Boston roots/garage-rockers Scruffy the Cat during the 1980s, Charlie Chesterman took a turn toward a somewhat more laid-back sound as a solo artist during the mid-1990s.

what to buy: *Studebakersfield* (Slow River, 1996, prod. Charlie Chesterman, Pete Weiss) ⅋⅋⅋⅋ reprises the Scruffy gem "Time Never Forgets" and includes a version of the late Jimmy Silva's "I've Got Time," along with 15 other cuts that stress the subtler qualities of Chesterman's songcraft and cast a warm, nostalgic glow.

the rest:

From the Book of Flames (Slow River, 1994) ⅋⅋⅋

influences:

◀◀ Hank Williams, Byrds

Peter Blackstock

KATHY CHIAVOLA

Born March 7, 1952, in Chicago, IL.

Formerly a professional opera singer, Chiavola (pronounced: *key ah' vo lah*) has sung on albums by Vince Gill, Garth Brooks, Emmylou Harris, Kathy Mattea and Ricky Skaggs. She's released two self-produced albums in the acoustic country and bluegrass vein.

The Chieftains **(Shanachie Records)**

what to buy: *Kathy Chiavola* (Demon/My Label, 1995, prod. Kathy Chiavola) ♫♫♫ contains a much harder bluegrass sound than on her debut recording, but with plenty of twists, like covering John Hiatt's "Thirty Years of Tears" and "Won't Be Long," which kicked off Aretha Franklin's debut album. It also features an all-star list of guests, including Bill Monroe, Emmylou Harris, Vince Gill, Bela Fleck, Chet Atkins and others.

the rest:
Labor of Love (My Label, 1990) ♫♫♫

influences:
◀◀ Doug Dillard Band, Emmylou Harris, Linda Ronstadt
▶▶ Cluster Pluckers, Claire Lynch, Kate McKenzie

Douglas Fulmer

THE CHIEFTAINS

Formed 1963, in Dublin, Ireland

Paddy Moloney, Uileann pipes; Martin Fay, fiddle; Sean Keane, fiddle; Derek Bell, harp; Kevin Conneff, bodhran; Matt Molloy, flute.

Often dismissed as a quaint bunch of old Irish folk musicians, the Chieftains are one of the most remarkably versatile groups around. For a bunch of scholarly looking, middle-aged Irish musicians, they've sure covered a lot of musical ground during their three-plus decades together. Formed by Paddy Moloney as a vehicle to preserve Ireland's Celtic music roots, the Chieftains eventually moved away from its traditionalism, finding links past and present and often in unlikely places such as Spain.

what to buy: *The Long Black Veil* (RCA Victor, 1995, prod. Paddy Moloney) ♫♫♫, the group's best-selling record, blends country and blues with heavyweight guest shots from the Rolling Stones, Sting, Van Morrison, Ry Cooder and others.

what to buy next: The Grammy-winning *Another Country* (RCA Victor, 1992, prod. Paddy Moloney) ♫♫♫ fully explores the country-Celtic connection. With help from Emmylou Harris, Willie Nelson, Chet Atkins and Don Williams, the group tackles "The Wabash Cannonball," "I Can't Stop Lovin' You," "Goodnight, Irene" and even "Cotton-Eyed Joe" with its usual battery of flutes, whistles, harps, fiddles and pipes.

the rest:
The Chieftains 10: Cotton-Eyed Joe (Shanachie, 1981) ♫♫♫
The Bells of Dublin (RCA, 1991) ♫♫♫♫

influences:
◀◀ Clancy Brothers, Carolan, Ceoltori Chuolann
▶▶ Maura O'Connell, Nanci Griffith, Altan, Clannad

Doug Pullen

THE CHIPMUNKS /ALVIN & THE CHIPMUNKS

Created 1958, in Hollywood, CA, by David Seville (born Ross Bagdasarian, 1919, in Fresno, CA; died 1972 in Beverly Hills, CA).

Oddly enough, this is where many adults got their initiation to contemporary music. The Chipmunks are an anonymous vocal trio whose Munchkin-like voices (the result of recording at half speed and playing back at full speed) graced a slew of hit records from 1958 to the present. The group is the handiwork of Bagdasarian, a composer, author, actor and cousin of playwright William Saroyan who, under the pseudonym David Seville, wrote a number of novelty records during the early 1950s, including Rosemary Clooney's 1951 hit "Come On-A My House." By and large a children's sing-along act, the Chipmunks—individually named Alvin, Simon and Theodore—jumped on the Beatlemania bandwagon in 1964 with *The Chipmunks Sing the Beatles' Hits*. More recently, Bagdasarian's son revived the group for a million-selling series of albums covering punk and country classics. The hits just keep on coming.

what to buy: The versatile rodents' country side is showcased best on *Urban Chipmunk* (Epic, 1981, prod. Ross Bagdasarian) *♫♫♫*, which makes good fun of the early-1980s cowboy craze with redneck tunes like "The Gambler" and "On the Road Again." A tempting collection of classic children's songs, *Here's Looking at Me* (Sony Wonder, 1994, prod. various) *♫♫♫* is a 35-year retrospective that includes 1980s rock ("Uptown Girl," "Girls Just Wanna Have Fun"), country ("On the Road Again"), and the song that started it all, Bagdasarian's 1958 hit, "Witch Doctor."

what to buy next: What holiday season would be complete without *A Very Merry Chipmunk* (Sony Wonder, 1994, prod. Ross Bagdasarian, Janice Karman, Steve Lindsey) *♫♫♫*, on which the trio's cute performances even cover the adult-contemporary blather of Celine Dion, Patty Loveless and Kenny G.

what to avoid: And break all the kids' hearts? Forget it!

the rest:
Christmas with the Chipmunks (EMI America, 1962) *♫♫*
Christmas with the Chipmunks, Volume 2 (EMI America, 1963) *♫♫*
A Chipmunk Christmas (Sony Kids, 1981) *♫♫♫*
Chipmunks in Low Places (Sony Kids, 1992) *♫♫♫*
Sing-Alongs (Chipmunk Records, 1993) *♫♫♫♫*

influences:
◀◀ *The Wizard of Oz* and all of your favorite singers, from every generation

Christopher "il Rodento" Scapelliti

THE CHUCK WAGON GANG

Formed 1935, in TX.

David "Dad" Carter, tenor vocals (1935–55); Jim Carter, guitar, bass vocals (1935–53); Rose Carter, soprano vocals (1935–late 1970s); Anna Carter, alto vocals (1935–late 1970s); various other family members, including Ruth Ellen Carter, Roy Carter, Jim Carter, Eddie Carter and others.

Active intermittently from 1935 to the present, the Chuck Wagon Gang is one of the best-loved and best-selling gospel groups of all time. Although they first formed in Texas, their endearing and enduring sound harks back to the singing schools of the southeastern U.S. Their sound is simple, melodic and hauntingly plaintive. The earliest and best recordings feature only guitar accompaniment to their beautiful four-part harmonies.

For many years the sound remained substantially the same; in fact, it still does, although there is no longer any family connection between the Carters and the group who uses the name. Recording first for ARC (which became Columbia), they recorded over 400 songs between 1936 and 1975, when the Gang severed ties with Columbia. They were active only intermittently until 1987, when remnants of the group, led by Ruth Ellen Carter Yates and her brother, Roy Carter, began to record for Copperfield Records, hewing substantially to the old family sound. Since the early 1990s the group has recorded for the Arrival label.

what to buy: *The Chuck Wagon Gang Columbia Historic Edition* (Columbia, 1984) *♫♫♫♫* is the real stuff, reissued from recordings made between 1936 and 1957, featuring mostly the original group. It has 16 tracks, including such Chuck Wagon Gang classics as "We Are Climbing," "The Church in the Wildwood," "After the Sunrise," "A Beautiful Life" and "Get a Touch of Heaven in Your Soul." Presently available only on cassette, but it's well worth having in any form.

what to buy next: Many of the Copperfield recordings have been reissued by MCA, including *Family Tradition* (MCA, 1979) *♫♫♫* and *Keep On Keepin' On* (MCA, 1983) *♫♫♫*.

the rest:
A Golden Legacy (MCA, 1983) *♫♫♫*
16 Country Gospel Favorites (MCA, 1984) *♫♫♫*
Homecoming (MCA, 1986) *♫♫♫*
An American Tradition (MCA, 1988) *♫♫♫*
Greatest Hits, Volume 1 (Arrival, 1991) *♫♫*
Old-Time Hymns, Volume 2 (Arrival, 1991) *♫♫*
16 Golden Country Gospel Favorites (MCA, 1992) *♫♫♫*
Golden Gospel Greats, Volume 1 (MCA, 1994) *♫♫♫*
Golden Gospel Greats, Volume 2 (MCA, 1995) *♫♫♫*

influences:
◀◀ Carter Family
▶▶ Chestnut Grove Gospel Quartet

Randy Pitts

CINDY CHURCH

Born June 11, in Bible Hill, Nova Scotia, Canada.

Cindy Church began her career as a backup singer for fellow-Canadian Ian Tyson. She formed the Great Western Orchestra with another Tyson musician, Nathan Tinkham, when they left the band. As a solo performer, she has stayed close to the folk/Western roots of the Tyson fold, and she has also performed with Sylvia Tyson's Quartette group.

what's available: *Love on the Range* (Stony Plain, 1994, prod. Nathan Tinkham, Dave Hamilton) 🎵🎵 is an acoustic-based country album that gets into some low-key Western swing at times. In addition to her own songs and the ones by producer Tinkham, Church covers "My Wishing Room," an obscure Lefty Frizzell song. *Love on the Range* generated four hit singles in Canada, one of which, "This October Day," had a video that received some airplay on CMT in the States. Church stretches out a bit on the follow-up, *Just a Little Rain* (Stony Plain, 1995, prod. Nathan Tinkham, Cindy Church) 🎵🎵🎵, but keeps the cowboy and Western themes. This time the country chestnut comes from Floyd Tillman, who wrote "I Gotta Have My Baby Back," which Church turns into a torchy acoustic-blues number.

influences:
◀◀ Ian & Sylvia, Emmylou Harris
▶▶ Lisa Brokop

Brian Mansfield

GENE CLARK

Born November 17, 1941, in Tipton, MO. Died May 24, 1991.

Best known for his work as singer/songwriter for the original lineup of seminal folk-rock band the Byrds, Gene Clark grew up in the Ozarks playing folk, bluegrass and surf music. As a member of the New Christy Minstrels, he played on a couple of their albums before moving to Los Angeles and meeting Roger McGuinn. After playing as a duo, Clark and McGuinn were soon joined by David Crosby, and the nucleus of the Byrds was formed. Smartly melding the 12-string folky intensity of Bob Dylan with the infectious melodies of the Beatles and the British Invasion, the Byrds pretty much invented the jangly folk-rock sound that continues to thrive today. Clark wrote many of the key tracks on the Byrds' classic first three Columbia albums, including "I Feel a Whole Lot Better," "Set You Free This Time" and "Eight Miles High." The pressures of success were instrumental in Clark's leaving the band in 1966, just as its popularity was peaking, and he went on to record with the Gosdin Brothers (Vern and Rex) in 1967 and for a variety of labels (including A&M, Asylum and RSO) under his own name during the 1970s. Clark was also part of the reunion of the original five Byrds (Clark, McGuinn, Crosby, Chris Hillman and Michael Clarke) in 1973 and of McGuinn, Clark & Hillman in 1979. He continued to record sporadically before dying of natural causes in 1991. Over the years his songs have been

recorded by Willie Nelson, the Eagles, Tom Petty and Dinosaur Jr., to name a few.

what to buy: As part of its ambitious reissue series, Columbia/Legacy has released the first four Columbia Byrds albums, with bonus tracks. The first two, *Mr. Tambourine Man* (Columbia, 1965/1996, prod. Terry Melcher, reissue prod. Bob Irwin) 🎵🎵🎵🎵 and *Turn! Turn! Turn!* (Columbia, 1965/1996, prod. Terry Melcher, reissue prod. Bob Irwin) 🎵🎵🎵🎵, are full of Clark compositions and his pensive, slightly mysterious vocals.

what to buy next: *Echoes* (Columbia Legacy, 1991, Digital producer Bob Irwin) 🎵🎵🎵🎵 collects the *Gene Clark with the Gosdin Brothers* release with six Clark-penned Byrds songs and three unreleased nuggets and gives a pretty good idea of Clark's considerable contribution to the burgeoning folk-rock movement.

the rest:
Firebyrd (Making Waves, 1984) 🎵🎵🎵
(With Carla Olson) *So Rebellious a Lover* (Razor & Tie, 1987/1992) 🎵🎵🎵
This Byrd Has Flown (Monster Music, 1996) 🎵🎵🎵

worth searching for: *No Other* (Asylum, 1974, prod. Thomas Jefferson Kaye) 🎵🎵🎵, originally released by Asylum during that label's hit runs with Linda Ronstadt and Jackson Browne, is a brooding L.A. blend of country, folk and rock with instrumental accompaniment from Richard Greene, Chris Hillman, Russ Kunkel, Michael Utley and Stephen Bruton, among others. After topping the best-seller lists with the Byrds, it is the only Clark solo album to even dent the charts.

influences:
◀◀ Beatles, Bob Dylan
▶▶ R.E.M., Tom Petty & the Heartbreakers

David Sokol

GUY CLARK

Born November 6, 1941, in Monahans, TX.

With a soft, Southern voice and terrific storytelling details that artfully give the right impression at the right time, Clark has quietly become a hero for a generation of young country-folk songwriters. The key influence for Lyle Lovett, Robert Earl Keen Jr., Nanci Griffith and many others has never been flashy, but he can knock you over with a rickety four-second lyrical observation. "I Don't Love You Much Do I"—the love song at the heart of *Boats to Build*—is as simple and refreshingly unclichéd as the Beatles' "I Wanna Hold Your Hand." There's a reason he's nicknamed "The Craftsman"; it's easy to picture Clark sanding down a piece of wood in the back yard and humming new songs as he builds a deck or a boat. After a career detour recording for Asylum, Clark has returned to his original label, Sugar Hill.

what to buy: *Boats to Build* (Asylum/Elektra, 1992, prod. Guy Clark, Miles Wilkinson) ♫♫♫ contains wonderful stories about love, romance and the folk singer Ramblin' Jack Elliot (a friend and occasional musical guest on Clark's albums). The soft, short songs express a wide range of emotions without much effort or instrumentation. His best-known album remains his debut, *Old No. 1* (Sugar Hill, 1975, recorded by Al Pachucki, Tom Pick and Ray Butts) ♫♫♫, which features Clark's classic "Desperados Waiting for a Train" and fawning liner notes by pal Jerry Jeff Walker.

what to buy next: On *Dublin Blues* (Asylum, 1994, prod. Miles Wilkinson, Guy Clark) ♫♫♫, lines such as "I have seen the David, seen the Mona Lisa, too/And I have heard Doc Watson play 'Columbus Stockade Blues,'" show that Clark's knack for detail is just getting more potent as he gets older.

what to avoid: *Old Friends* (Sugar Hill, 1988, prod. Miles Wilkinson, Guy Clark) ♫♫♫ is overly cluttered with star cameos and, despite a few good songs, constrains Clark's natural voice and lyrics.

the rest:
Texas Cookin' (Sugar Hill, 1976) ♫♫♫
The Essential Guy Clark (RCA, 1997) ♫♫♫♫
Keepers (Sugar Hill, 1997)

worth searching for: Several of Clark's best albums, including *Guy Clark*, *The South Coast of Texas* and *Better Days*, are long out of print. The two-disc set *Craftsman* (Philo/Rounder, 1995, prod. various) ♫♫♫ brings them back, even if the experience isn't as rewarding as the concise, cohesive *Boats to Build*.

influences:

◀◀ Jerry Jeff Walker, Johnny Cash, Willie Nelson, Townes Van Zandt

▶▶ Lyle Lovett, Robert Earl Keen Jr., Emmylou Harris, Nanci Griffith, Rodney Crowell

Steve Knopper

ROY CLARK

Born Roy Linwood Clark, April 15, 1933, in Meherrin, VA.

Roy Clark will forever be associated with *Hee Haw,* the cornpone country comedy and variety show that was among the longest running series on television (1968–94). Clark got his share of laughs on the show—which came in handy when Johnny Carson tapped him to guest host *The Tonight Show*—but it also showcased his versatility as a singer and, especially, a musician. Adept at guitar, banjo, mandolin and just about anything else with strings attached to it, Clark's first instrument was a crudely made home job his dad—a dance band leader who helped Clark master three instruments by his teens—fashioned out of a cigar box, ukulele neck and four guitar strings for a school band his son played in. Young Clark won a national banjo competition in his teens, appeared on Arthur Godfrey's amateur talent show during the 1950s and signed on as Wanda Jackson's guitarist in 1960. He was headlining Las Vegas within a couple of years. Clark was an established recording artist by the time he agreed to co-host *Hee Haw* with Buck Owens in 1968. His "Tips of My Fingers" was a hit at country and pop radio. Thanks to the television exposure, Clark's recording career rebounded during the late 1960s, pushing "Yesterday When I Was Young," "I Never Picked Cotton" and "Thank God and Greyhound" into the Top 20. Clark branched into gospel music during the early 1980s, at one point forming a gospel quartet with Owens and fellow *Hee Haw* regular Grandpa Jones. He has the distinction of winning both the Academy of Country Music's Comedian and Instrumentalist of the Year awards, is known for his philanthropy and other goodwill work, and was the first country artist to open a theater in Branson, Missouri, when the country mainstream all but forgot him. He has since left that tourist Mecca but continues to tour and record.

what to buy: Clark's diverse output is amply represented on *Greatest Hits* (Varese Vintage, 1995, prod. various) ♫♫♫, which includes classics such as "Tips of My Fingers," "Yesterday When I Was Young," "Thank God for Greyhound" and "I Never Picked Cotton." It's also a fine showcase for Clark's sensitive voice, another of his often overlooked and underappreciated talents.

what to buy next: *Banjo Bandits* (MCA Special Products, 1978, prod. Jim Fogelsong) ♫♫♫ is a picker's delight, pairing the fleet-fingered Clark and Buck Trent on standards such as "Beer Barrel Polka" and "Down Yonder."

what to avoid: Live albums rarely do artists much justice, which is true of Clark's *Live in Branson, MO* (Laserlight, 1993, prod. Ralph Jungheim) ♫.

the rest:
The Best of Roy (MCA, 1971) ♫♫♫
The Best of Roy Clark (Curb, 1971) ♫♫♫

Roy Clark **(Archive Photos)**

(With Clarence "Gatemouth" Brown) *Makin' Music* (One Way, 1979) 🎵🎵🎵

My Favorite Hymns (Intersound, 1993) 🎵🎵

(With Joe Pass) *Plays Hanks Williams* (Ranwood, 1995) 🎵🎵🎵

Great Picks and New Tricks (Intersound International, 1995) 🎵🎵🎵

influences:

◀◀ Flatt & Scruggs, Bill Monroe

▶▶ Mark O'Connor, Jerry Douglas

see also: *Hee Haw Gospel Quartet*

Doug Pullen

TERRI CLARK

Born August 5, 1968, in Medicine Hat, Alberta, Canada.

When her first single, "Better Things to Do," reached #1, Terri Clark immediately became a symbol of the new, strong female singer. She sang traditional country music, played guitar, bass and drums and wrote 11 of the 12 songs on her debut album.

She also refused to wear anything but t-shirts and Wranglers, a look that has become her trademark.

Terri grew up in western Canada, in the heart of cattle country. Her grandparents were country singers in Quebec during the 1950s and 1960s, and she learned to play guitar at the knee of her mom. By the age of nine Terri was playing guitar, and all through high school she was obsessed with country music, especially strong women performers like Loretta Lynn, the Judds, Barbara Mandrell and Reba McEntire. As soon as she graduated she was in Music City, and promptly marched into the legendary Tootsie's Orchid Lounge and asked for a job. They gave her a shot, and she was hired immediately as their house singer. She then spent several years honing her songwriting and paying her dues, working a series of odd jobs around town. After seven years of odd jobs, Terri got her shot, and her debut album went gold.

what's available: *Terri Clark* (Mercury, 1995, prod. Chris Waters, Keith Stegall) 🎵🎵🎵 contains her hits "Better Things to Do," "When Boy Meets Girl," "If I Were You," and "Suddenly Single." Terri's singing improved immensely on her sophomore outing *Just the Same* (Mercury, 1996, prod. Keith Stegall, Chris Waters, Terri Clark) 🎵🎵🎵. Bonus: pictures of Terri without her hat!

influences:

◀◀ Loretta Lynn, Patty Loveless

▶▶ Anita Cochran

Cyndi Hoelzle

PHILIP CLAYPOOL

Born in Memphis, TN.

The cover photo of Philip Claypool's debut album is the first indicator that the Memphis native isn't cut from the standard hat act cloth. Dressed in faded jeans, suede jacket, t-shirt and cowboy hat (the latter of which is more genuine country by-product than raison d'etre), a guitar leaning against his hip, Claypool makes a case for the lived-in look.

what's available: Writing solo, Claypool penned three of the 11 cuts on his debut, *A Circus Leaving Town* (Curb, 1995, prod. Jerry Crutchfield), and they are far and away the best tracks, clear evidence of a songwriter who blooms under a free rein. The title cut, a majestic, wailing steel ballad of loss and regret, is nothing less than a contemporary classic, while "Yellow Rose" grooves easily into Marshall Tucker country-rock territory. "The Strength of a Woman" also showcases Claypool's integrity—instead of a typical paean to perfect parents, he offers up a cutting tale of a remote, cruel father, offset by the lasting legacy of a good-hearted mother. Through it all, Claypool's voice shifts into an earthy grain, heavy on warmth and believability factor. As far as the hired songwriting help goes, the rest of the cuts fall too frequently into radio-ready predictability, the exceptions being a surprisingly decent redux of Bad Company's "Feel Like Makin' Love" and a snapping rockabilly duet with Carl Perkins on "Mile Out of Memphis." Claypool's rocking ease on the latter tune makes an excellent case for his inherent smarts. He generally upgrades contemporary sounds, while displaying a deft sense of the past.

influences:

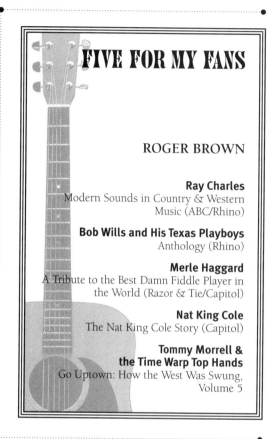

George Jones, Johnny Paycheck

Chris Dickinson

VASSAR CLEMENTS

Born April 28, 1928, in Kincaid, SC.

Fiddler extraordinaire Vassar Clements started out as a session player and, at age 14, got a steady gig with Bill Monroe's Blue Grass Boys. He honed his craft and soon developed a reputation not only for his blazing speed but also for his uncanny ability to make the instrument cry and sing. Other top bluegrass and country artists also enlisted his services, including Jim & Jesse, Faron Young and the Earl Scruggs Revue. During the early 1970s he turned a newer, younger audience on to bluegrass music when he was featured on the Nitty Gritty Dirt Band's *Will the Circle Be Unbroken* and as part of Old & In the Way, a bluegrass outfit formed by the Grateful Dead's Jerry Garcia. What's unique about Clements is he's never allowed himself to be pigeonholed into performing strictly bluegrass and country. He is equally the master of blues, rock and jazz and has graced the recordings of such diverse artists as Stephane Grappelli, the Allman Brothers, Paul McCartney and Woody Herman.

what to buy: *Crossing the Catskills* (Rounder, 1972, prod. Vassar Clements, Mike Melford) 𝄞𝄞𝄞, *Bluegrass Session* (Flying Fish, 1977/1992) 𝄞𝄞𝄞 and *Grass Routes* (Rounder, 1991, prod. Bil VornDick) 𝄞𝄞𝄞 all feature excellent musicianship.

what to buy next: *Vassar's Jazz* (Winter Harvest, 1996, prod. Vassar Clements) 𝄞𝄞𝄞 teams Clements with the Dixie Dregs' Stephen Davidowski for some interesting fusion-style jazz.

the rest:
Hillbilly Jazz (Flying Fish, 1974/1986) 𝄞𝄞𝄞𝄞
Hillbilly Jazz Rides Again (Flying Fish, 1986) 𝄞𝄞𝄞

FIVE FOR MY FANS

ROGER BROWN

Ray Charles
Modern Sounds in Country & Western Music (ABC/Rhino)

Bob Wills and His Texas Playboys
Anthology (Rhino)

Merle Haggard
A Tribute to the Best Damn Fiddle Player in the World (Razor & Tie/Capitol)

Nat King Cole
The Nat King Cole Story (Capitol)

Tommy Morrell & the Time Warp Top Hands
Go Uptown: How the West Was Swung, Volume 5

(With Old & In the Way) *Old & In the Way* (Grateful Dead Records, 1975) 𝄞𝄞𝄞

(With Stephane Grappelli) *Together at Last* (Flying Fish, 1987) 𝄞𝄞𝄞𝄞

worth searching for: *Superbow* (Mercury, 1975, prod. Buddy Killen) 𝄞𝄞𝄞 features some good, 1970-ish, country boogie à la Lynyrd Skynyrd.

influences:

Bill Monroe

Mark O'Connor, Kenny Kosek

Rick Petreycik

BILL CLIFTON

Born William August Marburg, April 5, 1931, in Riverwood, MD.

Vocalist, guitarist, and autoharpist Bill Clifton is an atypical bluegrass pioneer in that he didn't grow up with the music and he holds an M.B.A. from the University of Virginia. He brought many traditional country songs and tunes into the bluegrass repertoire via his recordings for Starday and Mercury during the late 1950s and early 1960s. Clifton's inclusion of Carter Family material and other traditional fare and his fondness for autoharp, clawhammer banjo, and other traditional influences appealed to folkboomers of the time. Clifton has lived overseas intermittently for long stretches since 1963, when he moved to England; he also lived in the Philippines as a Peace Corps administrator during the late 1960s. He's always served as an ambassador for bluegrass in his travels. He recorded three albums for County Records during the 1970s.

what's available: *The Early Years, 1957–1958* (Rounder, 1992, prod. Bill Clifton and/or Don Pierce) ♫♫♫ compiles many of Clifton's highly influential Mercury/Starday recordings, featuring all-star bands of both bluegrass pioneers (Ralph Stanley, Benny Martin, Curly Lambert), and prominent revivalists (Mike Seeger, John Duffey) and a decidedly folk-oriented repertoire, including "Dixie Darlin'," "Darlin' Corey," and "I'll Be There, Mary Dear."

influences:
◀◀ Carter Family, Stanley Brothers
▶▶ Country Gentlemen

Randy Pitts

CHARLIE CLINE

Born May 6, 1931, in Baisden, WV.

Multi-instrumentalist Charlie Cline (fiddle, banjo, mandolin, guitar, bass) has led a long and varied career in bluegrass; he, cousin Ezra and brothers Ned and Curly Ray were members of the Lonesome Pine Fiddlers from the late 1930s; he has also played and recorded extensively (Cline appears on myriad bluegrass classic cuts) with Jimmy Martin, Bill Monroe (playing every instrument in the band at one time or another), the Stanley Brothers, the Osborne Brothers, and the Warrior River Boys, as well as reviving the Lonesome Pine Fiddlers under his leadership from time to time.

what to buy: *Return of a Legend* (Hay Holler, 1995, prod. Charlie Cline, Kerry Hay) ♫♫♫, a recent album featuring Cline as leader, showcases his many talents, including lead singing and songwriting, not much in evidence elsewhere in his discography. He also plays fiddle, mandolin, and lead guitar.

what to buy next: *New Beginnings—The Warrior River Boys* (1990, Rounder, prod. Ken Irwin) ♫♫♫ features lots of Charlie's great fiddle and lead guitar work.

worth searching for: *Windy Mountain* (Bear Family, 1992) ♫♫♫, a Lonesome Pine Fiddlers reissue of the band's classic RCA material from their heyday, features Cline in a variety of roles, along with prominent bandmates Sonny Osborne, Melvin and Ray Goins, Curly Ray Cline, and Paul Williams.

influences:
◀◀ Jimmy Martin, Stanley Brothers, Osborne Brothers, Bill Monroe
▶▶ Warrior River Boys

Randy Pitts

PATSY CLINE

Born Virginia Patterson Hensley, September 8, 1932, in Winchester, VA. Died March 5, 1963, near Camden, TN.

One of music's great vocal stylists, Patsy Cline was the first woman to establish a career as a country solo artist, her popularity helping to render the barriers between country and pop useless. Although she never had a million-selling record during her short career, she remains a pervasive influence long after her death in an air crash at age 30. Cline recorded only 12 sessions (104 tracks) over eight years and had minimal control over her recordings and career. But her voice—alternately sassy and seductive, with emotionally charged swoops, chokes and catches—defined a new direction for female vocalists. In a sense, Cline was a pop singer more than a country singer, with nearly perfect breath control and a knack for making even a corny lyric profound. Nearly all her studio work was produced by Nashville veteran Owen Bradley, who recorded her in a variety of styles that, at their best, match her remarkable pop voice with the country-gal image she seemed reluctant to shed and, at their worst, sound so overproduced that you wonder what Cline might have been capable of if somebody had just lit a match under her bandmates.

Cline learned music at an early age and first came to Nashville in 1948 after winning an audition, returning there for good beginning in 1954. Her appearance in 1957 on Arthur Godfrey's popular *Talent Scouts* television program provided "Walkin' After Midnight," her first hit. As her career progressed, Bradley moved her away from her country roots, and at least one reason for her continued popularity is that you don't have to be a country fan to love her music.

what to buy: Given her short recording career and considering the depth of her influence, it's somewhat puzzling that there is only one decent comprehensive, chronological survey of Cline's recording career. Fortunately, it's a great one. *The Patsy Cline Collection* (MCA, 1991, prod. Owen Bradley, compilation prod. Country Music Foundation) 🎵🎵🎵🎵 doesn't include everything, but it touches all bases: her entire Decca catalog plus all but 10 tracks from her 4-Star Music period, interspersed with radio transcriptions and a few live tracks. The two versions of "Walkin' After Midnight" illustrate perfectly Cline's timeless appeal. The first could have been recorded with Hank Williams' band; the second, in stereo, punches up her vocals with a smoother pop backing, but Cline's voice soars over both. Besides "Crazy," "I Fall to Pieces" and the other classics, there are plenty of lesser-known gems—from "Stupid Cupid" and "Love Letters in the Sand" to "The Wayward Wind" and "Heartaches" —that Cline claims as her own. The 68-page booklet is a virtual primer of her recording career, with liner notes by Paul Kingsbury. *The Patsy Cline Story* (MCA, 1989, prod. Owen Bradley) 🎵🎵🎵🎵, a two-album, 24-track, greatest-hits set on one CD, offers the best overview for those unwilling to shell out for the box. There is no filler here.

what to buy next: *Her First Recordings Volumes 1-3* (Rhino, 1989) 🎵🎵🎵 fills in all but two of the boxed set's missing tracks and offers no-nonsense liner notes by compiler Jonny Whiteside. *The Birth of a Star* (Razor & Tie, 1996, prod. Mike Ragogna) 🎵🎵🎵 brings to light 17 performances—discovered in the attic of Cline's former Nashville home—from her appearances on *Talent Scouts*. They prove that she could even overcome the banality of Arthur Godfrey's settings.

what to avoid: There are an unfortunate number of Cline budget discs. Most include one or perhaps two classics and a lot of filler, often with backing tracks grafted onto the originals— ouch! Among those to steer clear of: *Cry Not for Me* (Starburst, 1996) 🎵🎵; *Walking After Midnight* (Kingfisher, 1996) 🎵🎵; and *Patsy Cline* (Collectables, 1994) 🎵.

the rest:
Here's Patsy Cline (MCA 1965) 🎵🎵🎵
Songwriters' Tribute (MCA, 1982) 🎵🎵🎵🎵
Sweet Dreams Soundtrack (MCA, 1985) 🎵🎵🎵
Greatest Hits MCA, 1988) 🎵🎵🎵
The Legendary Patsy Cline (Pair, 1988) 🎵🎵🎵
The Last Sessions (MCA, 1988) 🎵🎵
Patsy Cline Box (Laserlight, 1991) 🎵🎵🎵
In Care of the Blues (Rhino, 1993) 🎵🎵🎵
Loved & Lost (Drive Archive, 1994) 🎵🎵🎵
Faded Love (MCA, 1994) 🎵🎵🎵
Sings Songs of Love (MCA, 1995) 🎵🎵🎵

Patsy Cline **(Archive Photos)**

Classics (Sun, 1995) 🎵🎵🎵
The Essential Patsy Cline (RCA, 1997) 🎵🎵🎵

worth searching for: *Live at the Opry* (MCA, 1988, prod. Country Music Foundation) 🎵🎵🎵 contains live performances recorded between 1956–1962 and excellent liner notes by Jay Orr.

influences:
◀◀ Kitty Wells, Hank Williams, Bob Wills, Roy Acuff, Eddy Arnold, Texas Ruby Owens, Kay Starr, Webb Pierce, Ray Price, Faron Young, Lefty Frizzell

▶▶ Loretta Lynn, Linda Ronstadt, Reba McEntire, Tammy Wynette, Crystal Gayle, Mary Chapin Carpenter, Cowboy Junkies, k.d. lang, Dolly Parton, Lucinda Williams, LeAnn Rimes

Leland Rucker

ANITA COCHRAN
Born February 6, in Pontiac, MI.

Ever since Garth Brooks (and, to be fair, others) kicked open a mass-market door for country music, new performers have seemed to come from a cookie cutter, and the individualists are few and far between. We'll stake our best on Anita Cochran. How come? Mostly because she doesn't have to rely on the Nashville machine; Cochran wrote or co-wrote all but one song on her debut album, *Back to You*, co-produced with the head of her label, and played all the guitar leads, banjo, mandolin and dobro parts. Such self-contained talents are rare in country, particularly when they're women. Credit some of that to Cochran's upbringing. Born in Michigan—but exposed to country through her Kentucky-reared parents (who named her after Anita Carter and one of her brothers after Faron Young)—Cochran learned to make music away from Music City and, therefore, apart from the conventions that can coerce young performers into toeing a stylistic line. Cochran's music is fresh and explosive, which is what happens when you have twang on the home stereo and the legacies of Motown, Bob Seger and the MC5 in the air. Expect to hear lots more about her in the future.

what's available: *Back to You* (Warner Bros., 1997, prod. Anita Cochran, Jim Ed Norman) ♫♫♫♩ is the strong, stirring sound of an original voice. Whether playing blast-off rock ("I Could Love a Man Like That," "Girls Like Fast Cars") or tugging your heart strings ("Daddy Can You See Me," the title track), Cochran sounds as confident and in control as an established artist on her third or fourth album.

influences:

⏮ Carter Family, Bill Monroe, Johnny Cash, Loretta Lynn, Hank Williams, Chet Atkins, Wynonna Judd

Gary Graff

DAVID ALLAN COE

Born September 6, 1939, in Akron, OH.

One of country's most flamboyant and imaginative songwriter/performers, David Allan Coe spent much of his formative years in reform schools and, later, in the adult prison system, making his long-haired "outlaw" stage persona completely real. After being released from the Ohio State Correctional Facility in 1967, he started playing clubs in Nashville and was heard by Kris Kristofferson, who promptly introduced him to Willie Nelson, Webb Pierce, Billy Sherrill and others. Coe began recording for Columbia in 1974 and was billed as "The Mysterious Rhinestone Cowboy" for several years. Although his image was a little too left-of-center for mainstream country radio, there's always been a deep sensitivity just beneath the outrageous exterior, and Coe managed to reach the Top 10 three

times: first in 1975 with his rendition of Steve Goodman's "You Never Even Called Me by My Name" and later with the spooky "The Ride," which details a mysterious encounter with Hank Williams, and the edgy ballad "Mona Lisa Lost Her Smile." Many of his lesser-known singles and album cuts are equally worthy (with titles like "Jack Daniel's If You Please," "It's Great to Be Single Again," and "I'm Gonna Hurt Her on the Radio"). As a songwriter, Coe has been able to express his own visions through other performers, including Tanya Tucker and Johnny Paycheck, who topped the charts with Coe compositions "Would You Lay with Me (In a Field of Stone)" and "Take This Job and Shove It" respectively.

what to buy: Although almost all of his albums include at least a couple of under-appreciated gems, *17 Greatest Hits* (Columbia, 1985, prod. various) ♫♫♫ collects many of Coe's most memorable and popular sides and provides a comprehensive introduction to his vintage 1974–85 material.

what to buy next: *Just Divorced* (Columbia, 1984, prod. Billy Sherrill) ♫♫♫, with its hilarious cover photo of a black car parked in front of Tootsie's Orchid Lounge with dangling beer cans and the words "Just Divorced" and "I Won't Be Home Tonight" scrawled on it, finds the emotionally drained singer in top form, simultaneously mourning and celebrating his recent break up.

the rest:

Greatest Hits (Columbia, 1978) ♫♫♫♩
Castles in the Sand (Columbia, 1983) ♫♫♫
For the Record—The First Ten Years (Columbia, 1984) ♫♫♫
Biggest Hits (Columbia, 1991) ♫♫♫♩
Super Hits (Columbia, 1993) ♫♫♫♩
Super Hits, Volume 2 (Columbia, 1996) ♫♫♫

worth searching for: *Texas Moon* (Plantation, 1977, prod. Shelby S. Singleton Jr.) ♫♫♫ features some bare asses on the cover (hence the title) and a list of places where Coe has done time on the back, as well as compositions by Billy Joe Shaver, Guy Clark, Jackson Browne, Mickey Newbury and Johnny Cash inside. Like the cover, it's raw and real. Germany's Bear Family label has recently reissued the following albums in two-fer form: *The Mysterious Rhinestone Cowboy/Once upon a Rhyme* ♫♫♫♩; *Longhaired Redneck/Rides Again* ♫♫♫; *Tattoo/Family Album* ♫♫♫; *Human Emotions/Spectrum VII* ♫♫♫; *Compass Point/I've Got Something to Say* ♫♫♫; *Invictus (Means) Unconquered/Tennessee Waltz* ♫♫♫.

influences:

⏮ Merle Haggard, Hank Williams

▶▶ Johnny Paycheck, Hank Williams Jr.

David Sokol

LEONARD COHEN

Born September 21, 1934, in Montreal, Quebec, Canada.

While not strictly a country artist, Canadian singer/songwriter Leonard Cohen made his great 1960s records largely in Nashville, using the same producer (Bob Johnston) and many of the same musicians as Johnny Cash and Bob Dylan. Although he lived in a cabin outside Nashville for two years when these landmarks were recorded, the country music community never embraced the often morose poet. Nor have his songs exactly slipped into the easy repertoires of Nashville, where even someone as radical as Emmylou Harris would have trouble with the detail and darkness of Cohen's often elliptical folk-art songs. But Cohen evidently sees himself as working in the great songwriting tradition of the field. On his "Tower of Song," from his 1988 masterpiece album *I'm Your Man*, Cohen wonders aloud about Hank Williams; "But I can hear him coughing all night long," Cohen concludes, "about a hundred floors above me in the tower of song."

what to buy: Both of his Nashville albums, *Songs from a Room* (Columbia, 1969, prod. Bob Johnston) ♫♫♫ and *Songs of Love and Hate* (Columbia, 1971, prod. Bob Johnston) ♫♫♫♥, sympathetically capture Cohen's unique sensibilities in a spare, almost stark framework that underlines the basic bleak landscape of the songs.

the rest:
Songs of Leonard Cohen (Columbia, 1968) ♫♫♫♫♥
Best of Leonard Cohen (Columbia, 1975) ♫♫♫♫
New Skin for the Old Ceremony (Columbia, 1975/1995) ♫♫♫
Death of a Ladies' Man (Columbia, 1977) ♫♫
Recent Songs (Columbia, 1979/1990) ♫♫♥
Various Positions (Columbia, 1985/1995) ♫♫
I'm Your Man (Columbia, 1988) ♫♫♫♫
The Future (Columbia, 1992) ♫♫♫♫♥
Cohen Live (Columbia, 1994) ♫♫♫♥

influences:
◀◀ Hank Williams, Leadbelly, Jacques Brel, Bob Dylan
▶▶ Nick Cave, Sisters of Mercy, R.E.M., Morrissey

Joel Selvin and Doug Pippin

MARK COLLIE

Born January 18, 1956, in Waynesboro, TN.

Proof that singing and songwriting talent and stage presence won't necessarily make you a big star, Mark Collie has turned out one fine album after another since his sharp MCA Records debut in 1990. Collie is fond of describing his music by pointing out that he grew up roughly halfway between Nashville and Memphis. It's no marketing gimmick; Collie's music is a blend of the two music scenes, an aggressive mix of 1950s honky-tonk and a Memphis bent. Country, rockabilly and blues—it's Beale Street meets Music Row in a rural highway roadhouse.

what to buy: *Hardin County Line* (MCA, 1990, prod. Doug Johnson, Tony Brown) ♫♫♫♫ features arresting songs, killer hooks and a worldly-wise country voice on the quirky "Something with a Ring to It," the evocative warrior's tribute "Another Old Soldier," the road song "Bound to Ramble" and the anguished suicide cry for help "Deliver Me."

what to buy next: *Mark Collie* (MCA, 1993, prod. Don Cook) ♫♫♫♫ has a little more polish, a little less twang and a whole lot more rock 'n' roll. Collie's third album brought in a new producer and yielded some of his biggest hits, including "Even the Man in the Moon Is Cryin'" and "Born to Love You." Closer to his debut than album number three, *Born and Raised in Black & White* (MCA, 1991, prod. Doug Johnson, Tony Brown) ♫♫♫♥ continued the powerful, original songwriting of his debut while starting to polish some of his music's rougher edges. Hits included "She's Never Comin' Back," but radio missed the best tracks, the interracial friendship story of the title track, the outlaw-on-the-run tale of Robert Mitchum's "Ballad of Thunder Road" and "Johnny Was a Rebel," which portrayed a different view of the combat veteran's welcome home.

what to avoid: *Tennessee Plates* (Giant, 1995) ♫♫♥ emits the sound of Collie giving up and trying it everybody else's way.

the rest:
Unleashed (MCA, 1994) ♫♫♥

influences:
◀◀ Carl Perkins, Elvis Presley, John Hiatt
▶▶ David Lee Murphy

Bill Hobbs

THE COLLINS KIDS

Brother-and-Sister duo.

Lawrencine Collins (born May 7, 1942, in Tahlequah, OK), vocals; **Larry Collins** (born October 4, 1944, in Tulsa, OK), guitar, vocals.

Jessi Colter (© Ken Settle)

As the house teen rock 'n' roll stars on the 1950s country music television program *Town Hall Party*, Larry and Lorrie Collins found their way into a lot of homes during the popular series' run on Los Angeles television and in syndication. They never experienced commensurate success with their records, although the pair produced a dazzling procession of red-hot rockabilly discs. And, despite being absent from the scene for the better part of 35 years, their reputation continues to grow. Larry Collins twanged his Mosrite double-necked guitar with the kind of ferocity that made young surf guitar king Dick Dale a disciple. His older sister belted the often puerile lyrics with a swagger and raucous bon vivance that belied her youth and apparent innocence (the act fell apart, in fact, when teenaged Lorrie Collins eloped with the much older manager of Johnny Cash). Reels of their endless hours on 1950s television and persistent reissues of their early recordings have made the Collins Kids probably better known in historical fact than they were at their height. Although guitarist Larry went on to experience some success as a country songwriter during the 1970s ("Delta Dawn" was his biggest hit), his sister gave up performing to concentrate on motherhood. But in recent years, they have

emerged to headline rockabilly festivals in England and make sporadic appearances on the West Coast.

what to buy: The Collins Kids never released an album during the act's lifetime, but *Introducing Larry and Lorrie* (Columbia, 1983, prod. various) ♫♫♫ rectified that oversight with a blasting collection of the duo's 1950s recordings.

what to buy next: The entire Columbia oeuvre was collected across two CDs titled *The Collins Kids* (Bear Family, 1991, prod. various) ♫♫♫, although the additional tracks hardly seem worth the freight.

what to avoid: The bootlegs lifted off the *Town Hall Party* tapes sound like, well, like sound recordings from 1950s television. Stick with the studio versions.

influences:
◀◀ Joe Maphis
▶▶ Dick Dale

Joel Selvin

TOMMY COLLINS

Born Leonard Raymond Sipes, September 28, 1930, in Bethany, OK.

Tommy Collins was an important contributor to what became known as the Bakersfield Sound during the 1950s and 1960s. He wrote hit songs for contemporaries in the southern California country music scene of the time, most notably Merle Haggard, who had hits with his songs "High on a Hilltop," "Carolyn" and "The Roots of My Raisin'." Haggard, in turn, penned "Leonard" about Collins. Collins also wrote "If You Ain't Lovin'," a hit for both Faron Young and George Strait. Collins' own hits tended to have a comedic edge, titles like "Big Dummy," "I Made the Prison Band" and "You Better Not Do That," a #2 in 1954. Collins' career has moved in fits and starts for many years, plagued by drug and drinking problems and sidetracked by a religious conversion.

what's available: All Tommy's hits and many of his misses are contained on a five-CD set from Germany, *Leonard* (Bear Family, 1992, prod. Richard Weize) ♫♫♫, which contains all his hits for Morgan, Capitol and Columbia.

influences:
◀◀ Ferlin Husky, Buck Owens
▶▶ Roger Miller, Merle Haggard

Randy Pitts

JESSI COLTER

Born May 25, 1947, in Phoenix, AZ.

Jessi Colter started out as backup singer for twangmaster Duane Eddy in the early 1960s. She moved to Nashville in 1965, established herself as a songwriter and recorded the critically acclaimed *A Country Star Is Born* for RCA in 1966. Country artists who subsequently tapped her songwriting talents included Eddie Arnold, Dottie West, Anita Carter and Don Gibson. In 1969 she married renegade country artist Waylon Jennings, and in 1974 she scored big with the single "I'm Not Lisa"—a tune that shot to the top of the country charts and also became a huge pop crossover hit. In 1976 Jessi recorded the landmark album *Wanted: The Outlaws* with Jennings, Willie Nelson and Tompall Glaser. The album went platinum and earned Colter a Country Music Association Album of the Year Award.

what's available: *The Jessi Colter Collection* (Liberty, 1991, prod. Ken Mansfield, Richie Albright, Waylon Jennings) ✍✍✍ is the only available collection of Colter's unusual brand of piano-centered, pop-influenced country. Fortunately, it does a good job of assembling nearly all her charting singles, including the crossover hits "I'm Not Lisa" and "What's Happened to Blue Eyes," as well as interesting non-singles like her cover of Neil Young's "Hold Back the Tears." No serious country music fan should be without *Wanted: The Outlaws* (RCA, 1976/1996, prod. various) ✍✍✍✍. RCA's 1996 rerelease includes bonus tracks that didn't appear on the original.

worth searching for: *I'm Jessi Colter* (Capitol, 1975, prod. Waylon Jennings) ✍✍✍ contains the hit "I'm Not Lisa" and also highlights Colter's knack for clever songwriting.

influences:

◀◀ Linda Ronstadt, Waylon Jennings

▶▶ Shania Twain, Deana Carter

Rick Petreycik and Brian Mansfield

AMIE COMEAUX

Born December 4, 1976, in West Baton Rouge, LA.

Nashville label executive Harold Shedd first noticed Amie Comeaux when she was 11 and playing the lead in a production of *Annie* (she'd begun singing publicly at age 2.) He kept tabs on her progress, and when she got a little older he signed her to a record deal. Comeaux, who's just barely 5 feet tall, released her first record at 17 and hooked up with JC Penney to promote the album via a mall tour.

what's available: On *Moving Out* (Polydor, 1994, prod. Harold Shedd, David Malloy) ✍✍✍, 17-year-old Comeaux actually *sounds* like a teenager. The best parts of the album (such as the insouciant K.T. Oslin-penned title track) play to that effect. Sure, it's a substantial as puppy love, but it never pretends to be anything else.

influences:

◀◀ Tanya Tucker, Brenda Lee

▶▶ LeAnn Rimes, Mindy McCready

Brian Mansfield

COMMANDER CODY & HIS LOST PLANET AIRMEN

Formed 1967, in Ann Arbor, MI.

Commander Cody (George Frayne), piano, vocals; John Tichy, guitar; West Virginia Creeper, steel guitar (1967–70); Billy C. Farlow, harmonica, vocals (1968–76); Bill Kirchen, guitar (1968–76); Bruce Barlow, bass (1968–76); Lance Dickerson, drums (1968–76); Andy Stein, fiddles, saxophone (1968–76); Bobby Black, steel guitar (1970–76); others.

A band before its time, Commander Cody & His Lost Planet Airmen can be seen as the precursor to the Austin music scene of the 1980s. In fact, the Austin kingpins first moved to San Francisco under the influence of the Cody outfit and worked clubs there as a kind of satellite of the pioneering rockabilly/Western swing revivalists. The band's first four classic albums laid the groundwork for a whole wing of retro-revisionists in country-rock, as far away stylistically as possible from the slick Los Angeles hybrid practiced by the Byrds, Poco and others. Cody's crew specialized in a loose-jointed, rollicking brand of barroom boogie that sounded like it had been steeped in beer fumes in front of rowdy crowds as ready to fight as dance. Despite scoring a Top 10 hit ("Hot Rod Lincoln") off its debut album, Cody's band was never accorded appropriate acclaim, and the original players splintered in disarray in 1976—though the Commander continues to record and tour with an always changing squadron of Airmen.

what to buy: The first three albums have been cannibalized by an inconsistent collection, *Too Much Fun: The Best of Commander Cody & His Lost Planet Airmen* (MCA 1990, prod. various) ✍✍✍.

what to buy next: The fourth album, a jaunty concert recording originally titled *Live from Deep in the Heart of Texas* has been reissued as *Sleazy Roadside Stories* (Relix, 1995, prod.

S. Jarvis) ♫♫♫, hard evidence of the original lineup's swinging brand of country and rock 'n' roll.

what to avoid: Without the balance of the Lost Planet Airmen personalities, Cody's solo albums have suffered from contrivance and the unmitigated dominance of his personality, none more so than *Let's Rock* (Blind Pig, 1987) ♫♫, despite the presence of Airmen Barlow and Kirchen.

the rest:
We Got a Live One Here (Warner Bros., 1976) ♫♫
Lost in Space (Relix, 1995) ♫♫
Best of Commander Cody (Relix, 1995) ♫♫♫

worth searching for: The first two long-deleted albums, *Lost in the Ozone* (Paramount, 1971) ♫♫♫ and *Hot Licks, Cold Steel and Trucker's Favorites* (Paramount, 1972), qualify as certified classics in the field. During that period, the band cut a spectacular Christmas song, "Daddy's Drinking Up All Our Christmas," which has been rescued from obscurity by *Hillbilly Holiday* (Rhino, 1988, prod. various) ♫♫♫♫.

solo outings:
Commander Cody:
Ace's High (Relix 1990) ♫♫♫

Bill Kirchen:
Tombstone Every Mile (Black Top, 1994) ♫♫♫
Have Love, Will Travel (Black Top, 1996) ♫♫♫

influences:
◀◀ Bob Wills, Moon Mullican, Dave Dudley
▶▶ Asleep at the Wheel, Nick Lowe

Joel Selvin

RAY CONDO & HIS RICOCHETS

Formed 1994, in Vancouver, British Columbia, Canada.

Ray Condo, rhythm guitar, saxophone, vocals; Jimmy Roy, steel guitar, second lead guitar; Stephen Nikleva, lead guitar; Clive Jackson, bass fiddle, ukulele; Steve Taylor, drums.

The musical fringe is rich these days with young bands steeped in the past, outfits that specialize in precisely duplicating the classic sounds of vintage rockabilly, Western swing, honkytonk, jump blues and hillbilly boogie. The contingent includes California acts Big Sandy & His Fly-Rite Boys and the Dave & Deke Combo, Austin's High Noon and Chicago's Mighty Blue

Kings. At the top of the list you can safely place the Vancouver neo-traditional quintet Ray Condo & His Ricochets. Led by frontman Condo, this outfit tops all comers in terms of sterling musicianship, historical knowledge, and the power to rocket the past into the future.

what's available: The band's debut disc *Swing Brother Swing!* (Joaquin Records, 1996, prod. Marc L'Esperance, Stephen Nikleva, Jimmy Roy) ♫♫♫♫ features one original in the instrumental "Strathcona." The rest is split between classic swing and hillbilly bop numbers, including Hank Penny's 1952 "Hadicillin Boogie" and Henry "Red" Allen's "There's a House in Harlem for Sale." While all the musicians in this band are excellent, steelman Roy in particular is a standout.

worth searching for: Condo's pre-Ricochets outfit was Ray Condo & His Hardrock Goners. Two releases under that moniker, *Come On* and *Hillbilly Holiday*, are well worth seeking out. Also worth the investment is *5-Star Hop* by Condo's previous outfit, Jimmy Roy's 5-Star Hillbillies.

influences:
◀◀ Big Sandy & His Fly-Rite Boys
▶▶ High Noon, Dave & Deke Combo

Chris Dickinson

CONFEDERATE RAILROAD

Formed as Danny Shirley & the Crossroads Band, c. 1982, in Chattanooga, TN.

Danny Shirley, vocals, guitar; Chris McDaniel, keyboards; Wayne Secrest, bass; Mark DuFresne, drums; Gates Nichols, steel; Michael Lamb, guitar (left 1995); Jimmy Dormire, guitar (1995–present).

Confederate Railroad came out of that part of the South where people don't pay much attention to the distinctions that make Hank Williams Jr. a country singer and Lynyrd Skynyrd a rock band. The band that would evolve into Confederate Railroad formed during the early 1980s around lead singer Danny Shirley, Mark DuFresne and Chris McDaniel. That band often backed David Allen Coe and sometimes Johnny Paycheck. Shirley had a handful of inconsequential hits under his own name during the 1980s; in fact, he was signed to Atlantic as a

Confederate Railroad (© Ken Settle)

solo act and only later decided to release his album under the Confederate Railroad banner.

what to buy: *Confederate Railroad* (Atlantic, 1992, prod. Barry Beckett) 🎵🎵🎵, Confederate Railroad's first album, yielded six singles. The three that hit the Top 10—"Jesus and Mama," "Queen of Memphis," "Trashy Women"—staked out their turf as kinda rowdy, kinda sensitive rednecks.

what to buy next: Musically the group's most ambitious album, *Notorious* (Atlantic, 1994, prod. Barry Beckett) 🎵🎵🎵 had plenty of redneck novelty numbers ("Elvis and Andy," about the group's two favorite Southern icons, and "Move over Madonna"). But the ballads "Summer in Dixie" and "Three Verses" resonate more with Southern soul than any other songs the group has done.

the rest:
When and Where (Atlantic, 1995) 🎵🎵🎵
Greatest Hits (Atlantic, 1996) 🎵🎵🎵🎵

influences:
◀◀ David Allan Coe, Charlie Daniels Band
▶▶ Gibson/Miller Band, Big House

Brian Mansfield

JOHN CONLEE

Born August 11, 1946, in Versailles, KY.

Born and raised on a large Kentucky farm, John Conlee worked as a licensed embalmer in the funeral business for several years before becoming a pop music deejay and then moving to Nashville in 1971. He signed to ABC Records in 1976 and, with his beckoning, down-to-earth vocals, began a string of hits a couple of years later. After topping the charts with "Lady Lay Down," he was named the Academy of Country Music's Best New Artist of the Year in 1979. Conlee joined the Grand Ole Opry in 1981 and caught fire in 1983 with a string of #1 hits, including "Common Man" and "I'm Only in It for the Love" on MCA. He continued to choose quality material and make memorable singles through the 1980s with songs like Guy Clark's "The Carpenter," a 1986 hit that was one of his first singles after moving from MCA to Columbia. Conlee is on the board of directors of Farm Aid and was instrumental in creating the Family Farm Defense Fund.

what to buy: *20 Greatest Hits* (MCA, 1987, prod. Bud Logan) 🎵🎵🎵🎵 presents the backbone of this hardcore country singer's most successful period by chronologically collecting all of his

Top 20 hits except "Baby, You're Something" from his ABC/MCA period of 1978–1985.

what to buy next: *Best of* (Curb/Warner Bros., 1991) 🎵🎵🎵 combines a handful of the later MCA hits with marginally successful newer material originally released on the 16th Avenue label.

what to avoid: *Greatest Hits, Volume 2* (MCA, 1985, prod. Bud Logan) 🎵🎵🎵 became redundant when all but one of its tracks were collected on *20 Greatest Hits*.

the rest:
John Conlee's Greatest Hits (MCA, 1983) 🎵🎵🎵

worth searching for: *Harmony* (Columbia, 1986, prod. Bud Logan) 🎵🎵🎵, Conlee's first post-MCA album, contains the title track and two other Top 10 hits, "Got My Heart Set on You" and "The Carpenter," as well as songs by Jamie O'Hara and Bob McDill. But with the winds of change blowing around country music in 1986, Conlee's friendly and lushly familiar sound was getting dated and after this album, he enjoyed only one more Top 10 excursion.

influences:
◀◀ Merle Haggard, Freddy Fender
▶▶ Joe Diffie, John Anderson

David Sokol

EARL THOMAS CONLEY

Born October 17, 1941, in Portsmouth, OH.

The phrase "identity crisis" must have been coined with Earl Thomas Conley in mind. The Ohio native spent his entire recording career, from about 1975–92, as the faceless, Scotch-soaked baritone behind a slew of slow-burning country standards. While it was easy to hum his hits, it was much harder to name their singer. The topic of Conley's songs—whether he wrote them or not—was always cheating. Of course, cheating leads to drinking and thinking, all subjects of countless country tunes. But there's something in the way Conley sings them; his voice clings to every word like an adulterer embraces the bottle that's helping him forget the night's indiscretions. His deliveries reverberate with the echoes of experience, whether its facing the dilemma at the center of 1983's "Holding Her and Loving You" or expressing bitterness on the sobering "What I'd Say," a #1 hit in 1988. Eventually, it seemed to be a tumultuous lifestyle that ended Conley's mainstream country career. Rumored bouts with alcohol and the dollars-conscious 1990s country landscape—where radio hits should translate to record sales—proved more than Conley could surmount. After 12 years with RCA, he was dropped from the roster; today Conley tours clubs not unlike the Huntsville, Alabama, joints he frequented during the early 1970s, before he was discovered.

what to buy: The most complete compilation available is *The Essential Earl Thomas Conley* (RCA, 1996, prod. various) ✍✍✍✍. 20 cuts, ranging from "Fire & Smoke" to his duet with the late Keith Whitley on "Brotherly Love," trace his knack for transforming difficult—and painful—situations into hearty musical vignettes.

the rest:

Greatest Hits (RCA, 1985) ✍✍✍✍

worth searching for: The best of Conley's RCA albums is *The Heart of It All* (RCA, 1988, prod. Emory Gordy Jr., Randy Scruggs) ✍✍✍✍. From his single masterpiece "What I'd Say" to the surprisingly optimistic "We Believe In Happy Endings," a sweet duet with Emmylou Harris, this effort stands as Conley's most satisfying piece of work. For diehards, *Too Many Times* (RCA, 1986, prod. Earl Thomas Conley, Nelson Larkin, Don Mundo) ✍✍✍ is worth the trouble since the title cut, a cool duet with pop soulster Anita Pointer, is not included on any compilation.

influences:

◀◀ Conway Twitty, George Jones

▶▶ Keith Whitley, Wade Hayes

Mario Tarradell

STOMPIN' TOM CONNORS

Born Charles Thomas Connors, February 9, 1936, in Saint John, New Brunswick, Canada.

Stompin' Tom Connors has written more than 300 songs, his 40 albums have sold more than three million copies, and his autobiography recently soared high up the best-sellers lists. He has been the subject of at least one Masters thesis, been awarded an honorary Doctorate of Laws degree, and received a citation from Queen Elizabeth as well as the prestigious Order of Canada. He even got married live on national television. But chances are you have never heard of, much less heard, Stompin' Tom Connors, for the man has neither performed nor had a single record released outside of Canada during his 30-odd-year career. After winning an unprecedented six consecutive Junos (Canadian Grammys) as Male Country Singer of the Year, Stompin' Tom defiantly returned all of them in 1978 as a protest against "border jumpers"—Canadian artists who no longer live and rarely perform in their home and native land.

Soon afterwards, at the peak of his initial stardom, he enacted a one-year live-performance boycott of himself to further draw attention to Canada's mistreatment of its native artists. Ironically, this fervent, stubborn nationalism didn't help Connors' own career at home, as he inexplicably has yet to place a solitary song on a Canadian country music chart ("They told me in 1964 I didn't fit the format. They told me that in 1974. In 1984, they told me that again," Connors says. "I guess the format hasn't changed that much."). That Stompin' Tom has not only survived but actually thrived under such adverse conditions (by the way, that one-year boycott lasted 10) is a testament not only to the man's abundance of talent but also to his self-described "to-it-and-at-it-iveness."

Between 1968–73 Connors released six albums that are today rightly considered the Holy Grail of Canadian country. Rich in character studies as vivid as those of Hank Williams, but etched as always with Connors' fierce sense of Canadiana, the classic tone poems that fill these records stand today as nothing less than national totems, part of the Canadian cultural lexicon, yet they still perversely receive little if any radio airplay. Finally ending his decade-long exile in 1989 (singing a tribute to his most high-profile prodigy, "Lady k.d. lang"), Connors continues to tour and record proud and unbowed, continues to remain stubbornly loyal to his beliefs and ideals, and still hasn't had an album released outside of Canada. This should not for one second deter you from seeking out any of his two dozen releases newly available on CD from Capitol/EMI Canada, and all produced by—who else?—Stompin' Tom Connors himself.

what to buy: *A Proud Canadian* (Capitol/EMI Canada, 1990, prod. Stompin' Tom Connors) ✍✍✍✍, a 20-song compilation, is the place to start, though with a legacy—and catalog—as vast as Connors', this will only serve to scratch the surface and, hopefully, whet your appetite.

what to buy next: *On Tragedy Trail* (Capitol/EMI Canada, 1968, prod. Stompin' Tom Connors) ✍✍✍, *Bud the Spud* (Capitol/EMI Canada, 1969, prod. Stompin' Tom Connors) ✍✍✍✍✍, *Stompin' Tom Connors Meets Big Joe Mufferaw* (Capitol/EMI Canada, 1970, prod. Stompin' Tom Connors) ✍✍✍✍, *My Stompin' Grounds* (Capitol/EMI Canada, 1971, prod. Stompin' Tom Connors) ✍✍✍✍, *Stompin' Tom and the Hockey Song* (Capitol/EMI Canada, 1972, prod. Stompin' Tom Connors) ✍✍✍✍ and *To It and At It* (Capitol/EMI Canada, 1973, prod. Stompin' Tom Connors) ✍✍✍✍ is an astounding six-LP cycle-in-song that remains an unparalleled achievement in Canadian music, country or otherwise. Connors' "comeback" album, *Fiddle and Song* (Capitol/EMI

Canada, 1989, prod. Stompin' Tom Connors) 🎵🎵🎵🎵 shows an artist refreshed and vibrant, yet still as joyously cantankerous as ever, while this decade's releases—*More of the Stompin' Tom Phenomenon* (Capitol/EMI Canada, 1991, prod. Stompin' Tom Connors) 🎵🎵🎵🎵, *Believe in Your Country* (Capitol/EMI Canada, 1992, prod. Stompin' Tom Connors) 🎵🎵🎵, *Dr. Stompin' Tom—Eh?* (Capitol/EMI Canada, 1993, prod. Stompin' Tom Connors) 🎵🎵🎵🎵 and *Long Gone to the Yukon* (Capitol/EMI Canada, 1995, prod. Stompin' Tom Connors) 🎵🎵🎵🎵—demonstrate conclusively that the phenomenon known as Stompin' Tom thankfully shows no sign of abating any time soon.

the rest:

Northland's Zone (Capitol/EMI Canada, 1967) 🎵🎵🎵

Merry Christmas Everybody (Capitol/EMI Canada, 1970) 🎵🎵⅟

Live At the Horseshoe (Capitol/EMI Canada, 1971) 🎵🎵🎵🎵

Stompin' Tom and the Moon-Man Newfie (Capitol/EMI Canada, 1973) 🎵🎵🎵⅟

Stompin' Tom Meets Muk Tuk Annie (Capitol/EMI Canada, 1974) 🎵🎵🎵

The North Atlantic Squadron and Other Favourites (Capitol/EMI Canada, 1975) 🎵🎵🎵

The Unpopular Stompin' Tom (Capitol/EMI Canada, 1976) 🎵🎵🎵⅟

At the Gumboot Cloggeroo (Capitol/EMI Canada, 1977) 🎵🎵🎵

Once upon a Stompin' Tom (Capitol/EMI Canada, 1991) 🎵🎵🎵🎵⅟

Kick along with Stompin' Tom (Capitol/EMI Canada, 1993) 🎵🎵🎵🎵

influences:

◀◀ Wilf Carter, Hank Snow, Sir John A. MacDonald

▶▶ Steve Earle, k.d. lang, Tylin Whaler

Gary Pig Gold

PATRICIA CONROY

Born January 30 in Montreal, Quebec, Canada.

One of many female Canadian singers—Shania Twain, Terri Clark, k.d. lang, Michelle Wright—to make inroads to the U.S. audience, Conroy released her first Canadian album in 1990. She was named the Canadian Country Music Association's Female Vocalist of the Year in 1994. Her single "Somebody's Leavin'" gained her attention in the U.S.A., most notably from CMT, which led to Intersound picking her up for south-of-the-border distribution.

what's available: Up in Canada, where they don't know any better, it seems like a good idea to cut Lyle Lovett's "You Can't Resist It" and songs by Nashville rocker Tom Kimmel. Surprise! It is, and Conroy's smoldering alto finds the heart of these songs, making *You Can't Resist* (Intersound, 1996, prod. Mike Wanchic,

Justin Niebank) 🎵🎵🎵 a country-pop record that wouldn't shame fans of either genre.

influences:

◀◀ Trisha Yearwood, Michelle Wright

▶▶ Jo Dee Messina

Brian Mansfield

CONTINENTAL DIVIDE

See: David Parmley, Scott Vestal & Continental Divide

RY COODER

Born Ryland Peter Cooder, March 15, 1947, in Los Angeles, CA.

Eschewing trends and sticking stubbornly to the roots, guitarist Ry Cooder was exploring indigenous North American and world music long before it became fashionable. But Cooder's no scholarly purist. From his first recordings with Taj Mahal and Rising Songs during the 1960s, his guitar work—particularly his slide playing—has been as earthy and intuitive as the deepest blues and has led to countless "hired gun" studio gigs with the Rollings Stones, Eric Clapton and Little Feat, among others. On his solo outings, Cooder invariably uncovers and reinterprets lost gems of country and urban blues, R&B, gospel and Tex Mex, often blending textures and mixing styles from a global melting pot of rootsy sources. He is one of the few musicians who could bring Pearl Jam's Eddie Vedder and Pakistani singer Nusrat Fateh Ali Khan together—as he did for the *Dead Man Walking* soundtrack—and make the synthesis work. Cooder also has composed numerous film scores, and in 1992 he joined longtime cohorts Jim Keltner, John Hiatt and Nick Lowe in the band Little Village. He remains one of America's truest musical treasures.

what to buy: Of his many fine solo records, *Paradise & Lunch* (Reprise, 1974, prod. Lenny Waronker, Russ Titelman) 🎵🎵🎵🎵⅟ is Cooder's warmest and most enduring, a peerless collection of remakes ("Fool for a Cigarette," "It's All Over Now," "If Walls Could Talk") performed by an extraordinary group of musicians from widely divergent backgrounds—a Cooder trademark. With its rougher-edged mix of vintage blues, barroom laments, Tex-Mex accordion and Hawaiian slack-key guitar, *Chicken Skin Music* (Reprise, 1976, prod. Ry Cooder) 🎵🎵🎵🎵 is also highly recommended.

what to buy next: *Music by Ry Cooder* (Warner Archives, 1995, prod. various) 🎵🎵🎵🎵 is a superb two-CD sampler of Cooder's atmospheric film-score work from such movies as *Paris, Texas,*

The Long Riders and *Southern Comfort*. Some of Cooder's greasiest guitar playing can be heard on *Live & Let Live* (Rounder, 1993, prod. Ry Cooder) ♫♫♫, a record he produced for bluesmen Bobby King & Terry Evans.

what to avoid: Compared to his usual high standards, *The Slide Area* (Reprise, 1982, prod. Ry Cooder) ♫♫ falls flat.

the rest:
Ry Cooder (Reprise, 1970) ♫♫♫
Into the Purple Valley (Reprise, 1972) ♫♫♫♫
Boomer's Story (Reprise, 1972) ♫♫♫♫
Jazz (Reprise, 1978) ♫♫♫
Bop till You Drop (Reprise, 1978) ♫♫♫♫
Borderline (Reprise, 1980) ♫♫♫
Alamo Bay: Music from the Motion Picture (Slash, 1985) ♫♫♫♫
Paris, Texas: Original Motion Picture Soundtrack (Warner Bros., 1985) ♫♫♫♫
Blue City: Motion Picture Soundtrack (Warner Bros., 1986) ♫♫♫
Crossroads: Original Motion Picture Soundtrack (Warner Bros., 1986) ♫♫♫
Get Rhythm (Reprise, 1987) ♫♫♫
(With Robin Williams) *Pecos Bill* (Windham Hill, 1988) ♫♫♫♫
Johnny Handsome: Original Motion Picture Soundtrack (Warner Bros., 1989) ♫♫♫
Trespass: Original Motion Picture Soundtrack (Sire, 1992) ♫♫♫
Geronimo: An American Legend (Columbia, 1993) ♫♫♫♫
(With Vishwa Mohan Bhatt) *A Meeting by the River* (Water Lily Acoustics, 1993) ♫♫♫♫
(With Ali Farka Toure) *Talking Timbuktu* (Hannibal, 1994) ♫♫♫♫
(With Little Village) *Little Village* (Reprise, 1992) ♫♫♫

influences:
◀◀ Blind Willie Johnson, Golden Gate Quartet, Gabby Pahinui, Sleepy John Estes, Joseph Spence, Little Walter

▶▶ John Hiatt, Los Lobos, Daniel Lanois, Robbie Robertson

Doug Pippin

SPADE COOLEY

Born Donnell Clyde Cooley, February 22, 1910, in Grand, OK. Died November 23, 1969, in Oakland, CA.

His tragic "extra-curricular" activities (convicted in 1961 for the first-degree murder of his second wife, largely on the testimony of his 14-year-old daughter who'd witnessed, at Cooley's insistence, her mother's fatal beating) often overshadow the King of Western Swing's abundant musical achievements. However, with a character so much larger-than-life as Cooley, the fire-

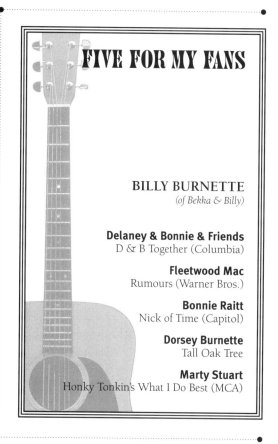

FIVE FOR MY FANS

BILLY BURNETTE
(of Bekka & Billy)

Delaney & Bonnie & Friends
D & B Together (Columbia)

Fleetwood Mac
Rumours (Warner Bros.)

Bonnie Raitt
Nick of Time (Capitol)

Dorsey Burnette
Tall Oak Tree

Marty Stuart
Honky Tonkin's What I Do Best (MCA)

works can sometimes get in the way. Of Scottish-Irish and Cherokee descent, both Cooley's father and grandfather were violinists of renown, and young Donnell's first musical instrument, not surprisingly, was the cello. As so many did during the Depression, the Cooleys headed west in 1931, and Hollywood beckoned Cooley like the proverbial moth to the flame: soon he was hired by Republic Pictures as a stand-in for the latest Singing Cowboy sensation, Roy Rogers. So impressed was Rogers by Cooley's fiddling ability that he quickly hired the would-be thespian to tour with his band between pictures. Later, Cooley joined Cal Shrum's combo and made his first-ever trip to the recording studio with them in 1941. It was really only a matter of time, though, before Cooley formed his own band—a monstrous (up to 22 members at times) aggregation that brought its own unique blend of country, jazz and pure wartime dance music to the booming southern California ballroom circuit, drawing crowds of 5,000 a night at its regular Santa Monica residency. Cooley's first session for Columbia Records in December 1944 produced his biggest-ever hit, "Shame on You," and he also found time to appear in several motion pictures and host his own highly rated local television series well into the 1950s. A long-time investor in California real estate, Cooley's plan to develop a mammoth recreational park called Water Wonderland in the middle of the Mojave Desert (go figure) was derailed when he discovered his wife bragging of an affair with old pal Roy Rogers. Rogers survived this incident relatively unscathed, but on August 22, 1961, Cooley was sentenced to life imprisonment for the murder of Ella Mae Cooley. Due to be paroled for good behavior from Vacaville Prison in 1970, he died of a massive heart attack several weeks prior to his scheduled release following a benefit performance for the Alameda Deputy Sheriff's Association.

what's available: Although he later recorded for RCA and Decca, Cooley's legend rests with his Okeh and Columbia recordings from the mid-1940s, the best of which are lovingly restored, annotated and compiled on *Spadella!: The Essential Spade Cooley* (Columbia, 1994, prod. various) *♪♪♪*. Although the biggest hits, crooned for the most part by vocalist Tex Williams, are somewhat lackluster, the instrumentals jump and cook as few others of their ilk did, or could, in their day.

influences:
◀◀ Cass County Boys
▶▶ Tex Williams, Dan Hicks & His Hot Licks

Gary Pig Gold

RITA COOLIDGE

Born May 1, 1944, in Nashville, TN.

During the late 1960s, Rita Coolidge was one of the most sought-after backup vocalists in rock. Her silky, smooth tenor graced the recordings of Joe Cocker, Eric Clapton and Delaney & Bonnie. In 1970 she signed with A&M Records, and in 1971 the label released *Rita Coolidge,* which highlighted the singer's bluesy, impassioned vocal style, augmented by an all-star backup band that included Clarence White, Leon Russell, Stephen Stills, Jim Keltner and Jerry McGee. She married singer-songwriter Kris Kristofferson in 1974 and began to focus more on an acting career than her music. Subsequent releases failed to live up to the promising future hinted at in her sparkling debut.

what to buy: *Greatest Hits* (A&M, 1980, prod. David Anderle) *♪♪♪* is a solid collection of Coolidge's pop hits, including the gold-selling "(Your Love Keeps Lifting Me) Higher and Higher" and "We're All Alone."

what to buy next: Not much else worth having is available, except perhaps for Coolidge's album with then-husband Kris Kristofferson, *Breakaway* (Monument, 1974/1991) *♪♪♪* and the recent *Out of the Blues* (Beacon, 1996, prod. David Anderle) *♪♪♪*, a blues album that relies heavily on standards such as "Am I Blue," "Bring It on Home to Me" and "The Man I Love," as well as a handful of Kristofferson songs.

the rest:
Love Lessons (Critique, 1992) *♪♪*

worth searching for: *Rita Coolidge* (A&M, 1971, prod. Booker T. Jones) *♪♪♪*, like the singers' other A&M recordings, is out of print. But this one is worth checking out, especially for her steamy rendition of "Born Under a Bad Sign."

influences:
◀◀ Delaney & Bonnie
▶▶ Kim Carnes, Shania Twain

Rick Petreycik

ROGER COOPER

Born in KY.

Roger Cooper is a Kentucky fiddler in the tradition of such regional legends as Buddy Thomas, Morris Allen and Jimmy Wheeler. He has won numerous fiddling contests in Kentucky, Ohio, Pennsylvania and Tennessee, and he is also an accomplished guitarist and banjo player.

what's available: *Going Back to Old Kentucky* (Rounder, 1996, prod. John Harrod, Mark Wilson) *♪♪♪* is a fine collection of 25 fiddle tunes, many of them traditional, in the old-time Lewis County fiddling style. Cooper is accompanied by guitarist Mike Hall.

influences:
◀◀ Bob Prater, Buddy Thomas

Brian Mansfield

WILMA LEE & STONEY COOPER

Formed c. 1940s, in WV.

Wilma Lee Cooper (born Wilma Lee Leary, February 7, 1921, in Valley Head, WV), vocals, guitar, banjo, piano; Dale T. "Stoney" Cooper (born October 16, 1918, in Harmon, WV; died March 22, 1977), vocals, fiddle.

This West Virginia husband-and-wife duo and their band, the Clinch Mountain Clan, helped keep alive the raw, acoustic hard-country sound popular in the Southeast during the 1930s for many years past its heyday, through their recordings and appearances at the Grand Ole Opry. From 1949–55, they cut many classic sides for Columbia. Subsequently, they recorded for Hickory with some success, and for Decca, Starday and others, with less success. After her husband's death, Wilma Lee continued to perform and record alone, never straying from the hard-core country stylings that first brought she and Stoney to prominence.

what's available: The gospel set *Walking My Lord up Calvary Hill* (Hollywood, c. 1974) ✶✶✶, the only Wilma Lee & Stoney readily available on CD, is a fair indicator of what they sounded like. Their style never changed much, but this isn't their best material.

worth searching for: *Wilma Lee and Stoney Cooper and the Clinch Mountain Clan—Early Recordings* (County, 1979) ✶✶✶✶, a reissue of Columbia recordings from 1949–53, is their prime stuff, including the classics "Thirty Pieces of Silver," "Sunny Side of the Mountain," "You Tried to Ruin My Name" and nine more.

solo outings:

Wilma Lee Cooper:
Classic Country Favorites (Rebel, 1996) ✶✶✶✶
Wilma Lee Cooper (Rounder, 1982) ✶✶✶

influences:
⏪ Molly O'Day, Roy Acuff
⏩ Carl & Pearl Butler, Delia Bell

Randy Pitts

COWBOY COPAS

Born Lloyd Estel Copas, July 15, 1913, in Muskogee, OK. Died March 5, 1963, near Camden, TN.

Tied forever to the Patsy Cline crash, Cowboy Copas was a Grand Ole Opry star whose biggest records were behind him when the plane that his son-in-law was piloting went down, with Copas in it, in 1963. He'd grown up a fiddler and a guitarist, backing a famed Native American fiddler named Natchee in many competitions. He came into his own during the post-World War II honky-tonk boom; his first two singles, "Filipino Baby" (1946) and "Signed, Sealed and Delivered" (1948) were both Top Five hits, but they each were also hits for three other artists during the years Copas released them. He recorded one of the early versions of "Tennessee Waltz" in 1948, but his career fell off during the 1950s. He revived it briefly with "Alabam" in 1960, which featured his flat-top picking and spent 12 weeks at #1.

what to buy: *24 Greatest Hits* (Deluxe) ✶✶✶ is hands-down the place to start, since it's the only album that collects most of Copas' hits in one place. Of course, Copas had only 14 Top 40 singles, so *24 Greatest Hits* is more than most people will need.

what to buy next: *Tragic Tales of Love & Life* (King, 1960) ✶✶ is the best CD reissue of an original Copas album, with a version of Grandpa Jones' "Tragic Romance" and some other good songs that never were hits. *Filipino Baby* (Country Road, 1976) ✶✶ is the most hit-packed of a number of budget cassette collections, with the title track, "Flat Top" and "Sunny Tennessee." It also contains a screamingly funny live track called "Thinkin' Tonight," which spoofs one of the most frequently plagiarized melodies in country music history.

what to avoid: *Opry Star Spotlight on Cowboy Copas* (Starday, 1962) ✶ and *Mister Country Music* (Starday, 1962) ✶ are mildly interesting because they're CD reissues of original albums, but they come from late in Copas' career and lack anything in the way of hits.

the rest:
Satisfied Mind (Country Road, 1976) ✶✶
Alabam (Richmond, 1985) ✶✶
Alabam (King EP, 1994) ✶✶

influences:
⏪ Pee Wee King, Ernest Tubb
⏩ T. Texas Tyler

Brian Mansfield

JEFF COPLEY

Born in WV.

Jeff Copley grew up in the coal-mining Appalachian hills of West Virginia before coming to Nashville. He was signed to Polydor by Harold Shedd, the same man who had signed Billy Ray Cyrus to sister label Mercury.

what's available: *Evergreen* (Polydor, 1995, prod. Donnie Canada, Russ Zavitson) ✶✶ contains pedestrian, rock-influenced country that usually reflects the singer's rural background. It's one of the few places besides Billy Ray Cyrus albums where you can find a song by Don Von Tress, the writer of "Achy Breaky Heart."

influences:
⏪ Keith Whitley, Billy Ray Cyrus

Brian Mansfield

Elvis Costello (© Ken Settle)

LARRY CORDLE

See: Lonesome Standard Time

ELVIS COSTELLO

Born DeClan McManus August 25, 1954, in Liverpool, England.

Hardly a country artist, Elvis Costello instead emerged as the chief songwriting voice of the New Wave movement. He quickly outgrew that tag, though, and has evolved into something of a songwriting icon in the pop field, though his U.S. success (only 1983's "Every Day I Write the Book," a minor number by most Costello fans' standards, reached the Top 40) has not matched his reputation. He's long had an affinity with Nashville, recording there and also duetting with George Jones on Jones' 1979 *My Very Special Guests* album.

what to buy: *King of America* (Rykodisc, 1986/1995, prod. De-Clan McManus, T-Bone Burnett) ♫♫♫♫ was a brilliant move—backing Elvis Costello with the Costello Show: drummer Ron Tutt, bassist Jerry Scheff and guitarist James Burton, the heart of the *other* Elvis' famed T.C.B. band. Costello got to the roots

of his love affair with American music, and made what is arguably his best album.

what to buy next: *Almost Blue* (Rykodisc, 1981/1994, prod. Billy Sherrill) ♫♫♫, recorded in Nashville with super-producer Billy Sherrill, is far from Costello's best album. But with covers ranging from George Jones to Gram Parsons, it does show his deep love of country music. If you're a country fan coming to Costello's music through the back door, *Very Best of Elvis Costello & the Attractions (1977–86)* (Rykodisc) ♫♫♫♫ is a fine introduction to his music.

what to avoid: *The Juliet Letters* (Warner Bros., 1993, prod. Kevin Killen, Elvis Costello, Brodsky Quartet) ♫♫ features Costello with the Brodsky Quartet performing a song cycle based on the story of a professor who answered letters addressed to Juliet Capulet. Some would say ambitious, some would say tuneless.

the rest:

My Aim Is True (Rykodisc, 1977/1993) ♫♫♫♫
This Year's Model (Rykodisc, 1978/1993) ♫♫♫♫
Armed Forces (Rykodisc, 1979/1993) ♫♫♫♫
Get Happy!! (Rykodisc, 1980/1994) ♫♫♫
Trust (Rykodisc, 1981/1994) ♫♫
Imperial Bedroom (Rykodisc, 1982/1995) ♫♫♫♫
Punch the Clock (Rykodisc, 1983/1995) ♫♫♫♫
Goodbye Cruel World (Rykodisc, 1984/1995) ♫♫
Blood & Chocolate (Rykodisc, 1986/1995) ♫♫♫
Out of Our Idiot (Demon, 1987) ♫♫♫♫
Spike (Warner Bros., 1989) ♫♫♫
Girls, Girls, Girls (Columbia, 1990) ♫♫♫
Mighty Like a Rose (Warner Bros., 1991) ♫♫♫
2 1/2 Years (Rykodisc, 1993) ♫♫♫♫
Brutal Youth (Warner Bros., 1994) ♫♫♫
Kojak Variety (Warner Bros., 1995) ♫♫♫
All This Useless Beauty (Warner Bros., 1996) ♫♫♫♫

worth searching for: *Mighty Like a Rose* (Warner Bros., 1991, prod. Mitchell Froom, Kevin Killen, D.P.A. MacManus) ♫♫♫, a specially packaged, limited edition version of the album, contains no additional music.

influences:
◀◀ Bob Dylan, Randy Newman, Gram Parsons
▶▶ T-Bone Burnett, Richard Thompson, Rockpile

Brian Mansfield

THE COUNTRY GENTLEMEN

Formed 1957, in Washington, DC-area.

Charlie Waller, guitar; John Duffey, mandolin, dobro (1957–69); Bill Emerson, banjo (1957–58, 1969–72); Larry Leahy, bass (1957); Tom Morgan, bass (1957); Jimmy Gaudreau, mandolin (1969–72, 1981); Doyle Lawson, mandolin (1972–79); Rick Allred, mandolin (1979–81); Pete Kuykendall, banjo, guitar, bass, fiddle (1958–59); Tom Morgan, bass (1957–59); Jim Cox, bass (1959–60;) Tom Gray, bass (1960–64); Ed Ferris, bass (1964–69); Bill Yates (1969–80); many more, including Ricky Skaggs, Jerry Douglas, Mike Lilly, Walt Hensley, Kevin Church, Jimmy Bowen, Keith Little, Norman Wright.

The first really influential urban bluegrass band, the early Country Gentlemen featured John Duffey's tart tenor voice and amazing range (his father was an opera singer), guitarist Charlie Waller's pleasantly light baritone lead vocals, Eddie Adcock's banjo virtuosity, fine three- and four-part harmonies, innovative choices of material, imaginative arrangements and humorous, friendly stage banter. They made bluegrass more immediate and more accessible to a large, young, urban audience, and their presence is felt today. Waller, the only remaining original member, leads the band into its fourth decade in 1997.

what to buy: *Country Songs Old and New* (Smithsonian/Folkways, 1960, prod. Mike Seeger) 🎵🎵🎵🎵 provides a full dose of tough, progressive bluegrass by this highly influential group early in their careers. *Folk Songs and Bluegrass* (Smithsonian/Folkways, 1961, prod. Pete Kuykendall, John Duffey) 🎵🎵🎵🎵 was the first album for Folkways by what came to be known as the "Classic Country Gentlemen," as bassist Tom Gray joins Duffey, Waller, and Adcock; it features extremely tight harmonies and innovative vocal arrangements of traditional songs. *25 Years* (Rebel, 1982, prod. Dave Freeman) 🎵🎵🎵 is a good overview of the band in various groupings and includes many favorites and a fair number of obscurities.

what to buy next: *Calling My Children Home* (Rebel, 1977, prod. Charles Freeland) 🎵🎵🎵 is wonderful gospel from a group that included Doyle Lawson and features several a cappella gospel quartets.

the rest:
Nashville Jail: Classic Country Gentlemen (Copper Creek, 1964/1990) 🎵🎵🎵
The Award-Winning Country Gentlemen (Rebel, 1971) 🎵🎵🎵
Live in Japan (Rebel, 1972) 🎵🎵🎵
Featuring Ricky Skaggs on Fiddle (Vanguard, 1987) 🎵🎵🎵
Return Engagement (Rebel, 1988) 🎵🎵🎵

Duffey, Waller, Adcock & Gray—*Classic Country Gents Reunion* (Sugar Hill, 1989) 🎵🎵🎵🎵
New Horizons (Rebel, 1992) 🎵🎵
Souvenirs (Rebel, 1995) 🎵🎵🎵
Sugar Hill Collection (1995) 🎵🎵🎵

worth searching for: *Folk Session Inside* (Mercury, 1963, prod. Pete Kuykendall) 🎵🎵🎵🎵, an outstanding and very popular album in its time, features the "Classic" configuration of the band. Great versions of "This Morning at Nine," "I Am Weary, Let Me Rest," and "Can't You Hear Me Calling." A big favorite of urban folkniks. *Bluegrass at Carnegie Hall* (Hollywood, 1962) 🎵🎵🎵🎵 is a great album by the early group recorded for Starday. (It's not a live album.)

solo outings:
Eddie Adcock:
Dixie Fried (CMH, 1991) 🎵🎵🎵
Eddie Adcock & His Guitar (CMH) 🎵🎵🎵
(With Talk of the Town) *The Acoustic Collection* (CMH) 🎵🎵🎵🎵
(With the Eddie Adcock Band) *Talk to Your Heart* (CMH, 1994) 🎵🎵🎵

influences:
◄◄ Stanley Brothers, Bill Monroe
►► Seldom Scene, Laurel Canyon Ramblers

Randy Pitts

COWBOY COPAS

See: Copas, Cowboy

COWBOY JUNKIES

Formed 1979, in Toronto, Ontario, Canada.

Margo Timmins, vocals; Michael Timmins, guitar; Peter Timmins, drums; Alan Anton, bass.

Folk singer Luka Bloom once said he'd never opened for so many people making so little noise on stage. The Cowboy Junkies are usually stamped with such labels as Valium-enhanced and narcoleptic, which is true on their most boring songs. They're slow, of course, but when they're good, you barely notice the tempo. The band merges songwriting styles culled from country (most notably Townes Van Zandt and Hank Williams), blues and punk (their cover of the Velvet Underground's "Sweet Jane" is what first got the group on college radio) and at best the results are charming and hypnotic. At worst, when the Junkies start to rely on their sound and let their considerable songwriting qualities play a lesser role, you

really can't get through an album or concert without developing a yawn addiction.

what to buy: *The Trinity Session* (RCA, 1988, prod. Peter
Moore) 𝄞𝄞𝄞 is the perfect starting place, mostly because its
cover songs ("Sweet Jane," Patsy Cline's "Walking after Midnight" and Hank Williams' "I'm So Lonesome I Could Cry") ease
you gradually into the Junkies' slow-motion world. *Black Eyed
Man* (RCA, 1992, prod. Michael Timmins) 𝄞𝄞𝄞𝄞, their best and
most underrated album, succeeds because of its reverence for
true country music; John Prine makes a terrific duet appearance on the romantic ballad "If You Were the Woman and I Was
the Man," and Van Zandt's influence is obvious in both the
style and name of "Townes' Blues."

what to buy next: *Whites Off Earth Now* (RCA, 1990, recorded
by Peter Moore) 𝄞𝄞𝄞 is full of slow and tortured versions of familiar songs, including Bruce Springsteen's "State Trooper"
and Robert Johnson's "Crossroads" and "Me and the Devil."
The Junkies, perhaps overly aware of their reputation for
leisure, accelerated to rock speed on *Lay It Down* (Geffen,
1996, prod. Michael Timmins, John Keane) 𝄞𝄞𝄞.

what to avoid: *The Caution Horses* (RCA, 1990, prod. Peter
Moore, Michael Timmins) 𝄞𝄞 was supposed to be the band's triumphant leap from college cult heroes to mainstream country-
rock hitmakers, but it was so blandly written and overproduced
it sent the Junkies reeling commercially for most of the 1990s.

the rest:
Pale Sun, Crescent Moon (RCA, 1993) 𝄞𝄞𝄞
200 More Miles: Live Performances 1985–1994 (RCA, 1995) 𝄞𝄞

worth searching for: A haunting treatment of another sacred
country-rock cow, the Rolling Stones' "Dead Flowers," turns up
on the 12-inch promotional single for "'Cause Cheap Is How I
Feel" (RCA, 1990).

influences:
◀◀ John Prine, Townes Van Zandt, Bruce Springsteen, Lou
Reed, Patsy Cline, Hank Williams
▶▶ Mazzy Star, Lisa Germano

Steve Knopper

THE COX FAMILY

Formed 1976, in Cotton Valley, LA.

Willard Cox, fiddle, vocals; Evelyn Cox, guitar, vocals; Suzanne Cox,
mandolin, vocals; Evelyn Cox Hobbs, guitar, vocals; Sidney Cox, guitar, dobro, banjo; Lynn Cox Thurman, bass, vocals.

Cotton Valley is an oil town about 40 miles north of Shreveport—not exactly a hotbed of bluegrass music. But for Willard
Cox and the rest of his musical family, it was as good a place as
any to carry the torch while adding a few touches of their own,
such as Western swing. Though they've worked the festival circuit for years, the Coxes manage to make their shimmering harmonies and traditional sound fresh, attracting the attention of
Alison Krauss, who has recorded some of Sidney's songs. She,
in turn, has produced some of their albums.

what to buy: *Just When You're Thinking It's Over* (Asylum, 1996,
prod. Alison Krauss) 𝄞𝄞𝄞 is a rarity that manages to update traditional bluegrass in a way that should not disturb purists.
Grammy-winning buddy Krauss steers them on a course that
keeps one foot rooted firmly in the past, the other charging into
the future.

the rest:
Everybody's Reaching Out for Someone (Rounder, 1993) 𝄞𝄞𝄞
(With Alison Krauss) *I Know Who Holds Tomorrow* (Rounder, 1994)
𝄞𝄞𝄞𝄞
(With Krauss) *Beyond the City* (Rounder, 1995) 𝄞𝄞𝄞

influences:
◀◀ Chuck Wagon Gang, Mac Wiseman, Bill Monroe
▶▶ Alison Krauss

Doug Pullen

BILLY "CRASH" CRADDOCK

Born June 16, 1939, in Greensboro, NC.

Billy "Crash" Craddock's penchant for pop songs earned him
the nickname "Mr. Country Rock" (four of his first five hits were
covers of pop smashes—the other was "Ain't Nothin' Shakin'
(But the Leaves on the Trees)." He fronted a rock band called
the Four Rebels with his brother Ronald and originally recorded
for Colonial in 1957. Columbia tried to turn him into a teen idol
version of Elvis Presley during the 1950s, but it didn't take. He
had 34 Top 40 hits during the years 1971–82, however, for Cartwheel, ABC/Dot and Capitol. (And he still reminded folks of
Presley.) Craddock later cut records for MCA and Atlantic, but
had no hits with those labels. He is currently semi-retired from
recording.

Margo Timmins of the Cowboy Junkies (© Ken Settle)

what's available: Unlike most other country singers with pop inclinations, Craddock usually didn't make watered-down pop records. Instead, his hits—especially early ones for Cartwheel like "Knock Three Times" and "Dream Lover"—loaded on the fiddle and pedal steel. *Crash's Smashes: Billy "Crash" Craddock's Greatest Hits* (Razor & Tie, 1996) 🎵🎵🎵 contains all 19 of his Top 10 hits, so you couldn't get a much more comprehensive compilation without a serious quality drop. Craddock's best stuff has much more energy and much better arrangements than most other country-pop of the time, even if he doesn't sound much like what passes for "country rock" these days.

influences:

◀◀ Elvis Presley, Tom Jones

▶▶ Narvel Felts

Brian Mansfield

FLOYD CRAMER

Born October 27, 1933, in Samti, LA.

Pianist Floyd Cramer's technique introduced one of the most influential musical sounds in Nashville history: When he'd hit a note, he'd purposely hit an adjacent key then slip off it. It's such a distinctive sound that Cramer's playing is as easily recognizable as the singer's voice on many of the records on which he played after he starting coming to Nashville in 1952. The "slip note" style can be found on nearly ever RCA-Nashville record made during the 1960s and 1970s—Don Gibson's "Oh, Lonesome Me," Hank Locklin's "Please Help Me I'm Falling," Jim Reeves' "Four Walls" and Elvis Presley's "Heartbreak Hotel," to name just a few. The former Louisiana Hayride member has also made dozens of solo records, many of which remain in print, and almost all of which sound essentially alike except for the songs.

what to buy: Cramer is better known for the records he played on than for the ones he made. *The Essential Series: Floyd Cramer* (RCA, 1995, prod. Chet Atkins, comp. prod. Paul Williams) 🎵🎵🎵 contains his two most significant chart hits: 1960's "Last Date" (#11 country, #2 pop) and his 1961 rendition of "San Antonio Rose" (#8 country, #8 pop), as well as 18 more tunes cut for RCA between 1958 and 1966.

what to buy next: *The Best of Floyd Cramer* (Pair, 1988) 🎵🎵🎵 has a lot of overlap with *Essential*, but it's the best of a number of Pair reissues of Cramer's RCA recordings.

the rest:

Country Classics (Pair, 1986) 🎵🎵

Special Songs of Love (Step One, 1988) 🎵🎵
Country Gold (Step One, 1988) 🎵🎵
Just Me and My Piano! (Step One, 1988) 🎵🎵
Collector's Series (RCA, 1988) 🎵🎵
Forever (Step One, 1989) 🎵🎵
Originals (Step One, 1990) 🎵🎵
Gospel Classics (Step One, 1990) 🎵🎵
Piano Masterpieces 1900–1975 (RCA, 1990) 🎵🎵🎵
Easy Listening Favorites (Pair, 1991) 🎵🎵
Favorite Country Hits (Ranwood, 1995) 🎵🎵
The Piano Magic of Floyd Cramer Volume 2 (Ranwood, 1996) 🎵🎵
Super Hits: Floyd Cramer (RCA, 1996) 🎵🎵🎵
We Wish You a Merry Christmas (Step One) 🎵🎵
The Magic Touch of Floyd Cramer (Pair) 🎵🎵
The Piano Magic of Floyd Cramer (Ranwood) 🎵🎵

influences:

◀◀ Jerry Lee Lewis, Moon Mullican, Chet Atkins

▶▶ Boots Randolph, Hargus "Pig" Robbins

Brian Mansfield and Craig Shelburne

ROB CROSBY

Born Robert Crosby Hoar, April 25, 1954, in Sumter, SC.

Rob Crosby grew up in South Carolina playing folk and acoustic country-rock, the influences of which remain in his records. One of the first artists signed to Arista Nashville, a handful of his singles for that label reached the Top 40, but the most successful was his first, 1990's "Love Will Bring Her Around." Crosby co-wrote Lee Greenwood's last Top Five hit, "Holdin' a Good Hand."

what's available: Crosby's earnest, slightly sandy voice is one of the most appealing qualities of his albums, which have been consistent without being spectacular. All four of his Top 40 hits come from his debut, *Solid Ground* (Arista, 1991, prod. Scott Hendricks) 🎵🎵🎵; he wasn't as successful with his follow-up, *Another Time and Place* (Arista, 1992, prod. Scott Hendricks) 🎵🎵🎵, and his contract with Arista ended. *Starting Now* (River North, 1995, prod. Jerry Crutchfield) 🎵🎵🎵 found him with a new label and new producer, but not much difference in sound or style.

influences:

◀◀ Restless Heart, Garth Brooks

▶▶ Steve Azar

Brian Mansfield

CROWE & McLAUGHLIN

Formed 1992 in Cherokee, NC.

Josh Crowe (born in GA), vocals, guitar; David McLaughlin (born February 13, 1958, in VA), vocals, mandolin, guitar.

Josh Crowe left Raymond Fairchild to strike out on his own in 1992. He invited David McLaughlin, the mandolin player for the Johnson Mountain Boys, to appear with him in a two-guitar and voices arrangement at a North Carolina bluegrass festival. They sounded like they had been singing together for years and decided to turn the one-time appearance into a regular arrangement.

what's available: On *Going Back* (Rounder, 1993, prod. Nancy McLaughlin) ♫♫♫, close harmonies and intricate acoustic guitar interplay on 14 songs including the Louvin Brothers' "Are You Wasting My Time," the Everly Brothers' "All I Have to Do Is Dream" and McLaughlin's fine original "Going Back to Old Virginia."

influences:

◀◀ Everly Brothers, Louvin Brothers, Delmore Brothers

▶▶ Gibson Brothers, Whitstein Brothers

Douglas Fulmer

J.D. CROWE
/J.D. CROWE &
THE NEW SOUTH

Born August 27, 1937, in GA.

J.D. Crowe, banjo, vocals; Tony Rice, guitar, vocals; Ricky Skaggs, fiddle, mandolin; Keith Whitley, guitar, lead vocals; Doyle Lawson, mandolin, vocals; Jerry Douglas, dobro; Phil Leadbetter, dobro; Curt Chapman, bass; Greg Luck, guitar, lead vocals; Darrell Webb, mandolin, lead vocals; others.

Incorporating songs from country and rock sources and employing sideman the like of Ricky Skaggs, Tony Rice, Keith Whitley, Doyle Lawson and Jerry Douglas, J.D. Crowe & the New South became major trend-setters in contemporary bluegrass. Their self-titled 1975 album is rightly considered an all-time classic. Crowe himself came from a traditional background, appearing with Mac Wiseman and Jimmy Martin during the 1950s. Crowe all but retired from the music business during the late 1980s but returned to touring with a new version of the New South in 1994 (earning the International Bluegrass Music Association's "Banjo Player of the Year" award despite not releasing

an album) and released *Flashback* the following year. Crowe has also played with the Bluegrass Album Band.

what to buy: The classic *J.D. Crowe & the New South* (Rounder, 1975) ♫♫♫♫ features one of the best line-ups of musicians ever assembled on a bluegrass album: Ricky Skaggs on mandolin and fiddle; Tony Rice on lead vocals and guitar; and Jerry Douglas on dobro. Some fabulous instrumental work, and Rice's lead vocals never sounded better.

what to buy next: *Flashback* (Rounder, 1995, prod. J.D. Crowe) ♫♫♫♫, Crowe's comeback album, is a backwards glance at his developmental years with Jimmy Martin and the Osborne Brothers and during the early days of the New South.

the rest:

Blackjack (Rebel, 1978) ♫♫♫♫
Model Church (Rebel, 1978) ♫♫♫♫
Straight Ahead (Rounder, 1986) ♫♫♫

influences:

◀◀ Country Gentlemen, Jimmy Martin

▶▶ Ricky Skaggs, Boone Creek, Tony Rice, Jerry Douglas

Douglas Fulmer

RODNEY CROWELL

Born August 7, 1950, in Houston, TX.

Rodney Crowell, one of Nashville's most respected singers and songwriters, began his musical career at age 11, drumming in his father's Western band. When he moved to Nashville, he fell in with better musicians, playing guitar in Emmylou Harris's famed Hot Band (1975–77). Harris cut nine of his songs, and soon Crowell found his songs being performed by Crystal Gayle, the Oak Ridge Boys, the Dirt Band, Highway 101, even Bob Seger and Foghat. Crowell later took the Hot Band, and turned it into his own Cherry Bombs: Its members included Vince Gill, future MCA-record exec Tony Brown, and future producers Emory Gordy Jr. and Richard Bennett. Crowell signed with Warner Bros. in 1978 but didn't have significant success until he reunited with Brown to make *Diamonds and Dirt* in 1988. He produced many of Rosanne Cash's hits; the two were married from 1979 to 1992. He has also produced records by Brady Seals, Jim Lauderdale, Guy Clark, Lari White and Johnny Cash.

what to buy: When Crowell started having hits with his songs instead of just writing them for other artists to cover, he did so with a vengeance. *Diamonds and Dirt* (Columbia, 1988, prod. Tony Brown, Rodney Crowell) ♫♫♫♫ was the first country album to produce five #1 singles, and Crowell was the only

Billy Ray Cyrus (© Ken Settle)

artist to write, produce and sing four consecutive chart-toppers. *Diamonds and Dirt* is a thoroughly amazing album that updates the Bakersfield sound and Western swing into a contemporary context, and Crowell's writing is so dead-on he makes Harlan Howard's "Above and Beyond" (previously a hit for Buck Owens) seem like a weak spot. The song "After All This Time" won Crowell a Grammy, and songs like "I Couldn't Leave You If I Tried," "She's Crazy for Leaving" and "It's Such a Small World" (a duet with then-wife Rosanne Cash) make this an essential 1980s country album.

what to buy next: The collaboration of Crowell and his former Cherry Bombs piano player Tony Brown continues to be successful on *Keys to the Highway* (Columbia, 1989, prod. Rodney Crowell, Tony Brown) ♫♫♫♫. Crowell adds some rockabilly to the mix on songs like "Tell Me the Truth," and the two songs dealing with his father's death, "Many a Long & Lonesome Highway" and "Things I Wish I'd Said," lend emotional resonance to the album.

what to avoid: *Life Is Messy* (Columbia, 1992, prod. Rodney Crowell, Tony Brown) ♫♫♫, and so is this album, which reflects

the break-up of Crowell's 13-year marriage to Rosanne Cash. *Life Is Messy* isn't so much a bad album as it is tough to listen to, with Crowell's increasingly cryptic lyrics juxtaposed with apparently lighthearted, rousing numbers like "Lovin' All Night." Radio could find hardly anything to play from this rather depressing affair (only "What Kind of Love" and "Lovin' All Night" reached the Top 20); Crowell's commercial career has yet to recover.

the rest:
Street Language (Columbia, 1986) ♫♫♫
The Rodney Crowell Collection (Warner Bros., 1989) ♫♫♫
Greatest Hits (Columbia, 1993) ♫♫♫♫
Super Hits (Columbia) ♫♫♫
Let the Picture Paint Itself (MCA, 1994) ♫♫♫
Jewel of the South (MCA, 1995) ♫♫♫

worth searching for: *Ain't Living Long Like This* (Warner Bros., 1978, prod. Brian Ahern) ♫♫♫ isn't as good as Crowell's work for Columbia, but it provides an interesting lesson in the way Nashville works. Nothing on this album went above #90 on the charts, but Crowell's songs did provide later hits for Waylon Jennings ("I Ain't Living Long Like This"), Alan Jackson ("Song for the Life"), the Dirt Band ("Voile, an American Dream") and the Oak Ridge Boys ("Leaving Louisiana in the Broad Daylight"). The album's first track is an eccentric, bluesy arrangement of Dallas Frazier's "Elvira" that the Oaks would fix up and turn into a massive crossover hit.

influences:
◀◀ Emmylou Harris, Waylon Jennings, Guy Clark
▶▶ Rosanne Cash, Vince Gill

Brian Mansfield

BOBBIE CRYNER

Born September 13, 1961, in Woodland, CA.

All things considered, Bobbie Cryner should be regarded by Nashville as a triple threat: she is a stunning beauty who can write terrific songs yet whose smoky, sultry voice may be her best asset. Inexplicably, Cryner's star has yet to truly shine in Music City. A native Californian who grew up in the Flint Hills of Kansas, Cryner's music is dominated by no particular school of country, yet lyrically she conveys a particularly Midwestern sensibility, dwelling on quotidian disasters and heartbreak with a plainspokenness that is often devastating in effect.

what's available: Cryner's debut, *Bobbie Cryner* (Epic, 1993, prod. Doug Johnson, Carl Jackson) ♫♫♫♫, is the livelier of her two albums, containing hard-country flourishes on "He Feel

Guilty" and "I Don't Care" (which features a vocal cameo by Dwight Yoakam). The album also asserts Cryner's writing talent, notably on the rollicking "Daddy Laid the Blues on Me" and the brazen "You Could Steal Me." Her follow-up album *Girl of Your Dreams* (MCA, 1996, prod. Barry Beckett, Tony Brown) ♫♫♫ is equally fine, if slightly more ballad-heavy and a little too polished. Dealing almost exclusively with heartbreak and its aftermath, the album contains such songs as the complex, thought-provoking "You'd Think He'd Know Me Better," which suggests there's two sides to a breakup, and "I Didn't Know My Own Strength," which conveys the sort of quiet, yet assured feminism that has transformed country music—and not a moment too soon—these past few years.

influences:

 Loretta Lynn, Bobbie Gentry, K.T. Oslin

Daniel Durchholz

DICK CURLESS

Born March 17, 1932, in Fort Fairfield, ME. Died May 25, 1995.

He was known as the Baron of Country Music, an eyepatch-wearing cowboy from Maine. The title was truly fitting for Dick Curless, whose voice and spirit made him country royalty without the neon and rhinestones. Best known for the 1965 note-bending trucking anthem, "A Tombstone Every Mile," Curless' chart success was spotty. In fact, "Tombstone" was his only substantial hit, but he parlayed that into a touring stint with Buck Owens' All-American Show and a spot on the soundtrack to the 1968 film *Killer's Three*. When one thinks of country music history, Curless' name falls to the back of the line behind George Jones, Lefty Frizzell, Hank Williams and Johnny Cash. But his voice was as piercing and as resonant as any of those legends. He proved that on 1995's *Traveling Through*, an excellent album that taps into the soul of country music. Recorded in North Brookfield, MA, at the site of his first professional gig, *Traveling Through* truly delineates Curless' life journey. He died of cancer shortly after the album was released, leaving it as the final testament to a career that deserved more notice.

what's available: *Traveling Through* (Rounder, 1995, prod. Jake Guralnick) ♫♫♫ is the only full-length studio effort by Curless available in the United States. A quiet masterpiece, the album showcases Curless' still-powerful voice—weathered and not as smooth but still able to yodel and dip to the bowels of the heart. The melancholy edge that surrounded his robust pipes permeates this effort, making it a cathartic listening experience that ultimately celebrates life.

FIVE FOR MY FANS

KATE CAMPBELL

Dolly Parton
Coat of Many Colors (RCA)

Dan Fogelberg
Souvenirs (Epic)

James Taylor
Sweet Baby James (Warner Bros.)

Bobbie Gentry
Ode to Billie Joe (Capitol)

Kris Kristofferson
The Songs of Kris Kristofferson (Monument)

worth searching for: "A Tombstone Every Mile" can be found as one of 10 hearty trucking songs on *Country Shots: Gear-Jammin' Greats* (Rhino, 1994, prod. various) ♫♫♫. In addition to Curless' song, Dave Dudley's rocking "Six Days on the Road," Tom T. Hall's charismatic "Ravishing Ruby" and C.W. McCall's 1970s novelty hit "Convoy" help make this an irresistible collection.

influences:

◀◀ Buck Owens, George Jones, Lefty Frizzell

▶▶ C.W. McCall, Tom T. Hall, Dave Dudley

Mario Tarradell

BILLY RAY CYRUS

Born August 25, 1961, in Flatwoods, KY.

Billy Ray Cyrus' name will always be associated with his first hit, "Achy Breaky Heart." Like it or hate it (there's rarely a middle ground), that's an unfair association, because the platinum-selling single's Rolling-Stones groove and novelty hook is atypical of the rest of Cyrus' music. Cyrus would wear his heart on his sleeve (if he wore sleeves), and he leans more toward simple, roots-oriented rock with grand sentiments than he does toward traditional country. "Achy Breaky," named the Country Music Association Single of the Year in 1992, established Cyrus financially—his debut was the first by a country artist to open at #1 and has sold more than eight million copies. Of course, nothing he's done since then has matched that in terms of sales; by his fourth album, his singles were barely making the charts.

what to buy: *Trail of Tears* (Mercury, 1996, prod. Terry Shelton, Billy Ray Cyrus) 𝄞𝄞𝄞 is NOT the album with Cyrus' biggest hit. Instead, it's an album produced by Cyrus and his guitarist in a desperate attempt to rediscover himself after his overwhelming (and declining) success. It works, too, at least artistically. The title track evokes Bill Monroe and Jimmy Martin with bluegrass-like simplicity, and the rest of the album contains some Cyrus' best roots-oriented writing, as well as covers of favorite songs like Merle Haggard's "Sing Me Back Home" and Tom T. Hall's "Harper Valley P.T.A."

what to buy next: *Some Gave All* (Mercury, 1992, prod. Joe Scaife, Jim Cotton) 𝄞𝄞 has "Achy Breaky Heart," plus most of the rest of Cyrus' biggest hits, including "Could've Been Me" and "She's Not Cryin' Anymore." The title track became something of a theme for country fans who were also veterans.

what to avoid: *Storm in the Heartland* (Mercury, 1994, prod. Joe Scaife, Jim Cotton) 𝄞𝄞 is the weakest of Cyrus' albums, lacking hits and hooks.

the rest:
It Won't Be the Last (Mercury, 1993) 𝄞𝄞𝄞

influences:
◀◀ Kentucky HeadHunters, Lee Greenwood
▶▶ Jeff Copley, Shania Twain

Brian Mansfield

LISA DAGGS

Born February 28, in Hollywood, CA.

One of the most popular performers in the self-explanatory Positive Country format, singer-songwriter Lisa Daggs has built a country foundation with a touch of R&B; she was named the 1996 Christian Country Music Association Entertainer of the Year. Daggs first moved to Nashville from California during the late 1980s and immediately found success singing sessions and performing showcases for popular Nashville songwriters. During a short stint away from Music City, she became well known on the West Coast nightclub circuit; during this period Daggs waged a battle with alcoholism. Her first radio single, "Walls," dealt with her recovery and religious re-dedication. Daggs followed that with four #1 singles on the Positive Country chart and has opened for such artists as Susan Ashton.

what to buy: *Love Is the Bottom Line* (Cheyenne, 1995, prod. John Elefante, Dino Elefante) 𝄞𝄞𝄞 separated Daggs from her peers in the Positive Country field. The title track sounds like vintage Wynonna.

the rest:
Angel in Your Eyes (Pakaderm, 1994) 𝄞𝄞𝄞

influences:
◀◀ Wynonna, Trisha Yearwood, Kathy Mattea
▶▶ Mindy McCready

Dick Byington

LACY J. DALTON

Born Jill Byrem, October 13, 1946, in Bloomsburg, PA.

If George Jones and Tammy Wynette were actually only one person, they might just be Lacy J. Dalton. This vastly underrated, smoky-voiced singer/songwriter majored in art at Brigham Young University before heading on to California, where she performed folk music, then rock 'n' roll, and eventually settled on a career in country music. Upon hearing a demo she'd recorded, producer Billy Sherrill, who helped guide the careers of George and Tammy, among others, signed her to Columbia Records, where she recorded a string of major hits throughout the 1980s, highlighted by the smash, "16th Avenue" (#7, 1982). The hits continued through the decade, until her final chart appearance with "Black Coffee" (#15, 1990). Today, Lacy J. continues to tour, and is at work on an acoustic collection of her greatest hits. Early in her career, she also recorded under the name Jill Croston.

what's available: *Greatest Hits* (Columbia, 1983, prod. Billy Sherrill) 𝄞𝄞𝄞𝄞 is a solid collection of the edgy, yet accessible material that highlighted her hit-making years. At only 10 cuts, it's a bit skimpy, but with nothing else to choose from, it's essential for any fan.

worth searching for: *Survivor* (Universal, 1989, prod. Jimmy Bowen, Lacy J. Dalton, James Stroud) ♪♪♪♪ is a comeback of sorts, recorded after Dalton left CBS. A strong and personal statement, impeccably produced, with some well-chosen covers, and the autobiographical "Hard Luck Ace," this is vintage Dalton and should never have been allowed to go out of print.

influences:
◀◀ Janis Joplin
▶▶ Bobbie Cryner

Stephen L. Betts

DAVIS DANIEL

Born Robert Andrykowski, March 31, 1961, in Arlington Heights, IL.

Daniel is a journeyman country singer who was raised in Illinois, Montana, Nebraska and Colorado. Daniels has a solid country voice—it has often been compared to Lefty Frizzell, though he grew up a Willie Nelson fan—but apparently not enough of an ear to take advantage of it. He moved to Nashville in 1987.

what's available: *I Know a Place* (A&M, 1996, prod. Ed Seay, Harold Shedd) ♪♪, the only one of Daniel's three albums that remains in print, has a bigger, brighter sound than his other two albums, but little that distinguishes it from other recordings of the time.

influences:
◀◀ Lefty Frizzell, George Jones
▶▶ Daron Norwood ·

Brian Mansfield

CHARLIE DANIELS BAND

Formed 1970, in Nashville, TN.

Charlie Daniels (born October 28, 1936, in Wilmington, NC), vocals, fiddle, guitar; Joel "Taz" DiGregorio, keyboards, vocals; Jack Gavin, drums; Bruce Ray Brown, guitar, vocals; Chris Wormer, guitar, saxophone, vocals; Charlie Haywood, bass; others.

A North Carolina native who became a popular session fiddler in Nashville, Daniels is best known for his 1979 hit "The Devil Went Down to Georgia," which country music fans and detractors alike cite to support their cases. Daniels, along with Lynyrd Skynyrd and the Marshall Tucker Band, was one of the early Southern rockers, building his Charlie Daniels Band in the

Charlie Daniels **(AP/Wide World Photos)**

image of the Allman Brothers Band but keeping a little more twang in his guitars and a bit more weep in his fiddle. Hard touring during the 1970s led to radio play for "Uneasy Rider," "The Legend of Wooley Swamp" and the moving Vietnam vets' tribute "Still in Saigon." Unfortunately, Charlie's stay-out-of-my-backyard myopia and lunkheaded jingoism (his anti-drug diatribes would embarrass even Nancy Reagan) has helped undercut his earlier accomplishments. Daniels has been off the charts for well more than a decade and makes his living touring country bars.

what to buy: *A Decade of Hits* (Epic, 1983, prod. various) ♪♪♪♪ features many of the intermittent gems Daniels fiddled onto the radio. The consistent *Million Mile Reflections* (Epic, 1979, prod. John Boylan) ♪♪♪♪ has "The Devil Went down to Georgia."

what to buy next: *Full Moon* (Epic, 1980, prod. John Boylan) ♪♪♪ is Daniels' most successful album, featuring "In America" and "The Legend of Wooley Swamp."

what to avoid: *Super Hits* (Epic, 1994, prod. various) ♪ is a skimpy best-of. For all his flaws, Daniels deserves better.

the rest:

Te John, Grease and Wolfman (Kama Sutra, 1970) ♪

Honey in the Rock aka *Uneasy Rider* (Buddah-Kama Sutra, 1973/Epic, 1977) ♪♪♪

Fire on the Mountain aka *Simple Man* (Buddah-Kama Sutra, 1974/Epic, 1989) ♪♪♪

Way Down Yonder aka *Whiskey* (Buddah-Kama Sutra, 1974/Epic, 1977) ♪

Night Rider (Buddah-Kama Sutra, 1975) ♪♪♪

Saddle Tramp (Epic, 1976) ♪♪

High Lonesome (Epic, 1977) ♪♪

Midnight Wind (Epic, 1977) ♪♪

Volunteer Jam III and IV (Epic, 1978) ♪♪

Volunteer Jam VI (Epic, 1980) ♪♪

Windows (Epic, 1982) ♪♪

Me and the Boys (Epic, 1985) ♪♪

Powder Keg (Epic, 1987) ♪♪

Homesick Heroes (Epic, 1988) ♪♪♪

Christmas Time Down South (Epic, 1990) ♪♪

Renegade (Epic, 1991,) ♪♪

America, I Believe in You (Liberty, 1993) ♪♪

The Door (Sparrow, 1994) ♪♪

Same Ol' Me (Capitol, 1995) ♪♪

The Roots Remain (Columbia/Legacy, 1996) ♪♪♪

worth searching for: *Volunteer Jam* (Capricorn, 1976) ♪♪♪ chronicles the first of Daniels' long-running all-star festivals, an idea that sounded tapped out on subsequent editions.

solo outings:

Charlie Daniels:

Charlie Daniels (Capitol, 1971) ♪♪

Blues Hat (Blue Hat, 1997) ♪♪♪

influences:

◄◄ Allman Brothers Band, Waylon Jennings, Hank Williams Jr., Merle Haggard

►► Marshall Tucker Band, Lynyrd Skynyrd, Alabama, Oak Ridge Boys, Little Texas, Brooks & Dunn

Steve Knopper

HELEN DARLING

Born May 1, 1965, in Baton Rouge, LA.

Helen Darling's husky voice and never-ending charm have won her many fans within the music community, but she has yet to have a commercial hit—though she did score a few hit "commercials" during her time a jingle singer in Chicago. Darling was raised in Houston and attended Austin's University of Texas, singing in the school's vocal group, Ensemble 109. After college she saved enough money singing the praises of Heinz ketchup to be able to move to Nashville. Garth Brooks became a big fan after hearing her demo of "Whisper My Name" (later cut by Randy Travis.) As it often works, Brooks' interest in Darling's voice started a chain of events that led to her first record deal.

what's available: *Helen Darling* (Decca, 1995, prod. Mark Wright, Michael Omartian) ♪♪♪ includes guest appearances by Garth Brooks, Lee Roy Parnell and Delbert McClinton. The album produced no hits, and Darling left Decca before releasing a second record.

influences:

◄◄ Garth Brooks, Trisha Yearwood

Cyndi Hoelzle

DAVE & DEKE COMBO

Formed 1992, in Los Angeles, CA. Disbanded 1996.

Dave Stuckley, rhythm guitar, vocals; Deke Dickerson, lead guitar, vocals; Lance Ray Soliday, drums; Shorty Poole, bass.

For this Bay area quartet, music is meant to be fun. Sure, they take their rollicking mix of rockabilly and hillbilly styles seriously—their musicianship is solid—but these boys are concerned with having a good time. Borrowing the musical verve of the great rockabilly duos of the 1940s and 1950s (the Delmore Brothers, Rusty and Doug Kershaw) and fusing it with the hillbilly traditions of such West Coast stalwarts as Merle Travis, this foursome makes it all their own by spooning healthy doses of old-fashioned frolic into their repertoire. The boys have established themselves as a force in the U.K., where they released their debut CD in 1993. Stateside, the Combo's first full-length project came three years later, but it was worth the wait: *Hollywood Barn Dance* is a hoot, a slice of the past right down to the 1950s-era artwork that adorns the CD package.

what's available: *Hollywood Barn Dance* (Heyday Records, 1996, prod. Cousin Tim Maag, Brother Wally Hersom) ♪♪♪♪ is truly a welcomed rarity. Not only was the album recorded in "high fidelity monophonic"—created by putting Ampex 300 tape recorders, echo chambers and ribbon microphone into a shack, then playing—but it's one of few (maybe the only) CD released during the mid-1990s that boasts music for doing the jitterbug. Two-part harmonies, upright bass and a batch of cool songs with titles like "Henpecked Peckerwood" and "Slippin' and Slidin' (And Scootin' Around)." All you need now is the hardwood floor.

worth searching for: Several 7-inch singles and EPs are floating around in the U.K., and there's even one in Finland. But for those willing to explore, the Combo's first full-length CD, 1993's *Moonshine Melodies* on the London-based No Hit Records, is probably worth the time and money.

influences:

◀◀ Merle Travis, Delmore Brothers

▶▶ BR5-49, Big Sandy & His Fly-Rite Boys

Mario Tarradell

GAIL DAVIES

Born Patricia Gail Dickerson, June 5, 1948, in Broken Bow, OK.

Obscured by the inescapable fact that Gail Davies was truly a pioneer in Nashville as the first woman to write, produce and arrange her own albums, it's sometimes difficult to recall just how good those albums were. Melding blues and folk with hard-edged country, Davies had a string of hits during the 1970s and early 1980s that are none too easy to categorize. From the mountain-tinged "Grandma's Song" (#9, 1981) to the pop-flavored "Jagged Edge of a Broken Heart" (#20, 1984) Davies has explored much territory in her music, and opened many a door for women in the music business. During a stint as a staff writer for an L.A. music publisher Davies received invitations from both Roger Miller and Frank Zappa to join them on their respective tours. Choosing Miller, she made her national TV debut with him and shortly thereafter was moved by her publisher to Nashville. She soon signed with CBS as a solo artist. Moving to Warner Bros., Davies earned her first Top 10 hit with the bluegrassy "Blue Heartache" (#7, 1979), and entered the hit-making phase of her career, following up with "It's a Lovely, Lovely World" (#5, 1981) and the soulful K.T. Oslin-penned "Round the Clock Lovin'" (#9, 1982), her last Top 10. A side project during the mid-1980s was the country/rock band Wild Choir, with Davies covering John Hiatt's "Girl on a String" and other material that, in retrospect, may have been a few years ahead of its time. A few MCA and Capitol albums during the late 1980s and early 1990s came and went, with Davies eventually joining Liberty Records as staff producer from 1991–93. In 1995 she returned to performing and songwriting full-time with a critically acclaimed, entirely self-penned and self-produced project on her own label.

what's available: *Eclectic* (Little Chickadee, 1995) 🎵🎵🎵 hits its peak with the barrelhouse rave-up of "Your Mama Works So Hard," and continues Davies' experimentation with divergent musical styles.

worth searching for: *Wild Choir* (RCA, 1986, prod. Gail Davies, others) 🎵🎵🎵 is an out-of-print album that features Davies with a country and rock/pop outfit. *Best of Gail Davies* (1995, prod. Gail Davies) 🎵🎵🎵 is the only collection currently in print that includes Davies' hits on various labels presented in their original form. It's available, however, only through her fan club.

influences:

◀◀ Emmylou Harris, Linda Ronstadt

▶▶ Sweethearts of the Rodeo, Jann Browne

Stephen L. Betts

JIMMIE DAVIS

Born September 11, 1902, in Quitman, LA.

Born the oldest of 11 children to sharecroppers in northern Louisiana, Jimmie Davis began singing as a youngster in church. He also became interested in politics and was twice elected governor of Louisiana. Although he failed in his bid for a third term in 1971, he would be elected to the Country Music Hall Of Fame the following year. With a repertoire that included gospel standards, weepy ballads and sexually suggestive blues numbers, Davis' appeal was certainly broad.

what to buy: *Country Music Hall Of Fame Series* (MCA, 1991, prod. Country Music Foundation) 🎵🎵🎵🎵 is the only worthwhile collection of Davis' most familiar material currently available on CD. Compiled by the Country Music Foundation, the single disc mixes classics such as "You Are My Sunshine" and "Nobody's Darling but Mine" with a good cross-section of other chart toppers, plus a few of the racier records from his early Decca days.

what to buy next: *Greatest Hits—Finest Performances* (Sun Entertainment, 1995) 🎵🎵🎵 contains re-recordings of many of his classics, with Davis in fine voice, and a lively production that attempts to stay fairly close to the original versions.

influences:

◀◀ Jimmie Rodgers

▶▶ Ernest Tubb

Stephen L. Betts

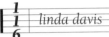
LINDA DAVIS

Born December 26, 1962, in Dodson, TX.

Linda Davis is a former jingle singer who kicked around Nashville in various roles until hooking up with Reba McEntire as a backup singer and duet partner on the 1993 smash "Does He Love You." Davis shares not only a vocal style with McEntire but a manager as well—McEntire's husband Narvel Blackstock. She first recorded for MDJ Records in 1982 with Skip Eaton, as Skip & Linda.

what to buy: Davis' fourth album, *Some Things Are Meant to Be* (Arista,1996, prod. John Guess) 🎵🎵, confirms that she is a singer with every bit of McEntire's vocal talent, but little of her scope. But with such songs as the insistent title cut and "Love Story in the Making," it does have better material than her other albums.

the rest:
Shoot for the Moon (Arista, 1994) 🎵🎵

worth searching for: Davis recorded two albums during the early 1990s, *In a Different Light* (Liberty, 1991, prod. Jimmy Bowen) 🎵🎵 and *Linda Davis* (Liberty, 1992, prod. Jimmy Bowen) 🎵🎵, both with onetime McEntire producer Jimmy Bowen. She also had three charting singles for Epic Records before that, though none was released on an album.

influences:
◀◀ Reba McEntire
▶▶ Faith Hill, Tammy Graham

Brian Mansfield

MAC DAVIS

Born January 21, 1942, in Lubbock, TX.

Like Eddie Rabbitt, guitarist/songwriter Mac Davis got a big lift by scoring a hit with Elvis Presley, the insightful "In the Ghetto," then quickly followed that success with yet another Presley smash, "Don't Cry Daddy." During that time, Davis also concocted another fine tune for Kenny Rogers and the First Edition, "Something's Burning." Those songs shed enough light on the former record company rep to help him parlay his good looks and songwriting smarts into a successful solo career capped by a TV variety show. But one enduring hit ("Baby Don't Get Hooked on Me") would be followed by a torrent of garden-variety schlock ("One Hell of a Woman," "It's Hard to Be Humble").

what's available: *Greatest Hits* (Sony, 1979, prod. various) 🎵🎵 sums it up in succinct fashion, including Davis' own rendering of "Something's Burning" and all the major hits, but you have to wade through some real tripe as well (including "Watchin' Scotty Grow," a cloying hit for Bobby Goldsboro). *Very Best and More* (Mercury Nashville, 1984, prod. various) 🎵🎵 contains mostly Davis' latter-day country fare, including a reading of Rodney Crowell's "Shame on the Moon."

influences:
◀◀ Elvis Presley, Neil Diamond
▶▶ Dan Seals, Eddie Rabbitt

David Simons

SKEETER DAVIS

Born Mary Frances Penick, December 30, 1931, in Dry Ridge, KY.

Although she's perhaps best known for the 1962 pop standard, "The End of the World," Skeeter Davis is a country girl at heart, a deeply spiritual, wide-eyed innocent but still worldly wise. From her earliest days as one half of the Davis Sisters (with friend Betty Jack Davis) to her still-frequent appearances on the Grand Ole Opry, Davis remains one of the most down-to-earth performers in country music and, surprisingly, one of the most innovative. As the Davis Sisters' sole hit, "I Forgot More Than You'll Ever Know" was topping the charts in 1953, Betty Jack died in an auto accident. Although Georgia Davis, Betty Jack's sister, joined Skeeter to continue the act, Skeeter finally went solo in 1957, with her first hit a year later. While girl groups such as the Crystals and the Shangri-La's were capturing the pop audience's attention during the early 1960s, Davis had already been experimenting vocally in that direction for some time. Working in Nashville's RCA studio with producer Chet Atkins, she multi-tracked her own vocals, with generally brilliant results. Davis' life is recounted with great style and passion in her 1993 autobiography, *Bus Fare to Kentucky*.

what to buy: *The Essential Skeeter Davis* (RCA, 1995, prod. various) 🎵🎵🎵🎵 collects all 10 of Davis' Top 10 hits and includes her only #1, "I Forgot More . . ." A real highlight of the set is her rendition of the Goffin/King tune "I Can't Stay Mad at You."

what to buy next: *She Sings, They Play* (Rounder, 1986) 🎵🎵🎵 is an entertaining, if not perfectly executed, project in collaboration with the band NRBQ. Davis married band member Joey Spampinato a year later; they divorced in 1996.

influences:
◀◀ Wanda Jackson, Patti Page
▶▶ Jann Browne

Stephen L. Betts

RONNIE DAWSON

Born Ronald Monroe Dawson, August 12, 1939, in Dallas, TX.

Ronnie Dawson owes his career resurgence almost entirely to obsessive rockabilly record collectors. Dawson was the youngest of the 1950s rockabillies, and like Jerry Lee Lewis (they both attended the Southern Bible Institute), he eschewed a career in religion to make music with a beat. His first band, Ronnie Dee & the D Men, played R&B and rockabilly to enthusiastic crowds in Waxahachie, Texas, where they won the Big D Jamboree talent contest 10 weeks in a row. In 1957 Dawson signed with Gene Vincent's manager, Jack Rhodes, who wrote his first two singles, "Rockin' Bones" and "Action Packed."

These two remarkably hot singles should've made Dawson a star; he was talented, fresh-faced and energetic, and his peroxide blonde crew-cut provided a distinct and recognizable image. Yet these records sold poorly outside of his hometown. After an unsuccessful stint at Dick Clark's Swan label, Dawson played Western swing with the Light Crust Doughboys, recorded under different names and did session work for eccentric Texas producer Major Bill Smith (Dawson played drums on Bruce Channel's "Hey Baby" and Paul & Paula's "Hey Paula"). During the mid-1960s, Dawson stopped playing full-time and started a career in radio & TV advertising. But more than a decade later, his early sides began to fetch high prices at auctions, while the Cramps and other neorockabillies recorded "Rockin' Bones" and "Action Packed." Rhino Records stirred interest by including "Action Packed" on its *Rock This Town* anthology. During the late 1980s Dawson reemerged, touring overseas to enthusiastic audiences and recording again. More than just a well-preserved legend from rock's golden era, Dawson (like Sleepy LaBeef) has actually improved with age. His voice is more powerful than ever, he's become an exciting lead guitarist, and he displays honest joy and intensity on stage. Though he's nearly 60, Dawson is just now reaching the peak of his powers.

what to buy: *Rockin' Bones: The Legendary Masters 1957–1962* (No Hit, 1993/Crystal Clear, 1996, prod. David Dennard) 𝄢𝄢𝄢𝄢 is a two-CD set that contains all of Dawson's 1950s work (including 20 previously unreleased tracks, demos, and outtakes) with a few icky early 1960s pop sides thrown in. It features a good booklet with great photos, too.

what to buy next: *Rockinitis* (No Hit, 1993/Crystal Clear, 1996, prod. Boz Boorer, Barney Koumis) 𝄢𝄢𝄢 was recorded in 1989, with backing provided by various members of the Planet Rockers and the Playboys. Proof positive that Dawson is the real deal.

the rest: *Monkey Beat* (No Hit/Crystal Clear, 1994) 𝄢𝄢𝄢
Just Rockin' & Rollin' (Upstart, 1996) 𝄢𝄢𝄢

influences:
◄◄ Gene Vincent, Johnny Carroll, Mac Curtis
►► Cramps, High Noon, Big Sandy & His Fly-Rite Boys

Ken Burke

CURTIS DAY

From Beaumont, TX.

Curtis Day has all the right ingredients for a male country singer during the 1990s. He's a young, good-looking, former-football-playing singer from Beaumont, which also produced Mark Chesnutt, Clay Walker and Tracy Byrd. So far, though, Day hasn't been able to turn that into stardom.

what's available: *Curtis Day* (Asylum, 1996, prod. Kevin Beamish, Kyle Lehning) 𝄢𝄢 starts off honky-tonking with the guitars cranked. But with songs like "My Baby's Cookin'," "Pull the Wool over My Heart" and "Athens Grease" there's little direction and even less depth to his music.

influences:
◄◄ Clay Walker, Tracy Byrd
►► David Kersh

Brian Mansfield

JESSE DAYTON

Born May 27, 1966, in Beaumont, TX.

In his early 30s, Jesse Dayton is already a quintessential Texas artist. He's been a member of two honky-tonk bands—the Alamo Jets (which once featured Austin's Dale Watson) and the rockabilly outfit the Roadkings—and he's shaped his musical vision with the help of influences such as George Jones, Lefty Frizzell, Hank Williams and bluesman Lightnin' Hopkins. At heart, Dayton is a honky-tonker in the Waylon Jennings/Willie Nelson vein, but he sprinkled his debut album with helpings of the blues, folkloric Mexican rhythms and rock 'n' roll. With a penchant for garb that makes him look like a cross between Elvis Presley and James Dean, and a fierce control of the electric guitar, he's been dubbed a rockabilly dude. Tireless touring and musical integrity—again, the Texas way—have carved him a respectable niche in clubs where the brew flows and cigarette smoke engulfs the air. Folks, that's anywhere real country music thrives.

what's available: Dayton wrote every song on his impressive debut, *Raising Cain* (Justice, 1995, prod. Randall Jamail) 🎵🎵🎵, and he obviously writes about what he knows—playing, loving and drinking. Standout tracks are "Blood Bucket Blues (Part One)," a song that would have made Lightnin' Hopkins holler, "Carmelita (Show Me How to Dance)," featuring legendary squeeze box master Flaco Jimenez, and "Boystown," a minor-chord rocker with a moody edge.

worth searching for: Dayton recorded a few albums released only in Europe that may be an expensive chore to find, so stick to stateside efforts. He plays guitars on nine of 13 tracks of Waylon Jennings' *Right for the Time* (Justice, 1996, prod. Randall Jamail) 🎵🎵🎵🎵. Dayton's gritty guitar riffs compliment Jennings' unmistakable baritone, an instrument that grows more authoritative with age. Dayton also co-wrote the great shuffle "Caught" from Dale Watson's excellent debut, *Cheatin' Heart Attack* (HighTone, 1995, prod. Bruce Bromberg) 🎵🎵🎵🎵.

influences:

◀◀ Lefty Frizzell, Billy Joe Shaver, Hank Williams

▶▶ Dale Watson, Derailers

Mario Tarradell

BILLY DEAN

Born April 2, 1962, in Quincy, FL.

Tall and ruggedly handsome, Billy Dean falls squarely in the romantic crooner category of country music. He's a Florida native who attended college in Mississippi on a basketball scholarship. He moved to Nashville after winning a Wrangler Starsearch talent contest. Before signing his record deal, he had songs cut by Ronnie Milsap, Randy Travis, Shelly West and Exile's Les Taylor. A string of romantic singles have made him a solid performer in the marketplace, and his most successful song, "Somewhere in My Broken Heart" got him a Grammy nomination and led to his being nominated for the Country Music Association's Horizon Award. Dean has also flirted with acting, making early appearances in commercials and more recently on such national television series as *Lois & Clark*.

what to buy: Dean's albums get silly or overly sentimental in places, which is not to say that *Greatest Hits* (Capitol, 1994, prod. various) 🎵🎵🎵does away with those weaknesses. But it does have two of his very best songs, "Somewhere in My Broken Heart" and "Billy the Kid," together.

what to buy next: Dean went through a slack period after 1993's "If There Hadn't Been You," but he found himself again when he reunited with producer Shapiro, who had worked on Dean's first two albums. *It's What I Do* (Capitol, 1996, prod. Tom Shapiro) 🎵🎵🎵 contains some of Dean's best love songs ever, including the title track and "In the Name of Love," written by Skip Ewing and Doug Stone.

what to avoid: Save for "Somewhere in My Broken Heart," *Young Man* (Capitol, 1990, prod. Chuck Howard, Tom Shapiro) 🎵🎵 falls prey to all of Dean's weakest tendencies. He would improve considerably by his second album, *Billy Dean*.

the rest:

Billy Dean (Capitol, 1991) 🎵🎵🎵
Fire in the Dark (Capitol, 1992) 🎵🎵
Men'll Be Boys (Capitol, 1994) 🎵🎵

influences:

◀◀ David Gates, Doug Stone

▶▶ Ty Herndon, Bryan White, Crystal Bernard

Brian Mansfield

JIMMY DEAN

Born August 10, 1928, in Plainview, TX.

At his peak, Jimmy Dean was a multi-media star who cut hit country records and hosted his own TV shows. Today, though, he's better known for his line of sausage products. Still, Dean was a Texas-raised singer who started a group called the Tennessee Haymakers while in the Air Force in 1948. By 1952 he was fronting a group called the Texas Wildcats; he recorded for 4-Star Records that same year and had his first hit single for that label, "Bumming Around," in 1953. Dean was given a national television series twice: a morning one for CBS (1957–58) and one in the afternoon with ABC (1963–66). During those years he also had a number of pop and country hits, most notably the gold-selling "Big Bad John" (#1 pop and country, 1961) and 1962's "P.T. 109," which was based on a story from John F. Kennedy's war days. The hits were smaller and more infrequent during the late 1960s and almost stopped by the 1970s, save for "I.O.U.," a spoken-word Mother's Day hit in 1976. But Dean had other sources of income: he had begun a restaurant chain, and the sausage had become very popular in certain regions. He married singer Donna Meade in 1991.

what to buy: *Greatest Hits* (Columbia, prod. Don Law) 🎵🎵🎵 features the most popular of Dean's early-1960s Columbia recitations—"Big Bad John," "P.T. 109," "To a Sleeping Beauty"—as well as more musical fare like "The First Thing Ev'ry Morning (And the Last Thing Ev'ry Night)."

Jimmy Dean (Archive Photos)

what to buy next: *24 Greats* (Deluxe, 1987) 🎵🎵 contains lots of music, but too few hits. This album includes songs that were minor hits for Dean during his RCA years, such as "A Thing Called Love" and "Born to Be by Your Side." It also has remakes of "I.O.U." and "Sleeping Beauty," two of Dean's most famous songs, but mainly it contains his versions of other people's hits, like "Okie from Muskogee," "Skip a Rope" and "All I Have to Offer You Is Me."

what to avoid: Like the other albums in K-Tel/Dominion's *Country Spotlight* series, the 10 tracks on *Country Spotlight* (Dominion, 1991) 🎵🎵 are remakes of the artist's hits, and not particularly good ones. Curb licensed some of these recordings for its *Greatest Songs* (Curb, 1995) 🎵🎵.

the rest:
Big Bad John and Other Fabulous Songs and Tales (Sony Music Special Products, 1993) 🎵🎵🎵

worth searching for: *American Originals* (Columbia, 1989) 🎵🎵🎵

is a 10-song collection that has serious overlap with Columbia's *Greatest Hits* album ("Big Bad John," "P.T. 109") but is a good hits survey nonetheless. *Big Bad John* (Bear Family, 1993, prod. Don Law) 🎵🎵🎵 is a 26-song disc consisting mainly of Dean's early-1960s output for Columbia that contains most of his hits and a lot more.

influences:
◀◀ Gene Autry, Little Jimmy Dickens
▶▶ Red Sovine

Brian Mansfield

THE DELEVANTES
Formed mid-1980s, in Hoboken, NJ.

Bob Delevante, vocals, guitar; Mike Delevante, lead guitar, vocals.

The story is really quite simple: two brothers born and bred in Hoboken, New Jersey making glorious roots-pop music. What else do you need to know? Brothers Bob and Mike Delevante developed their distinct harmony playing bluegrass as teens; by the time they were old enough to play in bars, they were writing catchy pop songs and calling themselves Who's Your Daddy. Though they were much beloved on the New Jersey club scene, they decided to move to Nashville to try and make records. Wouldn't you know the first person they hooked up with in Nashville was fellow Jersey boy and E-Street Band alum Garry Tallent (who, as it turns out, was anxious to try his hand at producing). Tallent volunteered to produce Who's Your Daddy's first singles, (including a version of "Big Love," which they later re-recorded for *Long About That Time*), and his interest in the band made other folks take notice. The brothers, now using their given name, the Delevantes, recorded their first album in 1995 and are working on their second for Capitol.

what's available: *Long About That Time* (Rounder, 1996, prod. Garry Tallent, Mike Porter, Michael Clute) 🎵🎵🎵 is the Delevantes' fine debut.

influences:
◀◀ Foster & Lloyd, Lonesome Strangers, Everly Brothers

Cyndi Hoelzle

THE DELMORE BROTHERS

Vocal duo from Elkmont, AL.

Alton Delmore (born December 25, 1908, in Elkmont, AL; died June 8, 1964), vocals, guitar; Rabon Delmore (born December 3, 1916, in Elkmont, AL; died December 4, 1952), vocals, guitar.

This very important duo melded the close harmonies common to brother acts with intricate, syncopated guitar and tenor guitar instrumental accompaniment to create a new and highly influential duet sound. Their 1930s-era Bluebird recordings featured such timeless numbers as "Brown's Ferry Blues," "Gonna Lay Down My Old Guitar," and "Weary Lonesome Blues." On their later records for King, they featured blues-influenced rhythms and lyrics, electric guitar, and Wayne Raney's harmonica accompaniment, creating many classics, including "Freight Train Boogie," "Hillbilly Boogie," and "Pan American Boogie," along with many other standards, including "Blues Stay Away from Me." They also recorded as members of the Brown's Ferry Four, a gospel quartet, along with Grandpa Jones and Merle Travis or Red Foley. The Delmore Brothers were early members of the Grand Ole Opry and remain an important influence in the music to this day.

what to buy: *Brown's Ferry Blues* (County, 1995, reissue prod. Gary B. Reid) 🎵🎵🎵🎵 is chock full of classic Bluebird material

from 1933 to 1940, including "Blue Railroad Train," "Gonna Lay Down My Old Guitar," "The Weary Lonesome Blues," and "Brown's Ferry Blues." On *Sand Mountain Blues* (County, 1986, reissue prod. Dave Freeman) 🎵🎵🎵🎵, early King recordings find the Delmores in a transitional mode between the pristine brother harmony duets they'd cut for Bluebird and the later, more raucous King boogies. Twenty classic blues and boogies are included on *Freight Train Boogie* (Ace, 1993) 🎵🎵🎵🎵, an English reissue of the Delmore's King material. This disc features topnotch instrumentalists of the day, including Wayne Raney, Homer & Jethro, Merle Travis and others.

what to buy next: *When They Let the Hammer Down* (Bear Family, 1984, prod. Richard Weize) 🎵🎵🎵🎵, a German reissue, features 18 tracks performed by the great country harmonica player Wayne Raney alongside the Delmores—classic stuff. There is some duplication with the Ace King compilation, but they're both well worth having.

influences:
◀◀ Blue Sky Boys, Jimmie Rodgers
▶▶ Louvin Brothers, O'Kanes

Randy Pitts

IRIS DeMENT

Born 1961, in Paragould, AR.

A songwriter with a distinctive voice that seems to embody the entire tradition of American folk music and an unerring ability to tell moving and believable stories, Iris DeMent is an anomaly in the music business. She was raised the youngest of eight children born in Arkansas and raised in California in a strict Pentecostal family. She had never thought of being a musician until she was in her late 20s; she now finds herself filtering such singer/songwriters as Joni Mitchell through her childhood love for the likes of Kitty Wells and delivers her story/songs with her charmingly unpolished, real voice cracking past notes without ever sounding like affectations. She's got fans in high places, including John Prine (who wrote the liner notes for her debut), Emmylou Harris and Nanci Griffith, who appreciate her songwriting and her unselfconscious style.

what to buy: DeMent's songs on her debut, *Infamous Angel* (Rounder, 1992/Warner Bros., 1992, prod. Jim Rooney) 🎵🎵🎵🎵, including "Let the Mystery Be" and "Our Town" (later used over the credits for the final episode of the TV show *Northern Exposure*), already sound like Smoky Mountain traditionals. Her debut's follow-up, *My Life* (Warner Bros., 1994, prod. Jim

Rooney) 𝄞𝄞𝄞𝄞, is a thoughtful though implacably sad and deeply moving collection of autobiographical songs and fictional sketches.

what to buy next: DeMent's third album, *The Way I Should* (Warner Bros., 1996, prod. Randy Scruggs) 𝄞𝄞𝄞, finds the vocalist broadening her stylistic base and adding frank political broadsides to her repertoire of self-observations and narrative vignettes. The sound is more commercial, but some of the songs are much less so.

influences:

◀◀ Kitty Wells, Joni Mitchell, Emmylou Harris, Nanci Griffith, Bruce Springsteen

▶▶ Kate Campbell

Gil Asakawa

WESLEY DENNIS

Born April 22, 1962, in Clanton, AL.

Wesley Dennis grew up Montgomery, Alabama, hometown of Hank Williams, but it's more recent artists whose work his recalls. Before landing his record deal, Dennis worked days for many years as an auto windshield repairman while singing almost every night in the nightclubs of southern Alabama.

what's available: *Wesley Dennis* (Mercury, 1995, prod. Keith Stegall, John Kelton) 𝄞𝄞𝄞 is a case where less could have been more. Dennis' debut album had some great tracks, including his dead-on cover of Mel Street's "Borrowed Angel" and some fine self-penned songs ("I Don't Know but I've Been Told" and "Leave Me a Picture of You"), but it suffers from the inclusion of the hokey numbers "Bubbaland" and "This Hat Ain't No Act."

influences:

◀◀ Randy Travis, Keith Whitley, Vern Gosdin, Mel Street

Bill Hobbs

JOHN DENVER

Born John Henry Deutschendorf, December 31, 1943, in Roswell, NM.

After being elevated to His Rocky Mountain Highness with such mid-1970s hits as "Take Me Home, Country Roads," "Thank God I'm a Country Boy" and "Annie's Song," John Denver: (1) starred as a confused grocery store clerk opposite George Burns in the movie *Oh God*; (2) made a TV Christmas special and album with the Muppets; (3) formed a record company called Windsong and signed the Starland Vocal Band, which was responsible for "Afternoon Delight"; and (4) approached

FIVE FOR MY FANS

DEANA CARTER

Fleetwood Mac
Rumours (Warner Bros.)

David Lee Murphy
Gettin' Out the Good Stuff (MCA)

Simon & Garfunkel
Greatest Hits (Columbia)

Nat King Cole
The Christmas Song (Capitol)

Matraca Berg
Lyin' to the Moon (RCA)

the Soviet Union about training for a space-station mission after being rejected by NASA. It was hardly the career path that you'd expect from 1975's Country Music Association Entertainer of the Year, but then Denver has often let his humanitarian passions and quirky interests distract him from his music. Beginning his career in 1965 as a member of the Chad Mitchell Trio, Denver wrote "Leaving on a Jet Plane" for the group, but it didn't become a hit until Peter, Paul & Mary covered it in 1969. Settling in Colorado, Denver started his solo career as a blissful protest singer/songwriter. After three albums that awkwardly mashed Beatles and James Taylor covers with political diatribes like Tom Paxton's "Ballad of Spiro Agnew," he took the gentler path with the country-flavored *Poems, Prayers and Promises*—which featured his career-making hit, "Take Me Home, Country Roads"—and his finest album, *Rocky Mountain High*. Ironically, these folk-based efforts (along with 1974's *Back Home Again*) were far more convincing stabs at country music than such later Nashville-pandering albums as *Some Days Are Diamonds*.

John Denver **(AP/Wide World Photos)**

By 1982 Denver was floundering from country to reggae, singing duets with everyone from Placido Domingo to Emmylou Harris in search of a niche. The only things that remained consistent were his humanitarian and spiritual convictions. Still active in the Windstar Foundation, an environmental education and research center that he co-founded, and a reforestation project called Plant-It 2000, Denver has continued releasing albums on his own Windstar label. He briefly resurfaced on Sony/Legacy in 1995 with the enjoyable *Wildlife Concert*, a two-CD set benefitting the Wildlife Conservation Society that marked one of the rare perfect marriages of his social consciousness and his art.

what to buy: Of his early works still in print, *Rocky Mountain High* (RCA, 1972, prod. Milton Okun) 🎵🎵🎵🎵 sounds the least dated, with fine musicianship, genuinely gorgeous ballads in "For Baby (For Bobbie)" and "Goodbye Again," and cool John Prine ("Paradise") and Beatles ("Mother Nature's Son") covers. *An Evening with John Denver* (RCA, 1975, prod. Milton Okun)

🎵🎵🎵🎵 captures him at the height of his fame, when all he had to do was utter "far out" to get applause. The between-song patter and notorious cover of New Christy Minstrels leader Randy Sparks' "Saturday Night in Toledo, Ohio" complement the faithful renderings of the hits. If you're not one of the 10 million who already own 1973's *Greatest Hits*, then the two-disc *Rocky Mountain Collection* (RCA, 1996, prod. various) 🎵🎵🎵🎵 is the best primer, with 39 tracks spanning Denver's career and his three greatest-hits collections.

what to buy next: The songs are familiar, but the rustic feel, acoustic band instrumentation and laid-back, Western-flavored arrangements on *The Wildlife Concert* (Sony/Legacy, 1995, prod. Bob Irwin) 🎵🎵🎵🎵 lend an infectious vitality to this two-disc set. We could do without the flutes, but former-Elvis Presley-guitarist James Burton adds some tasteful fuel to "Wild Montana Skies," "Back Home Again" and an Appalachian-style "Take Me Home, Country Roads."

what to avoid: In a weak attempt at a concept album about the environment, *Earth Songs* (Windstar, 1990, prod. Lee Holdridge) WOOF! gathers lackluster re-recordings of such 1970s favorites as "Rocky Mountain Suite," "Rocky Mountain High," "Sunshine on My Shoulders," "Eagle and the Hawk" and "Calypso" around new compositions like "Earth Day, Every Day."

the rest:

Poems, Prayers and Promises (RCA, 1971) 🎶🎶🎶
Farewell Andromeda (RCA, 1973) 🎶🎶
Greatest Hits (RCA, 1973) 🎶🎶🎶
Back Home Again (RCA, 1974) 🎶🎶🎶
Rocky Mountain Christmas (RCA, 1975) 🎶🎶
Spirit (RCA, 1976) 🎶🎶🎶
Windsong (RCA, 1976) 🎶🎶
I Want to Live (RCA, 1977) 🎶🎶
Greatest Hits, Volume 2 (RCA, 1977) 🎶🎶🎶
Some Days Are Diamonds (RCA, 1981) 🎶🎶
Seasons of the Heart (RCA, 1982) 🎶🎶
Greatest Hits, Volume 3 (RCA, 1984) 🎶🎶
Dreamland Express (RCA, 1985) 🎶🎶
One World (RCA, 1986) 🎶🎶
The Flower That Shattered the Stone (Windstar, 1990) 🎶🎶
Different Directions (Windstar, 1991) 🎶🎶
Higher Ground (Windstar, 1991) 🎶🎶

worth searching for: *Minneapolis Does Denver* (October, 1995, prod. John Strawberry Fields) 🎶🎶🎶 features such Minneapolis rock acts as the Honeydogs, Steeplejack, Tina & the B-Side Movement and the Delilahs paying surprisingly faithful tribute to Denver's 1970s material. If there's any doubt that he always knew how to write a memorable melody, check out Marlee McLeod and Kristin Mooney's duet on a jangly, uptempo rendition of "Follow Me."

influences:

◀◀ New Christy Minstrels, Tom Paxton, James Taylor, Bread
▶▶ Dan Fogelberg

David Okamoto

THE DERAILERS

Formed June 1993, in Austin, TX.

Tony Villanueva, vocals, rhythm guitar; Brian Hofeldt, lead guitar, vocals); Vic Gerard, bass, (1993–96); Terry Kirkendall, drums; Ethan Shaw, bass (1996–present).

In the thick of 1996, when Nashville took mainstream country to a new artistic low with the emergence of such slick pop acts as Mindy McCready, Ricochet and Mila Mason, this band of Bakersfield-influenced boys burst out of the Texas capitol with *Jackpot*, one of the best country records of the year. Lead singer and songwriter Tony Villanueva—whose thick baritone sports an engagingly mournful edge—crafts tunes modeled after the kicking West Coast country popularized by Merle Haggard and Buck Owens. Villanueva and writing partner Brian Hofeldt meld that style with the Western swing and honky-tonk traditions of the Lone Star state and the rebellious rockabilly beat. The results are shuffles, two-steppers, waltzes and ballads filled with irresistible hooks and a raw, authentic feel. But before you dub them a retro band, contemplate this; these guys have created a distinct image—elegant 1950s Western wear crowned by pompadour-meets-buzz-cut coifs—and an original repertoire that strides beyond the line separating gimmick from substance.

what to buy: *Jackpot* (Watermelon, 1996, prod. Dave Alvin) 🎶🎶🎶🎶 stands as the Derailers' masterpiece. Boasting a handful of such future country classics as the guitar-fueled "My Heart's Ready," the shuffling title cut and the West Coast country triumph "This Big City," *Jackpot* proves that a small budget and minimal independent-label promotion can still pack an artistic wallop.

the rest:

Live Tracks (Freedom, 1995) 🎶🎶🎶🎶

worth searching for: Although the Derailers' one contribution to *Austin Country Nights* (Watermelon, 1995, prod. Rob Patterson, Mike Stewart) 🎶🎶🎶🎶, the dance floor-ready "Just One More Time," can also be found on the *Live Tracks* CD, this compilation of Austin's brightest country artists merits attention. Great cuts by such stellar Texas acts as Mary Cutrufello, Dale Watson, the Cornell Hurd Band and Don Walser help make it a mini-treasure.

influences:

◀◀ Merle Haggard, Buck Owens, Hank Thompson
▶▶ BR5-49, Gary Allan

Mario Tarradell

THE DESERT ROSE BAND

See: Chris Hillman

DIAMOND RIO

Formed 1984, as the Tennessee River Boys, in Nashville, TN.

Marty Roe, lead vocals; Jimmy Olander, guitar; Brian Prout, guitar;

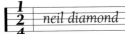

neil diamond

Gene Johnson, mandolin, fiddle; Dana Williams, bass; Dan Truman, keyboards.

Diamond Rio is a collection of super-pickers with backgrounds in bluegrass music who also harmonize extremely well with their lead vocalist. The band began life in the Opryland theme park under the name Tennessee River Boys with some different members, including, at one point, Ty Herndon. They played live for tourists at the theme park and also toured for several years. Marty Roe's sparkling high tenor now provides the lead vocals for the Country Music Association's Group of the Year from 1992–94.

what to buy: From the weird Southern-gothic tale of "It's All in Your Head" to the sentimental widow's ballad "She Misses Him on Sunday the Most" and the country hit "Walkin' Away," Rio's *IV* (Arista, 1996, prod. Michael Clute, Tim DuBois, Diamond Rio) 🎵🎵🎵 verged on art in a way their previous three hadn't. In fact, buy Diamond Rio's records in reverse order—the formula (middle-of-the-road country infused with highly accomplished and inventive picking and perfect harmonizing) doesn't change, but the songwriting gets better with each one. (Note: When the CD starts track one, push the rewind button and find a hidden track.)

what to buy next: *Diamond Rio* (Arista, 1991, prod. Monty Powell, Tim DuBois) 🎵🎵🎵, the group's debut, includes hits "Meet in the Middle," "Norma Jean Riley" and "Nowhere Bound.""

the rest:
Close to the Edge (Arista, 1992) 🎵🎵🎵
Love a Little Stronger (Arista, 1994) 🎵🎵🎵

worth searching for: *Greatest Hits: Nine Well-Cut Gems* (Arista, 1993, prod. Monty Powell, Tim DuBois) 🎵🎵🎵 is a promotional album featuring the group's first nine singles from *Diamond Rio* and *Close to the Edge*.

influences:
◀◀ Alabama, Exile, Shenandoah
▶▶ Lonestar, Ty Herndon

Bill Hobbs

NEIL DIAMOND
Born January 24, 1941, in Brooklyn, NY.

Neil Diamond is hardly a country artist, associated more closely with the Brill Building pop songwriters factory than Music City. But his music, particularly early in his career, was informed by country and folk influences. The twangy, ultra-cool "Girl, You'll Be a Woman Soon" (later covered by popsters Cliff Richard and Urge Overkill) and "Kentucky Woman" (an early Deep Purple staple) certainly draw from the native New Yorker's rural music tastes. After a couple of decades of MOR shmaltz, Diamond's recently returned to his country roots with *Tennessee Moon*, which he recorded in Nashville with such guests as Waylon Jennings and the Mavericks' Raul Malo. Coming fast on its heels was the *In My Lifetime* box set that brings his country/folk connection into sharper perspective.

what to buy: If you're willing to shell out the bucks, the triple-CD *In My Lifetime* (Columbia, 1996, prod. various) 🎵🎵🎵 is an excellent way to hear Diamond's music shine in all of its multi-faceted glory. The middle-of-the-road stuff is here in abundance, but so are such early, country-tinged classics as "Solitary Man," "Kentucky Woman," "Red, Red Wine," "Shilo," "Cracklin' Rosie," "Song Sung Blue," "Sweet Caroline" and the gospel-inflected "Brother Love's Traveling Salvation Show."

what to buy next: *Tennessee Moon* (Columbia, 1996, prod. Neil Diamond, James Stroud, Don Cook, Richard Landis, Paul Worley) 🎵🎵 could be seen as commercial opportunism, which, in some ways, it is considering country's considerable boom in popularity during the 1990s. Still one of the nation's biggest box-office draws, Diamond's last pop album was a mild flop and lacked the inspiration evident here. Diamond is aided and abetted by some of Nashville's top producers, writers and session men, but it's his enthusiasm, solid songwriting and warm performance that raise *Moon* above Music City formulaicism. Longtime label Columbia Records reissued songs from Diamond's fertile 1960s folk-rock period, when he recorded for Bang: *Classics: The Early Years (1966–67)* (Columbia, 1983, prod. various) 🎵🎵🎵 pulls together many of the songs that were among his first hits, including "Cherry, Cherry" and a slew of others since covered by the likes of the Monkees ("I'm a Believer"), UB40 ("Red, Red Wine"), Deep Purple ("Kentucky Woman"), Urge Overkill ("Girl, You'll Be a Woman Soon"), Cliff Richard (ditto) and Chris Isaak ("Solitary Man").

influences:
◀◀ Elvis Presley, Bob Dylan
▶▶ Michael Bolton, Barry Manilow, Chris Isaak

Doug Pullen

Marty Roe of Diamond Rio (© Ken Settle)

Joe Diffie (© Ken Settle)

HAZEL DICKENS

See: Hazel & Alice

LITTLE JIMMY DICKENS

Born December 19, 1920, in Bolt, WV.

Diminutive honky-tonk hitmaker, Country Music Hall of Famer and longtime Grand Ole Opry member Little Jimmy Dickens' first country hit, 1949's "Take an Old Cold Tater (And Wait)" typifies his output in the minds of most country fans; novelty hits "A-Sleepin' at the Foot of the Bed," and 1965's smash "May the Bird of Paradise Fly up Your Nose," (#1 Country, #15 Pop) have combined with his 4'11" stature to obscure his importance as a first-rate country balladeer and honky-tonker who has made excellent records for more than 50 years. Dickens' gems include such wonderful "heart" songs as "Pennies for Poppa," "My Heart's Bouquet," "We Could," "The Violet and the Rose," and "I've Just Got to See You Once More," and barroom boogies like "I've Got a Hole in My Pocket" and "Hillbilly Fever."

what to buy: *I'm Little but I'm Loud: The Jimmy Dickens Collec-*

tion (Razor & Tie, 1996, prod. Don Law, Harry Silverstein) ✎✎✎✎ is the best overview of Dicken's lengthy career, containing most of his hits, quality non-hits, and good notes.

what to buy next: Decidedly minimalist packaging (no dates, session info, or liner notes) can't obscure the fact that *"Little" Jimmy Dickens: Country Giant* (Sony Special Products, 1995) ✎✎✎✎, a budget reissue of 10 of the little giant's mostly novelty hits, is a good buy.

the rest:
Take an Old Cold Tater & Wait (Richmond, 1988) ✎✎
Straight ... from the Heart, 1949–1955 (Rounder, 1989) ✎✎✎✎

worth searching for: *Columbia Historical Edition* (Columbia, 1984) ✎✎✎✎ contains 11 of his best-known numbers, heavy on the novelties, but also including the classic "Slow Suicide," not on the Razor & Tie compilation.

influences:
▶▶ Joe Diffie

Randy Pitts

JOE DIFFIE

Born December 28, 1958, in Duncan, OK.

Joe Diffie is one of country's most unlikely looking stars, but that Regular Joe image is part of his appeal, along with his mix of quirky material and emotional power ballads. He sang in his high school gospel group and, after college, worked in an iron foundry before moving to Nashville to write songs and sing demos. Holly Dunn took his "There Goes My Heart Again" into the Top 5 in 1989, and a year later he signed with Epic. Each of the first four tracks on his debut album, *A Thousand Winding Roads* reached the #1 or #2 positions on *Billboard*'s Top Country Singles chart, and he made his first Grand Ole Opry appearance in 1991. Two years later, he became the cast's 71st member. Since then, Diffie's continued to distinguish himself with slightly off-the-wall material boasting such memorable titles as "Third Rock from the Sun" and "Bigger than the Beatles." He received a Grammy nomination for "Not Too Much to Ask," his duet with Mary Chapin Carpenter that appeared on her *Come On, Come On* album.

what to buy: *Honky Tonk Attitude* (Epic, 1993, prod. Johnny Slate) ✎✎✎✎, Diffie's third album, smartly captures the range of the singer's emotional sincerity and wacky humor. It's best exemplified in the three-and-a-half-minute "Prop Me Up Beside the Jukebox (If I Die)," which starts out as a mournful ballad and winds up with a rowdy barroom singalong. The album also includes the classic blue-collar love ode "John Deere Green" and Diffie's poignant version of "If I Had Any Pride Left at All," a big hit for John Berry in 1996.

what to buy next: *Third Rock from the Sun* (Epic, 1994, prod. Johnny Slate, Joe Diffie) ⱭⱭⱭ includes the sit-com-silly title track as well as "I'd Like to Have a Problem Like That," the poignant reflection of a Regular Joe wishing he had the tribulations of the rich and famous.

the rest:
A Thousand Winding Roads (Epic, 1990) ⱭⱭⱭ
Regular Joe (Epic, 1992) ⱭⱭⱭ
Mr. Christmas (Epic, 1995) ⱭⱭⱭ
Life's So Funny (Epic, 1995) ⱭⱭⱭ
Twice Upon a Time (Epic, 1997) ⱭⱭⱭ

influences:
◀◀ George Jones, Merle Haggard
▶▶ Doug Stone, Tim McGraw

David Sokol

THE DILLARDS

Formed c. 1962, in Salem, MO.

Doug Dillard, banjo, vocals (1963–68); Rodney Dillard, guitar, vocals; Dean Webb, mandolin, vocals; Mitch Jayne, bass, vocals; Herb Pedersen, banjo, vocals (1969–72); Billy Ray Lathum, banjo, vocals (1972–79); Steve Cooley, banjo.

Formed by two Illinois-born brothers, Doug and Rodney Dillard, the Dillards were a bona fide bluegrass band that borrowed the best of the folk-rock sound of the mid-1960s. The result was an ear-pleasing amalgam of corn-pone humor, greased-lightning soloing and pristine, country harmonizing (and a stint as the fictitious Darling Family on *The Andy Griffith Show*. In 1963 the group signed with Elektra and released *Backporch Bluegrass*, which included a smokin' version of "Duelin' Banjos" 10 years before *Deliverance*. That release was followed by *Live—Almost* in 1964 and *Pickin' and Fiddlin'* in 1965. Doug left the band in 1968 to start a group with former-Byrd Gene Clark and was replaced by banjoist Herb Pedersen. The band then cut *Wheatstraw Suite*—a landmark country-rock album that displayed some fiery playing and stunning vocal harmonies, especially on the Beatles' acoustic gem "I've Just Seen a Face" and the original composition "Nobody Knows." The band continued to push the bluegrass-country-rock envelope even further with its next release, *Copperfields*. Two mediocre albums appeared during the early 1970s—

Roots and Branches and *Tribute to the American Duck*—before the band packed it in. But only for a while. In 1979 the Dillards regrouped in Salem, Missouri for a reunion concert that was captured on tape and released by Flying Fish two years later.

what to buy: *There Is a Time: The Best of the Dillards 1963–1970* (Sierra, 1995, prod. Herb Pedersen, Rodney Dillard) ⱭⱭⱭⱭ contains the best of the Elektra years, from *Back Porch Bluegrass* to *Copperfields*. This is a must for any serious bluegrass and county-rock history buff.

what to buy next: *Homecoming and Family Reunion* (Flying Fish, 1981, prod. Herb Pedersen) ⱭⱭⱭⱭ features highlights from the historic August 1979 concert in Salem, MO, including "Old Joe Clark," "Ebo Walker" and "Tennessee Breakdown."

the rest:
Let It Fly (Vanguard, 1990) ⱭⱭⱭ
Take Me Along for the Ride (Vanguard, 1992) ⱭⱭⱭ

worth searching for: *The Fantastic Expedition of Dillard and Clark* (Edsel, 1990, prod. Henry Lewy) ⱭⱭⱭⱭ was originally released by A&M Records in 1969 and is a groundbreaking country-rock record that features Doug's sophisticated banjo playing and former-Byrd Gene Clark's wonderfully warm singing.

solo outings:
Doug Dillard:
(With Bernie Leadon, John Hartford and Gene Clark) *The Banjo Album* (Sierra, 1980) ⱭⱭⱭ
What's That (Flying Fish, 1986) ⱭⱭⱭ
Heartbreak Hotel (Flying Fish, 1989) ⱭⱭⱭⱭ
(With Rodney Dillard and Hartford) *Glitter-Grass/Permanent Wave* (Flying Fish, 1994) ⱭⱭⱭⱭ

Rodney Dillard:
Rodney Dillard at Silver Dollar City (Flying Fish, 1985) ⱭⱭⱭ
Let the Rough Side Drag (Flying Fish, 1992) ⱭⱭⱭ

influences:
◀◀ Flatt & Scruggs, Bill Monroe & His Blue Grass Boys
▶▶ Byrds, Flying Burrito Brothers, Eagles, Poco

Rick Petreycik

THE DIXIE CHICKS

Formed April 1989, in Dallas, TX.

Emily Erwin, dobro, banjo, rhythm guitar, vocals; Martie Seidel, fiddle, mandolin, vocals; Robin Macy, vocals, rhythm guitar (1989–92); Laura Lynch, vocals, upright bass (1989–95); Natalie Maines, vocals (1995–present).

The original concept for Dallas' Dixie Chicks was a stroke of genius—four female singer/songwriters and multi-instrumentalists with a penchant for conveying the peaceful yet picturesque quality of the Old West. It worked swingingly for the quartet's first two locally produced CDs, 1990's *Thank Heavens for Dale Evans* and 1992's *Little Ol' Cowgirl*. Working from its bluegrass base—banjo and mandolin figured prominently on those albums—the Dixie Chicks recorded Western songs, country classics and a few revamped pop and soul nuggets. Sam Cooke's "You Send Me" is a totally different song on *Little Ol' Cowgirl*. Patsy Montana's "I Want to Be a Cowboy's Sweetheart" is a wonderful part of *Thank Heavens for Dale Evans*. A few originals—particularly the haunting "Aunt Mattie's Quilt" and the sassy "Pink Toenails"—helped make them more than just a covers band. The package, though, was the Chicks' most irresistible selling point: picture four attractive women dressed in frilly Western wear, singing flawless four-part harmony and playing their fingers numb. Alas, internal strife took its toll on this ensemble by the middle of 1992. Robin Macy, who had done the bulk of the songwriting, rejected the new, slicker country-pop direction and exited in August. Down to a trio, the Chicks recorded another album, 1993's *Shouldn't a Told You That*, which presented a more commercial version of the original sound; essentially, the Chicks were trying to attract major label interest in Nashville. By the end of 1995 lead vocalist Laura Lynch was also gone, her departure shrouded in a myriad of rumors that she was booted out. Enter fresh-faced singer Natalie Maines, who radically changed the image of the group. Now, the Dixie Chicks is a trio of fresh-faced blondes dressed in 1990s clothing.

what to buy: *Thank Heavens for Dale Evans* (Crystal Clear Sound Distribution, 1990, prod. Dixie Chicks) 𝄢𝄢𝄢 distinctly draws the Chicks' musical concept. Such instrumental *tours de force* as "Brilliancy" and "Salty" work seamlessly with gorgeous ballads ("West Texas Wind"), smart Western rave-ups (the title cut) and the requisite country tune ("The Cowboy Lives Forever"). A true treat for the senses.

the rest:
Little Ol' Cowgirl (Crystal Clear Sound Distribution, 1992) 𝄢𝄢𝄢𝄢
Shouldn't a Told You That (Crystal Clear Sound Distribution, 1993) 𝄢𝄢𝄢𝄢

worth searching for: A few years back, the Chicks recorded a holiday season 7" vinyl single titled "Christmas Swing" b/w "The Flip Side." Erwin claims the song is so embarrassing they would rather keep it stacked on a shelf somewhere locked away. But should anyone want to pry a copy from the trio's hands, write a convincing letter to Dixie Chicks, 1450 Preston Forest Square, Suite 212, Dallas, TX 75230.

influences:
◀◀ Patsy Montana, Dale Evans, Forester Sisters
▶▶ Ranch Romance, Burns Sisters

Mario Tarradell

DERYL DODD

Born in April 1964, in Dallas, TX.

Judging from the album cover, Deryl Dodd looks more like he stepped off a Hollywood set than a Texas ranch. But look a little closer and you'll see that this guy is the real deal: he was born in a small town, the grandson of two Texas Pentecostal preachers. His mom, dad and uncle performed in a trio on the weekends, and Deryl took to music early. He began playing guitar at seven, banjo at 13 and pedal steel at 16. Yet, while he seemed to take to just about any stringed instrument, music was not Dodd's first career choice. He was a star football player in high school and planned to play college ball—until an injury sidelined him and he began to take his music seriously. Dodd began singing at a local club during his college years at Baylor University, and soon formed an in-demand club band in Dallas. Yet, even though he was a big shot in Dallas, Dodd knew he needed to move to Nashville if he really wanted to give it a shot. He did, and soon landed a job as a sideman in Martina McBride's band. He also continued to hone his songwriting, which led to his first record deal.

what's available: Dodd wrote or co-wrote eight of the songs on his traditional debut, *One Ride in Vegas* (Columbia, 1996, prod. Chip Young, Blake Chancey) 𝄢𝄢𝄢, which never strays far from honky-tonk themes. The standout is the title track, Dodd's haunting tale of the pull of the rodeo life.

influences:
◀◀ Radney Foster, George Strait, Tom T. Hall

Cyndi Hoelzle

MICHAEL DOUCET

See: Beausoleil

DOUGLAS, BARENBERG & MEYER

See: Jerry Douglas

JERRY DOUGLAS /DOUGLAS, BARENBERG & MEYER

Born May 28, 1956, in Warren, OH.

The undisputed master of the dobro resophonic guitar, Jerry Douglas first established his reputation in bluegrass, joining the Country Gentlemen in 1974 and later playing with both J.D. Crowe & the New South and Boone Creek, a band Douglas formed with Ricky Skaggs. Douglas became an in-demand session musician after moving to Nashville in 1979 to work with the Whites. Since leaving that band in 1986, he has worked in an astonishing array of formats and contexts, performing and recording with bands (The Bluegrass Album Band, Strength in Numbers and Douglas, Barenberg & Meyer), in duets with artists ranging from Peter Rowan to Vishwa Mohan Bhatt, on his own recordings and as a guest artist on literally hundreds (if not thousands) of albums by such artists as Paul Simon, James Taylor, the Nashville Bluegrass Band and Red Knuckles & the Trailblazers. Among Douglas' other career highlights are a stint in the house band on TNN's acclaimed *American Music Shop* series, several Grammy awards as an artist and producer (Alison Krauss, the Nashville Bluegrass Band), five International Bluegrass Music Association Dobro Player of the Year awards and enough other industry awards to stock a trophy shop.

what to buy: *The Great Dobro Sessions* (Sugar Hill, 1994, prod. Jerry Douglas, Tut Taylor) ✍✍✍✍, which won the Grammy for Best Bluegrass Recording in 1994, gathers 10 top dobro players for the most ambitious recorded survey of a single instrument in bluegrass history. Among the dobroists joining Douglas are Josh Graves, Mike Auldridge, Sally Van Meter and Rob Ickes. Douglas is featured on two cuts, the modern jazz standard "Birdland" and a solo "Abilene Gal." Douglas, Barenberg, & Meyer's *Skip, Hop & Wobble* (Sugar Hill, 1993, prod. Russ Barenberg, Jerry Douglas and Edgar Meyer) ✍✍✍✍ combines Douglas with guitarist Russ Barenberg and renowned bassist Edgar Meyer for an all-instrumental album of virtuoso music that's as accessible and enjoyable as it is challenging. Guest Sam Bush takes "Big Sciota" pretty close to bluegrass, but other highlights ("Big Bug Shuffle," "From Ankara to Izmir," "The Years Between") straddle genres with abandon and fiery aplomb. *Slide Rule* (Sugar Hill, 1992, prod. Jerry Douglas) ✍✍✍✍, described by Douglas as his return to "entertaining" music, made a big splash thanks to heavy airplay for cuts featuring guest vocalists Krauss ("I Don't Believe

You've Met My Baby"), Tim O'Brien ("Hey Joe") and the Brother Boys ("Pearlie Mae"). The solo "A New Day Medley" is Douglas at his best, though full-band cuts on "Ride the Wild Turkey," "Shenandoah Breakdown" and "Shoulder to Shoulder" aren't far behind.

what to buy next: *Under the Wire* (Sugar Hill, 1995, prod. Jerry Douglas) ✍✍✍✍, the first of a series of self-described non-entertaining (i.e., "art") albums Douglas recorded for MCA, is actually a very entertaining collection of tunes, most of them Douglas originals. "Two Friends," a duet with Bela Fleck, is a highlight, as are the tunes "Grant's Corner," "Redhill" and "T.O.B." *Everything Is Gonna Work Out Fine* (Rounder, 1989, prod. Jerry Douglas) ✍✍✍, a 19-track reissue drawn from his two Rounder albums (*Fluxology* and *Fluxedo*), presents Douglas in a more bluegrass-oriented setting than many of his later recordings. Guests such as Ricky Skaggs and Tony Rice add strong support on such standout cuts as "Randy Lynn Rag," "Dixie Hoedown" and "Wheel Hoss." Dreadful Snakes' *Snakes Alive* (Rounder, 1984) ✍✍✍ is a one-time supergroup project featuring Douglas, Bela Fleck, Pat Enright, Blaine Sprouse, Roland White and Mark Hambree.

the rest:

Fluxology (Rounder, 1979) ✍✍✍
Fluxedo (Rounder, 1982) ✍✍✍
(With the Bluegrass Album Band) *V. 6, The Bluegrass Album Band* (Rounder) ✍✍✍
(With Vishwa Mohan Bhatt) *Bourbon & Rosewater* (Water Lily Acoustics) ✍✍✍✍
(With Peter Rowan) *Yonder* (Sugar Hill, 1996) ✍✍✍

influences:

◀◀ Josh Graves, Mike Auldridge
▶▶ Rob Ickes, Kim Gardner

Jon Hartley Fox

PETE DRAKE

Born August 8, 1932, in Atlanta, GA. Died July 29, 1988.

A Hal Blaine of the country world, steel man Pete Drake became among the most sought-after session men in the business—and, like Blaine, nearly everything he played on for a time during the 1960s turned into a hit (including his own "Forever," a Top 30 back in 1964). When country began to infiltrate pop music during the late 1960s, Drake was there to add his bits to the likes of Bob Dylan's *Nashville Skyline* and George Harrison's opus *All Things Must Pass*. He also spent a fair amount of time on the other side of the talk-back, producing sessions for B.J. Thomas, Melba Montgomery and others.

worth searching for: Drake devoted a good chunk of studio time to numerous projects of his own, none of which remain in print. For the curious, though, *Amazing and Incredible Pete Drake* (Smash, 1964, prod. Pete Drake) 🎵🎵🎵 shows what Drake was capable of during his heyday, as well as containing his own renditions of the tunes he helped make famous on *Hits I Played On* (Smash, 1969, prod. Pete Drake) 🎵🎵🎵.

influences:
◀◀ Speedy West, Herbie Remington
▶▶ Rusty Young, Jerry Garcia

David Simons

DREADFUL SNAKES

See: Jerry Douglas

ROY DRUSKY

Born June 22, 1930, in Atlanta, GA.

Like many singers of his era, Roy Drusky came to record-making from radio. Though early in his life he was interested in professional sports and veterinary medicine, he learned to play guitar while in the Navy. He helped pay for his schooling by forming the Southern Ranch Boys, and later worked as a DJ in Decatur, Georgia and Minneapolis, Minnesota while playing in local clubs. In 1958 Faron Young's version of Drusky's "Alone with You" reached the top of the chart, and Drusky moved to Nashville and joined the Grand Ole Opry. He had his first charting single two years later with "Alone" and continued having hits through 1977, mostly for Decca and Mercury. Not only a singer, Drusky has written songs and produced records for other acts, has run his own publishing company and briefly headed the Nashville office of the performing-rights organization SESAC.

what to buy: Of Drusky's 42 charting singles, all but 13 of them came for Mercury Records between 1962 and 1973. *Songs of Love and Life* (Mercury, 1995, prod. Jerry Kennedy, compilation prod. Christine Ferreira) 🎵🎵🎵 includes the best-known of these, including the goofy "Peel Me a 'Nanner" and his sole #1, a shattering song about infidelity called "Yes, Mr. Peters." But the collection ignores lesser hits like Drusky's smooth-as-silk renditions of such standards as "Make the World Go Away" and "She Thinks I Still Care."

what to buy next: *Greatest Hits Volume 1* (Sun, 1980) 🎵🎵🎵 has considerable overlap with *Songs of Love and Life*, but it does contain one of Drusky's better records, "Three Hearts in a Tangle."

what to avoid: *16 Best of Roy Drusky* (Plantation, 1987) 🎵🎵 is a collection of remakes and inferior newer material.

influences:
◀◀ Jim Reeves, Bill Anderson
▶▶ Lee Greenwood, T.G. Sheppard

Brian Mansfield

DRY BRANCH FIRE SQUAD

Formed 1976, in Springfield, OH.

Current line-up features: Ron Thomason, mandolin, guitar, vocals; Suzanne Thomas, guitar, clawhammer banjo, vocals; Mary Jo Leet, guitar, vocals; Charlie Leet, bass, vocals; Bill Evans, banjo, vocals. Past members have included Dave Edmundson, guitar, fiddle, vocals; Dick Ervin, bass, vocals; John Hisey, banjo, vocals; Dan Russell, banjo, vocals; John Lee Baker, guitar, vocals.

A favorite attraction at bluegrass festivals for 20 years, Dry Branch Fire Squad is perhaps best known for the extemporaneous ramblings of their leader Ron Thomason during live shows. Not to be ignored as highly skilled musicians, however, their recorded output has included some mighty fine bluegrass. Thomason, the only remaining original member of the band, was mandolin player for Ralph Stanley for roughly a year in 1971, then joined Lee Allen and the Dew Mountain Boys for four years before forming DBFS. Their most recent album captures the band at its best.

what to buy: *Live! At Last* (Rounder, 1996, prod. Ken Irwin, Dry Branch Fire Squad) 🎵🎵🎵🎵 includes Ron Thomason's amusing (if mostly pointless!) introductions of band members, and of the songs fans have enjoyed for years. His duets with Thomas, including "We Believe in Happy Endings," are particularly good.

what to buy next: *Long Journey* (Rounder, 1991, prod. Ken Irwin) 🎵🎵🎵🎵 is the best studio record the band has yet recorded, the remainder of them lacking its cohesiveness and style.

the rest:
Tried & True (Rounder, 1987) 🎵🎵🎵
Fertile Ground (Rounder, 1989) 🎵🎵🎵
Just for the Record (Rounder, 1993) 🎵🎵🎵🎵

influences:

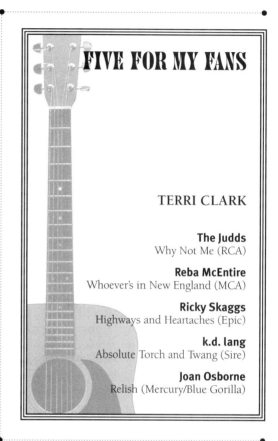

Ralph Stanley, Molly O'Day

Stephen L. Betts

GEORGE DUCAS

Born August 1, 1966, in Texas City, TX.

George Ducas has a handsome face half-hidden underneath that cowboy hat, which, in Nashville, is certainly a start. But in these video-driven days of countless hatted hunks, that attribute alone could make Ducas, in the words of one of his own songs, the "Invisible Man." That's not likely to happen, though, for Ducas' talent is real, his voice pleasant, and, importantly, he has proven writing ability (Ducas co-wrote Radney Foster's hit "Just Call Me Lonesome," as well as the lion's share of the songs on his own two albums). Ducas draws in large part on the music of the 1950s and early 1960s, especially country-inflected Texas pop and the Bakersfield sound. Like most new country acts, though, he knocks the hard edges off his source material, rocking it up a bit here, lounging amid washes of strings there. But Ducas is an act with a lot of potential and he's just one career-defining hit away from stardom.

what's available: Considering he's still a relative newcomer, Ducas' first two albums, *George Ducas* (Liberty, 1994, prod. Richard Bennett) 𝄇𝄇𝄇 and *Where I Stand* (Capitol, 1996, prod. Richard Bennett) 𝄇𝄇𝄇 are of surprisingly consistent—and consistently high—quality. Lyrically, Ducas' chief topic is heartbreak, while his musical reference points are Roy Orbison, Buddy Holly, and Buck Owens, each of whom could be considered an alternative-country emeritus act whose sound has become today's mainstream. But if "Lipstick Promises" and "Teardrops" (from *George Ducas*) or "Every Time She Passes By" and "You're Only My Everything" don't quite compare favorably to "Only the Lonely" or "Everyday," they'll at least convince you to give Ducas another crack at topping them. And with first-rate producer Richard Bennett adding wonderfully nostalgic retro touches to Ducas' tearful anthems, he may get there yet.

influences:

Roy Orbison, Willie Nelson, Dwight Yoakam, Buck Owens, Buddy Holly

Gary Allan, Ray Vega, Kim Richey

Daniel Durchholz

DAVE DUDLEY

Born David Pedruska, May 3, 1928, in Spencer, WI.

FIVE FOR MY FANS

TERRI CLARK

The Judds
Why Not Me (RCA)

Reba McEntire
Whoever's in New England (MCA)

Ricky Skaggs
Highways and Heartaches (Epic)

k.d. lang
Absolute Torch and Twang (Sire)

Joan Osborne
Relish (Mercury/Blue Gorilla)

Truck-driving songs had been a part of country music since Ted Daffan wrote "Truck Driver's Blues" in 1939, but Dave Dudley turned them into an art form. With a seemingly bottomless voice that conjured images of semi's barreling down the interstate, the former DJ and semi-pro baseball player rolled into the upper reaches of the country singles chart in 1963 with "Six Days on the Road," which inspired dozens of similar songs throughout the 1960s and early 1970s. Dudley had another 30 Top 40 singles after that, many of them truck-themed, including "Truck Drivin' Son-of-a-Gun," "Trucker's Prayer" and "One More Mile." He had charting hits for Vee, Jubilee, Golden Wing (the label for "Six Days") and United Artists, but most of his hits came for Mercury between 1963 and 1973.

what to buy: Dudley could stand a good reissue of his Mercury hits, but until then *Trucker Classics* (Sun, 1996, prod. Shelby S. Singleton Jr.) 𝄇𝄇 will have to do since it's on CD. Even though it's a collection of remakes, assorted trucking songs and non-hits, the songs and Dudley's rumbling bass voice are still entertaining.

what to buy next: *Best of the Trucks* (Richmond, 1985) ♫♫ is a cassette collection that at least has some different versions of the same songs.

what to avoid: When traveling, never buy more than one of the truck-stop cassette compilations on either Sun or Plantation. They're all repackages of the same remakes.

the rest:
Interstate Gold (Sun, 1980) ♫♫
Greatest Hits Volume 1 (Plantation, 1980) ♫♫
20 Truck Driver Favorites (Plantation, 1983) ♫♫
Six Days on the Road (Plantation, 1986) ♫♫
16 Best of Dave Dudley (Plantation, 1987) ♫♫
16 Greatest Hits (Plantation, 1987) ♫♫

influences:
◀◀ Red Sovine, Ted Daffan
▶▶ Dick Curless, Red Simpson

Brian Mansfield

STUART DUNCAN
Born April 14, 1964, in Quantico, VA.

Stuart Duncan is the fiddle player in the much-honored Nashville Bluegrass Band; he is also virtually everyone's favorite bluegrass fiddler these days, and is consequently the first call guy for most bluegrass and a lot of mainstream country sessions. He first gained widespread attention laying and recording in southern California with fellow-prodigy, banjo player Alison Brown as a pre-teen. He also logged time with the popular Southern California bluegrass band Lost Highway before taking Nashville by storm.

what's available: *Stuart Duncan* (Rounder, 1992, prod. Bela Fleck) ♫♫♫♫ is this fabulous fiddler's sole available effort as a leader, and it shows off his beautiful tone, control, articulation and imagination to great effect on a mixture of traditional fiddle tunes and Duncan originals.

influences:
◀◀ Chubby Wise, Byron Berline, Mark O'Connor
▶▶ Chris Thile

see also: *Nashville Bluegrass Band*

Randy Pitts

HOLLY DUNN
Born August 22, 1957, in San Antonio, TX.

The country music industry has yet to fully appreciate Holly Dunn's artistry. While she doesn't have a show-stopping voice, her sparkling soprano always rings authentic. Her background as a folk stylist with the Freedom Folk Singers during the mid-1970s and her Abiline Christian University education add subtle shades to her mountain-pure timbre. As a songwriter, Dunn, with the frequent help of brother Chris Waters, crafts thoughtful country songs with hints of pop, folk and gospel. Her professional recording career began during the mid-1980s on the now-defunct MTM Records label. Although small, MTM was able to establish Dunn as a hit-making act, particularly during her string of Top 10 tunes from 1986–89. She even nabbed the Country Music Association's Horizon Award in 1987. But MTM had only so much muscle—it made her a radio presence but failed to help her carve a durable identity. Switching to Warner Bros. in 1989 seemed like a great idea at the time, especially since so many of her compatriots at MTM found themselves in the vast, label-less wasteland after the imprint's demise. But Warner Bros.' early commitment to Dunn waned by her third album, and she exited the label at the end of 1992. After a self-imposed break from the biz, Dunn resurfaced in 1995 on the PolyGram-distributed River North Nashville and recorded the worthy *Life and Love and All the Stages*. Radio ignored it. She can now be found co-hosting a morning radio show in Detroit, though she continues to record.

what to buy: *Milestones—Greatest Hits* (Warner Bros., 1991, prod. various) ♫♫♫ culls her Warner Bros. hits, such as the rocking "You Really Had Me Going" and even includes the bittersweet album cut, "No One Takes the Train Anymore." It also features her big MTM songs, the best of which is the warm "Daddy's Hands," a song Dunn wrote as a Father's Day gift to her dad.

the rest:
Life and Love and All the Stages (River North Nashville, 1995) ♫♫♫
Leave One Bridge Standing (River North Nashville, 1997) ♫♫♫

worth searching for: All of Dunn's MTM albums were once available on CD, but it's her debut, *Holly Dunn* (MTM, 1986, prod. Tommy West) ♫♫♫, that's worth finding. While a bit too thematically innocent, *Holly Dunn* presents an artist who makes singing and songwriting sound really easy. Of her Warner Bros. output, the cleverly titled *Getting It Dunn* (Warner Bros., 1992, prod. Holly Dunn, Paul Worley, Ed Seay) ♫♫♫ showcases a more mature Dunn ready to vamp in seductive country-blues numbers then turn gentle in tender love songs.

influences:

◄◄ Brenda Lee, Deborah Allen

►► Judy Rodman, Girls Next Door

Mario Tarradell

BOB DYLAN

Born Robert Allen Zimmerman, May 24, 1941, in Duluth, MN.

No single songwriter since Hank Williams—save perhaps Harlan Howard—revolutionized Nashville more than Bob Dylan. His sweeping influence in the rock field has long been acknowledged, but Dylan isn't usually the first artist that comes to mind when people think about the dismantling of the Nashville establishment. But he struck a nerve in country songwriters that continues to this day. Of course, the country roots in Dylan's own music have long been ignored in favor of the Woody Guthrie connection that comfortably keeps his work within a stricter context. But the strains of early bluegrass harmonies, not to mention some of the Elizabethan lyricism, suffuse Dylan's early recordings, and he continues to toss off country standards during his live performances to this day. But even more, Dylan's casually sculpted lyrical touch, his phrase-twisting command of the vernacular, infected an entire generation of country songwriters, including Kris Kristofferson, who at least served an honest apprenticeship as janitor during the *Blonde on Blonde* recording sessions. Dylan's own songs continue to thrive in the repertoires of countless country singers. His association with country music's then-reigning star, Johnny Cash, signified the approval of the Nashville establishment. The pair recorded an album's worth of duets, although only "Girl From the North Country" surfaced on *Nashville Skyline* and Dylan made a crucial guest appearance on Cash's popular TV program.

what to buy: When Dylan came to Nashville to record what is arguably his masterpiece, *Blonde on Blonde* (Columbia, 1966, prod. Bob Johnston) ♪♪♪♪, he broke the mold at the onset, mixing established Nashville sidemen like Charlie McCoy and such young turks as Joe South and Charlie Daniels with members of his own backup band.

what to buy next: His two subsequent Nashville albums, *John Wesley Harding* (Columbia 1968, prod. Bob Johnston) ♪♪♪♫ and *Nashville Skyline* (Columbia 1969, prod. Bob Johnston) ♪♪♪♪, drew the association even more sharply, with Dylan leaning away from the blues-rock of his early Nashville sessions and moving increasingly toward a new folky country sound.

Bob Dylan (© Ken Settle)

what to avoid: *Dylan and the Dead* (Columbia, 1989) ♪ is the weakest entry among the scattershot plethora of live albums Dylan has released over the years.

the rest:

Bob Dylan (Columbia, 1962) ♪♪♪

The Freewheelin' Bob Dylan (Columbia, 1963) ♪♪♪

The Times They Are A-Changin' (Columbia, 1964) ♪♪♪

Another Side of Bob Dylan (Columbia, 1964) ♪♪♪♪

Bringin' It All Back Home (Columbia, 1965) ♪♪♪♪

Highway 61 Revisited (Columbia, 1965) ♪♪♪♪♪

Bob Dylan's Greatest Hits (Columbia, 1967) ♪♪♪

Self Portrait (Columbia, 1970) ♪♪♪♪

New Morning (Columbia, 1970) ♪♪♪

Bob Dylan's Greatest Hits Volume II (Columbia, 1971) ♪♪♪♫

Dylan (Columbia, 1973) ♪♪

Planet Waves (Asylum, 1974) ♪♪♪

Before the Flood (Asylum, 1974) ♪♪♪♪

Blood on the Tracks (Columbia, 1975) ♪♪♪♫

The Basement Tapes (Columbia, 1975) ♪♪♪♪

Desire (Columbia, 1976) ♪♪♪♫

Hard Rain (Columbia, 1976) 🎵🎵
Street Legal (Columbia, 1978) 🎵🎵🎵
Slow Train Coming (Columbia, 1979) 🎵🎵🎵
At Budokan (Columbia, 1979) 🎵🎵🎵🎵
Saved (Columbia, 1979) 🎵🎵🎵🎵
Shot of Love (Columbia, 1981) 🎵🎵🎵
Infidels (Columbia, 1983) 🎵🎵
Real Live (Columbia, 1984) 🎵🎵
Empire Burlesque (Columbia, 1985) 🎵🎵
Biograph (Columbia, 1985) 🎵🎵🎵
Knocked Out Loaded (Columbia, 1986) 🎵🎵🎵
Down in the Groove (Columbia, 1988) 🎵🎵
Oh Mercy (Columbia, 1989) 🎵🎵🎵
Under the Red Sky (Columbia, 1990) 🎵🎵🎵
Bootleg Series Volumes 1–3 (Columbia, 1991) 🎵🎵🎵🎵
Good As I Been to You (Columbia, 1992) 🎵🎵🎵🎵
World Gone Wrong (Columbia, 1993) 🎵🎵🎵🎵
Bob Dylan's Greatest Hits Volume III (Columbia, 1994) 🎵🎵🎵
MTV Unplugged (Columbia, 1995) 🎵🎵🎵🎵

worth searching for: *Forever Young* (Columbia, 1988, prod. various) 🎵🎵🎵🎵, an 18-song collection distributed to radio stations to promote the incidental "Silvio," the single from his indifferent *Down in the Groove* album, contains 17 other certified classics.

influences:

⏪ Woody Guthrie, Bill Monroe, Mississippi John Hurt

⏩ Johnny Cash, Kris Kristofferson, Willie Nelson

Joel Selvin

THE EAGLES

Formed 1971, in Los Angeles, CA. Disbanded 1981. Reunited 1994.

Glenn Frey, vocals, guitars, keyboards; Don Henley, vocals, drums; Randy Meisner, bass, vocals (1971–77); Bernie Leadon, guitar, banjo, mandolin, vocals (1971–76); Joe Walsh, guitar, vocals (1976–present); Don Felder, guitar, vocals (1974–present); Timothy B. Schmit, bass, vocals (1977–present).

Building their musical prowess in Los Angeles' fertile country-rock community during the late 1960s, the Eagles first came together in 1970 as the backing band for Linda Ronstadt's *Silk Purse* album; individually, the musicians had already played with the Flying Burrito Brothers, Poco, Rick Nelson's Stone Canyon Band and Bob Seger. But the Eagles' sound—smooth harmonies and polished, twangy arrangements—would define Southern California rock during the coming decade. As time went on, the sound became progressively more rock-oriented, and by the time they rolled out the groundbreaking *Hotel California* album in 1976, Henley and Frey had become astute social commentators—despite a bit of cynicism that lent a nasty edge to some of their songs. Always too serious, the Eagles succumbed to the pressures of success and called it quits in 1981. But the 1993 release of *Common Thread*, a tribute album featuring country stars doing Eagles songs, spurred the group to soar again—particularly after Travis Tritt reunited them to appear in the video for his version of "Take it Easy." Since then the Eagles have made a zillion dollars (or thereabouts) on the road, though the reunion has yet to produce any new material of note.

what to buy: A little inconsistent during their early years, the Eagles are best served by *Their Greatest Hits, 1971–1975* (Asylum, 1975, prod. Glyn Johns, Bill Szymczyk) 🎵🎵🎵🎵, an awesome collection of singles—from the hot picking of "Take It Easy" to the smooth pop polish of "One of These Nights"—that established the band as one of the top groups of the time.

what to buy next: *One of These Nights* (Asylum, 1975, prod. Bill Szymczyk) 🎵🎵🎵 is the apex of the Eagles' twang time with some truly gorgeous moments in "Lyin' Eyes" and "Take It to the Limit."

what to avoid: *Desperado* (Asylum, 1973, prod. Glyn Johns) 🎵🎵 is a misbegotten concept album about the Southwest whose best songs can be found on *Their Greatest Hits*.

the rest:
Eagles (Asylum, 1972) 🎵🎵🎵
On the Border (Asylum, 1974) 🎵🎵🎵
Hotel California (Asylum, 1976) 🎵🎵🎵🎵🎵
The Long Run (Asylum, 1979) 🎵🎵🎵🎵
Live (Asylum, 1980) 🎵🎵🎵
Greatest Hits, Volume 2 (Asylum, 1982) 🎵🎵🎵🎵
Hell Freezes Over (Geffen, 1994) 🎵🎵🎵

worth searching for: *Peaceful Easy Feeling* (Cuttlefish) is one of many bootleg recordings of a landmark 1974 show at New York's Bottom Line, at which Ronstadt and Jackson Browne joined the Eagles for a rendition of "Take It Easy." Recommended.

solo outings:
Glenn Frey:
No Fun Aloud (Asylum, 1982) 🎵🎵🎵

Best of (MCA, 1995) 🎵🎵🎵

Don Henley: 🎵🎵🎵
I Can't Stand Still (Asylum, 1982) 🎵🎵🎵
Building the Perfect Beast (Geffen, 1984) 🎵🎵🎵🎵
The End of the Innocence (Geffen, 1989) 🎵🎵🎵🎵
Actual Miles: Don Henley's Greatest Hits (Geffen, 1995) 🎵🎵🎵🎵

Joe Walsh:
(With Barnstorm) *The Smoker You Drink, the Player You Get* (ABC/Dunhill, 1973) 🎵🎵🎵
Look What I Did: The Joe Walsh Anthology (MCA, 1995) 🎵🎵🎵🎵

influences:

◀◀ Byrds, Gram Parsons, Beatles, Everly Brothers, Hank Williams, Louvin Brothers

▶▶ Travis Tritt, Restless Heart, Garth Brooks, Mavericks, Gin Blossoms, Uncle Tupelo, Jayhawks, Vince Gill, Judds

see also: *Flying Burrito Brothers, Rick Nelson, Poco, Linda Rondstadt*

Gary Graff

Don Henley of the Eagles (© Ken Settle)

influences:
◀◀ Bob Dylan, Neil Young
▶▶ Mary Chapin Carpenter, Robert Earl Keen Jr.

David Sokol

FRED EAGLESMITH

Born in Ontario, Canada.

One of nine children, Fred Eaglesmith grew up driving tractors and trucks on a southern Ontario farm. His music smartly marries the dusty town and far-off train whistle imagery of classic country music to his chilly, farm country north-of-the-border roots. The musical results are captivating, cinematic songs with a touch of humor and a folky edge. After recording several albums in Canada, he traveled to Nashville to become the first signee to the fledgling Vertical Records label.

what's available: *Drive-In Movie* (Vertical, 1996, prod. Scott Merritt, Fred Eaglesmith) 🎵🎵🎵🎵 is a beautifully coherent set of songs evoking more innocent times and happier days. But that's not to say that there isn't a fair share of humor and optimism in these sublimely catchy songs. Eaglesmith's voice can be mournful or uplifting, but it's never less than thoroughly convincing and totally inviting.

worth searching for: Fred J. Eaglesmith & the Flying Squirrels—*Things Is Changin'* (Sweetwater, 1993, prod. Scott Merritt) 🎵🎵🎵 and Fred J. Eaglesmith & the Flying Squirrels—*From the Paradise Motel* (Barbed Wire, 1994, prod. Dave Brogren) 🎵🎵🎵🎵, recorded live at the La Casa Music Series in Birmingham, Michigan, are two smartly crafted Canadian releases with living-room warmth.

JIM EANES

Born December 6, 1923, in Mountain Valley, VA. Died 1995.

Smilin' Jim Eanes celebrated 50 years in the music business in 1990; he was a prominent figure in both bluegrass and country circles, known for his smooth baritone vocal delivery and his songwriting prowess. He wrote several songs that became standards in country and bluegrass music, most notably "Missing in Action," "Your Old Standby," "Baby Blue Eyes" and "I Wouldn't Change You If I Could." He recorded prolifically for several labels from the late 1940s into the 1950s, including Capitol, Decca and Starday. Although his smooth vocal delivery was more country than bluegrass (he was a member of Bill Monroe's Blue Grass Boys briefly, but his baritone was an ill-fitting duet partner for Monroe's high tenor) and his major label recordings tended to be aimed at more mainstream audiences, Eanes did appear at many bluegrass festivals and made mostly bluegrass recordings during the later years of his career.

what's available: *Classic Bluegrass* (Rebel, 1992, prod. Gary B. Reid) ♪♪♪ is from several 1970s and 1980s Rebel sessions, including his excellent LP *50th Anniversary*, first released in 1990. He teamed with banjo player and singer Bobby Atkins on *Heart of the South* (Rural Rhythm, 1991, prod. Mike Swinson) ♪♪♪, an enjoyable collaboration that also features contributions from fiddler extraordinaire Vassar Clements and such outstanding pickers as dobro player Frank Poindexter and guitar flash Clay Jones.

worth searching for: Jim Eanes & the Shenendoah Valley Boys' *The Early Days Of Bluegrass, Volume 4* (Rounder, 1978, prod. Jack Tottle) ♪♪♪♪ hails from two 1950s sessions, featuring fine bands and outstanding Eanes vocals.

influences:

◀◀ Clyde Moody, Roy Hall

▶▶ Tony Rice, John Starling

Randy Pitts

STEVE EARLE

Born January 17, 1955, in Fort Monroe, VA.

The son of an air-traffic controller, Steve Earle infiltrated Nashville in 1986 with a twangy, hardcore-hillbilly sound filtered through the heartland rock 'n' roll of John Mellencamp and *Nebraska*-era Bruce Springsteen. Although signed to mainstream MCA Records, Earle quickly established himself as a rebel without a pause by worshipping Townes Van Zandt, covering the Rolling Stones and the Sir Douglas Quintet, opening shows for such alternative bands as the Replacements and battling cocaine and heroin addictions. Despite a string of powerful albums—capped by 1990's underrated *The Hard Way*—radio resisted the big, bad good ol' boy, and the back-to-back releases of a live album and a greatest-hits collection confirmed that even MCA had lost patience with him. But Earle has confronted and conquered his demons: now clean and sober, he released a 1996 comeback album called *I Feel Alright* that confirms the title with a hearty, hard-rocking relish. Simultaneously, such Nashville stalwarts as Travis Tritt, the Highwaymen, Gretchen Peters and Emmylou Harris are covering his songs, giving him a rare second chance for commercial redemption.

what to buy: *Guitar Town* (MCA, 1986, prod. Tony Brown, Emory Gordy Jr.) ♪♪♪♪ is an auspicious debut of small-town

frustration ("Someday") and romantic yearning ("Fearless Heart"). *The Hard Way* (MCA, 1990, prod. Steve Earle, Joe Hardy) ♪♪♪♪ slipped out when even his staunchest fans had forgotten about him, but "Promise You Anything," "The Other Kind" and "Billy Austin" are as trenchant as any songs he's recorded. *I Feel Alright* (E Squared/Warner Bros., 1996, prod. Richard Dodd, Ray Kennedy, Richard Bennett) ♪♪♪♪ finds Earle defiantly addressing his past in "Cocaine Can't Kill My Pain" and "The Unrepentant," but the brightest signs are the brash but breezy twang-pop confections "Hard-core Troubador," "More Than I Can Do" and "You're Still Standin' There" (a duet with Lucinda Williams).

what to buy next: For new fans who just discovered him via *I Feel Alright*, *Ain't Ever Satisfied: The Steve Earle Collection* (Hip-O/MCA, 1996, prod. various) ♪♪♪♪, a two-CD retrospective, renders obsolete 1993's *The Essential Steve Earle* by adding such album tracks as "Fearless Heart," "Nothing but a Child" and his promo-only live version of Springsteen's "State Trooper."

what to avoid: *Early Tracks* (Columbia, 1987, prod. Roy Dea, Pat Carter) ♪ is a hurriedly compiled collection of tepid, unreleased material designed to cash-in on Earle's *Guitar Town* accolades.

the rest:

Exit O (MCA, 1987) ♪♪♪♪

Copperhead Road (MCA, 1988) ♪♪♪

BBC Live (Windsong, 1988) ♪♪♪

Shut Up and Die Like an Aviator (MCA, 1991) ♪♪♪

Essential Steve Earle (MCA, 1993) ♪♪♪♪

Train a'Comin' (Winter Harvest, 1995/Warner Bros., 1997) ♪♪♪

worth searching for: Check out "Johnny Too Bad" (E Squared/Transatlantic, 1996, prod. Steve Earle, Ray Kennedy) ♪♪♪, a British CD single sporting a country-fried remake of reggae band the Slickers' title track, on which Earle is backed by Memphis' V-Roys.

influences:

◀◀ Townes Van Zandt, Waylon Jennings, Bruce Springsteen, Bob Dylan

▶▶ Travis Tritt, Todd Snider, Dale Watson

David Okamoto

Steve Earle (© Ken Settle)

DUANE EDDY

Born April 26, 1938, in Corning, NY.

"The Twangiest Guitar of Them All" was a red Gretsch 6120 wielded by Duane Eddy. Not well-remembered today, Eddy ruled the guitar scene of the late 1950s with his tremolo-heavy instrumentals. His shadow fell especially long in England, where a generation of young guitar players—from Hank Marvin of the Shadows to George Harrison of the Beatles—came under his spell. His records essentially came down to duets between Eddy, who scrupulously and carefully stated the melodic themes drenched in ringing, "twangy" tones, and saxophonist Steve Douglas, who replied in squawking, screeching blasts that came to define the sound of rock 'n' roll saxophone. Douglas went on to record all the solos on the famous Phil Spector records and, with King Curtis, supplied one of the two fountainheads of the instrument's rock vocabulary. The man behind the hits, producer Lee Hazlewood, parlayed his Eddy success into a career as one of Hollywood's masterful pop visionaries on records with Nancy Sinatra—work as fully realized and imaginative in scope as contemporary productions by such well-recognized *auteurs* as Spector and Brian Wilson. Eddy drifted into an uncomfortable obscurity, settling in Lake Tahoe, touring as guitarist for Italianate pop vocalist Al Martino and shunning the spotlight. Sporadic efforts to revive his career have been made—a 1976 single with then-hot Willie Nelson and Waylon Jennings providing lead vocals, a short-lived 1983 reformation of his vintage studio band with the addition of Ry Cooder on second guitar, a re-make of "Peter Gunn" in 1986 by the British dance band the Art of Noise, a 1987 album featuring help from Paul McCartney, John Fogerty, George Harrison, Steve Cropper and others. But as Eddy's contributions drift further beyond the horizon, he seems to be all the more neglected despite his work in the foundations of rock and country guitar.

what to buy: The double-disc retrospective, *Twang Thing: The Duane Eddy Anthology* (Rhino, 1993, prod. various) ♪♪♪♪♪ covers the full breadth of his career—from the earliest hits and album sides to 1980s recordings with McCartney, Harrison and Cooder.

what to buy next: Still want more? *Twangin' from Phoenix to Los Angeles* (Bear Family, 1994, prod. various) ♪♪♪♪ is a five-disc box from Europe that collects virtually the complete Jamie Records sessions and more.

what to avoid: Beware the abbreviated, cut-price collections that don't even scrape beneath the top of the surface of Eddy's remarkable body of work.

worth searching for: His debut album, *Have Twangy Guitar Will Travel* (Jamie, 1958, prod. Lee Hazlewood) ♪♪♪♪♪, is one of the keystone landmarks of modern rock guitar. Also, his comeback effort, *Duane Eddy* (EMI, 1987, prod. various) ♪♪♪♪ is not one to pass up in a cut-out bin.

influences:

◀◀ Chet Atkins, Les Paul, Jerry Byrd

▶▶ George Harrison, John Entwistle, John Fogerty, George Thorogood

Joel Selvin

JUDITH EDELMAN

Born November 14, 1964, in New York, NY.

An important new discovery in the field of acoustic music, Judith Edelman melds strong Celtic influences with progressive bluegrass instrumentation, and caps it off with some incisive songwriting. Although she began piano lessons at age five, it was a trip to Africa and a serious illness in her mid-20s that inspired her to take up the acoustic guitar. Joining the San Francisco Bay area band, Ryestraw, Judith toured with them throughout the 1980s.

what's available: *Perfect World* (Compass, 1996, prod. Bil VornDick) ♪♪♪♪ is a spectacular debut, highlighted by Edelman's cutting lyrics and the pervasive Celtic/bluegrass sound. It features virtuosi Jerry Douglas, Alison Brown and John Mock.

influences:

◀◀ Maura O'Connell, Shawn Colvin

Stephen L. Betts

DAVE EDMUNDS /ROCKPILE

Born April 15, 1943 in Cardiff, Wales.

Dave Edmunds is the quintessential musician's musician—a producer, performer, lead guitarist, sideman, frontman. He's done them all and all of them well, even if he's still a cult item to the masses. You'd never believe it from his early efforts in the band Love Sculpture, but his surprise first (and biggest) hit single, 1971's "I Hear You Knocking" contained the core of every track he recorded afterwards, a modern sound based in the rhythms of rockabilly that he made into his own. Edmund's name will always be associated with Rockpile—the super-players group that included Nick Lowe on bass, Terry Williams on drums and Billy Bremner on guitar. The band kick-started the retro '50s sound, equal parts Chuck Berry and the Everly Broth-ers, but adding a 1970s pub-rock sensibility. Rockpile released only one disappointing album under its own name, but due to contractual difficulties and solo career conflicts, the band en-joyed a fruitful period between 1977–80, recording on a total of six Edmunds and Lowe solo albums that still sound as fresh as the day they were recorded. Since Rockpile, Edmunds' solo al-bums seemed to lose direction. *Information*, for instance, em-braces synthesizers and computers in a clear bid for hit singles. His myriad production credits include the Stray Cats' first two (British) albums, the Everly Brothers' comeback effort *EB '84*, k.d. lang's *Angel with a Lariat* and Lowe's *Party of One*.

what to buy: Edmunds' Swan Song albums are uniformly excel-lent. *Get It* (Swan Song, 1977, prod. Dave Edmunds) ✍✍✍✍ is the first actual Rockpile collaboration and includes "I Knew the Bride," "Get Out of Denver" and "JuJu Man." *Tracks on Wax 4* (Swan Song, 1978, prod. Dave Edmunds) ✍✍✍✍ is Rockpile's hardest-rocking collection, while *Repeat When Necessary* (Swan Song, 1979, prod. Dave Edmunds) ✍✍✍✍ is amazingly sharp considering the band also recorded Lowe's *Labour of Lust* at the same time.

what to buy next: *The Dave Edmunds Anthology (1968–90)* (Rhino, 1993, prod. various) ✍✍✍, a 41-track overview, in-cludes too much Love Sculpture among its many gems. *D-E7* (Columbia, 1982, prod. Dave Edmunds) ✍✍✍ includes the Bruce Springsteen-composed "From Small Things, Big Things Come." *The Best of Dave Edmunds* (Swan Song, 1981, prod. Dave Edmunds) ✍✍✍ features all tracks from his classic period.

what to avoid: Anything by Love Sculpture, Edmunds' first real band, most of which approaches headache-inducing gui-tar music.

the rest:
Rockpile (MAM, 1972) ✍✍
Subtle as a Flying Mallet (RCA, 1975) ✍✍
(With Rockpile) *Seconds of Pleasure* (Columbia, 1980) ✍✍✍
Twangin' (Swan Song, 1981) ✍✍
Information (Columbia, 1983) ✍✍
Riff Raff (Columbia, 1984) ✍✍
I Hear You Rockin' (Columbia, 1988) ✍✍
Closer to the Flame (Capitol, 1990) ✍✍
Plugged In (Pyramid, 1994) ✍✍✍✍

worth searching for: Rockpile bootlegs—in particular *I Hear You Rocking* (GLR, 1991) ✍✍✍✍ and *Provoked Beyond En-durance* (Oh Boy) ✍✍✍—that capture the Rockpile experience

Dave Edmunds (© **Ken Settle**)

better than *Seconds of Pleasure. Rocking* features guest ap-pearances by Robert Plant and the Rolling Stones' Keith Richards.

influences:

◀◀ Les Paul & Mary Ford, Chet Atkins, Elvis Presley, Gene Vin-cent, Ricky Nelson, Smiley Lewis, Jerry Lee Lewis, Chuck Berry, Everly Brothers

▶▶ Stray Cats, Blasters, Bottle Rockets

Leland Rucker

DON EDWARDS

Born March 16, in NJ.

One of the most popular of the modern cowboy singers, Don Edwards became enamored with the black-and-white images of early film cowboy Tom Mix while a young child. He taught him-self guitar at age 10, then kicked around folk and country music scenes in various parts of the country as a young adult. He backed yodeler Elton Britt, released his first single on a small Dallas label in 1964 and recorded in Nashville during the late

1960s. Edwards hooked up with Michael Martin Murphey at a 1990 cowboy poetry gathering and later signed to Warner Western, which has released his four most recent albums.

what to buy: On *Songs of the Trail* (Warner Western, 1992, prod. Joey Miskulin, Michael Martin Murphey) ♫♫♫, Edwards' smooth cowboy crooning evokes Marty Robbins' gunfighter ballads on this collection of new and old Western tunes such as "I'd Like to Be in Texas When They Roundup in the Spring" and "Springtime in the Rockies."

what to buy next: *West of Yesterday* (Warner Western, 1996) ♫♫♫ won a Western Heritage "Wrangler" award for Edwards' performance of "The Freedom Song."

the rest:
Goin' Back to Texas (Warner Western, 1993) ♫♫♫
(With Waddie Mitchell) *The Bard and the Balladeer: Live from Cowtown* (Warner Western, 1995) ♫♫♫

influences:
◄◄ Red Steagall, Rex Allen, Michael Martin Murphey
►► Waddie Mitchell

Brian Mansfield

JONATHAN EDWARDS

Born July 28, 1946, in Minneapolis, MN.

Jonathan Edwards was one of a bevy of folkie songwriters who hit paydirt during the winter of 1972—the tune was "Sunshine," a Top Five single that became a coffeehouse standard. Edwards never did better commercially than on his self-titled debut, but maintained a decent following well into the 1980s, when he dug deep into his country/bluegrass roots and resurrected himself as a Nashville songwriter and performer.

what to buy: *Jonathan Edwards* (Atco, 1971, prod. Peter Casperson) ♫♫♫ contains most of the songs that would become radio and concert staples for the singer through the years, including the hit "Sunshine," "Emma," "Everybody Knows Her" and "Athens County," as well as the Edwards doper anthem, "Shanty."

the rest:
Lucky Day (Atlantic, 1974) ♫♫

worth searching for: *Rockin' Chair* (Atlantic, 1976) ♫♫ and *Sailboat* (Atlantic, 1977) ♫♫ are notable for the musical contributions of Emmylou Harris and Rodney Crowell.

influences:
◄◄ Jerry Jeff Walker
►► Michael Martin Murphey

David Simons

STONEY EDWARDS

Born December 24, 1929, in Seminole, OK.

Stoney Edwards is one of those anomalous figures in country music who turns up every once in awhile and makes people shake their heads in wonder. Edwards is of African American, Native American and Irish ancestry. He never wanted to be anything but a country singer, and he became a very good one, although he has never been more than moderately successful in a commercial sense. Born in Oklahoma, he knocked around the San Francisco Bay area for years, playing music part time until he was spotted at a benefit and encouraged to go to Nashville. He made four albums for Capitol during the early 1970s, two of which are minor classics and collector's items. Vocally, he seems to have distilled the essence of Merle Haggard and Lefty Frizzell into his own signature style, and, at his best, he is very good. In recent years, diabetes, which led to a partial amputation of one leg, has slowed him down considerably, but there are those two albums to look for.

worth searching for: *Mississippi You're on My Mind* (Capitol, 1975, prod. Earl Ball, Biff Collie) ♫♫♫♫ contains the title song, Jesse Winchester's love song to the South, and the classic Dallas Frazier-Doodle Owens song "Hank and Lefty Raised My Country Soul," plus perhaps Edwards' biggest hit, "She's My Rock," and his own "A Two Dollar Toy." *Blackbird* (Capitol, 1976, prod. Chip Taylor) ♫♫♫ is almost as good, with another Jesse Winchester song, "Yankee Lady," three by producer Taylor and a nice reading of Leonard Cohen's "Bird on A Wire." Probably a little too folky for some.

influences:
◄◄ Lefty Frizzell, Merle Haggard
►► David Ball

Randy Pitts

RAMBLIN' JACK ELLIOTT

Born August 1, 1931, in Brooklyn, NY.

Ramblin' Jack Elliott was Woody Guthrie's traveling companion as the folk troubador made his way across America during the late 1940s and early 1950s. A disciple of eastern mysticism and the beat writings of Allen Ginsburg, Jack fled city life and hooked up with a rodeo before becoming a folk minstrel. Bob Dylan, a disciple of Elliott's, invited the folksinger to join his Rolling Thunder Revue as they barnstormed across the U.S. in late 1975 and early 1976.

what to buy: *The Essential Ramblin' Jack Elliott* (Vanguard, 1976/1993) 🎸🎸🎸 features Elliott performing spirited renditions of tunes by Leadbelly and Jimmy Driftwood.

what to buy next: *Hard Travelin': Songs by Woody Guthrie and Others* (Fantasy, 1989) 🎸🎸🎸 is a *tour de force* that combines two great releases from the 1960s—*Jack Elliott Sings the Songs of Woody Guthrie* and *Ramblin' Jack Elliott*.

the rest:
Ramblin' Jack Elliott Sings Woody Guthrie and Jimmie Rodgers (Monitor, 1962) 🎸🎸🎸
Me & Bobby McGee (Rounder, 1995) 🎸🎸🎸
South Coast (Red House, 1995) 🎸🎸🎸

influences:
◀◀ Woody Guthrie
▶▶ Bob Dylan, Kevin Welch, Jimmie Dale Gilmore

Rick Petreycik

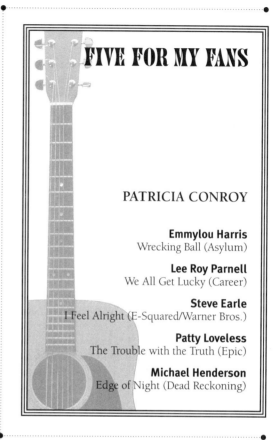

FIVE FOR MY FANS

PATRICIA CONROY

Emmylou Harris
Wrecking Ball (Asylum)

Lee Roy Parnell
We All Get Lucky (Career)

Steve Earle
I Feel Alright (E-Squared/Warner Bros.)

Patty Loveless
The Trouble with the Truth (Epic)

Michael Henderson
Edge of Night (Dead Reckoning)

JOE ELY

Born February 9, 1947, in Amarillo, TX.

Joe Ely blew out of the hot, windy, brown plains of Lubbock, Texas—where Buddy Holly grew up—during the late 1970s. His new wave honky-tonk baffled the country music establishment, which seemed more concerned with rhinestone suits and string arrangements, and fringe rockers alike. Ely was too rock for country, too country for rock, and he's never turned his critical acclaim into gold. A prolific songwriter who wandered the wilds of the Southwest as a teenager, Ely sang stories about drifters, not-so-star-crossed lovers and some of life's more colorful characters. His voice bad boy gritty, his bands always an overly aggressive mix of punkish roots rockers and straight-ahead country musicians, Ely turned his soulful but raucous blend of honky tonk, rock 'n' blues and Tex-Mex into vivid songs about life. He lists Merle Haggard and the Clash's Joe Strummer among his biggest fans.

what to buy: *Love and Danger* (MCA, 1992, prod. Joe Ely, Tony Brown) 🎸🎸🎸 was a return to form for the Texas singer, who'd ventured a little too far from his honky-tonk roots to a rootsy blues-rock sound during a stretch with HighTone Records. That

stuff was good, but a little too one-dimensional. Ely's at his best when he's writing compelling narratives, interpreting songs by wonderful but overlooked Texas writers like Robert Earl Keen Jr. (and buddy Butch Hancock) and using all of his musical tools.

what to buy next: Smoky, sweaty bars, hot summer nights and romantic desperadoes drip from *Honky Tonk Masquerade* (MCA, 1978, prod. Chip Young) 🎸🎸🎸, the product of Ely's restless spirit and his tenure as the king of the West Texas honky tonks during the late 1970s. Ely classics "West Texas Waltz" and "Fingernails" (opening line: "I keep my fingernails long so they click when I play the piano") are among its most colorful inclusions.

what to avoid: The raucous rockabilly of *Musta Notta Gotta Lotta* (MCA/Southcoast, 1981, prod. Joe Ely, Michael Brovsky) 🎸🎸 is fun but not as memorable as his best work.

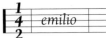

emilio

the rest:

Joe Ely (MCA, 1977) 🎵🎵🎵
Down on the Drag (MCA, 1979) 🎵🎵🎵
Live Shots (MCA/Southcoast, 1980) 🎵🎵🎵
Lord of the Highway (HighTone, 1987) 🎵🎵🎵
Dig All Night (HighTone, 1988) 🎵🎵
Live at Liberty Lunch (MCA, 1990) 🎵🎵🎵
Letter to Laredo (MCA, 1995) 🎵🎵🎵

worth searching for: All but one of Ely's albums are available on CD. The exception: the experimental *Hi-Res* (MCA, 1984, prod. Joe Ely, Michael Brovsky) 🎵🎵, issued on vinyl and cassette. It was Ely's one and only plunge into the world of computers and synthesizers, which, like many of his musical moves, was ahead of its time and hardly in character for a roots country-rocker. It was a clunker, but there are some superb songs under the layers of electronics, including "Cool Rockin' Loretta" and "Letter to Laredo," later recast as the title song of his newest, flamenco-inflected album.

influences:

◀◀ Buddy Holly, Hank Williams
▶▶ Alejando Escovedo, Son Volt

see also: *Flatlanders*

Doug Pullen

EMILIO

Born Emilio Navaira, August 23, 1963 in San Antonio, TX.

In the Latin music world, Texan Emilio Navaira is known as the King of Tejano, a jaunty blend of German polka, folkloric Mexican music and traditional country styles with a modern, rock-oriented touch. He stuck to the accordion-fueled *conjunto* sound—the rootsier predecessor of Tejano—and struck gold. But with his George Strait garb, photogenic look and penchant for singing English-language country and rock tunes on his albums and in concert, Navaira dropped the last name and recorded a mainstream country album in Nashville, away from the San Antonio, Texas base he's accustomed to.

what to buy: *SoundLife* (EMI Latin, 1994, prod. Raul Navaira, Emilio Navaira, Stuart Dill) 🎵🎵🎵 crosses the boundaries dividing old-school Mexican rhythms and new, pop-edged hybrids. *Quedate* (EMI Latin, 1996, prod. Michael Morales, Ron Morales, Raul Navaira, Emilio Navaira, Stuart Dill) 🎵🎵🎵 delivers the familiar stuff, then successfully experiments with 1970s rock elements and flamenco guitar-laced ballads.

what to avoid: *Life Is Good* (Capitol, 1995, prod. Barry Bockett) 🎵🎵 doesn't do Emilio justice. His robust, raspy voice struggles to remain vital in the midst of gutless production. Singing a batch of middle-of-the-road songs safely aimed at mainstream country radio, Emilio sounds like he walked into the studio and followed every order given by the producer, not once offering any original ideas.

influences:

◀◀ Roberto Pulido, George Strait, Little Joe
▶▶ Rick Trevino, Rick Orozco

Mario Tarradell

TY ENGLAND

Born December 5, 1963, in Oklahoma City, OK.

Ty England played guitar in the road band of his former college buddy, Garth Brooks, for five years before launching out on his own solo career.

what's available: A Ty England record doesn't sound like a Garth Brooks record (as you might have expected given his resume), which means he's not a clone of his former boss. Unfortunately, it's not as memorable, either. *Ty England* (RCA, 1995, prod. Garth Fundis) 🎵🎵🎵, England's first album, spawned a minor hit, the dance hall swing tune "Should've Asked Her Faster," and includes two memorable ballads, "It's Lonesome Everywhere" and "Smoke in Her Eyes," and the touching "The Blues Ain't News to Me." However, his remake of "Her Only Bad Habit Is Me" shows that England can't do George Strait, either. *Two Ways to Fall* (RCA, 1996, prod. James Stroud, Byron Gallimore) 🎵🎵🎵 finds Ty similarly un-Garthlike.

influences:

◀◀ Garth Brooks, George Strait
▶▶ Trace Adkins, David Kersh

Bill Hobbs

ALEJANDRO ESCOVEDO

Born January 10, 1951, in San Antonio, TX.

At first, nattily dressed Escovedo's concerts sound like any singer/songwriter who has studied Merle Haggard and George Jones—the songs are a bit downbeat, a bit rocking. By the time he reaches his droning version of rocker Iggy Pop's "I Wanna Be Your Dog," though, he gives himself away. Despite three moody, pristinely written solo albums, Escovedo hangs tightly to his roots as a Texas punk rocker. Escovedo—whose niece,

Sheila E, was a Prince percussionist and a solo artist—played in the Nuns, Rank & File and the True Believers (with his brother, Javier) throughout the 1980s. He has never, unfortunately, tasted any significant commercial success.

what to buy: *Gravity* (Watermelon, 1992, prod. Stephen Bruton) 𝄞𝄞𝄞𝄞, a hushed, moody album written after Escovedo's first wife committed suicide, contains the explosive rocker "One More Time" and the chanting tear-jerker "Bury Me." Escovedo co-founded the terrific New York City country-punk band Rank & File, with Dils members Tony and Chip Kinman, in 1981, and stuck around for the band's terrific debut, *Sundown* (Slash/Warner Bros., 1982, prod. David Kahne) 𝄞𝄞𝄞.

what to buy next: Escovedo's second solo album, *Thirteen Years* (Watermelon, 1993, prod. Stephen Bruton) 𝄞𝄞𝄞, is overly repetitive and harder to listen to than *Gravity*, but "Ballad of the Sun and the Moon" is one of many well-written highlights.

the rest:

With These Hands (Rykodisc, 1996) 𝄞𝄞𝄞𝄞.

worth searching for: Both catchy, rocking self-titled True Believers' albums (the first is out-of-print, the second never released) came out on the *Hard Road* reissue (Rykodisc, 1994, prod. Jim Dickinson, Jeff Glixman) 𝄞𝄞𝄞𝄞.

influences:

◀◀ Blasters, Jimmie Dale Gilmore, Buddy Holly, Ritchie Valens, Iggy Pop, X

▶▶ Uncle Tupelo, Jason & the Scorchers, Wilco, Bottle Rockets, Son Volt

Steve Knopper

GERALD EVANS & JOE MULLINS

See: Traditional Grass

THE EVERLY BROTHERS

Vocal duo from KY.

Don Everly (born February 1, 1937, in Brownie, KY), vocals, guitar; Phil Everly (born January 19, 1939, in Brownie, KY), vocals, guitar.

Having begun their singing careers as children on their parents' radio program, brothers Don and Phil Everly qualified as country music veterans by the time their first rock 'n' roll records hit the charts eight years later, their deeply entwined high-mountain harmonies practically instinctual. The blood harmonies of the Everly Brothers may be the main tributary feeding all rock vocal styles; the Beatles, among many others, styled their harmony sound after the Everlys. But the Everly Brothers were not only the children of long-standing members of the country music community. They were also an officially sanctioned Nashville project. Guitarist Chet Atkins conducted the sessions and Acuff-Rose frontliners Boudleaux and Felice Bryant supplied the material. Though they may have slipped off the charts during the 1960s, the brothers never stopped making heart-stoppingly beautiful records. When matched with the right piece of material and sympathetic production, the Everlys cut records that matched the finest work of their early years, right up to the modest 1984 comeback with Paul McCartney's "On the Wings of a Nightingale" (produced by Dave Edmunds) and beyond. And the Everlys never strayed far from the country field; one of their best-loved albums of their wilderness years was, in fact, the country-oriented *Roots*, not unlike the *Songs Our Daddy Taught Us* album of many years earlier. The duo split—bitterly—in 1973, breaking up literally in front of a Knott's Berry Farm audience when Don splintered a guitar across his brother's back and walked offstage, only to discover nobody wanted to hear one Everly brother singing alone. They rejoined forces for a sentimental 1983 Royal Albert Hall concert, recorded and filmed, and apparently found an uneasy truce that allowed them to continue to perform and record together.

what to buy: *Cadence Classics: Their 20 Greatest Hits* (Rhino, 1985, prod. Archie Bleyer) 𝄞𝄞𝄞𝄞 contains the basic fundamentals of the Everlys repertoire, from the acoustic guitar-accented rockabilly of "Wake Up Little Susie" and "Claudette" to almost ethereal ballads such as "Let It Be Me."

what to buy next: *Walk Right Back: The Everly Brothers on Warner Bros. 1960–1969* (Warner Archives, 1993, prod. various) 𝄞𝄞𝄞𝄞 is a 50-song survey that begins where the Cadence era left off and takes the Everlys through the flowering of Los Angeles country-rock that their early work did so much to inspire. The four-disc box set *Heartaches and Harmonies* (Rhino, 1994, prod. various) 𝄞𝄞𝄞𝄞 offers a detailed retrospective that smoothly covers nearly 40 years of Everlys' recordings.

what to avoid: During the mid-1960s, the brothers re-recorded a set of their Cadence hits for Warners, released as *The Very Best of the Everly Brothers* (Warner Bros., 1964, prod. various) 𝄞𝄞, which pales vastly in comparison to the original versions.

the rest:

Songs Our Daddy Taught Us (Cadence, 1958/Rhino, 1988) 𝄞𝄞𝄞𝄞

The Fabulous Style of the Everly Brothers (Cadence, 1960/ Rhino, 1988) 𝄢𝄢𝄢𝄢

Roots (Warner Bros., 1968) 𝄢𝄢𝄢

Reunion Concert (Mercury, 1984) 𝄢𝄢

EB 84 (Mercury, 1984/Razor & Tie, 1994) 𝄢𝄢𝄢𝄢

The Mercury Years (Mercury, 1993) 𝄢𝄢𝄢

worth searching for: In assembling the label's Everlys reissues of the Cadence material, Rhino Records researchers unearthed a set of unreleased demo tapes. The resulting CD, *All They Had to Do Was Dream* (Rhino, 1985, prod. Archie Bleyer) 𝄢𝄢𝄢𝄢, showcases the pure vocal sound of the brothers. Perhaps some of rock's first "unplugged" sessions, these songs glisten with the maturity and depth of artists far beyond their years when they were actually recorded.

influences:

◀◀ Stanley Brothers, Louvin Brothers

▶▶ Foster & Lloyd, O'Kanes, Marty Brown

Joel Selvin

SKIP EWING

Born Donald R. Ewing, March 6, 1964, in Redlands, CA.

Skip Ewing is a prime example of someone who's never quite been able to parlay his songwriting successes into a recording career. Ewing has been one of the top writers in Music City since moving to Nashville in 1984, with cuts by George Jones, George Strait, Kenny Rogers, Willie Nelson, Bryan White and Lorrie Morgan. He's had a half-dozen Top 40 hits on his own, but none of them have matched what other performers have done with his songs. Ewing worked in the Opryland USA theme park before signing with MCA, then with Liberty Records. He currently records for Word Nashville.

what's available: With his boyish looks and smooth tenor, he tends toward romantic numbers as a singer. *Greatest Hits* (MCA, 1991) 𝄢𝄢𝄢 culls the best material from Ewing's three MCA albums, including "Burnin' a Hole in My Heart" and "It's You Again," both of which made the Top Five.

worth searching for: Ever the pro songwriter, Ewing's albums possess consistency if nothing else. Among the more notable: *Coast of Colorado* (MCA, 1988) 𝄢𝄢𝄢𝄢 might as well be Ewing's *Greatest Hits*; it contains five of his six Top 40 singles, including the beautiful "I Don't Have Far to Fall." *A Healin' Fire* (MCA, 1990) 𝄢𝄢𝄢 contains Ewing's version of "Rebecca Lynn," later a #1 hit for Bryan White. *Following Yonder Star* (MCA, 1990, prod. Skip Ewing, Randy Scruggs) 𝄢𝄢𝄢 is a mostly traditional Christ-

mas album that contains Ewing's "It Wasn't His Child," one of Nashville's best new holiday tunes.

influences:

◀◀ Mac McAnally

▶▶ Bryan White

Brian Mansfield

EXILE
/LES TAYLOR
/J.P. PENNINGTON

Formed as the Fascinations 1963, in Lexington, KY. Disbanded 1995.

Jimmy Stokely (died 1978), vocals (1963–78); J.P. Pennington (born James Preston Pennington), vocals, lead guitar (1963–89); Buzz Cornelison, keyboards (1963–73); Marlon Hargis, keyboards (1973–85); Steve Goetzman, drums (1977–95); Les Taylor, rhythm guitar (1978–89); Sonny Lemaire, bass (c. 1983–95); Lee Carroll, keyboards (1985–95); Paul Martin, vocals, guitar (1989–95); Mark Jones, guitar, vocals (1989–95); others.

Following some disco-pop success in 1978 with "Kiss Me All Over," the members of Exile switched genres and watched 10 of their first 12 country singles, most of which leaned heavily on sentiment, top the Billboard country chart. The group had formed as the Fascinations in 1963, changed its name to the Exiles in 1965 and finally to Exile in 1973. The group became one of the most successful country bands of the 1980s while recording for Epic Records. Hoping for results twice as nice, J.P. Pennington (whose mother sang for the Coon Creek Girls) and Les Taylor attempted solo careers in 1989. Their efforts fell as flat as those of the revamped Exile, which signed to Arista Nashville for two albums. The group lost its deal in 1991 and disbanded three years later. It reunited briefly to record *Latest & Greatest* in 1995. Bassist Sonny LeMaire later formed the group Burnin' Daylight.

what to buy: During Exile's heyday, probably only Alabama was a more popular band. Much of the group's music sounds tame compared to today's rockin' country (or Alabama's records, for that matter), but the group's biggest singles, including "Woke Up in Love" and "I Don't Want to Be a Memory," can be found on *Exile's Greatest Hits* (Epic, 1986) 𝄢𝄢𝄢.

Phil (l) and Don Everly: The Everly Brothers
(UPI/Corbis-Bettmann)

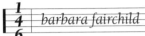

what to buy next: *The Complete Collection* (Curb, 1991) 🎵🎵, a second collection of hits, is only a notch down from the first batch.

what to avoid: Exile's reunion album, *Latest & Greatest* (Intersound, 1995, prod. Exile) 🎵🎵, includes remakes of hits such as "Woke Up in Love" and "Kiss You All Over," as well as some new material that made absolutely no impact on the charts.

the rest:
Still Standing (Arista, 1990) 🎵🎵
Keeping It Country (Curb, 1990) 🎵🎵
The Best of Exile (Curb, 1990) 🎵🎵
Justice (Arista, 1991) 🎵🎵
Super Hits (Epic, 1993) 🎵🎵🎵

solo outings:
J.P. Pennington:
Whatever It Takes (MCA, 1991) 🎵🎵

Les Taylor:
That Old Desire (Epic, 1990) 🎵🎵🎵
Blue Kentucky Wind (Epic, 1991) 🎵🎵

influences:
◀◀ Alabama
▶▶ Restless Heart, Burnin' Daylight

Brian Mansfield and Craig Shelburne

BARBARA FAIRCHILD

Born November 12, 1950, in Lafe, AR.

A singer noted for the childlike hits "Teddy Bear Song," "Kid Stuff" and "Baby Doll," Barbara Fairchild had to leave country music to grow up effectively. Raised in Knobel, Arkansas, Fairchild later moved to St. Louis, where she made her first record at age 15. Her first hit, 1970's "A Girl Who'll Satisfy Her Man," came before she turned 20, and Fairchild would record for Columbia Records through 1977. After she hit #1 with "Teddy Bear Song" in 1973, she was never able to eradicate the little-girl image in listener's minds, despite recording songs like "Cheatin' Is" and "Let Me Love You Once Before You Go" (later covered by Emerson, Lake & Palmer's Greg Lake). After Columbia dropped her contract in 1977 (she was 26), she divorced,

rediscovered her Christian faith and remarried, living in Texas during the first half of the 1980s. Fairchild later returned to Nashville, working first as a waitress, then as a gospel singer. She formed Heirloom in 1990 with Tanya Goodman and Candy Hemphill, women from two important Southern gospel families; Sheri Easter later joined the group. Heirloom won a Dove Award with its first album, and Fairchild released her gospel debut, *The Light*, in 1991. She has since become a fixture in the Christian music field.

what's available: None of Fairchild's Columbia recordings remain in print under her name. What is available is her most recent Christian album, *Stories* (Chapel, 1995, prod. Michael Sykes) 🎵🎵🎵, which contains songs with a country and Southern gospel influence. Glen Campbell duets with her on "Jezebel." Heirloom—*Hymns That Last Forever* (Chapel, 1995, prod. Michael Sykes) 🎵🎵🎵 is a collection of such familiar religious songs as "Faith of Our Fathers," "In the Sweet By and By" and "Cryin' Holy unto the Lord" with four-part harmonies and minimal acoustic instrumentation.

influences:
◀◀ Brenda Lee, Connie Smith
▶▶ Cristy Lane

Brian Mansfield

DONNA FARGO

Born Yvonne Vaughan, November 10, 1949, in Mount Airy, NC.

Early in 1972 Donna Fargo had her first hit, a #1 record, and continued the streak for a year and a half with three more hitting the top spot on the country charts, and enjoying pop chart success as well. Once a school teacher in California while she played in clubs at night, Fargo quit teaching only after "Happiest Girl in the Whole U.S.A." (#1, 1972) became a country and pop smash. It was eventually named Country Music Association Single of the Year and won her a Grammy, while her next hit, "Funny Face," (#1, 1972) hit the Top Five on the pop chart. Four #1 songs and eight additional Top 10 hits later, Fargo had switched from Dot Records to Warner Bros., and eventually Mercury, with short spells at RCA and Columbia as well. With her career retrospective on Varese Sarabande representing the best of her ABC/Dot years, Fargo doesn't have a great deal of product currently available, but what does exist is a lovingly captured, though relatively brief chapter in country music history. Today, in spite of being diagnosed with multiple sclerosis in 1978, she remains an active performer with a loyal following.

what's available: *The Best of Donna Fargo* (Varese Sarabande, 1995, prod. Stan Silver) ✍✍✍✍, a comprehensive, entertaining collection of monster hits and lesser-known tracks, contains "The Happiest Girl," "Funny Face" and 16 other cuts from her ABC/Dot and MCA years.

influences:

◀◀ Loretta Lynn, Tammy Wynette

▶▶ Becky Hobbs, Barbara Fairchild

Stephen L. Betts

CHARLIE FEATHERS

Born June 12, 1932, in Hollow Springs, MS.

Though never blessed with any real commercial acceptance, Charlie Feathers nonetheless made his mark as one of the most singular and respected practitioners of 1950s rockabilly. Hooking up with Sam Phillips' Sun Records during the early part of that decade, Feathers made the transition from straight country to rock 'n' roll by the time Elvis Presley began cutting sides (Feathers supposedly co-wrote Presley's "I Forgot to Remember to Forget"). Feathers made his most enduring music with King Records, including the tough "One Hand Loose" as well as other rockabilly staples like "I Can't Hardly Stand It" and "Tongue-Tied Jill." He has remained active through the years, surfacing here and there with the verve of his 1950s recordings intact.

what to buy: *Tip Top Daddy* (Norton, 1991, prod. various) ✍✍✍✍ and *Uh Huh Honey* (Norton, 1992, prod. various) ✍✍✍✍ both contain essential Feathers tracks ranging from 1958–73, including "Bottle to the Baby," "This Lonesome Feeling," "Fireball Mail" and others.

what to buy next: Feathers returned to the studio for *Charlie Feathers* (Elektra, 1991, prod. Ben Vaughn) ✍✍✍, which shows the man in fine form after all this time, teamed with former Sun cohorts Stan Kesler and Roland Janes.

the rest:

That Rock-A-Billy Cat! (Edsel, 1979) ✍✍✍✍
Good Rockin' Tonight (Edsel, 1979) ✍✍✍✍
Rock-a-Billy (Zu Zazz, 1991) ✍✍✍✍

worth searching for: Feathers recorded a pair of late-1970s albums, *Charlie Feathers, Volume I* (Feathers Records, 1979, prod. Charlie Feathers) ✍✍✍ and *Charlie Feathers, Volume II* (Feathers Records, 1979, prod. Charlie Feathers) ✍✍✍, each containing more than a few choice moments of rockabilly fever.

influences:

◀◀ Elvis Presley, Hank Williams

▶▶ Al Anderson, Dave Edmunds

David Simons

NARVEL FELTS

Born Albert Narvel Felts, November 11, 1938, near Keiser, AR.

Nicknamed "Narvel the Marvel" for his dramatic falsetto voice, Narvel Felts was one of many singers with a rockabilly background who rose to prominence in the country world of the 1970s. Felts began his recording career playing sessions at Sun, and he spent much of his career on independent labels like Cinnamon, Collage, GMC, Lobo, Compleat and Evergreen. His first recordings aimed for the pop market, but not until he started recording country records for Cinnamon during the 1970s did he have any success. His biggest hit was 1975's "Reconsider Me" (#2 country, #67 pop), but he reached the country Top 40 with covers of such pop staples as "Drift Away," "Lonely Teardrops" and "Runaway."

what's available: The only two Felts albums available in the United States come only on cassette. *Raindrops* (Starday, 1985) ✍✍ features eight songs from Felts' Cinnamon/ABC/Dot recordings. *The Very Best* (Deluxe) ✍✍ expands the number to 16. Though he had almost two dozen Top 40 hits during the 1970s, Felts' music hasn't dated very well. The vibrato in his voice is so overwhelming that he seems to have a hard time staying anywhere near pitch, and the arrangements of songs like "To Love Somebody," "Crying" and "Everlasting Love," at least on these low-budget tapes, sound like they're straight off a programmed rhythm track.

influences:

◀◀ Conway Twitty, Billy "Crash" Craddock

▶▶ Billy Joe Royal

Brian Mansfield

FREDDY FENDER

Born Baldemar G. Huerta, June 4, 1937, in San Benito, TX.

If Texas likes your style, a struggling musician can make a career touring its vast reaches. Freddy Fender, a Mexican-American raised in a South Texas border town, had a chance to do just that, but a 1960 drug bust landed him a three-year jail term. Nobody seemed to remember the balladeer's music upon his release, so he started at ground zero. Working with famed

$\frac{1}{4}$ *filé*
8

Freddy Fender **(Archive Photos)**

Texas/Louisiana R&B producer Huey Meaux, Fender turned a regional hit called "Before the Next Teardrop Falls" into one of the biggest hits of 1975 (it topped both the country and pop charts). He had three subsequent country #1 songs: "Wasted Days and Wasted Nights," "Secret Love" and "You'll Lose a Good Thing." In 1990 Fender joined with accordion wizard Flaco Jimenez and Doug Sahm and Augie Meyers (formerly of the Sir Douglas Quintet) to create a stirring Tex-Mex fiesta known as the Texas Tornados. He has continued to record with them and on his own, though he tends to reprise his old hits on solo albums.

what to buy: *Best of Freddy Fender* (MCA, 1996, prod. Huey P. Meaux) 🎵🎵🎵 has Fender's four chart-topping hits, plus fun versions of familiar country and R&B songs like "Wild Side of Life" and "Since I Met You Baby," all done in his inimitable Tejano-triplet style.

what to buy next: *The Freddy Fender Collection* (Reprise, 1991, prod. Steve Gibson) 🎵🎵🎵 reprises Fender's big hits with crisp new versions, plus Fender's renditions of such standards as "It's All in the Game," "Pledging My Love" and "Tell It Like It Is."

the rest:
Greatest Hits (Hollywood/IMG) 🎵🎵🎵
(With Delbert McClinton) *Sometimes Country, Sometimes Blue* (Quicksilver) 🎵🎵🎵
Before the Next Teardrop Falls (MCA, 1994) 🎵🎵🎵

worth searching for: Fender has occasionally recorded in Spanish, but those albums tend to be available only through Latin distributors and are therefore very difficult to find outside of Texas. *Canciones de Mi Barrio* (Arhoolie, 1993) 🎵🎵, which is in keeping with Fender's Tex-Mex R&B style, actually is one of the easier to find.

influences:
◀◀ Ivory Joe Hunter
▶▶ Johnny Rodriguez

see also: *Texas Tornados*

Brian Mansfield and Craig Shelburne

FILÉ

Formed 1983, in LA.

Ward Lormand, accordion, vocals; David Egan, piano, vocals; D'Jalma Garnier, fiddle, guitar, banjo, vocals; Kevin Shearin, bass; Peter Stevens, drums; others.

Combining elements of zydeco, blues and swing, Filé is one of the most progressive bands playing any form of Cajun music.

what to buy: *La Vie Marron (The Runaway Life)* (Green Linnet, 1996, prod. Filé, David Rachou) 🎵🎵🎵 boasts a new lineup, and finds Filé leaning more heavily on its blues roots without sacrificing any of its Cajun boisterousness.

the rest:
Cajun Dance Band (Flying Fish, 1987) 🎵🎵🎵🎵
2 Left Feet (Flying Fish, 1990) 🎵🎵🎵

influences:
◀◀ Beausoleil, Hackberry Ramblers, Zachary Richard
▶▶ Beau Jocque & the Zydeco Hi-Rollers, Evangeline

Bob Cannon

FIREFALL

Formed 1974, in Boulder, CO.

Rick Roberts, guitar, vocals (1974–83); Jock Bartley, guitar, vocals (1974–present); Larry Burnett, guitar, vocals (1974–83); Mark Andes, bass (1974–80); Michael Clarke, drums (1974–83); David Muse, sax,

flute, (1977–83); Steven Weinmeister, vocals, guitars (1983–present); Sandy Ficca, drums (1983–present); Bil Hopkins, bass, vocals (1983–present); Stephen Thomas Manshel, vocals, guitars (1983–present); Dan Clawson, saxophone, flute, harmonica, keyboards (1983–present).

Firefall is perhaps the nadir of the folk- and country-rock evolution sparked by the Byrds. The formula was perfect; bring together veteran country-rockers from the Byrds (Clarke), Flying Burrito Brothers (Roberts, who took over the Burritos after Gram Parsons went solo), Gram Parson's Fallen Angels Band (Bartley, who had been jamming with Tommy Bolin before joining Parsons in mid-tour) and even the psychedelic band Spirit (Andes), and give them a flawlessly glossy commercial surface for the hits to skate on. The formula was too good: Skate is exactly what they did, with Top 40 hits from the harmless "You Are the Woman" and the amazingly misogynistic "Cinderella" to the wimpy "Just Remember I Love You" and the weird "Strange Way." The music was catchy but insincere, and it doesn't come close to matching the quality of any of these guys' original bands. At best, they helped perpetuate a breezy, beautiful Boulder, Colorado ethos by capturing something of the town's freewheeling spirit. Andes left the band to join Heart full-time in 1980; Roberts was last heard writing children's music; Bartley still leads a harder-rocking version of Firefall in the Boulder area.

what to buy: *The Best of Firefall* (Atlantic, 1981, prod. various) 𝄞𝄞𝄢 gathers together the hits, and is mostly listenable.

what to buy next: *Firefall* (Atlantic, 1976, prod. Jim Mason) 𝄞𝄞 is the best of the rest, although it's nearly fatally flawed by some really dumb such songs as "Cinderella," "No Way Out" and "Sad Ol' Love Song" (all written by the machismo-stricken Burnett).

what to avoid: *Messenger* (Redstone, 1994, prod. Jim Mason, Jock Bartley) **WOOF!** is a completely lame collection under Bartley's leadership. Though it has all the right stylistic elements, the songs are empty-headed—including one wretched, unsubtle ode against child abuse.

the rest:
Luna Sea (Atlantic, 1977) 𝄞
Elan (Atlantic, 1978) 𝄞
Undertow (Atlantic, 1980) 𝄞
Clouds across the Sun (Atlantic, 1981) 𝄢
Break of Dawn (Atlantic, 1983) 𝄢

solo outings:
Rick Roberts:
Windmills (A&M, 1972) 𝄞𝄞
She Is a Song (A&M, 1973) 𝄞𝄢

influences:
◀◀ Byrds, Flying Burrito Brothers, Poco
▶▶ Brooks & Dunn, Shenandoah

see also: *Byrds, Flying Burrito Brothers, Gram Parsons*

Gil Asakawa

FIVE CHINESE BROTHERS

Formed 1987, in New York, NY.

Tom Meltzer, vocals, rhythm guitar, mandolin; Paul Foglino, bass, vocals, banjo; Neil Thomas, piano, organ, accordion, vocals; Kevin Trainor, lead guitar, vocals, ocarina (1987–94); Stephen B. Antonakos, guitars, vocals (1994–present); Dave Helberg, drums (1987–91); Charlie Shaw, drums (1991–95); Pete DeMeo, drums (1996–present).

The core of this urban country band met at Columbia University during the early 1980s, when Meltzer and Foglino played in the Special Guests (not a country group). Trainor and Thomas at that time were in Elmo & the Doobers, mixing country classics, humorous originals, jazzy jams and "Amazing Grace." Meltzer does the majority of the Brothers' singing and songwriting, specializing in a convincing astonishment at the passage of time and a general bemusement regarding the opposite gender. The music looks back to classic 1950s models without sounding self-consciously retro, with bluesy slide guitar and lots of accordion for variety.

what to buy: After the quintet released a number of singles on the Diesel Only label (in earlier versions than appeared on album), its debut *Singer Songwriter Beggerman Thief* (Prime CD, 1994, prod. Five Chinese Brothers) 𝄞𝄞𝄞𝄢 contains many songwriting gems, including "Paul Cezanne," perhaps the only country song about Cubism. (The label's name is also its 800 number).

what to buy next: *Let's Kill Saturday Night* (Prime CD, 1997, prod. Five Chinese Brothers) 𝄞𝄞𝄞𝄢 returns to the strong level of songwriting found on the debut, while sounding more energetic than ever.

the rest:
Stone Soup (Prime CD, 1995) 𝄞𝄞𝄞

influences:
◀◀ Merle Haggard, George Jones, Gram Parsons, Rolling Stones

Steve Holtje

THE FLATLANDERS

Formed 1970, in Lubbock, TX.

Jimmie Dale Gilmore, vocals, guitar; Joe Ely, vocals, harmonica, dobro, guitar; Butch Hancock, vocals, guitar; Tommy Hancock, fiddle; Syl Rice, string bass; Tony Pearson, mandolin; Steve Wesson, musical saw.

Spawned during roughly the same era as the *Sweetheart of the Rodeo* Byrds and the Flying Burrito Brothers, the Flatlanders represented that period's clash between traditional and radical values: the attempt to build on the legacies of Jimmie Rodgers and Hank Williams while gaining a higher consciousness and rejecting the outdated symbols of a bygone era. Perhaps the group's fatal error was to attempt this in Nashville, which didn't want to hear about such nonsense, rather than L.A., which likely would have taken to the band's lonesome West Texas warblings like it took to the Eagles and the Nitty Gritty Dirt Band.

what's available: *More a Legend Than a Band* (Rounder, 1990, prod. Royce Clark) 𝄞𝄞𝄞𝄞, is a reissue of the Flatlanders' original album, which, in 1972, only saw the light of day on 8-track tape. It's one of the great lost albums and contains the seeds of a generation of West Texas talent that has since gone on to fame, if not fortune. Gilmore's tremulous voice hovers above the proceedings on most of the tracks, which include two of his finest songs, "Dallas" and "Tonight I'm Gonna Go Downtown." Wesson's musical saw may as well be a sitar amidst these country & Eastern musings. Hancock contributes a handful of tunes, including the mournful "She Had Everything," while Ely settles mostly for being the session's hot-shot guitarist. Prompted by the growing reputation of these three as solo artists, Charly reissued the album in 1980, and Rounder a decade later in a slightly different configuration. Shelby S. Singleton Jr., who owned the original sessions, got into the act in 1995, re-releasing the album under the moniker Jimmie Dale Gilmore and the Flatlanders, with the then-trendy title *Unplugged* (Sun, 1995, comp. prod. Jim Wilson, Shelby S. Singleton Jr.) 𝄞𝄞𝄞. It includes two fewer tracks than the Rounder and substitutes for two others. The Rounder is the better reissue.

influences:

◀◀ Jimmie Rodgers, Hank Williams, Eastern Religion 101

▶▶ Joe Ely, Butch Hancock, Jimmie Dale Gilmore

see also: *Joe Ely, Butch Hancock, Jimmie Dale Gilmore*

Daniel Durchholz

FLATT & SCRUGGS

Formed in 1948. Disbanded 1969.

Lester Flatt (born Lester Raymond Flatt, June 19, 1914, in Overton County, TN; died May 11, 1979), guitar, mandolin; Earl Scruggs (born January 6, 1924, in Flintville, NC), banjo.

Does there exist a country music lover who hasn't heard "Foggy Mountain Breakdown" by Lester Flatt & Earl Scruggs? Their instrumental virtuosity still has everyone else playing catch-up. Flatt got his start with Charlie Monroe's band before joining younger brother Bill Monroe's band in 1944. Earl Scruggs played banjo and guitar on radio, jamming with the Morris Brothers as a teenager and with John Miller and His Allied Kentuckians as an adult before joining Monroe's Blue Grass Boys in late 1944. Flatt & Scruggs heightened the quality of Monroe's sound considerably: Lester's steady, subtle guitarwork and mandolin trilling perfectly supported and offset Earl's arpeggiated three-fingered banjo work, an "overdrive" technique now known as "Scruggs"-style picking. When the duo left to form the Foggy Mountain Boys in 1948, Monroe became so embittered that he didn't speak to either of them for decades.

Flatt & Scruggs signed with Mercury records and made their first solo recordings, "Rollin' in My Sweet Baby's Arms" and "Salty Dog Blues" among them. They joined Columbia Records in 1951 and increased their exposure when they began their regular show for Martha White Flour on WSM in 1953. "'Tis Sweet to Be Remembered," "Cabin in the Hills," "Cryin' My Heart Out over You," and "Goin' Home" were solid hits, but by the late 1950s, bluegrass was a novelty on country radio playlists. Flatt & Scruggs had to build their career upon the flashy innovation of their music and the unusually high quality of their band (which through the years featured Mac Wiseman, Curly Seckler, Cedric Rainwater, Jim Shumate, Josh Graves and Paul Warren). Flatt & Scruggs achieved snob appeal when they were "discovered" by the college folk crowd of the early 1960s, and their concerts at Vanderbilt University and Carnegie Hall were mainstream career highlights. In 1962 their version of *The Beverly Hillbillies'* theme, "The Ballad of Jed Clampett," became the first bluegrass song to hit #1. A song written for Bea Benederet's character, "Pearl, Pearl, Pearl," also charted highly. Though the CBS sitcom demeaned country people with its ironic tone, Flatt & Scruggs made several good-natured appearances on the program, which did more for their career than all their years on the road or the radio. In 1967 the soundtrack of the film *Bonnie & Clyde* featured Flatt & Scruggs' 1948 recording of "Foggy Mountain Breakdown"; the recording was an enormous hit and sparked a new bluegrass boom in the United States. Ironically, it was also the last career peak for the duo. While Scruggs wanted to extend traditional bluegrass music into pop, rock and jazz, Flatt resisted, as did many of the group's hard-core fans. Lester left, taking the Foggy Mountain Boys—renamed the Nashville Grass, the band would be the training ground for the young Marty Stuart—with him. Though they became friendly again shortly before Flatt's death in 1979, the duo never worked together again. Flatt cemented his position as a traditionalist and publicly made up with Monroe (Scruggs would do so in 1994). Scruggs grew his hair long and (with his sons Gary and Randy) started the Earl Scruggs Revue. Both musicians recorded many critically acclaimed LPs through the years, though Scruggs' sold much better.

what to buy: *The Mercury Sessions, Volume 1* (Rounder, 1988) ♫♫♫♫ and *The Mercury Sessions, Volume 2* (Rounder, 1988) ♫♫♫♫♫ are both essential collections.

what to buy next: *The Essential Flatt & Scruggs: 'Tis Sweet to Be Remembered* (Columbia Legacy, 1997, comp. Bob Irwin) ♫♫♫♫ contains their biggest hits and most memorable work for Columbia.

what to avoid: *Golden Hits* (Hollywood/IMG, 1987) ♫ is a poorly made, low-budget collection.

the rest:
Foggy Mountain Banjo (Sony Music Special Products, 1961) ♫♫♫♫
Songs of the Famous Carter Family (Columbia, 1961) ♫♫♫
At Carnegie Hall (Columbia, 1962) ♫♫♫♫
Live at Vanderbilt University (Sony Music Special Products, 1964) ♫♫
Columbia Historic Edition (Columbia, 1982) ♫♫♫
20 All-Time Great Recordings (Columbia, 1983) ♫♫♫♫
20 Greatest Hits (Deluxe) ♫♫
You Can Feel It in Your Soul (County, 1988) ♫♫♫♫
Blue Ridge Cabin Home (County, 1990) ♫♫♫♫
The Complete Mercury Sessions (Mercury, 1992) ♫♫♫♫
Don't Get above Your Raisin' (Rounder, 1992) ♫♫♫♫
Golden Era (Rounder, 1992) ♫♫♫♫

worth searching for: *Lester Flatt & Earl Scruggs with the Foggy Mountain Boys* (Sandy Hook) ♫♫♫♫ is a live 1953 broadcast from their Martha White Biscuit Time portion of the Grand Ole Opry show. *Flatt & Scruggs 1959–1963* (Bear Family, 1992) ♫♫♫♫ has everything they recorded in those years, with 19 previously unreleased live tracks from the Carnegie Hall concert.

solo outings:
Lester Flatt:

At His Best (Hollywood/IMG) ♫♫
Bluegrass Festival (CMH, 1986) ♫♫♫
Greatest Bluegrass Hits, Volume 1 (CMH) ♫♫♫♫
Greatest Performance (CMH) ♫♫♫
Heaven's Bluegrass (CMH) ♫♫
Lester Raymond Flatt (Flying Fish) ♫♫
Living Legend (CMH)
Pickin' Time (CMH) ♫♫♫
(With the Nashville Grass) *Fantastic Pickin'* (CMH) ♫♫♫

Earl Scruggs:
Dueling Banjos (Columbia, 1973/1984) ♫♫♫♫
(With Gary & Randy Scruggs) *All the Way Home* (Vanguard, 1970/1994) ♫♫♫

influences:
◀◀ Bill Monroe, Mac Wiseman, Ralph Stanley

▶▶ Osborne Brothers, Reno & Smiley, Ricky Skaggs, Ghost Rockets, Steve Martin, Marty Stuart

Ken Burke

LESTER FLATT
See: Flatt & Scruggs

BELA FLECK /BELA FLECK & THE FLECKTONES

Born July 10, 1958, in New York, NY. Flecktones formed 1990, in Nashville, TN.

Bela Fleck, banjo; Howard Levy, keyboards, harmonica (1990–92); Victor Lemonte Wooten, bass guitar; Roy "Future Man" Wooten, Synth-axe Drumitar.

Banjo player Bela Fleck is widely regarded as one of the most innovative and influential musicians to ever pick up the five-string. Beginning in bluegrass, Fleck was a key member of the influential New Grass Revival before taking the banjo into jazz fusion with the Flecktones and demonstrating a versatility many thought the instrument didn't possess. Born in New York, Fleck began learning the banjo at 15 and played with Tasty Licks and Spectrum before joining the New Grass Revival in 1982. He formed the Flecktones soon after the Revival disbanded in 1988.

what to buy: *Flight of the Cosmic Hippo* (Warner Bros., 1991) ♫♫♫♫ contains piano- and harmonica-driven jazz incorporating influences from Irish waltzes to African drumming. From the ethereal "Star of the County Down" to the soaring "Turtle Rock," this is the best Flecktones album.

what to buy next: In *Tales from the Acoustic Planet* (Warner Bros., 1995) ♫♫♫, Fleck took a break from the Flecktones to record with what he called "some of my all-time favorite guys." Jazzmen Chick Corea and Branford Marsalis and pop pianist Bruce Hornsby are among those joining bluegrassers Tony Rice, Jerry Douglas and Sam Bush for 14 songs rooted in jazz fusion coupled with infectious grooves.

the rest:

Crossing the Tracks (Rounder, 1980) ♫♫♫

(With Tony Trischka and Tom Adams) *Rounder Banjo Extravaganza* (Rounder, 1988) ♫♫♫♫

(With the Flecktones) *Bela Fleck and the Flecktones* (Warner Bros., 1990) ♫♫♫♫

(With the Flecktones) *UFO TOFU* (Warner Bros., 1992) ♫♫♫

(With the Flecktones) *Three Flew over the Cuckoo's Nest* (Warner Bros., 1993) ♫♫♫

(With the Flecktones) *Live Art* (Warner Bros., 1996) ♫♫♫

worth searching for: *Drive* (Rounder, 1988) ♫♫♫ is worth a listen.

influences:

◀◀ Tony Trischka, Earl Scruggs, Charlie Parker

▶▶ Alison Brown, Pete Wernick

Douglas Fulmer

BENTON FLIPPEN

Born July 18, 1920, in Surry County, NC.

Not simply an old-time fiddle player, Benton Flippen plays a style all his own that can express the anguish of the blues, the inspiration of gospel and the joy of a square dance. Benton has played since the late 1940s with a number of bands, including the Green Valley Boys, the Camp Creek Boys, the Smokey Valley Boys and the Dryhill Draggers.

what's available: *Old Time, New Times* (Rounder, 1994) ♫♫♫♫ features powerful fiddle, banjo and string band music on 27 songs recorded between 1949–93, including new and old recordings and previously unreleased radio transcriptions.

influences:

◀◀ Fiddlin' Arthur Smith, Camp Creek Boys, Smokey Valley Boys

▶▶ Kirk Sutphin, Fred Cockerham & Tommy Jarrell

Douglas Fulmer

ROSIE FLORES

Born September 10, 1950, in San Antonio, TX.

Dwight Yoakam's *Guitars, Cadillacs, Etc., Etc.* is often held up as the "alternative" linchpin of the late 1980's new-traditionalist movement, but the real dust was kicked up by Rosie Flores' self-titled 1987 solo debut. A sassy Southern California-based Texan who had apprenticed in an all-woman rock band called the Screamin' Sirens, Flores sings with a raspy authority and a fiery grace capable of straddling Tex-Mex, blues, rockabilly and even girl-group pop. After Warner Bros. dropped her in 1988, Flores moved to Austin, Texas and eventually signed with Oakland, California-based HighTone. Despite living in a city that helped trigger the current alternative-country boom, Flores has forsaken country-rock in favor of exploring the rawer rockabilly roots she flaunted in a late-1970s bar band called Rosie & the Screamers. She collaborated with childhood heroes Wanda Jackson and Janis Martin on 1995's *Rockabilly Filly* and Ray Campi on 1997's *A Little Bit of Heartache*.

what to buy: *A Honky Tonk Reprise*, aka *Rosie Flores* (Warner Bros., 1987/Rounder, 1996, prod. Pete Anderson) ♫♫♫♫♫, is a reissue of her stunning 1987 self-titled Warner Bros. debut, which ranges from such neo-traditional romps as "Crying over You" and "Heartbreak Train" to such sobering ballads as "Somebody Loses, Somebody Wins" and "God May Forgive You (But I Won't)." The latter—a Harlan Howard/Bobby Braddock composition that eclipses Lyle Lovett's similar "God Will"—has been resurrected as a Flores-inspired fixture in Iris DeMent's live show. The Rounder reissue comes with six bonus tracks, including a heartmelting cover of Skeeter Davis' "End of the World."

the rest:

After the Farm (HighTone, 1992) ♫♫♫♫

Once More with Feeling (HighTone, 1993) ♫♫♫

Rockabilly Filly (HighTone, 1995) ♫♫♫

(With Ray Campi) *A Little Bit of Heartache* (Watermelon, 1997) ♫♫♫

worth searching for: Rosie's faithful cover of "My Own Kind of Hat" appears on the Merle Haggard tribute *Tulare Dust* (HighTone, 1994, prod. Tom Russell, Dave Alvin) ♫♫♫♫

influences:

◀◀ Wanda Jackson, Brenda Lee, Patsy Cline

▶▶ Iris DeMent, k.d. lang

David Okamoto

FLYING BURRITO BROTHERS

Formed 1968, in Los Angeles, CA.

Gram Parsons, vocals, guitar (1968–70), Chris Hillman, vocals, guitar, bass (1968–72); Chris Etheridge, bass (1968–75); "Sneaky" Pete Kleinow, steel guitar (1968–71, 1974–present); Michael Clarke, drums, harmonica (1969–72); Bernie Leadon, guitar, banjo, dobro, vocals (1969–71); Rick Roberts, guitar, vocals (1970–73); Al Perkins, pedal steel (1971–72); Byron Berline, fiddle (1971–73); Roger Bush, bass (1971–73); Kenny Wertz, guitar (1971–73); Al Munde, banjo, guitar (1972–73); Don Beck, pedal steel (1972–73); Erik Dalton, drums (1972–73); John Beland, guitar (1981–present); Joe Scott Hill, bass, vocals (1974–present); Floyd "Gib" Gilbeau, fiddle, guitar, vocals (1974–present); Gene Parsons, drums, (1974–present); Skip Battin, bass, (1976–present); Ed Ponder, drums; Jim Goodall (1985–88).

Formed by ex-Byrds Chris Hillman and Gram Parsons, the Flying Burrito Brothers are generally considered a transition period for Parsons between the Byrds and his solo work. But the group, arguably the first to play what's now considered country-rock, still performs despite the absence of its two founders. During the early 1980s a version of the group relocated to Nashville and released a series of moderately successful country singles as the Flying Burrito Brothers and, simply, the Burrito Brothers (the biggest of which, "She Belongs to Everyone but Me," reached #16 in 1981). A group including Sneaky Pete, Skip Battin, Greg Harris and Jim Goodall also recorded as the Flying Brothers.

what to buy: *The Gilded Palace of Sin* (A&M, 1969, prod. Flying Burrito Brothers, Larry Marks, Henry Lewy) 🎵🎵🎵🎵 was a grand experiment that fused notions of country music, California hippie rock and Southern soul. Parsons and Hillman were writing some of their best songs—among them "Sin City" (later cut by Dwight Yoakam) and "Hot Burrito #1" (covered by Elvis Costello)—and also covered Muscle Shoals classics "Do Right Woman" and "Dark End of the Street." For a thorough overview, *Farther Along: The Best of the Flying Burrito Brothers* (A&M, 1988, prod. various) 🎵🎵🎵🎵 contains 21 cuts, including nine from *The Gilded Palace of Sin* and some rare outtakes.

what to buy next: Not quite the groundbreaker that *Gilded Palace* was, *Burrito Deluxe* (A&M/Edsel, 1970, prod. Jim Dickson, Henry Lewy) 🎵🎵🎵🎵 nevertheless offers some fine moments in the same vein. It also contains the Burritos' version of "Wild Horses," which Mick Jagger and Keith Richards allegedly wrote for Parsons (according to the same legend, he re-arranged "Honky Tonk Woman" as "Country Honk" for the Rolling Stones).

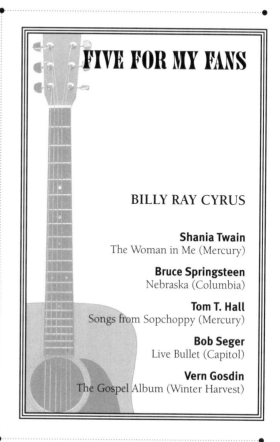

FIVE FOR MY FANS

BILLY RAY CYRUS

Shania Twain
The Woman in Me (Mercury)

Bruce Springsteen
Nebraska (Columbia)

Tom T. Hall
Songs from Sopchoppy (Mercury)

Bob Seger
Live Bullet (Capitol)

Vern Gosdin
The Gospel Album (Winter Harvest)

what to avoid: The quality of the band's recordings took a sharp drop after Parsons left, so all but the most die-hard fans could live without anything recorded after the group left A&M. Be especially wary of *Eye of a Hurricane* (One Way, 1994) 🎵🎵, a European-only release that finds the band a shell of its former self.

the rest:
The Flying Burrito Bros (A&M/Mobile Fidelity, 1971) 🎵🎵🎵🎵
Last of the Red Hot Burritos (A&M/Rebound, 1972) 🎵🎵🎵
Airborne (Columbia, 1976) 🎵🎵
Flying Again (Columbia, 1975) 🎵🎵
Close Up the Honky Tonks (A&M, 1974) 🎵🎵🎵
Sleepless Nights (A&M, 1976) 🎵🎵🎵
From Another Time (Shiloh, 1976)
Close Encounters to the West Coast (Relix, 1978) 🎵🎵
Live from Europe (Relix, 1986) 🎵🎵
Back to the Sweethearts of the Rodeo (Appaloosa, 1987) 🎵🎵
Cabin Fever (Relix, 1989) 🎵🎵

Sin City (Relix) ♫♫
Best of the Flying Burrito Brothers (Relix) ♫♫♩

worth searching for: Byrd fanatics can seek out the import *Dim Lights, Thick Smoke and Loud, Loud Music* (Edsel, 1993) ♫♫♩.

influences:

◀◀ Byrds, Hank Williams, Memphis/Muscle Shoals soul

▶▶ Eagles, Gram Parsons, Desert Rose Band, Jayhawks, Uncle Tupelo, Wilco, Son Volt

see also: *Byrds, Gram Parsons, Chris Hillman, Alan Munde*

Brian Mansfield

DAN FOGELBERG

Born August 13, 1951, in Peoria, IL.

Dan Fogelberg was raised in the Midwest, rose to prominence on the West Coast amidst Southern California's burgeoning folk-rock singer-songwriter scene of the early 1970s and ended up in Boulder, Colorado—a fitting final destination for a "quiet man of music," to borrow one of his better-known lyrics. He dropped out of art school at the University of Illinois in 1971 and moved to Los Angeles to try his hand at a music career; he earned a deal with Columbia (eventually settling on the CBS subsidiary Full Moon/Epic). As Fogelberg's career progressed, his music veered away from the West Coast's country-pop stylings and more toward an unlikely mix of sentimental ballads and atmospheric pro-rock. The ballads are what eventually made him famous, likely on the strength of Fogelberg's distinctive high-tenor voice. He became a staple of adult-contemporary radio stations during the late 1970s and early 1980s with hits such as "Longer" and "Leader of the Band." Since the mid-1980s, Fogelberg has shown an increasing and generally healthy willingness to experiment with other styles—sometimes with refreshing results, such as 1985's bluegrass-oriented *High Country Snows*, other times less successfully (1993's world-music-influenced *River of Souls*).

what to buy: Even after more than a quarter century and a dozen albums, Fogelberg's debut, *Home Free* (Columbia, 1972, prod. Norbert Putnam) ♫♫♫♫, still stands as his best work, simply because it's so unaffected by the more commercial considerations of his subsequent efforts. Songs such as "To the Morning" and "Hickory Grove" capture the innocence of his Illinois youth at an early enough stage in his career that he could still feel it pulling on him.

what to buy next: *High Country Snows* (Full Moon/Epic, 1985,

prod. Dan Fogelberg, Marty Lewis) ♫♫♫ was a welcome venture into bluegrass, with guest appearances by the likes of Doc Watson, David Grisman, Chris Hillman and Herb Pedersen. For a straightforward collection of chart successes, *Greatest Hits* (Full Moon/Epic, 1982, prod. various) ♫♫♫ is a serviceable document despite its revealingly yuppified cover photo.

what to avoid: *Windows and Walls* (Full Moon/Epic, 1984, prod. Dan Fogelberg) ♫ represents the depths of Fogelberg's shallowness; hardly a song on here is even worth hearing. *Love Songs* (Full Moon/Epic, 1995, prod. various) ♫♫ isn't so much bad as it is unnecessary, an apparent attempt by the label to rehash Fogelberg's hits one more time after he'd moved on to a different record company.

the rest:

Souvenirs (Full Moon/Epic, 1974) ♫♫♫
Captured Angel (Full Moon/Epic, 1975) ♫♫♩
Nether Lands (Full Moon/Epic, 1977) ♫♫♫
(With Tim Weisberg) *Twin Sons of Different Mothers* (Full Moon/Epic, 1978) ♫♫
Phoenix (Full Moon/Epic, 1979) ♫♫
The Innocent Age (Full Moon/Epic, 1981) ♫♫♫♩
Exiles (Full Moon/Epic, 1987) ♫♩
The Wild Places (Full Moon/Epic, 1990) ♫♫♩
Greetings from the West (Full Moon/Epic, 1991) ♫♫♫♫
River of Souls (Full Moon/Epic, 1993) ♫♫
(With Weisberg) *No Resemblance Whatsoever* (Giant, 1995) ♫♫

influences:

◀◀ Cascades, Jackson Browne, James Taylor, Bruce Cockburn

▶▶ Garth Brooks, Billy Dean, David Wilcox, James McMurtry

Peter Blackstock

JOHN FOGERTY

Born May 28, 1945, in Berkeley, CA.

Creedence Clearwater Revival mastermind John Fogerty fell in love with old-fashioned country & western while the band, reduced to a trio after the 1971 departure of his older brother Tom, recorded one of the worst albums ever made by a major American rock band, *Mardi Gras*. Hints of his growing infatuation could be heard on Fogerty's "I'm Looking for a Reason" and his steel guitar licks on his remake of "Hello Mary Lou" on that otherwise largely dismal album. But nothing could have prepared anyone for what followed. Fogerty went into the studio by himself and produced and recorded a *tour de force*, a straight-forward set of traditional country songs under the moniker the Blue Ridge Rangers.

John Fogerty (© **Ken Settle**)

what to buy: The repertoire on *The Blue Ridge Rangers* (Fantasy, 1973, prod. John Fogerty) 🎵🎵🎵🎵 ranges from the Hank Williams evergreen "Jamabalaya" and Webb Pierce's "I Ain't Never," to the 1961 Bobby Edwards hit "You're the Reason" and the Merle Haggard standard, "Today I Started Loving You Again." Although the set's third single nicked the bottom end of the Top 40 charts, the entire release was greeted with a thud and Fogerty soon retreated to making rock and roll records, re-emerging in 1985 as one of the great comeback stories in pop music. But this one album, a full heartfelt commitment to a radical departure for a brilliant artist, remains behind as a stunning product of an obsessive musical mind sorting through personal portraits of Americana that finds its wobbly, awkward way straight to the heart of the matter.

what to buy next: *Chronicle* (Fantasy, 1976, prod. John Fogerty) 🎵🎵🎵🎵 offers a fairly comprehensive overview of Creedence's hits, showing more than a few twangy roots in such songs as "Bad Moon Rising," "Lodi," "Who'll Stop the Rain" and "Lookin' out My Back Door."

what to avoid: Give a wide berth to *Mardi Gras* (Fantasy, 1971, prod. John Fogerty) **WOOF!**.

the rest:

(With Creedence Clearwater Revival) *Creedence Clearwater Revival* (Fantasy, 1968) 🎵🎵🎵

(With Creedence Clearwater Revival) *Green River* (Fantasy, 1969) 🎵🎵🎵🎵

(With Creedence Clearwater Revival) *Born on the Bayou* (Fantasy, 1969) 🎵🎵🎵🎵

(With Creedence Clearwater Revival) *Willy and the Poor Boys* (Fantasy, 1969) 🎵🎵🎵🎵

(With Creedence Clearwater Revival) *Cosmo's Factory* (Fantasy, 1970) 🎵🎵🎵🎵🎵

John Fogerty (Asylum, 1975) 🎵🎵🎵

Centerfield (Warner Bros., 1985) 🎵🎵🎵🎵

Eye of the Zombie (Warner Bros., 1986) 🎵🎵

red foley

(With Creedence Clearwater Revival) *Live in Europe* (Fantasy, 1987) **WOOF!**

(With Creedence Clearwater Revival) *The Concert* (Fantasy, 1980) ♪

(With Creedence Clearwater Revival) *Chronicle, Volume 2* (Fantasy, 1986) ♪♪♪

Blue Moon Swamp (Warner Bros., 1997)

worth searching for: A couple of Fogerty's Warner Bros. singles contain highly worthwhile non-LP B-sides, especially his rollicking take on the zydeco hit "My Toot Toot," on the flip of "Change in the Weather."

influences:

◀◀ Elvis Presley, Little Richard, Hank Williams, Merle Haggard, Booker T. & the MGs

▶▶ Bob Seger, Bruce Springsteen, Hollies, Dave Edmunds

Joel Selvin

RED FOLEY

Born Clyde Julian Foley, June 17, 1910, in Blue Lick, KY. Died Sept. 19, 1968, in Fort Wayne, IN.

Possessed of a smooth, trained baritone voice and an easy manner, Red Foley is often credited with making country music more palatable to the mainstream audience; he had several country hits that also charted on the pop hit parade, including 1950's "Chattanoogie Shoeshine Boy," which charted #1 both pop and country. Other of his #1 country hits that also were successful as pop fare were "Smoke on the Water," "Birmingham Bounce" and "Goodnight, Irene" (with Ernest Tubb). He was equally at home with country boogies, sentimental traditional fare, pop-styled ballads, and such gospel numbers as "Peace in the Valley." An early country radio star on WLS' *National Barn Dance* and the *Renfro Valley Barn Dance,* Foley became host of the Prince Albert segment of the Grand Ole Opry beginning in 1946; he left in 1954 to host ABC's *Ozark Jubilee,* one of the first nationally televised country music shows. He was elected to the Country Music Hall of Fame in 1967.

what to buy: *Country Music Hall of Fame Series* (MCA, 1991, prod. Country Music Foundation) ♪♪♪♪ contains a good sampling of the versatility of this important country star, with original versions of such landmark hits as "Old Shep," "Tennessee Saturday Night," "Tennessee Border," "Peace in the Valley," "Alabama Jubilee," "Midnight," and "Sugarfoot Rag."

what to avoid: For years, *The Red Foley Story* (Decca/MCA, 1964) **WOOF!**, a two-LP set of treacly remakes, was the only greatest-hits package available of this great and important artist. Avoid it.

influences:

◀◀ Bradley Kincaid, Rev. Thomas Dorsey

▶▶ Jim Reeves, Willie Nelson

Randy Pitts

THE FORBES FAMILY

Formed 1976, in PA.

Homer Forbes, vocals, banjo, fiddle; Lisa Forbes Roberts, vocals; Lori Forbes Slate, vocals, bass; Jay Forbes, vocals, mandolin.

This group of siblings recorded several country/bluegrass albums in its home state until eventually relocating to North Carolina to focus more on bluegrass gospel music. By the late 1980s, after four albums on Rebel Records, family obligations led to the Forbes Family's breakup. In 1994, following the release of a collection of their earlier material, they returned to record two remarkable albums.

what's available: *Best of the Early Forbes Family* (Rebel, 1994, prod. Homer Forbes) ♪♪♪♪ is 18 tracks long and includes a couple of standouts written by Claire Lynch among its many treasures. *I'll Look to Him* (Rebel, 1995, prod. Ron Rhoads Jr.) ♪♪♪♪ is distinguished by the group's gorgeous *a cappella* rendition of the Molly O'Day gospel number, "I'll Face Nobody's Record but Mine." *In the Shadow of Your Wings* (Rebel, 1996, prod. Ron Block, Forbes Family) ♪♪♪♪ is the latest and most polished effort by the group, aided by the members of Alison Krauss' band Union Station (minus Krauss).

influences:

◀◀ Marshall Family, Claire Lynch

▶▶ Alison Krauss, Cox Family

Stephen L. Betts

MARY FORD

See: Les Paul & Mary Ford

TENNESSEE ERNIE FORD

Born February 13, 1919, in Fordtown, TN. Died October 17, 1991.

Perhaps best-known for his mammoth 1956 hit "Sixteen Tons" and his prime-time network television show, Tennessee Ernie was a force in country music for many years before and after that giant hit. Based on the West Coast, Ford recorded for Capitol after 1949; he recorded a series of uptempo bluesy and "boogie" numbers during the 'Fifties, many of them charting quite high on the country charts—both "Mule Train" and "Shotgun Boogie" charted #1. He hosted NBC's College of Musical Knowledge from 1954, the show on which he first sang "Sixteen Tons." This giant hit and his general likeability led Ford to a weekly prime-time spot on NBC from 1956–61. His booming, trained baritone voice sounded less and less country on recordings as the years went by; he sold increasing numbers of albums–particularly gospel–through the 1960s than he had in the past, but most could hardly be called country. Ford was elected to the Country Music Hall of Fame in 1990.

what to buy: *Sixteen Tons* (Capitol, 1960, prod. Lee Gillette) *ƯƯƯƯƯ* contains the hit title song, one of the biggest country singles ever, along with 11 songs more typical of what ol' Ern' had recorded up to that time. *16 Tons of Boogie: The Best of Tennessee Ernie Ford* (Rhino, 1990, reissue prod. Rich Kienzle) *ƯƯƯƯ* offers an attractive alternative to the set above; also most of the early hits, but also contains duets with labelmates Ella Mae Morse, Kay Starr and the Dinning Sisters; a more wide-ranging overview. *Sixteen Tons* (Bear Family, 1990, reissue prod. Richard Weize) *ƯƯƯƯ* is another excellent retrospective, with more cuts (25), more oddities, complete with booklet, discography and detailed notes. *Masters, 1949–1976* (Capitol, 1995, prod. various) *ƯƯƯƯ* is a four-disc box set for the completist.

what to buy next: *Ernie Sings & Glen Picks* (Liberty, 1975, prod. Steve Stone) *ƯƯƯ* is a fine and unique album from late in Ernie's career, when he returns to spare arrangements of bluesy material, accompanied only by string bass and Glen Campbell's guitar. *Songs of the Civil War* (Capitol, 1961, prod. Lee Gillette) *ƯƯƯ* was recorded during the Civil War's Centennial and re-released to capitalize on the success of the PBS series. This set (originally two LPs) finds Ern embracing hits from both sides of the Civil War conflict.

the rest:
Favorite Hymns (Ranwood, 1987) *ƯƯ*
All-Time Greatest Hymns (Curb, 1990) *ƯƯƯ*
Country Gospel Classics, Volume 1 (Liberty, 1991) *ƯƯƯ*
Country Gospel Classics, Volume 2 (Capitol, 1991) *ƯƯƯ*
Red, White, and Blue (Liberty, 1991) *ƯƯƯ*
Collector's Series (Capitol, 1991) *ƯƯƯ*
Vintage Collections (Capitol, 1997) *ƯƯƯƯ*

influences:
◀◀ Merle Travis
▶▶ Junior Brown

Randy Pitts

THE FORESTER SISTERS

Formed 1982, in Lookout Mountain, GA.

Kathy Forester, lead vocals; Kim Forester, second lead vocals; June Forester, harmony vocals; Christy Forester, harmony vocals.

During their mid-1980s heyday, the Forester Sisters epitomized the flowery and feminine side of being Southern. They looked and sounded as though the term "Southern belle" was coined just for them. With their flowing four-part harmony and penchant for songs about the peaches-and-cream stage of love, this sibling quartet dominated the country charts from early 1985 to late 1989. Although they are not songwriters and don't really play any instruments, the Forester Sisters carefully crafted their images, both physical and musical. Such hits as "I Fell in Love Again Last Night," "Mama's Never Seen Those Eyes" and their sweet cover of the McGuire Sisters' "Sincerely" are ear candy. Sometimes, though, too much sugar is repugnant: "(I'd Choose) You Again" and "(That's What You Do) When You're in Love" took the formula to cloying levels. The Sisters were most effective when they channeled melancholy and realism into their soothing harmonies: "Letter Home," about one woman's therapeutic note to her mother; and their cover of Brenda Lee's torrid "Too Many Rivers" packed tranquil power. By 1991 the Sisters decided to experiment with their trademark country-pop-bluegrass hybrid. "Men," their last Top 10 hit, showcased a bluesier, sassier ensemble comfortable vamping about the pros and cons of the male sex. It was a resounding victory, a fresh transfusion into a dying style. But it was short-lived; "I Got a Date," from the Sisters' 1992 album of the same name, attempted to bank on "Men's" success with a dash of self-deprecating humor to go with the frankness. But radio rejected the song and Warner Bros. dropped the act from its roster. Four years later the Sisters resigned with Warner Bros., but this time with its Nashville-based religious music imprint, Warner Resound. Tapping into their gospel background, which they had done before for two specialty CDs, and delivering their signature sound in sparer arrangements, the Foresters crafted an elegant, cohesive project titled *More Than I Am*. Their days of radio hits are gone, but maybe the Forester Sisters can be more than a has-been group banking on past glories.

what to buy: *Greatest Hits* (Warner Bros., 1989, prod. various) *ƯƯƯƯ* is a must-buy for Forester Sisters novices; it's the only CD available that collects the bulk of the Sisters' staples. While anyone would survive just fine without a couple of sugary confections, especially "(I'd Choose) You Again," such quality stuff as "Letter Home," "Just in Case" and the ultra-catchy duet with the Bellamy Brothers, "Too Much Is Not Enough," are worth the price.

what to buy next: Unlike much of today's contemporary Christian pap, *More Than I Am* (Warner Resound, 1996, prod. Gary Smith, Forester Sisters) 𝅘𝅥𝅘𝅥𝅘𝅥 delivers its message without heavy-handed lyrics and weighty production. Such cuts as "Another Shoulder at the Wheel," "Have You Seen Me?" and the classic "Let's Get Together" extol the virtues of unity and compassion. You don't need any dogma to understand that.

what to avoid: If record companies would slap all their Christmas albums out of print, the holidays should be much less commercial. We don't need *The Christmas Card* (Warner Bros., 1987, prod. Jim Ed Norman) 𝅘𝅥𝅘𝅥. How many times can one human being possibly hear "White Christmas," "The First Noel" and "I'll Be Home for Christmas?" Somebody please write a new batch of holiday standards.

the rest:
Talkin' 'bout Men (Warner Bros., 1991) 𝅘𝅥𝅘𝅥𝅘𝅥
Sunday Meetin' (JCI/Warner Special Products, 1993) 𝅘𝅥𝅘𝅥𝅘𝅥

worth searching for: The "Men" phenomenon should have translated to wide acceptance for the title cut of *I Got a Date* (Warner Bros., 1992, prod. Robert Byrne, Alan Schulman) 𝅘𝅥𝅘𝅥𝅘𝅥, which explores the Forester's more mature side. The title cut is a hoot, "Redneck Romeo" is played for laughs, "Wanda" is touching storytelling and "Their Hearts Are Dancing" is Southern sentimentalism as its most endearing.

influences:
◀◀ Brenda Lee, McGuire Sisters
▶▶ Wild Rose, Dixie Chicks

Mario Tarradell

FOSTER & LLOYD

Formed 1987, in Nashville, TN. Disbanded 1992.

Radney Foster (born July 20, 1959 in Del Rio, TX), vocals, guitar; Bill Lloyd (born December 6, 1955 in Bowling Green, KY), vocals, guitar.

Foster & Lloyd's run was short-lived but of high quality. They specialized in country-tinged romantic angst cut with a healthy dose of wry detachment. Listening to the three albums they made together summons up wistful memories of one of those heady five-minute timeouts in Nashville (in this case, post-Barbara Mandrell, pre-Garth Brooks) when it seemed as if off-center artists might possibly find a niche. Lyle Lovett, Dwight

Yoakam and Steve Earle were shaking things up; Rosanne Cash hadn't fled to New York. Out of this interesting atmosphere came acts like Foster & Lloyd and the O'Kanes, sharp-eyed songwriting teams who turned to performing with the blessing—and creative license—of major recording labels. Foster, a lawyer's son, and Lloyd, an army brat and communications major, didn't fit the traditional country-act mold, coveting greater pop and rock influences than Nashville tolerated at the time. They were, however, writers of hit songs for the likes of the Sweethearts of the Rodeo and Holly Dunn, which gave them strong potential as a recording act.

what to buy: *Foster & Lloyd* (RCA, 1987, prod. Radney Foster, Bill Lloyd) 𝅘𝅥𝅘𝅥𝅘𝅥𝅘𝅥 is a charmer—deft songwriting, tight arrangements, enough rockabilly backbeat to keep things hopping and enough engaging harmony singing to keep things down-home. The pleading "Don't Go Out with Him," for instance, almost sounds like something the Ronettes could have sung. For those who'd like their Foster & Lloyd in one neat, easy-to-remember place, *The Essential Foster & Lloyd* (RCA, 1996) 𝅘𝅥𝅘𝅥𝅘𝅥𝅘𝅥 collects their career highlights.

the rest:
Faster and Llouder (RCA, 1989) 𝅘𝅥𝅘𝅥𝅘𝅥𝅘𝅥
Version of the Truth (RCA, 1990) 𝅘𝅥𝅘𝅥𝅘𝅥𝅘𝅥

solo outings:
Bill Lloyd:
Set to Pop (ESD, 1994) 𝅘𝅥𝅘𝅥𝅘𝅥𝅘𝅥

influences:
◀◀ Beatles, Eagles, Alabama, Big Star
▶▶ Brooks & Dunn

see also: *Radney Foster*

Elizabeth Lynch

RADNEY FOSTER

Born July 20, 1959 in Del Rio, TX.

"I love traditional country," Radney Foster said upon the release of his second solo album. "But there's always something creative and different that comes along in country music and shakes the trees." As part of the rock/pop-influenced duo Foster & Lloyd, Radney certainly knew a thing or two about shaking the trees. After signing as a solo act with Arista in 1992, he placed a heavier emphasis on the traditional—although his iconoclastic streak is still in evidence. The playful rockabilly riffs that distinguished the Foster & Lloyd sound are largely absent from Foster's solo outings. In their place is a stripped-down, foursquare sound with plenty of pedal steel, solid guitar work and close harmonies. To round things out, Foster hasn't been shy about gathering top-notch guest talent, including Kim Richey, John Hiatt, Lee Roy Parnell and Mary Chapin Carpenter.

what's available: *Del Rio, TX 1959* (Arista, 1992, prod. Steve Fishell, Radney Foster) 🎵🎵🎵 features Foster's usual strong songwriting and spawned three Top 10 hits, though it sounds a bit too self-consciously retro in spots. The underappreciated *Labor of Love* (Arista, 1994, prod. Steve Fishell, Radney Foster) 🎵🎵🎵🎵 displays a more confident array of styles, from the intro-spective and tender "Never Say Die" to a honky tonk drive that rivals Dwight Yoakam on "Walkin' Talkin' Woman." And the lyrics of "Making It Up" ("People think you know what you're talking about/All because you wrote some song/I ain't no smarter than the rest of the these clowns/I'm just making it up as I go along") prove that Foster's sardonic way with a lyric hasn't deserted him.

worth searching for: Foster's version of "The Running Kind" on *Mama's Hungry Eyes* (Arista, 1994, prod. various), one of two all-star tributes to Merle Haggard's songs.

influences:
◀◀ Merle Haggard, Ray Price, Waylon Jennings
▶▶ Kim Richey, George Ducas, Deryl Dodd

see also: *Foster & Lloyd*

Elizabeth Lynch

4 RUNNER

Formed 1995, in Nashville, TN.

Craig Morris, lead vocals; Jim Chapman, bass vocals; Lee Hilliard, vocals; Billy Crittenden, baritone vocals (1995–96); Billy Smith, baritone vocals (1996–present).

The only country group named for a sport-utility vehicle, 4 Runner became the first vocal quartet to chart a song since the Oak Ridge Boys. However, founding baritone Billy Crittenden, a former Tanya Tucker backup singer who co-wrote Diamond Rio's big hit "Love a Little Stronger," left the group after one album and was replaced by Billy Smith. Other members of the group include Lee Hilliard, a former gospel singer and former backup singer for Loretta Lynn, Vern Gosdin and Reba McEntire; bass singer Jim Chapman, a singer/songwriter and elementary school art teacher; and lead vocalist Craig Morris, whose re-

sume includes writing songs cut by John Conlee, the Oak Ridge Boys, McEntire, Ray Charles, Gary Morris and Gene Watson.

what's available: *4 Runner* (Polydor, 1995, prod. Buddy Cannon, Larry Shell) 🎵🎵🎵 is worth having for the good-versus-evil tale of the throbbing, menacing "Cain's Blood" and the hilarious small-town gossip of "Ripples."

influences:
◀◀ Oak Ridge Boys

Bill Hobbs

THE FOX FAMILY

Family group formed 1993.

Kim Fox, guitar, vocals; Barb Fox, bass, vocals; Joel Fox, banjo, vocals; Ron Feinberg, fiddle.

The Fox Family consists of three siblings and a fiddling friend who have earned a formidable reputation for consistently winning bluegrass talent shows in upstate New York. What makes the group so refreshing and appealing is its blending of tightly knit harmonizing with an intuitive feel for instrumental improvisation—the hallmark of truly great bluegrass. In 1994 the band was nominated for the Emerging Artist of the Year award by the International Bluegrass Music Association.

what's available: *Follow My Lead* (Sierra Records, 1995, prod. Kevin Short) 🎵🎵🎵🎵 brilliantly showcases the extraordinary singing and songwriting talents of Kim Fox. Her vivid, plaintive narrative approach is especially evident on "Widow Janie" and "I'm Your Papa." Patsy Montana's chestnut "Cowboy Sweetheart" is cleverly set to a lilting swing rhythm. *When It Comes to Blues* (Sierra Records, 1996, prod. Kevin Short, Fox Family) 🎵🎵🎵🎵 features "The Dream," a moving tribute to bluegrass greats Bill Monroe, Lester Flatt and Earl Scruggs.

influences:
◀◀ Bill Monroe, Cox Family
▶▶ New Vintage

Rick Petreycik

JEFF FOXWORTHY

Born September 6, 1958, in Atlanta, GA.

Jeff Foxworthy, riding his "You might be a redneck if . . ." joke all the way to the best-seller lists and prime-time television, almost singlehandedly restored pride to the silent hillbilly majority. Until sales of his books and CDs reached the million plus

Jeff Foxworthy **(Parallel Entertainment)**

mark, rednecks were portrayed as the racists in Randy Newman's song "Rednecks," as murderers and victims in the movie *Deliverance*, or as hapless bumpkins a la *The Beverly Hillbillies*. Foxworthy is a friendly, charismatic comedian whose paycheck comes from such lines as "you might be a redneck if you prefer car keys to Q-Tips" and "you might be a redneck if you know the Hooters menu by heart." Though his standup routines too frequently lapse into Jerry Seinfeld-like observations about the differences between men and women, he makes a perfect change of pace for any country-music festival.

what to buy: Both his comedy albums, *You Might Be a Redneck If . . .* (Warner Bros., 1993, prod. Jeff Foxworthy) 𝄞𝄞𝄞 and *Games Rednecks Play* (Warner Bros., 1995, prod. Doug Grau, Scott Rause) 𝄞𝄞, laugh *with* white Southerners instead of at them. There's a lot of boring filler beyond the redneck zingers, though.

what to buy next: A pre-stardom comedy album, *Live 1990* (Laughing Hyena, 1990, prod. Jeff Foxworthy) 𝄞𝄞 showcases Foxworthy developing his shtick and is a nice addition to diehard fans' collections.

what to avoid: *Crank It Up: The Music Album* (Warner Bros., 1996, prod. Jeff Foxworthy) 𝄞 is country's equivalent of the Blues Brothers; musicians do funny country songs already, so why (aside from money) glut the marketplace with the boring "Redneck Stomp" or "Redneck 12 Days of Christmas"?

influences:

⏮ Baxter Black, Bob Wills, George Carlin, Jerry Seinfeld

⏭ Bill Engvall, Ron White, Bill Clinton

Steve Knopper

MICHAEL FRACASSO

Born February 10, 1952, in Stubbenville, OH.

Through events that shaped his life, Michael Fracasso has been able to draw from three distinct musical landscapes to create his rootsy folk-country sound. A native of mill town-area Ohio, Fracasso was educated in Catholic schools and reared in working class neighborhoods, which explains his songs' frequent subject matters—religious mores and Midwestern life. In 1978 Fracasso relocated to New York City, where he soaked up the folk coffeehouse scene frequented by Steve Forbert, Suzanne Vega and Cliff Eberhardt. His songwriting reflected the thoughtfulness and the introspective spirit of his folk surroundings. But by 1991 Fracasso was on the move again; this time, he ended up in Austin, where he lives today. Naturally, the Texas connection provided Fracasso with the country kick that embellishes his compositions. The gorgeous country waltz, "Door #1," a duet with fellow-Austinite Lucinda Williams, makes his first album, *Love & Trust*, a must. His second set, *When I Lived in the Wild*, has a folkier feel, although the sneering "How Very Inconvenient" rocks as hard as any Rolling Stones song. His ability to travel through various territories and still maintain his melodic ground, which in turn smooths his nasal-tinged voice, makes Fracasso an artist on the verge of conquering more than just Lone Star state soil.

what to buy: *Love & Trust* (Dejadisc, 1993, prod. Michael Fracasso, Mike Hardwick) 𝄞𝄞𝄞𝄞 offers Fracasso's folk-country hybrid with elegance and depth. Whether he's questioning the effects of religion on "Wise Blood," examining the perils of love on "Door #1" or telling a story about Mama's little girl turned high-fashion model in "Apple Pie," Fracasso always has something important to say.

the rest:

When I Lived in the Wild (Bohemia Beat, 1995) 𝄞𝄞𝄞

worth searching for: Fracasso joined Austin buddies Iain Matthews and Mark Hallman to form the Hamilton Pool side project, a Buddy-Holly-meets-Beatles-with-harmonica group. The trio recorded an album, *Return to Zero*, but if you want a quick taste of their work and a slew of other cool acts like Webb Wilder, Timbuk 3, Alejandro Escovedo and Don Walser, pick up *The Watermelon Sampler Volume 1* (Watermelon, 1995, prod. various) ♫♫♫.

influences:

◀◀ Steve Forbert, Bob Dylan, Buddy Holly

▶▶ Jimmy LaFave, Iain Matthews, Silos

Mario Tarradell

J.P. & ANNADEENE FRALEY

Vocal duo formed in KY.

J.P. Fraley (born c. 1922), vocals, fiddle; Annadeene Fraley (born July 15, 1913; died April 12, 1996), vocals, guitar.

Though their two available recordings were made 20 years apart, J.P. & Annadeene Fraley manage to reach far beyond the walls of time with their emotion-filled, deftly delivered fiddle tunes, borne out of the hills surrounding their Northeastern Kentucky home. She had been a featured vocalist on numerous radio programs since age 13; he had a local reputation as a skilled fisherman as well as a fine fiddler. The couple married in 1946, but wouldn't begin playing together on a regular basis until the late 1950s. J.P. had beaten famed fiddler Buddy Spicher in a contest he had entered on a whim. More contests followed, and the couple also made numerous appearances at folk festivals as well. The couple made their first recording during 1973, while J.P. was working in brickyards and as a troubleshooting expert on coal-cutting equipment for the National Mine Service. Retired by the early 1990s, they resurfaced in 1995 to record what would be their second, and final album.

what to buy: *Maysville* (Rounder, 1995, prod. Mark Wilson) ♫♫♫♫ boasts more than two dozen fiddle tunes, both covers and Fraley originals. It's perfect music for a cool summer evening, relaxing on the front porch.

what to buy next: *Wild Rose of the Mountain* (Rounder, 1973, prod. Guthrie T. Meade, Mark Wilson) ♫♫♫ features fewer tunes than the other collection, but at 18 cuts, it's still packed with tradition and excellence.

worth searching for: Although it doesn't contain performances by the Fraleys, the collections *Traditional Fiddle Music Of Kentucky, Volumes One and Two* (Rounder, 1997, prod. John Harrod, Mark Wilson) ♫♫♫♫ are indicative of the pervasive music of the Kentucky and Ohio River regions that influenced, and was

ultimately influenced by, J.P and Annadeene Fraley. Guthrie "Gus" Meade, who helped compile the Fraley's recordings, gathered more than 70 field recordings for these two indispensable collections.

influences:

◀◀ Roy Acuff, Ed Haley

▶▶ Buddy Thomas, J.B. Miller

Stephen L. Betts

CONNIE FRANCIS

Born Concetta Rosa Maria Franconero, December 12, 1938, in Newark, NJ.

Connie Francis had only a couple of country hits, but she was one of the many pop singers of the 1950s and 1960s who recorded in Nashville. Along with Brenda Lee and Annette Funicello, Francis was one of America's teen idols of that time period, and her popularity crossed from pop not only into country but also into the R&B and film markets as well. She was also an international star, frequently recordings new vocal tracks for her hit singles in Italian, Spanish and other languages. Her best-remembered hits include her debut, 1958's "Who's Sorry Now," "Stupid Cupid" and 1961's "Where the Boys Are."

what to buy: *The Very Best of Connie Francis* (Polydor, 1986, compilation prod. Tim Rogers) ♫♫♫♫ contains most of Francis' biggest pop singles, including the chart-topping "My Heart Has a Mind of Its Own" and "Don't Break the Heart That Loves You." "Everybody's Somebody's Fool," from 1962, was one of her country crossover singles, and "Second-Hand Love," a Phil Spector tune recorded in Nashville, has a distinctive Floyd Cramer piano introduction.

what to buy next: With its four discs, the boxed set *Souvenirs* (Polydor, 1996, compilation prod. Don Charles, Bill Levenson, Patrick Niglio) ♫♫♫ provides a wide-ranging overview of Francis' recordings during her heyday. Many of these tracks were recorded in Nashville: during her career, Francis was produced by Danny Davis (of the Nashville Brass), Shelby S. Singleton Jr. and a young Norro Wilson. *Souvenirs* contains not only "Everybody's Somebody's Fool," but also Francis' other Top 40 country single, 1969's "Wedding Cake," as well as covers of the George Jones' classic "He Thinks I Still Care" and Tammy Wynette's "I Don't Wanna Play House."

what to avoid: Too many of Francis' original recordings remain in print to settle for the remakes on *Greatest Hits* (Dominion, 1994) ♫♫.

the rest:

Christmas in My Heart (Polydor, 1987) 🎵🎵🎵

Greatest Hits (Polydor) 🎵🎵🎵

Greatest Italian Hits (Polydor) 🎵🎵🎵

The Very Best of Connie Francis, Volume II (Polydor, 1988) 🎵🎵

Solid Gold (Pair) 🎵🎵🎵

Where the Hits Are (Malaco) 🎵🎵

De Coleccion (Latin/PolyGram, 1995) 🎵🎵🎵

worth searching for: The German label Bear Family has issued the duets Francis recorded in 1964 with Hank Williams Jr. on *Sing Great Country Favourites* (Bear Family) 🎵🎵🎵, which is mainly worth hearing just for the sheer strangeness of the concept.

influences:

◀◀ Kay Starr, Jo Stafford

▶▶ Brenda Lee

Brian Mansfield

FRAZIER RIVER

Formed 1992, in Cincinnati, OH.

Danny Frazier, lead vocals, guitar; Chuck Adair, guitar; Bob Wilson, bass, vocals; Jim Morris, keyboards, vocals; Brian "Gigs" Baverman, drums; Greg Amburgy, guitar, keyboards, vocals.

This Ohio-based sextet was formerly the house band at Cincinnati's River Saloon. Instead of seeking their fortune in Nashville, they built a strong following in their home state, eventually attracting the attention of Music City labels. They recorded one album for Decca with minimal success. Guitarist/vocalist Danny Frazier, who was born in California and grew up in Texas, played for Becky Hobbs in Nashville before moving to Cincinnati.

what's available: On *Frazier River* (Decca, 1996, prod. Mark Wright) 🎵🎵 the group plays energetic modern country with hints of heartland rock. Jimmy Webb and former Fleetwood Mac guitarist Billy Burnette are among the songwriters covered.

influences:

◀◀ Restless Heart, Steve Wariner, Glen Campbell

Brian Mansfield

FREAKWATER

Formed 1989, in Louisville, KY.

Catherine Irwin, vocals, guitar; Janet Beveridge Bean, vocals, guitar, percussion; Dave Gay, bass; Bob Egan, pedal steel, National guitar.

Freakwater's Catherine Irwin and Janet Bean have been singing close harmony together for 15 years and it shows—without coming across as studied or archival, their hillbilly folk music sounds as if it was recorded on the Tennessee–Virginia border during the late 1920s. What sets Freakwater apart from other spirited traditionalists, though, is Irwin's singular voice as a songwriter, especially her eye for gender and class politics and her ear for the rhythms of everyday life and speech.

what's available: *Feels Like the Third Time* (Thrill Jockey, 1993, prod. Brad Wood, Freakwater) 🎵🎵🎵 is a set of tragic songs of life that evokes the spare, earthy music of a bygone era. *Old Paint* (Thrill Jockey, 1995, prod. Brad Wood, Freakwater) 🎵🎵🎵🎵 is an achingly beautiful record that confronts sexism, violence, longing and loss through the stories of desperate, resilient women. *Dancing Under Water* (Thrill Jockey, 1997) 🎵🎵🎵 is a straight reissue of the band's more bluegrass-oriented second album.

influences:

◀◀ Carter Family, Hazel Dickens & Alice Gerrard

Bill Friskics-Warren

JANIE FRICKE

Born December 19, 1947, in South Whitney, IN.

It's not surprising that although Janie Fricke enjoyed 19 Top 10 hits over a nine-year stretch, today she's considered a footnote of the barren, 1980s country period. While Fricke is a capable singer with a fluid voice able to express emotions at the right times, she's not a particularly distinctive stylist. Spending her early career as an in-demand background vocalist for such legendary artists as Dolly Parton, Elvis Presley and Johnny Duncan, Fricke understands the strength of a song. But since she's not a songwriter, she's totally dependent on the song to shape her artistry. She did record a handful of memorable ones: "Don't Worry 'bout Me Baby," "You Don't Know Love," "Let's Stop Talkin' about It," "Always Have, Always Will" and the snappy "He's a Heartache (Looking for a Place to Happen)." But a decade after her rise, which included Country Music Association awards, much of her material comes off as pedestrian. "Do Me with Love," "The First Word in Memory Is Me" and "I'll Need Someone to Hold Me," to name a few, are lovey-dovey drivel. With time, Fricke learned to choose better songs—and she, in turn, delivered better performances. Her last album for Columbia, 1989's *Labor of Love*, is her strongest studio effort, making the best of tunes written by such revered songwriters as Steve Earle, Kevin Welch, Pam Tillis and Holly Dunn. In 1992, after Fricke signed with Georgia-based indepen-

Janie Fricke **(AP/Wide World Photos)**

dent label Intersound, she recorded *Crossroads*, a heartfelt collection of spiritual songs and traditional hymns. To present its own set of Fricke standards, the label also released *Now & Then*, a CD of re-recorded versions of her popular 1980s repertoire. She sometimes has spelled her surname "Frickie," presumably to aid pronunciation.

what to buy: The most comprehensive collection of Fricke singles is *17 Greatest Hits* (Columbia, 1986, prod. various) &ZZZZ. It serves as a potent starting point for Fricke's evolving artistry and a revealing look at the state of mainstream country radio during the early 1980s. Plus, "He's a Heartache (Looking for a Place to Happen)" still has an effervescent melody and great lyrics.

what to buy next: Fricke took control of the mixing board on *Crossroads: Hymns of Faith* (Intersound, 1992, prod. Janie Fricke) &ZZZZ, an impressive batch of country-flavored gospel songs. What made this album stand out from other old-school religious projects was her command of various styles. She took Eric Clapton's "Tears from Heaven" and gave it even more

depth, then transformed Curtis Mayfield's "People Get Ready" into a passionate call for eternal faith.

what to avoid: Since *17 Greatest Hits* is the only gathering of Fricke's Columbia cuts one would need, the other two compilations are completely useless. *Greatest Hits* (Columbia, 1982, prod. Jim Ed Norman, Billy Sherrill) &ZZ and *The Very Best of Janie Frickie* (Columbia, 1985, prod. Bob Montgomery) &ZZ concentrate on her early and latter periods, respectively.

the rest:
Janie Frickie (Intersound, 1991) &ZZZ
Now & Then (Intersound, 1993) &ZZZ

worth searching for: *Labor of Love* (Columbia, 1989, prod. Chris Waters) &ZZZZ widens Fricke's scope by forcing her to stretch vocally on a batch of stellar songs. Anybody who can carry Steve Earle's "My Old Friend the Blues" and Pam Tillis' "One of Those Things" with verve deserves merit. Too bad this album encountered an uninterested audience.

influences:

◀◀ Crystal Gayle, Louise Mandrell, Lynn Anderson

▶▶ Terri Gibbs, Faith Hill, Linda Davis

Mario Tarradell

KINKY FRIEDMAN

Born Richard Friedman, October 31, 1944, in Palestine, TX.

Everything about Kinky Friedman is a joke. He's a Jew born on Halloween in Palestine—Texas, that is. His take on country music is both reverent and irreverent. A University of Texas grad with a degree in psychology, Friedman opted to psyche out the country music establishment with his band Kinky Friedman and the Texas Jewboys. The band released three albums during the 1970s, filled with Friedman's razor wit and affectionate nod to Texas swing and traditional country. The song titles alone were worth a good laugh—"Ride 'Em Jewboy," "Let Saigons Be Bygones," "They Ain't Making Jews Like Jesus Anymore" and his signatory "Asshole from El Paso," renamed "Lasso from El Paso" to appease delicate sensitivities. Friedman's popularity didn't stretch out much beyond the Texas border, though he was a favorite on college campuses across the country. He incurred the wrath of many a stiff-necked country music exec, but Friedman and the Jewboys were also invited to perform at the venerable Grand Ole Opry in 1975 and later toured as part of Bob Dylan's Rolling Thunder Revue. His reign of terror ended with the 1970s as Friedman turned his attentions to writing detective novels in which he's the main character. His first eight books have been translated into 14 languages; his ninth, *The Love Song of J. Edgar Hoover*, was published in late 1996.

what to buy: Fortunately, a recent revival of interest in Friedman's off-color music has resulted in the reissue of two of his first three albums and two new, mostly live recordings. He was at the peak of his powers and his cultish popularity when *Kinky Friedman* (Varese Vintage, 1974, prod. Kinky Friedman) ♫♫♫ came out. It features some of his most incisive smarmy humor, with songs such as "Home Erectus," "Something's Wrong with the Beaver" and "They Ain't Makin' Jews Like Jesus Anymore," plus guest shots from fellow mavericks Willie Nelson and Waylon Jennings, who were only slightly more well-known at the time.

what to buy next: Aficionados might want to track down *Old Testaments & New Revelations* (Fruit of the Tune, 1992, prod. Kinky Friedman, Chinga Chavin) ♫♫♫. The anthology features mostly live recordings and is a fairly uneven career retrospective stretching from his first recording, "Schwinn 24," in 1964

to an in-studio performance of "They Ain't Makin' Jews Like Jesus Anymore" on the Don Imus radio show.

the rest:

Sold American (Vanguard, 1973) ♫♫♫

From One Good American to Another (Fruit of the Tune, 1995) ♫♫

worth searching for: Arguably his best album, *Lasso from El Paso* (Epic, 1976, prod. Kinky Friedman) ♫♫♫, is also one of the hardest to find. It's out of print and hasn't been reissued domestically on CD. Since there's not much call for Friedman's offbeat music, it might stay that way.

influences:

◀◀ Bob Wills and the Texas Playboys, Raymond Chandler, Doug Sahm

Doug Pullen

DAVID FRIZZELL & SHELLY WEST

Formed mid-1970s.

David Frizzell (born September 26, 1941, in El Dorado, AR), vocals; Shelly West (born May 23, 1958, in Cleveland, OH), vocals.

The offspring of two country music superstars, David Frizzell (Lefty's brother) and Shelly West (Dottie's daughter) had moderately successful careers as individual artists. Each of them had a single #1 hit—Frizzell with "I'm Gonna Hire a Wino to Decorate Our Home" in 1982 and West with "Jose Cuervo" in 1983. Together, though, they did well enough with hits such as "I Just Came Here to Dance," "A Texas State of Mind" and "You're the Reason God Made Oklahoma" (from the Clint Eastwood film *Any Which Way You Can*) to win the Country Music Association's Vocal Duo of the Year award in 1981 and 1982. Frizzell and West were brother- and sister-in-law at the time: West was married to Frizzell's younger brother Allen.

what's available: *Greatest Hits—Alone & Together* (K-Tel, 1994, prod. Snuff Garrett, Steve Dorff) ♫♫♫ is a recent collection of Frizzell and West's best-known songs, including solo numbers such as "Jose Cuervo" and "I'm Gonna Hire a Wino." Watch out, though: the two songs at the end, both of them non-hits written by the album's producers, give this away as a re-make album.

influences:

◀◀ Lefty Frizzell, Dottie West

▶▶ John & Audrey Wiggins

Brian Mansfield

LEFTY FRIZZELL

Born William Orville Frizzell, March 31, 1928, in Corsicana, TX. Died July 19, 1975.

Before George Jones and Merle Haggard, there was Lefty Frizzell, whose famous "blue yodel" and curlicued vocal style has influenced generations of country singers who followed him, including Jones, Haggard, Willie Nelson, Garth Brooks, Alan Jackson and Randy Travis. Frizzell got his nickname after a schoolyard fight in the Texas oil town where he grew up. Determined to be a country singer, Frizzell cut his teeth on the music of Jimmie Rodgers, Ernest Tubb and such honky-tonk artists of the 1940s as Ted Daffan. He parlayed a demo session at a Dallas studio into a deal with Columbia Records, which released the first of his many signature songs, "If You've Got the Money, I've Got the Time" to popular acclaim in 1950. It was the beginning of a revolution in country music, as Frizzell's resonant honky-tonk sound replaced the more traditional, unadorned vocal style common at the time. At the height of his popularity during the early 1950s, Frizzell became the first artist to place four songs in Billboard's Top 10 country singles charts. Immensely popular throughout the decade, he made some bad career moves—like leaving the Grand Ole Opry shortly after joining—that derailed his momentum for a few years. But the "Lefty Sound" didn't disappear for long, with songs such as "The Long Black Veil" and "Saginaw, Michigan" reviving his commercial fortunes and returning him to the good graces of Nashville's power elite. After the mid-1960s, Frizzell—whose younger brother David formed a popular 1970s duo with Dottie West's daughter, Shelly—seldom enjoyed the kind of commercial success his legend would suggest. But his name and influence have lived on, thanks to the dozens of singers who've cited him (Willie Nelson cut an album of his music) and recorded his songs.

what to buy: With so few of his records available now, it's best to pick up *The Essential Lefty Frizzell: Look What Thoughts Will Do* (Columbia/Legacy, 1996, prod. various) 𝄞𝄞𝄞𝄞, as comprehensive a collection of the influential singer's work as you'll find on these shores. The 34-track, two-CD set rounds up his biggest hits and a few B-sides, including "If You've Got the Money, I've Got the Time," "Saginaw, Michigan" and "Long Black Veil."

what to buy next: The archival Rhino label does a nice job of summarizing Frizzell's chart hits on one 18-song disc with *The Best of Lefty Frizzell* (Rhino, 1991, comp. prod. James Austin)

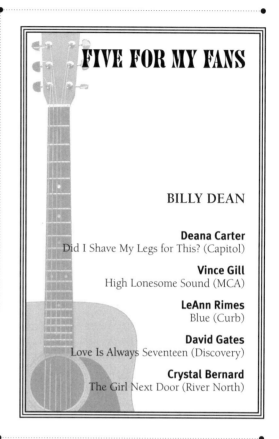

FIVE FOR MY FANS

BILLY DEAN

Deana Carter
Did I Shave My Legs for This? (Capitol)

Vince Gill
High Lonesome Sound (MCA)

LeAnn Rimes
Blue (Curb)

David Gates
Love Is Always Seventeen (Discovery)

Crystal Bernard
The Girl Next Door (River North)

𝄞𝄞𝄞𝄞, which features remastered versions of 14 hits and four B-sides recorded between 1950–65.

the rest:

American Originals (Columbia, 1993) 𝄞𝄞𝄞

That's the Way Love Goes: The Final Recordings of Lefty Frizzell (Varese Vintage, 1996) 𝄞𝄞𝄞

worth searching for: The German label Bear Family, known for its exhaustive collections and reissues, has assembled a dozen CDs' worth of Frizzell's recordings into the sprawling boxed set *Life's Like Poetry* (Bear Family, 1985, prod. various) 𝄞𝄞𝄞𝄞, which includes just about everything he ever recorded.

influences:

◀◀ Jimmie Rodgers, Ernest Tubb, Ted Daffan

▶▶ Merle Haggard, George Jones, Randy Travis, Garth Brooks, Willie Nelson

Doug Pullen

THE FRONT PORCH STRING BAND

See: Claire Lynch

FRONT RANGE

Formed late 1980s, in Denver, CO.

Bob Amos, guitar, lead vocals; **Mike Lantz**, mandolin, vocals; **Peter Schwimmer**, banjo (left band, 1989); **Ron Lynam**, banjo, vocals (1989–present); **Duane Webster**, bass (left band, 1986); **Pat Carbone**, bass (1986–1991); **Bob Dick**, bass, vocals (1991–present).

One of the more fascinating bluegrass success stories of the early 1990s, Front Range parlayed a pair of self-distributed albums (*So Many Pathways* and *The Road Home*), extensive regional touring and radio airplay and a wealth of distinctive original material into a significant national presence and a high-profile recording deal with Sugar Hill. The Colorado band, noted for its tradition-oriented sound, the powerful banjo picking of Ron Lynam, tight vocal-trio harmonies and the songwriting of Bob Amos, has since recorded three critically acclaimed albums.

what to buy: *Back to Red River* (Sugar Hill, 1993, prod. Charles Sawtelle, Front Range) ♬♬♬, the most fully realized of the band's albums, seamlessly blends traditional bluegrass power, Western themes and material and Bob Amos originals into a distinctive package. The title song and "The Hills That I Call Home" received considerable—for a bluegrass band—radio airplay.

what to buy next: *The New Frontier* (Sugar Hill, 1992, prod. Charles Sawtelle, Front Range) ♬♬♬, the band's national debut, showcased original material by Amos, Lynam and Lantz alongside classics by Charlie Monroe and the Stanley Brothers. *One Beautiful Day* (Sugar Hill, 1995, prod. Front Range) ♬♬♬, which features seven Bob Amos originals, is the band's first all-gospel recording.

influences:

◀◀ Hot Rize, Stanley Brothers

▶▶ Loose Ties, Left Hand String Band

Jon Hartley Fox

ROBBIE FULKS

Born March 25, 1963, in York, PA.

Gangsta rap gets all the headlines. But when it comes to violence and dysfunctional family values, country music ranks right up there with Snoop Doggy Dogg—why do ya think they call 'em murder ballads? Robbie Fulks mines country's darker side on *Country Love Songs* (Bloodshot, 1996, recorded by Steve Albini) ♬♬♬, a baker's dozen of demented song sketches. He sings in an earnest Buck Owens-derived croon, backed up by very fine period Bakersfield arrangements (Buckaroos veteran Tom Brumley's pedal steel lends authenticity to the proceedings). The main attraction is the manic humor and pathos of songs like "The Buck Starts Here" (punchline: "with Hank sure to follow"), "Papa Was a Steel-Headed Man" and "She Took a Lot of Pills (and Died)." Just sick enough.

influences:

◀◀ Buck Owens, Dwight Yoakam, Louvin Brothers, Roger Miller

David Menconi

TONY FURTADO

Born October 18, 1967, in Oakland, CA.

Tony Furtado twice (1987 and 1991) won the national Banjo Championship and played with Laurie Lewis & Grant Street between 1987–90. Furtado has been sporadically picking with Sugarbeat since that time. He also spent time with the Rounder Records Banjo Extravaganza tour, beginning in 1990.

what to buy: On *Full Circle* (Rounder, 1994, prod. Stuart Duncan) ♬♬♬, Furtado assembled a first-rate group of musicians—including David Grier, Stuart Duncan, Jerry Douglas and John Reischman—for 12 songs ranging from traditional to contemporary and relying on a full ensemble sound. Highlights include John Jackson's blues guitar and vocals on "Trouble in Mind" and Furtado's duet with clawhammer banjoist Mark Schatz on "Turned Around."

what to buy next: *Within Reach* (Rounder, 1992, prod. Jerry Douglas, Mike Marshall, Tony Furtado) ♬♬♬ finds Furtado still taking the banjo to new frontiers with a collection of originals, traditional songs and an inspired cover of the Beatles' "I Will," with Alison Krauss handling the lead vocals.

the rest:

Swamped (Rounder, 1989) ♬♬♬

(With others) *Rounder Banjo Extravaganza "Live!"* (Rounder) ♬♬♬

Roll My Blues Away (Rounder, 1997) ♬♬♬♬

influences:

◀◀ Laurie Lewis & Grant Street, Sugarbeat

▶▶ Alison Brown, Scott Vestal, Tony Trischka

Douglas Fulmer

G

CHRIS GAFFNEY

Born October 3, 1950, in Vienna, Austria; raised in Tucson, AZ.

As adept at covering Charlie Louvin's "See the Big Man Cry" as he is Philly soul numbers like the Intruders' 1968 hit, "Cowboys to Girls," Chris Gaffney is a versatile country-based accordion player and singer who revels in mixing a number of different musical strains including norteño, roadhouse blues-a-billy, cajun, roots rock and swamp pop along with country music from George Jones to Hank Williams. In 1983 he formed the band the Cold Hard Facts: Greg Gaffney, bass (1983–96); Wyman Reese, keyboards; Tucker Fleming, drums, Danny Ott, guitar, Doug Livingstone, steel guitar (1992–present) and Mike Berry, bass (1996–present).

what to buy: *Loser's Paradise* (1995, HighTone, prod. Dave Alvin) ♪♪♪, with his most mature playing and songwriting, is also an all-star outing that includes Alvin, Austin bassist Sarah Brown, Lucinda Williams, Ponty Bone, Ian McLagan (Faces), Rosie Flores and Dale Watson and Jim Lauderdale.

what to buy next: *Chris Gaffney & the Cold Hard Facts* (1990, ROM, prod. Wyman Reese) ♪♪♪ is the purest, most countrified Gaffney with the first and most energized version of the Cold Hard Facts. It has the original version of the Gaffney tune "Glass House," which was later redone on *Loser's Paradise*, as well as "The Gardens," a tune later covered by the Texas Tornados.

the rest:
Mi Vida Loca (HighTone, 1992, prod. Wyman Reese) ♪♪♪

worth searching for: *Road to Indio* (Cactus Club Records, 1986, prod. Wyman Reese) ♪♪♪, Gaffney's debut EP, has a cover of Lefty Frizzell's "Old, Old Man" and an appropriately woozy take of one of his best-ever originals, "Alcoholidays."

influences:
◀◀ Johnny Cash, Merle Haggard, Otis Redding, Little Willie G.
▶▶ Rosie Flores, Dave Alvin, Jim Lauderdale

Robert Baird

HANK GARLAND

Born Walter Louis Garland, November 11, 1930, in Cowpens, SC.

One of the most innovative guitarists in the entire history of country music, Hank Garland is also one of the few country artists whose nickname—"Sugarfoot"—came from his biggest hit, "Sugarfoot Rag." A guitar prodigy from an early age, Garland was asked to join the Opry in 1945 at the age of 15. He later played in Cowboy Copas' band before recording as a soloist for Decca in 1949. It was during his first session that Garland unveiled his original instrumental "Sugarfoot Boogie"; the next year he recorded the same tune—now called "Sugarfoot Rag"—with Red Foley singing added lyrics (Junior Brown recently covered this version on his 1993 disc *Guit with It*). For his solo recordings Garland assembled an ever-changing group of Nashville studio pros that usually included Owen Bradley on piano, Harold Bradley on guitar, Jack Shook, on left-handed rhythm guitar, and Farris Coursey on drums. While he never became a big solo star, Garland did find a measure of fame as one of Nashville's top sessionmen, crafting the intro to Patsy Cline's "I Fall to Pieces" and playing on Elvis' "Little Sister" and Don Gibson's "Sea of Heartbreak," among many others. In 1960, after an appearance at the Newport Jazz Festival and a resulting jazz LP (made with Boots Randolph and Floyd Cramer), Garland recorded a solo jazz album, *Jazz Winds from a New Direction*. His playing career was cut short when he was severely injured in an automobile crash in September 1961. He has since retired to South Carolina.

what's available: *Hank Garland and His Sugarfooters* (Bear Family, 1992, reissue prod. Richard Weize) ♪♪♪ is the cream of Garland's solo output recorded between 1949 and 1951, all remastered in brilliant sound. Both "Sugarfoot Boogie" and "Sugarfoot Rag," as well as "Flying Eagle Polka" and the "Third Man Theme." A superb booklet is also included.

worth searching for: *Jazz Winds from a New Direction* (Columbia, 1960) ♪♪♪ is a surprisingly masterful and convincing jazz LP that shows how much talent Garland had and some of the possible directions he might have gone.

influences:
◀◀ Maybelle Carter, Arthur "Guitar Boogie" Smith
▶▶ James Burton, Junior Brown, Lee Roy Parnell

Robert Baird

MARVIN GASTER

Born December 21, 1934, in Sanford, NC.

Gaster is the last in a line of old-timey two-finger banjo pickers from Lee County, North Carolina. He bought his first banjo when he was about 12 and learned the style from his uncle, the great Henry Gaster. Played at square dances and other events

david gates

in the area until the 1950s when he stopped performing to concentrate on being a father, farmer and teacher. Marvin picked up the banjo and fiddle again during the late 1960s.

what's available: Backed by some of the best pickers in and around Lee County, the 24 songs on *Uncle Henry's Favorites* (Rounder, 1995, prod. Bob Carlin) ♫♫♫ were recorded informally in the musicians' homes. An important recording documenting the local traditional musical styles of Lee County.

influences:
◀◀ Skillet Lickers, Bascom Lamar Lunsford
▶▶ Benton Flippen, Kirk Sutphin

Douglas Fulmer

DAVID GATES
/BREAD

Born December 11, 1940, in Tulsa, OK. Bread formed 1969, in Los Angeles, CA. Disbanded 1973. Reunited 1976.

David Gates, vocals, guitar, bass, keyboards, violin; James Griffin, vocals, guitar, keyboards; Larry Knechtel, keyboards, bass, guitar, harmonica (1971–77); Jim Gordon, drums (1969); Mike Botts, drums (1970–77); Robb Royer, guitar, bass, keyboards, flute (1969–71).

Though he's had tunes cut by Joe Stampley, the Kendalls and Connie Stevens and written arrangements for Merle Haggard, Buck Owens and Pat Boone, David Gates has never had a country hit on his own. Instead, he was the main vocalist and songwriter for Bread, a middle-of-the-road pop group that created romantic standards like "If," "Make It with You" and "Baby I'm-a Want You" during the late 1960s and 1970s. Gates also penned "Popsicles and Icicles," a 1964 pop hit for the Murmaids, among other things.

Bread's songs, and Gates' solo hits, had an enormous impact on romantically inclined country singers of the next generation, so when Gates returned to recording in 1993 after a decade-long absence (he'd turned ranching into a full-time vocation), he made a country album in Nashville.

what to buy: Gates' sweet tenor seems hardly to have aged at all on *Love Is Always Seventeen* (Discovery, 1994) ♫♫♫, his first solo album in more than a decade. Recorded in Nashville with the likes of Billy Dean, Jerry Douglas, and Lee Roy Parnell (and Larry Knechtel on piano), the album shows how much the music of modern MOR country singers owe to Gates' songs. Both the title track and "Save This Dance for Me" are particularly evocative of Gates' earlier hits.

what to buy next: Bread's *Retrospective* (Elektra Traditions/Rhino, 1996) ♫♫♫, a two-disc compilation, contains just about as much Bread as any but the most dedicated fan could desire. It also has 10 of Gates' solo recording, including "Goodbye Girl," "Never Let Her Go" and "Took the Last Train."

the rest:
Bread (Elektra Traditions/Rhino, 1969/1995) ♫♫
On the Waters (Elektra Traditions/Rhino, 1970/1995) ♫♫
Manna (Elektra Traditions/Rhino, 1971/1995) ♫♫♫
Baby I'm-a Want You (Elektra, 1972) ♫♫♫
Guitar Man (Elektra, 1972) ♫♫♫
The Best of Bread (Elektra Asylum, 1973) ♫♫♫♫
The Best of Bread, Volume II (Elektra Asylum) ♫♫♫
Anthology of Bread (Elektra Asylum, 1985) ♫♫♫♫

worth searching for: Gates has recorded five other solo albums, though all are out of print. *Goodbye Girl* (Elektra, 1979, prod. David Gates) ♫♫♫, which contains both the title hit and "Took the Last Train," Gates' last Top 40 pop hit, is easily the best. The other albums are *First* (Elektra, 1973) ♫♫; *Never Let Her Go* (Elektra, 1975) ♫♫♫; *Falling in Love Again* (Elektra, 1980) ♫♫; and *Take Me Now* (Arista, 1981) ♫♫.

influences:
◀◀ Chet Atkins, James Taylor
▶▶ Billy Dean, Bryan White

Brian Mansfield

LARRY GATLIN &
THE GATLIN BROTHERS

Formed c. 1973, in Nashville, TN. Disbanded 1992.

Larry Gatlin (born May 2, 1948, in Seminole, TX), tenor vocals; Steve Gatlin (born April 4, 1951, in Olney, TX); Rudy Gatlin (born August 20, 1952, in Olney, TX).

One of country's great tenors (he once beat Roy Orbison in a Texas talent contest), Larry Gatlin had the advantage of being one of the best songwriters of the 1970s and early 1980s. An English major at the University of Houston, he moved to Nashville in 1972 at the suggestion of Dottie West, who was impressed enough with some songs he had sent her to record two of them. When Larry's career began to take off, he convinced his two younger brothers to make the move as well, and the three of them recorded together under various names (Larry Gatlin, Larry Gatlin with Brothers & Friends, The Gatlin Bros., etc.) for the next two decades. Gatlin's songs invariably featured his soaring tenor and the brothers' harmonies relating one of Larry's vignettes. Their singles were among the best of the time: the Grammy-winning "Broken Lady"; 1976's "Statues without Hearts," with its Beach Boys-like falsetto part; 1978's achingly sad "I've Done Enough Dyin' Today"; and 1979's "All the Gold in California," with its three-part *a cappella* intro.

Larry Gatlin had his first Top 40 solo hit in 1973, and either he or the trio would place in the Top 40 every year but two until 1989. After the Gatlins went into semi-retirement following their 1992 farewell tour, Larry began acting in film, television and Broadway (*The Will Rogers Follies*), Steve became a Christian country artist, and Rudy did some theater, as well as staying behind the scenes to oversee the Gatlins' various business interests.

what to buy: *The Best of the Gatlins: All the Gold in California* (Legacy, 1996, prod. various) 🎧🎧🎧 is a solid, 18-song collection of Larry Gatlin and the Gatlin Brothers' hits for Monument and Columbia. It starts with Gatlin's early 1970s hits such as "Sweet Becky Walker" and "Delta Dirt," and ends with 1988's "Love of a Lifetime." In between, though, is the good stuff—songs like "Broken Lady," "Statues without Hearts" and "I've Done Enough Dyin' Today." When folks start re-discovering the top-shelf material in 1970s country, this will be among the best finds.

what to buy next: *Greatest Hits* (Columbia Legacy, 1991) 🎧🎧🎧 is a shorter collection, more tightly concentrated on the Gatlin's great 1970s hits.

what to avoid: The trio recorded during the early 1990s for Intersound and Branson. Stay far away from the two Branson albums—*Greatest Hits* (Branson, 1991, prod. Steve Gatlin) 🎧 and *Moments to Remember* (Branson, 1993, prod. Jim Foglesong) 🎧. This is what happens when a love of tradition turns into nostalgia. The two Intersound albums, *Cool Water* (Intersound) 🎧🎧 and *Sincerely* (Intersound) 🎧🎧, aren't much better.

the rest:
Biggest Hits (1981–1988) (Columbia, 1989) 🎧🎧🎧
Greatest Hits, Volume II (Columbia, 1991) 🎧🎧🎧

solo outings:
Steve Gatlin:
Love Can Carry (Cheyenne, 1993) 🎧🎧

influences:
◀◀ Statler Brothers, Oak Ridge Boys, Imperials, Dottie West
▶▶ Dave & Sugar, BlackHawk

Brian Mansfield

KEITH GATTIS

Born May 26, 1970, in Austin, TX.

A honky-tonk singer who grew up in Austin, Gattis moved to Nashville and played guitar with the remnants of Ernest Tubb's Texas Troubadours before signing with RCA Records.

what's available: On his debut disc *Keith Gattis* (RCA, 1996, prod. Norro Wilson) 🎧🎧🎧, Gattis shows an athletic voice on some high-energy honky tonk. He's got plenty of spunk, but hasn't forged much of an original style. Once he gets over his George Jones jones, he'll be on to something.

worth searching for: Gattis sings "(Going Down Like the) Titanic" on the soundtrack to *Going West Across America*.

influences:
◀◀ George Jones, Travis Tritt

Bob Cannon

CRYSTAL GAYLE

Born Brenda Gail Webb, January 9, 1951, in Paintsville, KY.

Crystal Gayle, the younger sister of Loretta Lynn, was raised in Wabash, Indiana and gained her first performing experience singing at age 16 in her sister's traveling show. Her debut single, "I've Cried (The Blues Right out of My Eyes)," reached #23 in 1970, leading to a career that was decidedly more pop than her sister's. Crystal's soft, lilting voice was the perfect instrument for MOR ballads and soft rockers, climaxing with "Don't It Make My Brown Eyes Blue," a huge crossover hit that reached #2 on the pop charts in 1977.

what to buy: Gayle's music has been repackaged to death, but *Classic Crystal* (Capitol, 1979, prod. Allen Reynolds) 🎧🎧🎧 is still the best collection of hits and better moments, including "Why Have You Left the One You Left Me For," "Somebody Loves You" and, of course, "Don't It Make My Brown Eyes Blue."

what to buy next: You'd think with four extra years to add new hits, *Greatest Hits* (Capitol, 1983, prod. TK) 🎧🎧 would be an improvement, but instead some crucial tracks are left off.

what to avoid: *What If We Fall in Love* 🎧, Gayle's link-up with Gary Morris, may have gotten plenty of attention, but lame material and Morris' persistent oversinging sinks it. *Best Always* (Branson, 1993) 🎧🎧 contains tepid re-recordings of Gayle's hits and other country standards.

the rest:
All-Time Greatest Hits (Curb/CEMA, 1990) 🎧🎧🎧

Crystal Gayle **(AP/Wide World Photos)**

The Best of Crystal Gayle (Curb/CEMA, 1993) 🎵🎵
Someday (Intersound, 1995) 🎵🎵

influences:
◀◀ Barbara Mandrell, Loretta Lynn
▶▶ Reba McEntire, Sylvia

Bob Cannon

BOBBIE GENTRY

Born July 27, 1944, in Chickasaw County, MS.

In July 1967, a tune by an unknown singer/songwriter from the Mississippi Delta was making as much noise as the Beatles' *Sgt. Pepper's Lonely Hearts Club Band*, which had been released only a month earlier. The artist was Bobbie Gentry, and the song was "Ode to Billie Joe"—a Deep South, Faulknerian folk-epic rife with themes of love and suicide set to a slow, swampy, syncopated beat accentuated by a matter-of-fact, smoky vocal delivery. Within weeks of its release, the song climbed to the upper reaches of both the country and pop charts, and Gentry became an international star. Subsequent

releases, however, failed to capture the magic of "Ode." During the 1970s Gentry won a Grammy for a duet with Glen Campbell on "Let It Be Me" and also received a Country Music Association award for her remake of the Everly Brothers chestnut "All I Have to Do Is Dream." However, after those accomplishments, Gentry and her musical career lapsed into obscurity.

what's available: *Greatest Hits* (Curb, 1990, prod. various) 🎵🎵🎵 contains the enigmatic hit "Ode to Billie Joe," as well as the Gentry-penned "Fancy," a tune that was successfully covered by Reba McEntire during the early 1990s.

influences:
◀◀ Dusty Springfield
▶▶ Deana Carter

Rick Petreycik

MARK GERMINO

Born in NC.

Possibly because of his rebellious streak, this stellar Nashville singer/songwriter has never tasted much commercial success, despite one truly classic country-rock song. "Rex Bob Lowenstein," his opus, is the story of a beloved old-fashioned (and crotchety) Southern DJ who gets replaced by a computerized playlist and locks himself in the studio playing thrash music. Though it applies to all kinds of radio stations, the song was most prophetic about country radio, which became hugely successful and blandly regimented right around 1991. Germino, a Vietnam veteran, sings with the punch and twang of Steve Earle, but he has a much more explicit social conscience. His backing band, the Sluggers, plays with the rocking consistency of the E Street Band.

what to buy: *Radartown* (Zoo, 1991, prod. R.S. Field) 🎵🎵🎵 contains "Rex Bob Lowenstein" and a lot of funny songs, including "Lerdy and Bo's Totalitarian Showdown," about love, freedom and injustice; it never went anywhere commercially.

what to buy next: With humor and hillbilly eloquence, Germino spins great tales on *Rank and File* (Winter Harvest, 1995, prod. Owsley Manier, Steve Roberts) 🎵🎵🎵, including "Rosemary's New Constitution," about a black woman standing in line to vote and fantasizing about being elected president.

what to avoid: *London Town & Barnyard Remedies* (RCA, 1986, prod. Paul Samwell-Smith) 🎵🎵🎵, Germino's debut, isn't quite as fleshed-out as his later releases.

worth searching for: *Rex Bob Lowenstein* (Zoo, 1991, prod. R.S. Field) 🎵🎵🎵 is an EP culled mostly from *Radartown*, but its highlight is a killer cover of Bob Dylan's "Highway 61 Revisited."

influences:

◀◀ Steve Earle, Bob Dylan, Carl Perkins, Johnny Cash, Bruce Springsteen

▶▶ Dan Bern, John Wesley Harding, Todd Snider

Steve Knopper

ALICE GERRARD

See: Hazel & Alice

TERRI GIBBS

Born June 15, 1954, in Augusta, GA.

Terri Gibbs wasn't quite a one-hit wonder, but nothing she cut topped the impact of her first record. "Somebody's Knockin'," with its darkly seductive storyline and piano groove, reached the Top 20 on both the pop and country charts in 1980, propelling the blind vocalist/pianist into instant stardom. She even won the Country Music Association's first Horizon Award in 1981. As it turned out, "Somebody's Knockin'" was such a huge record that Gibbs was never able to follow it up adequately. She had another dozen hits, none of them making the Top 10, for MCA, Warner Bros. and Horizon before moving first into contemporary Christian music and then semi-retirement.

what's available: *The Best of Terri Gibbs* (Varese Sarabande, 1996, prod. Ed Penney, Rick Hall, comp. prod. Cary Mansfield) 🎵🎵🎵 culls 10 songs—including "Somebody's Knockin'"—from Gibbs' four albums for MCA. Nearly all the songs show the same kind of R&B influence as her biggest hit, from Johnny Mercer's "I Wanna Be Around" to a rockabilly-gospel cover of the Etta James R&B hit "Tell Mama."

influences:

◀◀ Ronnie Milsap, Bobbie Gentry

▶▶ Kathy Mattea

Brian Mansfield

DON GIBSON

Born April 3, 1932, in Shelby, NC.

Recognized as the writer of Patsy Cline's "Sweet Dreams" and the Ray Charles pop chart-topper "I Can't Stop Loving You,"

Don Gibson had his own sizable hits with these and dozens of others throughout the 1950s, 1960s and even into the 1970s. Yet, he somehow remains under-appreciated and not very well served on CD. The son of a railroad worker, Gibson was in his first band at age 16, followed by a second shortly thereafter. Both outfits earned recording contracts, but scored no hits. In 1955 Wesley Rose offered Don a songwriter deal with powerful Acuff-Rose Publishing on the strength of "Sweet Dreams" (#9, 1956) which, released on MGM, became his first Top 10 record, seven years before Patsy Cline hit #5 with it. When his "Oh Lonesome Me" (#1, 1958) was released, it marked a major change for Gibson, as well as for Music City. The song ushered in the "Nashville Sound": under the guidance of producer Chet Atkins, fiddle and steel guitar gave way to lush orchestration and backing vocals by the Anita Kerr Singers. Not only was the song a pop Top 10, but "Oh Lonesome Me" became the first gold-certified single recorded in Nashville's legendary RCA Studio B. Gibson would hit #1 only twice more in his career, but managed to place hits into the Top 10 through the mid-1970s, by which time he was recording for the Hickory label. Although his performances are less frequent, he still appears from time to time on the Grand Ole Opry, which welcomed him as a member in 1958. In 1993 Mark Chesnutt had a hit with Gibson's final chart-topper, "Woman (Sensuous Woman)" (#1, 1972). Gibson's an important artist, and ought to be better represented.

what to buy: If you can find it and don't mind paying a bit more for the imported *A Legend in His Time* (Bear Family, 1987, prod. Chet Atkins, Richard Weize) 🎵🎵🎵🎵, you'll be rewarded with 26 of Gibson's original hits.

what to avoid: *Country Spotlight* (K-Tel, 1992) 🎵🎵 rehashes 10 hits without any of their original spark.

the rest:

18 Greatest Hits (Curb, 1990) 🎵🎵🎵
Best Of, Volume 1 (Curb, 1991) 🎵🎵🎵
The Singer, the Songwriter: 1949–1960 (Bear Family, 1991) 🎵🎵🎵🎵
Singer–Songwriter, 1961–66 (Bear Family, 1991) 🎵🎵🎵🎵

worth searching for: *All-Time Greatest Hits* (RCA, 1990) 🎵🎵🎵🎵🎵 is a nice compilation of original RCA hits, but has been out a print for a while.

influences:

◀◀ Eddy Arnold, Jim Reeves

▶▶ Ronnie Milsap, Ricky Van Shelton, Mark Chesnutt

Stephen L. Betts

The Gibson/Miller Band (© Ken Settle)

THE GIBSON/MILLER BAND

Formed 1992, in Nashville, TN. Disbanded 1995.

Dave Gibson, guitar, vocals; Blue Miller, guitar, vocals; others.

The Gibson/Miller Band was a briefly incendiary pairing of country songwriter Dave Gibson and Blue Miller — a Motown rock 'n' roller and former sideman for Bob Seger and Isaac Hayes. Mixing Detroit rock and Music City country, they graduated from playing a nightclub with a bullet hole in the window to center-stage performances of songs on their way up *Billboard*'s country charts. Gibson left the band after the group's second album, no longer in print.

what's available: On *Where There's Smoke* (Epic, 1992, prod. Doug Johnson) ♫♫♫ the band's biker bar-lite musical approach spawned the hits "Texas Tattoo," "High Rollin'" and "Where There's Smoke."

worth searching for: *Red, White and Blue Collar* (Epic, 1994, prod. Doug Johnson, Blue Miller) ♫♫ features more of the same, including a revved-up cover of "Mammas Don't Let Your Babies Grow up to Be Cowboys."

influences:
◄◄ Bob Seger, Lynyrd Skynyrd, Travis Tritt, Confederate Railroad
►► Big House

Bill Hobbs

VINCE GILL

Born April 5, 1957, in Norman, OK.

If Vince Gill didn't exist, it's unlikely Nashville would have been able to create him. The very definition of a regular guy, Gill doesn't rely on a hat, tight jeans or regular trips to the publishing houses to get by. Instead, there's simply talent. Gill's high, honeyed voice harmonized on countless songs during his stint as a backup singer during the 1980s. Eventually, it became obvious that Gill belonged out front. A gifted songwriter, Vince is also a dynamic guitarist who can play his own leads. Add to that his surprising lack of pretension, and you have proof that, yes, occasionally, nice guys can finish first.

After kicking around various bluegrass bands in Oklahoma, Gill toured with several different groups, including one of Ricky Skaggs' early outfits. Eventually he joined country-rock band Pure Prairie League, where he sang lead on its 1980 hit, "Let Me Love You Tonight." Signed to RCA, Gill had several hits but failed to click with the pre-New Traditional audience. Resurfacing on MCA under the guidance of Tony Brown—a former fellow bandmate in Rodney Crowell's hot band, the Cherry Bombs—Gill has recorded a string of albums that are astounding for their overall high quality and eclecticism, combining elements of country, folk, bluegrass, middle-of-the-road balladry and even some rock. He may just be the perfect country star.

what to buy: After his unsuccessful run at RCA, the album that announced Gill as an artist of substance and grace was *When I Call Your Name* (MCA, 1989, prod. Tony Brown) ♪♪♪♪♪. The album included the charming, rootsy "Oklahoma Swing" (featuring Reba McEntire), and the hits "Never Knew Lonely" and "When I Call Your Name," the latter of which won Country Music Association honors as 1990's single of the year. *I Still Believe in You* (MCA, 1992, prod. Tony Brown) ♪♪♪♪♪ finds the tenor vocalist at the apex of his career; only Gill could make such an astonishing, soulful achievement as the title track seem so effortless. But he can also rock ("One More Last Chance") and play it straight down the middle ("Don't Let Our Love Start Slippin' Away"). *Souvenirs* (MCA, 1995, prod. Tony Brown) ♪♪♪♪♪ collects an extraordinary string of singles from his early MCA years, duets "The Heart Won't Lie" and "I Will Always Love You" (which originally appeared on albums by Reba McEntire and Dolly Parton, respectively) and Gill's take on the Eagles' "I Can't Tell You Why" from the *Common Thread* tribute.

what to buy next: Gill's string of terrific albums just doesn't stop. *When Love Finds You* (MCA, 1994, prod. Tony Brown) ♪♪♪♪ features the singer's heartrending tribute to his late brother, "Go Rest High on That Mountain." The title track, one of Gill's trademark ballads, is one of his finest. *High Lonesome Sound* (MCA, 1996, prod. Tony Brown) ♪♪♪♪ features two versions of the title song, one of them a funky guitar workout and the other a bluegrass ballad with Alison Krauss and Union Station. *The Essential Vince Gill* (RCA, 1995, prod. various) ♪♪♪♪ collects the best of his RCA years, and it's a more generous package than any of the other collections from the period.

what to avoid: The holiday outing *Let There Be Peace on Earth* (MCA, 1993) ♪♪ is the only Gill album afflicted with humbug.

the rest:
Turn Me Loose (RCA, 1984) ♪♪♪
The Things That Matter (RCA, 1985) ♪♪♪
The Way Back Home (RCA, 1987) ♪♪♪
The Best of Vince Gill (RCA, 1989) ♪♪♪
Pocket Full of Gold (MCA, 1991) ♪♪♪♪
I Never Knew Lonely (RCA, 1992) ♪♪♪
Vince Gill and Friends (RCA, 1994) ♪♪♪
Super Hits (RCA, 1996) ♪♪♪

worth searching for: Gill has sung his share of duets, but none so unusual as the one he sings with Muppet Kermit the Frog on *Kermit Unpigged* (Jim Henson Records, 1994) ♪♪♪.

influences:
◀◀ Bill Monroe, Jim Reeves, Eagles, Don Rich, Albert Lee
▶▶ Collin Raye, Bryan White

Daniel Durchholz

MICKEY GILLEY

Born March 9, 1936, in Natchez, LA.

Mickey Gilley is first cousin to both rock/country legend Jerry Lee Lewis and televangelist Jimmy Swaggert. (Mickey's the one who isn't self-destructive.) They all learned to play a mix of gospel, country and boogie-woogie on the same piano during the days when Gilley's last name was pronounced with a soft "G." Gilley didn't get serious about a career in music until cousin Jerry Lee hit it big with "Whole Lotta Shakin' Goin' On" in 1957. Yet despite their sound-a-like status, Gilley had to wait much longer than Lewis did for a taste of success. When a Sun Records audition set up by Lewis brought him no offers, Gilley began recording for even smaller labels such as Goldband, Paula and Astro. Although his first recordings were blatant rip-offs of his more famous cousin, with Gilley's voice sounding weak and thin, as he progressed, he brought his own stamp to the style that Lewis originated. Instead of moaning a lyric Gilley learned to croon it; in place of leering a note Gilley made his voice glide. At the piano his work with the left hand is almost identical to Lewis', but Mickey's right hand technique was better suited to ballads and pop numbers than his cousin's. Gilley eventually achieved some regional chart success with "Drive-In Movie Show" and "Now I Can Live Again" (1968), and he was a popular performer around Houston. In 1971 he and Sherwood Cryer opened Gilley's, the world's largest honky-tonk, in

Pasadena, Texas. In 1974 the Playboy label (bought out by Epic in 1978) released Gilley's Lewis-styled version of "Roomful of Roses," which hit #1. He followed it up with hit reworkings of other country standards, such as "Window Up Above," "I Overlooked an Orchid" and "City Lights."

At the time, many fans claimed that Gilley's newfound stardom came solely at the expense of Jerry Lee Lewis, but Lewis' country career was already on the wane before 1974. Erratic in the studio, Lewis was either cutting rock too salacious for radio airplay or indifferent, drunk-sounding country. By contrast, Gilley's output was tight, enthusiastic, and reliably country. As his spot on radio playlists became secure, Gilley even began to out-rock Lewis with "Don't the Girls All Get Prettier at Closing Time" and "The Power of Positive Drinking." The 1980 movie *Urban Cowboy* used Gilley's nightclub as a backdrop and featured its namesake singing some of his biggest hits. The career boost was enormous, and Gilley used the opportunity to ditch his honky-tonk piano style for a more upscale adult contemporary-country crossover sound. His reworkings of "Stand by Me," "Talk to Me," "True Love Ways" and "You Don't Know Me," along with such original songs as "That's All That Matters" and "A Headache Tomorrow (Or a Heartache Tonight)" all hit #1. He also cut some successful duets with Charly McClain (Scott Faragher's book *Music City Babylon* details the petty bickering that killed their partnership). By the mid-1980s Gilley's run of big hits was over, and he left Epic in 1988. The following year, amid bitter disputes over the running of the famous honky tonk, Cryer and Gilley dissolved their partnership; Gilley's eventually burned down. These days Gilley records for independent labels, owns a popular theater in Branson, Missouri, tours as often as he wants and, when asked about his famous cousin, replies cheerfully: "I wouldn't even be in the business today if it weren't for Jerry Lee."

what to buy: *Biggest Hits* (Columbia, 1989, prod. Eddie Kilroy, Jim Ed Norman) ♪♪♪♫ is a nice compilation of Gilley's early honky tonk and later country-pop recordings. *Greatest Hits, Volume 1* (Epic, 1987, prod. Eddie Kilroy) ♪♪♪♫ and *Greatest Hits Volume 2* (Playboy, 1979, prod. Eddie Kilroy) ♪♪♪♪ document Gilley's hits just before the *Urban Cowboy* phase. *Ten Years of Hits* (Epic, 1987, prod. Eddie Kilroy, Jim Ed Norman) ♪♪♪♪ offers an impressive collection of #1 hits.

Vince Gill (© Ken Settle)

what to avoid: A number of albums that feature re-recordings of his big hits: *With Love from Pasadena, Texas* (Intermedia, 1988) ♪; *Ultimate* (Bransounds, 1994) ♪♪; *Make It Like the First Time* (Branson, 1993) ♪; and *Talk to Me* (Intersound, 1995) ♪♪.

the rest:
Christmas at Gilley's (Sony, 1981) ♪♪♪
Mellow Country (Sony, 1996) ♪♪♪♪
I Saw the Light (Arrival, 1996) ♪♪♪

worth searching for: On *Mickey Gilley at His Best* (Paula, 1974, prod. Mickey Gilley) ♪♪♪, Gilley does Jerry Lee with a flair that Jason D. Williams can only dream about. *Mickey Gilley* (Crazy Cajun, 1974, prod. Huey P. Meaux) ♪♪♪ captures the beginnings of Gilley's successful country style—along with the Jerry Lee Lewis rip-off "Whole Lotta Twistin' Goin' On" (retitled "Shake It for Mickey Gilley").

influences:
⏪ Jerry Lee Lewis, Moon Mullican, Eddy Arnold
⏩ Jason D. Williams

Ken Burke

JIMMIE DALE GILMORE

Born May 6, 1945, in Amarillo, TX.

Blessed with a voice of extraordinary range and expressiveness—think Roy Orbison if he'd wanted to be Jimmie Rodgers instead of Mario Lanza—and a lyrical vision that is equal parts West Texas lonesome and the sound of one hand clapping, Jimmie Dale Gilmore is a unique presence in contemporary music. Silent for nearly two decades after his abortive debut with the supergroup-in-retrospect Flatlanders, Gilmore's solo career began in fairly conventional country territory and moved further left-of-center with each release. His interpretive skills have led him to become the definitive performer of songs by fellow Texas visionary (and former Flatlander) Butch Hancock, while Gilmore's own songs have been covered by Natalie Merchant and David Byrne.

what to buy: *After Awhile* (Elektra Nonesuch American Explorer Series, 1991, prod. Stephen Bruton) ♪♪♪♪♪ is a stunning showcase for Gilmore's original artistry, notably the elliptical, Zen-like "Tonight I Think I'm Gonna Go Downtown" and "Treat Me Like a Saturday Night." But the album's otherworldly feel is nicely undercut by the gentle humor of Gilmore's own "Go to Sleep Alone" and the not-so-gentle humor of Butch Hancock's "My Mind's Got a Mind of Its Own." To complete the package, the blazing "Midnight Blues" proves Gilmore can play with intensity. Just try keeping your jaw from dropping repeatedly while listening to this one. *Spinning Around the Sun* (Elektra, 1993, prod. Emory Gordy Jr.) 🎵🎵🎵🎵 relies more heavily on covers than its predecessor, and it would rate as a superior work if Gilmore's near-definitive take on Hank Williams' "I'm So Lonesome I Could Cry" was its only selection. But there's also a loping cover of the Elvis B-side "I Was the One" and Butch Hancock's devastating lover's putdown, "Just a Wave." If anything proves Gilmore's artistic mettle, it's his cover of his ex-wife Jo Carol Pierce's "Reunion," which imagines a couple sundered on earth to be reunited in the hereafter.

what to buy next: If *Magical Mystery Tour* had been recorded in Austin, Texas, it might sound something like *Braver Newer World* (Elektra, 1996, prod. T-Bone Burnett) 🎵🎵🎵🎵. Producer Burnette removes Gilmore almost entirely from a country context, surrounding him instead with saxophones, echo-laden drums and stinging, sitar-like guitar leads, making explicit Gilmore's country & Eastern leanings. It's a radical experiment, but it works.

the rest:
Fair & Square (HighTone, 1988) 🎵🎵🎵
Jimmie Dale Gilmore (HighTone, 1989) 🎵🎵🎵

worth searching for: *Mudhoney/Jimmie Dale Gilmore* (Sub Pop EP, 1994, prod. various) 🎵🎵🎵 is a peculiar artifact on which Gilmore and the Seattle grunge pioneers cover each others' songs and team up for the late Townes Van Zandt's "Buckskin Stallion Blues." Also, Gilmore and Hancock's *Two Roads: Live in Australia* (Virgin Records Australia, 1990/Caroline 1993, prod. Keith Glass, Jimmie Dale Gilmore, Butch Hancock) 🎵🎵🎵🎵, which finds the two performing solo and in tandem, is an immensely satisfying live album from way, way south of the border.

influences:
◀◀ Hank Williams, Roy Orbison, Buddy Holly, Jimmie Rodgers, Willie Nelson
▶▶ Jim Lauderdale, Kevin Welch, Iris DeMent, Gillian Welch

see also: *Flatlanders*

Daniel Durchholz

THE GOINS BROTHERS

Formed c. 1950, in WV.

Melvin Goins (born December 30, 1933, in Bramwell, WV), vocals, guitar, bass; Ray Goins (born January 3, 1936, in Bramwell, WV).

The Goins Brothers began performing on a Saturday morning radio program in Bluefield, West Virginia, in 1951. They moved to Pikeville, Kentucky in 1953 and worked with the Lonesome Pine Fiddlers until that group disbanded in 1958. The brothers worked with Bill Monroe, the Stanley Brothers and Hylo Brown before forming their own band in 1969.

what to buy: *Still Goin' Strong* (Hay Holler Harvest, 1993, prod. Goins Brothers) 🎵🎵🎵 is a blast of no-holds-barred traditional bluegrass with exceptional vocal and instrumental work. Includes standards like "If I Should Wander Back Tonight" and fine originals including "I Guess I'll Do Without."

what to buy next: Due to illness, Buddy Griffin replaces Ray Goins on all but four songs on *We'll Carry On* (Hay Holler Harvest, 1995, prod. Kerry Hay) 🎵🎵🎵, and some of the chemistry is missing. The song selection is not nearly as strong on their first Hay Holler Harvest release and the presentation isn't as energetic.

influences:
◀◀ Stanley Brothers, Lonesome Pine Fiddlers
▶▶ Traditional Grass, Gillis Brothers

Douglas Fulmer

GOLDEN SMOG

Formed 1992, in Minneapolis, MN.

Gary Louris, guitar, vocals; Dan Murphy, guitar, vocals; Kraig Johnson, guitar, vocals; Marc Perlman, bass, vocals; Chris Mars, vocals (1992); Jeff Tweedy, guitar, vocals (1994–present); Noah Levy, drums (1994–present).

Initially an inter-band collective from such Minneapolis groups as Soul Asylum (Murphy), the Jayhawks (Louris, Perlman), the Replacements (Mars) and Run Westy Run (Johnson), Golden Smog was formed for the sole purpose of hanging out and goofing on such tunes as Bad Company's "Shooting Star" and Thin Lizzy's "Cowboy Song," both of which are on the debut EP. In the band's second incarnation, which includes Wilco's Tweedy and the Honeydogs' Levy, the Smog became alternative country's first supergroup (though the record sales of the various bands in question may be too modest to make that appellation stick). The group conveys spontaneity and a charming, homespun feel—attributes considered manna from heaven by the alt-country crowd—even if it lacks consistency. Due to contractual obligations (or mere perverseness), Golden Smoggers go, not by their own names, but by monikers consisting of their middle name in place of their first name, and the street they grew up on in place of their last name. For example, Jeff Tweedy is Scott Summit. Cute, no?

what to buy: A batch of fine songs thrown together with almost no rehearsal, *Down by the Old Mainstream* (Rykodisc, 1995, prod. James Bunchberry Lane, Golden Smog) 𝄞𝄞𝄞 is a potentially great album that wound up being just an average one. The vocals are particularly ragged, and while that may be considered the album's general aesthetic, you only have to listen to records by the group's forbears, the Byrds and the Flying Burrito Brothers, to see what was possible here. Some songs come off better than others: Louris' "V" and "Won't Be Coming Home" would fit well on any Jayhawks album; Murphy's contributions capture the energy and drama of his work with Soul Asylum; and Tweedy's "Pecan Pie" is completely charming. But Johnson's vocals aren't merely out of tune; they have no relationship whatsoever to the songs. The best advice on this group is to catch it live, where it rarely disappoints. Or wait for the next album.

the rest:

On Golden Smog EP (Crackpot, 1992/Rykodisc, 1995) 𝄞𝄞

worth searching for: Hardcore fans will no doubt want the promo-only version of *Down by the Old Mainstream* (Rykodisc, 1994) 𝄞𝄞𝄞, made up to look like a three-disc box set containing two phony discs and a booklet that, in a convoluted and occasionally hilarious manner, explains the fake history of the band.

influences:

◀◀ Byrds, Flying Burrito Brothers, Buffalo Springfield

see also: *Uncle Tupelo, Son Volt, Wilco, Honeydogs, Jayhawks*

Daniel Durchholz

GOOD OL' PERSONS

Formed 1975, in Berkeley, CA.

Kathy Kallick, guitar, vocals; Laurie Lewis, fiddle, vocals (1975–77); Dorothy Baxter, guitar, vocals (1975–77); Barbara Mendelsohn, banjo, hammered dulcimer, vocals (1975–77); Sue Shelasky, mandolin, vocals (1975); Paul Shelasky, fiddle, vocals (1975–88); Kevin Wimmer, fiddle (1988–present); Sally Van Meter, dobro, banjo, vocals (1977–present); John Reischman, mandolin, vocals (1978–present); Markie Sanders, bass, vocals (1977–80); Bethany Raine, bass, vocals (1980–90); Beth Weil, bass, vocals (1991); Todd Phillips, bass (1991–present).

A musical institution in the San Francisco Bay area for more

FIVE FOR MY FANS

JUDITH EDELMAN

Richard Thompson
Hand of Kindness (Hannibal)

Pierce Pettis
Chase the Buffalo (High Street)

Tim O'Brien
Red on Blonde (Sugar Hill)

Fairport Convention
Liege and Lief (A&M)

Kathy Kallick
Matters of the Heart (Sugar Hill)

than two decades, the Good Ol' Persons began life as an all-women band that blended bluegrass, folk, old-time country and swing music. Although the gender line would be breached the first year, musical eclecticism has remained a hallmark of this influential group. After recording a self-titled debut for Bay in 1977, the Persons made three albums during the 1980s for Kaleidoscope, all of which have recently been reissued by Flat Rock. Though relatively inactive in recent years, the band celebrated its 20th anniversary in 1995 with a live career-retrospective album on Sugar Hill and a gala two-night concert in Berkeley that reunited many of the band's past line-ups.

what to buy: *Good 'n' Live* (Sugar Hill, 1995, prod. Pieter Groenveld, Peter Thompson) 𝄞𝄞𝄞, which draws from live recordings spanning the years 1985–91, presents a satisfying overview of the band's career. Highlights include John Reischman's fiery playing on virtually every cut, Kathy Kallick's sassy lead vocals and such band favorites as "Part of a Story" and "I Can't Stand to Ramble." *I Can't Stand to Ramble* (Kaleidoscope, 1983/Flat Rock, 1995, prod. Tom Diamant) 🎵🎵🎵 features the group's signature version of "You Don't Miss Your Water," a half-dozen Kallick originals and a couple of cool Reischman-penned tunes: "Itzbin Reel" and "Get Up, Go to Work."

what to buy next: *Anywhere the Wind Blows* (Kaleidoscope, 1989/Flat Rock, 1995, prod. Tom Diamant) 🎵🎵🎵 showcases strong Kallick lead vocals on "Waking up Alone" and the title song. Other highlights include Bethany Raines' swinging take on "Walking the Floor over You" and a pair of Reischman's original tunes.

the rest:
Part of a Story (Flat Rock, 1996) 🎵🎵🎵

solo outings:
Kathy Kallick:
See individual entry

Laurie Lewis:
See individual entry

Todd Phillips:
In the Pines (Gourd, 1996)
Time Frame (Compass, 1996)

John Reischman:
North of the Border (Rounder, 1993) 🎵🎵🎵🎵

Sally Van Meter:
See individual entry

influences:
◀◀ Vern & Ray, High Country
▶▶ Laurie Lewis & Grant Street, All-Girl Boys

see also: *Kathy Kallick, Laurie Lewis, Sally Van Meter*

Jon Hartley Fox

STEVE GOODMAN

Born July 25, 1948, in Chicago, IL. Died Sept. 20, 1984, in Seattle, WA.

Steve Goodman was a folk singer from Chicago and a good friend of John Prine who emerged during the early 1970s with a gift for blues guitar playing and, like Prine, compassionate and humorous songwriting. His compositions have been recorded often, by Jimmy Buffett, Prine, David Allen Coe and the Clancy Brothers; Arlo Guthrie, John Denver and Willie Nelson are among those who have covered Goodman's best-known song, "The City of New Orleans." After a bout with major labels,

Goodman settled into a groove with his own Red Pajamas label until he died of leukemia at age 36.

what to buy: *No Big Surprise* (Red Pajamas, 1994, prod. various) 🎵🎵🎵🎵, a worthy anthology with a disc each of Goodman in the studio and onstage, offers more than a taste of him at his best. *Santa Ana Winds* (Red Pajamas, 1980, prod. Steve Goodman) 🎵🎵🎵🎵 showcases his strongest song collection—produced the way it ought to be.

what to buy next: *Affordable Art* (Red Pajamas, 1983, prod. Steve Goodman, Dan Einstein) 🎵🎵🎵🎵 includes "Talk Backwards," "Watching Joey Glow" and "A Dying Cub Fan's Last Request," one of the most poignant of all baseball songs. *Tribute to Steve Goodman* (Red Pajamas, 1985, prod. Al Bunetta) 🎵🎵🎵🎵🎵 features lots of special guests—including John Prine, Arlo Guthrie, John Hartford, Bonnie Raitt and David Bromberg—doing some of Goodman's best tunes.

the rest:
Artistic Hair (Red Pajamas, 1983) 🎵🎵🎵
Unfinished Business (Red Pajamas, 1987) 🎵🎵🎵
The Best of the Asylum Years, Volume 1 (Red Pajamas, 1988) 🎵🎵🎵
The Best of the Asylum Years, Volume 2 (Red Pajamas, 1989) 🎵🎵🎵

worth searching for: *Somebody Else's Troubles* (Buddah, 1972, prod. Arif Mardin) 🎵🎵🎵🎵🎵 is an early collection that includes "The Dutchman," "The Loving of the Game" and the powerful "The Ballad of Penny Evans."

influences:
◀◀ Bob Gibson, Josh White, Woody Guthrie, Bob Wills, Hank Williams, Big Bill Broonzy, Jethro Burns, Bob Dylan
▶▶ James McMurtry, Michael Penn, Steve Forbert

Leland Rucker

ROBERT GORDON

Born 1947, in Bethesda, MD.

Robert Gordon emerged on the New York City club scene of the 1970s as a contemporary artist whose dress and stylistic approach were rooted deep in rockabilly and country. After a stint fronting the glam-punk group the Tuff Darts, Gordon resumed his pursuit of music that owed nothing to current trends. He recorded a string of albums during the 1970s and 1980s for Private Stock and RCA, accompanied by respected guitarists such as Link Wray, Chris Spedding and Danny Gatton. Gordon has never laid claim to significant commercial success, though he did record early versions of Bruce Springsteen's "Fire" and

Marshall Crenshaw's "Someday, Someway," songs that later reached the pop Top 40 for other artists. His influence can be seen in later acts like the Stray Cats.

what to buy: Private Stock and RCA haven't seen fit to release CD versions of Gordon's original albums, such as *Fresh Fish Special* or *Rock Billy Boogie*, but *Red Hot 1977–1981* (Razor & Tie, 1995, prod. various) 🎜🎜🎜 gives a great overview of Gordon's best recordings ("Fire," covers of Conway Twitty's "It's Only Make Believe" and Roy Orbison's "Uptown").

what to buy next: *King Biscuit Flower Hour Presents Robert Gordon* (King Biscuit, 1996) 🎜🎜🎜 is a previously unreleased concert from 1979 that captures Gordon and Spedding promoting *Rock Billy Boogie* with ferocious live interpretations of rock 'n' roll and country classics, as well as Gordon's trademark songs. The sound quality is pretty good for a live recording and showcases the quality that made Gordon a cult hero.

what to avoid: *All for the Love of Rock 'n' Roll* (Viceroy, 1994, prod. Robert Gordon) 🎜 doesn't live up to Gordon's previous work. Marred by uneven material, it lacks the earlier albums' spontaneity and raucousness.

worth searching for: *Greeting from New York City* (New Rose) 🎜🎜, a French release of a 1989 live recording from New York's Lone Star Roadhouse, contains 14 songs, mostly covers.

influences:

⏮ Elvis Presley, Gene Vincent, Carl Perkins

⏭ Stray Cats, Blasters

Judy Rabinovitz

JOHN GORKA

Born July 27, 1958, in Edison, NJ.

Championed by the new folk movement of the late 1980s and early 1990s, Gorka is hardly a straight country artist. But his dark, emotionally honest songs fit in perfectly with classic country paradigms. Gorka's characters typically feel out of place or out of step with the world around them. In his songs, this can make for some harrowing or sometimes just plain funny stories. That his music sometimes blurs the lines between the two is further evidenced by his collaborations and tours with country stars Mary Chapin Carpenter and Kathy Mattea, not to mention work with Nanci Griffith, another singer-songwriter with feet planted firmly in both traditions. With a voice as deep as his hair is dark, the New Jersey-born, Pennsyl-

vania-based Gorka has quietly carved out a niche for himself as a writer and vocalist who sings about the process of living.

Gorka was a mainstay at the club Godfrey Daniels in Bethlehem, Pennsylvania before winning the 1984 New Folk Award at Texas' Kerrville Folk Festival, recognition that helped him sign with independent Red House Records three years later. His fame spread after Will Ackerman signed him to his Windham Hill label and released *Land of the Bottom Line* in 1990. While his earliest albums were stark, unadorned affairs, Gorka began recording with a full band with 1994's *Out of the Valley*. Gorka now records for Windham Hill's High Street imprint.

what to buy: Nowhere is Gorka's mordant wit more apparent than on *Land of the Bottom Line* (Windham Hill, 1990, prod. Bill Kollar) 🎜🎜🎜🎜, an evocative indictment of society—and relationships—run amok.

what to buy next: *Jack's Crows* (High Street, 1991, prod. Dawn Atkinson, William Ackerman) 🎜🎜🎜 is the most critically acclaimed of Gorka's six albums and one of his most intimate. The video for "Houses in the Fields" was a moderate hit on CMT.

the rest:

I Know (Red House, 1987) 🎜🎜🎜
Temporary Road (High Street, 1992) 🎜🎜🎜
Out of the Valley (High Street, 1994) 🎜🎜🎜
Between Five and Seven (High Street, 1996) 🎜🎜🎜

influences:

⏮ Stan Rogers, Woody Guthrie, Nanci Griffith

⏭ Shawn Colvin, Dar Williams, Bill Morrissey

Doug Pullen

SKIP GORMAN

Born May 18, 1949, in Providence, RI.

Skip Gorman is an accomplished bluegrass mandolinist, traditional fiddle player, and a onetime member of the old-timey group the Desert String Band, as well as being one half of the traditional duo Rabbit in a Log. He also recorded two albums of traditional cowboy songs for Folk Legacy in the 1970s, and has performed Western songs for a quarter century. Lately, Gorman has toured and recorded as a solo, performing traditional cowboy songs exclusively.

what's available: *Greener Prairie* (Rounder, 1994, prod. Skip Gorman) 🎜🎜🎜 features Gorman's fine instrumentals and melodic vocals on a repertoire of mostly traditional western fare. *Lonesome Prairie Love* (Rounder, 1996, prod. Skip Gorman) ♪♪♪♪ is just as good as the first, and just as true to the traditions from whence the songs are drawn.

influences:
◀◀ Carl Sprague, Eck Robertson
▶▶ Don Edwards

Randy Pitts

VERN GOSDIN

Born August 5, 1934, in Woodland, AL.

Dubbed "The Voice" because of the devastating power of his dramatic vocals, Vern Gosdin grew up singing in church and in a family gospel quartet. Early on, he moved to Chicago and worked as a machinist while singing nights in smoky clubs. During the mid-1960s Gosdin moved to Los Angeles and joined the Golden State Boys, a bluegrass band that would also include brother Rex and Chris Hillman. Gosdin first hit the charts with "Hangin' On" (on the Bakersfield Sound label) and performed with Rex as a member of the Gosdin Brothers in 1967. The brothers would sing harmony on the Byrds' classic country-rock album, *Sweetheart of the Rodeo*. After failing to take their own recording career to the next level, the Gosdins parted ways in 1972 and Vern moved to Atlanta with his wife and two sons and started a glass business. Despite the success of that endeavor, music drew him to Nashville in 1976; Gosdin asked Emmylou Harris to sing with him on his first Music City session. She agreed and he was offered a deal with Elektra. He had his first Top 10 hit in 1977, at the age of 42, and for the next decade recorded for a variety of labels, finally scoring a #1 in 1984 with "I Can Tell by the Way You Dance (You're Gonna Love Me Tonight)" on Compleat. After signing with Columbia in 1986 Gosdin's reputation as a master of heartache and harmony was cemented by brilliant ballads, including "Do You Believe Me Now" and "Chiseled in Stone," the Country Music Association Song of the Year in 1989.

what to buy: *Chiseled in Stone* (Columbia, 1987, prod. Bob Montgomery) ♪♪♪♪♪ is a masterwork of vocal balladry and songwriting artistry, with Gosdin collaborating with songwriting aces Max D. Barnes and Hank Cochran to craft the heart-stretching immortal country of the title track, "Do You Believe Me Now," "Set 'em Up Joe" (an Ernest Tubb tribute), "Is It Raining at Your House" and "Who You Gonna Blame It on This Time," all Top 10 hits.

what to buy next: *Warning: Contains Country Music (The Great Ballads of Vern Gosdin)* (American Harvest, 1996, prod.

Gary S. Paxton, Vern Gosdin, Ron Oates, Blake Mevis, Robert John Jones) ♪♪♪♪♪ is a stellar 19-track collection containing key tracks and re-recordings of material from his stints at Elektra, Compleat and Columbia as well as new single "The Number" and the non-ballad, "Dream of Me," a 1981 Top 10 hit originally recorded for Ovation. *The Gospel Album* (American Harvest, 1995, prod. Vern Gosdin, Robert John Jones) ♪♪♪♪ is the reissue of the Compleat album *If Jesus Comes Tomorrow (What Then)*, a collection of gospel standards that Gosdin had sung in church and some newer Gosdin/Barnes collaborations.

the rest:
Alone (Columbia, 1989) ♪♪♪♪
10 Years of Greatest Hits—Newly Recorded (Columbia, 1990) ♪♪♪♪
Out of My Heart (Columbia, 1991) ♪♪♪♪
The Truly Great Hits of Vern Gosdin (American Harvest, 1994) ♪♪♪♪
Super Hits (Columbia, 1994) ♪♪♪♪
If You're Gonna Do Me Wrong (Do It Right) (American Harvest, 1996) ♪♪♪♪
24-Carat Heartache (1997)

influences:
◀◀ Blue Sky Boys, Byrds
▶▶ George Jones, Vince Gill

David Sokol

GRANDPA JONES

Born Louis Marshall Jones, October 20, 1913, in Niagara, KY.

Born to a musically talented family, Louis Jones won a talent contest on the guitar at 16, then launched his career as a country singer, comedian and banjo player with radio appearances in 1929. Billed as "The Young Singer of Old Songs" while paired with ballad singer Bradley Kincaid, Jones became "Grandpa" at 22, wearing an old man disguise because he sounded so much older on the radio. Tall tales about mountain folk accompanied by the banjo became Jones' trademark as he struck out on his own in 1937. Although World War II interrupted Jones' career, he cut his first records during the mid-1940s with "It's Raining Here This Morning," "Eight More Miles to Louisville" and "Mountain Dew." After beginning work on the Grand Ole Opry show in 1946, Grandpa worked on radio and TV shows in Virginia and Washington, D.C., until returning to Nashville and a regular stint on the Opry in 1959. That year he had a Top 25 hit with Bobby Bare's "The All-American Boy," then hit the Top 5 with Jimmy Rodgers' "T for Texas." Grandpa's popularity continues today, having been boosted by a regular slot on *Hee Haw*, induction into the Country Music Hall of Fame in 1978 and continued Opry appearances.

what to buy: Though the 16 recordings on *Country Music Hall of Fame* (MCA, 1992, prod. Country Music Foundation) &&&& don't come from Jones' heyday (that would come later for Monument), this is certainly the best-assembled collection available on Jones. Recorded between 1956–59, these 15 studio tracks and one live cut from the Opry find Jones flirting with country (Johnny Cash's "Pickin' Time") as well as recording old tunes such as Bascom Lamar Lunsford's "Mountain Dew" and Jimmie Rodgers' "Waiting for a Train."

what to buy next: Recorded in Cincinnati during 1969, *Grandpa Jones Live* (Sony, 1969/1992, prod. Ray Pennington) &&&& captures Jones in all his hillbilly-vaudevillian glory just as a whole new audience was rediscovering him through *Hee Haw*. It's a wonderful introduction to Jones' style and charm—particularly his famed cowbell routine on "My Bonnie Lies over the Ocean," though that's a better sight gag.

the rest:
16 Greatest Hits (Hollywood) &&&
24 Country Hits (Hollywood/IMG, 1988) &&&
Family Album (CMH) &&&
Family Gathering (CMH) &&&
(With Ramona) *Grandpa Jones Story* (CMH) &&&
Old Time Country Music Collection (CMH) &&&

worth searching for: Details about release dates and such are extremely sketchy, but Jones has released a number of cassettes on his own. Among them are *Poems and Songs* &&, *Poems and Songs Volume 2* && and *Fifty Years of Country* &&.

influences:
◀◀ Uncle Dave Macon, Bascom Lamar Lunsford, Jimmie Rodgers
▶▶ Stringbean

see also: *Hee Haw Gospel Quartet*

Randall T. Cook

THE GRASS IS GREENER

See: Richard Greene

THE GRATEFUL DEAD

Formed 1965, in San Francisco, CA. Disbanded 1995.

Jerry Garcia, guitar, vocals (died August 9, 1995); Bob Weir, guitar, vocals; Phil Lesh, bass, vocals; Bill Kreutzmann, drums; Mickey Hart, drums (1967–69, 1974–95); Ron "Pig Pen" McKernan (died March 8, 1973), vocals, keyboards (1965–72); Keith Godchaux (died July 23, 1980), keyboards (1972–79); Donna Godchaux, vocals (1972–79); Brent Mydland (died July 26, 1990), keyboards, vocals (1979–90): Vince Welnick, keyboards, vocals (1990–95).

Under the spell of the Band's *Music from Big Pink*, the Grateful Dead returned to its own roots in bluegrass, folk and jug band music with the 1970 album *Workingman's Dead*. The acoustic, folky mood also flavored the subsequent album, *American Beauty*, but the Dead have always sidled up alongside country rather than wholeheartedly embraced it. The elemental music stream trickled through the band's electric rock improvisations—such as Merle Haggard's "Mama Tried" or Marty Robbins' "Big Iron"—but it was only on Dead side projects that guitarist and figurehead Jerry Garcia got to fully indulge his passion for traditional American country music.

what to buy: *Workingman's Dead* (Warner Bros., 1970, prod. Grateful Dead) &&&&& remains the crucial studio work in the band's entire oeuvre. *American Beauty* (Warner Bros., 1970, prod. Grateful Dead) &&&&& also manages to convey the band's fluid lyricism, although with somewhat darker undertones. On the solo side, Garcia's collaborations with longtime associate David Grisman—one of the key figures in the modern bluegrass movement—would be the means by which the late guitarist expressed his love and affinity for old timey music. Garcia's bluegrass prowess is best heard on *Jerry Garcia/David Grisman* (Acoustic Disc, 1991) &&&& and *Shady Grove* (Acoustic Disc, 1996) &&&&.

what to avoid: Despite their occasionally rootsy forays, the Dead's hackneyed attempts at commercial relevance during the late 1970s—*Terrapin Station* (Arista, 1977, prod. Keith Olsen), *Shakedown Street* (Arista, 1978, prod. Lowell George, Dan Healy) and *Go to Heaven* (Arista, 1980, prod. Gary Lyons) **WOOF!**—should be avoided at all costs.

the rest:
The History of the Grateful Dead, Volume 1 (Bear's Choice) (Warner Bros., 1973) &&&&
Two from the Vault (Grateful Dead Records, 1992) &&&&&
Dick's Picks, Volume 4 (Grateful Dead Records, 1996) &&&&

Jerry Garcia of the Grateful Dead (© Ken Settle)

solo outings:

Jerry Garcia:

(With Vassar Clements, Richard Greene, and David Grisman) *Old & In the Way* (Grateful Dead Records, 1975) 🎵🎵🎵

(With Grisman) *Not for Kids Only* (Acoustic Disc, 1993) 🎵🎵🎵

(With Old & In the Way) *That High Lonesome Sound* (Acoustic Disc, 1996) 🎵🎵🎵🎵

influences:

◀◀ Cannon's Jug Stompers, Jimmy Reed, Bob Dylan, Rolling Stones

▶▶ Allman Brothers Band, Los Lobos, Spin Doctors, Phish, Blues Traveler

Joel Selvin and Gary Graff

GREAT PLAINS

Formed 1991, in Nashville, TN.

Jack Sundrud, vocals, acoustic guitar; Russ Pahl, electric guitar (1991–93); Denny Dadmun-Bixby, bass; Michael Young, drums

(1991–93), Lex Browning, guitar, fiddle, mandolin, vocals (1995–present).

A guitarist for Great Plains once described them as "a band of character actors." That's not a bad description for this faceless band, whose members have backed singers ranging from George Jones to Mark Knopfler (and all of them, at some point, Michael Johnson) before coming together. None of the singles from the group's now-out-of-print 1991 debut, *Great Plains* (Columbia, 1991, prod. Brent Maher, Don Potter) 🎵🎵, made a significant impact on the charts, and by 1993 the group had shrunk to a duo. They eventually reunited with producer Brent Maher at Magnatone Records for an album (as a trio, having added a new guitarist) in 1996.

what's available: Acoustic guitarist Jack Sundrud has a slight hoarseness to his voice that evokes the Eagles' Don Henley, which often lands Great Plains a country-rock categorization. If the band's songwriting was as good as Henley's, *Homeland* (Magnatone, 1996, prod. Brent Maher, Great Plains) 🎵🎵 might be a more substantive album. But it does have an entertaining version of Claude King's 1962 smash "Wolverton Mountain."

influences:

◀◀ Eagles, Restless Heart

▶▶ BlackHawk

Brian Mansfield

THE GREENBRIAR BOYS

Formed 1958, in Madison, WI.

John Herald, guitar, vocals; Bob Yellin, banjo, vocals; Eric Weissberg, banjo, vocals (1958–59); Ralph Rinzler, mandolin, vocals (1959–64); Frank Wakefield, mandolin, vocals (1964–67); Jim Buchanan, fiddle (1964–67).

This band of young urban bluegrass enthusiasts played a small but important role in the folk revival of the 1960s, and must particularly be cited for bringing bluegrass music to urban audiences that may not otherwise have heard it. They won the band contest at the famed Union Grove Fiddler's Convention in 1960, a fair indication of the seriousness with which they approached the music. Guitarist John Herald was a product of the Washington Square folk jams in New York's Greenwich Village; he, Eric Weissberg, and Bob Yellin formed the first version of the band while students in Wisconsin. Mandolinist Ralph Rinzler joined in 1969, when Weissberg left. The band played a frenetic, skittery band of bluegrass; their repertoire was marked by the inclusion of traditional music from many traditions, from

"Stewball" to "Amelia Earhart's Last Flight." In addition to their own recordings, they backed Joan Baez on some bluegrass selections and also recorded with West Coast singer Di'an James on a bluegrass and traditional country record. After Rinzler left the band in 1964, ace pickers Frank Wakefield (mandolin), and Jim Buchanan (fiddle) joined the group for a time.

what's available: One reissue compilation is currently available, entitled *The Best of the Greenbriar Boys* (Vanguard, 1992) 𝄞𝄞𝄞.

worth searching for: *Di'an & the Greenbriar Boys* (Elektra, 1963, prod. Jim Dickson) 𝄞𝄞𝄞𝄞 is a quirky, long out-of-print album on which both the band and vocalist James are shown to best advantage on an adventurous repertoire of bluegrass, traditional country, and folk material.

influences:
◀◀ Red River Dave McEnery, Ramblin' Jack Elliott
▶▶ David Grisman, Jody Stecher

Randy Pitts

JACK GREENE

Born January 7, 1930, in Maryville, TN.

Jack Greene had excellent training to be a country star: playing drums with Ernest Tubb's prestigious Texas Troubadours during the early 1960s. "The Jolly Giant" could hold his own behind the mike as well, as evidenced by his four Country Music Association Awards in 1967, including one for Male Vocalist of the Year. "There Goes My Everything," written by Dallas Frazier, is Greene's best-remembered song, and anybody who listens to the Grand Ole Opry (which Greene joined in 1967) on a given weekend is likely to hear it again.

what to buy: *20 Greatest Hits* (Deluxe, 1987) 𝄞𝄞𝄞 contains Greene's biggest hits, among them the dramatic ballads "There Goes My Everything" and "Statue of a Fool" (which Ricky Van Shelton covered in 1989), but this album is slightly misleading. Though Greene's name appears alone on the jacket, the album contains a number of recordings by Jeannie Seely, a frequent duet partner of Greene's. Not that this is a bad thing, but it's disconcerting to hear Seely's "Don't Touch Me" come out of nowhere after Greene's "Until My Dreams Come True." The album also has three Greene/Seely duets.

what to buy next: Greene and Seely often recorded together and they reached the Top 40 together three times, most notably with 1969's "Wish I Didn't Have to Miss You." *Jack Greene & Jeannie Seely: Greatest Hits* (Hollywood/IMG) 𝄞𝄞𝄞 has many

of those duets and more, but the best stuff's available on the Deluxe set.

the rest:
Sings His Best (EMH) 𝄞𝄞
He Is My Everything (Step One, 1991) 𝄞𝄞
Highway to the Sky (Step One, 1995) 𝄞𝄞

influences:
◀◀ Ernest Tubb
▶▶ Ricky Van Shelton, Jeannie Seely

Brian Mansfield and Craig Shelburne

RICHARD GREENE /THE GRASS IS GREENER

Born November 9, 1942, in Hollywood, CA.

Fiddle/violin virtuoso Richard Greene started out with Bill Monroe's Blue Grass Boys and in 1969 formed the country-rock fusion band Seatrain with bluegrass crony Peter Rowan, also a Monroe alumnus. During the early 1970s he returned to his bluegrass roots, co-starring with David Grisman and Jerry Garcia in the legendary Old & In the Way and producing as well as accompanying Muleskinner. During the late 1980s Greene recorded two albums with a group known as The Grass Is Greener, whose lineup over the years has included Bill Keith, David Grier, Kenny Blackwell, Tim Emmons, Butch Baldassari, Tony Trischka and Buell Neidlinger.

what to buy: *The Greene Fiddler* (Sierra, 1995, prod. Richard Greene) 𝄞𝄞𝄞𝄞 spans Greene's musical career from 1967 through the 1990s and showcases the fiddler's mastery of styles ranging from bluegrass to Bach. Especially noteworthy are "Soldier's Joy" and his version of "Blue Rondo a la Turk." *Muleskinner: A Potpourri of Bluegrass Jam* (Sierra, 1974/Warner Bros., 1994, prod. Richard Greene, Joe Boyd) 𝄞𝄞𝄞𝄞 is a landmark of the "newgrass" era that features some stellar call-and-response fiddle and guitar playing on "Muleskinner Blues."

what to buy next: *Seatrain* (Capitol, 1969, prod. George Martin) 𝄞𝄞𝄞𝄞 was produced by legendary Beatles collaborator Martin and represents his first project after the last Fab Four album. On this recording Greene unleashes a psychedelic version of "Orange Blossom Special" that has to be heard to be believed.

the rest:
(With Seatrain) *Marblehead Messenger* (Capitol, 1971) 𝄞𝄞𝄞𝄞
The Grass Is Greener (Rebel, 1995) 𝄞𝄞𝄞𝄞

(With Old & In the Way) *That High Lonesome Sound* (Acoustic Disc, 1996) 🎵🎵🎵
(With The Grass Is Greener) *Wolves A' Howlin'* (Rebel, 1996) 🎵🎵🎵🎵

worth searching for: *Blue Rondo* (Sugar Hill, 1979/1992) on LP and cassette.

influences:
◀◀ Bill Monroe, Seatrain, Scotty Stoneman
▶▶ Peter Rowan, John McEuen, Butch Baldassari, Mark O'Connor

Douglas Fulmer

LEE GREENWOOD

Born Melvin Lee Greenwood, October 27, 1942, in Southgate, CA.

With experience ranging from an early Dixieland jazz combo gig at Disneyland to dealing cards in Las Vegas casinos, Lee Greenwood is country music's slickest entertainer. That reputation hasn't kept him in favor during these neo-traditionalist times, but it did make for an impressive run of hits, including seven #1 songs, during the 1980s. A saxophone and piano player, Greenwood's early days contained stints with Del Reeves and a pre-Young Rascals Felix Cavaliere. After Vegas, he came to Nashville, where he was the Country Music Association's Male Vocalist of the Year in 1983 and 1984. Today he has a revue in his own theater in the tourist town of Pigeon Forge, TN.

what to buy: *Greatest Hits* (MCA, 1985, prod. Jerry Crutchfield) 🎵🎵🎵 aren't always the biggest hits, but they're the ones people remember: "God Bless the U.S.A.," "Ring on Her Finger, Time on Her Hands," "I.O.U." It's definitely Greenwood's most solid collection of work.

what to buy next: Say what you will about Greenwood's later records, his first couple of albums were pretty solid collection of songs in the Kenny Rogers vein, marred only by what, in retrospect, are cheesy keyboard and string sounds. The hits on *Somebody's Gonna Love You* (MCA, 1983, prod. Jerry Crutchfield) 🎵🎵🎵, his second record, include "I.O.U.," "Somebody's Gonna Love You" and "Going, Going, Gone"; the album also contains his rendition of "Wind Beneath My Wings."

what to avoid: The only one of Greenwood's Liberty albums still in print (probably because the label hasn't been able to get rid of them), *American Patriot* (Liberty, 1992) 🎵 finds Greenwood continuing to mine the patriotic vein he stripped with "God Bless the U.S.A."

the rest:
Greatest Hits Volume 2 (MCA, 1988) 🎵🎵
At His Best (Richmond) 🎵🎵
Best of Lee Greenwood (Dominion, 1995) 🎵🎵
Totally Devoted to You (Arrival, 1995) 🎵🎵
Super Hits (Epic, 1996) 🎵🎵
Best of Lee Greenwood: God Bless the USA (Curb, 1996) 🎵🎵

influences:
◀◀ Kenny Rogers, Del Reeves
▶▶ Collin Raye

Brian Mansfield and Craig Shelburne

RICKY LYNN GREGG

Born August 22, 1961, in Henderson, TX.

Beginning in his teens, Ricky Lynn Gregg fronted a number of popular country and rock bands in the Dallas/Ft. Worth area (including Head East from 1986–89) before moving to Nashville to pursue a country career.

what's available: Neither of Gregg's albums has much to recommend it over other country albums of the period. *Ricky Lynn Gregg* (Liberty, 1993, prod. Chuck Howard) 🎵🎵 contains Gregg's lone Top 40 hit, "If I Had a Cheatin' Heart," which sounds like a knock-off of the Kentucky HeadHunters' "Walk Softly on This Heart of Mine." *Get a Little Closer* (Liberty, 1994, prod. Chuck Howard, Ricky Lynn Gregg) 🎵🎵 contains a revved-up version of the Loretta Lynn/Conway Twitty chestnut "After the Fire Is Gone" and a cover of Merle Haggard's "Silver Wings."

influences:
◀◀ Billy Ray Cyrus, Kentucky HeadHunters
▶▶ Jeff Copley

Brian Mansfield

CLINTON GREGORY

Born March 1, 1964, in Martinsville, VA.

As a fiddler, Clinton Gregory is an exuberant showman, and as a vocalist he's every bit as evocative as Keith Whitley was during his hitmaking years. As a package, however, Gregory has eluded star status beyond a few memorable videos and minor chart hits. A fifth-generation fiddler, Gregory began performing at age four. By age 12 he'd determined to make music his career, and won numerous fiddle contests over the next few years. With a number of family problems plaguing him, Clinton moved to North Carolina to live with John and Audrey Wiggins and their parents. He performed regularly with the Wiggins siblings, who are now successful recording artists in their own right. By 1987, when the three had moved to Nashville, Clinton hit the road, playing fiddle with Suzy Bogguss, then joined another sibling act, the McCarters, for a while, still playing fiddle. Pursuing a solo career during the early 1990s he came to the attention of independent Step One Records, signed with them and recorded a string of moderately successful albums before moving on briefly to the Polydor label in 1995. None of Gregory's records have really done him justice, but he's a powerful singer and expert fiddler, with loads of untapped potential.

what to buy: *(If It Weren't for Country Music) I'd Go Crazy* (Step One, 1991, prod. Ray Pennington) 𝄞𝄞𝄞 is the best bet here. The record offers some hard-core country, including the Top 20 title track.

what to buy next: *Freeborn Man* (Step One, 1992, prod. Ray Pennington) 𝄞𝄞𝄞 is slicker, but no less effective.

the rest:
Music 'n' Me (Step One, 1990) 𝄞𝄞𝄞
Master of Illusion (Step One, 1993) 𝄞𝄞𝄞
For Christmas (Step One, 1993) 𝄞𝄞𝄞
Clinton Gregory (Polydor, 1995) 𝄞𝄞𝄞

influences:
◀◀ Keith Whitley, Merle Haggard
▶▶ Tim McGraw, Tracy Lawrence

Stephen L. Betts

FIVE FOR MY FANS

VINCE GILL

Little Feat
Dixie Chicken (Warner Bros.)

Bonnie Raitt
Sweet Forgiveness (Warner Bros.)

Sonny Landreth
South of I-10 (Zoo)

Joni Mitchell
Court and Spark (Elektra)

Emmylou Harris
Pieces of the Sky (Reprise)

DAVID GRIER

Born September 23, 1961, in Washington, D.C.

The preeminent bluegrass lead guitar player of the 1990s, David Grier was exposed to the music early, through his father Lamar Grier, banjo picker for Bill Monroe during the mid-1960s. A devotee of the idiosyncratic playing of Clarence White, Grier first made himself know on a national level through recordings with the Doug Dillard Band and Country Gazette. Since launching his solo career during the late 1980s, Grier has become the highest-profile guitarist in bluegrass, thanks to tours and recordings with the Rounder Banjo Extravaganza, the Grass Is Greener and Psychograss; a pair of well-received solo albums and an outstanding duet album with mandolinist Mike Compton; guest appearances on literally scores of bluegrass, folk and country recordings; and three Guitar Player of the Year awards from the International Bluegrass Music Association (1992, 1993 and 1995).

what's available: *Freewheeling* (Rounder, 1991, prod. Jim Rooney, David Grier) 𝄞𝄞𝄞 acknowledges Grier's debt to the late Clarence White with dazzling versions of "Alabama Jubilee" and "The New Soldier's Joy." Solo performances on "Gold Rush" and "Fog Rolling Over the Glen" are especially nice, but most of the album features a first-rate band that includes Stuart Duncan and Sam Bush. *Lone Soldier* (Rounder, 1995, prod. Stuart Duncan) 𝄞𝄞𝄞 casts Grier in a jazzier light on "Porkchops & Applesauce" and "Alphabet Soup," but the more traditional-sounding tunes, particularly his originals "Smith Chapel" and "R Somethin'," suit him better. The superb backing band includes Bela Fleck, Craig Smith, Stuart Duncan and Sam Bush. *Climbing The Walls* (Rounder, 1991, prod. David Grier, Mike Compton) 𝄞𝄞𝄞𝄞, which pairs Grier with former Nashville Bluegrass Band mandolinist Mike Compton, is a sparkling all-instru-

mental romp through a set that includes original tunes, lesser-known gems from Bill Monroe ("Honky Tonk Swing" and "Going up Caney") and a killer duet on "Black Mountain Rag."

influences:

◀◀ Clarence White, Tony Rice

▶▶ Wyatt Rice, Chris Thile

Jon Hartley Fox

NANCI GRIFFITH

Born July 16, 1954, in Seguin, TX.

Nanci Griffith has spent a career bridging the uneasy gap between country and folk, earning critical praise, devoted fans and minimal mass market success. Emerging from the Austin folk scene during the mid-1970s, she recorded two albums for tiny labels and crisscrossed the country performing at festivals. By the time she cut her first Nashville album during 1984, she had a reputation as a writer of tight, insightful songs. Griffith released her first work for MCA in 1987, but big-label backing did not translate into chart success for her idiosyncratic style (in the U.S., anyway; Griffith has consistently topped charts in Ireland and Britain). Her songs, meanwhile, became Top 10 country hits for other singers like Kathy Mattea and Suzy Bogguss. Along with fellow Texan Lyle Lovett, Griffith just couldn't seem to carve out a niche in Nashville, even as her music was perceived in other quarters as too countrified to be rock. Fortunately, a move to MCA's pop division in 1989 pointed Griffith toward a grown-up pop emphasis that better suited both her distinctive voice and the burgeoning adult-contemporary format. Griffith held this course while changing labels to Elektra and remains in demand as a collaborator for everyone from the Chieftains to R.E.M. Still, she's best known as a musical storyteller whose slice-of-life vignettes like "Trouble in the Fields," "Love at the Five & Dime" and "It's a Hard Life" only gain impact with repeated handlings by other singers.

what to buy: Merely mentioning *Last of the True Believers* (Rounder/Philo, 1986, prod. Jim Rooney, Nanci Griffith) 𝄞𝄞𝄞𝄞𝄞 reduces many Griffith fans to mindless babbling. It is a beauty, with a supporting cast of musicians' musicians (Bela Fleck, Roy Huskey Jr., Maura O'Connell, Lyle Lovett) and a fistful of classic Griffith songs ("Love at the Five & Dime," "More than a Whisper," "Lookin' for the Time"). Another fine introduction to the

Nanci Griffith (© Ken Settle)

Griffith songbook is the live *One Fair Summer Evening* (MCA, 1988, prod. Nanci Griffith, Tony Brown) 𝄞𝄞𝄞𝄞, with moving versions of much of her best material and an understated reading of Julie Gold's "From a Distance" that eclipses Bette Midler's mawkish rendition.

what to buy next: *Other Voices, Other Rooms* (Elektra, 1993, prod. Jim Rooney) 𝄞𝄞𝄞𝄞, a Nanci Griffith record devoid of Nanci Griffith material, is a study of her interpretative abilities, featuring 17 songs by everyone from Woody Guthrie to John Prine to (yep) Janis Ian. On *Late Night Grande Hotel* (MCA, 1992, prod. Peter Van-Hooke, Rod Argent) 𝄞𝄞𝄞𝄞, the most successful-to-date of Griffith's VH1-style albums, Phil Everly duets on the nervous, driving "It's Just Another Morning Here," and Griffith continues her tradition of incisive political commentary with "One Blade Shy of a Sharp Edge."

what to avoid: The problem with *Lone Star State of Mind* (MCA, 1987, prod. Tony Brown, Nanci Griffith) 𝄞𝄞 isn't material; nor is it collaborators (Fleck, Huskey et. al.). It's MCA's production, which attempts to jam Griffith's music into a pair of pink sequined cowboy boots. Bad move. Griffith is many things, but a good ole girl ain't one of 'em.

the rest:

Poet in my Window (Philo/Rounder, 1982) 𝄞𝄞𝄞
Once in a Very Blue Moon (Philo/Rounder, 1984) 𝄞𝄞𝄞𝄞
Little Love Affairs (MCA, 1988) 𝄞𝄞𝄞𝄞
Storms (MCA, 1989) 𝄞𝄞𝄞
Flyer (MCA, 1995) 𝄞𝄞𝄞𝄞
Blue Roses From the Moon (Elektra, 1997) 𝄞𝄞𝄞

worth searching for: *There's a Light Beyond These Woods* (MCA U.K., 1982) 𝄞𝄞𝄞 is a rerelease of Griffith's first album from 1978, recorded live in an Austin studio.

influences:

◀◀ Carolyn Hester, Bill Staines, Weavers, Judy Collins, Tom Paxton

▶▶ Lucinda Williams, Iris DeMent

Elizabeth Lynch

DAVID GRISMAN

Born March 23, 1945, in Hackensack, NJ.

Dubbed "The Paganini of the Mandolin" by the *New York Times,* David Grisman is also a well-known champion of the "new acoustic music" movement, which draws heavily from traditional bluegrass, blues, ethnic music and jazz. David discovered the mandolin as a teenager and soaked up the stylings of bluegrass pioneers Bill Monroe and Frank Wakefield. His recording career began during the mid-1960s with the Even Dozen Jug Band, and during the late 1960s he hooked up with Bill Monroe-alumnus Peter Rowan to form the rock group Earth Opera, which was based in Boston. During the early 1970s, as a member of Old & In the Way and Muleskinner, David wowed critics and fans at bluegrass festivals and college campuses with his fast-as-lightning picking style and mastery of jazz and classical music as well as bluegrass. In 1977 the floodgates opened when Kaleidoscope Records released *The David Grisman Quintet*. The record brilliantly captured the breadth and depth of David's playing, helped no doubt by the top-notch accompaniment of guitarist Tony Rice and fiddler Darol Anger. Jerry Garcia gave David the nickname "Dawg," which has since been adopted by the manic mandolinist to describe his unique brand of music.

what to buy: *DGQ-20* (Acoustic Disc, 1996, prod. David Grisman) ♫♫♫♫ is a three-disc, 20-year David Grisman Quintet retrospective. What's unique is it's made up entirely of previously unreleased tracks from both live and studio performances. Among the outstanding DGQ alumni featured on the collection—and who established impressive careers of their own—are Darol Anger, Mike Marshall, Mark O'Connor and Tony Rice. The set also contains memorable collaborations with Jethro Burns, Vassar Clements, Jerry Garcia, Stephane Grappelli, Svend Asmussen and the Kronos Quartet.

what to buy next: *David Grisman Quintet* (Kaleidoscope, 1977, prod. David Grisman) ♫♫♫♫ is the one that started it all and subsequently set the stage for new-agey "Dawg" music. The interplay between David and guitarist Tony Rice is awesome.

the rest:
Hot Dawg (A&M, 1979/1987) ♫♫♫♫
Early Dawg (Sugar Hill) ♫♫♫♫
David Grisman Quintet 1980 (Warner Bros., 1980) ♫♫♫♫
(With Vince Gill, Herb Pedersen, Jim Buchanan and Emory Gordy Jr.)
    Here Today (Rounder, 1982/1992) ♫♫♫♫
Mondo Mando (Warner Bros./Zebra Acoustic, 1983) ♫♫♫♫
Home Is Where the Heart Is (Rounder, 1988) ♫♫♫
Dawg '90 (Acoustic Disc) ♫♫♫♫
Dawgwood (Acoustic Disc, 1993) ♫♫♫♫
(With Jerry Garcia) *Not for Kids Only* (Acoustic Disc, 1993) ♫♫♫
(With Daniel Kobialka) *Common Chord* (Cymekob, 1993) ♫♫♫♫
(With Tony Rice) *Tone Poems: The Sounds of the Great Vintage Guitars & Mandolins* (Acoustic Disc, 1994) ♫♫♫♫

(With Martin Taylor) *Tone Poems II* (Acoustic Disc, 1995) ♫♫♫♫
Dawganova (Acoustic Disc, 1995) ♫♫♫♫
The David Grisman Rounder Album (Rounder) ♫♫♫♫
(With Andy Statman) *Mandolin Abstractions* (Rounder)
Songs of Our Fathers (Acoustic Disc)
(With Garcia) *Shady Grove* (Acoustic Disc, 1996) ♫♫♫♫

influences:
◀◀ Bill Monroe, Frank Wakefield

▶▶ Bela Fleck, Jerry Douglas, Darrol Anger, Mike Marshall, Tony Rice

Rick Petreycik

ARLO GUTHRIE

Born July 10, 1947, in Coney Island, NY.

Much like Hank Williams Jr., Arlo Guthrie grew up in the shadow on a giant. Also like "Bocephus", Guthrie has honored the legacy while creating a distinct musical tradition. Still best known for his Vietnam-era satire/commentary "Alice's Restaurant" (which inspired the like-titled 1969 movie that he starred in), Guthrie has created a body of work over the last three decades that melds American roots/folk/country music into a rich contemporary setting. As early as his live 1968 second album, *Arlo*, he was dipping into classic country (in this case, Ernest Tubb's "Try Me One More Time"), and he was the first to bring Steve Goodman's "City of New Orleans" to a wide audience. He appeared with Bob Dylan during his "Rolling Thunder Revue" during the mid-1970s and, after a long career of releasing intelligent and heartfelt neo-folk albums for Warner Bros., continues to record for his own Massachusetts-based Rising Son label.

what to buy: *Outlasting the Blues* (Rising Son, 1979/1986, prod. John Pilla) ♫♫♫♫ gives Shenandoah (no, not *that* Shenandoah), his band at the time, co-billing, but the songs (except for one by Pete Seeger and one by Hoyt Axton) are Arlo all the way. Coming at a time of religious reawakening for Guthrie, *Outlasting the Blues* is a spirited set pondering life, compassion and mortality with rootsy melodicism and a touch of his trademark humor.

what to buy next: *Amigo* (Rising Son, 1976/1986, prod. John Pilla) ♫♫♫♫ is a gorgeously cohesive and warm collection spanning folk and rock and featuring collaborations with Linda Ronstadt and Leah Kunkel as well as a smokin' version of the Rolling Stones' "Connection."

what to avoid: *Together in Concert* (Warner Bros., 1975, prod. John Pilla) ♫♫, a live collaboration with Pete Seeger, lacks the spirit and energy that such a prodigious pairing promises.

the rest:
Alice's Restaurant (Reprise/Rising Son, 1967) ♫♫♫
Arlo (Rising Son, 1968) ♫♫
Running Down the Road (Rising Son, 1969) ♫♫
Washington County (Rising Son, 1970) ♫♫
Hobo's Lullaby (Warner Bros./Rising Son, 1972) ♫♫♫
Last of the Brooklyn Cowboys (Rising Son, 1973) ♫♫♫
Arlo Guthrie (Rising Son, 1974) ♫♫♫
One Night (Rising Son, 1978) ♫♫
Power of Love (Rising Son, 1981) ♫♫
(With Pete Seeger) *Precious Friend* (Warner Bros., 1982) ♫♫
Someday (Rising Son, 1986) ♫♫
Son of the Wind (Rising Son, 1992) ♫♫
Mystic Journey (Rising Son, 1996) ♫♫♫

worth searching for: *The Best of Arlo Guthrie* (Warner Bros., 1977, prod. various) ♫♫♫ is an early career overview that assembles the 18 1/2-minute "Alice's Restaurant Massacree," the hit single "City of New Orleans," the slightly left-of-center "Motorcycle (Significance of the Pickle) Song" and "Coming into Los Angeles" into one place. For that it's worthwhile, but far from cohesive. *All Over the World* (Rising Son, 1991, prod. John Pilla, Lenny Waronker) ♫♫♫ reprises some of Guthrie's most memorable material, here thematically connected by geography and titles like "Massachusetts," "Miss the Mississippi and You," "City of New Orleans" and Richard Thompson's "When I Get to the Border."

influences:
◄◄ Woody Guthrie, Pete Seeger
►► John Prine, Bob Dylan

David Sokol

JACK GUTHRIE

Born November 13, 1915, in Olive, OK. Died January 15, 1948, in Livermore, CA.

Jack Guthrie was the cousin and sometime performing partner of the legendary Woody Guthrie, with whom he shares composer credit for the oft-covered "Oklahoma Hills," the song with which he is most closely identified. The song was a big hit for Jack in 1945, when, ironically, he was serving in the army on Iwo Jima. Guthrie's music was an infectious blend of cowboy music, Western swing, country boogie, and the newly emerging

Woody Guthrie **(Archive Photos)**

honky tonk. The records he made for Capitol between 1945 and 1948 are among the finest examples of the post-depression country music recording scene in southern California. Guthrie died of tuberculosis at the age of 33.

what's available: *Oklahoma Hills* (Bear Family, 1991, prod. Lee Gillette) ♫♫♫ contains everything Guthrie cut for Capitol, including his biggest hits, "Oklahoma Hills" and "Oakie Boogie," plus eight previously unreleased titles. Also contains a thoroughly annotated 32-page booklet with discography: the definitive Jack Guthrie reissue.

influences:
◄◄ Al Dexter, Ernest Tubb
►► Hank Thompson, Arlo Guthrie

Randy Pitts

WOODY GUTHRIE

Born Woodrow Wilson Guthrie, July 14, 1912, in Okemah, OK. Died October 3, 1967, in Queens, NY.

Woody Guthrie is unquestionably the most important folk

singer of the 20th century. Guthrie's greatest gift was perhaps his ability to invest everything from protest songs and populist anthems to outlaw ballads with unfailing humor, compassion and insight. Indeed, his paeans to migrant workers, hobos and dustbowl refugees convey America's restless, expansive heart no less than the writings of Walt Whitman or Mark Twain. Guthrie's influence on Bob Dylan, Bruce Springsteen and countless others is immeasurable; his children's albums are second-to-none.

what to buy: *Dust Bowl Ballads* (Victor, 1940/Rounder, 1988, prod. Frank Driggs) 🎵🎵🎵🎵 represents the earliest flowering of Guthrie's social conscience and narrative sweep. Guthrie's song paintings are as vivid and gut-wrenching as the prose of James Agee and the photographs of Walker Evans.

what to buy next: *Library of Congress Recordings* (Rounder, 1988, prod. Alan Lomax) 🎵🎵🎵🎵 contains three volumes of conversation, songs and humanity that offer the most complete portrait of America's greatest folksinger.

what to avoid: *Worried Man Blues* (Collectables, 1990) 🎵🎵, *The Immortal Woody Guthrie* (Collectables, 1990) 🎵🎵🎵 and *Woody Guthrie & Cisco Houston: Volumes 1 & 2, the Stinson Collectors Series* (Collectables) 🎵🎵 all present classic Guthrie material with inferior sound quality and packaging.

the rest:
Songs to Grow On (Folkways, 1951) 🎵🎵🎵🎵
Songs to Grow On, Volume 2 (Folkways, 1958) 🎵🎵🎵🎵
Songs to Grow On, Volume 3 (Folkways, 1961) 🎵🎵🎵🎵
Woody Guthrie Sings Folk Songs (Smithsonian/Folkways, 1962/1989) 🎵🎵🎵🎵
Woody Guthrie Sings Folk Songs, Volume 2 (Folkways, 1964) 🎵🎵🎵🎵
Bound for Glory (Folkways, 1967) 🎵🎵🎵🎵🎵
Poor Boy (Folkways, 1968) 🎵🎵🎵🎵
Struggle (Smithsonian/Folkways, 1976/1990) 🎵🎵🎵🎵
Columbia River Collection (Smithsonian/Folkways, 1987) 🎵🎵🎵🎵
The Greatest Songs of Woody Guthrie (Vanguard, 1988) 🎵🎵🎵
(With Pete Seeger and Leadbelly) *Folkways: A Vision Revisited* (Legacy) 🎵🎵🎵🎵

influences:
◄◄ Elizabeth Cotten, Carter Family
►► Bob Dylan, Bruce Springsteen

Bill Friskics-Warren

MARTY HAGGARD

Born June 18, 1958.

Like Hank Williams Jr. or David Frizzell, Marty Haggard knows that having a famous family name is like a double-edged sword. The son of the legendary Merle Haggard, Marty was named after another country music legend—Marty Robbins—pretty much setting his career path in stone. Marty toured with his father during the 1970s and set out on his own in the 1980s, recording charting singles for Dimension and MTM between 1981–88, though none of them reached the Top 40. He still performs and records occasionally, but he's never been able to emerge from the family shadow.

what's available: If a totally unknown singer had recorded *Borders & Boundaries* (BMG/Critique, 1996, prod. David Briggs, Wade Conklin) 🎵🎵🎵, people would have praised him for how well he'd learned the lessons of Merle Haggard's emotional singing. There's a definite family resemblance in songs such as "Lovin' Time" and "Hello God," though Marty has a softer edge to his voice than his father.

influences:
◄◄ Merle Haggard, David Frizzell

Brian Mansfield

MERLE HAGGARD

Born April 6, 1937, in Bakersfield, CA.

Merle Haggard, a 1994 Country Hall of Fame inductee, is one of the greatest songwriters ever. He has amplified his reputation by consistently going his own way, keeping his distance from Nashville's power structure, paying eloquent tribute to his favorite predecessors in a business that's often uncomfortable with its past and, for a long time, keeping his music about as pure as country gets. A one-time hellraiser who served nearly three years in San Quentin for burglary, he's ironically best known to mainstream America for the ultra-conservative, anti-hippie "Okie from Muskogee" and "The Fightin' Side of Me." In the beginning of his remarkable career Haggard was known for criminal portrayals ("The Legend of Bonnie and Clyde," "Branded Man," "The Fugitive"), but he eventually became seen as a spokesman for the working class ("Workin' Man Blues," "A Working Man Can't Get Nowhere Today"). At first glimpse he seems easy to sum up, but Haggard is actually full of depth and contradictions—an ironic iconoclast. One thing he's always had a knack for is songs of plainspoken heartbreak. From his first hit, "Sing a Sad Song," to his classic "Today I Started Loving You Again" to his prototype drinking songs "The Bottle Let Me Down" and "I Threw Away the Rose," Haggard knows how to express despair. He only slips over the line into bathos, ironically, in his nostalgic family songs, such as "Daddy Frank (The Guitar Man)," where he lays on the tearjerking details to excess. The secret of Merle's success may be that no matter what the subject, even being a bum ("I Take a Lot of Pride in What I Am"), he projects an inner nobility.

what to buy: *Down Every Road* (Capitol, 1995, prod. various) ΔΔΔΔ is an altogether exemplary career overview that covers his Tally and Capitol years on three CDs and his subsequent stays at MCA (10 tracks), Epic (9 tracks) and Curb (1 track) on the last CD. This may be all the post-Capitol Hag most people will need—and enough of a taste for fanatics-to-be to decide that for themselves. A few previously unreleased tracks surface, so even fans with all the albums (like anybody has that many!) will find it worth getting. *The Lonesome Fugitive: The Merle Haggard Anthology (1963–1977)* (Razor & Tie, 1995, prod. various) ΔΔΔΔΔ is for those who only want the essential material but can't be satisfied with a one-CD set. The well-chosen collection's first CD entirely overlaps the Capitol box, but the second diverges plenty. Those who own no Hag and want to explore could find no better starting point. *A Tribute to the Best Damn Fiddle Player in the World (or, My Salute to Bob Wills)* (Capitol, 1970/Koch, 1995, prod. Earl Ball) ΔΔΔΔΔ might be the most musically and historically successful tribute album ever made. Certainly the excitement of the performances, while not equal to the Wills originals, is tangible and enhanced by the improved sonics.

what to buy next: *Same Train, a Different Time: Merle Haggard Sings the Great Songs of Jimmie Rodgers* (Capitol, 1969/Koch, 1995, prod. Ken Nelson) ΔΔΔΔ doesn't have quite the assurance and natural fit of the Wills tribute, but Haggard clearly loves the music. Such Rodgers classics as "Waitin' for a Train" even sound like Haggard could have written them. The five betweensongs narrations can be easily skipped on repeat listening.

what to avoid: At least on his mediocre 1980s material there's a sense that many of the songs are good and the production is annoying. But in the next decade's *1996* (Curb, 1996, prod. Merle Haggard, Abe Manuel Jr.) Δ, the songs are annoying and built around generalities. And Haggard's singing, on a long

Merle Haggard **(AP/Wide World Photos)**

downward decline for years, is so throaty it hardly seems like the same man. There is one great song amid the dreck: Hag's original version of "Untanglin' My Mind," which Clint Black later revised. The rest is as imaginative and repetitive as the recycled album title.

the rest:
Strangers (Capitol, 1965) ΔΔΔΔ
Land of Many Churches (Capitol, 1972/Razor & Tie, 1997) ΔΔΔΔ
I Love Dixie Blues (Capitol, 1973) ΔΔΔ
I'm Always on a Mountain When I Fall (MCA, 1978) ΔΔΔ
Serving 190 Proof (MCA, 1979) ΔΔΔ
Back to the Barrooms (MCA, 1980) ΔΔΔΔ
The Way I Am (MCA, 1980) ΔΔΔΔ
Rainbow Stew: Live at Anaheim Stadium (MCA, 1981) ΔΔΔΔ
Greatest Hits (MCA, 1988) ΔΔΔΔ
Big City (Epic, 1981) ΔΔΔΔ
Going Where the Lonely Go (Epic, 1982) ΔΔΔ
(With George Jones) *A Taste of Yesterday's Wine* (Epic, 1982) ΔΔΔ
That's the Way Love Goes (Epic, 1983) ΔΔ
Epic Collection (1983 live) (Epic, 1983) ΔΔΔΔ

(With Willie Nelson) *Pancho & Lefty* (Epic, 1983) ♪♪♪

It's All in the Game (Epic, 1984) ♪♪♪

Kern River (Epic, 1985) ♪♪♪♪

A Friend in California (Epic, 1986) ♪♪♪

Chill Factor (Epic, 1987) ♪♪♪

(With Nelson) *Seashores of Old Mexico* (Epic, 1987) ♪♪

5:01 Blues (Epic, 1989) ♪♪♪♪

Greatest Hits of the 1980s (Epic, 1990) ♪♪♪♪

His Epic Hits: The First 11/To Be Continued (Epic, 1984) ♪♪♪

Blue Jungle (Curb, 1990) ♪♪♪

A Christmas Present (Curb, 1992) ♪♪♪

1994 (Curb, 1994) ♪♪

worth searching for: *Untamed Hawk* (Bear Family, 1995, prod. various) ♪♪♪♪ contains all Haggard's work on Tally and Capitol from 1962–68 with the exception of the Rodgers tribute album. If you can find this import from Germany and have $140 available, you can have every track from his most important period on five jam-packed CDs.

influences:

◀◀ Jimmie Rodgers, Bob Wills & the Texas Playboys, Lefty Frizzell, Woody Guthrie, Hank Williams, Marty Robbins, Buck Owens

▶▶ James Talley, Stoney Edwards, Vince Gill, Dwight Yoakam, George Strait, Jayhawks, Five Chinese Brothers

Steve Holtje

BILL HALEY

Born July 6, 1925, in Highland Park, MI. Died February 9, 1981, in Harlingen, TX.

As a country singer with a fondness for cutting R&B songs, Haley first dabbled in cultural miscegenation with a 1951 recording of the Jackie Brenston hit "Rocket 88" under the moniker Bill Haley and the Saddlemen. The first record by the renamed Bill Haley and the Comets, "Crazy Man Crazy," on the independent Essex Records label became the first rock 'n' roll record to make the nationwide Top 20, which led Haley to drop the cowboy hats and the steel guitar. After signing to Decca Records in 1954, he recorded the epochal "Rock Around the Clock," which failed on its initial release but scorched up the charts after a film, *The Blackboard Jungle*, used the song as a theme the following year.

Rock 'n' roll's first monarch reigned only briefly; but from 1955, when "Rock Around the Clock" became the first #1 rock 'n' roll hit, until the ascendancy of Elvis the following year, Haley was the undisputed king. Virtually forgotten today, he would seem to have been an unlikely figure to wear the crown: 30 years old at the time, with cherubic features, a spit curl on his forehead, and invariably dressed in a tuxedo. But blaze the rock trail he did, singing the energetic refrain "one o'clock, two o'clock, three o'clock rock . . ." for the remainder of his career.

what to buy: *From the Original Master Tapes* (MCA, 1985, prod. various) ♪♪♪ provides adequate detail for most libraries.

what to buy next: The evolution of Haley from a country singer to the first rock 'n' roll star is examined in fine detail on *Rock the Joint! The Original Essex Recordings 1951–1954* (Schoolkids', 1994) ♪♪♪, an historic 24-song collection that hews closely to Haley's developing rock 'n' roll style.

what to avoid: An unilluminating late 1960s interview with Haley, interspersed with snatches of music, *The Haley Tapes* (Jerden, 1995) **WOOF!** does not make an interesting or rewarding CD.

the rest:

Bill Haley's Greatest Hits! (MCA, 1991) ♪♪♪

worth searching for: The German reissue specialists Bear Family did produce a five-disc boxed set, *The Decca Years and More*, although that may be overkill in this case.

influences:

◀◀ Big Joe Turner, Bob Wills, Louis Jordan

▶▶ Pat Boone

Joel Selvin

TOM T. HALL

Born May 25, 1936, in Tick Ridge, KY.

It's a testament to Tom T. Hall's songwriting capabilities that his efforts have reached #1 nearly 30 years apart. Known as "The Storyteller," Hall recounted the escapades of some folks he knew from his youth in Olive Hill, Kentucky in the 1968 smash, "Harper Valley, P.T.A.," a dark saga that Jeannie C. Riley would take to the top of both the country and pop charts. The tune inspired a film and TV series as well. About that time, Hall's own solo career grew on the strength of hits such as "Ballad of 40 Dollars" (1968), "Homecoming" and "A Week in a County Jail" (both 1969). His reputation as a performing songwriter was quickly founded on the consistency of his albums. In the strange days of the late 1960s and most of the 1970s, Hall unabashedly wrote with a liberal outlook, especially in brilliant cuts such as "I Washed My Face in the Morning Dew," "Mama Bake a Pie" and "The Monkey That Became President." His works are so concise that they have barely aged. Hall has also written novels and short-story collections. In 1996 Alan Jackson topped the charts with Hall's recent "Little Bitty."

what to buy: For the most comprehensive collection, *Storyteller, Poet, Philosopher* (Mercury, 1995, comp. Robert K. Oermann) 🎵🎵🎵🎵 is unbeatable. The biggest hits are here ("Old Dogs, Children and Watermelon Wine," "I Like Beer"), as are dozens of lesser-known wonders, such as "Strawberry Farms," and "I'm 40 Now." An excellent essay by compiler Oermann accompanies the affordable, two-CD, 50-song set.

what to buy next: Two other compilations, taken together, also form a solid presentation of Hall's work. *Greatest Hits, Volumes I and II* (Mercury, 1983) 🎵🎵🎵 is now available on one disc. *Loves Lost and Found* (Mercury, 1995, comp. Robert K. Oermann) 🎵🎵🎵, with 13 cuts, never overlaps with *Storyteller* and is notable for "I Love" and "Your Man Loves You Honey."

the rest:
Greatest Hits (Mercury, 1972) 🎵🎵🎵
Greatest Hits, Volume II (Mercury, 1975) 🎵🎵🎵
The Essential Tom T. Hall (Mercury, 1988) 🎵🎵🎵🎵
Country Songs for Kids (Mercury, 1988) 🎵🎵🎵
Songs from Sopchoppy (Mercury, 1996) 🎵🎵🎵
The Hits (Mercury, 1997) 🎵🎵🎵

influences:

◀◀ Floyd Carter, Roger Miller

▶▶ John Denver, John Gorka

Craig Shelburne

BUTCH HANCOCK

Born July 12, 1945, in Lubbock, TX.

When the Flatlanders broke up, it was kind of like the Beatles—if they'd released only one album. The founding members, all Texas country outlaws who knew how to play the rock 'n' roll, went on to prolific solo careers with varying degrees of commercial success. Butch Hancock, the weary folkie Flatlander—as opposed to Joe Ely's strident, rocking Flatlander or Jimmie Dale Gilmore's dignified, friendly Flatlander—took longest to grow his name in the music world. At first he focused on his architecture career, helping to design an amphitheater in Clarendon, Texas. During the late 1970s Hancock formed his own underground record label, Rainlight, and put out eight albums full of old-fashioned country songs about boxcars, junkyards and dustbowls. In 1991 he did something extraordinary, even by the standards of fellow prolific artists like Prince or They Might Be Giants. He did a six-night stand, "No Two Alike," at an Austin cafe, during which he performed (and recorded) more than 200

songs; then he released 140 of them on 14 one-hour Rainlight cassettes. A switch to the more established Sugar Hill Records, if anything, re-energized Hancock, who had squeezed in a couple of tepid albums among the gems at Rainlight. His most recent, *Eats Away the Night*, sounds like Bob Dylan died just after *Nashville Skyline* and was reincarnated into Hancock's body.

what to buy: The best of Hancock's Rainlight albums are the live party tape *Firewater Seeks Its Own Level* (Rainlight, 1981, prod. Butch Hancock, Joe Gracey) 🎵🎵🎵, the relentlessly catchy *Diamond Hill* (Rainlight, 1981, prod. Butch Hancock, Joe Gracey) 🎵🎵🎵 and the dry, twangy solo debut *West Texas Waltzes & Dust Blown Tractor Tunes* (Rainlight, 1978, prod. Butch Hancock, Joe Gracey) 🎵🎵🎵. *Eats Away the Night* (Sugar Hill, 1995, prod. Gurf Morlix) 🎵🎵🎵 is the best of Hancock's Sugar Hill career, full of unashamed Americana imagery, including "Moanin' of the Midnight Train" and "Junkyard in the Sun." Finally, the Hancock–Gilmore (along with the original Flatlanders producer) reunion *Two Roads: Live in Australia* (Virgin, 1990, prod. Royce Clark) 🎵🎵🎵 is more consistent than almost any Merle Haggard–Willie Nelson collaboration.

what to buy next: *Own and Own* (Sugar Hill, 1991, prod. various) 🎵🎵🎵 has moments of brilliance, but it's uneven.

what to avoid: Maybe he was too busy designing new buildings, but Hancock clearly phoned in a few of his Rainlight albums, including the tepid *Yella Rose* (Rainlight, 1985, prod. Butch Hancock, Royce Gracey) 🎵 and *Cause of the Cactus* (Rainlight, 1987, prod. Butch Hancock, Wayne Gracey) 🎵🎵.

the rest:
1981: A Spare Odyssey (Rainlight, 1981) 🎵🎵🎵
Split and Slide II (Rainlight, 1986) 🎵🎵🎵
Own and Own (Sugar Hill, 1991) 🎵🎵🎵
The Wind's Dominion (Rainlight, 1979) 🎵🎵

worth searching for: Why search? Call (512) 478-1688, and ask the nice people at Lubbock or Leave It for all 14 volumes of the amazing *No Two Alike Tape of the Month Club* (Rainlight, 1990s, prod. Butch Hancock) 🎵🎵🎵; but be sure not to ask about the weather in Lubbock, because the company is located in Austin.

influences:

◀◀ Willie Nelson, Johnny Cash, Jimmie Rodgers, Bob Dylan, Merle Haggard, Patsy Cline, Carl Perkins, Elvis Presley, Woody Guthrie

▶▶ Guy Clark, Lyle Lovett, Joe Ely, Jimmie Dale Gilmore, Bruce Springsteen, John Mellencamp, Rosanne Cash, Townes Van Zandt

Steve Knopper

WAYNE HANCOCK

Born May 1, 1965, in Dallas, TX.

A lot of people try to carry on the Hank Williams tradition, but few get it as right as Wayne "The Train" Hancock. He doesn't just have Williams' vocal mannerisms down cold, he's also got swagger and attitude to spare.

what's available: Hardcore honky-tonk doesn't get much more convincing than Hancock's debut *Thunderstorms and Neon Signs* (DejaDisc, 1995, prod. Lloyd Maines), 14 songs that sound classic yet not the slightest bit dated. Hancock has a lean, piercing voice that will put you in mind of wind rippling across a lonesome prairie, evoking "the juke joints, honey, where I learned how to sing/Where they honky-tonk all night and honky-tonk is king." Upright bass, no drums; perfect.

influences:

◀◀ Hank Williams, Jimmie Rodgers, Bob Wills, Jimmie Dale Gilmore, Joe Ely

David Menconi

EMMYLOU HARRIS

Born April 2, 1947, in Birmingham, AL.

While her musical trademark is a pure, aching soprano, Emmylou Harris' defining musical characteristic is curiosity. It's led her to traditional country; it's led her to new songwriters and maverick producers. Practically every hotshot on the country scene today, from Garth Brooks on down, claims Harris as an inspiration, but few can match her creative daring.

Harris began as a 1960s-style folkie, working clubs around Washington, D.C. Through ex-Byrd Chris Hillman, she met Gram Parsons. Their duets on Parsons' *Grievous Angel* are pioneering moments in country-rock and brought Harris' voice to the big time. Parsons' death in 1973 left Harris fiercely committed to continuing his vision in her solo work. With her 1975 major-label debut, *Pieces of the Sky*, she unveiled the sound that would become an influential trademark: classic country touches like galloping rhythm guitar and heartfelt vocals were cut with a driving rock backbeat. Early on, Harris demonstrated both her interest in country's past (the Louvin Brothers) and her commitment to new or unconventional material (the Beatles' "Here, There and Everywhere" or "Easy from Now On," by the young Carlene Carter). Harris' Hot Band, which toured with her through the 1980s, was an incubator of top talent; alumni include Ricky Skaggs, Vince Gill, Rodney Crowell and Albert Lee, as well as producers Emory Gordy Jr. and Tony Brown. Opting for a bare-bones traditional sound during the 1990s, Harris formed the Nash Ramblers and released the acclaimed *At the Ryman* in 1992. Her fan base is solid enough to offset country radio's indifference, and her most recent work reflects an increasing rock flavor and a continued willingness to stretch the boundaries.

what to buy: For a warp-speed trip through Harris' career, start with *Profile: The Best of Emmylou Harris* (Warner Bros, 1978, prod. various), the cream of her early studio work. High points: covers of Dolly Parton's "To Daddy" and the Louvins' "If I Could Only Win Your Love." Low point: a screechy "You Never Can Tell," which naturally remains the one Harris song most likely to be played on country radio. Fast-forward to 1995's daring *Wrecking Ball* (Asylum, 1995, prod. Daniel Lanois) to hear a Harris now completely confident in her musical impulses. Within rock producer Lanois' otherworldly arrangements, she pushes her voice to a raw, urgent edge and continues to dig up great material by underappreciated writers (Lucinda Williams, Gillian Welch, etc.). Two live albums provide excellent introductions to important phases of Harris' music. *Last Date* (Warner Bros., 1982, prod. Brian Ahern), an exuberant country-rock manifesto, summarizes why Harris' Hot Band work had such impact. She finds fresh drive in classics by Carl Perkins and Hank Cochran, pays tribute to Parsons with three of his songs and points the way forward with a startling yet stone-country cover of Bruce Springsteen's "Racing in the Streets." *At the Ryman* (Reprise, 1992, prod. Allen Reynolds, Richard Bennett) offers Harris as acoustic purist, extending and refining ideas first explored in *Roses in the Snow*. With the Nash Ramblers Harris achieves an unplugged sound that is firmly traditional and astoundingly flexible, encompassing everything from Steve Earle to Stephen Foster.

what to buy next: Any would-be country traditionalist should own *Roses in the Snow* (Warner Bros., 1980, prod. Brian Ahern), Harris' valentine to old-timey music (with assists from the likes of Parton, Skaggs, Linda Ronstadt and Johnny Cash). The ambitious concept album *The Ballad of Sally Rose* (Warner Bros., 1985, prod. Emmylou Harris, Paul Kennerley) doesn't meld into a convincing dramatic whole, but features wonderful songwriting by Harris and Kennerley on such songs as "Woman Walk the Line." The spiritual, introspective *Cowgirl's Prayer* (Asylum, 1993, prod. Allen Reynolds, Richard Bennett) features an eerie, ethereal version of Leonard Cohen's "Ballad of a Runaway Horse." And while Harris anthologies will probably always spark arguments over what was left out, the three-disc boxed set *Portraits* (Warner Bros., 1996, prod. various) ♪♪♪♪ does a respectably thorough job of collecting her Warner Bros. work.

what to avoid: *Cimarron* (Warner Bros., 1982, prod. Brian Ahern) ♪♪ is mostly listless Nashville-by-the-book—and Harris is infinitely better when she chucks the rulebook.

the rest:

Pieces of the Sky (Reprise, 1975) ♪♪♪♪

Elite Hotel (Reprise, 1976) ♪♪♪

Luxury Liner (Warner Bros., 1977) ♪♪♪

Quarter Moon in a Ten Cent Town (Warner Bros., 1978) ♪♪♪

Blue Kentucky Girl (Warner Bros., 1979) ♪♪♪

Light of the Stable (Warner Bros., 1980) ♪♪♪♪

Evangeline (Warner Bros., 1981) ♪♪♪

White Shoes (Warner Bros., 1983) ♪♪♪

Profile II: The Best of Emmylou Harris (Warner Bros., 1984) ♪♪♪♪

Thirteen (Warner Bros., 1986) ♪♪♪

Angel Band (Warner Bros., 1987) ♪♪♪♪

(With Linda Ronstadt and Dolly Parton) *Trio* (Warner Bros., 1987) ♪♪♪♪♪

Bluebird (Reprise, 1989) ♪♪♪

Brand New Dance (Reprise, 1990) ♪♪♪

Duets (Reprise, 1990) ♪♪♪

Songs of the West (Warner Bros., 1994) ♪♪♪

worth searching for: *Gliding Bird* (Jubilee, 1969) ♪♪♪, Harris' very first album, reportedly turns up from time to time in the record collections of Harris junkies; see if they'll let you tape it, though Harris herself—who sued for and won the rights to the masters after Jubilee folded—would probably prefer you don't.

influences:

◀◀ Carter Family, Buck Owens, Louvin Brothers, Hazel & Alice, Tom Rush, Gram Parsons

▶▶ Alison Krauss, Mavericks, Cowboy Junkies

see also: *Gram Parsons*

Elizabeth Lynch

FREDDIE HART

Born December 21, 1926, in Loachapoka, AL.

Freddie Hart has led a rich and varied life in country music, one that has seen him work as a roadie for Hank Williams, tour with Lefty Frizzell, become a regular on Compton, California's legendary *Town Hall Party* television show, and write hit songs for others ("Loose Talk" was a smash for Carl Smith in 1955). De-

Emmylou Harris **(AP/Wide World Photos)**

spite record deals with Capitol and Columbia, however, Freddie's own recording career languished until 1971, when he had a gigantic hit with "Easy Lovin'." From that time until 1976 he was seldom out of the Top 10, although the songs he wrote and recorded during this period were more countrypolitan than honky-tonk and artistically inferior to the things he had done for Columbia during the 1960s: songs like "The Key's in the Mailbox," "Drink Up and Go Home," "The Wall," "Chain Gang" and others, which are unfortunately not readily available today.

what's available: *The Best of Freddie Hart* (Capitol, 1997, prod. various) ♪♪♪♪ contains Freddie's biggest hits, from his very successful early 1970s recordings, beginning with "Easy Lovin'," which saved him from being dropped by the label.

influences:

◀◀ Hank Williams, Lefty Frizzell

▶▶ David Houston, Kenny Rogers

Randy Pitts

JOHN HARTFORD

Born December 30, 1937, in New York, NY.

If John Hartford were known only for his most famous song, "Gentle on My Mind," that would certainly be enough. One of the most performed and recorded songs of all time—it's been done by everyone from Glen Campbell, who used it as the opening theme of his *Goodtime Hour* TV show during the 1960s, to Aretha Franklin—it has earned Hartford sufficient royalties to play whatever music he chooses, regardless of commercial considerations, and to spend time as a riverboat pilot, his true passion. Hartford is an astonishing talent on both fiddle and banjo, but the entertainment quotient is kicked to a whole other level when he throws in the trick that has made him unique: he provides his own percussion, clog-dancing on a piece of amplified plywood he refers to as the "whomper stomper." It may not be much on record, but you should see him live. Hartford's artistic freedom led him to become Nashville's version of a hippie—respectful of his elders (so long as they can play), but stoned enough to record a twisted version of the Lord's Prayer on his best album, *Mark Twang*. Hartford has mellowed over the years, and many of his albums are interchangeable. As a rule, he's at his best and most entertaining when he's letting his eccentricities run wild.

what to buy: *Mark Twang* (Flying Fish, 1976, prod. Mike Melford) 🎵🎵🎵🎵 is the album on which Hartford's eccentric style came to its full fruition. Sawing the fiddle, pickin' the banjo, tapping his feet and singing about steamboats, the Mississippi river, his bluegrass heroes and reefer, Hartford sounds like he's singing for no one so much as himself. But it offers a glimpse at a worldview so fully formed and so compelling that you can't help forgive him his self-indulgence. Or, at the very least, tap your foot in time. *Me Oh My, How the Time Does Fly* (Flying Fish, 1987, prod. various) 🎵🎵🎵🎵 is a generous best-of disc that covers his years on the Flying Fish label, which marked the creative apex of his career.

what to buy next: *Aereo-Plain* (Warner Bros., 1971, prod. David Bromberg) 🎵🎵🎵 has a wonderful, old-timey feel, abetted by an amazing backup trio of Tut Taylor, Norman Blake and Vassar Clements. This album would sound best played through an old cathedral radio. *Nobody Knows What You Do* (Flying Fish, 1977, prod. Mike Melford) 🎵🎵🎵 is one of Hartford's more eccentric efforts, but it contains the wistful "In Tall Buildings," one of his best songs, plus some low humor in "The Golden Globe Awards" and even a brief tribute to the jazz-fusion guitar hero "John McLaughlin." After many soft albums, notably those on

his own label, Small Dog a Barkin', *Wild Hog in the Red Brush and a Bunch of Others You Might Not Have Heard* (Rounder, 1996, prod. John Hartford, Bob Carlin) 🎵🎵🎵, with the Hartford String Band, is a heartening return to form, featuring engaging arrangements of 19 old fiddle tunes.

what to avoid: A pair of albums, now available as the two-fer *Glitter-Grass from the Nashwood Hollyville Strings/Permanent Wave* (Flying Fish, 1977, 1980/1995) **WOOF!**, with Doug and Rodney Dillard, are filled with dreadful country-pop. The bizarre song selection—"Boogie on Reggae Woman," "No Beer in Heaven"—doesn't help.

the rest:
Morning Bugle (Warner Bros., 1972/Rounder, 1995) 🎵🎵🎵
Annual Waltz (MCA, 1987) 🎵🎵
(With the Hartford String Band) *Down on the River* (Flying Fish, 1989) 🎵🎵
(With Jamie Hartford) *Hartford & Hartford* (Flying Fish, 1991) 🎵🎵
(With Mark Howard and the Hartford String Band) *Cadillac Rag* (Small Dog a Barkin', 1992) 🎵🎵
The Walls We Bounce Off Of (Small Dog a Barkin', 1994) 🎵🎵🎵
Live at College Station, PA. (Small Dog a Barkin', 1994) 🎵🎵🎵
(With Bob Carlin) *The Fun of Open Discussion* (Rounder, 1995) 🎵🎵🎵
No End of Love (Small Dog a Barkin', 1996) 🎵🎵

worth searching for: Hartford's original version of "Gentle on My Mind" can be found on the out-of-print *Earthwords and Music* (RCA, 1967, prod. Felton Jarvis) 🎵🎵 and is a true artifact of the 1960s.

influences:
◄◄ Flatt & Scruggs, Stringbean, Tater Tate, Allen Mundy
►► Mark O'Connor, Bela Fleck

Daniel Durchholz

HAWKSHAW HAWKINS

Born Harold Franklin Hawkins, December 22, 1921, in Huntington, WV. Died March 5, 1963, near Camden, TN.

Standing 6'8" (in his cowboy boots), Hankshaw Hawkins was a country music traditionalist whose career was marked by such hits as "I Love You a Thousand Ways," "Slow Poke" and "Soldier's Joy." A versatile baritone who never received the acclaim his talents deserved until after his death, Hawkins was one of the Ernest Tubb-influenced singers who flocked to country music during the late 1940s. He grew up in West Virginia and started working on local radio at age 15; by 1946 he was a member of the popular Wheeling Jamboree. Two years later he had his first big hit, a train song called "Pan American" that played off the famous "Wabash Cannonball."

Hawkins had moderate hits throughout the next decade, primarily for King, though he also recorded for Columbia and RCA. He joined the Grand Ole Opry cast in 1955 and married Jean Shepard in 1960. Hawkins favored honky-tonk and Western music, but he could sing almost anything effectively, be it boogie or ballads. The song that would become his biggest hit, "Lonesome 7-7203," entered the country charts on March 2, 1963—three days before Hawkins was killed in a plane crash with Cowboy Copas and Patsy Cline.

what to buy: Though it's available only on cassette, *16 Greatest Hits* (Hollywood/IMG, 1978) ♫♫♫ is the single best choice to hear Hawkins' music. It's the only place that collects all of the influential honky-tonker's Top 10 singles—"Pan American," "Dog House Boogie," "I Love You a Thousand Ways," "I'm Waiting Just for You," "Slow Poke" and "Lonesome 7-7203."

what to buy next: *Hawkshaw Hawkins Volume 1* (King, 1988) ♫♫♫ is the only U.S. CD issue of Hawkins' music. It's short on hits (his 1951 version of Pee Wee King's "Slow Poke" is the only Top 40 single here) but it has good versions of familiar old country songs like "Barbara Allen" and "Sunny Side of the Mountain."

the rest:
His Everlasting Hits (IMG) ♫♫♫
Lonesome 7-7203 (King EP, 1994) ♫♫

worth searching for: If money's no object, *Hawk 1953–61* (Bear Family, 1991, prod. various) ♫♫♫ is a great three-disc, box-set summary that includes all his RCA and Columbia sides, along with in-depth liner notes.

influences:
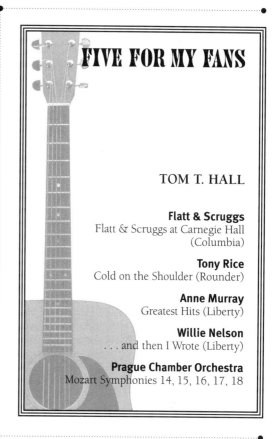 Red Foley, Ernest Tubb
▶▶ Jack Greene, Lefty Frizzell, Marty Robbins

Brian Mansfield and Bob Cannon

RONNIE HAWKINS

Born January 10, 1935, in Huntsville, AR.

There was once one brief shining moment, circa 1960, when "Rompin'" Ronnie Hawkins was poised to take over the world. All the crucial elements were in place: he and drummer Levon Helm were slowly assembling one of the greatest bands of all time (someday to become legendary in its own right as The Band); the head of Hawkins' label, Roulette, was spreading the

---

FIVE FOR MY FANS

TOM T. HALL

Flatt & Scruggs
Flatt & Scruggs at Carnegie Hall
(Columbia)

Tony Rice
Cold on the Shoulder (Rounder)

Anne Murray
Greatest Hits (Liberty)

Willie Nelson
. . . and then I Wrote (Liberty)

Prague Chamber Orchestra
Mozart Symphonies 14, 15, 16, 17, 18

---

word that his boy "moved better than Elvis, looked better than Elvis, and SANG better than Elvis" (he wasn't that far off the mark!); and, most important of all, the current mainstreaming of Music City simply begged for a talent like Hawkins' to grab it by the horns and shake it back to life. Unfortunately, Rompin' Ronnie chose instead to remain in his adopted home of Toronto, Canada where he spent the 1960s buying up nightclubs and making money as opposed to making history. Sure, he made great music and even had a few hits ("Mary Lou," "Forty Days"), but unless you happened to be spending your Saturday nights on Toronto's Yonge Street, you'd never know that the kind of rumble Willie Nelson was busy producing outside Nashville and that Buck Owens was starting in Bakersfield was already well under way wherever Ronnie & the Hawks were performing. Sadly, as one by one his musicians left to seek their deserved fortunes outside of Toronto (guitarists Robbie Robertson and Roy Buchanan among them), Hawkins stubbornly remained in Canada, only occasionally committing to

Ronnie Hawkins (© Ken Settle)

tape his special brand of razor-backed country-rock. Still, when Toronto recently threw him a 60th birthday bash, Carl Perkins and even Jerry Lee Lewis felt they owed it to the Hawk to make an appearance, and that night the rafters shook as they had back in 1960. Still not convinced Ronnie Hawkins is one of the greatest talents ever to sing country—or rock, for that matter? Name one other singer Jerry Lee would fly a thousand miles to play piano for.

what to buy: *The Best of Ronnie Hawkins & the Hawks* (Rhino, 1990, prod. various) ♪♪♪♪ contains a decade's worth of the sounds Ronnie said "took us from the hills and the stills and on to the pills," culminating with his 1970 comeback hit "Down in the Alley," produced in Muscle Shoals with Duane Allman. And speaking of ferocious guitar solos, Robbie Robertson's on "Who Do You Love" sounds no less awe-inspiring now as it must have back in 1963.

what to buy next: *Ronnie Hawkins: The Roulette Years* (Sequel, 1994, prod. various) ♪♪♪♪ fleshes out the years 1959–63 and is of particular interest in that it demonstrates just how fully

The Band's own unique approach to music was in evidence long before Mr. Dylan hijacked them.

the rest:

Let It Rock (Quality, 1995) ♪♪♪

Rock 'n' Roll Resurrection/Giant of Rock 'n' Roll (One Way, 1996) ♪♪♪

worth searching for: *Mr. Dynamo/Ronnie Hawkins Sings the Songs of Hank Williams* (TNT, 1992, prod. Joe Reisman) ♪♪♪♪ gathers on one CD Hawkins' second and fourth albums, the latter a surprisingly reverent tribute to the work of the Hillbilly Shakespeare. Also recommended in this same rootsy vein is *Folk Ballads of Ronnie Hawkins* (Roulette, 1960, prod. Joe Reisman) ♪♪♪.

influences:

◀◀ Bo Diddley, Conway Twitty

▶▶ Creedence Clearwater Revival, Redneck Greece Delux

Gary Pig Gold

TED HAWKINS

Born 1936, in Biloxi, MS. Died January 1, 1995.

Born into poverty, soulful country/blues singer Ted Hawkins developed his rich, poignant vocal style singing in reform school and on street corners. He learned how to play guitar at age 12, but it wasn't until 1971, while busking in Los Angeles, that he came to the attention of producer Bruce Bromberg. A longtime Venice Beach regular who bared his soul to the young and the restless for pocket change, Hawkins became an international cult hero before succumbing to a stroke at age 58. His trademark milk carton, on which he performed, traveled with him until the end, a constant reminder of the hard times that informed the gentle voice.

what to buy: *The Next Hundred Years* (DGC, 1994, prod. Tony Berg) ♪♪♪♪ released just months before his death, brims with optimism and proves that Hawkins' love for music overshadowed his troubled past. Searching and mystical originals mingle with gorgeously arranged covers of songs by Jesse Winchester, John Fogerty and Webb Pierce.

what to buy next: *Happy Hour* (Rounder, 1986/1994, prod. Bruce Bromberg, Dennis Walker, Dale Wilson) ♪♪♪♪ is an inviting and thoroughly dignified set of country blues in its purest form. *Watch Your Step* (Rounder, 1982/1994, prod. Bruce Bromberg, Dennis Walker) ♪♪♪♪ is unabashed soul music, born out of hardship, but rendered with spark and humor. These are the earliest available Hawkins sides, recorded not for a spot on a best-seller list, but because of their compelling and universal honesty.

influences:

◀◀ Sam Cooke, Otis Redding

▶▶ Sam Moore, Johnny Adams

David Sokol

WADE HAYES

Born April 20, 1969, in Bethel Acres, OK.

The son of a country singer who once came to Nashville and lost everything in a bad management deal, Hayes came to Music City at the age of 22 and worked construction—but not for long. He met a songwriter, got signed to write, and then landed a record deal in quick succession, as much for his deep older-than-his-years voice as his deft songwriting. One of a crop of new "hat acts" to debut during the 1990s, Hayes immediately stood out from the rest.

what's available: *Old Enough to Know Better* (Epic/DKC, 1994, prod. Don Cook, Chick Rains) ♫♫♫ spawned the hit ballads "I'm Still Dancin' with You," "What I Meant to Say" and the lusty rocker "Don't Stop," but the gems are the uptempo "Steady as She Goes" and "It's Gonna Take a Miracle," along with the poignant "Family Reunion" and his winning remake of Keith Whitley's "Kentucky Bluebird." On *On a Good Night* (Epic/DKC, 1996, prod. Don Cook, Chick Rains) ♫♫♫ Hayes continued his winning streak. Although it has fewer standout tracks, *On a Good Night* does have the rowdy title track, his cover of the Hank Cochran/Willie Nelson composition "Undo the Right" and a driving Kix Brooks/Ronnie Dunn song "Our Time Is Coming." The biographical "This Is the Life for Me" describes the hold honky-tonks have had on Hayes from his younger days—mercifully, without resorting to any of the "that's country, I'm country" bravado to which many supposedly more seasoned artists fall prey.

influences:

◀◀ Keith Whitley, Merle Haggard, Waylon Jennings

▶▶ Paul Brandt

Bill Hobbs

HAZEL & ALICE /HAZEL DICKENS /ALICE GERRARD

Formed early 1960s, in Baltimore, MD/Washington, DC area.

Wade Hayes (© Ken Settle)

Hazel Dickens (born June 1, 1935, Mercer County, WV), vocals; Alice Gerrard, fiddle, banjo, guitar, vocals.

Hazel Dickens and Alice Gerrard began playing bluegrass together informally, and soon made history in this heretofore largely male bastion of traditional music. With their songwriting skills, imaginative arrangements of traditional and original numbers, and, in particular, their impassioned and heartfelt vocal harmonies, working-class West Virginian Hazel and middle-class/West-Coast-reared Alice became a highly influential and successful bluegrass and traditional country duet. Their pioneering efforts helped bring countless young women artists into bluegrass and traditional country music, and their landmark recordings have influenced the repertoires of artists as diverse as Emmylou Harris (who adopted their arrangement of the Carter Family's "Hello Stranger") and the Judds, for whom their harmonizing served as an early inspiration.

Performing for the first time in 1962, the two recorded their best-known work for Rounder in 1973. Hazel & Alice's wild and fiercely emotional vocal harmonies breathed new life into the traditional material they recorded, and several of their original songs became bluegrass and traditional standards. Since 1981 they have performed together infrequently, but each has continued to perform solo and in other musical contexts. Dickens is widely regarded as among the finest traditional country songwriters in the business, penning such classics as "Won't You Come and Sing for Me," "Mama's Hands," "My Better Years," "A Few Old Memories," "These Old Pictures" and many more. She has also been involved in several movie projects, contributing music to the films *Harlan County, U.S.A.* and *Matewan*, in which she also appeared. Gerrard, a gifted fiddler, banjo player and guitarist, has been publisher of the *Old-Time Herald*, a quarterly magazine devoted to the preservation of old-time music, since 1987.

what to buy: *Hazel & Alice* (Rounder, 1973/1995, prod. Hazel & Alice) ��������, the duo's classic album, was extremely popular and influential in traditional music circles when it was released, due in part to the working woman's slant given to the material, but mostly because of the fierceness and raw, heartfelt emotion conveyed in the duo's harmonies. It contains three originals by Hazel and three by Alice, each imbued with the traditional feel of songs by Utah Phillips, the Carter Family, Wilma Lee Cooper, J.B. Coates, and Trixie Smith, which make up the remainder of the album's tracks.

what to buy next: *Pioneering Women of Bluegrass* (Smithsonian/Folkways, 1965/1996, prod. Peter K. Siegel) ��������, a reissue of Hazel & Alice's first recordings—26 cuts in all—contains more numbers from the traditional bluegrass repertoire and fewer originals than their first Rounder recording, with bands that include David Grisman, Lamar Grier, Chubby Wise and Billy Baker. One notable exception to the traditional repertoire here is Hazel's "Won't You Come and Sing for Me," which during the years since this recording was originally released has achieved classic status.

worth searching for: *Hazel Dickens & Alice Gerrard* (Rounder, 1976) �������� isn't the classic that the first Rounder album is, but it's still very worthwhile. *The Strange Creek Singers* (Arhoolie, 1975, prod. Mike Seeger, Chris Strachwitz) features Hazel & Alice along with Alice's then-husband Mike Seeger and his New Lost City Ramblers-bandmate Tracy Schwarz.

solo outings:

Hazel Dickens:
A Few Old Memories (Rounder, 1987) ��������

Alice Gerrard:
Pieces of My Heart (Copper Creek, 1994) ��������

Influences:

◄◄ Carter Family, Wilma Lee Cooper, Stanley Brothers

►► Iris DeMent, Judds, Emmylou Harris, Lynn Morris, Kate Brislin

Stephen L. Betts and Randy Pitts

THE HEALTH & HAPPINESS SHOW

Formed 1990, in New York, NY.

James Mastro, vocals, guitar, bouzouki, harmonica; Vincent DeNunzio, drums, vocals; Dave de Castro, bass, vocals (1995–present); Graham Maby, bass, vocals (1990–91); Tony Shanahan, bass, vocals, keyboards (1992–94); Sean Grissom, cello (1990–91); Todd Reynolds, fiddle (1992–94); Kerryn Tolhurst, mandolin, lap steel, dobro, guitar (1992–94); additional guitarists: Richard Lloyd, Ivan Julian, Erik Della Penna.

Finding himself in dire need of some honest, simple music-making after the sour break-ups of his two bands, the Bongos and Strange Cave, songwriter James Mastro initiated a series of kitchen-table hoots alongside old pal Vincent DeNunzio (ex-Feelies, the Richard Hell Band). The modern-day jug music that resulted as additional friends joined in led to the formation of a bona fide band several months later. Naming themselves after the Hank Williams radio show sponsored by half alcohol/half laxative elixir Hadacol ("The music was the laxative and beer was the alcohol," Mastro recalls) the Health & Happiness Show wasted no time committing to tape their uniquely countrified brand of pop.

what's available: *Tonic* (Bar/None, 1993, prod. James Mastro, Tony Shanahan) ���� mixed the Gram Parsons-plays-*Revolver* sound that H&H were already becoming known for with refreshing hints of Fairport Convention-styled neo-folk. The combination immediately won high praise from both traditional and New Country quarters, as did a subsequent tour alongside Butch Hancock. For the follow-up, *Instant Living* (Bar/None, 1995, prod. James Mastro, Tony Shanahan) ����, a louder, leaner, almost Crazy Horse approach was apparent, thanks in no small part to the guitar interplay between Mastro and new recruit Richard Lloyd (ex-Television).

worth searching for: Most recently, the band contributed "Stupefaction" to the Graham Parker tribute album *Piss and Vinegar* (Buy or Die, 1996, prod. various) ���.

influences:

◀◀ Hank Williams, Howlin' Wolf, Television

▶▶ Delevantes, Demolition String Band

Gary Pig Gold

THE HEE HAW GOSPEL QUARTET

Roy Clark; Buck Owens; Kenny Price; Grandpa Jones.

A popular segment on the long running *Hee Haw* TV series, the "quartet" actually came into being with seven members during a break in taping. Guest performer Tennessee Ernie Ford was gathered off camera with regulars Owens, Clark, Jones, Merle Travis and Archie Campbell when they ran through a few traditional gospel songs. The show's production staff recognized the possible audience appeal, and the idea stuck.

what's available: *The Best of the Hee Haw Gospel Quartet* (Ranwood, 1995) 𝄞𝄞𝄢 and *The Best of the Hee Haw Gospel Quartet Volume 2* (Ranwood, 1996) each boast 12 familiar gospel songs. *Volume 1* contains "Dust on the Bible," "Shall We Gather at the River" and "Amazing Grace"; *Volume 2* has "The Glory Land Way," "No Tears in Heaven" and "The Unclouded Day."

influences:

◀◀ Statesmen, Blackwood Brothers

see also: *Roy Clark, Buck Owens, Grandpa Jones*

Randall T. Cook

THE HELLECASTERS

Formed 1989, in Los Angeles, CA.

John Jorgenson, guitar; Jerry Donahue, guitar; Will Ray, guitar.

The Hellecasters are one of the most exciting guitar-based instrumental bands to emerge from L.A.'s thriving roots music community of the late 1980s. Its unique blend of outrageous string-bending techniques, fast-as-lightning picking, searing harmonics and whammy bar torturing made it *the* instrumental band of the 1990s, according to leading music publications and guitar aficionados. In 1992 former Monkee Mike Nesmith happened to hear a fiery performance by these guys at a club in L.A. and was completely bowled over; he subsequently offered the trio a recording contract, and the band has recorded two killer albums for his Pacific Arts label. The members' individual musical resumes are also quite impressive. John Jorgenson, in addition to being a founding member of the Desert Rose Band, has backed up artists such as Bob Seger, the Byrds, Bonnie Raitt, Roy Orbison, Bob Dylan and Elton John. During the mid-1980s Jerry Donahue filled Richard Thompson's shoes in the acoustic-based Celtic outfit Fairport Convention, while Will Ray, in addition to backing such country artists as Carlene Carter, ran a successful L.A. recording studio.

what's available: *The Return of the Hellecasters* (Pacific Arts, 1993, prod. Hellecasters) 𝄞𝄞𝄞𝄞 showcases the band's impeccable twanging and bending, including an exquisite treatment of Don Gibson's "Sweet Dreams" and a smokin' version of the theme from "Peter Gunn." *Escape from Hollywood* (Pacific Arts, 1994, prod. Hellecasters) 𝄞𝄞𝄞𝄞 picks up where *Return* left off but displays even more of a rhythmic openness and tightness.

influences:

◀◀ Duane Eddy, Ventures, Shadows, James Burton, Albert Lee

see also: *Desert Rose Band*

Rick Petreycik

MIKE HENDERSON

Born July 7, 1951, in Yazoo City, MS.

Mississippi-born, Missouri-raised Mike Henderson's music is a high-octane mix of country, blues and rock 'n' roll. A former member of the Missouri blues-rock outfit the Bel-Airs, Henderson kicked around Nashville, doing session work for such artists as Kevin Welch and Tracy Nelson and writing songs (including the Fabulous Thunderbirds' "Powerful Stuff"). His RCA debut was well above average, but the company didn't know how to market Henderson's renegade sound. Judging from his two more recent efforts, he's more at home on his new label, the artist-run Dead Reckoning.

what to buy: *First Blood* (Dead Reckoning, 1996, recorded by Peter Coleman) 𝄞𝄞𝄞𝄞, with the Bluebloods, is, for all intents and purposes, a scorching blues album, but it shares a roadhouse sensibility with country, and besides, a song titled "When I Get Drunk" can surely fit in either genre.

the rest:

Country Music Made Me Do It (RCA, 1994) 𝄞𝄞𝄞𝄢
Edge of Night (Dead Reckoning, 1996) 𝄞𝄞𝄞𝄞

influences:

◀◀ Jerry Lee Lewis, Merle Haggard, Dave Alvin

Daniel Durchholz

JOE HENRY

Born December 2, 1960, in Charlotte, NC.

That Joe Henry remains best known to the public at large as Madonna's brother-in-law is nothing short of criminal. He's a fine singer and drop-dead brilliant songwriter, responsible for some of the finest country-rock of the 1990s. Plus he has never shied away from pushing himself in unexpected or even difficult directions, as his body of work shows.

what to buy: While it's not fair to say it came out of nowhere, *Short Man's Room* (Mammoth, 1992, prod. Joe Henry) ♫♫♫♫ is still a startling record that makes absolute mincemeat of Henry's preceding three albums. Originally recorded as demos (with the Jayhawks as his backup band), the album has an offhanded freshness Henry has never duplicated, plus a timelessly airy sound that should ensure that it will age well. *Short Man's Room* also comes with Henry's best-ever set of songs, from the title track (a waltz!) to the doom-laden "A Friend to You." Magnificent, and a landmark.

what to buy next: *Kindness of the World* (Mammoth, 1993, prod. Joe Henry) ♫♫♫♫ tries to duplicate its predecessor's formula, with the Jayhawks again on board. Its only real flaw is that it's a shade too predictable, with material not quite as start-to-finish strong as *Short Man's Room*. But it's still intermittently stunning, especially "Third Reel" and the "Fireman's Wedding" single. Henry bounced back strong with *Trampoline* (Mammoth, 1996, prod. Patrick McCarthy, Joe Henry) ♫♫♫♫, the bravest album in his catalog. Just when alternative country was catching on, Henry chose to make his Tom Waits move, ditching the Jayhawks and enlisting Helmet guitarist Page Hamilton. While the results are strange and clattery (an opera sample adorns one track), *Trampoline* is also mesmerizing.

what to avoid: Henry's amateurish debut, *Talk of Heaven* (Profile, 1986, prod. Joe Henry) ♫♫, is most notable as proof of how far he's come—and that what he does ain't near as easy as he makes it look. It is the only black mark on an otherwise honorable career.

the rest:
Murder of Crows (Coyote/A&M, 1989) ♫♫♫
Shuffletown (Coyote/A&M, 1990) ♫♫♫♫

worth searching for: Henry appears on the Vic Chesnutt tribute album *Sweet Relief II: Gravity of the Situation* (Columbia, 1996, prod. various) ♫♫♫♫. A predictable enough place for him to be, right? The punchline is his duet partner—sister-in-law Madonna on a cover of "Guilty by Association," a song Ches-

null originally wrote about Michael Stipe. It has a terrifyingly high irony quotient.

influences:
◄◄ Steve Forbert, John Prine, Bob Dylan, Tom Waits, Van Morrison, the Band, Charlie Rich, T-Bone Burnett
►► Uncle Tupelo, Son Volt, Wilco

David Menconi

TY HERNDON

Born May 2, 1962, in Butler, AL.

A product of a Baptist/Assembly of God musical upbringing, Ty Herndon performed mostly in Tennessee and Texas before signing his record deal. In Nashville, he worked at the Opryland USA theme park, where he fronted an early version of the band that would eventually become Diamond Rio. On the strength of its shattering title hit, his *What Mattered Most* had the largest initial shipment of any debut album in Sony Music Nashville's history to that time. Herndon was arrested for felony drug possession and indecent exposure in 1995 and sentenced to five years' probation.

what's available: Herndon's an impressive vocalist, but his albums seem to be built around the old one-hit-and-some-filler formula. *What Mattered Most* (Epic, 1995, prod. Doug Johnson, Ed Seay) ♫♫♫ and *Living in a Moment* (Epic, 1996, prod. Doug Johnson) ♫♫♫ both have marvelous title tracks (especially "What Mattered Most"), but everything else is strictly by-the-numbers.

influences:
◄◄ Billy Dean, Collin Raye, Diamond Rio
►► James Bonamy

Brian Mansfield

DAN HICKS

Born December 9, 1941, in Little Rock, AR.

Dan Hicks polished the old-timey style of the Charlatans, a little-known but influential San Francisco band in which he served as drummer, into a campy, acoustic-flavored cabaret act, Dan Hicks & His Hot Licks. The group would presage such full-blown period pieces as Bette Midler, the Pointer Sisters and the Manhattan Transfer by several years. Hicks' sarcastic persona and well-developed sense of irony gave him a determined deadpan attitude and helped obscure the fact that his songwriting was really first-rate. With his jazzy mien and caustic air, he made a modest splash with his Blue Thumb albums of the early 1970s, which had the zippy nonchalance of an R. Crumb cartoon come to life. Hicks continues an active performing career, although his recordings have been few and far in between since the heyday of the Hot Licks.

what to buy: *Where's the Money* (MCA, 1971/1989, prod. Tommy LiPuma) *ʾʾʾʾ* probably best reflects the zany intransigence of Hicks & company.

what to buy next: *Striking It Rich* (MCA, 1972, prod. Tommy LiPuma) *ʾʾʾ* captures the live ambiance of the band's appearances.

the rest:
Last Train to Hicksville (MCA, 1973) *ʾʾ*
Shootin' Straight (On the Spot, 1994) *ʾʾʾ*

worth searching for: His debut album, *Dan Hicks & His Hot Licks* (Epic, 1969/1995, prod. Bob. Johnston) *ʾʾʾʾ* is his best, with such signature songs as "How Can I Miss You When You Won't Go Away," "Canned Music" and "I Scare Myself" (later covered by Thomas Dolby).

influences:
◄◄ Le Hot Club de France, Andrews Sisters, Charlatans
►► Pointer Sisters, Thomas Dolby

Joel Selvin

HIGH NOON

Formed 1988, in Austin, TX.

Sean Mencher, lead guitar; Shaun Young, vocals, acoustic guitar; Kevin Smith, electric/stand-up bass.

Like Elvis Presley's early band with Scotty Moore and Bill Black, this group's sound is a lot bigger than their three pieces suggest. Less rockabilly revivalists than Texas Troubadours with a beat, High Noon combines instrumental mastery with enthusiastic (but never harsh) vocals and a modern lyrical sense that is intelligent but never preachy. At the start, these guys were playing in separate bands, and High Noon was just a side project. Once together full-time, they played 20 gigs a month and jammed with Austin heavyweights Big Sandy & His Fly-Rite Boys, Wayne Hancock and the Derailers. In 1995 they opened and provided backing for comebacking rockabilly legend Ronnie Dawson and appeared with him on NBC-TV's *Late Night with Conan O'Brien*. High Noon makes the type of music that should be welcome on country radio–but isn't. You have to go to a CD shop or roadhouse to find stuff this good.

what to buy: *Stranger Things* (Watermelon, 1996, prod. Pete Hakonen, Jaane Haavisto) *ʾʾʾ* contains 15 tracks of self-written rockabilly, Western bop and old-timey country.

the rest:
Slow and Dance—The Rockabilly Trio (DOJCD, 1990) *ʾʾʾ*
Glory Bound (Goofin', 1993) *ʾʾʾ*
Live In Texas & Japan (Watermelon, 1997) *ʾʾʾ*

influences:
◄◄ Elvis Presley, Ronnie Dawson, Charlie Feathers
►► Big Sandy & His Fly-Rite Boys, Dave & Deke Combo

Ken Burke

HIGHWAY 101

Formed 1986, in Los Angeles, CA. Disbanded 1993. Reformed 1995.

Paulette Carlson, vocals (1986–90, 1995–present); Jack Daniels, guitar, vocals (1986–93, 1995–present); Curtis Stone, bass, vocals; Nikki Nelson, vocals (1990–93); Cactus Moser, drums, vocals (1986–95).

Taking their name from a lengthy stretch of California coast road, Highway 101, as a group, has traveled quite a long and winding path itself. Lead vocalist Paulette Carlson grew up in Minnesota and moved to Nashville in 1978, working as staff writer for the Oak Ridge Boys publishing company. Also in 1978, Jack Daniels and Curtis Stone, who had met earlier in L.A., began touring together with Canadian singer Burton Cummings, formerly of the Guess Who. Stone is the son of Country Music Hall of Famer and media entrepreneur Cliffie Stone and had lots of studio experience, working with artists like Tennessee Ernie Ford and Brian Wilson. Daniels, who grew up in the San Francisco area, moved to L.A. during the late 1970s, and previous to the invitation from Stone to join Highway 101, had appeared in the films *The Jazz Singer* and *One from the Heart*. Cactus Moser grew up on a Colorado cattle ranch and, during the 1970s, moved to California to become a member of the country-rock band Firefall.

It was the idea of Nitty Gritty Dirt band manager Chuck Morris to bring these four individuals together as Highway 101, after he'd heard some of Carlson's smoky vocals on demo tapes. The group recorded their smash debut and placed a string of 10 consecutive hits in the Top 10, including the Rodney Crowell-Harlan Howard-penned "Somewhere Tonight," (#1, 1987) the first of their four #1's. In 1988 and 1989 they were named Country Music Association Vocal Group of the Year, a title they also earned twice from the Academy of Country Music. In 1990, however, as the hits became less frequent, Carlson left for a solo career, signing with Capitol, but cracking the country Iop 40 only once. Highway 101 continued, with new singer, Nikki Nelson, faring little better, but still managing a few hits before switching labels. With the label change came the departure of Jack Daniels, and soon thereafter the trio called it quits. In 1995, however, minus Moser, who was previously committed, Carlson and Highway 101 reformed, releasing *Highway 101 & Paulette Carlson Reunited*. While the group toured again, but failed to return to the country charts with any impact, Highway 101 will be remembered as an important part of the mid-1980s neo-traditionalist movement in country music.

what to buy: *Greatest Hits* (Warner Bros., 1990) 𝄞𝄞𝄞𝄞 collects the group's early hits and one new track. Sadly, nothing remains in print from their later work, and the exclusion of some material keeps this from being absolutely essential.

what to buy next: *Highway 101* (Warner Bros., 1987, prod. Paul Worley) 𝄞𝄞𝄞𝄞 is their landmark debut and remains in print because of the number of hits included. Even outside the hits it's a strong collection, focusing on the group's boundless energy as well as their musical talent. *Highway 101 & Paulette Carlson Reunited* (1996, Willow Tree/Intersound, prod. Larry Butler, Paul Worley, Ed Seay) 𝄞𝄞𝄞 is a collection of hits plus a few new tracks.

influences:

◀◀ Desert Rose Band, Emmylou Harris

▶▶ Molly & the Heymakers, Twister Alley

Stephen L. Betts

THE HIGHWAYMEN

Formed 1985, in Nashville, TN.

Johnny Cash; Willie Nelson; Kris Kristofferson; Waylon Jennings.

In theory, these country superstar pals ought to weave their creaky voices into strands of gold every time they open their mouths. In reality, more turns out to be less, and the beautiful moments are rare. The quartet's first single, 1985's "The Highwayman," offers a stellar series of historical vignettes about a mystical working man that gained strength with each new voice. You can argue that Kristofferson, whose singing star faded as soon as "Me and Bobby McGee" slipped off the charts, isn't worthy of this quartet, but his gravely baritone fits between Cash's impossibly deep, serious register and Jennings' more amiable rumble. The single is essential for any country collection, but avoid most of the quartet's studio al-

burns, because the material just doesn't equal the foursome's individual talents.

what to buy: You need the single "The Highwayman" from the otherwise mediocre debut *Highwayman* (Columbia, 1985, prod. Chips Moman) 𝄞𝄞.

what to buy next: For the first time, possibly enlivened by Cash's lucrative new career with producer Rick Rubin and Nelson's fresh experimental stage, the Highwaymen put out a consistent batch of songs (written by Robert Earl Keen Jr., Steve Earle and Billy Joe Shaver, among others) on *The Road Goes on Forever* (Liberty, 1995, prod. Don Was) 𝄞𝄞𝄞.

what to avoid: Steer clear of the bland cash-in *Highwayman 2* (Columbia, 1990, prod. Chips Moman) 𝄞.

the rest:

Michael, Row Your Boat Ashore: The Best of the Highwaymen (EMI, 1992) 𝄞𝄞

worth searching for: It's better to buy the first single on the various artists set *Columbia Country Classics Volume 3: Americana* (Columbia, 1990, prod. various) 𝄞𝄞𝄞𝄞 than on the Highwaymen's debut. The collection also contains essential songs by Marty Robbins, Lefty Frizzell, Little Jimmy Dickens, Flatt & Scruggs and, of course, Cash.

influences:

◀◀ Carter Family, Flatt & Scruggs

▶▶ Little Texas, Shaver, Texas Tornados, Traveling Wilburys

see also: *Johnny Cash, Willie Nelson, Kris Kristofferson, Waylon Jennings*

Steve Knopper

HIGHWOODS STRING BAND

See; Walt Koken

FAITH HILL

Born Audrey Faith Perry Hill, September 21, 1967, in Jackson, MS.

Faith Hill's stunning good looks cannot be denied, but her talent is more than skin-deep. Her voice combines the same sort of spunkiness employed by her idol, Reba McEntire, with a slight tremelo reminiscent of Dolly Parton. In terms of material, however, Hill has yet to claim a niche that's all her own. On the one hand, she's already a master of breezy, throwaway singles, best typified by her debut smash, "Wild One." On the other hand, she delivers a number of heavy "message" songs, most of them having to do with cataloging the evils men do to

Willie Nelson (l) and Waylon Jennings of the Highwaymen. (© Ken Settle)

women. Hill is not really a writer, so chances are she'll continue to be blown whichever way the next hit single takes her.

what to buy: Hill's debut, *Take Me As I Am* (Warner Bros., 1993, prod. Scott Hendricks, Michael Clute, Gary Burr) 𝄢𝄢𝄢𝄢 took the public by storm, but it's hardly a perfect disc. "Wild One," whose protagonist is yet another rebel without a cause, sounded fine on the radio, but because it is a morality play with no real resolution, it lacks the resonance required for it to stand up to repeated listenings. Worse is "Piece of My Heart"; Janis Joplin's classic version was a complex, gut-wrenching tale of a woman unable to escape a relationship she knows is poison, while Hill's breezy offer to "take another little piece of my heart" sounds about as self-abnegating as a request for a drink of water. Only the closing ballad, "I Would Be Stronger than That" (better heard in Maura O'Connell's version, really) raises issues worth considering at length.

the rest:

It Matters to Me (Warner Bros., 1995) 𝄢𝄢𝄢𝄢

influences:

◀◀ Reba McEntire, Dolly Parton

▶▶ Mila Mason

Daniel Durchholz

KIM HILL

Born December 30, 1964, in MS.

As a Christian singer, Mississippi-born/Memphis-raised Kim Hill got more than her fair share of attention from the mainstream press and audience. Hill was also successful in her chosen field: she was the first contemporary Christian artist to have her debut single reach #1. Each of her first three albums took dramatic leaps, so by the early 1990s it was obvious she'd try her hand in the larger market. Hill signed with country label BNA and released one album, *So Far So Good*, in 1994. It won few new fans. By 1997 she was back in Christian music, recording for StarSong.

what to buy: Aided by members of the Christian rock group Whiteheart (one of whom would go on to play bass for Bruce Springsteen), Hill made *Talk about Life* (Reunion, 1989, prod. Brown Bannister) 🎵🎵🎵, an album that combined folk-rock and power-pop. Hill's dark, expressive alto placed her somewhere between Kathy Mattea and the Pretenders' Chrissie Hynde. The Christian hits ("Testimony," "Secret Place," "Charm Is Deceitful") came from her softer side, but moody power-pop cuts like "Closer to a Broken Heart" and "Inside of You" helped make this her best album to date.

what to buy next: *Testimony* (Reunion, prod. various) 🎵🎵🎵 collects Hill's biggest records in the Christian arena. At 10 songs it covers the hits but not the breadth of Hill's music.

what to avoid: When she "went country" on *So Far So Good* (BNA, 1994, prod. Wayne Kirkpatrick) 🎵🎵, Hill sounded like she was making a record for the marketplace instead of for herself.

the rest:
Kim Hill (Reunion, 1988) 🎵🎵🎵
Brave Heart (Reunion, 1991) 🎵🎵🎵
The Fire Again (StarSong, 1997) 🎵🎵🎵

influences:
◄◄ Kathy Mattea, Carly Simon

Brian Mansfield

CHRIS HILLMAN /THE DESERT ROSE BAND

Born December 4, 1943, in Los Angeles, CA. Desert Rose Band formed 1985.

Chris Hillman has been an integral part of country-rock's more notable groupings, with great skills as a collaborator. Already an accomplished mandolin player by the time he picked up the bass and joined the Byrds in 1964, Hillman began picking professionally with the Scottsville Squirrel Barkers, joining Rex and Vern Gosdin in the Golden State Boys by the time he was 16 (together, these musicians would later be known as the Hillmen). His contributions to the Byrds helped push that band in a country direction, climaxing with the seminal, country-flavored *Sweetheart of the Rodeo* in 1968. He left the Byrds to found the Flying Burrito Brothers with ex-Byrds-mate Gram Parsons in 1969; the Brothers' debut, *The Gilded Palace of Sin*, is another country-rock essential. Hillman spent the rest of the 1970s partnering with Stephen Stills (Manassas and Stephen Stills Band), John David Souther and Richie Furay (S.H.F. Band), and former Byrds Roger McGuinn and Gene Clark, along with an occasional solo record. During 1986 he formed, with Herb Pedersen and John Jorgenson, the Desert Rose Band, a more professional version of the Flying Burrito Brothers, which lasted through 1993.

what to buy: Chris Hillman & Herb Pedersen's *Bakersfield Bound* (Sugar Hill, 1996, prod. Herb Pedersen) 🎵🎵🎵🎵 is a stone-country record with Buck Owens overtones and excellent ensemble playing that takes the Desert Rose Band concept one step forward. *Desert Rose* (Sugar Hill, 1984, prod. Al Perkins) 🎵🎵🎵🎵 is prototypical of the Desert Rose Band as well as Hillman's best solo collection of country songs. *The Desert Rose Band* (Curb, 1987 prod. Paul Worley) 🎵🎵🎵🎵 features the same kind of kinetic energy and solid writing as *The Gilded Palace of Sin*, with the added bonus of experience.

what to buy next: *Manassas* (Atlantic, 1972/1995, prod. Stephen Stills) 🎵🎵🎵, which includes "It Doesn't Matter," written with Stills, along with some underrated instrumental contributions from Hillman, especially on the second half's country/bluegrass pastiche. *The Hillmen* (Sugar Hill, 1964/1995 prod. Jim Dickson) 🎵🎵🎵 offers spirited bluegrass recorded during 1963 and 1964, before Hillman, the Gosdin brothers and Don Parmley became well known. *Morning Sky* (Sugar Hill, 1982, prod. Jim Dickson) 🎵🎵🎵 is a country/rock fusion record with a formidable selection of songs, including Hillman's take on Parsons' classic "Hickory Wind."

what to avoid: The Souther-Hillman-Furay Band, a "supergroup" blues/country concept, ultimately didn't suit any of the participants' musical personalities. For proof, take an earful of *Trouble in Paradise* (Elektra/Asylum, 1975, prod. Tom Dowd) 🎵🎵.

the rest:
Clear Sailin' (Geffen, 1978) 🎵🎵🎵
(With Roger McGuinn and Gene Clark) *McGuinn, Clark & Hillman* (Capitol, 1979) 🎵🎵🎵
(With the Desert Rose Band) *Running* (Curb, 1988) 🎵🎵🎵
(With the Desert Rose Band) *Pages Of Life* (Curb, 1990) 🎵🎵🎵
(With the Desert Rose Band) *True Love* (Curb, 1991) 🎵🎵🎵
(With the Desert Rose Band) *A Dozen Roses: Greatest Hits* (Curb, 1991) 🎵🎵🎵
Traditional (Curb, 1993) 🎵🎵🎵

worth searching for: *Slippin' Away* (Geffen, 1976, prod. Ron Albert, Howard Albert) 🎵🎵🎵 is still the best collection of Hillman-penned songs in a polished 1970s-style production.

influences:

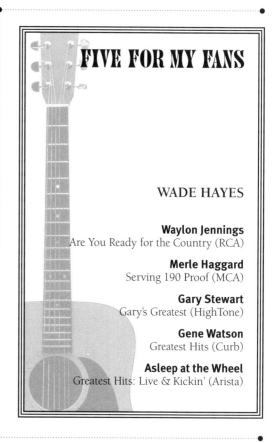

◀◀ Pete Seeger, Weavers, Flatt & Scruggs, Gosdin Brothers, Hank Williams

▶▶ Eagles, Gram Parsons, Jayhawks, Uncle Tupelo, Wilco, Son Volt

see also: *Byrds, Flying Burrito Brothers, Gram Parsons, Herb Pedersen, Hillmen*

Leland Rucker

THE HILLMEN

Formed c. 1963, in Los Angeles, CA.

Chris Hillman, mandolin, vocals; Vern Gosdin, guitar, lead vocals; Rex Gosdin, bass, vocals; Don Parmley, banjo, vocals.

Originally known as the Golden State Boys, the Hillmen was one of the first bluegrass bands in California. As a short-lived band with only one album to its name, the historical significance of the Hillmen comes mainly from what the band members accomplished after the band broke up: Chris Hillman, a member of the Rock & Roll Hall of Fame, helped found the Byrds, the Flying Burrito Brothers and the Desert Rose Band; Vern Gosdin, long known as one of country music's best singers, racked up a ton of hits and industry awards during the 1980s; the late Rex Gosdin (Vern's brother) was a respected country music songwriter; and Don Parmley, who provided much of the banjo music heard on *The Beverly Hillbillies*, has led his own band, the Bluegrass Cardinals, since the early 1970s.

what's available: *The Hillmen* (Sugar Hill, 1981, prod. Jim Dickson) ♪♪♪, recorded in 1963–64 but not released until 1969, sounds something like a West Coast version of the Country Gentlemen, with smooth, folk-influenced harmonies, punchy Scruggs-style banjo playing, solid original songs by the Gosdin brothers and covers drawn from such non-bluegrass sources as Bob Dylan, Woody Guthrie and Pete Seeger. The CD includes several songs not on the original LP.

worth searching for: The original LP version of *The Hillmen* (Together Records, 1969), sometimes referred to as "Redmen's Pow-Wow," is highly collectible. Chris Hillman completists might also be interested in *Blue Grass Favorites* (Crown, c. 1962/P-Vine) ♪♪♪ by the Scottsville Squirrel Barkers, the band Hillman was in before he joined the Golden State Boys; the all-instrumental album is available on CD from Japan's P-Vine Records.

FIVE FOR MY FANS

WADE HAYES

Waylon Jennings
Are You Ready for the Country (RCA)

Merle Haggard
Serving 190 Proof (MCA)

Gary Stewart
Gary's Greatest (HighTone)

Gene Watson
Greatest Hits (Curb)

Asleep at the Wheel
Greatest Hits: Live & Kickin' (Arista)

influences:

◀◀ Country Gentlemen, Dillards, Bill Monroe, Bob Dylan

▶▶ Kentucky Colonels, Byrds, Desert Rose Band, Chris Hillman, Vern Gosdin, Bluegrass Cardinals, Country Gazette

see also: *Chris Hillman, Vern Gosdin*

Jon Hartley Fox

TISH HINOJOSA

Born Leticia Hinojosa, December 6, 1955, in San Antonio, TX.

You'd think Tish Hinojosa's facility for singing in both English and Spanish would double her chances of stardom, but it's probably held her back. That, and the fact that her music may be too folksy and occasionally too political for country radio. Too bad, too, because Hinojosa's crystalline voice is captivating, as are her songs—many of them autobiographical sketches of growing up as the child of Mexican immigrants. Later albums find Hinojosa trying to make a more conventional pop/country/folk hybrid, and they're fine, but they lack the elements of daring and discovery that mark her earlier efforts. An exception is *Cada Nino/Every Child*, which makes a case for bilingualism in the form of a children's album with lyrics sung in both English and Spanish.

what to buy: The album that best sums up Hinojosa's appeal is *Culture Swing* (Rounder, 1992, prod. Tish Hinojosa) ����, which showcases her beautiful voice as she surveys Tex-Mex, Western swing, folk, pop and country, and addresses timeless themes of family, social issues and ecology. An all-around winner. The earlier *Homeland* (A&M, 1989, prod. Steve Berlin) ���� is a pleasing folk/country outing but has a slightly political edge, thanks to the opening salvo, "Border Trilogy," which details the hardships faced by illegal immigrants. "Donde Voy (Where I Go)" is another heartrending meditation on the subject.

what to buy next: Hinojosa's debut, *Taos to Tennessee* (self-released, 1987/Watermelon, 1992, prod. Michael Hearne, Tish Hinojosa, Craig Barker) ���� reveals the genesis of her bilingual folk-country style. The album includes "Amanecer," her first all-Spanish composition, several English originals, plus covers of songs by Peter Rowan ("Midnight Moonlight"), James Mc-Murtry ("Crazy Wind and Flashing Yellows"), and Irving Berlin ("Always"). The Spanish language *Frontejas* (Rounder, 1995, prod. Tish Hinojosa) ���� gains considerable bounce from its all-star cast, including Brave Combo, Flaco Jimenez, Santiago Jimenez Jr., Ray Benson and Eva Ybarra.

the rest:
Memorabilia Navidena (Watermelon, 1991) ���
Aquella Noche (Watermelon, 1991) ���
Destiny's Gate (Warner Bros.1994) ���
Dreaming from the Labyrinth (Warner Bros., 1996) ���
Cada Nino/Every Child (Rounder, 1996) ����

influences:
◀◀ Bob Dylan, Joan Baez, Linda Ronstadt
▶▶ Eva Ybarra

Daniel Durchholz

BECKY HOBBS

Born January 24, 1950, in Bartlesville, OK.

Becky Hobbs has had a successful career as a songwriter, penning hits for Alabama, Helen Reddy, Shirley Bassey, George

Jones and Loretta Lynn, among others. As a solo artist, however, she has had limited chart success with her own singles and albums, in spite of her energetic stage persona and her skills as a musician, especially on keyboards. Recording for several labels through the years, including MCA, Tattoo, Columbia, EMI America, MTM and RCA, Hobbs has amassed a loyal fan base and has traveled all over the world, achieving great success in Europe. The album *All Keyed Up* almost made Becky Hobbs a star in 1988, but independent label MTM folded before the recording could be promoted properly. Even RCA, upon reissuing the album with an additional track—the Top 40 hit "Do You Feel the Same Way Too?"—couldn't promote the record with any real fervor. So Hobbs moved on, landing at Curb, briefly, to record a remake of Ernie Ashworth's 1963 chart-topper "Talk Back Trembling Lips." In recent years Hobbs has played shows in far-reaching locales such as Switzerland and Africa. The experiences stemming from her involvement in a serious car accident led her to write the song, "Angels Among Us," which became a hit for Alabama and was included in a network television profile on Hobbs' experience with angels following the accident. The track also appears on her most recent album, *The Boots I Came to Town In*.

what to buy: *All Keyed Up* (MTM, 1988/RCA, 1989, prod. Richard Bennett) ���� is a near-perfect country album. Featured tracks include the honky-tonk tune "Jones on the Jukebox" and the sweet ballad "She Broke Her Promise," but there's not a weak song in the bunch, even on the revamped version, which is worth searching for if the original can't be found.

what to buy next: *The Boots I Came to Town In* (Intersound, 1994) ��� is highlighted by the well-known track, "Angels among Us," also a hit for Alabama.

influences:
◀◀ Skeeter Davis, Jerry Lee Lewis
▶▶ Ruby Lovett

Stephen L. Betts

ROBIN HOLCOMB

Born 1954, in GA.

Country is just one ingredient in Robin Holcomb's uncategorizable sound, an element most pronounced in the singer/songwriter's rural imagery (right down to a verse about trading roadkill), quavery Appalachian vibrato voice and general desolation of mood. Though now thought of as a denizen of the New York avant-garde scene, Holcomb once worked as a sharecropper in North Carolina. As ethereal as her music can often sound, it retains that grounded earthiness and deals with common concerns.

what to buy: The rootsy yet arty songs on *Robin Holcomb* (Elektra Nonesuch, 1990, prod. Wayne Horvitz, Peter Holsapple) ♫♫♫♫ are built from the simplest, sparest materials, but with extremely imaginative production. Guitarist Bill Frisell's slippery style relates to slide and pedal steel sounds without being either, while Horvitz (Holcomb's husband) contributes a surprisingly varied palette of gray and beige tones with his keyboard work. A couple of songs are almost straightforward country-rock, though even the fiddle-adorned "Troy" stands somewhat apart from country due to a pronounced New Orleans second-line rhythm on the verses, strongly suggesting the Band instrumentally.

what to buy next: *Rockabye* (Elektra Nonesuch, 1992, prod. Wayne Horvitz) ♫♫♫ has only one outright country track, a cover of Bruce Phillips' "The Goodnight-Loving Trail," but the album begins exploring more distant strains of Americana—not only gospel and folk but also 19th-century balladry—and makes Holcomb's spare piano playing more of a musical focus. The latter two aspects culminate in *Little Three* (Elektra Nonesuch, 1996, prod. Judith Sherman) ♫♫♫♫. A gorgeous solo piano album (Holcomb sings on only two tracks), it combines the feel of Civil War ballads, Indonesian gamalan, minimalism, the polytonality and song quotes of Charles Ives, and many beautiful melodies. The two long tracks sound like suites, with a procession of moods including a strong hoedown rhythm nine minutes into "Wherein Lies the Good." Some moments suggest a deeper, less saccharine George Winston. It's not even remotely a country album, yet very sympathetic to the feelings and impulses of country.

influences:
◀◀ Stephen Foster, Joni Mitchell, the Band, Charles Ives
▶▶ Tori Amos

Steve Holtje

GREG HOLLAND
Born in Douglas, GA.

Greg Holland grew up performing in Georgia, acting in local plays, singing on television at age 10 and making his first demo at 11. He's a versatile musician, playing guitar, trumpet, french horn and saxophone and having sung jazz and barbershop during a three-year stint in the Army.

what's available: Maybe Holland's wide-ranging talents made it difficult for him to stand out in one area, because his debut, *Let Me Drive* (Warner Bros., 1994, prod. Mark Wright) ♫♫, is assembly-line Southern-rockin' hat-act country.

influences:
◀◀ John Michael Montgomery, Garth Brooks
▶▶ David Kersh, Rhett Akins

Brian Mansfield

KEN HOLLOWAY
Born in Lafayette, LA.

Ken Holloway might have become a mainstream country star, except that at some point during his days of singing in Louisiana honky-tonks, he committed his life and music to Christianity. Today his music straddles the line between country and contemporary Christian music better than any of his contemporary Christian country singers, with the exception of Paul Overstreet, because his songwriting tackles real life rather than some sweet by and by.

what's available: *He Who Made the Rain* (Brentwood Music, 1995, prod. John Rotch) ♫♫♫ is standard country fare, except no celebrating of booze, brawlin' or one-night stands. Mainstream Nashville kicked in some help, with singer Lari White dueting on "I'm Not Gonna Fall to Pieces," and songwriters Chuck Cannon and Allen Shamblin helping write the title track. Two songs, "Not Enough Amazing Grace" and Holloway's own composition, "Momma Left the Light On," serve as thematic bookends, telling the story of a prodigal son, a worried mom and, finally, redemption. *Ken Holloway* (Brentwood Music, 1994, prod. John Rotch) ♫♫♫, Holloway's debut, eschewed contemporary gospel clichés in favor of new-traditionalist country music loaded with hooks and positive messages that speak to current life issues.

influences:
◀◀ Keith Whitley, Vern Gosdin, George Jones

Bill Hobbs

BUDDY HOLLY
Born Charles Hardin Holley, September 7, 1936, in Lubbock, TX. Died February 3, 1959, near Clear Lake, IA.

As a young country singer, Buddy Holly fell under the sway of the soon-to-be-King when Elvis Presley made one of his early concert stops in Holly's hometown of Lubbock; a home movie caught the suddenly transformed Holly and his pals backstage

Buddy Holly **(Archive Photos)**

at this crucial turning point in his life. His initial 1956 recording sessions under the sway of Nashville stalwart Owen Bradley transcend the steely hand of a producer unsympathetic to the emerging new music, but they mostly serve as an example of the uneasy borders between country music and rock 'n' roll during that era. Under the less restraining influence of Norman Petty in his Clovis, New Mexico, studios, Holly found the free rein he needed to write his page in rock 'n' roll history. The re-recorded version of "That'll Be the Day," literally remade in its second incarnation, launched the chart career of the Crickets, as Holly and his associates were known by the record label. With "Peggy Sue" three months later, producer Petty used the same group of musicians to establish Holly as a solo artist, as the single rose on the same charts the Crickets' single was slipping down. During the mere 22 months of his life that Buddy Holly spent on the pop charts, he etched his name indelibly into the music's history through his easy charm and his tuneful mastery of the basics of rock 'n' roll. Guileless but not naive, Holly captured the essential angst of young love with wit and an underlying aggressive edge that gave his simple songs a durability none of his contemporaries could match.

Holly left a lasting mark on country music, too. Not only did his music deeply effect a generation of country performers, but musicians Holly played alongside in his lifetime—such as songwriter Sonny Curtis or Waylon Jennings, who gave up his seat on the fatal plane ride that cost Holly his life—went on to become major country figures. Perhaps Holly himself, had he lived, would have turned country in face of growing pop chart indifference to his rugged brand of rock 'n' roll.

what to buy: Although at least three different boxed sets were released during the 1970s covering, to different degrees, the complete works of Holly, the existing two-disc set, *The Buddy Holly Collection* (MCA, 1993, prod. various) ♪♪♪♪, distills the essence into an admirable 50-song package.

what to buy next: Both of Holly's first two post-Nashville albums, *The Chirping Crickets* (MCA, 1958, prod. Norman Petty) ♪♪♪♪ and *Buddy Holly* (MCA, 1958, prod. Norman Petty) ♪♪♪♪, have been made available as compact discs.

what to avoid: The over-produced tribute album *Not Fade Away* (Decca, 1996, prod. various) ♪♪ may boast some big names, but the Holly spirit just doesn't survive these mostly ham-fisted covers.

the rest:
From the Original Master Tapes (MCA, 1985) ♪♪♪♪

worth searching for: During a brief 1995 dalliance with audiophile vinyl pressings, MCA put out an absolutely gorgeous edition of *Buddy Holly* on its so-called "heavy vinyl" series—a breathtaking audio experience, like listening to the playbacks in the studio control room.

influences:
◀◀ Hank Williams, Hank Ballard, Elvis Presley
▶▶ Bobby Vee, Waylon Jennings, Beatles, Rolling Stones

Joel Selvin

THE HOLY MODAL ROUNDERS

Formed 1963, in New York. Disbanded 1965. Reformed 1968 and recorded periodically until 1981.

Peter Stampfel, banjo, fiddle, vocals; Steve Weber, guitar, vocals.

The Holy Modal Rounders were a loose aggregation of beat-generation holdovers organized around the inspired lunacy of co-founders Peter Stampfel and Steve Weber. The duo recorded two albums of old-timey music and blues for Folklore and Prestige between 1963-64 before hooking up with fellow cultural anarchists the Fugs in 1965. Following a mid-1960s breakup that found Weber retaining the band's original name and Stampfel forming the Moray Eels, the two men—aided and abetted by playwright Sam Shepard on drums, as well as folk stalwarts Michael Hurley, Luke Faust, Robin Remaily and others—reunited for a psychedelic sidetrip from which they almost didn't return (even though their recording of "Bird Song," included on the soundtrack to the movie *Easy Rider,* exposed their acid-folk to a wider audience). After reclaiming their string-band roots, Stampfel, Weber, Hurley & company joined forces with Jeffrey Frederick for *Have Moicy!,* a bacchanalian fantasy that proved the high point of the group's 18-year career.

what's available: *Indian War Whoop* (ESP, 1967) ♫♫ makes a strong case for the argument that you had to be there, especially the indulgent, side-long "Jimmy and Crash Survey the Universe." *Have Moicy!* (Rounder, 1976, prod. John Nagy) ♫♫♫♫ is a lost classic, an undeniable collection of folk, country and bluegrass that lovingly embraces—and has fun at the expense of—the hippie lifestyle and myth.

worth searching for: *The Holy Modal Rounders* (Folklore, 1964, prod. Peter Stampfel, Steve Weber) ♫♫♫♫, the duo's debut, contains left-of-center covers of blues and old-timey tunes that never push the album so far overboard that it loses its edge or appeal.

influences:

◄◄ Charlie Poole, Grandpa Jones

Bill Friskics-Warren

HOMER & JETHRO

Henry D. "Homer" Haynes (born July 27, 1920, in Knoxville, TN; died August 7, 1971); Kenneth "Jethro" Burns (born March 10, 1920, in Conasuga, TN; died February 4, 1989, in Evanston, IL).

The clown princes of country music, Homer and Jethro first began performing together when they were 12 years old and had become veteran radio professionals, specializing in song parodies, by the time they enlisted in the military during World War II. It was cornball satires of pop hits—most notably the 1959 smash, "The Battle of Kookamonga"—that the pair recorded for RCA Victor and staked their reputation on during the 1950s and 1960s. They made a series of "Ooh, that's corny" television commercials for Kellogg's Corn Flakes that further enhanced that delicious image of rube punsters. But underneath all the hick shtick, Haynes and Burns were gifted instrumentalists whose album, *Playing It Straight* (RCA Victor, 1962) ♫♫♫♫ has long been prized by collectors. They also made a

number of recordings with virtuoso guitarist Chet Atkins during the 1970s as the Nashville String Band. After Haynes' death, Burns pursued a jazzier direction as a mandolin player, wrote mandolin instructional manuals and recorded for the folk-based independent label Flying Fish. Neither their classic comedic send-ups—a Nashville parallel to the kind of records Stan Freberg was making in Hollywood—nor their instrumentals have yet been made available on compact disc.

worth searching for: Jethro's solo outing, *Swing Low, Sweet Mandolin* (Acoustic Disc, 1995, prod. David Grisman, Don Stiernberg) ♫♫♫♫, is an aptly named instrumental album of mandolin-and-guitar duets with Don Stiernberg, recorded in 1987–88. Songs include "Stella by Starlight," "Body and Soul" and "Corrina Corrina."

influences:

◄◄ Uncle Dave Macon

►► Minnie Pearl, Ray Stevens

Joel Selvin

THE HONEYDOGS

Formed 1994, in Minneapolis, MN.

Adam Levy, guitar, vocals; Noah Levy, drums, vocals; Trent Norton, bass, vocals; Tommy Borschied, guitar (1995–present).

Falling more on the rock side of the roots-rock equations, the Honeydogs' sound is informed as much by the high-energy antics of their Twin Cities forebears the Replacements as by the high-harmonies of their other Twin Cities forebears, the Jayhawks. Songwriter Adam Levy has a knack for memorable melodies and simple but affecting lyrics, and the band falls in behind him with a memorable brand of bash, twang and pop.

what to buy: The group's debut, *The Honeydogs* (October, 1995, prod. John Strawberry Fields, Honeydogs) ♫♫♫♫ attests to the 'Dogs' versatility, scoring on the one hand with such rockers as "What I Want" and "That's Me," both of them supercharged pleas of naked need, and on the other with "Lost Again" and "Can I Change Your Mind," country-flavored 'plaints that purposely pour salt into old wounds. The sharply-rendered "Those Things Are Hers" is the highlight, though, detailing through a catalog of left-behind artifacts—a dress, a leather coat—how one relationship is haunted by a previous one that splintered, but won't quite disappear. Levy is a songwriting talent to watch.

the rest:

Everything I Bet You (October, 1996) 🎵🎵🎵🎵

influences:

⏪ Replacements, Jayhawks, Gear Daddies

see also: *Golden Smog*

Daniel Durchholz

THE HOOSIER HOT SHOTS

Formed 1932, in Fort Wayne, IN.

Paul "Hezzie" Trietsch, song whistle, alto horn, washboard, drums; Ken "Rudy" Trietsch, bass horn, banjo, guitar; Otto "Gabe" Ward, clarinet, saxophone, fife. Other members included: Frank Kettering; Gil Taylor; Nate Harrison; Keith Milheim; Skip Farrell.

Country music's answer to Spike Jones & His City Slickers, the Hot Shots began on radio in Fort Wayne, Indiana, and made their way to Chicago's *WLS National Barn Dance* in 1933. Soon they joined WLS act Uncle Ezra, who had his own radio show on the NBC network. "Are you ready, Hezzie?" became the trademark opening to most of these recordings, and the act incorporated a vast array of musical instruments including whistles, a washboard and even a pie plate or two. ARC, which later became part of Columbia Records, was their recording home for seven years beginning in 1935, with future Country Music Hall of Famer Uncle Art Satherley overseeing the production of their broadly comical but tastefully orchestrated body of work. Following their success with ARC, the Hot Shots achieved great chart success on Decca from 1944–46, with three singles all hitting the Top Three during those years. Appearing in a number of Hollywood films during the 1940s, the Hot Shots continued to perform for the next three decades, until Hezzie's death.

what's available: *Rural Rhythm 1935–1942* (Columbia Legacy, 1992, comp. Michael Brooks) 🎵🎵🎵🎵 is an uproarious collection that showcases, in equal measure, the humor and the musical proficiency of the Hot Shots. It's a non-stop riot, with tunes such as "I Like Bananas Because They Have No Bones" and "From the Indies to the Andies in His Undies."

influences:

⏪ Spike Jones & His City Slickers

⏩ Homer & Jethro, Lonzo & Oscar

Stephen L. Betts

JOHNNY HORTON

Born April 3, 1925, in Los Angeles, CA. Died November 5, 1960, in Milano, TX.

Although it was ultimately saga songs such as "North to Alaska" or "The Battle of New Orleans" that made him famous, Johnny Horton was one of country music's great links between honky-tonk and rockabilly. He arrived on the cast of the weekly *Louisiana Hayride* radio show in time to watch Hank Williams made his final appearances, and stayed long enough to see Elvis Presley change the face of music. Horton had recorded extensively for a variety of smaller labels by the time he released his first record on Columbia Records. 1956's "Honky-Tonk Man," a rumbling, driving number later revived by Dwight Yoakam, served as a kind of bridge between Hank and Elvis. Although he experienced some modest success with his early Columbia recordings, it wasn't until Horton cut Jimmy Driftwood's "The Battle of New Orleans" that he exploded onto the pop charts with the biggest-selling record of 1959. By the time he recorded "North to Alaska"—the title song to a John Wayne movie the following year, his career was already in decline. The week the record was released Horton died in a car crash. Horton may be seen as a somewhat peripheral figure from today's vantage point, but the fierce determination behind his best work elevated him well above his more parochial country-circuit contemporaries.

what to buy: The two-disc set *Honky-Tonk Man: The Essential Johnny Horton 1954–1960* (Columbia Legacy, 1995 prod. various) 🎵🎵🎵🎵 captures Horton at his peak: the first disc, all monaural, leans toward rockabilly while the second reaches a satisfying crescendo of the saga songs that made him famous.

what to buy next: The German reissue specialists, Bear Family, have compiled extensive (and expensive) boxed sets on both Horton's earlier recordings and his Columbia years, in addition to distilling 20 of his most rockin' Columbia sides on a single disc, *Rockin' Rollin' Johnny Horton* (Bear Family) 🎵🎵🎵🎵.

worth searching for: His early albums could be spotty, but *The Spectacular Johnny Horton* (Columbia, 1960) 🎵🎵🎵 contains some key hits and overlooked gems. The vinyl *Honky-Tonk Man* (Columbia, 1963) 🎵🎵🎵 collects his mid-1950s rockabilly-infected sessions.

influences:

⏪ Hank Williams

⏩ Marty Stuart, Dwight Yoakam

Joel Selvin

HOT RIZE /RED KNUCKLES & THE TRAILBLAZERS

Formed 1978, in CO. Disbanded 1990.

Tim O'Brien, vocal, mandolin, fiddle; Pete Wernick, banjo; Nick Forster, bass; Charles Sawtelle, guitar. Former members include: Mike Scap, guitar, vocals.

Hot Rize and their zany alter-egos, Red Knuckles & the Trailblazers, managed to walk a fine line between folk, country, pop, jazz and bluegrass, and surprisingly, rarely alienated anyone in the process. The group's lineup changed only once in nearly 15 years, even as they continued to diversify. Led by Tim O'Brien's folksy vocals and supplemented by the skillful playing of Pete "Dr. Banjo" Wernick, Hot Rize (named for the secret ingredient in Martha White flour, long-associated with bluegrass music) first recorded in 1979. Three years later they introduced their counterparts, the Trailblazers (the name comes from Martha White's brand of dog food!) with "Waldo Otto" (Wernick) on steel guitar, "Wendell Mercantile" (Forester) playing lead guitar, "Slade" (Sawtelle) on bass, and the devilishly charming "Red Knuckles" (O'Brien) on lead vocals and rhythm guitar. Veering from bluegrass to explore more honky-tonk music and to showcase their gifts for humor, the Trailblazers were as much in demand (if not, they frequently joked, as well-treated) as Hot Rize. O'Brien had a Top 10 country hit in 1990, a duet with Kathy Mattea on "Battle Hymn of Love," and earlier, in 1986, Mattea had hit the Top 10 with O'Brien's "Walk the Way the Wind Blows." O'Brien also released solo albums and recorded duet albums with sister Mollie throughout the years Hot Rize was in existence. In 1996 the band held a short reunion tour, which was highlighted by their appearance on the Martha White Bluegrass Series at Nashville's historic Ryman Auditorium. Once again, Red Knuckles & the Trailblazers threatened to steal the show, but all ended well as fans were reminded why Hot Rize will be remembered as one of the most innovative and important bluegrass/traditional bands of the 1980s.

what to buy: *Untold Stories* (Sugar Hill, 1987, prod. Hot Rize) ♫♫♫♫♪ is an absolutely beautiful record with some solid bluegrass picking and O'Brien in fine voice.

what to buy next: The immensely entertaining *Take It Home* (Sugar Hill, 1990, prod. Hot Rize) ♫♫♫♫ is a thoroughly satisfying collection, and sadly, the band's last.

the rest:
Hot Rize (Flying Fish, 1979) ♫♫♫♪
Radio Boogie (Flying Fish, 1981) ♫♫♫♪

Red Knuckles & the Trailblazers/Hot Rize in Concert (Flying Fish, 1982/1984) ♫♫♫♪
Hot Rize Presents Red Knuckles & the Trailblazers: Shades of the Past (Sugar Hill, 1988) ♫♫♫♪
Traditional Ties (Sugar Hill, 1988) ♫♫♫♫♪

solo outings:
Pete Wernick:
(With others) *Dr. Banjo Steps Out* (Flying Fish, 1978) ♫♫♫♪
On a Roll (Sugar Hill, 1993) ♫♫♫♪
I Tell You What! (Sugar Hill, 1996) ♫♫♫♪

influences:
◄◄ Tim & Mollie O'Brien, Pete Wernick
►► BR5-49, Jeff White

see also: *Tim O'Brien*

Stephen L. Betts

JAMES HOUSE

Born March 21, 1955, in Sacramento, CA.

While growing up, James House was influenced by the California country of the 1960s. Though his musical career would start in Los Angeles, where, among other things, he served as Dustin Hoffman's vocal coach for the film *Ishtar*, House ultimately made his way to Nashville in 1988. He released two albums for MCA beginning the following year, though neither made significant commercial impact. He wrote Dwight Yoakam's "Ain't That Lonely Yet" and Diamond Rio's "In a Week or Two" before returning to the studio himself.

what's available: With a new label and a new producer, House found a dramatic rockabilly-influenced sound that suited him perfectly. Backed by the likes of Trisha Yearwood and the Mavericks' Raul Malo, *Days Gone By* (Epic, 1995, prod. Don Cook) ♫♫♫♪ was one of the surprise successes of 1995, producing the moody hits "Little by Little" and "This Is Me Missing You."

worth searching for: *James House* (MCA, 1989, prod. Tony Brown) ♫♫♫ and *Hard Times for an Honest Man* (MCA, 1990, prod. Tony Brown) ♫♫♫ produced one hit between them— 1989's "Don't Quit Me Now"—but they're solid, if unspectacular albums. *James House* also contains a version of Jesse Winchester's "Oh What a Thrill," which the Mavericks also would record.

influences:
◄◄ Roy Orbison, Gene Pitney, Marty Robbins
►► Dwight Yoakam, Mavericks

Brian Mansfield

CISCO HOUSTON

Born Gilbert Vandine Houston, August 18, 1918, in Wilmington, DE. Died April 29, 1961, in San Bernardino, CA.

A contemporary of Woody Guthrie and Pete Seeger, Cisco Houston somehow survived during the Depression as a traveling minstrel. He later found fame on the college and folk club circuit and as a member of the Weavers. A significant influence on the likes of Bob Dylan, Ramblin' Jack Elliott and Tom Paxton, Houston was truly a master of the folk genre.

what to buy: Houston was one of the best pure vocalists of the folk movement, though that didn't always work to his advantage with fans of the era. It has helped his recordings stay fresh with time, however. His easygoing baritone makes the versions of "Dark as a Dungeon," "Saint James Infirmary," the humorous "The Cat Came Back" and more than two dozen other tunes on *The Folkways Years, 1944–1961* (Folkways, 1994, comp. Guy Logsdon) 🎵🎵🎵🎵 thoroughly enjoyable.

the rest:

Cisco Houston Sings Woody Guthrie (Vanguard) 🎵🎵🎵

influences:

◀◀ Woody Guthrie

▶▶ Tom Paxton, Ramblin' Jack Elliott, Bob Dylan

Randall T. Cook

DAVID HOUSTON

Born December 9, 1938, in Bossier City, LA. Died November 30, 1993.

These days, you'd expect somebody descended from Robert E. Lee and Sam Houston to be a kick-butt honky-tonker. Not David Houston, a countrypolitan tenor most often associated with producer Billy Sherrill. The godson of pop singer Gene Austin, Houston appeared on the *Louisiana Hayride* at age 12. He began a long association with Epic Records in 1963 when he hit with a cover of Harold Dorman's pop hit "Mountain of Love." Houston recorded duets with Tammy Wynette ("My Elusive Dreams," 1967) and Barbara Mandrell ("After Closing Time," 1970). Though he was a significant artist in his day, with 45 Top 40 hits between 1963 and 1979, his legacy boils down to two songs, "My Elusive Dreams" and the 1966 hit "Almost Persuaded," which spent nine weeks at #1 and won Houston a Grammy; his records are now all but out of print. Houston died in late 1993 following a brain aneurysm.

what's available: *At His Best* (Power Pak, 1984, prod. Moe Lytle, Tommy Hill) **WOOF!** contains a remake of Houston's 1971

Top 10 single "Maiden's Prayer" (not one of his better records) and nine other non-hit tracks, including the hoary "I'll Take You Home Again Kathleen" and "Because." *David Houston* (Richmond, 1986, prod. Moe Lytle, Tommy Hill) **WOOF!** is the same album minus two tracks.

worth searching for: *American Originals* (Columbia, 1989, prod. Billy Sherrill) isn't much, but it's a far sight better than the in-print recordings. At least it has recordings of "Almost Persuaded" and "My Elusive Dreams."

influences:

◀◀ Jim Reeves

▶▶ Charlie Rich, Barbara Mandrell

Brian Mansfield

HARLAN HOWARD

Born September 8, 1929, in Lexington, KY.

Almost certainly the most successful songwriter in the history of country music, Harlan Howard has written countless country hits, several songs that have crossed over into the pop and/or R&B charts ("Busted" by Ray Charles and "The Chokin' Kind" by Joe Simon come to mind), and #1 hits in every decade from the 1950s (Guy Mitchell's pop hit in 1958 of "Heartaches by the Number") to the 1990s (Patty Loveless' 1993 country #1 "Blame It on Your Heart"), with many more chart hits in between. He even had a small hit of his own, "Sunday Morning Christian," on Nugget, in 1971. But if Howard had to make a living as a singer he might still be struggling, particularly since he has never enjoyed performing in public. He has cut several albums over the years and, while they indicate that, for a songwriter, his voice possesses a sincerity ideal for pitching material, not much more can be said for it.

what's available: *All-Time Favorite Country Songwriter* (Koch, 1996, prod. Fred Foster, Bobby Bare) 🎵🎵🎵 is a reissue of an album originally recorded for Monument in 1967, when Howard was still in the middle of one of the hottest streaks as a writer anyone can remember. He does his versions of 12 of his biggest, including "Busted," "Heartaches by the Number," "Too Many Rivers," "I've Got a Tiger by the Tail" and "Pick Me Up on Your Way Down," backed by Nashville's finest pickers. In musical terms, it couldn't be called anything more than pleasant, but it is interesting to hear the man who wrote these great songs interpret them.

influences:

◀◀ Ernest Tubb, Buck Owens

▶▶ Billy Joe Shaver, Sonny Throckmorton

Randy Pitts

RAY WYLIE HUBBARD

Born November 13, 1946, in Soper, OK.

Ray Wylie Hubbard is best be remembered (saddled?) by his 1970s anthem, "Up against the Wall, Redneck Mother"—not that it does him a lick of good. Unlike the outlaw triumvirate of Willie Nelson, Waylon Jennings and Kris Kristofferson, Hubbard's boozin' and general lawlessness have cost him recording contracts and years of inactivity. Perhaps most crippling is that all of his early work has been out of print for years, never having been issued on CD. Hubbard recently put a cork in the bottle and became rejuvenated enough to venture back into the studio during the early 1990s.

what to buy: *Loco Gringo's Lament* (Dejadisc, 1994, prod. Lloyd Maines, Brian Hardin) ৶৶৶ finds a lean and confident Hubbard rambling through dusty tales of experience. Its highlight is "Wanna Rock and Roll," a bruiser in which he handles two-timers with clear adrenalin-pumping intent. Let's just say it involves knifeplay and leave it at that.

the rest:

Lost Train of Thought (Dejadisc, 1995) ৶৶৶

influences:

◀◀ Jerry Jeff Walker

Allan Orski

MARCUS HUMMON

Born December 28, 1960, in Washington, DC.

Marcus Hummon grew up the globe-trotting son of a state-department diplomat, coming of age in Washington, D.C., and New England, but also spending time in Africa, Italy and the Philippines. He moved to Nashville in 1986, after spending two fruitless years in Los Angeles. As a writer, he has penned "Only Love" for Wynonna Judd and "Every Little Word" for Hal Ketchum, as well as tunes recorded by the Nitty Gritty Dirt Band, Patty Loveless, Doug Stone and Michael Martin Murphey.

what's available: Marcus Hummon wrote "Cheap Seats," an ode to minor-league baseball that was one of the most fun things Alabama ever recorded. He should have saved it for *All*

FIVE FOR OUR FANS

HIGH NOON

Merle Travis
Walking the Strings (Capitol)

Lenny Breau & Chet Atkins
Standard Brands (One Way)

Billy Haley & His Comets
Rock This Joint! The Original Essex
Recordings 1951–1954 (Schoolkids')

Milt Hinton
Old Man Time (Chiaroscuro)

The Everly Brothers
Heartaches and Harmonies (Rhino)

in Good Time (Columbia, 1995, prod. Monroe Jones) ৶৶৶, a folk-rock album that dives into wimpy introspection way too often.

influences:

◀◀ Mary Chapin Carpenter, Hal Ketchum

Brian Mansfield

THE CORNELL HURD BAND

Formed 1977, in Berkeley, CA.

Cornell Hurd, vocals, guitar; Frank X. Roeber, bass; Paul Skelton, guitar; Ralph Power, drums; Bobby Snell, steel guitar; Cody Nicolas, rhythm guitar; Danny Roy Young, rubboard.

Mashing the heartfelt traditionalism of Asleep at the Wheel's Ray Benson with the raucous humor of the Beat Farmers' Country Dick Montana, Cornell Hurd has emerged as a tumultuous, towering presence on the Texas honky-tonk circuit since moving to Austin in 1989. While the performance of such satirical Hurd-penned numbers as "Your Ex-Husband Sent Me Flowers ('Cause He Feels Sorry for Me)" and "I Cry, Then I Drink, Then I Cry" and their hilarious cover of Red Simpson's "I Bought the Shoes That Just Walked on Me" have earned them the self-inflicted reputation as "Garth Brooks' worst nightmare," Hurd and his bandmates never let their spiked punchlines overwhelm their prowess as swinging, swaggering torchbearers. The band's repertoire spans such touchstones as Bob Wills, Floyd Tillman, Spade Cooley, Louis Jordan, Moon Mullican, Johnny Paycheck and Otis Blackwell, all played with a steel-guitar-driven, kick-up-the-sawdust gusto that makes the group easy to take seriously even when it's just having fun.

what to buy: With help from such Lone Star legends as Tommy Morrell, Lucky Oceans and "Whiskey River"-composer Johnny Bush, *Cool and Unusual Punishment* (Behemoth, 1996, prod. Rex Jones, James Willett, Kim Butler, Jim McCaskill) ♪♪♪♪ blurs the line between the past and present with irreverent relish. The covers are deliciously obscure (Spade Cooley's "Crazy 'Cause I Love You," Lalo Guerrero's "Do You Believe in Reincarnation") and Hurd's own songs—including the two-stepping, tongue-twisting "I Don't Care What It Is That You Did When You Lived in Fort Worth" and the surprisingly tender "She'll Always Love Me"—suggest that Junior Brown soon may have some competition for the title of kingpin of country's Deadpan Alley.

the rest:
Honky-Tonk Mayhem (Behemoth, 1993) ♪♪♪
Live! At the Broken Spoke (Behemoth, 1994) ♪♪♪

influences:
◄◄ Bob Wills, Asleep at the Wheel, Moon Mullican, David Allan Coe
►► Junior Brown

David Okamoto

FERLIN HUSKY

Born December 3, 1925, in rural MO (on a farm equidistant from Flat River, Hickory Grove and Cantwell).

Ferlin Husky was arguably the first star to emerge from the Bakersfield, California, scene. After five years in the Merchant Marines during WWII, he worked at radio stations in his home state and in California, with a stint in Hollywood landing him some bit parts in Western movies. Husky became a disk jockey in Bakersfield, and in 1950–51 recorded singles under the name Terry Preston (because, ironically, "Ferlin Husky sounded too

made-up") for the 4 Star label, which eventually led to a contract with Capitol. It wasn't until his 1953 duet with Jean Shephard on "A Dear John Letter" under his real name that Husky found success—going all the way to #1 on the country chart. After he reached #6 by himself with the honky-tonkish "I Feel Better All Over (More than Anywhere's Else)" in 1955, he was invited to fulfill a childhood dream by joining the Grand Ole Opry and moved to Nashville.

In 1956 Husky, with legendary Capitol producer Ken Nelson, reworked "Gone" (which Husky had recorded in 1952 as Terry Preston), stripping it of fiddles and steel guitar in favor of a vibraphone and using the Jordanaires and a female vocal to back Husky's lead. It reached #1 country and #4 pop and inaugurated a new, slicker production sound that helped Nashville compete with rock 'n' roll on the charts. In fact, for a while some of Husky's work took on a slight rockabilly feel (though more ornate), as on "Prize Possession." Husky stayed with Capitol until 1972, finding little success after switching to ABC but staying somewhat active to the present day. With his rich, highly emotive light baritone vocals, replete with melodramatic sobs and catches, Husky was perfectly suited to be a mainstream pop singer, and that's more or less what he became in Nashville, though there were always some country accouterments in his accompaniment. His great gift was that no matter how schmaltzy the material, he put it across with utter sincerity, even such prefab tearjerkers as "A Room for a Boy . . . Never Used" (from ABC's *Freckles and Polliwog Days*, not worth searching for). The unabashed sentimentality and slick production (sometimes strings, almost always background choruses) of his many albums have not aged well, and very little of his work remains available considering his discography of around 30 albums. But what is in print (mostly his 1950s Capitol work) stands up better than the records of many of Husky's contemporaries.

what to buy: *Vintage Collections* (Capitol Nashville, 1996, prod. various) ♪♪♪♪ includes both versions of "Gone" (as well as three other Terry Preston performances), the rollicking "I Feel Better All Over," the country-gospel crossover hit "Wings of a Dove" and a good sampling of Husky's interpretive range, from "I'm So Lonesome I Could Cry" to "Stormy Weather" to "I've Got the World on a String" (complete with horn chart). Some of the early Capitol tracks are notable for the imaginative work of guitarist Jimmy Bryant and pedal steel legend Speedy West, and, in an odd bonus, after the last listed track there's a smokin' uptempo instrumental cover of Duke Ellington's "Caravan" that pretty obviously features the pair. All but four of the 20 listed tracks here were recorded from 1951–60.

what to buy next: *Greatest Hits* (Curb/CEMA, 1990, prod. various) ♪♪♪ is largely superseded by Capitol's *Vintage Collections*, but four of its ungenerous 11 tracks aren't on the bigger collection and are worth the $10 by themselves, especially "I Can't Stop Loving You" (the other three are "Every Step of the Way," "Heavenly Sunshine" and "I Really Don't Want to Know"). *Country Music Is Here to Stay* (Laserlight, 1993) ♪♪♪ also duplicates the biggest hits on *Vintage Collections* but in re-recorded versions of undocumented vintage. However, it includes a few good songs that Capitol doesn't—("Divorce Lawyers, Funeral Directors and Jailers," "Dammit I'm Lonely," "If I Can't Have All of You (Just Give Me What You Think Is Fair)"—and at least allows a glimpse of Husky's comic alter ego, Simon Crum, on "(Good Ole) Country Music Is Here to Stay." And Laserlight is a super-budget label ($4), though the playing time is skimpy at 27+ minutes.

worth searching for: *The Heart and Soul of Ferlin Husky* (Capitol, 1963, prod. Ken Nelson) ♪♪♪♪ has fairly unadorned production beyond the inevitable backing vocals, and the material is an unbeatable collection of country standards: "I Can't Stop Loving You," "She Thinks I Still Care," "Silver Threads and Golden Needles," "I Really Don't Want to Know," "Cotton Fields" and more. If you can find this 12-song, out-of-print LP, which has pretty good sonics, you won't need the Curb collection.

influences:

◀◀ Frankie Laine, Hank Thompson

▶▶ Jim Reeves, Jim Nabors, George Jones

Steve Holtje

SYLVIA HUTTON

See: Sylvia

WALTER HYATT
/UNCLE WALT'S BAND

Born October 25, 1949, in Spartanburg, SC. Died May 11, 1996, in FL.

In 1990 Lyle Lovett persuaded MCA to sign soulful Austin, Texas, crooner Walter Hyatt and produced his first solo album, the gorgeous *King Tears*. It seemed like a strange way to wield his new-found clout, but Lovett had some debts to repay. As the leader of the regionally revered Uncle Walt's Band—a genre-defying, harmony-laden acoustic trio featuring David Ball and Champ Hood— Hyatt often invited the young Lovett to open the group's Texas A&M campus concerts during the late 1970s. Lovett's esoteric blend of Texas swing, gospel, folk and jazz clearly stems from Hyatt's daring vision, which flew in the face of Nashville convention and Austin's then-thriving Jerry Jeff Walker-led "Cosmic Cowboy" scene. Signing with Sugar Hill in 1993, Hyatt started drifting back to his Western swing roots on *Music Town*. He was benefiting from renewed interest in his music via Sugar Hill reissues of his influential 1974–82 recordings with Uncle Walt's Band and had started touring with a new band called King Tears when he was killed in the 1996 ValuJet crash in the Florida Everglades.

what to buy: Reissued at Lovett's request after Hyatt's death, the romantic *King Tears* (MCA, 1990/1996, prod. Lyle Lovett) ♪♪♪♪ is an exquisite collection of gentle swing numbers and jazz-tinged ballads highlighted by the swaying "Tell Me Baby" and a faithful take on Ray Charles' "Ruby." This is the album Harry Connick Jr. always wanted to make.

what to buy next: Culled from three Uncle Walt's Band releases recorded between 1979–82, *An American in Texas Revisited* (Sugar Hill, 1991, prod. various) ♪♪♪♪ contains the trio's liveliest music, partly the result of a temporary breakup that gave each member an opportunity to explore other styles. Although the country influences abound, such Hyatt numbers as "Motor City Man," "Deeper than Love" and "Desiree" also resonate with the melodic stamp of the *Rubber Soul*-era Beatles.

the rest:

The Girl on the Sunny Shore (Sugar Hill, 1991) ♪♪♪
Music Town (Sugar Hill, 1993) ♪♪♪♪

worth searching for: Lovett fans who own *Lyle Lovett and His Large Band* (MCA, 1989, prod. Lyle Lovett, Tony Brown, Billy Williams) ♪♪♪♪ can hear the influence and reunited voices of Uncle Walt's Band on the jazzy closing track, "Once Is Enough."

influences:

◀◀ Bob Wills, Django Reinhardt, Ray Charles, Beatles, Grateful Dead

▶▶ Lyle Lovett

David Okamoto

JACK INGRAM

Born November 15, 1970, in Houston, TX.

Jack Ingram's story is a source of inspiration for any upstart country artist who feels they must buckle to Nashville's computer-processed method of making and marketing records. Ingram hails from Texas, where country, rock, folk and blues are stripped of pretensions and overproduction. A graduate of Dallas' Southern Methodist University, Ingram began playing open-mike nights at Adair's Saloon, a dive located in the alternative-rock mecca of Deep Ellum. He slowly drew an audience, became a regular act at Adair's and took his music seriously enough to record his original material—a kicking, honky-tonk-based blend of country and rock. He released two independent CDs and sold 20,000 copies out of his truck at weekly gigs.

After he had established a loyal following in the Lone Star state, Ingram made a few trips to Nashville and played a few gigs. Eventually, he got introduced to manager Ken Levitan, who had carved a reputation for his work with such Texas originals as Lyle Lovett, Joe Ely and Nanci Griffith. Under Levitan's tutelage, Ingram inked a recording contract with Warner Bros. But before Ingram began recording his debut, he exited the label and followed Levitan to Rising Tide, a new MCA-distributed imprint. As president of the label, Levitan gave Ingram creative control and hooked him up with second-generation outlaw Steve Earle. Earle, whose gritty sound and stellar songs are undoubtedly an influence on Ingram, co-produced Ingram's first studio album for Rising Tide, *Livin' or Dyin'*, with Ray Kennedy. So at a mere 26, Ingram accomplished what takes many artists years to attain—artistic freedom within the major-label assembly line.

what to buy: *Livin' or Dyin'* (Rising Tide, 1997, prod. Steve Earle, Ray Kennedy) ↗↗↗↗ has prompted the heaviest Nashville buzz since BR5-49 were discovered singing originals and Hank Williams covers in the store window of Robert's Western World. The attention is not surprising; at a time when Nashville continues to dodge critical bullets for its flashy pop products, Ingram is the bold outsider who managed to get it done his way. One listen to this outstanding effort is enough to merit the hype; shuffles, hard-core honky-tonk numbers and honest ballads with nary a keyboard flourish abound. Highlights include the contemplative ballad "Don't You Remember," the carefree dance-floor staple "Make My Heart Flutter" and the cowpunk corker "I Can't Leave You." And it's so gratifying to hear Jerry Jeff Walker back in the Music City; his refreshingly at-home duet stint on "Picture on My Wall" assures us that the generation gap isn't so wide after all.

the rest:
Live at Adair's (Rising Tide, 1996) ↗↗↗↗

worth searching for: Ingram's two independent releases, *Jack Ingram* (Rhythmic Records, 1993, prod. Terence Slemmons, Cary Pierce) ↗↗↗↗ and *Lonesome Questions* (Rhythmic Records, 1994, prod. Terence Slemmons, Reed Easterwood) ↗↗↗↗ can easily be found anywhere in Texas. If he garners enough commercial success, Rising Tide may even pick up the CDs for national distribution. Both display a fully formed artist with a clear musical vision and a fearless grasp of his influences.

influences:

◄◄ Willie Nelson, Jerry Jeff Walker, Steve Earle

▶▶ Robert Earl Keen Jr., Dale Watson, Gary Allan

Mario Tarradell

ALAN JACKSON

Born Alan Eugene Jackson, October 17, 1958, in Newnan, GA.

Alan Jackson didn't look like much when he released his first single in the fall of 1989 on the heels of big successes by Garth Brooks and Clint Black—just a lanky, modestly handsome country singer in a cowboy hat. But the former car salesman and carpenter has gone on to fashion a career that will have singers 20 years from now looking back on him the way the ones now think about Merle Haggard or George Strait. He joined the Grand Ole Opry in 1991 and was named the Country Music Association's Entertainer of the Year in 1995. Working quietly and subtly, Jackson has created a body of work as strong as anybody's during the decade of the 1990s (during which he's had more than 13 chart-topping hits), and he's the only singer that appeared during country's boom of 1989 who doesn't seem to have reached his creative peak.

what to buy: *A Lot about Livin' (And a Little 'bout Love)* (Arista, 1993, prod. Keith Stegall, Scott Hendricks) ↗↗↗↗, Jackson's third album, was his breakthrough album and contained the hit "Chattahoochee," a coming-of-age celebration that won just about every award available. Jackson came into his own a singer here, too, turning songs ranging from the reconciliation

ballad "Tonight I Climbed the Wall" to K.C. Douglas' obscure "Mercury Blues" into major hits. The album has sold more than 6 million copies.

what to buy next: As best-of collections go, Jackson's *The Greatest Hits Collection* (Arista, 1995, prod. Keith Stegall, Scott Hendricks) 𝄞𝄞𝄞𝄞 is hard to beat, containing 20 songs, including two new ones, "I'll Try" and a cover of the Roger Miller/George Jones song "Tall, Tall Trees." *Everything I Love* (Arista, 1996, prod. Keith Stegall) 𝄞𝄞𝄞𝄞 solidified Jackson's position as the premier traditional country singer of his generation. Not only did he continue to best legends with their own material (in this case, a Cajun-flavored rendition of Tom T. Hall's "Little Bitty"), he added depth to his repertoire with the apocalyptic love song "Between the Devil and Me."

the rest:

Here in the Real World (Arista, 1990) 𝄞𝄞𝄞
Don't Rock the Jukebox (Arista, 1991) 𝄞𝄞𝄞
Honky-Tonk Christmas (Arista, 1993) 𝄞𝄞𝄞
Who I Am (Arista, 1994) 𝄞𝄞𝄞

worth searching for: *A Lot about Livin' (And a Little 'bout Love): Music Row Theater World Premier* (Arista, 1992, prod. Tim Riley) 𝄞𝄞𝄞. Arista co-produced this radio show with the American Radio Network and sent promotional copies to press. Charlie Chase interviews the normally taciturn Jackson between songs.

influences:

◀◀ George Jones, Merle Haggard, George Strait, Randy Travis
▶▶ Wade Hayes, Paul Brandt, Tracy Lawrence

Brian Mansfield

CARL JACKSON

Born September 18, 1953.

Multi-instrumentalist Carl Jackson (banjo, guitar, mandolin, dobro, fiddle) was hired at age 14 by Jim & Jesse McReynolds to become one of their Virginia Boys. After five years he worked for the bluegrass gospel group the Sullivan Family, and then was in Glen Campbell's band for 12 years. Jackson also recorded solo albums for Capitol during the 1970s, Columbia during the 1980s, and three albums for Sugar Hill during the early 1990s. He is a-much-in-demand session player and harmony singer and has had considerable success as a songwriter, both in country and bluegrass; he co-wrote Vince Gill's #3 hit "No Future in the Past" in 1993, and his bluegrass gospel number, "Little Mountain Church House," has rapidly achieved standard status in that realm.

what's available: *Spring Training* (1991, Sugar Hill, prod. Carl Jackson, John Starling) 𝄞𝄞𝄞, Jackson's 1991 collaboration with longtime Seldom Scene vocalist and guitarist John Starling and Emmylou Harris' acoustic band the Nash Ramblers received the 1991 Best Bluegrass Album Grammy.

influences:

◀◀ Earl Scruggs, Jim & Jesse
▶▶ Ricky Skaggs, Herb Pedersen

Randy Pitts

STONEWALL JACKSON

Born November 6, 1932, in Emerson, NC.

North Carolina-born, Georgia-raised Stonewall (his real name) Jackson is one of the rare artists signed to be a member of the Grand Ole Opry without a recording contract. His wide-open vocal style and talent for writing heartfelt songs contributed to his considerable success through the late 1950s and 1960s, including "Don't Be Angry," "Life to Go," 1959's #1 "Waterloo," "Why I'm Walkin'," "A Wound Time Can't Erase," "Leona," 1964's #1 "B.J. the D.J.," and "I Washed My Hands in Muddy Water." His last Top 10 hit to-date was 1971's "Me and You and a Dog Named Boo." A throwback even during the period of his greatest success, Jackson remains an anomalous figure in the country music scene of the 1990s, but his best recordings hold up as among the finest pure country recordings ever made in Nashville.

what to buy: All the big ones are included on *Stonewall Jackson's Greatest Hits* (Columbia, 1965, prod. Don Law, Frank Jones) 𝄞𝄞𝄞𝄞, in their original versions.

what to buy next: *The Dynamic Stonewall Jackson* (Sony Music Special Products, 1959) 𝄞𝄞𝄞 contains some of his earliest, rawest and best stuff.

what to avoid: *Waterloo* (Laserlight, 1993) 𝄞𝄞 doesn't feature very good remakes.

the rest:

American Originals (Columbia, 1989, prod. various) 𝄞𝄞𝄞
Waterloo—19 Great Country Stars (Country Stars, 1995) 𝄞𝄞𝄞

worth searching for: *Stonewall Jackson Recorded Live at the Grand Ole Opry* (Columbia, 1971, prod. Frank Jones) 𝄞𝄞𝄞 features a fine representation of his live show, recorded where the legend began.

influences:
◀◀ Hank Williams, George Jones
▶▶ Gary Stewart, Marty Brown

Randy Pitts

TOMMY JACKSON

Born March 31, 1925, in Birmingham, AL. Died December 9, 1979.

Nashville's first great session fiddler, Tommy Jackson grew up in Nashville listening to the Grand Ole Opry. A child prodigy, he went on tour with Johnny Wright and Kitty Wells at age 12; by the time he was 17, Jackson appeared regularly on the Opry with Curly Williams & His Georgia Peach Pickers. After World War II he became a member of Red Foley's Cumberland Valley Boys (guitarist Zeke Turner, steel player Jerry Byrd and rhythm guitarist Louis Innes), who became the first great "A" team of studio musicians in Nashville. During this period Jackson played fiddle on countless country classics, including Hank Williams' "I Saw the Light" and "Lovesick Blues" and Foley's "Satisfied Mind." The Cumberland Valley Boys then moved to Cincinnati in 1948, became the Pleasant Valley Boys, and continued to do studio work, primarily for King Records, while remaining a member of Foley's band. Jacksons began cutting records under his own name in Cincinnati, capitalizing on the then-current square-dance craze. He recorded first for Mercury, then signed a long-term contract with Dot Records and made 11 albums for them. He broke with Foley and, from 1954 on, made his living exclusively as a studio musician, pretty much inventing, then refining and redefining standard country back-up fiddle style. Jackson was the most imitated country fiddler of the time, and popularized the shuffle fiddle sound heard to great effect on the vastly influential recordings of Ray Price, among countless others.

what's available: Lamentably, the only currently available examples of Tommy Jackson's incredibly influential lead fiddle style are the 10 tunes on *Good Old Fiddle Music* (MCA,1995) 𝄞𝄞𝄞𝄞. Titles include "Little Ida Red," "Bitter Creek Breakdown," "Acorn Hill Breakdown," "Big Sandy," "Snowflake Breakdown," "Stay a Little Longer" and "Done Gone."

worth searching for: Two of Jackson's instrumental albums have served as primers for fledgling bluegrass fiddlers. They are *Greatest Bluegrass Hits* (Dot, 1962) 𝄞𝄞𝄞𝄞 and *Square Dances without Calls* (Decca, 1959) 𝄞𝄞𝄞.

influences:
◀◀ Fiddling Arthur Smith, George Wilkerson

▶▶ Gordon Terry, Vassar Clements

Randy Pitts

WANDA JACKSON

Born October 20, 1937, in Maud, OK.

A country/rockabilly pioneer, often called the "female Elvis," Wanda Jackson really had two careers throughout the 1950s and 1960s. Her professional career began when Hank Thompson invited her to sing on the weekends with his Brazos Valley Boys in Oklahoma City, 50 miles from her home. At 16 she earned her first hit, a Top 10 country duet with Billy Gray, "You Can't Have My Love" (#8, 1954). With her growling voice out front and some fiery rock rhythms behind her, Jackson became a rockabilly sensation, touring with Elvis and appearing on TV shows like *Ozark Jubilee* and *Town Hall Party*. Her pop hits were few ("Let's Have a Party," later featured in the film *Dead Poet's Society*, hit only #37 in 1960), but her influence is unquestionable. By 1962 Jackson was a successful country artist with two songs charting in Top 10, "Right or Wrong" (#9, 1961) and "In the Middle of a Heartache" (#9, 1962). For the next decade she would be present on the country charts, although she never hit the Top 10 again. Gospel recordings, on a much less visible scale, followed, and today Jackson is enjoying somewhat of a career revival. She continues to be a popular touring act in Europe, mixing her shows, like the best of her recently reissued recordings, with the country and rock hits she's made famous.

what to buy: Although it's really a toss-up, *Vintage Collections Series* (Capitol, 1996) 𝄞𝄞𝄞𝄞 prevails because the liner notes are better. And as far as song selection, you can't go wrong with this one.

what to buy next: The aptly titled *Rockin' in the Country/The Best of Wanda Jackson* (Rhino, 1990) 𝄞𝄞𝄞𝄞 really doesn't have a bad track on it.

the rest:
Greatest Hits (Curb, 1990) 𝄞𝄞𝄞
Right or Wrong (Bear Family, 1992) 𝄞𝄞𝄞𝄞

influences:
◀◀ Janis Martin, Brenda Lee
▶▶ Jann Browne, Rosie Flores

Stephen L. Betts

KATE JACOBS

Born January 11, 1959, in Alexandria, VA.

A winsome folkie with a melancholy streak, Kate Jacobs can sing about loss and regret with the best of them, but her ability to occasionally express contentment, happiness and love truly sets her apart. After all, who writes songs about feeling good anymore? Jacobs' songs are as fully fleshed-out as quality fiction, but her lilting, girlish voice lifts them off the page. Backed by an austere three-piece band, Jacobs comes off as an East Coast answer to Iris DeMent (*The Calm Comes After* even contains a song about DeMent, "Iris Has Faith"). Jacobs' EP *A Sister* is a companion recording to her children's book, *A Sister's Wish* (Hyperion, 1994).

what to buy: On the surface, *What about Regret* (Bar/None, 1995, prod. Gary Arnold, Kate Jacobs & band members) ♪♪♪♪ seems straightforward and breezy, but look a little closer and you'll find some of the richest, most complex songs written during the last decade. "See the Moon" seems to be about an old couple planning a dinner party, until you realize what they're contemplating is double suicide. Even the slightest songs, such as "Indiana," are carried along on such beautiful melodies that they seem instantly memorable. And there's even a touch of comic relief in "Three Years in Nebraska," about marijuana farming during the 1970s, and "A Sister," about a girl with too many brothers and no one on her side.

the rest:
The Calm Comes After (Bar/None, 1993) ♪♪♪♪
A Sister (Bar/None EP, 1996) ♪♪♪

influences:
◀◀ Nanci Griffith, Dolly Parton

Daniel Durchholz

BRETT JAMES

Born June 5, 1968, in Columbia, MO.

Brett James was one of many young, good-looking singers in cowboy hats signed by Nashville labels during the mid-1990s. A native of Oklahoma, he left medical school to pursue his music career and was the first new artist signed to Career Records, a spin-off from Arista.

what's available: For the most part, *Brett James* (Career, 1995, prod. Steve Bogard, Michael Clute) ♪♪♪ is standard-issue 1990s country, with references to honky-tonks and rodeos, marred only by the first single, the mildly obnoxious "Female Bond-ing." James almost redeemed it with "Dark Side of the Moon," a better than average ghost-of-Hank-Williams song.

influences:
◀◀ John Michael Montgomery, Garth Brooks
▶▶ David Kersh, Chris Ward

Brian Mansfield

MICHAEL JAMES

Born Michael James Murphy, in TX.

Michael James is a Christian country singer whose music tends to run to James Taylor more than Merle Haggard. He recorded for the small Christian label Milk & Honey as Michael James Murphy during the 1980s. Michael moved to Nashville in 1988 and has had songs cut by Lee Greenwood and Highway 101.

what's available: James has consistently made albums that reflect the most Christian elements of country. So *Shoulder to the Wind* (Reunion, 1992, prod. Gary Chapman, J.D. Cunningham) ♪♪ contains lots of moralistic story songs about tilling the soil, finding time for the family and forgiveness. (James co-wrote nine of 10 songs on the album.) *Closer to the Fire* (Reunion, 1994, prod. Gary Chapman, J.D. Cunningham) ♪♪ offers more of the same. By his third album, *Where Love Runs Deep* (Reunion, 1995, prod. Michael James) ♪♪, James was getting songs from major country writers Tony Arata and Mike Reid.

influences:
◀◀ Gary Chapman, Paul Overstreet
▶▶ Ken Holloway

Brian Mansfield

SONNY JAMES

Born James Hugh Loden, May 1, 1929, in Hackleburg, AL.

Billed as "The Southern Gentleman," Sonny James was one of the few 1950s pop-country crooners able to parlay his first hits into a lengthy career. James grew up singing in a family group and had his own radio show in Alabama while still a teenager. He had his first country hit in 1953 with "That's Me without You," but his breakthrough came four years later with "Young Love," which topped both the pop and country charts in 1957. James would have one more crossover hit that year, "First Date, First Kiss, First Love" and then drop off the pop chart, but he remained a staple on country radio for decades. James' middle-of-the-road adaptability brought him great success throughout the 1960s and 1970s and occasionally into the 1980s. Between

1967 and 1971 he had 16 consecutive #1 singles, including versions of such pop hits as "Only the Lonely," "Running Bear" and "It's Just a Matter of Time." James spent his most productive years with Capitol, but he also has recorded for Columbia, Monument and Dimension. The singer had parts in a number of country music B-movies, including *Second Fiddle to a Steel Guitar* and *Hillbillies in a Haunted House*. He has done occasional producing, most notably of Marie Osmond's 1973 hit "Paper Roses."

what's available: Both *Greatest Hits* (Curb, 1991) 𝄢𝄢𝄢 and *The Best of Sonny James* (Curb, 1991) 𝄢𝄢𝄢 contain a good selection of James' hits, apparently assembled at random. *Greatest Hits* contains "Young Love," James' biggest hit, and tends to focus on earlier hits like "The Minute You're Gone," "Baltimore" and "You're the Only World I Know." *Best Of*, on the other hand, goes into the 1970s often with singles like "Endlessly," "Empty Arms" and "Here Comes Honey Again." It also, inexplicably, has a non-charting duet with unknown Karla Taylor. Put together, they cover just about all of James' 23 chart-topping hits, and they're both preferable to *Young Love* (Pair, 1991) 𝄢𝄢, an even sloppier compilation.

influences:

◀◀ Eddy Arnold, Chet Atkins

▶▶ Jack Scott, Gene Pitney, Conway Twitty

Brian Mansfield

DUANE JARVIS

Born August 22, 1957, in Astoria, OR.

A guitarist whose resume includes stints with country/folk songwriting greats John Prine and Lucinda Williams as well as the Australian rock band the Divinyls, Duane Jarvis stepped out on his own in 1994 with rootsy, twangy pop songs that reflect the diversity of his background.

what to buy: *D.J.'s Front Porch* (Medium Cool, 1994, prod. Duane Jarvis, Peter Jesperson) 𝄢𝄢𝄢𝄢, Jarvis' debut, boasts a solid selection of originals, a few worthy of being covered by better-known artists, plus a dead-on cover of the Kinks' "This Is Where I Belong."

the rest:

Far from Perfect (D'Ville, 1997)

influences:

◀◀ Rolling Stones, Kinks, Beatles

Peter Blackstock

JASON & THE SCORCHERS

Formed 1981, in Nashville, TN.

Jason Ringenberg, vocals, harmonica, guitar; Warner Hodges, guitar, vocals; Jeff Johnson, bass (1981–97); Perry Baggs, drums, vocals; Andy York, guitar (1989); Ken Fox, bass (1989).

Jason & the Scorchers, along with the Mekons and other punkish 1980s bands, decided they understood Hank Williams better than the Eagles did. So they re-created "country-rock" in their own image. The Scorchers' name was not an exaggeration: Led by Jason Ringenberg's frenzied energy and herky-jerky stage movements, the band cranked up the guitars and turned Williams' music back into the honky-tonking classics they are. Ringenberg, as legend goes, grew up on his family's hog farm in Sheffield, Illinois, then moved to Nashville to become a star. He hooked up with a few hillbillies who shared his love for Bob Dylan and the Ramones, and they set about crashing punk and country into each other. After opening for Dylan during his 1990 tour, the Scorchers were fed up with each other and the lack of commercial attention, so they broke up. They reformed, with a still-blazing reunion album, in 1995, and Mammoth Records decided to re-release the band's early albums.

what to buy: *Essential Jason & the Scorchers, Volume 1: Are You Ready for the Country?* (EMI, 1992, prod. Jeff Daniel, Adam Block) 𝄢𝄢𝄢𝄢 collects two early albums, *Fervor* and *Lost & Found*, as well as a bunch of rarities and live tracks.

what to buy next: The reunion album, *A-Blazing Grace* (Mammoth, 1995, prod. Jason & the Scorchers) 𝄢𝄢𝄢, is built around an incredible version of John Denver's formerly corny "Take Me Home, Country Roads" and George Jones' "Why Baby Why." The debut EP *Reckless Country Soul* (Praxis, 1992/Mammoth, 1996, prod. Jack Emerson, Jason & the Scorchers, Jim Dickinson) gets repetitive, but its barnstorming country-punk breathes life into Williams' "I'm So Lonesome (I Could Cry)," plus the consummate Scorchers' classic, "Help! There's a Fire."

what to avoid: *Thunder and Fire* (A&M, 1989) 𝄢𝄢 is the sound of all the thunder and fire slipping away, just before the band broke up.

the rest:

Still Standing (EMI America, 1986) 𝄢𝄢𝄢

Clear Impetuous Morning (Mammoth, 1996) 𝄢𝄢𝄢

worth searching for: *Lost & Found* (EMI America, 1985, prod. Terry Manning) 𝄢𝄢𝄢 and the *Fervor* EP (EMI America, 1983, prod. Jim Dickinson, Jack Emerson, Chuck Ainlay, Terry Manning) 𝄢𝄢𝄢 are great but hard to find, and *Essential* is a better deal.

Jason Ringenberg of Jason & the Scorchers (© Ken Settle)

solo outings:

Jason Ringenberg:
One Foot in the Honky-Tonk (Liberty, 1992) ♪♪

influences:

◀◀ Hank Williams, Johnny Cash, Ramones, Mekons, Gram Parsons

▶▶ Social Distortion, Uncle Tupelo, Golden Smog, Bottle Rockets

Steve Knopper

THE JAYHAWKS

Formed 1985, in Minneapolis, MN.

Gary Louris, guitar, vocals; Mark Olson, guitar, vocals (1985–95); Marc Perlman, bass; Thad Spencer, drums (1985–90); Ken Callahan, drums (1990–95); Karen Grotberg, keyboards; Tim O'Regan, drums (1995–present).

Hailed as the second coming of the Flying Burrito Brothers, the Jayhawks actually have the goods to hold up to the comparison. Not that the notion is completely off the mark: Mark Olson played Gram Parsons to Gary Louris' Chris Hillman, and the band plays a musically sparse, emotionally packed music that taps into the spirit of country music without ever reflecting Nashville's infatuation with the mainstream. Olson, who married singer/songwriter Victoria Williams, left the band in November 1995; the remaining line-up (Louris, Perlman, Grotberg and O'Regan) considered changing the band's name but eventually decided to keep it.

what to buy: On *Tomorrow the Green Grass* (American, 1995, prod. George Drakoulias) ♪♪♪♪ the Jayhawks effectively start shaking off the Flying Burrito Brother comparisons, replacing it with—of all things—1970s power-pop. With songs such as "Blue" and a cover of Grand Funk Railroad's "Bad Time," the Jayhawks produce their best hooks without forsaking their country soul.

what to buy next: *Hollywood Town Hall* (American, 1993, prod. George Drakoulias) 𝄢𝄢𝄢 established the Jayhawks as the premiere country-rock (for lack of a better term) band of its time. The album made best-of lists in the *Village Voice, Entertainment Weekly* and just about everywhere else.

the rest:

The Jayhawks (Bunkhouse, 1986) 𝄢𝄢𝄢
Blue Earth (Twin/Tone, 1989) 𝄢𝄢𝄢𝄢
Sound of Lies (American, 1997) 𝄢𝄢𝄢𝄢

worth searching for: The import CD-5 for "Waiting for the Sun" (American, 1993) 𝄢𝄢𝄢𝄢 features four live songs, including a cover of Tim Hardin's "Reason to Believe."

influences:

◀◀ Gram Parsons, Neil Young

▶▶ Golden Smog, Wilco, Son Volt, Victoria Williams, Joe Henry

see also: *Golden Smog*

Brian Mansfield

PAUL JEFFERSON

Born in Woodside, CA.

Paul Jefferson grew up in California listening to the music of Waylon Jennings and Willie Nelson. As an adult, he did the only thing that seemed natural: he moved to Nashville. Jefferson worked as a demo singer and songwriter (he co-wrote Aaron Tippin's hit "That's as Close as I'll Get to Loving You") before signing to the fledgling ALMO Sounds label.

what's available: Jefferson makes smart, mainstream country music, and his debut, *Paul Jefferson* (ALMO Sounds, 1996, prod. Garth Fundis) 𝄢𝄢𝄢𝄢, was one of the most underappreciated records of 1996. His warm voice is more than capable of conveying a sense of humor (the saucy "Check Please," the ambitious "I Might Just Make It") and romance ("I Will," "Unconditionally").

influences:

◀◀ Kevin Welch, Vince Gill

Brian Mansfield

HERB JEFFRIES

Born September 24, 1916, in Detroit, MI.

Herb Jeffries' musical career was built around his singing with jazz groups (most notably Duke Ellington's orchestra, with which he had the big hit "Flamingo") and in sophisticated pop contexts, but he also gained fame as the first and most famous black singing cowboy on the silver screen. During the mid-1930s he proposed the idea of black Westerns, not to feature himself (though his handsome looks led to starring roles), but to correct the received image that all cowboys were white when in fact African Americans had a major role in taming the West. Jeffries wrote many of the songs heard in his five B-movie Westerns, backed by the vocals of the Four Tones. Though his albums up until the Warner Western release were jazz and pop, it's good that he returned to the country context, because in all of country music history, the only vocalist who could match Jeffries' bass-baritone in suave elegance with a touch of bluesy swagger was Tennessee Ernie Ford.

what to buy: *The Bronze Buckaroo (Rides Again)* (Warner Western, 1995, prod. Jim Ed Norman, Eric Prestidge) 𝄢𝄢𝄢𝄢 is full of guest stars from a broad range of genres (Little Texas, Michael Martin Murphey, Take 6, Sons of the San Joaquin, the Mills Brothers, Cleve Francis and Rex Allen Jr. all contribute vocals), but the spotlight is always on Jeffries' mellifluous tones. The arrangements are fairly down-home, if hardly rough, and the classic tunes include "Back in the Saddle Again," "Cow Cow Boogie" and "Tumbling Tumbleweeds." Jeffries' own compositions (some from his movie days, some new), including his long-time theme song, "I'm a Happy Cowboy," can stand alongside anyone's for unpretentious fun, and "Lonesome Rider Blues" deserves to be a classic itself.

worth searching for: *A Brief History of Herb Jeffries 1934–1995* (Warner Western, 1995, prod. various) 𝄢𝄢𝄢𝄢 is difficult to track down because it was never commercially released. It is, in fact, a sampler put together by the label to help promote awareness of Jeffries' long career at the time *The Bronze Buckaroo* came out. Besides selections from the latter album, it gathers together samples of his jazz (including "Flamingo") and R&B singing and also, most valuably, two of his 1930s Western recordings.

influences:

◀◀ Gene Autry, Billy Eckstine

▶▶ Ray Charles, Michael Martin Murphey

Steve Holtje

JOHN JENNINGS

Born November 22, 1953, in Harrisburg, VA.

John Jennings is a multi-instrumentalist with a background in jingle and session singing who grew up in the Northern Virginia suburbs of Washington, D.C. He first came to the attention of the country audience via his successful collaborations with Mary Chapin Carpenter, for whom he has served as producer and guitarist. He also co-wrote her hits "Never Had It So Good" and "Goin' out Tonight." Jennings has also produced records by Janis Ian, Beausoleil, John Gorka and Robin & Linda Williams; played on recordings by Tony Rice and the Indigo Girls; and toured with Lyle Lovett.

what's available: *buddy* (Vanguard, 1997, prod. John Jennings, Bob Dawson) ♪♪♪, Jennings' solo debut, contains the same suburban refinement of folk and rock that have made his recordings with other artists so well received. With a vocal and writing style reminiscent of Lyle Lovett's, Jennings primarily plays guitar, but also ventures onto bass, synthesizer, even dobro.

influences:

◀◀ Mary Chapin Carpenter, Lyle Lovett

Brian Mansfield

WAYLON JENNINGS

Born June 15, 1937, in Littlefield, TX.

The quintessential Outlaw, Waylon Jennings spent his early days in Littlefield where he and his musician father, whose favorite singer was Bill Monroe, would eat parch peanuts and listen to the Grand Ole Opry. Young Jennings began working for a local radio station at the age of 12 and at 17 moved to Lubbock, where he met Buddy Holly and played bass in his band from 1958 to 1959. Holly produced Jennings' first single, "Jole Blon"/"When Sin Stops" at Norman Petty's Studios in Clovis, New Mexico. In appreciation, Waylon gave up his seat to the Big Bopper—on the fatal February 4, 1959, charter flight that would kill Holly, Ritchie Valens, the Big Bopper and others. After relocating to Phoenix and becoming a local hero with the Waylors, Jennings moved to Nashville in 1965.

Jennings got his first major-label break when Herb Alpert signed him, but it would be with RCA and Chet Atkins that he entered into a long-term musical relationship. Not knowing exactly which direction to take, Jennings' RCA debut was titled *Folk-Country*. Released in 1966, the album coincided with Jennings' starring role in the movie *Nashville Rebel*. Waylon first hit the country Top 10 with "For Lovin' Me," a Gordon Lightfoot song that was a pop hit for Peter, Paul & Mary. Forging friendships with Johnny Cash, Willie Nelson and other musical mavericks, Jennings married Jessi Colter in 1969. He veered toward harder-edged country during the early 1970s with the release of seminal albums like *Ladies Love Outlaws* and *Honky-Tonk*

Heroes. The Outlaw movement reached critical mass when *Wanted: The Outlaws* (with Nelson, Colter and Tompall Glaser) became a huge hit in 1976. With the Outlaw movement supplying country music much of its spark, Jennings landed an impressive string of chart-topping hits between 1974 and 1983. He won the Country Music Association's Male Vocalist of the Year honor in 1975 and he and Nelson were the Vocal Duo of the Year in 1976. Jennings recorded the first of three albums as a member of the Highwaymen in 1985, and recorded his first MCA release, *Will the Wolf Survive*, in 1986. After four albums for MCA and a hits compilation *New Classic Waylon* from the MCA period (1986–88), he's continued to record for Epic, RCA and Justice, and to tour and make records with the Highwaymen, with his distinctive voice and style very much still intact. In the fall of 1996 his autobiography, *Waylon*, written with Lenny Kaye, was released. It's must reading for any serious country music fan.

what to buy: *Only Daddy That'll Walk the Line: The RCA Years* (RCA, 1993, prod. various) ♪♪♪♪ collects 40 of Jennings' most important recordings from 1965–84 in one place. While it doesn't have the cohesion and experimental friskiness of many of his time-pieces like 1977's *Ol' Waylon* or 1982's *Waylon*, it's the best place for one-stop shopping Jennings' most recognizable nuggets.

what to buy next: *Honky-Tonk Heroes* (RCA, 1973/1994, prod. Waylon Jennings, Tompall Glaser, Ronny Light, Ken Mansfield) ♪♪♪♪ is an outlaw classic with Jennings singing the songs of a feisty young Billy Joe Shaver.

what to avoid: *WW II* (RCA, 1982, prod. Chips Moman, Waylon Jennings) ♪♪♪, with Willie Nelson, is the duo's least inspired collaboration, with the sum of two very dynamic parts not adding up quite right.

the rest:
(With Willie Nelson) *Waylon & Willie* (RCA, 1978) ♪♪♪♪
Greatest Hits (RCA, 1979) ♪♪♪♪♪
Waylon's Greatest Hits, Volume 2 (RCA, 1984) ♪♪♪♪
Collector's Series (RCA, 1985) ♪♪♪♪
Will the Wolf Survive (MCA, 1986)
(With Johnny Cash) *Heroes* (Razor & Tie, 1986)
A Man Called Hoss (MCA, 1988) ♪♪♪
New Classic Waylon (MCA, 1989) ♪♪♪♪

Waylon Jennings (© Ken Settle)

The Eagle (Epic, 1990) 🎵🎵🎵

(With Nelson) *Clean Shirt* (Columbia, 1991) 🎵🎵🎵

Too Dumb for New York City, Too Ugly for L.A. (Epic, 1992) 🎵🎵🎵

Thanks to Buddy (Drive, 1994) 🎵🎵🎵

Waymore's Blues (Part II) (RCA, 1994) 🎵🎵🎵🎵

Super Hits: Waylon Jennings (RCA, 1996) 🎵🎵🎵🎵

(With Nelson, Jessi Colter, and Tompall Glaser) *Wanted: The Outlaws* (RCA, 1976/1996) 🎵🎵🎵🎵🎵

The Essential Waylon Jennings (RCA, 1996) 🎵🎵🎵🎵

Right for the Time (Justice, 1996) 🎵🎵🎵🎵

(With Cash, Nelson, and Kris Kristofferson) *Highwayman* (Columbia, 1985) 🎵🎵🎵🎵

Highwayman 2 (Columbia, 1990) 🎵🎵🎵

The Road Goes On Forever (Capitol, 1995) 🎵🎵🎵🎵

worth searching for: In his autobiography, Jennings calls *Dreaming My Dreams* (RCA, 1975, prod. Waylon Jennings, Jack Clement) 🎵🎵🎵🎵 "my favorite album I've ever done." It came at a time when Jennings' musical possibilities seemed endless, and with tracks like "Are You Sure Hank Done It This Way?" and a live "Bob Wills Is Still the King," the magic and energy of that period is time-capsuled here.

influences:

◀◀ Buddy Holly, Johnny Cash, Billy Joe Shaver

▶▶ Billy Joe Shaver, Travis Tritt

David Sokol

JIM & JESSE

Jim McReynolds (born February 13, 1927, in Coeburn, VA), guitar, vocals; Jesse McReynolds (born July 9, 1929, in Coeburn, VA), mandolin, vocals.

Jim & Jesse are a pivotal duo in the history of bluegrass music. They and their band the Virginia Boys illustrated early on that the tight harmony vocals featured in much early country music could be adapted to bluegrass and be a very viable commercial force. Additionally, Jesse was and is an important influence as a mandolinist; his patented crosspicking style has added a dimension to bluegrass that hadn't previously existed. Jim & Jesse's band, the Virginia Boys, has also hosted many important musicians over the years, from fiddlers Vassar Clements and Jim Buchanan to banjo players Allen Shelton, Bobby Thompson, Vic Jordan, Carl Jackson and many more. For a period during the late 1960s, they attempted with some success to adopt a more mainstream country sound, but, with the ad-

vent of bluegrass festivals, the duo has returned, for the most part, to the earlier, bluegrassier sound.

what to buy: The best single collection of Jim & Jesse material we are likely to see in the near future is *Jim & Jesse: Bluegrass and More* (Bear Family, 1993, prod. Don Law, Frank Jones, Jerry Kennedy, Billy Sherrill, Glenn Sutton) 🎵🎵🎵🎵, which contains everything the brothers recorded for Columbia and Epic between 1960 and 1970. The five-CD collection includes much classic bluegrass, but also their tribute to Chuck Berry (*Berry Pickin' in the Country*) and their more mainstream recordings, mainly from 1967 to 1972, when they had a country hit with "Diesel on My Tail." *Jim & Jesse* (Bear Family, 1992, prod. Ken Nelson) 🎵🎵🎵🎵 is a reissue of all the McReynolds' early Capitol material, from 1952 to 1955.

what to buy next: *The Jim & Jesse Story* (CMH, 1990, prod. Bobby Thompson) 🎵🎵🎵🎵 contains excellent remakes of 24 of the brothers' biggest hits with excellent accompanists and exhaustive liner notes. *In the Tradition* (Rounder, 1987, prod. Jim & Jesse) 🎵🎵🎵 is a good representative mix of classic older material revisited and newer stuff, featuring an outstanding band that includes Allen Shelton, Glen Duncan, Charlie Collins and Roy Huskey. *Music among Friends* (Rounder, 1991, prod. Carl Jackson) 🎵🎵🎵 is a nice set featuring many guest stars, including Bill Monroe, Emmylou Harris, Jim Buchanan, Porter Wagoner, and more.

worth searching for: *Border Ride* (King, 1996) 🎵🎵🎵🎵🎵, a minimally packaged, scantily programmed (10 cuts, 23 minutes) budget CD contains Starday singles circa the late 1950s and features one of the best groups of Virginia Boys (fiddler Vassar Clements and banjoist Bobby Thompson among them, although the cut that purportedly includes Carl Story probably doesn't). Overlook the cheesy packaging; this stuff has been hard to find for years.

solo outings:

Jesse McReynolds:

A Mandolin Christmas (Double J Entertainment) 🎵🎵🎵

influences:

◀◀ Delmore Brothers, Louvin Brothers

▶▶ O'Kanes, Wilburn Brothers

Randy Pitts

FLACO JIMENEZ

Born March 11, 1939, in San Antonio, TX.

The undisputed king of *conjunto* music and son of the influential

Santiago Jimenez, Flaco Jimenez is a squeezebox master who plays a rousing mix of American folk and country and Mexican rancheras and polkas. In addition to his own records, his colorful accordion work and straightforward vocals have graced albums by Ry Cooder (who helped introduce Jimenez to the rest of America), the Mavericks, Dwight Yoakam and the Rolling Stones. A *norteno* music veteran of more than three decades, Jimenez has branched out into American country both as a solo act and as a member of the Texas Tornados alongside Freddy Fender, Doug Sahm and Augie Meyers (both of the Sir Douglas Quintet).

what to buy: Jimenez's most accessible solo work has been with Arista Texas, which released his best Tex-Mex album, *Flaco Jimenez* (Arista, 1994, prod. Bill Halverson) ♪♪♪. It includes the Grammy-winning "Cat Walk" and features contributions from the Mavericks' Raul Malo, Lee Roy Parnell and Radney Foster.

what to buy next: *Buena Suerte, Senorita* (Arista, 1996, prod. Cameron Riddle, Flaco Jimenez) ♪♪♪ leans more heavily toward updating the Mexican side of his music. The rollicking *Partners* (Warner Bros., 1992, prod. Bill Halverson) ♪♪♪ features some big-name friends, including Linda Ronstadt, Emmylou Harris, Dwight Yoakam and Los Lobos.

the rest:

El Senido de San Antonio (Arhoolie, 1980) ♪♪♪

Ay Te Dejo en San Antonio y Mas (Arhoolie, 1986) ♪♪♪

Flaco's Amigos (Arhoolie, 1987) ♪♪♪

Arriba el Norte (Rounder, 1988) ♪♪♪

Entre Humor & Batellas (Rounder, 1989) ♪♪♪

San Antonio Soul (Rounder, 1991) ♪♪♪

Un Mojado sin Licencia (A Wetback without a Green Card) (Arhoolie, 1993) ♪♪♪

Flaco's First (Arhoolie, 1995) ♪♪♪

influences:

◀◀ Santiago Jimenez

▶▶ Ry Cooder, Doug Sahm

see also: *Texas Tornados*

Doug Pullen

JOHNNIE & JACK

Formed in Nashville, TN.

Johnnie Wright (born May 13, 1914, in Mount Juliet, TN); Jack Anglin (born May 13, 1916, in Franklin, TN; died March 7, 1963).

Unique in their day for combining hard country arrangements and instruments with surprisingly uptown lyrics and rhythms,

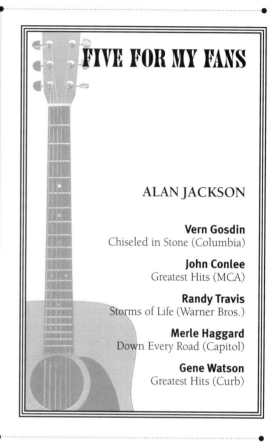

FIVE FOR MY FANS

ALAN JACKSON

Vern Gosdin
Chiseled in Stone (Columbia)

John Conlee
Greatest Hits (MCA)

Randy Travis
Storms of Life (Warner Bros.)

Merle Haggard
Down Every Road (Capitol)

Gene Watson
Greatest Hits (Curb)

this exuberantly raw and raucous duo often featured rhumba figures in their arrangements. They also favored fairly sophisticated vocal harmonies, often featuring a third male voice in their arrangements. Their biggest hits for RCA Victor, songs like "Poison Love," "Crying Heart Blues," "Slow Poison," "Ashes of Love," and "South in New Orleans," were suffused with Latin rhythms and their unique, hard edged vocals, making for an infectious, very appealing sound. Johnny Wright is the husband of female country legend Kitty Wells; before she became a star in her own right, Wells often toured with the Johnnie & Jack road show. Since the death of Jack Anglin in 1963 (he was killed in an auto accident on the way to Patsy Cline's funeral), Wells has often toured with her family; in recent years, son Bobby Wright has often performed old Johnnie and Jack material with his father on live shows. Johnnie Wright had a fairly substantial recording career for years after the death of Anglin, reaching his peak commercially with the #1 hit "Hello Vietnam" in 1965.

what's available: *Johnnie & Jack* (Bear Family, 1992, prod. Sidney Prosen, Syd Nathan, Chet Atkins, Steve Sholes, Paul Cohen, Owen Bradley) ♪♪♪♪ contains everything commercially recorded by this unique duo for Apollo, King, RCA Victor and Decca. *Johnnie and Jack with Kitty Wells At KWKH* (Bear Family, 1994, prod. Richard Weize) ♪♪♪ provides a fascinating look at what a country radio show was like in 1949. This recording, taken from a live broadcast from Shreveport, Louisiana, also features Wells, not yet a star, as just another member of the show's cast.

influences:

◀◀ Anglin Brothers, Wilma Lee & Stoney Cooper

▶▶ Farmer Boys, Wilburn Brothers

Randy Pitts

MICHAEL JOHNSON

Born August 8, 1944, in Alamosa, CO.

Michael Johnson is a singer/songwriter whose mellow folk-pop has enabled him to have success in a number of markets. Having learned guitar by listening to early rock and jazz, Johnson spent a year studying in Italy and later played alongside John Denver in the Mitchell Trio. He had three Top 40 pop hits during the 1970s, the biggest being 1978's "Bluer than Blue." Johnson recorded for the Nashville divisions of RCA and Atlantic during the 1980s and 1990s with even more success.

what's available: *Departure* (Vanguard, 1995, prod. Michael Johnson, Randy Goodrum) ♪♪ doesn't have "Bluer than Blue" or "Give Me Wings." Instead, it's an album from Johnson's latest incarnation as a folkie. Which doesn't mean it's substantially different from his days as a pop or country singer. It is, however, one of Johnson's weakest albums, with songs like the electro-pop "Software," which would have sounded silly even in 1984. Note of interest: "Cain's Blood" became a minor hit in 1995 for country vocal quartet 4 Runner.

worth searching for: Johnson had nine charting singles for RCA between 1985 and 1988. His two #1 songs, "Give Me Wings" and the exquisitely romantic "The Moon Is Still over Her Shoulder," appear on *Wings* (RCA, 1986, prod. Brent Maher) ♪♪♪, which has yet to be issued on CD.

influences:

◀◀ James Taylor

▶▶ Billy Dean, David Wilcox

Brian Mansfield

JOHNSON MOUNTAIN BOYS

Formed 1978, in Washington, DC, area. Disbanded 1995.

Dudley Connell, guitar, vocals; David McLaughlin, mandolin, vocals; Tom Adams, banjo, vocals; Eddie Stubbs, fiddle, vocals; Richard Underwood, banjo, vocals; Larry Robbins, bass; Marshall Willborn, bass; Ed Ferris, bass; Earl Yager, bass; others.

Guitarist Dudley Connell formed this hard-driving traditional bluegrass band and, with the 1978 release of its debut single on Copper Creek, the Johnson Mountain Boys became an instant success on the D.C. bluegrass circuit. The group quickly widened its fan base once its Rounder debut came out in 1981. Four superb albums followed during the next five years, with the group touring the U.S. extensively, even playing the Grand Ole Opry. It's of great interest, to Opry fans especially, to note that the band's exemplary fiddle player is WSM/Grand Ole Opry announcer Eddie "Deep Catalog" Stubbs, who's not only one of the finest fiddlers you'll ever hear, but one of old-time and bluegrass music's best friends. Stubbs' radio shows are loaded with lovingly chosen old songs from classic performers. In 1988 the JMB (as many fans are likely to refer to them) decided to retire, but instead merely scaled down their performance schedule, and shifted personnel slightly. Their 1993 album was highly praised, but would also be their last studio recording (at this point, anyway). The Boys finally went their separate ways in 1995, following the release of a live album.

what to buy: *Blue Diamond* (Rounder, 1993, prod. Ken Irwin, Ronnie Freeland, Johnson Mountain Boys) ♪♪♪♪ features "Duncan and Brady," along with several other great tunes. It's a real treat, when you consider the band had been close to breaking up by this point. (And, since they now have, it's an even more essential purchase!)

what to buy next: *Favorites* (Rounder, 1987, prod. various) ♪♪♪♪ is another great mix of JMB-brand bluegrass.

the rest:

Let the Whole World Talk (Rounder, 1987) ♪♪♪♪
Requests (Rounder, 1988) ♪♪♪♪
At the Old Schoolhouse (Rounder, 1989) ♪♪♪♪
Live at the Birchmere (Rounder, 1994) ♪♪♪♪

influences:

◀◀ Bill Monroe, Warrior River Boys

▶▶ Del McCoury Band

Stephen L. Betts

JOLENE

Formed 1994, in NC.

John Crooke, guitar, vocals, banjo; Mike Mitschele, bass, vocals; Dave Burris, guitar, vocals, mandolin; Bill Ladd, pedal steel guitar; Mike Kenerly, drums.

Born of the Southeast indie-rock scene and named after Dolly Parton's famous arch rival, this band of North Carolinians are what the Lord intended when he invented the term "country rock." Though Jolene would rather be dipped in oil than saddled with that now-meaningless moniker, they will admit that their music is inspired by a mixture of R.E.M., the Stanley Brothers, Echo & the Bunnymen and Merle Haggard. The result is an thoroughly and haunting impassioned debut album, with equal parts loud swirly guitars, weeping steel and haunting, Southern lyrics. (These guys have obviously read their share of Flannery O'Connor and William Faulkner—one of the members was once in a band called Light in August).

what's available: *Hell's Half Acre* (Ardent, 1995, prod. Jeff Powell) ♫♫♫, the band's full-length debut, doubles as an Enhanced Audio Visual CD and features guest vocals by Kim Richey on the soulful "I Read What You Wrote Today."

worth searching for: Jolene released an earlier EP, *Jolene*, which now is out of print, but if you can find it, by all means snatch it up (if only for their cover of Jimmie Dale Gilmore's "Tonight I Think I'm Going to Go Downtown").

influences:
◀◀ R.E.M., Uncle Tupelo, Jayhawks, Gin Blossoms, Gram Parsons, Bob Woodruff

Cyndi Hoelzle

GEORGE JONES

Born George Glenn Jones, September 12, 1931, in Saratoga, TX.

George Jones—"The Possum"—is one of the few real living legends in country music today. He has been cited as a major influence by just about every popular country singer of the day, from Garth Brooks to Tanya Tucker. Even though he can't compete with most of them for space on the radio these days, Jones' hurtful nasal tones and honest delivery is all over contemporary country music. And they don't call Jones the "Rolls-Royce of country singers" for nothing. Nobody can cry in their beer more pitifully, bemoan the loss of their woman more painfully or put himself down more severely than Jones can. He has pretty much stuck to what works over the 40-plus years

he's been a recording artist, though he has dabbled briefly with rock 'n' roll (he cut "Heartbreak Hotel" as Hank Smith and "Rock It" as Thumper Jones) and has tried his hand at gospel occasionally. But Jones is at his best when he's singing those honky-tonk blues. His ability to convey pain and regret has made him an excellent duet partner, too; the team-up of the Possum and ex-wife Tammy Wynette was the most formidable male-female duo in country, and one of its most colorful. The key to the Texan's success has been his ability to pick material that mirrors his own messy life—three divorces, years of drinking and hard living—though the man who once earned the nickname "No-Show Jones" because of his frequently canceled shows has settled down since the early 1980s, living a relatively clean and uneventful life with current wife Nancy. Now in his mid-60s, Jones keeps on plugging away, with tributes and honors still coming his way, including induction into the Country Music Hall of Fame, a tribute duets album featuring everyone from Alan Jackson to Rolling Stone Keith Richards and a recent reunion with Wynette. Numerous of Jones' songs are considered definitive country, and one of them, "He Stopped Loving Her Today," was voted the #1 country song in a *Country America* magazine reader's poll.

what to buy: Jones has recorded for several labels during the past 40 years, which makes it hard to own the more than five dozen albums he's released since 1955. Compilations are your best bet, but with so many of them, stick to *The Essential George Jones* (Columbia Legacy, 1994, prod. various) ♫♫♫♫. Most of his best known hits are here, along with guest performers like Johnny Paycheck, James Taylor, Melba Montgomery and, of course, Wynette.

what to buy next: *The Best of George Jones* (Rhino, 1991, comp. prod. Bill Inglot) ♫♫♫ covers top hits between 1955 ("Why Baby Why") and the late 1960s, before Jones dumped producer Pappy Daily for the broader palette of Billy Sherrill and the wider distribution of Epic Records. *The Bradley Barn Sessions* (MCA, 1994, prod. Brian Ahern) ♫♫♫ is a loving tribute to the man, with a diverse array of roots country and rock people contributing to this upbeat, loving collection of modern remakes of some of his greatest songs.

what to avoid: Several of Jones' early recordings are out of print, though some have been saved by reissue labels like Razor & Tie and Hollywood/Rounder. Still, there's a lot of bad hits packages and compilations out there that conform to the same formula: throw a couple of widely known hits in with a bunch of average or mediocre stuff and call it a hits album.

George Jones (© Ken Settle)

Among them: *Greatest Country Hits* (Curb, 1990) 🎵🎵; *All-Time Greatest Hits* (Liberty, 1994) 🎵🎵; *Golden Hits* (Hollywood/Rounder, 1965) 🎵🎵; *Party Pickin'* (Hollywood/Rounder, 1967) 🎵🎵; *14 Greats* (Hollywood/Rounder, 1992) 🎵🎵; and *Greatest Hits, Volume 2* (Hollywood/Rounder, 1966) 🎵🎵. Some of his thematic albums don't fare much better, such as the gospel records *Homecoming in Heaven* (Razor & Tie, 1962, prod. Pappy Daily) 🎵🎵 and *24 Gospel Greats* (Deluxe, 1993, prod. various) 🎵🎵, or the salute *George Jones Sings Bob Wills* (Razor & Tie, 1963, prod. Pappy Daily) 🎵🎵.

the rest:

The New Favorites of George Jones (Liberty, 1962) 🎵🎵🎵
George Jones Sings the Hits of His Country Cousins (Razor & Tie, 1962) 🎵🎵
George Sings Like the Dickens! (Razor & Tie, 1963) 🎵🎵🎵
My Favorites of Hank Williams (Liberty, 1963) 🎵🎵🎵
The Race Is On (Razor & Tie, 1965) 🎵🎵🎵
At His Best (Hollywood/Rounder, 1967) 🎵🎵
Life Turned Her That Way (Hollywood/Rounder, 1967) 🎵🎵🎵

(With Tammy Wynette) *We Love to Sing about Jesus* (Epic, 1972) 🎵🎵🎵
George Jones Sings the Great Songs of Leon Payne (Hollywood/Rounder, 1973) 🎵🎵🎵
The Grand Tour (Razor & Tie, 1973) 🎵🎵🎵🎵
(With Wynette) *Golden Ring* (Razor & Tie, 1976) 🎵🎵🎵🎵
(With Wynette) *Greatest Hits* (Epic, 1977) 🎵🎵🎵🎵
All-Time Greatest Hits, Volume 1 (Epic, 1977) 🎵🎵🎵
Bartender's Blues (Razor & Tie, 1978) 🎵🎵🎵
My Very Special Guests (Columbia/Legacy, 1979) 🎵🎵🎵
I Am What I Am (Epic, 1980) 🎵🎵🎵🎵
(With Johnny Paycheck) *Double Trouble* (Razor & Tie, 1980) 🎵🎵🎵
(With Wynette) *Together Again* (Razor & Tie, 1980) 🎵🎵🎵
(With Wynette) *Encore: George Jones & Tammy Wynette* (Epic, 1981) 🎵🎵🎵
Still the Same Old Me (Epic, 1981) 🎵🎵🎵
Anniversary—Ten Years of Hits (Epic, 1982) 🎵🎵🎵
Who's Gonna Fill Their Shoes (Epic, 1984) 🎵🎵🎵
By Request (Epic, 1984) 🎵🎵🎵
George Jones Salutes Hank Williams (Polydor, 1984) 🎵🎵🎵
Wine-Colored Roses (Epic, 1986) 🎵🎵
Super Hits (Epic, 1987) 🎵🎵🎵
I'm a One-Woman Man (Epic, 1988) 🎵🎵🎵
First Time Live (Epic, 1989) 🎵
You Oughta Be Here (Epic, 1990) 🎵🎵🎵
Hallelujah Weekend (Columbia, 1990) 🎵🎵
And Along Came Jones (MCA, 1991) 🎵🎵🎵
20 Greatest Hits (Deluxe, 1991) 🎵🎵🎵
Friends in High Places (Epic, 1991) 🎵🎵🎵
Walls Can Fall (MCA, 1992) 🎵🎵🎵
(With Wynette) *George & Tammy's Greatest Hits, Volume 2* (Epic, 1992) 🎵🎵🎵🎵
High-Tech Redneck (MCA, 1993) 🎵🎵🎵
Super Hits Volume 2 (Epic, 1993) 🎵🎵🎵
(With Melba Montgomery) *Vintage Collections* (Capitol/EMI, 1993) 🎵🎵🎵
A Cup of Loneliness (Mercury, 1994) 🎵🎵🎵
(With Wynette) *The President & The First Lady* (TeeVee, 1995) 🎵🎵🎵
(With Wynette) *One* (MCA, 1995) 🎵🎵🎵
(With Wynette) *Super Hits* (Epic, 1995) 🎵🎵🎵
I Lived to Tell It All (MCA, 1996) 🎵🎵🎵
She Thinks I Still Care: The George Jones Collection (Razor & Tie, 1997) 🎵🎵🎵🎵🎵

worth searching for: *Ladies' Choice* (Epic, 1984, prod. Billy Sherrill) 🎵🎵🎵 teamed the duet master with a formidable (in its day) cast of partners that included Loretta Lynn, Barbara Mandrell, Emmylou Harris and Lacy J. Dalton. It's currently available only as an import.

influences:

◀◀ Lefty Frizzell, Hank Williams, Roy Acuff

▶▶ Garth Brooks, Alan Jackson, Randy Travis, Mark Chesnutt, Vern Gosdin, Sammy Kershaw

Doug Pullen

SCOTT JOSS

Born May 1, 1962, in Santa Monica, CA.

Scott Joss is a multi-talented instrumentalist discovered by Tiny Moore, mandolin player with Bob Wills & His Texas Playboys. At 17 Joss joined Merle Haggard & the Strangers on tour, and has since toured several times with Dwight Yoakam. While he's best known as a fiddler, Joss is an accomplished mandolin and rhythm guitar player as well.

what's available: Joss' debut *Souvenirs* (Little Dog, 1996, prod. Pete Anderson, Dusty Wakeman) ♫♫♫♪ features mainstream country reminiscent of John Anderson's best work of the 1980s, combined with some brilliant, quirky touches, typical of a Pete Anderson production. A strong follow-up could establish Joss as a solid country act to be reckoned with.

influences:

◀◀ Merle Haggard, John Anderson, Dwight Yoakam

Stephen L. Betts

CLEDUS "T." JUDD

Born in Crowe Springs, GA.

Think of parodist Cledus "T." Judd as a white-trash version of "Weird" Al Yankovic. Or perhaps as the anti-Shania (Twain), since his video for "If Shania Was Mine," a parody of her "Any Man of Mine," gave him more notoriety than he ever could have imagined. He is destined to spend eternity in the land of the Morning Zoo radio shows.

what's available: A little of Judd goes a long way—and there's quite a bit of him. Figure about two good laughs every three songs, but Judd's squalling voice makes listening to more than two songs at a sitting difficult. *Cledus "T." Judd (No Relation)* (Razor & Tie, 1995, prod. Cledus "T." Judd) ♫♪ has parodies of "Gone Country" ("Gone Funky") and Tim McGraw's "Indian Outlaw" (the equally offensive "Indian In-Laws"). His second—believe it or not—album, *I Stoled This Record* (Razor & Tie, 1996, prod. Cledus "T." Judd) ♫♪, contains "If Shania Was Mine," two

other Shania Twain spoofs and "(She's Got a Butt) Bigger than the Beatles," a parody of Joe Diffie's "Bigger than the Beatles."

influences:

◀◀ "Weird" Al Yankovic, Ray Stevens

Brian Mansfield

WYNONNA JUDD
See: Wynonna

THE JUDDS
Mother-daughter vocal duo from Ashland, KY.

Naomi Judd (born Diana Ellen Judd, January 11, 1946, in Ashland, KY); Wynonna Judd (born Christina Claire Ciminella, May 30, 1964, in Ashland, KY).

One of the most successful musical duos of all time, the Judds made their way to the top of the charts with a combination of talent, determination and a batch of songs that, for the most part, harken back to a simpler time when love was true and families prayed together—and stayed together. That this all occurred during the Reagan years hardly seems coincidental. And not to get moralistic about it, but for the Judds—whose lives have hardly been modeled on *The Donna Reed Show*— this seems as hypocritical as the political tenor of the times. Still, such concerns can't detract that much from their music: acoustic-based folk/country, often with a bluesy touch, deftly produced by Brent Maher, who flouted Nashville convention by avoiding smothering choruses and washes of strings. With Wynonna's force-of-nature voice out front and Naomi often providing harmonies, the duo is tough to top. The endless tour that accompanied Naomi's retirement due to chronic hepatitis (if she was that sick, how could she stay on the road so long?) left a bad taste in the mouth, but a quick spin of one of their hits collections cures that. After all, as the Judds and Ronald Reagan amply proved, phony nostalgia can be a powerful thing.

what to buy: Nothing wrong with sticking with the hits, and *Greatest Hits* (Curb/RCA, 1988, prod. Brent Maher) ♫♫♫♫ has got 'em in abundance—"Why Not Me," "Mama He's Crazy," "Girls' Night Out," "Love Is Alive" and others. The set also includes one previously unreleased track, "Give a Little Love." *Greatest Hits Volume Two* (Curb/RCA, 1991, prod. Brent Maher) ♫♫♫♫ picks things up from there, featuring "I Know Where I'm Going," "Maybe Your Baby's Got the Blue" and the career summation "Love Can Build a Bridge." Fans with deep pockets may want to spring for the three-disc boxed set *The Judds Collection 1983–1990* (Curb/RCA, 1992, prod. Brent Maher) 𝄞𝄞𝄞𝄞, which contains the hits on two CDs and adds a live-in-the-studio disc of outtakes later released in a different configuration as *Live Studio Sessions*.

what to buy next: Dealing almost exclusively with love and the lack of it, *River of Time* (RCA, 1989, prod. Brent Maher) 𝄞𝄞𝄞𝄞 comes across almost as a concept album. Highlights include the bluesy opener "One-Man Woman," the Dixified "Not My Baby" and the rockabilly raveup "Let Me Tell You about Love." Dire Straits' Mark Knopfler sits in on the Judds version of his song "Water of Love." The theme continues on the duo's final album, *Love Can Build a Bridge* (RCA, 1990, prod. Brent Maher) 𝄞𝄞𝄞𝄞, which includes the momentous title track, plus the spirited "Born to Be Blue" and "Rompin' Stompin' Blues," whose scorching slide guitar lead comes courtesy of guest Bonnie Raitt.

what to avoid: Don't give yourself the gift of *Christmas Time with the Judds & Alabama* (RCA, 1994) 𝄞𝄞, which is cobbled together from the groups' separately released holiday albums.

the rest:
The Judds—Wynonna & Naomi (Curb/RCA, 1984) 𝄞𝄞𝄞
Why Not Me (Curb/RCA, 1984) 𝄞𝄞𝄞𝄞
Rockin' with the Rhythm (Curb/RCA, 1985) 𝄞𝄞𝄞
Heart Land (Curb/RCA, 1987) 𝄞𝄞
Christmas Time with the Judds (Curb/RCA, 1987) 𝄞𝄞𝄞
Collector's Series (Curb/RCA, 1990) 𝄞𝄞𝄞
Reflections (RCA, 1991) 𝄞𝄞𝄞𝄞
Talk about Love (RCA, 1993) 𝄞𝄞𝄞
This Country's Rockin' (RCA, 1993) 𝄞𝄞𝄞𝄞
Girls' Night Out: The Essential Collection of #1 Hits (Curb/RCA, 1994) 𝄞𝄞𝄞𝄞
Live Studio Sessions (RCA, 1994) 𝄞𝄞𝄞𝄞
The Essential Judds (RCA, 1995) 𝄞𝄞𝄞𝄞

worth searching for: The promotion-only sampler *Judd Music* (RCA, 1992, prod. Brent Maher) 𝄞𝄞𝄞𝄞 offers a 15-song taste of the boxed set.

influences:
◀◀ Bonnie Raitt, Elvis Presley
▶▶ Wynonna, Sweethearts of the Rodeo

see also: *Wynonna*

Daniel Durchholz

KATHY KALLICK

Born September 19, 1952, in Chicago, IL.

Singer/songwriter Kathy Kallick first made a name for herself in 1975 as a co-founder of the Bay area bluegrass band the Good Ol' Persons. Originally comprised of five women (including Laurie Lewis) the band incorporated swing, Latin and folk music into their bluegrass sound. Kallick released a solo children's album in 1987 and has since released one children's and two "adult" albums.

what to buy: *Use a Napkin (Not Your Mom)* (Sugar Hill, 1995, prod. Alan Senauke, Kathy Kallick) 𝄞𝄞𝄞𝄞 is considered by many to be among the best children's album in recent years. It mixes old-timey country/bluegrass songs with elements of jazz, swing and zydeco. It contains great originals like the title song, as well as traditional numbers ("Liza Jane") and historic pieces ("Did You See Jackie Robinson Hit That Ball?").

what to buy next: *Matters of the Heart* (Sugar Hill, 1993, prod. Todd Phillips) 𝄞𝄞𝄞𝄞, Kallick's first solo album, was a bit of a change of pace from her music with the Good Ol' Persons. The 13 original songs are played on bluegrass instruments plus drums and/or percussion. Piano and accordion appear in spots. Jazz progressions and a rock beat make this something other than a bluegrass album.

the rest:
What Do You Dream About? (Sugar Hill, 1990/1997) 𝄞𝄞𝄞𝄞
(With Laurie Lewis) *Together* (Rounder, 1991/1995) 𝄞𝄞𝄞𝄞
Call Me a Taxi (Sugar Hill, 1996) 𝄞𝄞𝄞𝄞

influences:
◀◀ Good Ol' Persons, Doc Watson
▶▶ Laurie Lewis, Sally Van Meter

Douglas Fulmer

KIERAN KANE
/THE O'KANES
/JAMIE O'HARA

Born October 7, 1949, in Queens, NY. O'Kanes formed 1986, in Nashville, TN. Disbanded 1990.

Kieran Kane began his musical career as a rock 'n' roll drummer at age nine. He also worked as a Los Angeles session musician before moving to Nashville in 1979 and making a name for himself as a writer of songs for Alabama and other acts. Kane recorded for Elektra and Warner Bros. during the early 1980s, reaching the Top 20 six times with songs like "You're the Best" and "It's Who You Love." In 1986 he and songwriting partner Jamie O'Hara (born August 8, 1950, in Toledo, OH) formed the O'Kanes and recorded three albums for Columbia. The O'Kanes disbanded in 1990, and Kane began recording on his own. He started an artists' co-operative independent label, Dead Reckoning, in 1994 with Kevin Welch, Harry Stinson and Tammy Rogers and has become one of the leading voices of independent music in Nashville.

what's available: *Dead Reckoning* (Dead Reckoning, 1995, prod. Harry Stinson, Kieran Kane) ♫♫♫ was a ground-breaking album because it was one of the first Nashville albums produced by an artist-run independent label. Since Kane was working on his own terms, this is a stripped-down affair (even more so than his other records), with songs that may take a while to get under the skin but stay there longer. The instrumentals center around Kane on guitar, drummer Harry Stinson and fiddler Tammy Rogers (all co-owners of the label). Guitarist Mike Henderson brings his blues bite in on three cuts, including a cover of Buck Owens' "Love's Gonna Live Here." Emmylou Harris and Lucinda Williams contribute harmonies to "This Dirty Little Town."

worth searching for: The O'Kanes had only a half-dozen hits (and one #1, "Can't Stop My Heart from Loving You") in their four years together; the acts' influence has outstripped its success. *The O'Kanes* (Columbia, 1987, prod. Kieran Kane, Jamie O'Hara) ♫♫♫ has the lion's share of the hits. Jamie O'Hara's *Rise Above It* (RCA, 1994, prod. Garth Fundis) ♫♫♫♫ is a wonderfully moody solo album by Kane's former singing and songwriting partner. *Find My Way Home* (Atlantic, 1994) ♫♫♫♫ is Kane's first solo album after the breakup of the O'Kanes.

influences:

◀◀ Foster & Lloyd, John Prine

▶▶ Kevin Welch, Lucinda Williams

Brian Mansfield

ROBERT EARL KEEN JR.

Born January 11, 1956, in Houston, TX.

Less weirdly fascinating than his old Texas college buddy Lyle Lovett, this singer/songwriter has penned a handful of the best (and unfortunately unknown) country songs of the past decade. He's friendly and straightforward and brags about his love of old-fashioned Texas hats, food and style. His songs occasionally match his personality, especially when he weighs in on funny, dysfunctional Christmas tales and (of course) barbecue. But more frequently they're dark outlaw story-songs about men who've snapped or hard-luck couples wavering between a serene future or becoming Bonnie and Clyde. Among his Austin peers, Keen's writing commands respect; Joe Ely did a great rock 'n' roll version of "The Road Goes on Forever" (later recorded by the Highwaymen) and Lovett continues to perform "This Old Porch," which he co-wrote with Keen during their Texas A&M days.

what to buy: Many of the characters on *A Bigger Piece of Sky* (Sugar Hill, 1993, prod. Garry Velletri) ♫♫♫♫ are as hopeless as those on Bruce Springsteen's *Nebraska*, but they have a distinctly Texas edge, such as the frustrated narrator who wants to blow you away or the stud with the trunkful of Pearl beer.

what to buy next: *West Textures* (Sugar Hill, 1989, prod. Jim Rooney) ♫♫♫♫ is an early portrait of the still-developing artist; "The Road Goes on Forever" is a classic story song, and there's some great youthful energy in the rock songs, but it's a little cluttered and filled with clunky phrases. *Gringo Honeymoon* (Sugar Hill, 1994, prod. Garry Velletri) ♫♫♫ contains Keen's live romp "Barbecue," but it doesn't quite have the focused power of *Bigger Piece of Sky*.

what to avoid: *No. 2 Live Dinner* (Sugar Hill, 1996, prod. Lloyd Maines) ♫♫♫ is an interesting but not particularly meaty album that serves as a holding pattern until Keen can go back to the studio.

the rest:

No Kinda Dancer (Philo/Rounder, 1984) ♫♫♫
The Live Album (Sugar Hill, 1988) ♫♫♫
Picnic (Arista Austin, 1997) ♫♫♫♫

worth searching for: The two great cover versions of "The Road Goes on Forever" are on Joe Ely's *Love and Danger* (MCA, 1992, prod. Tony Brown, Joe Ely) ♫♫♫♫ and the Highwaymen's *The Road Goes on Forever* (Liberty, 1995, prod. Don Was) ♫♫♫.

influences:

◀◀ Lyle Lovett, Joe Ely, Townes Van Zandt, Johnny Cash, Waylon Jennings

▶▶ Richard Buckner, Billy Ray Cyrus, Bottle Rockets, Tracy Byrd

Steve Knopper

Toby Keith (© Ken Settle)

TOBY KEITH

Born Toby Keith Covel, July 8, 1961, in Clinton, OK.

Though Toby Keith looks like a natural-born honky-tonker—he's a 6-foot-4-inch former oil-field worker, rodeo hand and semi-pro football player—his music often sounds more like ruggedly romantic pop than two-steppin' country. Keith came out of the Texas-Oklahoma dancehall circuit and tapped into Western fantasy with his first hit, 1993's "Should've Been a Cowboy." Subsequent hits show him at his most successful as the sympathetic romantic of mid-tempo songs like "He Ain't Worth Missing" and "Who's That Man."

what to buy: *Boomtown* (Polydor, prod. Harold Shedd, Nelson Larkin) 𝄞𝄞𝄞 wasn't quite as successful as Keith's first album when it came to hit singles, but with songs like "Boomtown," in which a young man watched his town close up around him, Keith's writing definitely matured. And it was no slouch in the singles department, either, with "Who's That Man," "Upstairs Downtown" and "You Ain't Much Fun" all making the Top 10.

what to buy next: *Blue Moon* (Polydor, 1996, prod. Nelson

Larkin, Toby Keith) 𝄞𝄞𝄞 got overlooked since Keith's label changed its name and then went out of business during the months following its release (it can now be found on Mercury), but it's a solid album that yielded a hit ballad, "Does That Blue Moon Ever Shine on You," which Keith wrote before he made his first record.

the rest:
Toby Keith (Mercury, 1993) 𝄞𝄞𝄞
Christmas to Christmas (Polydor, 1995) 𝄞𝄞𝄞

influences:
◀◀ Hank Williams Jr., John Conlee
▶▶ John Berry, BlackHawk

Brian Mansfield

THE KENDALLS

Father-daughter duo from St. Louis, MO.

Royce Kendall (born September 25, 1934, in AR); Jeannie Kendall (born November 30, 1954, in St. Louis, MO).

When it comes to discussions about great cheating songs, there's always room in the conversation for the Kendalls, who made a career of such songs during the 1970s and 1980s. With songs like "Heaven's Just a Sin Away," "It Don't Feel Like Sinnin' to Me" and "You'd Make an Angel Want to Cheat," the Kendalls—who, unlike most male-female duos, were father and daughter—made some of the best traditional-sounding country records of the era. Royce Kendall had originally sung in a brother duo called the Austin Brothers before giving up music to run a beauty shop with his wife in St. Louis, Missouri. As his daughter Jeannie grew up, the pair began singing together and eventually were encouraged to make a record. An early cover of John Denver's "Leaving on a Jet Plane" did well enough to gain interest in Nashville. After a few singles with Dot, the Kendalls wound up on Ovation, where they had their first #1 in 1977 with "Heaven's Just a Sin Away." The single won the Kendalls a Country Music Association Award and a Grammy and even made the pop singles chart. Future singles played on similar themes—"The Pittsburgh Stealers," "Sweet Desire," a cover of Dolly Parton's "Put It Off until Tomorrow"—and continued to feature Jeannie's angelic voice. The group later had singles with Mercury, MCA/Curb, Step One and Epic, but the hits slowed considerably after the duo left Ovation and cheating songs went out of style.

what to buy: *20 Greatest Hits* (Deluxe, 1986) 𝄞𝄞𝄞𝄞 doesn't actually have that many hits (more like 14), but it does contain the Kendalls' best records—"Heaven's Just a Sin Away," "Pittsburgh Stealers" and a lesser-known 1979 love song called "Just Like Real People" that's nothing short of devastating. Versions of "Leavin' on a Jet Plane" and "You've Lost That Lovin' Feelin'" show the duo's pop influences, which come through more subtly on the hits. It's hardly complete, but *20 Greatest Hits* is still an impressive collection.

what to buy next: The Kendalls' albums from their hit-making days are out of print, but three budget-line collections—*Just Like Real People* (Richmond, 1988) *ƎƎƎ*, *Heaven's Just a Sin Away* (Richmond, 1988) *ƎƎƎ* and *It Don't Feel Like Sinnin'* (Richmond, 1988) *ƎƎƎ*—go deeper into those original recordings, using a couple of big hits as teasers.

what to avoid: Almost all of the Kendalls albums have something to recommend them, though many of their recent albums are little more than remakes of their classic singles. *So Many Hits It's Sinful* (American Harvest, 1996) *ƎƎƎ* is a release of re-rerecordings made during the late 1980s. *Heaven's Just a Sin Away* (Kingfisher, 1996) *ƎƎƎ* is a similar collection licensed from Sony/ATV Music Publishing; they're not the originals, but the sound's pretty good.

the rest:

Best Country Duo—1978 Grammy Award Winners (Hollywood, 1987) *ƎƎƎ*

Break the Routine (Step One, 1987) *ƎƎ*

Make a Dance (Lonesome Dove, 1994) *ƎƎƎ*

Best of the Kendalls (Curb, 1994) *ƎƎƎ*

worth searching for: The Kendalls' days with Mercury are poorly documented now, but they included some good material, including the 1984 #1 "Thank God for the Radio" (later covered by Alan Jackson). *Thank God for the Radio . . . and All the Hits* (Mercury, 1985) *ƎƎƎ* contains that song plus "Dark End of the Street," an R&B cheating classic so great you knew the Kendalls would get around to singing it some day.

influences:

◀◀ Porter Wagoner & Dolly Parton, Conway Twitty & Loretta Lynn

▶▶ Judds

Brian Mansfield

THE KENTUCKY COLONELS

Formed 1958 as the Country Boys; became the Kentucky Colonels in 1963. Disbanded 1965.

Roland White, mandolin, banjo, vocals (1958–65); Clarence White, guitar, vocals (1958–65); Eric White, bass (1958–1961); Billy Ray Lathum, banjo (1958–65); LeRoy Mack, dobro (1959–65); Roger Bush, bass (1961–65); Bobby Sloane, fiddle (1963–65); Scott Stoneman, fiddle (1965).

One of the most storied bluegrass bands of all time, the Kentucky Colonels were build around three brothers, Roland, Clarence and Eric White, who were born in Maine and raised in Los Angeles. With an average age of 18, the young group became a fixture on local L.A. television shows *Town Hall Party* and *Hometown Jamboree*. They also recorded four tracks on an Andy Williams album on Capitol and appeared on his television show. After changing their name in 1963 to avoid confusion with Mac Wiseman's band, the Colonels recorded their first album for Briar Records. During this time they made their name as regular performers at L.A.'s famed Ash Grove folk club and benefited from folk music's then soaring popularity. Traditional songs like "Shady Grove" and "Sally Ann" and gospel numbers like "A Beautiful Life" made up the bulk of the group's repertoire. The years 1964–65 were the band's peak period; they appeared at folk clubs and bluegrass festivals all over the U.S. and Canada. In 1964 they recorded their best known album, *Appalachian Swing!* for the World Pacific label. Creative differences (primarily over electrification of the band's instruments), exacerbated by the onslaught of the Beatles, forced the group to break up in 1965. Several different pickup bands continued to use the name Kentucky Colonels through 1967. There were several reunions during the early 1970s but no serious reconciliation ever took place. After the Colonels, Roland White moved on, first to Bill Monroe's band in 1967, and two years later to Lester Flatt's band. Today he plays with the Nashville Bluegrass Band and records solo for Sugar Hill Records. Lathum played with the Dillards throughout the 1970s before retiring. Bush became a mainstay in the group Country Gazette before he, too, retired.

The Colonels' greatest claim to fame lies in the brilliant guitar-work of Clarence White, who left to join the Byrds in 1968. During the early 1970s White also became a much-sought-after sessionman contributing to a myriad of recordings, including Arlo Guthrie's *Last of the Brooklyn Cowboys*, Jackson Browne's *Late for the Sky* and Randy Newman's *12 Songs*. Unfortunately, White was killed by a drunk driver in 1973 while loading out of a club.

what to buy: The Colonels' finest hour, the instrumental *Appalachian Swing!* (Rounder, 1964/1993, prod. Richard Bock, Ed Pearl) *ƎƎƎƎ* showcases Clarence White's increasingly inventive guitarwork, which, while not always bluegrass, was always astonishing. The group's versions of "I Am a Pilgrim," "Nine Pound Hammer" and "Sally Goodin" are near-definitive.

what to buy next: *Long Journey Home* (Vanguard, 1991, prod. Mary Katherine Aldin) 🎸🎸🎸🎸 is a live recording of the group's high water mark: their 1964 appearance at the Newport Folk Festival. Especially wonderful are four duets featuring Clarence White and Doc Watson.

the rest:

Livin' in the Past (Briar, 1975/Sierra, 1997) 🎸🎸🎸
1965–67 w. R. & C. White (Rounder, 1976) 🎸🎸🎸
The Kentucky Colonels Featuring Clarence White (Rounder, 1980) 🎸🎸🎸
On Stage (Rounder, 1984) 🎸🎸🎸

solo outings:
Roland White:
Trying to Get to You (Sugar Hill, 1994) 🎸🎸🎸

influences:

◀◀ Bill Monroe & His Blue Grass Boys, Doc Watson
▶▶ Nashville Bluegrass Band, Hot Rize

Robert Baird

THE KENTUCKY HEADHUNTERS /BROTHER PHELPS

Formed 1986, in Metcalfe County, KY.

Richard Young, guitar; Fred Young, drums; Greg Martin, guitar; Doug Phelps, bass, vocals (1986–92, 1996–present); Ricky Lee Phelps, vocals (1986–92); Anthony Kennedy, vocals (1992–present); Mark Orr, vocals (1992–96).

With apologies to Donny and Marie, the Kentucky HeadHunters are a little bit country, a little bit rock 'n' blues. A ragtag group of hillbillies that, in one form or another, have been playing together for nearly three decades, the HeadHunters set Nashville on its ear with their debut album, *Pickin' on Nashville*, which shot to platinum status and won a passel of awards. The combination of country-leaning vocals, a swinging blues-rock beat, and Greg Martin's fluid lead guitar is darn near irresistible. And the group's taste in covers—everything from Bill Monroe to the Beatles to "The Ballad of Davy Crockett"—is eclectic in the extreme. After the success of their debut, the HeadHunters took a more rock-oriented approach, which alienated a good portion of their fans. Apparently Doug and Rickie Lee Phelps agreed; they left the band to form the more conventional country Brother Phelps in 1992; Mark Orr, who had sung with some of

the HeadHunters In an early group, took Ricky Lee's place as lead singer. Doug Phelps returned to the band as lead vocalist in 1996, and the group signed to BNA Records.

what to buy: From the very first track, which steamrollers Bill Monroe's "Walk Softly On This Heart of Mine," you can tell that *Pickin' on Nashville* (Mercury, 1989, prod. Kentucky Head-Hunters) 🎸🎸🎸🎸 is something new under the sun. "Dumas Walker" revels in redneck fun and slawburgers, and "Rag Top" rocks like nobody's business. Meanwhile, "Skip a Rope" proves the HeadHunters aren't above pickin' and grinnin' with the rest of Nashville. Almost a decade earlier, Alabama had opened the country music's door to a self-contained band of rock-influenced players; *Pickin' on Nashville* blew the door clean off.

what to buy next: *The Best of the Kentucky HeadHunters: Still Pickin'* (Mercury, 1994, prod. Kentucky HeadHunters) 🎸🎸🎸🎸 contains a judicious mix of material from the group's three discs, plus a cover of "Let's Work Together" from the soundtrack of *Harley Davidson and the Marlboro Man* and a previously unreleased version of the Beatles' "You've Got to Hide Your Love Away." Fans who object to the group's blues/rock-leaning direction are advised to stick with *Pickin' on Nashville*. Brother Phelps' debut can't top the HeadHunters at their best, but for those who miss that band's more country-leaning direction, *Let Go* (Asylum, 1993, prod. Ricky Lee Phelps, Doug Phelps) 🎸🎸🎸🎸 will have to do. It features the Top 10 title track and such songs as the boot-scootin' "Hot Water" and the Buddy Holly-inspired "Four Leaf Clover."

the rest:
Electric Barnyard (Mercury, 1991) 🎸🎸🎸
Rave On!! (Mercury, 1993) 🎸🎸🎸
(Brother Phelps) *Any Way the Wind Blows* (Asylum, 1995) 🎸🎸🎸
Stompin' Grounds (BNA, 1997) 🎸🎸🎸

worth searching for: *Johnnie Johnson & the Kentucky Head-Hunters* (Elektra Nonesuch American Explorer Series, 1993) 🎸🎸🎸🎸, a collaborative effort with the legendary pianist who co-wrote (uncredited) the many Chuck Berry hits that are the very foundation of rock 'n' roll, offers a rollicking good time, especially on the instrumental "Johnnie's Breakdown" and "That'll Work," on which the usually microphone-shy Johnson sings the lead vocal.

Greg Martin of the Kentucky HeadHunters **(© Ken Settle)**

Sammy Kershaw (© Ken Settle)

influences:
◀◀ Alabama, Lynyrd Skynyrd, Albert King
▶▶ Pirates of the Mississippi, Big House, Confederate Railroad

Daniel Durchholz

DAVID KERSH

Born Charles David Kersh, December 9, 1970, in Houston, TX.

One of many young singers to come out of the Texas dancehall circuit during the late 1980s and 1990s, David Kersh has the distinction of being one of the first major country singers to be directly influenced by hearing Garth Brooks' records during his teen years. Kersh's father was a musician as well and once played in a band with Rodney Crowell.

what's available: *Goodnight Sweetheart* (Curb, 1996, prod. Pat McMakin) ♪♪♪ has all the high-energy honky-tonk you'd expect from a young hatted singer, with the guitars cranked up higher than usual. But Kersh also has a way with a ballad, as evidenced by his 1996 Top 10 hit, "Goodnight Sweetheart."

influences:
◀◀ George Strait, Garth Brooks

Brian Mansfield

DOUG KERSHAW /RUSTY & DOUG

Born January 24, 1936, in Tiel Ridge, LA.

With his fancy fiddling and on-stage flamboyance, Doug Kershaw was the first major artist to expose Cajun music to a wide audience that included long-haired college students as well as mainstream country fans. In 1948 Doug and his younger brothers Rusty (born February 2, 1938, in Tiel Ridge, LA) and Pee Wee became part of the Continental Playboys, and in 1953 they hosted their own regional TV show. Rusty & Doug had their first hit record in 1955 with "So Lovely Baby," and in 1957 they cracked the charts again with "Love Me to Pieces." Their watershed year was 1961, when Doug's composition "Louisiana Man" exploded onto the regional and national charts. To this day, the song remains a Cajun and country standard. The duo split up in 1964, and Doug recorded a few mildly interesting albums for Warner Bros.

what to buy: *The Best of Doug Kershaw & Rusty Kershaw* (Curb, 1991) ♪♪♪♪ comes from the recordings the duo made for Roy Acuff's Hickory label during the 1950s and 1960s. The album contains the hit versions of "Louisiana Man" and "Diggy Liggy Lo," which Doug Kershaw would re-record throughout his career. There are also versions of Hank Williams' "Kaw-Liga" and "Why Don't You Love Me" that the sparse instrumentation, sibling harmonies and heavy slapback turn into an odd Cajun hillbilly rock. Strangely, it doesn't contain two of the duet's biggest hits from that time, "So Lovely, Baby" and "Love Me to Pieces," but it's still a heck of a lot of fun.

what to buy next: *The Best of Doug Kershaw* (Warner Bros., 1989, prod. various) ♪♪♪♪ contains versions of Doug's breakthrough hits from the 1960s, including "Louisiana Man" and "Diggy Diggy Lo," as well as spicy remakes of Hank Williams' "Jambalaya (On the Bayou)" and Fats Domino's "I'm Walkin'."

the rest:
The Cajun Way (Warner Bros., 1969) ♪♪♪
Alive & Pickin' (Warner Bros., 1975) ♪♪♪
The Louisiana Man (Warner Bros., 1978) ♪♪♪
(With Rusty Kershaw) *Now and Then* (Domino, 1992) ♪♪

worth searching for: *The Ragin' Cajun* (Warner Bros., 1976) ♪♪♪ doesn't let up for a second. A great party album.

influences:

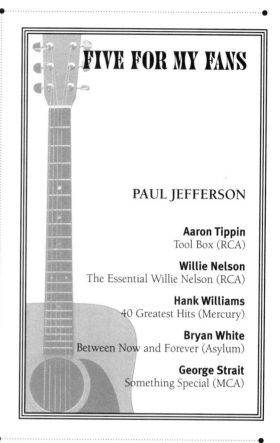

◀◀ Iry LeJeune

▶▶ Charlie Daniels, Beausoleil, Wayne Toups, Zachary Richard

Rick Petreycik and Brian Mansfield

SAMMY KERSHAW

Born February 24, 1958, in Kaplan, LA.

Born into a poor family in rural Louisiana, Kershaw became a roadie at age 12 after his father died. Later, he started performing regionally, even opening some concerts for singers like George Jones and Mel Street, whose songs and singing style his own work closely recalls. But living the stereotypical hard-drinking honky-tonk life took its toll and Kershaw, his third (and current) marriage on the rocks, chucked his musical ambitions during the late 1980s and took a job as a remodeling supervisor for Wal-Mart. Then his luck and life changed. One of his demo tapes found its way to Mercury Nashville and a label executive invited him to perform a showcase. Kershaw drove all night to Music City, played the show and was offered a recording contract the next day. His son-of-George Jones voice and wise-cracking attitude made him an almost instant hit at country radio with both light-hearted songs and hard-country ballads.

what to buy: On *Haunted Heart* (Mercury, 1993, prod. Buddy Cannon, Norro Wilson) ♪♪♪♪ Kershaw is at his best on both exquisite ballads ("Still Lovin' You," "Cry, Cry Darling," "I Can't Reach Her Anymore") and the up-tempo hit "She Don't Know She's Beautiful," as well as the over-the-top funny "Queen of My Double-Wide Trailer."

what to buy next: A compilation of the biggest hits off Kershaw's first three albums, *The Hits, Chapter 1* (Mercury, 1995, prod. Buddy Cannon, Norro Wilson) ♪♪♪♪ doesn't contain any of his best non-singles, but is still worth having as a one-disc dose of Kershaw's magic.

the rest:

Don't Go Near the Water (Mercury, 1991) ♪♪♪♪
Feelin' Good Train (Mercury, 1994) ♪♪♪♪
Christmas Time's a Comin' (Mercury, 1994) ♪♪♪
Politics, Religion and Her (Mercury, 1996) ♪♪♪

influences:

◀◀ George Jones, Mel Street

Bill Hobbs

FIVE FOR MY FANS

PAUL JEFFERSON

Aaron Tippin
Tool Box (RCA)

Willie Nelson
The Essential Willie Nelson (RCA)

Hank Williams
40 Greatest Hits (Mercury)

Bryan White
Between Now and Forever (Asylum)

George Strait
Something Special (MCA)

HAL KETCHUM

Born April 9, 1953, in Greenwich, NY.

A cabinet maker by trade and a country singer by instinct, Hal Ketchum was thinking more of woodworking than woodshedding when he moved to Gruene, Texas, in 1981. Discovering the richly textured story songs of the late Townes Van Zandt, Butch Hancock and Lyle Lovett inspired Ketchum to concentrate on songwriting, and he eventually caught the attention of composer Pat Alger and producer Jim Rooney, both of whom worked with Nanci Griffith during her Rounder/Philo era. Since moving to Nashville in 1990 and signing with Curb, Ketchum has surrounded himself with a reliable stable of collaborators that include Rooney and co-producer Allen Reynolds to help him stretch out without sacrificing his folk roots. The quavering power of his Lyle Lovett-like voice and the soulful simplicity of his intimate narratives about homeless families and small-town desperation usually prevent his sensitivity from turning into saccharine—even on "Hang in There Superman," his uplifting tribute to actor Christopher Reeve.

what to buy: His major-label debut, *Past the Point of Rescue* (Curb, 1991, prod. Allen Reynolds, Jim Rooney) �������� is a brooding but bracing introduction built around Ketchum's Texas country-folk influences. Such hard-hitting originals as "I Miss My Mary" blend with well-chosen covers of Pat Alger and Hank DeVito's "Small Town Saturday Night," Irish singer Mick Hanly's title track and producer Reynolds' blue-collar anthem "Five O'Clock World" (a 1965 Allen Reynolds hit for the Vogues recently turned into the theme for TV's *Drew Carey Show*) to create a seamless examination of lost love and dashed hopes.

what to buy next: Although it's more polished and pop-oriented than its predecessor, *Sure Love* (Curb, 1992, prod. Allen Reynolds, Jim Rooney) ������ also rocks harder ("Mama Knows the Highway," "Hearts Are Gonna Roll") and features two of his most touching story songs written from a child's point of view: "Daddy's Oldsmobile," about a homeless family living in a car; and "Someplace Far Away," a goldrush-era tale of watching a father's dream literally go up in smoke.

what to avoid: The uptempo tracks, particularly two songs written with Al Anderson ("Tonight We Just Might Fall in Love," "That's What I Get for Losin' You"), help *Every Little Word* (Curb, 1994, prod. Allen Reynolds, Jim Rooney) ����� stand out. But most of the ballads fall short of Ketchum's trademark urgency. And let's hope the cocktail-lounge jazz of "No Easy Road" and pallid blues of "Drive On" are dabblings rather than new directions.

the rest:
Threadbare Alibis (Watermelon, 1989) ������
The Hits (Curb, 1996) ������

worth searching for: The original British pressings of *The Hits* (Curb, 1996, prod. Allen Reynolds, Jim Rooney), a best of collection with three new songs, including "Hang in There Superman," come with a bonus CD of 14 live tracks.

influences:
◀◀ Lyle Lovett, Rodney Crowell, Jonathan Edwards

David Okamoto

KILLBILLY

Formed 1987, in Dallas, TX. Disbanded 1994.

Alan Wooley, vocals, guitar, mandolin; Craig "Niteman" Taylor, vocals, harmonica; Richard Hunter, vocals, bass (1990–94); Michael Schwedler, drums; Steve Lutke, banjo (1993–94); Harris Kirby, guitar; Stephen Trued, banjo; Mark Rubin, string bass; others.

On its face, the idea of "killer hillbilly" music is an appealing one. Take some old traditional bluegrass tunes—the subject matter of which is probably closer to punk rock and heavy metal sensibilities than hardcore devotees of any of the concerned genres would care to admit—and play them as fast and with as much attitude as is humanly possible. When it works, the juxtaposition of genres produces jaw-dropping and often funny results. But when it misses, it misses by a mile. That's the problem encountered by Killbilly, whose first album wasn't played cleanly enough for bluegrass aficionados, and whose metallic k.o. was more perception than reality. They calmed down a little on the follow-up, resulting in a much better album, but still no real interest from an audience. Had the alternative-country revolution happened a decade earlier, they might have had a chance. But it didn't, and the group split up in 1994.

what to buy: A considerable improvement over the group's debut, *Foggy Mountain Anarchy* (Crystal Clear Records, 1994, prod. Sam Berkow, Killbilly) ���� satisfactorily mates the band's bluegrass ambitions and punk rock sensibility. The title "Mountain Dew or Die" is evidence of their sense of humor, but the group can play it straight, too, as they do on "Heaven Is a Small Town" and "Shame the Devil." Unfortunately, their cover of Hüsker Dü's "Hare Krishna" was probably a better idea on paper than it turns out to be in practice.

the rest:
Stranger in this Place (Flying Fish, 1992) ��

worth searching for: *Alive from the City of Hate in the Lone Star State* (self-released, 1989) �� collects live recordings from Ft. Worth and Dallas that feature future Bad Livers leader Mark Rubin on string bass.

influences:
◀◀ Ralph Stanley, Stooges
▶▶ Bad Livers, Old 97's

Daniel Durchholz

ROYAL WADE KIMES

Born March 3, 1951, in AR.

Royal Wade Kimes got a late start in country music, working at his father's sawmill until he was well into his 30s. When he finally did come to Nashville, he wrangled horses at Loretta

Hal Ketchum (© Ken Settle)

Lynn's ranch before getting a break in the business. The break came when he approached Eddy Arnold at a hardware store, and Arnold agreed to listen to his songs. Arnold helped Kimes get a publishing deal and a better job (selling cars). Kimes penned Garth Brooks' "We Bury the Hatchet" and got his record deal when the label executive who had been in charge of marketing Brooks' album got a job running Asylum Records. Kimes is a natural storyteller with bank-robbing relatives from the Ozarks. His music has a strong sense of tradition, and his songs are full of stories and hard virtues. He got his name from Royal Crown Cola and cartoon character Ben Wade.

what's available: Kimes cut his first album, *Royal Wade Kimes* (Asylum, 1996, prod. Michael Clute) *ルルル*, when he was in his 40s. His old-fashioned approach makes this completely out of step with the music of its time, but nobody's ever going to accuse him of being anything but hardcore country.

influences:
◄◄ Ed Bruce, Aaron Tippin

Brian Mansfield

JAMES KING

Born September 9, 1958, in Martinsville, VA.

One of the strongest bluegrass/country music vocalists to emerge from the fertile Virginia soil (he shares his hometown, for instance, with Clinton Gregory), James King is a singer whose deep blue and lonesome voice can tackle strident bluegrass and honky-tonk tunes with equal brilliance. He's not afraid, for instance, to attach an even greater sense of urgency and sadness to Vince Gill's "When I Call Your Name," from his most recent album. An ex-marine, King became engrossed in the bluegrass scene in Delaware during the late 1970s. Influenced by Ted Lundy, a banjo picker from Virginia who had moved to Delaware, King began recording after relocating to Virginia, in 1985. His partners on his first album were none other than his idol, Ralph Stanley, Stanley's band, and Johnson Mountain Boys fiddler Eddie Stubbs. In 1988 King formed the Misty Valley Boys and recorded for Webco. In 1993 he made his Rounder debut with the acclaimed *These Old Pictures*, followed up in 1995 by his award-winning *Lonesome & Then Some*.

what to buy: *Lonesome & Then Some* (Rounder, 1995, prod. Ken Irwin) *ルルルル* is hard to beat. Along with the Gill cover, there are songs written by Hank Cochran, Harlan Howard *and* Ernest Tubb! And the true bluegrass tunes are kept strictly bluegrass. A pleasure from start to finish, King's voice is the star here.

what to buy next: *These Old Pictures* (Rounder, 1993, prod. Ken Irwin) *ルルル* is *Lonesome*'s worthy predecessor.

the rest:
Volume 2, Webco Classic Series (Webco, 1990/1995) *ルルル*

influences:
◄◄ Stanley Brothers, Ted Lundy
►► Dudley Connell, Del McCoury

Stephen L. Betts

PEE WEE KING

Born Julius Frank Kuczynski, February 18, 1914, in Abrams, WI.

Accordionist and bandleader Pee Wee King introduced Western music to the Grand Ole Opry during the 1930s, so his music is not the freewheeling swing of Bob Wills or Milton Brown. Instead, King, who was born in polka country and also lived in Louisville, Kentucky, often gives his music a refined gentility. King's Golden West Cowboys appeared on the Opry from 1937–47 and served as training grounds for Ernest Tubb, Eddy Arnold and Cowboy Copas. Henry Ellis "Redd" Stewart, however, was the vocalist on most of King's biggest hits, which came during the late 1940s and early 1950s for RCA. The Golden West Cowboys were probably the most popular country band during that period, with hits like "Slow Poke," "Bonaparte's Retreat" and "Bimbo." But King's greatest quality may be his gift of melody—he co-wrote "Tennessee Waltz," which with Patti Page's help became one of the biggest hits of the recording era, and "You Belong to Me," a smash for Jo Stafford and the pop group the Duprees. King was inducted into the Country Music Hall of Fame in 1974.

what's available: Joined by Redd Stewart on *Tennessee Waltz & Slow Poke* (Country Road, 1976) *ルルル*, King polishes off two of his biggest tunes. Those, plus nine other songs, almost surely come from King's Starday recordings of the 1960s, so they're not the original singles. But it's still a decent collection, with such well-written obscurities as "When the Lights Go Dim Downtown" and "Goodbye New Orleans." *Pee Wee King & the Golden West Cowboys* (Bear Family) *ルルルル* is available as an import and has many of the hit recordings.

influences:
◄◄ Bob Wills, Sons of the Pioneers
►► Ernest Tubb, Eddy Arnold, Cowboy Copas, Owen Bradley

Brian Mansfield

SID KING &
THE FIVE STRINGS

Formed 1952, in Denton, TX. Disbanded 1958.

Sid King (born Sid Erwin, October 15, 1936, in Denton, TX), lead vocals, guitar; Billy King (born Billy Erwin), lead guitar; Mel Robinson, steel guitar, sax; Ken Massey, bass; Dave White, drums.

It's all too easy to say rock 'n' roll was invented on Sam Phillips' studio floor the day Elvis Presley crossed Bill Monroe with Arthur Crudup. In truth, during the post-War years the Southland was positively teeming with musical visionaries blindly adapting what they'd hear on late-night "race radio" to their daytime C&W pursuits. As early as 1952 KDNT out of Dallas was sponsoring a radio show featuring one such combo busy mixing Lefty Frizzell with Fats Domino. Named the Western Melody Makers, the group's brave devotion to R&B, highly unusual for a Texas band at the time, won them a contract with the then-fledgling Starday label in 1953. Their lone release, a bizarre Harry Gibson parody entitled "Who Put the Turtle in Myrtle's Girdle?," not surprisingly failed to garner much airplay. But it did bring the band, newly rechristened Sid King & the Five Strings, to the attention of Don Law and Columbia Records. Over the next three years they cut dozens of sides together, running the gamut from Western swing to what would soon be called rockabilly, including historic early versions of "Blue Suede Shoes" and "Ooby Dooby" as well as several original compositions of unusual merit. Although their startlingly originality probably did more to harm than help sales and airplay at the time, to hear this material today is absolutely revelatory. Under Law's firm but lenient hand the Five Strings were free to indulge their every musical whim, from Hank and Elvis to the Drifters, Spike Jones and beyond, and the body of work they created is without equal in both its polish and its perversity. Unfortunately, it was most likely this very eccentricity that caused confusion and ultimately indifference amongst the record-buying public, to say nothing of Columbia's top brass. After a final single for Dot Records (a deal made possible, coincidentally, due to the kind-heartedness of Sid's pal, Pat Boone), the Five Strings disbanded. Although Sid and his brother Bill continue to perform when not tending to their barber shop in Richardson, Texas (they recently toured the Orient fronting a Japanese rockabilly band called the Rollin' Rocks), King's tale is a sad but textbook case of the perils of being too ahead-of-your-time in a behind-the-times industry.

what to buy: The exemplary *Gonna Shake this Shack Tonight* (Bear Family, 1991, prod. various) 🎵🎵🎵 contains literally every note the Five Strings recorded, including the initial Columbia A-side, King's own "I Like It," which sounds as if Frank Zappa had hijacked a Bob Wills session. I kid you not.

what to buy next: *Rockin' on the Radio* (Schoolkids', 1996) 🎵🎵🎵 presents two live broadcasts from 1954–55 that fully capture the evolution of the Five Strings' sound from accomplished Western cut-ups to trail-blazing proto-rockabillies.

worth searching for: *Let's Get Loose* (Rockhouse, 1987, prod. Jim Colegrove) 🎵🎵🎵 contains an interesting selection of cuts recorded in 1979 and 1980 by the King Brothers & Friends—ironically, just as the rockabilly revival was about to rear its immaculately coifed head.

influences:

◀◀ Milton Brown, Dewey Phillips, Bill Haley

▶▶ Buddy & Bob, Commander Cody, BR5-49

Gary Pig Gold

THE KINGSTON TRIO

Formed 1957, in San Francisco, CA. Disbanded 1967.

Bob Shane, guitar, vocals; Nick Reynolds, guitar, vocals; Dave Guard, banjo, vocals (1957–61; died March 22, 1991); John Stewart, banjo, guitar, vocals (1961–67).

The Kingston Trio made it look so easy, that it's no wonder the group was reviled by folk music colleagues who watched it leap over them to the top of the charts. The Trio—three glib, fun-loving West Coast guys with guitars, banjos, bongos, three-part harmonies and matching striped shirts and chinos—were big stuff during the late 1950s and early 1960s, when five of its first six albums went to #1 on the *Billboard* charts, occupying the top spot for a total of 50 weeks. The Trio's basic sound was deceptively simple and its albums were much better than its detractors were ready to admit. The group's this-business-is-easy attitude influenced many of its followers to pick up guitars and start groups of their own in country and rock. Dave Guard, the most gifted Trio member, left in 1961 and was replaced by John Stewart, who would go on to a prolific solo career.

what to buy: The best place to start is *The Kingston Trio* (Capitol Collector's Series, 1990, prod. Voyle Gilmore) 🎵🎵🎵🎵. It contains 20 of their best-known tunes on one CD, including all the Top 10 hit singles. If you're really interested, try *The Capitol Years* (Capitol, 1995, prod. Voyle Gilmore) 🎵🎵🎵🎵, an extensive four-CD collection that favors outtakes and unreleased tracks to offer a more sympathetic look at the Trio's place in history.

The original Kingston Trio (from left): Bob Shane, Dave Guard and Nick Reynolds (AP/**Wide World Photos**)

New Frontier (Capitol, 1962, prod. Voyle Gilmore) ♫♫♫♫, the group's finest album with Stewart, centers around the enthusiasm over John F. Kennedy's presidency.

what to buy next: *Live at the Hungry I* (Capitol, 1959, prod. Voyle Gilmore) ♫♫♫♫♫ captures a club show that includes "Zombie Jamboree," "The Merry Minuet" and "They Call the Wind Maria," plus lots of stage patter. *At Large* (Capitol, 1959, prod. Voyle Gilmore) ♫♫♫♫♫ features Bess Hawes' "M.T.A.," Guard's "Getaway John," "The Long Black Rifle" and Jane Bowers' "Remember the Alamo." *String Along* (Capitol, 1960, prod. Voyle Gilmore) ♫♫♫♫ includes Tom Drake's "The Escape of Old John Webb," Cisco Hayes and Lee Hays' "Bad Man's Blunder" and Harlan Howard's "Everglades."

what to avoid: *Once Upon a Time* (Tetragrammaton, 1969) ♫ was recorded live at Lake Tahoe near the end of the group's career in 1966, and it shows. Although the singing is fine, the jokes have gone flat and the song selection is questionable.

the rest:
The Kingston Trio (Capitol, 1958) ♫♫♫♫

Stereo Concert (Capitol, 1959) ♫♫♫
Here We Go Again (Capitol, 1959) ♫♫♫
Sold Out (Capitol, 1960) ♫♫♫♫
Make Way (Capitol, 1961) ♫♫♫
Goin' Places (Capitol, 1961) ♫♫♫
Encores (Capitol, 1961) ♫♫
Close-Up (Capitol, 1961) ♫♫♫
College Concert (Capitol, 1962) ♫♫♫
Something Special (Capitol, 1962) ♫♫♫♫
The Kingston Trio #16 (Capitol, 1963) ♫♫♫
Sunny Side (Capitol, 1963) ♫♫
Time to Think (Capitol, 1963) ♫♫♫
Back in Town (Capitol, 1964) ♫♫
Nick-Bob-John (Capitol, 1964) ♫♫
Stay Awhile (Capitol, 1965) ♫♫♫
Somethin' Else (Capitol, 1965) ♫♫♫
Children of the Morning (Capitol, 1966) ♫♫

worth searching for: *Live at Newport* (Vanguard, 1994, prod. Mary Katherine Aldin) ♫♫♫♫♫ was recorded live at the 1959 Newport Folk Festival before a demanding East Coast audience.

solo outings:
John Stewart:
(With Buffy Ford) *Signals through the Glass* (Capitol, 1968) ♫♫
Chilly Winds (Folk Era) ♫♫♫
Lonesome Picker Rides Again (Warner Bros., 1971) ♫♫♫♫
Sunstorm (Warner Bros., 1972) ♫♫♫♫
Cannons in the Rain/Wingless Angels (Capitol, 1973, 1975/Bear Family, 1990) ♫♫♫
The Complete Phoenix Concerts (Capitol, 1974/Bear Family, 1990) ♫♫♫♫♫
Fire in the Wind (RSO, 1977) ♫♫♫♫
Bombs Away Dream Babies (RSO, 1979/Razor & Tie, 1993) ♫♫♫
Dream Babies Go Hollywood (RSO/PolyGram, 1980) ♫
John Stewart in Concert (RCA, 1980) ♫♫♫
Blondes (Allegiance, 1982) ♫♫♫♫
(With Nick Reynolds) *Revenge of the Budgie* (Takoma, 1983) ♫♫♫
Trancas (Affordable Dreams, 1984) ♫♫♫♫
The Gathering (Homecoming, 1984) ♫♫
Centennial (Homecoming, 1984) ♫♫
Secret Tapes '96 (Homecoming, 1986) ♫♫♫♫
(With the Cumberland Three) *Trio Years* (Homecoming, 1983) ♫♫♫
Punch the Big Guy (Shanachie, 1987) ♫♫♫
Secret Tapes II (Homecoming, 1987) ♫♫♫
California Bloodlines/Willard Minus 2 (Bear Family, 1989) ♫♫♫♫♫
(With the Cumberland Three) *Songs of the Civil War* (Rhino, 1991) ♫♫
American Originals (Capitol, 1992) ♫♫♫
(With Ford) *The Essential John and Buffy* (Feegie, 1994) ♫♫♫
Airdream Believer (Shanachie, 1995) ♫♫♫♫

influences:

◀◀ Weavers, Pete Seeger, Gateway Singers

▶▶ Peter, Paul & Mary, Brothers Four, Chad Mitchell Trio, Limelighters, Journeymen, Serendipity Singers, New Christy Minstrels, Roger McGuinn, Bob Dylan, Simon & Garfunkel

Leland Rucker

BEECHER KIRBY

See: Bashful Brother Oswald

BUDDY KNOX

See: Jimmy Bowen

WALT KOKEN

Walt Koken was a banjo player in the Highwoods String Band, an influential group during the old-time music revival of the 1960s. After playing with that group, he entered a self-imposed playing hiatus, re-emerging in 1994 with the album *Banjonique* on Rounder.

what's available: Both of Koken's recent albums, *Banjonique* (Rounder, 1994, prod. Walt Koken) ♫♫♫ and *Hei-wa Hoedown* (Rounder, 1995, prod. Walt Koken) ♫♫♫, are fine examples of old-time solo banjo. Playing in a clawhammer style, Koken breathes fresh life into traditional tunes as well adding some songs of his own to the canon. The songs are mostly instrumental, but Koken occasionally sings as well. Also recommended listening is *Feed Your Babies Onions: Fat City Favorites* (Rounder, 1994) ♫♫♫♪ by the Highwoods String Band.

Brian Mansfield

STEVE KOLANDER

Born November 15, 1961.

Steve Kolander is a roots-oriented singer who was part of the music scenes in Austin, Texas, and Los Angeles before moving to Nashville. He has a degree from the University of Texas at Austin and worked in advertising before signing his record deal. Kolander also trains dogs for disabled people.

what's available: *Steve Kolander* (River North, 1994, prod. Joe Thomas) ♫♫♪ specializes in forlorn, rockabilly-influenced songs, sort of like a less haunted Chris Isaak. On *Pieces of a Puzzle* (River North, 1996, prod. Buddy Cannon) ♫♫♫ Kolander

hooks up with some of the great musical figures of Nashville past (pianist David Briggs, songwriter Hank Cochran). The result is an album that builds on the strengths of the previous effort, even recasting that album's "Scoot over, Move Closer" as a cocktail-jazz number with an 18-piece string orchestra.

influences:

◀◀ Mavericks, Stacy Dean Campbell

▶▶ Ray Vega, Dean Miller

Brian Mansfield

FRED KOLLER

Born c. 1950, in Chicago, IL

There's a gruff sweetness to his voice that falls somewhere between Louis Armstrong and John Hiatt, but Fred Koller writes tight folksy songs perfectly suited for the smart, friendly coffeehouse environment. With penpals like Hiatt, John Prine, John Gorka, Pat Alger and Shel Silverstein, the Nashville songwriter's also written some classic country-radio friendly songs, including the big Kathy Mattea hits "Goin' Gone," "She Came from Fort Worth" and "Life as We Knew It" (all Top 5); "Lone Star State of Mind," one of Nanci Griffith's best known tracks; and "Angel Eyes," the gorgeous pop hit for the bluesy Jeff Healey Band. The industry vet is also the author of the book *How to Pitch and Promote Your Songs.*

what to buy: *Where the Fast Lane Ends* (Alcazar, 1990, prod. Fred Koller, Steve O'Brien) ♫♫♫ has a cozy, living-room vibe. Koller's songs are provocative, even chilling sometimes, and his voice is warm and inviting on this set of originals (including "Goin' Gone" and "Lone Star State of Mind") written with luminaries including Al Anderson, Pat Alger, John Hiatt and Sonny Throckmorton.

what to buy next: *Songs from the Night Before* (Alcazar, 1989, prod. Fred Koller, Steve O'Brien) ♫♫♫♪ contains another generous helping of the songwriter's economic, off-color musical observations, including an otherworldly Presley invocation, "King and I," a frightening "Dentist Blues" and a hilariously goofy Prine co-write, "Let's Talk Dirty" (as in "Let's talk dirty in Hawaiian").

the rest:

Night of the Living Fred (Alcazar, 1989) ♫♫♫

influences:

◀◀ Tom Waits, Bruce Springsteen

▶▶ Randy Newman, John Hiatt

David Sokol

2/4/8 *kenny kosek*

KENNY KOSEK

Born August 18, 1949, in New York, NY.

Kenny Kosek grew up in the Southwest Bronx with a love of hill-billy fiddle while those around him listened to doo-wop and Tito Puente. That wide array of sounds informed his music with a beautifully eclectic style, and he has played sessions with artists ranging from Jerry Garcia and Red Allen to James Taylor and Chaka Khan, as well as performing in a number of commercials and New York City musicals.

what's available: *Angelwood* (Rounder, 1997, prod. Kenny Kosek, Edward Haber) ♪♪♪♪ shows Kosek playing in a variety of styles, from jazz and rock to bluegrass and Western swing. Whether he writes the tunes or gets them from the public domain, his arrangements are always informed by his sense of tradition—even as he gleefully leaps into new musical territory.

influences:
◀◀ Mark O'Connor, Stephane Grappelli

Brian Mansfield

ALISON KRAUSS

Born July 23, 1971, in Champaign, IL.

No one will ever be more important to bluegrass music than its progenitor, Bill Monroe. But it took Alison Krauss, a pre-teenager when she started her stellar career, to bring it to the masses. And the way she did it involved no gimmickry, but merely being herself—a fiddle champ who could share the stage with Monroe himself and hold her own, but also a young woman who's been exposed to pop culture and wants to reflect it in her own music. Thus the covers of rock and pop tunes, and guesting on albums by former Doobie Brother Michael McDonald and neo-hippie rock group Phish. In addition to being a world-class instrumentalist, Krauss possesses an angelic voice that recalls Dolly Parton and Emmylou Harris and is an accomplished bandleader and record producer. There may be no stopping her—nor should there be.

what to buy: Krauss is known for flouting stogy bluegrass conventions, but she shows just how far she's willing to go on *Now That I've Found You: A Collection* (Rounder, 1995, prod. various) ♪♪♪♪♪, which collects tracks from her five albums plus songs from other projects and previously unreleased material. Among the latter, there are covers of Sidney and Suzanne Cox, as well as the Foundations. No problem there. But what's this? "Oh Atlanta" by . . . Bad Company? Indeed, and Krauss pulls it off with aplomb. There's also a version of John Lennon & Paul McCart-

ney's "I Will," recorded for Tony Furtado's album *Within Reach*, and "When You Say Nothing at All," from a 1994 Keith Whitley tribute album. Krauss' collaboration with the gospel/bluegrass unit the Cox Family, *I Know Who Holds Tomorrow* (Rounder, 1994, prod. Alison Krauss) ♪♪♪♪ is nearly perfect. The arrangements are both traditional ("Will There Be Any Stars?") and innovative ("Walk Over God's Heaven"), and they turn in lively performances on Loretta Lynn's "Everybody Wants to Go to Heaven" and Paul Simon's "Loves Me Like a Rock."

what to buy next: Krauss' confidence as a bandleader and producer really shows on *Every Time You Say Goodbye* (Rounder, 1992, prod. Alison Krauss & Union Station) ♪♪♪♪. Every move seems assured, and her relationship with her band, Union Station, is symbiotic. The traditional material is fine, particularly the instrumental "Cluck Old Hen," and Krauss steps out with a pair of pop tunes, Shawn Colvin's "I Don't Know Why" and Karla Bonoff's "Lose Again."

the rest:
Too Late to Cry (Rounder, 1987) ♪♪♪♪
(With Union Station) *Two Highways* (Rounder, 1989) ♪♪♪♪
I've Got That Old Feeling (Rounder, 1990) ♪♪♪♪
So Long So Wrong (Rounder, 1997) ♪♪♪♪

worth searching for: Krauss contributes vocals to "If I Could" from rock band Phish's album *Hoist* (Elektra, 1994) ♪♪.

influences:
◀◀ Bill Monroe, Dolly Parton, Emmylou Harris
▶▶ Alison Brown, Laurie Lewis, Cox Family

Daniel Durchholz

KRIS KRISTOFFERSON

Born June 22, 1936, in Brownsville, TX.

This former army man and Rhodes scholar tried nearly everything to break into the country-music business during the late 1960s, including hanging out as a recording-studio janitor and, armed with a demo tape, piloting a borrowed helicopter onto Johnny Cash's estate. When he finally did break through in 1970, the waters ran mighty deep—Cash relented and scored big with "Sunday Morning Coming Down," Ray Price hit with "For the Good Times," Janis Joplin posthumously reached the top with "Me and Bobby McGee" and Sammi Smith recorded "Help Me Make It Through the Night." That quartet of songs was enough to make Kristofferson an instant star, and though he never again equalled the enormity of those classics, he's continued to write, act and perform up to the present day. His own versions of his work are limited by his rudimentary vocal ability, and the left-wing musings of the latter portion of his career turned off more than a few country listeners. Still, Kristofferson's importance as an insightful, sexual, rebellious songwriter at a time when country had grown staid can never be underestimated.

what to buy: The most obvious collection of Kristofferson in print is the comprehensive *Singer/Songwriter* (Columbia Legacy, 1991) 🎵🎵🎵, in which the compelling deliveries of Joplin, Price et al. are juxtaposed with the writer's ragged approach on "Why Me" and "Loving Her Was Easier."

what to buy next: *Me and Bobby McGee* (Monument, 1971/1988, prod. Fred Foster) 🎵🎵🎵, Kristofferson's recording debut, is essential for the inclusion of "Law Is for Protection of the People" and one of his early greats, "To Beat the Devil."

the rest:
The Silver-Tongued Devil and I (Monument, 1971) 🎵🎵🎵
Border Lord (One Way, 1972/1995) 🎵🎵
Jesus Was a Capricorn (Sony, 1972) 🎵🎵
(With Rita Coolidge) *Breakaway* (Monument 1974/1988) 🎵🎵
Who's to Bless and Who's to Blame (One Way, 1976/1996) 🎵🎵
Surreal Thing (One Way, 1976/1996) 🎵🎵
Songs of Kristofferson (Monument, 1977/1988) 🎵🎵
Easter Island (One Way, 1977/1995) 🎵🎵
To the Bone (One Way, 1981/1996) 🎵🎵
Live at the Philharmonic (Sony, 1992) 🎵🎵
Shake Hands with the Devil (One Way, 1995) 🎵🎵
Moment of Forever (Justice, 1995) 🎵🎵

influences:
⏪ Bob Dylan, Hank Williams
⏩ Any songwriter in Nashville alive today

David Simons

Kris Kristofferson (© Ken Settle)

SLEEPY LaBEEF

Born Thomas Paulsley LaBeef, July 20, 1935, in Smackover, AR.

Though his degree of stardom has never come close to matching his gargantuan talents, Sleepy LaBeef is one of the most amazing musicians in America. A dramatic singer with a big, booming baritone voice and a guitarist of dazzling versatility, LaBeef broke into the Houston country/rockabilly scene of the early 1950s, recording for Wayside and other obscure labels before moving on to Plantation, Sun, Columbia and, beginning in 1980, Rounder. Despite a couple of minor hits, LaBeef's records have never really captured his true genius, which is revealed only on stage. It is there that LaBeef, who's blessed with an encyclopedic knowledge of American music, gives free rein to his muse, combining the collective histories of country, blues, gospel, bluegrass, rockabilly, R&B and whatever else catches his fancy into a unique genre-straddling LaBeefian stew he calls "goosebump music." The music comes out in guitar-driven torrents, often in extended stream-of-consciousness medleys that leave listeners gaping in astonishment. Anyone who ever witnessed one of those shows understands just what the *New York Times* meant when it called Sleepy LaBeef a "national treasure."

what to buy: *Nothin' but the Truth* (Rounder, 1987, prod. Scott Billington) 🎵🎵🎵 has the right idea; instead of trying to capture the magic in a studio, record LaBeef in his natural element, on stage at a smoky, sweaty honky-tonk. It's not perfect, but it does a good job of explaining LaBeef's musical worldview, in which Hank Williams, Howlin' Wolf, Nancy Sinatra, Chuck Berry, Bill Monroe and the Five Blind Boys not only exist as equals, but also share space in the same medley. High points include smoking versions of "Tore Up over You" and "Let's Talk about Us" and the droll, autobiographical "Boogie at the Wayside Lounge."

what to buy next: *Strange Things Happening* (Rounder, 1994, prod. Jake Guralnick, Peter Guralnick) 𝄞𝄞𝄞 is a pretty apt title for a LaBeef album, as this one veers from nods to Ernest Tubb ("Waltz across Texas") to Muddy Waters ("Young Fashioned Ways"), with stops along the way for Sister Rosetta Tharpe (the title song) and Elvis ("Trying to Get to You"). *I'll Never Lay My Guitar Down* (Rounder, 1996, prod. Jake Guralnick) 𝄞𝄞𝄞, while a bit uneven and restrained, has its moments, ranging from the "Mystery Train" shuffle of "Treat Me Like a Dog" to the swampy "Roosevelt & Ira Lee" to the closing "The Open Door," which sounds like Brother Claude Ely updated for the late-1990s.

worth searching for: Though neither of LaBeef's first two Rounder albums has been issued on CD, both are cool, especially his 1980 debut, *It Ain't What You Eat It's the Way How You Chew It.*

influences:

⏪ Sister Rosetta Tharpe, Elvis Presley, Hank Williams

⏩ John Fogerty, Blasters

Jon Hartley Fox

JIMMY LaFAVE

Born July 12, 1955, in Wills Point, TX.

Rising to the top of the always competitive Austin singer/songwriter scene, Jimmy LaFave began his musical career as a drummer. During his teens, LaFave switched to guitar and began singing and writing songs. Moving with his family to Stillwater, Oklahoma, the budding musical talent took inspiration from a wide variety of Okie musical forbearers, such as J.J. Cale, Chet Baker, Leon Russell and, of course, Woody Guthrie. Mixing blues, jazz and country influences with the lessons learned from his musical hero, Bob Dylan, LaFave is both a perceptive songwriter and an appealing singer. Slowly but surely he was drawn back to his home state and the bustling music scene in Austin. In 1992 he signed with Colorado-based (and Rounder-distributed) Bohemia Beat Records, LaFave formed the first edition of his ever-changing backup band Night Tribe and recorded his debut, *Austin Skyline*. That album featured four

Dylan covers, including "Shelter from the Storm" and "Girl from the North Country." Two more Bohemia Beat albums followed: *Highway Trance* (1994) and *Buffalo Return to the Plains* (1995). In December 1995 LaFave won the Songwriter of the Year Award at the Kerrville Music Awards. In March 1996 he won the same award at the annual Austin Music Awards.

what to buy: *Buffalo Return to the Plains* (Bohemia Beat, 1995, prod. Jimmy LaFave) 𝄞𝄞𝄞 is his most distinguished collection of originals. Highlights include the title tune, "Foolish Pride" and the exquisitely sad "Never Be Mine." The obligatory Dylan cover is "Sweetheart Like You."

what to buy next: On his second album, *Highway Trance* (Bohemia Beat, 1994, prod. Jimmy LaFave) 𝄞𝄞𝄞, LaFave mixes it up more, blending more rockin' numbers such as "Shakin' Your Hips" and "Austin after Midnight" with gentle ballads like "Dark Dancing Eyes."

the rest:

Austin Skyline (Bohemia Beat, 1992) 𝄞𝄞𝄞𝄞
Road Novel (Bohemia Beat, 1997) 𝄞𝄞𝄞𝄞

influences:

⏪ Bob Dylan, Butch Hancock, Townes Van Zandt

Robert Baird

BARBARA LAMB

See: Ranch Romance

LAMBCHOP

Formed 1993, in Nashville, TN.

Kurt Wagner, vocals; others.

A quixotic cowboy orchestra that reinvents the lush Nashville Sound for the 1990s, Lambchop is one of Music City's best-kept secrets. Frontman Kurt Wagner's bemused, dreamlike lyrics illuminate seemingly mundane events with a painterly eye for detail.

what to buy: *How I Quit Smoking* (Merge, 1996, eng. Robb Earls) 𝄞𝄞𝄞𝄞 is an enchanting, string-laden outing that resembles no other country music being made today.

what to buy next: *I Hope You're Sitting Down* (Merge, 1994, eng. Robb Earls, Hank Tillbury) 𝄞𝄞𝄞𝄞 rocks more than its successor and finds Wagner's ruminations displaying a darker, sexier bent.

the rest:

Hank (Merge, 1996) ♪♪♪

influences:

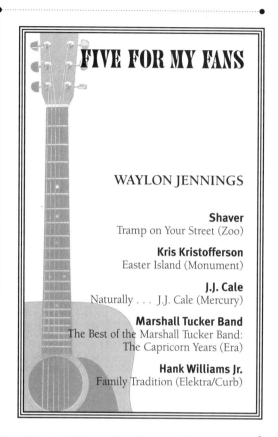 Jim Reeves, Yo La Tengo

Bill Friskics-Warren

k.d. lang

Born Kathryn Dawn Lang, November 2, 1961, in Consort, Alberta, Canada.

Can a vegetarian lesbian from north of the border make it in Music City? The answer seems so obvious that it's a measure of k.d. lang's moxie that she even bothered to ask. But lang—who, in campy garb and rhinestone spectacles, initially approached crooning countrypolitan tunes as performance art, and for a time even claimed to be the reincarnation of Patsy Cline (thus, the name of her band, the reclines)—is a singer/songwriter of rare talent and determination who eventually won the war, even if she lost the battle. After her U.S. debut mistakenly cast lang as a Canadian cowpunk, she brought legendary Cline producer Owen Bradley out of retirement for *Shadowland*, a triumphant album that proved lang could take Nashville on its own terms and succeed. After her next album took her torch-and-twang sound to its logical conclusion, lang progressed to a more expansive pop sound, a move that coincided with her declaring her lesbianism in the *Advocate* during 1992. Her continuing interest in other types of performance led her to a bold starring role in Percy Aldon's 1991 film *Salmonberries*, and she co-composed and performed the soundtrack to Gus Van Sant's 1993 film *Even Cowgirls Get the Blues*. Her political and social views—notably her 1990 "Meat Stinks" ads for People for the Ethical Treatment of Animals (PETA)—often draw more attention than her music, but they're part and parcel of lang's iconoclastic personality. And besides, her music continues to speak for itself.

what to buy: On *Absolute Torch and Twang* (Sire, 1989, prod. Greg Penny, Ben Mink, k.d. lang) ♪♪♪♪♪ lang and the reclines invented the perfect tag for her particular brand of music. lang also made her best album by internalizing her influences enough to come up with a sound all her own. Such songs as "Luck in My Eyes," "Big Boned Gal" and "Big Big Love" derive their energetic spunk from the raucous cowpunk of *Angel with a Lariat*, while "Three Days," "Wallflower Waltz" and especially the transcendent "Pullin' Back the Reins" reveal how much she'd learned from her sophisticated crooning on *Shadowland*. *Shadowland* (Sire, 1988, prod. Owen Bradley) ♪♪♪ is the

album on which lang realized the full range of her powerful voice, but also learned to sing with restraint and nuance. Bradley's careful production returns countrypolitan to its former luster, and the material is first rate, particularly the aching "Western Skies" and the weary, after-hours "Black Coffee." The "Honky-Tonk Angel" medley is something of an event, matching lang with three of Bradley's former charges, Loretta Lynn, Kitty Wells and Brenda Lee.

what to buy next: lang jokingly called *Ingenue* (Sire, 1992, prod. Greg Penny, Ben Mink, k.d. lang) ♪♪♪ her "stalker" album, for it is full of songs about desire and obsession. Despite such onerous implications, the album is a charmer, thanks to her sincerity and passion and the (forgive me) langorous arrangements of such songs as "Constant Craving," "The Mind of Love" and even the campy "Miss Chatelaine." Switching genres is no small thing. On *Ingenue* lang moves from country to adult-contemporary pop with admirable elan.

FIVE FOR MY FANS

WAYLON JENNINGS

Shaver
Tramp on Your Street (Zoo)

Kris Kristofferson
Easter Island (Monument)

J.J. Cale
Naturally . . . J.J. Cale (Mercury)

Marshall Tucker Band
The Best of the Marshall Tucker Band:
The Capricorn Years (Era)

Hank Williams Jr.
Family Tradition (Elektra/Curb)

k.d. lang

what to avoid: There's nothing really wrong with lang's U.S. debut, *Angel with a Lariat* (Sire, 1987, prod. Dave Edmunds) ♫♫. It's just that lang and the reclines never really click with producer Edmunds, and with the exception of the opening track, "Turn Me 'Round," nothing ever really takes off. And who needs a remake of Lynn Anderson's hit "Rose Garden"?

the rest:

Even Cowgirls Get the Blues (soundtrack) (Sire/Warner Bros., 1993) ♫♫♫
All You Can Eat (Warner Bros., 1995) ♫♫♫♫
Drag (Warner Bros., 1997)

worth searching for: lang's Canadian debut *a truly western experience* (Bumstead, 1984, prod. Jamie Kidd, k.d. lang, Gary Delorme) ♫♫ is an interesting look at lang and the reclines before k.d. truly hit her stride. The high-stepping "Bopalena" and "Hanky Panky" are standouts.

influences:

◀◀ Patsy Cline, Marshall Chapman, Roy Orbison, Gertrude Stein

▶▶ Shelby Lynne, Mandy Barnett, LeAnn Rimes, Lee Ann Womack

Daniel Durchholz

JONBOY LANGFORD & THE PINE VALLEY COSMONAUTS

See: Waco Brothers

NICOLETTE LARSON

Born July 17, 1952, in Helena, MT.

Best known for her work as a high-profile backup singer (Neil Young, Emmylou Harris, Jimmy Buffett, Linda Ronstadt, Commander Cody, the Doobie Brothers, among others) Nicolette Larson's career as a solo artist has been star-crossed at best. She's had her share of hits, from version of Neil Young's "Lotta Love" to "Let Me Go, Love," a duet with Michael McDonald, and a remake of the chestnut "I Only Want to Be with You." On the downside, her albums typify the laid-back L.A. style of the 1970s, and for the most part, they haven't aged well. Larson's interests have widened, though, and in recent years she's performed in musicals, movies, become a race car driver and recorded a children's album.

k.d. lang (© Ken Settle)

what's available: The only Larson album currently in print is *Sleep, Baby, Sleep* (Sony Wonder, 1994, prod. Andrew Gold, Nicolette Larson) ♫♫, an album of children's lullabies. Proving old friends still stick together, guests on the album include David Crosby, Graham Nash, Linda Ronstadt and producer Gold.

worth searching for: Her debut album, *Nicolette* (Warner Bros., 1979) ♫♫, contains "Lotta Love." The more country-flavored *Rose of My Heart* (MCA, 1986) ♫♫♫ contains "That's How You Know When Love's Right," a hit duet with Steve Wariner.

influences:

◀◀ Linda Ronstadt, Emmylou Harris, Mary Kay Place

▶▶ Trisha Yearwood, Wynonna

Daniel Durchholz

LAST ROUNDUP

See: Amy Rigby

JIM LAUDERDALE

Born April 11, 1957, in Statesville, NC.

For lack of a term that accurately describes the rootsy and increasingly soulful music of California-raised Jim Lauderdale, the singer/songwriter has been lumped in with the wildly diverse "Western Beat" crowd. And while such artists as Dave Alvin, Chris Gaffney and Kevin Welch are fine company, it can hardly be said to be a homogeneous or instantly identifiable sound. Lauderdale has entertained Nashvillian ambitions, but his sensibility is closer to those who have observed Music City as outsiders—rockers Dave Edmunds, Nick Lowe and Marshall Crenshaw—and those who've had nothing whatsoever to do with it, such as Otis Redding, one of Lauderdale's heroes. Country artists, notably George Strait, have covered Lauderdale's songs, but he's yet to break through as an artist. One spin of any of his fine albums will have you believing he deserves it. Just don't hold your breath.

what to buy: Lauderdale's most conventionally country album—which is to say that there's some twang amid the rootsy rock 'n' pop—is his debut, *Planet of Love* (Reprise, 1991, prod. Rodney Crowell, John Leventhal) ♫♫♫♫. A critical triumph, it vanished before an uncaring public. Highlights include "The King of Broken Hearts," Lauderdale's tribute to George Jones, and the high-stepping "Where the Sidewalk Ends," both of which have been covered by George Strait. *Planet of Love* remains one of the great undiscovered albums of the decade.

the rest:

Pretty Close to the Truth (Atlantic, 1994) ♪♪♪♪
Every Second Counts (Atlantic, 1995) ♪♪♪♪
Persimmons (Upstart, 1996) ♪♪♪

influences:

◀◀ Gram Parsons, Buck Owens, Marshall Crenshaw, Otis Redding

▶▶ Buddy Miller, Mandy Barnett

Daniel Durchholz

THE LAUREL CANYON RAMBLERS

Formed 1994, in Los Angeles, CA.

Herb Pedersen, banjo, vocals; Bill Bryson, bass, vocals; Kenny Blackwell, mandolin; Billy Ray Lathum, guitar (1994–96); Roger Reed, guitar, vocals (1996–present); Gabe Whitaker, fiddle (1996–present).

In 1993, when the country chart-topping Desert Rose Band formally disbanded, members Herb Pedersen and Bill Bryson got the bluegrass fever once again. They hooked up with Kentucky Colonels/Dillards alumnus Billy Ray Lathum and mandolinist Kenny Blackwell to form the Laurel Canyon Ramblers. Rather than focus on grand flourishes and extended jams, the band hones in on tight harmonizing, crisp solos and complementary instrumental accompaniment. Many of their arrangements follow in the Desert Rose Band style.

what's available: *Rambler's Blues* (Sugar Hill, 1994, prod. Herb Pedersen) ♪♪♪♪ contains the hot instrumental "Yellowhead" and the gorgeous bluegrass gospel "He Said If I Be Lifted Up." A bluegrass reworking of "Love Reunited," a Top 40 country hit for the Desert Rose Band, is also worth checking out; fiddler Byron Berline and dobroist LeRoy McNees guest. The somewhat more traditional *Blue Rambler 2* (Sugar Hill, 1996, prod. Herb Pedersen) ♪♪♪♪ features a blistering bluegrass mix of Ralph Stanley's "Bad Case of the Blues" and Herb's achingly beautiful "Wait a Minute."

influences:

◀◀ Bill Monroe & His Blue Grass Boys, Flatt & Scruggs, Kentucky Colonels, Dillards, Desert Rose Band, Country Gazette

▶▶ Blue Highway, IIIrd Tyme Out, Unlimited Tradition, Fox Family

see also: *Desert Rose Band, Chris Hillman*

Douglas Fulmer and Rick Petreycik

CHRISTINE LAVIN

Born January 2, 1952, in Peekskill, NY.

Having learned to play guitar from a public TV program while growing up, Christine Lavin quit her day job at a hospital in 1984 to pursue music full-time. She has gone on to become the doyen of the Manhattan folk scene, promoting many others' talents in various ways, including a local weekly radio program. Four Bitchin' Babes, a female singer/songwriters roundtable that she organized, has proven to have a long life—practically a career unto itself—with regulars Sally Fingerett and Megon McDonough and a rotating fourth chair that's been filled by Patty Larkin, Julie Gold and Debi Smith; temporary "guest Babes" have included Cheryl Wheeler, Kristina Olsen, Janis Ian and Mary Travers. Though Lavin's many humorous songs have typecast her as a comic singer, she also writes about relationships with an acute observatory eye and can be as deep and sincere as any other songwriter—she just doesn't take herself as seriously.

what to buy: *Attainable Love* (Philo/Rounder, 1990, prod. Christine Lavin) ♪♪♪♪ contains two of Lavin's most lasting humorous songs, "Sensitive New Age Guys" and "Shopping Cart of Love: The Play," and one of her most heart-rending plaints, "The Kind of Love You Never Recover From."

what to buy next: *Good Thing He Can't Read My Mind* (Philo/Rounder, 1988, prod. Bill Kollar) ♪♪♪♪ features "Mysterious Woman," which simultaneously laments Lavin's failure to be Suzanne Vega and lampoons Vega's willful obscurantism. Four Bitchin' Babes' *Buy Me Bring Me Take Me: Don't Mess My Hair!!! Volume 2* (Philo/Rounder, 1993, prod. Bitchin' Babes, Steve Rosenthal) ♪♪♪♪ offers the opportunity to hear the massively successful ballad "From a Distance" performed by its writer, Julie Gold, in a spare setting that doesn't overstate its pieties. Among Lavin's tracks is a charming cover of "Sealed with a Kiss."

what to avoid: *Please Don't Make Me Too Happy* (Shanachie, 1995, prod. Steve Rosenthal) ♪♪, while not a bad record, is flawed. The humor is more shaggy-dog than quirky observations and doesn't wear well on repeated listenings. But those who wish Lavin would lean more toward rock on occasion will like the denser production.

the rest:

Future Fossils (Philo/Rounder, 1986) ♪♪♪
Beau Woes and other Problems of Modern Life (Philo/Rounder, 1987) ♪♪♪♪
Compass (Philo/Rounder, 1991) ♪♪♪♪

Live at Cactus Cafe (Philo/Rounder, 1993) 🎵🎵🎵
Shining My Flashlight on the Moon (Shanachie, 1997) 🎵🎵🎵
(With Four Bitchin' Babes) *Fax it! Charge it! Don't Ask Me What's for Dinner!* (Shanachie, 1995) 🎵🎵🎵

worth searching for: *Another Woman's Man* (Philo/Rounder, 1987/92, prod. Christine Lavin) 🎵🎵🎵 is a seven-song EP that at one time was available on LP but is now only on cassette. Formerly called *Husbands and Wives*, it contains 1983 recordings ranging from the bitter/funny "If You Want Space, Go to Utah" to "If I Could Be Sonja Henie," an obsession Lavin retains to this day. With a couple of exceptions, the arrangements are pleasingly spare.

influences:
◀◀ Joni Mitchell, Peter, Paul & Mary, Loudon Wainwright III, Dave Van Ronk
▶▶ Debi Smith, Cheryl Wheeler, Shawn Colvin

Steve Holtje

TRACY LAWRENCE

Born January 27, 1968, in Atlanta, TX.

Born in Texas and raised in Arkansas, Tracy Lawrence gave regular performances on a Kentucky radio show, *Live at Libby's*, and showcased at Nashville's Bluebird Cafe before landing his record deal. Then he almost didn't live long enough to see his first album released. In May 1991 he was shot four times in a hotel parking lot. His record label, Atlantic, delayed releasing his debut, *Sticks and Stones*, while Lawrence recuperated. It was worth the wait, as the first two songs became #1 hits and solidly established Lawrence among the best of the early 1990s neo-traditional honky-tonk singers. To date, Lawrence has sold more than 6 million albums, enjoyed a dozen or more chart-topping hits and won several national awards, including two from the Academy of Country Music: 1993's Top New Male Vocalist and Best New Country Artist.

what to buy: *Sticks and Stones* (Atlantic, 1991, prod. James Stroud) 🎵🎵🎵 is packed with the first handful of Lawrence's string of chart-topping hits, including "Today's Lonely Fool" and the title track.

what to buy next: *Alibis* (Atlantic, 1993, prod. James Stroud) 🎵🎵🎵 continued Lawrence's success, with the hits "Runnin' Behind," "My Second Home," "Can't Break It to My Heart" and "If the Good Die Young."

the rest:
I See It Now (Atlantic, 1994) 🎵🎵🎵
Tracy Lawrence Live (Atlantic, 1996) 🎵🎵🎵
Time Marches On (Atlantic, 1996) 🎵🎵🎵
The Coast Is Clear (Atlantic, 1997) 🎵🎵🎵

influences:
◀◀ George Jones, George Strait
▶▶ Trace Adkins

Bill Hobbs

DOYLE LAWSON /QUICKSILVER

Born April 20, 1944, in Kingsport, TN. Quicksilver formed 1979.

Mandolinist and bandleader Doyle Lawson is considered one of the most influential forces in modern bluegrass; his bands are marked by their extremely well-honed vocal harmonies and bright, powerful renditions, especially of gospel material. Trained as a member of Jimmy Martin's Sunny Mountain Boys, Doyle also worked in groundbreaking bluegrass bands with J.D. Crowe and Red Allen and spent seven years as part of the Country Gentlemen making classic bluegrass recordings. In 1979 Lawson formed his band, Quicksilver, with banjoist Terry Baucom, guitarist Jimmy Haley, and Lou Reid on bass. Doyle Lawson & Quicksilver quickly established themselves as among the most innovative vocal bands in bluegrass and became particularly well known for their gospel efforts, including an increasing number of a cappella efforts. The turnover in Quicksilver has been frequent and rapid—on at least three occasions, versions of the band have left virtually en masse to form new bands (The New Quicksilver, Lou Reid, Terry Baucom & Carolina and IIIrd Tyme Out)—but Lawson inevitably finds replacements who are wonderful musicians and continues to make great and influential recordings.

what to buy: Quicksilver's breakthrough album is still one of the finest and most influential modern bluegrass albums. *Rock My Soul* (Sugar Hill, 1981, prod. Doyle Lawson) 🎵🎵🎵🎵 features inventive arrangements, inspired harmony singing and a far reaching and adventurous repertoire. A classic.

what to buy next: *There's a Light Guiding Me* (Sugar Hill, 1996, prod. Doyle Lawson) 🎵🎵🎵 is an outstanding recent all-gospel effort. *Heaven's Joy Awaits (A Cappella Quartets)* (Sugar Hill, 1987, prod. Doyle Lawson) 🎵🎵🎵 includes one of Lawson's finest vocal aggregations; Russell Moore, Scott Vestal and Ray Deaton have all gone on to success in other bands. *I'll Wander*

Back Someday (Sugar Hill, 1988, prod. Doyle Lawson) ♪♪♪♪ is a recording of mostly traditional secular numbers that show-cases that side of Quicksilver. *Never Walk Away* (Sugar Hill, 1995, prod. Doyle Lawson) ♪♪♪♪ is a good recent secular effort with a young band; it includes a superior version of the soon-to-be-classic "In the Gravel Yard."

the rest:

Doyle Lawson & Quicksilver (Sugar Hill, 1980) ♪♪♪
Quicksilver Rides Again (Sugar Hill, 1981) ♪♪♪
Heavenly Treasures (Sugar Hill, 1981) ♪♪♪
Once and for Always (Sugar Hill, 1985) ♪♪♪
Beyond the Shadows (Sugar Hill, 1986) ♪♪♪
The News Is Out (Sugar Hill, 1987) ♪♪♪
Hymn Time in the Country (Sugar Hill, 1988) ♪♪♪♪
I Heard the Angels Singing (Sugar Hill, 1989) ♪♪♪
My Heart Is Yours (Sugar Hill, 1990) ♪♪♪
Treasures Money Can't Buy (Brentwood, 1990) ♪♪♪♪
Pressing On Regardless (Brentwood, 1990) ♪♪♪
Doyle Lawson & Quicksilver Gospel Collection, Volume 1 (Sugar Hill, 1990) ♪♪♪♪

influences:

◀◀ Jimmy Martin, Country Gentlemen

▶▶ J. D. Crowe & the New South, Ricky Skaggs

Randy Pitts

CHRIS LeDOUX

Born October 2, 1948, in Biloxi, MS.

Funny thing: Chris LeDoux makes some of the wildest, loudest music to come out of Nashville in recent years, but you never hear anybody complaining about him selling out to rock 'n' roll. (Okay, maybe radio program directors, but who listens to them?) That's because LeDoux actually has lived the life he sings about. A former world-champion bareback bronc rider who started riding in rodeos and writing songs at age 14, LeDoux may be the only country singer this side of George Strait who's earned the hat he wears. LeDoux came to national attention when Garth Brooks sang about listening to "a worn-out tape of Chris LeDoux" on his first single, "Much Too Young (To Feel This Damn Old)," but he'd sold more than $4 million worth of 22 independently released albums on the rodeo cir-cuit. He made his first records in Wyoming, but started record-ing in Nashville when his parents moved to the town. He be-came such a cowboy icon that a biography, *Gold Buckle Dreams—The Rodeo Life of Chris LeDoux,* was published in

1987. As a result of Brooks' song (and some nudging on the singer's part), Capitol Records not only signed LeDoux in 1991, the label reissued his independent albums. He's sometimes had a tough go at radio, but his albums sell well in the West and among rodeo fans. LeDoux is possibly the finest musical scribe of modern cowboy life; he has also had gallery shows of his bronze sculptures.

what to buy: Only two of LeDoux's singles—"Cadillac Ranch" and "Watcha Gonna Do with a Cowboy," his duet with Garth Brooks—have reached the Top 40. *Best of Chris LeDoux* (Lib-erty, 1994, prod. Jimmy Bowen, Jerry Crutchfield, Allen Reynolds) ♪♪♪♪ has both of these, plus some great examples of country-rock that actually rocks: Joe Ely's "For Your Love" and his own "County Fair" and "Hooked on an 8-Second Ride." *Stampede* (Capitol, 1996, prod. Gregg Brown) ♪♪♪♪ doesn't have much in the way of hits, but it's probably LeDoux's finest single album. Working with producer Gregg Brown, who pro-duced Travis Tritt's early records, LeDoux's performances kick up more dirt than usual, particularly on the self-penned songs "Take Me to the Rodeo" and "Stampede."

what to buy next: *American Cowboy* (Liberty, 1994) ♪♪♪♪ is a three-CD box set that provides a fair overview of LeDoux's early music (including the cult hit "Copenhagen"), as well as his biggest singles for Capitol/Liberty.

what to avoid: LeDoux's early albums, like most independent country recordings, occasionally suffer from subpar sound and iffy songs. It's a little more than occasional on *Life as a Rodeo Man* (Capitol, 1975/1991, prod. Al LeDoux) ♪♪ and *Melodies and Memories* (Capitol, 1984/1991, prod. Al LeDoux) ♪♪.

the rest:

Rodeo Songs, Old & New (Capitol, 1973/1991) ♪♪♪
Rodeo and Living Free (Capitol, 1974, 1991) ♪♪♪
Songs of Rodeo Life (Capitol, 1977, 1991) ♪♪♪
Sing Me a Song Mr. Rodeo Man (Capitol, 1977/1991) ♪♪♪♪
Used to Want to Be a Cowboy (Capitol, 1981/1992) ♪♪♪♪
Old Cowboy Classics (Capitol, 1983/1991) ♪♪♪♪
Gold Buckle Dreams (Capitol, 1987/1991) ♪♪♪
Chris LeDoux & the Saddle Boogie Band (Capitol, 1988/1991) ♪♪♪
Powder River (Capitol, 1989) ♪♪♪
Radio & Rodeo Hits (Capitol, 1990) ♪♪♪
Whatcha Gonna Do with a Cowboy (Capitol, 1992) ♪♪♪
Under This Old Hat (Capitol, 1993) ♪♪♪
Haywire (Capitol, 1994) ♪♪♪♪
Rodeo Rock and Roll Collection (Capitol, 1995) ♪♪♪
Live (Capitol, 1997) ♪♪♪

influences:
◀◀ Charlie Daniels, Waylon Jennings, Bruce Springsteen
▶▶ Garth Brooks, Royal Wade Kimes

Brian Mansfield

BRENDA LEE

Born December 11, 1944, in Lithonia, GA.

Standing less than 5 feet tall, Brenda Lee nevertheless possesses a gargantuan set of vocal pipes that, like contemporary Pasty Cline, are able to wring every last drop of energy out of a melody. Beginning as a spry 11-year-old during the mid-1950s cutting country sides in Nashville, "Little Miss Dynamite" became a teenage pop sensation by 1960 and for the next three years scored repeatedly with "Sweet Nothin's," "I'm Sorry," "Break It to Me Gently" and many others, with high quality control provided by Cline-producer Owen Bradley. Lee's output would diminish to a few final chart hits by the later 1960s (including one last smash, "Coming On Strong"), before she returned to her country roots during the early 1970s, releasing a handful of Top 10s.

what to buy: The absolute best (as well as interesting obscurities) of Lee can be found on the tandem collection *The Brenda Lee Anthology, Volume I 1956–1961* and *The Brenda Lee Anthology, Volume II 1962–1980* (MCA, 1991, comp. prod. Andy McKaie) 𝄢𝄢𝄢𝄢, which contains all her hits from both sides of the tracks.

what to buy next: *Merry Christmas from Brenda Lee* (MCA, 1964, prod. Owen Bradley) 𝄢𝄢𝄢 has the standard "Rockin' Around the Christmas Tree" and other great yuletide tunes.

the rest:
Brenda Lee Story: Her Greatest Hits (MCA, 1974) 𝄢𝄢𝄢
Wiedersehn Ist Wunderschon (Bear Family, 1990) 𝄢𝄢𝄢𝄢
Brenda Lee (MCA, 1991) 𝄢𝄢𝄢

worth searching for: *Greatest Country Hits* (MCA, 1990, prod. Owen Bradley, Don Chancey) 𝄢𝄢𝄢 compiles her later—though lesser—material from the 1970s country charts.

influences:
◀◀ Edith Piaf, Davis Sisters
▶▶ Lesley Gore, LeAnn Rimes

David Simons

Brenda Lee **(AP/Wide World Photos)**

JOHNNY LEE

Born John Lee Ham, July 3, 1946, in Texas City, TX.

An ambitious, hopeful Johnny Lee finally met Mickey Gilley one night at Gilley's popular Pasadena, Texas, bar, but he never let on that it was their first encounter. Lee wove such an entrancing story about how the two singers had shared a stage on a local TV show and about how much he'd appreciate sitting in with Gilley that night that Gilley figured no harm would come of a reunion. The deception eventually led to friendship and musical collaboration. Later, Lee owed much of his success to Gilley's honky-tonk when the 1980 film *Urban Cowboy*, shot there, set the country scurrying for fringe shirts and Lee's gold single "Lookin' for Love."

what to buy: Because of *Urban Cowboy*, Lee practically defined country for an entire audience. Fortunately, "Lookin' for Love" was a decent representation, as were a couple of Lee's followups, "Pickin' up Strangers" and Michael Martin Murphey's "Cherokee Fiddle." *Greatest Hits* (Warner Bros., 1983, prod. various) 𝄢𝄢𝄢 has all these songs, of course, but it also shows Lee's middle-of-the-road tendencies getting the best of him on other hits like "Prisoner of Hope" and "When You Fall in Love." Lee's a passable singer, but a honky-tonk hero he's not.

what to buy next: *Best Of* (Curb, 1990, prod. various) 🎵🎵🎵 counts on people not remembering that Lee had hits other than "Lookin' for Love" and "Cherokee Fiddle." After those two cuts, this album is filled with modest numbers like "I Can Be a Heartbreaker, Too" that barely saw the bottom half of the singles charts during the late 1980s.

what to avoid: *Ramblin' Rose* **WOOF!** is merely a bad album, with Lee's Muzak-like versions of "Red Sails in the Sunset" and "Ramblin' Rose" (his two Top 40 hits). But when he then has the nerve to sing "If memories are all I sing, I'd rather drive a truck," while turning Rick Nelson's bitter "Garden Party" into the unfathomably dumb "Country Party," you know the guy has no clue what he's doing.

the rest:
New Directions (Curb, 1989) 🎵🎵

worth searching for: For two lessons on just how far afield one-time stars can go, check out Lee's attempt to cash in on the attention the O.J. Simpson criminal trial received. "911 O.J." (Hot Country Cafe, 1995, prod. Richard Feldman) **WOOF!** donated some of what few proceeds it generated to shelters for battered women.

influences:
◄◄ Mickey Gilley

Craig Shelburne and Brian Mansfield

LEGENDARY STARDUST COWBOY

Born Norman Carl Odam, Esq., September 5, 1947, in Lubbock, TX.

He has been hailed as a "cathartic genius"; others call his 1968 recording "Paralyzed" the worst record ever made. Whatever the case may be, the story of the Legendary Stardust Cowboy is, with no question, one of the strangest in all of country music. Stranger still is that every single word of it is true. This self-described singer/songwriter/dancer/actor/poet and "all 'round whoop-de-do guy" knew by the age of seven that he was destined for fame—just how exactly to achieve this goal he was not so certain of until he acquired his first guitar. He began emulating the styles of his favorite singers (Ray Price, Marty Robbins and Johnny Cash) and the dance steps of the young Elvis Presley. Joe Ely, who has gone on to pronounce "The Ledge" as no less than "West Texas' greatest jazz musi-

cian," remembers watching the teenager singing Everly Brothers songs on the steps of their high school; another friend, Jimmie Dale Gilmore, recalls Odam, atop a car with the words "NASA Presents the Legendary Stardust Cowboy" spray-painted across its sides, giving impromptu performances at the local Hi-D-Ho Drive-In. Not surprisingly, in these dark ages before the likes of Willie Nelson, some townsfolk took offense at the sight of a young man with shoulder-length hair, mutton-chop sideburns and bright orange cowboy get-ups singing the C&W hits of the day at the local burger joint. So in the summer of 1968 the Ledge decided Lubbock could no longer contain a talent and a vision of his magnitude and, with $160 in his pocket and a broken dobro, and without a manager, agent, record contract or even an invitation, he set out for New York City to perform on no less than Johnny Carson's *The Tonight Show*. He only made it as far as Fort Worth, though, where some vacuum cleaner salesmen caught his act and immediately took him to their neighbor T-Bone Burnett's recording studio. T-Bone, gamely offering his services on drums, began committing the Ledge's repertoire direct to quarter-inch tape, two minutes of which were spliced off and rushed upstairs to the town's only Top 40 radio station. That piece of tape, of a song called "Paralyzed," went on the air that night, and within a week was #38 on KXOL's All-American Hit List. Singles were hurriedly pressed (on the newly christened Psycho Suave label), one of which came to the attention of a local promoter who quickly licensed it to Mercury Records. One month later, the Legendary Stardust Cowboy was performing his breakaway smash, with every one of its fierce rebel yells and bugle solos intact, on the nation's most popular television show, *Rowan & Martin's Laugh-In*.

This appearance, rightly hailed by *Rolling Stone* magazine as one of the 25 Greatest Musical Moments in TV history, led to offers from *American Bandstand*, Joey Bishop and Ed Sullivan. It was at this most inopportune of moments that a four-month musician's strike, banning live music from network television, halted the phenomenal rise of "Paralyzed" and dealt the Cowboy's momentum a crippling blow. Two more singles were released in 1969, but within a year of first leaving Lubbock, Odam's career seemed to be prematurely dead. An arrest soon afterwards—on a trumped-up vagrancy charge—only served to add insult to injury. The Legendary Stardust Cowboy was reduced to working the night shift at the Dunes Hotel in Vegas—and not as a performer. His influence festered throughout the 1970s, however. Rocker David Bowie, having caught a BBC rerun of the notorious *Laugh-In* episode, admits to being inspired enough to create his Ziggy Stardust persona partially in the Ledge's honor. Norman Odam's former classmates Ely and Gilmore continued to sing his praises as their own careers took off, and all of this belated recognition coaxed the Cowboy back into the studio during the early 1980s to cut his first full-length album, *Rock-It to Stardom,* and then hit the road for long-awaited tours of the U.S., Europe and Australia—recordings of which were finally set for release during 1997. He is also the subject of an absolutely delightful documentary film by Anthony Philputt entitled *Cotton Pickin' Smash: The Story of the Legendary Stardust Cowboy.* At last report, he was sighted opening a Chris Isaak show at San Francisco's Fillmore Auditorium, and the less musically and socially adventurous part of Isaak's audience was suitably shocked and outraged by the Ledge's fierce-as-ever act. But Odam still hasn't gotten an invitation to appear on *The Tonight Show.*

what's available: *Retro Rocket Back to Earth* (New Rose, 1996, prod. Frank Novicki, Gary Stillens) 🎵🎵🎵🎵 is a CD re-issue of the Ledge's second and third albums, and Norton Records (PO Box 646, Cooper Station, New York, NY 10003) also has pressed two singles from these sessions.

worth searching for: *Rock-It to Stardom* (Amazing, 1984, prod. Jim Yanaway) 🎵🎵🎵 is the first "comeback" album, also issued in Europe on the Big Beat and Virgin labels. As for the song that started it all? "Paralyzed," although it deserves to be made Required Listening for every man, woman and child in America, is usually only available on novelty-record compilations, the easiest to find of which is *Wild, Weird & Wacky* (Time/Life, 1990, prod. various) 🎵🎵🎵🎵🎵.

influences:

⏮ Elvis Presley, Tom Jones, Herb Alpert

⏭ Wild Man Fisher, Eugene Chadbourne, Jack Pedler

Gary Pig Gold

THE LeROI BROTHERS

Formed 1981, in Fort Worth, TX.

Steve Doerr, guitar, vocals; Mike Buck, drums; Don Leady, guitar, vocals (1981–84); Joey Doerr, vocals (1984–85); Evan Johns, guitar, vocals (1984–85); Rick "Casper" Rawls, guitar, vocals (1986–present); Jackie Newhouse, bass (1983–88); Speedy Sparks, bass (1989–present).

The LeRoi Brothers have always suffered the bar band's curse: better seen (live) than heard (over your speakers or headphones). They are first and foremost a performing band, even though the core of the group first came together as a studio band to back up the Legendary Stardust Cowboy on his *Rock-It to Stardom* album. Doerr, Leady and ex-Fabulous Thunderbirds drummer Buck stuck together and subsequently moved a few hours south down Interstate 35 to Austin, where they fell in with that city's thriving blues scene (playing with singer Lou Ann Barton, among others) and matured into one of the best roadhouse bands in Texas by the time they began recording.

what to buy: Their debut album *Check This Action!* (Jungle, 1983/Rounder, 1994, prod. Vince McGarry, Gary Rice) 🎵🎵🎵🎵 is still the quintessential LeRoi Brothers album, going heavy on the country-blues raunch twang. It also has a manic garage-punk edge reminiscent of Roky Erikson's 13th Floor Elevators, especially "Ballad of a Juvenile Delinquent" and "Are You with Me Baby (Say Yeah)." Point of interest: Keith Ferguson, an old bandmate of Buck's in the Fabulous Thunderbirds, serves as guest bassist.

what to buy next: *Forget about the Danger . . . Think of the Fun* (Columbia, 1984, prod. Craig Leon, Denny Bruce) 🎵🎵🎵 is the only LeRoi Brothers record to grace a major label. This six-song EP is also as close as they've ever sounded, and they're a surprisingly convincing pop band. "Pretty Little Lights of Town" was the should've-been-a-hit single.

what to avoid: *Lucky Lucky Me* (Profile, 1985, prod. Vince McGarry) 🎵🎵 was recorded too soon after the departure of Don Leady, before his replacement Evan Johns had fully settled into the lineup. Consequently, it sounds rushed and half-baked, with demo-quality sound. (Note: Also released on Demon Records in England under the title *Protection from Enemies.*)

the rest:

Open All Night (Profile, 1986) 🎵🎵🎵
Viva LeRoi (New Rose, 1989) 🎵🎵🎵
Rhythm and Booze (New Rose EP, 1990) 🎵🎵🎵

worth searching for: After their stints in the band, various LeRoi Brothers have done worthy work elsewhere. Don Leady formed the Cajun-rock band the Tailgators, Evan Johns went on to a well-regarded solo career and Joey Doerr wound up in Ballad Shambles and, later, Hand of Glory. Leady, Johns and Mike Buck also turn up as the core of an ad hoc all-star band on the supersession album *Big Guitars from Texas* (Jungle, 1985, prod. Vince McGarry) 🎵🎵🎵; improbably, it earned the group a Grammy Award nomination, but don't hold that against them, because it's great—especially the scorching version of Ennio Morricone's *The Good, the Bad and the Ugly* theme.

influences:

◀◀ Joe Ely, Blasters, Fabulous Thunderbirds, Delbert McClinton, Jerry Lee Lewis, Dave Edmunds

▶▶ Beat Farmers, Old 97's

David Menconi

THE LEWIS FAMILY

Formed 1951, in Lincolnton, GA.

James Roy "Pop" Lewis, vocals; Pauline "Mom" Lewis, vocals; Roy "Little Roy" Lewis Jr., banjo, vocals; Wallace Lewis, guitar, vocals; Miggie Lewis, vocals; Polly Lewis Williams, vocals; Janis Lewis Phillips, vocals; Travis Lewis, bass; Lewis Phillips, guitar, banjo, mandolin.

Known as the First Family of Bluegrass Gospel, the Lewis clan has been keeping the flame alive for three generations, adding new members whenever an interested family member was old enough to pick or sing. Pop Lewis was a singer and musician who recruited his three oldest sons to perform with him during the 1940s. They brought along Little Roy Jr. and called themselves the Lewis Brothers for awhile before their sisters joined in 1951. They initially performed at churches, school houses and community functions in the Georgia/North Carolina area before they got their own radio show and, eventually, a TV show in the region. Though their membership has changed, their woodsy sound hasn't. Known for soaring female harmonies and Little Roy's virtuoso musicianship and screwball stage antics, the Lewises have made their name primarily on the busy bluegrass festival circuit.

what's available: Although the Lewises have cut more than 45 albums over the years, most are out of print and hard to find—though some are usually on sale at their shows. The family still records periodically, but its new album, *Bluegrass Country Club* (Thoroughbred, 1997) ♫♫ is the only one you're likely to find at a record store (and even then you'll probably have to order it). Their records, this one included, seldom do justice to the family group's tight harmonies and Southern fried playing. They have to be seen to be appreciated.

influences:

◀◀ Flatt & Scruggs

▶▶ Cox Family, Alison Krauss

Doug Pullen

JERRY LEE LEWIS

Born September 29, 1935, in Ferriday, LA.

The conventional take on this rock 'n' roll pioneer by the Nashville establishment, after he crashed the country charts during the late 1960s, was that Jerry Lee Lewis always had "one leg in" the country field. Indeed, his first Sun rockabilly 78 found him warbling, honky-tonk style, a Hank Williams number on the B-side of "Whole Lotta Shakin' Goin' On." But in a most amazing comeback, after a most public fall from grace, Lewis re-invented himself as a country music chart regular during the late 1960s with hits such as "She Even Woke Me Up to Say Goodbye" and "What Made Milwaukee Famous." He never changed his raucous, uninhibited live performances one wild hair, but he capitulated to the assembly-line process of Nashville's hit factory under the aegis of Mercury producer Jerry Kennedy. Of course, his raw nerve personality brimmed over the top of even the most pedestrian productions in which he and Kennedy engaged; like some freak force of nature, Jerry Lee Lewis cannot be restrained.

what to buy: The collection of his Mercury Records-era Nashville recordings, *Killer Country* (Mercury, 1995, prod. Jerry Kennedy) ♫♫♫, ranks with the finest of Buck Owens, Merle Haggard, George Jones and the other country kings of the era.

what to buy next: Europeans have pumped out so many bewildering boxed sets and multi-disc reissues of Lewis' abundant recordings that virtually every scrap of tape he imprinted during his lengthy stay with Sun Records may be available somewhere. But most people will happily suffice with the two disc set *The Jerry Lee Lewis Anthology: All Killer, No Filler* (Rhino, 1990, prod. various) ♫♫♫.

what to avoid: *The Golden Rock Hits of Jerry Lee Lewis* (Smash, 1967/1987) ♫♫, an album of remakes that seems unnecessary since he got it right the first time.

the rest:

Jerry Lee Lewis (Rhino, 1958/1989) ♫♫♫♫

Jerry Lee's Greatest! (Rhino, 1961/1989) ♫♫♫♫

Original Sun Greatest Hits (Rhino, 1984) ♫♫♫♫♫

Milestones (Rhino, 1985) ♫♫♫♫♫

20 Classic Jerry Lee Lewis Hits (Original Sound Entertainment, 1986) ♫♫♫♫

The Complete Palomino Club Recordings (Tomato, 1989) ♫♫♫♫

Heartbreak (Tomato, 1989) ♫♫♫

Rare Tracks: Wild One (Rhino, 1989) ♫♫♫♫♫

Best of Jerry Lee Lewis (Curb, 1991) ♫♫♫

Rockin' My Life Away: The Jerry Lee Lewis Collection (Warner Bros., 1991) ♪♪♪♫
Live at the Star Club, Hamburg (Rhino, 1992) ♪♪♪♪
Rocket '88 (Tomato, 1992) ♪♪♪
Greatest Hits—Finest Performances (Sun, 1995) ♪♪♪♫
Young Blood (Sire, 1995) ♪♪♫

worth searching for: His early country albums on Mercury are all pretty great, but *Another Place, Another Time* (Mercury, 1969, prod. Jerry Kennedy) ♪♪♪♪ is an especially fine piece from the period. A 1973 interview disc was issued to radio stations promoting his dud comeback album *Southern Roots,* and a few quick comments from Jerry Lee can spice up any home taping projects.

influences:

◀◀ Meade Lux Lewis, Moon Mullican

▶▶ Mickey Gilley, Jason D. Williams

Joel Selvin

LAURIE LEWIS

Born in 1950.

Laurie Lewis grew up in the San Francisco Bay area, where she gained valuable exposure at area folk music festivals to the likes of Doc Watson and the Greenbriar Boys. Performing in fiddle contests, she was a two-time winner of the California State Women's Championship. Her involvement in the predominantly female groups Blue Rose and Good Ol' Persons was helpful in expanding women's roles in bluegrass music, but it's her stylistic diversity that has kept Lewis an interesting and vital artist to watch, especially in the last decade. Her recording career took off in 1986, when her Flying Fish debut won the National Association of Independent Record Distributors (NAIRD) Album of the Year award. The 1987 addition of mandolin player Tom Rozum to her Grant Street String Band (originally formed in 1979) was a turning point; in 1995 the pair released a highly acclaimed duet album. A year before that, Lewis was named the International Bluegrass Music Association's Female Vocalist of the Year. A gifted songwriter, Nashville producers and artists would do well to comb through her albums for material.

what to buy: *True Stories* (Rounder, 1993, prod. Mike Marshall, Laurie Lewis) ♪♪♪♪♫ is highlighted by IBMA Song of the Year "Who Will Watch the Home Place?" and also includes Lewis' beautiful "Knocking on Your Door Again."

what to buy next: Lewis and Tom Rozum collaborated on *The*

Jerry Lee Lewis **(AP/Wide World Photos)**

Oak & the Laurel (Rounder, 1995, prod. Laurie Lewis, Tom Rozum) ♪♪♪♪, a nice duet album with some great original songs alongside well-chosen covers. A high point is Rozum's vocal on Dave Olney's "Millionaire."

the rest:
Restless Rambling Heart (Flying Fish, 1986) ♪♪♪♫
Love Chooses You (Flying Fish, 1989) ♪♪♪♪
(With Grant Street) *Singin' My Troubles Away* (Flying Fish, 1990) ♪♪♪♫
(With Kathy Kallick) *Together* (Rounder, 1991) ♪♪♪♫

influences:

◀◀ Good Ol' Persons, Blue Rose

▶▶ Kate MacKenzie, Mollie O'Brien

see also: *Scott Nygaard, Good Ol' Persons, Kathy Kallick*

Stephen L. Betts

LINDA GAIL LEWIS

Born July 18, 1947, in Ferriday, LA.

Though she has recorded only a handful of albums, Linda Gail

Tim Rushlow of Little Texas (© Ken Settle)

Lewis sings and plays piano with much of the swagger and abandon of her legendary brother, Jerry Lee Lewis.

what's available: *Love Makes the Difference* (Icehouse, 1996) 𝄞𝄞 is a watered-down mainstream country outing that rarely shows Lewis' considerable talents to best advantage. *International Affair* (Sharecropper, 1991, prod. Maury O'Rourk) 𝄞𝄞𝄞𝄞, which features inspired covers of Bob Dylan, Nick Lowe and Billy Swan originals, is a more rock-oriented effort than her late 1960s country recordings.

worth searching for: *Together* (Smash, 1970, prod. Jerry Kennedy) 𝄞𝄞𝄞𝄞, recorded with brother Jerry Lee, is perhaps the most incendiary country duet album of all time. The duo's ardent renditions of "Jackson" and "Don't Let Me Cross Over" are all the more arresting when you consider that Linda Gail and Jerry Lee are siblings, not lovers.

influences:
◀◀ Rose Maddox, Wanda Jackson
▶▶ Rosie Flores

Bill Friskics-Warren

THE LILLY BROTHERS /DON STOVER

Formed 1952, in Boston, MA.

Everett Lilly (born July 1, 1924, in WV), mandolin, fiddle; Michell Burt "Bea" Lilly (born December 15, 1921, in WV), guitar.

Everett and Bea Lilly were West Virginia natives with a long history of performing live and on radio when, in 1952, fiddler Tex Logan talked them into joining him in Boston; there, with the addition of fellow West Virginian Don Stover on banjo, the brothers became, for a time, the Confederate Mountaineers and began a regular live gig at Boston's famed Hillbilly Ranch. They were one of the few true bluegrass bands in New England during that period, and as such were immensely important to the growth of bluegrass in the Northeast, exposing such future stars of the genre as Bill Keith, Jim Rooney, Joe Val, Peter Rowan and members of the Charles River Valley Boys to the real stuff. The death of Everett's son in an auto accident prompted the return of the brothers to West Virginia; they performed sporadically with Stover and/or Logan at festivals throughout the 1970s and into the 1980s. Stover, an outstanding old-time, or clawhammer, banjo player—as well as one of the best bluegrass pickers—died November 11, 1996. Their early recordings continue to exert an influence through reissues.

what to buy: *Live at Hillbilly Ranch* (Hay Holler, 1996, prod. Kerry Hay) 𝄞𝄞𝄞𝄞, made at the Lilly's famous gig alongside Don Stover, features 23 tracks of traditional bluegrass. The trio (accompanied by an unknown bassist) are in fine fettle throughout. *Early Recordings* (Rebel Records, 1991, prod. Dave Freeman) 𝄞𝄞𝄞𝄞, a reissue of recordings from 1956 and 1957 that also feature Stover, presents the trio performing 11 examples of the finest traditional bluegrass imaginable.

worth searching for: *Folk Songs from the Southern Mountains* (Folkways, 1962, prod. Mike Seeger) 𝄞𝄞𝄞𝄞 was highly influential to roots-seeking folkies of the 1960s.

solo outings:

Don Stover:
Things in Life (Rounder, 1972) 𝄞𝄞𝄞𝄞

influences:
◀◀ Monroe Brothers, Blue Sky Boys
▶▶ Joe Val, Charles River Valley Boys

Randy Pitts

LITTLE TEXAS /BRADY SEALS

Formed 1989, in Nashville, TN.

Tim Rushlow, lead vocals; Dwayne O'Brien, guitar, vocals; Porter Howell, guitar; Duane Propes, bass, vocals; Brady Seals, lead vocals, guitar, keyboards (1989–95); Del Gray, drums; Jeff Huskins, keyboards, fiddle, vocals (1995–present).

Named for a holler south of Nashville, Little Texas became one of the most popular (and most maligned) groups in country music during the early 1990s. To some they represented a new generation of country players and listeners; to others, they were a bunch of pop-influenced hacks whose biggest asset was their hair. The group formed around Tim Rushlow and Dwayne O'Brien, who met in 1984 in Arlington, Texas, and later moved to Nashville. There they met Porter Howell and Duane Propes, also from Texas, who were attending the music-business program at Nashville's Belmont University. The final lineup came together after they found Brady Seals and Del Gray at a show in Springfield, Massachusetts. Seals is the nephew of songwriter Troy Seals and cousin to singer Dan Seals. "What Might Have Been," from the group's second album, *Big Time*, charted on *Billboard*'s pop and adult-contemporary charts. The group won the Academy of Country Music's Top Vocal Group award in 1994.

what to buy: Stand or fall, the members of Little Texas do it on their own merits: the only cut on *Greatest Hits* (Warner Bros., 1995, prod. various) 🎵🎵🎵 a member of the band *didn't* have a hand in writing is a version of "Peaceful Easy Feeling" from the Eagles tribute *Common Thread*. It's a pretty smooth collection, though the ballads ("What Might Have Been," "My Love") hold up better than the uptempo songs ("God Blessed Texas," "Kick a Little"). You'd think that a greatest-hits package after only three albums wouldn't give you much to pick from, but Little Texas had a dozen hits by then and even left two of those songs off. Funny thing is, two of the new songs on the album never even made the Top 40.

what to buy next: On the aptly-titled *Kick a Little* (Warner Bros., 1994, prod. Christy DiNapoli, Doug Grau, Little Texas) 🎵🎵, the group tries to push (ever so gently) at the boundaries of their hair-boys image.

the rest:
First Time for Everything (Warner Bros., 1992) 🎵🎵
Big Time (Warner Bros., 1993) 🎵🎵

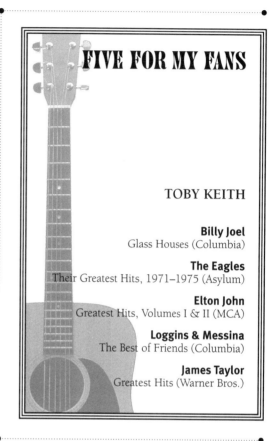

FIVE FOR MY FANS

TOBY KEITH

Billy Joel
Glass Houses (Columbia)

The Eagles
Their Greatest Hits, 1971–1975 (Asylum)

Elton John
Greatest Hits, Volumes I & II (MCA)

Loggins & Messina
The Best of Friends (Columbia)

James Taylor
Greatest Hits (Warner Bros.)

worth searching for: A promotional copy of *Big Time* featured a tuxedoed cover and a copy of the "What Might Have Been" single.

solo outings:
Brady Seals:
The Truth (Reprise, 1997) 🎵🎵🎵

influences:
◀◀ Eagles, Restless Heart
▶▶ Lonestar, Ricochet, Frazier River

Brian Mansfield

HANK LOCKLIN

Born Lawrence Hankins Locklin, February 15, 1918, in McLellan, FL.

Hank Locklin's soaring tenor made him one of the most popular country crooners of the 1950s and 1960s, both at home in

Maria McKee (© Ken Settle)

the United States and in Ireland. He had his first hit, "The Same Sweet Girl," for 4 Star in 1949, but had his greatest success with RCA from 1956 to 1969, with such songs as "Why Baby Why," "Geisha Girl" and "Send Me the Pillow You Dream On." He joined the Grand Ole Opry in 1960, the same year he had his biggest hit, "Please Help Me, I'm Falling," which featured the distinctive piano of Floyd Cramer. After his recording career waned, Locklin was elected mayor of his Florida hometown.

what's available: Locklin is one of many victims of RCA's disinterest in its non-Elvis Presley country catalog, so his U.S. output is limited to two cassettes of re-recordings, *Greatest Hits Volume 1* (Plantation) ♪ and *16 Best of Hank Locklin* (Plantation, 1987) ♪♪, made for Shelby Singleton's Nashville company around 1977. Germany's Bear Family label does have a box set of RCA recordings called *Please Help Me I'm Falling* for the dedicated and well-heeled.

influences:
◀◀ Eddy Arnold, George Morgan

▶▶ Jim Ed Brown, Jim Reeves

Brian Mansfield

LONE JUSTICE /MARIA McKEE

Formed 1983, in Los Angeles, CA. Disbanded 1987.

Maria McKee (born August 17, 1964), vocals, guitar; Ryan Hedgecock, guitar, vocals (1983–86); Marvin Etzioni, bass, vocals (1983–86); Don Heffington, drums (1983–86); Shayne Fontayne, guitar (1986–87); Gregg Sutton, bass (1986–87); Rudy Richman, drums (1986–87); Bruce Brody, keyboards (1986–87).

Before it was a rock 'n' roll movement, Lone Justice played rock with a countrified twang, taking a spirited, rootsy approach that in 1985 was fresh, not trendy. With her powerful voice and eye-catching presence, it wasn't long before Maria McKee became the group's focal point—and, in fact, the group, as an entirely different band of musicians, came on board for Lone Justice's second and final album. The group split up following a tour in which it opened for U2, and McKee (working with Lone Justice keyboardist Bruce Brody) took a solo path that's been nothing if not fascinating, as she's changed styles from the ethereal *Maria McKee* to the Lone Justice soundalike *You Gotta Sin to Get Saved* and the more eclectic *Life Is Sweet*. Marvin Etzioni, meanwhile, has recorded some albums of his own and produced titles for Peter Case and Toad the Wet Sprocket.

what to buy: *Lone Justice* (Geffen, 1985, prod. Jimmy Iovine) ♪♪♪♪ is an exceptional debut, the arrival of a fresh new sound via exuberant performances and a tremendous batch of songs such as "East of Eden," "Sweet, Sweet Baby (I'm Falling)" and Tom Petty's "Ways to Be Wicked."

what to buy next: Lone Justice's *BBC Radio 1 Live in Concert* (Windsong, 1993) ♪♪♪ gives a sense of Lone Justice's—and particularly McKee's—strength on a concert stage. McKee's second solo album, *You Gotta Sin to Get Saved* (Geffen, 1993, prod. George Drakoulias) ♪♪♪♪ is nearly as good as *Lone Justice* and features the original band's rhythm section as well as members of the Jayhawks.

what to avoid: McKee's *Life Is Sweet* (Geffen, 1996, prod. Maria McKee, Bruce Brody, Mark Freegard) ♪♪ is all over the place to the point where even the force of her singing can't bring the album back into focus.

the rest:

Shelter (Geffen, 1986) ♫♫♫

worth searching for: McKee's guest appearance for a duet on "Temple and Shine," with Marvin Etzioni on his album *Weapons of the Spirit* (Restless, 1994) ♫♫♫.

solo outings:

Maria McKee:

Maria McKee (Geffen, 1989) ♫♫♫

Marvin Etzioni:

The Mandolin Man (Restless, 1992) ♫♫♫

influences:

◀◀ Tom Petty & the Heartbreakers, Byrds, Flying Burrito Brothers, Janis Joplin, Aretha Franklin

▶▶ Sheryl Crow, Uncle Tupelo, Jayhawks, Cowboy Junkies

see also: *Tammy Rogers*

Gary Graff

LONESOME RIVER BAND /RONNIE BOWMAN

Formed 1983 in VA.

Ronnie Bowman, bass guitar, vocals (1990–present); Sammy Shelor, banjo, guitar, vocals (1990–92, 1993–present); Don Rigsby, mandolin, vocals; Kenny Smith, guitar, vocals; Tim Austin, guitar, vocals (1983–95); Dan Tyminski, mandolin, lead vocals (1988–92, 1993–94); Adam Steffey, mandolin; others.

Though they were formed in 1983, the Lonesome River Band didn't really come into its own until the release of *Carrying the Tradition*, which won the International Bluegrass Music Association's Album of the Year nod for 1992. Two more critically acclaimed albums have followed, as well as an award-winning solo effort from lead vocalist/bass guitarist Ronnie Bowman. The band is noted for traditionally rooted, contemporary bluegrass.

what to buy: *Carrying the Tradition* (Rebel, 1992, prod. Lonesome River Band) ♫♫♫♫, the album that turned the band into one of the biggest acts in bluegrass, is a mix of standards, including "Sitting on Top of the World," "Fireball Mail" and "My Sweet Blue-Eyed Darlin'," along with newer material like the original "Money in the Bank."

what to buy next: *Old Country Town* (Sugar Hill, 1994, prod. Lonesome River Band) ♫♫♫♫, a much-anticipated follow-up to *Carrying the Tradition*, earned the band a second IBMA Album

of the Year award. This one includes classics from Flatt & Scruggs and Don Reno.

the rest:

One Step Forward (Sugar Hill, 1996) ♫♫♫♫

solo outings:

Ronnie Bowman:

Cold Virginia Nights (Sugar Hill, 1995) ♫♫♫

influences:

◀◀ Boone Creek, J.D. Crowe

▶▶ IIIrd Tyme Out, Blue Highway, Hot Rize

Douglas Fulmer

LONESOME STANDARD TIME /LARRY CORDLE

Formed 1990, in Nashville, TN.

Larry Cordle (born November 16, 1949, in Cordell, KY), guitar, lead vocals; Glen Duncan, fiddle, guitar, vocals; Butch Baldassari, mandolin; Wayne Southards, bass, vocals (1991–92); Billy Rose, bass, vocals (1993–94); Robin Smith, bass (1994–95); Mike Bub, banjo, bass (1991-92); Larry Perkins, banjo (1993–94); Keith Little, banjo, guitar, vocals (1994–95).

Formed by songwriter Larry Cordle and ace fiddler Glen Duncan (who's worked with most of the top country and bluegrass acts), Lonesome Standard Time was one of the bluegrass success stories of the early 1990s. Cordle's mountain-inflected lead singing and Duncan's strong tenor harmonies gave the band a potent vocal sound, most often put to the service of Cordle's distinctive original songs. With a stage presentation and musical ethos reminiscent of 1950s-era Flatt & Scruggs, LST played many of the major festivals and venues, recorded a trio of well-received albums and had a few singles reach the top ranks of the bluegrass charts. By 1996, however, the band had scaled back its personal appearances and was largely inactive.

In addition to his work with Lonesome Standard Time, Larry Cordle has been a successful Nashville songwriter since the early 1980s, when boyhood friend Ricky Skaggs had a #1 country hit with Cordle's "Highway 40 Blues." A CPA in east Kentucky until he became a full-time songwriter, Cordle has had songs recorded by such artists as Garth Brooks, Trisha Yearwood, George Strait, Reba McEntire, Alison Krauss, Kathy Mattea and John Anderson. Cordle shared the International Bluegrass Music Association's 1993 Song of the Year award with co-writer Jim Rushing for their song "Lonesome Standard Time."

what's available: *Larry Cordle, Glen Duncan & Lonesome Standard Time* (Sugar Hill, 1992, prod. Glen Duncan, Larry Cordle) 𝄇𝄇𝄇 introduced the band and got a ton of radio airplay, thanks to "Lonesome Standard Time," "Lower on the Hog" and "Kentucky King," a tribute to Bill Monroe that featured the bluegrass patriarch guesting on mandolin. *Mighty Lonesome* (Sugar Hill, 1993, prod. Lonesome Standard Time) 𝄇𝄇𝄇, which includes the #1 bluegrass hit "The Bigger the Fool (The Harder the Fall)," showcased some of Cordle's more poignant songs, notably "The Tracks We Leave" and "Kentucky Thunder." Covers of Flatt & Scruggs and the Stanley Brothers honor the band's roots. *Lonesome As It Gets* (Sugar Hill, 1995, prod. Glen Duncan, Larry Cordle) 𝄇𝄇𝄇 is sparked by a pair of Duncan-penned instrumentals, "Duncan's Blues" and "Blue Field," a handful of Cordle originals and covers of Jimmie Rodgers and John Prine classics.

solo outings:
Butch Baldassari:
Old Town (Rebel, 1990) 𝄇𝄇𝄇
Evergreen/Mandolin Music for Christmas (Cactus/CMH, 1990) 𝄇𝄇𝄇
What's Doin'? (Cactus, 1991) 𝄇𝄇𝄇
(With the Nashville Mandolin Assembly) *Plectrasonics* (CMH, 1995) 𝄇𝄇𝄇
Gifts (Columbia, 1996) 𝄇𝄇𝄇

Larry Perkins:
A Touch of the Past (Pinecastle, 1993) 𝄇𝄇𝄇

influences:
◀◀ Flatt & Scruggs, Bill Monroe
▶▶ Wyatt Rice & Santa Cruz, Blue Highway

Jon Hartley Fox

LONESOME STRANGERS
Formed 1984, in Los Angeles, CA.

Jeff Rymes, vocals, guitar; Randy Weeks, vocals, guitar; Jeff Roberts, bass, backing vocals; Greg Perry, drums.

Although they are often thrown in with the California "cowpunk" movement (Dwight Yoakam, Rank & File, Lone Justice), the Lonesome Strangers owe a much bigger debt to the hillbilly boogie of the late 1940s. In fact, it was the Delmore Brothers that first brought Jeff Rymes and Randy Weeks together. The two met in Los Angeles during the early 1980s and soon discovered they had mutual love of old-time country music, rockabilly and hillbilly bop. They also found their voices blended together naturally, with a cool nasal harmony usually found only in blood kin. Pete Anderson included them on 1985's *Town*

South of Bakersfield compilation, which also featured Dwight Yoakam and Rosie Flores. That cut led to their debut effort, *Lonesome Pine*, now out-of-print. HighTone signed the band in 1989, and the Strangers scored a minor country hit that year with "Goodbye Lonesome, Hello Baby Doll" (a cover of the Johnny Horton song).

what's available: *The Lonesome Strangers* (HighTone, 1989, prod. Bruce Bromberg, Wyman Reese) 𝄇𝄇𝄇 contains "Goodbye Lonesome, Hello Baby Doll" and a revved-up version of the Delmore Brothers' "Lay Down My Old Guitar." On *Land of Opportunity* (Little Dog Records, 1997, prod. Dusty Wakeman) 𝄇𝄇𝄇, the band is again reunited with Dusty Wakeman, who produced *Lonesome Pine*. Rymes and Weeks wrote all of the songs, except for a rockin' cover of "Tobacco Road."

influences:
◀◀ Delmore Brothers, Everly Brothers, Foster & Lloyd

Cyndi Hoelzle

LONESTAR
Formed 1993, in Nashville, TN.

John Rich, lead vocals, bass guitar; Richie McDonald, lead vocals, guitar, keyboards; Michael Britt, guitar, vocals; Dean Sams, keyboards, guitar, vocals; Keech Rainwater, drums.

Lonestar basically took the Garth Brooks concept of country and applied it to a five-man band. The group's single "No News" spent three weeks at #1 in 1996 and was the first country hit to mention rock group Pearl Jam. The band played its first gig in 1993 under the name Texasee, since its members are from Texas, but they got together in Nashville. Drummer Keech Rainwater is a former member of Canyon.

what's available: *Lonestar* (BNA, 1996, prod. Don Cook, Wally Wilson) 𝄇𝄇𝄇 features big-beat country music, highlighted by "No News," a hard-driving talking blues.

worth searching for: *Lonestar/Live* (Lonestar, 1995, prod. Wally Wilson) 𝄇𝄇, a live EP recorded at Nashville's Wildhorse Saloon, led to Lonestar's signing with BNA Records. Among its six songs are early versions of "Heartbroke Every Day" and "When Cowboys Didn't Dance," as well as a cover of Kenny Loggins' "Danny's Song."

influences:
◀◀ Garth Brooks, Perfect Stranger
▶▶ Ricochet

Brian Mansfield

JOHN D. LOUDERMILK

Born March 31, 1934, in Durham, NC.

After trying his luck and largely failing as a pop recording artist during the 1950s (under the name Johnny Dee), John D. Loudermilk settled in Nashville, hooked up with Chet Atkins and began penning songs in earnest. "Tobacco Road"—his most enduring piece of work—was a gritty country-blues tune that became a pop smash for England's Nashville Teens. Though Loudermilk would continue to put out records, he would find more success as a songwriter during the 1960s. The Everly Brothers' "Ebony Eyes," Stonewall Jackson's "Waterloo" and the Raiders' #1 pop hit "The Lament of the Cherokee Reservation Indian (Indian Reservation)" are among his more notable songs (the latter was covered in excerpted form as the coda to Tim McGraw's "Indian Outlaw," giving Loudermilk his most recent country credit).

worth searching for: *Best of John D. Loudermilk* (1973) 🎵🎵🎵 reprises 1962's *12 Sides Of*, including "Tobacco Road," "Road Hog" and "Big Daddy," and includes Loudermilk's rendering of "The Lament of the Cherokee Reservation Indian (Indian Reservation)."

influences:

◀◀ Hank Williams

▶▶ Tony Joe White

David Simons

LOUVIN BROTHERS /CHARLIE LOUVIN

Brother duo from AL.

Lonnie Ira Louvin (born April 21, 1924, in Rainesville, AL; died June 28, 1965); Charlie Elzer Louvin (born July 7, 1927, in Rainesville, AL).

Without question, the Louvin Brothers are country music's most successful and most influential brother duo. Their two complementary voices, in contrast with their divisive personal battles, made for some incredible music and have cemented their place in the annals of country music history two decades after the Blue Sky Boys and the Delmore Brothers paved the way. Growing up in Henagar, Alabama, the pair began singing together as boys and had a radio program on WDEF in Chattanooga in 1942, where they were known as "The Radio Twins." Charlie went into the army while Ira worked with Charlie Monroe. In 1946 the Louvins were reunited, making their first record the following year on the Apollo label. Recordings followed in fairly rapid succession for Decca and MGM and, finally, Capitol in 1952. For three years they remained on the label without a hit until they scored with "When I Stop Dreaming" in 1955. Their next hit, 1956's "I Don't Believe You've Met My Baby," was their only chart-topper. By this time the brothers were established stars on the Grand Ole Opry, where they performed off and on until 1959. Their last Top 10 hit was "My Baby's Gone" in 1959. Although their music continued to showcase their harmonies, their relationship became quite strained during the next few years. In 1963 they broke up the act, both going on to pursue solo careers.

As tragic as if it were torn from one of their songs, Ira was killed in a car accident in 1965, on his way back to Alabama from a show in Missouri. Today, Charlie continues to perform on the Grand Ole Opry, and has benefited from the admiration of fans such as Emmylou Harris, whose first chart hit was the Louvin's "If I Could Only Win Your Love." Alison Krauss, along with Jerry Douglas, recorded a gorgeous version of "I Don't Believe You've Met My Baby," which she included on her double platinum *Now That I've Found You: A Collection*. The Everly Brothers and many other acts have also acknowledged the debt they owe to the Louvins. As a solo artist, Charlie Louvin had a pair of Top 10 hits and recorded duets with Harris, Roy Acuff and Melba Montgomery, also pairing with Louvin aficionado Charles Whitstein. In addition to appearances on the Grand Ole Opry, Charlie has opened the Louvin Brothers Museum in Bell Buckle, Tennessee.

what to buy: *When I Stop Dreaming: The Best of the Louvin Brothers* (Razor & Tie, 1995, comp. Marshall Crenshaw) 🎵🎵🎵🎵🎵 is just what it says, an extensive collection of hits and standout tracks, with comprehensive liner notes.

what to buy next: *Tragic Songs of Life* (Capitol, 1996) 🎵🎵🎵🎵🎵 is stark and beautiful. If you make it through any of these tracks without choking up, see your doctor; there's something seriously wrong with you. *Radio Favorites 1951–57* (Country Music Foundation, 1987) 🎵🎵🎵🎵 spans more years than any of the other radio show discs, and the sound quality, as expected from the CMF, is superior.

the rest:

Satan Is Real (Capitol, 1959/1996) 🎵🎵🎵🎵
Tribute to the Delmore Brothers (Capitol, 1960/1996) 🎵🎵🎵🎵
Songs That Tell a Story (Rounder, 1991) 🎵🎵🎵🎵
Live at New River Ranch (Copper Creek, 1996) 🎵🎵🎵🎵

worth searching for: Unless you've just got to have it all, the exhaustive eight-CD *Close Harmony* (Bear Family, 1992) 🎵🎵🎵🎵🎵

is more Louvin Brothers than you'd get through in one sitting. For completists only.

solo outings:

Charlie Louvin:

The Longest Train (Watermelon, 1996) 𝄞𝄞𝄞
(With Charles Whitstein) *Hoping That You're Hoping* (Copper Creek) 𝄞𝄞𝄞𝄞

influences:

◀◀ Delmore Brothers, Blue Sky Boys
▶▶ Whitstein Brothers, Flying Burrito Brothers

Stephen L. Betts

PATTY LOVELESS

Born Patricia Ramey, January 4, 1957, in Pikeville, KY.

It took Patty Loveless a decade to finally enjoy the critical and commercial success she's deserved. She achieved that lofty combination without having to compromise her musical integrity. If anything, perseverance has rewarded Loveless with the clout to sing better material and to avoid the superficial massacre of traditional country so prevalent in Nashville. Raised on bluegrass and country, Loveless and her brother Roger started performing as a duo when she was 14. While still in high school she toured with the Wilburn Brothers before working the club circuit in North Carolina and landing a job as a staff songwriter for Acuff-Rose. Two of her tunes, "I Did" and "Sounds of Loneliness," appear on her self-titled debut, but for subsequent albums Loveless relied on Nashville songwriters while she strengthened her expressive pipes. The improvement is noticeable: there's no other woman in contemporary country music whose voice has the power to evoke such deep emotions in those who hear it. Through her unerring song selection and elegant, restrained vocal delivery, Loveless has been able to bridge the gaps separating country, bluegrass, rock 'n' roll and the blues. She can travel from spunky country-rock such as Steve Earle's "A Little Bit in Love" to Patsy Cline-influenced balladry on "Can't Stop Myself from Loving You" and back to bluegrass-tinged country on the stellar "A Thousand Times a Day" without losing focus of the song.

what to buy: Loveless' creative rise is most evident on her three albums for Epic. The first, *Only What I Feel* (Epic, 1993, prod. Emory Gordy Jr.) 𝄞𝄞𝄞𝄞, includes the affecting ballad "How Can I Help You Say Goodbye," a farewell song long on heart but short on sap, and the piercing "Nothin' but the Wheel," an intelligent tune that raises loneliness to an art

form. The Country Music Association award-winning *When Fallen Angels Fly* (Epic, 1994, prod. Emory Gordy Jr.) 𝄞𝄞𝄞𝄞 proves Loveless can inject a frolicking spirit into a silly song, "I Try to Think about Elvis," without dumbing it any further. And she puts the definitive stamp on Gretchen Peters' gut-wrenching "You Don't Even Know Who I Am." *The Trouble with the Truth* (Epic, 1996, prod. Emory Gordy Jr.) 𝄞𝄞𝄞𝄞 finds her expanding her muse on a kicking cover of Richard Thompson's Cajun-spiced "Tear-Stained Letter" and Tony Arata's solemn "Someday I Will Lead the Parade." But even those don't compare to her gorgeous reading of Jim Lauderdale's ballad, "To Feel That Way at All."

what to buy next: For a quick look at Loveless' five-album tenure with MCA, pick up the *Greatest Hits* collection (MCA, 1993, prod. Tony Brown, Emory Gordy Jr.) 𝄞𝄞𝄞. But that album omits her best performance of that period, "Can't Stop Myself from Loving You," which appears on the equally worthy *Up Against My Heart* (MCA, 1991, prod. Emory Gordy Jr., Tony Brown) 𝄞𝄞𝄞.

what to avoid: *Patty Loveless Sings Songs of Love* (MCA, 1996, prod. Tony Brown, Emory Gordy Jr.) 𝄞𝄞 is an exploitative collection released after Loveless left MCA for Epic. It's skimpy on songs (eight) and short on hits.

the rest:

If My Heart Had Windows (MCA, 1988) 𝄞𝄞𝄞
Honky-Tonk Angel (MCA, 1988) 𝄞𝄞𝄞
On down the Line (MCA, 1990) 𝄞𝄞𝄞

worth searching for: Loveless has appeared as a background vocalist on countless records by better- and lesser-known country artists. Her guest-singer apex remains on the title cut of Vince Gill's *When I Call Your Name* (MCA, 1989, prod. Tony Brown) 𝄞𝄞𝄞𝄞. As her aching alto interlaces Gill's mournful tenor the listener is introduced to the sound of heartache. For those who feel like digging some more, Loveless slips a new song, the sassy blues-rocker "Where Are You Boy," into the *Tin Cup* soundtrack (Epic Soundtrax, 1996, prod. various) 𝄞𝄞𝄞.

influences:

◀◀ Loretta Lynn, Patsy Cline, Dolly Parton
▶▶ Bobbie Cryner, Mandy Barnett

Mario Tarradell

Patty Loveless (© Ken Settle)

Lyle Lovett **(MCA Records)**

LYLE LOVETT

Born November 1, 1957, in Houston, TX.

Originally a Houston folkie, Lyle Lovett went to Nashville during the mid-1980s, when alternative-leaning country acts like Steve Earle, k.d. lang and Lovett could get a fair hearing. While he did have some country hits and won a country Grammy, Nashville never could figure out what exactly was so intriguing or funny about a guy who wore an "Eraserhead" hairdo instead of a Stetson and sang Tammy Wynette's "Stand by Your Man" with a straight face. It's their loss; Lovett's albums have surveyed jazz, Texas swing, folk and country. Stylistically, he is, to use his own words, "What Hank Williams is to Neil Armstrong." But Lovett's lyrical bent—witty, ironic and sometimes unsettlingly direct—is his music's most memorable quality.

what to buy: *Pontiac* (MCA/Curb, 1987, prod. Tony Brown, Lyle Lovett) ∫∫∫∫ is quintessential Lovett. Few could turn the subject matter of a wedding that ends in double murder or a surreal seagoing horseback rider to their advantage, but that's what he accomplishes on "L.A. County" and "If I Had a Boat," respectively. "She's No Lady" and "She's Hot to Go" earned him

charges of misogyny, but the songs are as self-deprecating as they are chauvinistic. *Lyle Lovett* (MCA/Curb, 1986, prod. Tony Brown, Lyle Lovett) ∫∫∫∫ is a spectacular debut featuring the utterly unsentimental "God Will" and Lovett's wry reportage of nuptials held at a funeral parlor, "An Acceptable Level of Ecstasy (The Wedding Song)." On *Joshua Judges Ruth* (MCA/Curb, 1992, prod. George Massenburg, Billy Williams, Lyle Lovett) ∫∫∫∫ the melancholy streak that has run through Lovett's music from the beginning nearly takes over on such songs as "North Dakota" and "She's Already Made Up Her Mind," but injections of fiery gospel ("Church") and Lovett's arid wit ("Since the Last Time," which is narrated by a corpse) make the album one of his deepest and most diverse.

what to buy next: *The Road to Ensenada* (MCA/Curb, 1996, prod. Lyle Lovett, Billy Williams) ∫∫∫∫ is Lovett's most country-flavored album in a while, and while it contains plenty of upbeat humor ("That's Right (You're Not from Texas)") it's also his most somber album, perhaps reflecting obliquely on his split with ex-wife Julia Roberts. *Lyle Lovett and His Large Band* (MCA/Curb, 1989, prod. Tony Brown, Billy Williams, Lyle Lovett) ∫∫∫∫ spotlights his quirkiness with a string of non-sequiturs ("Here I Am") and plays the country numbers strictly for yuks ("I Married Her Just Because She Looks Like You," "Stand by Your Man").

what to avoid: Lovett's weakest album, *I Love Everybody* (MCA/Curb, 1994, prod. Lyle Lovett, Billy Williams) ∫∫∫, is the musical proof of your high-school football coach's imprecation that "women weaken legs." Lovett's only recording made during his brief tenure as Mr. Julia Roberts has its moments of wry humor, but it mostly consists of stale leftovers and trifles like "La to the Left" and "Penguins," which are more strange than funny.

worth searching for: The Oscar-nominated hit "You've Got a Friend in Me" from the *Toy Story* soundtrack (Disney, 1995) ∫∫∫ is a boisterous duet with Randy Newman.

influences:

◀◀ Townes Van Zandt, Guy Clark, Ray Charles, Randy Newman

▶▶ Robert Earl Keen Jr., Hayden Beck

Daniel Durchholz

RUBY LOVETT

Born February 16, 1967, in Laurel, MS.

Ruby Lovett grew up singing gospel and was a three-time winner of the True Value Hardware Country Music Showdown. Her music leans toward traditional country, with echoes of bluegrass and gospel.

what's available: *Ruby Lovett* (MCG/Curb, 1997, prod. Allen Reynolds) ♪♪♪, Lovett's debut, is a feisty country-rock collection. While Lovett hasn't yet developed her vocal personality, she's got a pure country instrument, handling rockers such as Kevin Welch's "True Love Never Dies" as easily as classic country ballads like Dallas Frazier's "I'm So Afraid of Losing You."

influences:

◀◀ Pam Tillis, Lorrie Morgan, Tim O'Brien, Kevin Welch

Bob Cannon

BASCOM LAMAR LUNSFORD

Born 1882, in Mars Hill, NC. Died 1973, in Asheville, NC.

Known to many as the "Minstrel of the Appalachians," Bascom Lamar Lunsford was an Asheville, NC, lawyer and virtually inexhaustible source of Southern culture and folklore. Lunsford wrote, collected and performed dozens of ballads, banjo tunes and sacred songs during the years immediately preceding and following World War II. His most famous compositions include "Old Mountain Dew" and "I Wish I Was a Mole in the Ground," a song that employs surrealistic imagery to convey vague but almost unbearably intense emotions.

what's available: *Smokey Mountain Ballads* (Folkways, 1953) ♪♪♪♪ is a charming collection of field recordings, including "Old Mountain Dew," made for the Smithsonian Institution. *Ballads, Banjo Tunes, and Sacred Songs of Western North Carolina* (Smithsonian/Folkways, 1996) ♪♪♪♪ is an exemplary single-disc collection of Lunsford's best-known material recorded for the Archive of American Folk Song in March 1949.

influences:

◀◀ Bob Dylan, the Band, Holy Modal Rounders

Bill Friskics-Warren

CLAIRE LYNCH /THE FRONT PORCH STRING BAND

Born February 20, 1954, in Poughkeepsie, NY.

Singer/songwriter Claire Lynch, along with her Front Porch String Band, has brought a touch of gentle grace to each of her recordings, combining powerfully performed bluegrass with gentle gospel tunes and acoustic country music. Born in upstate New York, Lynch relocated to Alabama at age 12, and has

remained there. In 1973 she became a member of Hickory Wind, a band that included her future husband, mandolin and fiddle player Larry Lynch. By 1975 they were called the Front Porch String Band. By 1981 when the Front Porch disbanded, they'd recorded three albums. Claire soon became acquainted with Music City, and began writing songs and pitching them to several artists. Among those who discovered her talent early on were Kathy Mattea, who recorded "Hills of Alabam," and Patty Loveless, who cut "Some Morning Soon" in 1990. These days, with her Rounder album earning a Grammy nomination, and the Front Porch String Band re-formed, playing numerous festivals and appearing on the Opry frequently, Lynch has also been in demand as a back-up vocalist for Pam Tillis, Dolly Parton and Linda Ronstadt, among others.

what to buy: *Moonlighter* (Rounder, 1995, prod. Bil VornDick) ♪♪♪♪ explores bluegrass, folk, and Cajun music with great success. The title track is a testament to the busy life of a working mother, something to which Claire—and millions of other women—can easily relate.

what to buy next: *Friends for a Lifetime* (Brentwood, 1993, prod. Bil VornDick) ♪♪♪♪ is an inspiring collection of bluegrass/gospel tunes that could convert just about anyone!

the rest:

(With the Front Porch String Band) *Lines and Traces* (Rebel, 1991) ♪♪♪♪
(With the Front Porch String Band) *Front Porch String Band* (Rebel, 1991) ♪♪♪♪

influences:

◀◀ Emmylou Harris, Linda Ronstadt

▶▶ Forbes Family

Stephen L. Betts

LORETTA LYNN

Born April 14, 1935, in Butcher's Hollow, KY.

Simply one of the most influential and colorful artists in country music, Loretta Lynn's life story would have been legendary even if she had not been the subject of a best-selling book and an Academy Award-winning film. Raised in "Butcher Holler," Kentucky, her father worked in the coal mines while Loretta helped raise her younger siblings. Married at 14 to the late Oliver "Mooney" Lynn (also nicknamed "Doolittle"), Loretta moved to Custer, Washington, and had four children by the time she was 18. Her first exposure as a singer came via a Tacoma-based TV show hosted by Buck Owens. She recorded her first single on L.A.-based Zero Records with steel-guitar

Shelby Lynne (© Ken Settle)

whiz Speedy West producing. A trip across country (one of the classic segments of the film, *Coal Miner's Daughter*) gained Loretta enough exposure to place her record, "I'm a Honky-Tonk Girl" (#14, 1960), in the Top 15. Shortly thereafter, Loretta and "Doo" moved to Nashville, where she signed as a songwriter with the Sure-Fire publishing company owned by the Wilburn Brothers. In 1962 Lynn became a Decca recording artist and began a 21-year streak of hits with the label. In all, she earned 16 #1 records through the years, and 50 Top 10s. Her close relationship with Patsy Cline, and the loss of her close friend just as both of their careers were taking off, was perhaps a catalyst for the very personal and strong-willed songs that Loretta peppered the country charts with through the next two decades. Titles like "You Ain't Woman Enough (To Take My Man)" (#2, 1966) and "Don't Come Home a Drinkin' (With Lovin' on Your Mind)" (#1, 1967) were indicative of the burgeoning feminist movement in full flower during the mid-1970s, by which time Loretta had charted with somewhat controversial material like "The Pill" (#5, 1975), and the earlier "One's on the Way" (#1, 1971). A member of the Grand Ole Opry since her debut in 1962, Lynn was part of the Wilburn Brothers' road

show for nearly a decade and frequented their IV series as well. In 1967 she became the first Country Music Association Female Vocalist of the Year, and its first female Entertainer of the Year in 1972. Her duets, first with Ernest Tubb, then with Conway Twitty, hit the charts regularly alongside her solo efforts. In 1988 she became one of only a handful of women inducted into the Country Music Hall of Fame. The death of her beloved husband in 1996 was the most recent, and perhaps most devastating, in a series of losses Lynn has suffered in the last few years, including the deaths of her brother and Twitty. Still, she is a fighter and a survivor. While she's increasingly curtailed her recording activity (the notable exception being the *Honky-Tonk Angels* project with Dolly Parton and Tammy Wynette), she plans to resume performing on a regular basis and is reportedly at work on the sequel to her best-selling autobiography, *Coal Miner's Daughter*. Few artists can claim the icon status that Lynn has achieved over the years. Her simplistic approach to life, her gift for picturesque lyrics and her ringing honky-tonk voice have become a true American treasure.

what to buy: *Honky-Tonk Girl: The Loretta Lynn Collection* (MCA, 1994, prod. various) ♪♪♪♪♪ is one of the few absolutely essential purchases of anyone searching for a primer in country music history. This three-disc set is simply without equal: the notes and photos are above average, and even the lesser material from the later MCA years is passable in this context. A great historical document.

what to buy next: If you can't spring for the three CD's, *Country Music Hall of Fame* (MCA, 1991, prod. Country Music Foundation) ♪♪♪♪♪ is the best deal on one disc, with superior song selection and great liner notes. *Coal Miner's Daughter* (MCA, 1971) ♪♪♪♪♪ is the only complete, non-greatest-hits album available on CD, and for good reason. It's a classic!

what to avoid: Pass on *Greatest Hits Live* (K-Tel, 1978) ♪♪. Loretta tries hard, but in spite of the hits included here, the musicianship sinks it.

the rest:
Loretta's Greatest Hits (MCA, 1968) ♪♪♪♪
Greatest Hits, Volume 2 (MCA, 1974) ♪♪♪
20 Greatest Hits (MCA, 1987) ♪♪♪

influences:
◄◄ Kitty Wells, Molly O'Day
►► Patty Loveless, Reba McEntire

Stephen L. Betts

SHELBY LYNNE

Born Shelby Lynn Moorer, October 22, 1968, in Quantico, VA.

A torch country balladeer, Lynne's music also includes elements of Western swing and jazz—elements that have come to the fore since she left Epic for a smaller label. Lynne was named the best new female artist in 1991 by the Academy of Country Music.

what to buy: Mixing Lynne's penchant for a full, big band-swing sound with producer Brent Maher's more sparse production style produced *Restless* (Magnatone, 1995, prod. Brent Maher) 𝄞𝄞𝄞. Clearly the best album of Lynne's career, it contains both straight country songs like "Talkin' to Myself Again" and "Another Chance at Love" and lounge-perfect jazz and swing numbers like "Wish I Knew" and "Swingtown."

what to buy next: *Sunrise* (Epic, 1989, prod. Bob Montgomery, Billy Sherrill) 𝄞𝄞 showcases Lynne's athletic voice fitted to a plush Nashville Sound for the 1990s.

the rest:
Tough All Over (Epic, 1990) 𝄞𝄞𝄞
Soft Talk (Epic, 1991) 𝄞𝄞𝄞

worth searching for: The least country of Lynne's albums, *Temptation* (Morgan Creek, 1993, prod. Brent Maher) 𝄞𝄞 mixes big-band and Western swing sounds.

influences:
◀◀ k.d. lang

Bill Hobbs

LYNYRD SKYNYRD

Formed 1965, in Jacksonville, FL. Disbanded 1977. Re-formed 1987.

Ronnie Van Zant (died October 20, 1977), vocals (1965–77; Gary Rossington, guitar; Allen Collins (died January 23, 1990), guitar; Ed King, guitar (1973–75, 1987–93); Billy Powell, keyboards; Leon Wilkeson, bass; Bob Burns, drums (1965–74); Artimus Pyle, drums (1974–91); Steve Gaines (died October 20, 1977), guitar (1976–77); Johnny Van Zant, vocals (1987–present); Randall Hall, guitar, (1991–93); Custer, drums (1991–96); Hughie Thomasson, guitar (1996–present); Rick Medlocke, guitar (1996–present); Owen Hale, (1996–present).

Lynyrd Skynyrd was the most commercially successful, critically acclaimed and hardest rocking of the Allman Brothers-influenced Southern rock bands to emerge during the early 1970s. With fierce regional pride, the Florida natives always evinced tremendous creativity and originality, mixing All-

FIVE FOR MY FANS

ALISON KRAUSS

Shawn Colvin
Steady On (Columbia)

Ella Fitzgerald & Louis Armstrong
Stars Fell on Alabama (Verve)

Maura O'Connell
Helpless Heart (Warner Bros.)

Boone Creek
One Way Track (Sugar Hill)

Bonnie Raitt
The Glow (Warner Bros.)

manesque guitar harmonies with crunchy Stones-style rhythms and overdriven, Cream-influenced distortion. At the heart of the band's sound was a three-guitar juggernaut of Gary Rossington, Ed King (later Steve Gaines) and Allen Collins, as well as the forceful presence of vocalist Ronnie Van Zant, who successfully combined a country voice with heavy metal swagger. And while some of its southern rock peers went over the edge into boogie excess, Skynyrd never did, in large part because—in addition to being a ferocious live band—its members wrote great songs, including "Sweet Home Alabama," "Gimme Three Steps," "What's Your Name" and the seminal guitar orgy "Free Bird." After a short dry spell the band was reenergized by the 1976 addition of the phenomenally talented guitarist Gaines, who infused the band with new energy that led to its finest album, *Street Survivors*. But before Lynyrd Skynyrd could reap the fruits of its second coming, its charter plane crashed into a Mississippi swamp, killing Van Zant and Gaines and two others, and seriously injuring the other members. The group re-formed during the late 1980s, with Van Zant's brother Johnny taking over as a vocalist.

what to buy: It doesn't get much better than *Street Survivors* (MCA, 1977, prod. Lynyrd Skynyrd, Jimmy Johnson, Tim Smith) ♪♪♪♪, a molten slab of fiery three-guitar Southern rock with just the right amount of country and a fantastic collection of songs—including "You Got That Right," "That Smell" and "What's Your Name." *One More from the Road* (MCA, 1977, prod. Tom Dowd) ♪♪♪♪ is an awesome live document that includes the famous "What song is it you want to hear?!" "Freeee-bird!!!" dialogue. *Pronounced Leh-Nerd Skin-Nerd* (MCA, 1973, prod. Al Kooper) ♪♪♪♪ introduced the band with a bang, though it's occasionally weighed down by Kooper's excessive production. The three-CD *Lynyrd Skynyrd* (MCA, 1991, comp. prod. Ron O'Brien, Andy McKaie) ♪♪♪♪ is everything a boxed set should be; it's not over-stuffed and it features all the essential tracks, as well as a host of previously unreleased material, most of which is actually good—including the demo of "Free Bird."

what to buy next: Both *Second Helping* (MCA, 1974, prod. Al Kooper) ♪♪♪♪ and *Nuthin' Fancy* (MCA, 1975, prod. Al Kooper) ♪♪♪♪ follow the same path as the band's debut. The former includes "Sweet Home Alabama," "Don't Ask Me No Questions," "Call Me the Breeze" and "The Needle and the Spoon," classics all, while the latter includes "Saturday Night Special" and the surprisingly introspective "Am I Losin'." *Gold & Platinum* (MCA, 1979, prod. various) ♪♪♪♪ is a thorough greatest hits collection with an annoying lack of notes or credits.

what to avoid: The band was sounding a little strained and creatively dry by *Gimme Back My Bullets* (MCA, 1976, prod. Tom Dowd) ♪♪♪, its fourth album in as many years. *Lynyrd Skynyrd 1991* (Atlantic, 1991, prod. Tom Dowd) ♪♪ was an outright embarrassment.

the rest:
Skynyrd's First and ... Last (MCA, 1978) ♪♪♪♪
Best of the Rest (MCA, 1986) ♪♪♪
Legend (MCA, 1987) ♪♪♪
Southern by the Grace of God (MCA, 1988) ♪♪♪
Skynyrd's Innyrds (MCA, 1989) ♪♪♪
The Last Rebel (Atlantic, 1992) ♪♪♪♪
Endangered Species (Capricorn, 1994) ♪♪♪
Freebird: The Movie (Cabin Fever/MCA, 1996) ♪♪♪
Twenty (CMC International, 1997)

worth searching for: *The King Biscuit Flower Hour Presents Lynyrd Skynyrd* (King Biscuit, 1995) ♪♪♪♪ was mistakenly re-

leased and quickly recalled, making this 1975 concert broadcast a collector's item.

solo outings:
Johnny Van Zant:
Brickyard Road (Atlantic, 1990) ♪♪
The Johnny Van Zant Collection (Polydor, 1994) ♪♪♪

Rossington Collins Band:
Anytime, Anyplace, Anywhere (MCA, 1980) ♪♪♪♪

influences:
◄◄ Allman Brothers, Cream, Led Zeppelin, Rolling Stones, Yardbirds
►► Travis Tritt, Confederate Railroad, Molly Hatchet, Black Crowes, .38 Special

Alan Paul

KATE MacKENZIE

Born April 25, 1952, in IA.

Kate MacKenzie first gained notice as a regular performer on Garrison Keillor's *Prairie Home Companion,* where she was both a solo performer and a member of the Hopeful Gospel Quartet alongside Keillor and Robin and Linda Williams. She sang lead with the Minneapolis-based bluegrass band Stoney Lonesome for more than 15 years. Her solo recordings mix bluegrass with honky-tonk, country blues and swamp music.

what's available: Backed by the likes of Emmylou Harris, Alison Krauss, Bela Fleck, Sam Bush and the Fairfield Four, the all-acoustic *Let Them Talk* (Red House Records, 1994, prod. Nick Forster) ♪♪♪♪, MacKenzie's debut solo album, dances on the line between country and bluegrass. *Age of Innocence* (Red House Records, 1996, prod. Nick Forster) ♪♪♪♪ is similar in style to her first album, though it also demonstrates MacKenzie's growth as a songwriter. It is very similar to the sort of rootsy country/bluegrass blend for which Emmylou Harris was once noted.

influences:
◄◄ Stoney Lonesome, Emmylou Harris
►► Claire Lynch, Laurie Lewis

Douglas Fulmer

UNCLE DAVE MACON

Born David Harrison Macon, October 7, 1870, in Smartt Station, TN. Died March 22, 1952.

David Macon became better known as simply "Uncle Dave," but was also called "the Dixie Dewdrop." In his 50s Macon began performing banjo and, in 1925, joined the Grand Ole Opry, becoming one of its first real star attractions. Today he is a true legend in country music and was an early member of the Country Music Hall of Fame, elected in 1966.

Born near McMinnville, Tennessee, Macon moved with his family to Nashville at age 13. Inspired by banjoist and comedian Joel Davidson, he took up the banjo at 15. He moved to a farm near Readyville, Tennessee, and married Matilda Richardson. By 1900 Mason regularly hauled produce (and liquor) under the auspices of the Macon Midway Mule & Wagon Transportation Co., taking his banjo along to entertain folks in the towns of Woodbury and Murfreesboro and points in between. With the advent of the automobile, which he detested (Mason never learned to drive), his company went out of business. By age 53 Macon had begun performing at parties and other gatherings, and he soon received an invitation to play at a theater in Birmingham, Alabama. He began making records for the Vocalion label and, along the way, charmed audiences everywhere with his freewheeling banjo picking and wild storytelling. At 56 he joined the Opry and remained its brightest light for the next 15 years. In 1939 Macon made his motion picture debut in *Grand Ole Opry,* performing alongside his son Dorris. Legends such as Uncle Dave Macon are few and far between; the quintessential showman, he was revered by those who knew him and will continue to be by those who've only heard the many stories that are told about him to this day.

what to buy: In spite of the lesser sound quality of some of its tracks, *Country Music Hall of Fame Series* (MCA, 1992, prod. Country Music Foundation) 🎵🎵🎵🎵 is a spectacular selection of Macon's best-loved work. The notes are thorough and entertaining.

what to buy next: *Travelin' Down the Road* (County, 1995, prod. coor. Gary B. Reid) 🎵🎵🎵 duplicates some tracks on the CMF set, but these were all recorded (with fiddler Charlie Arrington) during 1937–38.

the rest:

(With the Fruit Jar Drinkers) *Go Long Mule* (County, 1972/1994) 🎵🎵🎵🎵

Original Records 1925–1935 (County, c. 1973)

influences:

◀◀ Joel Davidson, Sam & Kirk McGee

▶▶ Stringbean

Stephen L. Betts

THE MADDOX BROTHERS & ROSE /ROSE MADDOX

Formed 1937 in Modesto, CA.

Cliff Maddox, vocals, guitar, mandolin; Cal Maddox, vocals, guitar, harmonica; Fred Maddox, vocals, bass; Don Maddox, vocals, fiddle; Henry Maddox, vocals, mandolin, guitar; Rose Maddox (born August 15, 1925, in Boaz, AL), vocals, bass, snare drum.

Favorites in California from the time they formed until they finally disbanded in 1957, the Maddox Brothers & Rose were a raucous bunch who billed themselves as "the most colorful hillbilly band in America." They played a loud, infectious mix of country boogie, rockabilly, Western swing, honky-tonk and even gospel, were famous for their outrageous outfits, and recorded for 4 Star Records and Columbia. When the band broke up, Rose, who was a mere 11 years old when the family formed its band as an alternative to the itinerant fruit-tramp life that had been their lot since they had emigrated to California from Alabama, continued to perform as a soloist, a path she continues to this day. She's recorded for Columbia, Capitol (cutting several hit duets with Buck Owens during the 1960s), Portland, Starday, Takoma, Varrick and, most recently, Arhoolie, which has also released several volumes of Maddox Brothers & Rose reissues over the years. She is popular in the U.S. at bluegrass festivals and has quite a reputation in rockabilly circles in Europe. Ill health has slowed Rose down, but hasn't kept her from touring and recording extensively.

what to buy: *America's Most Colorful Hillbilly Band—Their Original Recordings 1946–1951* (Arhoolie, 1993, prod. Chris Strachwitz) 🎵🎵🎵🎵 and *Maddox Brothers & Rose, Volume Two* (Arhoolie, 1995, prod. Chris Strachwitz) 🎵🎵🎵🎵 offer the most comprehensive overview of the band at its peak.

what to buy next: *On the Air: The 1940s* (Arhoolie, 1996, prod. Chris Strachwitz) 🎵🎵🎵 presents intriguing live broadcasts from 1940 to 1949, including the band's 1949 appearance on the Grand Ole Opry. *A Collection of Standard Sacred Songs* (King, 1960) 🎵🎵🎵 reissues Starday gospel material.

Barbara Mandrell **(AP/Wide World Photos)**

worth searching for: *Rockin' Rollin' Maddox Brothers & Rose* (Bear Family, 1981, prod. Richard Weize) 🎵🎵🎵 is a German reissue of the band's more rockabillyish material. *Columbia Historic Edition* (Columbia, 1985) 🎵🎵🎵 is an excellent reissue of the band's Columbia material.

solo outings:
Rose Maddox:
Rose Maddox Sings Bluegrass (Capitol, 1962) 🎵🎵🎵🎵
Rose of the West Coast Country (Arhoolie, 1990) 🎵🎵🎵🎵
The One Rose: The Capitol Years (Bear Family, 1993) 🎵🎵🎵🎵
Thirty-Five Dollars and a Dream (Arhoolie, 1994) 🎵🎵🎵

influences:
◀◀ Hoosier Hotshots, Patsy Montana
▶▶ Ranch Romance, BR5-49

Randy Pitts

CHARLIE MAJOR

Born December 31, 1954, in Aylmer, Quebec, Canada.

One of Canada's most awarded songwriter/performers of the

1990s, Charlie Major wrote his first song when he was 14 and played coffeehouses and church basements as a teenager. It wasn't until the late 1980s that his poignant songs about life's marvels and mysteries, told from the perspective of a hardworker searching for answers, began to be heard by a significant audience. In 1989 his rollicking but wishful "I'm Gonna Ride in a Cadillac" received a Canadian Country Music Association Song of the Year nomination, and four years later the softspoken singer hit paydirt when Ricky Van Shelton took his "Backroads" to the top of the charts in his homeland and in the States. Major's first album, the BMG Canada release *The Other Side*, contains six Canadian #1 hits, and he won the Juno Award for Country Male Vocalist of the Year in 1994, 1995 and 1996. Major now lives in Nashville, the home of Imprint, his U.S. record company.

what's available: The singer's second album and first U.S. release, *Here and Now* (Imprint, 1996, prod. Steve Fishell) 🎵🎵🎵, originally released in Canada with the title *Lucky Man*, is an impressive collection of thoughtful and provocative tunes, sometimes with a dollop of humor. "Lucky Man," a reflection on feeling the satisfaction of raising a family and working hard but sensing that something big is missing, is a prime example of Major's keen skill at expressing complex but universal thoughts with articulate simplicity. Similarly, "(I Do It) For the Money," with its deceptive bouncy beat and singalong chorus, searches for a cosmic payback for a lifetime of waking up early and punching the clock. Like its predecessor, this album yielded a handful of charttopping singles in Canada.

worth searching for: *The Other Side* (Arista Canada, 1993, prod. Steve Fishell) 🎵🎵🎵, his Canadian breakthrough album, is a little less polished but equally tuneful, with songs reminiscent of Bruce Springsteen and even Steve Earle with the electricity turned down.

influences:
◀◀ Jackson Browne, Gordon Lightfoot
▶▶ Lee Roy Parnell, Keith Stegall

David Sokol

BARBARA MANDRELL

Born December 25, 1948, in Houston, TX.

Because of her dynamic stage show and glitzy persona, people often forget that Barbara Mandrell is a talented musician. At age five she pumped out an accordion gospel number in church; by 12 she had appeared on the national TV show *Five*

Star Jubilee. Two years later Barbara initiated a family group with father Irby and sister Mary Ellen. Ken Dudney wasn't a family member when he stepped in as drummer, but in 1966 he became "Mr. Barbara Mandrell."

Irby soon became the young pro's agent. In turn, Barbara hit the Top 10 a few times for Columbia Records between 1969 and 1975, most notably with 1973's "The Midnight Oil," 1975's "Standing Room Only" and a few duets with David Houston.

In 1975 she signed with ABC/Dot (eventually acquired by MCA), where she became one of country's biggest draws during the 1980s. Success came during the late 1970s with "Married but Not to Each Other," "Sleeping Single in a Double Bed" and her cover of Luther Ingram's 1973 soul hit "(If Loving You Is Wrong) I Don't Want to Be Right." These titles suggest a degree of honky-tonk purity, but Mandrell's pop approach came with impeccable timing. At the turn of decade the nation was swept up in the *Urban Cowboy* craze, and Mandrell rode the fad all the way to the top. In 1980 and 1981 the Country Music Association named Mandrell its Entertainer of the Year, though the industry bit its tongue when she sang "I Was Country When Country Wasn't Cool."

More TV appearances (including a 1983 variety series and an HBO special) led to a long-running Las Vegas gig in 1983. The following year a severe car collision threatened to curtail Mandrell's career, but she recovered—a development she largely credits to the seat belt she was wearing at the time of the wreck. Mandrell later signed with EMI America and Capitol Records, where she had a few more successful singles (her last Top Five hit was 1988's "I Wish That I Could Fall in Love Today"). Today she hawks Sunsweet Prunes and has her own gift shop and museum near Nashville's Music Row.

what to buy: *The Best of Barbara Mandrell* (MCA, 1979, prod. Tom Collins) &&&& is Barbara at her country-soul peak, with her biggest hits from her ABC/Dot years (1975–79). The album begins with her rendition of Shirley Brown's 1974 pop hit "Woman to Woman," in which a woman confronts her husband's mistress, but it also has "Sleeping Single in a Double Bed" and Denise LaSalle's "Married but Not to Each Other."

what to buy next: Mandrell appeared regularly in the country chart's upper reaches during the first half of the 1980s with songs like "I Was Country When Country Wasn't Cool" (which featured George Jones on vocals), "Years," "One of a Kind Pair of Fools" and "Crackers" (as in, what you can eat in her bed). Occasionally the songs get a little silly, but *Greatest Hits* (MCA,

1985, prod. Tom Collins) &&&& is Mandrell during her commercial peak.

what to avoid: *Greatest Country Hits* (Curb, 1990) && is a 10-song collection that combines singles like "I Was Country When Country Wasn't Cool" from Mandrell's days at MCA and Liberty. The songs are available on better collections from the individual labels.

the rest:
He Set My Life to Music (MCA, 1982) &&
The Barbara Mandrell Collection (Capitol, 1995) &&&
It Works for Me (Razor & Tie, 1997) &&

worth searching for: *The Best of Barbara Mandrell* (Columbia, 1977) &&& contains the biggest of Mandrell's early 1970s singles for Columbia, including covers of R&B songs associated with Joe Tex ("Show Me"), Roy Head ("Treat Him Right") and Aretha Franklin ("Do Right Woman—Do Right Man").

influences:
◀◀ Dolly Parton, Lynn Anderson
▶▶ Louise Mandrell, Reba McEntire

Brian Mansfield and Craig Shelburne

CARL MANN
Born August 24, 1942, in Huntingdon, TN.

Carl Mann is a minor rockabilly-pop singer who had one Top 40 pop hit at age 16 with a rockabilly remake of "Mona Lisa" for the Sun subsidiary Phillips. About 15 years later Mann had a minor country hit with a remake of "Twilight Time."

what's available: The teenaged Mann justifiably was never the sensation that Elvis Presley or Ricky Nelson were. His tastes ran more to Tin Pan Alley pop than hillbilly boogie, and the recordings on *Like—MANN* (Sun, 1975) && sound gimmicky now (they probably did then too). There's only so much you can take of sped-up versions of songs like "Mona Lisa," "Mexicali Rose," "South of the Border," "Too Young" and "Don't Let the Stars Get in Your Eyes." Though it is fairly amusing the first time through.

influences:
◀◀ Elvis Presley, Ricky Nelson
▶▶ Charlie Rich, Bob Luman

Brian Mansfield

THE MARSHALL TUCKER BAND

Formed 1971, in Spartanburg, SC.

Toy Caldwell (died February 23, 1994), guitar, vocals (1971–83); Doug Gray, vocals; George McCorkle, guitar (1971–83); Paul Riddle, drums (1971–83); Jerry Eubanks, reeds, keyboards, vocals; Tommy Caldwell (died April 28, 1980), bass, vocals (1971–80); Frank Wilkie, bass (1980–83); Rusty Milner, guitar (1983–present); Tim Lawter, bass (1983–present).

Marshall Tucker is a unique entity in Southern rock; the group could boogie with the best of them, but it had a jazzier sensibility that gave Doug Gray's flutes and saxophones a berth alongside the dueling guitars. The group was also a little more Southern and more country, with a bit more twang in its sound than compatriots such as the Allman Brothers Band and Lynyrd Skynyrd; Waylon Jennings was even able to turn MTB's first hit, "Can't You See," into a country hit for himself in 1976. The group's heyday came to an end during the mid-1970s, and it was never the same after the 1983 schism that took three of the original members—including the indispensable Toy Caldwell—out of the picture. You'll still find Marshall Tucker trucking itself out on the road though, stretching hits such as "24 Hours at a Time" to just about that length.

what to buy: With a series of generally interchangeable albums, it's the comprehensive *The Best of the Marshall Tucker Band: The Capricorn Years* (Era, 1995, prod. various) 𝄞𝄞𝄞𝄞 that gives the band its due, though it chooses the occasional live track over the preferable studio version.

what to buy next: Though the biggest hits are on other albums, *Searchin' for a Rainbow* (Capricorn/AJK, 1975, prod. Paul Hornsby) 𝄞𝄞𝄞𝄞 is the group's most consistent outing.

what to avoid: The criminally skimpy *Greatest Hits* (Capricorn, 1978/AJK, 1989, prod. Paul Hornsby) 𝄞 offers just eight selections from the band's 1972–77 heyday.

the rest:

The Marshall Tucker Band (Capricorn, 1973/AJK, 1988) 𝄞𝄞𝄞
A New Life (Capricorn, 1974/AJK, 1988) 𝄞𝄞𝄞
Where We All Belong (Capricorn, 1974/AJK, 1988) 𝄞𝄞𝄞
Long, Hard Ride (Capricorn, 1976/AJK, 1988) 𝄞𝄞𝄞
Carolina Dreams (Capricorn, 1977/AJK, 1988) 𝄞𝄞𝄞
Southern Spirit (Cabin Fever, 1990) 𝄞𝄞𝄞
Still Smokin' (Cabin Fever, 1992) 𝄞𝄞
Walk Outside the Lines (Cabin Fever, 1993) 𝄞𝄞

worth searching for: The out-of-print *Dedicated* (Warner Bros., 1981) 𝄞𝄞𝄞 finds the band, deeply moved by Tommy Caldwell's death, delving deeper into the country side of its sound.

influences:

◀◀ Allman Brothers Band, Waylon Jennings, Johnny Cash, Grateful Dead

▶▶ Sea Level, Atlanta Rhythm Section, Black Crowes

Gary Graff

JIMMY MARTIN

Born August 10, 1927, in Sneedviille, TN.

Despite the fact that his impetuous stage behavior often overshadows his considerable musical skills, guitarist Jimmy Martin is almost universally recognized as among the finest lead singers and most influential bandleaders in bluegrass music. His unabashedly brash "good 'n' country" approach to his material and penchant for corny novelty fare can sometimes obscure the fact that he has contributed to many classic bluegrass records over the years, first as lead singer with Bill Monroe, later with the Osborne Brothers and, since 1955, with his own Sunny Mountain Boys, a band that has employed such future stars as J.D. Crowe, Bill Emerson, Alan Munde, Doyle Lawson and Paul Williams. From 1956 to 1974 Martin recorded many classic tracks for Decca; since then he has recorded for Starday/Gusto, mostly revisiting old hits.

what to buy: *You Don't Know My Mind* (Rounder, 1990, reissue prod. Ken Irwin, Hazel Dickens) 𝄞𝄞𝄞𝄞𝄞, a collection of material licensed from MCA, is the best one-disc overview of Jimmy's genius, featuring the original versions of 14 of his classic hits and bands that include a young J.D. Crowe on banjo and Paul Williams on mandolin.

what to buy next: The handsomely boxed, 146-song, five-CD set *Jimmy Martin & the Sunny Mountain Boys* (Bear Family, 1994, prod. Paul Cohen, Owen Bradley, Harry Silverstein, Steve Sholes) 𝄞𝄞𝄞𝄞𝄞 is the fanatical Jimmy Martin fan's dream, containing all the material he cut with the Osborne Brothers for RCA and everything he cut for Decca between 1956 and 1974. The box also contains a lavishly produced, comprehensively annotated 42-page book with a complete discography of the years covered.

the rest:

Me 'n' Ole Pete (Hollywood, 1978) 𝄞𝄞𝄞
Greatest Bluegrass Hits (Hollywood, 1978) 𝄞𝄞
One-Woman Man (Hollywood, 1995) 𝄞𝄞

Will the Circle Be Unbroken (Hollywood, 1995) 🎵🎵

Jimmy Martin & Ralph Stanley—First Time Together (Hollywood, 1995) 🎵🎵🎵

influences:

◀◀ Roy Acuff, Bill Monroe

▶▶ John Duffey, Little Roy Lewis

Randy Pitts

MILA MASON

Born August 22, 1963, in Murray, KY.

Could Mila Mason have avoided a singing career in these pop-culture days? Not likely: When she was six years old her picture appeared on the Kenner toy jukebox, an augury of fate if ever there was one. A divorced mother of two, Mason didn't catch her big break until she was past 30. Before that she sang demos and jingles, appeared in music videos and spritzed mallgoers with perfume. She also sang in a band with Deana Carter for a brief time.

what's available: Mason brings a husky passion to the songs on *That's Enough of That* (Atlantic, 1996, prod. Blake Mevis) 🎵🎵🎵, which includes the Top 40 title track, an example of countrified 1980s girl-singer New Wave. On ballads like "Tonight I Know I Will," her singing is reminiscent of Tanya Tucker's, but Mason shows every indication of coming into her own.

influences:

◀◀ Tanya Tucker

▶▶ Deana Carter

Brian Mansfield

KATHY MATTEA

Born June 21, 1959, in Cross Lanes, VA.

Originally a bluegrass singer and guitarist, Kathy Mattea's music found a home on country radio during the 1980s return to traditional sounds. A double Grammy winner, Mattea also has twice been named Female Vocalist of the Year by the Country Music Association. With her bluegrass-shaded country increasingly leaning on Scottish and Celtic influences, Mattea also organized the *Red, Hot + Country* AIDS benefit album project.

what to buy: *A Collection of Hits* (Mercury, 1990, prod. Allen Reynolds) 🎵🎵🎵 features most of her early hits.

what to buy next: *Walk the Way the Wind Blows* (Mercury, 1987, prod. Allen Reynolds) 🎵🎵🎵, Mattea's first real break-through, includes the title cut, "Train of Memories," and "Love at the Five and Dime." Other tracks include the big hits "Eighteen Wheels and a Dozen Roses" and "Goin' Gone."

the rest:

Kathy Mattea (Mercury, 1984) 🎵🎵

From My Heart (Mercury, 1985) 🎵🎵

Untasted Honey (Mercury, 1987) 🎵🎵🎵

Willow in the Wind (Mercury, 1989) 🎵🎵🎵

Time Passes By (Mercury, 1991) 🎵🎵🎵

Lonesome Standard Time (Mercury, 1992) 🎵🎵🎵

Walking Away a Winner (Mercury, 1993) 🎵🎵🎵

Good News (Mercury, 1994) 🎵🎵🎵

Love Travels (Mercury, 1997) 🎵🎵🎵

influences:

◀◀ Nanci Griffith

▶▶ Suzy Bogguss, Deana Carter

Bill Hobbs

THE MAVERICKS

Formed 1990, in Miami, FL.

Raul Malo, vocals, guitar; Robert Reynolds, bass; Paul Deakin, drums; Ben Peeler, guitar, mandolin (1990–91); David Lee Holt, guitar (1992–93); Nick Kane, guitar (1994–present).

Since they hail from Miami rather than Nashville or Texas, the Mavericks were greeted more as cool novelties than conquering heroes. But 1992's *From Hell to Paradise* introduced a vital, visionary outfit that foreshadowed the current alternative country boom by matching a traditional sound with a contemporary, hard-rocking edge. More important, the Mavericks wisely avoid lapsing into the redneck rowdiness of the Kentucky HeadHunters or the costume-heavy shtick of BR5-49 and the Derailers; Cuban-American lead singer Raul Malo, who combines the rich, soulful voice of a young Roy Orbison and the captivating, sweat-soaked stage presence of *Sun Sessions*-era Elvis, is the only attention-grabbing hook they need. Since their breakthrough with 1994's Orbinson-like "What a Crying Shame," the Mavericks have been embracing their retro-country roots with the help of such hook-for-hire co-writers as Kostas and Al Anderson. As result, Malo's songs have sacrificed the social consciousness that marked the Mavericks' early work but have helped the band join Dwight Yoakam as purveyors of a hard-nosed 1950s-inspired sound that alternately recalls and yearns for an era when the differences between country and rock weren't so easy to distinguish.

what to buy: The Mavericks come across as a thinking-man's bar band on *From Hell to Paradise* (MCA, 1990, prod. Steve Fishell, Raul Malo, Richard Bennett) ⵒⵒⵒⵒ, mixing honky-tonk raveups of Buck Owens' "Excuse Me (I Think I've Got a Heartache)" and Hank Williams' "Hey Good Lookin'" with Malo originals that address the hopes of Cuban refugees ("From Hell to Paradise"), the fall of Jim Bakker ("The End of the Line") and the plight of the homeless ("Mr. Jones").

what to buy next: The tongue-in-cheek, cosmo-country swing of *Music for All Occasions* (MCA, 1995, prod. Raul Malo, Don Cook) ⵒⵒⵒ may be poker-faced, tremelo guitar-laced fun, but it also demonstrates how much poise and authority Malo has developed as a singer. The Orbison influence is now an indelible echo, not a crutch, and the band proves it can still raise a convincing ruckus on "All You Ever Do Is Bring Me Down," a Tex-Mex romp featuring Flaco Jimenez.

what to avoid: The platinum bridge between their two finest albums, *What a Crying Shame* (MCA, 1994, prod. Don Cook) ⵒⵒⵒ is the pleasant but shaky sound of a band searching for a focus. Highlight: a splendid cover of Bruce Springsteen's "All That Heaven Will Allow."

worth searching for: Their frenetic Miami debut, *The Mavericks* (Y&T, 1990, prod. Raul Malo, Mavericks) ⵒⵒⵒⵒ, leans more toward acoustic guitars, fiddles, banjos and lap steels, but hints at the hard-rocking side to come. Four of the 13 tunes resurfaced on *From Hell to Paradise*, but the honky-tonk-flavored "You'll Never Know" and "Tomorrow Never Comes" are as strong as anything the band has recorded. The album was later reissued on Three Crosses Records.

influences:

◀◀ Roy Orbison, Elvis Presley, Dwight Yoakam, Joe Ely

▶▶ BR5-49, George Ducas

David Okamoto

MAC McANALLY

Born July 15, 1957, in Belmont, MS.

Most country fans know Mac McAnally as the composer of such hits as Alabama's "Old Flame," Sawyer Brown's "All These Years," Shenandoah's "Two Dozen Roses" and Linda Davis' "Company Time," to name but a few. But before his behind-the-scenes Nashville success, the former Muscle Shoals session guitarist with the Randy Travis-like baritone and Randy Newman-like wit was on the cutting edge of the singer/songwriter movement. McAnally became the first artist David Geffen signed

to his then-fledgling Geffen Records roster during the early 1980s, but he proved to be a hard sell: the Mississippi-reared redhead delivered his Southern small-town character studies and biting examinations of life's unfair, ever-changing rules with a droll delivery and a melodic breeziness that cloaked the irony and darkness of his deliciously devious sense of humor. Among his early subjects were the revenge of a rape victim ("Bad Boy"), society's indifference to death ("Real People"), how guilt can be assuaged by writing a check ("Hush Money") and a definition of life as "nothing more than to eat and excrete and die" ("Cuttin' Corners"). In between session stints with longtime supporter Jimmy Buffett (who covered his "It's My Job" on 1981's *Coconut Telegraph*), McAnally continues to write disarmingly lovely hit songs for Nashville's gold and platinum elite. Even though age has tempered his edge, he remains one of country music's warmest, most insightful clutch composers.

what to buy: All of his pre-MCA albums for Ariola, RCA, Geffen and Warner Bros. are out of print, but *Knots* (MCA, 1994, prod. Mac McAnally, Tony Brown) ⵒⵒⵒⵒ is an accurate snapshot of his humanity and humor. It includes a remake of "Miracle," originally recorded on his 1980 album, *Cuttin' Corners*.

the rest:
Live and Learn (MCA, 1992) ⵒⵒⵒ

worth searching for: McAnally's best albums never made it to CD, so used record stores are the most likely place to uncover his marvelous 1977 debut *Mac McAnally* (Ariola America, prod. Clayton Ivey, Terry Woodford) ⵒⵒⵒⵒ. It is highlighted by his Top 40 hit, "It's a Crazy World," and the bittersweet "Barney," perhaps the weirdest and most accurate song ever written about the aging process.

influences:

◀◀ John Prine, Randy Newman, James Taylor

▶▶ Sawyer Brown

David Okamoto

McBRIDE & THE RIDE /TERRY McBRIDE & THE RIDE

Formed 1989, in Nashville, TN.

Terry McBride, (born September 16, 1958, in Austin, TX) vocals, bass; Ray Herndon, guitar (1990–93); Billy Thomas, drums (1990–93). For-

Martina McBride (© Ken Settle)

mer members: Rick Gerken, keyboards; Keith Edwards, drums; Bob Britt, guitar; Kenny Vaughn, guitar; Randy Frazier, bass; Gary Morse, steel guitar; Jeff Roach, keyboards.

McBride & the Ride was brought together by Tony Brown, then head of MCA's A&R department. Frontman Terry McBride had played with Delbert McClinton. (His father, Dale McBride, had two Top 40 hits during the 1970s for Con Brio Records.) Arizonan Ray Herndon was a one-time member of Lyle Lovett's Large Band. Drummer Billy Thomas, a Florida native, had worked as a touring and session musician in Nashville and L.A. Though it had been conceived as a picker's band, the Ride quickly became noted for the harmony-loaded songs that featured McBride's vocals, eventually leading to Herndon's and Thomas' exodus from the group. McBride debuted the retooled Ride, which was basically McBride and a backing band with changing membership, on New Year's Eve 1993.

what's available: You get some idea of what Tony Brown was thinking from McBride & the Ride's first album, *Burnin' Up the Road* (MCA, 1990, prod. Tony Brown, Steve Fishell) ????, which features a number of bluesy, guitar-oriented tunes (though nothing that sounds like great shakes in a world containing Garth Brooks, Travis Tritt and Dwight Yoakam). The slow songs, "Same Old Star" and "Can I Count on You," were the ones that hit the charts, though. The lesson had sunk in by the second album, *Sacred Ground* (MCA, 1992, prod. Steve Gibson, Tony Brown) ????, which produced three Top 5 hits, "Sacred Ground," "Going Out of My Mind" and "Just One Night." All of them were harmony ballads, and it was becoming obvious that McBride's songs were best-suited for success. He had six cuts on the album; the other two members of the band didn't have any. The subsequent change in personnel brought a change in producers and a change in sound. *Terry McBride & the Ride* (MCA, 1995, prod. Josh Leo) ???? is a more rock-oriented album with backing vocals from the likes of the Eagles' Timothy B. Schmit and former .38 Special singer Max Carl. Ironically, it probably sounds more like Brown's original vision for the band. None of the songs became hits of significance.

worth searching for: *Hurry Sundown* (MCA, 1993, prod. Steve Gibson, Tony Brown) ????, the band's third album, features the hits "Love on the Loose, Heart on the Run" and "Hurry Sundown."

influences:
◀◀ Lyle Lovett, Delbert McClinton, Restless Heart
▶▶ Little Texas, Frazier River

Brian Mansfield

MARTINA McBRIDE

Born July 29, 1966, in Sharon, KS.

Martina McBride toured regionally with her parent's band, the Schiffters, before coming to Nashville, where she graduated quickly from selling T-shirts at Garth Brooks concerts to making records and opening for Brooks, to headlining her own shows and being inducted into the Grand Ole Opry. Winner of a Country Music Association award for her risky "Independence Day" video with its bare-boned portrayal of domestic violence, McBride's song selection took a more personal tone on her third album, *Wild Angels*, recorded after the birth of her first child.

what's available: Generally overlooked, McBride's first album, *The Time Has Come* (RCA, 1992, prod. Paul Worley, Ed Seay) ????, features songs and production almost as good as her later hits. *The Way That I Am* (RCA, 1993, prod. Paul Worley, Ed Seay, Martina McBride) ???? is the album that boosted McBride's career with its catchy pop-country "My Baby Loves Me" and the risky, Springsteenish abused woman's anthem "Independence Day." *Wild Angels* (RCA, 1995, prod. Martina McBride, Paul Worley, Ed Seay) ???? is country with elements of the Band, the Beatles and Creedence Clearwater Revival. Featured are the hits "Safe in the Arms of Love" and "Wild Angels," a nice cover of Delbert McClinton's "Two More Bottles of Wine," and a bevy of other fine cuts, including the country two-stepper "Swingin' Doors."

influences:
◀◀ Patty Loveless
▶▶ Jo Dee Messina, Deana Carter

Bill Hobbs

C.W. McCALL

Born William Fries, November 15, 1928, in Audubon, IA.

"C.W. McCall" was the brainchild of advertising executive Bill Fries and Chip Davis, who originally created the character for the Mertz Bread Company. Eventually the two would take McCall to the radio arena, recording not just 1975's "Convoy"—the gold-selling single for which McCall is best-known—but eight other Top 40 country hits as well. Fries, who provided McCall's voice, remained with his ad company, the Bozell Jacobs Agency, throughout McCall's recording career; he later was elected mayor of Ouray, Colorado. Davis went on to further recording success under the name Mannheim Steamroller.

what's available: It's not surprising that "Convoy" was such a big hit, since it cashed in on the CB radio craze of the 1970s.

What's amazing is that McCall had enough success with ersatz trucking songs like "Crispy Critters," "Wolf Creek Pass" and "'Round the World with the Rubber Duck" (the international sequel to "Convoy") to fill a greatest-hits album like *Greatest Hits* (Mercury, 1978) ♫♫. And if the common roots of McCall and the contemporary-instrumental act Mannheim Steamroller sound just too weird to believe, just listen to the pseudo-classical strings on "The Silverton."

influences:

◀◀ Dave Dudley, Red Sovine

▶▶ Mannheim Steamroller

Brian Mansfield

DARRELL McCALL

Born April 30, 1940, in New Jasper, OH.

A honky-tonker in the Ray Price mold, shuffle-beat aficionados revere Darrell McCall as a "picker's singer," even though he's charted only three Top 30 singles—including "Lily Dale," a 1977 duet with Willie Nelson—during his lengthy career. McCall has recorded extensively since the early 1960s, and many of the results are now available only as high-priced imports through Germany's Bear Family label.

what to buy: *A Way to Survive* (Artap, 1995, prod. Buddy Emmons, Darrell McCall) ♫♫♫♫ is a hard-country tour de force that finds McCall's soulful phrasing meshing seamlessly with strains of fiddle and steel guitar.

the rest:

Reunion (BGM) ♫♫♫

(With Johnny Bush) *Hot Texas Country* (Step One, 1986) ♫♫♫

All She Did Was Fall in Love (Artap, 1992) ♫♫♫♫

worth searching for: *The Real McCall* (Bear Family, 1996) ♫♫♫♫ is a five-CD career retrospective that establishes McCall as a prodigiously talented, if unsung, honky-tonk singer-songwriter.

influences:

◀◀ Ray Price, Faron Young

▶▶ Johnny Bush

Bill Friskics-Warren

MARY McCASLIN

Born December 22, 1946, in Indianapolis, IN.

Mary McCaslin was making musical Americana—in her case, a beguiling mix of mountain music and singer/songwriter folk—

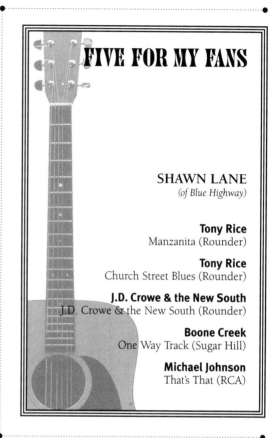

FIVE FOR MY FANS

SHAWN LANE
(*of Blue Highway*)

Tony Rice
Manzanita (Rounder)

Tony Rice
Church Street Blues (Rounder)

J.D. Crowe & the New South
J.D. Crowe & the New South (Rounder)

Boone Creek
One Way Track (Sugar Hill)

Michael Johnson
That's That (RCA)

long before the term became the name of a catch-all radio format. McCaslin's dulcet soprano and lilting acoustic guitar-based melodies are the perfect foil for her wry, incisive social commentary.

what to buy: *Way Out West* (Philo, 1974, prod. Mary McCaslin, Bill Schubart) ♫♫♫♫ features three-quarter-time ballads and clear-eyed proto-feminist explorations of the lure of the Western frontier. It also boasts the definitive version of Randy Newman's "Living without You."

what to buy next: *Things We Said Today* (Philo, 1992) ♫♫♫♫ is an almost flawless career retrospective, even though it doesn't supplant the near-classic *Way Out West*.

the rest:

Prairie in the Sky (Philo, 1976) ♫♫♫

Old Friends (Philo, 1977) ♫♫♫

The Bramble and the Rose (Philo, 1978) ♫♫♫♫

Sunny California (Mercury, 1979) 🎵🎵🎵
Broken Promises (Philo, 1994) 🎵🎵🎵

influences:

⏪ Marty Robbins, Joni Mitchell

Bill Friskics-Warren

CHARLY McCLAIN

Born Charlotte Denise McClain, March 26, 1956, in Jackson, TN.

Although she became known in later years for a series of television commercials with her husband, singer/actor Wayne Massey, soulful pop/country singer Charly McClain began her road to stardom as a cast member of the Mid-South Jamboree from 1973 to 1975. She then toured with O.B. McClinton and signed with Epic Records, with her first hit charting in 1978. During the nine years following, she would chart an additional 26 times, reaching the Top 10 14 times, and the #1 spot three times, including her biggest hit "Who's Cheatin' Who" (#1, 1981), later covered by Alan Jackson. Along the way Charly recorded duets with Massey (reaching the Top 10) and with Johnny Rodriguez, but her greatest duet success was with Mickey Gilley ("Paradise Tonight," #1, 1983). A short stint with Mercury Records in 1989 yielded no hits. Along with commercials, McClain has made numerous appearances on episodic television.

what's available: *Ten-Year Anniversary* (Legacy, 1987, prod. various) 🎵🎵🎵🎵 features most of McClain's Top 10 solo hits and representative duets, but at 10 tracks it's pretty skimpy.

influences:

⏪ Juice Newton

⏩ Deana Carter

Stephen L. Betts

DELBERT McCLINTON

Born November 4, 1940, in Lubbock, TX.

Delbert McClinton has been kicking around for years, playing a decidedly unfashionable mix of blues, rock, country and R&B that has rarely dented the charts. Highly regarded as a raspy, Southern-fried vocalist, an adroit songwriter and harmonica player and a performer par excellence, McClinton got his start on the Texas honky-tonk circuit, of which he is still a fixture. His early years were filled playing blues and breaking racial barriers—one of his bands, the Straitjackets, crossed the color line on a Fort Worth black station in 1960 with a cover of Sonny Boy Williamson's "Wake Up Baby." He played harmonica on Bruce Channel's 1962 hit "Hey Baby" and taught a then-unknown John Lennon a few licks while on tour in England. He fronted another group, the Ron Dels, during the 1960s, then formed a duo with Glen Clark that released two acclaimed albums during the early 1970s. The label-jumping, style-bending singer has been plugging ever since, cutting albums for ABC (now MCA), Capricorn, Alligator, Capitol (which issued his 1980 Top 40 hit "Givin' It Up for Your Love") and, more recently, Curb. His songs have been covered by artists as diverse as Emmylou Harris ("Two More Bottles of Wine") and the Blues Brothers ("B Movie Boxcar Blues"), and in 1991 he won a Grammy for his duet with Bonnie Raitt on "Good Man, Good Woman."

what to buy: Few of McClinton's studio albums have done him justice because it's onstage where he excels. His *Live from Austin* (Alligator, 1989, prod. Delbert McClinton) 🎵🎵🎵, taped during an *Austin City Limits* TV appearance, is a rock-solid example of what this guy can do.

what to buy next: McClinton, no doubt frustrated at his lack of commercial success, called in the big guns for *Never Been Rocked Enough* (Curb, 1992, prod. Don Was, Jim Horn, Delbert McClinton, Bonnie Raitt) 🎵🎵🎵, which includes his Grammy-winning version of "Good Man, Good Woman" (sung with Raitt) and guest shots from Melissa Etheridge, Tom Petty, Paul Shaffer and members of David Letterman's house band.

what to avoid: Pass on the weak *Honky-Tonk 'n' Blues* (MCA, 1994, prod. various) 🎵🎵.

the rest:

Second Wind (Mercury, 1978) 🎵🎵🎵
I'm with You (Curb, 1990) 🎵🎵🎵
The Best of Delbert McClinton (Curb, 1991) 🎵🎵🎵
Delbert McClinton (Curb, 1993) 🎵🎵🎵
Classics Volume 1: The Jealous Kind (Curb, 1994) 🎵🎵🎵
Classics Volume 2: Plain from the Heart (Curb, 1994) 🎵🎵🎵
The Great Songs: Come Together (Curb, 1995) 🎵🎵🎵

worth searching for: The two McClinton and Clark albums, *Delbert & Glen* (Clean, 1972, prod. Daniel J. Moore, T-Bone Burnett) 🎵🎵🎵 and *Subject to Change* (Clean, 1973, prod. Geoffrey Haslam) 🎵🎵🎵, foresaw the fusion of country, rock and blues that is common today. They still hold up well.

influences:

⏪ Jimmy Reed, Sonny Boy Williamson, Bobby "Blue" Bland

⏩ Lee Roy Parnell, McBride & the Ride, Mike Henderson

Doug Pullen

MAUREEN McCORMICK

Born c. 1956, in CA.

Best-known as *The Brady Bunch*'s Marcia Brady, Maureen Mc-Cormick tried to revive her career in 1994 by recording a country album in Nashville.

what's available: *When You Get a Little Lonely* (Phantom Hill, 1995, prod. Barry Coffing) ♪ is exactly what you'd expect from an actress making her first country album as she nears 40: McCormick gets enough name songwriters and musicians to draw attention (Pam Tillis, Barry Beckett, Wendy Waldman), but she doesn't have the voice to hold it.

worth searching for: The Brady Bunch's *It's a Sunshine Day: The Best of the Brady Bunch* (MCA, 1993, prod. various) ♪ contains all those big Brady Bunch hits, plus a McCormick solo single, "Truckin' Back to You."

influences:

◀◀ Partridge Family, Monkees, Florence Henderson

▶▶ Crystal Bernard

Brian Mansfield

THE DEL McCOURY BAND /RONNIE & ROB McCOURY

Formed as Del McCoury & the Dixie Pals, 1967, in TN; changed name to Del McCoury Band in 1987.

Del McCoury (born Delano Floyd McCoury, February 1, 1939, in Bakersville, NC), vocals, guitar; Ronnie McCoury, mandolin, vocals (1981–present); Rob McCoury, banjo (1987–present); Jason Carter, fiddle (1992–present); Mike Bub, bass (1992–present); others.

They don't get any more bluegrass than Del McCoury. With a voice that will unhinge every last good nerve within, Del takes "high lonesome" to a whole new level. Watching him perform with his young band is an education in how to sing with pure conviction, and how to wring the most out of every note, every phrase. Del is a genius, and if there's any justice, he will someday (very soon) be held in the same high regard as Bill Monroe.

Del McCoury spent most of his growing up years in York County, Pennsylvania. As a teenager he worked in a quartet with his brother, playing banjo with the Blue Ridge Ramblers and the Virginia Playboys during the 1950s and 1960s. A move to the Blue Grass Boys in 1963 found Del thinking he'd be playing banjo for leadman Monroe—until he learned that Bill Keith had been hired at the same time, leaving Del with guitar-playing and vocal duties instead. However, Del's real talent came through once he

Delbert McClinton (© Ken Settle)

joined Monroe and started singing lead. His voice, the very epitome of "high lonesome," has aged like the finest of wines. Today, Del McCoury is probably the most soulful singer on the planet, although his own son Ronnie, who joined his father's band in 1981, is running a close second. Ronnie, a multi-award winnIng mandolin player, has every bit of his father's bluesy voice, and shows even more control and emotion than his dad did at his age. The talent hardly stops there, however, as another acclaimed instrumentalist rounds out the McCoury clan. Rob, who made his debut with his dad in 1987, is a banjo player every bit as skillful as his older brother, and as dedicated to his craft as all of the McCourys. The tradition continues with young Jacob, Ronnie's preschool-aged son, who frequently steps on stage with dad, uncle and granddaddy McCoury, to "play" a small toy fiddle. The band's real fiddler, Kentuckian Jason Carter, is an amazing young player who is expected to begin making his own solo recordings soon. The group is immeasurably aided by Mike Bub, their bass player from Arizona.

The current configuration of Del's band has been together since 1992, when the group was signed to Rounder, but the band-

neal mccoy

leader's recording career stretches back to the early 1960s. Several Del McCoury albums are available, as is a duet album with brother Jerry McCoury and some by his former band, the Dixie Pals. Ronnie and Rob have also recorded their own album, and Ronnie was previously a member of the Nashville Station Inn-based Sidemen. The International Bluegrass Music Association awards the band has racked up, the perfectly constructed and executed records they've released and the impression they've left with countless fans have gone a long way toward keeping the Bill Monroe-based bluegrass tradition alive, even when the Del McCoury Band dares to include some non-bluegrass tunes in its uniformly excellent performances.

what to buy: *A Deeper Shade of Blue* (Rounder, 1993, prod. Ronnie McCoury) ♪♪♪♪ contains one great track after another, including Del's not-soon-forgotten take on "What Made Milwaukee Famous." For an intense understanding of the everlasting link between the blues and bluegrass, start here. The early years of Del & the Dixie Pals are distinctly documented in *Classic Bluegrass* (Rebel, 1991, prod. various) ♪♪♪♪, an 18-song set covering Del's 11 years with the Rebel label.

what to buy next: The young brothers McCoury have taken their roles seriously as keepers of the bluegrass flame passed down from dad. But they're individuals, too, as *Ronnie & Rob McCoury* (Rounder, 1995, prod. Ronnie McCoury) ♪♪♪♪♪ shows. With well-chosen covers and kicking originals, this is fantastic stuff! And with Tom Petty and Robert Cray covers to fan the flames, *Cold Hard Facts* (Rounder, 1996, prod. Jerry Douglas, Ronnie McCoury) ♪♪♪♪♪ is a real barn-burner.

the rest:
The McCoury Brothers (Rounder, 1978/1995) ♪♪♪♪
Live in Japan (Copper Creek, 1980/1992) ♪♪♪♪
Don't Stop the Music (Rounder, 1990) ♪♪♪♪
Blue Side of Town (Rounder, 1992) ♪♪♪♪

worth searching for: The Del McCoury Band, along with Doc Watson, Mac Wiseman and dobroist Gene Wooten, created a country version of the dance hit "Macarena" (Imprint, 1996, prod. Scott Rouse) ♪♪♪ as the Groovegrass Boys. It's good, strange fun hearing McCoury sing the tune, and, what's more, it actually sold pretty well.

solo outings:
Del McCoury:
I Wonder Where You Are Tonight (Arhoolie, 1968) ♪♪♪♪
Livin' on the Mountain (Rebel, 1971/1992) ♪♪♪♪
(With the Dixie Pals) *High on a Mountain* (Rounder, 1972/1995) ♪♪♪♪
(With the Dixie Pals) *Sawmill* (Rebel) ♪♪♪

influences:
◀◀ Bill Monroe
▶▶ Sidemen

Stephen L. Betts

NEAL McCOY

Born Hubert Neal McGauhey Jr., July 30, 1958, in Jacksonville, TX.

Neal McCoy didn't start having big hit singles until his third album. He was lucky—most male singers of the 1990s didn't get to take that long. A Texan of partial Filipino descent, McCoy began singing professionally at age 20. Eventually he won a talent show that led to opening slot for Charley Pride and provided his entry to a national audience. McCoy's sense of humor makes him an entertaining performer, but he's had trouble capturing that essence on record. He also has a tendency to rely on successful formulas, which give his albums a sameness and suggest that he's not a good bet for lengthy success.

what to buy: McCoy likes ditties, but he goes easy on his fourth album, *You Gotta Love That!* (Atlantic, 1995, prod. Barry Beckett) ♪♪♪, which contained the Top Five hits "No Doubt About It" and "For a Change." Still, it's pretty much indistinguishable from the previous album, *No Doubt About It*, except for "If I Was a Drinking Man," which has more depth than everything else he's ever recorded put together.

what to buy next: McCoy's breakthrough, *No Doubt About It* (Atlantic, 1994, prod. Barry Beckett) ♪♪♪ was also the first album he recorded with former Muscle Shoals keyboardist Barry Beckett producing. The title track took him to the top of the singles chart, but the songs "Wink" and "The City Put the Country Back in Me" gave him the first decent fast songs he'd ever had.

what to avoid: McCoy's first album *At This Moment* (Atlantic, 1990) ♪, is highlighted by a cover of Billy Vera's prom night standard "At This Moment." And that's the *best* part.

the rest:
Where Forever Begins (Atlantic, 1992) ♪♪
Neal McCoy (Atlantic, 1996) ♪♪

influences:
◀◀ Charley Pride
▶▶ David Kersh

Brian Mansfield

MINDY McCREADY

Born Malinda Gayle McCready, November 30, 1975, in Ft. Meyers, FL.

One year—no more, no less. That's the amount of time that Mindy McCready gave herself to "make it" in Music City. She had moved to Nashville at age 18 and promised her mother that if she hadn't made any progress in the music business in a year, that she would move back to Florida and study pre-law. As the story goes, exactly 51 weeks after arriving, McCready performed a live audition for the brass at RCA and landed a record deal that day. Three years later her debut album has sold platinum.

McCready is full of contradictions. The "bad girl" who likes to wear leather halter tops is also the girl who began taking vocal lessons at age 10 and attended summer school and night school so she could graduate from high school early—at age 16. She's also the same little girl who played quarterback on the co-ed football team in Little League—which isn't hard to picture at all. Don't you know she loved calling those plays.

what's available: On *Ten Thousand Angels* (BNA, 1996, prod. David Malloy, Norro Wilson) 🎵🎵🎵, which contains her hits "Ten Thousand Angels," "Guys Do It All the Time" and "Maybe He'll Notice Her Now," McCready seems to still be struggling to find her style. The highlight is the album's closer, a cover of Mark Germino's "Breakin' It," which was a minor hit for Loretta Lynn in 1983.

influences:
◀◀ Shania Twain
▶▶ Regina

Cyndi Hoelzle

RICH McCREADY

Born in Seneca, MO.

Rich McCready grew up on a cattle ranch near the Missouri/Oklahoma border. He used that experience when he moved to Nashville in 1992; his day job found him on a horse ranch belonging to Magnatone Records-president Brent Maher. Maher's son, Brian, began writing songs with McCready, and eventually the elder Maher signed the Missourian to a record deal. Rich is no kin to Mindy McCready, who released her first album about the same time.

what's available: *Rich McCready* (Magnatone, 1996, prod. Brian Maher) 🎵🎵🎵 contains capable rockin' honky-tonk, but nothing distinctive.

influences:
◀◀ John Michael Montgomery, Garth Brooks

Brian Mansfield

MEL McDANIEL

Born September 6, 1942, in Checotah, OK.

When people talk about how forgettable many of the male singers of the 1990s are, they forget about people like Mel McDaniel, who had a string of moderate hits—and one #1, 1984's "Baby's Got Her Blue Jeans On." Working with a little bit of Okie honky-tonk, a little rockabilly and a lot of malleability, the former staff writer and demo singer had more than 41 charting singles between 1976 and 1989, but only 10 of them reached the Top 10. The Hat Act Invasion of 1989 sent him packing for Branson, and he still plays the country oldies circuit.

what's available: *Baby's Got Her Blue Jeans On* (Branson, 1993, prod. Jerry Kennedy) 🎵🎵 contains remakes of McDaniels' best-known hits (the title track, "Stand Up," a cover of the Bruce Springsteen B-side "Stand on It") and a handful of new tunes. Since he's still working with producer Jerry Kennedy, these are pretty much indistinguishable from McDaniels' original recordings.

worth searching for: *Greatest Hits* (Capitol, 1987, prod. Jerry Kennedy) 🎵🎵 contains most, but not all, of McDaniel's biggest singles.

influences:
◀◀ Joe Stampley, Moe Bandy

Brian Mansfield

RONNIE McDOWELL

Born March 26, 1950, in Fountain Head, TN.

As a boy growing up in Portland, Tennessee, Ronnie McDowell spent most of his time picking berries and doing farm chores. He liked music, especially Elvis Presley, and learned how to play guitar, never thinking he'd one day have a musical career. After high school Ronnie enlisted in the navy and was stationed in the Pacific, where he started to perform publicly. In 1969, after his discharge, he formed his own band, the Nashville Road, and played small clubs on the country music circuit. The turning point in McDowell's career came in 1977, when Presley died and McDowell wrote and recorded a tribute song called the "The King Is Gone." It sold more than 500,000 copies, and

McDowell began making television appearances promoting the single. Dick Clark approached him to sing the soundtrack on a TV movie about Presley's life, and McDowell's vocals on it bore an amazingly close resemblance to those of the King. Though he would develop his own style on subsequent recordings, he never quite shook the association with Presley. McDowell topped the country chart twice, with "Older Women" in 1981 and "You're Gonna Ruin My Bad Reputation" in 1983, although none of his singles sold as well as "The King Is Gone." He recorded first for Scorpion, had most of hits on Epic and, in 1986, settled in with Curb, where he remains to this day. Mc-Dowell has had a long association with producer and former publishing magnate Buddy Killen.

what to buy: *All Tied Up in Love* (Curb 1986, prod. various) 𝄞𝄞𝄞 captures McDowell's own voice and sound rather than the Presley and 1950s doo-wop influences.

what to buy next: For *Unchained Melody* (Curb, 1991, prod. various) 𝄞𝄞𝄞, McDowell teamed with artists such as Conway Twitty, Jack Scott and Bobby Vinton to record reverb-heavy duet versions of their hits. *Greatest Hits* (Curb, 1994, prod. Various) 𝄞𝄞𝄞 is the most recent and best of all McDowell's compilations. It contains strong versions of "You're Gonna Ruin My Bad Reputation," "Older Women" and "It's Only Make Believe," a duet with Conway Twitty.

what to avoid: *Greatest Hits* (Epic, 1988, prod. various) 𝄞𝄞 contains many of the same songs as *Older Women and Other Greatest Hits*, as well as the Curb *Greatest Hits* set.

the rest:
Older Women and Other Greatest Hits (Epic, 1987) 𝄞𝄞
The Best of Ronnie McDowell (Curb, 1990) 𝄞𝄞
Your Precious Love (Curb, 1991) 𝄞𝄞
When a Man Loves a Woman (Curb, 1992) 𝄞𝄞
Country Dances (Curb, 1993) 𝄞
Greatest Gospel Songs (Curb, 1996) 𝄞𝄞

worth searching for: *I'm Still Missing You* (Curb, 1988) 𝄞𝄞 and *American Music* (Curb, 1989) 𝄞𝄞 aren't particularly good albums, but McDowell's backing band at the time featured future members of the Kentucky HeadHunters.

influences:
◀◀ Elvis Presley, Conway Twitty, Bobby Vinton
▶▶ Kentucky HeadHunters, Six Shooter

Ronnie McDowell (no relation)

REBA McENTIRE
Born March 28, 1954, in Chockie, OK.

Discovered singing the national anthem at an Oklahoma City rodeo in 1974 by Red Steagall, Reba McEntire suffered through a six-year string of meandering, overproduced songbird sessions for Mercury before landing at MCA in 1984. Credit often goes to producer Jimmy Bowen for rescuing her, but the key to McEntire's artistic rebirth was her discovery of how to fuse her strong-willed Oklahoma attitude with that powerful voice. Sassy and soulful, sardonic and seductive, McEntire embodied the feminist stance of such heroines as Loretta Lynn and Tammy Wynette, and by 1985 she was co-producing her own albums—a rarity in male-dominated Nashville. Grammys and Country Music Association trophies have made her the most powerful woman in country music. But instead of wielding her triple-platinum clout to challenge and change the industry, McEntire has chosen to bask in the spotlight and flaunt her success via flashy covers of Aretha Franklin's "Respect" and Vicki Lawrence's "The Night the Lights Went Out in Georgia"; commercial endorsements for Frito-Lay; elaborately choreographed videos; and lavish, wardrobe-driven stage shows more suitable for Las Vegas than the Grand Ole Opry. Still, just when you think she's sold her soul, McEntire throws an artistic curveball—like releasing 1994's chilling AIDS ballad, "She Thinks His Name Was John," as a single, or drafting her road band to cut 1996's full-throttled *What If It's You*—and rediscovers the difference between breaking through and raking it in.

what to buy: Recorded after the plane crash that killed seven of her band members, *For My Broken Heart* (MCA, 1991, prod. Tony Brown, Reba McEntire) 𝄞𝄞𝄞𝄞 channels her sorrow into a touching, well-crafted pop-country album about searching for closure in the face of loneliness ("Is There Life out There"), despair ("For My Broken Heart"), abandonment ("All Dressed Up with Nowhere to Go") and death ("Bobby," "The Greatest Man I Never Knew"). *Read My Mind* (MCA, 1994, prod. Tony Brown, Reba McEntire) 𝄞𝄞𝄞𝄞 is marked by such feisty rockers as the gospel-inflected "I Won't Stand in Line," the twangy "The Heart Is a Lonely Hunter" and the bluesy "Why Haven't I Heard from You." But the emotional centerpiece is "She Thinks His Name Was John," about a woman who contracts AIDS after a one-night stand. Fiddles and steel guitars keep her commercial breakthrough, *Whoever's in New England* (MCA, 1986, prod.

Reba McEntire (© Ken Settle)

Jimmy Bowen, Reba McEntire) 𝄞𝄞𝄞𝄞 anchored in country even though the bopping "Little Rock" and such heart-aching ballads as "Don't Touch Me There" and the title track hint at the pop detour lying ahead.

what to buy next: As the title suggests, *My Kind of Country* (MCA, 1984, prod. Harold Shedd) 𝄞𝄞𝄞𝄞 is McEntire's heartfelt take on traditional country reflected by the fiddle-driven sound and sentiments of "Somebody Should Leave," Connie Smith's "You Got Me (Right Where You Want Me)," Faron Young's "He's Only Everything" and "I Want to Hear It from You," written by Deana Carter's father, Fred Carter Jr.

what to avoid: From its gauzy cover photo to such cheesy vehicles as "I Don't Want to Be a One-Night Stand" and "(There's Nothing Like the Love) Between a Woman and a Man," *Reba McEntire* (Mercury, 1977, prod. Jerry Kennedy, Glenn Keener) **WOOF!** is the sad sound of a naive 22-year-old singer overwhelmed by clunky, reverb-heavy production that employs backing singers with the subtlety of the cavalry.

the rest:

Out of a Dream (Mercury, 1979) 𝄞
Feel the Fire (Mercury, 1980) 𝄞𝄞
Heart to Heart (Mercury, 1981) 𝄞𝄞
Unlimited (Mercury, 1982) 𝄞𝄞
Behind the Scene (Mercury, 1983) 𝄞𝄞
Just a Little Love (MCA, 1984) 𝄞𝄞
Have I Got a Deal for You (MCA, 1985) 𝄞𝄞𝄞
Best of Reba McEntire (Mercury, 1985) 𝄞𝄞
Reba Nell McEntire (Mercury, 1986) 𝄞𝄞
What Am I Gonna Do about You (MCA, 1986) 𝄞𝄞𝄞
The Last One to Know (MCA, 1987) 𝄞𝄞𝄞
Greatest Hits (MCA, 1987) 𝄞𝄞𝄞
Merry Christmas to You (MCA, 1987) 𝄞𝄞
Reba (MCA, 1988) 𝄞𝄞𝄞
Sweet 16 (MCA, 1989) 𝄞𝄞𝄞
Live (MCA, 1989) 𝄞𝄞
Rumor Has It (MCA, 1990) 𝄞𝄞𝄞
It's Your Call (MCA, 1992) 𝄞𝄞𝄞
Greatest Hits Volume 2 (MCA, 1993) 𝄞𝄞𝄞𝄞
Starting Over (MCA, 1995) 𝄞𝄞𝄞
What If It's You (MCA, 1996) 𝄞𝄞𝄞𝄞

worth searching for: Part of the label's Chronicles retrospective series, *Oklahoma Girl* (Mercury, 1994, comp. prod. Hazel Smith, Kira Florita) 𝄞𝄞 collects the "best" of McEntire's ill-fated Mercury era and adds six previously unreleased tracks,

including "She Came on Like Lightnin'" and "The Blues Don't Care Who's Got 'Em."

influences:

◀◀ Loretta Lynn, Bobbie Gentry, Dolly Parton, Crystal Gayle

▶▶ Linda Davis, Faith Hill, Jo Dee Messina

David Okamoto

JOHN McEUEN

Born December 19, 1945, in Garden Grove, CA.

John McEuen was a founding member of the Nitty Gritty Dirt Band. His precision-like mastery of acoustic guitar, dobro, fiddle, mandolin and banjo won legions of fans—and critical acclaim—throughout the band's 25-year history. But during the mid-1980s, as the Dirt Band began moving away from its acoustic-based roots in favor of a more country-pop flavor, McEuen became disenchanted. He left and began to focus on the acoustic-based music that had always been so dear to his heart.

what to buy: *Acoustic Traveller* (Vanguard, 1996, prod. John McEuen) 𝄞𝄞𝄞𝄞 is a new-agey, newgrass gem where McEuen plays a battery of acoustic instruments. Especially noteworthy are "Gypsy Knights" and his take on the bluegrass standard "I Am a Pilgrim."

what to buy next: *String Wizards II* (Vanguard, 1994, prod. John McEuen) 𝄞𝄞𝄞 contains the Flatt & Scruggs classic "The Ballad of Jed Clampett."

the rest:

John McEuen (Warner Bros., 1988) 𝄞𝄞
The Wild West (soundtrack) (Aspen Recording Society, 1993)
String Wizards (Vanguard, 1991) 𝄞𝄞𝄞

influences:

◀◀ Earl Scruggs, Doc Watson

▶▶ Bela Fleck

see also: *Nitty Gritty Dirt Band*

Rick Petreycik

ELEANOR McEVOY

Born in Dublin, Ireland.

That the roots of country and Celtic music are entwined is well known, although contemporary exponents of both Irish and Nashville sensibilities are few and far between. Eleanor McEvoy is one such artist, combining the Celtic-tinged pop/rock of her homeland with the brand of smart, singer/songwriter country-pop in the Mary Chapin Carpenter mold. Her overall sound may be too rockish for country radio, but someone in Nashville should seriously consider covering her songs, particularly the feminist anthem (and huge Irish hit) "Only a Woman" from her debut album.

what to buy: On *What's Following Me?* (Columbia, 1996, prod. Kevin Moloney, Eleanor McEvoy) 𝄞𝄞𝄞, the guitars are revved up a little too much for Nashville tastes, but adventurous country fans will find an album that they can certainly understand and appreciate. The soaring "A Glass Unkissed" crystallizes heartbreak as well as any honky-tonk song. And the vulnerable ballad "My Own Sweet Bed Tonight" offers pertinent commentary on the subjects of sleeping single and drinking doubles.

the rest:
Eleanor McEvoy (Geffen, 1993) 𝄞𝄞𝄞

influences:
◀◀ R.E.M., Bob Dylan, Mary Black

Daniel Durchholz

KATE & ANNA McGARRIGLE
Sister vocal duo from Canada.

Kate McGarrigle (born 1946, in Montreal, Canada); Anna McGarrigle (born 1944, in Montreal, Canada).

The McGarrigle sisters are folk artists, not country, but contemporary country audiences should recognize their work if only because Linda Ronstadt tapped Anna's "Heart Like a Wheel" for the title track of one of her million-selling 1970s country-rock albums. She also covered Kate's "Talk to Me of Mendocino" and "You Tell Me That I'm Falling Down." And because these Quebecois siblings often sing in French, don't look for them to make it in Nashville—at least not until restaurants there begin serving croissants with everything instead of grits. The McGarrigles' reedy voices are quirky and endearing, their harmonies are close in a way that only siblings' can be, and their songwriting is austere and staggeringly beautiful. Buy one of their albums and you'll want them all.

what to buy: Their debut, *Kate & Anna McGarrigle* (Warner Bros., 1976/Hannibal, 1994, prod. Joe Boyd, Greg Prestopino) 𝄞𝄞𝄞𝄞, contains their original versions of "Heart Like a Wheel" and "Talk to Me of Mendocino" within a compelling mix of genres—gospel harmonies here, a jazz saxophone there, plus folk-country touches of banjo and harmonica. They also turn in a lovely version of "Swimming Song" by Loudon Wainwright,

Kate's ex-husband. Twenty years later, this album still holds up. *French Record* (Warner Bros., 1981/Hannibal, 1992, prod. various) 𝄞𝄞𝄞𝄞 is an entrancing collection of the sisters' previously released French-language songs, plus a newly recorded version of the French Canadian folk song "C'est Magnifique."

what to buy next: *Dancer with Bruised Knees* (Warner Bros., 1977/Hannibal, 1994, prod. Joe Boyd) 𝄞𝄞𝄞𝄞 is intimate, engaging and arty. "Southern Girls" has a Randy Newman feel and sensibility, while "No-Biscuit Blues" rocks gently with gospel-style vocals. The album contains the original version of Kate's lovely "Come a Long Way," later covered by Wainwright.

the rest:
Love Over and Over (Polydor, 1983/Hannibal, 1997) 𝄞𝄞𝄞𝄞
Heartbeats Accelerating (Private, 1990) 𝄞𝄞𝄞𝄞
Matapedia (Hannibal, 1996) 𝄞𝄞𝄞𝄞

worth searching for: *Pronto Monto* (Warner Bros., 1978) 𝄞𝄞𝄞𝄞, their most conventional folk-pop album, is currently out of print.

influences:
◀◀ Bob Dylan, Joan Baez, Randy Newman, Fairport Convention
▶▶ Linda Ronstadt, Emmylou Harris

Daniel Durchholz

TIM McGRAW
Born May 1, 1967, in Delhi, LA.

Son of former baseball pitcher Tug McGraw, Tim McGraw grew up in Start, Louisiana, and taught himself to play guitar at age 20. He moved to Nashville two years later on the day Keith Whitley died and soon was singing in a nightclub on seedy Printers Alley. McGraw borrowed $3,000 from a family friend to record two songs; the demo got him a record deal. The politically incorrect "Indian Outlaw," which includes a snippet of the Raider's 1971 pop hit "Indian Reservation," became a huge smash hit, propelling McGraw's second album past 5 million sold and making it the sixth-biggest selling album of 1994, according to *Billboard* magazine. He married country singer Faith Hill in 1996.

what to buy: Rock radio hooks and finely written country songs ranging from arena rockers like "I Like It, I Love It" to tear-pulling numbers like "Can't Be Really Gone" and "Maybe We Should Just Sleep on It" pepper *All I Want* (Curb, 1995, prod. James Stroud, Byron Gallimore, Tim McGraw) 𝄞𝄞𝄞.

what to buy next: While "Indian Outlaw" offended many, its pummeling hooks made it a huge hit. Other non-novelty singles

musicHound COUNTRY

2
9
2

mcguinn, clark & millman

Tim McGraw (© Ken Settle)

"Don't Take the Girl" and the title cut off *Not a Moment Too Soon* (Curb, 1994, prod. James Stroud, Byron Gallimore) 𝄞𝄞𝄞 solidified McGraw's stardom. The album has sold more than 4 million copies. The low-octane *Tim McGraw* (Curb, 1993, prod. James Stroud, Byron Gallimore) 𝄞𝄞𝄞 is fueled by fewer hooks, less pandering and no hits.

influences:
◀◀ Garth Brooks
▶▶ Jo Dee Messina

Bill Hobbs

McGUINN, CLARK & HILLMAN
See: Chris Hillman

DON McLEAN
Born October 2, 1945, in New Rochelle, NY.

After graduating from Iona College in 1968, folk-singing trouba-dour Don McLean enrolled at Columbia Graduate School, but didn't attend, choosing instead to work dates with childhood hero Pete Seeger. McLean's first album, *Tapestry*, was released in 1970 on the Mediarts label after being turned down by 34 other companies. It contained the original version of "And I Love You So," a song that became a moderate country hit for Bobby Goldsboro, a pop smash for Perry Como and an album cut for Elvis Presley. McLean's breakthrough came with his sec-ond album, *American Pie*, which spent nearly two months atop the pop album charts in late 1971 and 1972 and was dedicated to Buddy Holly. In addition to the epic title song, that album also contained "Vincent." After *American Pie*, McLean made a series of inspired folk-rock albums, but never recaptured the magic of his eight-and-a-half minute blockbuster, though he was the inspiration for the song "Killing Me Softly with His Song," a chart-topping smash for Roberta Flack and, more re-cently, the Fugees. McLean, whose lengthy list of influences in-cludes Hank Williams and Johnny Cash, traveled to Nashville in 1978 to record *Chain Lightning*, the album yielding his only Top 10 country hit, a remake of Roy Orbison's "Crying" that didn't chart until 1981. In 1981 he released another Nashville album, *Believers*, which, like *Chain Lightning*, was engineered by Billy Sherrill and featured some of Music City's prime players. He had one of his last hits with "He's Got You," a remake of Patsy Cline's "She's Got You," in 1987.

what to buy: *The Best of Don McLean* (EMI, 1988, prod. vari-ous) 𝄞𝄞𝄞 is a 10-song career overview containing all of his key tracks as well as his loving remake of hero Buddy Holly's "Every Day."

what to buy next: *American Pie* (EMI-Manhattan, 1971, prod. Ed Freeman) 𝄞𝄞𝄞 is the original breakthrough album that made such a big noise during the winter of 1971, the pure and unpretentious work of a troubadour who had no idea that a chart-topping classic was in his future.

the rest:
Head Room (Curb, 1991) 𝄞𝄞𝄞
Don McLean Christmas (Curb, 1991) 𝄞𝄞𝄞
Classics (Curb, 1992) 𝄞𝄞𝄞𝄞
The River of Love (Curb, 1995) 𝄞𝄞𝄞

worth searching for: *Chain Lightning* (Millennium, 1978, prod. Larry Butler) 𝄞𝄞𝄞 features his compassionate vocals on mater-ial like "Crying" and "Your Cheatin' Heart," recorded in Nashville. A country singer he wasn't, but with his impassioned but tasteful deliveries, McLean makes you believe every word he sings.

influences:

◀◀ Pete Seeger, Johnny Cash

▶▶ Mary Chapin Carpenter, Steve Forbert

David Sokol

KEN MELLONS

Born July 10, in Kingsport, TN.

Ken Mellons grew up in suburban Nashville, where most kids his age listened to rock 'n' roll. But Mellons grew up to sing twangy hard-core country with more than a hint of his idols Keith Whitley and Vern Gosdin in his voice.

what's available: Mellons co-wrote most of the cuts on *Ken Mellons* (Epic, 1994, prod. Jerry Cupit) 🎵🎵🎵 including "Honky-Tonk Heroes," which pays homage to his favorite bygone stars. *When Forever Begins* (Epic, 1995, prod. Jerry Cupit) 🎵🎵🎵 is Mellons' followup.

influences:

◀◀ Keith Whitley, Vern Gosdin, John Anderson

▶▶ Kenny Chesney

Bill Hobbs

D.L. MENARD

Born April 14, 1932, in Erath, LA.

"The Cajun Hank Williams," D.L. Menard is highly regarded in Cajun circles as a songwriter (he has written several Cajun honky-tonk standards, the best known of which is "La Porte d'en Arriere" or "The Back Door"). Menard cites Hank Williams as his biggest single influence, both as a singer and songwriter. Menard is a forceful, moving vocalist, and his powerful rhythm guitar-playing is legendary in Cajun country. (Cajun bands routinely play dances without the benefit of bass to keep time.) He often records with a pedal steel, and his vocal approach owes as much to Hank Williams, Lefty Frizzell and other honky-tonkers as it does to traditional Cajun music; Menard's high, keening vocal style blends admirably with the bluesy lyrics of the best honky-tonk, something he seems to understand instinctively.

what to buy: *D.L. Menard & the Louisiana Aces* (Rounder, 1974, prod. Ken Irwin, Dick Spottswood) 🎵🎵🎵🎵 contains mostly traditional waltzes and two-steps sung in Cajun French in front of an outstanding band. *No Matter Where You At, There You Are* (Rounder, 1988, prod. Ken Irwin, D.L. Menard) 🎵🎵🎵🎵 is a mixture of traditional numbers and Menard originals with a killer band

(Eddie Lejeune, Blackie Forestier and Ken Smith). *Cajun Saturday Night* (Rounder, 1984, prod. Ken Irwin) 🎵🎵🎵🎵 is a country-oriented session. Menard sings in English, including five Hank Williams numbers and other honky-tonkers, plus a couple of Menard originals. His band includes Ricky Skaggs, Jerry Douglas, Don Helms and Buck White.

what to buy next: *The Swallow Recordings* (Ace, 1994) 🎵🎵🎵🎵 an English import, contains Menard's early Swallow material (some of his best) plus an album's worth of material from fiddler Austin Pitre. *Louisiana Cajun Music—Underneath the Green Oak Tree* (Arhoolie, 1977, prod. Chris Strachwitz) 🎵🎵🎵🎵 captures a traditional Cajun supersession featuring Menard, accordionist Marc Savoy, and fiddler Dewey Balfa working their magic on a completely acoustic set of traditional music.

the rest:

D.L. Menard's Cajun Memories (Swallow, 1996) 🎵🎵🎵

worth searching for: *The Back Door* (Swallow, 1980, prod. Floyd Soileau) 🎵🎵🎵🎵 contains the original versions of D.L. 's early hits, including his biggest, "The Back Door."

influences:

◀◀ Hank Williams, Aldus Roger

▶▶ Steve Riley & the Mamou Playboys, Rusty & Doug Kershaw

Randy Pitts

JO DEE MESSINA

Born August 25, 1970, in Holliston, MA.

After years of competing in local talent contests and performing every weekend with her country band, Jo Dee Messina left her small New England hometown at age 19 to move to Nashville. Eventually introduced to a record executive at the International Country Music Fan Fair in Nashville, she jokingly told him, "What you guys really need over there is a redhead." As fate would have it, just then a well-known producer walked up and praised her demo tape. Messina was signed shortly after to Curb, where she recorded her debut album in the same studio, during the same timeslot, and with the same musicians that co-producer Tim McGraw was using to record his own third album.

what's available: Recorded at the same time, with the same team, as Tim McGraw's *All I Want*, Messina's debut has the same mix of quality writing with rock radio hooks. *Jo Dee Messina* (Curb, 1996, prod. Byron Gallimore, Tim McGraw) 🎵🎵🎵

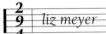
includes the debut hit "Heads Carolina, Tails California" among a slew of surefire cuts.

influences:
◀◀ Tim McGraw

Bill Hobbs

LIZ MEYER

Born March 7, 1952, in Munich, Germany.

A singer/songwriter whose music is folksy with strong bluegrass overtones, Liz Meyer grew up in Northampton, Massachusetts, and moved to Melbourne, Florida, at age seven, and finally to Washington, D.C., at 12. There she played in a band with guitar wizard Danny Gatton from 1972 to 1974, and in another alongside Bob Siggins (formerly of the Jim Kweskin Jug Band and Charles River Valley Boys). In 1985, after the abortive release of her debut album, Meyer moved to Holland and briefly retired to raise a family from 1987-94. In the meantime she gained a large European following and has continued to produce several acts there.

what's available: Recorded in 1976, *Once a Day* (Adelphi, 1982, prod. Liz Meyer, Obie O'Brien) ♫♫♫, Meyer's first album, was rushed out against her wishes, but nevertheless won unanimous critical raves. *Womanly Arts* (Strictly Country/Munich, 1995, prod. Liz Meyer) ♫♫♫, her first album in more than a decade, is a kinetic folk-bluegrass collection that features her warm vocal style and such ace players as fiddler Byron Berline and guitarist Steuart Smith, plus a fiery appearance by the New Grass Revival on "Get in the Wind."

worth searching for: Kate MacKenzie recorded Meyer's "Blue Lonesome Wind" on *Age of Innocence*.

influences:
◀◀ Emmylou Harris, New Grass Revival
▶▶ Nicolette Larson, Robin & Linda Williams

Bob Cannon

BILL MILLER

Born 1940, in WI.

Don't trouble yourself trying to label the music of Native American singer/songwriter Bill Miller; he's happy to do it himself. It's not alternative, he's fond of saying: it's altered-Native. And so it is. Miller can shift gears rapidly between Neil Young-style folkie reveries and tradition-based Native American chants. His 1996 release was a rock album, much of which draws on the

kind of energy Miller saw when he shared a concert bill with alternative rockers Pearl Jam. Having grown up on a northern Wisconsin reservation, Miller was exposed to the vagaries of racism and all its attendant violence. And while his music occasionally gives in to bitterness and a thirst for revenge, it is mostly about hope, dignity and compassion. Miller's is an important and genuinely wise voice.

what to buy: On *Raven in the Snow* (Reprise, 1995, prod. Richard Bennett) ♫♫♫♫, Miller switches from his gentle folkie stance to full-bore rock arrangements—a good idea since, for the first time, the music reflects the fury behind such songs as "The Final Word" and the title track. Others—such as the defiant "Brave Heart" and "Listen to Me," which pleads for understanding between generations—are more reflective and have an ethereal quality. Altogether, *Raven* is Miller's most fully realized work. To get a glimpse of Miller's other abilities, check out *The Red Road* (Warner Western, 1993, prod. Richard Bennett) ♫♫♫♫, which combines acoustic-based folk music with Native American flutes and chants. It includes the haunting instrumental "Dreams of Wounded Knee," plus "Praises," which is based on a Menominee prayer to the Creator, and "Reservation Road," a gritty memoir of Miller's birthplace.

the rest:
(With Robert Mirabal & the Smokey Town Singers) *Native Suite* (Warner Western, 1996) ♫♫♫♪

worth searching for: Miller's earlier, self-released albums, which he sells at shows and by mail order, include a pair of folk outings: *Old Dreams and New Hopes* (Rosebud, 1987) ♫♫♪ and *The Art of Survival* (Rosebud, 1990) ♫♫♫, as well as the Native American/New Age-leaning *Loon, Mountain and Moon: Native American Flute Songs* (Rosebud, 1991) ♫♫♪.

influences:
◀◀ Neil Young, Dan Fogelberg, XIT

Daniel Durchholz

BUDDY MILLER

Born in OH.

Buddy Miller's career, in large part, has been that of the roaming singer/songwriter. He's based himself, at various times, in San Francisco, New York, Austin, Los Angeles and, currently, Nashville. He has worked as a guitarist for folk/rock singer Shawn Colvin, and had a loose writing and performing partnership with Jim Lauderdale. He has recorded with Lauderdale, Heather Myles and Victoria Williams. Miller came into his own in 1995 when he finally released an album under his own name. His wife, Julie Miller, is also a recording artist.

what's available: *Your Love and Other Lies* (HighTone, 1995) 🎵🎵🎵 features appearances by Jim Lauderdale, Emmylou Harris, Lucinda Williams and others. Within a year of its release, every song on the album had been covered, recorded for future release, or put on hold by a major-label artist.

influences:
◀◀ Jim Lauderdale

Brian Mansfield

EMMETT MILLER

Born 1903 in Macon, GA. Date of death is unknown.

A little-known figure said to have taught Hank Williams his first hit, "Lovesick Blues," given Bob Wills his entire western swing style and who remains an idol of no less than Merle Haggard to this day, Emmett Miller first gained notoriety via Nick Tosches' 1977 book *Country*. Miller was a minstrel performer who cut some rare Okeh 78s during 1927–28 in New York with the Dorsey brothers and some other respected jazzmen. Bootleg editions of his recordings fueled his legend and fostered more disciples, notably Leon Redbone, who based a considerable part of his whole act on Miller's unnatural, guttural sound. Biographical details are thin, and he disappeared into the ether of history without so much as a fare-thee-well; nobody knows when or where he died. But his cult continues.

what's available: *Emmett Miller: The Minstrel Man from Georgia* (Columbia/Legacy, 1996) 🎵🎵🎵 is a masterpiece in musical archeology, a collection of 20 selections from those long-ago sessions. While falling somewhat short of establishing Miller conclusively as this great missing link in country music (too often the songs are little more than trite exercises in racial slander that passed as humor at the time), these recordings do show Miller to be a stylist of great originality and a vocalist with singular vitality—an altogether fascinating and rewarding unrevealed chapter in music history.

influences:
▶▶ Hank Williams, Bob Wills, Merle Haggard, George Jones, Bob Dylan

Joel Selvin

JO MILLER & LAURA LOVE

See: Ranch Romance

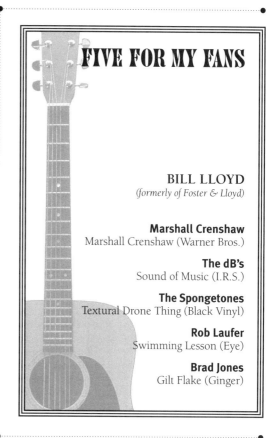

FIVE FOR MY FANS

BILL LLOYD
(formerly of Foster & Lloyd)

Marshall Crenshaw
Marshall Crenshaw (Warner Bros.)

The dB's
Sound of Music (I.R.S.)

The Spongetones
Textural Drone Thing (Black Vinyl)

Rob Laufer
Swimming Lesson (Eye)

Brad Jones
Gilt Flake (Ginger)

NED MILLER

Born Henry Ned Miller, April 12, 1925, in Raines, UT.

Ned Miller is a former pipe fitter who found moderate success in country music as both a singer and songwriter. He wrote numerous songs for other artists, usually with his wife, Sue. The most famous of those is probably "Dark Moon," a 1957 pop hit for both Gale Storm and Bonnie Guitar. On his own, Miller favored ballads, the biggest of which was "From a Jack to a King," which reached #2 in 1963 and later became a hit for Ricky Van Shelton. He had Top 40 hits for Fabor, Capitol and Gene Autry's Republic label.

what's available: Miller had barely enough hits for those three labels to fill one hits disc, so all that's currently available under his own name is *From a Jack to a King* (Sun, 1981) 🎵, but that doesn't feature the hit version of his most famous song. In fact, only two of these songs—"From a Jack to a King" and "One among the Many"—were ever hits for Miller. The others are versions of songs like "Mona Lisa" and "You Belong to Me."

influences:

◀◀ Jim Reeves, Sonny James

▶▶ Jack Greene, Ricky Van Shelton

Brian Mansfield

ROGER MILLER

Born January 2, 1936, in Fort Worth, TX. Died October 25, 1992, in Los Angeles, CA.

If he had left us with nothing more than "King of the Road," his place in the pantheon of American musical giants would be assured. But Roger Miller's remarkable body of work contains literally dozens of songs its equal and beyond—songs that remain as vibrant, funny, poignant and thought-provoking today as they were more than three decades ago when they first set the country music world on its ear. To the undiscriminating listener, Miller is best remembered for his mid-1960s string of light-hearted classics ("Dang Me," "England Swings," "Engine Engine #9"), songs that also sold in Beatle-like quantities to pop and folk audiences as few releases out of Music City did in those days. But behind the rubber-faced, often crazed performer who threw these tunes so effortlessly up the charts lurked a deep and often dark spirit that, just as easily and as eloquently, sang of the harsher sides of life. Miller's own life and career saw plenty from both sides.

Taught to play fiddle and guitar by family friend Sheb ("Purple People Eater") Wooley, Miller came out of the Korean War to haunt the honky-tonks and music offices of Nashville. Between stints playing fiddle for Minnie Pearl and drums for Faron Young, Miller was helped by George Jones to connect with Mercury/Starday Records, which released Miller's first single in 1957. Ray Price, Ernest Tubb, Jim Reeves and old pal Young began scoring hits with Miller material, though the songwriter's own recordings sank without a trace. That would change in early 1964 when Miller scored hits with "Dang Me" and "Chug-a-Lug," and by the time he'd relocated to Hollywood he was in demand as a concert and TV attraction, his songs crossing over to folk and pop audiences. The hits and accolades came hard and fast, but by 1967 things started going awry. First, Miller's loyal label, Smash, was swallowed up by the giant Mercury corporation, affording the singer/songwriter less of a free reign inside the studio and less of a promotional push outside of it. A long-rumored amphetamine dependency also began to take its toll, most noticeably on his writing ability. He could still spot

and release a good song before anyone else ("Ruby, Don't Take Your Love to Town," "Little Green Apples," "Me and Bobbie McGee"); they just weren't his songs anymore.

Miller wisely lay low during the early 1980s. Surprisingly, when he next popped up it was as a Broadway composer, and his score for *Big River* duly won a Tony Award in 1985. Having now proved to himself and the world that he still had what it took, Miller spent his remaining years fishing, hanging with friends both old and new (his last hit, "It Only Hurts Me When I Cry," was a collaboration with Dwight Yoakam) and joking about the throat cancer that finally claimed him in 1992. As writer J.R. Taylor so perfectly eulogized, "Having conquered the sticks, the suburbs and the city, Roger Miller then put our country in his pocket and took it all with him."

what's available: The three-CD *King of the Road: The Genius of Roger Miller* (Mercury, 1995, comp. Daniel Cooper) ✍✍✍✍ says and includes it all. From the early stabs to the mega-hits, the should've-been hits ("My Uncle Used to Love Me but She Died," to name but one), the *Big River* score, and even a manic "Orange Blossom Special" with guitarist Danny Gatton, you owe it to yourself to take the wild and wonderful ride through these 70 songs.

worth searching for: *Roger and Out* (Smash, 1964, prod. Jerry Kennedy) ✍✍✍✍, *The Return of Roger Miller* (Smash, 1965, prod. Jerry Kennedy) ✍✍✍✍ and *Words and Music by Roger Miller* (Smash, 1966, prod. Jerry Kennedy) ✍✍✍✍ contain the absolute cream of his work, wonderfully veering from the ridiculous ("You Can't Roller Skate in a Buffalo Herd") to the sublime ("Train of Life") and then some. These albums show a man at the absolute peak of his creative and commercial powers, and a musician at least the equal of any operating anywhere, then or now.

influences:

◀◀ Bob Wills, Hank Williams, Sheb Wooley

▶▶ Mel Tillis, Tom Waits, Chris Isaak

Gary Pig Gold

RONNIE MILSAP

Born January 16, 1946, in Robbinsville, NC.

One of country music's most versatile performers, Ronnie Milsap has built a career that stands outside conventional country parameters. Born blind with congenital cataracts, Milsap spent his early years with his paternal grandparents and enrolled in North Carolina's State School for the Blind at age five. There he began to learn music, first playing the violin, then the piano, then guitar. He trained classically, but privately listened to a wide range of music, from country to Southern soul. Milsap studied pre-law in college and was offered a full scholarship to Emory University Law School, but he gave it up to concentrate on music. He started his recording career with the R&B label Scepter Records during the 1960s. He also backed a number of musicians, including J.J. Cale. He played piano on Elvis Presley's "Kentucky Rain" and other recordings. He signed with RCA Records' Nashville division in 1973 and had his first hit that year with "I Hate You." Named the Country Music Association's Male Vocalist of the Year in 1974, 1976 and 1977, Milsap also received Entertainer of the Year honors in 1977.

Conventional critical wisdom on Milsap has him starting out as a promising country-soul singer, only to wimp out when he started cutting ballads like "It Was Almost Like a Song" and "Let's Take the Long Way around the World." But Milsap's body of work, while uneven, has always defied easy categorization, and even some of those domesticated love songs have held up well compared to other country hits of the time. More recently, Milsap has been getting back in touch with his R&B roots, though his efforts have met with mixed commercial success.

what to buy: *Greatest Hits* (RCA, 1980, prod. Tom Collins, Jack D. Johnson, Ronnie Milsap) 𝄢𝄢𝄢𝄢 shows just how versatile Milsap is. Covering the years 1974–80, *Greatest Hits* includes a couple of Milsap's crossover hits ("It Was Almost Like a Song," "Smoky Mountain Rain"), old-fashioned country-soul (Don Gibson's "I'd Be a Legend in My Time") and Milsap's emotional performance of Kris Kristofferson's "Please Don't Tell Me How the Story Ends"—which may come as a jolt to those who consider Milsap nothing more than a sappy middle-of-the-road crooner.

what to buy next: The scope of *Greatest Hits, Volume 2* (RCA, 1985, prod. Ronnie Milsap, Tom Collins, Rob Galbraith) 𝄢𝄢𝄢𝄢 doesn't cover quite as much as the first volume, but it's an impressive collection of Milsap's crossover singles of the early 1980s. "(There's) No Gettin' Over Me," "I Wouldn't Have Missed It for the World," "Any Day Now" and "Stranger in My House" were all Top 40 hits on both the country and pop charts.

what to avoid: Actually, as re-recordings go, Milsap's *Sings His Best Hits for Capitol Records* (Capitol, 1996, prod. Rob Galbraith, Ronnie Milsap) 𝄢𝄢𝄢 isn't a bad record. But, with many of the original versions of these songs in print, these remakes don't bring enough new ideas to the songs to make them worth having.

Ronnie Milsap **(AP/Wide World Photos)**

the rest:
Super Hits (RCA) 𝄢𝄢𝄢𝄢
When It Comes to My Baby (Starday, 1985) 𝄢𝄢
Kentucky Woman (Starday, 1985)
The Legendary Ronnie Milsap (Pair) 𝄢𝄢𝄢
16 Greatest Hits Volume II (Deluxe) 𝄢𝄢𝄢
The Essential Series (RCA, 1996) 𝄢𝄢𝄢𝄢

worth searching for: Hardcore Milsap fans often like to tout his abilities as an R&B singer, but good examples aren't always easy to come by. But during the years before Milsap became a star, he recorded for small labels like Scepter and Chips. Three budget albums on Starday contain some of this early material. *Didn't We* (Starday, 1985) 𝄢𝄢𝄢, with its simple, Stax-like arrangements, shows Milsap at his rawest. No hits, but it's cool stuff. (It'd be rated even higher if the tape quality were better and it had any information about the recordings.) *Back to the Grindstone* (RCA, 1991) 𝄢𝄢𝄢𝄢, with its duet with Patti LaBelle, and *True Believer* (Liberty, 1993, prod. Ronnie Milsap, Rob Galbraith) 𝄢𝄢𝄢, with its title tune by John Hiatt, are good modern examples of Milsap's white R&B chops.

Not nearly enough of Milsap's recordings for RCA remain in print. While most of his hits appear on one or more compilations, two albums stand out on their own. *Ronnie Milsap Live* (RCA, 1976, prod. Tom Collins, Ronnie Milsap) came right before Milsap's huge mainstream success and was chosen as the Country Music Association's Album of the Year in 1977. And *Christmas with Ronnie Milsap* (RCA, 1986) ♫♫♫, which only recently has slipped out of print, is one of the better country Christmas records.

influences:

◀◀ Ray Charles, Charlie Rich, Elvis Presley, Conway Twitty

▶▶ Terri Gibbs, Rick Trevino, Tony Toliver

Brian Mansfield

WADDIE MITCHELL

Born in NV.

Cowboy poet Waddie Mitchell became a full-time cowboy starting at age 16 and later managed a 36,000-acre Nevada ranch. He was one of the organizers of the Elko Cowboy Poetry Gathering, which began in 1984. His many books and records eventually made him the recipient of the Nevada Governor's Arts Award for Literature. Mitchell was one of the original inductees into the Cowboy Poets and Singers Hall of Fame.

what's available: *Lone Driftin' Rider* (Warner Western, 1992, prod. Joey Miskulin, Michael Martin Murphey) ♫♫♫, Mitchell's first album for Warner Western, features some material recorded live in Sparks, Nevada, and other studio performances backed by a group of musicians led by accordionist/producer Joey Miskulin. *Buckaroo Poet* (Warner Western, 1993, prod. Joey Miskulin) ♫♫♫ features more of the same—Mitchell's cowboy poetry with musical backing. *The Bard and the Balladeer* (Warner Western) and *Live from Cowtown* (Warner Western) feature two of the most popular contemporary cowboy performers (Mitchell is joined by Don Edwards) together in Fort Worth, Texas, at a 1994 concert.

influences:

◀◀ Red Steagall, Michael Martin Murphey

Brian Mansfield

KATY MOFFATT

Born 1950, in Fort Worth, TX.

Katy Moffatt is one of those artists about whom those in the know constantly ask, "Why isn't her name a household word?"

She is a powerful and passionate vocalist and she writes great songs, but she's never really caught on commercially, despite having recorded since 1970, when she made her first album for Columbia. Moffatt's recent efforts for Philo and Watermelon have featured her strong vocals and fine original songs, often co-written with Tom Russell.

what to buy: *Walkin' on the Moon* (Philo, 1989, prod. Katy Moffatt, Andrew Hardin) ♫♫♫ contains mostly Moffatt originals, with two heart wrenching vocals—"Walkin' on the Moon" and "I'll Take the Blame"—that deserve classic status. *Evangeline Motel* (Philo, 1993, prod. Katy Moffatt, Tom Russell) ♫♫♫ continues the Moffatt–Russell musical partnership to good effect.

what to buy next: On *Kate Brislin & Katy Moffatt* (Rounder, 1996, prod. Jody Stecher) ♫♫♫, Brislin blends her traditional country harmonic sensibilities with Moffatt's pure, passionate vocal intensity to create an album of wonderful duets; the repertoire embraces the Louvins, the Everlys, two Moffatt originals, and Jimmy Martin. Classic harmonizing. *Dance Me Outside* (Philo, 1992, prod. Katy Moffatt, Hugh Moffatt) ♫♫♫ finds Katy and brother Hugh Moffatt, a Nashville songsmith, combining voices on a bunch of country and R&B classics and originals.

the rest:

Child Bride (Philo, 1990) ♫♫♫
Hearts Gone Wild (Watermelon, 1994) ♫♫♫
Midnight Radio (Watermelon, 1996) ♫♫♫

influences:

◀◀ Tracy Nelson, Bonnie Raitt

▶▶ Lucinda Williams, Gillian Welch, Hugh Moffatt

Randy Pitts

THE MOFFATTS

Brother vocal group from British Columbia, Canada.

Scott Moffatt; Clint Moffatt; Bob Moffatt; Dave Moffatt.

This vocal quartet was formed when two musician parents took their oldest son and his triplet brothers to a make-your-own-record booth to sing the Judds' "Grandpa (Tell Me 'bout the Good Ole Days)." They were touring Canada and opening for the Osmonds in Branson, Missouri, before they were 10. By the time the oldest was 12, they'd been signed to a major country label by Harold Shedd, who also brought the world the Kentucky HeadHunters and Billy Ray Cyrus.

what's available: For kids, the Moffatts are good singers, but the Jackson 5 they're not. *It's a Wonderful World* (Polydor, 1995)

𝄢 is a reissue of an album they released independently. *The Moffatts* (Polydor, 1995) 𝄢, the quartet's major-label debut, contains songs by Garth Brooks ("When God Made You") and Lennon-McCartney ("This Boy," natch), but it still sounds like an Alvin & the Chipmunks record.

influences:

◄◄ Osmonds, Amie Comeaux

►► LeAnn Rimes

Brian Mansfield

MOLLY & THE HEYMAKERS

Formed 1979, in Hayward, WI.

Molly Scheer (born April 6, 1958, in Rice Lake, WI), mandolin, fiddle; Andy Dee, guitar; Paul Bergen, guitar; Rick Berger, bass; Scott Tate, drums; others.

Founded by Molly Scheer and Andy Dee, this country-rock group's style is a combination of raucous rock influences and traditional country. The group played the club circuit in the Great Lakes region, toured Africa and played alternative clubs in Minneapolis during the 1980s; Scheer briefly toured in the Mavericks' road band in 1995. Throughout numerous personnel changes, Scheer and Dee have been the two constant members.

what to buy: *Big Things* (Mouthpiece, 1994, prod. Rob Feaster, Molly Scheer, Andy Dee) 𝄢𝄢𝄢𝄢 is a feisty collection that simultaneously recalls Linda Ronstadt and the Pretenders' Chrissie Hynde (no mean feat).

what to buy next: *B-Sides from the Milkhouse* (self-distributed, 1993, prod. Molly Scheer, Andy Dee) 𝄢𝄢𝄢 is more rowdy than the group's Reprise outing the previous year and is a truer representation of their sound.

worth searching for: *Molly & the Heymakers* (Reprise, 1992, prod. Paul Worley, Ed Seay, Gregg Brown) 𝄢𝄢𝄢, the group's debut album (now out of print), didn't capture all the band's edgier tendencies, but is nevertheless an energetic set that hinted at great things.

influences:

◄◄ k.d. lang, Long Ryders, Carlene Carter

►► Picketts, Pam Tillis

Bob Cannon

BILL MONROE & HIS BLUE GRASS BOYS /CHARLIE MONROE /THE MONROE BROTHERS

Bill Monroe (born September 13, 1911, in Rosine, KY; died September 9, 1996, in Springfield, TN), vocals, mandolin; Charlie Monroe (born July 4, 1903, in KY; died September 27, 1975), guitar, vocals; Chubby Wise, fiddle; Earl Scruggs, banjo; Lester Flatt, guitar; Cedric Rainwater, bass; and a legion of other bluegrass performers, including Stringbean, Del McCoury, Jimmy Martin, Sonny Osborne, Hubert Davis, Carter Stanley, Mac Wiseman, Peter Rowan, Kenny Baker, Byron Berline, Dale Potter, Tommy Jackson, Richard Greene, Bill Keith, Roland White, and Vassar Clements.

Truly the Father of Bluegrass Music, mandolinist Bill Monroe began his performing and recording career with brother and guitarist Charlie Monroe during the 1930s, recording 60 classic numbers for Bluebird that were cast in the then-standard country-brother duet style of the day. But even then, there was something different about Bill's approach to old-time country harmony duets. His mandolin playing was faster and fiercer, and his harmony vocals were pitched higher than the norm. The brothers split during the late 1930s; Charlie went on to lead his group, the Kentucky Partners, a popular and successful traditional country string band group, into the 1950s, coming out of retirement briefly during the 1970s.

Bill, meanwhile, formed his first group of Blue Grass Boys and made country music history; they soon became members of the Grand Ole Opry (October 1939) and had their first hit, an uptempo version of the Jimmie Rodgers standard "Mule Skinner Blues." The sound that would be known as "bluegrass" was taking shape, but the conventions that coalesced into a new kind of acoustic string-band music didn't come together until banjoist Earl Scruggs and guitarist Lester Flatt, along with fiddler Chubby Wise, joined Monroe in 1946. This band, along with either Howard Watts (alias Cedric Rainwater) or Bill's brother Birch Monroe on bass, is generally accepted as being the first true bluegrass band. With their arrival, this new form of music was complete.

Bluegrass, as Monroe envisioned it and brought it to life, featured a repertoire drawn from Appalachian roots, with a touch of blues, Scottish and Irish fiddle influences (including many tunes learned in childhood and remembered from his uncle, Pendleton "Uncle Pen" Vandiver) and protestant gospel vocal harmonies, with the occasional folk song or honky-tonk num-

Bill Monroe **(Archive Photos)**

ber thrown in for spice. Scruggs brought the syncopated, three-finger banjo style to the band, and various members added their individual talents. All the members except the bass player took instrumental breaks, Monroe sang tenor on the verses and lead on the choruses, the guitarists sang lead on the verses, and gospel three- and four-part harmonies were always a featured part of the show. This was the formula Monroe used for more than 50 years; he had his ups and downs, but he persevered. A star during the 1940s, he was largely overlooked during the 1950s, rediscovered during the 1960s, lionized during the 1970s and 1980s, and revered during the last years of his life. Countless great musicians apprenticed in his band as Blue Grass Boys; that designation became a badge of honor. Most of Monroe's musicians went on to illustrious careers in the music he invented; many of them left their individual marks on the music as well.

what to buy: *The Music of Bill Monroe from 1936 to 1994* (MCA, 1994, comp. John W. Rumble) ♫♫♫♫ is a monumental compilation that includes tracks from every period of Monroe's career (although it concentrates on the 44-year point with

MCA/Decca). The collection includes two Monroe Brothers tracks with brother Charlie from Bluebird, a live "Muleskinner Blues" from a Grand Ole Opry broadcast in 1939, two tracks from the first Blue Grass Boys group on Bluebird from 1940–41, six tracks from his classic Columbia period, various live tracks and previously unissued or hard-to-find material from throughout Monroe's career, including appearances on albums by others; 98 selections in all. An excellent effort to trace the arc of this American master musician's career and probably the best place to begin any attempt to understand the magnitude and significance of Monroe's musical accomplishments. It is with the recordings collected in *The Essential Bill Monroe & His Blue Grass Boys, 1945–1949* (Columbia/Legacy, 1992, comp. prod. Lawrence Cohn) ♫♫♫♫ that modern bluegrass music, with all its conventions, was defined. All the songs and tunes cut by Monroe's Blue Grass Boys for Columbia are here (although 16 tracks are alternate, originally unissued versions), including all 28 titles cut by the classic Flatt & Scruggs–Chubby Wise–Howard Watts version of the Blue Grass Boys. Definitive. *16 Gems* (Columbia, 1996, prod. Lawrence Cohn) ♫♫♫♫ contains the issued cuts from the classic 1940s Blue Grass Boys that were replaced by alternates on the boxed set. *Country Music Hall of Fame* (MCA, 1991, prod. various) ♫♫♫♫ is a valiant attempt to distill Monroe's 1950–1991 output for Decca and MCA into 16 songs and tunes. Although an impossible feat, this is the best one-disc overview of the man's 40-plus years of work for the label, and it's all great stuff. *Live Recordings, 1965–69: Off the Record, Volume 1* (Smithsonian/Folkways, 1993, prod. Ralph Rinzler) ♫♫♫♫ captures 26 tracks of live performances at festivals, clubs, parties and picking sessions featuring versions of the Blue Grass Boys never recorded, often doing versions of classic material much different than the more familiar recorded versions. It also includes an interview/music segment with Bill and his brothers Charlie and Birch from 1969. A companion piece is *Live Duet Recordings, 1963–1980: Off the Record, Volume 2* (Smithsonian/Folkways, 1993, prod. Ralph Rinzler) ♫♫♫♫, where Bill is joined by folk legend Doc Watson.

what to buy next: Excellent early Decca material from 1950–55, *In the Pines* (County, 1993, reissue prod. Gary B. Reid) ♫♫♫♫ includes a killer version of the title cut featuring Jimmy Martin's lead vocal. All Monroe's Decca and MCA recordings up to 1979 are collected on three boxed sets from Germany's Bear Family label, including: *Bill Monroe: Bluegrass, 1950–1958* (Bear Family, 1989, prod. Paul Cohen, Owen Bradley) ♫♫♫♫; *Bill Monroe: Bluegrass, 1959–1969* (Bear Family, 1991, prod. Owen Bradley, Harry Silverstein) ♫♫♫♫; and *Bill Monroe: Bluegrass,*

1970–1979 (Bear Family, 1994, prod. Harry Silverstein, Walter Haynes) 🎵🎵🎵.

the rest:
Beanblossom (MCA, 1973) 🎵🎵🎵
Columbia Historic Edition—Bill Monroe (Columbia, 1984) 🎵🎵🎵
Bluegrass '87 (MCA, 1987) 🎵🎵
Southern Flavor (MCA, 1988) 🎵🎵
At His Best (Hollywood, 1989) 🎵🎵
Live at the Opry: Celebrating 50 Years (MCA, 1989) 🎵🎵🎵
Cryin' Holy unto the Lord (MCA, 1991) 🎵🎵🎵
The Essential Bill Monroe & the Monroe Brothers (RCA, 1997) 🎵🎵🎵

worth searching for: *Bill Monroe & His Blue Grass Boys: Mule-skinner Blues* (RCA, 1991, prod. Billy Altman) 🎵🎵🎵 contains all the Blue Grass Boys material recorded for Bluebird in 1940–41; bluegrass in its infancy, or pre-bluegrass in its seminal stages. Either way, it's classic material, historically important as well. *Are You from Dixie? Great Country Brother Teams of the 1930s.* (RCA, 1988, prod. Billy Altman) 🎵🎵🎵 contains three Monroe Brothers songs along with material by the Delmore Brothers, the Allen Brothers, the Dixon Brothers and the Blue Sky Boys. *Feast Here Tonight* (RCA/Bluebird, 1975, reissue prod. Frank Driggs) 🎵🎵🎵🎵 is a two-LP set of the classic 1930s Monroe Brothers recordings.

influences:
◄◄ Jimmie Rodgers, Carter Family
►► Del McCoury, Peter Rowan

Randy Pitts

MONTANA SLIM

See: Wilf Carter

BILLY MONTANA

Born William Schlappi, in Voorheesville, NY.

One of the few country singers to come from Cornell University, Billy Montana grew up in New York, the son of a father who listened to country. He formed Billy Montana & the Long Shots with his brother Kyle; the group had a Top 40 hit in 1987 on Warner Bros. with "Baby I Was Leaving Anyhow." Montana had more success in Canada where he won a British Columbia Country Music Award for Single of the Year. He also has had songs cut by Tim McGraw and Darryl & Don Ellis. Montana was the first artist signed to independent Magnatone Records in 1994.

what's available: If Montana's *No Yesterday* (Magnatone, 1995, prod. Jim McKell, David Flint, Billy Montana) 🎵🎵🎵 had come out on a major label instead of an independent, it might have found the audience it deserved. On the slow stuff, Montana's sweet tenor sounds like a working-class Vince Gill, and "Didn't Have You" and "Everything She Needs" are exquisite ballads. Then again, maybe he wouldn't have found that audience: Montana's a smart songwriter, and his best material is insinuating, not immediate.

influences:
◄◄ Vince Gill, Restless Heart

Brian Mansfield

PATSY MONTANA

Born Ruby Blevins, October 30, 1912, in Hot Springs, AR. Died May 3, 1996.

Growing up the only girl in a family with 10 boys, it's no wonder that Patsy Montana's image became one of a lovable tomboy. After growing up in rural Arkansas, Montana performed in California with the Montana Girls (where she picked up the nickname Patsy and, later, the stage name Montana). Later, she backed Jimmie Davis on recordings and fronted the Prairie Ramblers on the *WLS Barn Dance*. The first woman in country music to sell a million copies of a record ("I Want to Be a Cowboy's Sweetheart" in 1935, the middle of the Depression), Montana continued to perform and record well into the 1990s, providing a standard against which nearly female singer that followed could measure herself against. She was posthumously inducted into the Country Music Hall of Fame in 1996.

what's available: Patsy Montana is probably more poorly represented by her available catalogue than any other recent inductee into the Country Music Hall of Fame. *The Cowboy's Sweetheart* (Flying Fish, 1988, prod. Cathy Fink) 🎵🎵🎵 was recorded when she was well into her 70s and features renditions of classic Western songs (including "Cowboy's Sweetheart" and Gene Autry's "That Silver-Haired Daddy of Mine") with new genre tunes like Laurie Lewis' "The Cowgirl Song." This record possesses plenty of charm, but though Montana receives sympathetic backing from Cathy Fink and Marcy Marxer's band Rhythm Ranch, there's little of the freewheeling vocal spunk of her pioneering records of the 1930s. For the original recording of "Cowboy's Sweetheart," try the excellent various-artists compilation *Columbia Country Classic, Volume 1: The Golden Age* (Columbia, 1990) 🎵🎵🎵🎵.

John Michael Montgomery (© Ken Settle)

influences:
◀◀ Sons of the Pioneers, Gene Autry
▶▶ Suzy Bogguss, Dixie Chicks

Brian Mansfield

JOHN MICHAEL MONTGOMERY

Born January 20, 1965, in Danville, KY.

John Michael Montgomery may wear a black hat, but that does-n't necessarily mean he's one of the bad guys. Still, it wouldn't be impossible to argue that his good looks (he was named one of *People* magazine's "50 Most Beautiful People in the World" in 1994) have as much to do with his fame as anything else. As a performer Montgomery seems to constantly be stuck in one of two gears: either he's in honky-tonk mode, lacing his vocals with the sort of twang he probably heard on a George Strait record, or he's singing syrupy middle-of-the-road ballads that have about as much to do with country music as the lights of Broadway. Montgomery is fond of treating his concert audi-

ences to extended versions of the Marshall Tucker Band's "Can't You See" and Bob Seger's "Turn the Page." If 20-year-old rock songs and 10-year-old country stylings are Mont-gomery's idea of innovation, he'd better think again. Or at least take a good long look in the mirror and decide if there's any-thing original he can contribute.

what to buy: The album that validated the instant success of Montgomery's debut is its follow-up, *Kickin' It Up* (Atlantic, 1994, prod. Scott Hendricks) 🎵🎵🎵, which was led by one of Montgomery's trademark ballads, "I Swear" (which, interest-ingly, also became a #1 hit for the R&B vocal group All-4-One). Because there's little variance in Montgomery's performance, deciding which album to buy first is largely a matter of song choices. Fans who prefer the hits "I Can Love You Like That" and "Sold (The Grundy County Auction Incident)"—again, one slow, one fast (ho-hum)—should start with *John Michael Mont-gomery* (Atlantic, 1995, prod. Scott Hendricks) 🎵🎵🎵.

the rest:
Life's a Dance (Atlantic, 1992) 🎵🎵🎵
What I Do the Best (Atlantic, 1996) 🎵🎵🎵

influences:
◀◀ George Strait, Eagles, Bob Seger

Daniel Durchholz

MELBA MONTGOMERY

Born October 14, 1938, in Iron City, TN.

George Jones once said of Melba Montgomery: "Melba fit my style of singin' more than Tammy did. . . . She is a down-to earth, hardcore country singer." Montgomery, who recorded duets with Jones from 1963–1968, was all that and more. She wrote some of the duo's best-known hits, including its biggest, 1963's "We Must Have Been out of Our Minds." Still, Mont-gomery's best known for the people she worked with. First there was Roy Acuff, with whom the young fiddler and guitarist toured for four years after winning the Pet Milk Amateur Con-test in 1958. Montgomery also had charting hits with Gene Pit-ney and Charlie Louvin, as well as Jones. But her only #1 record came on her own: the weepy spoken recording "No Charge," released just in time for Mother's Day 1974.

what's available: Montgomery still has her traditional country pipes on the recent *Do You Know Where Your Man Is* (Playback, 1992, prod. Jack Gale) 🎵🎵🎵, which commendably features origi-nal material instead of remakes of her old songs. The title track would become a hit for Pam Tillis the following year. The best of Montgomery's work with Jones is collected on the 20-song *Vintage Collections* (Capitol, 1996, prod. Pappy Dailey) 🎵🎵🎵.

influences:

◀◀ Kitty Wells, Jean Shepard

▶▶ Tammy Wynette

Brian Mansfield and Craig Shelburne

THE MORELLS

See: The Skeletons

GEORGE MORGAN

Born June 28, 1924, in Waverly, TN. Died July 7, 1975.

During the late 1940s and early 1950s, before the onslaught of rock 'n' roll and the "Nashville Sound," traditional artists like George Morgan thrived. Moving to Ohio as a small child, Morgan became known first as "Tennessee George" for radio appearances there. Morgan will forever be known for two achievements—his first hit record and his singing daughter. His first hit, "Candy Kisses" (#1, 1949), spent three weeks on top, and was followed by eight more Top 10 hits. Morgan was renamed the "Candy Kid" after he joined the Grand Ole Opry in 1948 and had that first hit. He stayed with the Opry until 1956, when he started his own TV show on WLAC in Nashville. The show lasted three years, after which he rejoined the Opry cast, remaining there for the remainder of his career. Although he left Columbia in 1966, Morgan continued having chart hits up to the time of his death, and even briefly beyond that point. In 1979 a duet with daughter Lorrie was released, although it failed to crack the Top 40. George had first introduced his daughter to the Opry audience during the early 1970s, when 13-year-old Lorrie sang "Paper Roses" and received a standing ovation. While she's traveled her own road musically, her success remains a loving tribute to the tradition adhered to by her father.

what's available: *Room Full of Roses* (Razor & Tie, 1996) 🎵🎵🎵🎵 is the most complete collection of George Morgan hits and miscellaneous tracks you'll ever want or need.

influences:

◀◀ Eddy Arnold, Red Foley

▶▶ Jim Reeves, Lorrie Morgan

Stephen L. Betts

FIVE FOR OUR FANS

LONESTAR

Tim McGraw
All I Want (Curb)

Jo Dee Messina
Jo Dee Messina (Curb)

Trace Adkins
Dreamin' Out Loud (Capitol)

George Strait
Blue Clear Sky (MCA)

Brooks & Dunn
Borderline (Arista)

LORRIE MORGAN

Born June 27, 1959, in Goodlettsville, TN.

Lorrie Morgan has spent most of her artistic life surrounded by influential men. She grew up the youngest daughter of Grand Ole Opry star George Morgan and later married doomed honky-tonk singer Keith Whitley, who died of alcohol poisoning in 1989. But instead of hiding behind their shadows, Morgan learned valuable lessons from each one: she picked up pointers on how to work within the Nashville country music industry and developed a liking for orchestrated pop from her late father. Whitley taught her the rules of the honky-tonk scene: everything from singing with attitude to growing a thick skin capable of surviving rejection. She was a good student. Although she doesn't have vast vocal range, Lorrie has unlimited emotional depth, which works beautifully for the love-on-the-line songs that have become her trademark. Morgan takes the spunk of Loretta Lynn, combines it with the drama of Tammy

Wynette and injects her own diva-in-waiting persona. She sometimes goes overboard; 1994's *War Paint* is a high-falutin' mess, and the two radio staples from her 1995 *Greatest Hits* CD are pop fodder that seem beneath her talents. But when she sinks her manicured fingernails into a big song—such as the show-stopping "Something in Red"—she's one of the best interpreters working in country music today. Morgan has a knack for channeling her own tumultuous life (her publicized affairs are the stuff soap opera writers would kill for) into her music—so even when she's at her torchiest, you get the feeling she's really been there. Coincidentally, Whitley's death marked the resurrection of her own star, which had floundered in the late 1970s and early 1980s while she wasted time recording lame pop covers and banal, slick country-lite. Still, Morgan's artistic output has been as erratic as her love life. After a couple of mostly pop-driven projects in the mid-1990s, she returned to her countrier roots for 1996's splendid *Greater Need*. She also married singer Jon Randall, with whom she recorded the Top 10 duet "By My Side" in 1996.

what to buy: For a complete sampling of Morgan's style, one needs to pick up the CDs that bookend her RCA Records catalog. *Leave the Light On* (RCA, 1989, prod. Barry Beckett) 🎵🎵🎵 at once captures the country, torch and pop singer. The no-nonsense power she injects into "Five Minutes" is indicative of her inner strength while the tenderness that laces "Out of Your Shoes" reveals a softer center.

what to buy next: *Greater Need* (RCA, 1996, prod. James Stroud) 🎵🎵🎵 brings Morgan full circle as she strips things down for a countrier flavor without losing her theatrical dynamics. The ballad "I Can Buy My Own Roses" is a masterpiece and the sassy "I Just Might Be" is quintessential Morgan.

what to avoid: Two early years compilations—*Classics* (Curb, 1991, prod. various) 🎵🎵 and *Tell Me I'm Not Dreaming* (Intersound, 1992, prod. various) 🎵🎵—aren't worth exploring. While you can hear the green stages of her vocal ability, there's nothing in either of these CDs to merit a second listen. *War Paint* (RCA, 1994, prod. Richard Landis) 🎵🎵 has one truly good moment, a duet with Sammy Kershaw on the country standard "A Good Year for the Roses," but the rest is pop cheese with barely a guilty pleasure in the batch.

the rest:

Something in Red (RCA, 1991) 🎵🎵🎵
Watch Me (RCA, 1992) 🎵🎵🎵
Merry Christmas from London (RCA, 1993) 🎵🎵🎵
Greatest Hits (RCA, 1995) 🎵🎵🎵

worth searching for: Morgan turns in a rich rendition of Buck Owens' "Crying Time" on the out-of-print soundtrack to *The Beverly Hillbillies* (Fox/RCA, 1993, prod. various) 🎵🎵🎵. She captures the melancholy of the tune without padding it with too much drama. The rest of the album, boasting a batch of country artists, is a surprisingly satisfying set.

influences:

◀◀ Loretta Lynn, Tammy Wynette
▶▶ Chely Wright, Tammy Graham

Mario Tarradell

GARY MORRIS

Born December 7, 1948, in Fort Worth, TX.

It's no surprise that Gary Morris parlayed a string of country hits into a career in theater. He starred with Linda Ronstadt in *La Boheme* in 1984, and four years later was in *Les Miserables*. Although he's a Texan, Morris' singing voice has no twang and his knack for making even the most insignificant lyrics sound like monumental statements is perfect for the grandiose musical theater style. He also has some of that gospel verve, a product of early church-going in his native Fort Worth. Discarding a potential athletic career for music, he moved to Nashville during the late 1970s and was soon on the Warner Bros. roster. He found success during the early 1980s with pop-laced country and sweeping ballads. His slow, melodramatic take on "The Wind beneath My Wings" was the precursor to Bette Midler's hit 1989 pop version, and 1986's "100% Chance of Rain" was overblown but addicting. But it's on the quieter songs that Morris really flexes his vocal muscle: "Leave Me Lonely" and "Plain Brown Wrapper" are mini-masterpieces, while "Finishing Touches," written in 1987 with country-folkie Kevin Welch, is five minutes of compelling understatement. That song was the beginning of Morris' chart downslide; Warner Bros. let him go by 1989 and contracts with Universal Records and Capitol produced a handful of hitless albums. Morris, who was intelligent enough to open his own publishing company, Gary Morris Music, early on, still tours. His annual Christmas show is a fixture in the Dallas-Fort Worth area.

what to buy: *Hits* (Warner Bros., 1987, prod. various) 🎵🎵🎵 is a well-compiled chronicle of Morris' career. By avoiding the pop piffle duets with Crystal Gayle—particularly the banal "Making

Up for Lost Time"—the album concentrates on what Morris does best. It includes the countrier side of the Texan ("That's the Way It Is") as well as the balladeer and the pop-country belter excursions. Plus, you even get a slice of his theater life in "Your Little Hand," the aria from *La Boheme*.

the rest:

Why Lady Why (Warner Bros., 1983) ♪♪♪

Greatest Hits Volume II (Warner Bros., 1990) ♪♪♪

worth searching for: Morris tossed aside the heavy production and took the reins for *Plain Brown Wrapper* (Warner Bros., 1986, prod. Gary Morris) ♪♪♪♪. The result is a subdued, traditional and brilliant effort. The wonderful title cut anchors the album, while versions of Jimmie Rodgers' "Honeycomb," Hank Williams' "I'm So Lonesome I Could Cry" and Duke Ellington's "Ain't Got Nothin' but the Blues" fill the center. "Leave Me Lonely," an almost-cheating song with soul, is the album's artistic peak.

influences:

◀◀ Ronnie Milsap, Charley Pride, Eddy Arnold

▶▶ John Berry, Collin Raye

Mario Tarradell

THE LYNN MORRIS BAND

Formed 1988.

Lynn Morris (born San Antonio, TX), vocals, guitar, banjo; **Tom Adams**, banjo; **Marshall Wilborn**, bass, vocals; **David McLaughlin**, mandolin, guitar, vocals.

Lynn Morris, a National Banjo Champion, grew up in, as is often said facetiously, "the great bluegrass state of Texas." Her college years in Colorado led to her first exposure to the genre in which she would eventually become something of a pioneer. As a writer, producer, skilled picker and vocalist, Morris has been rewarded by bluegrass associations for her playing, and she is regarded as one of bluegrass music's most versatile female performers. Her husband, bass player and songwriter Marshall Wilborn, served in two impressive bluegrass outfits—as a member of Jimmy Martin's band and also the Johnson Mountain Boys. The couple first met as members of Whetstone Run, a Pennsylvania-based band. Wilborn, also from Texas, was in the Johnson Mountain Boys with Gettysburg, Pennsylvania's Tom Adams. Another survivor of the Jimmy Martin experience, Adams picked banjo with Martin for two years, joining Morris and Wilborn in 1988. Bridging the gap between hard-edged country vocals and sweet bluegrass har-

mony, Morris is obviously influenced by much of the work of legends like Hazel Dickens, ensuring she won't be confused with too many of the more pop-edged bluegrass acts proliferating these days. A handful of hard country cover songs can be found on the group's three albums, along with lots of traditional bluegrass music.

what to buy: Between the first and latest offerings, *Mama's Hand* (Rounder, 1995, prod. Lynn Morris) ♪♪♪♪ and *The Lynn Morris Band* (Rounder, 1990, prod. Lynn Morris Band) ♪♪♪♪, there's plenty of heavy-duty bluegrass picking to be found. The Hazel Dickens-penned title track of the former has become a multi-award-winning signature song for Morris. The debut record features young Ronnie McCoury on mandolin.

what to buy next: *The Bramble & the Rose* (Rounder, 1992) ♪♪♪ is a strong collection with tunes by Tom T. Hall, Johnny Cash and Dolly Parton. You'll also hear Wilborn's original version of the Alison Krauss hit "Heartstrings"

influences:

◀◀ Hazel Dickens, Johnson Mountain Boys

▶▶ Laurie Lewis, Cox Family

Stephen L. Betts

BILL MORRISSEY

Born November 25, 1951, in Hartford, CT.

The most bizarre thing about this New England folkie is not his voice, which sounds like a frog eating sandpaper. It's that such a voice manages to be soulful, funny and moving all at the same time. Though Morrissey rarely tries to rock—or honkytonk for that matter—his songs about normal people doing slightly odd things evoke the natural spirit of both country and rock 'n' roll. "Grizzly Bear," one of his best early songs, is about a rich, stuck-up, beautiful woman who won't give the narrator the time of day until he gets her to dance something called the Grizzly Bear. And "Letter from Heaven" is a party song about Charlie Parker, Mama Cass and devil-plagued bluesman Robert Johnson ("Yeah, I know, everybody's always surprised to see him here") having a ball on a cloud someplace. Though his idiom isn't country per se, he records a Hank Williams song now and then, and his songwriting style is as down-to-earth and friendly as that of Johnny Cash.

what to buy: The darkly funny *Night Train* (Philo/Rounder, 1993, prod. Ellen Karas) ♪♪♪♪, with "Letter from Heaven" and the romantic "Ellen's Tune" ("I love the way she knocks upon my door"), is Morrissey's most consistent (and, not coincidentally, shortest) album. His debut, *Bill Morrissey* (1984/ Philo/Rounder, 1991, prod. Bill Morrissey, Ellen Karas) 🎵🎵🎵, has "Grizzly Bear" and a bunch of other wry love songs and was actually re-recorded in 1991.

what to buy next: Recorded with pal folk singer Greg Brown, *Friend of Mine* (Philo/Rounder, 1993, prod. Ellen Karas) 🎵🎵🎵 is a reverential collection of great old songs, including Willie Dixon's "Little Red Rooster," Hank Williams' "I'll Never Get out of This World Alive" and Chuck Berry's "Memphis, Tennessee."

what to avoid: Most of Morrissey's records are solid, but the weakest material is on *Inside* (Philo/Rounder, 1992, prod. John Jennings) 🎵🎵.

the rest:
Standing Eight (Philo/Rounder, 1989) 🎵🎵
You'll Never Get to Heaven (Philo/Rounder, 1996) 🎵🎵🎵

worth searching for: "Live Free or Die"/"Trailer Park" (Shoot the Cat Records, 1977), the funny and rebellious first single—released, coincidentally, in the same year as *Never Mind the Bollocks, Here's the Sex Pistols.*

influences:
⏪ Hank Williams, Pete Seeger, Woody Guthrie, Leadbelly
⏩ Shawn Colvin, Suzanne Vega, Patty Larkin, Christine Lavin

Steve Knopper

MULESKINNER

Peter Rowan, guitar, lead vocals; David Grisman, mandolin, harmony vocals; Bill Keith, banjo; Richard Greene, violin, bass vocals; Clarence White, lead and rhythm guitar, harmony vocals.

Muleskinner was a short-lived bluegrass supergroup born of its members' shared experience with 1960s counterculture and love of traditional hillbilly music.

what's available: *Muleskinner: A Potpourri of Bluegrass Jam* (Sierra, 1974, prod. Richard Greene, Joe Boyd) 🎵🎵🎵 is the quintet's sole outing. Originally released on Warner Bros. in 1974, this record predates both the classic edition of New Grass Revival and mandolinist David Grisman's groundbreaking mix of jazz and bluegrass. It also documents one of flatpicker extraordinaire Clarence White's final studio sessions.

influences:
⏪ Bill Monroe, Dillards
⏩ New Grass Revival

see also: *Peter Rowan, David Grisman, Richard Greene*

Bill Friskics-Warren

MOON MULLICAN

Born Aubrey Mullican, March 29, 1909, in Corrigan, TX. Died January 1, 1967, in Beaumont, TX.

A spiritual forebear of rock 'n' roll and a direct, obvious influence on Jerry Lee Lewis, pianist Moon Mullican remains a little-known country music pioneer. Bald and overweight, he hardly looked like the father of rock 'n' roll, but his 1956 classic "Seven Nights to Rock" captured the exact feel of the burgeoning idiom with ease for the master of hillbilly boogie. He was a Grand Ole Opry regular in the wake of his 1949 hit "I'll Sail My Ship Alone," and he co-wrote "Jambalaya" with none other than Hank Williams, although his contributions went uncredited. Mullican's barrelhouse style fell from favor in the country world and he suffered health problems. He described his own style in a self-effacing bit of hillbilly hyperbole: "You got to make those bottles bounce on the table."

what to buy: Although he recorded more than 100 sides for the King Records label during his 10 years with that Cincinnati-based company, the only collection of his vintage recordings currently available is a reissue of an old album, *Sings His All-Time Hits* (King, 1958) 🎵🎵🎵.

what to avoid: The German reissue specialists Bear Family have compiled a pricey set of his post-King recordings, *Moon's Rock* (Bear Family, 1994) 🎵🎵, but these were not his finest hours.

worth searching for: The 1981 compilation album *Seven Nights to Rock: The King Years 1946–56* (Western, 1981) 🎵🎵🎵🎵 captures Mullican's roughneck roadhouse, whiskey-belting best.

influences:
⏪ Milton Brown & His Brownies, Big Joe Turner
⏩ Hank Williams, Jerry Lee Lewis, Gary Stewart, Asleep at the Wheel

Joel Selvin

ALAN MUNDE

Banjoist.

Alan Munde was one of the first players to successfully stretch the banjo's tonal possibilities from traditional bluegrass accompaniment instrument to melodic powerhouse. During the late 1960s he joined Jimmy Martin's Sunny Mountain Boys and in 1972 he and his fiddling college classmate Byron Berline

David Lee Murphy **(© Ken Settle)**

were recruited to back up the Rick Roberts-era Flying Burrito Brothers. A couple of years later, Munde and Berline formed Country Gazette, subsequently adding former Burritos Kenny Wertz and Roger Bush to the lineup. The group disbanded in 1986 and today Munde is an assistant professor at South Plains College in Levelland, Texas. In addition, he has co-written a book with guitarist Joe Carr titled *Prairie Nights to Neon Lights: The Story of Country Music in West Texas.*

what to buy: *Blue Ridge Express* (Rounder, 1994, prod. Alan Munde) 𝄢𝄢𝄢𝄢 is a compilation of the best of Munde's three works released between 1975 and 1986: *Banjo Sandwich, The Banjo Kid* and *In the Tradition*. The styles featured on the disc range from bluegrass to traditional folk to jazz. Especially worth checking out is the cool banjo-mandolin interplay between Munde and Joe Carr on the fiddle tune "Leather Britches."

the rest:
Festival Favorites Revisited (Rounder, 1993) 𝄢𝄢𝄢𝄡

influences:
◀◀ Earl Scruggs

▶▶ Bela Fleck

see also: *Flying Burrito Brothers*

Rick Petreycik

DAVID LEE MURPHY

Born January 7, 1958, in Herrin, IL.

David Lee Murphy's first hit, "Party Crowd," climbed the charts slooooowly, but wound up reaching #1 and being the most played song on country radio in 1995, while his debut album, *Out with a Bang*, was the best-selling debut country album by any male singer in 1995. Murphy's success came after 10 years of hard work that began when he drove his pickup truck from his hometown of Herrin, Illinois, to Nashville in July 1983 to become a songwriter. In 1985 his "Red Roses (Won't Work Now)" was cut by Reba McEntire. Murphy and his band, the Blue Tick Hounds, eked a living playing honky-tonks around the southeast, eventually grabbing the attention of MCA Records. His first single, "Just Once," also appears on the soundtrack of the rodeo film *Eight Seconds*.

what to buy: It took "Party Crowd" the better part of a year to climb the charts to #1, but once it did, it became the most-played single of the year and launched *Out with a Bang* (MCA, 1994, prod. Tony Brown) 𝄢𝄢𝄢𝄢, the album that jump-started Murphy's career.

the rest:
Gettin' out the Good Stuff (MCA, 1996) 𝄢𝄢𝄢𝄡

influences:
◀◀ Mark Collie
▶▶ Rhett Akins

Bill Hobbs

MICHAEL MARTIN MURPHEY

Born May 5, 1938, in Dallas, TX.

Michael Martin Murphey's career path has been an odd one—from rock-band singer to progressive-cowboy country to country balladeer to Western-music historian. The common thread through all these phases is Murphey's thoroughly romantic dedication to the American West. The first place many of today's country listeners first heard Murphey's work was from the pop band the Monkees, who recorded Murphey's "What Am I Doin' Hangin' 'Round?," written while Murphey was performing as Travis Lewis of the Lewis & Clarke Expedition, which had their own hit album in 1967. During the early 1970s Murphey relocated to Austin, Texas, and became part of that city's country scene; he made some of his best, most free-spirited music while living there, including early albums such as 1972's *Geronimo's Cadillac* and 1973's *Cosmic Cowboy Souvenir*, which featured the talents of Austin musicians such as Gary P. Nunn and Willis Alan Ramsey. Murphey moved progressively to the middle of the road—first to the pop market, where he had hits with "Wildfire" and "Carolina in the Pines" (both from *Blue Sky, Night Thunder*) in 1975, then into country where he had a string of largely forgettable hits during the 1980s. As the 1980s and the hits ended, he returned to the music of the American West. He signed with Warner Western and became largely responsible for the direction of that label during its early days. His most recent albums have been collections of standard and original cowboy music.

what to buy: *Cowboy Songs III: Rhymes of the Renegades* (Warner Western, 1993, prod. Joey Miskulin, Michael Martin Murphey) 🎵🎵🎵 is the best of Murphey's recent cowboy offerings, with duets with Chris LeDoux, Hal Ketchum and the late Marty Robbins (an electronically altered version of "Big Iron"), plus original songs and public-domain material about Cole Younger and Birmingham jails.

what to buy next: Largely a collection of traditional songs like "The Yellow Rose of Texas" and "Spanish Is the Lovin' Tongue" and silver-screen cowboy numbers ("Happy Trails," "Tumbling Tumbleweeds"), *Cowboy Songs* (Warner Western, 1991, prod. Steve Gibson, Michael Martin Murphey) 🎵🎵🎵 is a pleasantly romanticized look back at the American West. Murphey has better albums than this, but not in print.

what to avoid: In between his phases as hippie-cowboy and historian-cowboy, Murphey spent seven years making the kind of sappy middle-of-the-road ballads that would've made even John Denver blush. Most of that stuff has fallen out of print, but *The Best of Michael Martin Murphey* (Liberty, 1995, prod. Jim Ed Norman) 🎵—half of which consists of re-recordings of early songs like "Geronimo's Cadillac" and "Carolina in the Pines"—stays as a sad reminder.

the rest:
Blue Sky, Night Thunder (Epic, 1975) 🎵🎵
Swans against the Sun (Epic, 1975) 🎵🎵
Cowboy Christmas: Cowboy Songs II (Warner Western, 1991) 🎵🎵
Sagebrush Symphony (Warner Western, 1995) 🎵🎵🎵

worth searching for: Even before his *Cowboy Songs* trilogy, Murphey (or Michael Murphey, as he was first called) was always fascinated by the American West; he just used to write

more songs of his own about it. The best of those is the title track from *Geronimo's Cadillac* (A&M, 1972, prod. Bob Johnston) 🎵🎵🎵, which has been re-recorded often but never improved. This album also has a slightly renegade take on the West with songs such as "Calico Silver" and "Natchez Trace." It also has Murphey's version of "What Am I Doin' Hangin' 'Round?"

influences:
◀◀ Roy Rogers, Jerry Jeff Walker
▶▶ John Denver, Don Edwards

Brian Mansfield

ANNE MURRAY

Born Moma Anne Murray, June 20, 1945, in Springhill, Nova Scotia, Canada.

Anne Murray's rich, warm alto voice is recognized by pop and country fans alike and has earned her four Grammys, 22 Juno Awards, and numerous country music awards. It's hard to believe that her first singing audition wasn't successful; the TV show *Singalong Jubilee* already had enough contralto singers. A couple of years later, however, series co-host and associate producer Bill Langstroth tracked her down, invited her to sing on the show and convinced her to pursue a record deal. Two years after she released her first album, her single "Snowbird" was on both the U.S. and British country *and* pop charts. Her next album reinforced her success and popularity. She and Langstroth married in 1975 and put her career on hold while she had two children, William and Dawn. In 1978 she returned her attention to her music, earning her second Grammy with "You Needed Me." Murray now has 30 albums plus numerous compilations to her credit, yet she still continues to develop her voice and her art, refusing to be defined by a genre.

what to buy: *The Best . . . So Far* (EMI America, 1994, prod. various) 🎵🎵🎵 is a far-reaching collection, with 20 of her biggest hits like "Snowbird," "Danny's Song" and "You Needed Me." The album shows why Murray's pleasant voice won over such a large following through the years—as well as why her puffy arrangements are heard most often these days in waiting rooms.

what to buy next: *Now & Forever* (SBK, 1994, compilation prod. Fraser Hill) 🎵🎵🎵 is a 64-track, three-disc box set that provides a comprehensive overview of Murray's 29 albums. *Croonin'* (SBK, 1993, prod. Tommy West, Anne Murray) 🎵🎵🎵 features Murray's adaptations of songs sung by her favorite singers from the 1950s. More contemporary pop than country, it features duets with Bryan Adams, Aaron Neville and Murray's daughter, Dawn.

the rest:

Anne Murray Christmas (Liberty, 1970) 🎵🎵🎵

Christmas Wishes (Liberty, 1981) 🎵🎵🎵

Best of the Season (SBK, 1994) 🎵🎵🎵

Anne Murray (SBK, 1996) 🎵🎵🎵

worth searching for: *Anne Murray's Greatest Hits* (Liberty, 1980, prod. Brian Ahern, Jim Ed Norman) 🎵🎵🎵 collects the essential early hits. A special edition of *Croonin'* (Heartland Music, 1994) 🎵🎵🎵 contains two bonus tracks.

influences:

◀◀ Brenda Lee, Rosemary Clooney, Perry Como, Buddy Holly, Elvis Presley

▶▶ Kathy Mattea, Bryan Adams, Mary Chapin Carpenter, Aaron Neville

Linda Andres

HEATHER MYLES

Born in Riverside, CA.

Having grown up imbibing the aroma of dusty left-coast country and manure (her family raises thoroughbred horses), Myles has smartly steered her career away from the country-music machinery and by-the-numbers Nashville songwriters. Her original tunes are worthy successors to those of Buck Owens and Merle Haggard, as well as Myles' pop-oriented heroes like Joni Mitchell. Better received in England than in the U.S. (could it be her uncanny resemblance to Princess Di?), Myles' genuine talent and tough-but-tender stance deserve attention on both sides of the pond.

what to buy: Myles' debut, *Just Like Old Times* (HighTone, 1992, prod. Bruce Bromberg) 🎵🎵🎵, reveals the singer's raison d'etre in its title. Recalling classic California country in a way that will appeal to traditionalists and alternative-country fans alike, such originals as "Make a Fool out of Me" and "The Other Side of Town," plus a cover of Stonewall Jackson's "Why I'm Walking," come across with sass, class, and conviction.

the rest:

Untamed (HighTone, 1995) 🎵🎵🎵

worth searching for: The import disc *Sweet Little Dangerous: Live at the Bottom Line* (Demon, 1996) 🎵🎵🎵 offers a taste of Myles' rip-snortin' live show.

influences:

◀◀ Patsy Cline, Merle Haggard, Buck Owens

Daniel Durchholz

THE NASHVILLE BLUEGRASS BAND

Formed 1985, in Nashville, TN.

Pat Enright, guitar, lead vocals; Alan O'Bryant, banjo, lead vocals; Roland White, mandolin (1989–present); Stuart Duncan, fiddle, (1985–present); Gene Libbea, bass (1989–present); Mike Compton, mandolin (1984–88), Mark Hembree, bass (1984–88).

The Nashville Bluegrass band is arguably the most important bluegrass act of the 1990s next to Alison Krauss & Union Station. Noted for their strong harmony singing, they are responsible more than anyone for bringing the sound of black a cappella gospel into bluegrass. The multiple Grammy- and International Bluegrass Music Association-award winners are stronger and more influential then ever entering their second decade.

what to buy: *Waitin' for the Hard Times to Go* (Sugar Hill, 1993, prod. Jerry Douglas) 🎵🎵🎵🎵, a Grammy winner for Best Bluegrass Recording, varies styles and manages the difficult task of sounding both traditional and contemporary. From the hard-driving "Kansas City Railroad Blues" through the swaying rhythms of "On Again, Off Again" to the a cappella gospel number "Father I Stretch My Hand to Thee," this is the rare album with no flaws.

what to buy next: The band's second Grammy winner, *Unleashed* (Sugar Hill, 1996, prod. Jerry Douglas) 🎵🎵🎵🎵, deftly mixes traditional numbers with new songs by Gillian Welch, Dave Allen, Harry Stinson and others. A special highlight is the band's harmonizing with gospel greats the Fairfield Four on "Last Month of the Year."

the rest:

The Nashville Bluegrass Band (Rounder, 1987) 🎵🎵🎵

To Be His Child (Rounder, 1987) 🎵🎵🎵🎵

(With Peter Rowan) *New Moon Rising* (Sugar Hill, 1988) 🎵🎵🎵🎵

The Boys Are Back in Town (Sugar Hill, 1990) 🎵🎵🎵🎵

Home of the Blues (Sugar Hill, 1991) 🎵🎵🎵🎵

solo outings:

Roland White:

Trying to Get to You (Sugar Hill, 1994) 🎵🎵🎵

influences:

◀◀ Fairfield Four, Country Gazette, Kentucky Colonels

▶▶ IIIrd Tyme Out, Lonesome River Band

Douglas Fulmer

THE NASHVILLE MANDOLIN ENSEMBLE

See: Lonesome Standard Time

THE NASHVILLE SUPER GUITARS

See: The Nashville Superpickers

THE NASHVILLE SUPERPICKERS /THE NASHVILLE SUPER GUITARS

Formed 1994, in Nashville, TN.

The Nashville Superpickers is a catch-all name for a loose aggregate of bluegrass pickers and session musicians who record instrumental versions of familiar songs. California's CMH Records released three albums with the moniker in 1994. In 1995 they decided to use the name the Nashville Super Guitars.

what to buy: There are no overlapping musicians on *Pickin' on the '50s* (CMH, 1994, prod. Wynn Osborne) ♪♪ and *Pickin' on the Eagles* (CMH, 1994, prod. Billy Troy) ♪♪, so the Superpickers can't really be called a group. The Eagles tribute is more bluegrass oriented, while the 1950s tribute usually features electric guitar as the lead instrument. At least with the bluegrass-oriented *Pickin' on Christmas* (CMH, 1994) ♪♪ people are used to hearing the tunes given this kind of treatment.

what to avoid: Well, all of these, really, but particularly The Nashville Super Guitars' *Searching for Elvis* (CMH, 1995, prod. Billy Troy) ♪. They don't find him.

influences:
◀◀ Eagles, 1950s rock, Christmas songs, Chet Atkins

Brian Mansfield

JOEL NAVA

Born in Port Lavaca, TX.

Versatile Joel Nava was one of the first artists signed when Arista Records started its Texas division. A bilingual native of South Texas, Nava grew up on the sounds of both tejano and Western swing, and he has combined the two styles throughout his career. His group Bobby Lee and the Night Riders made the national finals of the 1987 True Value Hardware Country Showdown.

what's available: *Joel Nava* (Arista Texas, 1995, prod. Michael Morales, Ron Morales, Chris Waters) ♪♪♪ tries to establish Nava in the country and tejano markets simultaneously. He sings a gorgeous traditional tejano song called "Ella," a song called "Four-Letter Word" that sounds like it comes straight from the Clay Walker songbook, even a Spanish-language rendition of John Berry's hit "Your Love Amazes Me." Nava is capable in all these areas, but he tries to do so much that he never sounds committed to any of it. Backed by his full band, Nava eschewed the country ballads on his second album, *Soy Otro* (Arista Texas, 1996) ♪♪♪, in favor of Spanish-language tejano with more consistent results.

influences:
◀◀ Freddy Fender, Johnny Rodriguez

Brian Mansfield

EMILIO NAVAIRA

See: Emilio

FRED NEIL

Born 1937, in St. Petersburg, FL.

A little-known but major talent of the American folk renaissance, Fred Neil is probably better recognized for other people's performances of his songs—such as "Everybody's Talkin'" (Harry Nilsson) or "The Dolphins" (Tim Buckley)—than his own long-out-of-print albums. He was a fixture on the Greenwich folk scene during the early 1960s, and his laid-back 12-string guitar style and unique singing voice, which slipped effortlessly from a mellow tenor to a haunting baritone, was a major influence on the scene. After recording four albums from 1965-71, Neil retreated to his home in Florida where, by all accounts, he lives in virtual seclusion.

what to buy: *Fred Neil* (Capitol, 1966, prod. Nick Venet) ♪♪♪♪ is highlighted by Neil's versions of the dreamlike "The Dolphins" and "Everybody's Talkin'."

the rest:
Bleecker and MacDougal (Elektra, 1964) ♪♪♪
Other Side of This Life (Capitol, 1971) ♪♪♪

influences:

◀◀ Pete Seeger, Woody Guthrie

▶▶ Bob Dylan, Tim Buckley, John Sebastian

Joel Selvin and Dan Weber

RICK NELSON

Born Eric Hilliard Nelson, May 8, 1940, in Teaneck, NJ. Died December 31, 1985, near De Kalb, TX.

As his teenage idol years disappeared into the past, the son of television's Ozzie & Harriet renewed his passion for performing music with a pair of albums of straight-forward country music featuring hotshot Hollywood sidemen—such as guitarist Glen Campbell—alongside Nelson's former *Louisiana Hayride* ace, guitarist James Burton. The two albums, while not successful, bridged the gap into a successful resurgence by Nelson as a country-rock performer in the Flying Burrito Brothers/Poco mode. Nelson, who first took up rock 'n' roll in 1957 on his parents' popular TV series, had been one of the top record sellers of the era. But like most of the first-generation rockers, he watched his career slowly ebb from the heights of "Hello Mary Lou" and "Travelin' Man." One of his first country-rock studio experiments, a cover of Bob Dylan's "She Belongs to Me" during 1969, put him back on the radio for the first time in years, and his new country-rock band—the Stone Canyon Band, modeled after Poco and featuring Buck Owens' pedal steel guitarist Tom Brumley—became a legitimate attraction at the Troubadour, the happening Hollywood rock club of the day, and was celebrated with a live album. Although his unexpected 1972 hit "Garden Party" placed Nelson solidly in the burgeoning soft rock singer-songwriter school, the original bass player from his Stone Canyon Band, Randy Meisner, went on to form the Eagles after meeting Don Henley and Glen Frey on a casual date backing Linda Ronstadt, securing Nelson a lasting position in the whole development of the Los Angeles country-rock sound. At the latter stage of his career, cut short by his death in a plane crash on New Year's Eve 1985, Nelson showed signs of returning to his Sun Records rockabilly roots, but never had a chance to see if these retrograde recordings could refresh his appeal with the modern market.

what to buy: Nelson's country period—either the early experiments or the country-rock of the Stone Canyon Band—have been digitally documented only overseas. A European set, *Country Music* (The Entertainers, 1994, prod. various) ⅍⅍, combines the two original 1966 country albums. The British release *Rick Nelson & the Stone Canyon Band 1969–1976* (Edsel,

1995, prod. various) ⅍⅍⅍ is drawn from singles sessions and the Stone Canyon Band's four studio albums.

what to buy next: The CD reissue of the 1968 Troubadour engagement, *Rick Nelson in Concert* (MCA, 1994, prod. Rick Nelson, J. Sutton) ⅍⅍⅍, teems with the palpable excitement of the Hollywood nightclub shows where former teen idol Ricky reclaimed his position in California rock.

the rest:

The Best of Rick Nelson 1963–1975 (Decca/MCA, 1990) ⅍⅍

influences:

◀◀ Carl Perkins, Elvis Presley, Bob Dylan

▶▶ Eagles, Fleetwood Mac

Joel Selvin

WILLIE NELSON

Born Willie Hugh Nelson, April 30, 1933, in Fort Worth, TX.

Willie Nelson is arguably the most influential figure of the past quarter century—first as a songwriter and then as a performer who rewrote the rules for what qualified as country. After landing in Nashville in 1960, he penned hits such as Ray Price's "Night Life," Faron Young's "Hello Walls" and Patsy Cline's "Crazy." When Music City found his style (and nasal voice) too unusual, Nelson retreated to Texas, where he became a cultural icon. During the early 1970s his audience was an unlikely mix of rednecks and hippies, both of whom related to his relaxed attitude and cosmic cowboy themes. His *Red Headed Stranger* album made him the nominal head of the so-called "Outlaw" movement. Stylistically, Nelson tried everything from honky-tonk to Tin Pan Alley, and with his distinctive approach it all somehow formed a cohesive American style. His film career includes roles in *The Electric Horseman, Honeysuckle Rose, Barbarosa* and others. During the 1980s he co-founded the annual Farm Aid benefit concerts. Unimpressed, the IRS socked him for back taxes in 1991, which cost Nelson most of his assets. Nevertheless, his social conscience and mastery of all forms of country music have made him one of the genre's true giants. If they ever carve a country-music version of Mount Rushmore, they'll have to include Nelson.

what to buy: *Red Headed Stranger* (Columbia, 1975, prod. TK) ⅍⅍⅍⅍ is Nelson's greatest "Outlaw" album, with admirably spare production and the timeless "Blue Eyes Crying in the Rain." Nelson's return to Texas yielded *Shotgun Willie* (Atlantic, 1973, prod. TK) ⅍⅍⅍⅍, an adventurous concept album that brought him together with rockers such as Leon Russell and Doug Sahm and made him hip outside the country music community. *Phases and Stages* (Atlantic, 1974, prod. TK) 🎜🎜🎜🎜🎜, Nelson's second concept album, cemented his status as a crossover star. (These two albums can sometimes be found packaged together as *Shotgun Willie/Phases and Stages* (Mobile Fidelity Sound Lab, 1993) 🎜🎜🎜🎜🎜.) *Who'll Buy My Memories? (The IRS Tapes)* (Sony, 1991, prod. TK) 🎜🎜🎜🎜🎜 was intended only as a method of paying off his tax debt, but it's one of Nelson's most evocative albums ever, featuring nothing but his voice and guitar—and his soul.

what to buy next: *Nite Life: Greatest Hits and Rare Tracks, 1959–1971* (Rhino, 1990, prod. various) 🎜🎜🎜🎜🎜, a great collection of Nelson's early years, includes "Half a Man" and "Funny How Time Slips Away." On *Stardust* (Columbia, 1978, prod. TK) 🎜🎜🎜🎜, Nelson takes on the Tin Pan Alley of George Gershwin and Hoagy Carmichael, and wins hands down.

what to avoid: *Pancho, Lefty and Rudolph* (Columbia, 1995) 🎜🎜🎜, a collaboration with Merle Haggard, is a cheapo repackage that has five holiday songs from each artist. The music's pretty good (Nelson's "Pretty Paper," Haggard's "If We Make It through December"), but hold out for full Christmas albums by each artist.

the rest:

... *and then I Wrote* (Capitol, 1962/1995) 🎜🎜🎜🎜

The Sound in Your Mind (Columbia, 1976) 🎜🎜🎜

(With Waylon Jennings, Jessi Colter, and Tompall Glaser) *Wanted! The Outlaws* (RCA, 1976/1996) 🎜🎜🎜

To Lefty from Willie (Columbia, 1977) 🎜🎜🎜🎜

Willie and Family Live (CBS, 1978) 🎜🎜🎜🎜

Willie Sings Kristofferson (Columbia, 1979) 🎜🎜🎜

(With Leon Russell) *One for the Road* (Columbia, 1979) 🎜🎜🎜

(With Ray Price) *San Antonio Rose* (Columbia, 1980) 🎜🎜🎜🎜

Original Soundtrack: Honeysuckle Rose (Columbia, 1980) 🎜🎜🎜

Greatest Hits (& Some That Will Be) (Columbia, 1981) 🎜🎜🎜

Somewhere over the Rainbow (Columbia, 1981) 🎜🎜🎜

Always on My Mind (Columbia, 1982) 🎜🎜🎜🎜

Tougher than Leather (Columbia, 1983) 🎜🎜🎜

Without a Song (Columbia, 1983) 🎜🎜🎜

(With Roger Miller) *Old Friends* (Columbia, 1983) 🎜🎜🎜🎜

City of New Orleans (Columbia, 1984) 🎜🎜🎜

(With Kris Kristofferson) *Music from* Songwriter (Columbia, 1984) 🎜🎜🎜

Me and Paul (Columbia, 1985) 🎜🎜🎜

Half Nelson (Columbia, 1985) 🎜🎜🎜

(With the Highwaymen) *Highwayman* (Columbia, 1985) 🎜🎜🎜🎜

Partners (Columbia, 1986) 🎜🎜🎜

Willie (RCA, 1986) 🎜🎜🎜

The Promiseland (Columbia, 1986) 🎜🎜🎜

(With Waylon Jennings) *Take It to the Limit* (CBS, 1987) 🎜🎜🎜

Island in the Seas (Columbia, 1987) 🎜🎜🎜

What a Wonderful World (Columbia, 1988) 🎜🎜🎜

Best (EMI, 1988) 🎜🎜🎜

All-Time Greatest Hits, Volume 1 (RCA, 1988) 🎜🎜🎜

Horse Called Music (Columbia, 1989) 🎜🎜🎜

(With the Highwaymen) *Highwayman 2* (Columbia, 1990) 🎜🎜🎜🎜

Born for Trouble (Columbia, 1990) 🎜🎜🎜

Greatest Songs (Curb, 1990) 🎜🎜🎜

The Best of Willie Nelson (RCA, 1991) 🎜🎜🎜

Super Hits (Columbia, 1991) 🎜🎜🎜🎜

Willie Sings 28 Great Songs (Hollywood/IMG) 🎜🎜🎜

Super Hits (CSI Classics, 1991) 🎜🎜🎜

(With Jennings) *Clean Shirt* (Epic, 1991) 🎜🎜🎜

Moonlight Becomes You (Justice, 1993) 🎜🎜🎜🎜

The Early Years: The Complete Liberty Recordings Plus More (Liberty, 1994) 🎜🎜🎜🎜

The Legend Begins (Pair, 1994) 🎜🎜🎜🎜

Peace in the Valley: The Gospel Truth Collection (Promised Land, 1994) 🎜🎜🎜

Healing Hands of Time (Liberty, 1994) 🎜🎜🎜🎜

The Early Years (Scotti Bros., 1994) 🎜🎜🎜🎜

(With Curtis Potter) *Six Hours at Pedernales* (Step One, 1994) 🎜🎜🎜

A Classic and Unreleased Collection (Rhino, 1995) 🎜🎜🎜🎜🎜

The Essential Willie Nelson (RCA, 1995) 🎜🎜🎜🎜🎜

Super Hits, Volume 2 (Epic, 1995) 🎜🎜🎜

Just One Love (Justice, 1995) 🎜🎜🎜🎜

Revolutions of Time ... the Journey (Columbia/Legacy, 1995) 🎜🎜🎜🎜🎜

(With the Highwaymen) *The Road Goes on Forever* (Liberty, 1995) 🎜🎜🎜🎜

Spirit (Island, 1996) 🎜🎜🎜

(With Billy Walker) *Charlie's Shoes* (DEC) 🎜🎜🎜🎜

(With Bobby Nelson) *How Great Thou Art* (Finer Arts, 1996) 🎜🎜🎜

(With Johnny Lee) *Willie Nelson & Johnny Lee* (Intermedia) 🎜🎜🎜🎜

worth searching for: Never one to stick with an image, Nelson turned to such modern writers as Lyle Lovett, Paul Simon and John Hiatt for *Across the Borderline* (Columbia, 1993, prod. Don Was) 🎜🎜🎜🎜, his most satisfying album in years. *Pretty Paper* (Columbia, 1979, prod. Booker T. Jones) 🎜🎜🎜🎜, Nelson's Christmas album, features extreeemely laid-back renditions of holiday favorites like "Rudolph the Red-Nosed Reindeer" and "Jingle Bells."

influences:

◀◀ Floyd Tillman, Gene Autry, Lefty Frizzell

▶▶ Waylon Jennings, Rodney Crowell, Billy Joe Shaver

see also: *Highwaymen*

Bob Cannon

Willie Nelson (© Ken Settle)

MICHAEL NESMITH

Born December 30, 1942, in Houston, TX.

Being tagged "the smart Monkee" may seem faint praise indeed, but Michael Nesmith was that, and more. A session musician and folkie when he was tapped to join the Prefab Four, Nesmith regularly contributed songs to the group and was its most accomplished musician (apologies to Peter Tork). Apart from the Monkees, Nesmith wrote Linda Ronstadt's first hit "Different Drum" and recorded innovative, if quirky, concept albums such as *The Prison*. And despite the odious implications of his day job, Nesmith was there at the dawn of country rock, and his contributions, such as the utterly lovely song "Joanne," are often overlooked. Maybe that's because Nesmith's most significant innovation is in the field of video. His clip for "Rio" was one of America's first conceptual music videos, and the terrific *Elephant Parts* the first conceptual long-form video. *Popclips,* a video show Nesmith produced for Nickelodeon, was the prototype of MTV. Finally, his company, Pacific Arts,

produced the brilliant cult films *Repo Man* and *Tapeheads.* So laugh at his past if you want (and his present, in the wake of the Monkees' reunion), but no one else descended from the Monkees has evolved quite so far.

what to buy: These days, you're pretty much limited to whatever you can find, since nearly all of Nesmith's music is out of print. *The Newer Stuff* (Rhino, 1989, prod. Michael Nesmith) ♪♪♪ is a collection of mostly quirky pop tunes, while *The Older Stuff; The Best of the Early Years* (Rhino, 1991, prod. Michael Nesmith) ♪♪♪ is better, containing more country-flavored material, including "Joanne" and "Different Drum."

worth searching for: The long-form video *Elephant Parts* (Pacific Arts, 1980) ♪♪♪♪ has it all—good music, plenty of laughs, and an energetic spirit of innovation not seen since Judy Garland and Mickey Rooney decided "Hey, let's put on a show!"

influences:
◄◄ Bob Dylan, Merle Travis, Ernie Kovacs

▶▶ Stone Poneys, the wool hat industry, MTV

Daniel Durchholz

THE NEVILLE BROTHERS

See: Aaron Neville

AARON NEVILLE /THE NEVILLE BROTHERS

Born January 24, 1941, in New Orleans, LA.

Aaron Neville is a member of New Orleans' musical institution the Neville Brothers, and he has performed and recorded both with them and on his own. Neville's success as a pop singer dates to 1966, when he had a hit with "Tell It Like It Is." He revived his solo career during the 1990s with a series of recordings with Linda Ronstadt and by himself. Neville's recent solo albums have covered a wide range of styles, and he had a Top 40 hit in 1993 with a version of "The Grand Tour." He has a supple falsetto voice that's one of the most beautiful sounds on earth.

what to buy: The title of *The Grand Tour* (A&M, 1993, prod. Steve Lindsey) 𝄞𝄞𝄞𝄞 isn't just a George Jones song, it's a description of the album, on which Neville ranges from L.A. song-mill material (Dianne Warren's "Don't Take Away My Heaven") to 1970s soul (the Stylistics' "Betcha by Golly Wow"). "The Grand Tour" is the only country song here, but Neville and producer Steve Lindsey play it straight out of the Billy Sherrill songbook. And Neville is one of the few singers with an instrument as incredible as Jones'.

what to buy next: Neville had so much luck with his first foray into Nashville that he recorded three of the songs on *The Tattooed Heart* (A&M) 𝄞𝄞𝄞𝄞 — "Why Should I Fall in Love," "In Your Eyes" and Kris Kristofferson's "For the Good Times" — with producer Keith Stegall.

what to avoid: Outside of that one big hit, Neville's later output is superior to his early recordings. *Tell It Like It Is: The Best of Aaron Neville* (LaserLight, 1996) 𝄞𝄞 is the weakest of numerous repackages. After the title track, there's nothing.

the rest:
The Neville Brothers: Fiyo on the Bayou (A&M, 1981) 𝄞𝄞𝄞𝄞
Neville–ization (Black Top/Rounder, 1984) 𝄞𝄞𝄞𝄞
Treacherous—A History of the Neville Brothers, 1955–1985 (Rhino, 1989) 𝄞𝄞𝄞𝄞𝄞
Orchid in the Storm (Rhino EP, 1985/1990) 𝄞𝄞𝄞

FIVE FOR MY FANS

RUBY LOVETT

Shenandoah
Under the Kudzu (RCA)

Hal Ketchum
The Hits (MCG/Curb)

Patty Loveless
Only What I Feel (Epic)

Patty Loveless
When Fallen Angels Fly (Epic)

Waylon Jennings
The Taker/Tulsa & Honky Heroes
(Mobile Fidelity)

Yellow Moon (A&M, 1989) 𝄞𝄞𝄞𝄞
Brother's Keeper (A&M, 1990) 𝄞𝄞𝄞𝄞
Greatest Hits (Curb, 1990) 𝄞𝄞𝄞
My Greatest Gift—The Classic Aaron Neville (Rounder, 1990) 𝄞𝄞𝄞𝄞
Tell It Like It Is (Curb, 1991) 𝄞𝄞𝄞
Warm Your Heart (A&M, 1991) 𝄞𝄞𝄞𝄞
Treacherous Too! History of the Neville Brothers, Volume 2 (Rhino, 1991) 𝄞𝄞𝄞𝄞
Family Groove (A&M, 1992) 𝄞𝄞𝄞𝄞
Aaron Neville's Soulful Christmas (A&M, 1993) 𝄞𝄞𝄞𝄞
Live on Planet Earth (A&M, 1994) 𝄞𝄞𝄞𝄞
Mitakuye Oyasin Oyasin (A&M, 1996) 𝄞𝄞𝄞𝄞

influences:
◀◀ Dobie Gray
▶▶ All-4-One

Brian Mansfield

THE NEW COON CREEK GIRLS

Formed 1979, in Renfro Valley, KY.

Kathy Kuhn, fiddle (1995–present); Ramona Church, banjo, vocals (1991–present); Dale Ann Bradley, guitar, lead vocals (1991–present); Vicki Simmons, electric bass, vocals (1979–present); Deanie Richardson, fiddle, mandolin (1988–90); Pam Perry, mandolin, vocals, (1985–88, 1992–95); Jan Cummins, banjo (1979–83); Kelly Cummins, guitar (1979–82); Betty Linn, fiddle (1979–81); Cathy Lavendar, guitar (1982–85); Pam Gadd, banjo (1983–87); Annie Kaser, banjo (1987–91); Carmella Ramsey, fiddle (1990–91); Phylliss Jones, guitar (1991); Jennifer Wrinkle, fiddle (1991–92); Michelle Birkby, fiddle (1994–95); Wanda Barnette, fiddle, guitar (1982–91).

This all-female bluegrass band was originally formed in 1979 to provide an "all-girl" group for the weekly *Renfro Valley Barn Dance* show. They took their name from the Coon Creek Girls string band, which was popular during the 1930s.

what to buy: *The L&N Don't Stop Here Anymore* (Pinecastle, 1994, prod. New Coon Creek Girls) ♫♫♫♫ features 15 songs, including four originals. Dale Ann Bradley comes into her own as a soulful lead vocalist on this album, which also includes songs by Ralph Stanley, Mel Tillis and others.

what to buy next: On *Everything You Do* (Pinecastle, 1996) ♫♫♫♫, an even dozen gospel songs are marked by fine lead and harmony vocal work. Songs range from the Carter Family's "Little Black Train" to Bradley's "Everything You Do (Touches Someone Else)."

the rest:
Ain't Love a Good Thing (Pinecastle, 1992) ♫♫♫

influences:
◀◀ Coon Creek Girls

Douglas Fulmer

THE NEW GRASS REVIVAL

Formed 1971, in Louisville, KY. Disbanded 1989.

Sam Bush, mandolin; John Cowan, bass guitar, lead vocals (1974–89); Bela Fleck, banjo, (1981–89); Pat Flynn, guitar, vocals, (1981–89); Courtney Johnson (died June 7, 1996), banjo (1971–81); Curtis Burch, guitar, dobro (1971–81); Ebo Walker, bass (1971–74).

Sam Bush put together the New Grass Revival when he was only 19 years old, but it wasn't until 10 years later, when banjo ace Bela Fleck and guitar player Pat Flynn joined, that the band

really took off. Their shows were nearly legendary, adding a decided rock 'n' roll energy and style to bluegrass.

what to buy: New Grass Revival was always better live than in the recording studio and *Live* (Sugar Hill, 1989, prod. New Grass Revival) ♫♫♫♫, recorded during their farewell tour, effectively captures the raucous energy of the group's live sets.

what to buy next: *Hold to a Dream* (Capitol, 1987, prod. Garth Fundis) ♫♫♫♫ was the best of New Grass Revival's attempts at mainstreaming for the country audience.

what to avoid: Like any New Grass Revival album, *Friday Night in America* (Capitol, 1987, prod. Wendy Waldman) ♫♫ has some high points, but overall it's not as loose and energized as their other efforts.

the rest:
Fly through the Country/When the Storm Is Over (Flying Fish, 1976/77) ♫♫♫♫
Barren County (Flying Fish, 1979) ♫♫♫
Commonwealth (Flying Fish, 1981) ♫♫♫
On the Boulevard (Sugar Hill, 1985) ♫♫♫♫
Anthology (Sugar Hill, 1990) ♫♫♫♫

influences:
◀◀ Country Gazette, Kentucky Colonels
▶▶ Bela Fleck & the Flecktones, Chesapeake

Douglas Fulmer

THE NEW LOST CITY RAMBLERS

Formed 1958, in New York, NY.

Multi-instrumentalists Mike Seeger; John Cohen; Tom Paley (1958–62); Tracy Schwarz (1962 present).

The most popular, most influential, and arguably the most important first-generation revival band of the folk boom in terms of presenting rural Southern string-band music both in concert and on recordings, the New Lost City Ramblers remain a force in traditional music circles to this day. Their music, which came to be known as old-time or old-timey (to distinguish it from bluegrass), explores the diversity of U.S. string-band music within Appalachian ballads, black and white gospel and blues, Cajun and countless other traditions. They have tended to concentrate on—and are most successful at performing—the string-band music of the Appalachian and Ozark cultures, their knowledge of which has been gleaned from 78's, Library

The New Grass Revival (from left): John Cowan, Bela Fleck, Pat Flynn and Sam Bush **(AP/Wide World Photos)**

of Congress field recordings and from hunting down traditional performers and learning their repertoires. The Ramblers' influence on generations of young musicians who have followed in their footsteps is incalculable; it's difficult to imagine a revival of old-time music of any consequence without them. Ethnomusicologists to a man, the Ramblers chose to perpetuate rather than preserve the music by performing it with grace, dignity and a sense of good fun. Although all band members have gone on to other endeavors (musical and otherwise), they have continued to perform in recent years on an infrequent basis.

what to buy: *The New Lost City Ramblers, the Early Years, 1958–1962* (Smithsonian/Folkways, 1991, prod. Mike Seeger, Moses Asch, Peter Bartok) ♫♫♫♫ contains 26 tracks from the 12 highly influential albums recorded for Folkways with the original members, before Tom Paley left the band and subsequently moved to England. These performances breathed new life into old traditions, sparking an interest in the traditions

presented here that live on. *The New Lost City Ramblers Volume 2, 1963–1973: Out Standing in Their Field* (Smithsonian/Folkways, 1993, prod. various) ♫♫♫♫ continues the traditions of the first recordings and incorporate the musical contributions of Tracy Schwarz who, among other talents and interests, brought his enthusiastic fiddling and knowledge of Cajun music to the band.

what to buy next: *The New Lost City Ramblers & Friends* (Vanguard, 1994, prod. Mary Katherine Aldin) ♫♫♫ gathers 31 live examples—from the 1963–65 Newport Folk Festivals—of the Ramblers performing with influential performers of days gone by, including Cousin Emmy, Maybelle Carter, Eck Robertson, Roscoe Holcomb, Sam & Kirk McGee and Dock Boggs. This collection illustrates the band's familiarity and expertise performing the repertoires of these older performers and at the same time underlines the group's rediscovery efforts on behalf of these important, although sadly neglected, artists. *New Lost City Ramblers' 20th Anniversary Concert* (Flying Fish, 1987, prod. Steve Rathe) 🎵🎵🎵 is a live recording of a Carnegie Hall concert from 1978, celebrating the group's first 20 years. It includes special guests the Highwoods String Band, Elizabeth Cotten, and Mike Seeger's brother, Pete.

influences:

◀◀ Carter Family, Eck Robertson, many more

▶▶ Highwoods String Band, Freight Hoppers

Randy Pitts

NEW RIDERS
OF THE PURPLE SAGE

Formed 1969, in Marin County, CA.

John "Marmaduke" Dawson, guitar, vocals (1971–81); David Nelson, guitar, vocals (1971-81); Jerry Garcia, guitar, pedal steel (1969–71); Mickey Hart, drums (1969–70); Phil Lesh, bass (1969–70); Spencer Dryden, drums (1970); David Torbert, bass, vocals (1971–75); Skip Battin, bass, vocals (1974–76); Buddy Cage, pedal steel (1972–82); Stephen Love, bass (1976–82); Allen Kemp, guitar (1977–85); Rusty Gauthier, guitar, violin, fiddle, mandolin, dobro (1982); Gary Vogensen, vocals, guitar (1985–93); Evan Morgan, guitar (1993).

The New Riders of the Purple Sage garnered a substantial cult-like following as the Grateful Dead's warmup band—not to mention a busman's holiday for Jerry Garcia, Mickey Hart and Phil Lesh—during the Dead's country-oriented, *Workingman's Dead—American Beauty* period. They were offered a recording deal with Columbia, and in 1971 the label released *New Riders of the Purple Sage*, which contained the romantic "Louisiana Lady" and "Henry," a humorous tale about a dope smuggler. Subsequent releases, however, were simply a rehashing of the same hippie-outlaw material. Although they haven't recorded an album since 1981, the New Riders still make club appearances throughout the U.S.

what to buy: *New Riders of the Purple Sage* (Columbia, 1971, prod. various) 🎵🎵🎵 contains "Louisiana Lady" and John Dawson's gliding "I Don't Know You," which features some tasty steel guitar licks courtesy of Jerry Garcia.

what to buy next: Some early New Riders demos featuring Garcia and Dead-mates Phil Lesh and Mickey Hart can be found on *Before Time Began* (Relix, 1990) 🎵🎵.

what to avoid: Pass on such reissued MCA albums as *Marin County Line* (One Way) 🎵, *New Riders* (One Way) 🎵 and *Who Are Those Guys?* (One Way) 🎵.

the rest:

The Adventures of Panama Red (Columbia, 1973) 🎵🎵🎵

The Best of New Riders of the Purple Sage (Columbia, 1976) 🎵🎵🎵

influences:

◀◀ Grateful Dead, Byrds, Flying Burrito Brothers, Seatrain, Gene Clark

▶▶ Eagles, Ozark Mountain Daredevils, Marshall Tucker Band

see also: *Grateful Dead*

Rick Petreycik

THE NEW TRADITION

Formed 1988, in Nashville, TN.

Daryl Mosley, bass, lead vocals (1988–93, 1996–present); Riche Dotson, banjo, vocals (1988–present); Danny Roberts, mandolin, vocals (1988); Ken White, guitar, vocals (1993–present); Fred Duggin, guitar, vocals (1988–93); Ray Cardwell, bass, vocals (1993–96); others.

The original members of New Tradition met while participating in instrumental competitions and none of the musicians had much of a bluegrass background. Four of the band's six albums have been all-gospel projects marked by hot-picking in a contemporary style with considerable country influences in spots.

what to buy: *Love Here Today* (Brentwood, 1992, prod. Jack Jezzro) 🎵🎵🎵 was quite a change of pace for the band; this secular album finds them covering songs from expected sources like Bill Monroe, Hank Williams and Merle Haggard, and surprises like the Beatles' "I Saw Her Standing There."

what to buy next: *Follow the Son* (1995) 🎵🎵🎵, the band's self-released gospel album, is a loose and fun effort highlighted by some fiery pickin' and Ray Cardwell's true-believer vocals.

the rest:

Bluegrass Gospel at Its Finest (Brentwood, 1991) 🎵🎵🎵

Seed of Love (Brentwood) 🎵🎵🎵

Closer than It's Ever Been (Brentwood, 1993) 🎵🎵🎵

Old Time Gospel Jamboree (Brentwood, 1994) 🎵🎵🎵

influences:

◀◀ New Grass Revival, Doyle Lawson & Quicksilver, Merle Haggard

▶▶ Tim Graves & Cherokee

Douglas Fulmer

NEW VINTAGE

Formed 1989, in NC.

Russell Johnson, vocals; Earl Lewellyn, guitar, vocals; Jan Johansson, fiddle; Gena Britt, banjo, vocals; Carl Caldwell, bass.

New Vintage was formed by singer Russell Johnson and guitarist/singer Earl Lewellyn. The band's current lineup features Sweden-born fiddler Jan Johansson, bassist Carl Caldwell and banjo player Gena Britt, who also sings tenor and occasional lead. The group gained its record contract by winning the 1993 Pizza Hut International Bluegrass Showdown.

what's available: *No Time for the Blues* (Pinecastle, 1995, prod. Butch Baldassari) ♬♬♬ contains a typical assortment of gospel tunes ("He's All These Things to Me"), a country song (Rodney Crowell's "Til I Gain Control Again") and bluegrass classics such as Bill Monroe's "Cheap Love Affair." The group's three singers trade off lead vocals, both individually and as duets.

influences:
◀◀ Bill Monroe

Brian Mansfield

JIMMY C. NEWMAN

Born Jimmy Yeve Newman, August 27, 1927, near Big Mamou, LA.

Nicknamed "The Alligator Man," Jimmy C. Newman is best known for bringing Cajun flair to country music. Inspired by Gene Autry, he integrated his signature "Aireee" to his country act. During the 1950s his hits "Cry, Cry, Darling," "Seasons of My Heart," "Blue Darling" and "Day Dreaming" made the charts. One of his best-remembered songs, "Falling Star," made Newman a star in 1956, the same year he joined the Grand Ole Opry. Newman's Bayou-rich songs—such as "Alligator Man," "Bayou Talk," "Louisiana Saturday Night," "City of Angels" and "Back in Circulation"—continued to be chartmakers through the 1960s. Although his recording career slowed during the 1970s, he continues to bring down the house with his spirited Louisiana-flavored shows.

what to buy: Though Newman's days as a hitmaker are long past, he can still make great records, and *Whatever Boils Your Crawfish* (Swallow, 1995, prod. Jimmy C. Newman) ♬♬♬♬ is an absolute blast. Newman, producing himself, gets great performances out of his band. The album kicks off with a great one-two punch: Loudon Wainwright's "Dead Skunk in the Middle of the Road" and the rollicking title tune.

what to buy next: Rounder wanted a traditional Cajun country sound when Newman recorded *The Alligator Man* (Rounder, 1991, prod. Jimmy C. Newman, Ken Irwin) ♬♬♬♬, and that's exactly what they got. Newman sings the songs largely in French, and the playing is marked by the spirited fiddle of Rufus Thibodeaux and dobro of Joe Rogers.

what to avoid: Don't buy *Jimmy C. Newman & Cajun Country* (Dot, 1986, prod. Stan Cornelius) ♬♬ or *More Cajun Music* (MCA, 1995, prod. Stan Cornelius) ♬♬, which are essentially the same album, although *More Cajun Music* has two fewer cuts. Recorded about the time Rockin' Sidney's rhythm-box zydeco tune "My Toot Toot" became a national sensation, *More Cajun Music* finds Newman trying for the same sound, even recording Rockin' Sidney's "Cochon de Lait." On *Jimmy C. Newman*, Newman did his own version of "My Toot Toot." It's not a comfortable fit.

the rest:
Louisiana Love (Ridgewood) ♬♬
Cajun and Country Too (Swallow) ♬♬♬♬
20 Cajun Country Classics (Plantation, 1985) ♬♬
16 Best of Jimmy C. Newman (Plantation, 1987) ♬♬
Cajun Classics (Sun, 1995) ♬♬

influences:
◀◀ Dewey Balfa & the Balfa Brothers
▶▶ Doug Kershaw, Eddy Raven, Jo-El Sonnier

Randall T. Cook

JUICE NEWTON

Born Judy Kay Newton, February 18, 1952, in Lakehurst, NJ.

One of the most successful pop/country crossover artists of the late 1970s and early 1980s, Juice Newton actually had more success initially on the pop charts. Her first four singles all reached the pop Top 10, with "Queen of Hearts" (#2 pop, #14 country, 1981) being the biggest. Country hits, however, continued well into the 1980s, and she scored a total of four #1 songs, including the Eddie Rabbitt duet "Both to Each Other (Friends & Lovers)" (#1, 1986). Through the years her music alternated between country and pop, although she's had no hits in either field since 1990. Influenced musically by folk artists like Joni Mitchell and Judy Collins, among others, Juice (a nickname from childhood) played in California coffeehouses during the late 1960s, where she met her longtime collaborator Otha Young. As the country-rock movement was getting underway, they formed the band Dixie Peach, followed in 1973 by the formation of Silver Spur. In 1975 the band, now billed as Juice Newton & Silver Spur, signed with RCA and released two albums. They switched to Capitol in 1977, but disbanded after one year, although Juice remained with the label and released her breakthrough album *Juice* in 1981, followed a year later by *Quiet Lies*. The bulk of her biggest hits came from these two albums. In 1984 she switched labels, returning to RCA and continuing to record pop records until 1985, when she returned to the country charts with three #1 hits. Follow-ups were less successful during the next couple of years and finally, in 1989, she released her last album to date, *Ain't Gonna Cry*. Today, Juice continues to tour some, while spending more time with her family, and a new album is reportedly in the works. Her influence on country/pop female vocalists will likely be acknowledged more readily in coming years, with a new generation of up and coming stars heartily embracing both genres.

what's available: With 15 tracks, including her pop and country hits (and near hits), *Greatest Hits (And More)* (1987, Capitol, prod. various) ♪♪♪♪ is the most complete retrospective available on her entire career. (None of her later country hits are available on CD at this point.) If you want the earliest country hits only, *Greatest Country Hits* (Curb, 1990, prod. various) ♪♪♪♪ will do; otherwise, stick with the first.

worth searching for: *Ain't Gonna Cry* (RCA, 1989) ♪♪♪♫ features tunes by Pam Tillis and Cheryl Wheeler among the standouts, and it should have been a bigger hit. There's nothing essential here, but it's worth a listen.

influences:

Bonnie Raitt, Linda Ronstadt

Paulette Carlson

Stephen L. Betts

OLIVIA NEWTON-JOHN

Born September 26, 1948, in Cambridge, England

Although she was hardly the first, Olivia Newton-John, along with John Denver, became one of the most controversial pop/country crossover acts of the 1970s. Her harmless, if sometimes vapid, renditions of country classics such as "Jolene" and "Blue Eyes Crying in the Rain" did little to advance country's credibility with pop audiences—but in hindsight they certainly didn't damage the source material to any great degree. Hits such as "If You Love Me (Let Me Know)" and "Please Mr. Please" were so widespread on the radio that country artists, stuck in their own rut and seeing little hope on the hori-

zon for the return to "real" country music, railed against the prospect of awarding Country Music Association awards to artists such as Newton-John, who was the organization's Female Vocalist of the Year in 1974, and Denver, who was, perhaps more surprisingly, Entertainer of the Year in 1975. Whatever scandal may have erupted, it was all over fairly quickly, when Newton-John made the more rock-oriented album *Totally Hot* in 1978 and followed that with film roles in *Grease* and *Xanadu*, forever distancing herself from the country audience. Today she records less frequently and works mostly as an activist, particularly in the fight against breast cancer, which she survived during the early 1990s. Her most recent projects include an album of lullabies for her young daughter.

what to buy: *Back to Basics: The Essential Collection 1971–1992* (MCA, 1992, prod. various) ♪♪♪ contains the country/pop hits along with later rock-tinged hits and some fairly boring new songs as well, which could have been excluded to make room for some glaring omissions. Rather disappointing, although fans will need it.

what to buy next: *Olivia's Greatest Hits, Volume 2* (MCA, 1982, prod. John Farrar, Jeff Lynne) ♪♪♪ is skimpy (10 tracks), but does fill in a few gaps in the hit singles department.

the rest:

Come on Over (MCA, 1976) ♪♪♪
Making a Good Thing Better (MCA, 1977) ♪♪♪
Physical (MCA, 1981) ♪♪♫
Soul Kiss (MCA, 1985) ♪♪♫
The Rumour (MCA, 1988) ♪♪♫
Warm and Tender (Geffen, 1989) ♪♪♪

influences:

◀◀ John Denver, Dolly Parton

▶▶ Sheena Easton, Marie Osmond

Stephen L. Betts

JOE NICHOLS

Born November 26, 1976, in Rogers, AR.

Joe Nichols was a part-time DJ and garage attendant when country songwriter Randy Edwards discovered him while Nichols was changing his oil. He signed with independent Intersound after developing a regional following in the Arkansas-Texas-Oklahoma region.

what's available: *Joe Nichols* (Intersound, 1996, prod. Todd

Wilkes, Randy Edwards, Lee Ogle) ♫♫ is typical, souped-up Nashville country of the 1990s—but not bad for a 19 year old.

influences:

Shenandoah, Tracy Lawrence

Brian Mansfield

THE NITTY GRITTY DIRT BAND

Formed 1966, in Long Beach, CA.

Jeff Hanna, vocals, guitar; Jimmie Fadden, vocals, drums; Les Thompson, vocals, mandolin (1966–73); Bruce Kunkel, guitar, violin, vocals (1966–67); Ralph Barr, guitar, clarinet, vocals (1966–68); Jackson Browne, guitar, vocals (1966); John McEuen, banjo, guitar, fiddle, (1967–86); Chris Darrow, guitar, fiddle (1968); Jimmy Ibbotson, bass, vocals; (1969–76, 1983–present); John Cable, guitar, bass, vocals (1976–77); Jackie Clark, bass, guitar (1976–77); Michael Buono, drums (1976–77); Bob Carpenter, keyboards, vocals (1979–present); Al Garth, saxophone, violin (1978–82); Richard Hathaway, bass (1978–82); Merle Brigante, drums (1978–79); Vic Mastriani, drums (1980–82); Michael Gardner, bass (1980–82); Bernie Leadon, guitar, banjo (1987–88).

The Nitty Gritty Dirt Band was the group that introduced many second-generation rock 'n' rollers to music outside of the bubblegum pop that AM Top 40 radio served during the late 1960s and early 1970s. With hits such as "Mr. Bojangles" (written by Jerry Jeff Walker), the NGDB lead interested fans to other singer/songwriters and the country-rock scene. Its sprawling, landmark 1972 three-record set, *Will the Circle Be Unbroken* brought unadulterated folk and roots country stars to rock fans' ears. The collection was a multi-generational gathering, including traditional musicians from Mother Maybelle Carter and Doc Watson to Opry founders Roy Acuff and Merle Travis, with the long-haired Dirt Band members playing backup and proving they listened to a wider range of music than many of their fans.

The band's catholic stylistic sense came from its roots in the halcyon L.A. folk-rock scene of the mid-1960s. The NGDB first formed as a jug-band. When multi-instrumentalist John McEuen joined, the core group was set for most of the rest of its career. Its records at various times were more rock than country (the 1975 *Dream* LP even included a spacey banjo opus that sounded like Pink Floyd for hillbillies), but by the 1980s, with myriad personnel changes and a stint officially calling themselves the Dirt Band, the core members settled in as something of a country-music institution; their music hadn't changed, but

in the post-punk era, twangy music found itself unhip and relegated to country radio. Although it wasn't as much of a revelation the second time around, the Dirt Band also released an updated version of *Circle* in 1989, a songfest featuring some of the original legends (Roy Acuff, Earl Scruggs) as well as the new Nashville set (Rosanne Cash, John Hiatt, Emmylou Harris, Marty Stuart, Bruce Hornsby). Having passed its 30th year, the band is without a major-label deal for the first time ever, but it's still a staple on the road and seems far from quitting.

what to buy: *Will the Circle Be Unbroken* (Liberty, 1972, prod. William E. McEuen) ♫♫♫♫ is the hands-down, must-own release by the NGDB, although it's not as much a reflection of the band's own music as it is a testament to its roots. The music was already old by then but sounded fresh in this context. And it hasn't aged in the quarter-century since.

what to buy next: *Uncle Charlie and His Dog Teddy* (Liberty, 1970, prod. William E. McEuen) ♫♫♫ includes the group's biggest hit, "Mr. Bojangles," as well as a minor-hit version of Michael Nesmith's great "Some of Shelley's Blues" (recently covered by the Continental Drifters) that's typical of its hippie eclecticism. The mid-career three-LP compilation *Dirt, Silver & Gold* (United Artists, 1976, prod. various) ♫♫♫ collects the good stuff and filters out the dross.

what to avoid: Outside of collections and concept albums, the NGDB's output has been tepid fodder, such as *Jealousy* (Liberty, 1981) ♫♫ and *Let's Go* (Liberty, 1983) ♫♫.

the rest:
Nitty Gritty Dirt Band (Liberty, 1967) ♫♫
Ricochet (Liberty, 1967) ♫♫
Rare Junk (Liberty, 1968) ♫♫
Alive (Liberty, 1968) ♫♫
All the Good Times (Liberty, 1971) ♫♫♫
Stars and Stripes Forever (Liberty, 1971) ♫♫♫♫
Dream (United Artists, 1975) ♫♫♫♫
Wild Nights (United Artists, 1978) ♫♫
An American Dream (United Artists, 1979) ♫♫
Make a Little Magic (United Artists, 1980) ♫♫
Plain Dirt Fashion (Warner Bros., 1984) ♫♫
Partners, Brothers and Friends (Warner Bros., 1985) ♫♫
20 Years of Dirt (Warner Bros., 1986) ♫♫♫
Hold On (Warner Bros., 1987) ♫♫
Workin' Band (Warner Bros., 1988) ♫♫
More Great Dirt (Warner Bros., 1989) ♫♫
The Rest of the Dream (MCA, 1990) ♫♫
Live Two Five (Capitol Nashville, 1991) ♫♫

Not Fade Away (Liberty, 1992) 🎵🎵
Acoustic (Liberty, 1994) 🎵🎵

solo outings:
John McEuen:
See individual entry

Jimmy Ibbotson:
Wild Jimbos (MCA, 1991)
Wild Jimbos Two (Resounding Records, 1993) 🎵🎵🎵

influences:
◀◀ Carter Family, Weavers, Buddy Holly, Jim Kweskin Jug Band, Byrds

▶▶ Rodney Crowell, Rosanne Cash, Foster & Lloyd, Travis Tritt, Hank Williams Jr., Michelle Shocked, Uncle Tupelo

see also: *John McEuen*

Gil Asakawa

THE NOTTING HILLBILLIES

Formed 1989, in London, England.

Mark Knopfler, guitars, vocals; Brendan Croker, guitars, vocals; Steve Phillips, guitars, vocals; Guy Fletcher, keyboards, vocals.

Just as American blues and R&B invaded England and informed the rock 'n' roll that was shipped back our way, so did country music. It influenced the Rolling Stones, to be sure, and the Beatles as well. The strains of country that seem to have made an impression on the Notting Hillbillies (a side project for Dire Straits guitar whiz Mark Knopfler) include the smooth sounds of countrypolitan, the harmony vocals of cowboy music and white gospel. Interesting as that may sound, the Hillbillies' one album underlined the fact that, despite their common language, the U.S. and England are divided by dialects, and some things just don't translate. It entered the charts at #2 in the U.K., but barely got a sideways glance here, where, presumably, we can get our country music uncut.

what's available: *Missing . . . Presumed Having a Good Time* (Warner Bros., 1990, prod. Mark Knopfler, Guy Fletcher) 🎵🎵🎵 is laid-back almost to the point of somnambulance. A handful of original tunes plus some choice cover material doesn't add up to much, as the Hillbillies fail to raise a spark, much less fire and brimstone, from the Louvin Brothers' "Weapon of Prayer" and sleepwalk through the standard "Bewildered." Only Knopfler's trademark picking draws some attention, as does the after-hours track "Your Own Sweet Way."

worth searching for: Knopfler collaborated with his idol, Chet Atkins, on *Neck and Neck* (Columbia, 1990, prod. Mark Knopfler) 🎵🎵🎵 and appeared on several of Atkins' albums. The duo has won three Grammy Awards for their collaborations.

influences:
◀◀ Chet Atkins, Louvin Brothers, Stanley Brothers

Daniel Durchholz

NRBQ

See: Al Anderson

SCOTT NYGAARD

Born July 30, 1955, in Champaign/Urbana, IL.

After serving his musical apprenticeship in the Pacific Northwest playing in jazz, Celtic and old-time country bands, guitarist Scott Nygaard stepped into the national spotlight when he joined Laurie Lewis & Grant Street in 1989. Nygaard made his recording debut on that band's *Singing My Troubles Away* and made his solo debut shortly after that. One of the most versatile and tasteful guitarists on the acoustic music circuit, Nygaard has played since 1992 with acclaimed singer/songwriter Tim O'Brien, touring and recording as one of the O'Boys. Nygaard has also done extensive session work, guesting on albums by such artists as Jerry Douglas, Tim & Mollie O'Brien, Linda Waterfall, John Reischman, Tony Furtado and Sally Van Meter.

what's available: *No Hurry* (Rounder, 1990, prod. Laurie Lewis, Scott Nygaard) 🎵🎵🎵 illustrates Nygaard's eclecticism, as the all-instrumental album ranges from the "Irish calypso" of "Mary and the Soldier" to the jazz original "It Happened," with stops along the way for old-time music ("Red Apple Rag" and "Fiddle Tune Medley") and a nod to Clarence White on "Bury Me beneath the Willow." *Dreamer's Waltz* (Rounder, 1996, prod. Scott Nygaard) 🎵🎵🎵, as diverse as its predecessor but a bit more cohesive, showcases Nygaard (and guests like Tim O'Brien, Jerry Douglas and Dirk Powell) on a program of mostly Nygaard originals. Stand-out cuts include "Crawfeet," "The Lost Word," "Beaten to the Puncheon" and the Brazilian choro-influenced "Fog and Flame."

influences:
◀◀ Clarence White, Russ Barenberg
▶▶ Peter McLaughlin, Chris Thile

Jon Hartley Fox

Mark Knopfler of the Notting Hillbillies (© Ken Settle)

THE OAK RIDGE BOYS

Formed as the Oak Ridge Quartet, c. 1940s, in Oak Ridge, TN.

William Lee Golden, baritone vocals (1965–1987, 1996–present); **Duane Allen**, lead vocals (1967–present); **Richard Sterban**, bass vocals (1972–present); **Joe Bonsall**, tenor vocals (1973–present); **Steve Sanders**, baritone vocals (1987–96); others.

For the past two decades, the Oak Ridge Boys have established themselves not only as a high-powered gospel quartet, but also as a solid mainstream pop group. The group formed originally as a gospel quartet during the 1940s with different membership; it survived temporary breakups in 1946 and 1956. The group changed its name from the Oak Ridge Quartet to the Oak Ridge Boys in 1965, and the members of the more familiar lineup created quite a stir when they began singing secular songs during the 1970s. Between 1978 and 1980 the Oaks, with their smooth, soaring harmonies and tight instrumentation, rolled out a slew of chart toppers, including "Crying Again," "I'll Be True to You," "Sail Away," the Rodney Crowell-penned "Leavin' Louisiana in the Broad Daylight," "Trying to Love Two Women" and "Beautiful You." Their biggest hit came in 1981, with Dallas Frazier's "Elvira," followed by "Bobbie Sue," "American Made," "I Guess It Never Hurts to Hurt Sometimes," "Make My Life with You" and "Come On In (You Did the Best You Could." (A number of these, most notably "Elvira" and "Bobbie Sue," became pop hits as well.) In 1987 William Lee Golden, who with his scraggly waist-length hair and beard resembled a mountain man more than a gospel crooner, was asked to leave the band due to mounting personality clashes (he rejoined the group in 1996). In 1991 the group cracked the country Top 10 again with "Lucky Moon," their last major hit to-date.

what to buy: *The Best of the Oak Ridge Boys* (Columbia, 1978) 🎵🎵🎵 features a collection of the Oak's most solid hits.

what to buy next: *Greatest Hits, Volume 1* (MCA, 1980) 🎵🎵🎵 contains more of the Oak Ridge Boys' best.

the rest:
Old Fashioned, Down Home, Hand Clappin', Foot Stompin', Southern Style, Gospel Quartet Music (Columbia, 1976) 🎵🎵🎵
Fancy Free (MCA, 1981) 🎵🎵🎵
Greatest Hits, Volume Two (MCA, 1984) 🎵🎵🎵
Christmas (MCA, 1982/1985) 🎵🎵🎵

Christmas Again (MCA, 1986) 🎵🎵🎵
American Dreams (MCA, 1989) 🎵🎵🎵
Greatest Hits, Volume 3 (MCA, 1989) 🎵🎵
Unstoppable (RCA, 1991) 🎵🎵🎵
Back to Back (Arrival, 1994) 🎵🎵
Old Time Gospel Favorites (Curb, 1996) 🎵🎵🎵
At Their Best (Deluxe) 🎵🎵🎵
Forever and Ever (Hollywood/IMG) 🎵🎵
Glory Train (Intermedia) 🎵🎵
Smokey Mountain Gospel (Columbia)
Best of Gospel (Richmond) 🎵🎵
The Oak Ridge Boys (Richmond) 🎵🎵
(With the Statler Brothers) *The Oak Ridge Boys/The Statler Brothers* (Arrival) 🎵🎵
(With J.D. Sumner & the Stamps) *The Oak Ridge Boys/J.D. Sumner & the Stamps* (Arrival) 🎵🎵
The Sensational Oak Ridge Boys (Hollywood/IMG) 🎵🎵

worth searching for: *The Oak Ridge Boys Have Arrived* (MCA, 1979, prod. Jimmy Bowen) 🎵🎵🎵🎵 contain's the group's excellent cover of Rodney Crowell's "Leavin' Louisiana in the Broad Daylight." *Monongahela* (MCA, 1988, prod. Jimmy Bowen) 🎵🎵🎵 features the bluesy, easy-rollin' "Gonna Take a Lot of River (Mississippi, Monongahela, Ohio)."

influences:
◄◄ Tennessee Ernie Ford, Statler Brothers
►► 4 Runner

Rick Petreycik and Brian Mansfield

TIM O'BRIEN /TIM & MOLLIE O'BRIEN

Tim O'Brien was the leader of the traditional bluegrass band Hot Rize (and their humorous, more countrified alter egos Red Knuckles & the Trailblazers) from 1978 to 1992. He later went on to record with guitarist Scott Nygaard and bassist Mark Schatz as Tim O'Brien & the O'Boys, and through the years with sister Mollie, whose soulful voice found a perfect harmony with her brother's clear-as-a-bell tenor. The pair have both moved in bluegrass and folk circles for years, involving themselves in their own solo and duet recordings, as well as those of other artists, whether in a writing or singing capacity. Their blended family harmony is a precious thing, and their albums together are a rare, enjoyable treat.

what to buy: *Oh boy! O'Boy* (Sugar Hill, 1993, prod. JerryDouglas) 🎵🎵🎵🎵, recorded with the O'Boys, is a stellar album.

The Oak Ridge Boys **(AP/Wide World Photos)**

what to buy next: Tim and Mollie O'Brien's *Away Out on the Mountain* (Sugar Hill, 1994, prod. Tim O'Brien) 𝄢𝄢𝄢𝄢 is another fine CD.

the rest:
Hard Year Blues (Flying Fish, 1984) 𝄢𝄢𝄢
(With Mollie O'Brien) *Take Me Back* (Sugar Hill, 1988) 𝄢𝄢𝄢
Odd Man In (Sugar Hill, 1991) 𝄢𝄢𝄢
Remember Me (Sugar Hill, 1993) 𝄢𝄢𝄢
Rock in My Shoe (Sugar Hill, 1995) 𝄢𝄢𝄢𝄢
Red on Blonde (Sugar Hill, 1996) 𝄢𝄢𝄢𝄢

solo outings:
Mollie O'Brien:
Tell It True (Sugar Hill, 1996) 𝄢𝄢𝄢

influences:
◀◀ Hot Rize, New Grass Revival
▶▶ John Gorka, Maura O'Connell

Stephen L. Betts

MAURA O'CONNELL

Born September 16, 1958, in Ennis, County Clare, Ireland.

Blessed with a rich, powerful voice and a talent for finding excellent songs and rendering them with heartfelt poignancy, O'Connell is one of country music's finest singers, though her insistence on exploring the full range of country music's possibilities has meant she has often been overlooked within the narrowcast center of the Nashville mainstream. O'Connell first rose to prominence with the Irish band De Danaan, recording on its album *Star Spangled Molly*, and becoming a celebrity in her home country before moving to Nashville in 1987 and falling in with the likes of New Grass Revival and other boundary-pushing pickers within the city's acoustic music scene. After a debut album on Rounder, Maura was picked up by Warner Bros. for three albums before settling at Rykodisc/Hannibal.

what to buy: *Helpless Heart* (Warner Bros., 1989, prod. Bela Fleck) 𝄢𝄢𝄢 remains O'Connell's most endearing effort; Paul

Brady's "Helpless Heart" became a signature song of sorts for her, while versions of Nanci Griffith's "Trouble in the Fields" and Karla Bonoff's "Isn't It Always Love" gave the originals a run for their money. Gerry O'Beirne's stunningly beautiful "Western Highway" is the best single song she's done to date. *A Real Life Story* (Warner Bros., 1990, prod. Greg Penny) ♫♫♫♫ featured an intriguing version of Tom Waits' "Broken Bicycles," as well as first-rate selections by John Hiatt, Shawn Colvin and Hugh Prestwood.

what to buy next: *Blue Is the Colour of Hope* (Warner Bros., 1992, prod. Jerry Douglas) ♫♫♫ is highlighted by the slowly burning "Blue Train" and also features songs written by Mary Chapin Carpenter and the team of Paul Carrack and John Wesley Harding. The standout on *Stories* (Rykodisc/Hannibal, 1995, prod. Jerry Douglas) ♫♫♫ is a gorgeous version of the Lennon/McCartney staple "If I Fell."

what to avoid: *Just in Time* (Rounder, 1988, prod. Bela Fleck) ♫♫ didn't live up to O'Connell's potential in terms of either song selection or the quality of her singing.

influences:
◀◀ Linda Ronstadt, New Grass Revival

Peter Blackstock

MARK O'CONNOR

Born August 5, 1961, in Seattle, WA.

Few musicians have done as much to blur the lines between what is perceived as high and low art as has Mark O'Connor. A child prodigy on the fiddle, O'Connor is also master of the mandolin, guitar and other instruments, and he has used them to play bluegrass, country, jazz, rock, fusion, classical and all kinds of music in between. For years O'Connor was part of Nashville's A Team of session players, and his credit can be found on literally hundreds of recordings made during the last couple of decades. As a solo artist O'Connor has been responsible for bringing divergent constituencies together in the recording studio and the concert hall, and for breaking down barriers between genres. A noble cause, perhaps, but the results sound great, too.

what to buy: At once a celebration of the Music City's session scene and his declaration of independence from it, *The New Nashville Cats* (Warner Bros., 1991, prod. Mark O'Connor, Jim Ed Norman) ♫♫♫♫ marked O'Connor's "retirement" from playing sessions in favor of playing his own music. *Cats* features a stellar cast, including Vince Gill, Steve Wariner, Ricky Skaggs,

Bela Fleck and Marty Stuart, plus lots of other musicians whose names you might not recognize, but whose work you've heard hundreds of times. *Heroes* (Warner Bros., 1993, prod. Mark O'Connor) ♫♫♫♫ takes O'Connor's genre-busting mission to a higher level, bringing him together with his favorite players from across the musical spectrum, including Jean-Luc Ponty, Bill Monroe, L. Shankar, Pinchas Zukerman, Stephane Grappelli, Vassar Clements, Johnny Gimble and others. The music ranges from a playful "Ain't Misbehavin'" (with Grappelli) to a beautiful reading of "Ashokan Farewell" (with Zukerman) to a scorching treatment of Charlie Daniels' "The Devil Came Back to Georgia" (with Daniels, Travis Tritt, Marty Stuart and Johnny Cash).

what to buy next: For fans willing to dabble a little in classical music, look no further than *Appalachia Waltz* (Sony Classical, 1996, prod. Edgar Meyer, Mark O'Connor) ♫♫♫♫, a triumphant collaboration with world-class cellist Yo Yo Ma and noted composer/bassist Edgar Meyer. The album mixes Celtic and Texas fiddle traditions with classical music in ways that are accessible, yet instructive. O'Connor's title track is intoxicatingly beautiful. If you get past that, try *The Fiddle Concerto* (Warner Bros., 1995, prod. Mark O'Connor) ♫♫♫♫. After all, are there two words that bespeak a hybrid of different styles any more than fiddle and concerto?

what to avoid: The early recording *On the Rampage* (Rounder, 1979) ♫♫ is a lesser light in a largely stellar catalog.

the rest:
Markology (Rounder, 1978) ♫♫♫
Soppin' the Gravy (Rounder, 1979) ♫♫♫
False Dawn (Rounder, 1982) ♫♫♫
Stone from Which the Arch Was Made (Warner Bros., 1987) ♫♫♫
Retrospective (Rounder, 1987) ♫♫♫♫
Elysian Forest (Warner Bros., 1988) ♫♫♫
On the Mark (Warner Bros., 1989) ♫♫♫
The Championship Years (Country Music Foundation, 1990) ♫♫♫

influences:
◀◀ Benny Thomasson, Vassar Clements, L. Shankar, Johnny Gimble, Stephane Grappelli

▶▶ Rob Hajacos, Chris Thile, Luke & Jenny Anne Bulla, Kenny Kosek

Daniel Durchholz

MOLLY O'DAY

Born July 9, 1923, in McVeigh, KY. Died December 5, 1987, in Huntington, WV.

Molly O'Day's legend is based on 36 songs recorded for Columbia between 1946 and 1951, when she renounced a successful recording and performing career to devote her life to her faith. With her powerful, evocative and sincere vocal style, she excelled at sentimental ballads and traditional songs of Appalachia. O'Day was an early interpreter of Hank Williams' work and recorded the most popular version of the classic "Tramp on the Street," along with many other old time and gospel standards, a few of which have entered the bluegrass repertoire as standards, including "The Drunken Driver," "At the First Fall of Snow," "Matthew Twenty Four," "Too Late, Too Late," "The Evening Train," "Poor Ellen Smith," and "Teardrops Falling in the Snow." After her last Columbia session in 1951, she vowed never to perform in public outside church again, although she and husband and performing partner Lynn Davis maintained a radio ministry for many years.

what's available: *Molly O'Day & the Cumberland Mountain Folks* (Bear Family, 1992, prod. Art Satherly) 𝄢𝄢𝄢𝄢 contains all 36 songs recorded for Columbia. Definitive.

influences:
◀◀ Lulubelle & Scotty, Lilly May Ledford
▶▶ Hazel Dickens, Laurie Lewis

Randy Pitts

JAMIE O'HARA

See: Kieran Kane

THE O'KANES

See: Kieran Kane

OLD & IN THE WAY

See: Grateful Dead

THE OLD 97'S

Formed 1993, in Dallas, TX.

Rhett Miller, vocals, guitar; Ken Bethea, guitar; Murry Hammond, bass, vocals; Philip Peeples, drums.

One of the leading lights of latterday insurgent country, the Old 97's take their name from the railroad ballad "Wreck of the Old 97," and their attitude from the punk bands in which they individually earned their spurs.

what's available: Much of *Wreck Your Life* (Bloodshot, 1995, prod. Chuck Uchida) 𝄢𝄢𝄢 could pass for rockabilly, with plenty of rough edges left in to keep things honest—not for nothing do the 97's call it "honky-skronk." Don Walser and Mekon/Waco Brother Jon Langford put in cameo appearances, and the track list encompasses overdrive covers of everybody from Bing Crosby ("You Belong to My Heart") to Bill Monroe ("My Sweet Blue-Eyed Darlin'"). More than promising.

influences:
◀◀ Gram Parsons, Uncle Tupelo, Beat Farmers, Jason & the Scorchers

David Menconi

ONE RIOT ONE RANGER

Formed 1990, in Columbus, OH.

Mark Wyatt, vocals, accordion, bass; Pete Remenyi, vocals, dobro, harmonica, bass; Chas Williams, vocals, fiddle, mandolin (1992–present); Carl Yaffey, banjo, bass (1994–present); Mark Gaskill, vocals, guitar (1994–present); Elizabeth Lewis, vocals, guitar (1990–93); Jack Shortlidge, vocals, guitar, mandolin (1990–92); Lance Cummins, bass, mandolin (1990–92); Bruce Dadisman, bass, mandolin (1992–94); Hank McCoy, vocals, guitar (1992–94).

After the break-up of his "garage-folk" group Great Plains in 1989, Mark Wyatt found himself left with an inexplicable urge to pick some bluegrass—odd, one might think, for a man hitherto known as one of the instigators behind the Columbus punk-rock scene. However, aided and abetted by dobro/harmonica whiz Pete Remenyi and musician/folklorist Jack Shortlidge, One Riot One Ranger soon began molding together their own particular brand of "faux Cowboy" music, early sets boldly mixing Roky Erickson and Duke Ellington with Ralph Stanley and Jim & Jesse. With the addition of multi-instrumentalist (and condominium lawyer by day) Chas Williams, the band now had a prolific composer in their ranks (his haunting "Adios My Amigo" appears in the motion picture *Snakes and Arrows*), helping the quintet win a Best Country Band honor at the Columbus Music Awards that same year.

what's available: *Faces Made for Radio* (Fundamental, 1996, prod. John Sherman) 𝄢𝄢𝄢, with its refreshingly non-hotdogging, vocal-heavy blend of the traditional ("Tennessee Coot") and not-so-traditional (a superb reading of rock band Pere Ubu's "Cloud 149"), not to mention many delightful originals by

Roy Orbison **(AP/Wide World Photos)**

Williams, assuredly continues the band's quest to "bring acoustic country and bluegrass to audiences that ordinarily wouldn't touch the stuff." Mission accomplished.

influences:

⏮ Louvin Brothers, Highwoods String Band, Roky Erickson

Gary Pig Gold

ROY ORBISON

Born April 23, 1936, in Vernon, TX. Died December 6, 1988, in Hendersonville, TN.

Perhaps the greatest pure singer that rock 'n' roll has produced, Roy Orbison brought an unsurpassed sense of melodrama and angst to the music that has had a huge influence on other performers. A native of Texas, Orbison began singing country and rockabilly music but found that the styles weren't particularly suited to his tremendous tenor voice, which seemed to have no upper limit. He recorded for Sun Records during the 1950s and then RCA, but he didn't achieve fame until he signed with Monument in 1960 and began working with

producer Fred Foster. Together they made records that were miniature pop operas—"Only the Lonely (Know How I Feel)," "Running Scared," "Crying" et al. He also recorded for MGM, Mercury, Elektra and Virgin. Orbison's 1987 induction into the Rock and Roll Hall of Fame—as well as membership in the superstar group the Traveling Wilburys (with Bob Dylan, George Harrison, Tom Petty and Jeff Lynne)—helped spark a career revival. He was finishing *Mystery Girl*, his first album of new material in a decade, when he died at his Tennessee home.

what to buy: Take your choice among three worthwhile anthologies. *The Legendary Roy Orbison* (CBS Special Products, 1990, prod. various) 𝄞𝄞𝄞𝄞 is a three-disc box set that outshines all other Orbison collections, but *For the Lonely: A Roy Orbison Anthology, 1956–1964* (Rhino, 1988, prod. Fred Foster, Sam Phillips) 𝄞𝄞𝄞𝄞 or *The All-Time Greatest Hits of Roy Orbison* (Monument, 1972, prod. Fred Foster) 𝄞𝄞𝄞 will do just fine as a starter set.

what to buy next: *Roy Orbison and Friends: A Black and White Night Live* (Virgin, 1989, prod. T-Bone Burnett) 𝄞𝄞𝄞 is an excellent concert document recorded for an HBO film and featuring guest performances by Bruce Springsteen, k.d. lang and others. *Mystery Girl* (Virgin, 1989, prod. various) 𝄞𝄞𝄞 shows how other performers, such as U2's Bono and the Electric Light Orchestra's Jeff Lynne, viewed Orbison's music.

what to avoid: *The RCA Days* (RCA, 1988, prod. Chet Atkins) 𝄞𝄞 and *Little Richard/Roy Orbison* (RCA, 1990, prod. Chet Atkins) 𝄞𝄞 cull material from Orbison's time with RCA in Nashville, among the least successful recordings (artistically and commercially) of his career. And if you buy *In Dreams: The Greatest Hits* (Virgin, 1987, prod. T-Bone Burnett) 𝄞𝄞𝄞, know what you're getting: these are re-recordings of Orbison's big songs, inspired by a new version of "In Dreams" for the film *Blue Velvet*. They're quite good as these things go, but they're not the originals.

the rest:

The All-Time Greatest Hits of Roy Orbison, Volume 1 (Monument, 1973/1988) 𝄞𝄞𝄞𝄞

Laminar Flow (Elektra, 1979) 𝄞𝄞

(With Johnny Cash, Carl Perkins and Jerry Lee Lewis) *Class of '55* (America/Smash, 1986) 𝄞𝄞𝄞

Interviews from the Class of '55 Recording Sessions (America/Smash, 1986) 𝄞𝄞

(With the Traveling Wilburys) *Traveling Wilburys Volume 1* (Warner Bros., 1988) 𝄞𝄞𝄞

For the Lonely: 18 Greatest Hits (Rhino, 1988) 𝄞𝄞𝄞𝄞

The Sun Years (Rhino, 1989) 𝄞𝄞𝄞

The Classic Roy Orbison (1965–1968) (Rhino, 1989) 🎵🎵🎵
King of Hearts (Virgin, 1992) 🎵🎵🎵
The Very Best of Roy Orbison (Virgin, 1997) 🎵🎵🎵🎵

worth searching for: *The Sun Story* (Rhino, 1987) 🎵🎵🎵🎵 is a sampler of Sun's glory days that prominently features early Orbison hits such as "Ooby Dooby" and "Devil Doll."

influences:
⏪ Elvis Presley, Hank Williams
⏩ Mavericks, Ray Vega

Brian Mansfield

ORION

Born Jimmy Ellis, 1945, in Orrville, AL.

In a most unsettling case of life-imitating-art-imitating-the-King, author Gail Brewer-Giorgio received a phone call in 1978 from a man claiming to be the living, breathing embodiment of the hero of her just-published novel *Orion,* the story of the life and fake death of an internationally famous singing star. Sound vaguely familiar? Although the caller, whose real name was Jimmy Ellis, had been working the nether regions of the music business since 1964 (including, at one point, re-recording Elvis Presley's first-ever single), it wasn't until he'd assumed the identity of Brewer-Giorgio's mythical character that his career too, ironically, showed signs of life. Signed to (you guessed it, Elvis' first label) Sun in 1978, his voice was clandestinely overdubbed onto a series of Jerry Lee Lewis, Carl Perkins and Charlie Rich outtakes for the *Duets* and *Trio Plus* compilations, and an electronic duet with Lewis on "Cold, Cold Heart" actually charted in 1979. That same year Orion appeared—dressed as a ghostly Elvis-like apparition, face masked, rising from a coffin—on his first "solo" LP, *Reborn.* And in one of *Cashbox* magazine's greatest-ever lapses of taste, he was voted one of the world's three most promising country male vocalists in 1980. Several more albums followed before Ellis, understandably beginning to tire of the whole farce, tore off his mask in 1983 and, just to make sure everyone was listening, released a song entitled "I'm Trying Not to Sound Like Elvis." Problem was, nobody *was* listening: by then, the already booming Cult of Elvis had many more colorful and outrageous characters to concern itself with, relegating Ellis once again into well-earned obscurity. In 1989, however, he reappeared on the tiny Aron label with the optimistically titled *New Beginnings* and, having apparently resigned himself to his fate, once again donned his mask, capes and dry-ice machine en route to the Rock 'n' Roll Heaven circuit.

what's available: Surprisingly enough, not one of Orion's seven original (gold vinyl!) LPs are in print, though true connoisseurs of musical necrophilia are directed towards the import-only compilation *Some Think He Might Be King Elvis* (Bear Family, 1992, prod. various) **WOOF!** Then again, some once thought similarly of Billy Ray Cyrus.

influences:
⏪ Ryder Preston, Conrad Birdie
⏩ El Vez, Janice K.

Gary Pig Gold

ORRALL & WRIGHT
/ROBERT ELLIS ORRALL
/CURTIS WRIGHT

Vocal duo formed 1993, in Nashville, TN. Disbanded 1995.

Robert Ellis Orrall (born May 4, 1955, in Winthrop, MA); Curtis Wright (born June 6, 1955, in Huntington, PA).

Robert Ellis Orrall and Curtis Wright wrote together so much that they inevitably had to record an album together. Wright had been a member of the Super Grit Cowboy Band and Cimarron. Orrall began his career as a pop singer/songwriter with the loosest of ties to New Wave (he even had a Top 40 hit called "I Couldn't Say No" with Carlene Carter in 1983). After they started co-writing in 1988, Orrall & Wright had hits with Clay Walker ("What's It to You"), Shenandoah ("Next to You, Next to Me") and others, either separately or together. They recorded one album together at the suggestion of Giant Records Nashville-head-James Stroud, but it didn't take.

what's available: *Orrall & Wright* (Giant, 1994, prod. Lynn Peterzell, Robert Ellis Orrall, Curtis Wright) 🎵🎵 is a typical songwriters-turned-artist album: plenty of tightly crafted tunes with hummable choruses but not a lot of personality, not even as much as these two have shown solo.

worth searching for: Both Wright and Orrall recorded solo albums in Nashville before pairing up. Frankly, they're both better than the duo album, but neither is in print. *Curtis Wright* (Liberty, 1992, prod. James Stroud, Lynn Peterzell) 🎵🎵🎵 didn't do much on its own, but it's become a motherlode of material for other singers. Clay Walker turned "What's It to You" into a #1 hit; "Phonographic Memory" and "If I Ever Love Again" also have been covered. Robert Ellis Orrall's *Flying Colors* (RCA, 1993, prod. Steve Marcantonio, Robert Ellis Orrall, Josh Leo) 🎵🎵🎵 gave Orrall two Top 40 singles, "Boom! It Was Over" and "A

Little Bit of Her Love." "I Couldn't Say No," Orrall's pop hit with Carlene Carter can be found on a vinyl Orrall EP titled *Special Pain* (RCA, 1983, prod. Roger Bechirian) ♪♪♪.

influences:

◀◀ Restless Heart, Cimarron

▶▶ Archer/Park, Clay Walker

Brian Mansfield

ROBERT ELLIS ORRALL

See: Orrall & Wright

THE OSBORNE BROTHERS

Formed 1953.

Bobby Osborne (born December 7, 1931, in Hyden, KY), mandolin, vocals; Sonny Osborne (born October 29, 1937, in Hyden, KY), banjo, vocals.

One of the few bluegrass acts to have a mainstream country following, Bobby and Sonny Osborne's progressive approach to their music—they used electric guitar, pedal steel, drums, even strings when it suited their purposes—brought them a number of radio hits during the late 1960s and early 1970s. Before the group formed in 1953 Bobby had played with the Lonesome Pine Fiddlers while Sonny had backed Bill Monroe and Jimmy Martin. Now together, the brothers went after any audience they could find: They joined the Grand Ole Opry in 1964, but also frequented college campuses and folk festivals. The duo's widespread appeal even brought them the Country Music Association's award for vocal group of the year in 1971.

Since leaving Decca, where they had most of their hits, for independent labels, the Osborne Brothers' music has grown more traditional. It's still not without its surprises, though; the group has recorded albums of songs associated with songwriters Felice and Boudleaux Bryant (1977's *From Rock Top to Muddy Bottom*) and Ernest Tubb (1995's *The Ernest Tubb Song Folio Volume 1*). The roster has changed frequently behind the two brothers; some of the more prominent members of their backup band have included Bennie Birchfield, Ronnie Reno, Gene Wooten and Bobby Osborne Jr.

what to buy: *The Best of the Osborne Brothers* (MCA, 1982) ♪♪♪♪ is a great collection of the group's recordings made during their peak commercial period, with all the hits: "Rocky Top," "Georgia Pineywoods," "Tennessee Hound Dog" and "The Kind

of Woman I Got." Even today, the Osborne's cross-pollination of bluegrass and electric country ideas sounds adventurous.

what to buy next: With most, if not all, of their Decca catalog out of print in the early 1990s, the Osbornes decided to revisit some of the songs they'd made during their stay at the label. *Once More Volumes I & II* (Sugar Hill, 1991, prod. Sonny Osborne) ♪♪♪♪ takes two albums issued separately and puts them on one CD with more than an hour of music. Singles like "Rocky Top" and "The Kind of Woman I Got" aren't here, but Osborne favorites like "My Favorite Memory," "I'll Be Alright Tomorrow" and "Blue Moon of Kentucky." The sound is more traditional, but this is still a fine, well-stocked collection.

the rest:

From Rocky Top to Muddy Bottom (CMH, 1977/1991) ♪♪♪♪
Bluegrass Collection (CMH, 1978/1989) ♪♪♪♪
The Osborne Brothers and Mac Wiseman (CMH, 1979/1987) ♪♪♪♪
I Can Hear Kentucky Calling Me (CMH, 1980) ♪♪♪
Once More, Volume 1 (Sugar Hill, 1986) ♪♪♪♪
Once More, Volume 2 (Sugar Hill, 1987) ♪♪♪♪
Singing, Shouting Praises (Sugar Hill, 1988) ♪♪♪
Hillbilly Fever (CMH, 1991) ♪♪♪
When the Roses Bloom in Dixieland (Pinecastle, 1994) ♪♪♪
Our Favorite Hymns (MCA, 1995) ♪♪♪
The Ernest Tubb Song Folio Volume 1 (Pinecastle, 1995) ♪♪♪♪
Greatest Bluegrass Hits Volume 1 (CMH, 1996) ♪♪♪♪
Country Bluegrass (MCA, 1996) ♪♪♪♪
Class of '96 (Pinecastle, 1996) ♪♪♪♪
Some Things I Want to Sing About (Sugar Hill) ♪♪♪♪
#1 (CMH) ♪♪♪♪
Bluegrass Concerto (CMH) ♪♪♪♪
Bobby and His Mandolin (CMH) ♪♪♪♪

worth searching for: The "Rocky Top '96" (Decca, 1996, remix prod. Scott Rouse) ♪♪♪ single contains the original 1968 version plus three remixes by Scott Rouse.

influences:

◀◀ Bill Monroe, Jimmy Martin

▶▶ New Grass Revival, Diamond Rio

Brian Mansfield

K.T. OSLIN

Born Kay Toinette Oslin, May 15, 1941, in Crossett, AR.

K.T. Oslin is the unlikeliest of country stars. She was well into her 40s when "80's Ladies" made her a star. She writes from a decidedly female point of view, and her characters are seldom waifs or mindless sex objects. Her extensive background in theater only partially explains her dramatic flair. Oslin is one of those singer-songwriters who's been around, and that "been there, done that" quality permeates her music. A Southern girl whose family moved around a lot after her father died when she was five, Oslin majored in drama at a small Texas college while singing in a folk group with fellow Texan Guy Clark. She went on to sing in national touring productions of such musicals as *Hello, Dolly!* (with Carol Channing) before settling in New York City, where she appeared in a revival of *West Side Story* at Lincoln Center and a Broadway production of *Promises, Promises*. Oslin sang on commercial jingles and as a backup singer, for Clark among others, before she started writing about her own experiences. A short-lived deal with Elektra didn't discourage her, and she began to make a name for herself during the early 1980s, writing songs for Dottie West, Gail Davis and Judy Rodman. K.T. was discovered by Alabama's producer, Harold Shedd, and throttled country's good ol' boy network with "80's Ladies," the first of several hits she had from the late 1980s to the early 1990s. Oslin's fortunes have cooled in recent years, but she's still capable of making potent music that talks about life from the vantage point of one who's lived it.

what to buy: *Love in a Small Town* (RCA, 1990, prod. Harold Shedd) 🎸🎸🎸🎸 isn't exactly a concept album, but its colorful songs conjure up vivid images of real people struggling with life and love, from the lovestruck heroine of "Cornell Crawford" to the determined woman of "Come Next Monday," one of Oslin's biggest hits.

what to buy next: Leave it to the ever provocative (and sexy) Oslin to title her hits album *Greatest Hits: Songs from an Aging Sex Bomb* (RCA, 1993, prod. various) 🎸🎸🎸. But it's an apt title, given her proclivity for frankness and drama. The collection includes her biggest hits, such as "80's Ladies" (a Grammy winner) and "Come Next Monday," and some new songs produced by Glen Ballard, who co-produced rocker Alanis Morissette's mega-selling *Jagged Little Pill* debut.

what to avoid: *My Roots Are Showing* (BNA, 1996, prod. Rick Will, K.T. Oslin) 🎸🎸, which, with its covers of material by writers ranging from the Louvin Brothers to Irving Berlin to Richard Thompson, lacks the bite of her earlier work.

the rest:
80's Ladies (RCA, 1987) 🎸🎸🎸

worth searching for: Inexplicably, RCA has deleted her second album, *This Woman* (RCA, 1988, prod. Harold Shedd) 🎸🎸🎸, from

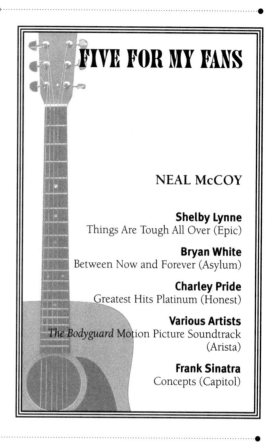

FIVE FOR MY FANS

NEAL McCOY

Shelby Lynne
Things Are Tough All Over (Epic)

Bryan White
Between Now and Forever (Asylum)

Charley Pride
Greatest Hits Platinum (Honest)

Various Artists
The Bodyguard Motion Picture Soundtrack
(Arista)

Frank Sinatra
Concepts (Capitol)

its catalog, despite the fact that it went platinum, produced five hits (including "Hold Me") and figured into two Grammys.

influences:
◀◀ Patsy Cline, Tammy Wynette
▶▶ Pam Tillis

Doug Pullen

MARIE OSMOND

Born October 13, 1959, in Ogden, UT.

Marie Osmond wasn't kidding when she sang "I'm a little bit country" every week on that 1970s television staple *The Donny & Marie Show*. When her career took off again during the mid-1980s, Osmond proved she truly was just a "little" bit country. With her thin, rangeless voice, she was a fixture on mainstream country radio during 1985–86, had three #1 hits and was awarded a Country Music Association award for Vocal Duo of the Year for her duet with Dan Seals on the melodic "Meet Me in Montana." But with precious few exceptions, Osmond's repertoire was disposable pop lightly brushed with a fiddle or steel guitar. She did, however, attempt to revamp her 1970s goody-goody image; the cover of 1985's *There's No Stopping Your Heart* CD featured a demure Osmond dressed in a slinky, low-cut black dress with a slit up to there. She even dared to sing songs with titles like "Needing a Night Like This" and "Read My Lips." But that message, too, was inconsistent. After going through a tabloid-publicized divorce and life as a single mother—perfect fodder for country songs—Osmond couldn't muster any deeper emotions than 1986's "Cry Just a Little." Still, maybe there was something stronger buried underneath those frothy pipes. On the lovely, mandolin-laced ballad "I'll Be Faithful to You," an album cut from *There's No Stopping Your Heart*, Osmond manages to emote in all the right places. Perhaps that song was the inspiration for her impressive vocal turn as Maria Von Trapp in 1993's traveling production of *The Sound of Music*.

what to buy: Osmond's Curb debut, *There's No Stopping Your Heart* (Curb, 1985, prod. Paul Worley, Kyle Lehning) ♫♫♫, is her best collection of ear candy. All three hits—the title cut, "Meet Me in Montana" and "Read My Lips"—are pleasantly hummable. Also, her song selection was at its shrewdest: Deborah Allen's "Needing a Night Like This" and Holly Dunn's "That Old Devil Moon" have aged surprisingly well.

what to buy next: *The Best of Marie Osmond* (Curb, 1990, prod. various) ♫♫ seems the logical follow-up to *There's No Stopping Your Heart*. In addition to her major 1980s hits, it also includes the career-launching "Paper Roses"—about as close to real country as Osmond ever came—and the slightly entertaining "Like a Hurricane," one of two new songs recorded for this compilation.

what to avoid: Osmond's last two studio albums are particularly abysmal. *All in Love* (Curb, 1988, prod. Paul Worley, Ed Seay) ♫♫ is watered-down pop with nary a hint of country. Ditto for *Steppin' Stone* (Curb, 1989, prod. Jerry Crutchfield) ♫, although this one doesn't even have a memorable song to call a guilty pleasure.

the rest:
I Only Wanted You (Curb, 1986) ♫♫♫
25 Hits-Special Collection (Curb, 1995) ♫♫♫

worth searching for: For those that must relive the *Donny & Marie Show*, there's *Donny & Marie Osmond: Greatest Hits* (Curb, 1993, prod. Mike Curb) ♫♫, a collection of the toothy duo's Top 40 hits and a few more cheesy, over-orchestrated slices from their 1970s pop repertoire. A warning: One listen is enough to last another two decades.

influences:
◄◄ Brenda Lee, Petula Clark, Connie Francis
►► Faith Hill, Mindy McCready, Mila Mason

Mario Tarradell

PETER OSTROUSHKO

Born August 12, 1953, in Minneapolis, MN.

Peter Ostroushko is an eclectic multi-instrumentalist whose style includes traditional folk, bluegrass, Eastern music and Ukrainian folk tunes. He has toured with Robin & Linda Williams and Dakota Dave Hull. In 1974 he played on Bob Dylan's *Blood on the Tracks* and started a 12-year run on the syndicated *Prairie Home Companion* radio show, the last five as musical director. He has also performed with the Minnesota and Rochester Symphony Orchestras and the St. Paul Chamber Orchestra. Since 1989 he has toured with guitarist Dean Magraw.

what to buy: In *Buddies of Swing* (Red House, 1990, prod. Peter Ostroushko) ♫♫♫♫, Ostroushko leads an all-star group—including Jethro Burns on mandolin and Johnny Gimble on fiddle—through original and traditional tunes, with a little George Gershwin and Fats Waller thrown in.

what to buy next: *Peter Ostroushko Presents the Mando Boys* (Red House, 1986, prod. Peter Ostroushko, Marge Friedrich Ostroushko) ♫♫♫♫ is a sparkling collection of tunes arranged for mandolin quartet that ranges from solemn fugues to fiery breakdowns.

what to avoid: *First Generation* (Flying Fish, 1986) ♫♫, a comic operetta featuring Bertram Levy, is closer to Gilbert & Sullivan than to Homer & Jethro.

the rest:
Blue Mesa (Red House, 1989) ♫♫♫♫
(With Dean Magraw) *Duo* (Red House, 1991) ♫♫♫
Heart of the Heartland (Red House, 1995) ♫♫♫

worth searching for: The early albums *Down the Streets of My Old Neighborhood* (Rounder, 1987) ♫♫♫ and *Slüz Düz Music* (Rounder, 1985) ♫♫♫ are rare treats, lessons in how to mix bluegrass, Dixieland and folk with some bone-dry humor.

influences:

◀◀ Bill Monroe, David Grisman

▶▶ Michael Hedges, Sam Bush

Bob Cannon

THE OUTLAWS

Formed 1974, in Tampa, FL. Disbanded 1995.

Hughie Thomasson, guitar; Billy Jones (died 1995), guitar (1974–81); Henry Paul, rhythm guitar, vocals (1974–77, 1983–86); Monte Yoho, drums (1974–80); Frank O'Keefe (died 1995), bass (1974–77); Harvey Arnold, bass (1977–79); Freddy Salem, guitar (1978–79); David Dix, drums (1977–95); Rick Cua, bass (1979); Chris Hicks, guitar (1983–95); Jeff Howell, drums (1983–95); Barry Borden, bass (1983–95); Timothy Cake, guitar, vocals.

One of the last of the Southern boogie bands to get a record deal during the early 1970s, the Outlaws often appeared to exist because Southern deejays could program only so much Lynyrd Skynyrd and Marshall Tucker. They developed a good reputation for their live, three-guitar jams, which could go on for 20 minutes, but 1975's "There Goes Another Love Song" would be their only original Top 40 rock hit. Eventually the group became a stopping point for musicians who wanted Southern rock credentials, and some Outlaws alumni went on to respectable careers: bassist Rick Cua became a contemporary Christian artist, and Henry Paul formed the platinum-selling country band BlackHawk. Thomasson now plays guitar with Lynyrd Skynyrd.

what to buy: Though many of their songs topped six minutes, the Outlaws were basically a singles band for Southern AOR radio, so *Greatest Hits of the Outlaws: High Tides Forever* (Arista, 1982, prod. various) ♪♪♪ adequately represents the band's output. Only eight tracks long, "High Tides Forever" still captures the Outlaws' best stuff—"There Goes Another Love Song," the "Free Bird"-wannabe "Green Grass & High Tides" and a live rendition of "(Ghost) Riders in the Sky."

what to buy next: The Outlaws were a fairly consistent band, at least until relegated to the Southern-rock oldies circuit, so any album's as good as another. But the best is probably *Outlaws* (Arista, 1975, prod. Paul Rothchild) ♪♪♪, recorded when the group still seemed like it might develop into something more than just another boogie band.

what to avoid: *Hittin' the Road—Live!* (Blues Bureau, 1993, prod. Mickey Mulcahy, Hughie Thomasson) ♪♪ is retread

Southern rock only for those needing a memento of their redneck youth.

the rest:

Lady in Waiting (Arista, 1976) ♪♪♪
Hurry Sundown (Arista/Collector's Pipeline, 1977) ♪♪♪
Playin' to Win (Arista, 1978) ♪♪♪
Bring It Back Alive (Arista, 1978) ♪♪♪
In the Eye of the Storm (Stodys, 1979) ♪♪
Ghost Riders in the Sky (Arista/Collector's Pipeline, 1980/1994) ♪♪♪
Los Hombres Malo (Arista, 1982) ♪♪
Soldiers of Fortune (Pasha, 1986) ♪♪

solo outings:

Henry Paul:
Grey Ghost (Atlantic, 1979) ♪♪
Feel the Heat (Atlantic, 1980) ♪♪
Anytime (Atlantic, 1981) ♪♪

influences:

◀◀ Poco, Eagles, Allman Brothers Band

▶▶ Henry Paul Band, BlackHawk, John Michael Montgomery

see also: *BlackHawk*

Brian Mansfield

PAUL OVERSTREET

Born March 17, 1956, in Newton, MS.

Paul Overstreet first dreamed of country stardom when he saw George Hamilton playing Hank Williams in the film *Your Cheatin' Heart.* He moved to Nashville in 1973 and released his first record, "Keep It in Mind," under the name Paul Overtone on the tiny Artistry label. He first tasted success as the writer of such songs as "On the Other Hand," "Forever and Ever Amen," "Deeper than the Holler" and "No Place Like Home" for Randy Travis. His success with Travis and other artists like the Judds ("Love Can Build a Bridge") and Keith Whitley ("When You Say Nothing at All," later recorded by Alison Krauss as well) led to his being named BMI's Songwriter of the Year for five consecutive years between 1987–91. "Forever and Ever Amen" won the Country Music Association's and Academy of Country Music's Song of the Year awards. As a performer, Overstreet first was part of the songwriter trio Schuyler, Knobloch & Overstreet (aka S-K-O), but went solo in 1987. He recorded for RCA from 1986–93 and his releases included the 1991 #1 "Daddy's Come Around." After leaving RCA, Overstreet focused on the Christian music market where he has won awards from the Gospel Music Association and the Christian Country Music Association.

what to buy: Overstreet shows that a songwriter is as good as his lyrics in *Best of Paul Overstreet* (RCA, 1994, prod. James Stroud, Brown Bannister, Paul Overstreet) ♫♫♫, and his voice is as explicit as his beliefs. Overstreet hit pay dirt by following the straight and narrow during the late 1980s and early 1990s with such songs as "Seein' My Father in Me," "Heroes" and "Daddy's Come Around," all contained here.

the rest:
Time (Scarlet Moon, 1996) ♫♫♫

worth searching for: Overstreet portrays day-to-day life, God, marriage and his values on the uplifting *Sowin' Love* (RCA, 1989, James Stroud) ♫♫♫, which includes the singles "Love Helps Those," "All the Fun," "Seein' My Father in Me," "Richest Man on Earth" and "Sowin' Love." *Heroes* (RCA, 1990, prod. Brown Bannister, Paul Overstreet) ♫♫♫ contains some of Overstreet's stronger writing and his only #1, "Daddy's Come Around," in which the lead character learns that he doesn't need to run around when he has good love at home. Overstreet turned "Billy Can't Read" into a public-service campaign against illiteracy.

influences:
◀◀ Randy Travis
▶▶ Ken Holloway, Skip Ewing

Denise Burgess

BUCK OWENS

Born Alvis Edgar Owens Jr., August 12, 1929, in Sherman, TX.

Such current Nashville industry catch-phrases as "twang-core" and "alternative country" could just as legitimately be applied in retrospect to the music and the attitude of Buck Owens & His Buckaroos. Owens was defiantly based in Bakersfield, California, throughout his 40-year career and, even at the height of his mid-1960s successes, never failed to assail the powers-that-be in Nashville for their narrow-mindedness. Owens and his band developed, perfected, then took around the world the highly characteristic honky-tonking, hard-country sound that to this day can be heard reverberating throughout "modern" C&W. For years remembered, if at all, as little more than the goobering co-star of television's *Hee Haw* series, the innovative Owens and his band are finally being fully appreciated.

At an early age the poor but music-obsessed Owens was play-

ing guitar and mandolin on local radio shows. But when his family relocated to Bakersfield in 1951 the young man began pursuing his passion with a vengeance. Soon after joining the Schoolhouse Playboys band he was not only fronting their act but also playing recording sessions with his newly acquired Fender Telecaster guitar—a revolutionary instrument for its time, especially in the hands of an innovator like Owens. It was one such session, for singer Tommy Collins, that led to Owens' own contract with Capitol in 1957, an association that didn't really begin bearing fruit until several years later. By then, having assembled (with musical right-hand man Don Rich) his first crack outfit of Buckaroos, Owens was ready to fully capitalize upon the hits that finally started coming during the early 1960s: 15 consecutive country #1 songs between 1963 and 1967, not to mention hit duets with Rose Maddox (during the early 1960s), Susan Raye (late 1960s) and Emmylou Harris (1979). Under the supervision of producer Ken Nelson, Owens and Rich's lyrically simple, musically focused and Telecaster-bright sound ensured that their records had sufficient punch on AM radio to take on all that the comparatively meek Music City releases had to offer. So pervasive was Owens' success in those years that Bakersfield was being called, grudgingly in some circles, Nashville West. Be it at Carnegie Hall, on the *Ed Sullivan Show* or at the Fillmore West, the Buckaroos' "Freight Train Sound" rolled on unchallenged until 1974, when a motorcycle accident claimed Rich, a loss from which the band, and Owens personally, never fully recovered.

Independently wealthy from his extensive business holdings, Owens made a few more half-hearted recordings for Warner Bros. during the mid-1970s and continued to ham it up with Roy Clark on *Hee Haw*, but he was clearly just going through the motions before eventually retiring in 1980. He was hardly heard from again for seven years, until Dwight Yoakam drew him back on stage, then into the studio for their 1988 hit duet on "Streets of Bakersfield." Owens then triumphantly re-signed with Capitol, re-recorded some old hits (including "Act Naturally" with Ringo Starr) and continues to proudly play the role of the undisputed, all-encompassing "Baron of Bakersfield." Long may he reign.

what to buy: They don't come much better than *The Buck Owens Collection, 1959–1990* (Rhino, 1992, comp. prod. James Austin) ♫♫♫♫, which is not only 62 of the man's greatest recordings, meticulously compiled and annotated with the assistance of Owens himself, but also an absolute honky-tonk music primer. In a word—essential.

what to buy next: *The Instrumental Hits of Buck Owens & His Buckaroos* (Capitol, 1965/Sundazed, 1995, prod. Ken Nelson) 𝄞𝄞𝄞 puts the spotlight not only on the ingenious Don Rich (guitars, fiddle) but the remainder of Buck's best-ever set of Buckaroos: Tom Brumley (steel guitar), Doyle Holly (bass) and Willie Cantu (drums). *Live at Carnegie Hall* (CMF, 1988, prod. Ken Nelson) 𝄞𝄞𝄞 is an expanded version of the original 1966 Capitol release which captured Bakersfield's finest, in all their Nudie-suited glory, sockin' it to 'em and at 'em at the corner of 57th and 7th.

what to avoid: A trio of skimpy collections—*All-Time Greatest Hits, Volume 1* (Curb, 1990) 𝄞𝄞; *All-Time Greatest Hits, Volume 2* (Curb, 1992) 𝄞𝄞; and *All-Time Greatest Hits, Volume 3* (Curb, 1993) 𝄞𝄞. Stick with the boxed set.

the rest:

Buck Owens (Capitol, 1961/Sundazed, 1995) 𝄞𝄞𝄞

You're for Me (Capitol, 1962/Sundazed, 1995) 𝄞𝄞𝄞

On the Bandstand (Capitol, 1963/Sundazed, 1995) 𝄞𝄞𝄞

Together Again/My Heart Skips a Beat (Capitol, 1964/Sundazed, 1995) 𝄞𝄞𝄞𝄞

I Don't Care (Capitol, 1964/Sundazed, 1995) 𝄞𝄞𝄞𝄞

I've Got a Tiger by the Tail (Capitol, 1965/Sundazed, 1995) 𝄞𝄞𝄞𝄞

Before You Go/No One but You (Capitol, 1965/Sundazed, 1995) 𝄞𝄞𝄞

Christmas with Buck Owens (Capitol, 1965/Curb, 1990) 𝄞𝄞

Roll out the Red Carpet (Capitol, 1966/Sundazed, 1995) 𝄞𝄞𝄞

Open up Your Heart (Capitol, 1966/Sundazed, 1995) 𝄞𝄞𝄞𝄞

The Very Best of Buck Owens, Volume 1 (Rhino, 1994) 𝄞𝄞𝄞𝄞

The Very Best of Buck Owens, Volume 2 (Rhino, 1994) 𝄞𝄞𝄞𝄞

Half a Buck: Greatest Duets (K-Tel, 1996) 𝄞𝄞𝄞

worth searching for: Owens' initial, pre-Buckaroo recordings for the tiny Pep and Chesterfield labels, including the searing rockabilly single "Hot Dog/Rhythm and Booze" from 1956 (released under the alias Corky Jones) are sporadically available on several semi-legitimate releases, the best of which is *You're for Me* (Creative Sounds, 1990) 𝄞𝄞𝄞.

influences:

◀◀ Bob Wills, Chuck Berry

▶▶ John Fogerty, Dwight Yoakam

Gary Pig Gold

THE OZARK MOUNTAIN DAREDEVILS

Formed 1971, in Springfield, MO.

Buck Owens **(Archive Photos)**

John Dillon, vocals, guitar, fiddle, mouthbow, mandolin, autoharp, dulcimer; Steve Cash, vocals, harmonica; Michael "Supe" Granda, vocals, bass; Randle Chowning, vocals, guitar, harmonica (1971–76); Buddy Brayfield, vocals, keyboards (1971–77); Larry Lee, vocals, drums, guitar, saw; Rune Walle, guitar, banjo (1977–78); Jerry Mills, mandolin (1977–78); Ruell Chappell, keyboards, vocals (1977–78); Steve Canaday, guitar, drums, vocals (1977–78).

The Ozark Mountain Daredevils started out as a group of Midwestern hippie pickers who drew on mountain music, country rock, and Southern boogie, but evolved into a pretty slick pop outfit before they were through. The group's two chart hits—"If You Wanna Get to Heaven" and "Jackie Blue"—couldn't be more dissimilar: "Heaven" is a choogling rocker with a countrified harmonica break; "Jackie Blue" is a lushly produced effort that actually bears some similarity to today's softer alternative rock. Somewhere in between lies the bulk of the group's material, mostly genial country-rock championing themes of love, nature and the country life. Ultimately, the group was too eclectic and too laid back for its own good, and its lineup proved too unstable. The Daredevils haven't recorded in almost a decade

and a half, yet they still tour with various musicians backing a core group of Steve Cash, John Dillon and Michael Granda.

what to buy: Weighing in at a mere 12 tracks, *The Best* (A&M, 1981, prod. Glyn Johns, David Anderle, David Kershenbaum) 𝄞𝄞𝄞 feels kinds of slight. But it contains both hits plus the pop ballad "You Know Like I Know" and the white-gospel tunes "Fly Away Home" and "You Made It Right." Too bad it's missing "Chicken Train," one of the group's most popular concert numbers.

the rest:

The Ozark Mountain Daredevils (A&M, 1973) 𝄞𝄞𝄞

worth searching for: They're probably pretty scarce in the used-LP bins by now, but the group's two best albums—*It'll Shine When It Shines* (A&M, 1974, prod. Glyn Johns, David Anderle) 𝄞𝄞𝄞𝄞 and *The Car over the Lake Album* (A&M, 1975, prod. David Anderle) 𝄞𝄞𝄞𝄞—show the band in top form. *Men from Earth* (A&M, 1976, prod. David Anderle) 𝄞𝄞𝄞 is worth finding just for the cover photograph of a pair of Missouri mule skinners—just about the scariest dudes you'll ever see.

influences:

◀◀ Allman Brothers Band, Lynyrd Skynyrd

▶▶ Travis Tritt

Daniel Durchholz

PATTI PAGE

Born Clara Ann Fowler, November 8, 1927, in Muskogee, OK.

Patti Page was the best-selling female singer of the 1950s and the kind of pop singer that rock 'n' rollers liked to think they saved the world from. But Page, who had grown up picking Oklahoma cotton with her 10 siblings, continued to appeal to more conservative country audiences long after she quit having pop hits. Page's watershed record was her version "Tennessee Waltz," a multi-million-selling crossover smash written by Western bandleader Pee Wee King and singer Redd Stewart. Page learned the song from a version by R&B trumpeter Erskine Hawkins, which shows something of the tune's across-the-board appeal. The song reached #2 on the country chart, though it topped the pop chart for 13 weeks. It has sold more than six million copies, exceeded only by Bing Crosby's "White

Christmas." Page didn't have another country hit for another 10 years (about the time she quite having pop hits), but after that she'd occasionally show up on the Top 40 all the way into 1981 with "No Aces."

what to buy: *Golden Hits* (Mercury, 1960/1994) 𝄞𝄞𝄞 contains the best of Page's pop hits, many of them featuring the double-track vocal technique she helped pioneer on songs like "Tennessee Waltz."

what to buy next: *Golden Hits* is by far the best single collection of Page's hits, but if you want to go deeper into her music, *The Patti Page Collection, Mercury Years, Volume 1* (Mercury, 1991) 𝄞𝄞𝄞 and *The Patti Page Collection, Mercury Years, Volume 2* (Mercury, 1991) 𝄞𝄞𝄞 have 20 songs each. *Volume 2* also tacks on three radio promotional spots from the 1950s.

what to avoid: Page has often re-recorded her material, and none of those sessions were as good as the originals. Deceptive remake packages include *16 Best of Patti Page* (Plantation, 1987) 𝄞; *16 Greatest Hits* (Plantation, 1987) 𝄞; and *Greatest Songs—Legendary Artist Series* (Curb, 1995) 𝄞𝄞, although the Plantation packages each contain a charting single or two recorded for that label during the early 1980s.

the rest:

Greatest Hits (Columbia) 𝄞𝄞

16 Most Requested Songs (Columbia/Legacy, 1989) 𝄞𝄞

Christmas with Patti Page (Mercury, 1995) 𝄞𝄞

Just a Closer Walk with Thee (Mercury, 1995) 𝄞𝄞

influences:

◀◀ Kay Starr, Jo Stafford, Dinah Shore

▶▶ Connie Francis, Anne Murray

Brian Mansfield

BILLY PARKER

Born July 19, 1937, in Okemah, OK.

Billy Parker has been a DJ for more than 25 years at KVOO in Tulsa, Oklahoma. He has won four Academy of Country Music awards and one Country Music Association award for Disc Jockey of the Year. As a performer, Parker, who had worked with Ernest Tubb, had a string of minor hits between 1976 and 1989 for such independent labels as SCR, Soundwaves and Canyon Creek. He is currently executive director of promotions and community affairs at KVOO.

what to buy: From its crying fiddles to its big-band sounds, *Swingin' with Bob* (Sims, 1996, prod. Russell Sims) 𝄞𝄞𝄞 is pure

Western swing. On his tribute to Bob Wills, Parker receives help from some great old-school musicians, including Tommy Allsup, Hargus "Pig" Robbins, Pete Wade and Buddy Spicher. Darrell McCall sings background vocals.

the rest:
I'll Speak Out for You, Jesus (Canyon Creek, 1991) 🎵🎵

worth searching for: *Billy Parker & Friends* (Bear Family, prod. Ray Ruff, Joe Gibson) 🎵🎵🎵, an album of duets, will please any traditional country-and-western fan. A former Texas Troubadour, Parker was trained by Ernest Tubb, who helps Parker out with "Tomorrow Never Comes," the next-to-last recording Tubb made before his death. Cal Smith, who goes back to Troubadour days with Parker, shares a song called "Too Many Irons in the Fire." Webb Pierce, Jack Greene and Johnnie Lee Wills also contribute to this project.

influences:
◀◀ Ernest Tubb, Bob Wills
▶▶ Gene Watson

Denise Burgess

CARYL MACK PARKER

Born February 12, in Abilene, TX.

After working the Portland, Oregon, music scene for a number of years (where she earned the Portland Music Association Songwriter of the Year accolade), Caryl Mack Parker and her musical partner, husband/guitarist Scott Parker, made the move to Nashville in 1994, where her strong sense of songcrafting and easy-on-the-ears vocals immediately brought her to the attention of Magnatone Records.

what's available: *Caryl Mack Parker* (Magnatone, 1996, prod. Caryl Mack Parker, Scott Parker, Brian David Willis, Christy DiNapoli) 🎵🎵🎵 contains the kind of strong melody and clever harmony that made the artist a West Coast favorite, typified by the single "Better Love Next Time" and the compelling album track "When I Come to My Senses."

worth searching for: While out West, Parker issued the independent release *Smoke and Mirrors*, which got a decent chunk of airplay in the Portland area.

influences:
◀◀ Karla Bonoff, Trisha Yearwood, Patty Loveless

David Simons

PARLOR JAMES

See: Amy Allison

DAVID PARMLEY, SCOTT VESTAL & CONTINENTAL DIVIDE /DAVID PARMLEY

Formed December 1994, in Nashville, TN.

David Parmley (born February 1, 1959, in Artesia, CA), guitar, lead vocals; Scott Vestal, banjo, vocals; Jimmy Bowen, mandolin, vocals; Mike Anglin, bass, vocals; Gail Rudisill, fiddle (1995); Aubrey Haynie, fiddle, mandolin (1995–96); Rickie Simpkins, fiddle, mandolin (1996–present).

Formed by young but veteran bluegrass pickers David Parmley (Bluegrass Cardinals) and Scott Vestal (Larry Sparks, Doyle Lawson & Quicksilver, Livewire), Continental Divide hit the ground running. Within the band's first twelve months, it had played many of the major bluegrass festivals, seen a single from its debut album go to the top of the bluegrass charts and capped the year by being named Emerging Artist of the Year by the International Bluegrass Music Association in 1995. The band's sound, which relies heavily on country-flavored ballads, has been described by Parmley as "traditional roots with a 1990s approach."

Prior to forming Continental Divide, Parmley was the lead singer/guitarist for the popular band the Bluegrass Cardinals, from the band's founding during the mid-1970s until 1993, when he left to pursue a solo career. Although Parmley made his solo debut in 1989 with *I Know a Good Thing*, his discography with the Bluegrass Cardinals has included albums on Briar, Rounder, CMH, Sugar Hill and BGC.

what's available: *David Parmley, Scott Vestal & Continental Divide* (Pinecastle, 1995, prod. David Parmley, Scott Vestal) 🎵🎵🎵 launched the band in fine fashion, with "Wing and a Prayer" topping the national bluegrass charts. The Vestal-penned instrumental "Benny Hill" displays the band's formidable bluegrass chops, but most of the focus here is on the group's smooth vocal sound. *On The Divide* (Pinecastle, 1996, prod. David Parmley, Scott Vestal) 🎵🎵🎵 showcases the band's winning country/bluegrass fusion on "New Tin Roof" and "On the Divide Tonight." A solid cover of Flatt & Scruggs' "I've Lost You" and the memorable instrumental "Andersonville March" keep the album anchored to traditional bluegrass.

Lee Roy Parnell (© Ken Settle)

solo outings:

David Parmley:
I Know a Good Thing (Sugar Hill, 1989) 🎵🎵🎵

influences:
◄◄ Bluegrass Cardinals, Alison Krauss & Union Station
►► IIIrd Tyme Out, Lonesome River Band

Jon Hartley Fox

LEE ROY PARNELL

Born December 21, 1956, in Abilene, TX.

Raised on a ranch in Stephenville, Texas, Lee Roy Parnell made his singing debut at the age of seven on a Fort Worth radio station, singing "San Antonio Rose" with the legendary Bob Wills, a friend of his father. After high school, he moved to Austin, where he played at honky-tonks like the Broken Spoke and, for awhile, was one of Kinky Friedman's Texas Jewboys. Several years later Parnell transferred to Nashville, where he got a publishing deal in six months and later was signed to Arista Records after label executive Tim DuBois heard him at Nashville's Blue-

bird Cafe. Nominated in 1996 for a Grammy for "Cat Walk," an instrumental collaboration with Flaco Jimenez, Parnell was also the first artist on Arista's spinoff label, Career Records.

what to buy: Country-soul numbers like "Hearts Desire," "A Little Bit of You" and "We All Get Lucky Sometimes," plus tasty numbers like the rousing "If the House Is Rockin'" and the gentle ballad "Saved by the Grace of Your Love," made *We All Get Lucky Sometimes* (Career, 1995, prod. Scott Hendricks, Lee Roy Parnell) 🎵🎵🎵🎵 Parnell's best yet.

what to buy next: *Lee Roy Parnell* (Arista, 1990, prod. Barry Beckett) 🎵🎵🎵🎵 mixes country, rock, Texas soul and R&B, plus horns. All this and whaddya get? No radio airplay. Still, Parnell's debut is well worth having, especially for cuts like "There Oughta Be a Law" and "Mexican Money."

the rest:
Love without Mercy (Arista, 1992) 🎵🎵🎵
On the Road (Arista, 1993) 🎵🎵🎵
Every Night's a Saturday Night (Career, 1997) 🎵🎵🎵

influences:
◄◄ Delbert McClinton
►► Stephen Bruton

Bill Hobbs

GENE PARSONS

Born September 4, 1944, in Los Angeles, CA.

Prior to joining the Byrds in 1969, Gene Parsons (no relation to Gram, another Byrd) was a member of the Castaways ("Liar, Liar") and Nashville West, arguably the first country-rock band in the United States. In addition to having played drums with the Byrds, Parsons also plays guitar and killer bluegrass banjo. What's more, he was blessed with an amazingly powerful voice and masterful songwriting skills; his "Gunga Din" and "Yesterday's Train" are absolutely brilliant. When the Byrds disbanded in 1973, Parsons returned to his bluegrass roots with *Kindling*. In 1975 he hooked up with a revamped Flying Burrito Brothers, recording two abysmal albums for Columbia (*Flying Again* and *Airborne*) before packing it in. In 1979 Parsons recorded *Melodies*, and in 1988 he teamed up with Meridian Green, daughter of folk legend Bob Gibson, to record *Birds of a Feather*.

what to buy: *The Kindling Collection* (Sierra, 1994, comp. John Delgatto) 🎵🎵🎵🎵 represents the perfect anthology of Parsons' career. It features Parsons' best work with the Byrds, including "Gunga Din," "Yesterday's Train" and the sizzling instrumental

"Nashville West," as well as the only good tunes on the Burritos disasters'—Parsons' own "Wind and Rain," "Sweet Desert Childhood" and "Out of Control," and a poignant version of songwriter Nickey Barclay's "Northbound Bus." *Collection* also features the entire *Kindling* album, originally released by Warner Bros. in 1973. Among the stellar musicians lending support to this gem are Vassar Clements, Ralph Stanley, Little Feat's Bill Payne and the late, great Clarence White—Parsons' Byrds-bandmate and best friend. *Melodies* (Sierra, 1979/1992, prod. Gene Parsons) ♫♫♫ features a bouncy version of Bob Nolan's "Way Out There" and a moving tribute to White titled "Melodies from a Bird in Flight."

what to buy next: *Birds of a Feather* (Sierra, 1988/1992, prod. Gene Parsons) ♫♫♫ was recorded with Meridian Green and features a breathtaking version of 1960s British folksinger Donovan's chestnut "Catch the Wind."

influences:

◀◀ Stanley Brothers, Flatt & Scruggs, Buck Owens

▶▶ Vidalias, Wilco

see also: *Byrds, Flying Burrito Brothers*

Rick Petreycik

GRAM PARSONS

Born Cecil Ingram Connor, November 5, 1946, in Winterhaven, FL. Died September 19, 1973, in Joshua Tree, CA.

A Harvard dropout who played with both the Byrds and the Flying Burrito Brothers before going solo, Parsons gave rock 'n' roll a country martyr it could claim as its own. Parsons serves much the same function for 1990s "alternative country" acts such as Son Volt and the Jayhawks that Hank Williams serves for mainstream country—he drank too much, wrote sad songs and died before he hit 30. Parsons's storytelling gift is enhanced by his tragic legend, and it didn't hurt that he helped introduce Emmylou Harris to the music world. When Parsons died, his road manager and a friend stole his body, cremated it and scattered the ashes at Cap Rock, a California national monument.

what to buy: *G.P./Grievous Angel* (Reprise, 1990, prod. Gram Parsons, Rick Grech) ♫♫♫♫ is a two-fer classic that combines Parsons' two solo albums. California country-rock doesn't come more influential than this.

what to buy next: *Sleepless Nights* (A&M, 1976, prod. various) ♫♫♫, a posthumous release, was compiled from solo material and tracks from Parsons' days with the Flying Burrito Brothers.

the rest:

Gram Parsons & the Fallen Angels Live (Sierra, 1992) ♫♫♫

worth searching for: *Safe at Home* (Shiloh, 1968) is an early record with the International Submarine Band that shows the direction Parsons would travel. Also worth uncovering is *Warm Evenings, Pale Mornings, Bottled Blues* (Raven, 1995), an Australian compilation.

influences:

◀◀ Hank Williams, Merle Haggard, Elvis Presley, Byrds

▶▶ Emmylou Harris, Eagles, Jayhawks, Uncle Tupelo, Wilco, Son Volt, Bottle Rockets

see also: *Byrds, Flying Burrito Brothers*

Brian Mansfield

DOLLY PARTON

Born January 19, 1946, in Sevier County, TN.

Simply put, Dolly Parton is the most recognized female country singer of the last 20 years. The story of her transformation from simple country girl to glittering superstar has been amply documented in her songs, numerous articles, interviews, countless talk show appearances and in her autobiography, *Finding Her Voice*. An actress, an entrepreneur and a darn fine banjo picker (in spite of her lengthy—and very real fingernails—), Parton's been ignored all too often, for her real gift is as a compelling storyteller. From the deeply personal songs that shaped the early years of her act to the universal appeal of her more recent material, Parton has been willing to not only accept, but to freely flaunt the fact that her appearance generates much of the attention she receives. It may, to paraphrase her, "cost a lot to make a person look this cheap," but even sometimes at the expense of her music, Parton has been a great risk taker, and has won a great deal more than she's lost.

Growing up in a family of 12, Parton knew early on she would be a star. Her classmates laughed at her declaration, yet the day after she graduated high school in tiny Locust Ridge in the Smoky Mountains of East Tennessee and left for Nashville, Parton had already appeared on television in Knoxville, singing on the *Cas Walker Show* there. She made her first appearance on the Grand Ole Opry at age 13 and had also recorded a single, "Puppy Love," on the Gold Band label out of Lake Charles, Louisiana, with the help of her uncle Bill Owens. Shortly after Parton arrived in Music City she sang in the early-morning *Eddie Hill Show,* also meeting her future husband, Carl Dean, outside the Wish-Washy laundromat. By 1967, signed to Monu-

Dolly Parton (© Ken Settle)

ment Records, Parton began her recording career in earnest, with a Top 30 single, the inappropriately titled "Dumb Blonde," and a Top 20 hit, "Something Fishy," both featured on the excellent album *Hello, I'm Dolly*, which was later reissued on CD as *The World of Dolly Parton, Volume 1*. Her next triumphs were an RCA recording contract and her role as replacement for singer Norma Jean on TV's popular *Porter Wagoner Show*, a move Norma Jean's fans first protested vehemently, but eventually accepted. Parton's business association with Porter would last until 1974, although they hit the country charts with duets well into 1980. There would be much speculation of romance between the two over the years, something Parton will neither confirm nor deny in her autobiography, although Wagoner attests to it in his. Their relationship, no matter how close, was obviously an integral part of both their careers. In fact, the song Parton wrote as a thank you to Wagoner when she struck out on her own has become, by way of two #1 versions of Parton's and one enormous pop #1 by Whitney Houston, Parton's best-known song, "I Will Always Love You."

By 1976 Parton had set her sights on a movie career, and began recording more pop-oriented material. In 1977 she began a streak of five #1 songs, with "Here You Come Again," her first pop hit (#3, 1977). Although she had only two more pop #1 songs, "9 to 5" (#1, 1981) and "Islands in the Stream" (#1, 1983), a duet with Kenny Rogers, Parton continued to rack up country chart toppers, hitting #1 18 times between 1977 and 1991. And, of course, her duet with Vince Gill on "I Will Always Love You" (#15, 1995) was historic, since no other artist had hit the charts with three different versions of the same song before. After the film *9 to 5* premiered in 1980, Parton followed with less successful ventures like *Best Little Whorehouse in Texas* and *Rhinestone*.

After she left RCA, and before she landed at Columbia Records, Parton teamed, at long last, with Emmylou Harris and Linda Ronstadt for the *Trio* album, which proved extremely successful and helped usher in her return (after the dreadful *Rainbow* album) to more acoustically oriented country music, with Ricky Skaggs as producer. A string of fairly successful and quite enjoyable albums followed, although Parton's chart success seems to be relegated to duets and, to a lesser degree, novelties like "Romeo" (#27, 1993). Parton again looked to an acoustic project in 1994, perhaps to make up for the fact that her scheduling conflicts sidetracked the anticipated recording of a *Trio* follow-up, though some tracks recorded for the sessions appeared on her 1996 album *Treasures*, with only Linda Ronstadt backing her. The 1995 chart appearance of "I Will Always Love You" was unique, not only because of the song's history, but also because it was a pretty big hit for an artist of Parton's age. In recent years, Parton has had a television sitcom in the works. Her own Nashville-based syndicated variety show was a big hit during the 1970s, although when she tried the same thing on ABC during the 1980s it didn't quite click. While she may not achieve greatness as an actress (especially if she never stretches beyond playing someone so close to herself), Dolly's role as Truvy the hairdresser in *Steel Magnolias* was well-received by audiences and critics alike.

Parton continues to explore new avenues and oversees several business ventures, including her Dollywood theme park in Pigeon Forge, Tennessee. Although her music may not be "cutting edge" anymore, early tunes like "To Daddy," and "Down from Dover" were unusual for their day and helped distinguish her long songwriting career. A shoo-in for future Hall of Fame honors, Dolly Parton is a true American icon.

what to buy: The two-CD *The RCA Years (1967–1986)* (RCA, 1993, prod. various) ♫♫♫♫ just barely scratches the surface, considering Parton's massive catalog of hits. But her best-known hits are here, covering nearly twenty years at RCA, during which she made her transition from country to pop. You can find this material elsewhere, but this particular compilation serves as a great starting point.

what to buy next: Okay, so *I Will Always Love You: The Essential Dolly Parton, Volume One* (RCA, 1995, prod. various) 🎵🎵🎵🎵 (once again) capitalizes on the success of THAT song. This is still a solid collection of genuine, if mostly later, hits, and even features Dolly's 1976 version of her own "To Daddy," later recorded by Emmylou Harris. Also notable: "Real Love" features a Parton solo, with Kenny Rogers having been erased from the track for its release here.

what to avoid: The transitional *Rainbow* (Columbia, 1988) 🎵🎵 is pretty much a stinker from the word "go." An indication of the yawn-inducing material included inside (with the possible exception of "The River Unbroken") is Parton's reclining pose on the front cover. *The Best There Is* (RCA, 1987) 🎵🎵 is among the shortest there is. You don't have to dig much deeper to find everything (and more) included here elsewhere. *Collector's Series* (RCA, 1985) 🎵🎵 is the same story, even more so, since it's got only eight tracks.

the rest:
The Best of Dolly Parton (RCA, 1975) 🎵🎵🎵🎵
Greatest Hits (RCA, 1982) 🎵🎵🎵🎵
(With Kenny Rogers) *Once upon a Christmas* (RCA, 1984) 🎵🎵🎵
Collector's Series (RCA, 1985) 🎵🎵🎵
The Best There Is (RCA, 1987) 🎵🎵🎵
(With Linda Ronstadt and Emmylou Harris) *Trio* (Warner Bros., 1987) 🎵🎵🎵🎵🎵
The World of Dolly Parton, Volume 1 (Columbia, 1988) 🎵🎵🎵🎵
The World of Dolly Parton, Volume 2 (Columbia, 1988) 🎵🎵🎵🎵
White Limozeen (Columbia, 1989) 🎵🎵🎵🎵
Eagle When She Flies (Columbia, 1991) 🎵🎵🎵🎵
Slow Dancing with the Moon (Columbia, 1993) 🎵🎵🎵🎵
Home for Christmas (Columbia, 1993) 🎵🎵🎵🎵
Golden Streets of Glory (RCA, 1993) 🎵🎵🎵🎵🎵
Heartsongs: Live from Home (Blue Eye/Columbia, 1994) 🎵🎵🎵🎵
(With Tammy Wynette and Loretta Lynn) *Honky-Tonk Angels* (Columbia, 1994) 🎵🎵🎵🎵
Something Special (Blue Eye/Columbia, 1995) 🎵🎵🎵🎵
I Will Always Love You & Other Greatest Hits (Blue Eye/Columbia, 1996) 🎵🎵🎵🎵
Super Hits (RCA, 1996) 🎵🎵🎵🎵
Treasures (Rising Tide, 1996) 🎵🎵🎵
(With Porter Wagoner) *The Essential Series* (RCA, 1996) 🎵🎵🎵🎵
The Essential Dolly Parton, Volume Two (RCA, 1997) 🎵🎵🎵🎵🎵

worth searching for: Any of Dolly's albums from the 1960s and early 1970s are worth buying, if only to trace the evolution of the artist. But, there's the added bonus of all those great cover shots, too!

influences:
◀◀ Kitty Wells, Porter Wagoner
▶▶ Alison Krauss, Emmylou Harris

Stephen L. Betts

STELLA PARTON
Born May 4, 1949, in Sevierville, TN.

Stella Parton followed her older sister, Dolly, to Nashville. Before she had her first country hit, though, she had her own gospel group, the Stella Parton Singers. The younger Parton (she was the sixth of 12 children) had eight Top 40 hits between 1975 and 1979, the biggest of which, "I Want to Hold You in My Dreams Tonight," came from her own label, Country Soul. She had the remainder of her biggest hits for Elektra but never again reached the Top 10. Parton was the one artist to go on record defending Olivia Newton-John with her single "Ode to Olivia," which said, in part, "We don't have the right to say you're not country."

what's available: You've got to admire Parton's do-it-yourself attitude: she co-produced and co-wrote everything on *A Woman's Touch* (SPPI, 1995, prod. Stella Parton, Greg Alexander) 🎵🎵, and it appeared on her own label. But it's just a mess, with poor production values, weak material and harmonies that sometimes stray painfully from tune.

influences:
◀◀ Dolly Parton, Crystal Gayle
▶▶ Louise Mandrell

Brian Mansfield

LES PAUL
Born Lester William Polsfuss, January 9, 1915, in Waukesha, WI.

An innovator and inventor of the caliber of Thomas Edison, it is sometimes hard to remember that the man who designed the world's first solid-body guitar and eight-track tape recorder is, and always has been, a musician first and foremost. Had Les Paul's head not first been filled with so many wondrous and unprecedented sounds, he never would have been driven to develop the hardware (or, as he so quaintly calls them, "toys") needed to realize this music. Had others been capable of imagining such sounds, the toys on which to perform them would have already existed.

At the precocious age of eight, the "Wizard of Waukesha" was already tampering with his mother's player piano rolls and distinctly remembers hearing a guitar come out of the first crystal radio set he ever built. By 13, using the name Red Hot Red, he was performing at local radio stations and barbecue stands on his own $4.50 Sears flat-top, a harmonica hanging around his neck on a customized clothes-hanger (the first of many inventions). After picking up a few chords from Gene Autry when the singing cowboy toured through town, Paul graduated to larger venues, amplifying his guitar with a crude pick-up fashioned from a phonograph needle. His first recording, a rendition of "Don't Send My Boy to Prison" performed over station WTMJ in 1929, was pressed onto an aluminum disc by way of a recording machine he'd built with a Cadillac flywheel and some dental belts.

Now calling himself Rhubarb Red, Paul toured the Midwest alongside country singer Sunny Joe Wolverton, a partnership that lasted through a stint at the 1933 World's Fair. Paul next found himself playing piano behind a young and struggling Jackie Gleason on Chicago's North Side while hosting a local radio show. What little spare time he could find was spent experimenting with disc-to-disc "multiples" of sound layering (today known as overdubbing). In May 1936 he cut his first commercially released recordings for Decca. Soon afterwards, becoming more enamored with (and accepted in) jazz over country, he dropped the Rhubarb moniker and formed his very first Les Paul Trio. When not on stage, he was busy developing his latest toy: the world's first solid-body electric guitar. It was at Bing Crosby's insistence in 1945 that Les built his first recording studio—for $415 in the garage of a newly purchased Hollywood bungalow (clients included Andy Williams and W.C. Fields). That same year, Paul met Colleen Summers, a young country singer who'd been working with his childhood idol, Gene Autry. Within four years they'd married, signed a 10-year pact with a then-new Capitol Records and launched a 23-week radio series for NBC. It was on these shows that the two, with Colleen now known as Mary Ford, developed the hitherto-unimaginable "Les Paul Sound"—a curious blend of jazz guitar, country-styled vocals and a slick, multi-tracked production style that soon launched a string of international hits ("The World Is Waiting for the Sunrise," "How High the Moon" and "Vaya Con Dios" among them). Eventually, as so many did, Les Paul and Mary Ford found themselves unable to compete in a marketplace increasingly saturated with the new sounds of rock 'n' roll (a sound, ironically, most often performed on Gibson Les Paul guitars). After several LPs for Columbia and London Records, Mary retired from show business, divorcing Les in 1964 (she died 13 years later). Paul began recording again during the mid-1970s with Chet Atkins (the delightful "Chester & Lester" series) and, despite heart surgery, still continues to perform and record regularly. And at his home in Mahwah, New Jersey, he continues to develop the toys that will enable him to take his music well into another century.

what to buy: *Les Paul: The Legend and the Legacy* (Capitol, 1991, prod. Les Paul) 🎸🎸🎸🎸 contains 75 stellar recordings from his golden decade with Capitol, including 34 unreleased gems and even some most illuminating (not to mention thoroughly entertaining) *Les Paul Show* radio airchecks not heard since their original broadcast. Absolutely essential listening.

what to buy next: *Chester & Lester* (RCA, 1976, prod. Chet Atkins) 🎸🎸🎸, the first and best of the recordings with his Music City soul-mate, marked Paul's return to the studio after 10 years of so-called retirement. And the sparks were flying.

influences:

◄◄ Sonny Terry, Gene Autry, Django Reinhardt

►► Practically anyone and everyone who's ever plugged in an electric guitar or stepped inside a recording studio

Gary Pig Gold

JOHNNY PAYCHECK

Born Donald Eugene Lytle, May 31, 1938, in Greenfield, OH.

Singer, songwriter, guitarist, bass player and harmony singer, Johnny Paycheck is among the most talented honky-tonkers ever to cut a record. But his checkered career, caused by drinking and drug problems, violence and constant run-ins with authority, has more than once found him teetering on the edge of oblivion. At a time during the early 1970s when there was much rhetorical posing about the "outlaw" presence in country music, Paycheck was the real thing. Both in his music and in his personal life, his stance toward the world at large reflected a belligerence that sometimes bordered on the psychotic.

As a teenager in the navy, Paycheck did hard time in the brig for striking an officer. After his release, he drifted to Nashville and recorded four singles for Decca under the name Donny Young. He also had success as a writer, penning "Apartment #9" for Tammy Wynette and "Touch My Heart" for Ray Price. In Nashville Paycheck began working as a sideman and harmony singer for such stars of the day as Porter Wagoner, Faron

Young, Ray Price and, most significantly, George Jones. In Jones' band he began to gain recognition as a harmony singer; he is present on much of Jones' finest material from the early 1960s. In 1965 he renamed himself Johnny Paycheck and had minor hits on the Hilltop label with "A-11" and "Heartbreak, Tennessee." He then formed Little Darlin' Records with producer Aubrey Mayhew. During the next two years, he cut some of the toughest honky-tonk records of the era, although they seldom reached higher than the lower rungs of the charts. The label folded and Johnny migrated to the West Coast, where he went into serious decline, singing for drinks and living on L.A.'s skid row until producer Billy Sherrill signed him to an Epic contract in 1971. "She's All I Got" became his biggest hit to that point, going to #2 on the country charts in 1971. That was followed by eight other Top 10 hits for Epic during the 1970s, topped by 1977's #1 song, the working-class anthem "Take This Job and Shove It."

After 1982 a period of label hopping ensued. It ended in 1985, when Paycheck became involved a shooting scrape in an Ohio bar that led to a conviction for aggravated assault and a sentence of up to nine years in prison. His sentence was commuted and he was released in 1991 on the condition that he tread the straight and narrow. Despite all his troubles, Paycheck has left his mark, both as singer and songwriter, in the annals of honky-tonk music.

what to buy: *The Real Mr. Heartache: The Little Darlin' Years* (Country Music Foundation, 1996, prod. Aubrey Mayhew) ♪♪♪♪ contains the best of the Hilltop and Little Darlin' material. While these are not Paycheck's biggest hits, they represent him at his best; it is easy to see why he is so highly regarded by insiders in the business after listening to such titles as "The Lovin' Machine" (#10, 1966), "The Real Mr. Heartache," "I'm Barely Hangin' on to Me," "He's in a Hurry (To Get Home to My Wife)" and, most ominously, "(Pardon Me) I've Got Someone to Kill." Twenty-four cuts of heartfelt honky-tonk.

what to buy next: *Biggest Hits* (Epic, 1987, prod. Billy Sherrill) ♪♪♪♪ is a truncated (10 cuts) greatest-hits collection covering only the late 1970s–early 1980s material and inexplicably not including 1977's #2, "Slide off Your Satin Sheets," one of his better efforts of the period. It does feature "She's All I Got," "I Can't Hold Myself in Line" (a duet with Merle Haggard), the violent "Colorado Cool-Aid," the countrypolitan "Friend, Lover, Wife" and "Take This Job and Shove It."

what to avoid: *Double Trouble* (Razor & Tie, 1996, prod. Billy Sherrill) ♪♪, a reissue from the early 1980s, features 10 Epic

duets with Paycheck and his old boss George Jones in a program (for some reason) of mostly rhythm-and-blues warhorses, featuring hokey asides from both parties.

the rest:
20 Greatest Hits (Deluxe, 1986) ♪♪
Golden Hits (Hollywood, 1987) ♪
Take This Job and Shove It (Richmond, 1988) ♪♪
Country Spotlight (Dominion, 1991) ♪

worth searching for: *Johnny Paycheck Sings George Jones* (K-Tel, 1996) ♪♪♪♪, a nice set of Jones' hits with a good country backing band, is an appropriate tribute to his old boss.

influences:
◀◀ Hank Williams, Faron Young
▶▶ Steve Earle, Dwight Yoakam

Randy Pitts

HERB PEDERSEN

Born April 27, 1944, in Berkeley, CA.

Herb Pedersen was a member of the Dillards, and his unmistakable high, sweet tenor and superb banjo playing graced two of the band's best-known recordings—the classic *Wheatstraw Suite* and *Copperfields*. He left the band during the mid-1960s and kicked around Los Angeles as a much sought-after session musician, supplying banjo accompaniment as well as harmonies for dozens of artists, such as James Taylor, Emmylou Harris, Gram Parsons, Bonnie Raitt and Chris Hillman. Pedersen recorded two solo albums during the mid-1970s, *Southwest* and *Sandman*, and in 1982 he teamed up with mandolinist David Grisman, fiddler Jimmy Buchanan, bassist Emory Gordy Jr. and a hot, young flatpicker named Vince Gill to record a breathtaking bluegrass album titled *Here Today*. Two years later Pedersen recorded another solo album titled *Lonesome Feeling*. In 1987 he hooked up with Hillman and guitarist John Jorgenson to form the Desert Rose Band, a group that enjoyed a string of country music chart-toppers during the late 1980s and early 1990s, including "Ashes of Love," "I Still Believe In You," "Summer Wind" and a brilliant take on John Hiatt's "She Don't Love Nobody." After the band broke up in 1993, Herb got the bluegrass fever once again and formed the Laurel Canyon Ramblers with bassist Bill Bryson and guitarist Billy Ray Lathum, formerly of the legendary Kentucky Colonels. In 1995 he regrouped with Hillman to record *Bakersfield Bound*, which rekindles the country sounds and spirit pioneered by Merle Haggard and Buck Owens.

3/4/4 *j.p. pennington*

Carl Perkins (© Ken Settle)

what's available: *Lonesome Feeling* (Sugar Hill, 1987, prod. Herb Pedersen) 🎵🎵🎵 is a classic precursor to the Desert Rose Band and features top-notch session playing by Hillman, steel guitarist J.D. Maness, bassist Lee Sklar and string-bender extraordinaire Bob Warford. Standout tracks include "Last Thing on My Mind" and "Lonesome Feeling."

worth searching for: The out-of-print *Southwest* (Epic, 1976, prod. Mike Post) 🎵🎵🎵 features a cool, Cajun reworking of the Beatles' "Paperback Writer" as well as the achingly beautiful "Wait a Minute."

influences:
◄◄ Flatt & Scruggs, Dillards
►► Desert Rose Band

see also: *Chris Hillman*

Rick Petreycik

J.P. PENNINGTON
See: Exile

PERFECT STRANGER
Formed in TX.

Steve Murray, vocals, acoustic guitar; Richard Raines, electric guitar, vocals; Shayne Morrison, bass, vocals; Andy Ginn, drums.

The East Texas quartet Perfect Stranger is proof that not all indie success stories hail from the rock ranks. Touring relentlessly and establishing itself as a popular club draw in Texas, Oklahoma, Louisiana and Arkansas, the band went on to cut its own CD in Nashville. Blending steel-driven honky-tonk and intelligent balladry, the group's crack, restrained playing complements lead singer steve Murray's Clint Black-influenced vocals.

what's available: That independent debut album, *It's Up to You*, did so well that the group was signed by Curb Records.

Substituting two songs and changing the track order, Curb reissued the release under the new title *You Have the Right to Remain Silent* (Curb, 1995, prod. Clyde Brooks) 🎵🎵🎵. The indie-to-biggie move paid off, with the title track sending Perfect Stranger up the country charts.

influences:

◀◀ Clint Black

▶▶ Lonestar, Ricochet

Chris Dickinson

CARL PERKINS

Born April 9, 1932, in Ridgeley, TN.

Like many Southerners of his generation, Carl Perkins is a country singer who heard the clarion call of rock 'n' roll on the first Elvis Presley record and headed straight for 706 Union Avenue in Memphis to sign up with the suddenly ascendant Sun label. When Sun owner Sam Phillips sold Presley's contract to RCA Victor, he did so under the assumption that he had another guy as good as Presley—and maybe even a little better, because Perkins wrote his own songs. But Perkins never followed "Blue Suede Shoes"—his version actually beat Presley's RCA debut, "Heartbreak Hotel," into the Top 10—with anything remotely that impactual. He spent the rest of his career making records that hewed closely to his original artistic vision, while the pop music world quickly left rockabilly—and Carl Perkins—behind. He conducted a few experiments with country, but, although obviously comfortable with the idiom, never achieved any great success in the field. Like Bill Haley, his career often boiled down to one record—the redoubtable "Blue Suede Shoes"—but Perkins, even more than Elvis, served as a role model for aspiring rockabilly kings. A badly timed car crash on the way to become the second rock 'n' roller ever to appear on *The Ed Sullivan Show* interrupted his career at a crucial juncture, but Perkins churned out a slew of classic sides for Sun Records, a body of work that stands like a mountain in the tiny realm of authentic rockabilly.

what to buy: His *Original Sun Greatest Hits* (Rhino, 1986, prod. various) 🎵🎵🎵🎵🎵 eloquently makes the case for Perkins as one of rock 'n' roll's greats. The wealth of material he cut during his few short years at Sun runs far deeper than just "Blue Suede Shoes."

what to buy next: Perkins continued to record in the same style for years to come, without much commercial success, alongside his Sun compatriot Johnny Cash at the Columbia label.

FIVE FOR MY FANS

MINDY McCREADY

Patty Loveless
The Trouble with the Truth (Epic)

Alanis Morissette
Jagged Little Pill (Reprise)

Joan Osborne
Relish (Mercury/Blue Gorilla)

Sting
Mercury Falling (A&M)

Kenny Chesney
Me and You (BNA)

Restless: The Columbia Recordings (Columbia/Legacy, 1992, prod. various) 🎵🎵🎵 chronicles the next decade of Perkins' recordings, rockabilly-in-exile.

what to avoid: Watch out for a chintzy *Best of Carl Perkins* (Curb, 1993), a 10-song rip-off featuring re-recordings of "Blue Suede Shoes" and lesser known pieces.

the rest:

Carl Perkins and NRBQ: Boppin' the Blues (Columbia, 1970) 🎵🎵🎵
Jive after Five (Rhino, 1991) 🎵🎵🎵
Friends, Family and Legends (Platinum Records Int., 1992) 🎵🎵

worth searching for: An obscure album, *Carl Perkins On Top* (Columbia, 1969, prod. B. Denny) 🎵🎵🎵, contains a rare, unreissued track, "Champagne, Illinois," that Perkins co-wrote with Bob Dylan. Proof of his enduring legacy can be found in the 1996 tribute album, *Go Cat Go!* (Dinosaur Entertainment, 1996), which includes recordings by such admirers as Paul McCartney,

George Harrison, Johnny Cash, John Fogerty, Ringo Starr, Paul Simon, Tom Petty and others.

influences:

◄◄ Ernest Tubb, Muddy Waters, Elvis Presley

►► Ricky Nelson, Beatles, John Fogerty

Joel Selvin

LARRY PERKINS
See: Lonesome Standard Time

GRETCHEN PETERS
Born November 14, in Brooklyn, NY

One of the most important Nashville songwriters of the 1990s, Gretchen Peters has had her songs recorded by George Strait ("Chill of an Early Fall"), Randy Travis ("High Lonesome"), George Jones ("Traveller's Prayer") and nearly every female singer in Music City. Her song "Independence Day," as recorded by Martina McBride, was chosen as the Country Music Association's Song of the Year in 1995. Peters began performing at clubs in Boulder, Colorado, and moved to Nashville in 1988. She made her recording debut in 1996.

what's available: *Secret of Life* (Imprint, 1996, prod. Green Daniel) 𝄞𝄞𝄞 has the same kind of soft rhythms that characterized much of Bruce Springsteen's *Tunnel of Love* and *Human Touch* albums. Coupled with Peter's lyrical insight, that makes for a wonderful listening experience, but not much of a country album, at least by traditional definitions. *Secret of Life* includes Peters' version of "On a Bus to St. Cloud," previously a single for Trisha Yearwood, and an unlikely cover of Steve Earle's "I Ain't Ever Satisfied."

Influences:

◄◄ Matraca Berg, Martina McBride

►► Deana Carter, Kim Richey

Brian Mansfield

THE PICKETTS
Formed 1990, in Seattle, WA.

Christy McWilson, vocals; Leroy Sleep, drums, vocals; John Olufs, guitar; Walt Singleman, bass; Jim Sangster, guitar.

Since they hail from Seattle and specialize in twangy reworkings of the Clash's "Should I Stay or Should I Go?," Yoko Ono's "Walking on Thin Ice" and Kyu Sakamoto's 1963 hit "Sukiyaki,"

the Picketts are often mistaken for just another beer-chugging bunch of smirking roots-rock revisionists. Despite their own roots in such pre-grunge Pacific Northwest acts as Young Fresh Fellows and Red Dress, the band writes original material that reflects a keen knowledge and genuine feel for country music's chugging Bakersfield and swinging Texas roots. Singer Christy McWilson, who shares lead vocals with stand-up drummer/songwriter Leroy Sleep, possesses a husky voice drenched with the down-home passion of Loretta Lynn and the longing ache of Patsy Cline; when she and Sleep lock horns on the choruses, their sweet-and-sour harmonies combine with the runaway freight-train rhythms and ragged guitars to create a spirited marriage of honky-tonk and bar-band rock 'n' roll that—contrary to most modern-day cowpunk acts—is more about heart than attitude.

what to buy: The tough-rocking *Euphonium* (Rounder, 1996, prod. Steve Berlin) 𝄞𝄞𝄞 features two of the band's trademark covers: "Should I Stay or Should I Go?" as a honky-tonk shuffle and an Appalachian-flavored take on the Who's "Baba O'Riley." But when McWilson throws herself into the rollicking "Same Town, Same Planet (Different World)" and delivers the chilling payoff verse ("Please tell me that the darkness is deceiving/And somewhere down this tunnel this is light") on the self-penned "Night Fell," you'll realize that the Picketts are more than just another roadhouse attraction.

the rest:

The Wicked Picketts (Rounder, 1995) 𝄞𝄞𝄞

worth searching for: *Paper Doll* (Popllama, 1992, prod. Jim Sangster) 𝄞𝄞𝄞 is their Seattle debut and includes their cover of Tom Waits' "Heart of Saturday Night."

influences:

◄◄ Buck Owens, Wanda Jackson, Rockpile

►► Old 97's

David Okamoto

JO CAROL PIERCE
Born July 20, 1944, in Wellington, TX.

Somewhere between the coffeehouse warblings of Phoebe, Lisa Kudrow's character on TV's *Friends*, and, say, Wittgenstein, there's the work of Jo Carol Pierce. The ex-wife of Jimmie Dale Gilmore, Pierce is a contemporary of the brighter lights along the Austin/Lubbock axis—Gilmore, Joe Ely, Butch Hancock, Terry Allen, Angela Strehli and David Halley. Pierce wrote her songs in secret during the 1970s, then began writing plays and screenplays. Her works include *Falling, Back to School, New World Tango* (with music by Ely), *Bad Girls Upset by the Truth* and *In the West* (which ran in Austin for five years). An infrequent performer, Pierce works by day as a counselor on a state child-abuse hotline.

what's available: Pierce's only recording, *Bad Girls Upset by the Truth* (Monkey Hill, 1995, prod. Frank Quintini, Troy Campbell) ♪♪♪♪, is a collection of monologues and music tracing a "bad girl's" complex romantic and religious history. Hilarious, outrageous and absolutely true to life, the play contains such philosophical musings as "Does God Have Us by the Twat or What?," "Secret Dan" and "I Blame God." Great stuff.

worth searching for: A slightly uneven tribute album, *Across the Great Divide: Songs of Jo Carol Pierce* (Dejadisc, 1992) ♪♪♪♪, finds such artists as Gilmore, Allen, Ely, Michael Hall, Darden Smith and David Halley, among others, performing Pierce's wonderful songs.

influences:

◀◀ Terry Allen, Mary Magdalene, Joan of Arc

▶▶ Shawn Colvin, Mary Chapin Carpenter

Daniel Durchholz

WEBB PIERCE

Born August 8, 1926, in West Monroe, LA. Died February 24, 1991.

Flashy suits, guitar-shaped swimming pool and clichéd excesses aside, Webb Pierce was a vocalist whose style not only embraced honky-tonk music, it clearly and irrefutably defined it. From 1952 to 1957 he had an incredible streak of 34 Top 10 records, 13 of which accumulated a staggering total of 118 weeks at #1. Now considered one of the Top 10 country artists of all time, he, somewhat surprisingly, has yet to be elected to the Country Music Hall of Fame. Born in Louisiana, in the heart of *Hayride* country, Pierce longed to appear on the Shreveport-based radio show for many years, finally making it in 1949. At the same time he was offered a contract with 4 Star Records, for whom he scored, regionally, with "Panhandle Rag." He also owned Pacemaker Records, which launched the careers of others, like Faron Young and Claude King. Signing with Decca in 1951, Pierce would dominate the country charts for weeks at a time. His hit "Slowly" (#1, 1954) was the first to feature pedal steel guitar, played by the legendary Bud Isaacs. In another important business venture, Pierce, with former Opry manger Jim Denny, founded Cedarwood Music. In 1955 Pierce left *Louisiana Hayride,* moved to Nashville and became a member of the

Grand Ole Opry. His hit records continued for another decade before trailing off, stopping altogether in 1971. In 1977 he signed with Plantation Records, but to no avail. Sadly, while he continued to oversee his business ventures in his final years, Pierce also fought battles with alcoholism and, ultimately unsuccessfully, with cancer. Webb Pierce died in 1991, but his impressive collection of pure, unadulterated, hard-driving honky-tonk music will live on.

what to buy: *King of the Honky-Tonk: From the Original Decca Masters 1952–1959* (Country Music Foundation/MCA, 1994, prod. Country Music Foundation) ♪♪♪♪ is a marvelous collection of the majority of Pierce's big hits. A vital addition to any country fan's collection.

the rest:

The One and Only (King) ♪♪

Webb Pierce & His Southern Valley Boys: The Unavailable Sides (1950–51) (Krazy Kat) ♪♪▽

worth searching for: *The Wondering Boy 1951–58* (Bear Family, 1990) ♪♪♪▽ is a four-disc set loaded with hits and otherwise unavailable material. It is worth the expense to get the full effect of Webb Pierce's impact on the world of honky-tonk music.

influences:

◀◀ Jimmie Rodgers, Ernest Tubb

▶▶ Lefty Frizzell, David Ball

Stephen L. Betts

PINKARD & BOWDEN

Comedic act formed c. 1975, in Nashville, TN.

James Sanford Pinkard Jr. (born January 16, 1947, in Abberville, LA); Richard Bowden (born September 30, 1945, in Linden, TX).

James Pinkard started his country music career writing (after a stint with the rodeo in Texas) for chart-toppers such as Tanya Tucker, Ray Charles, Mel Tillis and Brenda Lee. Richard Bowden, meanwhile, was an accomplished musician for Linda Ronstadt, Dan Fogelberg and Roger McGuinn. Pinkard & Bowden originally collaborated on mainstream writing projects, but their efforts left them cracking up. Fortunately, they recognized their comical compatibility and took their act on the road. They are best known for their satires of popular songs: "Blue Hairs Drivin' in My Lane," "Momma He's Lazy," "Somebody Done Somebody's Song Wrong," "She Thinks I Steal Cars," "Freeloading" and "Wind Beneath My Sheets." During the 1990s this

$\frac{3}{4}$
$\frac{}{8}$ *pirates of the mississippi*

off-color duo began to cross over, performing across the country on the comedy-club circuit.

what's available: Both *Live in Front of a Bunch of D**kh**ds* (Warner Bros., 1989, prod. Pinkard & Bowden, Jim Ed Norman) 🎵🎵🎵 and *Cousins, Cattle and Other Love Songs* (Warner Bros., 1992) 🎵🎵🎵 contain song parodies and comedy numbers that, as one might infer by the former album title, can get pretty raunchy. Humor for people who thought *Deliverance* was a comedy.

influences:
◀◀ Ray Stevens, Lenny Bruce
▶▶ Cledus "T." Judd

see also: *Austin Lounge Lizards*

Randall T. Cook

PIRATES OF THE MISSISSIPPI
Formed mid-1980s, in Nashville, TN.

Bill McCorvey, lead vocals; Rich Alves, guitar; Pat Severs, steel guitar; Dean Townson, bass; Jimmy Lowe, drums.

Pirates of the Mississippi formed as a side project to give its members a creative outlet from their day jobs (which included session musician and songwriter). The group released its first single—a cover of Hank Williams' "Honky-Tonk Blues"—shortly after the Kentucky HeadHunters released their version of Bill Monroe's "Walk Softly on This Heart of Mine" and never completely escaped the "clone" perception. Their "Feed Jake" was one of the first big country video hits and also the first country hit to specifically mention homosexuality.

what's available: *Pirates of the Mississippi* (Capitol, 1990, prod. James Stroud, Richard Alves) 🎵🎵🎵, the group's first album, is also its best musically. In addition to "Feed Jake," it contains some freewheeling Southern-rock-influenced honky-tonk and a pair of Guy Clark covers. *Best of the Pirates of the Mississippi* (Capitol, 1994, prod. James Stroud, Jimmy Bowen, Richard Alves, Mark Wright) 🎵🎵🎵 is a neat summary of the group's career and shows that their singles had more substance than people generally gave them credit for.

worth searching for: Most of the Pirates' catalog has fallen out of print and didn't really have much memorable material that's not on *Best Of*. But *Dream You* (Liberty, 1993, prod. Mark Wright) 🎵🎵🎵 was a solid but overlooked last-ditch effort for Liberty that contained a nifty cover of Hank Thompson's "The Wild Side of Life."

influences:
◀◀ Alabama, Kentucky HeadHunters
▶▶ Confederate Railroad

Brian Mansfield

GENE PITNEY
Born February 17, 1941, in Hartford, CT.

Gene Pitney had some huge hits during the early 1960s, thanks to a vibrant but pained tenor that could give the heartstrings a pretty good tug. Unlike many pop singers of his day, Pitney wrote many of his own songs and worked easily in a variety of styles and with a diversity of artists, including songwriters Burt Bacharach and Hal David (who wrote his wrenching hit "Only Love Can Break a Heart"), the Rolling Stones and George Jones. Pitney was much bigger in Europe than in the U.S., so by the mid-1960s he concentrated his recording and touring efforts there. The resilient singer had a #1 hit in the U.K. as recently as 1988 ("Something Gotten Hold of My Heart," a collaboration with Marc Almond) and made a triumphant return to the U.S. in 1993 with a sold-out show at Carnegie Hall. Mostly a singles artist, Pitney has racked up more than 20 hits during his career.

what to buy: There is no definitive Pitney collection that deftly covers the singer's long and varied career. The one that comes closest is *More Greatest Hits* (Varese Vintage, 1995, prod. various) 🎵🎵🎵, which rounds up 19 re-mastered versions of Pitney's biggest hits, including "Town Without Pity," "(The Man Who Shot) Liberty Valance," "Only Love Can Break a Heart" and the more recent "Something's Gotten Hold of My Heart."

what to buy next: *Anthology (1961–1968)* (Rhino, 1991, prod. various) 🎵🎵🎵 sums up his most prolific period, the 1960s, with the obvious hits, but also Pitney's versions of hits he wrote for other artists, including Ricky Nelson's "Hello Mary Lou."

what to avoid: With just 10 songs, *Greatest Hits* (Curb, 1995, prod. various) 🎵🎵🎵 is far too skimpy, particularly compared to what else is available.

the rest:
Best of Gene Pitney (K-Tel International, 1991) 🎵🎵🎵
Best of Gene Pitney (LaserLight Digital, 1995) 🎵🎵
The Great Recordings (Tomato, 1995) 🎵🎵🎵
20 Greatest Hits (Fest) 🎵🎵🎵
Best of Gene Pitney (Delta) 🎵🎵
Greatest Hits (Evergreen) 🎵🎵
The Collection (Griffin) 🎵🎵
The Best of Easy Listening (Richmond) 🎵🎵

Town Without Pity (Richmond) 🎵🎵

worth searching for: Pitney cut a number of sides with George Jones during the 1960s, one of which, "That's All It Took," actually hit the country charts under the name George & Gene in 1966. Some of their recordings can be found domestically on the budget cassettes *George Jones & Gene Pitney* (Starday, 1985) 🎵🎵 and *One Has My Name* (Starday, 1985) 🎵🎵, or on the higher quality import, *George Jones & Gene Pitney* (Bear Family) 🎵🎵🎵.

influences:

⏪ George Jones, Johnny Ray

⏩ Stacy Dean Campbell, Ray Vega, Mavericks

Doug Pullen

POCO

Formed 1968, in Los Angeles, CA.

Rusty Young, pedal steel, vocals (1968–84, 1989–present); Richie Furay, guitar, vocals (1968–73, 1989–91); Jim Messina, guitar, vocals, 1968–70, 1989–91); Randy Meisner, bass, vocals, (1968–69, 1989–91); Timothy B. Schmit, bass, vocals (1969–77); George Grantham, drums, vocals (1968–77); Paul Cotton, guitar, vocals, 1970–84; Steve Chapman, drums (1977–84); Kim Bullard, keyboards, (1977–84); Charlie Harrison, bass (1977–84).

Of all the original groups that tried to combine rock and country music in the wake of the Byrds' *Sweetheart of the Rodeo* album, Poco went farthest in creating a new kind of sound. Instead of just singing with a twang and adding pedal steel (they did that, too), Poco's members incorporated elements of bluegrass music but sang with a high-pitched fever that was matched by the group's electric performances, both on record and on stage. These guys just never sounded like a mere folkrock band (except in the band's later, more commercial years). Founded by former Buffalo Springfield members Jim Messina and Richie Furay, the group recruited several Colorado musicians—Randy Meisner (who left before the first album came out), pedal steel specialist Rusty Young (who brought a rock mentality to what was still considered a country instrument) and Geroge Grantham—and cut loose for a handful of breathless albums before attrition and a changing radio climate tamed the sound. Meisner was the first out, joining Rick Nelson's band, then Linda Ronstadt's, then the Eagles (he was replaced by Timothy B. Schmit, who later left to replace Meisner again, in the Eagles). Messina followed his muse to a successful duo career with Kenny Loggins. Furay left to form a "super-

group," the Souther–Hillman–Furay Band, and now is a pastor in Boulder, Colorado. Latter-day releases under Young's leadership are likable pop albums, with big production touches including horns and synthesizer strings on hits such as "Heart of the Night," "Keep on Tryin'" and "Crazy Love." Watch for Young's new career as one of the co-leaders of Sky Kings, a new group featuring Bill Lloyd and John Cowan. The original Poco lineup reformed in 1989 for the *Legacy* recording and tour.

what to buy: The group's purity of vision is clear as a bell on *Poco* (Epic, 1970, prod. Jim Messina) 🎵🎵🎵🎵. The album's sound is driven by Furay's cutting tenor, which gives the record a sonic edge that other country rockers didn't have. Even the harmonies are unbelievably high. But the music rocks (and also gets churchy when it needs to), and makes cool use of Young's pedal steel without ever sounding like a rock imitation of country music. *Deliverin'* (Epic, 1971, prod. Jim Messina) 🎵🎵🎵🎵 is the live flipside and shows how powerful a live group Poco was, even at its start.

what to buy next: *The Very Best of Poco* (Epic, 1975, prod. various) 🎵🎵🎵🎵 is a good choice—a non-stop fun-fest and a great overview of Poco's strengths up to mid-career. As for Poco's later work, after *Rose of Cimarron* (ABC, 1976, prod. Poco, Mark Harman) 🎵🎵🎵 the band sounded increasingly more pedestrian and middle-of-the-road despite its original uniqueness. Then again, this is the period when the big hits came—go figure. *Crazy Loving, the Best of Poco 1975–1982* (MCA, 1989, prod. various) 🎵🎵🎵 is a lean, no-fat collection of those pop chartmakers.

what to avoid: *Legacy* (RCA, 1989, prod. David Cole) 🎵🎵 was a calculated move at reigniting the fan base with a reunion of original members, but the music was too cynically aimed at middle-of-the-road radio. One of the hits (there were two) was co-written by lame-o rocker Richard Marx.

the rest:

Pickin' up the Pieces (Epic, 1969) 🎵🎵🎵
From the Inside (Epic, 1971) 🎵🎵🎵
A Good Feelin' to Know (Epic, 1972) 🎵🎵🎵
Crazy Eyes (Epic, 1973) 🎵🎵🎵
Seven (Epic, 1974) 🎵🎵🎵
Cantamos (Epic, 1974) 🎵🎵🎵
Head over Heels (Epic, 1975) 🎵🎵🎵
Live (Epic, 1976) 🎵🎵
Indian Summer (ABC, 1977) 🎵🎵🎵
Legend (ABC, 1978) 🎵🎵
Under the Gun (MCA, 1980) 🎵🎵

Blue and Gray (MCA, 1981) 🎵🎵

Cowboys and Englishmen (MCA, 1982) 🎵🎵

Ghost Town (Atlantic, 1982) 🎵🎵

Inamorata (Atlantic, 1984) 🎵🎵

The Forgotten Trail 1969–1974 (Epic/Legacy, 1990) 🎵🎵🎵🎵

worth searching for: The CD single for "Call It Love" (RCA, 1989, prod. David Cole) 🎵🎵 is worth hunting out, not so much for the fairly pedestrian song, but for the arresting fold-out graphics that feature a cut-out of the Poco horse emblem on the cover.

solo outings:

Richie Furay:

(With John David Souther and Chris Hillman): *The Souther, Hillman, Furay Band* (Asylum, 1974) 🎵🎵🎵

Trouble in Paradise (Asylum, 1975) 🎵🎵🎵

(With the Richie Furay Band) *I've Got a Reason* (Asylum, 1976) 🎵🎵

Jim Messina:

Oasis (Columbia 1979) 🎵🎵

Messina (Warner Bros., 1981) 🎵

Rusty Young:

(With the Sky Kings) *The Sky Kings* (Warner/Reprise, 1997) 🎵🎵🎵

influences:

⏪ Flatt & Scruggs, Everly Brothers, Byrds, Flying Burrito Brothers, Buffalo Springfield

⏩ New Grass Revival, Foster & Lloyd, Alison Krauss & Union Station, Uncle Tupelo, Son Volt, Wilco

see also: *Eagles, Chris Hillman*

Gil Asakawa

CHARLIE POOLE /CHARLIE POOLE & THE NORTH CAROLINA RAMBLERS

Born March 22, 1892, in Alamance County, NC. Died May 21, 1931, in Spray, NC.

Charlie Poole and his band, the North Carolina Ramblers, played breakdown dances in the Spray-Leaksville area of central North Carolina as early as 1918. From there they went on to record some of the most lilting, rhythmically dynamic stringband music of the 1920s. Poole's three-finger banjo style and vaudeville-inspired "story" songs sound remarkably fresh 70 years later.

what to buy: *Old Time Songs* (County, 1965) 🎵🎵🎵🎵 includes a handful of songs—"White House Blues," "Don't Let Your Deal Go Down" and "Take a Drink on Me" among them—that became staples in the repertoires of generations of country, bluegrass and folk performers.

what to buy next: *Old Time Songs: Volume 2* (County, 1974) 🎵🎵🎵🎵 contains more fine stringband music and tall tales, the best of the latter assaying the virtues and pitfalls of the sportin' life.

the rest:

Charlie Poole & the North Carolina Ramblers: Volume 1 (County, 1996) 🎵🎵🎵🎵

Charlie Poole & the North Carolina Ramblers: Volume 2 (County, 1996) 🎵🎵🎵🎵

influences:

⏩ New Lost City Ramblers, Nancy & Norman Blake

Bill Friskics-Warren

SANDY POSEY

Born Sandra Lou Posey, June 18, 1944, in Jasper, AL.

Born in Alabama and raised in Arkansas, Sandy Posey got her start in music as a studio receptionist, but soon became a backing singer for acts like Bobby Goldsboro, Joe Texa and Elvis Presley. Producer Chips Moman eventually cut some sides on her and got enough interest from MGM Records that Posey was signed to a contract. Her "Born a Woman," with lyrics like "If you're born a woman, you're born to be . . . treated like dirt," became a pre-feminist hit in 1966. It was recorded by a number of country singers, including Connie Smith, Jean Shepard and Jan Howard. (That song and its follow-up, "Single Girl," were penned by future Warner Bros. Nashville A&R executive Martha Sharp, who would later sign Randy Travis and other acts.) Posey had four Top 40 pop hits during 1966–67, then took some time off beginning in 1968. When she returned, she signed with Columbia Records as a country artist. She had three Top 40 country hits for Columbia during the early 1970s, including covers of Presley's "Don't" and the Tune Weavers' "Happy, Happy Birthday Baby." She also had charting hits for Monument, Warner Bros. and Audiograph. She continued backing other singers as well, including her husband Wade Cummins, better known as Elvis-impersonator "Elvis Wade."

what's available: *The Best of Sandy Posey* (Collectables, 1995, prod. Chips Moman) 🎵🎵 features Posey's big pop hits and 10 other songs in that vein. The litany of suffering in "Born a Woman" is so over the top that it's hard to hear these days; "I Take It Back," in which Posey repeatedly tries to break up with her boyfriend but can't bear to see him hurt, is nearly as bad. *The Best of Sandy Posey* (Columbia) 🎵🎵 collects some of her country hits. The five songs on *I Take It Back* (King, 1994, prod. Lou Lofredo) 🎵, recorded during the late 1970s at Starday/King studios, are remakes of some of Posey's hits.

influences:

◀◀ Lesley Gore, Dusty Springfield

▶▶ Linda Hargrove, Lynda K. Lance

Brian Mansfield

MC POTTS

Born Mary Christina Potts, June 7, 1968, in Pittsburgh, PA.

Growing up in Ohio, with musical influences as far-ranging as Stephen Sondheim and Loretta Lynn, MC Potts was involved in musical theater, but eventually studied nursing before making the trip to Nashville from New York City and landing work as a demo singer and staff writer for (Lee) Greenwood Music. Charming and funny, she's a dynamic live performer.

what's available: *Straight to You* (Avex-Critique, 1996, prod. Steve Gibson) 🎵🎵🎵 shows Potts has some emotion in her delivery, but there's little territory here that more mature artists like Lorrie Morgan haven't explored with greater results. With better-chosen material, she stands a pretty good chance of gaining a wider audience.

influences:

◀◀ Tammy Wynette, Crystal Gayle

Stephen L. Betts

PRAIRIE OYSTER

Formed 1974, in King City, Ontario, Canada.

Russell deCarle, vocals; Dennis Delorme, pedal steel; Keith Glass, guitar; Bruce Moffet, drums (1986–96); Joan Besen, keyboards (1985–present); John P. Allen, fiddle, mandolin (1985–present); Bohdan Hluszko, drums (1996–present).

When Prairie Oyster re-entered record stores with 1997's *Blue Plate Special*, it marked the return of one of country music's best-kept secrets. The Canadian ensemble has been kicking around since the mid-1970s, when it formed as a trio, earning acclaim in its homeland (Group of the Year six times running in the RPM Big Country Awards, along with five Juno Awards), but scant notice south of the border. In fact, all of its previous albums had fallen out of print when *Blue Plate Special* emerged. Hopefully, U.S. audiences will accept this second chance to check out the sextet's deft blending of country styles, which incorporates elements of other sounds—notably rock and R&B—but without diluting its country integrity.

what's available: *Blue Plate Special* (Velvel, 1997, prod. Mike Poole, Prairie Oyster) 🎵🎵🎵🎵 might just do the trick. As the first release on former Columbia mogul Walter Yetnikoff's new label, it's sure to get plenty of promotional punch. And it delivers the musical goods, too, with a mature, fully realized sound evident in the shuffling "She Won't Be Lonely Long," the poppy "One-Way Track" and the sing-time bent of "If My Broken Heart Would Ever Mend."

worth searching for: The group's second album, *Everybody Knows* (RCA Canada, 1991, prod. Richard Bennett, Josh Leo) 🎵🎵🎵🎵 was its most successful in its homeland.

influences:

◀◀ Blue Rodeo, the Band, Bob Wills, Oyster Band, Alabama, New Riders of the Purple Sage

Gary Graff

ELVIS PRESLEY

Born Elvis Aron Presley, January 8, 1935, in East Tupelo, MS. Died August 16, 1977, in Memphis, TN.

Elvis Presley—King of Rock 'n' Roll, movie star, tragic symbol of garish excess, paragon of moral decay, one of the best-selling pop artists of all time, even a pop-culture Jesus Christ figure—was at first a daydreaming hillbilly truck driver who learned to sing from listening to Hank Snow and Hank Williams on the radio. One of his first hits was "Blue Moon of Kentucky" by Bill Monroe, the father of bluegrass. Some said Presley's mythological linking of white country and black R&B was sacrilege. But he was eventually vindicated when the notoriously conservative Monroe recorded a new "Blue Moon of Kentucky" in the hopped-up Presley style.

Born to a poor Southern couple, Vernon and Gladys, Presley was initially destined to meet a pretty girl, marry her, possibly graduate from high school and fix plumbing or drive a truck the rest of his life. But his instincts and ambition wouldn't let him go in that direction, even after his parents upgraded their lifestyle slightly and moved to Memphis. Beginning in high school, the shy boy began greasing his hair into a tall pompadour, wearing long sideburns and carefully choosing his outlandish outfits in pinks, blacks and whites. Peers thought he was nuts. After a year of persistent hanging around the downtown Sun Records studio, record producer Sam Phillips saw an

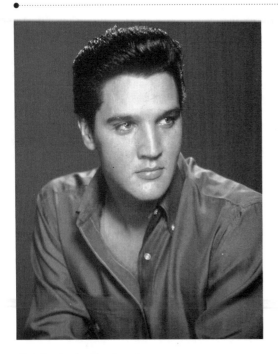

Elvis Presley **(Archive Photos)**

intangible quality in Presley and set him up for a session. (Phillips, a longtime recorder of black bluesmen and minor R&B stars from Junior Parker to Rufus Thomas, had long predicted that if he could get a white boy with "the Negro look and the Negro feel" to sing black music, he would make a million dollars. That turned out to be a major understatement.) With hungry sessionmen Scotty Moore on guitar and Bill Black on upright bass, the trio performed take after take until, while fooling around, they came up with re-worked versions of "Blue Moon of Kentucky" and Arthur "Big Boy" Crudup's "That's All Right (Mama)." They were fast and smooth, and they sounded like nothing anybody had ever heard. An excited Phillips dropped the cuts off to famous Memphis country DJ Dewey Phillips, who played "That's All Right" countless times in a row, thus creating Presley's first official buzz.

As Presley grew from poor Southern boy to the most famous rock singer who ever lived, he gradually turned away from his country roots. His unprecedented string of 1950s hits—including "You're So Square (Baby, I Don't Care)," "Good Rockin' Tonight" and "Mystery Train"—were firmly rooted in country

music. His followers, from Buddy Holly to Bill Haley to Carl Perkins, immediately picked up on the country-to-rock 'n' roll blueprint and sped up their twang from country to rockabilly. But during the 1960s Presley's shift towards slick movie music and Hollywood glamour (and, later, Las Vegas) pushed him away from hillbilly culture. He made it a point to return frequently to gospel music, but with just a few exceptions, his post-1950s forays into country were almost always part of commercial schemes.

It's possible to interpret Presley's death—on August 16, 1977, in his Graceland bathroom—as a slow shift from his roots to a lifestyle he never fully understood. His 1970s music contains very little trace of traditional country, unless you count his voice's natural twang and the Vegas-style showmanship that has come to dominate concerts by Dolly Parton, Reba McEntire and Garth Brooks.

what to buy: Four box sets in particular have been a godsend, because without them it would be impossible to navigate the record store's binfuls of studio albums and hits collections for the essential stuff. To hear Presley's early transformation from hillbilly crooner to the King you need *The King of Rock 'n' Roll: The Complete 1950's Masters* (RCA, 1992, prod. Ernst Mikael Jorgensen, Roger Semon) 🎵🎵🎵🎵. The other sets—*From Nashville to Memphis: The Essential '60's Masters I* (RCA, 1994, prod. Ernst Mikael Jorgensen, Roger Semon) 🎵🎵🎵🎵, *Command Performances: The Essential '60s Masters II* (RCA, 1995, prod. Ernst Mikael Jorgensen, Roger Semon) 🎵🎵🎵 and *Walk a Mile in My Shoes: The Essential '70s Masters* (RCA, 1995, prod. Ernst Mikael Jorgensen, Roger Semon) 🎵🎵🎵🎵—are great but stray from country. *The Complete Sun Sessions* (RCA, 1987, prod. Sam Phillips) 🎵🎵🎵🎵 is mostly revisited on the first box set, but it contains the fascinating sound of Elvis, guitarist Scotty Moore, bassist Bill Black and producer Phillips inventing rock 'n' roll in the Sun Records studio; "Milkcow Blues Boogie" has Elvis stopping a slow blues song, announcing "that don't MOVE me" and proceeding to change it before our ears into something completely different. *The Million Dollar Quartet* (RCA, 1990, prod. Sam Phillips) 🎵🎵🎵🎵 features Presley, Jerry Lee Lewis and Carl Perkins (plus a no-show Johnny Cash) doing 1950s rockabilly hits with spontaneity, style and fun.

what to buy next: These are his finest early studio albums, which are classic portraits of the innovative country singer: *Elvis Presley* (RCA, 1956, prod. Steve Sholes, Chet Atkins) 🎵🎵🎵🎵; the debut *Elvis* (RCA, 1956, prod. Elvis Presley, Steve Sholes) 🎵🎵🎵🎵; the first movie soundtrack, *Loving You* (RCA,

1957, prod. Elvis Presley, Hal Wallis) ✰✰✰✰; *Elvis' Christmas Album* (RCA, 1957, prod. Elvis Presley, Steve Sholes) ✰✰✰✰; *King Creole* (RCA, 1958, prod. Jerry Leiber, Mike Stoller) ✰✰✰✰; *For LP Fans Only* (RCA, 1959, prod. various) ✰✰✰✰; *A Date with Elvis* (RCA, 1959, prod. various) ✰✰✰✰; *Elvis Is Back!* (RCA, 1960, prod. Elvis Presley) ✰✰✰✰; and *His Hand in Mine* (RCA, 1960, prod. Elvis Presley) ✰✰✰✰, a gospel album that initially confused the record company. Finally, *Elvis Country* (RCA, 1971, prod. Jarvis Sholes, Steve Sholes) ✰✰✰✰ was decent proof that the 1970s Elvis wasn't just a fat druggie awaiting death.

what to avoid: Most of Presley's schlock, which became almost as famous as his greatest work, was in either the bad concert or icky movie soundtrack categories. His bad live albums were most prominent during the 1970s, including *As Recorded at Madison Square Garden* (RCA, 1972) ✰✰, *Recorded Live on Stage in Memphis* (RCA, 1974) ✰✰, *Having Fun with Elvis on Stage* (RCA, 1974) ✰ (just the King making bad jokes), *Elvis in Concert* (RCA, 1977) ✰ and *Elvis on Stage* (RCA, 1977) ✰. The wretched movie music was most prominent during the 1960s, on *Fun in Acapulco* (RCA, 1963) ✰✰, *Live a Little, Love a Little/Charro!/The Trouble with Girls/Change of Habit* (RCA, 1995) ✰✰, *Girl Happy/Harum Scarum* (RCA, 1965) ✰✰ and *Frankie and Johnny/Paradise, Hawaiian Style* (RCA, 1966) ✰✰. Also stay away from *It's Now or Never: The Tribute to Elvis* (Mercury, 1994, prod. various) ✰✰, which does have fan Dwight Yoakam but also such hacks as Michael Bolton and Wet Wet Wet.

the rest:

Elvis' Golden Records, Volume I (RCA, 1958) ✰✰✰✰✰

50,000,000 Elvis Fans Can't Be Wrong: Elvis' Golden Records, Volume 2 (RCA, 1960) ✰✰✰✰✰

Elvis' Golden Records, Volume 3 (RCA, 1963) ✰✰✰✰✰

Elvis' Golden Records, Volume 4 (RCA, 1968) ✰✰✰✰✰

50 World Wide Gold Award Hits, Volume 1, Nos. 1-2 (RCA, 1970/1988) ✰✰✰✰

50 World Wide Gold Award Hits, Volume 1, Nos. 3-4 (RCA, 1971) ✰✰✰✰✰

A Legendary Performer: Volume 1 (RCA, 1974) ✰✰✰✰

A Legendary Performer: Volume 2 (RCA, 1976) ✰✰✰✰

A Legendary Performer: Volume 3 (RCA, 1978) ✰✰✰✰

A Legendary Performer: Volume 4 (RCA, 1983) ✰✰✰✰

Elvis' Gold Records, Volume 5 (RCA, 1984) ✰✰✰

Elvis—A Golden Celebration (RCA, 1984) ✰✰✰

The #1 Hits (RCA, 1987) ✰✰✰

The Memphis Record (RCA, 1987) ✰✰✰✰

Essential Elvis (RCA, 1988) ✰✰✰✰

Stereo '57 (Essential Elvis Volume 2) (RCA, 1988) ✰✰✰✰

The Top Ten Hits (RCA, 1988) ✰✰✰✰

The Essential Elvis, Volume 3 (RCA, 1991) ✰✰✰✰

worth searching for: The soundtrack *Honeymoon in Vegas* (Epic, 1992, prod. Peter Afterman, Glen Brunman) ✰✰✰, despite the lifeless carbon-copy Billy Joel versions of "All Shook Up" and "Heartbreak Hotel," has terrific cover versions by Dwight Yoakam, Willie Nelson, Trisha Yearwood and Ricky Van Shelton. Also, great books about Elvis include *Last Train to Memphis: The Rise of Elvis Presley,* by Peter Guralnick (Little, Brown); *Dead Elvis,* by Greil Marcus (Anchor Books); and *The Elvis Reader,* by various writers, including rocker Mojo Nixon (St. Martin's Press).

influences:

◀◀ Bill Monroe, Hank Snow, Arthur "Big Boy" Crudup, Little Richard, Chuck Berry, Lowell Fulson, Big Mama Thornton, Frank Sinatra, Hank Williams, Roy Brown, Carter Family, Jimmie Rodgers, Ink Spots, Eddy Arnold

▶▶ Buddy Holly, Carl Perkins, Roy Orbison, Beatles, Johnny Cash, Bob Dylan, Beach Boys, Janis Martin, Bruce Springsteen, Billy Joel, Mojo Nixon, Dwight Yoakam, the Band, Blasters, Travis Tritt, Marty Stuart, Garth Brooks

Steve Knopper

RAY PRICE

Born January 12, 1926, in Perryville, TX.

One of the truly great honky-tonkers, Ray Price has been making hit records for over 40 years: early on with his band the Cherokee Cowboys, whose famous alumni include Roger Miller, Buddy Emmons, Jimmy Day, Johnny Bush, Johnny Paycheck and Willie Nelson, and later with a more uptown, countrypolitan sound. Price's early hits featured a chugging, bass-driven shuffle beat, Western swing-style fiddle and plenty of twittering pedal-steel guitar. His vocals, at first heavily reminiscent of Hank Williams, featured an affecting catch in his voice and a bluesy delivery, along with strong tenor harmony vocals on the choruses. "Crazy Arms," "You've Done Me Wrong," "My Shoes Keep Walking Back to You," "City Lights," "Heartaches by the Number," "Under Your Spell Again" and other honky-tonk hits virtually defined the genre during the era. Price's style gradually changed, becoming smoother, more urbane and sophisticated, as such hits as his version of "Danny Boy," "Take Me As I Am or Let Me Go" and, most notably, the Kris Kristofferson–penned "For the Good Times," a giant hit for Ray in 1970. By this time, of course, Price had reportedly become Johnny Carson's favorite singer, and many of his hits bore little resemblance to the honky-tonk classics of the 1950s and early 1960s. His major hitmaking days were over by the mid-1970s, but he has continued to tour and record successfully, often revisiting his hits on remakes for Step One Records. Price was elected to the Country Music Hall of Fame in 1996.

what to buy: *The Essential Ray Price: 1951–1962* (Columbia, 1989, prod. Gregg Geller) 🎵🎵🎵🎵 contains 20 of Ray's finest honky-tonk numbers from 1951 to 1962. *Ray Price's Greatest Hits* (Columbia, 1963, prod. various) 🎵🎵🎵 is a good collection of Price's early hits, but the fidelity leaves a lot to be desired.

what to buy next: *San Antonio Rose: Ray Price Sings a Tribute to the Great Bob Wills* (Koch, 1996, prod. Don Law, Frank Jones) 🎵🎵🎵🎵 is a reissue of the 1962 tribute to one of Ray's early influences, including 12 of Wills' best known songs. *Night Life* (Koch, 1996, prod. Don Law, Frank Jones) 🎵🎵🎵 is a reissue of a very nice 1963 album cut for Columbia, featuring his classic reading of Willie Nelson's "Night Life."

the rest:
Happens to Be the Best (Pair, 1983) 🎵🎵🎵
Portrait of a Singer (Step One, 1985) 🎵🎵
Greatest Hits, Volume 1 (Step One, 1986) 🎵🎵
Greatest Hits, Volume 2 (Step One, 1986) 🎵🎵
Greatest Hits, Volume 3 (Step One, 1986) 🎵🎵
A Revival of Old-Time Singing (Step One, 1986) 🎵
Heart of Country Music (Step One, 1987) 🎵🎵
Just Enough Love (Step One, 1988) 🎵
Greatest Hits, Volume IV: By Request (Step One, 1989) 🎵🎵
Hall of Fame Series (Step One, 1991) 🎵🎵
Sometimes a Rose (Columbia, 1992) 🎵🎵🎵
Los Dos (Amistad, 1994) 🎵🎵🎵

worth searching for: *American Originals* (Columbia, 1989, prod. various) 🎵🎵🎵 contains representative hits from both the honky-tonk and countrypolitan-crooner phases of Ray's career: a good one-disc overview. *Ray Price and the Cherokee Cowboys* (Bear Family, 1995, prod. Don Law, Frank Jones, Jim Beck) 🎵🎵🎵🎵 is a monumental, 12-CD German import reissue, including everything Price cut for Columbia between 1950 and 1966, plus an exhaustive 80-page book. Ideal for the Ray Price & the Cherokee Cowboys fanatic.

influences:
◀◀ Hank Williams
▶▶ Kris Kristofferson

Randy Pitts

TONI PRICE
Born in Philadelphia, PA.

Toni Price cut her musical teeth singing Led Zeppelin covers in a Nashville bar band, not worshipping at the shrine of Patsy, Tammy and Loretta. It wasn't until an encounter with a stack of Bonnie Raitt records that Price saw there might be other possibilities for her in music. Still, the tattoo on her shoulder that says "Keith" commemorates not an old boyfriend but Rolling Stone Keith Richards, so it's not surprising to find that her music is a hybrid of rock, blues and country. During the late 1980s, Price moved to Austin, Texas, where she remains rooted to the spot, refusing to tour, make videos, or do anything that might be deemed careerist. Instead, she holds down the Tuesday happy hour time-slot at a local watering hole, playing for tips and doing what she damn well pleases. One could do worse in life.

what to buy: Price's sophomore effort, *Hey* (Antone's/Discovery, 1995, prod. Derek O'Brien, Toni Price) 🎵🎵🎵🎵, is more country-inflected than her boozy, bluesy debut, though it still retains the genre-busting edge that is the singer's stock-in-trade. Not a songwriter herself, Price has a knack for picking choice material from the pens of others, and here she chooses seven songs by underrated Austin tunesmith Gwil Owen, plus a tender cover of Butch Hancock's "Bluebird" and a raucous run-through of Bob Dylan's "Obviously 5 Believers."

the rest:
Swim Away (Antone's/Discovery, 1993) 🎵🎵🎵🎵

influences:
◀◀ Bonnie Raitt, Aretha Franklin, Ray Charles, Lou Ann Barton

Daniel Durchholz

CHARLEY PRIDE
Born Charley Frank Pride, March 18, 1939, in Sledge, MS.

Charley Pride is one of country's most successful singers and certainly its most successful black singer. He cites Hank Williams as his main musical idol. Pride worked in many other areas before reaching stardom—cotton picker, construction worker, soldier, even pitcher/outfielder for the Negro League Memphis Red Sox. Pride tried his luck in Nashville after receiving encouragement from Red Foley and Red Sovine when they heard his unique, resonant baritone. He made his debut on the Grand Ole Opry stage on January 4, 1967; 30 years later the Country Music Association honored him for "three decades of contributions in country music." During those years, Pride had 60 Top 40 hits. He won several Grammy Awards and the CMA named him its Entertainer of the Year in 1971 and Male Vocalist of the Year in 1971 and 1972. Pride has been married for more than 40 years to his wife, Rozene. They have three children: sons Kraig and Dion (who now plays guitar in his father's band), and a daughter, Angela.

what to buy: Charley Pride issued more than 40 albums during his stay at RCA from 1966–1985, and the label has been notoriously bad about keeping his music in print. After issuing collections of such lesser artists as Floyd Cramer and Earl Thomas Conley, RCA finally got around to putting out a decent collection on Pride, who has more charting country hits than anybody in the label's history except Elvis Presley. At 20 cuts, *The Essential Charley Pride* (RCA, 1997, prod. various) 🎵🎵🎵🎵 is a healthy dose of Pride's hard-country, working-man music, and it includes his gold-selling "Kiss an Angel Good Morning" from 1971. Pride had 20 chart-toppers for RCA, so this is merely a good start. He deserves much, much more.

what to buy next: With his music nearly impossible to find in its original form, Pride took to re-recording his hits during the 1990s. *My Six Latest & Six Greatest* (Honest Entertainment, 1994, prod. Jim Long) 🎵🎵🎵 captures a refreshing blend of old and new material. Joe Diffie, Hal Ketchum, Marty Stuart and Travis Tritt joined Pride on this album, which includes new versions of "Kiss an Angel Good Morning" and "Hope You're Feelin' Me (Like I'm Feeling You)."

what to avoid: If they weren't the only way to get some of Pride's singles, RCA's cheapo hits packages such as *The Best of Charley Pride* (RCA, 1979/1985) 🎵🎵, *Greatest Hits* (RCA, 1988) 🎵🎵 and *The Best of Charley Pride, Volume II* (RCA, 1995) 🎵🎵 ought to be shunned just on principle. *Best of Charley Pride* (Curb, 1991) 🎵 is the worst, though—a repackaging of an album Pride recorded for the now-defunct 16th Avenue Records.

the rest:
Platinum Pride, Volume 1 & 2 (Honest, 1994) 🎵🎵🎵
Greatest Hits Volume 2 (RCA, 1995) 🎵🎵🎵
Super Hits (RCA, 1996) 🎵🎵🎵🎵

influences:
⏪ Hank Williams, Red Foley
⏩ Neal McCoy, Cleve Francis

Beth Lockamie and Brian Mansfield

JOHN PRINE

Born October 10, 1946, in Maywood, IL.

One of the first to be strapped as "the new Dylan," John Prine is one of the few to actually outgrow the tag and become a distinct, trenchant songwriting voice. Mostly because of his admittedly limited guitar skills, Prine often gets lumped in the folkie singer/songwriter genre, but as anyone who has ever listened carefully or heard him play with a band knows, he has the heart and soul of a rock 'n' roller. His 1971 self-titled debut alone includes astonishing songs such as: "Sam Stone," the first Vietnam protest song to examine the war's effect on soldiers' lives; an homage to the elderly wryly titled "Hello in There"; "Donald and Lydia," a touching ode to masturbation; the wicked social satire "Spanish Pipedream" with the oft-repeated chorus "Blow up your TV/Throw away your paper"; and "Angel from Montgomery," a longtime staple of Bonnie Raitt and dozens of country singers. Major labels gave up on Prine, which led him to start his own Oh Boy Records during the early 1980s. These days his edge, sharp eye for detail and feel for simple melodies, common language and popular culture seems, if anything, more intact—and he's even more effective in concert. His songs have been recorded by many diverse artists, including Joan Baez, Bette Midler, the Everly Brothers and Cowboy Junkies. But more importantly, Prine's influence can be heard whenever guitars are played on streets and living rooms around the world.

what to buy: *John Prine* (Atlantic, 1971, prod. Arif Mardin) 🎵🎵🎵🎵🎵, with its raw, harrowing, sometimes goofy tales of life, best reflects his talents. *The Missing Years* (Oh Boy, 1991, prod. Howie Epstein) 🎵🎵🎵🎵🎵 offers the same kind of worldview, undaunted by middle age. *Bruised Orange* (Asylum/Oh Boy, 1978, prod. Steve Goodman) 🎵🎵🎵🎵 offers Goodman's inspired arrangements. *John Prine Live* (Oh Boy, 1988, prod. John Prine, Dan Einstein, Jim Rooney) 🎵🎵🎵🎵 includes the stories and onstage charisma that's missing on some of his studio albums.

what to buy next: *Storm Windows* (Asylum, 1980, prod. Barry Beckett) 🎵🎵🎵🎵 offers Prine's best sound, courtesy of producer Beckett. *Aimless Love* (Oh Boy, 1984, prod. John Prine, Jim Rooney) 🎵🎵🎵🎵 is a pleasant, country flavored record. *Great Days* (Rhino, 1993, prod. various) 🎵🎵🎵🎵🎵 is as good a collection as you'll find, with all albums represented.

what to avoid: *Common Sense* (Atlantic, 1975, prod. Steve Cropper) 🎵🎵 is a classic example of mismatching producer and artist. The songs—and there are some good ones—often sound incomplete, and Prine sounds out of breath at the end of every one.

the rest:
Sweet Revenge (Atlantic, 1973) 🎵🎵🎵

Prime Prine (Atlantic, 1976) ♫♫
German Afternoons (Oh Boy, 1988) ♫♫♫
A John Prine Christmas (Oh Boy, 1993) ♫♫♫
Lost Dogs and Mixed Blessings (Oh Boy, 1995) ♫♫♫
Live on Tour (Oh Boy, 1997) ♫♫♫

worth searching for: *Pink Cadillac* (Asylum/Oh Boy, 1979, prod. Knox Phillips, Jerry Phillips) ♫♫♫♫ finds a primal Prine drawing a strange energy and vibe from Sam Phillips' kids in the famous Sun studios.

influences:

◄◄ Carter Family, Hank Williams, Chuck Berry, Jerry Lee Lewis

►► Nanci Griffith, Iris Dement, Cowboy Junkies

Leland Rucker

PSYCHOGRASS

Formed 1993. Reformed 1996.

Darol Anger, fiddle (1993, 1996); Mike Marshall, mandolin (1993, 1996); Todd Phillips, string bass (1993, 1996); Tony Trischka, banjo (1996); David Grier, guitar (1996); Joe Craven, percussion (1993).

Psychograss is a sort of supergroup of progressive acoustic musicians who mix bluegrass, jazz and other musical styles. The first incarnation in 1993 featured four musicians who had all played with David Grisman. The 1996 version strengthened the band by adding virtuoso players David Grier on guitar and Tony Trischka on banjo.

what to buy: *Like Minds* (Sugar Hill, 1996, prod. Darol Anger, Mike Marshall) ♫♫♫♫ is an all-instrumental effort more closely tied to bluegrass than its predecessor, featuring 12 originals and a cover of Jimi Hendrix's "Third Stone from the Sun." The focus is on the players' virtuosity and wild inventiveness, with plenty of ensemble improvisations.

what to buy next: *Psychograss* (Windham Hill, 1993, prod. Mike Marshall, Darol Anger) ♫♫♫ fuses jazz and bluegrass with folk, classical, rock and world music. The one vocal is handled by guest Tim O'Brien on a cover of Procol Harum's "Whiter Shade of Pale." Tony Trischka guests on his own "Flanders Rock."

influences:

◄◄ David Grisman, Turtle Island String Quartet

►► Modern Mandolin Quartet, Bela Fleck & the Flecktones.

see also: *Tony Trischka, David Grier*

Douglas Fulmer

RILEY PUCKETT

Born George Riley Puckett, May 7, 1894 (or possibly 1890), in Alpharetta, GA. Died July 13, 1946, in College Park, GA.

The first prominent guitarist in country music, and probably the first country singer to yodel on a recording, Riley Puckett (who was blinded as an infant) made his radio debut in 1922. He first recorded in 1924, as a duo with Georgia fiddler Gid Tanner, and was a charter member of Tanner's immensely popular and free-wheeling stringband, the Skillet Lickers. As lead singer and guitarist for that pioneering group until it disbanded during the mid-1930s, Puckett was enormously influential on young musicians in the South. As a solo artist, he recorded for Columbia, Bluebird and Decca and worked on radio stations in Georgia, Kentucky, West Virginia and Tennessee.

what's available: While the sound of the Skillet Lickers was raucous and wonderfully chaotic, Puckett's solo recordings were more restrained, featuring his mellow singing and distinctive guitar playing. Unfortunately, none of his solo recordings are available on CD (1970s-era LP reissues on County, Old Homestead and Bear Family are worth the search). The only Skillet Lickers CD available, *Old-Time Fiddle Tunes and Songs from North Georgia* (County, 1996) ♫♫♫, reissues 16 songs and tunes recorded between 1927 and 1931. Puckett is present on every cut, driving the fiddle tunes with his propulsive, bass-heavy guitar playing, singing on about half of the selections. Puckett's playing is most impressive on "Dixie" and "Molly Put the Kettle On"; of the vocals, "Dixie," "Devilish Mary" and "Pretty Little Widow" are the most enjoyable to modern ears.

influences:

◄◄ Roy Harvey, Maybelle Carter

►► Every other guitar player in bluegrass and old-time country music

Jon Hartley Fox

PURE PRAIRIE LEAGUE

Formed 1971, in Cincinnati, OH. Disbanded 1988.

Craig Fuller, vocals, guitars (1971–75, 1985–88); George Powell, guitars, vocals (1971–77); Jim Lanham, bass, vocals (1971–72); Jim Caughlan, drums (1971–72); John David Call, steel guitar (1971–75); Michael Connor, keyboards (1972–88); Michael Reilly, bass, vocals (1972–88); Billy Hinds, drummer (1972–88); Larry Goshorn, guitar (1975–77);

John Prine (© Ken Settle)

Timmy Goshorn, steel guitar (1975–77); Vince Gill, guitar, vocals (1978–81); Patrick Bolin, woodwinds (1979–80); Jeff Wilson, guitar, vocals (1980–88); Gary Burr, vocals (1981–85).

Pure Prairie League, which took its name from a women's temperance group in an Errol Flynn movie, was a Cincinnati country-rock group that drew influences from the California sounds of the Flying Burrito Brothers as well as from regional bluegrass. Neither of the group's first two albums, *Pure Prairie League* or *Bustin' Out*, did well upon their release in 1972, prompting RCA to drop the group. Craig Fuller, having draft problems, left the band (President Gerald Ford eventually pardoned him). Two years later, "Amie" began receiving national airplay, leaving the group in the unenviable position of having a hit and no frontman. RCA re-signed a revamped group, which continued evolving into the 1980s and eventually featured a young Vince Gill on the group's only Top 10 hit, 1980's "Let Me Love You Tonight." Fuller went on to form American Flyer and front a post–Lowell George version of Little Feat before rejoining PPL in 1985.

what to buy: At the time of its release, *Bustin' Out* (RCA, 1972, prod. Robert Alan Ringe) 𝄞𝄞𝄞 didn't quite seem to be either rock or country but rather a blend of the better parts of both. Fuller wrote and sang gentle pop-rock songs, which were accented by steel guitar and a largely acoustic background. The "Falling in and out of Love/Amie" medley that appears here became an FM radio hit before "Amie" turned into a Top 40 single on its own, suggesting possibilities to an entire generation of future country singers. Mick Ronson of David Bowie's Spiders from Mars contributed string arrangements.

what to buy next: Fuller left PPL before the group made *Two Lane Highway* (RCA, 1975, prod. John Boylan) 𝄞𝄞𝄞, so the songwriting suffers. But this album showcases the group's country licks, particularly on the concert favorite "Pickin' to Beat the Devil." Even though *Best of Pure Prairie League* (Mercury, 1995, prod. various) 𝄞𝄞𝄞 sequences the "Falling in and out of Love/Amie" medley backwards and favors the band's Mercury days over its better RCA material, the compilation is still the only place to get "Amie" and "Let Me Love You Tonight" on the same disc.

what to avoid: Pure Prairie League hasn't been well served by best-of compilations, partially because the group's two biggest hits came five years apart for different labels. Those singles aside, the band's albums are fairly consistent, *Dance* (RCA, 1976, prod. Alan Abrahams) 𝄞𝄞 being the weakest album from the early period and *Something in the Night* (Mercury, 1981, prod. Rob Fraboni) 𝄞𝄞 the weakest from the later.

the rest:
Mementos: 1971–1987 (Rushmore Productions, 1987) 𝄞𝄞𝄞
"Amie" and Other Hits (RCA, 1990) 𝄞𝄞𝄞

worth searching for: *Live! Takin' the Stage* (RCA, 1977) 𝄞𝄞𝄞 shows an adequate band on stage and offers live versions of the some of the band's early favorites

influences:
◀◀ Byrds, Flying Burrito Brothers, Creedence Clearwater Revival
▶▶ Little Feat, Garth Brooks, Clint Black

see also: *Vince Gill*

Brian Mansfield

R

EDDIE RABBITT
Born November 27, 1944, in Brooklyn, NY.

City-slicker-turned-Nashvillian Eddie Rabbitt waited several years before getting a shot at stardom, but made his mark in the meantime as the writer of Elvis Presley's comeback hit "Kentucky Rain" and Ronnie Milsap's "Pure Love." A staff writer for Nashville music publishers Hill & Range—and earning a meager $37.50 a week—Rabbitt hit the big time in 1970 when Presley turned his "Kentucky Rain" into a solid smash. Three years later Milsap scored with "Pure Love" and Elektra Records took notice, hiring Eddie in 1973. His first single for the label, "You Get to Me," did fairly well, and by 1975, Eddie's tunes began cracking the country Top 20. "Drinkin' My Baby (Off My Mind)" soared to #1, while "Rock Mountain Music" and "Two Dollars in the Jukebox" easily entered the Top 10. From the mid-1970s till the mid-1980s, Eddie continued to deliver chart-toppers, including "You Don't Love Me Anymore," "I Just Want to Love You," "Every Which Way but Loose," "Suspicions," "Gone Too Far," "Drivin' My Life Away," "I Love a Rainy Night," "Step by Step," "Someone Could Lose a Heart Tonight" and "Repetitive Regret."

what to buy: Between the two of them, *The Best of Eddie Rabbit/Greatest Hits, Volume II* (Warner Bros., prod. David Malloy) 𝄞𝄞𝄞𝄞 and *All-Time Greatest Hits* (Warner Bros., 1991, prod. David Malloy) 𝄞𝄞𝄞𝄞 contain most of the aforementioned tunes. Stripped of filler, *All-Time Greatest Hits* makes a good case for

Rabbitt's commercial appeal—it's hard to argue with the catchiness of "Someone Could Lose a Heart Tonight" and especially "Drivin' My Life Away."

what to buy next: Rabbitt lost his pop luster during the 1980s, but *Greatest Country Hits* (Curb, 1991, prod. David Malloy) 🐾🐾🐾 compiles his continued country hot streak through the end of that decade, including "I Wanna Dance with You" and his #1 remake of Dion & the Belmonts' "The Wanderer."

the rest:
The Best of Eddie Rabbitt (Elektra, 1979) 🐾🐾🐾
Step by Step (Capitol Nashville, 1981) 🐾🐾
The Best Year of My Life (Warner Bros., 1984) 🐾🐾🐾
#1's (Warner Bros., 1985) 🐾🐾🐾
Jersey Boy (Capitol Nashville, 1990) 🐾🐾🐾
Ten Years of Greatest Hits (Capitol Nashville, 1990) 🐾🐾🐾
Classics Collection (Capitol Nashville, 1991) 🐾🐾🐾
Ten Rounds (Capitol Nashville, 1991) 🐾🐾

influences:
◀◀ Bob Dylan, Elvis Presley, Neil Diamond
▶▶ Steve Wariner

Rick Petreycik and David Simons

WILLIS ALAN RAMSEY

Born March 5, 1951, in Birmingham, AL.

Wielding more influence than the meager sales of his lone album would indicate, Willis Alan Ramsey is seen today as a genuine forbear of the progressive country scene that has grown up around Austin, Texas, during the past two decades. Only 21 when he recorded his debut album, an effort that teemed with promise and a crack session team (Leon Russell, Ernie Watts, Leland Sklar, Russ Kunkel, Jim Keltner, Carl Radle), Ramsey inexplicably failed to follow it up. For a time he lived in England and Ireland, but has since relocated to Nashville. Rumors of a second album abound, but thus far none has appeared.

what's available: *Willis Alan Ramsey* (Shelter, 1972/DCC Compact Classics, 1990, prod. Denny Cordell, Willis Alan Ramsey) 🐾🐾🐾🐾 is an acoustic-based collection of literate and laid-back country/folk tunes, some of which have been covered by Leon Russell, Jimmy Buffett, America, Waylon Jennings, and, most recently, Shawn Colvin. Ramsey's best-known song, "Muskrat Love," which is included here, was a hit for America and for the Captain & Tennille.

Eddie Rabbitt **(AP/Wide World Photos)**

influences:
◀◀ Woody Guthrie, Bob Dylan, Gram Parsons
▶▶ Lyle Lovett, Nanci Griffith, Butch Hancock

Daniel Durchholz

RANCH ROMANCE

Formed 1989, in Seattle, WA. Disbanded 1994.

Jo Miller, guitar, vocals; Lisa Theo, vocals, mandolin (1989–91); Barbara Lamb, vocals, fiddle; Nancy Katz, vocals, bass; Nova Karina Devonie, accordion, vocals (1991–94); Michael Buono, drums (1991–93); David Keenan, vocals, guitar, mandolin, banjo (1992–94).

This hot, mostly female band (David Keenan, the man with longest tenure in the band was usually referred to onstage as the band's Ranch Ro-man), opened a series of shows for k.d. lang early in its existence, giving the group a nice push. They were a hot band, featuring the scintillating fiddle of Barbara Lamb, who went on to become a member of Asleep at the Wheel, the passionate lead vocals of Jo Miller, and for a time, Lisa Theo, plus the plucky Clevinger bass playing of Nancy

Katz. Nova Devonie added her accordion beginning with the second album, and the versatile hotpicking of David Keenan added to the mix. The band's repertoire featured a mixture of country boogie, Western swing, some cowboy yodeling, torchy country ballads, a little bluegrass, a lot of originals by the band and a strong spirit of good fun.

what's available: *Western Dream* (Ranch Hand Records, 1989/ Sugar Hill, 1991, prod. Ranch Romance, Michael Lord) ♪♪♪, the band's first album, represents their spirit of good fun very well. On *Blue Blazes* (Sugar Hill, 1991, prod. Michael Lord, Jo Miller) ♪♪♪♪, the band really hits its stride—a collection of scorching honky-tonkers, swing, cowperson yodeling and smoldering ballads, it includes the band's perverse take on roadhouse sin, "Buckaroo." *Flip City* (Sugar Hill, 1993, prod. Tim O'Brien) ♪♪♪ offers more hot honky-tonk, Western swing and country boogie.

solo outings:

Barbara Lamb:

Fiddle Fatale (Sugar Hill, 1993) ♪♪♪

Tonight I Feel Like Texas (Sugar Hill, 1996) ♪♪♪♪

Jo Miller:

(With Laura Love) *Jo Miller and Laura Love Sing Bluegrass and Old Time Songs* (Rockin' Octoroon Records, 1995) ♪♪♪

influences:

◄◄ Sons of the Pioneers, Patsy Cline

►► k.d. lang, Red Knuckles & the Trailblazers

Randy Pitts

JON RANDALL

Born Jon Randall Stewart, February 17, 1969, in Dallas, TX.

Winner of a Grammy as part of Emmylou Harris' band the Nash Ramblers, Randall's clear tenor and bluegrass-inflected sound is reminiscent of Vince Gill. He married country singer Lorrie Morgan, with whom he recorded the Top 10 duet "By My Side," in 1996.

what's available: *What You Don't Know* (RCA, 1995, prod. Garth Fundis, Sam Bush) ♪♪♪♪, Randall's debut, features a bouncy cover of Kevin Welch's "I Came Straight to You," along with a guest appearance by the Nash Ramblers on one cut, "Just Like You."

worth searching for: RCA issued promotional copies of a different version of *What You Don't Know* with three different tracks, as well as a second album the label never released.

influences:

◄◄ Vince Gill, Emmylou Harris

Bill Hobbs

BOOTS RANDOLPH

Born Homer Louis Randolph Jr., June 3, 1927, in Paducah, KY.

As part of a family possessing musical talent and the desire to survive the Depression, Boots Randolph grabbed a ukulele and joined the family band. They played any club, auditorium or run-down theater that would take them and often were paid with cans of food. While a teenager in Cadiz, Kentucky, he was presented with a trombone by his father. Thrust into the high school band, Randolph traded his trombone for a saxophone because it was easier to march with. After a stint with the army and while playing at a club in Illinois, Randolph and an associate, James "Spider" Rich, wrote "Yakety Sax." They sent a tape to an impressed Chet Atkins at RCA and before long, Randolph was a session musician in Nashville. He played for such greats as Al Hirt, Homer & Jethro, Perry Como, Roy Orbison, Eddy Arnold and Elvis Presley. A change to Monument Records in 1960 brought Randolph's *Yakety Sax* album to popularity with country fans. Appearances on the Grand Ole Opry, TV shows and the opening of the popular Boots Randolph Club in Nashville's Printers Alley continued to solidify his popularity. Today Randolph continues to entertain fans with limited performances and remains country music's best-known saxophonist.

what to buy: Boots Randolph never has had a charting country hit, and only "Yakety Sax" made the pop Top 40, so take the title of *The Greatest Hits of Boots Randolph* (Monument, 1976/1988) ♪♪♪ with a grain of salt. Still, these are the songs most associated with Randolph through his career, with plenty of Randolph's honking sax on tunes as dissimilar as "Charlie Brown" and "The Shadow of Your Smile."

what to buy next: You could put all of Randolph's albums on one long tape, play them continuously, and nobody'd be able to tell when one album ended and the next one started. *Country Boots* (Monument, 1974/1988) ♪♪♪ is recommended over other collections because of songs such as "Wabash Cannonball," "Tennessee Waltz" and "Behind Closed Doors."

the rest:

Homer Louis Randolph III (Monument, 1976/1991) ♪♪♪

Sunday Sax (Monument, 1976/1991) ♪♪

Yakety Sax! (Monument, 1988) ♪♪♪

Sentimental Journey (Monument, 1988) ♪♪

Live (Monument, 1992) 🎵🎵
Christmas at Boots' Place (LaserLight) 🎵🎵
Best of Boots Randolph (Curb, 1997) 🎵🎵

influences:

◀◀ King Curtis, Earl Bostic

▶▶ Ace Cannon, Jim Horn

Randall T. Cook

WAYNE RANEY

Born August 17, 1921, in Wolf Bayou, AR. Died January 23, 1993.

Harmonica player Wayne Raney enjoyed brief popularity during the late 1940s with a string of acoustic folk and boogie tunes recorded for King. The most popular of these, "Why Don't You Haul Off and Love Me" spent four weeks atop *Billboard* magazine's Juke Box chart. Raney worked with the Raney Family and the Brown's Ferry Four, two gospel groups, and the Delmore Brothers, and he was also an influential country and bluegrass DJ. He died of cancer in 1993.

what's available: *Songs from the Hills* (King, 1987) 🎵🎵 contains all three of Raney's Top 40 hits, "Lost John Boogie," "Jack and Jill Boogie" and "Why Don't You Haul Off and Love Me." This is folksy stuff, with arrangements featuring acoustic guitar, fiddles and Raney's harmonica. At 16 songs, there's plenty of music, but the master recordings are often scratchy and there are no liner notes.

influences:

◀◀ Raney Family, Delmore Brothers

▶▶ Doc Watson

Brian Mansfield

RANK & FILE

Formed 1981, in Austin, TX. Disbanded 1987.

Chip Kinman, vocals, guitar, harmonica; Tony Kinman, vocals, bass; Alejandro Escovedo, guitar (1981–83); Jeff Ross, guitar (1983–87); Slim Evans, drums (1981–83); Stan Lynch, drums (1983–85); R. Kahr, drums (1986–87).

Long before it became fashionable to hang bolo ties and Telecasters around one's neck, Rank & File were bravely bringing their own ferocious mixture of thrash and twang to an initially bewildered public—and in the process almost single-handedly kick-started the entire alternative-country movement (though they'd likely be loathe to admit to, or take credit for, such an achievement). Following the disbandment of their Bay Area

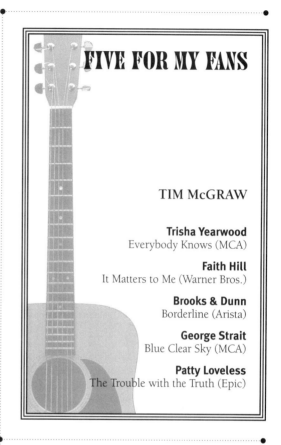

FIVE FOR MY FANS

TIM McGRAW

Trisha Yearwood
Everybody Knows (MCA)

Faith Hill
It Matters to Me (Warner Bros.)

Brooks & Dunn
Borderline (Arista)

George Strait
Blue Clear Sky (MCA)

Patty Loveless
The Trouble with the Truth (Epic)

punk combo the Dils in 1980, brothers Chip and Tony Kinman sought refuge in Austin alongside old pal Alejandro Escovedo and soon afterwards formed the initial incarnation of R&F. Their highly unusual—and at the time highly unfashionable—blend of Bakersfield-style swagger and Ramones-tempo fervor quickly landed them a deal with Warners' upstart Slash division.

what to buy: Their debut album, *Sundown* (Slash, 1982, prod. David Kahne) 🎵🎵🎵🎵, won widespread praise (no less than the *Los Angeles Times* called it "one of the strongest American debut records in a decade"), a headlining appearance on *Austin City Limits* and even a cover of one of its songs, "Amanda Ruth," by the Everly Brothers. Before fully capitalizing on this notoriety, however, the band splintered, leaving the Kinmans to record *Long Gone Dead* (Slash, 1984, prod. Jeff Eyrich) 🎵🎵🎵🎵🎵 with a bevy of competent, if "uninitiated" sidemen. Nevertheless, this album is even better than its predecessor: richer, more melodically adventurous and surprisingly more

John Fogerty than Johnny Cash in its overall approach. Unfortunately, outside of a small circle of friends and followers (a young Dwight Yoakam among them), nobody seemed to be listening, and after one final record, the Kinmans unceremoniously pulled the plug on the entire endeavor.

the rest:

Rank & File (Rhino, 1987) 🎵🎵

influences:

◀◀ Blasters, George Jones, Everly Brothers, Creedence Clearwater Revival

▶▶ Long Ryders, Lone Justice, Uncle Tupelo

Gary Pig Gold

THE RARELY HERD

Formed September 1989, in Albany, OH

Jim Stack, guitar, lead vocals; Alan Stack, mandolin, fiddle, vocals; Jeff Weaver, bass, vocals; Dan Brooks, dobro, vocals; Calvin Leport, banjo, guitar.

Fan favorites throughout the Midwest and upper South, the Rarely Herd (the name's a take-off on the bad-pun moniker of the Seldom Scene) is a hard-working young bluegrass band and one of the most entertaining outfits on the circuit. Taking their cue from past "show bands" like Flatt & Scruggs and the Boys from Indiana, the Herd combines crowd-pleasing novelty songs and stage antics with rock-solid musicianship (Leport, Brooks and Alan Stack are all impressive pickers) and an engaging vocal sound spearheaded by underrated lead singer Jim Stack. The band has won a number of major awards from the Society for the Preservation of Blue Grass Music in America and was featured in a documentary program on bluegrass aired on NHK, Japan's largest television network.

what's available: *Heartbreak City* (Pinecastle, 1994, prod. Butch Baldassari) 🎵🎵🎵, the band's most successful album in terms of radio airplay, features Jim Stack and company on covers of Elvis and Buddy Holly, the uptempo title cut and outstanding performances on "I Haven't Seen Mary in Years" and "I and Young Billy." *Pure Homemade Love* (Pinecastle, 1995, prod. Butch Baldassari) 🎵🎵🎵, graced by a nice Jim Stack–Kathy Chiavola duet on the title song, reflects the ongoing maturation of the band in such songs as "Once upon a Heartbeat" and Jeff Weaver's original "I Can Face the Rain." *Midnight Loneliness* (Pinecastle, 1992, prod. Butch Baldassari) 🎵🎵🎵, the band's debut, established the Ohio group with a diverse program that

ranges from original songs like "Feed My Sheep" and "Arizona" to bluegrass classics like "Darcy Farrow."

influences:

◀◀ Country Gentlemen, Boys from Indiana

▶▶ Blue Highway, New Vintage

Jon Hartley Fox

EDDY RAVEN

Born Edward Garvin Futch, August 19, 1944, in LaFayette, LA.

From his first single on the Cosmos label during the 1960s, to his RCA hits of the 1980s, Eddy Raven has been widely influenced by everything from the blues to Cajun music. Although he envisioned a baseball career, he was sidelined by a broken ankle and took up music instead, cutting his first single in Brunswick, Georgia, in 1962. With the help of Cajun Grand Ole Opry star Jimmy C. Newman, Raven signed a songwriting contract with Acuff-Rose, penning tunes for Roy Acuff and Don Gibson, among others. His "Thank God for Kids" later became a smash for the Oak Ridge Boys. Raven's first major-label deal, with ABC/Dot, lasted two years without much chart action, followed in rapid succession by stints with Monument, Dimension and Elektra, until he signed with RCA in 1983, where he amassed 13 Top 10 hits, four of which went to #1. In his move to Universal, run by Jimmy Bowen, his former boss at Elektra, Raven managed two consecutive #1 songs before the label was swallowed by Capitol, for whom he had his last chart hit to date, "Island" (#10, 1990).

what's available: *Wild Eyed and Crazy* (Intersound/Branson, 1994) 🎵🎵🎵 is an album of reworked hits that sound pretty much like they did originally, supplemented by new, decidedly lackluster material. Considering the backgrounds of both raven and Jo-El Sonnier, their joint effort, *Cookin' Cajun* (K-Tel, 1996) 🎵🎵🎵, should have worked. Considering the material, it doesn't really; the passable Cajun-style country mix fails to ignite.

influences:

◀◀ Oak Ridge Boys

▶▶ Doug Stone

Stephen L. Betts

COLLIN RAYE

Born Floyd Collin Wray, August 22, 1959, in DeQueen, AR.

Collin Raye began his recording career as "Bubba" Wray, the lead singer for an Oregon-based group called the Wrays that had four charting country singles during the mid-1980s. When the Wrays' career failed to take off, Raye spent the next years in the Top 40 clubs of Reno, Nevada, where he developed an extensive repertoire. He began making country records as a solo act in 1991, though he now lives in Greenville, Texas, rather than moving to Nashville, in order to live close to his children and ex-wife. A supple-voiced tenor who often brings to mind Vince Gill on first listen, Raye has a flair for the melodramatic, which serves him well when he chooses good material. He tends to have his biggest records with romantic ballads like "Love, Me," "In This Life" and "One Boy, One Girl."

what to buy: After making his reputation on a string of romantic ballads, Raye extended his reach on his third album, *Extremes* (Epic, 1994, prod. John Hobbs, Ed Seay, Paul Worley) 𝄞𝄞𝄞. It still contained plenty of slow songs, but they included "Little Rock," an intense tale of recovery from alcohol abuse that's the best thing Raye's cut, and a gorgeous cover of Waylon Jennings' "Dreaming My Dreams with You." Raye also included a couple of bar-band rockers, "That's My Story" and "My Kind of Girl."

what to buy next: In *I Think about You* (Epic, 1995, prod. Paul Worley, Ed Seay, John Hobbs) 𝄞𝄞𝄞 Raye continues to find songs with unusual approaches. In the title track, the singer personalizes society's sexual objectification by seeing his daughter in the women who flit by in TV commercials. In "What If Jesus Comes Back Like That," he imagines the reaction Jesus would get if he returned as a hobo or drug addict.

what to avoid: The title track of *In This Life* (Epic, 1992, prod. Garth Fundis, John Hobbs) 𝄞𝄞 became a huge wedding standard among country fans, but here, more than on any other of his albums, Raye too often succumbs to the sappiest elements of his nature.

the rest:
All I Can Be (Epic, 1991) 𝄞𝄞𝄞
The Gift (Epic, 1996) 𝄞𝄞𝄞

influences:
◀◀ Vince Gill, Lee Greenwood, Wrays
▶▶ Ty Herndon

Brian Mansfield

THE RED CLAY RAMBLERS
Formed 1972, in Chapel Hill, NC.

Tommy Thompson, banjo, guitar, vocals (1972–94); Jim Watson, mandolin, guitar, vocals (1972–86); Bill Hicks, fiddle, vocals (1972–81);

Collin Raye (© Ken Settle)

Clay Buckner, fiddle, vocals (1980–present); Mike Craver, piano, vocals (1973–86); Bland Simpson, piano, vocals (1986–present); Jack Herrick, bass, horns, vocals (1976–present); Chris Frank, piano, guitar, accordion, horns, vocals (1987–present).

To call the Red Clay Ramblers a bluegrass band is simply to acknowledge that there's nothing else *to* call them. Original fiddler Bill Hicks describes the Ramblers as "a band that might have existed in 1930, but didn't." They started out as an old-time stringband, self-consciously trying to recreate the musty 78 RPM ambience of Appalachian folk. Even during their early days, however, the Ramblers were never exactly purists about it. They're one of the most versatile bands in the business, drawing from Tin Pan Alley, Cajun, blues, Irish folk and even Broadway standards. Some of the Ramblers' best work has been in conjunction with theatrical productions, beginning with their stint in the acclaimed 1975 off-Broadway musical *Diamond Studs: The Story of Jesse James*. Through 25 years and myriad lineup changes (Shawn Colvin was a part-time member during the mid-1980s, although she does not appear on any of their recordings), the Ramblers have maintained a consistently high standard of quality.

what to buy: The Ramblers have enjoyed a long and fruitful association with writer/director Sam Shepard, starting with *A Lie of the Mind* (Rykodisc/Sugar Hill, 1986, prod. Jack Herrick, Gary Bristol) &&&&. The Ramblers served as pit band for this play about familial clashes, providing musical emphasis points. The score mixes originals with traditional covers like "In the Pines" and Stephen Foster's "Hard Times," and more than stands on its own apart from the play. It's the perfect Ramblers sampler, hitting just the right balance between old and new. The next best thing to seeing 'em live. (The Ramblers also play a medicine show band in Shepard's 1993 movie *Silent Tongue*.)

what to buy next: While it's true that the Ramblers can get a shade too cutesy at times, only the congenitally churlish won't be won over by the 1991 Flying Fish CD package that combines *Twisted Laurel* (1976, prod. Red Clay Ramblers, Alice Gerrard, Bruce Kaplan, Bill McElroy) and *Merchants Lunch* (1977, prod. Red Clay Ramblers, Bill McElroy) &&&&. The material ranges far and wide, from Jimmie Rodgers to W.C. Handy to originals that fit in seamlessly. If you have a hard time telling the difference between the Ramblers' originals and their covers, well, that's the point. *Rambler* (Sugar Hill, 1992, prod. Jack Herrick) &&&& is well-executed but not quite as loose—although its Irish jig take on "Cotton-Eyed Joe" is pretty amazing.

the rest:
The Red Clay Ramblers with Fiddlin' Al McCanless (Folkways, 1974) &&&
Stolen Love (Flying Fish, 1975) &&&&
Chuckin' the Frizz (Flying Fish, 1978) &&&
Meeting in the Air (Flying Fish, 1980) &&&&
Hard Times (Flying Fish, 1982) &&&&
It Ain't Right (Flying Fish, 1986) &&&
The Merry Wives of Windsor, Texas (Snappy, 1988) &&&
Music from Sam Shepard's A Lie of the Mind (Sugar Hill, 1989) &&&&

worth searching for: Of the Ramblers' many extracurricular projects, one of the most intriguing is Michelle Shocked's roots music travelogue *Arkansas Traveler* (Mercury, 1992, prod. Michelle Shocked) &&&, on which they back her up on the track, "Contest Coming." Singer Marti Jones' lost classic *Unsophisticated Time* (A&M, 1985, prod. Don Dixon) &&&& has a wonderful version of Bland Simpson's wistful "Follow You All Over the World." Simpson moonlights with Don Dixon and Jim Wann as the Coastal Cohorts, a trio that performs the musical *King Mackerel & the Blues Are Running* (Sugar Hill, 1996, prod.

Don Dixon) &&&; the production has been known to tour and is well worth seeing.

influences:
◀◀ Charlie Poole & His North Carolina Ramblers, Fats Waller, Louvin Brothers, the Band, Carter Family
▶▶ Hot Rize, Ry Cooder, Bela Fleck, Squirrel Nut Zippers

David Menconi

REDNECK GREECE
Lead singer born Greg Reece, July 18, 1961, in Ellijay, GA.

"Legend has it that Redneck Greece drifted out of the North Georgia mountains carrying nothing but a jug of corn liquor, a bag of songs and a vision," says this wily Southerner's only official press release. "The corn liquor is long gone and the songs and the vision have gotten twisted around, but Redneck is still climbing the stage like he ain't got nowhere else to go." His self-described swingin' hillbilly honky-tonk music is a ferocious blend of Bakersfield and swamp, with a wrong-side-of-the-tracks authenticity which is no doubt the result of Greece's hand-deep-in-dirt upbringing (born and raised on a farm, he was operating a tractor long before he'd ever picked up a guitar).

Following several years spent terrorizing Athens' fledgling college-rock scene, he raided the cream of the area's musicians to form his first of several back-up bands and quickly recorded the delightful *Good Eatin'*. To properly reproduce this record on stage, motorcycles, horses and plenty of "PBR" (Pabst Blue Ribbon, for the uninitiated) were required, and the Redneck Greece Delux Show quickly became a forbidden pleasure in the ballrooms and motor inns of the American Southeast. Most recently the man has not only been spotted playing his first solo shows in many years but has popped up on local cable television hawking his very own brand of Redneck Burgers for the one and only Loco's Deli. He also remains an outspoken critic of the current "alternative country" movement, spotting from a mile away the obvious lack of pedigree in some of its most high-profile practitioners. "Son Volt came and saw me at the Star Bar," recalls Redneck. "They thought I was crazy giving away all those panties." Case closed.

what to buy: *Cold Hard Facts* (SMBT, 1994, prod. Jeff Walls) &&&&, with its Hank Jr.–sings–*Exile on Main Street* bravado, further established the band as a force to be reckoned with, and Reece in particular as a fine songwriter capable of carrying the art of the story-song twisting and writhing into the next century.

the rest:

Good Eatin' (SMBT, 1992) ♫♫♫♪

worth searching for: Redneck Greece tracks also adorn several compilation discs, the most highly recommended being *Deep South, Volume One* (Spinning Mule, 1992, prod. various) ♫♫♫ and *Bubbapalooza, Volume One* (Ichiban, 1995, prod. various) ♫♫♫♪.

influences:

◀◀ Merle Haggard, George Jones, Jimmie Rodgers

▶▶ Bad Livers, James Richard Oliver

Gary Pig Gold

JERRY REED

Born Jerry Reed Hubbard, March 20, 1937, in Atlanta, GA.

If ever the phrase "Good things come to those who wait" applied to one man, it would be Jerry "Guitar Man" Reed. After over a decade spent toiling in obscurity, helping others acquire the very fame he himself so richly deserved, Reed finally burst upon the scene during the early 1970s with a flair for musicianship *and* for showmanship so undeniable it affected not only the record charts but also television and even motion pictures. While still in his teens, Reed was already proficient enough a guitarist to win a brief contract with Capitol Records, and his songs as well were worthy of covers by the stars of the day (most notably Gene Vincent, who recorded Reed's "Crazy Legs" in 1958, and Brenda Lee, who hit big with "That's All You Got to Do" in 1960). Settling in Nashville in 1962, Reed recorded a couple of minor hits for Columbia, but it was his growing notoriety as one of Music City's leading session players that brought him to the attention of Chet Atkins, who signed Reed to a long-term pact with RCA in 1965. No sooner had Elvis Presley hit big with versions of "U.S. Male" and Reed's signature tune "Guitar Man" than Hollywood came calling, and the real Guitar Man soon became a favorite on the Johnny Cash and Glen Campbell television series. He finally scored his own million-seller in 1970 with "Amos Moses," and the hits kept coming ("When You're Hot, You're Hot," "Lord Mr. Ford") for the next several years. By 1974 he was appearing alongside Burt Reynolds in a string of *Smokey and the Bandit* movies, and to this day, unfortunately, he remains more well known to the general public as the wise-cracking, gun-totin' good ol' guy he portrayed in these films than for the musical giant he really is. After one last #1 in 1982 with the brilliant "She Got the Goldmine (I Got the Shaft)," Reed bounced back to Capitol, then to Columbia (and Chet Atkins) in 1992. But it is for his exemplary pre-"Smokey" work with RCA that he should be best remembered today.

what to buy: *The Essential Jerry Reed* (RCA, 1995, prod. various) ♫♫♫♫ is exactly that: essential listening for all keen students of taut, gutbucket guitaring and clever song-styling—though for some unfathomable reason "U.S. Male" isn't included.

what to buy next: *The Best of Jerry Reed* (RCA, 1992, prod. various) ♫♫♫ is a shorter, budget compilation that includes not only "U.S. Male" but one of the better Elvis tributes, "Tupelo Mississippi Flash"—which was actually recorded while the King was still alive!

the rest:

Flyin' High (Southern Tracks, 1995) ♫♫♫

worth searching for: Reed recorded three now-hard-to-find albums over the years with his mentor Chet Atkins: *Me and Jerry* (RCA, 1970, prod. Chet Atkins) ♫♫♫♪, *Me and Chet* (RCA, 1972, prod. Chet Atkins) ♫♫♫♪ and *Sneakin' Around* (Columbia, 1992, prod. Chet Atkins) ♫♫♫. As you can well imagine, each contain sounds rarely coaxed, before or since, out of a pair of unsuspecting six-strings. Reed's early, rockin' 1950s sides make the compilation *Collector's Series* (Capitol, 1985, prod. various) ♫♫♫♫ worth the hunt as well.

influences:

◀◀ Merle Travis, Chet Atkins, James Burton

▶▶ Tony Joe White, Junior Brown, them Dukes of Hazzard

Gary Pig Gold

DEL REEVES

Born Franklin Delano Reeves, July 14, 1933, in Sparta, NC.

Del Reeves is the kind of guy that drives country purists crazy. He rarely sings tragic songs, preferring lighthearted fare that often contains his vocal signature, which goes something like, "doodle-oo-doo-doo." On top of that, he borrows liberally from pop and R&B music (he had a 1970 hit with Clyde McPhatter's "A Lover's Question").

A natural-born performer who specializes in impressions of other artists, Reeves had his own radio and TV shows before moving to Nashville in 1966, the same year he joined the Grand Ole Opry. He also appeared in such country-corn films as *Second Fiddle to a Steel Guitar* and *Forty-Acre Feud*. Reeves recorded for Capitol, Decca, Reprise, Columbia, Koala and Playback, but nearly all his biggest hits came for United Artists.

what to buy: His *Greatest Hits* (Razor & Tie, 1994) ✍✍✍ covers Reeves' United Artists years (1965–78). Songs like "Girl on the Billboard" and "The Philadelphia Fillies" give this collection an air of goofy fun, but it's definitely ephemeral stuff.

what to buy next: *The Silver Anniversary Album* (Playback, prod. Jack Gale) ✍✍ is pretty much a waste of time, but it contains a truly bizarre version of Reeves singing "Achy Breaky Heart" in the voices of Roy Acuff, Johnny Cash, Walter Brennan and Jimmy Stewart.

the rest:
Golden Good Time Hits, Volumes 1 & 2 (Playback) ✍✍

influences:
◀◀ Roger Miller, Bill Anderson
▶▶ Dave Dudley, Neal McCoy

Brian Mansfield

JIM REEVES

Born James Travis Reeves, August 20, 1924, in Panola County, TX. Died July 31, 1964, near Nashville, TN.

When Jim Reeves' single-engine plane went down near Nashville in 1964, the velvet-voiced baritone was one of Nashville's most successful crossover artists. His records regularly reached the upper levels of the country chart, and they usually made the pop chart as well (four even hit the pop Top 40). Though he'd grown up in Texas, Reeves refined his style in Nashville, where he moved in 1955, shortly after joining the Grand Ole Opry. He started out as a typical Texas honky-tonker, but when he hooked up with producer/guitarist Chet Atkins, Reeves basically defined the "Nashville Sound" of the 1960s (along with Owen Bradley and his stable of female singers that included Patsy Cline and Brenda Lee). He had his first hit in 1953 with "Mexican Joe," but 1957's "Four Walls" really established him, spending two months atop the country singles chart. At a time when rock 'n' roll was changing the rules even for country, Reeves made his mark with intimate ballads, often backed with vibes, strings and (almost always) the Anita Kerr Singers. His posthumous fame was, if anything, greater than what he knew when he was alive. "I Guess I'm Crazy," which was released less than three weeks before his death, spent seven weeks at #1 and five of the next seven singles RCA released topped the charts. Reeves' records would continue to chart well into the 1980s. He was elected to the Country Music Hall of Fame in 1967.

what to buy: *The Essential Series: Jim Reeves* (RCA, 1995, prod. Chet Atkins, comp. prod. Paul Williams) ✍✍✍✍ offers 20 cuts, including Reeves' smashes "He'll Have to Go," "Four Walls," "Welcome to My World" and "I Guess I'm Crazy." Well annotated and stocked full of music, this is the definitive single-disc Reeves collection.

what to buy next: Because Reeves' biggest hits for RCA were songs such as "He'll Have to Go" and "Four Walls," he is remembered primarily as a balladeer. *Four Walls (The Legend Begins)* (RCA, 1991, prod. various) ✍✍✍✍ shows a different side of the singer by focusing this collection on his recordings from 1953–57, including a couple of early hits for Abbott Records. By the time the album reaches "Am I Losing You" and "Four Walls," he's obviously found a niche with the ballads, but early songs such as "Mexican Joe," "Bimbo" and "Wagon Load of Love" show Reeves as a young honky-tonker.

what to avoid: Any of RCA's eight-song Reeves compilations, such as *The Best of Jim Reeves* (RCA, 1964) ✍✍ or *I Guess I'm Crazy* (RCA, 1991) ✍✍. They've got some good cuts, sure, but with so many albums out there with as many as 20 songs on them, why would you want to buy these?

the rest:
Live at the Opry (Country Music Foundation, 1986) ✍✍✍✍
The Intimate Jim Reeves (RCA, 1995) ✍✍✍✍
Whispering Hope (Pair, 1996) ✍✍✍
(With Patsy Cline) Greatest Hits (RCA) ✍✍✍

worth searching for: *Welcome to My World: The Essential Jim Reeves Collection* (RCA, 1993) ✍✍✍✍ is an excellent two-CD compilation that offers the biggest single dose of Reeves' music. If you can find this, you'll need hardly anything else that's currently in print.

influences:
◀◀ Eddy Arnold
▶▶ Vince Gill

Brian Mansfield

RONNA REEVES

Born September 21, 1966, in Big Spring, TX.

Ronna Reeves started her singing career at age nine and was

opening shows around Texas for George Strait at age 17. Signed to Mercury Records in 1991, she was nominated in the Best New Female Artist category by the Academy of Country Music a year later. She has appeared regularly on TNN's *The Statler Brothers Show*.

what's available: After having no hits from her Mercury albums, Reeves moved to a new label, but as *After the Dance* (River North Nashville, 1995, prod. Joe Thomas) 🎵🎵 shows, was still unable to find top-drawer songs to match her fine country voice.

worth searching for: *What Comes Naturally* (Mercury, 1993, prod. Clyde Brooks, Harold Shedd) 🎵🎵🎵 contains the best of Reeves' Mercury work. The album includes a solid version of a song later cut by Mandy Barnett ("That's All Right with Me"), a powerful wife-abuse tale ("Staying Gone") and a ballad, "He's My Weakness," that was made popular by a daytime soap opera.

influences:
◀◀ Crystal Gayle, Louise Mandrell
▶▶ Tammy Graham

Bill Hobbs

REGINA REGINA

Vocal duo formed March 1995, in Nashville, TN.

Regina Nicks (born in Houston, TX); Regina Leigh (born in Marshville, NC).

This singing duo formed in the halls of Reba McEntire's Starstruck Entertainment offices. Regina Nicks, who had sung some in Texas, worked as McEntire's personal assistant; Regina Leigh, once one of the female singers in Dave & Sugar, spent three years as one of McEntire's backup vocalists. Leigh also sang in the house band for the TNN television show *Prime Time Country*. Leigh is married to former Matthews, Wright & King member Tony King; Nicks is the wife of a fighter pilot.

what's available: *Regina Regina* (Giant, 1997, prod. James Stroud, Wally Wilson) 🎵🎵 comes post–Shania Twain, post–Mindy McCready. Which means the album has a bright, splashy sound and big hooks in songs like "More Than I Wanted to Know." But the duo never quite finds an identity that exists separately from producers, musicians and trends (like bare midriffs and navel rings).

influences:
◀◀ Reba McEntire, Linda Davis, Shania Twain

Brian Mansfield

LOU REID /LOU REID & CAROLINA

Born September 13, 1954, in NC. Carolina formed 1992.

Lou Reid, mandolin, guitar, lead vocals; Terry Baucom, banjo, vocals (1992–95); Marcus Smith, bass guitar, vocals (1992–95); Clay Jones, guitar, vocals (1992–95); Gena Britt, bass, banjo, vocals (1995–present); Randy Barnes, bass, vocals (1995–present); Alan Bibey, mandolin, vocals (1995–present).

Lou Reid began as a banjo player with the Atlanta-area Southbound Band before becoming a founding member of Doyle Lawson & Quicksilver in 1979. From there he joined Ricky Skaggs before becoming lead singer and guitarist with the Seldom Scene in 1986. He left the Scene in 1992, playing briefly with both Vince Gill and IIIrd Tyme Out before forming Lou Reid, Terry Baucom & Carolina in 1992. Baucom left in 1995.

what to buy: Carolina more than beats the sophomore-jinx with *Carolina Moon* (Rebel, 1994, prod. Lou Reid) 🎵🎵🎵, a collection of standards like Lester Flatt's "My Little Girl in Tennessee" and contemporary songs including Reid and T. Michael Coleman's "I Call Your Name." Baucom's Scruggs-style banjo keeps everything driving along.

what to buy next: *Carolina Blue* (Webco, 1993, prod. Lou Reid, Terry Baucom) 🎵🎵🎵 is the first paring of old Quicksilver bandmates Reid and Baucom. It's a fine example of traditionally rooted contemporary bluegrass, reaching #1 on the *Bluegrass Unlimited* album chart.

the rest:
Lou Reid & Carolina (Rebel, 1996) 🎵🎵🎵

influences:
◀◀ Seldom Scene, Doyle Lawson & Quicksilver
▶▶ Blue Highway, Lonesome River Band.

Douglas Fulmer

DON RENO & RED SMILEY

Formed 1951. Disbanded 1964.

Don Reno (born February 21, 1926, in Spartanburg, SC; died October 16, 1984), banjo, guitar, vocals; Red Smiley (born May 17, 1925, in Asheville, NC; died January 2, 1972), guitar, vocals.

Singer/songwriter and bandleader Don Reno was a long-time, influential musician from the first generation of artists to consciously play a music called bluegrass. With guitarist and singer Red Smiley and their band the Tennessee Cut-ups (a crack outfit that included fiddler Mack Magaha, bassist John Palmer and, from the age of nine, Reno's son, mandolin player Ronnie Reno), Reno made some of the most successful and enduring bluegrass albums of the early days of the music. He was recognized as among the most innovative banjo players around, was an outstanding bluegrass guitarist, and wrote "Feudin' Banjos" with sometime performing partner Arthur "Guitar" Smith. He replaced Earl Scruggs in Bill Monroe's band before forming a duo, and eventually a band, with Smiley. Together, they cut many classic bluegrass sides for King Records and others; the partnership dissolved in 1964 due to Smiley's ill health. Reno then formed a group with guitarist and vocalist Bill Harrell that lasted for a decade. From 1976 Reno performed mostly with his younger sons, Dale and Don Wayne, although oldest son Ronnie sometimes took time out from his job with Merle Haggard to appear with the family band.

what to buy: *Reno & Smiley & the Tennessee Cut-ups, 1951–1959* (King, 1993, reissue prod. Gary B. Reid) 🎵🎵🎵🎵 is a beautifully compiled and annotated collection of the duo's first eight years on King, featuring many classics, including "I'm Using My Bible for a Roadmap," "Drifting with the Tide," "I'm the Talk of the Town," "Country Boy Rock 'n' Roll," "I Know You're Married" and more, 115 in all. *Good Old Country Ballads* (King, 1959) 🎵🎵🎵 and *A Variety of Country Songs* (King, 1959) 🎵🎵🎵 are budget reissues of albums from the late 1950s; like most reissues from King and its subsidiaries, they offer no liner notes or other information, fidelity is iffy, and the track count is low—but the price is right and the music is classic and has been hard to find for years.

what to buy next: *Don Reno & Red Smiley on Stage* (Copper Creek, 1996) 🎵🎵🎵🎵 and *Don Reno & Red Smiley on the Air* (Copper Creek, 1996) 🎵🎵🎵🎵 present Don and Red during the late 1950s in a pair of live recordings, the first from concerts, the second from a variety of radio shows.

the rest:
Instrumentals (Hollywood, 1958) 🎵🎵🎵
New & Original Folk Songs Written in Commemoration of the Centennial of the American Civil War (King, 1961) 🎵🎵🎵
16 Greatest Gospel Hits (Gusto, 1996) 🎵🎵🎵

worth searching for: *Family & Friends* (Kaleidoscope, 1988, prod. Tom Stern) 🎵🎵🎵🎵, one of Reno's last sessions, finds him joined by top-notch pickers like Byron Berline, Tony Rice, and his sons Ronnie, Don Wayne and Dale on a program of mostly familiar Reno & Smiley material.

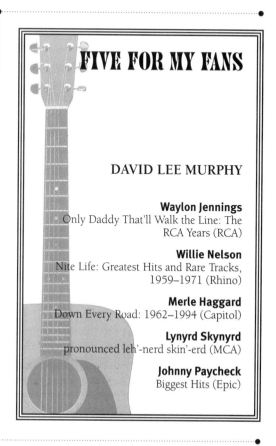

FIVE FOR MY FANS

DAVID LEE MURPHY

Waylon Jennings
Only Daddy That'll Walk the Line: The RCA Years (RCA)

Willie Nelson
Nite Life: Greatest Hits and Rare Tracks, 1959–1971 (Rhino)

Merle Haggard
Down Every Road: 1962–1994 (Capitol)

Lynyrd Skynyrd
pronounced leh'-nerd skin'-erd (MCA)

Johnny Paycheck
Biggest Hits (Epic)

solo outings:
Don Reno:
(With Eddie Adcock) *Sensational Twin Banjos* (Rebel, 1968/1992) 🎵🎵🎵
Fastest Five Strings Alive (Hollywood, 1969) 🎵🎵🎵
(With Arthur Smith) *The Original Dueling Banjos* (CMH, 1979) 🎵🎵

influences:
◀◀ Bill Monroe, Earl Scruggs
▶▶ Reno Brothers, Bluegrass Cut-ups

Randy Pitts

RESTLESS HEART /LARRY STEWART

Formed mid-1980s, in Nashville, TN. Disbanded January 1995.

Larry Stewart (born March 2, 1959, in Paducah, KY), vocals, guitar, keyboards (1985–92); **Dave Innis**, keyboards, guitar (1985–93); Greg

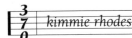

Jennings, guitar, vocals; Paul Gregg, bass, vocals; John Dittrich, drums, vocals.

Restless Heart's sleek-harmonied pop-country sound made them one of the most successful country groups of the 1980s. The group had an impressive string of hits, including six consecutive #1 singles released during 1986–88. Generally regarded as something of a manufactured band of session musicians, Restless Heart came together under the supervision of guitarist Greg Jennings and songwriter/producer/financier Tim DuBois. The band marked the first of DuBois' many successes at putting musicians together; he'd later have a hand in the formation of Brooks & Dunn and BlackHawk. Lead singer Larry Stewart left the group for a solo career in 1992; keyboardist Dave Inniss departed a year later. In Stewart's absence, the remaining three members of the group found they could share lead-vocal duties. They soon had their one crossover hit, "When She Cries," which was a Top 10 country single and a Top 20 pop record. Their pop success alienated many country fans, though, and the personnel changes took a psychic toll on the group. Restless Heart's label, RCA, dropped them in 1994, and the act broke up the following year. Drummer John Dittrich has since formed Buffalo Club with Charlie Kelley and former Imperials singer Ron Hemby.

what to buy: Restless Heart's biggest successes began with *Wheels* (RCA, 1986) 🎵🎵🎵, which produced four #1 singles, including the title track, "I'll Still Be Loving You" and "That Rock Won't Roll." *Fast Movin' Train* (RCA, 1990) 🎵🎵🎵 had the same sort of Eagles-influenced sound, but didn't have quite as much impact. Its singles included "Fast Movin' Train" and "Dancy's Dream." RCA has allowed much of Restless Heart's output to fall out of print, so *The Best of Restless Heart* (RCA, 1991) 🎵🎵🎵 will have to suffice as a source for the band's most popular recordings.

the rest:
Restless Heart (RCA, 1986) 🎵🎵🎵
Big Dreams in a Small Town (RCA, 1988) 🎵🎵🎵
Matters of the Heart (RCA, 1994) 🎵🎵

worth searching for: Like most of the group's other albums, the post-Stewart *Big Iron Horses* (RCA, 1992) 🎵🎵🎵 is now out of print, but it's the place to find "When She Cries."

solo outings:
Larry Stewart:
Down the Road (RCA) 🎵🎵🎵
Heart Like a Hurricane (Columbia, 1994) 🎵🎵🎵
Why Can't You (Columbia, 1996) 🎵🎵

influences:
◀◀ Alabama, Exile

▶▶ BlackHawk, Little Texas, Buffalo Club

Brian Mansfield

KIMMIE RHODES

Born March 6, 1954, in Wichita Falls, TX.

In an unassuming way, Kimmie Rhodes has managed to keep a silent hold on Nashville while creating music in her Lone Star home state. Two of Rhodes' compositions—sobering tales of love lost titled "Hard Promises to Keep" and "I Just Drove By"—were recorded by Trisha Yearwood and Wynonna, respectively. Undoubtedly these accomplished vocalists appreciate the caliber of Rhodes' talent. As a songwriter Rhodes crafts poignant vignettes with a soulful core and a lyrical power that conveys melancholy without resorting to melodramatics. "West Texas Heaven," the title cut of her excellent stateside debut album, communicates longing with a sense of resiliency. The equally beautiful "The Corner of the Bar" is both picturesque and transcendent. It's no wonder Rhodes has attracted a slew of respected and outspoken admirers, including Willie Nelson, Waylon Jennings, Joe Ely and Billy Joe Shaver. Nelson, Jennings and the late Texas songwriter Townes Van Zandt make guest appearances on *West Texas Heaven*, released in 1996 on the Houston-based independent Justice Records label.

what to buy: *West Texas Heaven* (Justice, 1996, prod. Joe Gracey, Kimmie Rhodes, John Leventhal) 🎵🎵🎵🎵 showcases Rhodes' seamless control of her artistry. The singer/songwriter runs the gamut from folk to country to blues. Her angelic voice, an instrument of stark beauty, turns sassy on "Git You a Job" and "Home John," then contemplative on "I'm Not an Angel" and the title cut. A quiet masterpiece.

the rest:
Jackalopes, Moons & Angels (Justice, 1997)

worth searching for: Pal Willie Nelson invited Rhodes to sing with him on two songs from Nelson's *Just One Love* (Justice, 1995, prod. Grady Martin) 🎵🎵🎵. The title cut and "I Just Drove By"—both written by Rhodes—are just two of the solid country tunes on Nelson's splendid album, an indie-label side project that captured the rich country history inherent in Nelson's native Texas.

influences:
◀◀ Emmylou Harris, Bobbie Gentry
▶▶ Kelly Willis, Libbi Bosworth

Mario Tarradell

TONY RICE

Born June 8, 1951, in Danville, VA.

Virginia-born, California-bred Tony Rice is a brilliant, innovative flat-picking guitarist who was introduced to bluegrass by his father. While knocking around the more popular West Coast bluegrass hangouts in the early- to mid-1960s, Rice learned a lot from superpickers such as Clarence White, Merle Watson, Norman Blake and Ry Cooder. Between 1970–81 the guitarist allied himself with a number of cutting-edge "newgrass" bands, including the Bluegrass Alliance, J.D. Crowe's New South, the David Grisman Quintet and the Bluegrass Album Band. As part of the David Grisman Quintet, Rice expanded his horizons beyond three-chord bluegrass, studying chord theory, learning to read charts and expanding the range of his playing. In 1979 he left the group to pursue his own music and recorded *Acoustics*, a guitar-oriented record. That was followed by *Manzanita*, which leaned more toward folk music and highlighted Rice's soulful vocal style. He subsequently formed a band called the Tony Rice Unit, which showcased his forays into jazz and experimental "spacegrass." In 1996 Rice was named Best Acoustic Pickstyle Guitarist by *Guitar Player* magazine's readers. The same year he also recorded *Out of the Woodwork*—a marvelously crafted album with brother Larry Rice and Desert Rose Band alumni Herb Pedersen and Chris Hillman.

what to buy: *Tony Rice Sings and Plays Bluegrass* (Rounder, 1996, prod. Tony Rice) ♪♪♪♪ shows Rice dipping into the bluegrass canon with Bill Monroe's "On and On" and Flatt & Scruggs' "I'll Stay Around." Also included is a tasteful rendition of Bob Dylan's "Girl from the North Country."

what to buy next: *Manzanita* (Rounder, 1979) ♪♪♪♪ and *Church Street Blues* (Sugar Hill, 1983) ♪♪♪♪ are two hugely influential bluegrass albums. *Manzanita* features the accompaniment of Sam Bush, Jerry Douglas and Ricky Skaggs on tunes with a largely old-time feel. *Church Street Blues* is more of a solo affair, with phenomenal picking by Rice.

the rest:
(With the Tony Rice Unit) *Acoustics* (Kaleidoscope, 1979/ Rounder, 1994) ♪♪♪♪
Backwaters (Rounder, 1982) ♪♪♪
Cold on the Shoulder (Rounder, 1984) ♪♪♪♪
Me & My Guitar (Rounder, 1986) ♪♪♪♪
(With Norman Blake) *Blake & Rice* (Rounder, 1987) ♪♪♪
Native American (Rounder, 1988) ♪♪♪♪
Devlin (Rounder, 1988) ♪♪♪♪

(As the Rice Brothers) *Tony, Larry, Ron & Wyatt Rice* (Rounder, 1989) ♪♪♪♪
California Autumn (Rebel, 1990) ♪♪♪♪
(With Blake) *Norman Blake and Tony Rice 2* (Rounder, 1990) ♪♪♪
Guitar (Rebel, 1991) ♪♪♪♪
(As the Rice Brothers) *Rice Brothers II* (Rounder, 1994) ♪♪♪♪
(With John Carlini) *River Suite for Two Guitars* (Sugar Hill, 1995) ♪♪♪
(With Larry Rice, Chris Hillman, and Herb Pedersen) *Out of the Woodwork* (Rounder, 1996) ♪♪♪♪

worth searching for: The Tony Rice Unit's *Mar West* (Rounder, 1980, prod. Tony Rice) ♪♪♪♪ is a splendid collection of the guitarist's spacegrass originals. Especially noteworthy is "Nardis," a Miles Davis tune that showcases Rice's uncanny ability to segue from jazz to bluegrass in a heartbeat.

influences:
◄◄ Doc Watson, Clarence White, Merle Watson
►► Bela Fleck

Rick Petreycik

CHARLIE RICH

Born December 14, 1932, in Forest City, AR. Died July 25, 1995, in Hammond, LA.

His rich, resonant baritone and poor, white Southern soul crossed all the customary boundaries of music. Perhaps the most powerfully talented of all his Sun Records compatriots, Charlie Rich always enjoyed the respect and appreciation of Elvis Presley, who clearly understood Rich's unique appeal. His career began during the late 1950s at Memphis' Sun label with the gospel-rock sound of "Lonely Weekends," turned toward his signature hybrid soul sound with "Mohair Sam" and cruised into jazz-inflected Ray Charles territory with "River Stay Away from My Door." But he only reached any sweeping popular acceptance with a series of recordings under Nashville producer Billy Sherrill, who produced big 1970s hits such as "Behind Closed Doors"—although sacrificing much of Rich's most singular appeal in the process. Rich receded from the limelight after riding into the ground the popularity of the slick, orchestrated pop-country hybrid called "countrypolitan" that Sherrill had designed around Rich's Nashville hits. He emerged from the seclusion of semi-retirement to make one final, brilliant and unnoticed album under the scrupulous supervision of authors Peter Guralnick and Joe McEwen. His death from a heart attack rated barely a mention in the media, but Rich was one of the true originals of American music whose career can be seen

Charlie Rich **(Archive Photos)**

as frustrating compromises between a deeply personal visionary and a streamlining industry.

what to buy: The two-disc, multi-label career retrospective *Feel Like Going Home: The Essential Charlie Rich* (Columbia Legacy, 1997, prod. various) *ANN* provides the only cross-licensed retrospective covering the entire expanse of his long career. His breakthrough album *Behind Closed Doors* (Columbia, 1972, prod. Billy Sherrill) *ANN* swells with lush strings at unwelcome times and the material veers into the saccharine and sentimental, but it remains Rich's best single album.

what to buy next: His first album for Epic, *The Fabulous Charlie Rich* (Epic, 1968/Koch, 1995, prod. Billy Sherrill) *ANN*, is a sturdy, spare piece with some strong ballads, including the undiscovered gem, "San Francisco Is a Lonely Town." But *Pictures and Paintings* (Sire/Warner Bros./Blue Horizon, 1992, prod. Scott Billington) *ANN* captures Rich as the barriers between soul, country, jazz and pop dissolve before him.

the rest:
Set Me Free (Epic, 1968/Koch, 1995) *AN*
Boss Man (Koch International, 1970/1994) *ANN*

Best of Charlie Rich (Epic, 1972/1986) *ANN*
Behind Closed Doors (Epic, 1973) *ANN*
Greatest Hits (Epic, 1976) *ANN*
Greatest Hits/Best of Charlie Rich (Epic, 1986) *ANNV*
American Originals (Epic, 1991) *AN*
The Very Best of Charlie Rich (Dominion, 1995) *AN*
Lonely Weekends: The Best Of the Sun Years (AVI, 1996) *ANNV*
The Sun Sessions (Varese Sarabande, 1996) *ANN*

worth searching for: In wake of his countrypolitan chart success, Rich's label pulled together *Charlie Rich* (Epic 1973, prod. various) *ANN*, a single-disc promotional retrospective that contained all the landmarks in his long and varied career.

influences:
◀◀ Elvis Presley, Mose Allison
▶▶ Ronnie Milsap

Joel Selvin

ZACHARY RICHARD

Born September 8, 1950 in Scott, LA.

Having both crusaded for Acadian traditional music and built a reputation as a rock showman, Zachary Richard embodies the best qualities of fusion. His original music unmistakably partakes of Cajun and zydeco without seeming dated or museumbound, while his more traditional efforts respectfully imbue the old songs with vigor. Despite his pure Acadian bloodlines, he was brought up outside of that culture and learned its musical folk roots retroactively during long stints in Quebec and France. His largely French-language recordings on Arzed (also known as RZ) reflect this quest, while his Rounder albums tend to be more zydeco and his A&M records successfully add rock and R&B performance and songwriting without watering down the music's primal power.

what to buy: *Looking Back* (Arzed, 1986, prod. various) *ANNN* provides an overview of his first seven French albums and a couple other sessions, showing his broad stylistic range and especially his winning ways with ballads. Among the star musicians are fiddler Michael Doucet and guitarist Sonny Landreth. Short liner notes explain each track. *Snake Bite Love* (A&M, 1992, prod. Bill Wray) *ANN*, mostly in English, shows Richard at the apex of his Cajun-rock hybrid, mixing classic rock hooks and stinging guitar with irresistible zydeco and R&B rhythms and plenty of his own accordion grooves.

what to buy next: *Live in Montreal* (Arzed, 1980, prod. Zachary Richard) *ANN* offers a burning set of classics ("Bon Temps

Rouler," "Jambalaya," "La Berceuse Creole" and many more) sung in French and features the extraordinary lead guitar of Sonny Landreth. *Mardi Gras Mambo* (Rounder, 1989, prod. Zachary Richard) ♪♪♪♪ is Richard's most "New Orleans" album, complete with horns, "Iko Iko" and "Big Chief," and the rollicking pianism of Craig Légé.

what to avoid: *Migration* (Arzed, 1978, prod. Zachary Richard) ♪♪ is hardly a bad album, but its experiment with synthesizer and the fact that Richard sticks to acoustic guitar and piano keep it from ranking with his other work.

the rest:
Bayou des Mysteres (Arzed, 1976) ♪♪♪
Mardi Gras (Arzed, 1977) ♪♪♪♪
Allons Danser (Arzed, 1979) ♪♪♪
Vent d'Eté (Arzed, 1981) ♪♪♪♪
Zack Attack (Arzed, 1984) ♪♪♪♪
Zack's Bon Ton (Rounder, 1988) ♪♪♪
Women in the Room (A&M, 1990) ♪♪♪

worth searching for: Richard recorded a rock album for Elektra in 1972–73 in New York City that got lost in the shuffle when Warner Bros. acquired the label. C'mon somebody, let this one see the light of day!

influences:
◀◀ Amedé Ardoin, Clifton Chenier, electric Bob Dylan
▶▶ Beausoleil, Terrance Simien, Wayne Toups

Steve Holtje

KIM RICHEY

Born December 1, 1956, in Zanesville, OH.

Like John Hiatt, Kim Richey has paid enough dues and sold enough songs to make her one of those rare "integrity" artists that a record company signs more for cachet value than sales figures—which means she gets a little more rope creatively and a little less pressure to "deliver." It's a comfortable situation that resulted in an impressive 1995 self-titled solo debut that showcased her natural instincts for blurring the lines between pop, rock, country and folk and for writing insightful, incisive lyrics about that gray area between heart-fluttering romance and ego-bandaging recovery. She might have leased out two of her catchiest songs to Radney Foster ("Nobody Wins") and Trisha Yearwood ("(Believe Me Baby) I Lied"), but Richey has saved her most personal material for herself, not out of greed but out of necessity. There's something about the way her quavering voice describes running away from a doomed re-

lationship ("It's just me and one good wiper blade up against the rain"), wondering whether to stick it out ("Lately we've been missing something/love is wearing at the seams") and acknowledging the futility ("After all was said and done/there was nothing left to do") that makes you appreciate the difference between hearing a song and truly feeling it.

what to buy: *Bitter Sweet* (Mercury Nashville, 1997, prod. Angelo, John Leventhal) ♪♪♪♪ substitutes the jangly crackle that producer Richard Bennett brought to her first album with a softer but equally compelling sound built around acoustic guitars, banjos and accordions that suits the longing passion of these songs. Her pop savvy comes through on "I Know," which echoes Joni Mitchell's *Court and Spark* era, and "Lonesome Side of Town," which could easily pass for an old Del Shannon hit. More important, Richey's voice hovers over the straightforward arrangements without reverb or other studio enhancements, lending a natural, comforting intimacy to such moving, melodic numbers as "Fallin'," the retro-country "To Tell the Truth" and the jaunty "I'm Alright."

the rest:
Kim Richey (Mercury Nashville, 1995) ♪♪♪♪

worth searching for: Before he formed a duo with Radney Foster, Bill Lloyd released a collection of Beatlesque pop demos, recorded between 1983–86, called *Feeling the Elephant* (Throbbing Lobster/Bar/None, 1987, prod. Bill Lloyd) ♪♪♪♪. The haunting last cut, "Everything's Closing Down," features one of Richey's first recorded vocals.

influences:
◀◀ John Hiatt, Mary Chapin Carpenter, Joni Mitchell
▶▶ Radney Foster, George Ducas, Trisha Yearwood

David Okamoto

RICOCHET

Formed 1993, in Nashville, TN.

Heath Wright, vocals, guitar, fiddle; Teddy Carr, steel guitar, dobro, lap steel; Junior Bryant, fiddle, vocals, mandolin, acoustic guitar; Eddie Kilgallon, keyboards, vocals, acoustic guitar, saxophone; Greg Cook, bass, vocals; Jeff Bryant, drums, vocals.

Ricochet sends talent shooting out in all directions. Consisting of six experienced musicians who share a vision of being a working band, they scored with high energy and exuberance mixed with a pure country sound. Brothers Jeff and Junior Bryant, both from Pecos, Texas, and Heath Wright from Vian,

Oklahoma, formed Ricochet a couple of weeks after their band Lariat broke up in 1993. The band spent a couple of years honing its skills in clubs across the country, carefully selecting material for its debut album. The group's second single, "Daddy's Money," topped the country chart in May 1996.

what's available: *Ricochet* (Columbia, 1996, prod. Don Chancey, Ed Seay) 🎵🎵🎵 is a promising debut, showcasing the band's extensive talent and diverse stylistic ability, including upbeat contemporary country, waltzes, honky-tonkers and poignant ballads.

influences:

◀◀ Merle Haggard, Bob Wills, Hank Williams, Marty Robbins, Restless Heart, Diamond Rio, Southern Pacific, Huey Lewis & the News

▶▶ Lonestar

Linda Andres

RIDERS IN THE SKY

Formed 1977.

Ranger Doug (Douglas B. Green), lead & baritone vocals, yodels, guitar; Woody Paul (Paul Chrisma), lead & tenor vocals, fiddle, guitar, accordion, harmonica, mandolin; Too Slim (Fred LaBour), melody vocals, stand-up bass, guitar, accordion.

Riders in the Sky are throwbacks to the silver-screen era of singing range riders, a day when cowboys were the idolized heroes of the Western world. Brimming with original music and a repertoire of classics, the trio is known equally for their music and their numerous radio and television endeavors, especially those geared toward children.

No hat act, Ranger Doug is a country music historian, while Woody Paul holds a Ph.D. in theoretical plasma. This makes for great conversation out on the prairie. The group's albums typically have some combination of music and Western skit comedy. The members of Riders in the Sky have been Grand Ole Opry members since 1982 and appeared in the 1985 Patsy Cline biopic *Sweet Dreams*.

what to buy: If you're new to the Riders, *Best of the West* (Rounder, 1987) 🎵🎵🎵🎵🎵 is a collection of their early recordings that makes an excellent introduction to the band.

what to buy next: *Best of the West Rides Again* (Rounder, 1987) 🎵🎵🎵🎵 is the second volume of the group's best-known material.

what to avoid. The Riders comedy shtick goes over best live or on radio. You've got to be a real fan to want *The Riders Go Commercial* (MCA, 1989) 🎵🎵, a spoken-word album packed with fake advertisements.

the rest:

Three on the Trail (Rounder, 1980) 🎵🎵🎵
Cowboy Jubilee (Rounder, 1981/1991) 🎵🎵🎵
Weeds & Water (Rounder, 1983/1991) 🎵🎵🎵
Live (Rounder, 1984) 🎵🎵🎵
New Trails (Rounder, 1986) 🎵🎵🎵
Saddle Pals (Rounder, 1987) 🎵🎵🎵
The Cowboy Way (MCA, 1987) 🎵🎵🎵🎵
Prairie Serenade (Rounder, 1991) 🎵🎵🎵🎵
Harmony Ranch (Columbia, 1991) 🎵🎵🎵
Merry Christmas from Harmony Ranch (Columbia, 1992) 🎵🎵🎵
Always Drink Upstream from the Herd (Rounder, 1995) 🎵🎵🎵
Public Cowboy #1: The Music of Gene Autry (Rounder, 1996) 🎵🎵🎵

influences:

◀◀ Gene Autry, Sons of the Pioneers

▶▶ Don Edwards, Wylie & the Wild West Show

Craig Shelburne and Brian Mansfield

AMY RIGBY /THE LAST ROUNDUP

Born January 27, 1959, in Pittsburgh, PA.

When Amy Rigby was a teenager she was bitten by the New Wave rock bug in a decidedly un–New Wave city (Pittsburgh). After high school she split for New York for college but quickly became immersed in the music scene, gained an interest in country stylings and wound up in the Last Roundup, a quartet dubbed alternately cowpunk and rockabilly, even though it sounds like a good roadhouse band to most ears. Rigby's next group, a female trio called the Shams, took their harmonies directly from country roots. After that group broke up in 1993, Rigby went solo with the evocative and entertaining *Diary of a Mod Housewife*.

what to buy: *Diary of a Mod Housewife* (Koch, 1996, prod. Elliot Easton) 🎵🎵🎵🎵 is a concept album in which Rigby tracks the travails of being a mom (at this juncture a single mom), a temp office worker and an aspiring musician. But rather than wallow, her songs display a down-to-earth realism that never forgets the joys and occasional humor of her situation. Best of all, former Cars guitarist Elliot Easton crafts a shimmering sound for these rich and fully realized songs.

what to buy next: The Last Roundup's *Twister* (Rounder, 1987, prod. Lou Whitney) 𝄢𝄢𝄢 is a joyful, almost innocent whoop-it-up that absolutely revels in its fresh-faced exuberance. Imagine the Brady Bunch after an encounter with the Cramps. Or Jerry Lee Lewis.

the rest:

(With the Shams) *Quilt* (Matador, 1991) 𝄢𝄢𝄢𝄢
(With the Shams) *Sedusia* (Matador EP, 1993) 𝄢𝄢𝄢

influences:

◀◀ Tanya Tucker, Patti Smith, Syd Straw, Continental Drifters

Gary Graff

BILLY LEE RILEY

Born October 5, 1933, in Pocahontas, AR.

Immortalized in the Johnny Cash song "I Will Rock 'n' Roll with You" ("Memphis 1955 on Union Avenue/Carl and Jerry and Charlie and Roy/And Billy Riley too . . ."), Riley is considered more of a rockabilly or Southern soul performer, though he too synthesized the same blend of country, blues and R&B that characterized the work of his Sun Records labelmates Carl Perkins, Elvis Presley, Warren Smith, Jerry Lee Lewis and Sonny Burgess. In 1956 Riley and future Sun producer Jack Clement recorded the brooding, Elvisy "Trouble Bound" for Slim Wallace's Fernwood label. When Clement leased the tape to Sam Phillips, both he and Billy were hired by Sun. Handsome, multi-talented and a crowd-pleaser on stage, Riley seemed destined for stardom, and with his band the Little Green Men (Roland Janes on guitar, Pat O'Neil on bass, J.M. Van Eaton on drums and Jerry Lee Lewis on piano), cut two of the wildest rock 'n' roll sides ever: "Flying Saucers Rock 'n' Roll" and "Red Hot." However, neither were more than regional successes, and Riley was caught in a classic small label conundrum. Only at a small label like Sun could he find a sympathetic home for his R&B/country rave-ups, but Phillips had limited resources. So at the same time Riley was producing his best work, Phillips was devoting most of his time and cash to Jerry Lee Lewis' booming career; Riley even overheard Phillips cancel pressings of his records so Sun could afford to ship more of Lewis'. Riley and his band continued cutting hot Little Richard–type rockers and jump blues that didn't sell, picking up eating money by backing nearly every act that came into the Sun studios until 1960. In 1961 Riley helped start Rita Records, but sold his interest in the label just before Harold Dorman hit it big with "Mountain of Love." In 1962 he moved to Hollywood and found work as the featured harmonica player for Sammy Davis Jr., Dean Martin and Johnny

Rivers, as well as fronting his own band. The Whiskey-a-Go-Go style matched well with Riley's, but no hits were forthcoming.

Through the 1960s he recorded under various names (Lightning Leon, Skip Wiley, Darren Lee, etc.) for a variety of labels big and small (Brunswick, Hip, Mojo, Home of the Blues, Mercury, etc.), some of which he partly owned. During 1972 Riley finally hit the charts with "I've Got a Thing about You Baby" on Chips Moman's Entrance label. Moman's lack of promotion doomed the release to mid-chart status, and the song was eventually covered more successfully by Elvis Presley, who copied the arrangement note-for-note. After Presley's death, fresh interest in the original rockers began to build, and Riley returned to Memphis to record for Sam Phillips' son Knox at Southern Rooster. His rockabilly reworking of "Blue Monday" earned Riley a favorable feature article in *Rolling Stone*, but the disc was poorly distributed and his moment seemed lost. Despite many frustrating years as an underpaid "cult hero," Riley somehow kept pumping, supplementing his day job in construction with further small label offerings, club dates and Sun Reunion tours. In 1992 he came back strong with a critically acclaimed release on the independent HighTone label. A respected figure in U.S. roots music, Riley is still out there, looking for that hit.

what to buy: *Red Hot—The Best of Billy Lee Riley* (AVI, 1995, prod. various) 𝄢𝄢𝄢𝄢 offers the cream of his work for Sun. *Classic Recordings 1956–1960* (Bear Family, prod. various) 𝄢𝄢𝄢𝄢 includes everything Riley recorded at Sun during the 1950s plus his first sides at Rita Records.

what to buy next: *Blue Collar Blues* (HighTone 1992, prod. Bruce Bromberg) 𝄢𝄢𝄢, a smart, convincing mix of Jimmy Reed–style blues, T. Graham Brown–style country and updated 1950s rockabilly.

what to avoid: On *Harmonica Beatlemania* (Mercury, 1964, prod. Nick Venet) **WOOF!**, Riley and company try to combat/co-opt/cash-in on the British Invasion by doing an LP of harmonica versions of hits by the Fab Four.

the rest:

Southern Soul aka *Twist 'n' Shout* (Mojo, 1968/Cowboy Carl Records, 1981) 𝄢𝄢𝄢
Reunion at 706 Union (Sun-Up, 1992) 𝄢𝄢
A Tribute to the Legendary Billy Lee Riley (BSC Records, 1996) 𝄢𝄢
Hot Damn! (Capricorn, 1997) 𝄢𝄢𝄢

worth searching for: *Vintage* (Mojo, 1978, prod. Billy Lee Riley) 𝄢𝄢𝄢𝄢 is a fun collection of rockabilly standards. Also worth checking out are *Billy Lee Riley in Action* (Vogue, 1966, prod.

Gene Norman) 🎵🎵🎵, a solid EP of folk and blues done Whiskey-a-Go-Go style, and *Harmonica & the Blues* (Crown, 1962) 🎵🎵🎵, which Riley regards as his best harmonica LP.

influences:

◀◀ Big Joe Turner, Elvis Presley, Little Richard, Jimmy Reed, Ricky Nelson, Johnny Rivers

▶▶ Delbert McClinton, Creedence Clearwater Revival, T. Graham Brown

Ken Burke

JEANNIE C. RILEY

Born Jeanne Carolyn Stephenson, October 19, 1945, in Anson, TX.

Jeannie C. Riley will always be remembered as the mini-skirted, go-go-booted singer of "Harper Valley P.T.A.," a country and pop smash in 1968. The song won Riley a 1968 Grammy for Best Female Country Vocal Performance and would sell some five million copies. Riley, who was raised in a strict Christian home, was miserable with the image, however. She'd release a number of brassy singles, none of them as successful as "Harper Valley," but she has seemed much happier since rediscovering religion during the early 1970s. She's now one of the grand dames of the Grand Ole Opry, where she can be seen nearly every weekend.

what to buy: *The Best of Jeannie C. Riley* (Varese Sarabande, 1996, prod. Shelby S. Singleton Jr., Eddie Kilroy, Billy Strange) 🎵🎵🎵 starts and ends with "Harper Valley P.T.A." and never once matches Tom T. Hall's brilliant lancing of small-town hypocrisy. It tries hard, though, on tough-minded numbers like "The Girl Most Likely" and "The Rib." The album contains mostly Riley's recordings for Plantation (where she was most successful), but it also has a couple of non-charting records she made for MCA during the 1980s.

what to buy next: *Here's Jeannie* (Playback, 1991, prod. Jack Gale, Jim Pierce) 🎵🎵 occasionally shows flashes of Riley's trademark spark, but, for some reason, peppy versions of "Blue Moon of Kentucky" and "Rockin' Pneumonia & the Boogie Woogie Flu" just don't measure up to "Harper Valley P.T.A." and "The Girl Most Likely."

what to avoid: In the wake of Varese Sarabande's compilation, steer clear of *16 Best of Jeannie C. Riley* (Plantation, 1987) 🎵🎵, which, despite its title, has very few of Riley's hits, instead concentrating on her renditions of songs like "Okie from Muskogee" and "Games People Play."

the rest:

Help Me Make It through the Night (Plantation, 1985) 🎵🎵

worth searching for: Dig around at enough truck stops and you can still find budget-cassette versions of Riley's original albums, including *Harper Valley P.T.A.* (Plantation, 1968, prod. Shelby S. Singleton Jr.) 🎵🎵🎵, *Yearbooks and Yesterdays* (Plantation, 1968, prod. Shelby S. Singleton Jr.) 🎵🎵, *Country Girl* (Plantation, 1970, prod. Shelby S. Singleton Jr.) 🎵🎵, *Jeannie* (Plantation, 1971, prod. Shelby S. Singleton Jr.) 🎵🎵 and *Greatest Hits Volume Two* (Plantation, prod. Shelby S. Singleton Jr.) 🎵🎵🎵.

influences:

◀◀ Dolly Parton, Loretta Lynn

▶▶ Jeanne Pruett, Billy Ray Cyrus

Brian Mansfield

LeANN RIMES

Born August 28, 1982, in Jackson, MS.

One song does not make a career, but "Blue" certainly helped then-13-year-old LeAnn Rimes make an impression. Originally written by Fort Worth, Texas, disc jockey Bill Mack for Patsy Cline (shortly before her death), the unrecorded ballad was offered to Rimes in 1994, when she was stunning Dallas sports, rodeo and concert audiences with the glass-shattering pyrotechnics and yodeling flexibility of her seven-octave voice. After generating a deafening hometown buzz, Rimes signed with Curb Records, becoming the youngest major-label country act since Tanya Tucker. Her 1996 single, the retro-country "Blue," met with some resistance from radio programmers who initially shrugged her off as a glee-club novelty act. But Country Music Television exposure, savvy interviews and her upbeat, down-home charm combined to send the accompanying album to the top of the country chart and to snare her Country Music Association nominations for Single of the Year and the Horizon Award. Rimes' most endearing trademark is the seemingly in-grained sense of poise and restraint that most vocal power-houses never develop—which makes it easier to overlook the fact that flawless technique is no substitute for the intimacy and urgency that naturally develops as one experiences the joys, disappointments and pains of everyday life. Good singers can hit all the right notes, but the great ones aim higher. When her age catches up with her voice, she should be one of the latter.

what to buy: Rimes' major-label debut, *Blue* (Curb, 1996, prod. Wilbur C. Rimes, Johnny Mulhair, Chuck Howard) 🎵🎵🎵, boasts confident readings of such retro-country ballads as "Blue" and

Deborah Allen's "Hurt Me" that belie Rimes' youth, along with such effervescent gems as "One-Way Ticket," which celebrates it. It also points to the ongoing struggle to find material that challenges her voice but also suits her age: Allen's "My Baby" is a fine song, but should a junior high student be singing "My baby . . . makes me feel like a natural woman/I know he's the only one who can"?

what to avoid: Recorded when she was 11 and featuring her first recording of "Blue," *All That* (NOR VA JAK, 1994, prod. Johnny Mulhair, Wilbur C. Rimes) *♫♫* is a glossy, pop-oriented hometown release on which she valiantly tackles Dolly Parton's "I Will Always Love You," Patsy Montana's "I Want to Be a Cowboy's Sweetheart" and the Beatles' "Yesterday" with mixed results—when she sings "Yesterday, all my troubles seemed so far away," she really means 24 hours ago, and that's not exactly what Paul McCartney had in mind. Seven songs from this album were repackaged with her show-stopping rendition of the Righteous Brothers' "Unchained Melody" and two *Blue* outtakes on *Unchained Melody/The Early Years* (Curb, 1997, prod. Johnny Mulhair, Wilbur C. Rimes, Chuck Howard) *♫♫*.

worth searching for: A CD single of her jaunty Christmas ditty, "Put a Little Holiday in Your Heart" (Curb, 1996, prod. Wilbur C. Rimes, Roger Wojahn) *♫♫♫*, was sold only through Target stores as a bonus gift with copies of *Blue*.

influences:

◀◀ Patsy Cline, Reba McEntire, Linda Ronstadt, Wynonna

David Okamoto

LeAnn Rimes (© Ken Settle)

TEX RITTER

Born Maurice Woodward Ritter, January 12, 1905, in Murvaul, TX. Died January 2, 1974.

Raised on a Texas ranch, Maurice Ritter enjoyed all the amenities that the lifestyle had to offer: riding, roping, swapping tall tales. The boy, nicknamed "Tex," could sing pretty well too, and he mesmerized fellow Texans by spinning legends about the wildest days of their beloved Lone Star State. A career in entertainment seemed natural, but Ritter attempted a law degree instead.

Ritter's storytelling led him all over the country, eventually to Chicago, where a fascination with radio won him over. After a heavy hand in writing and producing the legendary *Lone Ranger* series, Ritter landed on Broadway in 1931 in Lynn Riggs' *Green Grow the Lilacs* (a predecessor of the musical *Oklahoma!*). Hollywood lured Ritter away in 1936, and there he dabbled in movies

(he has 85 to his credit), radio and TV (he co-hosted the *Town Hall Party* series from 1953–60) and more music ("You Two-Timed Me Once Too Often" spent 11 weeks at #1 in 1945, and the theme song to *High Noon*, which he sang, won an Oscar). Ritter, who is the father of actor John Ritter, was elected to the Country Music Hall of Fame in 1965 and moved to Nashville the following year, where he became a regular on the Grand Ole Opry.

what to buy: The fabulously annotated *Country Music Hall of Fame* (MCA, 1991) *♫♫♫♫* contains more than half the 30 sides Ritter recorded for Decca during 1935–39. Many of these recordings, such as "I'm a Natural Born Cowboy" and "Ride, Ride, Ride," come from his movies. While these recordings weren't as popular as ones he'd later make, this is a fine package.

what to buy next: *Greatest Hits* (Curb, 1990) *♫♫♫* contains a pretty good selection of Ritter's best-known recordings for Capitol Records, including "Deck of Cards," "High Noon" and "Have I Told You Lately that I Love You." The liner notes are skimpy, so if you can find the out-of-print *Capitol Collector's Series*, it's a preferable buy. Until Capitol releases another reissue, this will do.

what to avoid: The recordings on *Conversation with a Gun* (Richmond, 1988) 🎵🎵, dating from late in Ritter's career, are hardly his best, and there's only eight of them here.

worth searching for: Ritter was Capitol Records first country signing, and he spent some 30 years with the label. *Capitol Collector's Series* (Capitol, 1992) 🎵🎵🎵 collects the best of that period; it's probably the best compilation of Ritter's work and can be found with some diligence. *High Noon* (Bear Family) 🎵🎵🎵 is a single-disc collection of cowboy songs.

influences:

◀◀ Gene Autry, Roy Rogers

▶▶ Rex Allen, Riders in the Sky

Brian Mansfield and Craig Shelburne

JIMMIE RIVERS

Born Jimmie Fewell, 1926, in Hockerville, OK.

A semi-legendary cult figure among country-jazz enthusiasts, half-Cherokee electric guitarist Jimmie Rivers became part of the Okie migration during the 1940s and led a popular Oakland-based Western swing band, the Cherokees, off and on for years without achieving more than workaday regional success. His legend is based almost entirely on tapes he and steel guitarist Vance Terry made during the 1960s in Brisbane, California. (Terry was an alumnus of Billy Jack and Bob Wills' bands and teamed up with Rivers in 1958.) Influenced both by fellow Oklahoma jazzers Charlie Christian and Barney Kessel, and country greats Eldon Shamblin and Jimmy Bryant, Rivers' technical virtuosity and wealth of solo ideas have been saved for posterity by the only surviving recorded examples of Jimmie Rivers and the Cherokees in full cry, *Brisbane Bop*.

what's available: *Brisbane Bop, Western Swing, 1961–1964* (Joaquin Records, 1995, reissue prod. Jeff Richardson) 🎵🎵🎵🎵 is essential to any fan of hot country jazz guitar. Featuring 19 examples of the finest Western swing, honky-tonk, and country jazz guitar, the album features interplay between Rivers and steel player Vance Terry that is incredibly exciting, reminiscent of Speedy West and Jimmy Bryant at their best. Vocalist and rhythm guitarist Gene Duncan is also great. Somewhat low-fi sound is only a minor annoyance considering the ambience of the live recordings and the scarcity and magnificence of the music.

influences:

◀◀ Charlie Christian, Jimmy Bryant

▶▶ Jim Campilongo, Wendell Mercantile

Randy Pitts

MARTY ROBBINS

Born Martin David Robertson, September 26, 1925, in Glendale, AZ. Died December 8, 1982.

One of the most versatile and progressive artists ever in country music, Marty Robbins was a trend-setter, not a follower. His 30 years as a recording artist encompassed a wide and often unexpected variety of styles, from the rockabilly of his early days to Hawaiian music, slick Nashville pop and, of course, the Western balladry that was a staple throughout most of his career. Robbins suffered three heart attacks in his life (he died after open heart surgery in 1982), little wonder considering the high-octane life he led. Robbins loved car racing and was a tireless craftsman who is regarded as one of the most talented singer/songwriters to emerge from Music City. He dabbled in movies and television but mostly won audiences over with his clear tenor, colorful songs and that uncanny ability to spot a trend in the making.

Robbins had a contentious relationship with his father, who left home when the boy was 12. His grandfather, Texas Bob Heckle, was a major influence, both personally and musically. Robbins took up the guitar while in the army, and upon his return to Arizona in the late 1940s began moonlighting as a musician. He scored his first #1 hit in 1953 with "I'll Go on Alone" and, soon after, began experimenting with his music. He added country fiddles to his version of Chuck Berry's rock standard "Maybelline," leaned toward pop with "A White Sport Coat (And a Pink Carnation)," then turned to Hawaiian music before trying his hand at Western music. The resulting *Gunfighter Ballads and Trail Songs* is considered one of his classic albums, and produced that alluring hit about a Mexican maiden, "El Paso." He dipped from that well many times after that 1959 hit but never stopped trying out new ideas and sounds. Robbins found success as a balladeer in the late 1960s and early 1970s, but when his career finally floundered he ventured into other areas, particularly movies and TV, including roles in Clint Eastwood's *Honkytonk Man* and the 1973 western *Guns of a Stranger*. Robbins was the last man to perform at the Grand Ole Opry at Ryman Auditorium and the first to play in its current location. His son, Ronnie, took a stab at music himself, but with far less success.

what to buy: If you like "El Paso," then you'll love *Gunfighter Ballads and Trail Songs* (Columbia, 1959, prod. Don Law) 𝄞𝄞𝄞𝄞, the first of his albums wholly devoted to Western music. It set a standard seldom matched since. The sequel, *More Gunfighter Ballads and Trail Songs* (Columbia, 1960, prod. Don Law) 𝄞𝄞𝄞 is almost as good.

what to buy next: There are several worthwhile retrospectives of Robbins' career, which is good since much of his album output is now out of print. Probably the most definitive collection is the two-CD *The Essential Marty Robbins: 1951–1982* (Columbia Legacy, 1992, prod. various) 𝄞𝄞𝄞𝄞, which reaches back to the beginning with "I'll Go on Alone." Though it covers the bulk of Robbins' recording career, this retrospective dwells most heavily on his best 1950s and 1960s hits.

what to avoid: *Super Hits* (Columbia, 1995, prod. various) 𝄞𝄞 is part of a low-budget reissue series that doesn't do his wide-ranging career the justice it deserves. *El Paso City* (Columbia, 1976, prod. Billy Sherrill) 𝄞𝄞 led to a commercial revival during the mid-1970s, but it was a little too self-aware and a little too calculated to help the failing Robbins get back on the track.

the rest:

The Song of Robbins (Columbia Legacy, 1957) 𝄞𝄞𝄞𝄞

A Lifetime of Song 1951–1982 (Columbia, 1983) 𝄞𝄞𝄞

Lost and Found (Columbia, 1993) 𝄞𝄞𝄞

More Greatest Hits (Columbia Legacy, 1993) 𝄞𝄞𝄞

All-Time Greatest Hits (Columbia Legacy, 1994) 𝄞𝄞𝄞

Rock 'n' Rollin' Robbins (Koch, 1996) 𝄞𝄞𝄞

The Story of My Life: The Best of Marty Robbins (Columbia Legacy, 1996) 𝄞𝄞𝄞

worth searching for: Germany's Bear Family label is a lot like our Rhino Records, only Bear Family focuses on country and roots performers and their catalogs. Bear Family has been reissuing Robbins' material since the 1950s in a series of volumes grouped either by theme or the time period in which they were created. Its five-volume *Marty Robbins Files* (Bear Family, 1983, prod. various) 𝄞𝄞𝄞 looks at his straight country and pop era, while the three-CD *Rockin' Rollin' Robbins* (Bear Family, prod. various) 𝄞𝄞𝄞 examines his rockabilly leanings. The five-CD *In the Wild West* (Bear Family, prod. various) 𝄞𝄞𝄞𝄞 lassos all of his cowboy songs in one package.

influences:

◀◀ Gene Autry, Jimmie Rodgers

▶▶ Michael Martin Murphey, Dwight Yoakam, Wylie & the Wild West Show

Doug Pullen

Marty Robbins **(AP/Wide World Photos)**

KENNY ROBERTS

Born October 14, 1926, in Lenoir City, TN.

Though he was born in Tennessee, Kenny Roberts spent much of his career working out of the Boston/New England region. He's generally considered one of country music's most accomplished yodelers, and his mainstream popularity was swift: he placed four records in the Top 20 during a 12-month period in 1949–50.

what's available: The recordings on *Indian Love Call* (Starday, 1992) 𝄞𝄞 come well after Roberts' heyday, but Roberts' voice is still fascinating. He sings the yodeling standard of measure, "Indian Love Call," of course, as well as Swiss-oriented material like "She Taught Me to Yodel" and a remake of his biggest hit, "I Never See Maggie Alone." But what's most impressive is how Roberts incorporates his yodel seamlessly into honky-tonk numbers like "Please Don't Turn Around" and "Maybe, I'll Cry Over You." The sound could be better, though; Roberts' high notes blow out the tape. Although there are only five songs on *Blue* (King, 1996) 𝄞𝄞𝄞, one of them's Roberts' original version of "Blue" (the same song LeAnn Rimes made a smash in 1996), and it's a fabulous version in which Roberts' imaginative yodeling just runs rings around the competition.

influences:
◄◄ Elton Britt, Wilf Carter
►► Slim Whitman, Don Walser

Brian Mansfield

CARSON ROBISON

Born August 4, 1890, in Oswego, KS. Died March 24, 1957, in Pleasant Valley, NY.

Carson Robison was a vaudeville performer who came to country music through his job as Vernon Dalhart's whistler. Nicknamed the "Kansas Jaybird" because of that talent, Robison eventually became a popular performer in his own right, particularly overseas. He wrote many popular tunes, including "Blue Ridge Mountain Blues," "Carry Me Back to the Lone Prairie" and "Barnacle Bill the Sailor." Robison was the first country singer to tour Great Britain and, next to Jimmie Rodgers, he was the most popular early country singer in Britain. In America he had some of his biggest success during World War II with his recordings of "1942 Turkey in the Straw" and "Hitler's Last Letter to Hirohito." He also had the first version of the popular 1948 novelty "Life Gets Tee-Jus Don't It," later recorded by Tex Williams. His backing groups were known as the Pioneers, the Buckaroos and the Pleasant Valley Boys.

what's available: *Home, Sweet Home on the Prairie* (Living Era, 1996, comp. prod. Peter Dempsey) ♫♫♫, which contains 25 recordings made between 1930–36, includes three of Robison's recordings with Dalhart and some tracks he cut in London during his first European tour. Modern notions of cowboy music have been shaped so completely by later Hollywood films that these recordings, made with an East Coast mentality, sound quite surprising.

influences:
◄◄ Vernon Dalhart, Wendell Hall
►► Sons of the Pioneers, Gene Autry

Brian Mansfield

ROCKPILE

See: Dave Edmunds

JIMMIE RODGERS

Born James Charles Rodgers, September 8, 1897, in Meridian, MS. Died May 26, 1933.

A childhood spent shuffling back and forth between relatives (and consequently sampling the life of music halls and vaudeville acts) aided Jimmie Rodgers in absorbing the rich music of Mississippi during the early 1900s. After winning a local talent contest at age 12, Rodgers was persuaded to pursue a more stable life and worked for more than a decade for the railroad. When diagnosed with tuberculosis in 1924 he ditched the railroad and plunged into his true calling—music. He broke records by selling more than a million copies of a recording that included his legendary "T for Texas." The following years were dotted with hits such as "Blue Yodel," "Way out on the Mountain" and "A Drunkard's Child." His vocal style, a distinct yodel, became the one to imitate, but Rodgers also experimented with eclectic back-up arrangements, tossing in jazz or Hawaiian bands to add a twist. In 1933 he finally lost his battle with TB. Often referred to as the "Father of Country Music" or "America's Blue Yodeler," Rodgers certainly earned his charter induction into the Country Music Hall of Fame in 1961 and into the Rock and Roll Hall of Fame in 1986.

what to buy: The recordings on *First Sessions, 1927–1928* (Rounder, 1990, prod. Ralph Peer) ♫♫♫♫, along with the Carter Family's first recordings, set the course for recorded country music. Rodgers accompanies himself on guitar for these songs (another musician occasionally adds banjo or ukelele), and the second his keening voice sets to wailing "Blue Yodel" (aka "T for Texas"), it's obvious something special is going on. This collection contains Rodger's first three "blue yodels," plus the classic "In the Jailhouse Now."

what to buy next: Rounder has released all of Rodgers' Victor recordings on CD, and *America's Blue Yodeler, 1930–1931* (Rounder, 1991, prod. Ralph Peer) ♫♫♫♫ is probably the place to go after Rodgers' historic first recordings. If the pop influence on modern country music strikes you as a betrayal of tradition, just listen to these fully arranged "Jimmie's Mean Mama Blues"—piano, clarinet, tuba, banjo and cornet, courtesy of Bob Sawyer's Jazz Band. And future jazz legend Louis Armstrong even plays trumpet on "Blue Yodel No. 9." But when the songs are this good—"T.B. Blues" is on this collection, as is "Blue Yodel No. 8" (aka "Muleskinner Blues")—it doesn't much matter how you play them.

what to avoid: On *Jimmie Rodgers* (RCA, 1991, prod. Ralph Peer) ♫♫♫ the songs are undeniable—"Blue Yodel No. 1 (T for

Texas)," "Muleskinner Blues"—but, geez, there's only eight of them. Many better collections exist.

the rest:

Country Legacy (Pair, 1989) 🎵🎵
Early Years, 1928–1929 (Rounder, 1990) 🎵🎵🎵
On the Way Up, 1929 (Rounder, 1991) 🎵🎵🎵
Riding High, 1929 (Rounder, 1991) 🎵🎵🎵
Down the Old Road, 1931–1932 (Rounder, 1991) 🎵🎵🎵🎵
No Hard Times, 1932 (Rounder, 1991) 🎵🎵🎵🎵
Last Sessions (Rounder, 1991) 🎵🎵🎵
Train Whistle Blues (ASV Living Era, 1992) 🎵🎵
The Essential Jimmie Rodgers (RCA, 1997) 🎵🎵🎵🎵🎵

influences:

◀◀ Riley Puckett, Tenneva Ramblers

▶▶ Ernest Tubb, Carson Robison, Gene Autry

Randall T. Cook

JOHNNY RODRIGUEZ

Born Juan Rodriguez, December 10, 1951, in Sabinal, TX.

Johnny Rodriguez was one of nine children born into a poor Texas family. As a teenager he was jailed for goat rustling. During his jail stay, a Texas Ranger noticed Rodriguez' singing and brought him to the attention of a promoter named Happy Shahan. Shahan began managing the young singer and introduced him to Tom T. Hall, who encouraged Rodriguez to move to Nashville, then hired him as his guitar player. Rodriguez soon signed with Mercury, Hall's label, and his first single, "Pass Me By," reached #4 (it was later covered by Paul Brandt). His next single, "You Always Come Back to Hurting Me," did even better, reaching #1. During 1974 Rodriguez appeared as a character on the television drama *Adam 12;* the acting credit later led to a part in the Western movie *Rio Diablo.* Rodriguez continued having success on Mercury throughout the 1970s with Top 20 singles such as "I Wonder If I Said Goodbye," "If Practice Makes Perfect," "Eres Tu" and "Love Put a Song in My Heart." In 1979 he left Mercury and signed with Epic Records, where he was produced by Billy Sherrill. He continued having hits during the early 1980s, including a duet with Charly McClain, "I Hate the Way I Love It."

what to buy: *You Can Say That Again* (HighTone, 1996, prod. Roy Dea, Jerry Kennedy) 🎵🎵🎵🎵 was produced by Rodriguez' early producers, the same ones he used during his peak career days with Mercury. It features material written by Merle Hag-

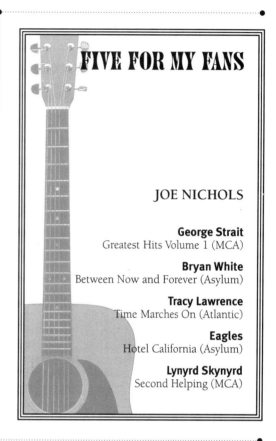

FIVE FOR MY FANS

JOE NICHOLS

George Strait
Greatest Hits Volume 1 (MCA)

Bryan White
Between Now and Forever (Asylum)

Tracy Lawrence
Time Marches On (Atlantic)

Eagles
Hotel California (Asylum)

Lynyrd Skynyrd
Second Helping (MCA)

gard, Whitey Shafer and Doodle Owem and is some of Rodriguez' best work since the 1970s.

what to buy next: *Greatest Hits* (Mercury, 1995) 🎵🎵🎵🎵 collects original recordings of Rodriguez' best work when he was at the peak of his singing career, with everything from "Pass Me By" to "Your Love Put a Song in My Heart."

what to avoid: Rodriguez' records took a big dip on the charts when he left Mercury for Epic in 1979. *Super Hits* (Epic, 1995) 🎵🎵 suggests why.

the rest:

Run for the Border (Intersound, 1993) 🎵🎵🎵

influences:

◀◀ Merle Haggard, George Jones

▶▶ Freddy Fender, Rick Trevino, Joel Nava

Ronnie McDowell

KENNY ROGERS

Born Kenneth Donald Rogers, August 21, 1938, in Houston, TX.

Kenny Rogers is fabulously wealthy now, having attained the kind of stardom in country music during the 1970s that only Garth Brooks has managed to surpass since. Rogers came from a poor family in Houston, where he played in a high school rockabilly band and eventually released a couple of singles, including the 1956 national hit "Crazy Feeling," that were popular enough to get him on *American Bandstand*. His circuitous route to the top included stints as a bass player in a couple of jazz groups during the mid-1960s, then a stint in the folk-pop group the New Christy Minstrels. Several of them formed First Edition, a folk-rock group that Rogers fronted. Though the group's first taste of success was a quasi-psychedelic reading of Mickey Newbury's "Just Dropped In (To See What Condition My Condition Was In)," it wasn't until a few years later, as Kenny Rogers & the First Edition, that they cracked the Top 10 with "Ruby, Don't Take Your Love to Town," a heartbreaking account of a wheelchair-bound Vietnam vet whose lover is unfaithful. It was written by Mel Tillis and was the group's introduction to the country charts.

Though the First Edition had more hits, notably "Something's Burning," Rogers left to go solo in 1973 with the help of producer Larry Butler, who had a knack for finding easy, light country songs that suited Rogers' pleasant but thin wisp of a voice. He had several hits, including "Lucille" and "Daytime Friends," but his popularity reached unprecedented heights after the story-song "The Gambler" paid huge dividends as both a country and pop hit in 1978. Rogers would rule those charts for nearly 10 years after that, teaming with duet partners like Dottie West and Sheena Easton while collaborating with such pop heavyweights as Lionel Richie, who wrote and produced Rogers' smash version of the ballad "Lady." By the time Rogers' *Greatest Hits* came out, retailers couldn't keep his records in the stores and his concerts typically sold out. Rogers, wary of fickle audience tastes, took measures to ensure his continued stardom, turning "The Gambler" into a series of TV movies (five in all) while branching out into such other areas as clothing lines. His career cooled considerably during the mid-1980s; his duet with Dolly Parton on the Barry Gibb-penned shlock ballad "Islands in the Stream" was one of his last big hits and his concert audiences dwindled. He keeps plugging away with popular Christmas tours, a chain of fast-food chicken restaurants and, most recently, a Christmas album, *The Gift*, which topped the contemporary Christian charts late in 1996. Rogers is living proof that a modicum of talent, a maximum of business savvy and a likable public persona can go a long way in country music.

what to buy: Rogers' career was at its zenith in 1980, when the singer with the peppery black and grey hair and raspy, woodsy voice could do no wrong. He had the pick of the best songs, the best production and an audience that couldn't get enough. His *20 Greatest Hits* (Liberty, 1983, prod. Larry Butler, Lionel Richie, David Foster, David Malloy, Kenny Rogers) ♪♪♪ is a pretty complete snap shot of that period in his career, spanning the best of the First Edition with his biggest hits up to that point, from "Just Dropped In . . .," "Ruby" and "Reuben James" to "Don't Fall in Love with a Dreamer," a duet with Kim Carnes.

what to buy next: *Kenny Rogers' Greatest Hits* (Liberty, 1980, prod. Larry Butler, Lionel Richie, Kenny Rogers) ♪♪♪ isn't as extensive, but this multi-platinum collection captures most of that period with fewer songs, while *Ten Years of Gold* (EMI America, 1977, prod. Larry Butler, Kenny Rogers) ♪♪♪ nicely sums up his First Edition and early country years.

what to avoid: *Timepiece: Orchestral Sessions with David Foster* (Atlantic, 1994, prod. David Foster) ♪ was an unabashed attempt to jump on Natalie Cole's career-rejuvenating *Unforgettable* bandwagon. It sounds just like what you'd expect at this point in his career: a desperate singer teamed up with a schmaltzy producer to tackle treacle like "You Are So Beautiful" and such classy standards as Rodgers & Hart's "My Funny Valentine."

the rest:
Kenny (Razor & Tie, 1979) ♪♪
Gideon (Razor & Tie, 1980) ♪♪
Share Your Love (Liberty, 1982) ♪♪
We've Got Tonight (Liberty, 1983) ♪♪♪
Greatest Hits (RCA, 1983) ♪♪♪
Eyes that See in the Dark (RCA, 1983) ♪♪♪
What About Me (RCA, 1984) ♪♪
Duets (EMI America, 1984) ♪♪
Once upon a Christmas (RCA, 1984) ♪♪♪
The Heart of the Matter (RCA, 1985) ♪♪
They Don't Make Them Like They Used To (RCA, 1986) ♪♪
I Prefer the Moonlight (RCA, 1987) ♪♪♪
25 Greatest Hits (EMI America, 1987) ♪♪♪
A Kenny Rogers Christmas (Capitol, 1987) ♪♪
(With the First Edition) *The Best of Kenny Rogers and First Edition* (K-Tel, 1987) ♪♪♪
(With the First Edition) *Greatest Hits* (MCA, 1987) ♪♪♪
20 Great Years (Reprise, 1988) ♪♪♪
Something inside So Strong (Reprise, 1989) ♪♪
Christmas in America (Reprise, 1989) ♪♪♪

Love Is Strange (Reprise, 1990) ♫♫

Back Home Again (Reprise, 1991) ♫♫

(With the First Edition) *Lucille and Other Classics* (CEMA Special Product, 1992) ♫♫♫

The Best of Kenny Rogers (CEMA Special Products, 1992) ♫♫

Heart to Heart (RCA Special Products, 1992) ♫♫

The Ultimate Kenny Rogers (Bransounds, 1994) ♫♫♫

The Gift (Magnatone, 1996) ♫♫♫

(With the First Edition) *Greatest Hits* (Hip-O, 1996) ♫♫♫

worth searching for: One of the first production jobs Rogers ever took was for a little-known band called Shiloh in 1970. He produced their debut album, *Shiloh*, which had been out of print in the United States for years before the Razor & Tie label recently reissued it. The group had two noteworthy members, a pianist and guitarist named Jim Ed Norman, who would become Rogers' producer and the head of Warner Bros. Nashville, and drummer Don Henley of Eagles fame.

influences:

◄◄ Kingston Trio, Merle Haggard

►► Dolly Parton, Neil Diamond, Bob Seger

Doug Pullen

ROY ROGERS

Born Leonard Franklin Slye, November 5, 1911, in Cincinnati, OH.

Roy Rogers is the only person to be inducted into the Country Hall of Fame twice. The group in which he rose to fame, the Sons of the Pioneers, was inducted in 1980, and Rogers was elected as a solo performer eight years later. Raised on Tom Mix movies, Rogers picked up acting naturally and starred in more than 100 films, usually as a genial singing cowboy. Hollywood couldn't get enough of the handsome hero, so Rogers and his screen partner/wife Dale Evans earned a green light for an NBC Saturday-morning TV series, which lasted from 1951–1957. Dale and Rogers, married since 1946, eventually retired to Apple Valley, California, in the Mojave Desert, where they maintain the Roy Rogers Museum. Rogers' other sidekick, Trigger the horse, is mounted and on display there.

what to buy: The recordings on *Country Music Hall of Fame* (MCA, 1992, prod. Country Music Foundation) ♫♫♫, made for Decca during the 1930s and 1940s, show Rogers as a smooth-voiced balladeer. After he left the Sons of the Pioneers in 1937, his music began to steer away from the strictly cowboy and Western themes—which could be one reason his music had such wide appeal.

Kenny Rogers (© Ken Settle)

the rest:

Best of Roy Rogers (Curb, 1990) ♫♫♫

(With Dale Evans) *Sweethearts of the West* (Star Line) ♫♫♫

(With Dale Evans) *Peace in the Valley* (Pair, 1996) ♫♫♫

worth searching for: *Tribute* (RCA, 1991, prod. Richard Landis) ♫♫, one of the first major-label country tribute albums, features a number of contemporary artists—most notably Clint Black, Randy Travis, Emmylou Harris and the Kentucky HeadHunters—singing songs with Rogers.

influences:

◄◄ Carson Robison, Gene Autry

►► Tex Ritter, Rex Allen

see also: *Sons of the Pioneers*

Brian Mansfield

TAMMY ROGERS

Born January 18, 1965, in Rogersville, TN.

Tammy Rogers' distinctive fiddle style has been heard on

records by folks from Neil Diamond to the Jayhawks (she's even on the soundtrack to the film, *So I Married an Axe Murderer!*). But with two albums to her credit, Rogers has established herself as one of the most versatile performers to emerge from Nashville during the 1990s. As business partner in the independent Dead Reckoning record label with Kevin Welch, Kieran Kane, Mike Henderson and Harry Stinson, Rogers is one of the few women in Nashville to assume such a role.

what's available: *In the Red* (Dead Reckoning, 1995, prod. Tammy Rogers, Don Heffington, Kieran Kane, David Vaught) 𝄢𝄢𝄢𝄢 is a predominately instrumental duet album with ex-Lone Justice drummer Don Heffington. *Tammy Rogers* (Dead Reckoning, 1996, prod. Harry Stinson, Tammy Rogers) 𝄢𝄢𝄢 is a pleasant, well-produced follow-up that leans more heavily on Rogers' vocals and songwriting. It's marred only by her somewhat dispassionate vocal performance.

influences:
◀◀ Mark O'Connor, Alison Krauss

Stephen L. Betts

LINDA RONSTADT

Born July 15, 1946, in Tucson, AZ.

Any assessment of Linda Ronstadt stands or falls upon how strongly you feel about songwriting as an artistic credential. If you believe that not writing your material is creative treason, this entry will guarantee ulcers. But the profound influence of Ronstadt's singing mandates a place for her, along with such artists as Emmylou Harris, as a major voice in the 1970s fusion of country and rock. Where Harris leaned toward country's mountain and bluegrass traditions, Ronstadt mined the throbbing, emotional territory once owned by Patsy Cline. In doing so, she established a model for any number of subsequent country-rock belters and future country divas.

Ronstadt arrived in Los Angeles at the end of the 1960s as singer for the Stone Poneys (Bobby Kimmel on guitar, Kenny Edwards on bass). With them she scored her first chart success, 1967's "Different Drum," but they broke up the following year. Ronstadt eventually emerged as princess of the California rock mafia that included the Eagles, John David Souther and Jackson Browne—a prominence that grew as she worked with producer Peter Asher. Their collaboration on 1974's *Heart Like a Wheel* produced a #1 hit in "You're No Good" and established Asher's trademark formula: torchy, country-tinged pop seasoned with oldies (Hank Williams, Buddy Holly) and untried

material (Karla Bonoff, Kate & Anna McGarrigle). This approach made Ronstadt a force on both the pop and country charts for most of the 1970s.

Nevertheless, Ronstadt's boredom with the game plan grew as the decade ended. Although she would release one more pure pop album (1982's *Get Closer*), she was beginning a period of experimentation that included a Broadway fling with Gilbert & Sullivan (*The Pirates of Penzance*), three big-band collections with conductor Nelson Riddle and two albums of mariachi music. Her departure from the mainstream, ironically, came as a new generation of Nashville talent (including Garth Brooks and Trisha Yearwood) was paying tribute to her as a formative influence. Traces of Ronstadt's emotion-laden style are evident in the balladeering of Yearwood and other such belters as Patty Loveless, while such artists as Kathy Mattea, with her mixing of rock, country and folk idioms, echo the eclectic approach to song selection Ronstadt took during the 1970s. And when Ronstadt chose to revisit country territory, the results were eminently satisfying.

what to buy: *Heart Like a Wheel* (Capitol, 1974, prod. Peter Asher) 𝄢𝄢𝄢𝄢𝄢 and *Prisoner in Disguise* (Asylum, 1975, prod. Peter Asher) 𝄢𝄢𝄢𝄢𝄢 exemplify Asher's influential production style and Ronstadt's emotional country rock. In the poignant title tunes, memorable duets with Harris and carefully chosen remakes (such as Smokey Robinson and the Miracles' "Tracks of My Tears"), Ronstadt successfully walks the line dividing sadness from sappiness. Some of Ronstadt's best singing of the 1980s is on the spare, mountain-acoustic arrangements of *Trio* (Warner Bros., 1987, prod. George Massenburg) 𝄢𝄢𝄢𝄢𝄢, her collaboration with Harris and Dolly Parton.

what to buy next: *Hasten Down the Wind* (Asylum, 1976, prod. Peter Asher) 𝄢𝄢𝄢𝄢 completes the 1970s trio of Ronstadt/Asher megasuccesses and spotlights excellent songwriting by Bonoff and Warren Zevon. Those interested in pre-Asher Ronstadt should seek out *A Retrospective* (Capitol, 1977) 𝄢𝄢𝄢, which collects the best of her early output.

what to avoid: *Mad Love* (Asylum, 1980, prod. Peter Asher) 𝄢𝄢 is an ill-advised foray into tough-posturing punk that kind of reminds you of the time the Girls' Citizenship president tried to smoke her first cigarette and swallowed instead of inhaling. Except for the rueful "Hurt So Bad," it's a yowl.

the rest:
(With the Stone Poneys) *Stone Poneys* (Capitol, 1967/1995) 𝄢𝄢
(With the Stone Poneys) *Evergreen Volume 2* (Capitol, 1967) 𝄢𝄢

Hand Sown Home Grown (Capitol/EMI, 1969) 🎵🎵🎵
Silk Purse (Capitol, 1970) 🎵🎵🎵🎵
Linda Ronstadt (Capitol, 1972) 🎵🎵🎵
Don't Cry Now (Capitol, 1973) 🎵🎵🎵🎵
Greatest Hits Volume 1 (Asylum, 1975) 🎵🎵🎵🎵
Simple Dreams (Asylum, 1977) 🎵🎵🎵🎵
Living in the USA (Asylum, 1978) 🎵🎵🎵
Greatest Hits Volume 2 (Asylum, 1980) 🎵🎵🎵
Get Closer (Asylum, 1982) 🎵🎵🎵
What's New (Asylum, 1983) 🎵🎵🎵🎵
Lush Life (Asylum, 1984) 🎵🎵🎵🎵
'Round Midnight: The Nelson Riddle Sessions (Elektra, 1986) 🎵🎵🎵🎵
(With Aaron Neville) *Cry Like a Rainstorm, Howl Like the Wind* (Elektra, 1989) 🎵🎵🎵
Mas Canciones (Elektra, 1991) 🎵🎵🎵
Frenesi (Elektra, 1992) 🎵🎵🎵
Winter Light (Elektra, 1993) 🎵🎵🎵🎵
Feels Like Home (Elektra, 1995) 🎵🎵🎵🎵
(With the Stone Poneys) *Stone Poneys and Friends, Volume 2* (Capitol, 1995) 🎵🎵🎵
Dedicated to the One I Love (Elektra, 1996) 🎵🎵🎵

worth searching for: Ronstadt has made myriad guest appearances on an assortment of albums. Two of the most interesting (and varied): Philip Glass' *1000 Airplanes* (Virgin Classics, 1989), on which her singing humanizes Glass' ethereal minimalism; and *Kermit Unpigged* (Jim Henson Records, 1994), on which she and the frog duet on "All I Have to Do Is Dream."

influences:

◀◀ Patsy Cline, Elvis Presley, Lola Beltran

▶▶ Trisha Yearwood, Kathy Mattea, Rosanne Cash

Elizabeth Lynch

PETER ROWAN

Born July 4, 1962, in Boston, MA.

Raised in a household of musical fanatics, multi-instrumentalist/songwriter Peter Rowan's career is filled with the gyrations of someone unwilling to settle into any one musical form and excelling at all of them. Reared on the Boston folk circuit in the outfit Mother Bay State Entertainers, Rowan first made his bluegrass mark nationally singing and playing guitar for Bill Monroe's Blue Grass Boys during the mid-1960s. Torn by the experimental musical offshoots of the latter part of that decade, Rowan hooked up with mandolinist David Grisman (the beginning of a 30-year relationship) and formed Earth

Opera, scoring a minor chart hit in 1969 with "Home to You." Rowan would find greater commercial viability with the acoustic-fusion Seatrain a few years later, before forming the on-again-off-again Rowan Brothers with siblings Chris and Lorin. A live 1973 bluegrass show at San Francisco's Boarding House featuring Rowan, Grisman, Jerry Garcia, Vassar Clements and John Kahn became the highly regarded one-off *Old & In the Way* album, highlighted by a pair of Rowan songwriting gems, "Midnight Moonlight" and "Panama Red" (both covered by New Riders of the Purple Sage, who also recorded Rowan's "L.A. Cowboy"). Since that time Rowan's projects have included yet another bluegrass amalgam, Muleskinner; Mexican Airforce featuring accordionist Flaco Jiminez (continuing a life-long love of Tex-Mex soundings); as well as the Wild Stallions.

what to buy: Proof of Rowan's durability is the fact that his most recent release, *Bluegrass Boy* (Sugar Hill, 1996, prod. Peter Rowan, Jim Rooney) 🎵🎵🎵🎵, is as satisfying as anything he's done, and therefore not a bad place to start. Joining Rowan on this set of quality bluegrass standards and originals are Laurie Lewis and Del McCoury, plus old Seatrain cohort Richard Greene.

what to buy next: Those who've longed for another set of Old & In the Way can run out and grab *High Lonesome Sound* (Acoustic Disc, 1996, prod. David Grisman) 🎵🎵🎵🎵, which unearths more supple sounds of Rowan, Garcia, Grisman, Clements and Kahn from the Boarding House in October 1973.

the rest:
Peter Rowan (Flying Fish, 1978) 🎵🎵🎵
Medicine Trail (Flying Fish, 1980) 🎵🎵🎵
Texican Badman (Appaloosa, 1981) 🎵🎵🎵
Walls of Time (Sugar Hill, 1981) 🎵🎵🎵🎵
Peter Rowan with the Red Hot Pickers (Sugar Hill, 1984/1995) 🎵🎵🎵🎵
First Whippoorwill (Sugar Hill, 1985) 🎵🎵🎵🎵
New Moon Rising (Sugar Hill, 1988) 🎵🎵🎵🎵
Dust Bowl Children (Sugar Hill, 1990) 🎵🎵🎵🎵
All on a Rising Day (Sugar Hill, 1991) 🎵🎵🎵
Awake Me in the New World (Sugar Hill, 1993) 🎵🎵🎵🎵
(With the Rowan Brothers) *Tree on a Hill* (Sugar Hill, 1994) 🎵🎵🎵
(With Jerry Douglas) *Yonder* (Sugar Hill, 1996) 🎵🎵🎵🎵

worth searching for: *The Great American Eagle Tragedy* (Elektra, 1969, prod. Peter K. Siegel) 🎵🎵🎵🎵, a sort of Boston-psychedelia-meets-acoustic-bluegrass set, includes the chart-scraper "Home to You."

influences:

◀◀ Bill Monroe, Beatles, Jerry Garcia

▶▶ John Dawson, Nashville Bluegrass Band

David Simons

BILLY JOE ROYAL

Born April 3, 1942, in Valdosta, GA.

Billy Joe Royal hit his stride during the mid-1960s with a series of candy-flavored pop hits, including the poor-boy lament "Down in the Boondocks" as well as "Hush," "Cherry Hill Park" and "I Knew You When." He vanished from the music scene completely during the 1970s, and then resurfaced during the early 1980s with a series of pop-country hits, such as "I Miss You Already," "I'll Pin a Note on Your Pillow," "Out of Sight and out of Mind" and "It Keeps Right on Hurtin'." In 1989 Billy Joe's remake of Aaron Neville's 1967 R&B smash "Tell It Like It Is" reached #2 on the country charts.

what to buy: *Greatest Hits* (Columbia, 1989, prod. various) 🎵🎵🎵 spans Billy Joe's musical career from mid-1960s bubble-gum pop to 1980s country. The collection contains "Down in the Boondocks," "Hush," "Cherry Hill Park," "Tell It Like It Is" and "Save the Last Dance for Me."

what to buy next: *The Best of Billy Joe Royal* (Atlantic, 1991, prod. Nelson Larkin) 🎵🎵 features Royal's searing, vibrato-charged delivery on "Till I Can't Take It Anymore."

the rest:

Looking Ahead (Atlantic, 1986) 🎵🎵

The Royal Treatment (Atlantic, 1987) 🎵🎵

Tell It Like It Is (Atlantic, 1989) 🎵🎵

Out of the Shadows (Atlantic, 1990) 🎵🎵

Greatest Hits (Special Music Co.) 🎵🎵

Greatest Hits (Hollywood/IMG) 🎵🎵

influences:

◀◀ Joe South, Dennis Yost, Ray Stevens, Tommy Roe

▶▶ Narvel Felts

Rick Petreycik

JOHNNY RUSSELL

Born John Bright Russell, January 23, 1940, in Sunflower County, MS.

An early bloomer, the bigger-than-life Johnny Russell left Mississippi with his family to settle in California at age 12. There he began his entertaining career, winning talent contests, working as a DJ and performing in clubs, bars and on local TV shows. His interest in writing was stronger than ever, and after successfully getting a handful of his tapes to Chet Atkins, Russell moved to Nashville in 1958. Atkins chose Russell's "In a Mansion Stands My Love" as the "B" side of a Jim Reeves single. While waiting for his country creations to hit, Russell returned to California and got good news: Buck Owens recorded Russell's "Act Naturally," a Top 10 hit for Owens in 1963. The song's success didn't end there: in 1965 the Beatles scored on the pop charts with the same song, and it surfaced again (complete with video) when Ringo Starr and Buck Owens paired up in 1989. Russell continued to churn out successful singles for Burl Ives, Patti Page, Loretta Lynn, the Wilburn Brothers and Del Reeves. During the 1970s Russell signed a contract with RCA and, before long, found himself on the country charts with "Mr. & Mrs. Untrue," "Rain Falling on Me," "Rednecks, White Socks and Blue Ribbon Beer," "Catfish John," "The Baptism of Jesse Taylor" and "Hello I Love You." After changing labels to Polydor in 1978, Russell made the Top 25 with "You'll Be Back (Every Night in My Dreams)." His talent as a songwriter continued through the 1980s with hits for the Statler Brothers, George Strait and Gene Watson. Russell joined the Grand Ole Opry in 1985 and continues to entertain with his humor and crowd appeal. A sought after guest for TV talk shows, he was a regular on *Hee Haw* and has earned many fans in Europe. Poor health during the late 1980s slimmed Russell down, but it never diminished his talent as a well-rounded country artist.

what to buy: Russell continues to make occasional recordings and to release them independently. *Here's Johnny!* (self-released, 1996) 🎵🎵🎵 captures him in his live element, mixing in his humorous asides with more than two dozen songs, including "Rednecks, White Socks and Blue Ribbon Beer," "Act Naturally" and "The Baptism of Jesse Taylor."

the rest:

Almost Alive (self-released) 🎵🎵

Somethin' Old Somethin' New (self-released) 🎵🎵

worth searching for: *Greatest Hits* (Dominion, 1993) 🎵🎵 contains recent stereo recordings of Russell's signature hits and country standards such as "Jambalaya," "Kaw-Liga" and "Blue Eyes Cryin' in the Rain."

Leon Russell (© Ken Settle)

influences:

◀◀ Conway Twitty, Wilburn Brothers, Buck Owens

▶▶ Mel McDaniel, Moe Bandy

Randall T. Cook

LEON RUSSELL

Born April 2, 1941, in Lawton, OK.

Though pianist Leon Russell hit his stride during the early 1970s with *Carney*, he'd spent his formative years sharpening his chops as a session man for L.A.'s notorious "Wrecking Crew" and writing hits like Gary Lewis' "Just My Style." His years fronting the Shelter People found him sharing stages and studios with the likes of Eric Clapton, Bob Dylan and George Harrison. Masquerading under the pseudonym Hank Wilson, Russell cut a double-sided tribute to Hank Williams, "Roll in My Sweet Baby's Arms"/"I'm So Lonesome I Could Cry" in 1973. In 1992 Russell hit the record racks once more with the Bruce Hornsby-produced *Anything Can Happen*.

what to buy: *Leon Russell & the Shelter People* (The Right Stuff, 1971/1995, prod. Denny Cordell) 𝄢𝄢𝄢𝄢 follows his strong self-titled debut and finds Russell solidifying his swamp-boogie style, featuring gritty covers of Dylan's "A Hard Rain's a Gonna Fall" (the reissue contains several previously unreleased Dylan tracks) plus George Harrison's "Beware of Darkness" (reprised in live form on 1972's *The Concert for Bangladesh*).

what to buy next: *Carney* (The Right Stuff, 1972/1995, prod. Denny Cordell) 𝄢𝄢𝄢 was Russell's commercial peak; the tracks have added polish (compared with the raw exuberance of *Shelter People*), but Russell is afforded a real hit in the form of "Tight Rope." Russell also added "This Masquerade"—later a smash for George Benson—to his list of middle-of-the-road balladry (joining the Carpenters' "Superstar" and B.B. King's "Hummingbird").

the rest:

Leon Russell (The Right Stuff, 1970/1975) 𝄢𝄢𝄢
Hank Wilson's Back (The Right Stuff, 1973/1995) 𝄢𝄢𝄢
Leon Live (The Right Stuff, 1973/1996) 𝄢𝄢𝄢
Stop All That Jazz (The Right Stuff, 1974/1995) 𝄢𝄢𝄢
Will o' the Wisp (The Right Stuff, 1975/1995) 𝄢𝄢

influences:

◀◀ Jerry Lee Lewis, Phil Spector

▶▶ Lee Roy Parnell

David Simons

TOM RUSSELL

Born February 8, 1955, in Oklahoma City, OK.

Tom Russell may be best known for "Outbound Plane," which he wrote with Nanci Griffith, but which became a Top 10 hit for Suzy Bogguss in 1993. However, his story is more complex than that. After growing up in California, he began his career playing strip joints in Vancouver, British Columbia, then moved to Austin, Texas, and recorded two albums with pianist Patricia Hardin. He then quit the business and moved to New York to write novels. Eventually he started playing again and later toured Europe as a cowboy singer in a Puerto Rican carnival. He recorded three albums in Norway before finally establishing himself in the States. Russell's songs are literate and literary: his best songs are narratives, often involving real people. "Blue Wing" is about a man who was once jailed with blues great Little Willie John; "William Faulkner in Hollywood" traces the novelist's disastrous run at writing screenplays to pay off Southern loan sharks; and "Haley's Comet" (written with Dave Alvin) traces the downward spiral of rock 'n' roll progenitor Bill Haley. Russell has also worked as a producer, and in 1995 he co-produced the best of the Merle Haggard tribute albums, *Tulare Dust*.

what to buy: *Poor Man's Dream* (Philo, 1989, prod. Andrew Hardin, Charles Caldarola, Tom Russell, Jonas Fjeld) 𝄢𝄢𝄢𝄢 contains Russell's original version of "Outbound Plane" plus the narrative "Blue Wing" and two salt-of-the-earth anthems, "The Heart of the Working Man" and "Veteran's Day." And don't discount "Gallo Del Cielo," perhaps the best song ever written about a cock fight. *Hurricane Season* (Philo, 1991, prod. Tom Russell, Andrew Hardin) 𝄢𝄢𝄢 cuts a wide cultural swath, name-checking Argentinean composer Astor Piazzolla and boxing legend Jack Johnson. The album also features Russell and Alvin's ode to Bill Haley and includes one of Russell's best non-narrative songs, "Beyond the Blues," co-written with Peter Case and Bob Neuwirth.

what to buy next: *Cowboy Real* (Philo, 1992, prod. Tom Russell) 𝄢𝄢𝄢𝄢 is a charming collection of mostly original cowboy-style songs, and it includes two duets with folk great Ian Tyson, notably "Navajo Rug," which was the 1987 Country Music Association single of the year. To get a feel for Russell's full range as a writer and performer, check out one of two albums he has recorded with R&B wildman Barrence Whitfield: *Hillbilly Voodoo* (East Side Digital, 1993, prod. Tom Russell) 𝄢𝄢𝄢𝄢 has a loose, roadhouse feel and a terrific song list that includes Bob Dylan's "Blind Willie McTell," Jesse Winchester's "Mississippi,

You've Been on My Mind" and Jimmy Driftwood's "What Is the Color of the Soul of a Man?"

the rest:

Road to Bayamon (Rounder, 1987) 🎵🎵🎵

Box of Visions (Philo, 1993) 🎵🎵🎵🎵

(With Barrence Whitfield) *Cowboy Mambo* (East Side Digital, 1994) 🎵🎵🎵

Rose of the San Joaquin (HighTone, 1995) 🎵🎵🎵🎵

worth searching for: The import-only release *The Early Years: 1975–79* (Dark Angel, 1994) 🎵🎵🎵, which Russell recorded with Patricia Hardin, combines the duo's early efforts, *Ring of Bone* and *Wax Museum*, plus bonus tracks. *Beyond St. Olav's Gate, 1979–92* (Round Tower, 1992) 🎵🎵🎵🎵 is an import-only best-of collection. Russell's debut as a solo artist, *Heart on a Sleeve* (Bear Family, 1984) 🎵🎵🎵, has never been issued in the U.S.

influences:

◀◀ Merle Travis, Merle Haggard, Bob Dylan, Gram Parsons, William Faulkner

▶▶ Nanci Griffith

Daniel Durchholz

DOUG SAHM

Born November 6, 1942, in San Antonio, TX.

The Sir Douglas Quintet was the brainchild of original cosmic cowboy Doug Sahm. A steel-guitar prodigy, Sahm began performing as Little Doug Sahm at age six. Though the music of the Quintet's two hits, "She's About a Mover" and "Mendocino," produced by Cajun wildman Huey Meaux, was a mixed bag of border conjunto and San Francisco psychedelia, the members' long hair and quasi-royal name had many convinced they were from England. Sahm's eclectic, checkered solo career has included recordings with Bob Dylan, Dr. John, Flaco Jimenez, David "Fathead" Newman, Yusef Lateef and, most recently, with Freddie Fender, Jimenez and Augie Meyers as the Texas Tornados. Sahm's wry blend of rock, country, conjunto, soul and horn-based R&B has grown even better with age, and he remains an understated master of all stringed instruments. In whatever incarnation, Sahm represents Texas music at its finest.

what to buy: *The Best of Doug Sahm and Friends: Atlantic Sessions* (Rhino, 1992, prod. various) 🎵🎵🎵🎵 is an eclectic selection from Sahm's two early 1970s Atlantic albums, which include his collaborations with Dylan.

what to buy next: *Juke Box Music* (Antone's, 1988, prod. Doug Sahm) 🎵🎵🎵🎵 offers a refreshing set of pure Texas soul classics, including Sahm's unforgettably tasty cover of Little Sunny's "Talk to Me." *The Last Real Texas Blues Band* (Antone's, 1994, prod. Doug Sahm, Derek O'Brien) 🎵🎵🎵🎵 forms a perfect bookend, reprising the R&B of the big horn bands that Sahm chewed up in San Antonio during the 1950s.

what to avoid: *Daydreaming at Midnight* (Elektra, 1994, prod. Doug Sahm, Doug Clifford) 🎵🎵 is a heavy-metal Quintet reincarnation with Sahm's son, Shawn, on second guitar.

the rest:

Live (Bear Family, 1988) 🎵🎵🎵

Amos Garrett, Doug Sahm, Gene Taylor (Rykodisc, 1989) 🎵🎵🎵

The Best of Doug Sahm & the Sir Douglas Quintet (Mercury, 1990) 🎵🎵🎵🎵

worth searching for: You can't go wrong with most of the Quintet's long-out-of-print vinyl albums, especially *Honkey Blues* (Smash, 1968) 🎵🎵🎵🎵, *Mendocino* (Smash, 1969) 🎵🎵🎵🎵 or *1+1+1=4* (Philips, 1970) 🎵🎵🎵🎵. They all sound like they came from a planet somewhere between Texas and Mars. Another period piece worth seeking out is *Groover's Paradise* (Warner Bros., 1974) 🎵🎵🎵🎵, a hilarious, stoned Tex-Mex trip through the middle 1970s recorded with the rhythm section from Creedence Clearwater Revival.

influences:

◀◀ Hank Williams, Freddy Fender, Santiago Jimenez, Little Sunny & the Skyliners, T-Bone Walker, Junior Parker, Bobby "Blue" Bland, Howlin' Wolf, Jimmy Reed

▶▶ Sam the Sham & the Pharaohs, ? & the Mysterians, Mouse & the Traps, Joe "King" Carrasco & the Crowns, Elvis Costello & the Attractions, Uncle Tupelo

see also: *Texas Tornados*

Leland Rucker

SALAMANDER CROSSING

Formed 1991, in Amherst, MA.

Andrew Kinsey, bass, vocals; Rani Arbo, fiddle, viola, vocals; Jeff Kelliher, guitar, harmonica, vocals; Tim Farnham, banjo.

This New England quartet infuses spirited and melodic originals and songs by artists ranging from Tim O'Brien to the Beatles with a strong respect for bluegrass tradition to evoke a folky back-porch friendliness. Its reverential but contemporary sound has made the group a favorite on the festival circuit. Dobro/banjo wizard Tony Furtado guests on *Passion Train*.

what's available: *Salamander Crossing* (Signature Sounds, 1995, prod. Guy DeVito) 🎵🎵🎵, the group's debut album, is an inviting collection of rootsy contemporary folk played with living room informality. *Passion Train* (Signature Sounds, 1996, prod. Brooks Williams) 🎵🎵🎵, the group's second album, reached the Top 10 of the Americana chart with its friendly mix of evocative original songs and nods to Bill Monroe and Bruce Springsteen.

influences:
◀◀ Bill Monroe, Seldom Scene
▶▶ Blue Highway

David Sokol

THE SAVOY-DOUCET CAJUN BAND
Formed 1978, in Lafayette, LA.

Marc Savoy, accordion, vocals; Ann Savoy, guitar, vocals; Michael Doucet, fiddle, vocals.

This occasional band is dedicated to the perpetuation of traditional Cajun music; their music is rooted in the sound of the Gulf Coast Cajun culture. They record and tour whenever member Michael Doucet's busy schedule (he is the leader of the popular progressive Cajun band Beausoleil) allows. Although well known for his inventive fiddle forays with Beausoleil, Michael's playing with Savoy-Doucet is firmly within the tradition; he is conversant with and mindful of the work of his fiddling forebears at all times. He has been particularly influenced by Dennis McGee and two great Creole fiddlers, Canray Fontenot and Amedé Ardoin. Marc Savoy is probably the most accomplished accordionist in traditional Cajun styles and is also well known as an accordion builder. His wife Ann, born in St. Louis and raised in Virginia, is a Cajun by marriage and has embraced the musical traditions of the Cajun culture enthusiastically. She is a forceful rhythm guitarist and singer. Their instrumental work is exemplary, and they are fine singers as well.

what to buy: *Home Music with Spirits* (Arhoolie, 1992, prod. Chris Strachwitz) 🎵🎵🎵🎵 contains classic waltzes, two-steps, stomps and blues from the Cajun repertoire. It also includes a wonderful version of the "Cajun national anthem," "Jolie Blonde." *Two-Step d' Amedé* (Arhoolie, 1988, prod. Chris Strachwitz, Savoy-Doucet Cajun Band) 🎵🎵🎵🎵 is a mix of live and studio cuts, just as good as *Home Music with Spirits* with the added excitement of seven live cuts. An all-live set from three dances, *Live! At the Dance* (Arhoolie, 1994, prod. Chris Strachwitz) 🎵🎵🎵🎵, effectively captures the palpable excitement of traditional Cajun dance music.

what to buy next: On *Now & Then* (Arhoolie, 1996, prod. Scott Ardoin) 🎵🎵🎵🎵, Ken Smith, another outstanding fiddler, less adventurous, perhaps, and more melodic than Doucet, sits in with the Savoys on another outstanding bunch of Cajun classics .

worth searching for: *Cajun Jam Session* (Arhoolie, 1989, prod. Chris Strachwitz) 🎵🎵🎵🎵 features Doucet along with guitarist Alan Senauke and accordionist Danny Poullard in an impromptu recording of a live radio show from 1983. It's an enjoyable, if occasionally ragged, set of traditional Cajun music.

solo outings:
Michael Doucet:
Beau Solo (Arhoolie, 1989) 🎵🎵🎵🎵

Marc Savoy:
Oh, What a Night (Arhoolie, 1981) 🎵🎵🎵🎵
(With Dewey Balfa and D.L. Menard) *Under a Green Oak Tree* (Arhoolie, 1977) 🎵🎵🎵🎵🎵
(With Wallace Read) *Cajun House Party* (Arhoolie, 1979) 🎵🎵🎵🎵

influences:
◀◀ Iry LeJeune, Harry Choates, Cleoma Falcon, Canray Fontenot, Amedé Ardoin, Dewey Balfa, Nathan Abshire, Dennis McGee
▶▶ Steve Riley, Balfa Toujours, California Cajun Orchestra

Randy Pitts

SAWYER BROWN
Formed 1981, in Nashville, TN.

Mark Miller, vocals; Gregg "Hobie" Hubbard, keyboards; Bobby Randall, guitar (1981–92); Jim Scholten, bass; Joe Smyth, drums; Duncan Cameron, guitar (1992–present).

You don't get much respect when you're a winner of the *Star Search* television talent contest. The members of Sawyer

Mark Miller of Sawyer Brown (© Ken Settle)

Brown have spent their career living down the very achievement that brought them their first success. The group's 1984 win on the show netted it $100,000 and a recording contract, but their outrageous costumes and singer Mark Miller's hyperactive performances made the group an object of ridicule from critics and within the music industry. Still, the group had a #1 hit with its second single, "Step That Step" and went on to win the Country Music Association's Horizon Award in 1985. Sawyer Brown named itself after a suburban street in southwest Nashville, and all its members except Miller had played backup for country singer Don King before setting out on their own. They made their reputation not on radio, which was reluctant to play their records, but in concert. The group began to mature around 1991 with songs like "The Walk" and "Some Girls Do," and found the reception at radio that previously had eluded them. Guitarist Bobby Randall left the group in 1992 to host TNN's *Be a Star*; Duncan Cameron replaced him. Despite all the negative reaction to the band, Sawyer Brown is one of the few acts (along with the likes of George Strait, Reba McEntire and John Anderson) to have had a chart-topping single before Randy Travis and after Garth Brooks.

what to buy: *Greatest Hits 1990–1995* (Curb, 1995, prod. Mark Miller, Randy Scruggs, Mac McAnally) 🎵🎵🎵 contains most of the band's best singles ("All These Years," "This Time," "Thank God for You") and very few of the bad ones. *This Thing Called Wantin' and Havin' It All* (Curb, 1995, prod. Mark Miller, Mac McAnally) 🎵🎵🎵 continues to hone the band's direction as "small town heroes" (even the name of a song on the album). The first three singles from the album—"(This Thing Called) Wantin' and Havin' It All," "'Round Here" and "Treat Her Right"—are probably the strongest trio of hits the group has ever had.

what to buy next: The best thing that ever happened to Sawyer Brown was hooking up with singer/songwriter Mac McAnally, who wrote two songs, "Cafe on the Corner" and the devastating "All These Years," on *Cafe on the Corner* (Curb, 1992, prod. Mark Miller, Randy Scruggs) 🎵🎵🎵. The group's music grew up almost immediately, and it began dealing with complex, adult issues. By the group's next album, *Outskirts of Town* (Curb, 1993, prod. Mark Miller) 🎵🎵🎵, McAnally was producing and writing regularly with Miller.

what to avoid: Steer clear of pretty much anything before 1990, but especially the group's first three albums, *Sawyer Brown* (Curb, 1985) 🎵, *Shakin'* (Curb, 1985) 🎵 and *Out Goin' Cattin'* (Curb, 1986) 🎵. Rule of thumb: the goofier they look on the cover, the worse the record.

the rest:
Somewhere in the Night (Curb, 1987) 🎵🎵
Wide Open (Curb, 1988) 🎵🎵
The Boys Are Back (Curb, 1989) 🎵🎵
Greatest Hits (Curb, 1990) 🎵🎵
Buick (Curb, 1991) 🎵🎵
The Dirt Road (Curb, 1992) 🎵🎵🎵
Six Days on the Road (Curb, 1997) 🎵🎵🎵

influences:
⏪ Alabama, Mac McAnally
⏩ John Schneider, Boy Howdy

Brian Mansfield

DAVID SCHNAUFER

See: The Cactus Brothers

JOHN SCHNEIDER

Born April 8, 1959, in Mount Kisco, NY.

John Schneider was the more successful of the two actors who turned their roles on the CBS TV series *The Dukes of Hazzard* into country music careers. During a two-year period beginning in 1984, Schneider actually topped the country charts four times, and he had Top Five hits dating back to 1981. (Tom Wopat, Schneider's TV brother, had hits for six years, but only three of them ever reached the Top 20.) The rise of new traditionalists like Dwight Yoakam and Randy Travis knocked Schneider out of the market: he had his last charting single in 1987.

what's available: *Greatest Hits* (MCA, 1987, prod. Jimmy Bowen, John Schneider) 🎵🎵🎵 is better than you'd expect from watching *Dukes* reruns on TNN (or from seeing the cover, on which Schneider is posed playing air guitar). Schneider's singing is nothing more than workmanlike, but some of the songs ("I've Been Around Enough to Know," "It's a Short Walk from Heaven to Hell") aren't half bad.

influences:
⏪ Merle Haggard
⏩ Tom Wopat, Sawyer Brown

Brian Mansfield

JACK SCOTT

Born Jack Scafone Jr., January 28, 1936, in Windsor, Ontario, Canada.

Jack Scott's deep, dark voice, coupled with the dreamlike backing vocals and prominent acoustic bass of his records, has made the Canadian singer a cult figure among rockabilly aficionados. He had a string of rockabilly-ballad hits for Carlton and Top Rank labels during 1958–60, the biggest of which was 1958's "My True Love" b/w "Leroy," a better-than-average "Jailhouse Rock" knock-off. Years later he had one minor country hit, "You're Just Gettin' Better."

what's available: *Greatest Hits* (Curb, 1990, prod. Harley Hatcher) 🎵🎵🎵 will cover the bases for most casual Scott fans. It contains not only "My True Love" and "Burning Bridges," his two biggest hits, but hepper numbers like "Leroy" and "The Way I Walk" and a version of Roy Orbison's "Running Scared" as well. Those who need more are pointed to the German imports *On Groove* (Bear Family) and *Classic Scott: The Way I Walk* (Bear Family).

influences:
⏪ Sonny James, Elvis Presley
⏩ Conway Twitty

Brian Mansfield

EARL SCRUGGS

See: Flatt & Scruggs

GARY & RANDY SCRUGGS

See: Flatt & Scruggs

THE SCUD MOUNTAIN BOYS

Formed 1991, in Northampton, MA.

Joe Pernice, guitar, vocals; Stephen Desaulniers, bass, vocals; Bruce Tull, guitar, lap steel, vocals; Tom Shea, drums, mandolin.

Born of late-night acoustic music sessions after their gigs as a rock band were over, the Scud Mountain Boys play a brand of lush, hypnotic country-pop that has been dubbed "slowcore."

Unabashedly drawing on strains of pop and country-rock found in such acts as the early Bee Gees, the Eagles and Bread, the Scuds play music that is pretty, but they're no saps—the lyrics, mostly written by guitarist/vocalist Joe Pernice, are stark and filled with quiet desperation. The group is fond of writing, recording and even performing around a kitchen table, and their work has an appealingly loose, but never sloppy, feel. It's reminiscent of the first few Cowboy Junkies albums, only informed more by "New York Mining Disaster 1941" and "Wichita Lineman" than "Sweet Jane."

what to buy: You know something is up from the very first song on *Massachusetts* (Sub Pop, 1996, prod. Thom Monahan, Mike Deming, Scud Mountain Boys) ♫♫♫, in which Pernice sings in a calm, measured voice—or is he under sedation?—about a girl-friend killed in a car crash and his subsequent emotional dis-connection ("It must have been so difficult to deal/I used to know her face/Broken on the steering wheel"). The rest of *Massachusetts* is much the same—gorgeous, but somehow fundamentally damaged, and ultimately hard to forget.

the rest:
Pine Box (self-released, 1994/Chunk, 1995) ♫♫♫
Dance the Night Away (Chunk, 1995) ♫♫♫

influences:
◄◄ Bee Gees, America, Uncle Tupelo, Palace

Daniel Durchholz

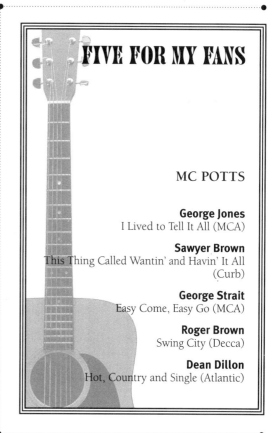

FIVE FOR MY FANS

MC POTTS

George Jones
I Lived to Tell It All (MCA)

Sawyer Brown
This Thing Called Wantin' and Havin' It All (Curb)

George Strait
Easy Come, Easy Go (MCA)

Roger Brown
Swing City (Decca)

Dean Dillon
Hot, Country and Single (Atlantic)

DAN SEALS

Born February 8, 1948, in McCamey, TX.

It's no surprise that Dan Seals has carved two notable music careers. His 1970s success as one half of the pop-folk duo England Dan & John Ford Coley precedes his 1980s country charts dominance. Part of his dual victory lies in his tender voice—a soothing instrument able to seamlessly blend country, pop, folk and Western influences that appeal to a wide cross-section of listeners. The rest can be attributed to his songwriting and keen ear for a powerful song. Such story tunes as the classics "Everything That Glitters (Is Not Gold)" and "They Rage On" and gut-wrenching ballads like "Addicted" and "You Still Move Me" have earned Seals a place in country folklore. But whereas today's crooners—John Berry and Collin Raye—tend to belt for effect, Seals finds his strength in hushed performances, al-though he does have a tendency to slide toward pop ditties. The Country Music Association award-winning "Bop" has not aged well, and his duet with Marie Osmond, "Meet Me in Mon-

tana," remains just a pleasant confection. But Seals' charm will never fade. A tall, imposing figure with a thick beard, mustache and wide-brimmed hat, he embodies the good-hearted singing cowboy that roams the West. That's an image engraved in American culture.

what to buy: Seals resurfaced during the mid-1990s with *In a Quiet Room* (Intersound, 1995, prod. Dan Seals) ♫♫♫♫, a collec-tion of mostly acoustic re-recordings of his solo hits and a cou-ple of England Dan & John Ford Coley standards. This setting best suits Seals' gentle voice and pop- and folk-laced songs. The two new numbers here, particularly the bluegrass-based "The Healing Kind," make this CD a welcomed return to form.

what to avoid: *Best of Dan Seals* (Curb, 1994, prod. various) ♫♫ is a haphazard, poorly compiled set of a few hits and filler ma-terial that completely belies its title, particularly when there are two other collections that truly represent Seals' creative peaks.

curly seckler

Dan Seals **(Warner Bros. Records)**

the rest:
The Best (Liberty, 1987) 𝄞𝄞𝄞𝄞
Greatest Hits (Capitol Nashville, 1991) 𝄞𝄞𝄞

worth searching for: The out-of-print *Rage On* (Capitol Nashville, 1988, prod. Kyle Lehning) 𝄞𝄞𝄞𝄞 stands as Seals' finest studio album to date. A concept album of sorts, *Rage On* focuses on small-town, blue-collar life and its unique set of problems. Although the entire effort is a wonderful listen, two cuts deserve special mention: Cheryl Wheeler's heartbreaking "Addicted" and John Scott Sherrill's stirring story song "Five Generations of Rock County Wilsons."

influences:
◀◀ Roy Rogers, James Taylor, Michael Martin Murphey
▶▶ Bryan White, Kevin Sharp, Ty Herndon

Mario Tarradell

CURLY SECKLER
Born December 25, 1919, in China Grove, NC.

Mandolinist and guitar player Curly Seckler (sometimes spelled

Sechler) has been in music since 1935; he joined Charlie Monroe's Kentucky Pardners in 1939, and made his first recordings (with Monroe) in 1946. He worked for Jim & Jesse briefly, but is best known for his long tenure as mandolinist and tenor singer for Flatt and Scruggs, his great bellowing tenor gracing many of their finest early records. He left music from 1962 to 1971, rejoining Lester Flatt and his new band, the Nashville Grass, in 1973. In 1979, following Flatt's death, Seckler took over leadership of Nashville Grass, and continues to lead them on a few dates a year even now, sharing band leadership with Lester Flatt soundalike Willis Spears.

what's available: Although Seckler's bellowing tenor voice can be heard on many fine Flatt & Scruggs reissues and on albums by others, the sole album under Seckler's name that is readily available today is *60 Years of Bluegrass with My Friends* (Vine Street Records, 1995, prod. Billy Henson) 𝄞𝄞𝄞, which features Seckler along with an array of guest stars, including Jim & Jesse, Josh Graves, Marty Stuart, Mac Wiseman, Ralph Stanley and many more. Also included is a version of "Shine on Me" from a 1950 radio program featuring Curly on guitar and harmony vocal with the Sauceman Brothers.

influences:
◀◀ Charlie Monroe, Stanley Brothers
▶▶ Red Allen, Jim & Jesse

see also: *Flatt & Scruggs*

Randy Pitts

JEANNIE SEELY
Born Marilyn Jeanne Seely, July 6, 1940, in Titusville, PN.

Jeannie Seely was such a consummate torch singer that for a while she became known as "Miss Country Soul." Seely took the radio and TV route from her native Pennsylvania to California, and she resettled in Nashville in 1965. A year later she had her first hit on Monument with "Don't Touch Me," which netted her a husband (the song's writer, Hank Cochran) and a Grammy. Seely performed with both Ernest Tubb and Porter Wagoner, but had her biggest duet successes with fellow Grand Ole Opry star Jack Greene ("Wish I Didn't Have to Miss You," "Much Oblige," "What in the World Has Gone Wrong with Our Love"). Seely has always stayed in touch with fashion, wearing mini-skirts and go-go boots on the Opry stage during the 1960s and hanging out with the outlaw crowd during the 1970s.

what's available: Sony apparently has allowed Seely's *Greatest Hits on Monument* (Sony Music, 1993) 🎵🎵🎵 to fall out of print, but it's still fairly easy to find. Seely's hits from the 1960s were prime countrypolitan, and at their best—"Don't Touch Me" or "It's Only Love"—they could be devastating. Jack Greene's *20 Greatest Hits* (Deluxe, prod. various) 🎵🎵🎵🎵 is the next best place to go. It mixes in a fair number of Seely's solo recordings along with her Decca duets with Greene.

influences:

◀◀ Hank Cochran, Jack Greene, Patsy Cline

▶▶ Lorrie Morgan, Trisha Yearwood

Brian Mansfield

THE SELDOM SCENE

Formed 1971, in Arlington, VA.

John Duffey (died December 10, 1996), mandolin, lead and harmony vocals (1971–96); Ben Eldridge, banjo, vocals (1971–present); Mike Auldridge, dobro (1971–95); John Starling, guitar, lead vocals (1971–77, 1992–94); Tom Gray, bass (1971–86); Lou Reid, guitar, lead vocals (1986–92); Phil Rosenthal, guitar, lead vocals (1977–85); T. Michael Coleman, bass guitar (1986–95); Moondi Klein, guitar, lead vocals (1994–95); Dudley Connell, guitar, lead vocals (1996–present); Ronnie Simpkins, bass, vocals (1996–present); Fred Travers, dobro, vocals (1996–present).

Former Country Gentlemen John Duffey and Ben Eldridge founded this influential band that's noted for mixing traditional tunes with country, pop and folk songs. The band has survived numerous personnel changes to remain one of the most influential bands in bluegrass for a quarter century. Mike Auldridge, T. Michael Coleman and Moondi Klein left in 1995 to work full-time with Chesapeake. Duffey's death in late 1996 leaves the band's future uncertain.

what to buy: *Scene 20: 20th Anniversary Concert* (Sugar Hill, 1991, prod. T. Michael Coleman) 🎵🎵🎵🎵 was recorded over two nights at the legendary Birchmere in Alexandria, Virginia, the group's regular home for many years. It reunites different line-ups of the band and features a guest appearance by Emmylou Harris.

what to buy next: For *Like We Used to Be* (Sugar Hill, 1994) 🎵🎵🎵🎵, John Starling briefly returned to the band and left behind this terrific collection of 13 songs, ranging from standards by the Stanley Brothers and Woody Guthrie to the original "I'll Take You Home."

the rest:

Act 3 (Rebel, 1973) 🎵🎵🎵🎵

Old Train (Rebel, 1974) 🎵🎵🎵🎵

Recorded Live at the Cellar Door (Rebel, 1975) 🎵🎵🎵🎵

The New Seldom Scene Album (Rebel, 1976/1989) 🎵🎵🎵

. . . At the Scene (Sugar Hill, 1983) 🎵🎵🎵

The Best of the Seldom Scene, Volume 1 (Rebel, 1986) 🎵🎵🎵🎵

A Change of Scenery (Sugar Hill, 1988) 🎵🎵🎵🎵

Scenic Roots (Sugar Hill, 1990) 🎵🎵🎵

Dream Scene (Sugar Hill, 1996) 🎵🎵🎵🎵

worth searching for: *Act II* (Rebel, 1973) 🎵🎵🎵🎵 is worth a look.

solo outings:

Mike Auldridge:

(With Lou Reid and T. Michael Coleman) *High Time* (Sugar Hill, 1989) 🎵🎵🎵

Mike Auldridge & Old Dog (Flying Fish) 🎵🎵🎵

Treasures Untold (Sugar Hill, 1990) 🎵🎵🎵🎵

Eight String Swing (Sugar Hill, 1992)

John Starling:

Long Time Gone (Sugar Hill, 1990) 🎵🎵🎵

Waitin' on a Southern Train (Sugar Hill, 1995) 🎵🎵🎵🎵

influences:

◀◀ Country Gentlemen, New Shades of Grass

▶▶ Alison Krauss & Union Station, Chesapeake

see also: *Country Gentlemen, Chesapeake*

Douglas Fulmer

ROBERT SHAFER

Born October 27, 1963, in Walton, WV.

Robert Shafer is a rising country guitar hero in the tradition of Danny Gatton who has been a major player at guitar contests for years. He won the National Flatpicking Championship in 1983 and has taken many other state guitar and mandolin awards as well. He also was Alison Krauss' accompanist of choice at several of her fiddle contests.

what's available: Shafer's electric and acoustic picking on his debut, *Hillbilly Fever* (Upstart, 1997, prod. Don Dixon) 🎵🎵🎵, is mind-boggling, and he makes clever choices of material (Kitty Wells' "Will Your Lawyer Talk to God," Tim Carroll's "Every Kind of Music"). But he could use a better singer than rough-voiced producer Don Dixon to complement his talent properly.

influences:

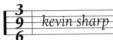 Danny Gatton, Albert Lee, Tony Rice

Brian Mansfield

KEVIN SHARP

Born December 10, 1970, in Redding, CA.

Kevin Sharp's story is a truly amazing one. At age 18 he was diagnosed with cancer and given no chance of survival. His bald head on the CD cover is not a fashion statement, it's the result of years of radiation and chemotherapy. Apparently there are plans in the works for a television movie about his struggle.

Sharp comes from a large family—seven brothers and sisters and numerous foster children. He began singing in choirs when he was three, and was auditioning for musicals when he was 10. He also loved sports, playing football, lifting weights and wrestling. He was the all-American high school kid, until he started having trouble getting out of bed. Doctors weren't sure what was wrong with him and kept telling him he was suffering from a sports injury. Sharp knew better, and soon the doctors discovered that he had bone cancer, which had spread throughout his body. When he was told he would have to have his leg amputated, he refused. That was when the Make-a-Wish Foundation, which grants "wishes" to terminally ill children, asked Sharp to name his heart's desire. He told them that what he wanted most in the world was to meet Grammy award-winning producer/composer David Foster (*The Bodyguard* soundtrack, Natalie Cole's *Unforgettable*). The friendship and encouragement Sharp gained from Foster quite literally gave him the will to live. Sharp went into remission in 1991, and made his debut album five years later.

what's available: Sharp's *Measure of a Man* (Asylum, 1996, prod. Chris Farren) ♫♫♫ is very contemporary. His debut single was a cover of the Tony Rich Project's R&B hit, "Nobody Knows," which topped the charts in 1997.

Cyndi Hoelzle

BILLY JOE SHAVER /SHAVER

Born August 16, 1939, in Corsicana, TX.

While most of his talented country friends have eventually hit big bucks on the pop charts, old songwriting hand Billy Joe Shaver continues to put out his speeding-train rockers and fragile tearjerkers in relative obscurity. A daunting roster of big stars—from Bob Dylan and Elvis Presley to the Highwaymen and Patty Loveless—have covered Shaver's songs; Waylon Jennings once put out *Honky Tonk Heroes*, an almost entirely Shaver-penned album. But where most country hitmakers write songs in Nashville offices, Shaver drives his truck around Texas and hopes to straighten out the financial problems that have kept him from enjoying his royalty checks. ("I was putting record companies out of business all through the 1970s," Shaver told critic Jimmy Guterman in 1995.) Meanwhile, after declaring himself a performer with 1993's impeccably written and blissfully honky-tonking *Tramp on Your Street*, Shaver has toured small clubs with his namesake band, featuring his son, hotshot guitarist Eddy Shaver.

what to buy: *Tramp on Your Street* (Zoo/Praxis, 1993, prod. R.S. Field) ♫♫♫♫ opens with three explosive songs, including "Heart of Texas" (with Waylon Jennings) and the instant classic "Georgia on a Fast Train." Bonuses include the heartwarming "Live Forever" and the singer's liner notes about seeing Hank Williams perform.

what to buy next: Upon listening to *Restless Wind: The Legendary Billy Joe Shaver 1973–1987* (Razor & Tie, 1995) ♫♫♫♫, a compilation of the singer-songwriter's solid albums for various record labels, you realize just how badly marketing and money people must have screwed up for not making this huge talent a superstar. *Highway of Life* (Justice, 1996, prod. Randall Jamail) ♫♫♫♫, the follow-up to *Tramp*, is sadly lacking a great Shaver stomper, but its romantic songs have a certain grizzled soul.

what to avoid: Don't knock yourself out trying to find Shaver's excellent but undiscovered and out-of-print early albums on Monument, Capricorn and Columbia; they're so impossible to dig up they've become major collector's items.

the rest:

Unshaven: Live from Smith's Olde Bar (Zoo/Praxis, 1995) ♫♫♫
Honky-Tonk Heroes (Bear Family, 1994) ♫♫♫♫

worth searching for: Waylon Jennings' *Honky Tonk Heroes* (1973/Mobile Fidelity Sound, 1991) ♫♫♫♫ is the closest any musician has come (aside from Shaver himself) to tapping the power and eloquence of this Texas stalwart's good old songs.

influences:

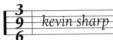 Johnny Cash, Kris Kristofferson, Hank Williams, Bob Dylan, Willie Nelson

▶▶ Waylon Jennings, Dwight Yoakam, Marty Brown, Steve Earle

Steve Knopper

VICTORIA SHAW

Born in Manhattan, NY.

A New York-born, California-bred veteran of piano bars and publishing companies, Victoria Shaw grew up in a house where her father gave up his singing career to manage her mother's. Shaw got her recording contract on the strength of her songwriting success, since she had penned chart-topping hits for Garth Brooks ("The River"), John Michael Montgomery ("I Love the Way You Love Me") and Doug Stone ("Too Busy Being in Love").

what's available: Shaw specializes in power-ballad anthems and clichéd uptempo numbers. That's fine when other artists cuts her material, because they also sing songs by different writers. But Shaw does the same thing song after song on *In Full View* (Reprise, 1995, prod. Andy Byrd, Jim Ed Norman) ♫♫, and her music rarely holds any surprises.

influences:

◀◀ Carole King, Juice Newton

▶▶ Gretchen Peters

Brian Mansfield

RICKY VAN SHELTON

Born January 12 1952, in Danville, VA.

Ricky Van Shelton was a frequent performer at the Nashville Palace nightclub at the same time Randy Travis washed dishes there—before both became part of the country explosion of the late 1980s. Some of Shelton's biggest hits were remakes of songs by such classic singers as Jack Greene, Charlie Rich and Elvis Presley. Shelton got his record deal after a newspaper columnist pitched his tape to a producer. Shelton, whose style runs to straight country and rockabilly-lite, later authored a children's book, *Tales of a Duck Named Quacker*. He was voted new male vocalist of the year by the Academy of Country Music in 1987 and won the Country Music Association's Horizon Award in 1988. As his sales and radio airplay declined, Shelton showed up more and more on religious programming on cable television. His gospel album, *Don't Overlook Salvation*, was reissued by a gospel label four years after its initial release and was nominated for a gospel Grammy in 1997. Shelton left Columbia Records in 1996 with plans to form his own record label and produce his own records in the future.

what to buy: Shelton's best material is on his first three albums, collected in one package in *Wild-Eyed Dream/Loving Proof/RVS III* (Legacy, 1986, 1987, 1988/1995, prod. Steve Buckingham) ♫♫♫. It contains most of his hits, including "Crime of Passion," "Life Turned Her That Way," "Don't We All Have the Right" and "From a Jack to a King."

what to buy next: *Super Hits, Volume 2* (Columbia, 1992, prod. Steve Buckingham) ♫♫♫, a solid collection of Shelton's later hits, includes "Backroads," "Wild Man" and "Wild-Eyed Dreams." It also brings Shelton's subtle rockabilly influence to the forefront with covers of "Wear My Ring Around Your Neck" and "Oh Pretty Woman."

what to avoid: Lots of folks wondered why *Don't Overlook Salvation* (Columbia, 1992) ♫♫ got a Grammy nomination four years after its original release, especially since its humdrum renditions of gospel songs stiffed the first time out.

the rest:

Wild-Eyed Dream (Columbia, 1987) ♫♫♫
Loving Proof (Columbia, 1988) ♫♫♫
RVS III (Columbia, 1990) ♫♫♫
Backroads (Columbia, 1991) ♫♫♫
Greatest Hits (Columbia, 1992) ♫♫♫
A Bridge I Didn't Burn (Columbia, 1993) ♫♫
Ricky Van Shelton Sings Christmas (Columbia, 1993) ♫♫
Super Hits (Columbia, 1995) ♫♫♫

influences:

◀◀ Randy Travis, Jack Greene

▶▶ Clay Walker, Daryle Singletary

Bill Hobbs

SHENANDOAH

Formed 1985, in Muscle Shoals, AL.

Marty Raybon, vocals; Jimmy Seales, guitar, vocals; Ralph Ezell, bass, vocals; Stan Thorn, keyboards, vocals; Mike McGuire, drums, vocals.

Despite the impressive pedigrees of its members—Marty Raybon sang bluegrass and Southern gospel for years and wrote songs for George Jones and Johnny Duncan; Jimmy Seales backed Bill Haley and David Allen Coe; Stan Thorn was a member of George Clinton's Funkadelic—this group has never been able to sustain any momentum. Shenandoah had a string of hits, including "Church on Cumberland Road" and "Mama Knows" during the late 1980s, culminating in an Academy of Country Music group of the year award. But they lost two critical years fighting for the rights to their name—foisted on them by their first producers (who thought the band's idea, Diamond Rio, wasn't commercial enough)—which they shared with three other groups, including Arlo Guthrie's backing band. Shenandoah won the court fight, but paid dearly, filing for bankruptcy in 1991. They re-emerged in 1992 with a new label (RCA), a new producer (hit-making machine Don Cook) and renewed determination. Danceable hits such as "Janie Baker's Love Slave" and "If Bubba Can Dance (I Can Too)" endeared them to audiences and country radio programmers all over again. But they've struggled since then, moving to Capitol, where they scored a hit and a Grammy with "Somewhere in the Vicinity of the Heart," featuring Alison Krauss on vocals.

what to buy: Most of Shenandoah's Columbia and RCA albums are out of print, though their best material has been rounded up on hits albums by their former labels. The group even resorted to re-recording seven of those songs for its new label, Capitol. But its second album, *The Road Not Taken* (Columbia, 1989, prod. Rick Hall, Robert Byrne) ♫♫♫, is still its best, a spirited blend of traditional country, pop, bluegrass and Southern gospel that includes three #1 hits, "The Church on Cumberland Road," "Sunday in the South" and "Two Dozen Roses."

what to buy next: The biggest hits from its brief tenure with RCA, including the goofy "Janie Baker's Love Slave" and the more earnest "Rock My Baby," are included on *The Best of Shenandoah* (RCA, 1995, prod. Don Cook) ♫♫♫.

what to avoid: *Shenandoah Christmas* (Capitol, 1996, prod. Don Cook) ♫ is another rote holiday release.

the rest:
Extra Mile (Columbia, 1990) ♫♫
In the Vicinity of the Heart (Liberty, 1994) ♫♫♫
Super Hits (Columbia, 1994) ♫♫♫
Now and Then (Capitol/EMI, 1996) ♫♫

influences:
◀◀ Alabama, George Jones, Merle Haggard
▶▶ Diamond Rio, BlackHawk

Doug Pullen

JEAN SHEPARD

Born Ollie Imogene Shepard, November 21, 1933, in Pauls Valley, OK.

Jean Shepard was born in Oklahoma, but she was raised in California, where she formed an all-girl band, the Melody Ranch Girls, as a teenager. Shepard's big break came in 1952. Hank Thompson heard her sing and, amazed that such a petite girl could have such a strong voice, he helped set up a recording deal. Shepard recorded her first session September 20, 1952, at age 18. Her first single, "A Dear John Letter," a duet with Fer-

lin Husky, spent six weeks at #1 and even hit the Top 5 on the pop charts; she followed that with "Forgive Me John," a duet answer record. She joined both Red Foley's Ozark Jubilee and the Grand Ole Opry in 1955. At the Opry she met Hawkshaw Hawkins, whom she married in 1960. (Hawkins died in the 1963 plane crash that also took the lives of Patsy Cline and Cowboy Copas.) Shepard is noted for her yodeling ability, and she is one of the pioneering women of country music. She still performs at the Opry, where she is well respected both by her fans and by her peers.

what to buy: The two dozen tracks on *Honky-Tonk Heroine: Classic Capitol Recordings (1952–1964)* (Country Music Foundation, 1995, prod. Country Music Foundation) ♫♫♫♫ show a confident, spirited honky-tonk singer. These are by far Shepard's best recordings, and they include "A Dear John Letter," "A Satisfied Mind," "Beautiful Lies" and "Second Fiddle (To an Old Guitar)," her first single released after Hawkins' death.

the rest:
Second Fiddle to an Old Guitar (Starday, 1985) ♫♫♫
Dear John (LaserLight) ♫♫

worth searching for: The five-CD set *The Melody Ranch Girl* (Bear Family, 1996, prod. Ken Nelson, Marvin Hughes) ♫♫♫♫♫ contains all of Shepard's Capitol recordings. Shepard cut a wide trail for female singers who succeeded her; the 151 tracks here offer an insight into how she did it. An example is her album *Songs of a Love Affair* (included here in its entirety), which is acknowledged by many country scholars as being the first concept album by a female singer.

influences:
◀◀ Kitty Wells
▶▶ Loretta Lynn, Dolly Parton

Denise Burgess

T.G. SHEPPARD

Born William Neal Browder, July 20, 1942, in Alamo, TN.

A high-school dropout, Bill Browder moved to Memphis in 1960 looking for a shot at pop music stardom. There he befriended Elvis Presley, who gave him a tour bus. The King's investment was unnecessary, as Browder gave up the rockabilly stage for a desk job, albeit one in the promotions end of the music industry.

In 1972 Browder found "Devil in a Bottle," which he considered a surefire hit. He couldn't find anybody in Nashville who wanted a song like that, so he recorded it himself. A Motown subsidiary released it, and the newly renamed T.G. Sheppard had his first #1 hit in 1975. Sheppard signed with Warner Bros. in 1977, and his pop influences complemented the *Urban Cowboy* trend of the early 1980s perfectly. From late 1979 to 1984 Sheppard racked up 11 chart-topping hits, including "Last Cheater's Waltz" and "I'll Be Coming Back for More." Even a novelty pairing with Clint Eastwood titled (what else?) "Make My Day" reached #12. These days Sheppard has retreated to the outlet store mecca of Pigeon Forge, Tennessee, where he has his own theater.

what to buy: Sheppard has had nearly 40 Top 40 hits, but most of them, in retrospect, weren't very substantial musically. *The Best of T.G. Sheppard* (Curb, 1992, prod. various) 🎵🎵🎵 does contain the best of them, having collected tracks from Sheppard's Melodyland, Hitsville and Warner Bros. days. This is the compilation that contains the powerful "Devil in a Bottle," Sheppard's first hit, as well as chart-toppers like "Party Time" and "Last Cheater's Waltz" and a version of Bryan Adams' "Everything I Do (I Do It for You)."

what to buy next: *All-Time Greatest Hits* (Warner Bros., 1991, prod. Buddy Killen, Jim Ed Norman) 🎵🎵🎵 goes deeper into Sheppard's Warner Bros. catalog, but it does have seven songs that overlap with the Curb collection.

the rest:

T.G. Sheppard's Greatest Hits (Warner Bros., 1983) 🎵🎵🎵

worth searching for: Though they're far from his best, Sheppard had a number of hits for Columbia during the mid-1980s. These can be found on *Biggest Hits* (Columbia, 1988) 🎵🎵.

influences:

◀◀ Eddie Rabbitt, Mickey Gilley, Johnny Lee

▶▶ Ricky Van Shelton

Craig Shelburne and Brian Mansfield

THE SHIVERS

Formed 1988, in Austin, TX.

Carey Kemper, guitar, vocals; Kelly Bell, guitar, acoustic and electric bass, vocals; Doug Spinks, drums (1988–89); Diesel Tucker, drums (1989–92); Barry Haney, drums (1992–93, 1994–96); Chris Wolf, drums (1993–94); Christian Famiglietta, drums (1996–present).

The Shivers' dark, snarling folk-rock has been called "Gothic country," at times recalling the thrash of X. Carey Kemper and Kelly Bell were married onstage in Austin, Texas, in 1989, and

have since been based in Minneapolis, Minnesota; Portland, Oregon; and Chattanooga, Tennessee, where they became a quartet.

what's available: *The Shivers* (Restless, 1994, prod. Tom Herbers,Shivers) 🎵🎵🎵, the band's first outing, establishes their brooding sound with a set of lonesome ballads and R.E.M.-style rockers. It's worth it just for the spooky duets "Never Leave Nevada" and "Red Cats." Much more somber than their debut, *The Buried Life* (Restless, 1996, prod. Tom Herbers, Shivers) 🎵🎵🎵 goes heavy on dark moments like "Shade the Light" and "The Wind in Abilene," but also contains the bouncy "Tumbledown Girl" and the horn-driven "Cry of Love," for which the Shivers are almost cheery.

worth searching for: The European import of their sophomore album, *The Buried Life* (Glitterhaus, 1996, prod. Tom Herbers, Shivers) 🎵🎵🎵, contains three tracks that aren't on the U.S. version.

influences:

◀◀ Cowboy Junkies, Knitters

Bob Cannon

THE SIDEMEN

Formed 1989, in Nashville, TN.

Mike Bub, bass, vocals; Jimmy Campbell, fiddle, vocals; Ed Dye, vocals, bones; Terry Eldredge, guitar, vocals; Ronnie McCoury, mandolin, vocals; Larry Perkins, banjo, guitar; Gene Wooten, dobro, vocals.

The Sidemen are an eclectic conglomeration of musicians rooted in the bluegrass tradition who began playing together in 1989, on Tuesday nights at Nashville's tiny but important bluegrass hangout, the Station Inn. Ronnie McCoury, the dynamic mandolin player and vocalist, no longer performs with the group on a regular basis, but, then again, the group isn't exactly adhering to a particular membership. Informal jam sessions, after all, are what led to the group's formation. If there's a star in the group, it's most likely Ed Dye. Dye, who's sort of a cross between Leon Redbone and Grandpa Jones (although he plays bones, not banjo), grew up in Montgomery, Alabama, and was once Hank Williams' paperboy. Ronnie McCoury and bass player Mike Bub, from Arizona and Pennsylvania, respectively, are members of the multi-award-winning Del McCoury Band. Jimmy Campbell, a Kenny Baker-style fiddler, is a former Blue Grass Boy who also played with Jim & Jesse McReynolds. Superb vocalist Terry Eldredge has worked with the Lonzo & Oscar show and Wilma Lee Cooper, in addition to a long stint with the

Osborne Brothers. Gene Wooten, "King of the Carolina Dobro Pickers," spent six years with Wilma Lee's band and then joined Country Gazette. He's currently working with the Osborne Brothers. And Larry Perkins is a former member of Lonesome Standard Time who also played banjo with Curly Seckler for several years. Together they have redefined what a band could be, staying focused on keeping up their musical chops by breaking loose from their day jobs to just have fun. The Japanese label Red Clay Records couldn't resist getting the experience on tape, and so the recording was born. Whether or not another album is ever released, this one does its job, capturing a group of supremely talented pickers at their best—and having a heck of a good time, too.

what's available: *Almost Live at the Station Inn* (Red Clay, 1994, prod. Sidemen) ♪♪♪ finds the boys cutting loose on some pretty traditional stuff, with equal doses of unconventionality and reverence.

influences:
◀◀ Nashville Jug Band
▶▶ Del McCoury Band

Stephen L. Betts

SHEL SILVERSTEIN

Born November 23, 1932, in Chicago, IL.

A man of varied talents, Shel Silverstein divided his creative life into two parts: a writer/cartoonist who wrote both children's books and social commentary for *Playboy*; and a witty songwriter who wrapped novel lyrics around simple folk tunes. In 1969 Johnny Cash recorded Silverstein's "A Boy Named Sue" live at San Quentin Prison, and the song eventually flew to #2 on the Hot 100 to become the commercial highlight of Cash's career. Loretta Lynn recorded "One's on the Way," and Dr. Hook and the Medicine Show got a pair of huge hits out of the writer's "Sylvia's Mother" and "Cover of the *Rolling Stone*."

what to buy: *Where the Sidewalk Ends* (Sony Kid's Music, 1976/1992) ♪♪♪ shows Silverstein's gift for penning kids tunes with stuff like "Ickle Me, Pickle Me, Tickle Me Too" and "Crocodile's Toothache."

the rest:
The Great Conch Train Robbery (Flying Fish)
A Light in the Attic (Sony Kid's Music, 1992) ♪♪♪

worth searching for: *Freakin' at the Freakers Ball* (CBS, 1969, prod. Roy Halee) ♪♪♪ became a 1969 cult classic due to its

abundance of counterculture/hippie themes, including the hilarious title track, "I Got Stoned and I Missed It" and "Don't Give a Dose to the One You Love Most," while 1972's *Songs and Stories* (Parachute, 1972, prod. Ron Haffkine) ♪♪♪ includes such commendable titles as "Never Bite a Married Woman on the Thigh" and "Someone Ate the Baby."

influences:
◀◀ Tom Lehrer
▶▶ Dr. Hook

David Simons

DARYLE SINGLETARY

Born March 10, 1971, in Whigham, GA.

Daryle Singletary lived every aspiring country singer's dream when hero Randy Travis acknowledged his talent and took him under his wing. The young singer was given the opportunity to open Travis' shows even before the release of "I'm Living Up to Her Low Expectations," the first single from Singletary's self-titled debut. Steeped in pure, traditional country, Singletary cites his grandfather right alongside George Jones and Merle Haggard as major influences in his life.

what's available: *Daryle Singletary* (Giant, 1995, prod. James Stroud, Randy Travis, David Malloy) ♪♪♪♪, the singer's first album, jump-started his career with the hits "I Let Her Lie" and "Too Much Fun," and shows off a young performer who's more comfortable with pure country in the style of his influences than with the flashier country pop of other hat acts. *All Because of You* (Giant, 1996) ♪♪♪ is a mixed affair that sinks below his high expectations with titles like "Liar Liar My Heart's on Fire" and "Redneckin'."

influences:
◀◀ Randy Travis, Keith Whitley
▶▶ Ken Mellons, Wesley Dennis

David Sokol

SIX SHOOTER

Gabe Dixon, keyboards, vocals; Jason Egly, guitar, vocals; J.P. King, lead guitar; Chris McDowell, vocals, percussion; Ronnie Dean McDowell, drums; Brian Zonn, bass.

The members of Six Shooter gained some notoriety during the early 1990s for being the only self-contained band with no members old enough to buy a drink. The group featured two sons of Ronnie McDowell, who co-produced the album and recorded for the same label as the band. On record they sound like a good gimmick for a marketing plan.

what's available: Depending on who's doing the singing, the music on *Six Shooter* (Curb, 1991, prod. Buddy Killen, Ronnie McDowell, Joe Meador) 🎵🎵 ranges from merely pedestrian to really juvenile. The band goes for teenybop rockabilly sounds on versions of Faron Young's "Goin' Steady" and Jerry Lee Lewis' "High School Confidential," but pulls mercilessly on the heartstrings with the originals "Love in the Heart (Peace in the World)" and "Daddy Don't You Sign the Papers."

influences:
◀◀ Ronnie McDowell
▶▶ Moffatts

Brian Mansfield

RICKY SKAGGS

Born July 18, 1954, in Cordell, KY.

One of the most successful country artists of the 1980s (and also one of the most influential), Ricky Skaggs is credited with bringing bluegrass and roots music back into vogue shortly after the troubling *Urban Cowboy* phase had mercifully been laid to rest. A mandolin whiz before he hit his teens, and a member of Ralph Stanley's Clinch Mountain Boys at age 15 with boyhood pal Keith Whitley, Skaggs retreated to the Washington, D.C., area by 19, tiring of life as a traveling bluegrass musician. However, his early retirement was short-lived after the Country Gentlemen invited him to tour with them. Following stints with J.D. Crowe & the New South and the Seldom Scene, Skaggs formed Boone Creek, adding electric instruments and drums to his band's sound. After Boone Creek's demise, he joined Emmylou Harris' Hot Band in 1977, replacing Rodney Crowell and putting his own bluegrass stamp on a string of Harris' late 1970s and early 1980s records, like the acoustic *Roses in the Snow*. Following a pair of critically acclaimed records on Sugar Hill during the late 1970s, Skaggs signed with Epic and began an impressive hitmaking streak, scoring 10 #1 singles in four short years, including his 1984 smash, "Uncle Pen," the first bluegrass song to hit the top since Flatt & Scruggs' "Ballad of Jed Clampett" in 1963.

Skaggs married Sharon White, of the Whites, in 1981 and joined the Grand Ole Opry in 1982. In 1985 the Country Music Association named him its Entertainer of the Year. After leaving Epic, Skaggs signed with Atlantic Records in 1995. Although some

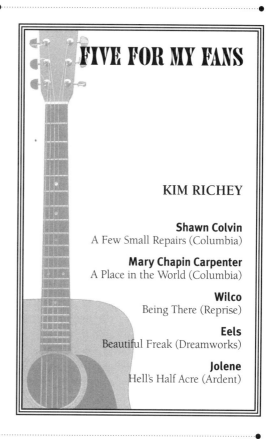

FIVE FOR MY FANS

KIM RICHEY

Shawn Colvin
A Few Small Repairs (Columbia)

Mary Chapin Carpenter
A Place in the World (Columbia)

Wilco
Being There (Reprise)

Eels
Beautiful Freak (Dreamworks)

Jolene
Hell's Half Acre (Ardent)

time has passed since Skaggs had a big charting single, he's still involved in several ventures musically, including a concert series taped for TNN at the historic Ryman Auditorium, as well as producing records for Dolly Parton and the Whites.

what to buy: *Highways and Heartaches* (Epic, 1982, prod. Ricky Skaggs) 🎵🎵🎵🎵 contains three #1 singles, including Guy Clark's "Heartbroke," and stands as simply one of the best country albums of the 1980s, though it's certainly rivaled by its predecessor, *Waitin' for the Sun to Shine* (Epic, 1981, prod. Ricky Skaggs) 🎵🎵🎵🎵.

what to buy next: Previous to his Epic signing, Skaggs was signed to independent Sugar Hill, where he made two exceptional records that leaned more heavily on bluegrass, but still showed Skaggs' penchant for experimentation. *Sweet Temptation* (Sugar Hill, 1979) 🎵🎵🎵🎵 is a bluegrass/honky-tonk mixture, and *Skaggs and Rice* (Sugar Hill, 1980) 🎵🎵🎵🎵, with gui-

Ricky Skaggs **(AP/Wide World Photos)**

tarist Tony Rice, is a pure delight, with spare instrumentation and an old-time sound.

the rest:

(With Keith Whitley) *Second Generation Bluegrass* (Rebel, 1990) 🎸🎸🎸🎸
Family and Friends (Rounder, 1982/1986) 🎸🎸🎸🎸
Don't Cheat in Our Hometown (Sugar Hill/Epic, 1983) 🎸🎸🎸🎸
Country Boy (Epic, 1984) 🎸🎸🎸🎸
Live in London (Epic, 1985) 🎸🎸🎸🎸
Love's Gonna Get Ya! (Epic, 1986) 🎸🎸🎸
Comin' Home to Stay (Epic, 1988) 🎸🎸🎸
Kentucky Thunder (Epic, 1989) 🎸🎸🎸🎸
My Father's Son (Epic/Word, 1991) 🎸🎸🎸🎸
Solid Ground (Atlantic, 1995) 🎸🎸🎸

worth searching for: With a band that includes Skaggs, Jerry Douglas, and Terry Baucom, *Boone Creek* (Sugar Hill, 1977) 🎸🎸🎸🎸 is pretty progressive stuff, featuring horns and synthesizers, and Skaggs taking a few lead vocals, including a fair Ralph Stanley impression on "Drifting Too Far from the Shore."

influences:

◀◀ Emmylou Harris, Bill Monroe, Ralph Stanley
▶▶ Jerry Douglas, Keith Whitley, Steve Wariner

Stephen L. Betts

THE SKELETONS /THE MORELLS

The Skeltons formed 1979, in Springfield, MO. The Morells formed 1983, in Springfield, MO; disbanded, 1987.

The Skeletons: Lou Whitney, bass, vocals; D. Clinton Thompson, guitar, vocals; Bobby Lloyd Hicks, drums, vocals; Randle Chowning, guitar, harmonica, vocals (1979); Nick Sibley, keyboards, guitar, harmonica, vocals (1979, 1988); Joe Terry, keyboards, vocals (1988, 1990–present); Kelly Brown, keyboards, vocals (1990–present). The Morells: Lou Whitney, bass, vocals; D. Clinton Thompson, guitar, vocals; Maralie, keyboards, vocals; Ron Gremp, drums, vocals; Joe Terry, keyboard, vocals (1983–87).

Purveyors of roots rock in nearly all its myriad guises, the Skeletons and Morells—different incarnations of roughly the same sensibility—are the greatest bar bands you never heard. Their members have assimilated an astounding array of influences—rockabilly, country, R&B, beach music, frat rock and Phil Spector are all in there someplace—making for an eclecticism that has cost them commercial success but left their fans agape on countless occasions. The Skeletons formed from the ashes of the Springfield, Missouri, group the Original Symptoms, then took a hiatus when Lou Whitney, Clinton Thompson and Bobby Lloyd Hicks backed Steve Forbert for a spell. Whitney and Thompson then chose to start the Morells before reactivating the Skeletons during the late 1980s. The Skeletons continue to work on their own and as a popular backing band for such artists as Dave Alvin, Jonathan Richman, Boxcar Willie and Syd Straw.

what to buy: The Morells' *Shake and Push* (Borrowed Records, 1982/East Side Digital, 1989, prod. Morells) 🎸🎸🎸🎸🎸 is an absolute masterpiece of what was not then called roots rock. Drawing on obscure sources from across the musical spectrum, *Shake and Push* is a rockin' dance floor delight, with lyrics that are smart and funny to boot. Of special note is "Red's," which pays tribute to their hometown's finest roadside diner, and a high-stepping version of the Maddox Brothers & Rose's hilarious "Ugly and Slouchy."

what to buy next: The Skeletons' *In the Flesh!* (East Side Digital, 1991, prod. Skeletons) 🎸🎸🎸🎸 compiles two albums issued during the 1980s on the Scottish label Next Big Thing. Featured numbers include Whitney's brilliant car anthem "Trans Am" and "Thirty Days in the Workhouse," as great a Johnny Cash-style tune as Cash ever wrote himself, plus Thompson's percussive pop gem "Outta My Way" and covers of Little Jimmy Dickens' "I'm Little but I'm Loud" and the Flying Burrito Brothers' "Older Guys."

the rest:

(As the Skeletons) *Waiting* (Alias, 1993) 𝄢𝄢𝄢𝄢

(As the Skeletons) *Nothing to Lose* (HighTone, 1997) 𝄢𝄢𝄢𝄢

worth searching for: The Skeletons turn in a rockin' Christmas classic by combining "Do You Hear What I Hear?" with the Kinks' "You Really Got Me" on the holiday compilation album *Christmas Party with Eddie G.* (Strikin' It Rich/Columbia, 1990, prod. Jeff Rosen) 𝄢𝄢𝄢𝄢.

influences:

◀◀ Swingin' Medallions, Arthur Conlee, Moon Mullican, Sonny Bono, Johnny Cash

▶▶ Ben Vaughan, Del Lords, Dave Alvin, Marshall Crenshaw

see also: *Boxcar Willie*

Daniel Durchholz

THE SKILLET LICKERS

Formed c. 1926.

James Gideon "Gid" Tanner (born June 6, 1885, in Thomas Bridge, GA; died May 13, 1960), fiddle, banjo; Clayton McMichen (born January 26, 1900, in Allatoona, GA; died in 1970), fiddle; Riley Puckett (born May 7, 1894, in Alpharetta, GA; died in 1946), guitar, vocals; Fate Norris, banjo; Lowe Stokes, fiddle; Berty Layne, fiddle.

The Skillet Lickers were the preeminent old-time string band of the 1920s. Led by Gid Tanner, with his wild red hair and wacky stage antics, the Skillet Lickers had a profound impact on musicians, as well as on radio and recording, both in their infancy and during the band's heyday. The group featured four fiddlers including Tanner, whose comic routines became as well known as his music. Riley Puckett, the blind singer and guitarist, played in a style that would be imitated successfully by groups like the Carter Family. Invited to record in New York in 1924, Tanner and Puckett were teamed up with Clayton McMichen and Fate Norris in order to give the band a bigger sound.

The combination worked immediately, and by 1926, when their first recordings were released, the Skillet Lickers were a hit. Recordings of their comic skits were bigger sellers than their

fiddle music, and Puckett's vocal recordings also sold well. This created a shift in the focus of the group and a name change, to the rather unwieldy "Gid Tanner & His Skillet Lickers with Clayton McMichen and Riley Puckett." The group began to splinter, and McMichen, who had worked in the studio with Jimmie Rodgers, left to form Clayton McMichen & His Georgia Wildcats. Tanner recorded with Puckett one last time in 1934 for Bluebird, with his teenage son joining them, along with mandolin player Ted Hawkins. McMichen would go on to form a Dixieland band in 1944, and couldn't escape the old-time/folk revival of the 1960s. Puckett worked for a number of years on various radio programs and recordings with only moderate success. Today few people understand the strong influence the Skillet Lickers had on the development of string band music.

what's available: Sadly, their catalog hasn't been treated with the respect it deserves, but, with a little hunting, fans will find music from this seminal outfit available. Among the recordings to look for are: *Old-Time Songs & Tunes* (County); *The Skillet Lickers with Tanner, McMichen, Stokes* (County); and *The Skillet Lickers with Tanner, McMichen, Stokes: Volume 2* (County).

influences:

◀◀ Clayton McMichen & His Georgia Wildcats, Fiddlin' John Carson

▶▶ Freight Hoppers, Mac Benford & His Woodshed All-Stars

Stephen L. Betts

ARTHUR "GUITAR" SMITH

Born April 1, 1921, in Clinton, SC.

One of the first country performers to see the potential of the electric guitar, Arthur "Guitar" Smith recorded "Guitar Boogie," one of the most influential instrumentals of all time. He recorded the song during the mid-1940s, and over the years it sold some three million copies, even making *Billboard*'s country Juke Box chart in 1948–49. The song had a huge impact on the young guitarists who would develop rockabilly during the next decade. Smith, who also played banjo, also recorded a song with Don Reno called "Feudin' Banjos." That tune became the basis for "Dueling Banjos" from the 1972 film *Deliverance*, though Smith and Reno had to wage a two-year legal battle to prove it. Smith has also been active in the radio, television and recording community in Charlotte, North Carolina.

what's available: The instrumentals on *Guitar Boogie* (IMG) 𝄢𝄢 range from the pre-rock 'n' roll of the title track to slow, organ-based blues to straight-ahead acoustic country picking. It's recorded on cheap tape, but it has good licks.

influences:

◀◀ Merle Travis, Charlie Christian

▶▶ Scotty Moore, rock 'n' roll

Brian Mansfield

BILLY & TERRY SMITH

Brother duo from VA.

Billy Smith, guitar, vocals; Terry Smith, bass, vocals.

Billy and Terry Smith grew up playing in a family band with their parents and later hit the bluegrass trail. Billy played guitar and sang with Jimmy Martin and Lester Flatt; Terry played upright bass for Martin, the Osborne Brothers and Wilma Lee Cooper. The duo recorded one album for Epic Records in 1990. Their mother is *Country Music* magazine columnist Hazel Smith.

what's available: Not that these acoustic versions of songs like "Friend of the Devil," "Alabama Getaway" and "Touch of Grey" measure up to the originals, but on *Long Live the Dead: A Tribute to the Grateful Dead* (K-Tel, 1996, prod. Billy Smith, Terry Smith) ✍✍✍ the Smiths do a good job pointing up the Dead's country influences. The duo is backed by guitarist David Grier and multi-instrumentalist Robert Bowlin.

worth searching for: *Billy & Terry Smith* (Epic, 1990) ✍✍✍ features bluesy, acoustic country with sibling harmonies. Not quite the O'Kanes, who were recording for sister label Columbia during the same period, but at times it's close.

influences:

◀◀ O'Kanes, Jimmy Martin

Brian Mansfield

CARL SMITH

Born March 15, 1927, in Maynardsville, TN.

By the time of his self-imposed retirement from the music business in 1977, Carl Smith had placed nearly 100 singles on the country charts. In fact, in his first four years at Columbia Records he never once failed to score a Top 10 record. While his chart feats were certainly impressive, it was his easygoing manner, his pure honky-tonk singing style and his great ear for a hit song that all added up to earn Smith an important place in country music history. Following high school and a short stint in the navy, Smith pursued his career in music during the late

1940s by working with various groups in North Carolina and Georgia. He then played bass with Skeets Williamson (brother of Molly O'Day) on WROL Radio in Knoxville, Tennessee. When a demo he had recorded made its way to officials at WSM, he was hired to perform on the Opry as well as on a WSM morning show. Signed to Columbia Records in 1950, Smith had an instant hit with "Let's Live a Little" (#2, 1951), and continued the hit-making streak in full force for the next five years. His band, the Tunesmiths, included famed Nashville session drummer Buddy Harman, who toured with him and played in the studio, but was not allowed to appear with him on the Opry at that time. Smith's repertoire included Western swing tunes and even touched on rockabilly. He quit the Opry in 1956 after his daughter, Carlene, now a famed country rocker in her own right, was born. His marriage to Carlene's mother, June Carter, lasted until 1957, when he married singer Goldie Hill, to whom he remains married today. During the 1960s, as his hits became fewer, Smith remained active as host of the TV shows *Four Star Jubilee* and, in Canada, *Carl Smith's Country Music Hall*. In 1974 he switched labels, leaving Columbia for Hickory, but spent more time on his ranch near Nashville until finally retiring in 1977.

Smith is often regarded as one of the few artists who knew when to call it quits. He's made only a few select appearances since then, but his music remains as vital and exciting as it was during the 1950s. Carl Smith will long be remembered for a substantial collection of pure country gems, and his influence has been felt by many through the years.

what to buy: "Essential" is right! *The Essential Carl Smith 1950–1956* (Legacy, 1991) ✍✍✍✍ covers seven years and collects only 20 tracks, but it's a fine introduction to the honky-tonk hits he had over this fertile period, including his five #1 songs that spent a combined total of 35 weeks on top!

what to buy next: *Best Of* (Curb, 1991) ✍✍✍ is a typical Curb release: decent songs buried with lesser material, wrapped in boring packaging. Still, if it's Carl Smith—the singer—you're after, this will suffice (it'll have to, as not much else is available!).

worth searching for: *Satisfaction Guaranteed* (Bear Family, 1996) ✍✍✍✍ is an expansive five-CD set, but for the full impact of Smith's appeal and influence, there's no more complete document.

influences:

◀◀ Hank Williams, Eddy Arnold

▶▶ Ray Price, Faron Young

Stephen L. Betts

CONNIE SMITH

Born August 14, 1941, in Elkhart, IN.

Connie Smith makes it all sound so easy. Her voice—an effortless blend of innocence and maturity wrapped in her trademark plaintive style—was the toast of Nashville from 1964–76: she charted twenty Top 10 hits during that fruitful period. But she might still be just a fresh-faced housewife from Ohio had singer/songwriter Bill Anderson not discovered her during the summer of 1963, after she won a talent contest at a country music park. After a stint on *Saturday Night Jamboree* on WSAZ-TV in Huntington, West Virginia, Anderson took her to Nashville, where RCA Records honcho Chet Atkins signed her in late 1963. Smith's first single, the bittersweet "Once a Day," spent eight weeks at the top of the charts, turning the unassuming vocalist into an overnight sensation. By 1971 she was a member of the Grand Ole Opry, where Opry godfather Roy Acuff dubbed her "The Sweetheart of the Grand Ole Opry."

Smith switched from RCA to Columbia Records during the early 1970s and continued enjoying singles success, even though her radio dominance had started to wane. A move to Monument Records during the late 1970s spelled the end of her chart career; her biggest Monument hit was a country-pop cover of Andy Gibb's smash "I Just Want to Be Your Everything." But Smith didn't seem to mind her gradual fade-out; indicative of her offhanded rise to stardom, she spent more time with her children and grandchildren before she ceased recording during the mid-1980s. Lately, her name has resurfaced in Nashville: Promising new vocalist Chely Wright mentions Smith as her main influence, Dolly Parton has been singing Smith's praises again and RCA Records recently released a long overdue collection of Smith's biggest hits. And Smith, who penned precious few of her career tunes, has been busy writing songs for a Warner Bros. album to be produced by fellow Opry member Marty Stuart.

what to buy: *The Essential Connie Smith* (RCA, 1996, prod. Steve Lindsey) ♪♪♪♪ clearly details Smith's charming way with a song. And you can hear all 20 cuts—some originally recorded 30 years ago—in surprising clarity. From the sad "Once a Day" to the rollicking "Nobody but a Fool (Would Love You)" and various country standards, including the heartbreaking "Cry, Cry, Cry," Smith is indeed a vocalist with restrained power and elegance.

the rest:

Greatest Hits on Monument (Monument/Sony, 1993) ♪♪♪
Live in Branson, Mo., USA (LaserLight, 1993) ♪♪♪♪

worth searching for: Smith's long-out-of-print RCA debut, *Connie Smith* (RCA, 1965, prod. Bob Ferguson) ♪♪♪♪, is a find for any traditional country collection. It showcased a 23-year-old with an uncanny talent for conveying emotions without resorting to melodrama. This must have been the album Patty Loveless and Chely Wright used to mold their singing styles.

influences:

◀◀ Patsy Cline, Lynn Anderson, Dottie West

▶▶ Dolly Parton, Patty Loveless, Chely Wright

Mario Tarradell

DARDEN SMITH

Born 1962 in Brenham, TX.

Darden Smith's music has grown by leaps and bounds since his first album in 1986. His sound has transformed itself from the country-folk of his debut release to country, country-rock and, with his latest album—the stark *Deep Fantastic Blue*—to a more raw, almost hard folk sound. A farm boy who moved to the big city of Houston as a teenager, Smith soaked up country, folk, rock and pop influences and developed a keen eye for observing the little details of live and love. He moved to Austin to attend the University of Texas and joined a burgeoning singer/songwriter scene, following in the footsteps of Lyle Lovett. He has worked with Lovett and fellow Texans Nanci Griffith and Chip Taylor, and he's found great inspiration in an ongoing partnership with English singer/songwriter Boo Hewerdine, with whom he released one album.

what to buy: Smith's most commercial record is also his most consistent. *Little Victories* (Chaos, 1993, prod. Richard Gottehrer, Jeffrey Lesser) ♪♪♪ reflects on life's ups and downs but never gives up hope.

what to avoid: Smith took an ill-advised left turn with the spare, monotonous *Deep Fantastic Blue* (Plump, 1996, prod. Stewart Lerman) ♪♪, with stripped-down production and Spartan arrangements that don't do his songs about transition and redemption much justice.

the rest:

Native Soil (Watermelon, 1986) ♪♪♪
(With Boo Hewerdine) *Evidence* (Compass, 1989) ♪♪♪
Trouble No More (Columbia, 1990) ♪♪♪

influences:

◀◀ Guy Clark, Rosanne Cash, Nanci Griffith

▶▶ Shawn Colvin, Lyle Lovett

Doug Pullen

SAMMI SMITH

Born Jewel Fay Smith, August 5, 1943, in Orange, CA.

Sammi Smith is a husky voiced singer whose seductive vocals on the Kris Kristofferson tune "Help Me Make It Through the Night" (#1, 1971) propelled her to stardom and eventually earned the song a Country Music Association award as Single of the Year. When she was 11 Smith dropped out of school; she was singing in nightclubs by age 12, and got married at 15. She had four children shortly thereafter. When her marriage failed in 1967, Smith moved to Nashville where, with the help of Marshall Grant (Johnny Cash's bassist in the Tennessee Three), she was signed to Columbia Records. A move to Mega Records would help Smith begin to finally crack the Top 40, first with "He's Everywhere" (#25, 1970), then "Help Me," which also landed at number eight on the pop chart. She hit the Top 10 only twice during the next five years, but during this time she relocated to Dallas and became involved in the "outlaw" movement along with Willie Nelson and Waylon Jennings—Jennings scored a hit with Smith's "Cedartown, Georgia" (#12, 1971). In 1975 she moved to an Apache reservation in Arizona and adopted three children. Her recording career continued to a much lesser degree with Elektra, and later with smaller independent labels. During the last decade Smith has had no chart hits, but a recent reissue of her best-known material returned her to the spotlight, albeit briefly.

what's available: *The Best of Sammi Smith* (Varese Sarabande, 1996) 𝄞𝄞𝄞 is a well-rounded collection of hits and assorted other tracks. Smith's sultry delivery helps even the mediocre material included here shine.

influences:

◀◀ Donna Fargo, Jeannie Seely

▶▶ Bobbie Cryner, Lacy J. Dalton

Stephen L. Betts

CHRIS SMITHER

Born 1945, in New Orleans, LA.

Although perhaps best known for writing "Love Me Like a Man" and "I Feel the Same," two of Bonnie Raitt's most enduring songs, Smither is a gifted folk-bluesman in his own right. His urgent vocals and finger-picked guitar come across best with little or no accompaniment.

what to buy: *Another Way to Find You* (Flying Fish, 1991, prod. John Nagy) 𝄞𝄞𝄞𝄞, an intimate solo acoustic album recorded live in the studio, is a career retrospective on which Smither reprises material from both of his excellent, long-out-of-print albums for Poppy.

what to buy next: *Up on the Lowdown* (HighTone, 1995, prod. Stephen Bruton) 𝄞𝄞𝄞, recorded with a sympathetic backing band, is further proof of Smither's unassuming brilliance as a singer, songwriter and guitarist.

the rest:

Happier Blue (Flying Fish, 1993) 𝄞𝄞𝄞

Small Revelations (HighTone, 1997) 𝄞𝄞𝄞𝄞

worth searching for: Smither recorded two albums during the early 1970s—*I'm a Stranger Too* (Poppy, 1971, prod. Ronald Frangipane, Michael Cuscuna) 𝄞𝄞𝄞𝄞 and *Don't It Drag On* (Poppy, 1972, prod. Michael Cuscuna) 𝄞𝄞𝄞𝄞—that eclipse virtually all of the rootsy singer/songwriter competition of the era.

influences:

◀◀ Mississippi John Hurt, Eric von Schmidt

Bill Friskics-Warren

THE SMOKIN' ARMADILLOS

Formed March 1993, in Bakersfield, CA.

Rick Russell, vocals; Aaron Casida, bass; Darrin Kirkindoll, drums; Scott Meeks, guitar, vocals; Josh Graham, guitar; Jason Theiste, fiddle.

Not so much the progeny of Buck Owens and Merle Haggard, the Smokin' Armadillos are a rockin' country band that more likely used the Charlie Daniels Band as a model than their Bakersfield heroes. Dreaming of arena-sized country from the start, the sextet booked its own concerts instead of playing clubs and recorded and released an EP that reportedly sold 150,000 copies before MCG/Curb signed them.

what's available: The famed EP that got the band its deal, *Out of the Burrow* (MCG/Curb, 1994, prod. Darrin Kirkindoll) 𝄞𝄞 shows all the signs of a band ready for the big time, but the hands-down highlight is "I'm a Cowboy," one of the better country-rap fusions, despite its novelty. The group's major-label debut, *Smokin' Armadillos* (MCG/Curb, 1995, prod. Chuck Howard) 𝄞𝄞𝄞 was a more polished affair, with the best parts intact—the unapologetic beat and "I'm a Cowboy." It turns out that the band has at least three members—Scott Meeks, Aaron Casida and Josh Graham—capable of writing songs. And in case there's any question about their musical allegiances, they cover Daniels' "The Legend of Wooley Swamp."

influences:

◀◀ Charlie Daniels, Garth Brooks

Brian Mansfield

TODD SNIDER

Born October 11, 1966, in Portland, OR.

One of the freshest voices on the alternative country scene, Todd Snider successfully mixes Dylanesque wordplay, Springsteen and Mellencamp populism, and Steve Earle's renegade country rock. He's a bit of an uncomfortable fit for Nashville, since he has no trouble occasionally tweaking the Religious Right, and, in "I Believe In," goes even farther that Garth-sanctioned tolerance ("I believe in gansta rap, gays, and geeks, and ghosts"). Snider is an adept storyteller, a moralist with a sense of humor and a ragged-but-right vocalist. A talent to watch, for sure.

what to buy: True to its title, Snider's debut, *Songs for the Daily Planet* (Margaritaville/MCA, 1994, prod. Tony Brown, Michael Utley) ✍✍✍✍, reads like dispatches from the newspaper of a modern Metropolis. The sardonic "My Generation (Part 2)" tweaks Generation X with a laundry list of its flash-in-the-pan iconography. "Easy Money" details a scam artist's dealings over a brassy R&B backing. On the serious side, the tempestuous rocker "This Land Is Our Land" offers the Native American spin on the white man's idea of progress. But lest he get too deep, Snider offers "Alright Guy," perhaps the ultimate "What? Me worry?" anthem. The album may be rough around the edges, but that's part and parcel of Snider's considerable charm.

the rest:

Step Right Up (Margaritaville/MCA, 1996) ✍✍✍✍

worth searching for: Snider portrays a naive hitchhiker in the radio-play-style audio version of Hunter Thompson's classic gonzo journalism screed, *Fear and Loathing in Las Vegas* (Margaritaville/Island, 1996, prod. Laila Nabulsi) ✍✍✍✍. He also wrote and performed incidental music for the production.

influences:

◀◀ Bruce Springsteen, Bob Dylan, John Mellencamp, Steve Earle

Daniel Durchholz

HANK SNOW

Born Clarence Eugene Snow, May 9, 1914, in Brooklyn, Nova Scotia, Canada.

If there was anyone in country music who, through the years, truly had it all, Hank Snow was probably the one. He could play the guitar with precision and intensity, and his singing was distinguished by careful phrasing and near perfect pitch. He wore, especially in later years, flashy Nudie suits, which Snow said he loved because they were "loud and beautiful." And in a 25-year chart career, Snow had eight #1 songs, including two that, between them, spent nearly 10 months at #1, "I'm Movin' On" (#1, 1950) and "I Don't Hurt Anymore" (#1, 1954). He's one of the most beloved entertainers on the Grand Ole Opry, and has been elected to the Hall of Fame.

Snow's early years, growing up in a remote fishing village in Canada, were far from the glittering spotlight to which he would escape later on. When he was eight years old, his parents divorced, and his new stepfather proved a violent foe. Leaving home to work on a ship as a cabin boy by age 12, Snow sailed the Arctic Ocean. Here, through records, he first learned many of the songs that would prove influential in years to come. Four years later he was working in a fish plant, then suffered a ruptured appendix. The turning point in young Snow's life came when his mother bought him some Jimmie Rodgers records. While continuing to do manual labor, Hank also pursued his love for music by teaching himself guitar, copying Rodgers' style. Soon he was performing on Canadian radio in Halifax, Nova Scotia, where he was eventually billed as "the Yodeling Ranger," changing his name to "Hank" once he earned sponsorship from the Crazy Water Crystals company. In 1936 in Montreal, Snow cut the first of what would eventually number more than 800 records in his career. Released only in Canada, he nevertheless had a 10-year string of hits for the Canadian Bluebird label.

Snow's success in the U.S. would have to wait until 1950, when he met Ernest Tubb, who helped him earn a spot on the Grand Ole Opry. With the enormous success of "I'm Movin' On," Snow was unstoppable throughout the 1950s, ranking with Webb Pierce and Eddy Arnold as the decade's biggest sellers. Snow's connection with Elvis Presley was an interesting sidebar to both star's careers. Presley made his solitary Opry appearance on a Snow-hosted segment of the Opry in 1954, then the pair toured together, due to their sharing the same manager at the time—Col. Tom Parker. Even with the onslaught of rock 'n' roll, Snow never left traditional country music far behind. Even as his hits decreased during the 1960s, he remained a top Opry attraction. In 1974, the year he had his last Top 40 country hit, Snow also had a #1 record, "Hello, Love." He was elected to the Country Music Hall of Fame in 1979, and is in semi-retirement today, though he remains an Opry cast member. Snow's music still holds strong appeal and has aged remarkably well. Most of his recorded material remains available, primarily in massive boxed sets. (Other collections are not as complete as they should be.) Hank Snow will be remembered as one of the great stylists in country music, even if his recordings are not afforded their proper respect.

what to buy: *The Singing Ranger 1949–1953* (Bear Family, 1989) 🎵🎵🎵🎵, the complete RCA collection of Hank's earliest hits and more, is four CDs long and worth the expense.

what to buy next: The 12-CD set *The Singing Ranger, Volume 3* (Bear Family, 1991) 🎵🎵🎵 may be too much to handle for the casual fan, but if you've got to have it all, go for it! This takes you right up to the last recordings Snow made for RCA.

the rest:
The Thesaurus Transcriptions (Bear Family, 1991) 🎵🎵🎵🎵
The Singing Ranger, Volume 2 (Bear Family, 1990) 🎵🎵🎵🎵
The Yodelling Ranger (1936–1947) (Bear Family) 🎵🎵🎵🎵
The Singing Ranger, Volume 4 (Bear Family) 🎵🎵🎵🎵
The Essential Hank Snow (RCA, 1997) 🎵🎵🎵🎝

worth searching for: If you're going to have one single CD of Hank Snow, *I'm Movin' On and Other Great Country Hits* (RCA, 1990) 🎵🎵🎵🎵 would have to be it. It's not currently in print, but it contains 20 essential tracks and is a fine place to start. RCA ought to be a bit more respectful and put it back out, along with other unavailable classic hits: "A Fool Such as I," "I've Been Everywhere" and "Rockin' Rollin' Ocean."

influences:
⏪ Ernest Tubb, Jimmie Rodgers
⏩ Lefty Frizzell, Webb Pierce

Stephen L. Betts

SON VOLT
See: Uncle Tupelo

JO-EL SONNIER
Born October 2, 1946, in Rayne, LA.

Jo-El Sonnier is an internationally known French-Cajun accordionist. He started playing accordion at the age of three, and by the time he was 13, he had already cut his first record—"Tes Yeaux Blues" ("Your Blue Eyes"), which became a regional hit. Between 1972–80 Sonnier bounced between Nashville and Los Angeles, establishing himself as a songwriter and studio musician. In 1975 he signed with Mercury Records and scored a few minor hits with "I've Been Around Enough to Know," "Always

Late (With Your Kisses)" and "He's Still All Over You." In 1980 he returned to his Cajun roots and recorded *Cajun Life*, which was sung entirely in Acadian French. Sonnier recorded a similar album, *Cajun Roots*, in 1994. During the 1980s he penned songs for George Strait, Johnny Cash, Conway Twitty, Loretta Lynn, Emmylou Harris and John Anderson, and he backed new wave rock icon Elvis Costello on his critically acclaimed album, *King of America*. In 1987 Sonnier signed with RCA and cracked the country Top 40 with "Come On Joe." The following year, his "No More One More Time" and the Cajun-inflected "Tear-Stained Letter" hit the country Top 10.

what to buy: *Cajun Roots* (Rounder, 1994, prod. Michael Doucet) 🎵🎵🎵🎝, which is sung entirely in old-world French, shows Sonnier covering the music of his native Louisiana with style, grace and expert musicianship, especially the artist's accordion playing and powerful tenor. Standout tracks include "Huppes Taiauts," "Amedee Two Step" and "La Chere Toute-Toute," which features dazzling guitar-fiddle interplaying between Jo-El and Beausoleil's Michael Doucet.

what to buy next: *Cajun Life* (Rounder, 1980, prod. Earl Ball, Alex Broussard) 🎵🎵🎵🎵 shows Sonnier reveling in the traditional Acadian sounds of Louisiana's bayou country.

the rest:
The Complete Mercury Sessions (Mercury, 1992) 🎵🎵🎵
(With Eddy Raven) *Cookin' Cajun* (K-Tel, 1996) 🎵🎵🎵
Cajun Pride (Rounder, 1997) 🎵🎵🎵

worth searching for: *Come on Joe* (RCA, 1988, prod. Bill Halverson, Richard Bennett) 🎵🎵🎵 and *Have a Little Faith* (RCA, 1990, prod. Bill Halverson, Richard Bennett, Josh Leo) 🎵🎵🎵🎝 were Sonnier's two best major-label albums. *Come On Joe* contains his biggest hits, "No More One More Time" and "Tear-Stained Letter." The hits from *Have a Little Faith*, "(Blue, Blue, Blue) Blue, Blue" and "If Your Heart Should Ever Roll This Way Again," didn't chart as high, but the album has excellent covers of John Hiatt's "Have a Little Faith in Me" and "I'll Never Get Over You."

influences:
⏪ Iry LeJeune, Amedé Ardoin
⏩ Michael Doucet, Beausoleil, Wayne Toups, Zachary Richard

Rick Petreycik

SONS OF THE PIONEERS
Formed as the Pioneer Trio, 1934, in Los Angeles, CA.

Bob Nolan (born April 1, 1908; died June 15, 1980), string bass, guitar,

vocals (1934–49); Leonard Slye, aka Roy Rogers, guitar, vocals (1934–37); Tim Spencer (died June 26, 1974), vocals (1934-37, 1937–49); Karl Farr (died September 20, 1961), guitar, vocals (1936–61); Hugh Farr, fiddle, vocals (1934–58); Lloyd Perryman (died 1977), guitar, vocals (1936–42, 1946–77); Pat Brady, bass, vocals (1937–43, 1947-59, 1959–67); Ken Carson, vocals (1942–47); Shug Fisher, bass, vocals (1943–46, 1949–53, 1955–59); Ken Curtis, vocals (1949–53); Tommy Doss, fiddle, vocals (1949–63); Dale Warren, vocals (1953–present); Deuce Spriggins, bass, vocals (1953–95); Roy Lanham, guitar, vocals (1961–present); Rusty Richards, vocals (1961–66, 1974–present); Billy Armstrong, fiddle (1964–72); Bob Mensor (1967); Luther Nallie, vocals (1968–74, 1980–present); Billy Liebert, accordian (1974–81); Rome Johnson, vocals (1977–80); Dale Morris (1981–present).

The Sons of the Pioneers certainly kept the "western" in country & western music throughout their celebrated career. Original members Bob Nolan, Tim Spencer and Roy Rogers created the group and soon added brothers Karl and Hugh Farr. Staff changes continued through the years, but the original trio was memorialized by induction into the Country Music Hall of Fame in 1980.

With a burgeoning film career during the 1940s and the advent of television a decade later, Rogers (also a solo Hall of Fame inductee in 1988) epitomized the dashing, heroic do-gooder. His singing cowboy image brought millions of dollars into Hollywood, mostly through a tally of dimes from afternoon matinees in Anytown, USA. Still, somebody had to play harmonica and provide the indispensable harmonies. More importantly, the music had to sound fresh, had to capture a dreamy youth's imagination. For that reason, Nolan and Spencer proved vital as well to the initial Sons of the Pioneers lineup. Nolan wrote and arranged the ensemble's signature pieces "Cool, Cool Water" and "Tumbling Tumbleweeds" with clear, infectious harmonies. Spencer, who quit singing in the group but still managed it until 1955, penned more hits, such as "Careless Kisses," "Cigarettes, Whisky and Wild, Wild Women" and "Roomful of Roses."

what to buy: *Country Music Hall of Fame* (MCA, 1991) 🎵🎵🎵🎵🎵 contains the group's classic performances, culled from more than 20 years' worth of recordings, including the original versions of "Tumbling Tumbleweeds" and "Cool, Cool Water."

what to buy next: The recordings on *Columbia Historic Edition* (Columbia, 1982, prod. Art Satherly) 🎵🎵🎵🎵 were made in 1937 for the American Recordings Corporation. Spencer had left the group temporarily and was replaced by Lloyd Perryman, who sings on these recordings, notable for the emphasis on the fine instrumental work of the Farr brothers and for some of Rogers'

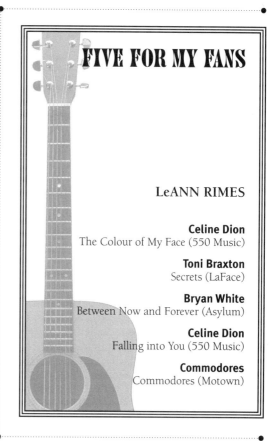

FIVE FOR MY FANS

LeANN RIMES

Celine Dion
The Colour of My Face (550 Music)

Toni Braxton
Secrets (LaFace)

Bryan White
Between Now and Forever (Asylum)

Celine Dion
Falling into You (550 Music)

Commodores
Commodores (Motown)

exquisite, fluid yodeling on "The Devil's Great Grandson" and "Cowboy Night Herd Song."

what to avoid: *Country & Western Memories* (Pair, 1991) 🎵🎵 has only two cowboy tunes and a bunch of smoothed-out country-pop. Why would anybody want to listen to the Sons of the Pioneers sing anything but cowboy songs?

the rest:
Cool Water (RCA Nashville, 1960) 🎵🎵🎵
Songs of the Trails (Pair, 1990) 🎵🎵🎵
Sunset on the Range (Pair, 1990) 🎵🎵🎵🎵

influences:
◀◀ Carson Robison & the Pioneers, Jimmie Rodgers
▶▶ Gene Autry, Tex Ritter, Riders in the Sky

see also: *Roy Rogers*

Craig Shelburne and Brian Mansfield

SONS OF THE SAN JOAQUIN
Formed 1989.

Joe Hannah, vocals; Jack Hannah, vocals; Lon Hannah, vocals.

Cowboy culture, particularly its poetry and music, kicked up some dust again during the 1990s thanks to such revivalists as Riders in the Sky and this trio, modeled after the Sons of the Pioneers, one of the great singing cowboy groups of the 1930s and 1940s. Joe and Jack Hannah are brothers, both retired schoolteachers in their 60s who formed the group with Joe's son Lon, expecting little more than to sell tapes out of their home. But the trio's exacting melodies and steadfast devotion to all things cowboy caught the ear of Michael Martin Murphey, who hooked them up with the Warner Western label for all three of their albums, and producer Joey Miskulin, known for his work with Riders.

what to buy: *Songs of the Silver Screen* (Warner Western, 1993, prod. Joey Miskulin) 𝄢𝄢𝄢 is a loving tribute to the movie music recorded by their idols, the Sons of the Pioneers, whose members included movie and TV hero Roy Rogers. Vintage stuff, including "Durango Kid," "The Wyoming Trail" and "South of the Santa Fe," is faithfully recreated.

the rest:
A Cowboy Has to Sing (Warner Western, 1992) 𝄢𝄢
From Whence Came the Cowboy (Warner Western, 1995) 𝄢𝄢

influences:
◀◀ Sons of the Pioneers, Gene Autry, Roy Rogers

Doug Pullen

SOUTHER-HILLMAN-FURAY BAND
See: Chris Hillman

SOUTHERN PACIFIC
Formed 1984, in Los Angeles, CA. Disbanded 1990.

John McFee, vocals, guitar, fiddle, mandolin; Jerry Scheff, bass, vocals (1984–85); Stu Cook, bass, vocals (1985–90); Tim Goodman, vocals, guitar (1985–87); Glenn D. Hardin, keyboards (1985–86); Keith Knudsen, drums; Kurt Howell, keyboards, vocals (1986–89); David Jenkins, vocals, guitar (1986–89).

Ahead of its time, Southern Pacific fashioned a marriage of rock and country that was a good five years before the whole Young Country movement took flight. The musicians' pedigrees were admirable—John McFee and Keith Knudsen from the Doobie Brothers, Jerry Scheff from Elvis Presley's bands and, later, Stu Cook from Creedence Clearwater Revival. Southern Pacific could twang and shuffle with the best of 'em (evidence "Reno Bound" from the band's debut album), but it was also adept at bringing country swing to rock numbers such as Bruce Springsteen's "Pink Cadillac," Del Shannon's "I Go to Pieces" and Tom Petty's "Thing About You," which was recorded with Emmylou Harris.

what's available: All that's left in print is *Greatest Hits* (Warner Bros., 1991, prod. Southern Pacific, Jim Ed Norman) 𝄢𝄢𝄢, a spirited collection of singles from all four albums, including "Midnight Highway," "New Shade of Blue" and the playfully reverent "A Girl Like Emmylou."

worth searching for: *Southern Pacific* (Warner Bros., 1985, prod. Jim Ed Norman) 𝄢𝄢𝄢 is the best single album distillation of the group's vision, which sounds much more in tune with the mid-1990s than it did a decade earlier.

influences:
◀◀ Eagles, Doobie Brothers, Creedence Clearwater Revival, Pure Prairie League, Poco, Alabama
▶▶ Mavericks, Garth Brooks, Tractors

Gary Graff

SOUTHERN RAIL
Formed 1979, in Watertown, MA.

Jim Muller, guitar, lead vocals; Sharon Horovitch, bass, vocals; Paul Muller, banjo, harmony vocals; Paul Trianosky, mandolin, vocals; Dave Dick, banjo.

A Boston-area bluegrass quartet with a contemporary, almost folkish edge to their sound, Southern Rail released their first album, *Looking for the Lighthouse*, on Track Records in 1987. The band is centered around the husband-and-wife team of lead vocalist/guitarist Jim Muller and bass player Sharon Horovitch.

what to buy: *Glory Train* (Pinecastle, 1996, prod. Bob Dick, Southern Rail) 𝄢𝄢𝄢, an all-gospel recording ranging from traditional bluegrass to a cappella Celtic, including four songs from the Stanley Brothers' repertoire. The group sings nice four-part harmonies and does a decent job of mixing tempos.

what to buy next: *Carolina Lightning* (1993, Turquoise Records) 𝄢𝄢 is a good second helping of Southern Rail.

worth searching for: *Drive by Night* (Turquoise, 1991) 𝄢𝄢𝄢, the band's first recording for Turquoise, is still their best work.

influences:

◀◀ Red, White & Bluegrass

Douglas Fulmer

RED SOVINE

Born Woodrow Wilson Sovine, July 17, 1918, in Charleston, WV. Died April 4, 1980.

Country fans love a singer with sentiment, and they don't come more sentimental than Red Sovine. Sovine specialized in two types of songs: truck driving tunes and melodramatic recitations, two forms that offer ample opportunity for romanticism. Sovine's baritone voice made him all the more effective when talking about reuniting with a long-lost son in "Giddyup Go" or the CB-wielding crippled child in "Teddy Bear." Sovine got his start performing with Jim Pike & the Carolina Tar Heels, and he formed his own band, the Echo Valley Boys, in 1947. He soon joined the *Louisiana Hayride*, and when Hank Williams left to join the Grand Ole Opry in 1949, Hayride officials gave Sovine his featured spot. Sovine followed Williams to Nashville five years later. Sovine's storytelling ability made him one of country's most popular performers during his career, though he hit the top of the singles chart only three times: with Webb Pierce in 1956 with "Why Baby Why," in 1966 with "Giddyup Go" and in 1976 with the gold single "Teddy Bear."

what to buy: Sovine's legacy has been cluttered by a series of cheap, mediocre reissues that package filler material around a couple of big hits. *The Best of Red Sovine* (Deluxe, 1986, prod. various) ♫♫♫ is the exception to the rule, containing most of his trucking hits ("Phantom 309," "Giddyup Go") and maudlin recitations ("Little Rosa," "Teddy Bear").

what to buy next: The sound's pretty awful, but the music on *The One and Only* (Starday, 1987) ♫♫♫ is classic, especially Sovine's hit duet with Webb Pierce on "Why Baby Why." *The One and Only* also shows Sovine's rarely seen honky-tonk side with great songs like "Color of the Blues" and "Invitation to the Blues."

what to avoid: One can take only so much of Sovine's maudlin side, which is over-indulged on the gospel set *Cryin' in the Chapel* (Hollywood, 1989) ♫.

the rest:

The Sensational Red Sovine (Starday/King, 1976) ♫♫
Truck Drivin' Son of a Gun (Starday, 1985) ♫♫
Phantom 309 (Hollywood, 1987) ♫♫♫
Teddy Bear (Hollywood, 1987) ♫♫♫
Giddy-Up-Go (Hollywood, 1987) ♫♫

Classic Narrations (Hollywood, 1988) ♫♫
Famous Duets with Minnie Pearl, Johnny Bond, and Others! (Hollywood, 1989) ♫♫
Golden Hits (Hollywood, 1989) ♫♫♫
Gone But Not Forgotten (Power Pak, 1994) ♫♫

influences:

◀◀ Hank Williams, Webb Pierce

▶▶ Dave Dudley, Dick Curless, Red Simpson, Charley Pride

Brian Mansfield

THE SPANIC BOYS

Formed 1987, in Milwaukee, WI.

Ian Spanic, vocals, guitar; Tom Spanic, vocals, guitar; Mike Fredrickson, bass (1987–93); Teddy Freese, drums (1987–91); Paul Schroeder, bass (1993–present); Curt Lefevre, drums (1991–present).

Best known as the band that replaced Sinead O'Connor when she refused to perform on *Saturday Night Live!* with offensive host Andrew "Dice" Clay in 1990, the Spanic Boys, it turns out, know exactly how to rock. The father-and-son team—both parts wearing horn-rimmed glasses goofier than Buddy Holly's—rehashes rockabilly and other roots music, but adds wailing, raging guitars that would fit on some Metallica songs. Tom, the elder Spanic, played in rock 'n' roll cover bands during the 1960s, then gave guitar lessons for two decades before forming the band with his son during early 1987. Though the Boys have never produced a followup as powerful as their debut or *Strange World*, they deserve far more commercial attention than they've received.

what to buy: *Strange World* (Rounder, 1991, prod. Ian Spanic, Mike Hoffman) ♫♫♫♫ is a wonderfully catchy mix of sharp rockabilly rhythms, spooky harmonies and fierce guitar playing. The group's debut, *Spanic Boys* (Rounder, 1990, prod. Scott Billington) ♫♫♫, is an out-of-nowhere update of Everly Brothers harmonies and 1950s-style rock 'n' roll songwriting.

what to buy next: *Dream Your Life* (Rounder, 1992, prod. Ian Spanic, Mike Hoffman) ♫♫♫ has "That Train" and a few other stomping songs, but it's not as explosive as *Strange World* or the debut.

the rest:

(As the Spanic Family) *Family Album* (East Side Digital, 1994) ♫♫♫

worth searching for: *Early Spanic Boys* (Rounder, 1992, prod. Mike Hoffman) ♫♫♫, a reissue of the band's tiny-label debut, showcases the band's developing Buddy Holly and Chet Atkins influence.

influences:

◀◀ Buddy Holly, Chet Atkins, Elvis Presley, Everly Brothers, Jimi Hendrix, Ritchie Valens, X, Los Lobos

▶▶ Blazers, Wayne Hancock, Rosie Flores, Big Sandy & His Fly-Rite Boys

Steve Knopper

LARRY SPARKS

Born September 15, 1947, in Lebanon, IN.

Larry Sparks is one of the most distinctive and compelling lead singers in bluegrass music. Probably the best of the traditional style lead guitarists, he and his band, the Lonesome Ramblers, have been in the forefront of traditional bluegrass for many years. Sparks filled in with the Stanley Brothers as lead guitarist while still in his teens, and after Carter Stanley's death he joined the Clinch Mountain Boys as lead vocalist and lead guitarist, his fierce, percussive flatpicking style much in evidence even then. In 1969 he left to lead his own band and has been a favorite of traditional bluegrass lovers ever since, cutting many songs that have become much identified with him. His rich, deep vocals and fiery guitar work, along with his penchant for bluesy material set to bluegrass, have made him a festival favorite for years, and he has cut many fine recordings, a handful of which ("A Face in the Crowd," "Blue Virginia Blues," "John Deere Tractor") have achieved modern classic status in bluegrass circles.

what to buy: *Classic Bluegrass* (Rebel, 1989, prod. Gary B. Reid) ♫♫♫♫♪ contains the three songs mentioned above, plus the standouts "Tennessee 1949," "Kentucky Girl" and "Great High Mountain." Spark's guitar workout on "Cannonball Blues" is mind-boggling. *Silver Reflections* (Rebel, 1988, prod. Larry Sparks) ♫♫♫♪ has "The Girl of My Dreams" and "The Natural Thing to Do," two of Sparks' cooler songs.

what to buy next: On *Sings Hank Williams* (Rebel, 1977, prod. Larry Sparks) ♫♫♫♪, Williams' lyrics and Sparks' voice and bluegrass arrangements go together very nicely. *The Rock I Stand On* (Rebel, 1994, prod. Larry Sparks) ♫♫♫ is a nice gospel set.

the rest:

(With the Lonesome Ramblers) *Thank You Lord* (Old Homestead, 1975, prod. John Morris) ♫♫♫
Travelin' (Rebel, 1992) ♫♫♫
Blue Mountain Memories (Rebel, 1996) ♫♫♫

influences:

◀◀ Carter Stanley, George Shuffler

▶▶ James King, David Parmley

Randy Pitts

BILLIE JO SPEARS

Born Billie Jean Spears, January 14, 1937, in Beaumont, TX.

Billie Jo Spears was the daughter of a guitarist in the Light Crust Doughboys, so perhaps it was inevitable that she'd be performing in clubs and on the Louisiana Hayride when she hit her teens. She moved to Nashville in 1964, though it took her awhile to break: She had her first hit with the working-woman song "Mr. Walker, It's All Over" in 1969. Her breakthrough single came six years later with the safely sexy "Blanket on the Ground," which hit #1 in the United States and also made her a popular figure in Great Britain. Spears' producers soon overwhelmed her with string sections and "ooh"-ing background singers, and her material—which once had included a murder song called "Stepchild" and one called "Marty Gray" about teen pregnancy—became more questionable. By 1979 she was covering Gloria Gaynor's "I Will Survive" and by 1985 she was off the American charts altogether.

what's available: *The Best of Billie Jo Spears* (Razor & Tie, 1994, prod. various) ♫♫♫ is an adequate overview of Spears' hits, though it also shows her creative slide in later years. The compilation includes important numbers like "What I've Got in Mind" and her version of "Misty Blue," but it leaves out early Capitol hits like "Marty Gray" and "Mr. Walker, It's All Over" in favor of weakly performing later singles like a cover of Hal David and Burt Bacharach's "What the World Needs Now Is Love."

influences:

◀◀ Loretta Lynn, Norma Jean

▶▶ Jeanne Pruett

Brian Mansfield

JIM STAFFORD

Born January 16, 1944, in Eloise, FL.

Jim Stafford turned a handful of mid-1970s novelty records ("Spiders and Snakes," "My Girl Bill," "Wildwood Weed"—a takeoff on the Carter Family's classic "Wildwood Flower") into a lengthy career appearing on television variety shows and hosting syndicated shows like *Those Amazing Animals*. He also wrote and performed three songs for the Walt Disney film *The Fox and the Hound*.

what's available: *Jim Stafford* (Polydor, 1974, prod. Phil Gernhard, Lobo) 🎵🎵 is Stafford's first album, and it contains nearly all his significant hits. "Swamp Witch" is a reasonable approximation of Tony Joe White, but Stafford's humorous songs, which are usually spoken, aren't that funny anymore. And it gets worse after the hits. *Greatest Hits* (Curb, 1995, prod. Phil Gernhard, Kent Lavoie) 🎵🎵 contains the three biggies, plus a few more almost-knowns like "Cow Patti" and "Turn Loose of My Leg."

influences:
◀◀ Tony Joe White, Ray Stevens

Brian Mansfield

TERRY STAFFORD

Born 1941. in Hollis, OK.

Terry Stafford's biggest country claim to fame is as the co-writer of "Amarillo by Morning." Stafford had a Top 40 hit with the song in 1973; George Strait took it to #4 a decade later. But Stafford, who grew up in Amarillo, Texas, started out as a pop singer in the mold of Elvis Presley and Roy Orbison. His "Suspicion" was a #3 pop hit in 1964; "I'll Touch a Star" reached #25 that same year. Stafford looked toward the country market when his pop singles faltered: Buck Owens' cut Stafford's "Big in Vegas," and Stafford had three Top 40 hits for Atlantic's country division in the early 1970s. He later recorded for the Casino and Player labels.

what's available: *Best of Terry Stafford* (Curb, 1996, prod. various) 🎵🎵 has Stafford's two Top 40 pop singles, a lot of filler and none of his country hits. Stafford's melodramatic, heavily reverbed voice gets tiresome after awhile, but it makes him sound like a dead-on prototype for rock singer Bryan Ferry of Roxy Music.

influences:
◀◀ Elvis Presley
▶▶ Roxy Music, George Strait

Brian Mansfield

JOE STAMPLEY

Born June 6, 1943, in Springhill, LA.

Joe Stampley merged honky-tonk with old fashioned rock and R&B sounds to become one of the most consistent hitmakers

Jim Stafford **(AP/Wide World Photos)**

of the 1970s and early 1980s. He'd grown up in the rock world, even having limited national success fronting a band called the Uniques. He left that group in 1970, though, and almost immediately began making country records for Dot and later Epic, Columbia and Evergreen. He hooked up with fellow honky-tonker Moe Bandy in 1980 for a series of successful duets, which included "Just Good Ol' Boys" and "Where's the Dress?" a spoof of Culture Club lead singer Boy George. The pairing won them the Country Music Association's Vocal Duo of the Year award in 1980.

what's available: Stampley had 45 Top 40 hits on his own and with Moe Bandy between 1972 and 1985, so there's little overlap (five cuts) between *The Best of Joe Stampley* (Varese Sarabande, 1995, prod. Norro Wilson, Ray Baker) 🎵🎵🎵 and *Good Ol' Boy: His Greatest Hits* (Razor & Tie, 1995, prod. various) 🎵🎵🎵, two compilations that were released the same year. *Good Ol' Boy* focuses on Stampley's early recordings for ABC/Dot, while *Best Of* concentrates more on his duet hits with Bandy and his association with producer Billy Sherrill at Epic. The Razor & Tie compilation probably gets the nod for covering more turf and having more songs, but it really comes down to a matter of individual preference. Both albums have Stampley's first hit ("If You Touch Me (You've Got to Love Me)") and his three #1 songs with Epic ("Roll On Big Mama," "All These Things" and "Just Good Ol' Boys," his first duet with Bandy).

worth searching for: *Joe Stampley & the Uniques—Golden Hits* (Paula, prod. Joe Stampley, Ron Diulio) 𝄞𝄞𝄞 is an interesting curiosity that collects the recordings Stampley made with his R&B-influenced rock band between 1961 and 1971. It includes the group's national hits, "Not Too Long Ago," and a prototype version of Art Neville's "All These Things."

influences:

◀◀ Conway Twitty, Hank Williams

▶▶ Travis Tritt, Moe Bandy

Brian Mansfield

THE STANLEY BROTHERS

Formed 1946, in VA.

Carter Stanley (born August 27, 1925, in McClure, VA; died December 1, 1966), guitar, vocals; Ralph Stanley (born February 25, 1927, in Stratton, VA), banjo, vocals.

Combining their true Appalachian mountain upbringing with the increasingly popular bluegrass sound emerging during the 1950s, Carter and Ralph Stanley became and remain one of the most influential duos in old-time, bluegrass, country and indeed American music in general. At 14 Carter got his first guitar and formed the Lazy Ramblers, with Ralph playing banjo. Following high school and stints in the service, the brothers began recording as a duet in 1946, working on various radio stations, including WCYB in the Tennessee/Virginia border city of Bristol. Forming the Clinch Mountain Boys, the Stanley Brothers began recording for the Rich-R-Tone label in nearby Johnson City, Tennessee, in 1947. They signed to Columbia Records in 1948, where they recorded 22 tracks. During this time Carter briefly left to sing lead for Bill Monroe. The brothers reunited in 1952 and resumed recording for Columbia until the next year, when they signed to Mercury, recording there for the next five years. The bulk of their recordings, however, were done for King and Starday, beginning in 1958, when they also relocated to Florida. Although they had few genuine hits, this era yielded some of their most highly regarded recordings. In 1966 the Stanley Brothers came to an abrupt end with the death of Carter at age 41. While Ralph carried on, the magic of their harmony singing was clearly gone. The Stanley Brothers are an American trea-

sure, however, and clearly influenced many musicians with their impressive body of work.

what to buy: *Angel Band: The Classic Mercury Recordings* (Mercury, 1995, comp. prod. Colin Escott) 𝄞𝄞𝄞𝄞 is one scary record! This is such beautiful, ghostly music, that it may take some getting used to, but the Stanleys didn't get much better.

what to buy next: *The Complete Columbia Stanley Brothers* (Legacy, 1996) 𝄞𝄞𝄞𝄞 collects all sides recorded for Columbia Records from 1949 to 1952, including classic performances like "Little Glass of Wine."

the rest:

Stanley Series, Volume 3, No. 3—May 4, 1958 (Copper Creek, 1990) 𝄞𝄞𝄞𝄞

The Early Starday/King Years (Starday/King, 1993) 𝄞𝄞𝄞𝄞

Stanley Series, Volume 2, No. 1—June 3, 1956 (Copper Creek, 1993) 𝄞𝄞𝄞𝄞

Shadows of the Past (Copper Creek, 1996) 𝄞𝄞𝄞𝄞

Stanley Series, Volume 4, No. 1—July 29, 1956 (Copper Creek, 1996) 𝄞𝄞𝄞𝄞

Old Country Church: Volume 1 (County)

Long Journey Home: Volume 2 (County)

Uncloudy Day: Volume 3 (County)

Stanley Brothers of Virginia: Volume 4 (County)

On Radio: Volume 1 (County)

On Radio: Volume 2 (County)

influences:

◀◀ Bill Monroe

▶▶ Ralph Stanley & the Clinch Mountain Boys

see also: *Ralph Stanley & the Clinch Mountain Boys*

Stephen L. Betts

RALPH STANLEY & THE CLINCH MOUNTAIN BOYS

Formed 1966, in VA.

Ralph Stanley (born February 25, 1927, in Stratton, VA), banjo, vocals; Curly Ray Cline, fiddle; Melvin Goins, guitar; George Shuffler, bass; Larry Sparks, guitar, lead vocals; other members have included Roy Lee Centers, vocals; Keith Whitley, vocals; Charlie Sizemore, vocals; Sammy Adkins, vocals; Ernie Thacker; Ralph Stanley II, vocals; Ricky Skaggs, mandolin; Ron Thomason, mandolin.

Although he continued to grieve his brother Carter Stanley's death, Ralph Stanley decided within weeks to return to performing. With former Lonesome Pine Fiddler Curly Ray Cline, Melvin Goins on guitar, and George Shuffler, Stanley re-formed the Clinch Mountain Boys, adding lead vocalist Larry Sparks. Through the years some impressive talent has moved through the ranks of the Clinch Mountain Boys. The basic premise for the band never changed, and Ralph has remained incredibly active as a touring act and recording artist. In 1980 Stanley was honored with a National Heritage fellowship by President Ronald Reagan and earned an honorary doctorate from Lincoln Memorial University, becoming "Dr. Ralph Stanley." While a great many of his recordings remain in print, many are available only on cassette. But the many CD reissues and new recordings available attest to Ralph Stanley's pure staying power. Keeping old-time bluegrass music alive and vibrant has been a lifelong quest, and he has more than contributed to the preservation of the style he and brother Carter (along with Bill Monroe and Flatt & Scruggs) helped define.

what to buy: *Bound to Ride* (Rebel, 1991, prod. various) 𝄞𝄞𝄞𝄞 is a sterling 20-song collection, dating mostly from the early 1970s, and featuring various band configurations.

what to buy next: *Ralph Stanley: Classic Bluegrass* (1990, Rebel, prod. various) 𝄞𝄞𝄞𝄞 covers even more ground, focusing on the group's 15 years and 20 albums with Rebel Records.

the rest:
Pray for the Boys (Rebel, 1991) 𝄞𝄞𝄞
Saturday Night, Sunday Morning (Freeland, 1992) 𝄞𝄞𝄞
Almost Home (Rebel, 1992) 𝄞𝄞𝄞
50th Anniversary Collection (Rebel, 1995) 𝄞𝄞𝄞
16 Years (Copper Creek, 1995) 𝄞𝄞𝄞
Short Life of Trouble: Songs of Grayson and Whitter (Rebel, 1996) 𝄞𝄞𝄞

influences:
◀◀ Bill Monroe, Flatt & Scruggs
▶▶ Keith Whitley, Ricky Skaggs, Bob Dylan

Stephen L. Betts

JOHN STARLING
See: The Seldom Scene

THE STATLER BROTHERS
Formed as the Four Star Quartet, 1948, in Staunton, VA. Became the Statler Brothers in 1963.

Lew DeWitt (born March 8, 1938; died August 15, 1990), tenor vocals

(1955–82); Don Reid (born June 5, 1945), lead vocals (1964–present); Philip Balsley (born August 8, 1939), baritone vocals; Harold Reid (born August 21, 1939), bass vocals; Joe McDorman, vocals (1948–64); Jimmy Fortune, tenor vocals (1982–present).

Country music's premier vocal group for more 30 years, the Statler Brothers possess an ability to imbue clever hook songs with the histrionics of country gospel that gives their work a unique and compelling edge. In 1948 Lew DeWitt, Harold Reid, Phil Balsley and Joe McDorman formed the Four Star Quartet and sang at local gospel concerts and churches. They changed the group's name to the Kingsmen (not the guys who sang "Louie Louie") in 1955. When the group's repertoire began including pop and country songs, there was a backlash from the gospel music community. So, as a way to differentiate their strictly gospel image from their new, more secular style, the Kingsmen changed their name to the Statler Brothers in 1963. (There's no one named Statler in the group; they took the name off a box of tissues at the Statler Hotel.)

McDorman left the group in 1964; his replacement was Harold's younger brother, Don Reid. The Statlers' live audition for Johnny Cash resulted in steady work on Cash's many tours and a contract with Columbia Records. Their first chart record, "Flowers on the Wall," is a classic song of a man kidding himself about the effects of heartache and dissipation; it hit the Top 5 on both the country and pop charts and won a Grammy for best pop song in 1965. Neither the Statlers nor Columbia could provide an appropriate follow-up to "Flowers on the Wall," and the group's career lost momentum. They had a few chart records, but no solid musical or career direction. That changed when they joined Mercury Records in 1971; producer Jerry Kennedy immediately found and helped them develop material that highlighted their serio-comic abilities and tastes. Traditional-type country releases such as "Bed of Roses," "Susan When She Tried," "I'll Go to My Grave Loving You" and "Do You Know You Are My Sunshine" were solid smashes. But when the Statlers started tackling baby boomer nostalgia, as in "The Class of '57," "Whatever Happened to Randolph Scott" and "Do We Remember These," they became a dominant force on the charts. This new clout allowed them the creative freedom to form a band within a band—Lester "Roadhog" Moran & the Cadillac Cowboys, a conceptual satire of country music that fell flat on the charts. DeWitt, suffering from complications of Crohn's Disease, left the group in 1982; he was replaced by Jimmy Fortune. In the 1980s hits such as "Elizabeth," "Atlanta," and "Hello Mary Lou" kept coming. The Statlers have released several strong-selling LPs of gospel material as well. By the end of the 1980s, country radio program directors were eliminating older artists from their playlists, and the Statler Brothers' string of hits came to an end. They bounced back in 1991, with a highly rated variety program on TNN. They still play to sellout crowds wherever they appear and sell hundreds of thousands of LPs via their TV offers. The Statler Brothers have received over 400 music industry awards, among them three Grammys, 11 Country Music Association awards for best vocal group and the *Music City News* Readers Poll Award 25 years in a row. Despite accolades, the hits and the worldwide star status, they are still based in the little town of Staunton, Virginia.

what to buy: *Best of the Statler Brothers* (Mercury, 1980, prod. Jerry Kennedy) ♫♫♫♫ contains their hot run of hits from the 1970s. It's essential.

what to buy next: The box set *A 30th Anniversary Celebration* (Mercury, 1994, prod. Jerry Kennedy) ♫♫♫♫ contains all the Statlers' Mercury hits and the *Pulp Fiction* soundtrack version of "Flowers on the Wall." *The Complete Lester "Roadhog" Moran & the Cadillac Cowboys* (Mercury, 1994, prod. Jerry Kennedy) ♫♫♫ has everything the Statler's comedy alter egos recorded, some hilarious satire and wonderfully goofy moments.

what to avoid: Considering the Statlers' background as a gospel quartet, and their normally sure commercial sense, the Scripture-based concept albums *Holy Bible: Old & New Testament* (Mercury, 1979, prod. Jerry Kennedy) ♫♫, *Holy Bible: New Testament* (Mercury, 1975, prod. Jerry Kennedy) ♫♫ and *Holy Bible: Old Testament* (Mercury, 1975, prod. Jerry Kennedy) ♫ should have turned out better that they did.

the rest:

Oh Happy Day (Columbia, 1969) ♫♫♫
The World of the Statler Brothers (Columbia, 1972) ♫♫
Entertainers: On & Off the Record (Mercury, 1978/1994) ♫♫♫
Christmas Card (Mercury, 1978) ♫♫
Best Of . . . Rides Again (Mercury, 1979) ♫♫♫♫
10th Anniversary (Mercury, 1980/1994) ♫♫♫
Years Ago (Mercury, 1981/1994) ♫♫♫
Pardners in Rhyme (Mercury, 1985) ♫♫♫
Christmas Present (Mercury, 1985) ♫♫♫
Radio Gospel Favorites (Mercury, 1986) ♫♫♫♫
Greatest Hits Volume 3 (Mercury, 1988) ♫♫♫
Live and Sold Out (Mercury, 1989) ♫♫♫♫
Music, Memories and You (Mercury, 1990) ♫♫
All-American Country (Mercury, 1991) ♫♫♫
Words and Music (Mercury, 1992) ♫♫♫
Home (Mercury, 1993) ♫♫

Today's Gospel Favorites (Mercury, 1993) ♫♫♫
Flowers on the Wall: The Essential Statler Brothers 1964–1969 (Columbia Legacy, 1996) ♫♫♫♫
The Hits (Mercury, 1997) ♫♫♫

worth searching for: *The Statler Brothers Sing Country Symphonies (in E Major)* (Mercury, 1972, prod. Jerry Kennedy) ♫♫♫♫ represents the precise time when the group found its formulaic balance of commercial sense and artistic vision.

influences:

◀◀ Kingsmen, Statesmen, Blackwood Brothers

▶▶ Oak Ridge Boys, 4 Runner, Alabama

Ken Burke

RED STEAGALL

Born Russell Steagall, December 22, 1937, in Gainesville, TX.

Red Steagall grew up in the ranching community of Sanford, Texas, north of Amarillo. He wanted to be a bullrider, but those dreams were dashed when he contracted polio as a teen. Instead, he began playing guitar and also learned mandolin, eventually graduating from West Texas State University with a degree in animal science and agronomy. Steagall wrote Ray Charles' hit "Here We Go Again," and he first recorded in 1969. He had many moderate hits for Capitol, ABC/Dot and Elektra between 1972 and 1980, the biggest being "Lone Star Beer and Bob Wills Music," which reached #11 in 1976.

Steagall has also worked as a rodeo rider, a breeder of quarter horses and an actor (his credits include *Benji, The Hunted* and *Dark before Dawn*). He began his own syndicated radio show, *Cowboy Corner,* in 1984 and once served as chairman of the board of the Academy of Country Music. He also once encountered a petite redhead belting out the national anthem at a rodeo in 1974 and introduced her to some of his music industry contacts. Reba McEntire has been grateful to him ever since.

what to buy: *Born to This Land* (Warner Western, 1993, prod. Steve Gibson) ♫♫♫ is a sentimental mix of story, poems and songs that won the National Cowboy Hall of Fame Western Heritage Award for original music.

what to buy next: *The Cowboy Code* (Eagle, 1996) ♫♫♫ is a two-disc collection of poems and songs that features many Steagall originals, plus familiar songs like Jimmy Driftwood's "Tennessee Stud," Gene Autry's "Ridin' Down the Canyon" and the traditional "I'd Like to Be in Texas for the Roundup in the Spring."

the rest:

For All Our Cowboy Friends (MCA) ♫♫♫
Faith and Values (Warner Western, 1995) ♫♫♫

The Statler Brothers **(AP/Wide World Photos)**

influences:
◀◀ Gene Autry, Rex Allen
▶▶ Don Edwards, Waddie Mitchell

Brian Mansfield and Craig Shelburne

KEITH STEGALL

Born November 1, 1954, in Wichita Falls, TX.

A writer-turned-recording-artist-turned-producer-turned-record executive, Keith Stegall wrote his first hit, "Sexy Eyes," for Dr. Hook in 1980. He hit the lower reaches of the country charts in the early 1980s with a series of singles for Capitol and EMI America, and had another sizable pop success when his "We're in This Love Together" hit for Al Jarreau in 1981. A solo album during the mid-1980s yielded two Top 15 successes, and Stegall has penned hits for Glen Campbell, Conway Twitty, Mickey Gilley, Travis Tritt, Clay Walker and Alan Jackson. He's produced or co-produced all of Jackson's albums, and he now serves as vice-president of A&R for Mercury Nashville Records, where he's signed artists Terri Clark, Kim Richey and Mark Wills. Stegall recorded *Passages*, his first album in more than a decade, in 1996.

what's available: *Passages* (Mercury, 1996, prod. Keith Stegall, John Kelton, Carson Chamberlain) ♫♫♫♫ has moments of brilliance as the singer grapples with mid-life by reflecting on the innocence and simplicity of the past and the complexities of being a "Middle Age Man."

worth searching for: *Keith Stegall* (Epic, 1985, prod. Kyle Lehning) ♫♫♫ finds the burgeoning songwriter doing palatable country pop with a Gatlin Brothers feel and includes "Pretty Lady," his only Top 10 hit as a solo artist. A year after its release, Stegall would produce two tracks ("On the Other Hand," "Reasons I Cheat") on Randy Travis' classic *Storms of Life* album with Lehning.

$\frac{4}{1}$
$\frac{1}{8}$ *ray stevens*

influences:
⏪ Kris Kristofferson, Aretha Franklin
⏩ Alan Jackson, John Anderson

David Sokol

RAY STEVENS

Born Ray Ragsdale, January 24, 1939, in Clarksdale, GA.

Besides being a top-notch recording artist, Ray Stevens has written, produced and arranged the vast majority of his recorded work. In 1954, at age 15, Stevens got a part-time job as a disc jockey. He was so technically skilled and zany, he earned his own show the following year. For a time, Stevens wanted to be a rock 'n' roll singer; he recorded unsuccessfully for the Prep label in 1957 but scored a regional hit with "Chickie-Chickie Wah-Wah" on Capitol Records in 1958. Stevens' big break came in 1961, when he took a job in the A&R department of Mercury Records. There, Shelby Singleton believed Stevens' humor would appeal to the wacky DJ's who dominated teen Top 40 radio. He was right; their first release, "Jeremiah Peabody's Polyunsaturated Quick Dissolving Fast Acting Pleasant Tasting Green and Purple Pills," was not just a clever send-up of patent medicine ads, but it also showcased some rather hip R&B chanting by Stevens as well. "Jeremiah" hit the Top 40, but "Ahab the Arab" made it to #1 and fully established Stevens' name. It wasn't all yuks; his plea for tolerance, "Everything Is Beautiful," was a major hit and Grammy winner. The follow-up, "America Communicate with Me," charted just as socially conscious AM-radio pop died out. But despite such serious-minded fare, it was such comedy records as "Bridget the Midget," "The Moonlight Special" (a vicious parody of Wolfman Jack's "The Midnight Special"), "The Streak" and "Would Jesus Wear a Rolex" that were popularly heard. During the 1990s Stevens seemed to run out of creative steam, and these days he seems content to lease out his massive music catalog, make tapes for the lucrative home video market and perform to sellout crowds in Branson, Missouri.

what to buy: *The Best of Ray Stevens* (Mercury, 1970, prod. Ray Stevens) 𝄢𝄢𝄢𝄢 contains his early 1960s run of comedy songs after "Ahab the Arab" and a couple of cuts of Spector/Orbison-type teen pop. It's a good place to start. *Even Stevens* (Monument, 1968/Varaese Sarabande, 1996, prod. various) 𝄢𝄢𝄢𝄢 offers the best of his message songs originally released on the Monument label.

what to buy next: *Greatest Hits* (MCA, 1987, prod. Ray Stevens, Jim Malloy, Fred Foster) 𝄢𝄢𝄢𝄢 has his series of comeback comedy singles and a bluegrass reworking of "Misty." *Great Gospel Songs* (Curb, 1996, prod. Ray Stevens) 𝄢𝄢𝄢𝄢 mixes such hits as "Everything Is Beautiful" and "Have a Little Talk with Myself" with some interesting productions on traditional gospel tunes. It's better than you'd think.

what to avoid: A few spoken bits are funny, but on *Live* (Curb, 1995) 𝄢 Stevens runs through his big hits so fast you get the impression he is bored by them. *Back to Back* (K-Tel, 1992) 𝄢𝄢 features five of Stevens' hits along with four of Jim Stafford's. There are much more complete budget collections out there.

the rest:
Gitarzan (Monument, 1969/Varese Sarabande, 1996) 𝄢𝄢𝄢𝄢
I Have Returned (MCA, 1985) 𝄢𝄢𝄢
Greatest Hits Volume 2 (MCA, 1987) 𝄢𝄢𝄢
I Never Made a Record I Didn't Like (MCA, 1988) 𝄢𝄢𝄢
Beside Myself (MCA, 1989) 𝄢𝄢𝄢
He Thinks He's Ray Stevens (MCA, 1990) 𝄢𝄢
Lend Me Your Ears (Curb, 1990) 𝄢𝄢
All-Time Greatest Comic Hits (Curb, 1990) 𝄢𝄢𝄢𝄢
Number 1 with a Bullet (Curb, 1991) 𝄢𝄢𝄢
Greatest Hits (Curb, 1991) 𝄢𝄢𝄢𝄢
Star Spangled Banner/Greatest Hits (Curb, 1991) 𝄢𝄢𝄢
At His Best (MCA Special Products, 1994) 𝄢𝄢𝄢
Crackin' Up (MCA Special Products, 1994) 𝄢𝄢𝄢
20 Comedy Hits Collection (Curb, 1995) 𝄢𝄢𝄢𝄢
Cornball (Warner Bros., 1995) 𝄢𝄢
The Serious Side of Ray Stevens (Warner Bros., 1995) 𝄢𝄢
Do You Wanna Dance (Warner Bros., 1995) 𝄢𝄢
Greatest Gospel Songs (Curb, 1996) 𝄢𝄢𝄢
Everything Is Beautiful (Rhino, 1996) 𝄢𝄢𝄢
Hum It (MCA, 1997) 𝄢𝄢𝄢

worth searching for: *1,837 Seconds of Ray Stevens Humor* (Mercury, 1962, prod. Ray Stevens) 𝄢𝄢𝄢𝄢 is Stevens' best comedy LP start to finish, featuring demented kiddie show vocals he has long since dropped. *All-Time Hits* (PolyGram Special Products, 1996, prod. Ray Stevens) 𝄢𝄢𝄢𝄢 has much of the material on *1,837.*

influences:
⏪ Stan Freberg, Dickie Goodman, Ray Charles, Allan Sherman
⏩ Weird Al Yankovic, Jeff Foxworthy, Cletus "T." Judd

Ken Burke

GARY STEWART

Born May 28, 1945, in Letcher County, KY.

Loved by critics, but shunned by both radio and mainstream buyers, Gary Stewart remains one of the greatest honky-tonk performers. With a high vibrato voice and a hard-to-pigeonhole style that mixes the honesty of honky-tonk with country rock guitars and adds a few dashes of outlaw country for good measure, it's not too surprising that Stewart is also one of country music's ultimate cult artists. Named for Gary Cooper (his mother's favorite film star), Stewart was born in Kentucky but raised in Fort Pierce, Florida. Joining his first band, the Tomcats, in high school, Stewart's first brush with fame came when Mel Tillis saw him perform at a club in Okeechobee and advised him to pitch his original songs in Nashville.

Along with his songwriting partner (and former Tomcat) Bill Eldridge, Stewart began making trips to Tennessee, also building his career as a performer. Unfairly compared to Jerry Lee Lewis (to whom at times he can bear an uncanny vocal resemblance), Stewart recorded his first single in 1964 for Corey Records. In 1968 he was signed to Kapp Records, where he recorded several more unsuccessful singles. Fortunately, Stewart's success as a songwriter was taking off; beginning in the mid-1960s, he and Eldridge wrote hits for Stonewall Jackson ("Poor Red Georgia Dirt," 1965), Nat Stuckey ("Sweet Thang and Cisco," 1969) and Billy Walker ("When a Man Loves a Woman (The Way I Love You)," 1970). In 1971 Stewart became an Allman Brothers fan, and his own songwriting took on a more country rock sound. At this same time he decided to move back to Florida, but before he left he made a tape of Motown covers that eventually fell into the hands of producer Roy Dea.

When Dea moved to RCA in 1972, he signed Stewart. The six ensuing albums and slew of singles—starting with a cover of the Allman Brothers' "Ramblin' Man"—became the basis of Stewart's enduring legacy. In 1975, his version of Wayne Carson's "She's Actin' Single (I'm Drinkin' Doubles)" became Stewart's only #1 country hit. Stewart himself played the slide in the fashion of his friend, the late Duane Allman, and between 1976–78, he had eight Top 20 country hits. But as the 1970s wound down, Stewart's fame also faded. In 1983 he was dropped by RCA and returned again to Florida to battle personal and financial demons. In 1988 he reemerged and signed with Oakland, California-based HighTone, which reissued many of his RCA hits as well as new albums such as *Brand New, Battleground* and *I'm a Texan.* In 1996 Stewart was dropped by HighTone.

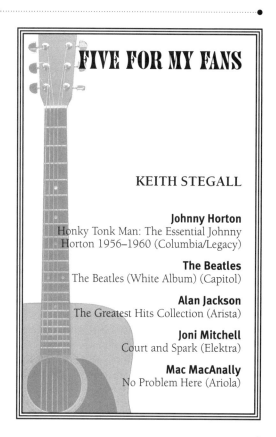

FIVE FOR MY FANS

KEITH STEGALL

Johnny Horton
Honky Tonk Man: The Essential Johnny Horton 1956–1960 (Columbia/Legacy)

The Beatles
The Beatles (White Album) (Capitol)

Alan Jackson
The Greatest Hits Collection (Arista)

Joni Mitchell
Court and Spark (Elektra)

Mac MacAnally
No Problem Here (Ariola)

what to buy: *Gary's Greatest* (HighTone, 1991, prod. Roy Dea, Glen Middleworth, Eddie Kilroy) 𝄢𝄢𝄢 is his most complete greatest hits collection yet issued. It contains hits from his RCA period such as "Drinkin' Thing" and "Your Place or Mine," as well as later tunes like "Brand New Whiskey."

what to buy next: *Out of Hand* (RCA, 1975/HighTone, 1991, prod. Roy Dea) 𝄢𝄢𝄢 is still the best single album Stewart ever released, with tunes such as "Honky-Tonkin'," "Out of Hand," "Drinkin' Thing" and "She's Actin' Single (I'm Drinkin' Doubles)." Everything here works: from Stewart's voice, which is by turns at its most lowdown and its most vulnerable, to the cheesy 1970s electric keyboards and multi-voice overdubs that are applied here in just the right dosage.

the rest:
Brand New (HighTone, 1988) 𝄢𝄢𝄢
Battleground (HighTone, 1990) 𝄢𝄢𝄢

I'm A Texan (HighTone, 1993) ♫♫♫♫
Greatest Hits (RCA, 1995)
The Essential Gary Stewart (RCA, 1997)

worth searching for: Any of the now-deleted RCA albums, such as *Cactus and a Rose* (RCA, 1980) ♫♫♫ and *Your Place or Mine* (RCA, 1977) ♫♫♫. The non-single material on these discs is where Stewart stretched out and got a lot grittier and rowdier than he would (or could) on the singles.

influences:
◀◀ Merle Haggard, Lefty Frizzell, Allman Brothers
▶▶ Tracy Byrd, Travis Tritt, Mark Chesnutt

Robert Baird

JOHN STEWART
Born September 5, 1939, in San Diego, CA.

John Stewart took a giant step upon leaving the Kingston Trio in 1967. His first album, *California Bloodlines*, recorded in Nashville at the same time as Bob Dylan's *Nashville Skyline*, set the standard for his subsequent work. Building on the enthusiasm of the New Frontier (he traveled with the 1968 Robert Kennedy presidential campaign), Stewart has always written with a liberal's unabashed love of country, good humor and a genuine love for the subjects of his songs. His only real hit was the strangely ironic "Gold," recorded in 1979 for RSO, better known for the Bee Gees and *Saturday Night Fever,* and his best-known song is the tongue-in-cheek "Daydream Believer," a hit for the Monkees in 1967. Stewart's images have turned more impressionistic over the years, but he remains a formidable songwriter and singer.

what to buy: You just can't beat *California Bloodlines/Willard* (Bear Family, 1989, prod. Nick Venet) ♫♫♫♫. *Bloodlines*, written mostly in 1968 on the road with Kennedy, has a strong, rural Midwestern flavor and still captures the yin and yang of that period as well as any record. It is now packaged with its equally charismatic 1970 follow-up (less two songs), *Willard,* on one CD, a bargain even at import prices. *The Complete Phoenix Concerts* (Bear Family, 1990 prod. Nick Venet) ♫♫♫♫ is a superb 1974 live recording with one of Stewart's best country ensembles. *Bullets in the Hourglass* (Shanachie, 1992, prod. John Hoke, John Stewart) ♫♫♫ shows the ever-widening direction and more impressionistic tone of his recent material.

what to buy next: *Airdream Believer* (Shanachie, 1995, prod. John Stewart) ♫♫♫ includes several new songs and a retrospective that even reaches back into his Trio days. *Lonesome*

Picker Rides Again (Warner Bros., 1971) ♫♫♫ and *Sunstorm* (Warner Bros., 1972) ♫♫♫ are both strong Americana song collections in the manner of *California Bloodlines* that got lost in the shuffle.

the rest:
Punch the Big Guy (Shanachie, 1987) ♫♫♫
Cannons in the Rain/Wingless Angels (Bear Family, 1990) ♫♫♫♫
American Originals (Capitol, 1992) ♫♫♫

worth searching for: *The Last Campaign* (Homecoming, 1985, prod. John Stewart) ♫♫♫♫ finally gathers together the songs written specifically about the ill-fated 1968 Robert Kennedy campaign.

influences:
◀◀ Cumberland Three, Kingston Trio, Dave Guard
▶▶ Lindsey Buckingham, Rosanne Cash, Beat Farmers

see also: *Kingston Trio*

Leland Rucker

LARRY STEWART
See: Restless Heart

WYNN STEWART
Born Wynnford Lindsey Stewart, June 7, 1934, Morrisville, MO. Died July 17, 1985.

Bakersfield, California, was a breeding ground during the late 1950s and early 1960s for future greats like Merle Haggard and Buck Owens, and to a lesser degree, Wynn Stewart. Not to diminish his immense talent, it's just unfortunate he never gained the reputation of his California-based counterparts. And, since he died at age 51, Stewart is no longer around to take part in the revival that has occurred in recent years, due in part to the development of the Americana radio format.

Although he envisioned a career in baseball, Stewart decided to pursue music instead. His first record deal was with Intro Records in 1954, followed by a short-term deal with Capitol, which earned him his first hit, the Top 20 "Waltz of the Angels" (#14, 1956). Switching to the independent Challenge/Jackpot label, Stewart recorded a string of hits, earning his biggest success there with "Wishful Thinking," (#5, 1960) and the Top 20 "Big Big Love" (#18, 1962), later covered by k.d. lang. He also recorded duets with Jan Howard. In 1963 he was performing in Las Vegas, playing bass in Merle Haggard's band. Stewart soon returned to Capitol and scored four consecutive Top 10 hits, beginning with the chart-topping "It's Such a Pretty World Today" (#1, 1967). He left Capitol in 1971 and had no chart hits for five years. But with his switch to Playboy Records, he scored his final Top 10, "After the Storm" (#8, 1976). In 1985, shortly after starting his own label, Pretty World, Stewart died suddenly of a heart attack. Neither terribly influential nor astoundingly successful, Wynn Stewart was still an innovative and extremely talented singer/songwriter who has finally been given his due.

what's available: *California Country: The Best of the Challenge Masters* (AVI, 1995) ♪♪♪♪♪ contains 29 tracks on a single CD, and there's not a weak one in the bunch. You can't go wrong here. Someday a Wynn Stewart revival may result in many of these tracks being covered by new artists; until then you'll marvel at these original honky-tonk classics.

influences:

◀◀ Buck Owens, Tommy Collins

▶▶ Dwight Yoakam, Chris Hillman

Stephen L. Betts

DOUG STONE

Born Douglas Jackson Brooks, June 19, 1956, in Marietta, GA.

Often called Conway Twitty's heir apparent, Doug Stone is best known for two things: romantic ballads and heart problems. Despite his relatively young age, Stone had emergency quadruple bypass surgery in 1992 and was hospitalized three years later after a mild heart attack. Fittingly, Stone's most popular songs are about affairs of the heart, though some, such as his breakthrough hit "I'd Be Better Off (In a Pine Box)," cut a little too close to the bone these days. Stone has blamed his medical problems on heavy smoking and fatty foods, but after a divorce early in his career, he's tended to other matters of the heart rather well. His chiseled good looks and soothing tenor are perfectly suited for the light ballads and bluesy country pop for which he has become known—and adored—by female fans. Stone hasn't had a brilliant career—he opened for Loretta Lynn at age seven and made his movie debut opposite a pig in the 1993 stinker "Gordy"—but he has a great country voice that occasionally wraps around the right song.

what to buy: Stone bounced back from heart surgery with his wit and romanticism intact, as evidenced by *From the Heart* (Columbia, 1992, prod. Doug Johnson) ♪♪♪, the most consistent of his five studio albums.

what to buy next: Most of Stone's albums features a handful of good songs and a lot of filler, which makes *Greatest Hits, Vol-*

ume One (Epic, 1994, prod. Doug Johnson, James Stroud) ♪♪♪ a must for the casual fan. His biggest hits also happen to be some of his best work, and this nicely packages together such staples as "A Jukebox with a Country Song," "Warning Labels" and "Pine Box" on one album.

what to avoid: *The First Christmas* (Epic, 1992, prod. Doug Johnson) ♪♪ is, unfortunately, not the first Christmas album to not make the grade.

the rest:

Doug Stone (Epic, 1990) ♪♪
I Thought It Was You (Epic, 1991) ♪♪
More Love (Epic, 1993) ♪♪♪
Faith in Me, Faith in You (Columbia, 1995) ♪♪♪
Super Hits (Columbia, 1997) ♪♪♪

influences:

◀◀ George Jones, Conway Twitty

▶▶ T. Graham Brown, Randy Travis

Doug Pullen

ERNEST STONEMAN /THE STONEMAN FAMILY

Born May 25, 1893, in Carroll County, VA. Died June 14, 1968.

Ernest "Pop" Stoneman, along with his wife Hattie and his progeny, bestrode the first 40 years of the history of recorded country music; he made more than 200 recordings before 1930, suffered a severe decline along with the country during the Depression and reemerged as a force in country music during the 1950s and 1960s. Ernest and Hattie recorded together during the 1920s—he as a singer, autoharpist, harmonica player, guitarist and clawhammer banjo stylist, she as fiddle accompanist—for many labels and took part in the famed Bristol Sessions. They had 15 children who lived to adulthood, and most of them played music at least semi-professionally. Patsy, Scott, Donna, Jimmy, Roni and Van all grew to be skilled multi-instrumentalists and members of the Stoneman Family for varying lengths of time. Scott is among the most influential bluegrass fiddle stylists ever; his influence far outreaches any personal commercial success he ever had. Donna is a very good bluegrass mandolin player, and Roni, who has gained some measure of notoriety as a comic on television's *Hee Haw*, is a first-rate bluegrass banjo picker. Patsy, Jimmy and Van are all skilled professionals as well, although none of them ever attained the level of virtuosity of Scott, Donna and Roni. Of them all, Scott, who died in 1973, was the true genius, and he is sadly underrepresented on recordings today—as is the whole family, although Ernest recorded for virtually every available label during his good years in the 1930s. The Stonemans as a family band have had a long recording history with everyone from MGM to RCA to Starday during the 1960s and 1970s, when they were a unique part of the folk revival going at the time. They never really successfully integrated themselves into either the folk or country mainstream, but they made some very odd records in the attempt, most of them out of print today.

what's available: Ernest V. Stoneman's *Edison Recordings— 1928* (County, 1996, reissue prod. Gary B. Reid) ♫♫♫ contains 22 samples of the songs that first made Pop Stoneman a star— the first time. From fiddle tunes to gospel favorites to sentimental parlor songs of the day to transplanted English ballads, these are the types of songs that made up the repertoire of early country music recording stars.

worth searching for: *Ernest V. Stoneman & the Blue Ridge Corn Shuckers* (Rounder, 1975) ♫♫♫ includes more of Stoneman's commercial recordings from the 1920s.

solo outings:

Scott Stoneman:
(With Bill Emerson) *Fiddle and Banjo Bluegrass* aka *20 Fiddle and Banjo Hits* (Arion, 1967/1990) ♫♫♫♫
Scotty Stoneman with the Kentucky Colonels (Sierra, 1976) ♫♫♫♫

influences:
▶▶ Freight Hoppers

Randy Pitts

GEORGE STRAIT

Born May 18, 1952, in Poteet, TX.

If you were asked to name one contemporary country artist that's bound for Hall of Fame induction, you'd best put your money on George Strait. Since his 1981 debut, *Strait Country*, this Texan has been cranking out albums filled with the foundations of pure country. Strait revels in the story song, the Western swing number, the heart-tugging ballad, the casual two-stepper, the rodeo staple and the occasional sexually charged corker. And from the start, Strait has not changed a lick of his sound. His voice—a combination of the hillbilly grit of such country legends as Lefty Frizzell and Hank Williams and the urban sophistication of famed stylists like Frank Sinatra and Perry Como—is as familiar and welcomed as a comfortable pair of Wranglers and broken-in Justin boots. In fact, Strait has even launched a legion of wardrobe clones: whenever you see cur-

rent singers wearing pressed jeans, starched button-down shirts and Stetson hats, rest assured they copied Strait. And let's not get into the slew of soundalikes that usually fall flat next to the original. But Strait does have one crucial downfall: he sticks closely to the formula he devised early in his career, which is essentially the only thing he knows how to do, making a Strait album a fairly predictable project. From a critical standpoint, a new Strait release is far from exciting. Still, while Garth Brooks changes and toys with his music for the sake of shock value—usually with poor results—Strait's sameness comes from the heart. This is the music he grew up with, and you have to respect an artist who refuses to chase trends. Perhaps that's the reason he won three Country Music Association awards in 1996, his first big victory since 1990. In Texas, where country music is holy and the competition for air time and concert space is fierce, Strait is royalty; one radio station in Dallas refers to him as "King George." Place your bets now, folks, 'cause in another 20 years George Strait will become the newest member of the Country Music Hall of Fame.

what to buy: Strait's best studio albums are all 1990s releases. *Livin' It Up* (MCA, 1990, prod. Jimmy Bowen, George Strait) ♫♫♫♫, *Chill of an Early Fall* (MCA, 1991, prod. Jimmy Bowen, George Strait) ♫♫♫♫ and *Blue Clear Sky* (MCA, 1996, prod. Tony Brown, George Strait) ♫♫♫♫ present a magnificent blend of old and new, fast and slow, raw and polished—simply put, the essence of George Strait.

what to buy next: *Greatest Hits* (MCA, 1985, prod. Jimmy Bowen, George Strait) ♫♫♫ and *Greatest Hits Volume Two* (MCA, 1987, prod. Blake Mevis, Ray Baker) ♫♫♫ provide the best synopses of Strait's early and mid-period chart successes. Both are perfect for the essential country music library.

what to avoid: A George Strait album can be only so weak, since he doesn't ever mess with the proven recipe. But *Holding My Own* (MCA, 1992, prod. Jimmy Bowen, George Strait) ♫♫ feels like a rushed piece of work. The songs (even the hits) aren't as strong or memorable, and Strait sounds strangely uncommitted to this effort.

the rest:
Strait Country (MCA, 1981) ♫♫♫
Strait from the Heart (MCA, 1982) ♫♫♫♫
Right or Wrong (MCA, 1983) ♫♫♫
Does Fort Worth Ever Cross Your Mind (MCA, 1984) ♫♫♫
Something Special (MCA, 1985) ♫♫♫
#7 (MCA, 1986) ♫♫♫♫
Ocean Front Property (MCA, 1987) ♫♫♫♫

If You Ain't Lovin' You Ain't Livin' (MCA, 1988) 🎵🎵🎵
Beyond the Blue Neon (MCA, 1989) 🎵🎵🎵
10 Strait Hits (MCA, 1991) 🎵🎵🎵🎵
Pure Country (MCA, 1992) 🎵🎵🎵🎵
Easy Come Easy Go (MCA, 1993) 🎵🎵🎵🎵
Lead On (MCA, 1994) 🎵🎵🎵
Strait out of the Box (MCA, 1995) 🎵🎵🎵
Carrying Your Love with Me (MCA, 1997) 🎵🎵🎵

worth searching for: After years of remaining in print, MCA has suddenly taken *Merry Christmas Strait to You* (MCA, 1986, prod. Jimmy Bowen, George Strait) 🎵🎵🎵 off the market. Sure, it's just a Christmas record, but it does contain the swinging title cut and serves as an example of Strait's fascination with Americana icons Frank Sinatra and Perry Como.

influences:

◀◀ Bob Wills, Lefty Frizzell, Hank Thompson

▶▶ Alan Jackson, Clay Walker, David Kersh

Mario Tarradell

MEL STREET

Born King Malachi Street, October 21, 1933, near Grundy, WV. Died October 21, 1978.

A rural West Virginia native who worked variously as an electrician, construction worker and mechanic, Mel Street cut a series of honky-tonk sides during the 1970s that are evocative in their simplicity and hard-country stance. Because much of Street's discography has fallen into disrepair, his name isn't as well preserved as it should be. During his career he recorded for various labels, independent and major, and all his individual album releases are out of print. Street committed suicide on his 45th birthday.

what's available: A couple of compilations—*Greatest Hits* (Deluxe, 1992) 🎵🎵🎵 and *Greatest Hits* (Capitol, 1994) 🎵🎵🎵—suffer from cheap package design, but they do contain a number of Street's classic sides. Many of Street's best songs are alternately weepy and brazen, wonderful steel-driven events that focus on the cheating side of marriage—"Borrowed Angel," "Lust Affair," "Slip Away," "I Met a Friend of Yours Today." An acolyte of George Jones, Street's voice never achieved the Possum's grand scale. But his utter lack of artifice and his subtle, uncanny phrasing are exceptional. He grows on you.

worth searching for: Mercury Records has put on hold plans to release a Street retrospective, executive produced by major Street fan Sammy Kershaw. Here's hoping that a largely unsung

George Strait **(MCA Records—Nashville)**

country great will eventually receive the reissue treatment he richly deserves.

influences:

◀◀ George Jones, Webb Pierce

▶▶ Sammy Kershaw, George Strait, Wesley Dennis

Chris Dickinson

STRENGTH IN NUMBERS

Formed c. mid-1980s.

Sam Bush, mandolin; Mark O'Connor, fiddle; Bela Fleck, banjo; Jerry Douglas, dobro; Edgar Meyer, bass violin.

A bluegrass supergroup where each member is considered a master of his instrument, Strength in Numbers has played in various combinations on each others' projects and appears regularly at the Telluride Bluegrass Festival.

what's available: While not as flashy as their live shows, the group's one studio album, *The Telluride Sessions* (MCA, 1989, prod. Strength in Numbers) 🎵🎵🎵, could be described as cham-

$\frac{4}{2}$ *stringbean*
$\frac{4}{4}$

ber bluegrass, stressing precise ensemble work over individual soloing.

worth searching for: O'Connor and Meyer team up with cellist Yo-Yo Ma on *Appalachia Waltz* (Sony Classical, 1996) ✧✧✧✧✧, a collection that combines bluegrass and classical in a truly original way. Sort of Copland-goes-country.

influences:

◀◀ David Grisman, New Grass Revival, Bela Fleck & the Flecktones

▶▶ Alison Brown, Russ Barenberg

see also: *Mark O'Connor, Bela Fleck, Jerry Douglas, Sam Bush*

Bob Cannon

STRINGBEAN

Born David Akeman, June 17, 1915, in Annville, KY. Died November 11, 1973, in Nashville, TN.

David Akeman—lovingly known as "Stringbean"—was raised on a Kentucky farm and taught to play banjo by his father, who gave him his first instrument at age 14. Soon Stringbean was playing on local radio shows and touring or performing with the likes of Bill Monroe, Ernest Tubb, Red Foley and Uncle Dave Macon. Macon particularly became a mentor to Stringbean, who picked up much of his picking style. Stringbean joined the Grand Ole Opry in 1942 and essentially took over Macon's role after his death in 1952. The 6-foot 2-inch Stringbean combined elements of vaudevillian comedy and old-time banjo playing in his shows, and he flip-flopped his proportions by wearing long shirts and small pants that made his torso appear to comprise three-fourths of his body. He was an audience favorite for his comedy, but he was also a fine banjo player, and he was an original member of the *Hee Haw* cast upon its TV debut in 1969. In one of the most shocking crimes in Nashville's history, Stringbean and his wife were murdered by burglars upon returning to their home after his Opry appearance November 11, 1973.

what's available: There's a lot of overlap, at least in song titles, on the three Stringbean albums currently in print. All of them, for instance, contain "I'm the Man That Rode the Mule Around the World," one of his most popular numbers. On *A Salute to Uncle Dave Macon* (Hollywood/IMG, 1963/1986, prod. various) ✧✧✧, Stringbean makes a nod to his mentor with an album of vaudevillian proportions: it includes humorous songs ("There'll Be Moonshine in the Old Kentucky Hills"), folk songs ("John Henry") and gospel ("Take My Hand, Precious Lord"). *Hee Haw Corn Shucker* (Country Road, 1976) ✧✧✧ plays off his associa-

tion with the syndicated TV series *Hee Haw* and features Stringbean's novelty songs, as does *Front Porch Funnies* (King Special, 1993) ✧✧✧, which is the only one of the three albums available on CD.

influences:

◀◀ Uncle Dave Macon

▶▶ Grandpa Jones

Brian Mansfield

MARTY STUART

Born John Marty Stuart, September 30, 1958, in Philadelphia, MS.

Marty Stuart has spent more than half his life on the stage. A versatile picker, singer and writer, Stuart has a reputation for being a party kind of guy, an image he doesn't try too hard to downplay thanks to his association with fellow rowdy Travis Tritt, with whom he has toured and recorded a handful of hits. But Stuart cut his teeth on Southern gospel and bluegrass, performing with the Sullivans, a gospel group from his native Mississippi, before Jim McReynolds (of Jim & Jesse fame) introduced him to the legendary Lester Flatt. Stuart joined Flatt's band at age 12, playing guitar and mandolin as they crisscrossed the country. He stayed until Flatt broke up the band in 1978. Stuart spent the next year with Doc and Merle Watson, then became Johnny Cash's guitarist. He went solo in 1982 with a largely instrumental album, *Busy Bee Cafe,* on Sugar Hill. Stuart then signed with Columbia, but his solo career floundered until MCA came along in 1989. It's been a slow, solid build ever since as country fans slowly embraced his mix of bluegrass, blues, honky tonk, rock, old and new country, which he calls "hillbilly music."

what to buy: *Honky Tonkin's What I Do Best* (MCA, 1996, prod. Tony Brown, Justin Niebank) ✧✧✧✧ has just the right balance between the party hearty Marty of the past and the deeper, more sensitive Stuart of recent years. The balance is tipped, of course, in favor of the former, with frequent recording and touring buddy Tritt checking in on the title cut and yet another of Stuart's offbeat songs, "The Mississippi Mudcat and Sister Sheryl Crow," which features various canines barking in the background.

what to buy next: Stuart's fourth solo record, *Tempted* (MCA, 1991, prod. Richard Bennett, Tony Brown) ✧✧✧, refined that amalgamation of styles he calls "hillbilly music" and helped him break through to country radio. *Love and Luck* (MCA, 1993, prod. Tony Brown, Marty Stuart) ✧✧✧ tempered his upbeat and

Marty Stuart **(AP/Wide World Photos)**

offbeat ways with a more sensitive side. Stuart's biggest MCA hits make up *The Marty Party Hit Pack* (MCA, 1995, prod. various) ♪♪♪, which includes his memorable version of "The Weight" recorded with the Staple Singers for the *Rhythm Country and Blues* all-star project that brought together prominent country and R&B artists.

what to avoid: *Marty Stuart* (Columbia, 1986, prod. Curtis Allen) ♪♪♪, with appearances by Duane Eddy and a then-unknown Vince Gill, finds Stuart still in a formative stage.

the rest:
Busy Bee Cafe (Sugar Hill, 1982) ♪♪♥
Hillbilly Rock (MCA, 1989) ♪♪♪
This One's Gonna Hurt You (MCA, 1992) ♪♪♪♥

worth searching for: Columbia tried to cash in on the star they let go with *Let There Be Country,* a 1992 compilation of material Stuart cut for the label during the 1980s, with guests including Emmylou Harris and Vassar Clements.

influences:
◀◀ Bill Monroe, Ernest Tubb, Hank Williams, Elvis Presley, Johnny Cash
▶▶ Travis Tritt

Doug Pullen

JERRY & TAMMY SULLIVAN /THE SULLIVAN FAMILY

Family act from AL.

Jerry Sullivan (born November 22, 1933, in St. Stephens, AL), guitar, vocals; Tammy Sullivan (born October 2, 1964, in St. Stephens, AL), vocals.

Jerry Sullivan performed with various family members as part of the bluegrass gospel group, the Sullivan Family, which at various times included Enoch and Emmett Sullivan (Jerry's nephews) and Enoch's wife, Margie. Jerry's daughter Tammy is

Doug Supernaw (© Ken Settle)

blessed with a voice that's both powerful and tender. Father and daughter began performing together in 1978, continuing in the "brush arbor" tradition. Marty Stuart has been involved with their most recent projects as well, producing the records and collaborating with Jerry as songwriter.

what's available: *A Joyful Noise* (Country Music Foundation, 1991, prod. Marty Stuart, Richard Bennett) 🎵🎵🎵🎵 is pure celebration from start to finish. The follow-up, *At the Feet of God* (New Haven, 1995, prod. Marty Stuart) 🎵🎵🎵✔, was well worth the four-year wait between albums.

worth searching for: *Live* (Loyal, c. 1972) is a Sullivan Family album, recorded in 1971, that doesn't feature Jerry (or Tammy) but does contain what may be the first commercially available recordings featuring Marty Stuart, who, according to Enoch Sullivan's flowery introduction on the record, was just 13 years and two months old at the time. Another young musician, Carl Jackson, also toured with the family during the making of the album, recorded in Stuart's hometown of Philadelphia, Mississippi, just prior to Stuart joining Lester Flatt's group.

influences:
◀◀ Wilma Lee Cooper, Dorothy Love Coats, J.B. Sullivan
▶▶ Marty Stuart, Connie Smith

Stephen L. Betts

DOUG SUPERNAW

Born in Houston, TX.

Doug Supernaw is an imposing singer whose best quality is the unabashed redness of his neck. That feature hasn't always made him friends or worked on record, but it's taken him as far as he's gotten. In addition to performing and writing, Supernaw briefly went to college on a golf scholarship and also promoted concerts. His backing band is called the Possum Eatin' Cowboys.

what's available: Supernaw actively looks for songs that are "too country," which has limited his success. *You Still Got Me* (Giant, 1996, prod. Richard Landis) 🎵🎵 has plenty of those songs, but it also has a hit single in the romantic "Not Enough Hours in the Night."

worth searching for: *Red and the Rio Grande* (BNA, 1993, prod. Richard Landis) 🎵🎵 produced a #1 single ("I Don't Call Him Daddy") and two other hits and sold half a million copies. Problems started for Supernaw when some people perceived his single "What'll You Do About Me," from *Deep Thoughts from a Shallow Mind* (BNA, 1994, prod. Richard Landis) 🎵✔, as a song about a stalker. Nothing else from the album hit the Top 40—not even a remake of Steve Goodman's "You Never Even Call Me By My Name" that featured Waylon Jennings, Merle Haggard, Charley Pride and David Allen Coe—and BNA dropped Supernaw.

influences:
◀◀ Jerry Jeff Walker, Con Hunley
▶▶ Trace Adkins

Brian Mansfield

BILLY SWAN

Born May 12, 1942, in Cape Giradeau, MO.

"A modern-day '50s" is how no less an expert than Elvis Presley-producer Felton Jarvis described Billy Swan upon the release of his 1974 chart-topper "I Can Help." True enough, Swan's roots reach deep into the sounds and styles of classic country and rockabilly. While still in high school, leading his first band Mirt Mirley & the Rhythm Steppers, Swan wrote

"Lover Please," which became a huge hit for Clyde McPhatter in 1962. Soon afterwards, Swan moved to Nashville on the recommendation of Kris Kristofferson (who offered him his job as janitor at the Columbia studios) and recorded several singles for the MGM and Rising Sons labels. His initial success, however, came as producer of Tony Joe White's early albums, including the hit "Polk Salad Annie," though Billy kept active onstage as well, joining old pal Kristofferson's road band (he continues to record and tour with Kris to this day). Then came the international country-crossover sensation "I Can Help," a song so charmingly absolute in its treatment of early rock that it earned Swan not only a cover version by Elvis himself, but an actual pair of the King's socks! Not bad for a kid who, not long before, had been crashing on Presley's uncle's living-room couch. It was Swan's last major hit, though he's remained active both in the studio and on the road with everyone from Kinky Friedman (during the mid-1970s) to Randy Meisner (with the band Black Tie a decade later) and, most recently, Peter Case.

what's available: *Billy Swan's Best* (Sony Special Products, 1993, prod. various) ✓✓✓, the most comprehensive of several retrospectives, includes not only the still timeless "I Can Help" but also Billy's own "Lover Please" and an other-worldly version of his idol's "Don't Be Cruel."

influences:

◀◀ Sun Records, Sir Douglas Quintet

▶▶ Nick Lowe, Rick Harper

Gary Pig Gold

SWEETHEARTS OF THE RODEO

Formed 1974, in southern CA.

Janis Gill, vocals; Kristine Oliver, vocals.

One of country's great disappointments, this talented vocal duo has been around a long time but seldom lived up to the potential of its first few records. Sisters Janis (Vince Gill's wife) and Kristine Oliver formed the duo in southern California during the early 1970s, when country-rock's popularity surged thanks to artists such as Linda Ronstadt and the Eagles. The Sweethearts stopped to raise families during the early 1980s but returned anew by the middle of the decade, securing a deal with Columbia just before they won the Wrangler Country Showdown in 1985. The Sweethearts' glittering harmonies and sparse, sweetly sung arrangements draw not only from their obvious traditional and new wave country roots, but also from 1960s folk, pop, rock and bluegrass. The duo scored such hits

as "Since I Found You" (written by Foster & Lloyd, another overlooked duo) and "Chains of Gold," and *Buffalo Zone* (complete with a Byrds-inspired cover) was a solid album. Sadly, their first four albums are no longer in print. North Carolina's Sugar Hill Label, home to many an iconoclastic singer and writer, signed the duo and has released a pair of albums that seemed to resuscitate them.

what's available: *Rodeo Waltz* (Sugar Hill, 1993, prod. Janis Gill) ✓✓ found them covering an array of rootsy songs, but not always as impressively. *Beautiful Lies* (Sugar Hill, 1996, prod. Janis Gill) ✓✓✓ is a more focused improvement.

worth searching for: No album showcased the sisters' natural harmonies, adroit song selection and effortless ability to blend traditional country with modern touches better than the out-of-print *Buffalo Zone* (Columbia, 1990) ✓✓✓.

influences:

◀◀ Byrds, Poco, Everly Brothers, Bob Seger

▶▶ Alison Krauss, Suzy Bogguss

Doug Pullen

SYLVIA

Born Sylvia Kirby, December 9, 1956, in Kokomo, IN.

Hovering somewhere between country and pop, Sylvia adequately managed the balancing act perfected by the likes of Dolly Parton and Crystal Gayle, but never quite convincingly enough. Sylvia moved to Nashville in 1975, and worked as a secretary at Tom Collins' music publishing firm. While there she also sang on demos and studied the music business from the inside, joining Collins in the studio as he produced Barbara Mandrell. Mandrell invited the singer to join her on tour, singing back-up in her Las Vegas show. An unsuccessful audition for the act Dave & Sugar on RCA led instead to Sylvia signing with the label as a solo artist. What followed was a series of successful country singles that included a pair of #1 songs. In 1982 she hit #15 on the pop chart with "Nobody," her second #1 country single ("Drifter" in 1981 was her first). From 1981 to 1986 Sylvia had at least one Top 10 record every year, then left RCA and the touring life to focus on songwriting. By 1992, as Sylvia Hutton, she returned to performing and in 1996 made an acoustically based, very enjoyable record on independent Red Pony Records.

what's available: *Greatest Hits* (RCA, 1987) ✓✓✓ contains most of Sylvia's big hits. *The Real Story* (Red Pony, 1996) ✓✓✓ is definitely worth a listen.

4
2
8
russ taff

influences:

◀◀ Charly McClain, Crystal Gayle

▶▶ Marie Osmond, Holly Dunn

Stephen L. Betts

RUSS TAFF

Born in AK.

Some folks place Russ Taff right up there with Vince Gill and the Mavericks' Raul Malo as one of Nashville's best vocalists. The son of a Pentecostal preacher who ministered to California's migrant community, Taff grew up listening to nothing but the gospel greats of the day—Mahalia Jackson, the Blackwood Brothers, etc. He also discovered Merle Haggard when an older brother brought his records into the Taff household after returning from Vietnam. Taff was a member of the inspirational/gospel group the Imperials (1977–81) before becoming a solo Christian artist. He won four Grammy awards either with the Imperials or as a solo act, but began feeling stifled within the Christian industry and signed with Warner Bros. in 1994 to make country records.

what's available: *We Will Stand: Yesterday and Today* (Word/Epic, 1994, prod. various) ♪♪♪, a compilation of Taff's Christian work both solo and with the Imperials. It has some spectacular stuff (a shattering statement of faith called "I Still Believe," for instance) and early versions of songs that would appear on his Warner Bros. debut, *Winds of Change* (Reprise, prod. Randy Scruggs, James Hollihan Jr., Russ Taff) ♪♪♪. Working with producer Randy Scruggs as well as his normal collaborator, guitarist James Hollihan Jr., Taff loses some of his edge on *Winds of Change* as he trades in Pentecostal passion for mundane tales of earthly romance. Still, when the spirit hits him, as it does on "Bein' Happy" and "Love Is Not a Thing," the results are inspired.

worth searching for: Much of Taff's Christian output is scarce, but *Under Their Influence Volume 1* (Word, 1991, prod. Russ Taff, James Hollihan Jr.) ♪♪♪♪ is a stone masterwork, as Taff and Hollihan fall into the spirit of classic gospel songs like "God Don't Never Change," "Everybody Shoulda Really Oughta Been There" and "There's a Hand." Released as a contract

filler, the album went on to sell more than 100,000 copies (a good number for the Christian market) and win a Grammy. Not all of Taff's albums have worn well, but *Russ Taff* (A&M/Myrrh, 1987, prod. Jack Joseph Puig) ♪♪♪ and *The Way Home* (Myrrh, 1989, prod. Russ Taff, James Hollihan Jr.) ♪♪♪, the first album Taff and Hollihan produced themselves, have moments of greatness.

influences:

◀◀ Imperials, John Hiatt

▶▶ Ashley Cleveland, Brian Barrett

Brian Mansfield

JAMES TALLEY

Born November 9, 1944, in Mehan, OK.

James Talley is a songwriter/singer whose thoughtful, compelling lyrics and folk/country/blues music documents and champions the lives and struggles of working-class people. Talley's family moved to the state of Washington before settling in Albuquerque, New Mexico. After graduating from the University of New Mexico, he began writing songs about the hopes, dreams, ambitions and fears of the working class. He traded his carpentry skills for studio time and recorded *Got No Bread, No Milk, No Money, but We Sure Got a Lot of Love* in 1975, which led to a contract with Capitol for three more critically acclaimed albums. He has lived in Nashville for many years, where he is in the real estate business and releases the occasional album.

what to buy: You simply can't go wrong with *Got No Bread/Tryin' Like the Devil* (Bear Family, 1989, prod. James Talley, Steve Mendell) ♪♪♪♪ or *Blackjack Choir/Ain't It Somethin'* (Bear Family, 1989, prod. James Talley) ♪♪♪♪, the four Capitol albums repackaged on two CDs. All are understated song treasure chests, with production touches that perfectly emphasize the country/blues amalgam for which Talley's expressive voice and lyrics are so well suited.

the rest:

American Originals (Bear Family, 1985) ♪♪♪♪

Love Songs and the Blues (Bear Family, 1989) ♪♪♪

Live (Bear Family, 1994) ♪♪♪

worth searching for: *"The Road to Torreon: Photographs of New Mexico Villages"* by Cavalliere Ketchum; Songs by James Talley (Bear Family, 1992, prod. James Talley) 🎵🎵🎵🎵, a song cycle written after a period Talley spent as a welfare worker among Chicanos in New Mexico. It includes a 107-page book of photos.

influences:

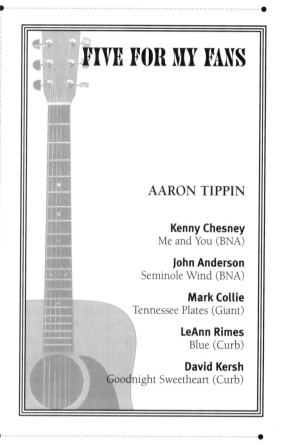 Lee O'Daniel & the Light Crust Doughboys, Bob Wills & the Texas Playboys, Jimmie Rodgers, Hank Williams, Woody Guthrie, Lefty Frizzell

Leland Rucker

TARNATION

Formed 1992, in San Francisco, CA.

Paula Frazer, lead vocals, guitar, bass; Matt Wendell Sullivan, guitar, steel guitar, bass, vocals; Lincoln Allen, guitar, banjo, vocals; Michelle Cernuto, drums, bass, vocals.

Paula Frazer, a veteran of Bay Area alternative rock bands, is the daughter of a preacher; she grew up singing in church choirs in small towns in Georgia and Arkansas. Her piano-playing mother introduced her to a wide variety of singers such as Billie Holiday, Patsy Cline and Roy Orbison. After stints in the rock bands and in a choir that specialized in Bulgarian folk music, Frazer formed Tarnation. Her soaring, mournful vocals are at the heart of the group's hushed, heavy-hearted sound.

what to buy: The second Tarnation album, *Gentle Creatures* (4AD/Reprise, 1995, prod. Tarnation, Warren Defever, Joshua Heller, Wally Sound) 🎵🎵🎵 toes the darker realms of heartbreak, with the angelic-voiced Frazer sounding like Patsy Cline in the depths of depression.

the rest:

I'll Give You Something to Cry About ('Nuf Sed, 1993) 🎵🎵🎵
Mirador (4AD/Reprise, 1997) 🎵🎵🎵🎵

influences:

◀◀ Patsy Cline, Hank Williams, Roy Orbison, Billie Holiday
▶▶ Cowboy Junkies, k.d. lang, Wilco

Doug Pullen

BARRY & HOLLY TASHIAN

Husband-and-wife duo from Westport, CT.

Barry and Holly Tashian both grew up in New England and attended the same high school. In 1964 Barry and his Boston-based rock 'n' roll band, the Remains, achieved near-stardom

when they toured with the Beatles. Barry and the Remains couldn't top that feat, however, and quickly disbanded. Tashian then joined Gram Parsons in the country/rock outfit the International Submarine Band and married Holly in 1972. Holly's musical experience encompasses both bluegrass and madrigal singing. The couple formed a country band, called the Outskirts, that was pretty far away from the sweet, acoustic music they're known for today. In 1980 Barry was asked to join Emmylou Harris' Hot Band, and began a nine-year stint with the group, replacing Ricky Skaggs, playing guitar and singing harmony. After Barry exited the Hot Band, the Tashians began their recording career, first with Northeastern Records, then with Rounder in 1993. Their records are marked not only by their tight harmony, but also by the fact that they write much of their material. They've also contributed vocals and songwriting skills to records by other artists. Favorites on the folk and bluegrass festival circuits, the Tashian's music is warm and gentle. It's not entirely bluegrass, and not strictly folk; enjoyable, if maybe a bit safe.

FIVE FOR MY FANS

AARON TIPPIN

Kenny Chesney
Me and You (BNA)

John Anderson
Seminole Wind (BNA)

Mark Collie
Tennessee Plates (Giant)

LeAnn Rimes
Blue (Curb)

David Kersh
Goodnight Sweetheart (Curb)

what to buy: *Ready for Love* (Rounder, 1993, prod. Jim Rooney) 🎵🎵🎵 showcases the best of the duo.

the rest:

Trust in Me (Northeastern, 1989) 🎵🎵🎵
Straw into Gold (Rounder, 1994) 🎵🎵🎵
Live in Holland (Strictly Country, 1995) 🎵🎵🎵

influences:

◀◀ Emmylou Harris, International Submarine Band

▶▶ Sweethearts of the Rodeo, Laurie Lewis & Tom Rozum

Stephen L. Betts

EARL TAYLOR /THE STONEY MOUNTAIN BOYS

Born June 17, 1929, in Rose Hill, VA. Died January 28, 1984.

Bluegrass mandolinist Earl Taylor led his Stoney Mountain Boys intermittently from the 1950s through the 1980s; he also performed and recorded with Jimmy Martin and Flatt & Scruggs. The Stoney Mountain Boys were the first bluegrass band to play Carnegie Hall, as part of a folk music evening produced by Alan Lomax. They made an album for United Artists shortly thereafter and in 1963 made another for Capitol, making them one of the few bands below the top echelon superstars to cut albums for major labels. Unfortunately, Earl and his fine bands are very underrepresented on recordings now, a particularly sorry state for an artist who was such an integral part of the music's early growth.

what's available: The compilation CD *Mountain Music Bluegrass Style* (Smithsonian/Folkways, 1959/reissued 1991, prod. Mike Seeger) 🎵🎵🎵🎵 features Taylor and the Stoney Mountain Boys on six cuts of the most raucous, heartfelt and exciting traditional bluegrass on disc, along with 17 similar cuts by such contemporaries as Tex Logan, the Lilly Brothers and Bob Baker.

influences:

◀◀ Stanley Brothers, Bill Monroe

▶▶ Don Stover, Vern Williams

Randy Pitts

JAMES TAYLOR

Born March 12, 1948, in Boston, MA.

Regardless of what he says in the song "Steamroller," of the many things that James Taylor is, has been or may someday be, a "churnin' urn of burnin' funk" is not one of them. Perhaps the quintessential sensitive male singer/songwriter, Taylor's confessional odes and gentle folk-inflected R&B covers to this day make whole amphitheaters full of baby boomers swoon. They've also been a primary influence on country singers who came to prominence during the 1980s—notably Garth Brooks, who was raised on 1970s FM radio, of which Taylor was a staple. His influence on Nashville has been—for better and worse—to inspire relationship songs of a kinder, gentler nature and to infuse a little introspection into the mix as well.

Taylor started out as one of the Beatles' initial signings to Apple Records, and he ushered in an era of, depending on your point of view, ruthless self-examination or hopeless navel-gazing. It's telling that he actually began his career as a songwriter after checking himself into a mental institution. Such songs as "Fire and Rain" were the result, but Taylor actually had greater success covering the work of others—notably Carole King's "You've Got a Friend." Once a dependable hitmaker, if an erratic songwriter, Taylor has, for the most part, vanished from the scene save for semi-annual summer tours, political campaigns and public-television pledge drives. But cut him some slack; he did, after all, write "Bartender's Blues," a nearly perfect country lament, with Ol' Possum in mind.

what to buy: *Greatest Hits* (Warner Bros., 1976, prod. various) 🎵🎵🎵 would seem the natural place to start, but "Carolina in My Mind" and "Something in the Way She Moves" are re-recorded versions, not the originals. If you're looking for Taylor's best single album, you have to go all the way back to *Sweet Baby James* (Warner Bros., 1970, prod. Peter Asher) 🎵🎵🎵🎵, which contains a number of songs that became his fans' favorites—including the title track, "Fire and Rain," "Country Road" and "Steamroller Blues," Taylor's own personal "Free Bird." Since Taylor lacks a hits package that covers his entire career (excepting the import *Classic Songs*), *(Live)* (Columbia, 1993, prod. Don Grolnick, George Massenburg) 🎵🎵🎵 will have to do. All the requisite songs are there, but Taylor's performance is disappointingly subdued. The set is also available in an abridged one-disc version, *(Best Live)* (Columbia, 1994, prod. Don Grolnick, George Massenburg) 🎵🎵🎵.

what to buy next: Taylor's debut, *James Taylor* (Apple, 1969, prod. Peter Asher) 🎵🎵🎵, lets you feel his pain as he helps establish the singer/songwriter genre. The album includes "Rainy Day Man," "Carolina in My Mind," "Something in the Way She Moves" and the upbeat "Knockin' Around the Zoo." *Gorilla* (Warner Bros., 1975, prod. Lenny Waronker, Russ Titelman) 🎵🎵🎵 was Taylor's comeback album after a self-imposed exile during the early 1970s. It contains the delightful original "Mexico," but also eased Taylor's transition from confessional singer/songwriter to craftsmanlike covers man with Marvin Gaye's "How Sweet It Is (To Be Loved By You)." One of his better mid-period albums, *J.T.* (Columbia, 1979, prod. Peter Asher) ✍✍✍ includes the sunny hit "Your Smiling Face," the requisite R&B cover "Handy Man" and the charming "Secret o' Life," plus "Bartender's Blues," which Taylor wrote for George Jones. Of his recent albums, *New Moon Shine* (Columbia, 1991, prod. Danny Kortchmar, Don Grolnick) ✍✍✍✍ stands out, thanks to Taylor's sharpest and most relevant set of lyrics in some time, notably on "Slap Leather" and "Shed a Little Light."

what to avoid: *Never Die Young* (Columbia, 1988, prod. Don Grolnick) ✍✍ is a slight collection, even by Taylor's sometimes lightweight standards.

the rest:

Mud Slide Slim and the Blue Horizon (Warner Bros., 1971) ✍✍✍
One Man Dog (Warner Bros., 1972) ✍✍
Walking Man (Warner Bros., 1974) ✍✍
In the Pocket (Warner Bros., 1976) ✍✍
Flag (Columbia, 1979) ✍✍✍
Dad Loves His Work (Columbia, 1981) ✍✍✍
That's Why I'm Here (Columbia, 1985) ✍✍
Hourglass (Columbia, 1997)

worth searching for: Curiosity seekers may want to find *James Taylor and the Original Flying Machine 1967* (Euphoria, 1971/Gadfly, 1996) ✍, which contains demos—studio chatter included—of "Night Owl," "Rainy Day Man" and "Brighten Your Night with My Day," which Taylor and guitarist Danny Kortchmar recorded during 1967. The seven-song album saw the light of day only after Taylor hit pay dirt elsewhere.

influences:

◀◀ Simon & Garfunkel, Bob Dylan, Carole King
▶▶ Garth Brooks, Clint Black

Daniel Durchholz

LES TAYLOR

See: Exile

S. ALAN TAYLOR

Born in Gilbert, SC.

S. Alan Taylor is a Nashville singer/songwriter who has had tunes cut by Alabama, Lee Greenwood, and Reba McEntire. He has also sung jingles for McDonald's, Miller Beer, Sears, Kellogg's Corn Flakes and others. He was the first country artist to release an album on the independent River North Nashville.

what's available: Taylor sounds a little like former Restless Heart lead singer Larry Stewart on his debut, *Forever Dance* (River North, 1994, prod. Joe Thomas, Ira Antelis) ✍✍. The music is competent, but nothing more.

influences:

◀◀ Restless Heart, Great Plains
▶▶ Steve Azar

Brian Mansfield

THE TEXAS TORNADOS

Formed 1989, in San Francisco, CA.

Doug Sahm, vocals, guitar; Freddy Fender, vocals, guitar; Flaco Jimenez, accordion, vocals; Augie Meyers, keyboards, vocals.

For those in pursuit of encyclopedic knowledge of Texas music over the past three decades or so, you could do a lot worse than to begin your search with a serious study of the Texas Tornados. From the Anglo side come rockers Doug Sahm and Augie Meyers, who brought arid border breezes to the rest of the nation during the 1960s with the Sir Douglas Quintet and songs like "She's About a Mover" and "Mendocino." From the Latino side come balladeer non pareil Freddy Fender, who charted with "Wasted Days and Wasted Nights" and "Before the Next Teardrop Falls," and accordionist Flaco Jimenez, who has enjoyed crossover success by rocking up traditional Mexican conjunto and Norteno styles. The Tornados play party music, pure and simple, with an occasional Fender ballad thrown in like a couple of swigs of cerveza between bites of hot Texas chili. As mercurial as the individual members of the group are, that they can get together to make music that is this engaging—aw, hell, just plain fun—is nothing short of awe-inspiring.

what to buy: The Tornados' best single album is their debut, *Texas Tornados* (Reprise, 1990, prod. Bill Halverson, Texas Tornados) ✍✍✍✍. Mixing Spanish and English throughout, the group scores with the Sir Douglas-style "Who Were You Thinkin' Of" and the high-stepping conjunto number "(Hey Baby) Que Paso." Fender contributes the heart-tugging ballad "A Man Can Cry," and Sahm takes an admirable run at Butch Hancock's brilliant "She Never Spoke Spanish to Me." The album is also available in a Spanish-only version, *Los Texas Tornados* (Reprise, 1990, prod. Bill Halverson, Texas Tornados) ✍✍✍✍.

The Texas Tornados (from left): Flaco Jimenez, Augie Meyers, Doug Sahm and Freddy Fender **(Reprise Records)**

what to buy next: *The Best of Texas Tornados* (Reprise, 1994, prod. Bill Halverson, Texas Tornados) 🎵🎵🎵 is just that, collecting tunes from each of their albums, including updates of Fender's "Wasted Days and Wasted Nights" and Sahm's "Is Anybody Goin' to San Antone."

what to avoid: *The Nada Mixes* (Reprise, 1997) **WOOF!** contains dance remixes of "A Little Bit Is Better than Nada" from 1995's *4 Aces*. In this case, nada would have been better.

the rest:
Hangin' on by a Thread (Reprise, 1991) 🎵🎵🎵🎵
Zone of Our Own (Reprise, 1992) 🎵🎵🎵
4 Aces (Reprise, 1995) 🎵🎵🎵🎵

influences:
⏮ Santiago Jimenez, Dave Clark Five, Ritchie Valens, Bob Dylan

⏭ Emilio, Los Lobos, Santiago Jimenez Jr.

see also: *Freddy Fender, Doug Sahm, Flaco Jimenez*

Daniel Durchholz

CHRIS THILE

Born February 20, 1981, in Oceanside, CA.

Chris Thile began playing mandolin at age five and added fiddle and guitar to his arsenal at ages eight and nine respectively. He won the prestigious Walnut Valley Championship in 1993 and released his first bluegrass-rich album in 1994, at the age of 13. Playing mandolin with a dexterity and sophistication that's jaw-dropping-unusual in someone so young, Thile performed and toured for several years with bluegrass/western band Nickel Creek and is a founding member of The Grass Is Greener with Richard Greene and David Grier.

what's available: *Leading Off* (Sugar Hill, 1994, prod. Pete Wernick) 🎵🎵🎵🎵 is a bluegrass showcase introducing an eighth-grader with the sensitivity, chops and musical friskiness of an adult. Thile wrote or arranged 11 of the 13 tracks here and is joined by luminaries, including fiddlers Byron Berline and Stuart Duncan and guitarist Scott Nygaard.

worth searching for: *Tinsel Tunes* (Sugar Hill, 1996, prod. Barry Poss) 𝄞𝄞𝄞𝄞 is a generous, various artists collection of bluegrassy holiday material performed by artists from the Sugar Hill roster. Thile arranged "Bring a Torch, Jeanette Isabella" for the project, which also includes tracks by Chris Hillman & Herb Pedersen, Sam Bush, Mollie O'Brien, Robert Earl Keen Jr., the Laurel Canyon Ramblers and others.

influences:

◀◀ Bill Monroe, Alison Krauss

▶▶ Dr. Banjo's Bluegrass Youth All-Stars

David Sokol

IIIRD TYME OUT

Formed 1991.

Russell Moore, guitar, lead vocals; Ray Deaton, bass guitar, vocals; Mike Hartgrove, fiddle; Wayne Benson, mandolin, vocals (1993–present); Steve Dilling, banjo, vocals (1994–present); Terry Baucom, banjo (1991–92); Alan Bibey, mandolin (1991–92); Barry Abernathy, banjo (1993).

Founded by veterans of Doyle Lawson & Quicksilver, IIIrd Tyme Out made an immediate impact on the bluegrass world when their debut album received an Album of the Year nomination from the International Bluegrass Music Association. A single from that album, "Erase the Miles," spent two months at #1 on the *Bluegrass Unlimited* chart. The band has won several awards for their vocal work and is noted for producing a contemporary sound while staying firmly within the genre's traditions.

what to buy: *Puttin' New Roots Down* (Rebel, 1992, prod. IIIrd Tyme Out) 𝄞𝄞𝄞𝄞, a more than worthy follow-up to their successful debut, once had four songs in *Bluegrass Unlimited*'s Top 30. Includes songs from Hank Williams, Jimmie Rodgers, Lionel Delmore and others.

what to buy next: The band's first Rounder album, *Letter to Home* (Rounder, 1995, prod. IIIrd Tyme Out) 𝄞𝄞𝄞𝄞, includes an inspired a cappella cover of the Platters' "Only You (And You Alone)" plus Wes Golding's classic "Raining in L.A."

the rest:

IIIrd Tyme Out (Rebel, 1991) 𝄞𝄞𝄞

Grandpa's Mandolin (Rebel, 1993) 𝄞𝄞𝄞

Across the Miles (New Haven, 1994) 𝄞𝄞𝄞

Living on the Other Side (Rounder, 1996) 𝄞𝄞𝄞𝄞

influences:

◀◀ Doyle Lawson & Quicksilver

▶▶ Blue Highway, Lonesome River Band

Douglas Fulmer

B.J. THOMAS

Born August 7, 1942, in Houston, TX.

Though Billy Joe Thomas first hit it big on the pop charts with a cover of Hank Williams' "I'm So Lonesome I Could Cry" in 1966, it would be nearly a decade before he would find real success in country music. Prior to that, though, Thomas' sinuous, Southern vocal style gave him one fabulous string of pop hits, including "I Just Can't Help Believing" and "Raindrops Keep Falling on My Head." Producer Chips Moman's "(Hey Won't You Play) Another Somebody Done Somebody Wrong Song" became a pop and country #1 for Thomas in 1975, jump-starting a series of forays onto the country singles chart that peaked with the early 1980s hits "Whatever Happened to Old Fashioned Love" and "New Looks from an Old Lover."

what to buy: There are numerous best-of packages that survive Thomas' three-decade's worth of recording, and *Greatest Hits* (Curb, 1972/1991, prod. various) 𝄞𝄞𝄞𝄞 makes the definitive statement on the singer's commercial impact, from his self-penned 1963 war story "Billy and Sue" to bigger hits like "I Just Can't Help Believing" and a final pop smash, a cover of the Beach Boys' "Don't Worry Baby."

the rest:

I'm So Lonesome I Could Cry (Richmond, 1966) 𝄞𝄞𝄞

Peace in the Valley (Word, 1982/Epic, 1991) 𝄞𝄞

Sings Hank Williams' Songs (Richmond, 1985) 𝄞𝄞

16 Greatest Hits (Deluxe, 1987) 𝄞𝄞𝄞

Greatest Hits (Rhino, 1991) 𝄞𝄞𝄞𝄞

Country Soul (King, 1994) 𝄞𝄞

Still Standing Here (Laurie, 1994) 𝄞𝄞𝄞

More Greatest Hits (Varese Sarabande, 1995) 𝄞𝄞𝄞𝄞

Precious Memories (Warner Bros., 1995) 𝄞𝄞

worth searching for: *New Looks* (Sony, 1983, prod. Pete Drake) 𝄞𝄞𝄞 marked Thomas' triumphant return to commercial acceptance on the country side following a nasty drug addiction, and contains his back-to-back #1's, "Whatever Happened to Old Fashioned Love" and "New Looks from an Old Lover," the latter co-written by his wife Gloria.

influences:

◄◄ Hank Williams, Jackie Wilson

►► Dan Seals

David Simons

THE THOMPSON BROTHERS BAND

Formed early 1990s, in Norwell, MA.

Andy Thompson, vocals, guitar; Matt Thompson, vocals, drums; Michael Whitty, vocals, bass.

A trio of young musicians who play country music filtered through the ethos of Boston-area clubs, the Thompson Brothers Band plays what might be called "garage country"—a rough style built more on power chords and raw energy than on studio-honed craftsmanship. The members of the group, who had cut their teeth on the likes of Steve Earle and Dwight Yoakam, won track scholarships to Nashville's Belmont University and enrolled in the school's music-business department before signing with RCA.

what's available: *Cows on Main Street* (RCA, 1996, prod. Steve Fishell) 𝄞𝄞𝄞 is a six-song EP with the trio augmented by a keyboardist, an additional guitarist and a steel player. It also contains two songs recorded live in Athens, Georgia, one of them a rave-up of Neil Diamond's "Solitary Man."

influences:

◄◄ Steve Earle, Dwight Yoakam, Foster & Lloyd

►► Keith Urban

Brian Mansfield

HANK THOMPSON

Born Henry William Thompson, September 3, 1935, in Waco, TX.

As a boy growing up in Waco, Texas, Hank Thompson was influenced by everything from Jimmie Rodgers to the Grand Ole Opry. His first instrument was the harmonica, and he later was inspired to learn guitar by watching Gene Autry in western movies. Thompson started performing in a Saturday youth program that was broadcast on a Waco radio station. That led to a show called *Hank the Hired Hand*, where Thompson was sponsored by a flour company. After six months of that, Thompson received his high school diploma and enlisted in the navy, attending Princeton University after his discharge. He then returned to Waco and put together a band called the Brazos Valley Boys; they became popular throughout the state and Thompson signed with Globe Records in 1946.

Thompson's recording caught Tex Ritter's ear, and Ritter introduced Thompson to Capitol Records executives. Thompson signed with Capitol in 1948, beginning an association that would last until 1966. That first year, Thompson had two songs—"Humpty Dumpty Heart" and "Today"—reach the Top 10. In 1952 he had his first #1 with "Wild Side of Life." The hits continued to pour in: during 1954 Thompson placed five singles in the Top 10. He averaged 240 personal appearances a year throughout much of the 1950s and 1960s, including regular performances at the Texas State Fair, where he often set attendance records. The pace slowed some during the 1970s, though Thompson still toured the U.S., Canada, the Far East and Europe. By the time Thompson signed with Warner Bros. in 1966, he had sold millions of records and had placed almost 50 singles on the charts. For most of his stay at Capitol he was ranked as the top country artist by polls in *Billboard* and *Cashbox*. He signed with ABC/Dot in 1968 and remained there until MCA absorbed the label at the end of the 1970s, at which point his releases appeared on that label. While Thompson has had more than 30 Top 10 hits, he hasn't had a charting single since 1983, though he still continues to record occasionally.

what to buy: *The Best of Hank Thompson 1966–1978* (Varese Sarabande, 1996, prod. Joe Allison, Larry Butler) 𝄞𝄞𝄞𝄞 contains some of Thompson's strongest stuff and covers his later performances. Eight of the 16 songs were written or co-written by Thompson.

what to buy next: *Vintage Collection Series* (Capitol, 1996, prod. various) 𝄞𝄞𝄞𝄞 is a 20-song collection that covers the biggest hits of Thompson & His Brazos Valley Boys from 1947–60.

what to avoid: Acquiring more than one of the redundant collections *All-Time Greatest Hits* (Curb, 1990, prod. various) 𝄞𝄞, *Greatest Hits Volume 2* (Curb, 1993, prod. various) 𝄞𝄞, *Greatest Songs, Volume 1* (Curb, 1995, prod. various) 𝄞𝄞 and *Greatest Songs, Volume 2* (Curb, 1995, prod. various) 𝄞𝄞 is unnecessary.

the rest:

Live at the Golden Nugget (Capitol, 1958/1995) 𝄞𝄞𝄞

Wild Side of Life (Richmond, 1985) 𝄞𝄞

Greatest Hits, Volume 1 (Step One, 1987) 𝄞𝄞𝄞

Greatest Hits, Volume 2 (Step One, 1987) 𝄞𝄞𝄞

Here's to Country Music (Step One, 1987) 𝄞𝄞

20 Greatest Hits (Deluxe, 1987) 𝄞𝄞𝄞

The Best of the Best of Hank Thompson (Hollywood, 1990) 𝄞𝄞

Country Music Hall of Fame (MCA, 1992) 🎵🎵🎵

influences:
◀◀ Bob Wills
▶▶ Kitty Wells, Asleep at the Wheel

Ronnie McDowell

SUE THOMPSON

Born Eva Sue McKee, July 19, 1926, in Nevada, MO.

Though Sue Thompson never had a solo country hit reach the Top 40, she spent much of her career on the edges of country. Raised in California, she performed country songs on radio and television there and then sang with Red Foley on the Grand Ole Opry during the 1950s. But when recording success came, it came on the pop charts: "Sad Movies (Make Me Cry)" and "Norman," both written by John D. Loudermilk, each reached the Top Five during the early 1960s. Thompson quit hitting the pop Top 40 in 1965 and later turned toward the country market. She released nine duets with Don Gibson between 1971 and 1976, three of which charted in the Top 40.

what's available: As *Greatest Hits* (Curb, 1991) 🎵🎵 makes clear, Thompson has a frothy, girlish voice—dubbed "itty bitty" in its time, it was perfect for pre-Beatles pop, so songs like "Norman" and "James (Hold the Ladder Steady)" have a certain adolescent sweetness. But Thompson's early 1970s solo country singles ("Candy and Roses," "Big Mable Murphy," "Never Naughty Rosie") have such cloying Dixieland arrangements it's amazing they managed to reach even the low end of the charts.

influences:
◀◀ Brenda Lee, Skeeter Davis
▶▶ Marion Worth

Brian Mansfield

THRASHER SHIVER

Formed in Nashville, TN.

Neil Thrasher (born July 13, 1965, in Birmingham, AL), vocals, guitar; Kelly Shiver (born July 19, 1963, in Savannah, TN), vocals, guitar.

The cool, bluegrassy harmonies and instrumentation of Thrasher Shiver's self-titled first album made this duo a critic's favorite, though they have yet to reach real commercial acceptance. Both men grew up around music, and got their start as songwriters. In the early 1990s they began writing together and recording demos of their songs. One of the tapes got into the hands of producer Kyle Lehning, who signed the duo to Asylum Records.

what's available: *Thrasher Shiver* (Asylum, 1996, prod. Justin Niebank, Neil Thrasher, Kelly Shiver) 🎵🎵🎵, the band's excellent debut, contains six songs written or co-written by the duo, who also co-produced the album.

influences:
◀◀ O'Kanes, Louvin Brothers

Cyndi Hoelzle

MEL TILLIS

Born Lonnie Melvin Tillis, August 8, 1932, in Tampa, FL.

Mel Tillis didn't get serious about music until he left the air force and dropped out of the University of Florida after two semesters. Then, while working odd jobs to make money, he wrote a song called "I'm Tired," which was recorded by Webb Pierce. Tillis came to Nashville in 1956 hoping to maximize his potential as a recording artist. (Although Tillis stuttered—the result of a childhood bout with malaria—his voice came through loud and clear when he sang.) Tillis cut his first record, a version of the folk classic "It Takes a Worried Man," in 1956, but industry people told Tillis he needed original material to succeed, so he penned more than 350 songs during the next six years. His writing caught the attention of other artists, and a who's who of country music recorded his songs during the late 1950s and 1960s. By the end of the 1960s, Tillis' "Detroit City" had been recorded more than 115 times (most successfully by Bobby Bare) and had sold a total of 4.5 million records. "Ruby Don't Take Your Love to Town" was also recorded by many artists, but it earned a gold record for Kenny Rogers & the First Edition. Tillis still had his sights set on a performing career, and though he recorded often for Columbia during the 1950s and 1960s, his singles weren't massive hits. He then tried at Decca, RIC and, finally, Kapp before taking Harlan Howard's "Life Turned Her That Way" to #11 in 1967. Later he scored his biggest hit of the decade with "These Lonely Hands of Mine." Meanwhile, Tillis and his band the Statesiders had become a major attraction on the country music circuit, averaging 250 dates a year. He also got a lot of national television exposure, which he parlayed into movie roles during the 1970s. Tillis' popularity increased during the 1970s, and he won the Country Music Association Entertainer of the Year award in 1976. That same year he moved to MCA and had a chart-topping single with "Good Woman Blues." He continued recording for MCA throughout the 1970s, moving to Elektra in 1979. Dur-

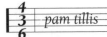

ing the 1980s Tillis also had charting singles for MCA (again), RCA, Mercury and Radio. He continues to perform frequently, and has had his own theater in Branson, Missouri.

what to buy: *The Very Best of Mel Tillis* (MCA, 1981, prod. Jimmy Bowen) 𝄞𝄞𝄞𝄞 captures the true and very best sound of Mel & the Statesiders. Cuts include "Coca-Cola Cowboy," "Charlie's Angel" and "Burning Memories."

what to buy next: *Greatest Hits* (Curb, 1991, prod. various) 𝄞𝄞𝄞𝄞 contains some original hits that aren't on every other Mel Tillis compilation.

what to avoid: *Best of Country* (Richmond, 1985) 𝄞𝄞 suffers from poor production quality. It contains some of Tillis' less popular hits, and there's a reason they weren't very popular. Give *The Great* (Hollywood/IMG, 1987) 𝄞𝄞 a wide berth for the same reasons.

the rest:
The Memory Maker (Mercury, 1995) 𝄞𝄞𝄞

worth searching for: *American Originals* (Columbia, 1990) 𝄞𝄞𝄞, one of the few places to find Tillis' early Columbia recordings.

influences:
◀◀ Bob Wills, Ray Price, Faron Young
▶▶ Pam Tillis, George Strait

Ronnie McDowell

PAM TILLIS

Born July 24, 1957, in Plant City, FL.

The daughter of singer and songwriter Mel Tillis, Pam Tillis grew up wanting to follow in her father's footsteps but not wanting to rely on his connections. During the early years of her career, she had problems establishing her own identity, experimenting with various permutations of rock and country before finally finding her niche with Arista Records in 1991. She'd previously spent five years with Nashville's Warner Bros. division, but nothing except four low-charting singles came of that. At Arista, Pam's career blossomed with fine, distinctive hits such as "Maybe It Was Memphis," "Shake the Sugar Tree" and "Cleopatra, Queen of Denial." She continued to evolve as an artist to the point where she felt comfortable including her father on her 1995 album *All of This Love*. Tillis is married to songwriter Bob DiPiero, who has co-written a number of her songs, including the 1992 single "Blue Rose Is."

what to buy: As fine a country album as any recorded by a woman during the 1990s, *Sweetheart's Dance* (Arista, 1994,

prod. Pam Tillis, Steve Fishell) 𝄞𝄞𝄞𝄞𝄞 is Tillis' artistic breakthrough. She got permission from Arista to co-produce herself, and the best songs were unlike anything else at the time—the sympathetic "Spilled Perfume," a cover of Jackie DeShannon's "When You Walk in the Room," a Diddley-beat rave-up "Mi Vida Loca (My Crazy Life)" and a waltz, "In Between Dances." Radio awarded her accordingly ("Mi Vida Loca" was her first Billboard #1), and so did her peers: This is the album that won her the 1994 Female Vocalist of the Year award from the Country Music Association.

what to buy next: All of Tillis' albums for Arista are worth having, but her Arista debut, *Put Yourself in My Place* (Arista, 1991, prod. Paul Worley, Ed Seay) 𝄞𝄞𝄞𝄞, offers her sultry signature song, "Maybe It Was Memphis," plus a bluegrass influence on songs such as "Put Yourself in My Place" and the semi-autobiographical "Melancholy Child" that would be absent on subsequent releases.

the rest:
Homeward-Looking Angel (Arista, 1992) 𝄞𝄞𝄞𝄞
The Pam Tillis Collection (Warner Bros., 1994) 𝄞𝄞𝄞
All of This Love (Arista, 1995) 𝄞𝄞𝄞𝄞
Greatest Hits (Arista, 1997) 𝄞𝄞𝄞𝄞

worth searching for: For an example of just how much Tillis' music has developed, check out her rock album *Above and Beyond the Doll of Cutey* (Elektra, 1983, prod. Jimmy Bowen, Dixie Bowen) 𝄞𝄞, which sometimes sticks its toes in the waters of synth-pop and new wave but never has the nerve to jump all the way in. It includes two songs co-written by future *Thelma and Louise* screenwriter Callie Khoury, a childhood friend of Tillis' (who was reportedly one of the inspirations for the film's characters).

influences:
◀◀ Mel Tillis, Gail Davies
▶▶ Deana Carter, Matraca Berg

Brian Mansfield

FLOYD TILLMAN

Born December 8, 1914, in Ryan, OK.

Oklahoma-born but living most of his life in Texas, Floyd Tillman has been an important figure in country, Western swing and honky-tonk music since 1933, when he joined Adolph and Emil Hofner's Western swing band. In 1935 he was a member, along with historic contemporaries Moon Mullican and Ted Daffan, of the Blue Ridge Playboys. Tillman recorded under his own name for a variety of labels during the 1930s, finally settling in with Decca in 1939. His composition "It Makes No Difference Now" was a hit for Cliff Bruner's Texas Wanderers around that time. Although an accomplished guitarist, mandolin player and banjoist, it is as a songwriter and song stylist that he has left his most indelible mark. His own hits include such World War II-era numbers as "They Took the Stars out of Heaven," "G.I. Blues," "Each Night at Nine" and "Drivin' Nails in My Coffin," as well as such enduring standards as "I Love You So Much It Hurts" (a #1 hit for Jimmy Wakely in 1949), "Slippin' Around" (popularly regarded as the first country cheatin' song) and others.

After leaving Columbia in 1954, Tillman recorded for a variety of labels, making nice records but never again having the giant hits he had enjoyed during the 1940s and 1950s. His influence, however, has been immense, both as a singer and songwriter, and his early hits have achieved classic status. As a singer, his whisky laced baritone voice, jazzy phrasing and languid, behind-the-beat approach to time have influenced many honky-tonkers who have followed in his wake. He was a charter member of the Nashville Songwriter's Hall of Fame in 1970 and was inducted into the Country Music Hall of Fame in 1984.

what to buy: *The Country Music Hall of Fame* (MCA, 1991, prod. Country Music Foundation) 🎵🎵🎵 contains Tillman's earliest hits under his own name but, with the exception of "Each Night at Nine," not his biggest, which were recorded for Columbia.

what to buy next: *Columbia Historic Edition* (Columbia, 1985, prod. various) 🎵🎵🎵🎵 contains 11 of Tillman's classic Columbia numbers, including "Slippin' Around" and "Drivin' Nails in My Coffin." For now, unavailable on CD.

worth searching for: The long out-of-print LP *The Best of Floyd Tillman* (Columbia, 1976) 🎵🎵🎵 features Tillman's original versions of 10 of his best, including the classics "I Love You So Much It Hurts," "I Gotta Have My Baby Back" and "This Cold War with You." Classic stuff.

influences:

◀◀ Adolph Hofner, Cliff Bruner

▶▶ Lefty Frizzell, Willie Nelson, Don Williams, Merle Haggard

Randy Pitts

JOHNNY TILLOTSON

Born April 20, 1939, in Jacksonville, FL.

One of the most versatile and consistent of the pre-Beatles teen-pop singers of the 1960s, Johnny Tillotson was a great

Pam Tillis **(Archive Photos)**

popularizer of country songs such as "Talk Back Trembling Lips," "Send Me the Pillow You Dream On" and "I Can't Help It (If I'm Still in Love with You)," which he turned into pop hits. The self-penned "It Keeps Right on a-Hurtin'" went Top 5 on both the pop and country charts during 1962, but 1960's "Poetry in Motion" was Tillotson's most successful pop hit, reaching #2 in 1960. Since at the time Tillotson recorded for Cadence (also home of country-pop sensations the Everly Brothers), he recorded even that song in Nashville with such musical luminaries as saxophonist Boots Randolph and pianist Floyd Cramer. The Beatles effectively ended Tillotson's run on pop radio, and he eventually turned to Las Vegas lounges. He would occasionally appear on the lower rungs of the country singles chart during the late 1960s, 1970s and 1980s. Unlike many other singers of his era whose quality of material drops off immediately after the hits, Tillotson's albums reflect a deep love and understanding of good songs.

what to buy: *Poetry in Motion: The Best of Johnny Tillotson* (Varese Sarabande, 1995, prod. Archie Bleyer, Paul Tannen) 🎵🎵🎵 contains all of Tillotson's biggest hits: "Poetry in Motion,"

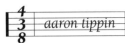
for sure, as well as the crossover singles "It Keeps Right on a-Hurtin'" and "Send Me the Pillow You Dream On." Though Tillotson's remembered on oldies radio for one or two songs, this collection shows a singer versatile enough to sing teeny-bop fluff such as "(Wait til' You See My) Gidget," but still turn in credible renditions of "Funny How Time Slips Away" or "Heartaches by the Number."

what to buy next: Tillotson had the good sense to get the rights to his master recordings, so his material is much more readily available than that of most other singers with similar successes during the early 1960s. The British label Ace has released a number of CD's containing two original Tillotson albums. The songs and performances are of consistent quality, but *Talk Back Trembling Lips/The Tillotson Touch* (Ace, 1963, 1964/1991, prod. Paul Tannen) 🎵🎵🎵 contains quite a few Nashville standards, including "Talk Back Trembling Lips," "I Can't Stop Loving You," "Then You Can Tell Me Goodbye" and "Cold, Cold Heart."

the rest:
The Fabulous Johnny Tillotson (Ace) 🎵🎵🎵
She Understands Me/That's My Style (Ace, 1964) 🎵🎵🎵
You're the Reason: Best of the MGM Years (Ace) 🎵🎵🎵
All His Early Hits: And More!!! (Ace) 🎵🎵🎵

influences:
◀◀ Pat Boone, Jimmie Rodgers
▶▶ Del Shannon

Brian Mansfield

AARON TIPPIN

Born July 3, 1958, in Pensacola, FL.

Aaron Tippin is an anomaly in modern country: A successful singer whose nasal twang actually recalls the style of Hank Williams rather than that of George Jones or Merle Haggard. A bodybuilder who specializes in blue-collar material, Tippin had his songs cut by Charley Pride before he started recording himself. His first single, "You've Got to Stand for Something" had the good fortune to come out about the same time the first fighter jets entered Iraqi air space in the Gulf War. Hardly a political commentator, Tippin's later singles have more often dealt with personal integrity and home-grown values. He gets into trouble when he tries to get metaphorical and comes up with titles like "Honky Tonk Superman" and "Working Man's Ph.D.," but he's built a respectable catalog of hits. His father was a jet-

pilot instructor, and Tippin has channeled that upbringing into becoming a collector of all sorts of large machinery.

what to buy: Tippin's records have always been a hard sell at radio, and he'd slacked off some until he released *Lookin' Back at Myself* (RCA, 1995, prod. Steve Gibson) 🎵🎵🎵. That album's change in producers (from Scott Hendricks to the more tradition-minded Steve Gibson) served him well. For the first time, Tippin's strongest material wasn't his ditties. Even though he didn't write it—and reportedly was reluctant to record it—the darkly obsessive "That's as Close as I'll Get to Loving You" turned into one of his biggest records.

what to buy next: Usually best-of compilations with a 9:4 hits-to-new-song ratio aren't a very good idea, but *Greatest Hits and then Some* (RCA, 1997, prod. various) 🎵🎵🎵 shows Tippin approaching his artistic peak. The four new songs, including "If Only Your Eyes Could Lie" and "That's What Happens When I Hold You," really are some of the best songs of his career, and with no silly filler holding them back, his hits shine.

what to avoid: "Working Man's Ph.D." is one thing: If nothing else, it's got a heckuva groove. But in country there's a fine line between clever and cornpone, and *Call of the Wild* (RCA, 1993, prod. Scott Hendricks) 🎵🎵 dishes out the latter in big, mushy spoonfuls. Did somebody really think "Honky-Tonk Superman" was a good idea for a song?

the rest:
You've Got to Stand for Something (RCA, 1991) 🎵🎵🎵
Read between the Lines (RCA, 1992) 🎵🎵
Tool Box (RCA, 1996) 🎵🎵🎵

influences:
◀◀ Hank Williams, Charley Pride
▶▶ Marty Brown, Royal Wade Kimes

Brian Mansfield

TONY TOLIVER

Born July 4, 1956, in Richards, TX.

The rare country singer who's a piano player instead of a guitarist, Tony Toliver grew up singing in a family gospel group, the influence of which still shows in his records. After moving to Nashville, he became a bandleader at the Nashville Palace (where a dishwasher named Randy Travis would sing during Toliver's breaks). Later he became Dottie West's bandleader. He held that job until her death, then began fronting his own band.

what's available: Both of Toliver's albums, *Tony Toliver* (Curb/Capitol, 1991, prod. James Stroud) ♫♫♫ and *Half Saint Half Sinner* (Curb/Rising Tide, 1996) ♫♫♫, are solid country records, though neither fared well in the marketplace. Toliver's music sounds like it's rooted in the country of the 1970s and early 1980s, partly because of his influences, partly because of the dominance of piano in his mix. As the title of his second record suggests, his songs have a strong spiritual presence; the highlight of *Tony Toliver* is "Mamaw's Song," which features his 86-year-old grandmother singing "Love Lifted Me."

influences:

◄◄ Dottie West, Ronnie Milsap

►► Rick Trevino

Brian Mansfield

THE TRACTORS

Formed 1990, in Tulsa, OK.

Steve Ripley, guitar, drums, vocals; Walt Richmond, keyboards, accordion, drums, horns, vocals; Ron Getman, guitar, mandolin, vocals; Casey Van Beek, bass, vocals; Jamie Oldaker, drums, percussion.

Perhaps more than most outfits, the Tractors are a band that has been fully road-tested, though they all paid their dues separately rather than as a unit. Steve Ripley played with Leon Russell, J.J. Cale and Bob Dylan, worked as a producer and built a widely used custom guitar. Walt Richmond toured with Bonnie Raitt; Ron Getman with Janis Ian and Leonard Cohen; Casey Van Beek with Linda Ronstadt and the Righteous Brothers; and Jamie Oldaker's drums saw Eric Clapton through his Okie period during the late 1970s. With a combination like that, it's no surprise the Tractors are well-versed in all kinds of music, but when they get together, they play Oklahoma roadhouse boogie with a fervor so real you can practically see the chicken wire stretched across the front of the bandstand. Amid the often phony glitz of Nashville, the Tractors come off as genuine salt-of-the-earth types. Their music is ragged, but decidedly right.

what to buy: On *The Tractors* (Arista, 1994, prod. Steve Ripley, Walt Richmond) ♫♫♫♫, the group goes a little over the top in trying to write a populist anthem. Nearly half of the album's dozen tracks address economic hardship, and three of them come complete with genuine fist-waving titles—"I've Had Enough," "The Blue Collar Rock" and "The Little Man," the latter of which sports platitudinous lyrics about putting bankers on John Deere tractors and politicians out in the street with the homeless. The Tractors fare far better when they stick to such boogie-woogie

FIVE FOR MY FANS

TONY TOLIVER

Ronnie Milsap
Live (RCA)

Ronnie Milsap
Stranger Things Have Happened (RCA)

Steve Wariner
Steve Wariner (RCA)

Elton John
Greatest Hits (MCA)

Charlie Rich
Behind Closed Doors (Epic)

roadhouse fare as "Baby Likes to Rock It" and the boot-scootin' "Tulsa Shuffle." Guests on the album include Bonnie Raitt, J.J. Cale, James Burton, Ry Cooder and Leon Russell.

the rest:

Have Yourself a Tractors Christmas (Arista, 1995) ♫♫♫♪

influences:

◄◄ J.J. Cale, John Mellencamp

Daniel Durchholz

THE TRADITIONAL GRASS

Formed 1983, in Middletown, OH. Disbanded 1995.

Joe Mullins, banjo, tenor vocals; Paul Mullins, fiddle; Mark Rader, guitar, lead vocals; Gerald Evans, mandolin, fiddle, baritone vocals; Mike Clevenger, bass.

After nearly a decade of relative obscurity, the Traditional Grass created a bit of a furor in the bluegrass world with several fine recordings of traditional bluegrass during the early 1990s. Unfortunately it was short-lived, and the group disbanded three years after its debut label release.

what to buy: Half of the generous 16 cuts on *10th Anniversary Collection* (Rebel, 1994, prod. Traditional Grass) ???? are originals, including the haunting gospel number "Lazarus." Eight covers, including classics such as "Weary Lonesome Blues" and "You Are My Flower," round out an album that manages to be both original and fresh while never losing the band's hard traditional sound.

what to buy next: *I Believe in the Old Time Way* (Rebel, 1993, prod. Traditional Grass) ???? is an all-gospel release with strong harmony vocals front and center. The instrumental work is tasteful, nicely underscoring the vocals while providing the occasional driving break.

the rest:
Howdy Neighbor, Howdy (Rebel, 1992) ????
Songs of Life and Life (Rebel, 1995) ????

solo outings:
Gerald Evans & Joe Mullins:
Just a Five-String and a Fiddle (Rebel, 1995) ???

influences:
◀◀ Stanley Brothers, Boys from Indiana
▶▶ Warrior River Boys, Del McCoury Band

Douglas Fulmer

MERLE TRAVIS

Born November 29, 1917, in Rosewood, KY. Died October 20, 1983, in Tahlequah, OK.

Beginning his career shortly after the Second World War, guitarist Merle Travis wrote, recorded and had covered some of the most enduring (and sometimes amusing) songs in the country collection, among them "Smoke, Smoke, Smoke That Cigarette," "So Round, So Firm, So Fully Packed" and "Dark as a Dungeon." His most memorable tune, "16 Tons," became a huge hit for Tennessee Ernie Ford and perhaps one of the biggest country standards of the century. That would be enough for anyone's resume, but Travis' ultimate claim to fame is his singular guitar fingerpicking style, known appropriately as "Travis picking," which he developed with a nod to Everly Brothers pop Ike Everly and which has been used far and wide by folkies and rockers alike for the past 50 years.

what to buy: *Best of Merle Travis* (Rhino, 1990, prod. James Austin) ???? is a 20-year collection of prime Travis, featuring the above-mentioned gems in addition to other blatantly misogynist and totally memorable entries like "I Like My Chicken Fryin' Size," "Fat Gal" and "Divorce Me C.O.D."

what to buy next: *Folk Songs of the Hills* (Capitol, 1947/1996, prod. Lee Gillette) ???? is the most worthwhile set of Travis songs recorded during the late 1940s, including his popular blue-collar ode "I Am a Pilgrim" plus his own rendition of the Hall of Famer "16 Tons."

the rest:
(With Joe Maphis) *Country Guitar Giants* (CMH, 1979) ???
Guitar Standards (CMH, 1980) ???
Light Singin' & Heavy Pickin' (CMH, 1980) ???
Travis Pickin' (CMH, 1981) ???
(With Mac Wiseman) *Clayton McMichen Story* (CMH, 1982) ???
(With Grandpa Jones) *Merle and Grandpa's Farm and Home* (CMH, 1985) ???
Rough Rowdy and Blue (CMH, 1986) ???
Merle Travis Story (CMH, 1989) ???
Guitar Rags and a Too Far Past (Bear Family, 1992) ????
Guitar Retrospective (CMH, 1995) ????
Walkin' the Strings (Capitol, 1996) ???

influences:
◀◀ Ike Everly
▶▶ Everly Brothers, Chet Atkins, Bob Dylan, David Bromberg

David Simons

RANDY TRAVIS

Born Randy Bruce Traywick, May 4, 1959, in Marshville, NC.

A reformed juvenile delinquent, Randy Travis has been a model of gentleman charm and aw-shucks civility during his reign as the soft-spoken king of the new-traditionalist movement. As a result, he's lost some of his marquee power to such brasher, more pop-oriented chart warriors as Garth Brooks and John Michael Montgomery. But since rescuing country music from its post-*Urban Cowboy* doldrums with 1986's *Storms of Life*, Travis has quietly upheld the legacy of Lefty Frizzell and George Jones, singers whose commanding delivery and distinctive phrasing were natural instincts, not polished techniques. Armed with a warm, comforting baritone, Travis knows how to hold back and avoid overselling a punchline like "On one hand, I could stay and be your lovin' man/But the reason I must go is on the other hand," just as he knows how to turn "amen" into a goosebump-raising four-syllable word without resorting to gospel pyrotechnics. Despite his diminishing sales clout—which peaked with a 1987–89 stretch of seven straight #1 singles—Travis continues making consistently commendable albums with help from such outside writers as Troy Seals, David Lynn Jones, Kevin Welch, Hugh Prestwood, Trey Bruce and Craig Wiseman. Some might compare such recent efforts as *This Is Me* and *Full Circle* with predecessors like *Storms of Life* and *Old 8 x 10* and charge that Travis is stuck in a rut. Others would say he's simply sticking to his guns.

what to buy: Remarkably timeless in both sound and feel, *Storms of Life* (Warner Bros., 1986, prod. Kyle Lehning, Keith Stegall) ♫♫♫♫♫ is a masterpiece of taste and restraint. The acoustic-based arrangements complement Travis' understated but authoritative singing, and the material—including "Diggin' Up Bones," "On the Other Hand" and "1982"—is unbeatable. The multiplatinum followup, *Always and Forever* (Warner Bros., 1987, prod. Kyle Lehning) ♫♫♫♫, is a little soft around the edges. But if you need proof of the calming charms of Travis' voice, listen to how he makes "What'll You Do About Me?" sound more like a harmless novelty song about a persistent lover than a scary narrative about a stalker ("What in the world are you plannin' to do/When a man comes over just to visit you/And I'm on the porch with a 2-by-2?").

what to buy next: The aptly titled *Full Circle* (Warner Bros., 1996, prod. Kyle Lehning) ♫♫♫♫ is a revelatory return to form as Travis rocks out ("Highway Junkie," "If It Ain't One Thing, It's Another"), breathes life into Roger Miller's dusty "King of the Road" and unearths two should-have-been-classics: Skip Ewing's "Ants on a Log" and Mark Knopfler's soulful "Are We in Trouble Now."

what to avoid: Recording "Happy Trails" on 1991's *Roy Rogers Tribute* was one thing, but *Wind in the Wire* (Warner Bros., 1993, prod. Steve Gibson) ♫♫ is a cakewalk collection of old-fashioned singing-cowboy odes crassly tied to a TV special co-starring Burt Reynolds and Chuck Norris.

the rest:
Old 8 x 10 (Warner Bros., 1988) ♫♫♫♫
No Holdin' Back (Warner Bros., 1989) ♫♫♫
An Old-Time Christmas (Warner Bros., 1989) ♫♫♫
Heroes and Friends (Warner Bros., 1990) ♫♫♫
High Lonesome (Warner Bros., 1991) ♫♫♫
Greatest Hits Volume 1 (Warner Bros., 1992) ♫♫♫♫
Greatest Hits Volume 2 (Warner Bros., 1992) ♫♫♫♫
This Is Me (Warner Bros., 1994) ♫♫♫

Randy Travis (© Ken Settle)

worth searching for: Before he signed with Warner Bros., Travis grazed the country charts with the Joe Stampley-produced single, "She's My Woman" (Paula, 1979), recorded under his real name.

influences:

⏪ Lefty Frizzell, Merle Haggard, George Jones, John Anderson

⏩ Ricky Van Shelton, Clint Black, John Michael Montgomery

David Okamoto

RICK TREVINO

Born May 16, 1971, in Austin, TX.

In the flood of so-called "hat acts" of the early 1990s, Trevino had an extra hook: He sang bilingually, producing his first album in both English and Spanish. A singer who melds the starched Texas cowboy approach of George Strait with the more rock-derived presentation of Garth Brooks, Trevino is also a classically trained pianist who has performed with Van Cliburn.

what to buy: *Rick Trevino* (Columbia, 1994, prod. Steve Buckingham) ♫♫♫ is an accomplished debut album, featuring the hits "Just Enough Rope," "She Can't Say I Didn't Cry" and "Honky Tonk Crowd," plus a bilingual version of "Just Enough Rope," and the all-Spanish "Un Momento Alla."

what to buy next: *Dos Mundos* (Columbia, 1993, prod. Steve Buckingham) ♫♫♫ includes Spanish versions of several songs on *Rick Trevino*.

the rest:
Looking for the Light (Columbia, 1995) ♫♫♫
Learning As You Go (Columbia, 1996) ♫♫♫

influences:
◀◀ George Strait, Johnny Rodriguez

Bill Hobbs

TONY TRISCHKA

Born January 16, 1949, in Syracuse, NY.

An innovative and influential banjo player, Tony Trischka was one of the first to play jazz on the five-string. In addition to working as a solo artist he's played with Country Cooking, Breakfast Special, Skyline, the Big Dogs and Psychograss and is currently putting together the Tony Trischka Band. Trischka was Bela Fleck's first banjo instructor.

what to buy: *Dust on the Needle* (Rounder, 1987) ♫♫♫♫, a collection of the best from Trischka's first six albums, documents his early experiments with jazz fusion.

what to buy next: Virtually a history of the banjo, *World Turning* (Rounder, 1993) ♫♫♫ traces the instrument's developments from its roots in Africa up though its most modern stylings.

the rest:
Banjoland (Rounder, 1978) ♫♫♫
Robot Plane Flys Over Arkansas (Rounder, 1982) ♫♫♫
Hill Country (Rounder, 1985) ♫♫♫
(With Tom Adams & Tony Furtado) *Rounder Banjo Extravaganza* (Rounder, 1988) ♫♫♫
(With Bela Fleck) *Solo Banjo Works* (Rounder, 1992) ♫♫♫
(With Joe Ayers, Clarke Buehling, Bob Carlin, Rob Flesher and Bob Winans) *Minstrel Banjo Style* (Rounder, 1994)
Glory Shone Around: A Christmas Carol (Rounder, 1995) ♫♫♫

worth searching for: *Fiddle Tunes for Banjo* (Rounder, 1981) features some interesting picking with fellow banjoists Bill Keith & Bela Fleck.

influences:
◀◀ Bill Keith, Country Cooking
▶▶ Bela Fleck, Tony Furtado, Alison Brown

Douglas Fulmer

TRAVIS TRITT

Born February 9, 1963, in Marietta, GA.

Since he refused to wear a hat and hailed from the Deep South, Travis Tritt was pegged as an ornery honky-tonk rebel when he broke onto the country charts in 1989. But what he really offered was a cunning bridge connecting the tradional values of Alan Jackson, the barnstorming spirit of Lynyrd Skynyrd and the hard-drinking, hard-rocking bluster of Hank Williams Jr.—only where Bocephus would lapse into sloppy cynicism, Tritt exuded Southern hospitality and stubborn pride ("I've been called hillbilly, I've been called a redneck, too/But I ain't backwards, dumb or poor/I'm just red, white and blue"). "The Whiskey Ain't Workin'," his first duet with Marty Stuart, and the sardonic "Here's a Quarter (Call Someone Who Cares)," made him a bona fide star, and Tritt was elevated to near-mythical status in 1992 when an off-the-cuff but on-the-money critique of Billy Ray Cyrus' overnight success got him lionized as an outspoken hero who would suffer no phonies. Tritt reveled in his newfound notoriety—his "No Hats" tour with Stuart seemed designed to ruffle Garth Brooks' feathers, and albums like *T-R-O-U-B-L-E* were more about noise than nuance. But *The Restless Kind*, a splendid 1996 collaboration with producer Don Was, put him back in touch with his country roots, focusing his talents and throttling back on the over-the-top blue-collar anthems that were starting to sound as empty as a church on Super Bowl Sunday.

what to buy: *It's All About to Change* (Warner Bros., 1991, prod. Gregg Brown) ♫♫♫ is Tritt's foot-stomping, keg-tapping breakthrough, highlighted by the infamous "Here's a Quarter (Call Someone Who Cares)," "If Hell Had a Jukebox" and a scorching Little Feat-backed rocker called "Bible Belt."

Travis Tritt (© Ken Settle)

what to buy next: Anchored by acoustic instruments, *The Restless Kind* (Warner Bros., 1996, prod. Travis Tritt, Don Was) ♪♪♪♪ still raises a roadhouse ruckus on the Atlanta Rhythm Section's Skynyrd-like "Back up Against the Wall" and "Double Trouble," a bluesy duet with Marty Stuart. But even more impressive are such dusty ballads as "Helping Me Get Over You" (with Lari White) and "Where Corn Don't Grow" (previously recorded by Waylon Jennings), which demonstrate his improving skills as a singer.

what to avoid: From its muscle-man sleeve photos to its Elvis Presley title track to the eight-minute Buddy Guy jam that closes the album, *T-R-O-U-B-L-E* (Warner Bros., 1992, prod. Gregg Brown) ♪♪ is all swagger and no sweat. When you have to hire Kostas to write your blue-collar anthem ("Lord Have Mercy on the Working Man"), you know you're in trouble.

the rest:

Country Club (Warner Bros., 1990) ♪♪♪
A Travis Tritt Christmas (Warner Dros., 1992) ♪♪♪
10 Feet Tall and Bulletproof (Warner Bros., 1994) ♪♪♪
Greatest Hits from the Beginning (Warner Bros., 1995) ♪♪♪♪

worth searching for: Before signing with Warner Bros., Tritt released an independent album called *Proud of the Country* (Copperhill, 1987) featuring "Don't Put Us Down," "Staying Power" and "Get a Little Rowdy."

influences:

◀◀ George Jones, Lynyrd Skynyrd, Allman Brothers, Hank Williams Jr.

▶▶ Marty Stuart, Kentucky HeadHunters, Tractors

David Okamoto

ERNEST TUBB

Born Ernest Dale Tubb, February 9, 1914, in Crisp, TX. Died September 6, 1984.

Ernest Tubb quite simply defined the term "hardcore honky-tonk." With his paint-peeling voice, his willingness to help other aspiring entertainers and his inescapable connection to the Jimmie Rodgers tradition, "E.T." cut a wide path across country music over his 50-year career. Tubb worked on radio in both San Antonio and Fort Worth during the mid-1930s and began his recording career with Bluebird in 1936. A visit with the widow of Jimmie Rodgers in 1935 was an important one for Tubb. Carrie Rodgers was so taken with E.T.'s devotion to her late husband's music that she helped secure a pair of recording dates with RCA for him. That year also brought him his first

son, Justin, who would later have a successful career of his own in country music. Next came a move to Decca Records in 1940, but little excitement was generated by initial releases, until the recording of his best-known tune, "Walkin' the Floor Over You." Tubb soon appeared in the film *Hollywood Barn Dance*, and made his way to Nashville in 1942, to appear on the Grand Ole Opry, earning three encores during his debut. Tubb's first Texas Troubadours took the stage with him in 1943, by which time he was recording hit after hit. Soon thereafter came the debut of the *Midnight Jamboree*, the radio show that followed the Opry on WSM, and originated from the recently opened Ernest Tubb Record Shop. Each year for the next decade there were at least two and, more often than not, several E.T. records in the Top 10, including duets with the Andrews Sisters and comic records with Decca labelmate Red Foley. Later collaborations with the Wilburn Brothers and Loretta Lynn also scored hits for Tubb. During the late 1950s, Tubb was hitting the charts less frequently, and his popularity started to wane. The 1963 hit "Thanks a Lot" was Tubb's final entry in the Top 10, although he continued to tour and record over the next two decades. Former Texas Troubadours who went on to successful solo careers include Jack Greene and Cal Smith. Also worth noting is Tubb's "Singing Bus Driver" during the early 1960s, Johnny Wiggins, who is the father of Mercury Records artist Audrey Wiggins. Tubb helped Audrey make her debut on the Grand Ole Opry at 12 years old, a full four years before meeting the age requirement of 16. Along the way Ernest Tubb was an ally to countless artists either seeking their big break or just a little advice. In 1984 he died in a Nashville hospital, his legend and his legacy by that time well-documented and well-preserved.

what's available: For the most complete collection, the best bet is *Country Music Hall of Fame* (MCA, 1991, prod. Country Music Foundation) ♪♪♪♪. *Ernest Tubb & Guests: Collection* (Step One, 1989) ♪♪♪ is a two-CD set, recorded mainly in 1978 and 1979, overdubbing Tubb's vocals with more than two dozen fans and friends, like Johnny Cash, George Jones and Marty Robbins. It's not all smooth sailing, but it's basically a tribute album anyway.

worth searching for: The three collections *Let's Say Goodbye Like We Said Hello* (Bear Family, 1994) ♪♪♪♪, *The Yellow Rose of Texas* (Bear Family, 1993) ♪♪♪♪, and *Walking the Floor Over You* (Bear Family), with more than a dozen discs between them, are much more than anyone, save for completists and researchers, would ever need. But they do well at telling most of the Ernest Tubb story on record. For a peek into an important aspect of Tubb's career, that of traveling Troubadour, you'll need to be on the lookout for the recently deleted *Live 1965* (1989, Rhino) ♪♪♪♪.

influences:
◀◀ Jimmie Rodgers, Hank Thompson
▶▶ Webb Pierce, Hank Snow

Stephen L. Betts

JUSTIN TUBB

Born Justin Wayne Tubb, August 20, 1935, in San Antonio, TX.

The Hall-of-Fame career of his father, Ernest Tubb, has always obscured the fact that Justin Tubb was a decent country singer in his own right. Though he was most popular during the mid-1950s, just as his father's popularity was beginning to slip, his five Top 40 hits cover more than a decade. He had his most successful recordings for Decca (his father's label), RCA and its subsidiary Groove, but he also recorded for Starday and other, smaller labels. He had more success as a songwriter, penning "Lonesome 7-7203" for Hawkshaw Hawkins, "Keeping Up with the Joneses" for Faron Young and Margie Singleton and "Love Is No Excuse" for Jim Reeves and Dottie West. A DJ during the early 1950s, he now manages the post-Opry *Ernest Tubb Midnight Jamboree Radio Show*.

what's available: Tubb may be only a minor artist, but he doesn't deserve *Star of the Grand Ole Opry* (Starday, 1987) ♪. The master's a mess, there are no liner notes, and the track listing on the jacket's not even right. The recordings, such as they are, show Tubb as a straight-ahead honky-tonk singer and include re-recordings of "Looking Back to See" and "I've Gotta Go Get My Baby," two of his biggest 1950s hits for Decca. There's a German import called *Rock It Down to My House* (Bear Family) that couldn't help but be better.

influences:
◀◀ Ernest Tubb

Brian Mansfield

TANYA TUCKER

Born Tanya Denise Tucker, October 10, 1958, in Seminole, TX.

Despite her nearly 25 years as a recording artist, sassy Texas native Tanya Tucker is younger than Reba McEntire and only a few years older than Garth Brooks, Alan Jackson and a slew of the other artists dominating country music today. She is a survivor, to say the least. Tucker broke into the big time at

the ripe old age of 14 with the smash hit "Delta Dawn" and has weathered various images, record companies, producers, fickle audiences, abuse problems and even more difficult lovers, yet she's seldom had a dry spell in her career. Remarkably, Tucker's career enjoyed an upswing during the 1990s, as other trendier acts competed for limited space on the airwaves. She has evolved from the vulnerable little girl with the big voice of her adolescent days to a passionate singer with a penchant for songs about strong women who can handle the pressure. LeAnn Rimes couldn't wish for a better role model.

what to buy: Tucker's return to the top of the charts during the 1990s was fueled by solid, back-to-back albums that showcased her powerful, emotionally supple voice and a smart song selection. Together, *What Do I Do with Me* (Liberty, 1991, prod. Jerry Crutchfield) ♪♪♪ and *Can't Run from Yourself* (Liberty, 1992, prod. Jerry Crutchfield) ♪♪♪ represent her finest one-two punch in years.

what to buy next: Like so many country veterans, Tucker has had tons of hits, but she's recorded them for various labels, all of whom have packaged them into hits collections when she's moved on to the competition. There are hits albums that correspond with just about every phase of her storied career, but the box set *Tanya Tucker* (Liberty, 1994, comp. prod. Jerry Crutchfield, John Allen) ♪♪♪♪ is the most exhaustive. Nearly 60 songs are jammed onto its four discs, including signature hits such as "Delta Dawn," "San Antonio Stroll," "It's a Cowboy Lovin' Night," "Call Me" and the more recent "Down to My Last Teardrop" and "Two Sparrows in a Hurricane," which helped Tanya earn the female vocalist award from the Country Music Association in 1992.

what to avoid: *Greatest Hits* (Columbia, 1975, prod. Billy Sherrill) ♪♪ is a thin and premature set that only seems more superfluous as time goes on.

the rest:
Lizzie and the Rain Man (MCA Special Products, 1975) ♪♪♪
Greatest Hits (MCA, 1978) ♪♪
The Best of Tanya Tucker (MCA, 1982) ♪♪
Live (MCA Special Products, 1982) ♪♪
Girls Like Me (Liberty, 1986) ♪♪♪
Love Me Like You Used To (Liberty, 1987) ♪♪
Strong Enough to Bend (Liberty, 1988) ♪♪♪
Greatest Hits (Liberty, 1990) ♪♪
Tennessee Woman (Liberty, 1990) ♪♪♪
Greatest Country Hits (Curb, 1991) ♪♪♪

4/4/6 *shania twain*

Tanya Tucker (© Ken Settle)

The Tanya Tucker Collection (MCA, 1992) 𝄞𝄞𝄞
Greatest Hits 1990–1992 (Liberty, 1993) 𝄞𝄞𝄞
Soon (Liberty, 1993) 𝄞𝄞𝄞
Fire to Fire (Liberty, 1995) 𝄞𝄞𝄞
Love Songs (Capitol, 1996) 𝄞𝄞𝄞
Complicated (Capitol, 1997) 𝄞𝄞𝄞

influences:
◀◀ Connie Smith, Elvis Presley, George Jones
▶▶ LeAnn Rimes, Mandy Barnett

Doug Pullen

SHANIA TWAIN

Born August 28, 1965, in Windsor, Ontario, Canada.

What a difference a producer/cowriter/husband makes. Before Shania Twain hooked up with Robert John "Mutt" Lange—who co-wrote, then produced her breakthrough album *The Woman in Me* (and in the process, fell in love with and married her)— she seemed headed for a career as a garden-variety female country singer, lovely of voice and visage but unspectacular in almost every other way. Lange, who previously was known as the producer of such 1980s arena-rock acts as Def Leppard, Bryan Adams and the Cars, brought out the best in Twain, both in terms of the material they co-wrote and the pop/rock sheen he lent the album via his production. The staggering success of the album marked the final stage of the mainstreaming of country music that began during the 1980s with rock-inspired acts like Garth Brooks. For better or worse, things will never be the same.

what to buy: Beyond its obvious value as the country music success story of the decade, *The Woman in Me* (Mercury, 1995, prod. Robert John "Mutt" Lange) 𝄞𝄞𝄞𝄞 actually marks a quantum artistic leap forward for Twain, who co-wrote the album's dozen songs with Lange and delivers them with a confidence that is almost completely absent on its predecessor. Especially affecting is the sweet, seductive drawl Twain has developed for her ballads like "Home Ain't Where His Heart Is (Anymore)" and "The Woman in Me (Needs the Man in You)." The album also presents Twain as the prototype of the 1990s Nashville woman on the assertive "Any Man of Mine" and "(If You're Not in It for Love) I'm Outta Here," which combine the lyrical moxie of, say, Loretta Lynn's "Fist City" with Lange's thunderdome production. The album, which won the 1996 Grammy for best country album, is a triumph on nearly every level.

the rest:
Shania Twain (Mercury, 1993) 𝄞𝄞𝄞

worth searching for: The single version of "God Bless the Child" (Mercury, 1996, prod. Robert John "Mutt" Lange) 𝄞𝄞𝄞𝄞 gussies up the a cappella rendering found on *The Woman in Me* with a gospelish backing track and a choir. Beautiful sentiment, beautiful song.

influences:
◀◀ Loretta Lynn, Dolly Parton, Juice Newton, Bryan Adams
▶▶ Mindy McCready, Regina Regina

Daniel Durchholz

TWISTER ALLEY

Formed c. 1986, in Paragould, AR. Disbanded 1995.

Shellee Morris, vocals; Amy Hitt, guitar, vocals; Steve Goins, guitar; Kevin King, drums; Randy Loyd, bass (1987–95); Lance Blythe, guitar (1990–95).

Fronted by two female singers, Twister Alley signed to Mercury in 1992. The group released one album, which spawned a moderate radio and video hit with "Dance" in 1993. After splitting up in 1995, Hitt and Morris remained in Nashville, Hitt to write songs and Morris to raise a family. The rest of the group returned to Arkansas to continue club work.

what's available: Although it veers toward country bubblegum in places, *Twister Alley* (Mercury, 1993, prod. Mike Lawler, Harold Shedd) ☪☪ is a spunky mix of two-step shuffle and out-and-out rockers, highlighted by Morris' soulful vocals.

influences:

◄◄ k.d. lang, Highway 101, Linda Ronstadt

►► Faith Hill, Martina McBride

Bob Cannon

CONWAY TWITTY

Born Harold Lloyd Jenkins, September 1, 1933, in Friars Point, MS. Died June 5, 1993, in Springfield, MO.

Conway Twitty was the most romantic, sensual-sounding singer in the annals of country music, but it took awhile for him to discover and refine his style. As a teenager, Harold Jenkins sang the songs of Roy Acuff, Bill Monroe and Eddy Arnold over KFFA (Helena, Arkansas) with the Arkansas Cotton Choppers and the Phillips County Ramblers, and was exposed to the sounds of the Delta blues. He was all set to play minor league baseball for the Philadelphia Phillies after his discharge from the army, but then he heard "Mystery Train" by Elvis Presley, and it changed his life. Jenkins moved to Memphis, formed a band and began hanging around Sun Records. While there, he wrote "Rockhouse" for Roy Orbison and recorded several tracks that Sam Phillips chose not to release. A deal with Mercury Records prompted Jenkins to change his name to the attention-grabbing Conway Twitty (from points on a map marking Conway, Arkansas, and Twitty, Texas). Another name he considered: Kane Tuckett.

Twitty's first Mercury single "I Need Your Lovin'" (1957), was rockabilly pop replete with Presleyesque vocals and Buddy Holly hiccups. The record stalled at #93 on the charts, and Mercury dropped him after several other singles stiffed. During a subsequent gig in Canada, Twitty signed with MGM Records and co-wrote the smash pop hit "It's Only Make-Believe" (1958), featuring the Brook Benton-style throaty growl that became his trademark. Twitty intentionally tried to sound like Elvis Presley, and his biggest hits came during Presley's stay in the army. Yet there was a maturity and low blues range in a few of Twitty's records that wouldn't appear in Presley's work for years to come. In 1960 Twitty appeared in three low-budget movies: *Platinum High School, College Confidential* and *Sex Kittens Go to College.* Considered camp classics today, Twitty found pride in having speaking parts in addition to providing the music. The rockin' "Danny Boy" (1959) and the brooding "Lonely Blue Boy" (1960) reached the pop Top 10, but Twitty's subsequent MGM releases sputtered in the middle to lower regions of the Top 40 until they stopped coming altogether in 1961. At that point, Twitty begged his MGM producer Jim Vienneau to let him record some of the country songs he had been writing, but the label turned him down.

Twitty's big country music break came when songwriter Harlan Howard played one of his demo tapes for Decca Records producer Owen Bradley, who was mightily impressed. Twitty's first six Decca releases fared poorly, but in 1968 "The Image of Me" reached the Top Five, and "The Next in Line" became his first #1 country record. Twitty's career really picked up momentum in 1970 when he wrote and recorded the classic "Hello Darlin'," which not only hit #1 on the country charts but received significant airplay on pop stations as well. In 1971 Twitty recorded his first duet with Loretta Lynn—"After the Fire Is Gone"—and it too hit #1. Twitty's amazing chart success during the 1970s was fueled by solid production values, vigorous promotion and great songwriting, most of which Twitty did himself. During this time he also crystallized his recording persona as the romantic singer who really understood women; in 1973 his erotic rendering of "You've Never Been This Far Before" evoked a storm of controversy from critics who labeled the record "porno-country," while Twitty's core audience of housewives loved it. He released an even hotter record in 1974, "I See the Want To in Your Eyes."

By the 1980s Twitty had stopped writing, but he still scored #1 hits with sensual covers of "Slow Hand" and "The Rose." His chart successes had slowed at the time an abdominal aneurysm ended his life, but Twitty had planned to revitalize his career by selling off his many business interests and concentrating full-time on writing and recording. During the course of his career, Twitty recorded more than 50 #1 hits, 17 of which he wrote himself. He was country music's most successful singer/songwriter, and modern country radio seems empty without him.

what to buy: *The Conway Twitty Collection* (MCA, 1994, prod. various) ☪☪☪☪ is a tremendous double-CD set of hits and previously unreleased demos. Also worthwhile are the budget collections *Greatest Hits Volume 1* (MCA, 1972, prod. Owen Bradley) ☪☪☪, *Greatest Hits Volume 2* (MCA, 1976, prod. Owen Bradley) ☪☪☪☪ and *Greatest Hits Volume 3* (MCA, 1990, prod.

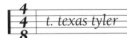
various) 🎵🎵🎵, as well as *Number Ones/The Warner Brothers Years* (Warners, 1993, prod. various) 🎵🎵🎵.

what to buy next: Though many tracks are larded with male choruses and burping saxophones, *Rockin' Conway—The MGM Years* (Mercury, 1993, prod. Jim Vienneau) 🎵🎵🎵 is worth it just to hear Twitty occasionally rock like a true Bop Cat.

what to avoid: *Super Hits Volume 2* (Epic, 1995, prod. various) 🎵🎵 contains some needless country remakes of Twitty's MGM material.

the rest:

Hello Darlin' (MCA, 1970) 🎵🎵🎵🎵
Conway Twitty (MCA, 1970) 🎵🎵🎵
(With Loretta Lynn) *Lead Me On* (MCA, 1971) 🎵🎵🎵
The Very Best of Conway Twitty (MCA, 1978) 🎵🎵🎵🎵🎵
Borderline (MCA, 1978) 🎵🎵🎵
Very Best of Conway Twitty & Loretta Lynn (MCA, 1979) 🎵🎵🎵🎵🎵
House on Old Lonesome Road (MCA, 1981) 🎵🎵🎵
A Bridge That Won't Burn (MCA, 1981) 🎵🎵🎵
Redneckin' Love Makin' Night (MCA, 1981) 🎵🎵🎵
Number Ones (MCA, 1982) 🎵🎵🎵🎵
Classic Conway (MCA, 1983) 🎵🎵🎵🎵
20 Greatest Hits: Making Believe (MCA, 1987) 🎵🎵🎵🎵
Crazy in Love (MCA, 1990) 🎵🎵🎵
Even Now (MCA, 1991) 🎵🎵🎵
It's Only Make-Believe (PolyGram Special, 1992) 🎵🎵🎵
20 Greatest Hits (K-Tel, 1993) 🎵🎵🎵🎵
(With Loretta Lynn) *Hey Good Lookin'* (MCA, 1993) 🎵🎵🎵🎵
Final Touches (MCA, 1993) 🎵🎵🎵
Final Recordings, Greatest Hits Volume 1 (Curb, 1993) 🎵🎵🎵
Final Recordings, Greatest Hits Volume 2 (Curb, 1993) 🎵🎵🎵
Super Hits (Epic, 1994) 🎵🎵🎵🎵
His Greatest Hits (LaserLight, 1994) 🎵🎵🎵🎵🎵
Greatest Hits (Dominion, 1994) 🎵🎵🎵🎵🎵
Sings Songs of Love (MCA, 1995) 🎵🎵🎵🎵🎵
Critique Country Classics Collection, Volume 4 (BMG/Critique, 1996) 🎵🎵🎵🎵

worth searching for: *The Best of Conway Twitty Volume I: The Rockin' Years* (Mercury, 1994, prod. various) 🎵🎵🎵🎵 is a hard-to-find but worthwhile collection of this period of Twitty's career.

influences:

◀◀ Roy Acuff, Elvis Presley, Brook Benton, Jack Scott
▶▶ Doug Stone, Lee Greenwood

Ken Burke

T. TEXAS TYLER

Born David Luke Myrick, June 20, 1916, in Mena, AR. Died January 28, 1972, in Springfield, MO.

Billed as "The Man with a Million Friends," T. Texas Tyler was an important country music figure during the 1940s and 1950s before he entered the ministry and devoted his voice to religious music. A native of Arkansas, Tyler was raised in Texas and educated in Philadelphia. He appeared on the *Major Bowes Amateur Hour* in New York during the 1930s and joined the *Louisiana Hayride* in 1942. His singing style was marked by a growl that he liked to throw into fast numbers. He was one of three singers that had their first Top Five hit in 1946 with "Filipino Baby" (Cowboy Copas and Texas John Robertson were the other two), but his biggest hit came two years later with "Deck of Cards," a spoken tale about how a deck of cards served as both Bible and almanac for a soldier. "Deck of Cards" would point the way for Tyler's career: Though he continued to hit the Top Five regularly through 1954, he felt drawn more strongly by his religious convictions. He eventually gave up his country career for the ministry and died of cancer in Springfield, Missouri, in 1972.

what to buy: *T. Texas Tyler* (King, 1959) 🎵🎵 is a CD reissue of one of Tyler's original albums, which means it has one big song ("Filipino Baby") and 11 less familiar tunes. It's not much of an overview of the singer's career, but it's the easiest place to start. *Remember Me* (Country Road, 1976) 🎵🎵 is a hard-to-find cassette with a number of Tyler's hits: "Deck of Cards," "Dad Gave My Dog Away" and "Courtin' in the Rain."

what to buy next: *The Great Texas* (King, 1960) 🎵🎵 is a collection of hymns and religious numbers like "What a Friend We Have in Jesus" and "Blessed Jesus Hold My Hand." Not surprisingly, Tyler drops the growl for a more reverent sound.

what to avoid: King released a whole series of "Moe's Mighty Mini's" cassettes in 1994, with only four or five songs and the same program on each side. The idea was to collect only the best of an artist onto a short tape for a budget price, but while *Deck of Cards* (King, 1994) 🎵🎵 has "Deck of Cards" and "Courtin' in the Rain," its other two songs weren't "Bumming Around" and "Filipino Baby," arguably Tyler's other biggest hits.

influences:

◀◀ Ernest Tubb
▶▶ Tennessee Ernie Ford

Brian Mansfield

IAN TYSON

Born Ian Dawson Tyson, September 25, 1932, in Victoria, British Columbia, Canada.

Ian Tyson is an iconoclast in contemporary country music, one of the few artists still mining the fertile but now overlooked ground of western music and culture. He's a much bigger star in his native Canada than in the United States, but his influence over the small but growing legion of western music makers is undeniable. Tyson is a former rodeo rider who took up the guitar while hospitalized with an injury. He got caught up in Toronto's burgeoning folk music scene during the 1960s, where he met his first wife and singing partner Sylvia Fricker. Ian & Sylvia became one of Canada's most popular and best-selling folk acts, thanks to signature songs such as his "Four Strong Winds" and her "You Were on My Mind." Their success opened doors for fellow Canadians Gordon Lightfoot, Joni Mitchell and Neil Young, and they presaged the neo-traditionalism of the late 1980s and early 1990s with their group Great Speckled Bird, named for the Roy Acuff classic. They released a dozen albums together and hosted their own popular TV show in Canada before separating during the mid-1970s. Tyson returned to western Canada, where he took up ranching and started writing songs about the western culture he soaked up as an avid reader of Will James' adventures and an admirer of 19th-century painter Charlie Russell. Tyson has cut his own swath in modern country and western, turning a grass roots following into a cottage industry.

what to buy: The album that established Tyson's unique voice was *Cowboyography* (Vanguard, 1987, prod. Adrian Chornowal) 𝄞𝄞𝄞𝄞, sort of a manifesto for the modern cowboy. The final installment of a so-called "cowboy trilogy," this understated masterpiece put into words and music the honesty, the simplicity, the romanticism and the magic that was and still is part of the West today.

what to buy next: *All the Good 'Uns* (Vanguard, 1996, prod. various) 𝄞𝄞𝄞 isn't as complete a retrospective as it could be. There's nothing from the Ian & Sylvia days, and, perhaps for contractual reasons, the gems from Tyson's self-titled 1984 Columbia album aren't here either. But what is included on this 19-song collection of audience and artist favorites represents a formidable body of work in a style and voice that is unique among today's assembly-line country stars. With songs such as "M.C. Horses," "Navajo Rug," "Will James" and " 'Til the Circle Is Through" (with Suzy Bogguss), Tyson casts a sentimental eye to the past and a wary glance to the future of a dying culture.

the rest:
I Outgrew the Wagon (Vanguard, 1989) 𝄞𝄞𝄞𝄢
And Stood There Amazed (Vanguard, 1991) 𝄞𝄞𝄢
Old Corrals and Sagebrush (1983–84) (Vanguard, 1993) 𝄞𝄞𝄞
18 Inches of Rain (Vanguard, 1994) 𝄞𝄞𝄞

worth searching for: All of Tyson's solo catalog is available in Canada, including complete versions of *Old Corrals and Sagebrush* (Stony Plain, 1983, prod. Ian Tyson) 𝄞𝄞𝄢 and *Ian Tyson* (Stony Plain, 1984, prod. Ian Tyson) 𝄞𝄞𝄞. Tyson's hardcore fans can trace the roots of his sound on two compilations of Ian & Sylvia songs, *Greatest Hits Volume 1* (Vanguard, 1970, prod. various) 𝄞𝄞𝄞 and *Greatest Hits Volume 2* (Vanguard, 1971, prod. various) 𝄞𝄞𝄢.

influences:
◀◀ Gene Autry, Roy Acuff, Marty Robbins
▶▶ Chris LeDoux, Michael Martin Murphey

Doug Pullen

UNCLE TUPELO /WILCO /SON VOLT

Formed 1987, in Belleville, IL.

Jeff Tweedy, vocals, guitar, bass; Jay Farrar, vocals, guitar, banjo, harmonica, mandolin; Mike Heidorn, drums (1987–92); Bill Belzer, drums (1992); Ken Coomer, drums (1992–94); John Stirratt, bass; Max Johnston, banjo, fiddle, mandolin, steel guitar (1993–94).

Like many important bands before them, Uncle Tupelo's reputation spread fastest after its breakup, and its influence far outdistanced the number of units sold—to the point where they are now seen by some as the Rosetta Stone of the alternative/roots/country movement sometimes called No Depression, after the title of the group's debut album (which itself was named for an A.P. Carter song). Rising from the factory- and farm-belt community of Belleville, Illinois (near St. Louis) during 1987, the band in its initial incarnation—Jeff Tweedy, Jay Farrar, and Mike Heidorn—drew equally on hardcore country and hardcore punk. Songwriting chores were split between Farrar, whose tunes are oblique and wistful, and Tweedy, who

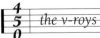
speaks more directly but is no less profound in describing the pair's favorite subject, small-town ennui. Heidorn left the band, and new members Ken Coomer, John Stirratt and Max Johnston signed on. But just as the new lineup was gaining steam, Farrar left the band to form Son Volt, while Tweedy soldiered on with the rest of Tupelo, switching its name to Wilco.

Son Volt, which also includes brothers Jim and Dave Boquist and original Tupelo drummer Heidorn, continues to survey Farrar's trademark brand of alt.country, switching back and forth between blistering rockers and bittersweet acoustic numbers. Wilco, which added guitarist Jay Bennett and cast off multi-instrumentalist Johnston after its first album, at first continued in the vein of pleasant, mid-tempo country rock, only to switch gears on their sprawling second album, which aspires to the range and gritty feel of the Rolling Stones' *Exile on Main Street.*

what to buy: *Anodyne* (Sire/Reprise, 1993, prod. Brian Paulson) 𝄞𝄞𝄞𝄞 is Uncle Tupelo's swan song but also its finest hour. Alternating between yearning, hard-bitten country-folk ("Slate," "Anodyne") and careening rockers ("The Long Cut," "We've Been Had"), it epitomizes the sound, pacing and texture of Tupelo's memorable live shows. The group's first two albums, *No Depression* (Rockville, 1990, prod. Paul Kolderie, Sean Slade) 𝄞𝄞𝄞𝄞 and *Still Feel Gone* (Rockville, 1991, prod. Paul Kolderie, Sean Slade) 𝄞𝄞𝄞𝄞, are of a piece, both of them raucous affairs featuring numerous anthems to booze and boredom.

what to buy next: *March 16–20, 1992* (Rockville, 1992, prod. Peter Buck) 𝄞𝄞𝄞 is a fine acoustic effort featuring Buck's minimal production, and spotlighting dour white-gospel tunes and equally grim originals. Farrar wrote the music for Son Volt's debut during long, searching sojourns up and down the highways along the Mississippi River. *Trace* (Warner Bros., 1995, prod. Brian Paulson, Son Volt) 𝄞𝄞𝄞𝄞𝄞 reflects the countryside that inspired it. Though lyrically obtuse, Farrar's tunes hit home hard, particularly the hard-country/folk numbers "Windfall" and "Tear-Stained Eye" and the slashing rockers "Drown" and "Loose String." Wilco's second album, *Being There* (Reprise, 1996, prod. Jeff Tweedy) 𝄞𝄞𝄞𝄞 jettisons the friendly mid-tempo country rock of its debut for a more aggressive stance, clearly inspired by the Stones' *Exile.* The two-disc set, a series of sketches from the road and fevered noise-rock experiments, succeeds on guts and sheer ambition.

the rest:
(As Wilco) *A.M.* (Reprise, 1995) 𝄞𝄞𝄞
(As Son Volt) *Straightaways* (Warner Bros., 1997) 𝄞𝄞𝄞

worth searching for: *The Long Cut + Five Live* (Sire/Reprise EP, 1993) 𝄞𝄞𝄞 offers the single from *Anodyne* plus a handful of live cuts featuring the full five-piece Tupelo lineup.

influences:
◀◀ Gram Parsons, Neil Young, Black Flag, Merle Haggard, Clash, Louvin Brothers

▶▶ Bottle Rockets, Blue Mountain, Old 97's, Honeydogs, Golden Smog

Daniel Durchholz

THE V-ROYS

Formed mid-1990s, in Knoxville, TN.

Scott Miller, guitar, vocals; Mike Harrison, guitar, vocals; Paxton Sellers, bass, vocals; Jeff Bills, drums.

Having the distinction as the first act signed to Steve Earle's E-Squared label is an enviable leg up in the business—and it gives you a pretty good sense of which direction the V-Roys are coming from. They play their country with a tough, roadhouse-rock edge, meaning there's a bit of grit in their twang. Scott Miller is a big fan of Roger Miller, and it shows in his narrative sense and gruff-but-sweet aesthetic. But the V-Roys just as easily ape the Beatles or other British Invasion rock bands, which makes for some entertaining diversity when they get to cranking out the tunes.

what's available: *Just Add Ice* (E-Squared, 1996, prod. Steve Earle, Ray Kennedy) 𝄞𝄞𝄞 is a snappy, live document of the V-Roys' broad-based sound, from the heartbreak of "Good Night Looser" and "Lie I Believe" to the 1960s Brit-pop jangle of "Around You" and *hee-ya!* fire of "Cold Beer Hello."

influences:
◀◀ Roger Miller, Beatles, Creedence Clearwater Revival, Buck Owens, Steve Earle, Dwight Yoakam, Replacements

Gary Graff

JOE VAL & THE NEW ENGLAND BLUEGRASS BOYS

Formed 1970, in MA. Disbanded 1985.

Joe Val (born Joseph Valiante, June 25, 1926, in Everett, MA; died June 13, 1985), mandolin, vocals; Herb Applin, guitar, vocals; Bob French,

Jeff Tweedy of Uncle Tupelo (© Ken Settle)

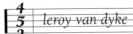

banjo, vocals; Bob Tidwell, bass. Later members included Dave Dillon, guitar, vocals; Paul Silvius, banjo, guitar, vocals; Eric Levenson, bass; Dave Haney, guitar, vocals; Roger Williams, dobro; Karl Lauber, banjo, guitar; Jim Buchanan, fiddle; Herb Hooven, fiddle.

Though his Massachusetts upbringing was a far cry from the hills of Kentucky, Joe Val managed to convincingly yodel, moan the blues and play mandolin as if he were a true Blue Grass Boy. Val began his professional career with the Radio Rangers, and soon discovered West Virginia transplants the Lilly Brothers and Don Stover playing bluegrass in Boston. Prior to joining the Charles River Valley Boys in 1963, Val performed with future Blue Grass Boy Bill Keith and folklorist/record producer (Nanci Griffith, Hal Ketchum) Jim Rooney at Club 47 in Cambridge. In 1970 Val formed the New England Bluegrass Boys, aided uniquely on high tenor vocals by Herb Applin. The group went through several personnel changes throughout the 1970s and early 1980s, playing their last show in December 1984. Six months later Val died of cancer.

what to buy: *One Morning in May* (Rounder, 1996) 🎵🎵🎵🎵 is the group's 1971 debut, chock full of high tenor singing and expert playing. The CD version features several unissued tracks and is highlighted by a heartstopping version of "Sparkling Brown Eyes."

what to buy next: *Diamond Joe* (Rounder, 1995) 🎵🎵🎵🎵 is basically a Joe Val retrospective, with several incarnations of the New England Bluegrass Boys providing solid support throughout. Five albums are well represented by an impressive 25 tracks.

the rest:
Live in Holland (Strictly Country, 1981) 🎵🎵🎵

influences:
◀◀ Charles River Valley Boys, Lilly Brothers
▶▶ Del McCoury Band

Stephen L. Betts

LEROY VAN DYKE

Born October 4, 1929, in Spring Fork, MO.

Leroy Van Dyke had only two significant hits, but they were memorable enough to earn him a lasting place in country lore. On the first, 1957's "Auctioneer," he used the rapid-fire delivery he'd learned in auctioneer training with hysterical results. The former reporter followed it in 1961 with "Walk on By," a cheating song with a guitar tremolo that resonated with pop and country audiences. "Walk on By" became one of the biggest

country hits of the rock 'n' roll era, but Van Dyke was never able to duplicate its success. Though he had singles chart through 1977, only five more reached the Top 40.

what's available: Van Dyke recorded "Auctioneer" and "Walk on By" for different labels, so finding both hits on one collection is practically impossible. *Walk on By* (Mercury, 1995, comp. prod. Colin Escott) 🎵🎵🎵 contains the title track, obviously, and a stereo re-recording of "Auctioneer." The album covers Van Dyke's recordings from 1961–65, during which he covered songs like "Party Doll," "Faded Love" and "Heartaches by the Number." He usually kept the guitar tremolo and the vibrato in his voice just as big. Van Dyke had only 19 singles to make the charts, so you can imagine that the budget compilation *20 Great Hits, Volumes I & II* (Playback) 🎵🎵🎵 gets thin fast.

worth searching for: Two German imports of Van Dyke's recordings are available: *The Auctioneer* (Bear Family), and *Hits and Misses* (Bear Family).

influences:
◀◀ Red Foley

Brian Mansfield

SALLY VAN METER

Born October 7, 1956, in Los Angeles, CA.

One of the few women instrumentalists in bluegrass to have recorded a solo album, California dobroist Sally Van Meter started her career in 1977 when she joined the Good Ol' Persons, a San Francisco band that also included Laurie Lewis and Kathy Kallick. With a reputation for vibrant tone, dexterity, expressiveness and creativity, Van Meter continues to play dobro with the G. O. P. today, in addition to a busy solo career, and has contributed to four Good Ol' Persons albums. Her other recording credits include albums by Laurie Lewis, Kathy Kallick, Tony Furtado, Sugarbeat, Peter Rowan & the Rowan Brothers, Sarah Elizabeth Campbell, Blue Rose and John Reischman. Van Meter made her solo recording debut in 1991, and in 1994 was one of 10 dobro players featured on the 1995 Grammy-winning *The Great Dobro Sessions*.

what to buy: *All in Good Time* (Sugar Hill, 1991, prod. Jerry Douglas) 🎵🎵🎵 shows Van Meter's versatility on the dobro as she adeptly handles both up-tempo bluegrass ("Road to Columbus," "Crazy Creek") and more atmospheric tunes like "Annie's Waltz" and "Amor de Mi Vida." Three of the tracks also feature vocals, the best of which is a soulful duet on "Blues for Your Own." Guests include producer Jerry Douglas, Kallick, Furtado and Scott Nygaard. Notable are "Crazy Creek" and "Anne's Waltz" with Van Meter and Douglas trading dobro licks.

what to buy next: *The Great Dobro Sessions* (Sugar Hill, 1994, prod. Jerry Douglas, Tut Taylor) ♪♪♪, which won the Grammy for Best Bluegrass Recording in 1995, presents 10 of the country's leading resophonic guitarists; Van Meter is featured on two cuts. *Blue Rose* (Sugar Hill, 1988, prod, Cathy Fink) ♪♪♪, a one-shot album by a folk/bluegrass all-star band of the same name, features Van Meter, Laurie Lewis, Cathy Fink, Marcy Marxer and Molly Mason.

influences:

◀◀ Josh Graves, Mike Auldridge, Jerry Douglas

▶▶ Rob Ickes, Kathy Barwick, New Grass Revival, Kathy Kallick

see also: *Good Ol' Persons*

Jon Hartley Fox and Douglas Fulmer

RICKY VAN SHELTON

See: Shelton, Ricky Van

TOWNES VAN ZANDT

Born March 7, 1944, in Fort Worth, TX. Died January 1, 1997, in Smyrna, TN.

Born into a wealthy and prestigious Texas oil family, Townes Van Zandt found his life's work to be a far more spiritual calling. Bent on hard living and heavy drinking, Van Zandt aged quickly and died early of a heart attack at age 52, but not before leaving behind an indelible legacy of American music. "Townes Van Zandt is the best songwriter in the world, and I'd stand on Bob Dylan's coffee table in my cowboy boots and say that," declared Steve Earle in an oft-repeated quote. And while Van Zandt's notoriety never approached Dylan's household-name status, it's worth noting that Dylan and Willie Nelson once dueted on Van Zandt's classic "Pancho & Lefty" on a prime-time network TV special. (Nelson and Merle Haggard took the same song to the top of the country charts in 1983.) While Van Zandt racked up a remarkable catalog of cuts covered by other artists (more than 100 versions of his songs have been recorded, by everyone from Hoyt Axton to the Walkabouts), his own recordings are a wellspring of considerable musical magic in their own right. A master lyricist considered by many to be one of the finest poets of his generation, Van Zandt also possessed a gift for darkly beautiful, often melancholy melodies, as well as a plaintive and personable voice, though his singing grew increasingly rougher and deeper in his later years.

what to buy: *The Late Great Townes Van Zandt* (Poppy, 1973, prod. Jack Clement) ♪♪♪♪ was in fact recorded a good quarter-century before his demise and caught Van Zandt at the peak of his artistic instincts. It contains his two best-known tunes, "Pancho & Lefty" and "If I Needed You" (a country smash duet for Emmylou Harris & Don Williams), as well as several other unforgettable songs. *Live at the Old Quarter, Houston, Texas* (Tomato, 1977, prod. Earl Willis) ♪♪♪♪♪ was recorded during July 1973, completely solo acoustic, and is a *de facto* overview of his oeuvre to that date, with 27 songs on the original vinyl (though eight are missing on the CD reissue).

what to buy next: *Rear View Mirror* (Sundown, 1993, prod. Townes Van Zandt) ♪♪♪♪ is a 17-song live recording from 1979 that covers some of the same ground as *Old Quarter* but in a slightly more augmented acoustic trio format. *At My Window* (Sugar Hill, 1987, prod. Jack Clement, Jim Rooney) ♪♪♪♪ shows that Van Zandt remained one of country-folk's finest songwriters a good 15 years past his supposed prime, introducing such classics as "Buckskin Stallion Blues" and "Still Lookin' for You." Whereas *At My Window* benefited from the wisdom of Van Zandt's years, his earliest efforts—*For the Sake of the Song* (Poppy, 1968) ♪♪♪, *Our Mother The Mountain* (Poppy, 1969) ♪♪♪♪ and *Townes Van Zandt* (Poppy, 1970) ♪♪♪—are equally marvelous for their youthful wonder.

what to avoid: *Live and Obscure* (Sugar Hill, 1987) ♪♪ doesn't have the coherence or quality of material that Van Zandt's other live recordings possess. *Roadsongs* (Sugar Hill, 1994) ♪♪, 15 covers of songs by artists ranging from Lightnin' Hopkins to Bruce Springsteen, is of interest to devoted fans but doesn't play to Van Zandt's obvious strengths, and the performances are spotty.

the rest:

Delta Momma Blues (Poppy, 1971) ♪♪♪
High, Low & In Between (Poppy, 1972) ♪♪♪
Flyin' Shoes (Tomato, 1978) ♪♪♪♪
The Nashville Sessions (Tomato, 1993) ♪♪♪
No Deeper Blue (Sugar Hill 1994) ♪♪♪
The Highway Kind (Sugar Hill, 1997) ♪♪

influences:

◀◀ Lightnin' Hopkins, Bob Dylan, Hank Williams, Elvis Presley, Woody Guthrie, Mickey Newbury

▶▶ Guy Clark, Steve Earle, Joe Ely, Jimmie Dale Gilmore, Butch Hancock, Steve Young, Rodney Crowell, Richard Dobson, Jerry Jeff Walker, Peter Rowan, Nanci Griffith, Lyle Lovett, Emmylou Harris, Garth Brooks, Hal Ketchum, Jonell

ben vaughn

Townes Van Zandt **(Keith Case & Associates)**

Mosser, Alejandro Escovedo, Will T. Massey, Son Volt, Walkabouts, Paul K., Tindersticks, Mudhoney

Peter Blackstock

BEN VAUGHN

Born April 6, 1955, in Camden, NJ.

Part musicologist, part goofball and all heart, Ben Vaughn is a rock 'n' roll purist who prefers AM radio to Surround Sound, the Goodwill to Tower Records and loves Tom T. Hall as much as "Johnny B. Goode." Ever since forming the short-lived Ben Vaughn Combo in 1984, the New Jersey singer-songwriter-producer has blended odes to facial hair ("Growin' a Beard"), vintage cars ("El Rambler Dorado") and convenience stores ("Lookin' for a 7-11") with hooks liberally lifted from Sun Records-era rockabilly, Buddy Holly, surf music, British Invasion pop and Muscle Shoals R&B. While Vaughn's quirky sense of humor makes him easy to shrug off as a clever novelty act, there's a genuine soul bubbling beneath the smirk: his passion for rock's roots shine through, whether he's recording base-

ment tapes of vintage 1960s instrumentals or cutting an entire album in his car. A distinct twang permeates most of his albums, but Vaughn generally prefers to celebrate his affection for country music with his tongue in his cheek, dabbling in obscure covers such as "Skip a Rope," Henson Cargill's spooky 1967 hit about parental misguidance, and titling one of his originals "I'm Sorry (But So Is Brenda Lee)."

what to buy: The presence of Marshall Crenshaw, Foster & Lloyd, John Hiatt and Peter Holsapple on *Dressed In Black* (Enigma, 1990, prod. Ben Vaughn) 🎵🎵🎵 lends a boys'-night-out exuberance to the Memphis undertones of "The Man Who Has Everything," the twangy pleading of "Doormat," the unrequited crush of "Cashier Girl" and the greasy punch of "Words Can't Say What I Want to Say." *Mood Swings ('90–'85 & More)* (Restless, 1992, prod. Ben Vaughn) 🎵🎵🎵 is a handy compilation drawn from his four Restless/Enigma releases, including such essentials as "Jerry Lewis in France," "I'm Sorry (But So Is Brenda Lee)," "Daddy's Gone for Good" and the prisoner lament "Big House with a Yard."

what to buy next: To appreciate the depths of Vaughn's record collection and country roots, check out *Mono U.S.A.* (Bar/None, 1993, prod. Ben Vaughn) 🎵🎵🎵, an all-mono collection of rollicking home-recorded 8-track covers of Ersel Hickey's "Goin' Down That Road," Henson Cargill's "Skip a Rope," Charlie Rich's "Just a Little Bit of You," Tom T. Hall's "That's How I Got to Memphis," Willie Nelson's "Suffer in Silence" and Joe South's "Dark Glasses." Equally obscure Dion, Ventures and Link Wray tunes round out the package.

what to avoid: *Kings of Saturday Night* (Sector 2, 1995, prod. Ben Vaughn, Kim Fowley) 🎵🎵 is a raucous, *Duets*-like collaboration between Vaughn and rock svengali Fowley, on which the latter simply rants over backing tracks that Vaughn mailed to him. We assume Sinatra wasn't available.

the rest:
The Many Moods of Ben Vaughn (Restless, 1986) 🎵🎵🎵
Ben Vaughn Blows Your Mind (Restless, 1988) 🎵🎵🎵
Instrumental Stylings (Bar/None, 1995) 🎵🎵🎵
Rambler '65 (Rhino, 1997) 🎵🎵🎵

worth searching for: Vaughn's tasteful production of the late Arthur Alexander's comeback album, *Lonely Just Like Me* (Elektra, 1993, prod. Ben Vaughn) 🎵🎵🎵, helped revive interest in the 1960s R&B singer's long-neglected career and the timeless country-soul blend that marked the Muscle Shoals, Alabama, sound. An obvious labor of love.

influences:

◀◀ Chuck Berry, Tom T. Hall, Sonny Bono, Kingsmen

▶▶ Rodney Crowell, Skeletons, John Hiatt

David Okamoto

RAY VEGA

Born in El Paso, TX.

Ray Vega grew up in Texas and studied at Boston's Berklee College of Music. He and his brother Robert had one minor hit, "Heartache the Size of Texas," as the Vega Brothers for MCA in 1993.

what's available: On *Remember When* (BNA, 1997, prod. Josh Leo) ♫♫♫, Vega and producer Josh Leo indulge their most melodramatic pop instincts for Vega's solo debut, which uses old Roy Orbison and Gene Pitney mini-operas for inspiration. Vega's got a stunning tenor range (think the Mavericks' Raul Malo on protein shakes), but he's still working up to material that'll match it.

influences:

◀◀ Roy Orbison, Gene Pitney, Mavericks

▶▶ Dean Miller

Brian Mansfield

THE VIDALIAS

Formed 1993, in GA.

Henry Bruns, pedal steel, lap steel; Jim Johnson, bass; David Michaelson, drums (1993–95); Randy Arrant, drums, percussion, vocals (1995–present); Page Waldrop, guitar; Charles Walston, guitars, harmonica, vocals.

Named after Georgia's famous onions, the Atlanta-based Vidalias were the brainchild of Chuck Walston, head onion and songwriter with the band. Upon hearing the Byrds' 1968 landmark recording *Sweetheart of the Rodeo*, Walston was blown away by the lyrical depth and tortured-but-assured delivery of guitarist Gram Parsons. After tooling around with some musician friends in a garage, he decided to form his own band. He subsequently enlisted the services of chicken pickin' Telecaster torturer Page Waldrop, bassist Jim Johnson, pedal steel player Henry Bruns and drummer Dave Michaelson, who was in the original lineup of the Georgia Satellites. The group landed a recording deal with Upstart, a division of Rounder, and recorded *Melodyland*—a blistering potpourri of country-rock, Memphis

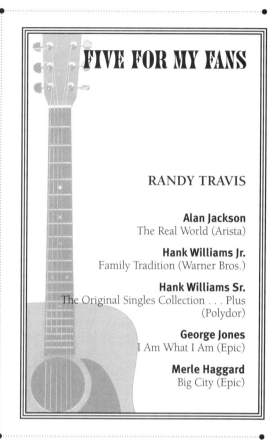

FIVE FOR MY FANS

RANDY TRAVIS

Alan Jackson
The Real World (Arista)

Hank Williams Jr.
Family Tradition (Warner Bros.)

Hank Williams Sr.
The Original Singles Collection . . . Plus
(Polydor)

George Jones
I Am What I Am (Epic)

Merle Haggard
Big City (Epic)

soul, blues and Texas swing. In September of 1996 Upstart released the group's second album, *Staying in the Doghouse*.

what's available: *Melodyland* (Upstart, 1995, prod. Donal Jones, Vidalias) ♫♫♫ features plenty of such good-time rockers as "Fakin' It" and "Something She Said" sprinkled with dark visions and gentle country sadness a la Gram Parsons in "End of the Night" and "Carry Me." *Staying in the Doghouse* (Upstart, 1996, prod. Donal Jones) ♫♫♫ picks up where *Melodyland* left off. Remarkable pedal steel guitar playing, muscular Telecaster licks and clever, heartfelt lyrics abound as the band stays clear of the sophomore jinx with the Rolling Stones-y rocker "Misery Loves Company" and a twangy cover of the Ramones' "Questioningly."

influences:

◀◀ Byrds, Flying Burrito Brothers, Gram Parsons, Flatlanders, Georgia Satellites, R.E.M.

Rick Petreycik

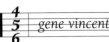

GENE VINCENT

Born February 11, 1935, in Norfolk, VA. Died October 12, 1971.

He had only one big hit, but with its compelling lead vocal, slap-back echo and burst of guitar, 1956's "Be Bop a Lula" secured Gene Vincent's place in music history. Taking their cue from Elvis Presley, Vincent and the Blue Caps became rockabilly standard-bearers whose initial sides for Capitol Records are among the most urgent recordings of their kind, sparked by the dynamic playing of Blue Cap guitarmeister Cliff Gallup. After the modest hit "Lotta Lovin'," numerous personnel changes followed and the band lost its spark. Vincent, who survived the same auto crash in England that claimed the life of Eddie Cochran, spent the rest of his young life trying for the comeback that would never happen and eventually succumbed to an alcohol-induced stomach hemorrhage. His impact on guitarists and vocalists from all walks of life would reverberate for years to come.

what to buy: *The Screaming End: The Best of Gene Vincent & His Blue Caps* (Razor & Tie, 1997, prod. Ken Nelson) 𝄞𝄞𝄞𝄞 concentrates on the absolute best that Vincent and the Blue Caps had to offer from 1956–67—before guitarist Gallup departed and while the band knew exactly what they were really doing. The recording utilizes original mono mixes.

what to buy next: The *Capitol Collectors Series* (Capitol, 1990, prod. Ken Nelson) 𝄞𝄞𝄞𝄞 has it all—21 tracks of the best, most unpretentiously pure rock that Vincent and the Blue Caps could muster, including the hits plus "Bluejean Bop," "Woman Love" and "Get It."

the rest:
Bird Doggin' (Fat Boy Specials, 1967/1996) 𝄞𝄞𝄞
Gene Vincent & the Blue Caps (Curb, 1993) 𝄞𝄞𝄞𝄞
Ain't That Too Much (Sundazed, 1993) 𝄞𝄞𝄞

influences:
◀◀ Elvis Presley, Link Wray
▶▶ Al Anderson, Robert Gordon

David Simons

RHONDA VINCENT

Born July 13, 1962, in Kirksville, MO.

Bluegrass- and gospel-influenced, Rhonda Vincent flirted briefly with Nashville stardom during the late 1980s and early 1990s. Although it seems she may have been overshadowed by the rise of newcomer Alison Krauss (who, interestingly, performed with Rhonda playing twin fiddles in the Vincent's family act, the Sally Mountain Show, at age 12), Rhonda remains a uniquely individual stylist and a favorite of many Nashville artists.

Much in demand for session work as a vocalist, she also plays mandolin, dobro, fiddle, bass, banjo and guitar, and was the drummer for the Sally Mountain Show by the time she was six, by which time she was already a stage veteran. A recording artist and TV star at age five with her family, then located in Iowa, Rhonda worked on the radio in Kirksville, Missouri, for a year after the family left Iowa. The Sally Mountain Show backed country artists like Ernest Tubb and Conway Twitty as the house band at the Frontier Jamboree in Marceline, Missouri. Rhonda recorded her first solo single in 1971, and recorded eight albums with her parents and her two brothers, Darrin and Brian. By the mid-1980s Vincent had competed on TNN's *You Can Be a Star* and came to the attention of Rebel Records, for whom she recorded three acclaimed solo albums before moving to Giant Records in Nashville, where she made her debut in 1993. Although she lost her deal with Giant after the release of her most recent album, Rhonda Vincent continues to perform, and will likely return to recording soon.

what to buy: *A Dream Come True* (Rebel, 1990, prod. Rhonda Vincent, Darrin Vincent, Bil VornDick) 𝄞𝄞𝄞𝄞½ is a near-perfect collection.

what to buy next: *Timeless and True Love* (Rebel, 1991) 𝄞𝄞𝄞𝄞 features the familiar title tune among several other highlights.

the rest:
New Dreams and Sunshine (Rebel, 1988) 𝄞𝄞𝄞𝄞
(With the Sally Mountain Show) *Bound for Gloryland* (Rebel, 1991) 𝄞𝄞𝄞½
Written in the Stars (Giant, 1993) 𝄞𝄞𝄞½
Trouble Free (Giant, 1996) 𝄞𝄞𝄞

influences:
◀◀ Sally Mountain Show, Marshall Family
▶▶ McCarters, Alison Krauss

Stephen L. Betts

RICK VINCENT

Born in San Bernadino, CA.

Growing up in Bakersfield, California, young Rick Vincent got a heavy dose of Buck Owens that has lasted his entire life. He began performing professionally at age 15, eventually playing the same West Coast clubs as Dwight Yoakam. He was one of the early regular performers on the "Western Beat Barndance," a popular, weekly country jam session that was started in Los Angeles by the Bum Steers' Billy Block.

what's available: *A Wanted Man* (Curb, 1993, prod. Wendy Waldman) 🎵🎵🎵 is one of the best examples of California country this side of Yoakam. Vincent's got a warm, appealing voice, and he's a top-notch songwriter whose lyrics are filled with wanderlust and broken hearts. The reasons that it produced only one Top 40 hit, "The Best Mistakes I Ever Made," and that Vincent has yet to follow it up remain mysteries.

influences:
◀◀ Dwight Yoakam, Buck Owens
▶▶ Gary Allan

Brian Mansfield

THE WACO BROTHERS

Formed 1995, in Chicago, IL.

Jon Langford, vocals, guitar; Dean Schlabowske, guitar; Tom Ray, bass (1995); Steve Goulding, drums; Tracy Dear, mandolin, vocals; Alan Doughty, bass (1995–present); Mark Durante, pedal steel.

The Waco Brothers come not to praise country music—well, sorta, maybe—but to bury it. A barroom brawl of a band, the Wacos are a ragtag outfit comprised of British and German rockers on holiday from groups such as the Mekons (Jon Langford, Steve Goulding), Jesus Jones (Alan Doughty) and KMFDM (Mark Durante), plus a couple of Americans (Tom Ray, who left to play full-time with the Bottle Rockets, and Dean Schlabowske of Wreck), all of whom are drunk on Hank Williams, Johnny Cash and, likely, a few pints of their favorite brew. The result has been described as half Cash/half Clash, and that's pretty accurate. But it's a combination that makes sense: after all, country's hell-raising honky-tonk heroes and punk rock's first generation had a lot more in common than either would care to admit. But be warned: the group's yowling vocals, ragged arrangements and relentlessly bleak outlook are more appropriate for those more inclined to pass out in a beer than cry in it.

what to buy: The country music that appeals to the Wacos' sensibilities is full of grim circumstances and losers with no future—but with terrific barroom stories despite that. *Cowboy in Flames* (Bloodshot, 1997, recorded by Ken Sluitar) 🎵🎵🎵 declares the "Death of Country Music" on one track, but their covers of Roy Acuff's "Wreck on the Highway," George Jones' "White Lightning" and Johnny Cash's "Big River" swears that it just ain't so. Harder, more musical and less cynical than their debut.

the rest:
. . . to the Last Dead Cowboy (Bloodshot, 1995) 🎵🎵🎵

worth searching for: Jonboy Langford & the Pine Valley Cosmonauts' *Misery Loves Company* (Scat, 1994) 🎵🎵🎵 is a precursor to the Wacos, featuring a lineup of Langford, Goulding, Dear and Ray. On this album the group steamrolls 14 Johnny Cash classics, rocking it up on "Cocaine Blues," pleading their case on "Sunday Morning Coming Down" and adding a reggae bass to "I Still Miss Someone."

influences:
◀◀ Hank Williams, Johnny Cash, Sex Pistols

Daniel Durchholz

WAGON

Formed 1992, in St. Louis, MO.

Ben Davis, guitar, vocals; Chris Peterson, fiddle, lap dulcimer; Danny Kathriner, drums, vocals; Steve Rauner, mandolin, Hammond organ, lap steel, accordion; Len Small, bass, vocals.

Born from the same fertile alt.country scene that spawned the formidable talents of Uncle Tupelo and the Bottle Rockets, Wagon is a band spilling over with potential, though it hasn't found its niche just yet. Lacking the gravitas of Tupelo and the go-for-broke attitude of the Bottle Rockets, Wagon instead lopes along in a mid-tempo groove that eventually becomes a rut. Still, there's much to be said for their laid-back harmony vocals, inventive folk/bluegrass instrumentation, and especially Chris Peterson's stellar fiddling (he was Arkansas state champ in 1990). A little more woodshedding, particularly in the songwriting department, and this could be a band to watch.

what's available: On *No Kinder Room* (HighTone, 1996, prod. Lloyd Maines) 🎵🎵🎵 the group distinguishes itself instrumentally, if not lyrically, on songs such as "Too Long Here" and "Three A.M.," which feature lovely backing tracks and solo sections. More distinctive in terms of subject matter are "Downtown Larry Brown" and "Rob Berry," a pair of laments regarding self-destructive personalities, and "She's Alone, She's Alright," about a spurned lover who's making it on her own.

influences:

◀◀ Uncle Tupelo, Jayhawks

Daniel Durchholz

PORTER WAGONER

Born Porter Wayne Wagoner, August 12, 1927, in Howell County, MO.

During the late 1950s and early 1960s, when the rest of country music was trying to downplay its rural origins, Porter Wagoner was a Nudie-suited aberration who played up his strong honky-tonk roots and smooth country balladry. Born into poverty in Howell County, Missouri, Wagoner moved to West Plains, Missouri, in 1943. He played bluegrass with a local group, the Hall Brothers, and got his start on radio in 1951, eventually landing on the *Ozark Jubilee* and on RCA Records in 1952. In 1957 he joined the Grand Ole Opry, and by 1960 had his own syndicated TV show, which eventually aired in more than 100 markets. The show featured Norma Jean as the designated "girl singer" until her departure in 1966. She was replaced by Dolly Parton in 1967, and under Wagoner's tutelage Parton blossomed as singer and solo artist. She left his touring entourage in 1974, and quit the show a year later to go solo. Wagoner remained a vital recording presence through 1980, by which time he had scored 66 Top 40 country hits on RCA, both by himself and in duets with Parton. By the 1990s he had become the *de facto* leader of the Grand Ole Opry.

what to buy: As a duo, Porter and Dolly were right up there with George Jones and Tammy Wynette, and *The Essential Porter Wagoner and Dolly Parton* (RCA, 1996, prod. various) ♫♫♫♫ gives a good idea why—their perfect vocal blend was as beautiful as their offstage relationship was tense.

what to buy next: Porter shares vocals with Parton on *Sweet Harmony* (Pair, 1992, prod. various) ♫♫♫. Not as complete as the RCA set, but still a fine sampling of their duets.

what to avoid: Although Wagoner could do some great hard country, he was also prone to some truly maudlin material. Unfortunately, *Heartwarming Songs* (Hollywood) ♫ stresses the latter.

the rest:

The Thin Man from the West Plains (Bear Family) ♫♫♫♪
Greatest Songs (Curb, 1995) ♫♫♪
The Essential Porter Wagoner (RCA, 1997) ♫♫♫♪

worth searching for: The budget disc *Pure Gold* (RCA, 1991) ♫♫♫ serves as a good overview of Wagoner's livelier hits.

influences:

◀◀ Hank Snow, Roy Acuff

▶▶ George Jones, Gram Parsons

Bob Cannon

JIMMY WAKELY

Born James Clarence Wakely, February 16, 1914, near Mineola, AR. Died September 25, 1982.

Though he made some 70 films and was a Gene Autry protege, Jimmy Wakely was a minor movie cowboy. But, nicknamed "The Melody Kid" for his smooth singing style, Wakely was a major recording star during the 1940s and 1950s with some two dozen hits for Decca and Capitol to his credit. In 1937 he formed a Sons of the Pioneers-influenced group called the Jimmy Wakely Trio with Johnny Bond and Dick Reinhart. After making a few solo records for Decca during the early 1940s, Wakely's film career laid the foundation for later country hits. In the early 1950s, after his singles quit charting, Wakely started his own label, Shasta, to sell his music directly through mail-order. He had his own radio show from 1952–57 and co-hosted the country music TV show *Five-Star Jubilee* with Tex Ritter in 1961. Wakely died of emphysema in 1982.

what's available: Wakely reprises many of his classics on *Beautiful Brown Eyes* (Richmond, 1985) ♫♪, including "Slipping Around" and "My Heart Cries for You." But the sessions sound slapped together, a sad state for Wakely, whose hit recordings always featured great musicians. *Vintage Collections Series* (Capitol, 1996, prod. Lee Gillette, Ken Nelson) ♫♫♫♫ shows Wakely during his prime, a Western singer every bit the equal of Gene Autry. These recordings cover Wakely's seven years with Capitol Records, a period during which he had more than 20 Top 10 hits, including "One Has My Name (The Other Has My Heart)" and "Slipping Around," which between them spent six months on top of *Billboard*'s country best-sellers chart. Wakely sings a Hollywoodized version of cowboy music and Western swing; he puts his Bing Crosby-like croon atop inventive arrangements that might use clarinet, accordion or organ in addition to fiddle, guitar or pedal steel.

influences:

◀◀ Gene Autry, Floyd Tillman

▶▶ Johnny Bond, Cliffie Stone

Brian Mansfield

BILLY WALKER

Born January 14, 1929, in Ralls, TX.

Something about Clovis, New Mexico, seems to attract young hopefuls. Buddy Holly recorded his earliest works there, as did LeAnn Rimes. Texas native Billy Walker felt the pull too. He hosted his own radio show in Clovis from age 15 until he graduated from high school. He returned briefly to Texas, then joined the *Louisiana Hayride* during the late 1950s. Standing 6-feet-3-inches tall, "The Tall Texan" achieved his first hit, "Thank You for Calling," in 1954. His 1960 induction into the Grand Ole Opry solidified future success, including the #1 "Charlie's Shoes," as well as "Cross the Brazos in Waco" and "A Million and One."

what to buy: Walker spent most of his hit-making career with four labels: Columbia, Monument, MGM and RCA. He felt most comfortable with ballads, and the records he made for Monument between 1966–70, collected on *Greatest Hits on Monument* (Columbia, 1993, prod. various) 🎵🎵, were generally unimaginative countrypolitan, though he did record Kris Kristofferson's "From the Bottle to the Bottom." His hits for the other labels have not been collected.

the rest:

Precious Memories (Step One) 🎵🎵
Law & Order (BMW, 1987) 🎵🎵
Let My Faith Begin to Move (Tall Texan, 1992) 🎵🎵
Larger than Life (Tall Texan, 1994) 🎵🎵
Greatest All-Time Cowboy Hits (Power Pak, 1995) 🎵🎵🎵

worth searching for: *Cross the Brazos at Waco* (Bear Family) is a German import of Walker's hits.

influences:
◀◀ Eddy Arnold

Craig Shelburne and Brian Mansfield

CHARLIE WALKER

Born November 2, 1926, in Copeville, TX.

Charlie Walker served in the Armed Forces Radio Network during World War II and used that experience to become one of the best country DJ's of the 1950s. His biggest hit was a pure honky-tonker, 1958's "Pick Me Up on Your Way Down," but other titles ("I Wouldn't Take Her to a Dogfight," "Don't Squeeze My Sharmon") say more about his choice of material. Walker joined the Grand Ole Opry in 1967.

what's available: Walker's a credible honky-tonker on *16 Best of Charlie Walker* (Plantation, 1987, prod. various) 🎵🎵 with songs like "Pick Me Up on Your Way Down," "San Antonio Rose," "Faded Love" and "My Shoes Keep Walkin' Back to You," even though these recordings were made late in his career for oldies-monger Shelby Singleton's Plantation label and aren't his hits. But you've really got to wonder what kind of guy thinks it's a good idea to cover Olivia Newton-John's "Please Mr. Please." (Answer: the same guy who thought "Don't Squeeze My Sharmon" was clever back in 1967.)

influences:
◀◀ Ernest Tubb, Hank Thompson
▶▶ Joe Diffie

Brian Mansfield and Craig Shelburne

CLAY WALKER

Born August 19, 1969, in Beaumont, TX.

Clay Walker came out of the same fertile East Texas nightclub circuit that produced fellow "hat-act" traditional country singers Mark Chesnutt and Tracy Byrd. Though only in his early 20s when he landed his record deal, Walker had already spent five years on the road, performing regionally and in Canada. His first two albums sold platinum, propelled by a series of #1 hits starting with his 1993 debut single, "What's It to You." Walker was diagnosed with multiple sclerosis in early 1996 but continues to record and perform. He was named the Academy of Country Music's Best New Male Vocalist in 1993.

what to buy: *Clay Walker* (Giant, 1993, prod. James Stroud) 🎵🎵🎵🎵, his debut album, produced several #1 hits, including "What's It to You," "Dreaming with My Eyes Open," and "Live Until I Die."

the rest:

If I Could Make a Living (Giant, 1994) 🎵🎵🎵
Hypnotize the Moon (Giant, 1996) 🎵🎵🎵
Rumor Has It (Giant, 1997) 🎵🎵

worth searching for: *Self-Portrait* (Nu. Millenia, 1996) 🎵🎵🎵 is an enhanced CD with videos, interviews, etc.

influences:
◀◀ Tracy Byrd, Mark Chesnutt
▶▶ Rick Trevino, David Kersh

Bill Hobbs

Jerry Jeff Walker **(AP/Wide World Photos)**

JERRY JEFF WALKER

Born Ronald Clyde Crosby (aka Paul Crosby), March 16, 1942, in Oneonta, NY.

Jerry Jeff Walker is one of music's most enduringly successful "cult" figures. His claims to national fame are his authorship of "Mr. Bojangles" (which hit the pop Top 10 for the Nitty Gritty Dirt Band in 1971) and his FM radio anthem "Up Against the Wall, Redneck Mother." Walker is also credited with being one of the architects of country music's Outlaw movement during the 1970s. Though his raspy, uneven vocal style is an acquired taste, Walker's sly, eclectic songs continue to resonate with his ever-expanding fan base. Born and raised in upstate New York, his musical roots are in the Greenwich Village folk scene. In 1967 he made his first recordings with Circus Maximus, a psychedelic folk-rock band, for Vanguard. His first solo LP, *Mr. Bojangles*, was well-received by critics, but it sold poorly. Subsequent releases on different labels fared even worse. After moving to Austin, Texas, in 1970, Walker signed with MCA and formed the Lost Gonzo Band (later incarnations would be dubbed the Bandito Band and the Gonzo Compadres). His pro-

gressive sound and style never caught on with country radio programmers, but he cultivated a reputation as an innovator and did manage to actually sell some albums; he received a gold record for *Viva Terlingua* in 1973. By the time the Outlaw movement died during the early 1980s, critics complained that Walker's LPs all sounded alike, and sales again fell off. His last major label outing was 1982's *Cowjazz*, which was an improvement over previous efforts, but didn't sell, either.

In 1986 Walker started his own label, Tried & True Music, and sold cassettes to his vast mailing list of fans, expanding its reach via a licensing deal with Rykodisc. Walker's 1989 release *Live at Gruene Hall* was his most highly regarded LP in nearly a decade. His "comeback" was furthered by his 1991–93 stint as host of TNN's *The Texas Connection*. At present, Walker's career is on a nice roll: He's planning new releases on Rykodisc, MCA has repackaged much of his old material and the crowds at his legendary birthday bashes get bigger every year. Iconography has its perks.

what to buy: *Great Gonzos* (MCA, 1991, prod. various) 𝄞𝄞𝄞𝄞 contains Walker's best-known songs: "L.A. Freeway," "Up Against the Wall, Redneck Mother," "Desperados Waiting for a Train" and more.

what to buy next: *Live at Gruene Hall* (Rykodisc, 1989, prod. Jerry Jeff Walker, Jim Rooney) 𝄞𝄞𝄞𝄞 is Walker's best live disc, featuring some funny and observant new material recorded in a Texas honky-tonk. It includes Chris Walls' "Trashy Women." Recorded in the mid-1970s, *A Man Must Carry On, Volume 1* (MCA, 1997, prod. Michael Brovsky) 𝄞𝄞𝄞𝄞 and *A Man Must Carry On, Volume 2* (MCA, 1997, prod. Michael Brovsky) 𝄞𝄞𝄞 show Walker at his most laid-back, with *Volume 1*'s busking version of *The Music Man*'s "Pick a Little/Goodnight Ladies" leading into the rollicking "Don't It Make You Wanna Dance?" and Rodney Crowell's classic "Song for the Life." *Volume 2* is mostly live, with lively versions of "Mr. Bojangles" and "L.A. Freeway," but is weighed down by several tracks of poetry readings. For a best-of set, *The Best of Jerry Jeff Walker* (MCA, 1980, prod. Michael Brovsky) 𝄞𝄞𝄞 is a pretty sparse affair, with only 10 tracks and no liner notes. Still, any collection with "L.A. Freeway" and "Desperados Waitin' for a Train" has two steps on the competition.

what to avoid: Walker's craggy vocal style doesn't mix well with the seasonal music selections on *Christmas Gonzo Style* (Rykodisc, 1994, prod. Lloyd Maines, Jerry Jeff Walker) 𝄞.

the rest:
Mr. Bojangles (Bainbridge, 1968/Rhino, 1993) 🎵🎵🎵
Driftin' Way of Life (Vanguard, 1968/1991) 🎵🎵🎵
Five Years of Gone (Line, 1969/1995) 🎵🎵
Viva Terlingua (MCA, 1973) 🎵🎵🎵
Ridin' High (MCA, 1975/1990) 🎵🎵🎵
Gypsy Songman (Rykodisc, 1987) 🎵🎵
Navajo Rug (Rykodisc, 1991) 🎵🎵
Hill Country Rain (Rykodisc, 1992) 🎵🎵
Viva Luchenbach (Rykodisc, 1994) 🎵🎵
Night after Night (Tried & True Music, 1995) 🎵🎵🎵
Scamp (Tried & True Music, 1996) 🎵🎵🎵

worth searching for: *It's a Good Night for Singin'* (MCA, 1976) 🎵🎵🎵 is one of Walker's better regarded LPs from his peak years, though it's currently out of print.

influences:
◀◀ Guy Clark, Bobby Bare, Townes Van Zandt
▶▶ Steve Earle, Chris Wall

Ken Burke

CHRIS WALL

Born February 26, 1952, in Hollywood, CA.

Chris Wall was a regular on the cowboy bar scene in Jackson Hole, Wyoming, during the late 1980s when Jerry Jeff Walker came across him and invited him to move down to Austin and record for his Tried & True record label. Wall's songwriting, singing and playing are all firmly rooted in traditional country, although the rowdy, sometimes gimmicky nature of his songs has made him a favorite with rural collegiate crowds as well. The cornier side of his craft paid off big-time during the mid-1990s, when Confederate Railroad had a chart smash with his song "Trashy Women." But Wall is really at his best on more heartfelt material that stresses the richness of his voice and the classic lyricism of his songwriting.

what to buy: *Cowboy Nation* (Cold Spring, 1994, prod. Lloyd Maines, Chris Wall, Pat Colgan) 🎵🎵🎵🎵 is Wall's most confident and assured album, from the near-perfect ballad "I Feel Like Hank Williams Tonight," to the brilliant lyric of "My Favorite Lies," to the more pop-oriented title track. *Honky Tonk Heart* (Tried & True/Rykodisc, 1989, prod. Pat Colgan) 🎵🎵🎵, Wall's debut, documented several of his best songs right out of the gate, including "Rodeo Wind" and "I Wish John Stetson Made a Heart," as well as his own version of "Trashy Women."

what to buy next: *No Sweat* (Tried & True/Rykodisc, 1991, prod. Chris Wall) 🎵🎵🎵 picks up where Wall's debut left off; the songs aren't quite as strong but the vibe is equally country-friendly, well-balanced between ballads and honky-tonkin' rave-ups.

the rest:
Any Saturday Night in Texas (Cold Spring, 1996) 🎵🎵🎵

influences:
◀◀ Guy Clark, Jerry Jeff Walker
▶▶ Confederate Railroad

Peter Blackstock

JERRY WALLACE

Born December 15, 1928, in Guilford, MS.

Like many singers of the 1950s, Jerry Wallace began his career as a pop vocalist and eventually moved over to country. He's most associated with his lone Top 10 pop hit, 1959's "Primrose Lane," but he had six other Top 40 pop hits and three times that many country singles. (Only 1972's "If You Leave Me Tonight I'll Cry," which he performed on the television series *Night Gallery*, made both charts.) Wallace also had an acting career, with roles on *Night Gallery*, *Hec Ramsey* and other TV shows. His year of birth is sometimes listed as 1938 (improbable, since he first recorded for Allied Records in 1951) and 1933.

what's available: *Best of Country* (Richmond, 1985) 🎵🎵 are remakes of his best-known pop and country songs. *Greatest Hits* (Curb, 1990, prod. Joe E. Johnson) 🎵🎵 has the original recordings, but leans more heavily on Wallace's pop hits of the late 1950s and early 1960s. It includes only three of his country Top 40s: "If You Leave Me Tonight," "To Get to You" and "Don't Give Up on Me." Often schlocky and over-produced, these weren't the greatest records of their time, and their only value now is nostalgic.

influences:
◀◀ Elvis Presley, Pat Boone
▶▶ Conway Twitty

Brian Mansfield

KATE WALLACE

Born March 11, in Pasadena, CA.

Singer/songwriter Kate Wallace made her first public performance at Los Angeles' Palomino Club and later was a New Folk Finalist at the Kerrville Folk Festival in Texas. Before making her debut album, she had songs recorded by Billy Ray Cyrus and Neal McCoy. Some of the songs for her debut were chosen by surveying users of on-line country-music bulletin boards, who listened to demos and selected their favorite songs for inclusion. Wallace also was the first country act to have a music CD that doubled as a CD-ROM.

what's available: *Kate Wallace* (Honest Entertainment, 1995, prod. Brent Rowan, Rocky Schnaars, Kate Wallace) ♫♫♯ is solid folk/rock-influenced country, and Wallace has a warm alto voice, but this album lacks the one knock-out song to make it special.

worth searching for: Keep an eye out for the promotional three-song CD-PLUS that contains music videos for "Dancin' on the Edge of a Heartache," "Hard Woman to Love" and "Saving It All for You."

influences:

◄◄ Mary Chapin Carpenter, Kim Richey

►► Stephanie Bentley, Caryl Mack Parker

Brian Mansfield

DON WALSER

Born September 19, 1934, in Braunfield, TX.

Tagged the Pavarotti of the Plains—for his pure tenor voice and his prodigious girth—Don Walser is a larger-than-life figure in more ways than one. Though he started playing in bands while still in his teens, Walser waylaid his music career until he retired from his day job as an accountant with the National Guard. Having grown up listening to the Grand Ole Opry and watching singing-cowboy movies, Walser remained determined to keep the music of his childhood alive. Now able to live his dream of being a touring and recording musician, Walser is doing just that. He's fond of saying he plays the Top 40—from 40 years ago. And so he does, mixing songs from Sons of the Pioneers, Faron Young, Merle Travis and Hank Williams in with his own songs, which stand up to the comparison. Walser's high-pitched yodel, perhaps his music's most distinctive attribute, would sound astonishing if it came from a man half his age. But that's true of all his vocals. While some contemporary singers might put a tear in your beer, a weeper in Walser's hands will have you crying buckets. And his uptempo tunes, with a little help from his Pure Texas Band, will have you thinking that the Texas Playboys are back in the saddle again. Perhaps the strangest thing about Walser's career, though, is that he has become an unlikely bridge between traditional country

and the alternative rock scene; Ministry's Al Jourgensen and the Butthole Surfers are among his fans, and Walser is one of the few non-rock acts that can hold his own on the stage of Austin, Texas' alt-rock hot spot, Emo's.

what to buy: They don't make 'em like *Rolling Stone from Texas* (Watermelon, 1994, prod. Ray Benson, T.J. McFarland) ♫♫♫♫♫ anymore, and that's too bad. Walser wrote the swinging title track when he was 18 years old and first recorded it during 1964. It still holds up as well as any other Lone Star state anthem and contains one of Walser's most astonishing yodeling performances. A hot, dusty wind blows through his version of Stan Jones' "Cowpoke," as well as Willie Nelson's "Three Days." Walser generously acknowledges one of his primary influences on "(The Party Don't Start) 'Til the Playboys Get Here," while "The John Deere Tractor Song" neatly pays tribute to family farming, a way of life that is fast disappearing. Altogether, *Rolling Stone* makes as strong a case as is possible for keeping traditional country music alive.

what to buy next: Nearly as fine is *Texas Top Hand* (Watermelon, 1996, prod. Ray Benson, T.J. McFarland) ♫♫♫♯, which features a gorgeous take of the Sons of the Pioneers' "Tumbling Tumbleweeds," plus a high-stepping big-band version of Bob Wills' "Whose Heart Are You Breaking Now?" As a finale, Walser pulls out all the stops on a near-operatic version of the traditional Irish tune "Danny Boy." Bring an extra handkerchief for this one.

the rest:

(With the Pure Texas Band) *The Archive Series Volume 1* (Watermelon, 1995) ♫♫♫

(With the Pure Texas Band) *The Archive Series Volume 2* (Watermelon, 1995) ♫♫♫

influences:

◄◄ Jimmie Rodgers, Bob Wills & the Texas Playboys, Slim Whitman, Eddy Arnold

►► Asleep at the Wheel, Wylie & the Wild West Show

Daniel Durchholz

THE MARTY WARBURTON BAND

Formed as a family band, mid-1970s, in southwestern NV.

Marty Warburton, banjo, mandolin, lead vocals; Kelly Warburton, guitar, harmony vocals; April Warburton-Wilkey, bass, lead and harmony vocals; Jay Buckey, mandolin, fiddle, guitar, dobro, banjo.

Though the Warburton family has been a bluegrass mainstay in Nevada for two decades, the group came to national attention by winning the Pizza Hut International Bluegrass Showdown in 1996. The group originally formed around Fon "Curly" Warburton, a contractor and Nevada State Legislature member who learned bluegrass from transplanted Appalachian miners. Marty Warburton became the *de facto* frontman after his father's death in 1991, but he and his sister April share lead vocal duties and three-part family harmonies factor strongly into the group's sound.

what's available: *Headin' Home* (Pinecastle, 1996, prod. Darrin Vincent) ♫♫♫, the Warburton's national debut, covers a wide range of territory: country covers ("Battle Hymn of Love"), nostalgic novelties (Marty Warburton's "Mayberry North Carolina"), gospel ("Voice of Eddie Lee") and tunes that showcase multi-instrumentalist Jay Buckey ("Sweet Memories of You," "Frailroad").

influences:
◄◄ Highstrung, Cox Family

Brian Mansfield

CHRIS WARD

Born June 27, 1959, in Columbia, SC.

Chris Ward, like many other country artists, is a former demo singer who got his deal after enough people heard his voice on tapes being pitched to other singers and said, "Who's that singing?" As a demo singer, he made the first recordings of "Not Enough Hours in the Night" and "Only on Days That End in Y," which were hits for Giant Records artists Doug Supernaw and Clay Walker, respectively. As a writer, Ward got a Confederate Railroad cut with "See Ya." He is also a former U.S. Marine Corps sergeant and California police officer who used to play drums for Bonnie Guitar.

what's available: On his debut, *One Step Beyond* (Giant, 1996, prod. Dann Huff) ♫♫, Ward encounters the same identity problem many other contemporary country singers have: put a hat on 'em, they all look (and sound) the same. Which is not to say this is a bad album; it's just that any of a dozen other singers could've made it.

influences:
◄◄ Garth Brooks, John Michael Montgomery

Brian Mansfield

MONTE WARDEN

Born April 26, 1967, in Houston, TX.

A fixture on the fertile Austin, Texas, music scene since he was a teenager, Monte Warden combines the giddy innocence of vintage Buddy Holly with the hard-nosed spirit of classic Lone Star honky-tonk. The result is an inspiring, irresistible sound reminiscent of an era when rock 'n' roll was more about joy than rebellion. Since breaking up the Wagoneers, a rootsy quartet that released two excellent, but out-of-print, late-1980s albums (*Stout and High* and *Good Fortune*) for A&M, Warden has developed into one of Austin's most revered writers and his upbeat, hook-laden songs have been covered by Kelly Willis and Patty Loveless. Now signed to River North, he continues to expand upon his remarkable melodic strengths with help from such co-writers as Bill Lloyd and Colin Boyd. A harder-rocking edge marks many of his newer compositions, including a brooding gospel-country ballad called "Child, I'm Not Finished with You Yet," which would have sounded right at home on Gillian Welch's debut.

what to buy: Echoing the heartbeat-accelerating bliss of "Peggy Sue"–era Buddy Holly, *Monte Warden* (Watermelon, 1993, prod. Dave McNair, Mas Palermo) ♫♫♫♫ is country's equivalent to pop singer Marshall Crenshaw's self-titled debut album. Such standout tracks as "Everyday We Fall in Love," "Forever from Now On" and "Don't Know a Thing" are yearning, heel-clicking celebrations of the boundless hopes and cherished dreams that accompany the noble pursuit of true love.

the rest:
Here I Am (Watermelon, 1995) ♫♫♫

worth searching for: With help from Jack Ingram's Beat-Up Ford Band, Warden transforms Prince's "Take Me with U" into a honky-tonk workout on a tribute album called *Do Me Baby: Austin Does Prince* (Fume, 1996, prod. J.P. Riedie) ♫♫♫.

influences:
◄◄ Buddy Holly, George Jones, Neil Diamond
►► Kelly Willis, George Ducas

David Okamoto

STEVE WARINER

Born December 25, 1954, in Noblesville, IN.

Steve Wariner fell into singing by chance. An accomplished guitarist who mentored with picking master Chet Atkins, Wariner was playing guitar in a local Indiana country band when he was cajoled into stepping in as the lead singer. It proved to be his big break; Atkins signed Wariner to RCA Records as a singer and the hits started coming. While he lacks the resonating twang of such greats as Hank Williams and Merle Haggard, Wariner has made do with his pop-laced tenor. A move to MCA established him as a hit-maker with an identity crisis; Wariner racked up one radio smash after another but couldn't sell an album. While most folks knew his monster songs—"Lynda," "The Weekend," "Small Town Girl"—they were hard-pressed to tell you who sang them. Perhaps those staples did him more harm than good in the long run. During the 1980s Wariner fell into a commercial trap that pushed him to record a slew of throwaway pop-country songs that distanced him from the guitar; consequently, it turned him into an underrated artist whose full potential was never heard on record. Enter Tim DuBois of Arista Nashville, who signed him to the label during the early 1990s. Wariner's first Arista album, 1991's *I Am Ready*, showcased his prowess—he sang and played a stellar batch of tunes that mined his country, pop, blues and rock influences. Not surprisingly, it is his only gold album. His creative freedom continued at Arista: 1993's *Drive* is a kicking slice of rock-charged country and pop. In 1996 Wariner recorded his dream record, *No More Mr. Nice Guy*, an instrumental album that zig-zags through jazz, country, pop, funk and blues.

what to buy: *I Am Ready* (Arista, 1991, prod. Scott Hendricks, Tim DuBois) 𝄞𝄞𝄞 finds Wariner flexing muscles long dormant during his RCA and MCA tenures. He's confident tackling a country classic (Bill Anderson's "The Tips of My Fingers"), a scorching blues number (his own "Crash Course in the Blues") and an absorbing country-pop ballad ("Leave Him out of This"). It's easy to see why this album did more for Wariner's career than two previous decades of radio hits.

what to buy next: *No More Mr. Nice Guy* (Arista, 1996, prod. Steve Wariner) 𝄞𝄞𝄞 is a festive gathering of such instrumental virtuosos as banjo player Bela Fleck, guitarists Larry Carlton, Chet Atkins and Richie Sambora and fiddle master Mark O'Connor, who drop the egos and play for sheer enjoyment. A daring record at a time when instrumentals at mainstream country radio are a thing of the past.

what to avoid: It's the album that contains Wariner's most recognizable numbers, but *Greatest Hits* (MCA, 1987, prod. Tony Brown, Jimmy Bowen, Emory Gordy Jr.) 𝄞𝄞 is also a reminder of the era when Wariner was filling country airwaves with one disposable pop song after another.

the rest:
Greatest Hits Volume II (MCA, 1991) 𝄞𝄞𝄞
Drive (Arista, 1993) 𝄞𝄞𝄞

worth searching for: Wariner's last album for MCA, *Laredo* (MCA, 1990, prod. Randy Scruggs, Tony Brown, Garth Fundis) 𝄞𝄞𝄞, is his most stripped-down, countriest outing for the label. Dobro, steel guitar, fiddle, mandolin, harmonica and Wariner's own guitar-playing figure prominently in this back-to-basics project. It was his first step toward gaining artistic respect.

influences:
◀◀ Chet Atkins, Bob Luman, Glen Campbell
▶▶ Bryan White, Kevin Sharp

Mario Tarradell

THE WARRIOR RIVER BOYS

Formed 1960, in AL. Reformed 1980.

David Davis, mandolin; Tom Ewing, guitar; Bill Sage, fiddle; Marty Hays, bass; Randy Lindley, banjo. Past members include: Garry Thurmond; Mitch Scott, guitar; Stan Wilemon, bass; Anthony Bailey, banjo; Tommy Chapman, fiddle; Gary Waldrep, banjo; Charlie Cline, fiddle, guitar; Jarrod Rains, bass; Al Lester, fiddle.

Bluegrass music, it seems, is built on endless connections. The Warrior River Boys found theirs as purveyors of staunch traditionalism. In 1980 bandleader Garry Thurmond, recently recovered from a serious illness, knew that the then-recently-reunited group would need a new leader. He handed the job to the band's mandolin picker, David Davis. Today, with Davis the only remaining member from the 1980s resurrection of the group, the Warrior River Boys have continued to perform and record straight-ahead bluegrass music. They're a popular festival attraction and feature some fine pickers from various other outfits, including Bill Sage, a former Blue Grass Boy and also one of Del McCoury's Dixie Pals, and Tom Ewing, also a former Blue Grass Boy.

what's available: Two Rounder albums featuring the previous lineup—including Charlie Cline, brother of former Clinch Mountain Boy Curly Ray Cline—remain in print: *Sounds Like Home* (Rounder, 1993) 𝄞𝄞𝄞 and *New Beginnings* (Rounder, 1990) 𝄞𝄞𝄞.

influences:
◀◀ Ralph Stanley & the Clinch Mountain Boys, Bill Monroe
▶▶ Johnson Mountain Boys

Stephen L. Betts

DALE WATSON

Born October 7, 1966, in Birmingham, AL.

Drawing on the pure honky-tonk tradition of icons such as Merle Haggard and Buck Owens, Dale Watson makes the kind of country that is most true to the spirit of the music, but is tragically out of step with the industry. "I'm too country now for country/Just like Johnny Cash," he sings in "Nashville Rash," and so he is. But that's Nashville's problem, not Watson's. For his part, Watson specializes in cheatin', drinkin' and truck-drivin' songs, and extols the virtues of "fast women and slow songs." But he's no retro relic. Many of his songs manage to strike a contemporary chord, notably "She Needs Her Mama," which approaches the aftermath of a breakup with the enlightened vision of a sensitive 1990s guy, and "A Real Country Song," which berates the current sad state of country radio. Watson's voice is authoritative, his crack backing band nearly flawless and his songwriting dead-on. And so much a man of the people is Watson that he spent part of 1996 touring truck stops, playing right alongside the racks of Sno-Balls and $3.99 cassettes. Now, what could be more country than that?

what's available: Watson's two albums—*Cheatin' Heart Attack* (HighTone, 1995, prod. Bruce Bromberg) ♫♫♫♫ and *Blessed or Damned* (HighTone, 1996, prod. Bruce Bromberg, Dale Watson) ♫♫♫♫—are the honkiest, tonkiest albums you'll likely get to hear at this late date. "List of Reasons," "Caught" and "South of Round Rock, Texas" (from *Cheatin'*) and "Truckin' Man," "Honkiest Tonkiest Beer Joint" and "That's What I Like about Texas" (from *Blessed*) are such perfect exponents of the form that, in listening to them, you can almost taste the cheap brew, pickled eggs and Slim Jims.

influences:

◄◄ Merle Haggard, Buck Owens, Ray Price, Waylon Jennings

Daniel Durchholz

DOC WATSON
/THE WATSON FAMILY
/DOC & MERLE WATSON

Born March 2, 1923, in Deep Gap, NC.

It's difficult to grasp the far reaching influence of Doc Watson on traditional American music; since his "discovery" by folklorist Ralph Rinzler and a subsequent appearance in New York as part of Clarence Ashley's String Band, he has bestrode the traditional music world like the colossus he is. A multi-instrumentalist (guitar, banjo, autoharp, harmonica, mandolin), a

FIVE FOR MY FANS

SHANIA TWAIN

Smashing Pumpkins
Mellon Collie and the Infinite Sadness
(Virgin)

Wynonna
Tell Me Why (MCA/Curb)

Alanis Morissette
Jagged Little Pill (Reprise)

Seal
Seal (Sire)

Wade Hayes
On a Good Night (Columbia)

wonderful singer with a rich, easy baritone voice, a treasure trove of traditional songs learned from family and friends, and an influence whose reach is incalculable (he popularized the practice of flatpicking fiddle tunes note for note on the guitar, for instance), nearly all Watson's recordings are worthwhile. He has recorded in a wide variety of styles and with a mind-boggling diversity of accompanists and partners, from family members—particularly son Merle (born 1949; died 1986), who became an accomplished slide guitarist and old-time banjo player in his own right—to Flatt & Scruggs, Chet Atkins, Jean Ritchie and many more. Doc's participation in the Nitty Gritty Dirt Band's *Will the Circle Be Unbroken* in 1972 exposed him to an ever widening audience.

what to buy: Where to begin? *Doc Watson and Clarence Ashley: The Original Folkways Recordings, 1960–1962* (Smithsonian/Folkways, 1994, prod. Ralph Rinzler) ♫♫♫♫ contains material from the period when Watson was first becoming known in the world of traditional music. It contains 20 previously unreleased tracks. *Doc Watson: The Vanguard Years* (Vanguard, 1995, prod. Mary Katherine Aldin) ����, four CDs worth of material from Vanguard's holdings recorded between 1963 and 1968, includes much unissued live material in various contexts. An example? Six duets with Watson's idol, Merle Travis, and three tracks with Clarence White, the young bluegrass guitar whiz whom Doc influenced greatly. *The Doc Watson Family* (Sugar Hill, 1994, prod. John Delgatto) ����� contains material recorded live during the 1960s and early 1970s, and features Watson surrounded by talented family members, including his father-in-law, fiddler Gaither Carlton, son Merle, wife Rosa Lee, brother Arnold, his mother and others, in a festival of traditional Appalachian material (for the most part). *Watson Country: Doc & Merle Watson* (Flying Fish, 1995, prod. Mitch Greenhill) ���� is a sampling of Doc and Merle's work together for Flying Fish during the 1980s.

what to buy next: The reissue of 1963's *The Watson Family* (Smithsonian/Folkways, 1990, prod. Ralph Rinzler) ����� with 11 new tracks makes it just as good as the Sugar Hill release that features Doc amid his talented family members. *Old Timey Concert: Doc Watson, Clint Howard and Fred Price* (Vanguard, 1977, prod. Manny Greenhill) ���� is a 1967 concert recording featuring Watson and frequent collaborators—guitarist Clint Howard and fiddler Fred Price—in a program of mostly traditional material. *Docabilly* (Sugar Hill, 1995, prod. T. Michael Coleman) ����, which shows off Doc's rock and commercial-country roots, features guests Marty Stuart, Duane Eddy and Junior Brown. *Riding the Midnight Train* (Sugar Hill, 1986, prod. Barry Poss) ����� finds Doc right at home, surrounded by many of the best young bluegrass pickers in the business and displaying his bluegrass chops. *Remembering Merle* (Sugar Hill, 1992, prod. T. Michael Coleman) ���� features Doc and son Merle in informal settings through the years. Although Watson and Monroe often performed duets live, the material on *Live Duet Recordings, 1963–1980: Off the Record, Volume 2* (Smithsonian/Folkways, 1993, prod. Ralph Rinzler) ����� was not available—except on a couple of rare bootlegs—until recently. Watson proves that he is a worthy duet partner for anyone, even the Father of Bluegrass Music.

what to avoid: With the caveat that Doc has never really made a bad record, he seems less comfortable with the mainstream country hotshots of the day in *Good Deal! Doc Watson in Nashville* (Vanguard, 1968, prod. Jack Lothrop) ��� than in nearly any other context.

the rest:

Jean Ritchie and Doc Watson at Folk City (Smithsonian/Folkways, 1963) ���

Doc Watson (Vanguard, 1964) ����

(With Merle Watson) *Doc Watson & Son* (Vanguard, 1965) ����

Southbound (Vanguard, 1966) ����

Home Again! (Vanguard, 1966) ����

Ballads from Deep Gap (Vanguard, 1967) ����

(With Flatt & Scruggs) *Strictly Instrumental* (Columbia, 1967/County 1995) �����

Doc Watson on Stage (Vanguard, 1970) ����

The Elementary Doc Watson (Poppy, 1972/Sugar Hill 1993) ����

(With Merle Watson) *Then and Now/Two Days in November* (Poppy, 1973, 1974/Sugar Hill, 1995) ���

The Essential Doc Watson (Vanguard, 1973) ����

Memories (United Artists, 1975/Sugar Hill, 1995) ���

The Watson Family (Rounder, 1977) ����

(With Merle Watson) *Red Rocking Chair* (Flying Fish, 1981) ����

(With Merle Watson) *Pickin' the Blues* (Flying Fish, 1983) ����

(With Merle Watson) *The Guitar Album* (Flying Fish, 1983) ����

(With Merle Watson) *Down South* (Sugar Hill, 1984) ����

Portrait (Sugar Hill, 1987) ���

On Praying Ground (Sugar Hill, 1990) ����

Sings Songs for Little Pickers (Sugar Hill, 1990) ���

Doc Watson & Family (Vanguard, 1991) �����

My Dear Old Southern Home (Sugar Hill, 1992) ����

worth searching for: *Favorites of Clint Howard: Doc Watson & the Blue Ridge Mountain Boys* (Rutabaga, 1988) ���� presents Doc playing the traditional repertoire he seldom tackles these days with a sympathetic band. *Reflections* (RCA Victor, 1980) ���, an interesting pairing of Doc and Chet Atkins, doesn't always work.

influences:

◀◀ Monroe Brothers, Merle Travis

▶▶ Clarence White, Tony Rice

Randy Pitts

GENE WATSON

Born Gary Rene Watson, October 11, 1943, in Palestine, TX.

Gene Watson, who spent most of his early life in Paris, Texas, came from a family with strong religious beliefs and musical ties. His father and brother played guitar and encouraged Watson to take up an instrument at an early age. Watson began singing in a local church, and as a teenager began performing professionally around the state. He cut his first record for a small label at age 18 and moved to Houston to seek greater opportunities. He found many club engagements there, but they didn't pay enough to support him. So, he got most of his income from working on automobiles; for a while, it seemed that his music would be a sideline at best. Watson's luck began to change after his manager and label owner Ross Reeder took him to Nashville to record a song called "Love in the Hot Afternoon." Released first on Reeder's Resco label, Capitol Records picked it up and signed Watson. Watson continued to have hits throughout the 1970s with "Her Body Couldn't Keep You off My Mind," "Paper Rosie," "The Old Man and His Horn" and "I Don't Need Anything at All." During the early 1980s Watson ended his affiliation with Capitol and moved to MCA, where his "14-Carat Mind" became his biggest hit. Nearly all of his singles for MCA, from 1981–84, reached the Top 10. Watson hasn't had that kind of success since, though he has recorded for Curb, Epic, Warner Bros. and Step One. Occasionally he still wraps his voice around a good song, and he's considered by many to be one of the most underrated country vocalists of his time.

what to buy: *Greatest Hits* (MCA, 1985, prod. Ross Reeder) ♫♫♫ contains some of Watson's best-known cuts. It's well produced, and Watson's vocals stand out as some of the best country music has to offer.

what to avoid: *At Last* (Warner Bros., 1990, prod. Gregg Brown) ♫♫ and *Uncharted Mind* (Step One, 1993) ♫♫ are Watson's two weakest albums.

the rest:
Greatest Hits (Curb, 1990) ♫♫
Best of Gene Watson (Curb, 1996) ♫♫
Good Ole Days (Step One, 1996) ♫♫♫

worth searching for: Scout the bins for *The Best of Gene Watson* (Liberty, 1989) ♫♫♫, a collection of late 1970s hits recorded for Capitol.

influences:
◄◄ George Jones, Merle Haggard
►► Keith Whitley

Ronnie McDowell

GILLIAN WELCH

Born October 2, 1967, in New York, NY.

With her Carter Family values, melancholy voice and gothic imagery, Gillian Welch stands out from the country music main-

stream like a black-and-white photograph in a Jackson Pollock exhibit. Mournful but never morose, the haunting originals that she pens with partner/guitarist David Rawlings recall old-timey country ballads, backwoods blues and traditional gospel hymns while her lyrics offer the soul-purging proclamations of emotionally spent, hard-luck cases unsure if they can muster the strength for one last stand. Welch's songs have been recorded by the likes of Kathy Mattea and Emmylou Harris, whose cover of "Orphan Girl" on her 1995 *Wrecking Ball* album set the stage for Welch's 1996 debut album, *Revival*. Welch's relentless touring with Rawlings—headlining club shows and opening for such stalwart troubadours as Guy Clark and Townes Van Zandt—has refined the forlorn harmonies and tortured textures of her music and produced one ringer for a forthcoming album: "Caleb Meyer," the spooky tale of a farmer's wife who kills her would-be rapist with a broken bottle.

what's available: *Revival* (ALMO Sounds, 1996, prod. T-Bone Burnett) ♫♫♫♫ is the riveting, relentless sound of hope draining out. But the darkness is tempered by striking imagery ("The night came undone like a party dress/and fell at her feet in a beautiful mess"), a knowing wink to country's roots ("Paper Wings" could pass for a Patsy Cline outtake) and the stark but comforting beauty of Welch's singing. The repeat button on your CD player was designed for the hymn-like "By the Mark" and the chilling "Tear My Stillhouse Down," the deathbed-plea of a cirrhosis-stricken bootlegger.

influences:
◄◄ Townes Van Zandt, Carter Family, Stanley Brothers
►► Parlor James

David Okamoto

KEVIN WELCH

Born August 17, 1955, in Long Beach, CA.

Born in California and raised in Oklahoma, Kevin Welch's alternative-leaning music has more to do with the sound of the Great Plains and left-coast country rock than it does with Nashville. Still, he made his reputation in the Music City song mills, cranking out hits for Gary Morris, Moe Bandy, the Judds, Don Williams, Ricky Skaggs and others before stepping to the microphone himself. Welch's songs carry a feeling of restlessness that's also conveyed in the term often used to describe them, "Western Beat." Also the name of his second album, Welch has said that the term is meant to convey not just an image of cowboys and campfires, but also "beat" in the sense of Jack Kerouac's constantly on-the-move Beat generation. A critical darling, Welch has yet to taste popular acclaim. But rather than play the game in the usual fashion, he has joined with fellow musicians Kieran Kane, Tammy Rodgers and Harry Stinson to form the artist-run record label, Dead Reckoning.

what to buy: Getting off of the major-label treadmill has been good for Welch. On his first effort recorded for his own imprint, *Life Down Here on Earth* (Dead Reckoning, 1995, prod. Harry Stinson, Kevin Welch) ♫♫♫♫, you can almost hear him relax, playing music he knows is good without having to write to whatever style or topic is currently in fashion. Welch draws on a wealth of sources, including Celtic music ("Pushing Up Daisies"), gospel ("Life Down Here on Earth"), folk ("Wilson's Tracks"), bluegrass ("The Love I Have for You") and hardbitten country ("Troublesome Times"). The cast includes fellow Dead Reckoners Rodgers, Stinson and Kane, Mike Henderson, former NRBQ guitarist Al Anderson and gospel group the Fairfield Four.

the rest:
Kevin Welch (Reprise, 1990) ♫♫♫♫
(With the Overtones) *Western Beat* (Reprise, 1992) ♫♫♫♫

influences:
◀◀ Gram Parsons, J.D. Souther, Eagles, Guy Clark, Billy Joe Shaver

Daniel Durchholz

KITTY WELLS

Born Muriel Deason, August 30, 1919, Nashville, TN.

The undisputed "Queen of Country Music," Kitty Wells (the name comes from an old folk song) took the role of women in country music to a then-unexplored level during the early 1950s, and became country's first genuine female star. During the 1930s, Wells sang on WSIX radio in Nashville. In 1938 she married Johnny Wright, with whom she performed in a trio, along with Wright's sister, Louise. When Jack Anglin entered the picture, forming a duo with Wright (backed by a band that featured a young fiddler by the name of Chet Atkins), Wells sang with the pair occasionally.

Wells' first records, released at the same time Johnnie and Jack were enjoying lots of success, were gospel records that didn't sell. Although she planned to retire to raise a family, Decca Records executive Paul Cohen asked her to record a song that

he felt would be an answer to Hank Thompson's hit, "The Wild Side of Life." In a move that would change the course of musical history for women, Kitty released the playful indictment of the male species, "It Wasn't God Who Made Honky Tonk Angels" (#1, 1952), which spent six weeks at the top of the country chart. During the eight-year history of the *Billboard* charts up to that time, Wells was the first woman to have a solo #1 hit. (She wouldn't have another chart-topper until 1961's "Heartbreak, U.S.A.") While the 1960s saw a steady decline in her record sales, Wells remained active, touring and recording for smaller labels. She was elected to the Country Music Hall of Fame in 1976 and remains one of the artists most often cited by female country acts as both an inspiration and a pioneer. In 1988, for a cut on her *Shadowland* CD, k.d. lang brought together producer Owen Bradley and three of the women whose classic music he had produced through the years: Loretta Lynn, Brenda Lee, and Kitty Wells.

what to buy: *Country Music Hall of Fame* (MCA, 1991) ♫♫♫♫♫ features the absolute best collection of the indomitable Kitty.

what to avoid: The best thing you can say about *Country Spotlight—Kitty Wells* (K-Tel, 1991) ♫♫ is that it's only 25 minutes long.

the rest:
Greatest Hits Volume 1 (Step One, 1989) ♫♫♫
Greatest Hits Volume 2 (Step One, 1989) ♫♫
Greatest Songs (Curb, 1995) ♫♫♫

worth searching for: *The Queen of Country Music* (Bear Family, 1993) ♫♫♫♫ is a four-disc box set that Kitty Wells fanatics will find indispensable.

influences:
◀◀ Carter Family, Johnnie & Jack
▶▶ Loretta Lynn, Iris DeMent

Stephen L. Betts

DOTTIE WEST

Born Dorothy Marie Marsh, October 11, 1932, in McMinnville, TN. Died September 4, 1991, in Nashville, TN.

One of the top female stars of the 1970s, Dottie West recorded briefly for Starday and Atlantic during the late 1950s and early 1960s, before finally catching some breaks in 1964 with "Love Is No Excuse," a duet with Jim Reeves, and "Here Comes My Baby," a solo hit that earned her a Grammy Award. That year brought West a career high and a tragic low: the

Grand Ole Opry welcomed her as a member shortly after Reeves' death, just four months after the release of "Love Is No Excuse." West had moderate but consistent chart success with RCA during the next 12 years, but her songwriting and career flourished after she hooked up with the Coca-Cola Company. West wrote a jingle for them in 1970, and an enthusiastic board of directors offered her a lifetime job writing Coke jingles. One of the results, 1973's "Country Sunshine," earned her a #2 hit and a Clio Award for best commercial—a first for a country artist.

West's career got another boost when Kenny Rogers, riding high on the success of "Lucille," joined her for the 1978 smash "Every Time Two Fools Collide"; the pair won the Country Music Association's Vocal Duet of the Year award in 1978 and 1979 (West's daughter Shelly captured the same trophy with David Frizzell in 1981 and 1982). West, who had previously enjoyed hits with Reeves, Don Gibson and Jimmy Dean, recorded a number of other songs with Rogers, including the chart-topping "All I Ever Need Is You" and "What Are We Doin' in Love." Her road band gave boosts to the careers of many aspiring singers, most notably Steve Wariner and Tony Toliver. After the hits stopped around 1984, West's finances hit the skids, too; she filed for bankruptcy in August 1991 and was forced to sell many of her possessions. A sprightly performer to the end, West found herself late to a 1991 Opry performance during slippery weather and with no reliable transportation. The neighbor who agreed to give her a ride lost control of his car near the Opry House, and West died from injuries sustained in the accident.

what to buy: *The Essential Series: Dottie West* (RCA, 1996, prod. various) 🎵🎵🎵 collects 20 songs from West's 12-year association with RCA and shows her progression from Patsy Cline clone to established individual talent. *Essential* contains most, but not all, of her Top 40 hits from 1963–75, including "Country Sunshine," "Paper Mansions" and 1974's "Last Time I Saw Him." It also has West's duets with Jim Reeves (1964's "Love Is No Excuse"), Don Gibson (1969's "Rings of Gold" and "There's a Story (Goin' 'Round)") and Jimmy Dean (1971's "Slowly").

the rest:
She's Got You (Richmond, 1985) 🎵🎵
Greatest Hits (Curb) 🎵🎵🎵

influences:
▶▶ David Frizzell & Shelly West, Larry Gatlin, Steve Wariner, Tony Toliver

Craig Shelburne and Brian Mansfield

Dottie West **(Archive Photos)**

SPEEDY WEST & JIMMY BRYANT

Instrumental duo formed in 1950. Disbanded 1953. Reunited 1975.

Speedy West (born Wesley Webb West), pedal steel guitar; Jimmy Bryant (born Ivy James Bryant; died 1980, in GA), guitar.

Few in the history of country music ever ignited the strings like Speedy West and Jimmy Bryant. While each had a successful, if brief, solo career, it was their partnership, first realized in 1950 when West Coast talent scout and radio show host Cliffie Stone hired them both for a new television show called *Hometown Jamboree,* that earned them the most notoriety. Paired on television as "The Flaming Guitars" the pair began recording for Capitol (on Stone's recommendation) in 1951. Fast, wildly inventive and a perfect match, this fleet-fingered duo waxed a total of 50 instrumentals for Capitol between 1951–56. Some, like "Stratosphere Boogie," "Arkansas Traveler" and "Midnight Ramble," remain among the finest (and fastest) country instrumentals ever conceived. Rarely written out, most of their numbers were head arrangements that the pair improvised while in the studio or during live shows. After Bryant quit *Hometown*

Jamboree in 1955, the partnership broke up. Speedy went on to record on over 6,000 recordings for 177 artists, including Frank Sinatra and Bing Crosby. He became one of the best known and most recorded pedal steel players in all of country music. His solo disc, *Guitar Spectacular,* remains one of the few power-house showcases for solo pedal steel. After his partnership with Speedy, Bryant made six solo discs for Imperial and became a spokesman for Vox guitars. The pair reunited in Nashville in 1975 for a final session. Bryant died in Georgia in 1980. West had a stoke the following year and has since retired to Oklahoma.

what to buy: After years of every disc they did being out-of-print, reissue label Razor & Tie collected 16 of the duo's most incendiary instrumentals for the single disc collection *Stratosphere Boogie: The Flaming Guitars of Speedy West & Jimmy Bryant* (Razor & Tie, 1995, comp. prod. Matt Goldman) 𝅘𝅥𝅘𝅥𝅘𝅥𝅘𝅥. One listen and you'll never think of the steel guitar the same way.

the rest:
For The Last Time (One Way, 1975/1992)

solo outings:
Speedy West:
Guitar Spectacular (Capitol, 1962) 𝅘𝅥𝅘𝅥𝅘𝅥𝅘𝅥

influences:
◀◀ Bob Dunn, Leon McAuliffe
▶▶ Buddy Emmons, Sneaky Pete Kleinow, Big Sandy & His Fly-Rite Boys

Robert Baird

WESTERN FLYER

Formed January 1992, in Nashville, TN.

Danny Myrick, lead vocals, bass, Steve Charles, guitar (1992–96); Roger Helton, guitar, banjo, fiddle; T.J. Klay, mandolin, guitar, harmonica; Chris Marion, keyboards; Bruce Gust, drums.

A country-rock band signed to Step One Records, Western Flyer's high-energy vocals and guitar work is very slick, reminiscent of 1970s southern California bands like the Eagles and Poco.

what's available: On *Western Flyer* (Step One, 1994, prod. Ray Pennington, Western Flyer) 𝅘𝅥𝅘𝅥 the band stakes out some solid country-rock turf with the title tune and the cautionary tale of racism, "Cherokee Highway." However, not all the songwriting is as substantive. Their second album, *Back in America* (Step One, 1996, prod. Ray Pennington, Western Flyer) 𝅘𝅥𝅘𝅥, lapses into bland balladeering, with an occasional stab at Spring-

steen-style roots-rock. Trouble is they sound more like a Chevy ad than they do the Boss.

influences:
◀◀ Eagles, Poco, Alabama
▶▶ Lonestar, Ricochet

Bob Cannon

CHERYL WHEELER

Born July 10, 1951, in Baltimore, MD.

Straddling the line between folk and country, Cheryl Wheeler's biggest challenge has been squeezing both of her musical personalities—sensitive songwriter and sinister satirist—onto one album. In concert, the husky-voiced vocalist relies on a wry, raucous sense of humor that sends fans in search of her CDs, only to discover that much of her recorded repertoire consists of introspective ballads. Wheeler's move out of the coffee-house circuit began in 1986 when Jonathan Edwards hired her to play in his band and produced her self-titled debut album. After releasing *Half a Book* (featuring the adult contemporary chart-grazer "Emotional Response") on the now-defunct Cypress label, Wheeler signed with Capitol's Nashville division in 1990. But even the Midas touch of noted Randy Travis producer Kyle Lehning couldn't help the label figure out how to promote *Circles and Arrows*, which ranged from the beautiful "Aces" (a 1992 hit for Suzy Bogguss) to the weird "Estate Sale," a riotous tune about the joys of rifling through dead people's houses in search of bargains. Wheeler has found a more supportive home with Rounder's Philo subsidiary, where she finally hit her stride in 1995 with *Mrs. Pinocci's Guitar,* the first album that makes her multi-faceted personality come across as a complex human being, not some guitar-toting Jekyll and Hyde.

what to buy: *Mrs. Pinocci's Guitar* (Philo, 1995, prod. Jonathan Edwards, Cheryl Wheeler) 𝅘𝅥𝅘𝅥𝅘𝅥𝅘𝅥 mixes playful full-band arrangements with spare, demo-like acoustic guitar performances. It also offers the ideal balance of moods and material: in between such love songs as "Further and Further Away" and "So Far to Fall," and the disarmingly vulnerable demo of "One Love," Wheeler copes with a midlife crisis on "Is It Peace or Is It Prozac?," mocks right-wing conservatism on the Jonathan Swift-like "Makes Good Sense to Me" ("In whose sick mind did it ever occur/that a choice like that should be up to her?") and rocks with surprising conviction on "Does the Future Look Black?"

what to buy next: *Circles and Arrows* (Capitol, 1990, prod. Kyle Lehning) 𝅘𝅥𝅘𝅥𝅘𝅥 is her most polished and country-sounding album, thanks to such guests as Mark O'Connor, Vince Gill (who sings harmonies on "Aces"), Pam Tillis and Jerry Douglas. Given the seamless sound and emotional clout of such acoustic ballads as "Don't Wanna," "Miss You More Than I'm Mad" and "Arrow," the irreverent "Estate Sale" might have worked better as a hidden bonus track. Reissued in 1995 by Rounder.

what to avoid: Her debut album, *Cheryl Wheeler* (North Star, 1986, prod. Jonathan Edwards) ♫♫, includes "Quarter Moon" and her original versions of "Arrow" and "Addicted" (later a hit for Dan Seals), but the cheesy production lends a goopy sentimentality to songs that are already pushing the emotional envelope.

the rest:
Half a Book (North Star, 1987) ♫♫♫
Driving Home (Philo, 1993) ♫♫♫

worth searching for: *Christine Lavin Presents: Laugh Tracks, Volume 1* (Shanachie, 1996, prod. Steve Rosenthal, Christine Lavin) ♫♫♥ collects live performances of neo-novelty songs by the Chenille Sisters, Vance Gilbert, Chuck Brodsky and others. Wheeler contributes "Potato," a silly ode to the starchy vegetable sung to the tune of "The Mexican Hat Dance."

influences:
◄◄ Phoebe Snow, Tracy Chapman, Christine Lavin
►► Mary Chapin Carpenter, Don Henry, Maura O'Connell

David Okamoto

ONIE WHEELER

Born November 10, 1921, in Senath, MO. Died May 26, 1984, in Nashville, TN.

Although singer, songwriter, guitarist, harmonica player and bassist Onie Wheeler worked in music from 1945 to his death (literally; he collapsed onstage and died at Opryland), and never achieved much financial success, he is highly regarded by a growing cult of history-minded country fans and rockabilly collectors. His music defied categorization while he lived, but in death his music has been embraced by hard country, bluegrass and rockabilly enthusiasts alike. Wheeler left behind a handful of inspired recordings that transcended genres, wrote songs that Lefty Frizzell covered, wrote songs for Flatt & Scruggs (and played bass with them), toured with Roy Acuff and Elvis Presley, and made several recordings destined to become minor classics, including "Run 'Em Off" (covered by Lefty Frizzell), "Onie's Bop" (a real rockabilly gem), "Jump Right out of This Jukebox" (a Sun single and another Wheeler classic), "I Saw Mother with God Last Night" (which has become a blue-

grass-gospel standard), and "John's Been Shuckin' My Corn," a single on Royal American highly regarded by rockabilly collectors. His truly inimitable vocal style and singular writing skills contributed to making Wheeler one of country music's true unheralded originals.

what's available: *Onie's Bop* (Bear Family, 1991, prod. Don Law, Bill Justis, Jack Clement) ♫♫♫♫ is a fantastic collection of all Onie's singles recorded during the 1950s for Okeh, Columbia and Sun, including the classics "Jump Right out of This Jukebox," "Onie's Bop," "Would You Like to Wear a Crown," "Run 'em Off," "I Saw Mother with God Last Night" and more, 31 tracks in all.

influences:
◄◄ Ernest Tubb, Roy Acuff
►► Johnny Cash

Randy Pitts

WHISKEYTOWN

Formed 1993, in Raleigh, NC.

Ryan Adams, vocals, guitars; Phil Wandscher, guitars, vocals; Caitlin Cary, violin, vocals; Skillet Gilmore, drums; Steve Grothman, bass.

Whiskeytown is primarily the brainchild of Ryan Adams, a frightfully charismatic young man given to obsessive ruminations on doomed romance, drinking and why George Jones is more of a punk than those poseurs in Rancid.

what to buy: Ryan Adams was only 21 when recording Whiskeytown's debut album, *Faithless Street* (MoodFood, 1995, prod. Whiskeytown, Greg Woods) ♫♫♫♥, but sounds twice his age on the achingly beautiful "Midway Park" (a song Freedy Johnston would kill to have written) and the on-a-bender raveup "Drank Like a River." His voice alternates between an earthy rasp and an angelic Gram Parsons tenor, and it's never less than convincing.

worth searching for: On *Who the Hell: A Tribute to Richard Hell* (Cred Factory, 1995, prod. various) ♫♫♫, Whiskeytown puts punk legend Hell's signature anthem "Blank Generation" through a hayride hoedown deconstruction that is pure, hilarious genius.

influences:
◄◄ Uncle Tupelo, Jason & the Scorchers, Replacements, Freedy Johnston, Tom T. Hall
►► Slobberbone

David Menconi

BRYAN WHITE

Born Bryan Shelton White, February 17, 1974, in Lawton, OK.

Sure, the girls go wild. Sure, a lot of them are 13. But don't let Bryan White's *Teen Beat* status cloud your judgment—this young Oklahoman is more than just another pretty face. White makes no apologies for his youth; in fact, his innocence and pure tenor voice let him get away with songs that might be sappy in the hands of another.

White was five when he started playing the drums. His parents, who divorced when he was very young, were both musicians and White backed them both on stage. He stayed behind the drum kit until he was 17, when he discovered it was easier to write songs with a guitar than a tom-tom. By that time, he knew what he was going to do. As soon as he graduated from high school, White loaded up his car and moved to Nashville to realize his dream. Within three months of arriving, he had a staff songwriting job and a management deal. The next year he had a record deal. He had just turned 20. Two years later, both of his albums had sold platinum.

what's available: *Bryan White* (Asylum, 1994, prod. Billy Joe Walker Jr., Kyle Lehning) 🎵🎵🎵 contains his breakthrough hit "Someone Else's Star," along with "Rebecca Lynn" and "Look at Me Now." White did a lot of growing up between his first album and *Between Now and Forever* (Asylum, 1996, prod. Billy Joe Walker Jr., Kyle Lehning) 🎵🎵🎵, and you can hear it on his sophomore release, which features "I'm Not Supposed to Love You Anymore," "So Much for Pretending" and "That's Another Song."

influences:
◀◀ Steve Wariner
▶▶ David Kersh

Cyndi Hoelzle

JEFF WHITE

Born August 2, 1957, in Syracuse, NY.

Jeff White is a highly effective bluegrass and country vocalist/guitar player, whose voice brings to mind the sweetness and clarity of Vince Gill or Tim O'Brien. Growing up in central New York State and Indiana, he was fascinated with bluegrass and folk music early on and learned guitar as a teenager, frequenting festivals where he studied the styles of heroes like Doc Watson and Tony Rice. His graduate studies were cut short by the opportunity to tour as a member of Alison Krauss' band, Union Station. The AK&US show favorite "Wild Bill Jones," which Krauss has called her favorite song of theirs, owes much of its initial appeal to the emotional delivery in White's lead vocal, featured on the group's 1988 album, *Two Highways*. White also contributed significantly to Krauss' next album, the Grammy-winning *I've Got That Old Feeling*, before moving on to perform with the Weary Hearts and then spending six months in rural Japan with the band Texas Rangers. He followed that up with a move to Nashville to begin his solo career, but was sidetracked by two gigs, first a stint with Tim O'Brien, then a more permanent position, in 1992, as guitarist for country superstar Vince Gill.

A much-sought-after studio musician and vocalist, White finally got his chance to record a fairly straight-ahead bluegrass record (and even got to give it a very cool title). Considering that both Krauss and Gill were willing participants in the recording of *The White Album* (during their respective reigns as the Country Music Association's top male and female vocalists, no less), White has obviously already established himself as a well-respected, top-flight musician. He is a true star on the country/bluegrass horizon.

what's available: His brilliant debut, *The White Album* (1996, Rounder) 🎵🎵🎵🎵, is an album you will want to play more than once the minute you first hear it. "I Never Knew," with Vince Gill and Alison Krauss on backing vocals, is a mournful masterpiece.

influences:
◀◀ Ricky Skaggs, Tim O'Brien, Alison Krauss

Stephen L. Betts

LARI WHITE

Born May 13, 1965, in Dunedin, FL.

Lari White has always been at ease on a stage. She grew up in central Florida and sang with her brothers and sisters at festivals, churches and community centers as part of the White Family Singers. She majored in music engineering and minored in voice at the University of Miami, and soon afterwards auditioned for a spot on TNN's *You Can Be a Star*. Yes, she won the grand prize—a singles contract with Capitol. Nothing came of those efforts, but White did sign a songwriting deal with Ronnie Milsap's publishing company, and soon became Rodney Crowell's opening act. Crowell became a huge fan of White's singing and went on to produce her debut RCA album. She released three albums for RCA, one of which sold gold on the strength of White's hit, "Now I Know."

what to buy: *Best of Lari White* (RCA, 1997, prod. various) 🎵🎵🎵, a 12-song overview of White's RCA years, includes tracks from her three albums plus a version of "Amazing Grace" and a duet with Travis Tritt, "Helping Me Get Over You."

what to buy next: *Wishes* (RCA, 1994, prod. Garth Fundis) 🎵🎵🎵 contains her breakthrough hit, "Now I Know," and her duet with Hal Ketchum, "That's How You Know (When You're in Love)."

the rest:
Lead Me Not (RCA, 1993) 🎵🎵🎵🎵
Don't Fence Me In (RCA, 1995) 🎵🎵🎵🎵

influences:
 Pam Tillis, Trisha Yearwood
▶▶ Jo Dee Messina, Deana Carter

Cyndi Hoelzle

ROLAND WHITE
See: Nashville Bluegrass Band

TONY JOE WHITE
Born July 23, 1943, in Oak Grove, LA.

Though Tony Joe White spent much of his career in Nashville and proudly played what his followers dubbed "country-swamp-blues," his 1969 hit "Polk Salad Annie" is a classic sloppy funk song. You can hear White's forehead sweating underneath the bizarre "whomper stomper" guitar and his deep, incomprehensible mumbles about Annie and her weirdly abusive polk-salad-picking family. Aside from that single, which Elvis Presley and Tom Jones covered, White has had a less-than-cult following his whole career. Though he lived in Nashville most of his career and wrote successful singles for Dusty Springfield, Brook Benton and others—and has more recently done commercials and put out successful albums overseas—he's a true, crazed one-hit wonder.

what to buy: Get ahold of anything with "Polk Salad Annie," most notably *The Best of Tony Joe White* (Warner Bros., 1993, prod. various) 🎵🎵🎵, where you don't have to listen to the embarrassing stuff. Also try his most successful solo album, *Continued* (Monument, 1969, prod. Billy Swan) 🎵🎵🎵.

what to buy next: The rest is a toss-up. The early *Black and White* (Monument, 1968, prod. Billy Swan) 🎵🎵🎵 or *Tony Joe* (Monument, 1970, prod. Billy Swan) 🎵🎵🎵, which contain so-so covers of Otis Redding and John Lee Hooker songs, are your best bets.

what to avoid: After a while, White's career wasn't worth much, though he continued to release albums, write songs and tour.

Lari White (© Ken Settle)

The schlock-filled *Real Thing* (Casablanca, 1980) 🎵🎵 and *Dangerous* (Columbia, 1983) 🎵 didn't even live up to the earlier Otis Redding covers.

the rest:
The Train I'm On (Warner Bros., 1972) 🎵🎵
Home Made Ice Cream (Warner Bros., 1973) 🎵🎵
Eyes (20th Century Fox, 1977) 🎵🎵
Tony Joe White (20th Century Fox, 1977) 🎵🎵

worth searching for: His 1990s albums, *Closer to the Truth* and *Path of a Decent Groove*, were mildly successful in Europe but didn't even come out in the U.S. There's no accounting for European nostalgia.

influences:
◀◀ Booker T. & the MGs, Otis Redding, Johnny Cash, Ernest Tubb, John Lee Hooker
▶▶ Lynyrd Skynyrd, Wet Willie, Bachman-Turner Overdrive, Alabama, Hank Williams Jr., Beat Happening, Country Dick Montana, Mojo Nixon

Steve Knopper

THE WHITES

Formed as Buck & the Down Home Folks, 1971, in Nashville, TN.

Buck White (born H.S. White, December 13, 1930, in OK), piano; Sharon White (born December 17, 1953, in Abilene, TX), guitar; Cheryl White (born January 27, 1955, in Abilene, TX), bass.

For 30 years, the Whites have functioned as a recording act and, even more amazingly, as a close-knit family, in spite of the obvious perils. Their bluegrass/gospel blend, enhanced by close family harmony, has remained relatively unchanged in those years, providing moments of pure pleasure for fans of fresh, acoustically based music. Buck White grew up in Texas, where he met his wife, Pat, who participated in the music until retiring during the early 1970s. In 1966, with the entire family involved, Buck and Pat, along with Arnold and Peggy Johnston, were the Down Home Folks, and the White and Johnston children formed the Down Home Kids. When the Whites moved to Nashville in 1971, they became Buck and the Down Home Folks, and made their first recording the following year. By the mid-1970s they had made a few more records, and in 1979 recorded with Jerry Douglas, Roland White, and the man who would later marry Sharon, Ricky Skaggs. They followed the album with a live record made in Japan, then soon embarked on a tour with Emmylou Harris, who had Skaggs in her Hot Band at the time. The group's 1981 Capitol debut didn't make much noise, but the next year they had the first of five Top 10 records with "You Put the Blue in Me" (#10, 1982). In 1983, the year they hit the Top 10 for the final time, the Whites became members of the Grand Ole Opry, where they remain a top attraction. Skaggs continues to be involved in their recordings and they contribute to his, as well as those of other artists, from time to time.

what to buy: Whether it's a bluegrass tune, a gospel number or a country standard, the Whites have made some great music through the years. But, sadly, too little of it remains in print. Among the best albums out there are *Greatest Hits* (Curb/MCA, 1986, prod. various) 🎵🎵🎵 and *Give a Little Back* (Step One, 1996, prod. Ray Pennington) 🎵🎵🎵.

the rest:
Doing It by the Book (Word/Epic, 1988) 🎵🎵🎵

solo outings:
Buck White:
More Pretty Girls Than One (Sugar Hill, 1980) 🎵🎵🎵
Poor Folks' Pleasure (Sugar Hill, 1978) 🎵🎵🎵

influences:
◀◀ Emmylou Harris

▶▶ Ricky Skaggs

Stephen L. Betts

DWIGHT WHITLEY

Born in KY.

Dwight Whitley's primary claim to fame is being Keith Whitley's brother. Which means he has about as much effect on country music as Roger Clinton and Billy Carter have had on national policy.

what's available: *Brotherly Love* (Neon, 1996, prod. Gene Waggoner) 🎵🎵 is a well-intentioned tribute album in which Dwight sings four of his brother's tunes plus songs like "I'm No Stranger to the Rain." Recommended only for the most devoted fans.

influences:
◀◀ Keith Whitley
▶▶ Hank Williams III

Brian Mansfield

KEITH WHITLEY

Born July 1, 1955, in Shady Hook, KY. Died May 9, 1989.

Keith Whitley lived a country cliché; he literally died from the bottle. His death from an alcohol overdose shocked the country music world at a time when the bluegrass veteran had crossed over very successfully into the considerably more profitable country music mainstream. Whitley was one of the most likable men in Nashville, and one of its most respected young, up-and-coming talents when he died. Whitley was just 14 when he formed one of his first bands with Ricky Skaggs, and three years later he was taping his own radio show in his family's garage. By then, he had been discovered by Ralph Stanley, who invited Whitley—then all of 15—to join his Clinch Mountain Boys. Whitley made his first appearance at the Grand Ole Opry that same year. He sang and played guitar on a dozen of the Boys' albums, recorded a duet album with Skaggs and spent time in at least three other groups, most notably silver-haired picker J.D. Sumner's progressive "newgrass" band, the New South. Longing to be his own man, Whitley set his sights on Nashville. He moved to Music City in 1983, when country slumped into a post-*Urban Cowboy* depression. He had a deal with RCA within a year and, with his appealing tenor and a knack for writing and/or picking distinctive songs, began making his ascent up the charts. "Miami My Amy" was his first real breakthrough, but it was 1988's "Don't Close Your Eyes" that became Whitley's signature hit, reigning as the most popular country song of that year. Tragically, Whitley died a year later. He cut five albums' worth of material for RCA, one of which was never issued, though elements of it have appeared on several posthumous albums—some of which cashed in on Whitley's commercial life after death rather than paying respects to the fallen singer. His music has continued to thrive: Alison Krauss' luscious version of "When You Say Nothing at All" was a huge hit in 1994, as was the tribute album from whence it came, with contributions from such stars as Alan Jackson, Tracy Lawrence and Whitley's widow, singer Lorrie Morgan.

what to buy: A concise, manageable compilation of Whitley's best and most popular work is *The Essential Keith Whitley* (RCA, 1996, comp. prod. Steve Lindsey) 𝄞𝄞𝄞, which serves up 20 of Whitley's songs, including such big hits as "Don't Close Your Eyes" and "I'm No Stranger to the Rain." It also contains RCA demo recordings from 1984–86, when yet more unreleased demos were spiffed up with new instrumentation.

what to buy next: *Don't Close Your Eyes* (RCA, 1988, prod. Garth Fundis) 𝄞𝄞𝄞 was Whitney's breakthrough album with "It's All Coming Back to Me Now," "When You Say Nothing at All" and the blockbuster title song.

what to avoid: *Wherever You Are Tonight* (BNA, 1995, prod. Steve Lindsey, Benny Quinn, Bill Caswell, Don Cook, Gary Nicholson, Max D. Barnes, Keith Whitley) 𝄞𝄞 is an interesting, spooky and ultimately unsuccessful attempt to lift the vocals from Whitley's 1984 audition tape and set them to fresh, new accompaniment from some of Nashville's top session players.

the rest:
L.A. to Miami (RCA, 1986) 𝄞𝄞𝄞
Greatest Hits (RCA, 1990) 𝄞𝄞𝄞
I Wonder Do You Think of Me (RCA, 1990) 𝄞𝄞𝄞
The Best of Keith Whitley (RCA, 1993) 𝄞𝄞𝄞
Super Hits (RCA, 1996) 𝄞𝄞𝄞

worth searching for: Whitley's popularity has ebbed as his death slowly fades into memory, which may explain why two of his albums are out of print. The six-song mini-album *A Hard Act to Follow* (RCA, 1985, prod. Blake Mevis) 𝄞𝄞𝄞 was Whitley's first non-single release for RCA, while *Kentucky Bluebird* (RCA, 1991, prod. various) 𝄞𝄞𝄞 features guest spots by Emmylou Harris and other prestigious country performers. Also of interest to fans is *Keith Whitley: A Tribute Album* (BNA, 1994) 𝄞𝄞𝄞.

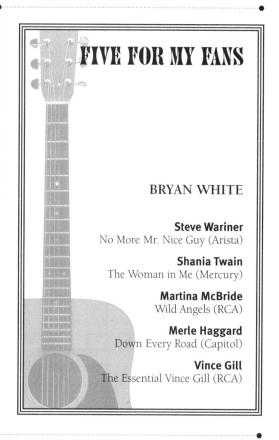

FIVE FOR MY FANS

BRYAN WHITE

Steve Wariner
No More Mr. Nice Guy (Arista)

Shania Twain
The Woman in Me (Mercury)

Martina McBride
Wild Angels (RCA)

Merle Haggard
Down Every Road (Capitol)

Vince Gill
The Essential Vince Gill (RCA)

influences:
◄◄ Lefty Frizzell, Ralph Stanley
►► Garth Brooks, Alan Jackson, Tim McGraw, Tracy Lawrence

Doug Pullen

SLIM WHITMAN

Born Otis Dewey Whiman, January 20, 1924, in Tampa, FL.

Cutting his teeth with the Light Crust Doughboys in 1949 and the *Louisiana Hayride* a year later, Slim Whitman had high hopes when RCA signed him around the same time. That deal was mostly fruitless, but Imperial Records hit a home run with the former semi-pro baseball player's "Indian Love Call," a thrilling, yearning, yodeling favorite, in 1952. Though Whitman would have hits for years, none was ever that popular again in the United States. Great Britain was another matter: He toured there frequently, and his single "Rose-Marie" had an astounding 11-week run at the top of the charts, a feat even the Beatles couldn't match. Whitman's warbling tenor still rises occasionally in the public conscious—through TV mail-order commercials during the 1980s and as the destroyer of invading aliens in Tim Burton's 1996 sci-fi comedy film *Mars Attacks!*

what to buy: *Greatest Hits* (Curb, 1990, prod. various) ♫♫♪ provides a wide sampling of Whitman's career, from the trio of hits that established him in 1952—"Indian Love Call," "Love Song of the Waterfall" and "Keep It a Secret"—to lesser-known later singles like 1966's "I Remember You" and 1970's "Shutters and Boards." But its 12 songs jump around in no apparent order, and it leaves off important early hits like "My Heart Is Broken in Three" in favor of less successful covers of pop songs.

the rest:
How Great Thou Art (Arrival, 1993) ♫♫
Vintage Collections (Capitol, 1997) ♫♫♫

worth searching for: Trends in modern U.S. country to the contrary, Slim Whitman still defines "country music" for many Europeans. Which is probably why you can get 10 years' worth of his early recordings for Imperial on the six-disc German import *Rose Marie—His Recordings 1949–1959* (Bear Family, 1996) ♫♫♫♪.

influences:
◀◀ Kenny Roberts
▶▶ Don Walser, Wylie & the Wild West Show

Brian Mansfield

THE WHITSTEIN BROTHERS
Brother vocal duo from LA.

Robert Whitstein (born March 16, 1944, in Pineville, LA); Charles Whitstein (born December 11, 1945, in Pineville, LA).

Bringing the Louvins and the Delmores clear into the 1990s, the Whitstein Brothers have put an old spin on some new music. That's because, along with standards like "Pitfall" and "Knoxville Girl," they've recorded things like Simon & Garfunkel's "Sounds of Silence" and recent tunes by Nashville writers like Dave Olney, although each time they've tackled a tune they've given it the feel of an old-time brother duet. Raised in central Louisiana, the brothers' dad, R.C., had a weekly radio show in Alexandria. His sons began appearing, winning local talent contests at 11 and 12 years old, and then moved to local TV. Their first record, a single called "Louisiana Woman," was enough of a success during the early 1960s to encourage the duo's move to Nashville. As the "Whitt Broth-

ers," Robert and Charles appeared on the Opry and toured with the likes of Faron Young and Porter Wagoner. Both were drafted into the marines and eventually returned home, where they recorded a gospel album of Louvin Brothers songs (re-released by Rounder in 1994). A contract with Rounder Records was offered when label head Ken Irwin received a tape via bluegrass artist Jesse McReynolds. Their 1992 release earned the duo a Grammy nomination. The next year Charles made an album with Charlie Louvin, then in 1994 reunited with Robert, which led to several Opry appearances and their most recent album.

what to buy: *Sweet Harmony* (Rounder, 1996, prod. Ken Irwin) ♫♫♫♫ and *Rose of My Heart* (Rounder, 1986/1994) ♫♫♫♫♪ show the Whitsteins holding to a grand tradition and instilling it with new and exciting life.

the rest:
Trouble Ain't Nothin' but the Blues (Rounder, 1987) ♫♫♫♪
Old Time Duets (Rounder, 1990) ♫♫♫♫
Sing Gospel Songs of the Louvins (Rounder, 1994) ♫♫♫♫

solo outings:
Charles Whitstein:
(With Charlie Louvin) *Hoping That You're Hoping* (Copper Creek, 1992) ♫♫♫♪

influences:
◀◀ Louvin Brothers, Blue Sky Boys
▶▶ Charlie Louvin

Stephen L. Betts

JOHN & AUDREY WIGGINS
Brother-sister duo from Nashville, TN.

John Wiggins (born October 13, 1962, in Nashville, TN); Audrey Wiggins (born December 26, 1967, in Nashville, TN).

Brother and sister duets are a rarity in country music, so John and Audrey Wiggins are a breath of fresh mountain air in that respect. Additionally though, this is an act brimming with unquestionable talent and obvious passion. Audrey's emotion-packed vocals and John's considerable songwriting skills highlight their outstanding 1994 debut. An interesting footnote to John and Audrey Wiggins' history is the fact that their father, the late Johnny Wiggins, was known as the "Singing Bus Driver" during the 1960s, when he performed with, and drove bus for, Ernest Tubb.

what to buy: The maturing of these two as artists comes through clearly on *The Dream* (Mercury, 1997, prod. Dann Huff) ♫♫♫♫, highlighted by the title track, penned by Harley Allen, which includes a snippet from an old Ernest Tubb record featuring Johnny Wiggins. A remake of Poco's "Crazy Love" suits their sweet family harmony perfectly. Look out Brooks & Dunn, here come John & Audrey!

what to buy next: *John and Audrey Wiggins* (Mercury, 1994, prod. Joe Scaife, Jim Cotton) 🎵🎵🎵 is a well-crafted debut, featuring the yodel song "Falling out of Love," the hit "Has Anybody Seen Amy" and the chilling John Wiggins original "Memory Making Night" among its many standouts.

influences:

◀◀ Everly Brothers, Whites

▶▶ Clinton Gregory, LeAnn Rimes

Stephen L. Betts

THE WILBURN BROTHERS

Duo from Hardy, AR.

Doyle Wilburn (born Virgil Doyle Wilburn, July 7, 1930; died October 16, 1981); Teddy Wilburn (born Thurman Theodore Wilburn, November 30, 1931).

The Wilburn Brothers haven't had the lasting impact on country that the Louvin Brothers or the Delmore Brothers did, but they were tremendously popular during the 1950s and 1960s due to their regular appearances on the Grand Ole Opry and their syndicated television series that introduced Loretta Lynn to many. They first joined the Opry in 1941 as part of the Wilburn Family, which featured two other brothers and a sister; they went to the *Louisiana Hayride* from 1948–51, then Doyle and Teddy entered the army. They formed the duo after leaving the service and rejoined the Opry. The Wilburn Brothers had all their biggest hits for Decca, including "Which One Is to Blame" (1959), "Trouble's Back in Town" (1962) and "Hurt Her Once for Me" (1966), and recorded with Webb Pierce and Ernest Tubb. None of the more than 25 LPs the duo recorded for Decca are currently in print.

what's available: *The Wonderful Wilburn Brothers* (King, 1988) 🎵🎵 is a sampling of the duo's early recordings from the days before they were recording stars. (The sound's not very good, either.) The songs, such as "Down in Dixie (Where They Say You All)" and "Bugle Call from Heaven," are more traditional than their later records.

worth searching for: *Retrospective* (MCA, 1990) 🎵🎵🎵 collects many of the Wilburn's biggest hits of the 1950s and 1960s.

influences:

◀◀ Delmore Brothers, Johnnie & Jack

▶▶ Louvin Brothers

Brian Mansfield

WILCO

See: Uncle Tupelo

WEBB WILDER

Born May 19, 1954, in Hattiesburg, MS.

A tall, balding, bespectacled white guy in a state trooper's hat might seem a man least likely to be a wild rock 'n' roller, but Wilder has turned his odd looks into an effective shtick. Playing deadpan with his deep baritone voice, Wilder has created a body of work he sometimes calls "hillbilly gothic"—a weird mixture of country, blues and psychedelic-era rock. His band has evolved from Webb Wilder & the Beatnecks to simply Webb Wilder, and most recently Webb Wilder & the NashVegans. But the elements have remained largely the same: power chords, wild twangy guitar and a large dose of novelty. He's also come up with one of the best credos in the business: "work hard, rock hard, eat hard, sleep hard, grow big, wear glasses if you need 'em."

what to buy: *It Came from Nashville* (Watermelon, 1986/1993, prod. R.S. Field) 🎵🎵🎵 , Wilder's first album, combines instrumentals and songs filled with deadpan Southern humor. The best is "Poolside" (co-written by Kevin Welch), in which Wilder lists his summertime rules: "no running, no pushing, no profanity and no dogs." The CD version of the album includes four extra tracks.

what to buy next: *Town & Country* (Watermelon, 1995, prod. R.S. Field, Mike Janas, Webb Wilder & the NashVegans) 🎵🎵🎵 was originally conceived as a driving tape in which one band performs all the songs. The result is a wild cover album that ranges from the Flamin' Groovies ("Slow Death") to Rodney Crowell ("I Ain't Living Long Like This").

what to avoid: The vinyl version of *It Came from Nashville* (Racket, 1986, prod. R.S. Field) is improved with the CD version's extra tracks.

the rest:

Hybrid Vigor (Demon, 1984) 🎵🎵🎵
Doo Dad (Praxis/Zoo, 1991) 🎵🎵🎵
Acres of Suede (Watermelon, 1996) 🎵🎵🎵

influences:

◀◀ Rolling Stones, ZZ Top, Howlin' Wolf

▶▶ Omar & the Howlers, LeRoi Brothers

Brian Mansfield

DON WILLIAMS

Born May 27, 1939, in Floydada, TX.

Don Williams rode his velvety smooth tenor to the top of the country charts during the late 1970s and early 1980s, a time when his gentle, breezy songs about love and devotion fit in comfortably alongside the pop stylings of lesser singers such as Kenny Rogers and the more aggressive, rocked-up country of upstarts like Alabama. The soft-spoken Texan is a throwback to country's simpler days, but his sound was commercial enough to cross over to the pop charts on occasion, particularly with his biggest hit, the buttery "I Believe in You," which topped the country charts and cracked pop's Top 30 in 1980. Not that Williams was a stranger to pop music; as a member of the Texas folk trio the Pozo Seco Singers, he'd visited the charts a few times during the 1960s folk boom. Their hits included the mid-1960s nuggets "Time," "I Can Make It with You" and "Look What You've Done." But the group broke up after moving to Nashville during the early 1970s.

Williams returned to Texas to work in his father's furniture business, but made the Music City trek soon after when former Pozo Seco member Susan Taylor invited him to write songs for her. Williams then launched a solo career and scored his first hit with "The Shelter in Your Eyes" in 1972. He went on to become one of Nashville's classiest, most laid-back singers. He's also a fine writer whose songs have been recorded by artists as diverse as Johnny Cash ("Down the Road I Go"), Eric Clapton ("Tulsa Time") and the Who's Pete Townshend ("'Till the Rivers All Run Dry"). His hitmaking ways continued through the 1980s, but country's growing emphasis on younger, faceless singers in the 1990s left little room for a guy like Williams, who moved to independent American Harvest Records in 1994 after more than 20 years with majors MCA, Capitol and RCA. Though forgotten in his native country, where many of his albums are no longer in print, Williams' popularity in Europe, particularly England, thrives.

what to buy: With so few of his studio albums available, the anthology *20 Greatest Hits* (MCA, 1987, prod. various) 🎵🎵🎵🎵 encapsulates the years he was with MCA Records, one of his most successful and consistent periods. The song selection is pretty

obvious, with "I Believe In You," "Tulsa Time" and the beautiful "Amanda" among them, but there's a timelessness to the material and a sincerity in Williams' voice that's hard to find in today's climate.

what to avoid: The performances on Williams' first live album, *An Evening with Don Williams: Best of Live* (American Harvest, 1995, prod. Don Williams) 🎵🎵 pale before the studio versions of recent and past hits.

the rest:

Don Williams Volume I (MCA, 1972) 🎵🎵🎵
Don Williams Volume III (MCA, 1974) 🎵🎵🎵
Greatest Hits, Volume 1 (MCA, 1975) 🎵🎵🎵
The Best of, Volume II (MCA, 1982) 🎵🎵🎵
The Best of, Volume III (MCA, 1984) 🎵🎵🎵
The Best of, Volume IV (MCA, 1986) 🎵🎵🎵
Greatest Country Hits (Curb, 1993) 🎵🎵🎵
The Ultimate Don Williams (Bransounds, 1995) 🎵🎵
Borrowed Tales (American Harvest, 1995) 🎵🎵🎵
Flatlands (American Harvest, 1996) 🎵🎵🎵

influences:

◀◀ Bob Dylan, Hank Williams

▶▶ John Anderson

Doug Pullen

HANK WILLIAMS

Born Hiriam King Williams, September 17, 1923, in Mount Olive, AL. Died January 1, 1953.

Though Hank Williams died before he turned 30 and recorded for barely six years, he created a mythology as large as those of Elvis Presley or the Beatles in rock. Every songwriter covets his ability to pierce the soul with minimally drawn lines. Every performer craves the kind of charisma that would get them a half-dozen encores at the Grand Ole Opry. And every singer with self-destructive tendencies uses Williams as the measuring glass against which he compares his ability to drink himself to death.

The Alabama-born son of a railroad engineer, Williams became a star of the Grand Ole Opry between 1949 and 1952, after stints with radio shows in Shreveport, Louisiana, and Montgomery, Al-

Hank Williams (Archive Photos)

abama. He has been inducted into both the Country Music and Rock and Roll Halls of Fame. He also recorded as Luke the Drifter.

what to buy: Every single—and then some—in Williams' catalog has become a standard in its genre, making *40 Greatest Hits* (Polydor, 1978, prod. Fred Rose) 𝄞𝄞𝄞𝄞𝄞 the best place to start delving into Williams' material, both musically and contextually.

what to buy next: It's up for grabs, depending on what you want, because most of Williams' compilations will include some cuts from *40 Greatest Hits*. *The Original Singles Collection . . . Plus* (Polydor, 1990, comp. prod. Colin Escott) 𝄞𝄞𝄞𝄞𝄞 expands the Williams oeuvre to three discs but, deceptively, doesn't include many of Williams' singles with his wife Audrey. *Health & Happiness Shows* (Mercury, 1993) 𝄞𝄞𝄞𝄞 contains eight radio performances from 1949.

what to avoid: *24 Greatest Hits* (PolyGram, 1976) 𝄞𝄞 and *24 Greatest Hits Volume 2* (Polydor, 1977) 𝄞𝄞, two collections of posthumously overdubbed recordings. The original versions of all these songs are available elsewhere, rendering these collections superfluous. Mercury targeted the alternative-rock crowd with *Alone and Forsaken* (Mercury, 1995) 𝄞𝄞𝄞, which features Williams' most angst-ridden tunes. British rocker Matt Johnson, who had recorded a Williams tribute album, *Hanky Panky* (Epic, 1995, prod. Matt Johnson, Bruce Lampcov) 𝄞𝄞𝄞, with his group the The, opened *Alone and Forsaken* with a monologue that insulted the many country fans who didn't need to have Williams' greatness explained to them.

the rest:
Greatest Hits (Polydor, 1963) 𝄞𝄞𝄞𝄞
Beyond the Sunset (Polydor, 1963) 𝄞𝄞𝄞
Very Best Of (Polydor, 1963) 𝄞𝄞𝄞
I Saw the Light (Polydor, 1968) 𝄞𝄞𝄞𝄞
Rare Demos: First to Last (Country Music Foundation, 1990) 𝄞𝄞𝄞𝄞
I Saw the Light (PolyGram Special Markets, 1994) 𝄞𝄞𝄞
The Hits Volume 1 (Mercury, 1994) 𝄞𝄞𝄞𝄞𝄞
The Hits Volume 2 (Mercury, 1995) 𝄞𝄞𝄞𝄞𝄞
Low Down Blues (Mercury, 1996) 𝄞𝄞𝄞𝄞

worth searching for: *The Collectors' Edition* (Mercury, 1987) 𝄞𝄞𝄞𝄞𝄞, an eight-disc, limited-edition set available only through Tower Records, collected the individual volumes that contained almost every recording Williams made for MGM in chronological order. *The Legend of Hank Williams* (Mercury, 1996, prod. Joseph Wilson) 𝄞𝄞𝄞 is an abridgment of Colin Escott's Williams biography, read by Sammy Kershaw, and includes Williams' music.

influences:
◀◀ Carter Family, Roy Acuff
▶▶ Hank Williams Jr., Jimmie Dale Gilmore, every male country singer since

Brian Mansfield

HANK WILLIAMS JR.

Born Randall Hank Williams, May 26, 1949, in Shreveport, LA.

Hank Williams Jr. has lived long enough to play out the complexities of the Williams bloodline on record in a way his father never got to. Not quite four years old when his father died, Hank Jr. had his first chart hit at age 14 with a rendition of daddy's "Long Gone Lonesome Blues." That record set the tone for his career: Williams had to emerge from one of the longest shadows in musical history, and it nearly killed him to do it. Nearly every one of Hank Jr.'s albums contains either a song written by Hank Sr. or one about his relationship to the father he barely knew—including the macabre posthumous duet on "There's a Tear in My Beer" that Hank Jr. fashioned in 1989. For a long time, it seemed that Hank Jr. would fall victim to the same substance abuse problems that killed his father, and many fans expected him to do just that to keep the legacy going. Eventually, Williams distinguished himself as a redneck Southern rocker, though he had recorded for more than a decade before he reached that point. He's actually a better singer than his dad, but his material varies wildly. His ability to draw rock and country crowds together—not to mention football fans, thanks to his theme song for ABC's *Monday Night Football*—made him one of country's biggest stars during the late 1980s, when he won the Country Music Association's Entertainer of the Year award twice.

what to buy: *Hank Williams Jr. & Friends* (MGM, 1975, prod. Dick Glasser) 𝄞𝄞𝄞𝄞𝄞 was the first of his Southern rock albums, and with it he began to tie the outlaw country of Willie Nelson and Waylon Jennings to the Southern rock of Lynyrd Skynyrd and Charlie Daniels. Daniels, the Marshall Tucker Band's Toy Caldwell and Chuck Leavell of the Allman Brothers Band appear on this album, which contains the hits "Stoned at the Jukebox" and "Living Proof."

what to buy next: *Family Tradition* (Elektra/Curb, 1979, prod. Ray Ruff, Jimmy Bowen, Phil Gernhard) 𝄞𝄞𝄞𝄞 continued in the Southern rock/outlaw vein, especially with the title-track hit.

Hank Williams Jr.'s Greatest Hits (Warner Bros./Curb, 1982, prod. Jimmy Bowen) 🎵🎵🎵 collects Williams' hits from 1979–82—among them "Whiskey Bent and Hell Bound" and "A Country Boy Can Survive"—and is probably the best single-disc Williams anthology.

what to avoid: *11 Roses* (Polydor, 1972, prod. Jim Vienneau) 🎵🎵 is one of Williams' weakest efforts from his early period, with none of the attitude that would show itself later. That attitude, though, only carries Williams so far and makes him wildly un-even. *Lone Wolf* (Warner Bros./Curb, 1990, prod. Barry Beckett, Hank Williams Jr., Jim Ed Norman) 🎵🎵 is dull, by-the-numbers Southern rock, while *America (The Way I See It)* (Warner Bros./Curb, 1990, prod. Jimmy Bowen, Barry Beckett, Hank Williams Jr., Jim Ed Norman) 🎵 is a collection of Williams' politically (feeble) minded material that rides the fence between blindly patriotic and offensive.

the rest:
14 Greatest Hits (Polydor, 1976) 🎵🎵🎵
One Night Stands (Warner/Curb, 1977) 🎵🎵🎵
The New South (Warner Bros., 1978) 🎵🎵🎵🎵
Whiskey Bent and Hell Bound (Elektra, 1979) 🎵🎵🎵🎵
Habits Old and New (Elektra, 1980) 🎵🎵🎵
Rowdy (Warner Bros./Curb, 1981) 🎵🎵🎵
High Notes (Warner Bros./Curb, 1982) 🎵🎵🎵
Man of Steel (Warner Bros./Curb, 1983) 🎵🎵🎵
Strong Stuff (Warner Bros./Curb, 1983) 🎵🎵🎵
Major Moves (Warner Bros./Curb, 1985) 🎵🎵🎵
Five-o (Warner Bros./Curb, 1985) 🎵🎵🎵
Greatest Hits, Volume 2 (Warner Bros./Curb, 1985) 🎵🎵🎵
The Early Years 1976–1978 (Warner Bros./Curb, 1986) 🎵🎵🎵🎵
Montana Cafe (Warner Bros./Curb, 1986) 🎵🎵🎵
Born to Boogie (Warner Bros./Curb, 1987) 🎵🎵🎵🎵
Hank "Live" (Warner Bros., 1987) 🎵🎵🎵
Hank Williams Jr.'s Greatest Hits (Polydor, 1987) 🎵🎵🎵
Standing in the Shadows (Polydor, 1988) 🎵🎵🎵🎵
Wild Streak (Warner Bros., 1988) 🎵🎵🎵
Greatest Hits III (Warner Bros./Curb, 1989) 🎵🎵🎵🎵
Pure Hank (Warner Bros., 1991) 🎵🎵🎵
The Pressure Is On (Warner Bros., 1991) 🎵🎵🎵🎵
The Best of Hank Williams Jr., Volume 1—Roots & Branches (Mercury, 1992) 🎵🎵🎵
Living Proof: The MGM Recordings, 1963–1975 (Mercury, 1992) 🎵🎵🎵🎵
The Bocephus Box: The Hank Williams Jr. Collection, 1979–1992 (Curb/Capricorn, 1992) 🎵🎵🎵
Maverick (Capricorn, 1992) 🎵🎵🎵
Hank Williams/Hank Williams Jr. (K-Tel, 1992) 🎵🎵🎵

The Best of Hank and Hank (Curb/CEMA, 1992) 🎵🎵🎵
Out of Left Field (Capricorn, 1993) 🎵🎵🎵🎵
Hog Wild (Curb, 1995) 🎵🎵
Aka Wham Bam, Sam (Curb, 1996) 🎵🎵
(As the Three Hanks) *Men with Broken Hearts* (Curb, 1996) 🎵🎵
The Hits (Mercury, 1997) 🎵🎵🎵

worth searching for: *Live at Cobo Hall, Detroit* (Polydor, 1969, prod. Jim Vienneau) 🎵🎵🎵🎵 is an impressive live album from Williams' pre-Southern rock days.

influences:
◀◀ Hank Williams, Charlie Daniels, Lynyrd Skynyrd, Marshall Tucker Band
▶▶ Steve Earle, Travis Tritt, Kentucky HeadHunters

Brian Mansfield

JASON D. WILLIAMS

Born January 28, 1967, in El Dorado, AR.

Rumor has it that Jason D. Williams was adopted, and that Jerry Lee Lewis once dated his natural mother, but the Killer refuses to take a DNA test to determine if he's Jason's biological father or not. Great story—if it's true. All anybody knows for sure (because Williams himself likes to speak with more tongue than truth) is that Williams plays hard-driving piano boogie in the style of Jerry Lee Lewis. His onstage repertoire contains mostly Lewis oldies, and he has been known to purchase and wear Lewis' old clothes! Also, some of Lewis' former associates (Roland Janes, Al Embry, Shelby S. Singleton Jr. and Roy Dea) have advised Williams' career and helped produce his first two discs. Williams deflects the inevitable comparisons with dead-pan humor, saying, "I'm not like Jerry Lee, 'cuz I can play *classical* music" (although Lewis has been known to bang out a few bars of Beethoven's Fifth himself).

There are genuine stylistic differences between the two. Williams' patter is affable, and he has an appealing, absurdist sense of humor. On stage, Williams is far more physical at the keyboard than Lewis ever was. Vocally, however, he has none of Lewis' depth, range or dramatic instincts; he is simply inca-pable of putting across a convincing ballad, and his stockpile of piano riffs aren't used as imaginatively as Lewis'. Still, if you like flat-out rock-a-beatin' boogie, with occasional semi-classi-cal interludes (which has the same effect as Buddy Hackett emoting poetry in between motel jokes), the recordings of Jason D. Williams are the place to go. President Clinton's late mother was a member of his fan club. A new independent release is slated for sometime in 1997.

what's available: Williams may be the only artist in history to start at RCA and wind up at Sun (which is little more than a regional mail-order service these days). He wrote most of the material on *Wild* (Sun, 1993, prod. Shelby S. Singleton Jr., Roy Dea) 🎵🎵🎵, much of it hot-tempo boogie, with a beautifully absurd sidestep into "Tubular Bells (Theme from *The Exorcist*)."

worth searching for: *Tore Up* (RCA/BMG, 1989, prod. Roy Dea, Mark Wright) 🎵🎵🎵 contains the Wright productions of "Waitin' on Ice" and "Where There's Smoke (You'll Find My Old Flame)," the best songs Williams has cut and his only legitimate shot at radio air play thus far.

influences:

◀◀ Jerry Lee Lewis, Mickey Gilley, Liberace, Freddie "Fingers" Lee

▶▶ Mark Collie

Ken Burke

LUCINDA WILLIAMS

Born January 26, 1953, in Lake Charles, LA.

Unfortunately, the same qualities that make Lucinda Williams' music so great also ensure that there isn't more of it put out for public consumption. The daughter of a poet/university professor, Williams is notoriously headstrong and has an artistic temperament ill-suited to issues of career logistics—stories of her clashes with labels and producers are legendary in the music business. Yet she is also one of the finest songwriters of her generation, with a writerly gift for nailing characters or situations with the perfect detail. Her earthy voice also makes Williams her own best interpreter; if only we got to hear more of her songs! In 1997 she planned to release her fifth full-length album in 17 years on American Recordings.

what to buy: Williams made two early albums before she found her own voice, both as a writer and singer, and they're most notable as acts of homage to her country and Delta blues roots. Her third album, *Lucinda Williams* (Rough Trade, 1988, prod. Lucinda Williams, Gurf Morlix) 🎵🎵🎵🎵, is one of the signpost albums of post-punk Americana. Drawing on Williams' failed marriage (to Long Ryders drummer Greg Sowders) and eight years of pent-up career frustrations, these songs cut with an unbelievable intensity. The tough-minded feminine perspective of "I Just Wanted to See You So Bad" and "Passionate Kisses" rings absolutely true, and it's as unusual as it is emotionally

rich. One measure of this album's songcraft is that other singers frequently raid it for material: Mary Chapin Carpenter had a hit with "Passionate Kisses"; Patty Loveless scored on the country charts with "The Night's Too Long"; and Tom Petty covered "Changed the Locks" on his soundtrack for the 1996 movie *She's the One.*

what to buy next: The follow-up, *Sweet Old World* (Chameleon, 1992, prod. Lucinda Williams, Gurf Morlix, Dusty Wakeman) 🎵🎵🎵🎵, is more self-conscious than its predecessor, but still damned fine. It's also grim, coursing with images of suicide, death and despair. Fitting, then, that it closes with a cover of the late English cult folkie Nick Drake's "Which Will."

the rest:

Ramblin' on My Mind (Smithsonian/Folkways, 1979/1991) 🎵🎵🎵
Happy Woman Blues (Smithsonian/Folkways, 1980/1990) 🎵🎵🎵
Passionate Kisses (Rough Trade EP, 1989) 🎵🎵🎵

worth searching for: Williams' "Main Road" is one of the high points of the Victoria Williams tribute, *Sweet Relief* (Chaos, 1993, prod. various) 🎵🎵🎵🎵. Her most recent recorded work is as duet partner with Steve Earle on "You're Still Standin' There," from his 1996 album *I Feel Alright.*

influences:

◀◀ Bob Dylan, Flannery O'Connor, Emmylou Harris, Robert Johnson, Rosanne Cash, Bonnie Raitt

▶▶ Victoria Williams, Joe Henry, Mary Chapin Carpenter, Iris DeMent, Amy Rigby

David Menconi

ROBIN & LINDA WILLIAMS

Husband and wife vocal duo formed 1973.

Robin Williams (born March 16, 1947); Linda Williams (born July 7, 1947).

This folk/country husband and wife duo began recording together in 1973 and first gained national exposure through their frequent guest appearances on Garrison Keillor's *Prairie Home Companion.* They specialize in a cross between folk and acoustic country, drawing heavily on bluegrass and classic country sources, including the Carter Family and Hank Williams.

what to buy: *All Broken Hearts Are the Same* (Sugar Hill, 1988, prod. T. Michael Coleman) 🎵🎵🎵🎵 is a superb collection of originals highlighted by the duo's intricate arrangements and electrifying harmony vocals. "Rollin' and Ramblin'" is a poignant tale about the death of Hank Williams.

what to buy next: *Turn Toward Tomorrow* (Sugar Hill, 1993) is toe-tapping country featuring pure, full country production, including a pedal steel guitar. Incudes a honky-tonk drinking song, "On the Day the Last Tear Falls."

the rest:
Rhythm of Love (Sugar Hill, 1990) 🎵🎵🎵
Robin & Linda Williams & Their Fine Group (Sugar Hill, 1994) 🎵🎵🎵
Live (Sugar Hill, 1994) 🎵🎵🎵
Good News (Sugar Hill, 1995)
Sugar for Sugar (Sugar Hill, 1996) 🎵🎵🎵🎵
Close As We Can Get/Nine 'till Midnight (Sugar Hill) 🎵🎵🎵🎵

worth searching for: *Harmony* (June Appal, 1981) was the couple's first album.

Douglas Fulmer

TEX WILLIAMS

Born Sollie Paul Williams, August 23, 1917, near Ramsey, IL. Died October 11, 1985.

A singer from Illinois nicknamed for the Lone Star state, Tex Williams first came to the attention of Western-swing fans by singing on fiddler Spade Cooley's Columbia Records hits "Shame on You" and "Detour." When Cooley fired him in 1946 Williams took a good chunk of Cooley's band with him and formed the Western Caravan, one of the more musically inventive swing bands. He had his first big hit under his own name with "Smoke! Smoke! Smoke! (That Cigarette)," a talking-blues novelty written by Merle Travis (Williams shared a writing credit for altering one line). The song was a country and pop smash, making Williams' Western Caravan one of the few Western bands to be popular on both sides of the Mississippi. Williams' reliance on the talking-blues gimmick (later singles included "That's What I Like about the West" and "Never Trust a Woman") denied him the critical credibility and the commercial longevity that other bands had. His heyday was 1946–1949 for Capitol Records; subsequent recordings for RCA and Decca were never as popular. The Western Caravan broke up in 1957, and Williams recorded solo into the 1970s. Ironically (considering the title of his biggest hit), Williams died of lung cancer in 1985 (and he smoked).

what's available: *Vintage Collections Series* (Capitol, 1996, comp. prod. Rich Kienzle, John Johnson) 🎵🎵🎵🎵 captures the essence of Williams' band with his 1940s talking-blues hits,

instrumental radio transcriptions and a healthy helping of previously unissued recordings. Despite his fondness for spoken numbers, Williams is a smooth singer, and the band, which might feature accordion, triple fiddles, vibes and/or trumpets, is top notch. "Wild Card," which features guest guitarist Jimmy Bryant, was co-written by actor Buddy Ebsen. This isn't all the good stuff Williams ever recorded, but it is his most successful.

influences:
◀◀ Jimmy Wakely, Spade Cooley
▶▶ Asleep at the Wheel, Dave & Deke Combo

Brian Mansfield

THE WILLIS BROTHERS
Family trio.

James "Guy" Willis (born July 15, 1915; died April 13, 1981); Charles "Skeeter" Willis (born December 20, 1907; died 1976), fiddle; Richard "Vic" Willis (born May 31, 1922; died January 15, 1995), accordion.

The Willis Brothers worked around country for years, first gaining a radio audience under the name the Oklahoma Wranglers. As the Oklahoma Cowboys, the trio backed Hank Williams on his first recordings. Later the group would back Eddy Arnold. The group was a Grand Ole Opry act from 1946–1949; they rejoined in 1960. The Willis Brothers found its biggest commercial success during the truck-driving-song craze of the 1960s, most notably with the 1964 hit "Give Me 40 Acres (To Turn This Rig Around)." Vic Willis later fronted the Vic Willis Trio.

what's available: The songs on *24 Great Truck Drivin' Songs* (Hollywood/IMG, 1987) 🎵🎵 aren't far removed from the vaudeville humor of performers like Grandpa Jones and Uncle Dave Macon, with titles like "Diesel Drivin' Donut Dunkin' Dan" and "Alcohol and #2 Diesel." "Give Me 40 Acres" is still mildly amusing after all these years, but the Willis' hammy performances get tiresome after awhile. *Diesel Smoke on Danger Road* (Starday, 1985) 🎵🎵 is an eight-song cassette, with only one song ("Truck Stop Cutie") that doesn't appear on the CD. Both albums contain "Give Me 40 Acres."

influences:
◀◀ Dave Dudley, Eddy Arnold, Grandpa Jones
▶▶ Dick Curless

Brian Mansfield

4
8
4 *kelly willis*

KELLY WILLIS

Born October 2, 1968, in Lawton, OK.

Of MCA's wisely signed but woefully marketed triumvirate of hard-rocking, hard-knocks Texans—anchored by Joe Ely and Steve Earle—Kelly Willis was always the most commercially viable: during the early 1990s, the honey-voiced, strawberry-blonde Austinite injected a refreshing urgency and energy into Nashville's bloodstream, mining the rich songbooks of John Hiatt, Kevin Welch and Jim Lauderdale long before they became fashionable fine print. Despite her shy stage demeanor, Willis can bowl over a crowd with the stunning clout and clarity of her singing, which can raise roofs without resorting to blues-mama growling. In 1995 she signed with A&M Records and cut some much-ballyhooed sessions with members of Son Volt that were destined for her label debut. But she severed ties with A&M before an album could be completed, leaving the Son Volt sessions to be piecemealed out on a promotional EP and various soundtracks and compilations, including Upstart's *Rig Rock Deluxe* (a take on Little Feat's "Truckstop Girl") and Reprise's *Red Hot + Bothered* (a duet with Volt leader Jay Farrar on Townes Van Zandt's "Rex's Blues").

what to buy: Her knockout MCA swan song, *Kelly Willis* (MCA, 1993, prod. Don Was, Tony Brown, John Leventhal) ♫♫♫♫, draws from left-field sources for both backing (Kieran Kane, Benmont Tench, ex-Rockpile guitarist Billy Bremner and members of Jellyfish) and songs. Her inspired covers of Marshall Crenshaw's "Whatever Way the Wind Blows" and the Kendalls' "Heaven's Just a Sin Away" snared some attention from country radio, but the defiant "Get Real"—written by Willis and co-producer John Leventhal—offers the most encouraging sign for her future.

what to buy next: The polished production and inconsistent song choices on *Bang Bang* (MCA, 1991, prod. Tony Brown) ♫♫♫ can't stop this album from occasionally living up to its title, especially on Joe Ely's ferocious "Settle for Love," Jim Lauderdale and Monte Warden's "I'll Try Again" and a cover of rockabilly singer Janis Martin's raucous title track.

what to avoid: *Well-Travelled Love* (MCA, 1990, prod. Tony Brown, John Guess) ♫♫♫ is the tough but tentative sound of a talented singer searching for her voice.

worth searching for: *Fading Fast* (A&M, 1996, prod. Kelly Willis, Brian Paulson) ♫♫♫ is a four-track promotional EP boasting three collaborations with Son Volt that don't throw the anticipated sparks but still radiate with an engaging warmth, especially on "What World Are You Living In?" (written by Willis and Gary Louris of the Jayhawks). The title track garnered so much

airplay on Americana stations that A&M eventually licensed the disc to indie Crystal Clear Sound (10486 Brockwood Road, Dallas, TX 75238) for regional commercial release.

influences:
◀◀ Loretta Lynn, Buddy Holly, Joe Ely, Rosie Flores
▶▶ Kim Richey, Jo Dee Messina

David Okamoto

BOB WILLS

Born James Robert Wills, March 6, 1905, near Kosse, TX. Died May 13, 1975.

Inducted into the Country Music Hall of Fame in 1968, Bob Wills never cared much for the fiddle as a youth—that is, until he stood before an anxious crowd. His father was late for the gig, and somebody had to play. So "Jim Rob" did what he could: repeated the same six songs until his dad showed up. The audience responded to the 10-year-old, and an entertainer was born. In 1931 Wills founded the Light Crust Doughboys, named after the sponsor of the group's radio show. Founding member Milton Brown couldn't take Wills' bawdy demeanor, and Brown was replaced by Tommy Duncan. Both Wills and Duncan left the Doughboys in 1933 and created the first of many incarnations of the Texas Playboys. Wills blended electric steel with standard guitar for a thrilling new sound, while Duncan supported his reputation as perhaps the greatest of the Playboys' vocalists. Oklahoma farmers and Texas ranchhands packed dancehalls throughout the region to see the Playboys, and at the end of the Depression Wills was among the most famous musicians alive. The band had broadened to 18 members under the supervision of guitarist Eldon Shamblin. A revamped vocal version of "New San Antonio Rose," the group's signature tune, swept the country.

World War II threatened to end all their careers, however. Duncan enlisted in the army shortly after Pearl Harbor, and other members followed right behind him. Wills temporarily disbanded the Playboys and joined the army himself in late 1943. Taking orders was never his strong suit, though, and he and Duncan were soon discharged. The two reunited and formed a smaller, tighter version of the Playboys. In 1943 Wills also married for the sixth time, to Betty Anderson; that union would last until his death.

Though Wills outsold the pop-oriented Tommy Dorsey and Benny Goodman for the next decade, the advent of television decimated the dancehall crowds. Poor health, due to his fondness for cigars and drink, kept Wills out of the spotlight as well (he would lead his last sessions from a wheelchair, after suffering a stroke during 1970). Country radio didn't play Wills much, either, but he never considered himself a country artist. Instead, he was "the King of Western Swing." To him, they were two separate styles of music. Merle Haggard had the opportunity to play fiddle on Wills' final project, and the singer championed the innovator with the 1982 album *Tribute to the Best Damn Fiddle Player in the World (Or My Salute to Bob Wills)*. Asleep at the Wheel paid similar tribute in 1994 with *Tribute to the Music of Bob Wills & the Texas Playboys*.

what to buy: Assembled with Rhino's usual flair and passion, the two-disc *Anthology, 1935–1973* (Rhino, 1991, comp. prod. James Austin, Bob Fisher) 🎵🎵🎵🎵 spans nearly 40 years of Wills' recordings, from his early days on the Vocalion label to his final sessions in December 1973, just a year and a half before his death. The compilation includes most of the Playboys' biggest hits, but it tends (probably rightly) to concentrate on the years when Duncan was the group's vocalist.

what to buy next: *Encore* (Capitol, 1994, comp. prod. John Johnson) 🎵🎵🎵🎵 surveys Wills' career another way. This three-disc box set compiles studio recordings made for Liberty Records between 1960–63, seven cuts from 1963–64 Ft. Worth, Texas, radio shows and Wills' final recordings, made in December 1973. (Wills had a stroke the night of the first session and remained in a coma for 15 months until his death; Haggard plays fiddle on the final four tracks, recorded the next day.) It's a fascinating look at the latter days of a legend. *Columbia Historic Edition* (Columbia, 1982) 🎵🎵🎵🎵 is an excellent one-disc collection of hits from the group's commercial heyday.

what to avoid: Bob Wills & the McKinney Sisters' *Tiffany Transcriptions* (Rhino, 1991) 🎵, a largely pop-oriented outing with yodeling sisters Dean and Evelyn McKinney.

the rest:
21 Golden Hits (Hollywood) 🎵🎵🎵
The Best of Bob Wills (MCA, 1973) 🎵🎵🎵
The Best of Bob Wills, Volume 2 (MCA, 1975) 🎵🎵🎵
King of Western Swing/Wills & His Playboys (MCA) 🎵🎵🎵
24 Greatest Hits (Mercury, 1977) 🎵🎵🎵
The Tiffany Transcriptions, Volume 1 (Rhino, 1982) 🎵🎵🎵🎵
The Tiffany Transcriptions, Volume 2 (Rhino, 1984) 🎵🎵🎵🎵
The Tiffany Transcriptions, Volume 3 (Rhino, 1984) 🎵🎵🎵🎵
The Tiffany Transcriptions, Volume 4 (Rhino, 1985) 🎵🎵🎵🎵
The Tiffany Transcriptions, Volume 5 (Rhino, 1986) 🎵🎵🎵🎵
The Tiffany Transcriptions, Volume 6 (Rhino, 1987) 🎵🎵🎵🎵
The Tiffany Transcriptions, Volume 7 (Rhino, 1987) 🎵🎵🎵🎵

Kelly Willis **(MCA Records—Nashville)**

The Golden Era (Columbia, 1987) 🎵🎵🎵🎵
Fiddle (Country Music Foundation, 1987) 🎵🎵🎵🎵
The Tiffany Transcriptions, Volume 8 (Rhino, 1988) 🎵🎵🎵🎵
The Tiffany Transcriptions, Volume 9 (Rhino, 1990) 🎵🎵🎵🎵
Country Music Hall of Fame (MCA, 1992) 🎵🎵🎵
The Essential Bob Wills & His Texas Playboys (1935–1947) (Legacy, 1992) 🎵🎵🎵
For the Last Time (Capitol, 1994) 🎵🎵🎵
Classic Western Swing (Rhino, 1994) 🎵🎵🎵🎵
Greatest Hits (Curb, 1990) 🎵🎵🎵

worth searching for: In the United States, only the misleadingly named *21 Greatest Hits* collects Wills' 1960s recordings for the Dallas, Texas-based Longhorn label. *The Longhorn Recordings* (Bear Family) 🎵🎵🎵, a German import, does a much better and more complete job.

influences:
◀◀ Milton Brown, Adolph Hofner
▶▶ Asleep at the Wheel, Merle Haggard, Spade Cooley, Johnny Gimble

Craig Shelburne and Brian Mansfield

MARK WILLS

Born Mark Williams, August 8, 1973, in Cleveland, TN.

Mark Wills started playing regular gigs at the Buckboard, a club near Atlanta, when he was 17. His music has a definite pop sensibility, but also contains hints of his traditional country influences, such as Keith Whitley and Conway Twitty.

what's available: *Mark Wills* (Mercury, 1996, prod. Keith Stegall, Carson Chamberlain) 𝄞𝄞𝄞 is a collection of mostly upbeat toe-tappers. His baritone is pure country, serving him well on the Top 5 hit "Jacob's Ladder" and such honky-tonk romps as "High Low and In Between."

influences:
◀◀ George Jones, Clay Walker, Keith Whitley

Deborah Barnes

JESSE WINCHESTER

Born May 17, 1944, in Shreveport, LA.

Early in his career, Jesse Winchester was known as much for his conscientious objection to the Vietnam War, that sent him up to Canada during the late 1960s, as for the sweet, finely edged country/folk songs, often invoking the American South, that he wrote and recorded beginning in 1970. His first album, produced by Robbie Robertson of the Band and engineered by Todd Rundgren, signaled the emergence of a sensitive and literate tunesmith with a lot on his mind. By his third album, the appropriately titled *Learn to Love It* (1974), Winchester was familiar with expressing the complexities and frustrations of his exile from the States and his Memphis home, but with his gentle bluesy style, he articulately told the story, sometimes even with a touch of humor, without complaining about it. He became a Canadian citizen in 1973 and still lives in Canada, but was able to return to the States and tour here after President Carter's amnesty for draft resisters in 1977. Though he recorded most prolifically between 1970 and 1981, Winchester's songs continued to be recorded by artists ranging from Wynonna ("Let's Make a Baby King"), Emmylou Harris and Chris Smither ("Thanks to You"), to dancefloor proponents the Weather Girls ("Well-a-Wiggy"). The Canadian label Stony Plain reissued the Jesse Winchester album catalog, originally released on Ampex and Bearsville, in 1994, 1995 and 1996.

what to buy: *The Best of Jesse Winchester* (Rhino, 1988, prod. various) 𝄞𝄞𝄞𝄞, compiled by Bill Flanagan, collects highlights from the seven albums Winchester recorded between 1970 and 1981, and includes his only Top 40 hit, "Say What" from 1981's *Talk Memphis* album.

what to buy next: *Jesse Winchester* (Stony Plain, 1970, prod. Robbie Robertson) 𝄞𝄞𝄞 and *Learn to Love It* (Stony Plain, 1974, prod. Jesse Winchester) 𝄞𝄞𝄞, his first and third album respectively, both recently reissued, were originally critical favorites by the tasteful, then reclusive folk/blues songwriter. His songs have gracefully withstood the test of time.

the rest:
Third Down, 110 to Go (Stony Plain, 1972) 𝄞𝄞𝄞
Let the Rough Side Drag (Stony Plain, 1976) 𝄞𝄞𝄞𝄞
Nothing but a Breeze (Stony Plain, 1977) 𝄞𝄞𝄞𝄞
A Touch on the Rainy Side (Stony Plain, 1978) 𝄞𝄞𝄞𝄞
Talk Memphis (Stony Plain, 1981) 𝄞𝄞𝄞

worth searching for: His most recent recording, 1988's *Humour Me* (Sugar Hill, 1988, prod. Jesse Winchester) 𝄞𝄞𝄞, is Winchester at his most relaxed. Recorded in Nashville, the album features 12 tracks and includes his laid-back readings of "Thanks to You," "Let's Make a Baby King" and "Well-a-Wiggy," with stellar accompaniment by Sam Bush, Bela Fleck, Jerry Douglas, Mark O'Connor and other top players.

influences:
◀◀ Bob Dylan, the Band
▶▶ John Prine, Lyle Lovett

David Sokol

REVEREND BILLY C. WIRTZ

Born September 28, 1954, in Aiken, SC.

A fast-talking, funky, blues/boogie-woogie piano man with a raunchy sense of humor, a keen sense of observation and a great big heart, the Reverend Billy C. Wirtz spent years playing country, blues, R&B and rock before combining it all into his own warp-a-billy style. His songs poke fun at religion, musical trends, tacky Americana and modern times; his best albums, recorded live, have an off-beat spontaneity that lends them to repeated listenings by fun-loving mature audiences.

what to buy: *Pianist Envy* (HighTone, 1994, prod. Rev. Billy C. Wirtz, Harry Simmons) 𝄞𝄞𝄞𝄞, recorded live at the Brewery in Raleigh, North Carolina, finds the Reverend in top form with irreverent pontifications on Elvis Presley in a Barney suit ("The King Gets a Day Job"), playing in a club for a bunch of unyielding Jimmy Buffett-loving yuppies ("Margarita Hell") and growing up in a Grateful Dead-loving home ("Mama Was a Dead-head"). Lots of Nashville references, too.

what to buy next: *Songs of Faith and Inflammation* (High-Tone, 1996, prod. Bruce Bromberg) ♫♫♫ is full of pokes at life as we know it and includes a hilarious but way too short "We Dismember These," in which the Reverend takes a nostalgic, Statler Brothers-like look back at the good old days—only the good old days are mid-1990s America and the memories are of drive-by shootings, pierced nipples and the O.J. Simpson murder trial. Recorded live at Be Here Now in Asheville, North Carolina.

the rest:
Backslider's Tractor Pull (HighTone, 1990) ♫♫♡
A Turn for the Wirtz (Confessions of a Hillbilly Love-God) (HighTone, 1992) ♫♫♫

worth searching for: The Reverend's first album, *Deep Fried and Sanctified* (HighTone, 1989, prod. Bob Greenlee, Rev. Billy C. Wirtz) ♫♫♫, finds the funnyman in sharp form, tackling everything from shopping malls and TV evangelists to modern stress and answering machines.

influences:
◄◄ Jerry Lee Lewis, Mark Russell
►► Root Boy Slim, Jeff Foxworthy

David Sokol

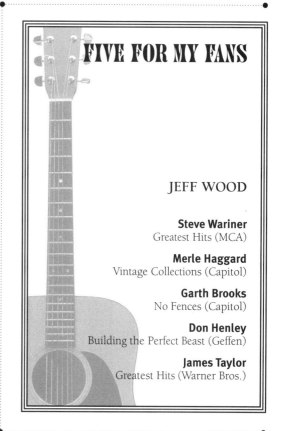

FIVE FOR MY FANS

JEFF WOOD

Steve Wariner
Greatest Hits (MCA)

Merle Haggard
Vintage Collections (Capitol)

Garth Brooks
No Fences (Capitol)

Don Henley
Building the Perfect Beast (Geffen)

James Taylor
Greatest Hits (Warner Bros.)

CHUBBY WISE

Born Robert Russell Wise, October 2, 1915, in Lake City, FL. Died January 6, 1996.

A fiddle player's fiddle player, Chubby Wise's music associations read like a who's who of country music. Performing and recording with the likes of Hank Snow (as a member of Snow's Rainbow Ranch Boys), Bill Monroe, Flatt & Scruggs, Mac Wiseman, Connie Gay, Howdy Forrester and Ervin Rouse (composer of "Orange Blossom Special"), Wise certainly left his mark on country music.

what's available: Wise's final album, *An American Original* (Pinecastle, 1995, prod. Sonny Osborne) ♫♫♫♫, features backing by the Osborne Brothers, plus guitarist David Crow and bassist Terry Smith. Wise's unique choice of songs makes this album stand out; in addition to public-domain fiddle favorites like "Cotton-Eyed Joe," "Little Liza Jane" and "Under the Double Eagle," Wise also lends his distinctive fiddle tone to the country ballads "I Can't Stop Loving You" and "I'm So Lone-

some I Could Cry," plus the beautiful gospel melody of "It Is No Secret (What God Can Do)." Wise's first album for Pinecastle, *Chubby Wise in Nashville* (Pinecastle, 1994) ♫♫♫, is almost as good, joined as he is by the Osbornes and members of the Del McCoury Band. The album was recorded in three days in a Nashville house in which Patsy Cline once lived.

worth searching for: There's not much to lead you on the trail to finding Chubby Wise and Mac Wiseman's *Chubby Wise and Mac Wiseman* ♫♫♫—a live recording from Gilley's in Texas—except for the song titles. It's a double-length cassette filled with country tunes such as "Faded Love," "Wabash Cannonball," "The Wreck of the Old '97" and "The Prisoner's Song."

influences:
◄◄ Bill Monroe, Howdy Forrester
►► Jimmy Campbell, Stuart Duncan

Randall T. Cook

MAC WISEMAN

Born May 23, 1925, in Crimora, VA.

Known as "The Voice with a Heart" because of his distinctive warm, burred tenor voice, renowned bluegrass singer and guitarist Malcolm "Mac" Wiseman began his career playing bass with mountain singer Molly O'Day. An early member of Flatt & Scruggs' Foggy Mountain Boys, Wiseman spent most of 1949 playing guitar with Bill Monroe before launching his own band in 1950. He signed with Dot the following year; that association was long and fruitful, producing a number of best-selling singles and the recordings that earned Wiseman his enduring reputation. Working as a sometimes A&R man for Dot, Wiseman was a prolific recording artist during his career, cutting also for Capitol, Vetco, MGM, RCA Victor and CMH. One of the few bluegrass singers who didn't maintain a regular band, Wiseman often worked with the Osborne Brothers during the 1980s and 1990s. His pioneering contributions to bluegrass were officially acknowledged in 1994 with his induction into the International Bluegrass Music Association's Bluegrass Hall of Honor.

what to buy: *Early Dot Recordings, Volume 3* (County, 1992, reissue prod. Gary B. Reid) 𝄞𝄞𝄞𝄞, drawn from Wiseman's early-1950s Dot material, gives a good feel for the singer's unique and highly enjoyable take on bluegrass. Includes such Wiseman favorites as "Don't Let Your Sweet Love Die," "Goin' Like Wildfire" and "I'll Still Write Your Name in the Sand." Volumes one and two also come highly recommended but are unavailable on CD.

what to buy next: *Classic Bluegrass* (Rebel, 1989, prod. Lou Ukelson, Fred Bartenstein) 𝄞𝄞𝄞, which reissues mid-1970s Vetco recordings, displays Wiseman's facility with sentimental "heart" songs like "Mary of the Wild Moor," "Letter Edged in Black" and "Black Sheep," along with excellent backup from the Shenandoah Cut-ups. *The Mac Wiseman Story* (CMH, 1991, prod. Arthur Smith) 𝄞𝄞𝄞, a slightly stronger set also drawn from mid-1970s recordings, includes solid remakes of many of Wiseman's biggest songs, including "'Tis Sweet to Be Remembered," "Love Letters in the Sand," "I Wonder How the Old Folks Are at Home" and "Jimmie Brown, the Newsboy." The backing band includes Billy Edwards and Tater Tate from the Shenandoah Cut-ups.

what to avoid: *Teenage Hangout* (Bear Family, 1993, prod. Richard Weize) **WOOF!** is a bizarre reissue that brings together Dot singles from the 1950s aimed at the newly developing teen rock 'n' roll market. It's difficult to imagine a more ill-conceived or badly executed marketing ploy—and the music is bad, too.

the rest:
Grassroots to Bluegrass: A Very Special Collection (CMH, 1990) 𝄞𝄞𝄞
The Osborne Brothers and Mac Wiseman (CMH, 1979) 𝄞𝄞𝄞
24 Greatest Hits (Deluxe, 1987) 𝄞𝄞𝄞

influences:
◄◄ Bradley Kincaid, Blue Sky Boys, Wilf Carter
►► Glenn Yarborough, Bobby Osborne, Charlie Waller, Peter Rowan

Randy Pitts and Jon Hartley Fox

LEE ANN WOMACK

Born August 19, 1966, in Jacksonville, TX.

Texas native Lee Ann Womack grew up between the speakers of her stereo, listening to the Grand Ole Opry and picking songs for her father, a part-time DJ, to play on the air. As a result, Womack's own music has a strong traditional bent. She completed her first album before she graduated from college at Nashville's Belmont University.

what's available: Pick a song from Womack's debut, *Make Memories with Me* (Decca, 1997, prod. Mark Wright) 𝄞𝄞𝄞, and chances are it'll be worth a listen. Still, 11 songs do not an album make. Cohesiveness is at a minimum here, and there's no singular memory to be made. However, a few cuts stand out, including "Never Again, Again" and "Get up in Jesus' Name."

influences:
◄◄ Vince Gill, Ricky Skaggs

Craig Shelburne

JEFF WOOD

Born May 10, 1968, in Oklahoma City, OK.

Singer/songwriter Jeff Wood took a lot of inspiration from Garth Brooks, whom Wood befriended while the two attended Oklahoma State University. It was Brooks who helped get Wood's feet planted in Nashville, where Wood would eventually pen a big hit for John Michael Montgomery ("Cowboy Love"), paving the way for his fledgling recording career.

what's available: *Between the Earth and the Stars* (Imprint, 1996, prod. Mark Bright) 𝄞𝄞𝄞 shows the signs of Wood's Brooksian influence in the emotive lead-off track, "You Call That a Mountain," and Wood gets top-shelf compositional help from the likes of John Scott Sherrill and Gary Burr as well.

influences:

◀◀ Merle Haggard, Garth Brooks

David Simons

BOB WOODRUFF

Born March 14, 1961, in Suffern, NY.

Spending his early childhood in Greenwich Village amidst the folk music explosion, and then coming of age in upstate New York and New Hampshire, Bob Woodruff was smitten with the genuine country purity of Buck Owens and George Jones and the grassroots reality and heartbreak of the souls inhabiting the songs of Hank Williams, Merle Haggard, Otis Redding and Al Green. Woodruff played drums in various garage bands as a teenager, then switched over to guitar to write songs during the early 1980s. Gram Parsons proved a major influence with his brilliant forging of country, rock and R&B, and Woodruff's own growth as a songwriter and singer has paralleled his own ability to sculpt roots and twang into an engagingly original sound.

what's available: *Desire Road* (Imprint, 1997, prod. Ray Kennedy) ♫♫♫, with its share of rootsy country, personal, evocative storytelling and jangly folk-rock, is a big-hearted and uncluttered collection of originals (with co-writers including Gary Nicholson, Gwil Owen and Vince Melamed) and covers. "That Was Then," about a long-past-his-prime guitar picker who just wants to go to the corner bar, plug in his amp and crank it up so he can feel young again, is typical of Woodruff's colorful, bittersweet vision. Of the covers, he nails John Fogerty's exuberant country-hit wannabe "Almost Saturday Night," but falls a little short of the requisite heartbreak on Arthur Alexander's soulful chestnut "Every Day I Have to Cry."

worth searching for: *Dreams & Saturday Nights* (Asylum, 1994, prod. Steve Fishell) ♫♫♫ dodged the glossy trend at a time when most Nashville record labels were obsessed with jumping on the goldrush bandwagon, so its simultaneously edgy and reflective sound was a hopeful breath of fresh air. Despite critical raves, sales were unspectacular and radio play for the shoulda-been-a-hit "Bayou Girl" was underwhelming. It would be nearly three years before Woodruff would resurface on the songwriter-friendly Imprint label.

influences:

◀◀ Gram Parsons, Creedence Clearwater Revival

David Sokol

CHELY WRIGHT

Born October 25, 1970, in Kansas City, MO.

Chely Wright grew up in a small Kansas town where, she says, she never wanted to do anything else but go to Nashville, make traditional country records and be inducted into the Grand Ole Opry. Wright co-wrote half the songs on her 1994 debut album, music she aptly calls "a jacked-up 1990s version of Connie Smith and Loretta Lynn," and had her first hit with a song master country tunesmith Harlan Howard wrote three years before she was born. She was named the best new female vocalist by the Academy of Country Music in 1995 and moved to MCA Records after her first label closed.

what to buy: *Woman in the Moon* (Polydor, 1994, prod. Barry Beckett, Harold Shedd) ♫♫♫ features songs written by Alan Jackson, "Whisperin'" Bill Anderson, Keith Whitley and Harlan Howard, as well as Wright's own tunes. One, "The Last Supper," an eerie murder tale that uses biblical imagery, held up to the competition especially well.

the rest: *Right in the Middle of It* (Polydor, 1996) ♫♫♫

influences:

◀◀ Patty Loveless, Connie Smith
▶▶ Sara Evans

Bill Hobbs

CURTIS WRIGHT

See: Orrall & Wright

MICHELLE WRIGHT

Born July 1, 1961, in Morpeth, Ontario, Canada.

Canadian Michelle Wright grew up equally enamored with the country music her parents performed and the sounds of Motown soul emanating from nearby Detroit, Michigan, radio stations. As a result, her best music has a sultry, soulful sound. Wright is one of Canada's top country artists (winning the Canadian Country Music Association's Fan Choice Entertainer of the Year Award in 1993), though she's struggled more to break the U.S. market. Despite winning the Academy of Country Music's award for best new female vocalist in 1993, Wright has had only one song, "Take It Like a Man," make the U.S. Top 10 (as of early 1997).

what to buy: *Michelle Wright* (Arista, 1990) 𝄞𝄞𝄞𝄞 is Wright's best album, a torchy mix of soul and country that didn't win her many fans at radio but set her up as a voice to watch.

what to buy next: *Now and Then* (Arista, 1992, prod. Steve Bogard) 𝄞𝄞𝄞 dropped most of the soul influences and very nearly became Wright's stateside breakthrough, with singles such as "Take It Like a Man" and the tear-jerker "He Would Be Sixteen."

what to avoid: Wright spent almost four years working and re-working *For Me It's You* (Arista, 1996, prod. various) 𝄞𝄞𝄞, which ended up with five different producers. The album wasn't the cobbled-together mess that most such albums are, but while it contained some good songs (Gretchen Peters' "Nobody's Girl," Pam Tillis' "Cold Kisses") and some smoldering performances, it still didn't establish Wright as anything more than a singer with great pipes.

worth searching for: Arista released *The Reasons Why* (Arista, 1995, prod. various) 𝄞𝄞𝄞 in Canada only. Parts of the album would show up eventually on *For Me It's You*, but the original album also includes the single "One Good Man" and a version of "Safe in the Arms of Love," which became a hit for Martina McBride.

influences:

◀◀ k.d. lang, Reba McEntire

▶▶ Linda Davis, Lisa Brokop, Tammy Graham

Brian Mansfield

WYLIE & THE WILD WEST SHOW

Formed 1990, in Los Angeles, CA.

Wylie Gustafson, vocals, bass; Ray Doyle, guitar, vocals (1990–96); Larry Mitchell, drums (1990–92); Will Ray, steel guitar (1990–92); Dennis Crouch, double bass; Mark Thornton, guitar, vocals (1996–present); Kenny Griffin, drums (1992–96); John Shelley, drums (1996–present); Mike Fried, steel guitar (1992–present).

It's near impossible not to notice Wylie & the Wild West Show. First off, the group is fronted by Wylie Gustafson, a redheaded Howdy Doody look-alike with a wiry frame and thick glasses. Most importantly, the ensemble plays a pure, eclectic mix of classic country, neo-Western music and 1950s-era rock 'n' roll. Emerging from the same West Coast environment that spawned legends Merle Haggard and Buck Owens, Wylie and his boys turned in an auspicious self-titled debut album on the small Cross Three label. It was a perfect homage to all things

American, with a quirky charm that enthralled the few who heard it. How could anyone dislike a band with songs bearing such titles as "Yodeling Fool," "Black Boots & Blue Jeans" and the undiscovered classic, "All Hat, No Cattle"? But while there's a comical edge to Wylie & the Wild West Show's repertoire, particularly the sardonic "Ugly Girl Blues" from *Get Wild*, the musicianship is no joke. These guys can play, Wylie can sing and the songs have memorable hooks as well as grit, spirit and style. By 1996, two years after the release of the second album, the band had experienced personnel changes and parted ways with Cross Three. Not to worry, however; Connecticut's Rounder Records has signed them. Wylie and company will prevail.

what to buy: *Wylie & the Wild West Show* (Cross Three, 1992, prod. Will Ray) 𝄞𝄞𝄞𝄞 is akin to a four-star art-house film: you know it won't get mainstream attention but that's just as well; those that do partake will appreciate it even more. There's not a bad cut here: the slow shuffle, "This Time," and the rousing "Wild Hair Boogie," an instrumental that Junior Brown would kill for, deserve special attention. Just pop this CD in, grab a partner and stir up some sawdust.

the rest:

Get Wild (Cross Three, 1994) 𝄞𝄞𝄞

worth searching for: The group's third album, *Way Out West* (Massive Records, 1996, prod. Ray Benson), was initially released only in Australia. But Rounder had plans to put out the set stateside sometime in 1997.

influences:

◀◀ Buck Owens, Merle Haggard, Buddy Holly

▶▶ Derailers, BR5-49

Mario Tarradell

TAMMY WYNETTE

Born Virginia Wynette Pugh, May 5, 1943, in Itawamba County, MS.

Nobody sings about domestic discord quite the way Tammy Wynette does. Her confidential vocal tone and the little catch in her voice combine to create the illusion of a woman who's trying hard not to frighten you to death while she's telling you something horrible. This schism gives her work undeniable power. Wynette did her first singing in church, and she liked it

Tammy Wynette (© Ken Settle)

so well that she began attending two different churches so she could sing even more. By age 17, starved for independence, she married Euple Byrd. By age 24 she had already experienced a nasty divorce, a vicious custody battle and an emotional breakdown. Supporting three small children on her salary as a beautician, Wynette still harbored dreams of a career in country music. A stint on WBRC-TV's *Country Boy Eddie Show* in Birmingham, Alabama, and a 10-day tour with Porter Wagoner built her confidence sufficiently so she could pack up the kids and move to Nashville.

After several rejections, Epic Records' staff producer Billy Sherrill took pity on Wynette Byrd and signed her to his label. After commenting that the bottle blonde's ponytail made her "look like a Tammy," Sherrill rechristened the singer Tammy Wynette. Their first offering, a cover of Bobby Austin's regional hit "Apartment #9," was so successful Wynette received hundreds of letters of sympathy from fans who thought the song was her true story. The follow-up, "Your Good Girl's Gonna Go Bad," was shrill sass on the order of Loretta Lynn, and it became Wynette's first of 16 straight #1 records. In 1967 Wynette married songwriter Don Chapel, who tried to cash in on Wynette's fame by making himself a prominent (and unpopular) addition to her stage show. When a dispute with David Houston's manager left her without a band and an onstage partner for their hit duet "My Elusive Dreams," Wynette first sang with her hero George Jones. Their infatuation grew as Wynette's marriage to Chapel disintegrated. Wynette's great records—"I Don't Wanna Play House," "D-I-V-O-R-C-E," "Kids Say the Darndest Things" and the immortal "Stand by Your Man"—resonated with American women, who felt she was singing about their lives. Wynette credits her success to producer Billy Sherrill; though an uncommunicative autocrat, Sherrill knew how to make hit records. He wrote or co-wrote many of Wynette's biggest hits and groomed her to be a great songwriter on her own. In 1968 Wynette married George Jones, and when Jones joined Epic they began recording their great run of duet hits, such as "We're Gonna Hold On," "Golden Ring" and "We're Not the Jet Set." In 1969 Wynette became the first female country artist to sell a million copies of an album and was dubbed "The First Lady of Country Music."

Singles like "There Are So Many Ways to Love a Man," "My Man" and "My Song" perpetuated Wynette's mythology as a woman triumphing over adversity because she was well loved. In truth, her marriage to Jones was falling apart due to his lengthy, drunken absences and vile temper. When they divorced in 1974 the media laid the blame on Wynette, crowing in

headlines: "The Woman Who Sings 'Stand by Your Man' Is Getting a D-I-V-O-R-C-E!" Despite the acrimony that led up to it, Jones and Wynette had a happy aftermath to their divorce; Wynette wrote the hit "These Days I Barely Get By" for her ex-husband, and Jones gave her his touring band. In 1982 they reunited to record Wynette's "Two-Story House," which hit #1. Her third marriage, to real estate broker Michael Tomlin, lasted only 44 days. Her 1977 hit " 'Til I Can Make It on My Own" became her personal anthem of survival.

Dogged by health problems, the departure of Billy Sherrill, bad press and changing trends in country music, Wynette's hits tapered off during the early 1980s. But there were bright spots. Her 1978 marriage to songwriter/producer George Richey has turned out to be a lasting one. In 1987 her LP *Higher Ground* was critically acclaimed. In 1992 she teamed up with British synth-pop group KLF and recorded the international smash "Justified & Ancient." And in 1993 Wynette, Loretta Lynn and Dolly Parton released *Honky Tonk Angels*, which achieved instant gold record status. As Wynette was enjoying her commercial resurgence, a recurrent health problem nearly took her life; the national media, which had previously treated her with scorn, provided vigilant coverage of her condition. Wynette recovered and went on tour to more favorable publicity than she ever had in her career. She even recorded with George Jones again, and their longtime fans were ecstatic. Wynette has won two Grammy Awards and 16 BMI songwriter awards, and she has 39 Top 10 hits, 20 #1 records and nearly a dozen chart-topping LPs to her credit. They are the trophies of a career that is finally bringing her some happiness.

what to buy: *Anniversary: 20 Years Of Hits* (Epic, 1987, prod. Billy Sherrill, George Richey) 𝄞𝄞𝄞𝄞 contains her biggest and best hits, the ones that made her a cultural icon.

what to buy next: *Tears Of Fire: The 25th Anniversary Collection* (Epic, 1992, prod. various) 𝄞𝄞𝄞𝄞 is a nice boxed set featuring her big hits, first demo and some strong duets.

what to avoid: *Best Loved Hits* (Epic, 1992, prod. Billy Sherill) 𝄞𝄞 contains only two hits and a bunch of recycled LP tracks. *Without Walls* (Epic, 1994, prod. Barry Beckett) **WOOF!** is an all-star collaboration with Elton John, Joe Diffie, Sting, Smokey Robinson, Wynonna and Lyle Lovett that seldom sounds genuine.

the rest:
Your Good Girl's Gonna Go Bad (Epic, 1967/Legacy, 1996) 𝄞𝄞𝄞
Greatest Hits (Epic, 1969) 𝄞𝄞𝄞𝄞
(With George Jones) *We Love To Sing About Jesus* (Epic, 1972) 𝄞𝄞𝄞
(With Jones) *Golden Ring* (Razor & Tie, 1976) 𝄞𝄞𝄞𝄞

Wynonna (© Ken Settle)

(With Jones) *George & Tammy's Greatest Hits* (Epic, 1977) 𝄞𝄞𝄞𝄞

(With Jones) *Together Again* (Razor & Tie, 1980) 𝄞𝄞𝄞

(With Jones) *Encore: George Jones & Tammy Wynette* (Epic, 1981) 𝄞𝄞𝄞

Biggest Hits (Legacy, 1983) 𝄞𝄞𝄞

Heart over Mind (Epic, 1990) 𝄞𝄞𝄞

(With Jones) *George & Tammy's Greatest Hits, Volume 2* (Epic, 1992) 𝄞𝄞𝄞𝄞

(With Dolly Parton and Loretta Lynn) *Honky Tonk Angels* (Columbia, 1993) 𝄞𝄞𝄞

(With Jones) *The President & The First Lady* (TeeVee, 1995) 𝄞𝄞𝄞

(With Jones) *One* (MCA, 1995) 𝄞𝄞𝄞

(With Jones) *Super Hits* (Epic, 1995) 𝄞𝄞𝄞

Super Hits (Epic, 1996) 𝄞𝄞𝄞𝄞

Christmas with Tammy (Sony Music Special, 1995)

Greatest Hits Volume 3 (Epic) 𝄞𝄞𝄞𝄞

worth searching for: *D-I-V-O-R-C-E* (Epic, 1968, prod. Billy Sherrill) 𝄞𝄞𝄞𝄞 is the LP where Wynette's vocal style really came of age; solid song selections, too.

influences:

◀◀ George Jones, Loretta Lynn, Connie Smith

▶▶ Trisha Yearwood, Mindy McCready

Ken Burke

WYNONNA

Born Christina Ciminella (aka Wynonna Judd), May 30, 1964, in Ashland, KY.

Considering the success that Wynonna has enjoyed as a solo act, the trepidation that preceded her mother Naomi's much ballyhooed retirement (Can Wy make it without Mama by her side?) now seems overstated. A bold and brassy vocalist, Wynonna's solo albums reveal a soulfulness and depth of character only hinted at on the Judds' albums. Credit producer Tony Brown for much of this, for between daring song selection and edgy musical backing, Wynonna is pushed in directions she may never have explored otherwise. The result has been an almost unbroken string of hits and a confidence in her own ability that her identity as the singing daughter never would have allowed.

what to buy: On her sophomore set, *Tell Me Why* (MCA, 1993, prod. Tony Brown) 🎵🎵🎵, Wynonna steps out of the conservatism that marked her career thus far, turning in an album that is progressive, soulful and even a little funky, stretching her talent and plainly believing in her abilities with every new move. Sheryl Crow's "Father Sun" is plainly pop, while Jesse Winchester's "Let's Make a Baby King" and "Just Like New" add an appealing blues strut to her walk. Mary Chapin Carpenter's "Girls with Guitars" makes for a timely feminist anthem, and mother Naomi's "That Was Yesterday" is an assertive vocal tour-de-force.

the rest:
Wynonna (MCA, 1993) 🎵🎵🎵
Revelations (MCA, 1996) 🎵🎵🎵
Collection (MCA, 1997) 🎵🎵🎵🎵

influences:
◀◀ Patsy Cline, Bonnie Raitt, Elvis Presley, Naomi Judd
▶▶ Mindy McCready, Terri Clark

see also: *Judds*

Daniel Durchholz

TRISHA YEARWOOD

Born September 19, 1964, in Monticello, GA.

A Nashville session singer who got her big break when Garth Brooks hired her to sing on *No Fences*, Trisha Yearwood knew better than to let coat-tails become apron strings. Brooks, Vince Gill, Emmylou Harris and Don Henley offered their voices and marquee value to her first two albums, but Yearwood had already devised an admirable game plan that balanced Nashville's commercial expectations with her own vision of an infectious, inspiring sound that seamlessly mixed country, pop and folk. She eschewed the usual songwriting suspects for a young talent pool that included Kim Richey, the O'Kanes, Beth Nielsen Chapman, Matraca Berg and Gretchen Peters, and she spiked her albums with such deliciously left-field choices as Texas newcomer Kimmie Rhodes' "Hard Promises to Keep" and Melissa Etheridge's "You Can Sleep While I Drive." If she wrote

more of her own material like Mary Chapin Carpenter, she might get more respect and more crossover exposure. Instead, like Linda Ronstadt during her late-1970s heyday, Yearwood is content to look for good songs in unexpected places and to lead her own subtle revolution that's as unobtrusive as the Bible passages she lists in fine print at the end of every album's liner notes.

what to buy: From the soaring jangle of Kim Richey's "Believe Me Baby (I Lied)" to the comforting balladry of Craig Carothers' "Little Hercules" and Steve Goodman's "A Lover Is Forever," *Everybody Knows* (MCA, 1996, prod. Garth Fundis) 🎵🎵🎵🎵 captures Yearwood's voice at its most assured and her choice of material at its most astute. The relentless ache of romantic longing is expressed with passion and remarkable restraint on the spare, mostly acoustic *Thinkin' about You* (MCA, 1994, prod. Garth Fundis, Harry Stinson) 🎵🎵🎵🎵. The elegant arrangements of Etheridge's "You Can Sleep While I Drive" and Peters' "On a Bus to St. Cloud" enhance their haunting beauty, but the album is docked half a bone for MCA's decision to shoehorn the upbeat stopgap single, "XXX's and OOO's (An American Girl)," into the otherwise thematically cohesive lineup.

what to buy next: The heel-clicking "She's in Love with the Boy" and "That's What I Like about You" are charming introductions, but the telling treasures on her exuberant debut, *Trisha Yearwood* (MCA, 1991, prod. Garth Fundis) 🎵🎵🎵🎵, are "Fools Like Me," a soulful Hal Ketchum-Kostas composition bolstered by organist Al Kooper, and Pat McLaughlin's rollicking "You Done Me Wrong (And That Ain't Right)."

what to avoid: The string-drenched, overdramatic ballads and stiff throwaways by the usually reliable Kostas and Rodney Crowell drag down *The Song Remembers When* (MCA, 1993, prod. Garth Fundis) 🎵🎵, a strained attempt to establish Yearwood as a "mature" artist before she was ready.

the rest:
Hearts in Armor (MCA, 1992) 🎵🎵🎵
The Sweetest Gift (MCA, 1994) 🎵🎵🎵

worth searching for: Check out her swaggering take on Elvis' 1963 hit "You're the Devil in Disguise," from the all-star soundtrack *Honeymoon in Vegas* (Epic, 1992, prod. various) 🎵🎵🎵.

influences:
◀◀ Linda Ronstadt, Kathy Mattea, Patty Loveless
▶▶ Kim Richey, Suzy Bogguss, Jo Dee Messina

David Okamoto

DWIGHT YOAKAM

Born October 23, 1956, in Pikesville, KY.

Though country trends have dramatically shifted around him, Yoakam has never been anything other than an Elvis Presley and Buck Owens worshipper who always wears a cowboy hat and impossibly tight blue jeans. He writes the meanest honky-tonk grooves—notably "Fast As You" and "Never Hold You"—this side of Hank Williams and the Rolling Stones. During the mid-1980s he was part of the "neo-traditionalist" tradition, an outlaw type who, with Lyle Lovett and Steve Earle, was prepared to shake Nashville into a punkish brand of country. Gradually, as Garth Brooks rose to prominence, Yoakam became a cuddly figure for both rockers and the country establishment. He racked up hits almost from the start, with a couple of lucrative Presley covers like "Little Sister" and "Suspicious Minds," then became sort of a cult superstar. He dated actress Sharon Stone, appeared in a few movies, drove a motorcycle and made people ignore the fact that underneath his hat, he's as bald as Telly Savalas.

what to buy: Yoakam has always been a consistent artist, from his debut country-stomp album *Guitars, Cadillacs, Etc., Etc.* (Reprise, 1986, prod. Pete Anderson) 🎸🎸🎸🎸 to his dark, irresistibly grooving *Gone* (Reprise, 1995, prod. Pete Anderson) 🎸🎸🎸🎸. The best part of *Just Lookin' for a Hit* (Reprise, 1989, prod. Pete Anderson) 🎸🎸🎸🎸 is its impeccable selection of cover songs, including the Doc Pomus-Mort Shuman classic "Little Sister" and the Blasters' "Long White Cadillac."

what to buy next: *This Time* (Reprise, 1993, prod. Pete Anderson) 🎸🎸🎸🎸, despite the wonderful "Fast As You," is slightly uneven.

what to avoid: One of Yoakam's few recorded missteps was *Dwight Live* (Reprise, 1987, prod. Pete Anderson) 🎸🎸, which doesn't begin to capture the live energy that comes from seeing the hat's shadow across his face and the black leather pants wrapped around his bowed legs.

the rest:
Hillbilly Deluxe (Reprise, 1987) 🎸🎸🎸
Buenas Noches from a Lonely Room (Reprise, 1988) 🎸🎸🎸🎸
If There Was a Way (Reprise, 1990) 🎸🎸🎸

worth searching for: *La Croix D'Amour* (Reprise, 1992) 🎸🎸🎸🎸 is a European hits compilation containing covers of the Beatles' "Things We Said Today," the Grateful Dead's "Truckin'" and Them's "Here Comes the Night." It hasn't been issued stateside. Yoakam's explosive take on "Suspicious Minds" rescues

Trisha Yearwood (© Ken Settle)

the otherwise boring *Honeymoon in Vegas* (Epic, 1992, prod. various) 🎸🎸🎸 Elvis-cover soundtrack.

influences:
◀◀ Buck Owens, Elvis Presley, Hank Williams, Blasters
▶▶ Marty Brown, Mavericks, Mary Chapin Carpenter, BR5-49

Steve Knopper

FARON YOUNG

Born February 25, 1932, in Shreveport, LA. Died December 10, 1996.

Despite his later protests, Faron Young was something of a rockabilly; his scene-stealing appearance in *Country Music Holiday* (1958) is highlighted by gestures and histrionics that made Elvis Presley seem catatonic. Yet that was Young's personal style; he was cocky, contradictory and really quite shrewd. Just a farm boy when he made his first appearances on the *Louisiana Hayride*, Young initially recorded for Webb Pierce's Pacemaker label, where he saw limited success. His move to Capitol Records and the greater exposure of the Grand

Dwight Yoakam (© Ken Settle)

Ole Opry in 1952 resulted in his first chart appearances. On leave from the U.S. Army in 1953, he recorded his first Top Five record, "Goin' Steady." After his discharge a year later, Young's style became more confident and boisterous. A honky-tonk version of Frank Sinatra, Young could belt out an up-tempo number laden with sly sexuality one minute, then croon a ballad heavy with emotion the next. Such hits as "If You Ain't Lovin' (You Ain't Livin')," "Live Fast, Love Hard, Die Young" and "I've Got Five Dollars (And It's Saturday Night)" heavily influenced the rockabillies who would become his competition. "Sweet Dreams," on the charts for 33 weeks, established Young as a romantic singer as well. Young could also write a good song, and despite his reputation as a real hard-ass, he helped nurture the careers of such singer/songwriters as Don Gibson, Roy Drusky, Roger Miller and Willie Nelson. Young's version of Nelson's "Hello Walls" is the defining achievement of his career. He sings most of the song blithely, almost self-mockingly as he talks to the inanimate objects in his home; then, at song's end, he let's just enough emotion leak into his voice to give the impression of a man on the verge of a major emotional breakdown.

During his peak years, Young appeared in 11 motion pictures, mostly cheap westerns that did little for his career but resulted in his nickname, "The Singing Sheriff." Young's switch to Mercury in 1962 led to a fertile period; he was a regular fixture in the Top Five and "It's Four In The Morning," a 1972 ballad drenched with longing and regret, hit #1 and won the Country Music Association's Single of the Year award. Mercury dropped him from its roster during the late 1970s, and shortly thereafter Young cut a duet LP with the then-hot Willie Nelson that was well-reviewed, but sold poorly. Young's investments had made him wealthy, and being co-founder of *Music City News*, he was still something of a power broker in Nashville. But he couldn't stay away from making music. He recorded several LPs for the independent Step One label, but their chief value were as items to sell at Young's increasingly rare live shows. In December 1996, depressed over the state of his career and suffering from complications of prostate cancer and other health problems, Young died of a self-inflicted gunshot wound. It was an ironic ending for a man who put so much vigor into singing "Live Fast, Love Hard, Die Young (And Leave a Beautiful Memory)."

what to buy: *Faron Young: Live Fast, Love Hard—Original Capitol Recordings, 1952–1962* (Country Music Foundation, 1995, comp. prod. Country Music Foundation) 𝄢𝄢𝄢𝄢 includes his biggest hits for Capitol Records.

what to buy next: *Golden Hits* (Mercury, 1995, comp. prod. Bob Allen) 𝄢𝄢𝄢𝄢 contains the cream of Young's Mercury material.

what to avoid: Several re-recordings have been made obsolete by the Country Music Foundation and Bear Family packages. *Greatest Hits Volume 1* (Step One, 1989, prod. Ray Pennington) 𝄢𝄢, *Greatest Hits Volume 2* (Step One, 1989, prod. Ray Pennington) 𝄢𝄢, and *Greatest Hits Volume 3* (Step One, 1989, prod. Ray Pennington) 𝄢𝄢 all pale in comparison.

the rest:
Here's to You (Step One, 1989) 𝄢𝄢
All-Time Greatest Hits (Curb, 1990) 𝄢𝄢𝄢
Best Of Young Country (Step One, 1991) 𝄢𝄢𝄢
Country Christmas (Step One, 1991) 𝄢𝄢
(With Ray Price) *Memories That Last* (Step One, 1991) 𝄢𝄢𝄢
Country Spotlight (Dominion, 1991) 𝄢𝄢𝄢
20 Greatest Hits (Deluxe, 1993) 𝄢𝄢𝄢
Live in Branson, MO, USA (LaserLight, 1993) 𝄢𝄢𝄢
20 Best Hits (Deluxe, 1993) 𝄢𝄢

worth searching for: *The Classic Years 1952–1962* (Bear Family) 𝄢𝄢𝄢𝄢 features nearly everything Young recorded for Capitol.

influences:

◄◄ Webb Pierce, Ferlin Husky, Ray Price

►► Willie Nelson, Roger Miller, Sonny James, Don Gibson

Ken Burke

NEIL YOUNG

Born November 12, 1945, in Toronto, Ontario, Canada.

Because Neil Young is an extremist who never sticks with any one extreme for very long (not to mention that he's a brilliant artist), the length and breadth of his influence is enormous. Who else can claim Sonic Youth as well as Uncle Tupelo as his spiritual progeny? Of course, the rather profound downside is that many of his stylistic shifts seem about as well thought out as drunken moodswings. From style to style, the consistent thread in Young's work is his catalog of ongoing obsessions—cars, highways, Indians, ch-ch-changes—with his own stylistic restlessness serving as musical metaphor for his thematic variations on motion. Like an erratic home run hitter, even Young's whiffs are at least somewhat entertaining.

His initial impact in the country field was as lead guitarist in the pioneering California country-rock band Buffalo Springfield during the mid-1960s. Since then, even with his early-1970s stint with premier hippie band Crosby, Stills, Nash & Young, Young has never gone too long in his wandering without returning to some variation of roots rock. Unfortunately for country fans, his folksy singer/songwriter side tends to be less interesting than his primordial guitar-mangling side. His best work comes on those occasions when he unites both halves. Someday, if Young really does put out *Decade II* (the much-rumored multi-disc retrospective that has been in the works since the late 1980s), maybe it will all make sense.

what to buy: *Tonight's the Night* (Reprise, 1975, prod. David Briggs, Neil Young) 🎵🎵🎵🎵 is the spookiest album Young (or anyone else) has ever made. Haunted by images of death and decay, this is macabre honky-tonk music that lands in a pitch-black netherworld somewhere between Robert Johnson and Hank Williams. The best albums Young has made since then are all, in some way, Young battling the ghosts he conjured up on *Tonight*. *After the Gold Rush* (Reprise, 1970, prod. Neil Young, David Briggs, Kendall Pacios) 🎵🎵🎵🎵 goes down smoother and is almost as powerful as *Tonight*. *Everybody Knows This Is Nowhere* (Reprise, 1969, prod. David Briggs, Neil Young) 🎵🎵🎵🎵 is in the same mold as Buffalo Springfield, just with the guitars turned up to 11. *Rust Never Sleeps* (Reprise, 1979, prod. Neil

FIVE FOR MY FANS

TRISHA YEARWOOD

Kim Richey
Kim Richey (Mercury)

Matraca Berg
Lying to the Moon (RCA)

Linda Ronstadt
Hasten Down the Wind (Elektra)

Ron Sexsmith
Ron Sexsmith (Interscope)

Catie Curtis
Truth from Lies (Guardian)

Young, David Briggs, Tim Mulligan) 🎵🎵🎵🎵 is folksier, yet was also the album that cemented Young's credibility with the punk generation. It has one of his best songs ever, "Pocahontas."

what to buy next: *Harvest* (Reprise, 1972, prod. Elliot Mazer, Neil Young, Jack Nitzsche, Henry Lewy) 🎵🎵🎵🎵 is one of the landmarks of 1970s-vintage California country-rock and also Young's most popular album. The sequel, *Harvest Moon* (Reprise, 1992, prod. Neil Young, Ben Keith) 🎵🎵🎵🎵, is surprisingly successful, in part because of the dark imagery lurking within the music's pretty placid surfaces. Of Young's handful of live albums, country fans will probably get the most mileage out of *Unplugged* (Reprise, 1993, prod. David Briggs) 🎵🎵🎵🎵, which offers a career-spanning lineup of songs.

what to avoid: Of all Young's schizoid 1980s genre experiments, *Old Ways* (Geffen, 1985, prod. Neil Young, Ben Keith, David Briggs, Elliot Mazer) 🎵🎵 is the one that should've worked.

Neil Young (© Ken Settle)

American Stars 'n' Bars (Reprise, 1977) ♪♪♪
Decade (Reprise, 1978) ♪♪♪♪
Comes a Time (Reprise, 1978) ♪♪♪♪
Live Rust (Reprise, 1979) ♪♪♪♪
Hawks & Doves (Reprise, 1980) ♪♪♪
Re-ac-tor (Reprise, 1981) ♪♪♪
Trans (Geffen, 1982) ♪♪♪
Landing on Water (Geffen, 1986) ♪♪♪
Life (Geffen, 1987) ♪♪♪♪
(With Crosby, Stills and Nash) American Dream (Atlantic, 1988) ♪♪♪♪
This Note's for You (Reprise, 1988) ♪♪♪
Freedom (Reprise, 1989) ♪♪♪♪
Ragged Glory (Reprise, 1990) ♪♪♪♪
Weld (Reprise, 1991) ♪♪♪
Lucky 13 (Geffen, 1993) ♪♪♪
Sleeps with Angels (Reprise, 1994) ♪♪♪♪
Mirror Ball (Reprise, 1995) ♪♪♪♪
Broken Arrow (Reprise, 1996) ♪♪♪
The Year of the Horse (Reprise, 1997)

worth searching for: Among the best of Young's array of "lost albums" is *Chrome Dreams* ♪♪♪♪, a bootleg made from an acetate copy of an album Young worked on during 1975–76. The album never came out, but the songs—including "Pocahontas," "Too Far Gone," "Sedan Delivery" and "Powderfinger"—made their way onto other albums.

influences:

◀◀ Bob Dylan, Byrds

▶▶ Uncle Tupelo, Jayhawks, Bruce Springsteen, T-Bone Burnett, Joe Henry, R.E.M., Sidewinders, Beat Farmers

David Menconi

Young's live shows from that period, with his band International Harvester, were great, and Young has a better feel for straight country than the technopop and blues he was dabbling with before and after. Instead, it's slick and lifeless (although *Old Ways* is notable because it's the album that got Young sued by his record label for making uncommercial records). Even worse is the rockabilly caricature *Everybody's Rockin'* (Geffen, 1983, prod. Elliot Mazer, Neil Young) ♪♪, which sounds like Young flailing around in desperate search of God only knows what.

the rest:

Neil Young (Reprise, 1969) ♪♪♪
(With David Crosby, Stephen Stills and Graham Nash) Deja Vu (Atlantic, 1970) ♪♪♪♪♪
(With Crosby, Stills and Nash) 4 Way Street (Atlantic, 1971) ♪♪♪♪
Journey through the Past (Warner Bros., 1972) ♪♪
Time Fades Away (Reprise, 1973) ♪♪♪♪
(With Crosby, Stills and Nash) So Far (Atlantic, 1974) ♪♪♪♪
On the Beach (Reprise, 1974) ♪♪♪♪
Zuma (Reprise, 1975) ♪♪♪♪
Long May You Run (Reprise, 1976) ♪♪♪

STEVE YOUNG

Born July 12, in GA.

Steve Young's songs have bolstered the careers of others—notably the Eagles, Hank Williams Jr. and Waylon Jennings—but the Southern singer/songwriter has never come close to tasting fame on his own. That's hardly surprising, since Young's eclectic style draws on blues, folk, country, rock and mountain styles; it's simply too diverse to package and sell to the masses. Which is not to say it's not worth checking out. A native Southerner, Young moved to the West Coast during the late 1960s, where he was an integral part of the California country-rock movement (Gram Parsons, Chris Hillman, Bernie Leadon and Gene Clark all appeared on Young's 1969 debut, *Rock Salt*

& *Nails*). From there he has gravitated toward Austin, Texas, Nashville and, once again, Los Angeles, with varying degrees of success. His songs alone make him well worth checking out, but he's also an agile guitarist and an expressive singer.

what to buy: A *de facto* best-of release, *Solo/Live* (Watermelon, 1991, prod. Heinz Geissler) &&&&, contains acoustic performances of Young's songs that have been made famous by others, including "Seven Bridges Road" (the Eagles) and "Montgomery in the Rain" (Hank Williams Jr.), plus some that have influenced him—the traditional "Go to Sea No More" and Bob Dylan's "Don't Think Twice, It's All Right." Young proves himself more than a great songwriter, though; he's also a terrific guitarist and vocalist. *Switchblades of Love* (Watermelon, 1993, prod. J. Steven Soles) &&&& puts him in a full-band setting with impressive results. Highlights include "Angel of Lyon," co-written with Tom Russell, and the harrowing title track.

the rest:

Honky Tonk Man (Mountain Railroad, 1975/Drive Archive, 1994) &&&
Seven Bridges Road (Reprise, 1971/Rounder, 1982) &&&&
To Satisfy You (Rounder, 1982) &&&

worth searching for: The best-of collection *Lonesome, On'ry & Mean: Steve Young, 1968–1978* (Raven, 1994) &&&& is available as an Australian import. Of Young's older, out-of-print material, look for *Rock Salt & Nails* (A&M, 1969) &&&&, *Renegade Picker* (RCA, 1976) &&&& and *No Place to Fall* (RCA, 1978) &&&&.

influences:

◄◄ Bob Dylan, Hank Williams

►► Steve Earle, Townes Van Zandt, Gary Stewart, Tom Russell

Daniel Durchholz

RESOURCES
AND OTHER INFORMATION

Can't get enough country? Here are some books and magazines you can check out for further information. Happy reading!

BOOKS

Biographies

Almost Like a Song
Ronnie Milsap, with Tom Carter (McGraw/Hill, 1990)

Back In the Saddle Again
Gene Autry, with Mickey Herskowitz (Doubleday,1978)

The Barbara Mandrell Story
Charles Paul Conn (Berkley Books, 1988)

Bill Monroe and His Blue Grass Boys: An Illustrated Discography
Neil V. Rosenberg (Country Music Foundation, 1974)

By the Seat of My Pants
Buddy Killen, with Tom Carter (Simon & Schuster, 1993)

The Carter Family
John Atkins, ed. (Old Time Music, 1973)

Coal Miner's Daughter
Loretta Lynn, with George Vecsey (Contemporary Books, 1976)

Country Gentleman
Chet Atkins, with Bill Neely (Henry Regnery, 1974)

Dark Star: The Roy Orbison Story
Ellis Amburn (Lyle Stuart, 1990)

Dead Elvis
Greil Marcus (Doubleday, 1991)

Dolly: My Life and Other Unfinished Business
Dolly Parton (HarperCollins, 1994)

Elvis
Dave Marsh (Times Books, 1982)

Elvis
Albert Goldman (McGraw-Hill, 1981)

Elvis and Gladys
Elaine Dundy (Macmillan, 1985)

Elvis and Me
Priscilla Beaulieu Presley and Sandra Harmon (G.P. Putnam's Sons, 1985)

Elvis and the Colonel
Dirk Vellenga, with Mick Farren (Delacorte Press, 1988)

Elvis: What Happened?
Red West, Sonny West and Dave Hebler (Ballantine Books, 1977)

Ernest Tubb: The Texas Troubador
Ronnie Pugh (Duke, 1996)

Everybody's Grandpa
Louis M. "Grandpa" Jones, with Charles K. Wolfe (University of Tennessee Press, 1984)

From the Heart
June Carter Cash (Prentice-Hall Press, 1987)

Garth Brooks
Michael McCall (Bantam, 1991)

Garth Brooks: One of a Kind, Working on a Full House
Rick Mitchell (Simon & Schuster, 1993)

Garth Brooks: Platinum Cowboy
Edward Morris (St. Martin's, 1993)

Garth Brooks: The Road Out of Santa Fe
Matt O'Meilia (University of Oklahoma Press, 1997)

George Jones: The Life and Times of a Honky Tonk Legend
Bob Allen (Birch Lane Press, 1994)

Get to the Heart
Barbara Mandrell, with George Vecsey (Bantam Books, 1990)

Hank Williams
Colin Escott (Little, Brown, 1994)

Happy Trails: Our Life Story
Roy Rogers and Dale Evans, with Jane and Michael Stern (Simon & Schuster, 1994)

Hear My Song: The Story of the Celebrated Sons of the Pioneers
Ken Griffis (Norken, 1986)

Hellfire: The Jerry Lee Lewis Story
Nick Tosches (Delacorte, 1982)

Hickory Wind: The Life and Times of Gram Parsons
Ben Fong-Torres (Pocket Books, 1991)

I Hope You're Living as High on the Hog as the Pig You Turned Out to Be
Bill Anderson (Longstreet, 1993)

I Lived to Tell It All
George Jones, with Tom Carter (Villard, 1996)

Jimmie Rodgers: The Life and Times of America's Blue Yodeler
Nolan Porterfield (University of Illinois Press, 1979)

Johnny Cash
Sean Dolan (Chelsea House, 1995)

The Judds
Bob Millard (Dolphin/Doubleday, 1988)

Last Train to Memphis: The Rise of Elvis Presley
Peter Guralnick (Little, Brown, 1994)

Lefty Frizzell: The Honky-Tonk Life of Country Music's Greatest Singer
Daniel Cooper (Little-Brown, 1995)

The Life and Times of Hank Williams
Arnold Rogers and Bruce Gidoll (Haney-Jones Books, 1993)

The Man in Black
Johnny Cash (Warner Books, 1975)

Memories: The Autobiography of Ralph Emery
Ralph Emery, with Tom Carter (Macmillan, 1991)

Minnie Pearl: An Autobiography
Minnie Pearl, with Joan Dew (Simon & Schuster, 1980)

More Memories
Ralph Emery, with Tom Carter (G.P. Putnam's Sons, 1993)

My Years with Bob Wills
Al Stricklin, with Jon McConal (Naylor Press, 1976)

Nickel Dreams
Tanya Tucker, with Patsi Cox (Hyperion, 1997)

Patsy Cline: An Intimate Biography
Ellis Nassour (Tower Books, 1981)

Queen of Country Music: The Life Story of Kitty Wells
A.C. Dunkleburger (Ambrose Printing, 1977)

Ramblin' Rose: The Life and Career of Rose Maddox
Jonny Whiteside (Vanderbilt University Press/Country Music Foundation, 1997)

Reba: My Story
Reba McEntire, with Tom Carter (Bantam, 1994)

Ricky Nelson: Idol for a Generation
Joel Selvin (Contemporary Books, 1990)

Rockabilly Queens: The Careers and Recordings of Wanda Jackson, Janis Martin, Brenda Lee
Bob Garbutt (Robert Garbutt Productions, 1979)

Roy Acuff: The Smoky Mountain Boy
Elizabeth Schlappi (Pelican Publishing, 1978)

San Antonio Rose: The Life and Music of Bob Wills
Charles R. Townsend (University of Illinois Press, 1976)

Sing a Sad Song: The Life of Hank Williams
Roger M. Williams (University of Illinois Press, 1980)

Sing Me Back Home
Merle Haggard, with Peggy Russell (Times Books, 1981)

Stand By Your Man: An Autobiography
Tammy Wynette, with Joan Dew (Simon & Schuster, 1979)

Still in Love with You
Lycrecia Williams and Dale Vinicur (Rutledge Hill Press, 1989)

The Storyteller's Nashville
Tom T. Hall (Doubleday, 1979)

Ten Feet Tall and Bulletproof
Travis Tritt, with Michael Bane (Warner Books, 1994)

Waylon: An Autobiography
Waylon Jennings, with Lenny Kaye (Warner Books, 1996)

Whisperin' Bill: An Autobiography
Bill Anderson (Longstreet, 1989)

Whole Lotta Shakin' Going On: Jerry Lee Lewis
Robert Cain (Dial Press, 1981)

Willie Nelson Family Album
Lana Nelson Fowler, compiler (H.M. Poirot and Co., 1980)

Your Cheatin' Heart: A Biography of Hank Williams
Chet Flippo (Simon & Schuster, 1981)

General Interest and Reference

All Music Guide to Country Music
Michael Erlewine, ed. (Miller Freeman, 1997)

Behind Closed Doors: Talking with the Legends of Country Music
Alanna Nash (Alfred A. Knopf, 1988)

The Best of Country Music
John Morthland (Doubleday Dolphin, 1984)

The Big Book of Country Music: A Biographical Encyclopedia
Richard Carlin (Penguin, 1995)

The Billboard Book of Top 40 Country Hits
Joel Whitburn (Billboard Books, 1996)

The Blackwell Guide to Recorded Country Music
Bob Allen, ed. (Blackwell, 1994)

Bluegrass: A History
Neil V. Rosenberg (University of Illinois Press, 1985)

Border Radio
Gene Fowler and Bill Crawford (Texas Monthly Press, 1987)

The Comprehensive Country Music Encyclopedia
Country Music Magazine, ed. (Times Books, 1994)

Country: The Biggest Music in America
Nick Tosches (Scribner's, 1985)

Country: The Music and the Musicians
Country Music Foundation (Abbeville Press, 1988)

The Country Music Book
Michael Mason, ed. (Scribner's, 1985)

Country Music Culture: From Hard Times to Heaven
Curtis W. Ellison (Mississippi, 1995)

Country Music U.S.A.
Bill C. Malone (University of Texas Press, 1968, rev. 1985)

Country on Compact Disc:
The Essential Guide to the Music
Country Music Foundation, with Paul
  Kingsbury, ed. (Grove Press, 1993)

Country Reader:
25 Years of the Journal of Country Music
(CMF, 1996)

Country Roots:
The Origins of Country Music
Douglas B. Green (Hawthorn Books, 1976)

Definitive Country:
The Ultimate Encyclopedia of Country
Music and Its Performers
Barry McCloud (Perigee, 1995)

Devil's Box: Masters of Southern Fiddling
Charles Wolfe (CMF/Vanderbilt, 1997)

Dixie Rising: How the South Is Shaping
American Values, Politics and Culture
Peter Applebome (Times Books, 1996)

The Encyclopedia of Folk,
Country and Western Music
Irwin Stambler and Grelun Landon (St.
  Martin's Press, 1983)

Finding Her Voice:
The Saga of Women in Country Music
Mary A. Bufwack and Robert K. Oermann
  (Crown Publishers, 1993)

Giants of Country Music
Neil Haislop, Tad Lathrop and Harry Sum-
  rall (Billboard Books, 1995)

Good Rockin' Tonight:
Sun Records and the Birth of Rock 'n' Roll
Colin Escott and Martin Hawkins (St. Mar-
  tin's Press, 1991)

Grand Ole Opry
Jack Hurst (Harry N. Abrams, Inc., 1975)

The Grand Ole Opry History of Country
Music: 70 Years of the Songs, the Stars
and the Stories
Paul Kingsbury (Villard, 1995)

The Grand Ole Opry:
The Early Years, 1925–1935
Charles K. Wolfe (Old Time Music, 1975)

Grand Ole Opry WSM Pictures-History
Book
Jerry Strobel, ed. (Opryland USA, 1984)

The Illustrated History of Country Music
Patrick Carr, ed. (Doubleday, 1979)

The Improbable Rise of Redneck Rock
Jan Reid (Heidelberg Publishers, 1974)

In the Country of Country
Nicholas Dawidoff (Pantheon, 1997)

Mountaineer Jamboree:
Country Music in West Virginia
Ivan M. Tribe (University Press of Ken-
  tucky, 1984)

Nashville: Music City U.S.A.
John Lomax III (Harry N. Abrams, Inc., 1985)

The Nashville Sound:
Bright Lights and Country Music
Paul Hemphill (Simon & Schuster, 1970)

The New Folk Music
Craig Harris (Whitecliffs Media, 1991)

The Outlaws:
Revolutions in Country Music
Michael Bane (Country Music Magazine
  Press/ Doubleday/ Dolphin, 1978)

Sing Your Heart Out, Country Boys
Dorothy Horstman (Country Music Foundation, 1975)

Singers & Sweethearts
Joan Dew (Dolphin/Doubleday, 1977)

The Singing Cowboys
David Rothel (A.S. Barnes & Company,
  1978)

The Sound of the City
Charlie Gillett (Pantheon, 1983)

Stars of Country Music
Bill C. Malone and Judith McCulloh, ed.
  (University of Illinois Press, 1975)

Top Country Singles, 1944–1993
Joel Whitburn (Record Research, 1994)

We Wanna Boogie: An Illustrated History
of the American Rockabilly Movement
Randy McNutt (HHP Books, 1988)

MAGAZINES AND NEWSPAPERS

Billboard
One Astor Plaza
1515 Broadway
New York, NY 10036
    *$275/1 year. International magazine of
    music and home entertainment geared
    toward professionals in the music and*

*home video industries and related
fields.*

Bluegrass Unlimited
PO Box 111
Broad Run, VA 22014
    *$22/1 year. Covers bluegrass and old-
    time country music.*

Cash Box
50 Music Square West, Suite 804
Nashville, TN 37203
    *$185 /1 year. Magazine for members of
    the record and music industries.*

Country America
1716 Locust St.
Des Moines, IA 50309-3023
    *$16.97/1 year. Entertainment and
    lifestyle magazine for people who
    enjoy country music and opt for the
    country way of life.*

Country Music
329 Riverside Ave., Suite 1
Westport, CT 06880
    *$15.98/1 year. Covers country music,
    especially as it relates to the profes-
    sional and personal lives of the per-
    formers. Includes interviews, record
    reviews, and more.*

Country Music People
225A Lewisham Way
London SE4 1UY, England
    *Reports on American country music,
    including artist features and record re-
    views.*

Country Music Round Up
PO Box 111
Waltham, Grimsby DN37 0YN, England
    *Country music magazine for Britain
    and abroad. Includes artist profiles,
    record reviews, tour schedules, and
    regional reports.*

Country Wave
20461 Douglas Crescent, Suite 4
Langley, BC V3A 436, Canada
    *$35/1 year. Covers country music in
    Canada, the U.S., and abroad. In-
    cludes features, interviews, album re-
    views, and more.*

Country Weekly
600 S. East Coast Ave.
Lantana, FL 33462
    *$46.50/1 year. Covers country music
    artists and their lives. Includes inter-*

views, concert and appearance schedules, album reviews, and more.

Goldmine
700 E. State St.
Jola, WI 54990
$39.95/1 year. Magazine for record/CD/tape collectors and music fans. Covers collecting and selling recordings in all music fields and features discographies, interviews, and album reviews.

International Bluegrass
International Bluegrass Association
207 E. 2nd St.
Owensboro, KY 42303
$20/1 year. Reports on business aspects of the bluegrass music industry.

Journal of Country Music
4 Music Square East
Nashville, TN 37203
$18/1 year. Features biographical reviews of performers and their musical development, question-and-answer interviews with performers and music business people, and essays on the historical development of specific styles of music.

Kountry Korral
6031 S-791 06
Falun, Sweden

Scandinavia's country music magazine.

Modern Screen's Country Music
Sterling/McFadden
233 Park Ave. South
New York, NY 10003
$22.50/1 year. Magazine for country music fans.

Music City News
PO Box 22975
50 Music Square West
Nashville, TN 37202-2975
$23.50/1 year. Country music magazine containing interviews, new record releases, artist itineraries, and other news for entertainment professionals and their fans.

Music Row
PO Box 158542
Nashville, TN 37215
$80/1 year. Covers Nashville's music industry. Features current news items, album reviews, interviews, and more.

New Country
86 Elm St.
Peterborough, NH 03458
$107.40/1 year. Covers all facets of country music: the superstars and the legends, the fringe-dwellers and the up-and-comers. Encompasses honky-

tonk and bluegrass, Cajun and Tejano, folk and Americana. Features comprehensive album review section. Full-length compilation CD or cassette included with each issue.

Old-Time Herald
PO Box 51812
Durham, NC 27717
$34/1 year. Dedicated to old-time music. Discusses folk music, bluegrass, cabin songs, and ballads.

Radio & Records
10100 Santa Monica Blvd., 5th Floor
Los Angeles, CA 90067
$299/1 year. Covers the radio and recording industries. Features news, information on sales and marketing, airplay data, and more.

Tradition
Prairie Press
Country Opera House
PO Box 438
Walnut, IA 51577
$15/1 year. Covers traditional American acoustic music, including country, bluegrass, folk, mountain, and hillbilly music.

Country music is everywhere, even out in cyberspace. Point your Web browser to these pages and you won't be disappointed.

ARTISTS

Eddie Adcock
http://www.banjo.com/Profiles/
Adcock.html

Trace Adkins
http://www.Nashville.Net/~sarepta/
adkins.htm

Rhett Akins
http://www.decca-nashville.com/ra/
raalbum.htm

Alabama
http://www.public.iastate.edu/
~skramer/stuff/music/alabama/
alabama.html
http://www.countrystars.com/artists/
alabama.html

Gary Allan
http://www.decca-nashville.com/ga/
gaalbum.htm

John Anderson
http://www.plix.com/~users/ab7iz/
andersonpage.htm

Archer/Park
http://www.traveller.com/archpark/

Chet Atkins
http://www.chetatkins.com/

Hoyt Axton
http://www.eyekon.com/hoytaxton/

Bad Livers
http://www.hyperweb.com/badlivers

Joan Baez
http://baez.woz.org/
http://www.execpc.com/~henkle/
fbindex/b/baez_joan.html

Matraca Berg
http://www.atv.com/~fleming/
matraca/index.html

John Berry
http://www.john-berry.com/
index.html

Clint Black
http://it.stlawu.edu/~mdoyle/clint/
clint.html

BlackHawk
http://www.webcom.com/autobuy/
country_music/blackhaw.html

The Blasters
http://www.cs.uit.no/Music/View/
Blasters

Bluebloods
http://songs.com/deadreck/
bluebloods.html

Suzy Bogguss
http://www.bogguss.com/

BR5-49
http://www.br5-49.com/home.htm

Lisa Brokop
http://www.lisabrokop.org/

Brooks & Dunn
http://www.geocities.com/Broadway/
5125/

Garth Brooks
http://www.inlink.com/~brandon/
http://www.coastside.net/USERS/
termite/gb-page.htm#info
http://www.roughstock.com/garth/
http://www.westworld.com/
~garthbrk/

Brother Phelps
http://plix.com/~users/ab7iz/
phelpspage.htm

Jimmy Buffett
http://www.soasoas.com/

T-Bone Burnett
http://www.niweb.com/tony/sam/
burnett/tbone.html

Tracy Byrd
http://hcc.cc.fl.us/services/staff/
dawn/tbyrd.htm

The Byrds
http://members.aol.com/byrdsonlne/
byrdsstuff/byrds.htm
http://www.q-net.net/~rrussell/
Byrds/

Glen Campbell
http://www.glencampbellshow.com/

Mary Chapin Carpenter
http://members.aol.com/djcoplien/
mcc/index.html
http://www.servtech.com/public/
mrs7764/MCC/

The Carter Family
http://bmi.com/CARTER.html

Carlene Carter
http://grendel.partyline.net/~carlene/
index.html

Deana Carter
http://www.angelfire.com/id/deana/
index.html

Johnny Cash
http://american.recordings.com/
American_Artists/Johnny_Cash/
cash_home.html
http://www.odysseygroup.com/cash/
legend1.htm

Rosanne Cash
http://www.rollanet.org/~hbeydler/
rosecash.html

Ray Charles
http://www.raycharles.com/

Kenny Chesney
http://www.dbaadv.com/tour95/
Kenny.html

Mark Chesnutt
http://www.Nashville.Net/~chesnutt/

The Chieftains
http://www.escape.ca/~skinner/
chieftains/chief.html

Guy Clark
http://www.physitron.com/~topher/
guyclark/

Terri Clark
http://www.countrystars.com/artists/
terri.html

Patsy Cline
http://www.patsy-cline.com/
http://www.mca-nashville.com/
pcbox/pcbox.htm

Leonard Cohen
http://www.music.sony.com/Music/
ArtistInfo/LeonardCohen.html
http://www.vsonic.fi/~ja/cohen/

Mark Collie
http://www.hotcc.com/1countrycorner/
collie.html

Commander Cody
http://www.globerecords.com/
Cody.html

Confederate Railroad
http://www.countrylightning.com/
confed.html

Rita Coolidge
http://users.aol.com/rcfan/private/
rita.html

Elvis Costello
http://www.wbr.com/elvis/
http://east.isx.com/~schnitzi/elvis.
html

Cowboy Junkies
http://www.oberlin.edu/~wfleming/
CowboyJunkies.html
http://www.glue.umd.edu/~dcrane/
junky.html

Cox Family
http://www.banjo.com/BG/Profiles/
Cox.html

J.D. Crowe & the New South
http://www.banjo.com/BG/Profiles/
JDCrowe.html

Rodney Crowell
http://it.stlawu.edu/~mdoyle/rodney/
rodney.html

Billy Ray Cyrus
http://home.earthlink.net/
~poeticpage/

Charlie Daniels
http://members.aol.com/mattsmith/
matt.html
http://www.a2znet.com/cdb/cdbfan.
html
http://www.a2znet.com/cdb/

Linda Davis
http://www.lindadavis.com

Billy Dean
http://204.96.208.1/services/staff/
dawn/bdean.htm

Iris DeMent
http://www.he.net/~jarmode/
DeMent.html

John Denver
http://www.sky.net/~emily/

The Derailers
http://www.derailers.com/

Diamond Rio
http://www.countrystars.com/artists/
diamond.html

http://www.diamondrio.com/

Neil Diamond
http://www.superdiamond.com/
http://users.aol.com/klerxt/
diamondhome.html
http://www.worldaccess.nl/
~hogensti/

Joe Diffie
http://www.joediffie.com/

Jerry Douglas
http://www.alternetcomm.com/
moonlight/doug.html

George Ducas
http://www.lookup.com/Homepages/
75687/ducas.html

Bob Dylan
http://bob.nbr.no/
http://www.ideasign.com/~nh/
http://www.execpc.com/~billp61/
boblink.html

The Eagles
http://members.aol.com/ivyrain/
fastlane.html
http://www.dreamscape.com/esmith/
dansm/eagles.htm

Steve Earle
http://www.mcs.net/~lisa/EARLE/
steve.htm

Joe Ely
http://www.ely.com/Joe.home.html

Ty England
http://www.nashville.net/~tyland

The Everly Brothers
http://www.xs4all.nl/~owjasonb/

Exile
http://www.geocities.com/Hollywood/
5362/

Freddy Fender
http://www.freddyfender.com

Bela Fleck/Bela Fleck & the Flecktones
http://www.ubl.com:80/artists/
002504.html

The Flying Burrito Brothers
http://www.primenet.com/~klugl/
gpgilded.html

Dan Fogelberg
http://www.treehouse.org/fogelberg/

Jeff Foxworthy
http://www.jeff-foxworthy.com

Fox Family
http://www.banjo.com/Profiles/fox.
htm

Lefty Frizzel
http://www.bizniz-web.com/lefty/

Front Range
http://www.banjo.com/BG/Profiles/
FrontRange.html

The Gatlin Brothers
http://www.patricia.com/entertain/
gatlins.html

Vince Gill
http://www.vincegill.com/
http://www.mca-nashville.com/vg/
vgalbum.htm

Mickey Gilley
http://www.branson.com/branson/
gilley/gilley.htm

Jimmie Dale Gilmore
http://m2.monsterbit.com/jdg/index2.
html

John Gorka
http://www.windham.com/ourmusic/
artist_pages/gorka.empty.byartist.
html

Nancy Griffith
http://www.sover.net/~rschrull/
ngriffith/gchpnet3.html
http://www.rahul.net/frankf/nanci.
html
http://www.socsci.umn.edu/
~worthen/nanci/nanci.high.html

Arlo Guthrie
http://www.clark.net/pub/downin/
cgi-bin/arlonet.html

Woody Guthrie
http://www.artsci.wustl.edu/~davida/
woody.html

Merle Haggard
http://miso.wwa.com/~travel96/
http://www.TheHag.com/

Tom T. Hall
http://www.cnct.com/~tomthall/

Butch Hancock
http://207.226.241.14/mi/jeffmiller/

Emmylou Harris
http://nashville.net/~kate/

John Hartford
http://www.techpublishing.com/
hartford/

Ty Herndon
http://tyherndon.com/

Dan Hicks
http://www.ns.net/~chaler/hicks.
html

High Noon
http://members.aol.com/noontunes/
highnoon.htm

Highway 101
http://www.hiway101.com/

Faith Hill
http://fly.hiwaay.net/~shanek/
FaithHill/faith.htm
http://www.faith-hill.com/

Tish Hinojosa
http://.wbr.com/tishhinojosa/index.
html

Buddy Holly
http://www.idm.co.uk/buddy/buddy.
htm
http://www.geocities.com/
SunsetStrip/Towers/5236/

Hot Rize
http://www.banjo.com/BG/Profiles/
HotRize.html

Alan Jackson
http://www.geocities.com/
Heartland/Plains/5753/
http://www.geocities.com/Broadway/
4404/

Jason & the Scorchers
http://edge.edge.net/~hpeek/scorch.
html

The Jayhawks
http://american.recordings.com/
American_Artists/Jayhawks/
jayhawks_home.html

Waylon Jennings
http://waylon.com/

George Jones
http://www.countrylightning.com/
jones.html

Scott Joss
http://www.littledogrecords.com/

The Judds
http://www.mpimedia.com/Judds/
index.html

Kathy Kallick
http://www.banjo.com/Profiles/
kallick.html

Toby Keith
http://www.ifco.org/tobykeith.htm

The Kentucky HeadHunters
http://www.plix.com/~users/ab7iz/
headpage.htm

Sammy Kershaw
http://www.Nashville.Net/~krshwknr/
http://pages.nyu.edu/~sqt1073/

Hal Ketchum
http://www.hotcc.com/1countrycorner/
ketchum.html

Royal Wade Kimes
http://www.nashville.net/~troppo/
royal.htm

Alison Krauss
http://www.dotmusic.co.uk/
MWtalentkrauss.html
http://www.countrystars.com/artists/
alison.html

Kris Kristofferson
http://www.wu-wien.ac.at/usr/h92/
h9225291/kris/intro1.html

Sleepy LaBeef
http://www.bear-family.de/tabel1/
neuheit/sep/internat/LABEEF/
sleepy.htm

Jimmie LaFave
http://www.rounder.com/bobeat/
JimmyLafaveHome.htm

k.d. lang
http://members.aol.com/oink454737/
home/kdlang.htm
http://www.infohouse.com/
obviousgossip/
http://www.wbr.com/kdlang/

Laurel Canyon Ramblers
http://www.banjo.com/Profiles/
LaurelCanyon.html

Christine Lavin
http://www.automatrix.com/~lavin/

web pages

Tracy Lawrence
http://www.edge.net/tle/

Chris LeDoux
http://www.cowgirls.com/

Brenda Lee
http://www.voy.net/~brenlefn/
fanclub.html

Jerry Lee Lewis
http://www.student.tdb.uu.se/
~m93aum/jerry.html

Laurie Lewis
http://www.banjo.com/Profiles/
LaurieLewis.html

Little Texas
http://www.iuma.com/Warner/html/
Little_Texas.html

Patty Loveless
http://www.music.sony.com/Music/
Nashville/PattyLoveless/
http://www.cbvcp.com/c2/patty.html

Lyle Lovett
http://www.geocities.com/SoHo/
1192/lyle.html
http://www.curb.com/Artists/ll.html

Loretta Lynn
http://www.ols.net/~cass/Loretta.
html

Kate MacKenzie
http://www.gotech.com/performr.dir/
mackenzi/katemck.htm

Charlie Major
http://www.songnet.com/cmajor/

Barbara Mandrell
http://www.geocities.com/Heartland/
Plains/9532/
http://www.midtod.com/9512/
mandrell.html

Mila Mason
http://www.Nashville.Net/~mila/

Kathy Mattea
http://www.mattea.com/

The Mavericks
http://www.mca-nashville.com/mav/
mavalbum.htm
http://www.the-mavericks.com

Martina McBride
http://martina-mcbride.com/

http://members.aol.com/naterothen/
index.htm

Del McCoury Band
http://www.banjo.com/BG/Profiles/
DelMcCoury.html
http://www.techpublishing.com/
johnson/cj4.htm

Neal McCoy
http://www.luvneal.com/
http://204.96.208.1/services/staff/
dawn/nmccoy.htm

Reba McEntire
http://www.reba.com/
http://www.ziplink.net/~darkfire/
http://www.geocities.com/Hollywood/
Set/5952/

John McEuen
http://www.banjo.com/BG/Profiles/
JohnMcEuen.html

McGarrigle Sisters
http://www.glen-net.ca/mcgarrigles/

Tim McGraw
http://www.funzone4mcgraw.com/

Maria McKee/Lone Justice
http://www.hgs.se/~nd93men/Maria.
McKee/
http://www.hgs.se/~nf95166/index.
htm

Don McLean
http://www.rdg.ac.uk/%7esgshowrd/
DonMcLean/home.htm
http://www.mbhs.edu/~bconnell/
cty/american-pie.html

Jo Dee Messina
http://wwwcurb.com/Artists/jdm.html

The Moffatts
http://www.themoffatts.com/

Bill Monroe
http://www.banjo.com/BG/Profiles/
BillMonroe.html

John Michael Montgomery
http://www.cbvcp.com/c2/john.html
http://www2.johnmichael.com/cow/
jmm/html/jm1a.html

Lorrie Morgan
http://www.lorrie.com/
http://www.nmt.edu/~nguyenm/
lorrie.html

Alan Munde
http://www.banjo.com/Profiles/
MundeCarr.html

David Lee Murphy
http://www.webcom.com/autobuy/
country_music/DavidLee/
DavidLee.html

Anne Murray
http://www.emimusic.ca/am/html/

Heather Myles
http://www.iac.net/~sharonv/
heather.html

The Nashville Bluegrass Band
http://www.newportfolk.com/
bluegras.html

Willie Nelson
http://www.justicerecords.com/
~nancy/arp16.html
http://www.countrystars.com/artists/
wnelson.html

Michael Nesmith
http://www.flexquarters.com/main/
nesmith.html

New Coon Creek Girls
http://www.banjo.com/Profiles/
cooncrk.htm

Juice Newton
http://www.juicenewton.com/

Olivia Newton-John
http://www-leland.stanford.edu/
~clem/
http://www.geocities.com/WallStreet/
7015/olivia.htm
http://members.tripod.com/
~Devoted_Fan/index.html

The Nitty Gritty Dirt Band
http://www.missouri.edu/~c570492/
ngdb.html

The Oak Ridge Boys
http://www.plix.com/~users/ab7iz/
oakspage.htm
http://members.aol.com/BryanTyson/
oaks.htm

Tim & Mollie O'Brien
http://www.banjo.com/Profiles/
Obrien.html

Mark O'Connor
http://www.markoconnor.com/

One Riot One Ranger
http://members.aol.com/oneriot/
oneriot.html

Roy Orbison
http://stm1.chem.psu.edu/~krk/
orbison/RoyOrbison.html

Marie Osmond
http://www.osmond.com/

Buck Owens
http://www.geocities.com/Heartland/
Plains/5040/home.htm

Ozark Mountain Daredevils
http://www.cowgirls.com/dream/jan/
ozarks.htm

**David Parmley, Scott Vestal &
Continental Divide**
http://www.banjo.com/BG/Profiles/
ContinentalDivide.html

Lee Roy Parnell
http://www.tiac.net/users/twostep/
parnell.htm

Gram Parsons
http://www.primenet.com/~klugl/
gramhome.html

Dolly Parton
http://www.geocities.com/Hollywood/
Set/2836/
http://www.bestware.net/spreng/
dolly/index.html
http://www.aber.ac.uk/~daa93/Dolly/
dolly.html

Johnny Paycheck
http://www.nashville.com/~paycheck

Carl Perkins
http://erc.jscc.cc.tn.us:80/jfn/
exchange/carl.html

Gretchen Peters
http://www.gretchenpeters.com/

MC Potts
http://www.mcpotts.com

Prarie Oyster
http://www.io.org/~oyster/

Elvis Presley
http://sunsite.unc.edu/elvis/elvishom.
html
http://users.aol.com/elvisnet/index.
html

John Prine
http://www.execpc.com/~oos/
prinemain.htm

Psychograss
http://catalog.com/psygrass/

The Rarely Heard
http://www.banjo.com/Profiles/
RarelyHerd.html

Collin Raye
http://www.seark.net/~kerbear/Raye/

Ronna Reeves
http://www.cris.com/~jevers/ronna/
rrid.html

Lou Reid & Carolina
http://www.banjo.com/Profiles/
LRCarolina.html

Kimmie Rhodes
http://www.kimmierhodes.com/

Kim Richey
http://www.u.arizona.edu/~nam/kim.
html

Jeannie C. Riley
http://www.teleport.com/~luckylg/
sirius/jeannie_c_riley.html

LeAnn Rimes
http://members.aol.com/fanofleann/
home.html
http://www.leann.com/
http://www.angelfire.com/tx/rimes/

Jimmie Rodgers
http://www.discover-texas.com/
jimmie/
http://www.cmgww.com/music/
rodgers/rodgers.html

Kenny Rogers
http://www.roasters.com/krrsing2.
html
http://www.epn.com:80/rogers/
kenny.htm

Roy Rogers
http://www.vivanet.com/~blues/roy/
rogers.html

Linda Ronstadt
http://www.wco.com/~sashlock/

Peter Rowan
http://BGR.ee/ROWAN/
http://www.rtpnet.org/~bith/
peter_rowan.html

Leon Russell
http://users.aol.com/leonrussel/
leonaol.htm

Salamander Crossing
http://www.banjo.com/Profiles/
SalamanderCrossing.html

Sawyer Brown
http://www.acton.com/country/
sawyerbrown.html

Scud Mountain Boys
http://www.subpop.com/bands/scud/
scudboys.html

Brady Seals
http://bradyseals.com

Seldom Scene
http://www.banjo.com/Profiles/
SeldomScene.html

Billy Joe Shaver
http://www.billyjoeshaver.com/

Ricky Skaggs
http://www.jii.com/countrystars/
artists/rskaggs.html

Bryan Smith
http://www.members.aol.com/
bryanmusik/bryansmith.html

Chris Smither
http://www.intermarket.net/~stessa/
smither/

Southern Pacific
http://www.geocities.com/Hollywood/
5362/sppage.html

Southern Rail
http://world.std.com/~muller/SR/

Ralph Stanley/The Stanley Brothers
http://www.banjo.com/Profiles/
RalphStanley.html

The Statler Brothers
http://www.dreamscape.com/statler

Keith Stegall
http://www.songnet.com/stegall/

Ray Stevens
http://www.raystevens.com/
~rstevens/

Doug Stone
http://ally.ios.com/~khulet19/

George Strait
http://www.georgestraitfans.com/

http://www.concom.com/patriot/
george.htm

http://www2.pair.com/tsniff/
George_Strait/

Marty Stuart
http://www.martyparty.com/
http://www.mca-nashville.com/ms/
msfront.htm

James Taylor
http://www.westworld.com/~gregb/
jt.html

Texas Tornados
http://www.xanadu2.net/rrogers/
ttnet.html
http://www.repriserec.com/
Reprise_HTML_Pages/TexasTDir/
TexasTornados.html

Chris Thile
http://www.banjo.com/Profiles/
ChrisThile.html

Hank Thompson
http://www.preferred.com/~ics/hank/

Pam Tillis
http://www.instantweb.com/~omega/
starweb/pamt.html

Aaron Tippin
http://pages.prodigy.com/
CountryMusic/aaron1.htm

Tractors
http://www.thetractors.com/

Randy Travis
http://www.randy-travis.com/
http://www.geocities.com/Hollywood/
1548/

Rick Trevino
http://www.music.sony.com/Music/
ArtistInfo/RickTrevino.html

Travis Tritt
http://www.wbr.com/travistritt/
http://www.countrystars.com/artists/
ttritt.html

Tanya Tucker
http://www.gorgon.com/users/
~ron2nina/tanyatuc.htm

Shania Twain
http://homepages.enterprise.net:80/
sque/shania/
http://www.shania.com/

Conway Twitty
http://bizweb.lightspeed.net/
~Conway_Twitty/

Ian Tyson
http://www.nucleus.com/~cowboy/

Uncle Tupelo
http://www.eos.ncsu.edu:80/eos/
users/s/sdhouse/Mosaic/
uncle-tupelo.html

Townes Van Zandt
http://www.cleaf.com/~marq/
townsdex.html

Gene Vincent
http://www.athenet.net/~genevinc/
index.html

Wagon
http://www.wagon1.com/

Clay Walker
http://www.claywalker.com/
http://pages.prodigy.com/
kountrykris/clay.htm

Jerry Jeff Walker
http://www.jerryjeff.com/

Doc Watson
http://www.rootsworld.com/folklore/
doc.html
http://sunsite.unc.edu/doug/DocWat/
DocWat.html

Gillian Welch
http://www.geffen.com/almo/gillian/

Cheryl Wheeler
http://www.gv.psu.edu/personal/
wrp103/wheeler/home.htm

Bryan White
http://www.zmc.com/bw/index.html
http://ourworld.compuserve.com/
homepages/bryan_white/

Lari White
http://www.hcc.cc.fl.us/services/
staff/dawn/lwhite.htm

Don Williams
http://www.universal.nl/users/
welling/

Hank Williams
http://www.cmgww.com/music/hank/
hank.html

Hank Williams Jr.
http://paris.aeneas.net/hank/
Welcome.html

www.hank-williamsjr.com

Lucinda Williams
http://www.cleaf.com:80/~marq/
lucinda.html

Robin & Linda Williams
http://www.dn.net/williams/

Kelly Willis
http://www.zoomnet.net/~michaelp/
kelly.html

Michelle Wright
http://members.aol.com/rbotsford/
michelle/michelle.html

Wylie & the Wild West Show
http://www.telalink.net/~buckskin/
wylie/

Tammy Wynette
http://www.music.sony.com/Music/
ArtistInfo/TammyWynette.html

Wynonna
http://www.curb.com/artists/wn.html
http://www.Nashville.Net/~wifc/
http://www.america.net/~mwise/

Trisha Yearwood
http://www.geocities.com/Hollywood/
hills/4619/
http://www.users.dircon.co.uk:80/
~kozzey/trisha/credits.html
http://www.epn.com:80/yearwood/
index.htm-ssi

Dwight Yoakam
http://www.iac.net/~sharonv/dwight.
html
http://www.tpoint.net/~wallen/
country/dwight-yoakam.html

Neil Young
http://HyperRust.org/
http://ourworld.compuserve.com/
homepages/nyas/
http://www.capetech.co.uk/
Aurora_Borealis/ny_index.html

OTHER COUNTRY AND MUSIC RELATED SITES

Alabama Music Hall of Fame
http://www.alamhof.org/mustour.htm

All Things Country
http://www.eng.rpi.edu/~bonurn/
Country/chome.html

Austin City Limits
http://austin-city-limits.org

Back Porch Country Show
http://castaway.cc.uwf.edu/~rpollard/

Basket Full of Country
http://www.hcc.cc.fl.us/services/
staff/dawn/basketc.htm

Behind Closed Doors
http://www.cybercape.com/alandale/
legends/

Billboard Magazine
http://www.billboard-online.com/

Bluegrass Connection
http://www.gotech.com/

BMG Music Service
http://www.bmgmusicservice.com

Bradley's Country
http://ro.com/~bwalker/

Brian's Music Home Page
http://www.owlnet.rice.edu/~briwahl/

Cash Box OnLine
http://cashbox.com

Chili Beans
http://www.kiis.or.jp/kjk/jdm/pure/
eng/purece.html

A CMT Page in England
http://www.sky.co.uk/cmt.htm

Columbia House Music Club
http://www.columbiahouse.com

Corey's Country Corner
http://web.syr.edu/~cojackso/
country.html

Country Artists on the Web!
http://members.gnn.com/Demon/
cmalist1.htm

Country Connection
http://digiserve.com/country/

Country Fans Page
http://www.hcc.cc.fl.us/services/
staff/dawn/cfans.htm

Country Music Association
http://www.countrymusic.org/

Country Music at Galaxy
http://galaxy.einet.net/EINet/staff/
wayne/country/country.html

Country Music
http://www.tpoint.net/Users/wallen/
country/country.html

Country Music Fan Page
http://www.catt.ncsu.edu/users/
drmellow/public/www/country.
html

Country Music Northern Ontario
http://www.cyberbeach.net/~country/

Country Music Picture Page
http://qrp.cc.nd.edu/country/szabo/
index.html

Country Music Review Page
http://www.ozemail.com.au/~fiddling/

Country Music UK
http://dspace.dial.pipex.com/town/
square/aat96/index.htm

Country Music USA
http://www.LawtonNet.com/
country-music

Country Music Viewpoint
http://pages.prodigy.com/GWPM57A/
stevelind.html

Country Online World Wide
http://www2.johnmichael.com

The Country Page
http://infoweb.magi.com/~jamesb/
country/country.html

Country Standard Time
http://www1.usa1.com/~cst/CST.html

Country Wave Magazine
http://www.textorcom.com/
countrywave/

Country Weekly
http://www.countryweekly.com/

Cowboy's Country Music Page
http://www.oz.net/~roper1/music.
html

Cowgal's Home on the Web
http://www.enteract.com/~cowgal/
cowhome/index.html

Cowgirl's Dream Trading Post
http://www.cowgirls.com

Create a Generic Country Song
http://www.catt.ncsu.edu/users/
drmellow/public/www/
generic-country.html

Crook & Chase's Top 40
http://www.rronline.com/

Cybergrass
http://www.banjo.com/BG/

Dawn's Country Page
http://www.hcc.cc.fl.us/services/
staff/dawn/dawnmain.htm

Debbie's Country Music Page
http://data.gc.peachnet.edu/
stu_home/dmar1171/country.htm

Digital Country
http://www.sfm.com/
digital-country/althome.html

Dr. Mellow
http://www.infi.net/~drmellow/
country/index.html

Dustin's Country Homepage
http://www.nashville.net/~country/

EINet's Country Music
http://www.einet.net/EINet/staff/
wayne/country/country.html

Gaylord Entertainment
http://www.country.com

Gene's Country Music Page
http://www.cs.orst.edu/~moorege/
country.html

Gibson Guitars
http://www.gibson.com/

Glade's Songwriting Page
http://www.zapcom.net/~glade

Gone Country
http://edge.edge.net/~nwinton/

Great American Country
http://www.countrystars.com/index.
html

Great American Country—Artist Information
http://www.countrystars.com/artists.
html

Great American Country—Crook and Chase Country Countdown
http://www.countrystars.com/top40.
html

Gypsy Heart Music
http://www.usa.net/~jadams/gypsy.
html

web pages

History of Country Music
http://orathost.cfa.ilstu.edu/classes/
ORAT389.88Seminar/exhibits/
JohnWalker/ohome.html

Hitdude
http://users.the-link.net/hitdude/

ICE Magazine
http://www.icemagazine.com

IFCO's Fan Club Directory
http://www.ifco.org/fanclubdir.htm

JAM! Music's Country Music
http://www.canoe.ca/
JamMusicCountry/home.html

Janet's Rocky Mountain Home Page
http://www.interealm.com/p/ratzloff/
jan/

Josie's Country Music Page
http://duke.usask.ca/~nobeljos

Kickin' Country
http://kickincountry.com

Kountry Kris' Two-Step Thru Cyperspace!
http://pages.prodigy.com/
kountrykris/index.htm

Kris and Chris
http://www.amug.org/~djdeity/

Macreena's Music Links
http://it.stlawu.edu/~mdoyle/

Marie's Country Music Island
http://www.webcom.com/autobuy/
country_music/cwel.html

Mike's Country Page
http://www.dsu.edu/~kesslerm/
country.html

Miller Creek
http://www.wp.com/MillerCreek/

Music City News
http://www.hsv.tis.net/mcn/

NASCAR's Official Site
http://www.nascar.com/

The Nashville Country Music Scene
http://www.geocities.com/Heartland/
3829/

Nashville Music Link
http://www.nashville.net/~troppo/
muslink.htm

Nashville Online
http://www.nol.com/

Nashville Singer-Songwriter Information
http://www.musiccity.net/demos.htm

New Country Magazine
http://www.newcountrymag.com/

Online-country.com
http://online-country.com/

The Original Roughstock Home Page
http://www.roughstock.com/
roughstock/index.html

Peer Music's Historical Country
http://www.peermusic.com/country/

Pollstar Magazine
http://www.pollstar.com/

PolyGram—Country
http://www.media.philips.com/
polygram/indexes/g-country.shtml

Pure Country
http://www.westworld.com/
~garthbrk/country.html

Radio & Records
http://www.rronline.com/

Real Country
http://www.netcom.com/~djsteve/

Rebel Country
http://www.uc.edu./~roundsda/
INDEX.HTML

Rhymes and Cliches Dictionary
http://www2.eccentricsoftware.com/
eccentric/ZKDemo.html

Ricochete's Country Page
http://members.aol.com/ricochete/
index.htm

Robert's Country Music Page
http://www.il.ft.hse.nl/~robbert/
country.html

The Roughstock Country Pages
http://www.roughstock.com/
roughstock/country.html

Sandra's Country Music Site
http://www.opus1.com/emol/music/
country/country.html

Songwriter's Goldmine
http://windworld.com/gallery/
richman/

Steve's Massive Country Music Roundup—Australia
http://www.nor.com.au/users/
stevefw/music_main.html

Sun Studio Memphis
http://www.sunstudio.com/Welcom.
html

Taz's Country Corner
http://www.sihope.com/~terryb/

Texas Music on the Internet
http://www.auschron.com/txmusic.
html

TicketMaster Online
http://www.ticketmaster.com/

TicketMaster Online—Canada
http://www.ticketmaster.ca/HOME.
HTM

Today's Country
http://www.connect.ca/country/

Twangin!
http://www.well.com/user/cline/
twangin.html

The Ultimate Band List Country/Western
http://american.recordings.com/
WWWoM/ubl/cou_list.shtml

The Unofficial Country Music Homepage
http://pages.prodigy.com/country/

USA TODAY (Music Page)
http://www.usatoday.com/life/enter/
music/lem99.htm

Vic's Country Music Page
http://value.net/~vb/country.html

Wall of Sound
http://www.wallofsound.com/

Way Out West
http://www.alinc.com/~jorgill/wow/
wow.html

Western Wear Shopping Mall
http://www.airmail.net/westernwear/

Young Country
http://www.angelfire.com/pages5/tif/
index.html

If you're looking for more information on your favorite country artist, or if you want to correspond with other country music fanatics, these fan clubs might be a good place to start.

Trace Adkins Fan Club
PO Box 121889
Nashville, TN 37212-1889

Alabama Fan Club
101 Glen Blvd. SW
Fort Payne, AL 35967
(205) 845-1646
Fax: (205) 845-5650

Harley Allen Fan Club
c/o Mercury Nashville
66 Music Square W
Nashville, TN 37203

Bill Anderson Fan Club
PO Box 85
Watervliet, MI 49098
(616) 468-3976

John Anderson Fan Club
PO Box 1129
Smithville, TN 37166
(615) 597-2828

Lynn Anderson Fan Club
PO Box 90454
Charleston, SC 29410
(803) 797-0802

Asleep at the Wheel World Headquarters
PO Box 463
Austin, TX 78767
(512) 444-9885

Chet Atkins Appreciation Society
1224 E. Hancock Dr.
Deltona, FL 32725-6428
Fax: (615) 579-5567

Steve Azar Fan Club
PO Box 5098
Greenville, MS 38704

Moe Bandy Fan Club
3540 Garland St.
Mulberry, FL 33860
(813) 425-3348

Bellamy Brothers Fan Club
PO Box 801
San Antonio, FL 33576

John Berry's Pack
1807 N. Dixie Ave., Ste. 116
Elizabethtown, KY 42701
(900) 454-PACK

Big House Fan Club
9 Music Square South, Ste. 325
Nashville, TN 37203

Clint Black Fan Club
PO Box 299386
Houston, TX 77299-0386
(713) 498-2734
WWW: http//lt.stlawu.edu/
   -mdoyle/clint/clint.html

BlackHawk Fan Club
PO Box 121804
Nashville, TN 37212-1804
(615) 320-8545
Fax: (615) 320-8800

Suzy Bogguss Fan Club
PO Box 7535
Marietta, GA 30065
(770) 565-2432
E-mail: sbprez@bellsouth.net

James Bonamy Fan Club
PO Box 587
Smyma, TN 37167
Fax: (904) 677-4092

BR5-49 Fan Club/The Hayloft Gang
PO Box 23288
Nashville, TN 37202
(888) 96BR5-49
Fax: (615) 255-1209
E-mail: tenten@ix.netcom.
   com
WWW: http://www.br5-49.com

Paul Brandt Fan Club
PO Box 57144
Sunridge Postal Outlet
Calgary, AB T1Y 5T0 Canada

Brooks & Dunn Honky Tonk Fan Club
PO Box 120669
Nashville, TN 37212-0669
(615) 248-6772
WWW: http://www.
   brooks-dunn.com

Garth Brooks/The Believer Magazine
PO Box 507
Goodlettsville, TN 37070-0507
(615) 859-5336

Junior Brown Fan Club
PO Box 180763
Utica, MI 48318-0763
(810) 566-0827
E-mail: bjpruett@clark.net
WWW: http://www.clark.net/
   pub/bjpruett/jbweb/
   jbhome.htm

The Bullas Fan Club
PO Box 1369
Northport, WA 99157
(615) 329-4878

Tracy Byrd Fan Club
PO Box 7703
Beaumont, TX 77726-7703
(409) 729-BYRD
E-mail: TByrdClub@aol.com

Jeff Carson Fan Club
PO Box 121056
Nashville, TN 37212

Carter Family Fan Club
PO Box 1371
Hendersonville, TN 37077

Johnny Cash & June Carter Cash Fan Club
430 Oaklawn Rd.
Winston-Salem, NC 27107
(910) 769-2816)

Kenny Chesney Fan Club
PO Box 22847
Nashville, TN 37202
(615) 292-8134

Mark Chesnutt Fan Club
PO Box 128031
Nashville, TN 37212-8031
(615) 320-7820
WWW: http://www.nashville.
net/-chesnutt/fanclub/htm

Friends of Guy Clark
PO Box 173
Yorkville, CA 95494-0173
(707) 894-5446

Roy Clark Fan Club
PO Box 148258
Nashville, TN 37214-8258

Terri Clark Fan Club
PO Box 1079
Gallatin, TN 37066
Fax: (615) 230-7553

Always Patsy Cline
PO Box 2236
Winchester, VA 22604

David Allan Coe Fan Club
PO Box 1387
Goodlettsville, TN 37070

Mark Collie Fan Club
PO Box 120311
Nashville, TN 37212

**Confederate Railroad Fan
Club**
PO Box 128185
Nashville, TN 37212-8185
(615) 320-7820

Earl Thomas Conley Fan Club
48 Music Sq. E.
Nashville, TN 37202
(615) 256-1936

**Billy "Crash" Craddock Fan
Club**
PO Box 1585
Mt. Vernon, IL 62864-1585
(618) 244-0149

Billy Ray Cyrus Spirit
PO Box 1206
Franklin, TN 37065-1206
(615) 595-0272
Fax: (615) 595-0275

Lacy J. Dalton Fan Club
915 Millbury Ave.
La Puente, CA 91746
(818) 337-2552

Davis Daniel Fan Club
PO Box 121377
Nashville, TN 37212-1377
(615) 832-6826

**Charlie Daniels Band
Volunteers**
17060 Central Pike
Lebanon, TN 37090
(615) 799-8923

Linda Davis Fan Club
PO Box 121027
Nashville, TN 37212
(900) 288-9393
Fax: (615) 259-5354

Curtis Day Fan Club
922 Lynn Ct.
Hermitage, TN 37076

Billy Dean Fan Club
PO Drawer T-1150
Nashville, TN 37244
(900) 288-9393
Fax: (615) 259-5354

Diamond Rio Fan Club
242 W. Main St. #236
Hendersonville, TN 37075
(615) 672-3326
E-mail: driofanclub@juno.com

Joe Diffie Fan Club
PO Box 279
Velma, OK 73091
(405) 444-2315

**George Ducas Coast To Coast
Club**
PO Box 22299
Nashville, TN 37202
(615) 259-4500
E-mail: TSaviano@aol.com

Ty England Fan Club
PO Box 120964
Nashville, TN 37212-0964
(615) 320-7820
WWW: http://www.nashville.
net/-tyland/fanclub/htm

Skip Ewing Connection
PO Box 40185
Nashville, TN 37204

Donna Fargo Fan Club
PO Box 233
Crescent, GA 31304
(912) 832-2463
E-mail: donnafargo@hotmail.
com

Forester Sisters Fan Club
PO Box 1456
Trenton, GA 30752
(706) 657-7056

Frazier River Fan Club
PO Box 36184
Cincinnati, OH 45236
(513) 731-3381

Janie Fricke Fan Club
PO Box 798
Lancaster, TX 75146

**Larry Gatlin and the Gatlin
Brothers Fan Club**
1302 Zermatt Ave.
Nashville, TN 37211-8303

Vince Gill Fan Club
PO Box 1407
White House, TN 37188
(615) 230-7553

Vern Gosdin Fan Club
2509 W. Marquette Ave.
Tampa, FL 33614
(813) 932-8075

Grand Ole Opry Fan Club
2804 Opryland Dr.
Nashville, TN 37214
(615) 251-1025
Fax: (615) 871-5719

Ricky Lynn Gregg Fan Club
PO 8924
Bossier City, LA 71113
(318) 742-1293
Fax: (318) 742-1498
WWW: http://www.utopianet.
com/rigregg/rlgregg/htm

Merle Haggard Fan Club
3009 Easty St.
Sevierville, TN 37862
(423) 429-3534

Wade Hayes Fan Network
PO Box 128546
Nashville, TN 37212
Hotline: (615) 329-0599
Fax: (615) 385-3636

Ty Herndon and Friends
PO Box 120658
Nashville, TN 37212
(615) 329-8017
WWW: http://www.tyherndon.
com

High Noon Fan Club
Watermelon Records
PO Box 49056
Austin, TX 78765-9598
(512) 472-6192
Fax: (512) 472-6249

Faith Hill Fan Club
PO Box 24266
Nashville, TN 37202
Hotline: (615) 297-1500

Alan Jackson Fan Club
PO Box 121945
Nashville, TN 37212-1945

Stonewall Jackson Fan Club
3253 W. Green Ave.
Milwaukee, WI 53221
(414) 282-3517

**Jim & Jesse (McReynolds) Fan
Club**
8574 Tram Road
Tallahassee, FL 32311-9354
(904) 877-5431
Fax: (904) 877-5431

George Jones Fan Club
Rt. 3, Box 150
Murphy, NC 28906
(704) 837-7622

Wynonna Judd Fan Club
PO Box 682068
Franklin, TN 37068
(900) 370-JUDD
E-mail: wifc@nashville.net
WWW: http://www.nashville.
net/-wifc

Toby Keith Fan Club
PO Box 8739
Rockford, IL 61126-8739
Fax: (815) 234-7109
E-mail: tkfanclub@aol.com

Doug Kershaw Fan Club
PO Box 24762
San Jose, CA 95154

Sammy Kershaw Fan Club
PO Box 121739

Nashville, TN 37212-1739
(615) 320-7820
WWW: http://www.nashville.
net-krshwknr/fanclub/htm

Hal Ketchum Fan Club
PO Box 120205
Nashville, TN 37212

Alison Krauss Fan Club
Union Station Land
PO Box 121711
Nashville, TN 37212

Tracy Lawrence Fan Club
9 Music Square, S., Ste. 110
Nashville, TN 37203
(615) 329-0966
Fax: (615) 329-0977
WWW: http://www.songs.
com/tle/

Chris LeDoux Fan Club
Box 253
Sumner, IA 50674
(319) 578-8600

Brenda Lee Fan Club
4720 Hickory Way
Antioch, TN 37013
E-mail: brenleefan@aol.com

Little Texas Fan Club
PO Box 589
Hendersonville, TN 37077-
0589
Hotline: (900) 737-TEXAS

Lonestar Fan Club
PO Box 128467
Nashville, TN 37212
(615) 356-8969

Patty Loveless Fan Club
PO Box 1423
White House, TN 37188

Barbara Mandrell Fan Club
PO Box 620
Hendersonville, TN 37077-
0620

Mila Mason Fan Club
PO Box 2797
Hendersonville, TN 37077-
2797
WWW: http://www.nashville.
net/-mila
E-mail: milafanclub@aol.com

Kathy Mattea Fan Club
PO Box 158482
Nashville, TN 37215
(615) 259-4382
E-mail: KMPREZ@aol.com

Tommy Matthews Fan Club
PO Box 1514
Yorktown, VA 23692
(757) 988-1739

The Mavericks Fan Club
PO Box 22586
Nashville, TN 37202
Hotline: (615) 254-3665

Martina McBride Fan Club
PO Box 291627
Nashville, TN 37229-1627
Hotline/Fax: (615) 872-7642

Delbert McClinton Fan Club
PO Box 40185
Nashville, TN 37204

Neal McCoy Fan Club
PO Box 9610
Longview, TX 75608-9610
(903) 297-9000
Fax: (903) 759-7977

**Friends Through Ronnie
McDowell**
PO Box 215
Romeo, MI 48065

**On The Road With Ronnie
McDowell**
4200 Balmoral Ave., #4823
Richmond, VA 23228

Reba McEntire Fan Club
Drawer T-REBA
Nashville, TN 37244
(900) 454-REBA
WWW: http://www.reba.com

**Tim McGraw/
Mcgrawfunaddicts**
PO Box 128138
Nashville, TN 37212
WWW: http://www.
funzone4mcgraw.com

Jo Dee Messina Fan Club
PO Box 8031
Hermitage, TN 37076

Ronnie Milsap Fan Club
PO Box 121831
Nashville, TN 37212-1831
Hotline: (615) 327-7796

Moffatts Fan Club
PO Box 270337
Nashville, TN 37227-0337

Patsy Montana Fan Club
226 Hunt Ln.
Madisonville, TN 37354
(423) 442-6794

**John Michael Montgomery
Fan Club**
PO Box 639
Danville, KY 40423-0639
(606) 548-3500
E-mail: fmmfc@seamet.com
WWW: http://www.
johnmichael.com

Lorrie Morgan Fan Club
PO Box 78
Spencer, TN 38585
(615) 946-7700

Gary Morris Fan Club
607 W. Church Drive
Sugar Land, TX 77478
(713) 494-2598

David Lee Murphy Fan Club
PO box 25333
Nashville, TN 37202

Willie Nelson Fan Club
PO Box 7104
Lancaster, PA 17604-7104
Hotline: (717) 653-0204

Oak Ridge Boys Fan Club
329 Rockland Rd.
Hendersonville, TN 37075
(615) 824-4924

Gram Parsons Foundation
3109 N. Ola Ave.
Tampa, FL 33603
(813) 221-0596
Fax: (813) 221-0596

Stella Parton Fan Club
PO Box 120295
Nashville, TN 37212
(615) 385-9922
Fax: (615) 385-5040
WWW: http://www.preferred.
com/-ics/stella/

Perfect Stranger Fan Club
PO Box 330
Carthage, TX 75633
(903) 694-2911

MC Potts Fan Club
PO Box 120161
Nashville, TN 32712
(615) 352-8103
E-mail: MCFanClub@aol.com
WWW: http://www.mcpotts.
com

Fans and Friends of Ray Price
PO Box 61
Harrisburg, PA 17108

Charley Pride Fan Club
PO Box 670507
Dallas, TX 75367
(214) 350-8477

Eddie Rabbitt Fan Club
PO Box 35286
Cleveland, OH 44135

Eddy Raven Fan Club
PO Box 2476
Hendersonville, TN 37077-
2476
(615) 230-8217

Del Reeves Fan Club
Rte. 2, 12615 U.S. 30, W
Upper Sandusky, OH 43351
(419) 294-4264

Ronna Reeves Fan Club
PO Box 80424
Midland, TX 79709-0424

Kim Richey Fan Club
c/o Mercury Nashville
66 Music Square W
Nashville, TN 37203

Ricochet Fan Club
PO Box 128468
Nashville, TN 37212

Tex Ritter Fan Club
15326 73rd Ave. SE
Snohomish, WA 98290
(360) 668-2429

Marty Robbins Pen Friends
3307 Saindon St.
Nashville, TN 37211-2859
(615) 831-0250
Fax: (615) 834-9297

Friends of James Rogers
PO Box 621
Hixson, TN 37343
(615) 875-2671

Roy Rogers-Dale Evans
Collectors Association
PO Box 1166
Portsmouth, OH 45662
(614) 353-0900

Billy Joe Royal Fan Club
4063 E. Plantation Ave.
Terre Haute, IN 47805

Tom Russell Fan Club
25 Springfield Dr.
Oklahoma City, OK 73149
(405) 632-2955

Sawyer Brown Fan Club
4219 Hillsboro Rd. #318
Nashville, TN 37215
(615) 799-0850
Fax: (615) 292-3328
Hotline: (615) 298-1027

John R. Schneider #1 Fan Club
PO Box 2277
Mountain Lake Park, MD
21550-0677

Kevin Sharp Fan Club
PO Box 888
Camino, CA 95709
(916) 647-1312

Victoria Shaw Fan Club
PO Box 120512
Nashville, TN 37212-0512
WWW: http://www.hotcc.
com/1countrycorner/shaw

Shenandoah Fan Club
PO Box 120086
Nashville, TN 37212-0086
Hotline: (615) 356-8744

T.G. Sheppard Fan Club
3341 Arlington #F206
Toledo, OH 43614

Daryle Singletary Fan Club
PO Box 121377
Nashville, TN 37212

Ricky Skaggs Fan Club
PO Box 121799
Nashville, TN 37212-1799

Smokin' Armadillos Fan Club
PO Box 81805
Bakersfield, CA 93380

Smokin' Armadillos Fan Club
PO Box 770129
Houston, TX 77214
(713) 498-3031

Doug Stone/Stone Age Fan
Club
PO Box 128
Orlinda, TN 37141
(900) 73-STONE

Geroge Strait Fan Club
PO Box 2119
Hendersonville, TN 37077
(615) 824-7176
E-mail: fanclub@george
straitfans.com
WWW: http://www.george
straitfans.com

Marty Stuart Fan Club
PO Box 24180
Nashville, TN 37202-4180
Hotline: (423) 790-6120
WWW: http://telalink.net/
-martys/

B.J. Thomas Fan Club
PO Box 1632
Whittier, CA 90609-1632

Mel Tillis National Fan Club
PO Box 1626
Branson, MO 65615-1626
(417) 335-5715
(417) 335-8089
Fax: (417) 335-3735

Pam Tillis Fan Network
PO Box 128575
Nashville, TN 37212
Hotline: (615) 329-0599
Fax: (615) 385-3636

Aaron Tippin Fan Club
PO Box 121709
Nashville, TN 37212-1709
(615) 292-8134

Randy Travis Fan Club
PO Box 38
Ashland City, TN 37015
(615) 792-6873
Fax: (615) 792-6873

Rick Trevino Fan Club
PO Box 500148
Austin, TX 78750
Fax: (512) 258-0390

Travis Tritt Country Club
PO Box 2044
Hiram, GA 30141
(770) 439-7401

Justin Tubb Fan Club
PO Box 500
Nashville, TN 37202
(615) 868-6887

Tanya Tucker Fan Club
5200 Maryland Way, Ste. 103
Brentwood, TN 37027
(615) 371-0073

Shania Twain Fan Club
PO Box 1150
Timmins, Ont. P4N 7H9 Canada

Leroy Van Dyke Fan Club
1400 Topping Ave., No. 707
Kansas City, MO 64126-2089

Rhonda Vincent Fan Club
PO Box 31
Greentpo, MO 63546
(816) 766-2522

Jerry Jeff Walker Fan Club
PO Box 39
Austin, TX 78767
(512) 477-0036
Fax: (512) 477-0095
e-mail: ttm@inetport.com

Steve Wariner Fan Club
PO Box 1667
Franklin, TN 37065-1667

Kitty Wells-Johnny Wright-
Bobby Wright Fan Club
PO Box 477
Madison, TN 37116
(615) 226-2892
Fax: (615) 865-1900

Special Friends of Dottie West
PO Box 61
Harrisburg, PA 17108

Bryan White Fan Club
PO Box 120162
Nashville, TN 37212

Lari White Fan Club
PO Box 120086
Nashville, TN 37212

Dwight Whitley Fan Club
HC 77, Box 340

Stephens, KY 41177
(606) 738-5292

Friends of Keith Whitley
PO Box 222
Sandy Hook, KY 41171
(606) 738-5292

Slim Whitman Appreciation
Society of the United States
1002 W. Thurber St.
Tucson, AZ 85705
(602) 887-8384

Hank Williams Intl. Society &
Fan Club
PO Box 280
Georgiana, AL 36033

Hank Williams Jr. Fan Club
PO Box 850
Paris, TN 38242
(800) FOR-HANK

Jett Williams/Club Jett
PO Box 177
Hartsville, TN 37074
(615) 655-5549
Fax: (615) 655-5525

Mark Wills Friends Club
2094 Cobb Parkway
Smyrna, GA 30080

Jeff Wood Fan Club
PO Box 7052
Oklahoma City, OK 73038-7052

Chely Wright Fan Club
PO Box 120876
Nashville, TN 37212-0876

Michelle Wright Fan Club
PO Box 22953
Nashville, TN 37202
(615) 329-4700
E-mail: wrightstff@aol.com

Tammy Wynette International
Fan Club
PO Box 121926
Nashville, TN 37212
(615) 321-5308
Fax: (615) 327-4925

Trisha Yearwood Fan Club
PO Box 65
Monticello, CA 31064
(706) 468-9933

If you want to see some country music performed live, we suggest you check out some of these North American music festivals. (For more information on these and other music festivals, consult Visible Ink Press' Music Festivals from Bach to Blues.)

UNITED STATES

ALABAMA

Athens
Tennessee Valley Old-Time Fiddlers Convention
First weekend in October
(205) 233-8100

Birmingham
City Stages
Father's Day weekend
(800) 277-1700
(205) 715-6000
WWW: http://www.citystages.
org/1996

Brierfield
Brierfield Music Festival
First weekend in May
(205) 665-1856

Cullman
Bluegrass Superjam

First weekend in April, first weekend in November, Friday and Saturday
(205) 747-1650
(205) 734-0454

Fairhope, Gulf Shores, Orange Beach
Frank Brown International Songwriters Festival
First Thursday–second Sunday in November
(334) 981-5678
(904) 492-7664
E-mail: songfest@amaranth.
com
WWW: http://www.amaranth.
com/~ken/fbrown.html

Fort Payne
Alabama June Jam
First or second Saturday in June
(205) 845-9300

Georgiana
Salute to Hank Williams Sr.
Day
First weekend in June
(334) 376-2396

Huntsville
Annual State Fiddling and Bluegrass Convention
Third weekend in September
(205) 859-4471
(205) 883-4576

Montgomery
Jubilee City Fest

Memorial Day weekend
(334) 834-7220

ALASKA

Fairbanks
Athabascan Old-Time Fiddlers' Festival
First or Second weekend in November, Thursday–Saturday
(907) 452-1825

Fairbanks Summer Folk Fest
Second or third weekend in June
(907) 488-0556
E-mail: FNKEC@aurora.alaska.
edu

Haines
Bald Eagle Music Festival
Second weekend in August, Wednesday–Sunday
(907) 766-2476
WWW: http://haines.ak.us

Juneau
Alaska Folk Festival
First or second week in April, Monday–Sunday
(907) 789-0292

Sutton
Sutton Summer Music Festival
Third weekend in July
(907) 745-3395
(907) 745-4527

ARIZONA

Casa Grande
Arizona Old Time Fiddlers Jamboree
First weekend in January
(520) 723-5242

Lake Havasu City
Sandpoint's Fiddler's Jamborina
Weekend before Thanksgiving Day
(520) 855-0549

Payson
State Championship Old Time Fiddlers' Contest
A weekend in late September, Saturday and Sunday
(520) 474-5242
(520) 474-3397

Phoenix
Phoenix Folk Traditions Acoustic Music Festival
A weekend in late March or early April
(602) 495-5458

Wickenburg
Four Corner States Bluegrass Festival and Fiddle Championship
Mid-November
(520) 684-5479

ARKANSAS

Jacksonport
Port Fest
Last full weekend in June
(501) 523-3618

Moodus
Connecticut River Valley Bluegrass Festival
Second weekend in August
(860) 347-5007

Morris
Morris Bluegrass Festival
Second Sunday in August
(860) 567-0270

Mountain View
Arkansas Old-Time Fiddle Championships
Third weekend in September
(501) 269-3851

CALIFORNIA

Agoura
Topanga Banjo-Fiddle Contest, Dance & Folk Arts Festival
Third Sunday in May
(818) 354-3795

Blythe
Colorado River Country Music Festival
Third weekend in January
(800) 445-5513
(619) 922-6037
(619) 922-4354

Buck Meadows/Camp Mather, near Yosemite
Strawberry Music Festival
Memorial Day weekend and Labor Day weekend, Thursday–Sunday
(209) 533-0191

Calico Ghost Town
Calico Spring Festival
Second weekend in May
(800) 862-2542

Felton
Saw Players' Picnic and Music Festival
Third Sunday in July
(510) 523-4649

Grass Valley
Grass Valley Bluegrass Festival
Father's Day weekend, Thursday–Sunday
(209) 293-1559
(707) 762-8735

Needles
Bluegrass River Revel
Presidents' Day weekend
(619) 326-9222

Santa Clarita
Cowboy Poetry and Music Festival
Last weekend in March
(800) 305-0755
(805) 255-4910

Yucaipa
Bluegrass Festival
Labor Day weekend, Friday–Monday
(909) 790-3127

COLORADO

Fort Collins
Colorado Mid-Winter Bluegrass Festival
Third weekend in February
(970) 482-0863

Grand Junction
Country Jam
Third weekend in June, Thursday–Sunday
(800) 530-3020
(715) 839-7500

Lyons
Rockygrass
First weekend in August
(800) 624-2422
(970) 449-6007
E-mail: planet@bluegrass.com
WWW: http://www.bluegrass.com/planet

Telluride
Telluride Bluegrass Festival
Third weekend in June, Thursday–Sunday
(800) 624-2422
(970) 449-6007

E-mail: planet@bluegrass.com
WWW: http://www.bluegrass.com/planet

Winter Park
Winter Park Jazz and American Music Festival
Third weekend in July, Saturday and Sunday
(970) 830-8497
(970) 726-4221

CONNECTICUT

Mountain View
Tribute to Jimmie Rodgers
Last weekend in August
(501) 269-3851

Tribute to Merle Travis & National Thumbpicking Guitar Championship
Fourth weekend in May
(501) 269-3851
(501) 269-8068

Preston
Strawberry Park Bluegrass Festival
First weekend in June
(860) 886-1944

Springdale
Albert E. Brumley Memorial Sundown to Sunup Gospel Sing
First full weekend in August, Thursday–Saturday
(417) 435-2225

DELAWARE

Harrington
Eastern Shore Bluegrass Association Festival
Third weekend in June
(302) 492-1048

FLORIDA

Auburndale
Carl Allen's Annual State Championship Bluegrass Festival
Third weekend in March

(941) 967-4307
(941) 299-9489
(941) 665-0062

Live Oak
Suwannee River Country Music Jam
Second weekend in October
(904) 364-1683

Perdido Key, Pensacola, Pensacola Beach
Frank Brown International Songwriters Festival
First Thursday through second Sunday in November
(334) 981-5678
(904) 492-7664
E-mail: songfest@amaranth.com
WWW: http://www.amaranth.com/~ken/fbrown.html

Tallahassee
Swamp Stomp
A Saturday in mid-July
(904) 575-8684

GEORGIA

Blue Ridge
Sugar Creek Bluegrass Festival
Second weekend in October
(706) 632-2560

Dahlonega
Dahlonega Bluegrass Festival
Third weekend in June, Thursday–Saturday
(706) 864-7203

Hiawassee
Georgia's Official State Fiddlers Convention
Ten days in mid-October
(706) 896-4191

Spring Music Festival
Third weekend in May, Friday and Saturday
(706) 896-4191

Jekyll Island
Annual Country by the Sea Music Festival
First Saturday in June
(800) 841-6586
(912) 635-3636

New Year's Bluegrass Festival
New Year's weekend, Thursday–Saturday
(706) 864-7203

Lincolnton
Lewis Family Homecoming and Bluegrass Festival
First weekend in May, Thursday–Saturday
(706) 864-7203

Tifton
Folk Life Festival & Fiddlers' Jamboree
Fourth Saturday in April
(912) 386-3344

IDAHO

McCall
McCall Summer Music Festival
Third weekend in July, Thursday–Sunday
(208) 634-5259

Moscow
Rendezvous in the Park
Second and third weekends in July
(208) 882-3581
(208) 882-1800

Rexburg
Idaho International Folk Dance Festival
Last weekend in July through first weekend in August
(208) 356-5700

Weiser
National Oldtime Fiddlers' Contest
Third full week in June, Monday–Saturday
(800) 437-1280
(208) 549-0452

ILLINOIS

Berwyn
American Music Festival
Weekend closest to July 4, Thursday–Sunday
(708) 788-2118
E-mail: FitzMail@aol.com

Chicago
Chicago Country Music Festival
Weekend in late June
(312) 744-3370
(312) 744-3315
WWW: http://www.ci.chi.il.us

Decatur
Greater Downstate Indoor Bluegrass Music Festival
Second weekend in November
(217) 243-3159

Grand Detour
June Jam
Last Sunday in June
(815) 652-4551

INDIANA

Battle Ground
Indiana Fiddlers' Gathering
Last full weekend in June
(317)742-1419
E-mail: khallman@dcwi.com

Bean Blossom
Bean Blossom Bluegrass Festival
Third weekend in June, Thursday–Sunday
(615) 868-3333
(812)988-6422

Converse
Bluegrass Festival
First weekend in July, Thursday–Sunday and weekend following Labor Day
(317) 674-5117

Indianapolis
Midsummer Festival
First Saturday following the Summer Solstice (June 21 or 22)
(317) 637-4574

IOWA

Avoca
Avoca Old-Time Country Music Contest & Festival
Six days preceding Labor Day and Labor Day
(712) 784-3001

Burlington
American Music Festival (Burlington Steamboat Days)
Six days ending the third Sunday in June (Father's Day)
(800) 827-4837
(319) 754-4334

Medora/Indianola
Hickory Hills Hoedown
Third Sunday in September
(515) 961-6169

Oskaloosa
Bluegrass Music Weekend
Third Saturday in August, Thursday–Sunday
(816) 665-7172

Stratford
Bluegrass and Old-Time Country Music
Second weekend in July
(515) 838-2311

KANSAS

Clifton
Country Music Festival
Third weekend in August
(913) 455-3660

Lawrence
Kansas State Fiddling & Picking Championships
Last or second-to-last weekend in August
(913) 841-7817
(913) 842-3321

Winfield
Walnut Valley Festival and National Flat-Picking Championship
Third weekend in September
(316) 221-3250

KENTUCKY

Ashland
Summer Motion
July 4 and nearest weekend
(800) 416-3222, (304) 522-8141

Carter Caves State Resort Park/Olive Hill
Carter Caves Gathering
Weekend after Labor Day, Thursday Sunday
(606) 286-4411

Central City
Everly Brothers Homecoming
Saturday of Labor Day Weekend
(502) 754-9603
(502) 754-2360

Merle Travis Festival
Saturday following Thanksgiving Day
(502) 754-9603
(502) 754-2360
(502) 754-2881

Falls of Rough
Official KY State Championship Old-Time Fiddlers Contest
Third full weekend in July
(502) 259-0450

Hyden
Osborne Brothers Homecoming
First weekend in August
(606) 266-1991

Lexington
Festival of the Bluegrass
Second full weekend in June
(904) 364-1683
(606) 846-4995

Red Mile Bluegrass Festival
Third weekend in May
(606) 266-1991

Louisville
Otter Creek Park Bluegrass Festival
Memorial Day weekend
(502) 583-3577

Owensboro
IBMA Bluegrass Fan Fest
Last full weekend in September
(502) 684-9025

Pikeville
Hillbilly Days
Third weekend in April, Thursday–Saturday
(800) 844-7453

Renfro Valley
Old Joe Clark Bluegrass
Festival
First weekend in July
(800) 765-7464

Somerset
Master Musicians Festival
First week after Labor Day
(606) 678-2225

LOUISIANA

Abita Springs
Abita Springs Water Festival
*A Saturday in mid- or late Oc-
tober*
(504) 892-0711

Athens
Bluegrass Festival
*Second weekend in Septem-
ber*
(318) 258-4943

Monroe
Louisiana Folklife Festival
*Second full weekend in Sep-
tember*
(318) 329-2375

Shreveport
Red River Revel Arts Festival
*Last Saturday in September
through the first Saturday in
October*
(318) 424-4000

MAINE

Brunswick
Thomas Point Beach Blue-
grass Festival
Labor Day weekend
(207) 725-6009

Cambridge
Salty Dog Bluegrass Music
Festival
Last weekend in August
(207) 277-5624

East Benton
East Benton Fiddlers Convention
Last Sunday in July
(207) 453-2017

Natick
New England Folk Festival
*Weekend following the third
Monday in April*
(617) 354-1340

South Paris
Record Family's Oxford County
Bluegrass Festival
Third weekend in August
(207) 743-2905

MARYLAND

Centreville
Bay Country Music Festival
Second Saturday in June
(410) 827-4810
(410) 626-2208

Crisfield
Tangier Sound Country Music
Festival
Fourth Saturday in June
(800) 521-9189
(410) 651-2968

Cumberland
Rocky Gap Music Festival
First weekend in August
(800) 424-2511
(301) 724-2511

Friendsville
Friendsville Fiddle and Banjo
Contest
Third Saturday in July
(301) 746-8194

Leonardtown
Little Margaret's Bluegrass
and Old-Time Country Music
Festival
Second weekend in August
(301) 475-8191

Upperco, Arcadia
Arcadia Bluegrass Festival
Last weekend in September
(410) 374-2895

Westminster
Deer Creek Fiddlers' Convention
Second Sunday in June
(410) 848-7775
(800) 654-4645

MICHIGAN

Brethren
Spirit of the Woods Folk Festival
Third Saturday in June
(616) 477-5381

Cheboygan
Cheboygan Fiddler's Jamboree
Second Saturday in October
(616) 627-5811

Davison
Banjo-Rama
First Saturday in May
(810) 687-1573

East Lansing
Michigan Festival
*First Friday through the sec-
ond Sunday in August*
(800) 935-3378
email: SMyers3745@aol.com

Grand Rapids
Annual Fiddlers Jamboree
Last weekend in April
(616)361-3444

Nirvana
Whispering Winds
First weekend in October
(810) 546-7424

Port Austin
Country-Cajun-Polish Music
Festival
Last weekend in July
(517) 738-2267

Portage
Great Lakes Folk & Bluegrass
Festival
Second Saturday in July
(616) 329-4522

Saginaw
KCQ Country Music Fest
Mid-June
(517) 752-8161

MINNESOTA

Bloomington
Summerfolk
Fourth Sunday in June
(800) 695-4687
(612) 379-1089
E-mail: rhrpub@aol.com

Detroit Lakes
We Fest
First full weekend in August
(218) 847-1340
WWW: http://www.tnnet.com

New Ulm
Minnesota Festival of Music
*First or second weekend in
April, Saturday and Sunday*
(507) 354-7305

MISSISSIPPI

Meridian
Jimmie Rodgers Festival
*Last week in May, always in-
cluding May 26*
(800) 396-5882
(601) 693-5353
(601) 483-5763

MISSOURI

Branson
Great American Music Festival
*Late May or early June for two
weeks*
(800) 952-6626

Camdenton
Ozarks Dogwood Music
Festival
Third weekend in April
(573) 346-2227

Kahoka
Kahoka Festival of Bluegrass
Music
Second weekend in August
(573) 853-4344

Patterson
Sam A. Baker Bluegrass
Festival
*Fourth weekend in July, Thurs-
day–Saturday*
(800) 334-6946

MONTANA

Columbus
Musicians Rendezvous
First full weekend in July
(406) 322-4143

Emigrant
R & R Music Festival
Second weekend in July
(800) 499-4021
(406) 686-4021

Hamilton
Bitterroot Valley Bluegrass
Festival
Second weekend in July
(406) 363-2400
(406) 363-1250

Lincoln
Wilderness Bar Fiddlers Contest
Last weekend in August
(406) 362-9200

Missoula
Marshall Mountain Music Festival
A Saturday in late July or early August
(406) 258-6000

Polson
Montana State Fiddlers Contest
Fourth full weekend in July, Thursday–Saturday
(406) 323-1198

Troy
Big Sky Rendezvous
Third weekend in August
(406) 295-4358

NEBRASKA

Ainsworth
Annual National Country
Music Festival
Second weekend in August, Saturday and Sunday
(402) 387-2740

Elgin
Bluegrass Festival
Second-to-last weekend in August
(402) 843-5307

Fremont
Elkhorn Valley Country Music
Festival
Last full weekend in April, Thursday–Sunday and first weekend in September
(402) 727-7626

Syracuse
Nebraska State Country Music
Championship
Second weekend in June
(402) 234-5277

NEVADA

Fallon
Desert Oasis Bluegrass Festival
Second or third weekend in May
(702) 423-7733

Logandale
Bluegrass & Old Time Music
Festival
A weekend in early October
(702) 564-5455

Pahrump
Jazz, Bluegrass, & Barbecue
Weekend after Labor Day
(800) 368-9463

NEW HAMPSHIRE

Campton
Pemi Valley Bluegrass Festival
First weekend in August
(603) 726-3471

Lincoln
Old-Time Fiddlers Contest
Last Saturday in June
(603) 745-3563

Stark
Stark Fiddlers' Contest
Last Sunday in June
(603) 636-1325

NEW JERSEY

Bridgeton
Bridgeton Folk Festival
Second or third Saturday in June
(609) 451-9208

Lebanon
Bluegrass Festival at Round
Valley
Second weekend in August
(908) 638-8400

Woodstown
Delaware Valley Bluegrass
Festival
Labor Day weekend
(302) 475-3454
WWW: http://www.sas.
upenn.edu/~jlupton/bfotm.
html

NEW MEXICO

Cloudcroft
Cloudcroft Bluegrass Festival
Fourth weekend in June
(505)746-9351

Farmington
Riverfest
Memorial Day weekend
(800) 448-1240

Santa Fe
Santa Fe Banjo and Fiddle
Contest
Last weekend in August or first weekend in September
(505) 471-3462

Truth or Consequences
International Fiesta Fiddle
Contest
Last weekend in April
(505) 894-3536
(800) 831-9487

New Mexico Old-Time Fiddlers' State Championship
Third weekend in October
(505) 894-2847

NEW YORK

Altamont
Old Songs Festival of Traditional Music and Dance
Last full weekend in June
(518) 765-2815
E-mail: fennig@aol.com

Ancramdale
Winterhawk Bluegrass Festival
Third weekend in July
(518) 390-6211
E-mail: mgdoub@aol.com

Clayton
Thousand Islands Bluegrass
Festival

First weekend in June
(315) 686-5385

Corinth
Corinth Bluegrass Festival
Second full weekend in August
(518) 654-9424

Long Lake
Bluegrass Festival
Third Saturday in August
(518) 624-3077

McDonough
Del-Se-Nango Fiddle & Bluegrass Festival
First Sunday following July 4
(607) 847-8501

Old Forge
Fox Family Bluegrass Festival
Weekend following the first Sunday in August
(315) 369-6983

Orleans
Old-Time Music Festival
Third Sunday in July
(315) 788-2882

Shinhopple
Peaceful Valley Bluegrass Festival
Third weekend in July
(607) 363-2211

South Fallsburg
Bluegrass with Class
Third weekend in March
(607) 363-2211
(914) 434-6000

Stony Brook
Long Island Fiddle and Folk
Music Festival
Second Sunday in September
(516) 751-0066, ext. 212

NORTH CAROLINA

Beaufort
Beaufort Music Festival
Last full weekend in April
(919) 728-6894

Burnsville/Celo
Music in the Mountains Folk
Festival

Third Saturday in September
(704) 682-7215

Cherokee
Cherokee Bluegrass Festival
Fourth weekend in August,
Thursday–Saturday
(706) 864-7203

Denton
Doyle Lawson & Quicksilver's
Bluegrass Festival
Weekend after July 4, Thurs-
day–Sunday
(704) 252-1233

Salisbury
Fall Jamboree
Weekend after Labor Day
(704) 636-7170

Statesville
Old Time Fiddlers and Bluegrass Convention
First Saturday night in March
(704) 872-6776
(704) 628-9704

Union Grove
Ole Time Fiddler's and Bluegrass Festival
Memorial Day weekend
(704) 539-4417

Wilkesboro
Merle Watson Festival
Last full weekend in April
(800) 343-7857
(800) 666-1920
(910) 838-6291

NORTH DAKOTA

Fargo
Froggy 99.9's Country Jam
Second Sunday in August
(701) 241-8160
(218) 233-1522

Hensler
Missouri River Bluegrass and
Old-Time Music Festival
Labor Day weekend, Saturday
and Sunday
(701) 794-3731

Medora
Country Western Jamboree
Last Sunday in July

(701) 623-4444
(701) 623-4310

West Fargo
Old-Time Fiddlers Contest and
Jamboree
First weekend in July, Satur-
day and Sunday
(701) 282-2822
(800) 700-5317

OHIO

Glenmont
Mohican Bluegrass Festival
Second weekend after Labor
Day
(614) 599-6741

Lisbon
Columbiana County Bluegrass
Festival
Third weekend in June, Friday
and Saturday
(304) 387-1103

St. Clairsville
Jamboree in the Hills
Third full weekend in July,
Thursday–Sunday
(800) 624-5456

OKLAHOMA

Gene Autry
Gene Autry Film and Music
Festival Weekend
Friday and Saturday closest to
September 29 (Gene Autry's
birthday)
(405) 389-5335

Guthrie
Jazz Banjo Festival
Memorial Day weekend
(800) 652-2656

Hugo
Grant's Bluegrass Festival
Five days beginning the first
Wednesday in August
(405) 326-5598

McAlester
Sanders Family Bluegrass Festival

Second full weekend in June,
Wednesday–Saturday
(918) 423-4891

OREGON

Portland
North by Northwest
A weekend in September or
October
(512) 467-7979
E-mail:
72662.2465@compuserve.
com

Sweet Home
Oregon Jamboree
Fourth weekend in September
(541) 367-8909
(541) 367-8800

PENNSYLVANIA

Gettysburg
Gettysburg Bluegrass Cam-
poree
First full weekend in May
(717) 642-8749

Kempton
Blue Mountain Gospel Festival
Last Saturday in August
through the first Sunday in
September
(717) 872-5615

Lake Harmony
Poconos Country Music Festi-
val
Third or fourth weekend in
June
(717) 722-0100

Wagontown
Chester County Old Fiddlers'
Picnic
Second Saturday in August
(610) 344-6415
(610) 384-0290
E-mail: c-snowberger@mail.
co.chester.pa.us

Wellsboro
Canyon Country Bluegrass
Festival
Second weekend in July
(800) 724-7277

RHODE ISLAND

Escoheag
Cajun & Bluegrass Music-
Dance-Food Festival
Labor Day weekend
(401) 351-6312
(800) 738-9808

SOUTH CAROLINA

Mountain Rest
Hillbilly Day
July 4 (Independence Day)
(803) 638-6871

Myrtle Beach
South Carolina State Blue-
grass Festival
Fourth Thursday in November
(Thanksgiving Day) through
Saturday
(706) 864-7203

SOUTH DAKOTA

Deadwood
Deadwood Jam
Second Saturday after Labor
Day
(605) 578-1102

Rockerville
Black Hills Bluegrass Festival
Last full weekend in June
(605) 394-4101

Yankton
Great Plains Old-Time Fiddlers
Contest
Third weekend in September
(605) 665-3636

TENNESSEE

Chattanooga
Riverbend Festival and Bessie
Smith Strut
Nine days ending the last Sat-
urday in June
(423) 756-2212

Cosby
Cosby Dulcimer and Harp Festival

Second Friday in June
(423) 487-5543

Eastview
Mid-South Jammin' Jamboree
Labor Day weekend
(901) 645-3797

Memphis
International Elvis Tribute
Week
Nine days in mid-August
(800) 238-2000
WWW: http://www.
elvispresley.com/~king

Memphis Music & Heritage
Festival
Second weekend in July
(901) 525-3945

Murfreesboro
Uncle Dave Macon Days
Second weekend in July
(615) 848-0055

Nashville
Reno Revival
*First or second weekend in
October*
(615) 889-4197

Summer Lights in Music City
Weekend after Memorial Day
(615) 259-3956

Smithville
Smithville Fiddlers' Jamboree
*Weekend closest to July 4, Fri-
day and Saturday*
(615) 464-6444
(615) 597-4163

TEXAS

Athens
Texas Fiddlers' Association
Contest
*First Thursday and Friday in
May*
(903) 675-2325

Austin
Traditional Music Festival
*A Saturday or Sunday in mid-
January*
(512) 454-9481
E-mail: john beatty@mail.
utexas.edu

Acoustic Music Festival
Third weekend in November
(512) 499-8497
(512) 404 4368
WWW: http://mosterbit.com/
aamf/

South by Southwest
*Third week in March, Wednes-
day–Sunday*
(512) 467-7979
E-mail: 72662.2465
@compuserve.com
WWW: http://monsterbit.
com/sxsw.html

**Austin, Luckenbach, and
Environs**
Jerry Jeff Walker Birthday
Weekend
Last weekend in March
(512) 477-0036
E-mail: ttm@inetport.com
WWW: http://www.io.com/
-ccamden/jjw/

Canton
Texas State Bluegrass Festival
*Fourth weekend in June, Tues-
day–Saturday*
(903) 567-6004

Texas State Bluegrass Kickoff
*Fourth weekend in April, Fri-
day and Saturday*
(903) 567-6004

Corsicana
Lefty Frizzell Country Music
Festival
*Saturday closest to March 31
(Lefty Frizzell's Birthday)*
(903) 654-4846

El Paso
Border Folk Festival
Weekend following Labor Day
(915) 532-7273

Glen Rose
Glen Rose Bluegrass Reunion
*Memorial Day weekend,
Thursday–Sunday, and first
weekend in October, Fri-
day–Sunday*
(817) 897-2321

Lone Star State Dulcimer Festival
Mother's Day weekend
(817) 275-3872

Halletsville
Texas State Championship
Fiddlers' Frolics
*Fourth weekend in April,
Thursday–Sunday*
(512) 798-2311
(512) 798-2662

Kerrville
Kerrville Folk Festival
*Last weekend in May and the
first three weekends in June*
(800) 435-8429

**Kerrville, Austin, Dallas, and
Bandera**
Texas Heritage Music Festival
Third weekend in September
(210) 896-3339

Meridian
John A. Lomax Gathering
Fourth Saturday in April
(817) 435-2966

Mineola
Pickin' in the Pines
Third weekend in May
(903) 857-2253

Overton
Overton Bluegrass Festival
*Second weekend in July,
Thursday–Saturday*
(903) 843-3171

Port Arthur
Pleasure Island Music Festival
Last weekend in April
(409) 962-6200

Round Rock/Austin
Old Settlers' Bluegrass &
Acoustic Music Festival
*Last weekend in March, Satur-
day and Sunday*
(512) 443-5001
(512) 416-7827

San Antonio
Fiesta San Antonio
*Ten days surrounding and in-
cluding April 21 (San Jacinto
Day)*
(210) 227-5191

Great Country River Festival
Fourth weekend in September
(210) 227-4262

Snyder
Legends of Western Swing Reunion
*Fourth week in June, Wednes-
day–Saturday*
(405) 376-4939

Texarkana
Strange Family Bluegrass Festival
*Memorial Day weekend and
Labor Day weekend, Thurs-
day–Sunday*
(903) 792-9018

Turkey
Bob Wills Day
Last Saturday in April
(806) 423-1033

Weslaco
South Texas Music Fest & International Bull Chip Throw-
ing Contest
*Second week in March, Thurs-
day–Sunday*
(210) 464-7767

VERMONT

Barre
National Traditional Old-Time
Fiddlers & Stepdancers Con-
test
*Third or fourth weekend in
September*
(802) 879-1536
(802) 862-6708

Hardwick
Old-Time Fiddler's Contest
Last Saturday in July
(802) 472-6425
(802) 472-5501

Newbury
Cracker Barrel Fiddlers Contest
*Friday of the last full weekend
in July*
(802) 866-5518

Weston
Bluegrass Music Show
Third Saturday in February
(802) 824-6674

VIRGINIA

Camp Pendleton/Virginia Beach
Pendleton Bluegrass Festival
Third weekend in July
(800) 253-7842
(804) 853-1608

Galax
Old Fiddlers' Convention
Second weekend in August
(540) 236-8541
(540) 236-6355

Mineral
Mineral Bluegrass Festival
Third weekend in July
(706) 864-7203

Syria
Graves' Mountain Festival of Music
Weekend after Memorial Day
(540) 923-4231

Virginia Beach
Viva Elvis Festival
First weekend in June
(804) 437-4700
(800) 822-3224

Warsaw
Northern Neck Bluegrass Festival
Memorial Day weekend
(804) 333-4038

WASHINGTON

Port Townsend
Festival of American Fiddle Tunes
Late June and early July
(800) 733-3608
(360) 385-3102

Richland
Washington State Fiddle Contest
Second weekend in May
(509) 586-2843
(509) 575-6320

Tacoma
Wintergrass
Last weekend in February
(360) 871-7354

Tenino
Old Time Music Festival
Third weekend in March
(360) 264-4590

WEST VIRGINIA

Charleston
Vandalia Gathering
Memorial Day weekend
(304) 558-0220

Elkins
Augusta Old-Time Week and Fiddlers' Reunion
A week in mid- or late October
(304) 637-1209
(304) 636-1903
E-mail: augusta@dne.wvnet.edu

Fairmont
Traditional Music Weekend
Second weekend in May
(800) 225-5982
(304) 363-3030

Fairmont/Bunner Ridge
Bluegrass! At the Sagebrush Roundup
Third weekend in May
(304) 387-1103

Sagebrush Roundup Country Music Festival
Third weekend in June, second weekend in September, Friday and Saturday
(304) 363-6366
(304) 363-4864

New Manchester
Memorial Day Music Festival
Memorial Day weekend
(304) 564-3651

Petersberg
Spring Mountain Festival
Last weekend in April
(304) 257-2722

Summersville
Music in the Mountains
Last full weekend in June
(304) 872-3145

Walker
West Virginia Bluegrass Festival

Third weekend in July
(304) 387-1103

WISCONSIN

Beloit
Beloit Riverfest
First or second weekend in July, Thursday–Sunday
(800) 423-5648

Cadott
Chippewa Valley Country Fest
Last weekend in June, Thursday–Sunday
(800) 326-3378
(715) 289-4401

Eau Claire
Country Jam USA
Third weekend in July, Thursday–Sunday
(800) 780-0526

Green Bay
Bayfest
Second full weekend in June
(414) 465-2145

Kaukauna
River Jam
First weekend in June
(414) 766-6300

Manitowish
Midsummer in the Northwoods Bluegrass Festival
Last weekend in July, Thursday–Sunday
(715) 543-2166

Marinette
Porterfield Country Music Festival
Fourth weekend in June
(715) 789-2130

Milwaukee
Summerfest
Eleven days beginning the last Thursday in June
(800) 273-3378
(414) 273-3378

Prescott
Rockin' on the River
A weekend in early July
(715) 262-3512
(715) 262-3284
(715) 262-3950

WYOMING

Douglas
High Plains Old Time Country Music Show and Contest
A weekend in mid- or late April
(307) 358-9006

Grand Targhee Ski and Summer Resort (Alta)
Grand Targhee Bluegrass Festival
Second weekend in August
(800) 827-4433
(307) 353-2300

CANADA

ALBERTA

Calgary
Calgary Folk Music Festival
Last weekend in July
(403) 233-0904

Camrose
Big Valley Jamboree
First or second weekend in August, Thursday–Sunday
(403) 672-0224
(800) 667-7899

Nanton
Shady Grove Bluegrass and Old Tyme Music Festival
Third weekend in August
(403) 646-2076

Stony Plain
Blueberry Bluegrass and Country Music Festival
First weekend in August
(403) 963-5217

BRITISH COLUMBIA

Merritt
Merritt Mountain Music Festival
Second week in July, Thursday–Sunday
(604) 525-3330

Vancouver
Granville Island Bluegrass Festival

Third weekend in May, Saturday–Monday
(604) 535-0362

Whistler
Whistler Country, Roots & Blues Festival
Third or fourth weekend in July
(800) 944-7853
(604) 644-5625
(604) 932-4222

MANITOBA

Dauphin
Dauphin's Countryfest
Last weekend in June
(204) 638-3700
(800) 361-7300

Selkirk
Sun Country Jam
Second weekend in August
(204) 780-7328
(800) 465-7328

NEW BRUNSWICK

Fredericton
New Brunswick Gospel Music Festival
Second weekend in August
(506) 459-7419

St. John
Festival by the Sea
Ten Days beginning the Friday after New Brunswick Day
(506) 632-0086

NEWFOUNDLAND

Grand Falls-Windsor
Exploits Valley Salmon Festival

Third weekend in July, Thursday–Monday
(709) 489-2728

Stephenville
Musicfest
Third full weekend in July, Thursday–Sunday
(709) 643-9123

NORTHWEST TERRITORIES

Aklavik
Pokiak River Festival
Third weekend in June
(403) 978-2252
(403) 978-2239

Fort McPherson
Midway Lake Music Festival
First weekend in July
(403) 952-2330

Fort Smith
South Slave Friendship Festival
Third weekend in August, Thursday–Sunday
(403) 872-2014

Inuvik
Break up Break down Weekend
Last weekend in May
(403) 979-2476

NOVA SCOTIA

Caledonia
Country Music Weekend Featuring the Hank Snow Tribute
Third full weekend in August
(902) 354-4675

Mount Denson
Avon River Bluegrass and Old-time Music Festival
First weekend in June
(902) 684-1046

ONTARIO

Toronto
Canadian Music Festival
One week in early March, Monday–Sunday
(416) 695-9236
E-mail: cmw@cmw.com

North by Northeast
Third weekend in June, Thursday–Saturday
(416) 469-0986
(512) 467-7979
E-mail: 72662.2465 @compuserve.com

PRINCE EDWARD ISLAND

Fairview
PEI Bluegrass and Old Time Music Festival
First or second weekend in July
(902) 675-3061

SASKATCHEWAN

Big River
Ness Creek Festival
Third full weekend in July, Thursday–Sunday
(306) 652-6377
(306) 343-5671

Dinsmore
Coors Country Bandstand
Second Sunday in August
(306) 846-4511

Govan
Govan Olde Tyme Fiddle Festival
First weekend in July
(306) 484-4566
(306) 484-2119

Regina
Regina Folk Festival
Last weekend in June
(306) 757-6196
(306) 569-8966

Watrous
Manitou Country Music Jamboree
Third weekend in June, Saturday and Sunday
(306) 946-3369

Weyburn
Country Music Jamboree
Last Sunday in July
(306) 842-4738

YUKON TERRITORY

Dawson City
Dawson City Music Festival
Third or fourth weekend in July
(403) 993-5584

Whitehorse
Frostbite Music Festival
Weekend before the last full week in February
(403) 668-4921

If you're driving through the United States or Canada, tune in to one of the following radio stations to hear some country music. (Warning: radio formats often change like the weather, so if you're looking for Alan Jackson and end up with Michael Jackson, don't blame us!)

UNITED STATES

ALABAMA

Birmingham
WFMH (101.1 FM)
WOWC (102.5 FM)
WSMQ (1450 AM)
WYDE (850 AM)
WZZK (610 AM)
WZZK (104.7 FM)

Dothan
WDJR (96.9 FM)
WGEA (1150 AM)
WOAB (104.9 FM)
WTVY (95.5 FM)
WXUS (100.5 FM)
WZTZ (101.1 FM)

Huntsville
WBHP (1230 AM)
WDRM (102.1 FM)

WHOS (800 AM)
WPZM (93.3 FM)

Mobile
WASG (550 AM)
WBCA (1110 AM)
WDWG (104.1 FM)
WHXT (102.1 FM)
WKSJ (1270 AM)
WKSJ (94.9 FM)
WXBM (102.7 FM)

Montgomery
WBAM (98.9 FM)
WJCC (101.9 FM)
WLWI (92.3 FM)

Tuscaloosa
WACT (105.5 FM)
WOWC (102.5 FM)
WTXT (98.1 FM)

ALASKA

Anchorage
KASH (1080 AM)
KASH (107.5 FM)
KBRJ (104.1 FM)

ARIZONA

Phoenix
KCWW (1580 AM)
KMLE (107.9 FM)
KNIX (102.5 FM)
KXLL (105.9 FM)

Tucson
KAVV (97.7 FM)
KCDI (97.5 FM)

KCUB (1290 AM)
KIIM (99.5 FM)

ARKANSAS

Fayetteville-Springdale
KAMO (1390 AM)
KAMO (94.3 FM)
KBRS (104.9 FM)
KFAY (98.3 FM)
KKIX (103.9 FM)
KUOA (1290 AM)

Fort Smith
KMAG (99.1 FM)
KOMS (107.3 FM)
KRWA (103.1 FM)
KTCS (1410 AM)
KTCS (99.9 FM)

Little Rock
KDDK (100.3 FM)
KLRA (1530 AM)
KLRA (96.5 FM)
KMVK (106.7 FM)
KSSN (95.7 FM)

CALIFORNIA

Bakersfield
KCNQ (102.5 FM)
KCWR (550 AM)
KTIE (107.1 FM)
KTPI (103.1 FM)
KUZZ (107.9 FM)

Chico
KALF (95.7 FM)
KHSL (103.5 FM)

Fresno
KJUG (106.7 FM)
KNAX (97.9 FM)
KRBT (101.1 FM)
KSKS (93.7 FM)
KTNS (1090 AM)

Los Angeles
KIKF (94.3 FM)
KYKF (94.3 FM)
KZLA (93.9 FM)

Merced
KUBB (96.3 FM)

Modesto
KATM (103.3 FM)
KMIX (100.9 FM)
KUBB (96.3 FM)

Monterey/Salinas/Santa Cruz
KAXT (93.5 FM)
KLUE (106.3 FM)
KRKC (1490 AM)
KTOM (1380 AM)
KTOM (100.7 FM)

Oxnard/Ventura
KHAY (100.7 FM)
KTND (105.5 FM)

Palm Springs
KPLM (106.1 FM)

Redding
KALF (95.7 FM)
KEWB (94.7 FM)
KNCQ (97.3 FM)

Riverside/San Bernardino
KFRG (95.1 FM)
KMET (1490 AM)
KOOJ (92.7 FM)

Sacramento
KNCI (105.1 FM)
KRAK (98.5 FM)

San Diego
KOWF (92.1 FM)
KSON (97.3 FM)

San Francisco
KNEW (910 AM)
KSAN (94.9 FM)
KYCY (93.3 FM)

San Jose
KRTY (95.3 FM)
KSAN (94.9 FM)
KYCY (93.3 FM)

San Luis Obispo
KDDB (92.5 FM)
KIXT (107.3 FM)
KKJG (98.1 FM)
KSNI (102.5 FM)

Santa Barbara
KHAY (100.7 FM)

Santa Rosa
KRAZ (100.9 FM)
KRPQ (104.9 FM)

Stockton
KATM (103.3 FM)
KMIX (100.9 FM)

Visalia/Tulare/Hanford
KJUG (1270 AM)
KJUG (106.7 FM)

COLORADO

Colorado Springs
KCCY (96.9 FM)
KHII (105.5 FM)
KKCS (1460 AM)
KKCS (101.9 FM)

Denver/Boulder
KGLL (96.1 FM)
KLMO (1060 AM)
KYGO (1600 AM)
KYGO (98.5 FM)

Grand Junction
KEKB (99.9 FM)
KKNN (95.1 FM)

KKXK (94.1 FM)
KQIL (1340 AM)
KZKS (105.3 FM)

Pueblo
KCCY (96.9 FM)
KKCS (101.9 FM)
KYZX (104.5 FM)

CONNECTICUT

Bridgeport
WGSM (750 AM)

Danbury
WINE (940 AM)
WPUT (1510 AM)

Hartford/New Britain/Middletown
WWYZ (92.5 FM)

New Haven
WWYZ (92.5 FM)

New London
WCTY (97.7 FM)
WJJF (1180 AM)

DELAWARE

Wilmington
WDSD (94.7 FM)
WXCY (103.7 FM)

DISTRICT OF COLUMBIA

Washington
WAGE (1200 AM)
WMZQ (98.7 FM)
WRCY (107.7 FM)

FLORIDA

Daytona Beach
WDXD (103.3 FM)
WGNE (98.1 FM)

Fort Myers/Naples/Marco Island
WCKT (107.1 FM)
WFSN (100.1 FM)
WIKX (92.9 FM)
WMYR (1410 AM)
WWGR (101.9 FM)

Fort Pierce/Stuart/Vero Beach
WAVW (101.7 FM)

WCLB (95.5 FM)
WPAW (99.7 FM)

Fort Walton Beach
WAAZ (104.7 FM)
WJSB (1050 AM)
WMMK (92.1 FM)
WYZB (105.5 FM)

Gainesville/Ocala
WMOP (900 AM)
WOGK (93.7 FM)
WTRS (102.3 FM)
WYGC (100.9 FM)

Jacksonville
WJQR (105.5 FM)
WJXR (92.1 FM)
WKBX (106.3 FM)
WQAI (1570 AM)
WQIK (99.1 FM)
WROO (107.3 FM)

Lakeland/Winter Haven
WBAR (1460 AM)
WPCV (97.5 FM)

Melbourne/Titusville/Cocoa
WGNE (98.1 FM)
WHKR (102.7 FM)
WWKA (92.3 FM)

Miami/Fort Lauderdale/Hollywood
WKIS (99.9 FM)

Orlando
WPCV (97.5 FM)
WWKA (92.3 FM)

Panama City
WAKT (105.1 FM)
WPAP (92.5 FM)

Pensacola
WDWG (104.1 FM)
WXBM (102.7 FM)

Sarasota/Bradenton
WCTQ (92.1 FM)
WFSN (100.1 FM)

Tallahassee
WAIB (103.1 FM)
WGWD (93.3 FM)
WTNT (94.9 FM)

Tampa/St. Petersburg/Clearwater
WQYK (99.5 FM)
WRBQ (104.7 FM)

West Palm Beach/Boca Raton
WCLB (95.5 FM)
WIRK (107.9 FM)
WKIS (99.9 FM)

GEORGIA

Albany
WKAK (101.7 FM)
WOBB (100.3 FM)

Atlanta
WKHX (590 AM)
WKHX (101.5 FM)
WYAY (106.7 FM)

Augusta
WKBG (107.7 FM)
WKXC (99.5 FM)
WTHO (101.7 FM)

Columbus
WKCN (99.3 FM)
WSTH (106.1 FM)

Macon
WDEN (1500 AM)
WDEN (105.3 FM)
WMKS (92.3 FM)

Savannah
WCHY (1290 AM)
WCHY (94.1 FM)
WHVL (104.7 FM)
WJCL (96.5 FM)

IDAHO

Boise
KCID (107.1 FM)
KIZN (92.3 FM)
KQFC (97.9 FM)

ILLINOIS

Bloomington
WBWN (104.1 FM)

Champaign
WCZQ (105.5 FM)
WIAI (99.1 FM)
WIXY (100.3 FM)
WWHP (98.3 FM)

Chicago
WCCQ (98.3 FM)
WKKX (94.7 FM)
WLLI (96.7 FM)
WUSN (99.5 FM)

Danville
WHPO (100.9 FM)
WIAI (99.1 FM)
WIXY (100.3 FM)

**Marion/Carbondale
(Southern Illinois)**
KEZS (102.9 FM)
WDDD (810 AM)
WDDD (107.3 FM)
WMCL (1060 AM)
WOOZ (99.9 FM)

Peoria
WFYR (97.3 FM)
WXCL (104.9 FM)

Rockford
WJVL (99.9 FM)
WLUV (1520 AM)
WLUV (96.7 FM)
WXXQ (98.5 FM)

Springfield
WFMB (104.5 FM)
WWTE (93.9 FM)

INDIANA

Evansville
WBKR (92.5 FM)
WBNL (1540 AM)
WKDQ (99.5 FM)
WRAY (98.1 FM)
WRUL (97.3 FM)
WYNG (105.3 FM)

Fort Wayne
WBTU (93.3 FM)
WQHK (105.1 FM)

Indianapolis
WCBK (102.3 FM)
WFMS (95.5 FM)
WGRL (104.5 FM)
WIRE (100.9 FM)

Lafayette
WGBD (95.7 FM)
WKOA (105.3 FM)

South Bend
WBYT (100.7 FM)
WGTC (102.3 FM)

Terre Haute
WACF (98.5 FM)
WTHI (99.9 FM)

IOWA

Cedar Rapids
KBOB (99.7 FM)
KHAK (98.1 FM)
KXMX (102.9 FM)

Des Moines
KDLS (1310 AM)
KHKI (97.3 FM)
KJJC (106.9 FM)
KJJY (92.5 FM)
KWWT (540 AM)

Dubuque
KIKR (103.3 FM)
WGLR (1280 AM)
WGLR (97.7 FM)
WJOD (107.5 FM)

**Quad Cities (Davenport/Rock
Island/Moline)**
KBOB (99.7 FM)
KWCC (93.1 FM)
WLLR (1230 AM)
WLLR (101.3 FM)

Sioux City
KKYA (93.1 FM)
KMNS (620 AM)
KOLK (102.3 FM)
KSUX (105.7 FM)
WNAX (570 AM)

Waterloo/Cedar Falls
KKCV (98.5 FM)
KOEL (92.3 FM)

KANSAS

Topeka
KTPK (106.9 FM)
WIBW (97.3 FM)

Wichita
KFDI (1070 AM)
KFDI (101.3 FM)
KSOK (107.9 FM)
KSPG (98.7 FM)
KYQQ (106.5 FM)
KZSN (1480 AM)
KZSN (102.1 FM)

KENTUCKY

Lexington/Fayette
WKXO (106.7 FM)
WVLK (92.9 FM)
WWYC (100.1 FM)

Louisville
WAMZ (97.5 FM)
WCND (940 AM)
WHKW (1080 AM)
WKJK (98.9 FM)
WTHQ (101.7 FM)
WTMT (620 AM)

Owensboro
WBIO (94.7 FM)
WBKR (92.5 FM)
WKDQ (99.5 FM)
WYNG (105.3 FM)

LOUISIANA

Alexandria
KAPB (1370 AM)
KAPB (97.7 FM)
KICR (98.7 FM)
KRRV (100.3 FM)

Baton Rouge
KXKC (99.1 FM)
WHMD (107.1 FM)
WKJN (103.3 FM)
WYCT (94.1 FM)
WYNK (1380 AM)
WYNK (101.5 FM)

Lafayette
KCRL (106.7 FM)
KMDL (97.3 FM)
KROF (960 AM)
KXKC (99.1 FM)
WYNK (101.5 FM)

Lake Charles
KJEF (92.9 FM)
KYKZ (96.1 FM)

Monroe
KJLO (104.1 FM)
KMYY (106.1 FM)
KXKZ (107.5 FM)

New Orleans
KLEB (1600 AM)
WNOE (101.1 FM)
WYLA (94.7 FM)
WYLK (104.7 FM)

Shreveport
KITT (93.7 FM)
KRMD (1340 AM)
KRMD (101.1 FM)
KWKH (1130 AM)
KWKH (94.5 FM)

MAINE

Augusta/Waterville
WEBB (98.5 FM)
WKCG (101.3 FM)
WMCM (103.3 FM)
WQCB (106.5 FM)
WTHT (107.5 FM)
WTVL (1490 AM)

Bangor
WQCB (106.5 FM)

Portland
WPOR (1490 AM)
WPOR (101.9 FM)
WTHT (107.5 FM)

MARYLAND

Baltimore
WANN (1190 AM)
WGRX (100.7 FM)
WPOC (93.1 FM)

Frederick
WFRE (99.9 FM)
WQSI (820 AM)

**Hagerstown/Chambersburg/
Waynesboro**
WAYZ (101.5 FM)
WCHA (800 AM)
WFRE (99.9 FM)
WHGT (1380 AM)
WKSL (94.3 FM)
WYII (95.9 FM)

Salisbury/Ocean City
WDSD (94.7 FM)
WICO (94.3 FM)
WSBL (97.9 FM)
WWFG (99.9 FM)
WXJN (105.9 FM)

MASSACHUSETTS

Boston
WBCS (96.9 FM)
WCAV (97.7 FM)
WKLV (105.7 FM)

New Bedford/Fall River
WCTK (98.1 FM)

Springfield
WPKX (97.9 FM)

Worcester
WARE (1250 AM)

WQVR (100.1 FM)

MICHIGAN

Ann Arbor
WSDS (1480 AM)

Battle Creek
WBHR (94.1 FM)
WNWN (98.5 FM)
WRCC (104.9 FM)

Detroit
CHYR (96.7 FM)
WWWW (106.7 FM)
WYCD (99.5 FM)

Flint
WKCQ (98.1 FM)

Grand Rapids
WBCT (93.7 FM)
WCUZ (101.3 FM)
WMUS (106.9 FM)

Kalamazoo
WBCT (93.7 FM)
WNWN (98.5 FM)

Lansing/East Lansing
WBHR (94.1 FM)
WITL (100.7 FM)

Saginaw/Bay City/Midland
WCEN (94.5 FM)
WIXC (97.3 FM)
WKCQ (98.1 FM)

**Traverse City/Petoskey
(Northwest Michigan)**
WKJF (92.9 FM)
WMKC (102.9 FM)
WTCM (103.5 FM)

MINNESOTA

Duluth/Superior
KKCB (105.1 FM)
KTCO (98.9 FM)
KUSZ (107.7 FM)
WKKQ (650 AM)

Minneapolis/St. Paul
KEEY (102.1 FM)
WBOB (100.3 FM)
WQPM (106.1 FM)

Rochester
KAUS (99.9 FM)
KMFX (102.5 FM)

KNFX (970 AM)
KNFX (104.3 FM)
KWWK (96.5 FM)

St. Cloud
KASM (1150 AM)
KMSR (94.3 FM)
KZPK (98.9 FM)
WQPM (106.1 FM)
WWJO (98.1 FM)

MISSISSIPPI

Biloxi/Gulfport/Pascagoula
WGCM (1240 AM)
WKNN (99.1 FM)
WXOR (92.5 FM)
WZKX (107.9 FM)

Jackson
WBKJ (105.1 FM)
WIIN (780 AM)
WJKK (98.7 FM)
WKTF (95.5 FM)
WMSI (102.9 FM)

Laurel/Hattiesburg
WBBN (95.9 FM)
WESV (96.5 FM)
WHER (103.7 FM)
WZKX (107.9 FM)

Meridian
WMYQ (97.9 FM)
WOKK (97.1 FM)

Tupelo
WBIP (1400 AM)
WCNA (95.9 FM)
WFTO (1330 AM)
WWMS (97.5 FM)
WWZD (106.7 FM)
WZLQ (98.5 FM)

MISSOURI

Columbia
KCLR (99.3 FM)
KFAL (900 AM)
KRES (104.7 FM)
KWWR (95.7 FM)

Joplin
KBTN (1420 AM)
KBTN (99.7 FM)
KDMO (1490 AM)
KIXQ (93.9 FM)
KJKT (102.5 FM)
KKOW (860 AM)

KKOW (96.9 FM)

Kansas City
KBEQ (104.3 FM)
KFKF (94.1 FM)
WDAF (610 AM)

Springfield
KCTG (92.9 FM)
KGMY (100.5 FM)
KLTQ (96.5 FM)
KTTS (1260 AM)
KTTS (94.7 FM)
KYOO (1200 AM)

St. Louis
KLPW (101.7 FM)
KWRE (730 AM)
WIL (92.3 FM)
WKKX (106.5 FM)

MONTANA

Billings
KBKO (103.7 FM)
KCTR (102.9 FM)
KDWG (970 AM)
KGHL (790 AM)
KIDX (98.5 FM)

Great Falls
KMON (560 AM)
KMON (94.5 FM)

NEBRASKA

Lincoln
KZKX (96.9 FM)

Omaha/Council Bluffs
KFMT (105.5 FM)
KISP (101.5 FM)
KXKT (103.7 FM)
WOW (590 AM)
WOW (94.1 FM)

NEVADA

Las Vegas
KFMS (101.9 FM)
KWNR (95.5 FM)

Reno
KBUL (98.1 FM)
KHIT (630 AM)
KHWG (107.7 FM)
KQNV (100.9 FM)

NEW HAMPSHIRE

Manchester
WOKQ (97.5 FM)
WSMN (1590 AM)

Portsmouth/Dover/Rochester
WOKQ (97.5 FM)

NEW JERSEY

Atlantic City/Cape May
WKOE (106.3 FM)

Monmouth/Ocean
WJLK (1310 AM)

Morristown
WKMB (1070 AM)

NEW MEXICO

Albuquerque
KARS (860 AM)
KASY (103.3 FM)
KRST (92.3 FM)
KRZY (105.9 FM)

Santa Fe
KASY (103.3 FM)
KNYN (95.5 FM)
KRST (92.3 FM)
KRZY (104.9 FM)
KYBR (92.9 FM)

NEW YORK

Albany/Schenectady/Troy
WBUG (1570 AM)
WBUG (101.1 FM)
WGNA (1460 AM)
WGNA (107.7 FM)
WPTR (96.3 FM)
WZZM (93.5 FM)

Binghamton
WCDW (100.5 FM)
WHWK (98.1 FM)

Buffalo/Niagara Falls
WNUC (107.7 FM)
WWKB (1520 AM)
WXRL (1300 AM)
WYRK (106.5 FM)

Elmira/Corning
WOKN (99.5 FM)
WPGI (100.9 FM)
WQIX (820 AM)

Ithaca
WPCX (106.9 FM)

Nassau/Suffolk (Long Island)
WGSM (750 AM)
WMJC (94.3 FM)

Newburgh/Middletown,
(Mid-Hudson Valley)
WDLC (1490 AM)
WRWD (107.3 FM)
WTHN (99.3 FM)
WVOS (1240 AM)
WVOS (95.9 FM)

Poughkeepsie
WHVW (950 AM)
WPUT (1510 AM)
WRWD (1170 AM)
WRWD (107.3 FM)
WTHN (99.3 FM)

Rochester
WBEE (92.5 FM)

Syracuse
WBBS (104.7 FM)
WFRG (104.3 FM)
WPCX (106.9 FM)
WSCP (101.7 FM)

Utica/Rome
WBUG (101.1 FM)
WFRG (104.3 FM)
WLFH (1230 AM)

Watertown
CFMK (96.3 FM)
WBBS (104.7 FM)
WLKC (100.7 FM)
WLLG (99.3 FM)

NORTH CAROLINA

Asheville
WFNQ (93.3 FM)
WKSF (99.9 FM)
WPTL (920 AM)
WWNC (570 AM)
WZQR (1350 AM)

Charlotte/Gastonia/Rock Hill
WFMX (105.7 FM)
WLON (1050 AM)
WSOC (103.7 FM)
WTDR (96.9 FM)

Fayetteville
WAGR (1340 AM)
WEGX (92.9 FM)

WJSK (102.3 FM)
WKML (95.7 FM)
WRRZ (880 AM)

Greensboro/Winston
Salem/High Point
WFMX (105.7 FM)
WGOS (1070 AM)
WHSL (100.3 FM)
WKSI (98.7 FM)
WKTE (1090 AM)
WPCM (101.1 FM)
WTQR (104.1 FM)

Greensville/New
Bern/Jacksonville
WKTC (96.9 FM)
WRNS (960 AM)
WRNS (95.1 FM)

Raleigh/Durham
WETC (540 AM)
WKIX (96.1 FM)
WKTC (96.9 FM)
WMPM (1270 AM)
WPCM (101.1 FM)
WQDR (94.7 FM)

Wilmington
WKXB (99.9 FM)
WWQQ (101.3 FM)

NORTH DAKOTA

Bismarck
KBMR (1130 AM)
KKCT (97.5 FM)
KQDY (94.5 FM)

Fargo/Moorhead
KFGO (790 AM)
KFGO (101.9 FM)
KVOX (99.9 FM)

Grand Forks
KFGO (790 AM)
KNOX (1310 AM)
KNOX (94.7 FM)
KYCK (97.1 FM)

OHIO

Akron
WQKT (104.5 FM)
WQMX (94.9 FM)

Canton
WNPQ (95.9 FM)
WQKT (104.5 FM)
WQMX (94.9 FM)

WQXK (105.1 FM)

Cincinnati
WHKO (99.1 FM)
WPFB (105.9 FM)
WUBE (105.1 FM)
WYGY (96.5 FM)

Cleveland
WGAR (99.5 FM)
WKKY (104.7 FM)
WOBL (1320 AM)

Columbus
WCLT (100.3 FM)
WCOL (92.3 FM)
WHOK (95.5 FM)
WHTH (790 AM)
WLLD (98.9 FM)
WMNI (920 AM)
WMRN (106.9 FM)

Dayton
WBZI (1500 AM)
WHKO (99.1 FM)
WKSW (101.7 FM)
WPFB (105.9 FM)
WYGY (96.5 FM)

Lima
WDOH (107.1 FM)
WIMT (102.1 FM)

Toledo
WKKO (99.9 FM)
WTOD (1560 AM)

Youngstown/Warren
WICT (1470 AM)
WICT (95.1 FM)
WQXK (105.1 FM)
WWIZ (103.9 FM)

OKLAHOMA

Lawton
KFXI (92.1 FM)
KLAW (101.5 FM)
KRHD (1350 AM)
KRPT (103.7 FM)
KTJS (1420 AM)
KYYI (104.7 FM)

Oklahoma City
KTST (101.9 FM)
KXXY (1340 AM)
KXXY (96.1 FM)

Tulsa
KCKI (99.5 FM)
KREK (104.9 FM)

KTFX (102.3 FM)
KVOO (1170 AM)
KVOO (98.5 FM)
KWEN (95.5 FM)

OREGON

Eugene/Springfield
KFAT (106.1 FM)
KKNU (93.1 FM)
KNND (1400 AM)
KUGN (97.9 FM)

Medford/Ashland
KAKT (105.1 FM)
KROG (96.9 FM)
KRRM (94.7 FM)
KRWQ (100.3 FM)

Portland
KUPL (98.5 FM)
KWJJ (1080 AM)
KWJJ (99.5 FM)

PENNSYLVANIA

Allentown/Bethlehem
WRNJ (107.1 FM)

Altoona
WBRX (94.7 FM)
WFGY (98.1 FM)
WMTZ (96.5 FM)
WVAM (1430 AM)

Erie
WEYZ (1530 AM)
WXTA (97.9 FM)
WZPR (100.3 FM)

Harrisburg/Lebanon/Carlisle
WGTY (107.7 FM)
WHYL (102.3 FM)
WRKZ (106.7 FM)
WWSM (1510 AM)

Johnstown
WFGY (98.1 FM)
WFRB (560 AM)
WFRB (105.3 FM)
WMTZ (96.5 FM)
WVSC (990 AM)

Lancaster
WIOV (105.1 FM)

Philadelphia
WXTU (92.5 FM)

Pittsburgh
WASP (94.9 FM)

WDSY (1080 AM)
WDSY (107.9 FM)

Reading
WIOV (105.1 FM)

State College
WBLF (970 AM)
WFGI (94.5 FM)

Wilkes Barre/Scranton
WEMR (1460 AM)
WGGY (101.3 FM)
WKXP (95.9 FM)

Williamsport
WILQ (105.1 FM)
WQBR (99.9 FM)

York
WGRX (100.7 FM)
WGTY (107.7 FM)
WOYK (1350 AM)
WRKZ (106.7 FM)

RHODE ISLAND

**Providence/Warwick/
Pawtucket**
WCTK (98.1 FM)
WHIM (1450 AM)

SOUTH CAROLINA

Charleston
WAZS (980 AM)
WBUB (107.5 FM)
WEZL (103.5 FM)
WHLZ (92.5 FM)
WXTC (1390 AM)

Columbia
WCOS (97.5 FM)
WHKZ (96.7 FM)

Florence
WDAR (105.5 FM)
WDSC (800 AM)
WEGX (92.9 FM)
WHLZ (92.5 FM)

Greenville/Spartanburg
WAGI (105.3 FM)
WESC (660 AM)
WESC (92.5 FM)
WFIS (1600 AM)
WFNQ (93.3 FM)
WRIX (103.1 FM)
WSSL (100.5 FM)

Myrtle Beach
WGTN (100.7 FM)
WGTR (107.9 FM)
WJXY (93.9 FM)
WLSC (1240 AM)
WTAB (1370 AM)
WVCO (94.9 FM)
WYAK (103.1 FM)
WYNA (104.9 FM)

SOUTH DAKOTA

Rapid City
KBHB (810 AM)
KIQK (104.1 FM)
KOUT (98.7 FM)
KRCS (93.1 FM)

Sioux Falls
KIKN (100.5 FM)
KJAM (1390 AM)
KJAM (103.1 FM)
KKYA (93.1 FM)
KLQL (101.1 FM)
KTWB (101.9 FM)
KXRB (1000 AM)
WNAX (570 AM)

TENNESSEE

Chattanooga
WDOD (96.5 FM)
WEPG (910 FM)
WKWN (1420 AM)
WQCH (1590 AM)
WQRX (870 AM)
WSDQ (1190 AM)
WSGC (101.9 FM)
WUSY (100.7 FM)

Jackson
WDXL (1490 AM)
WHHM (107.7 FM)
WTBG (95.3 FM)
WTNV (104.1 FM)
WWYN (106.9 FM)
WZLT (99.3 FM)

**Johnson City/
Kingspot/Bristol**
WBEJ (1240 AM)
WEMB (1420 AM
WGOC (640 AM)
WIKQ (94.9 FM)
WMEV (93.9 FM)
WRGS (1370 AM)
WXBQ (96.9 FM)

Knoxville
WDLY (105.5 FM)
WECO (101.3 FM)
WGAP (1400 AM)
WGAP (95.7 FM)
WIVK (107.7 FM)
WKCE (1120 AM)
WLIL (93.5 FM)
WOKI (100.3 FM)
WSEV (930 AM)
WXVO (98.7 FM)
WYSH (1380 AM)

Memphis
KHLS (96.3 FM)
WGKX (105.9 FM)
WOGY (94.1 FM)

Nashville
WAKM (950 AM)
WANT (98.9 FM)
WBOZ (104.9 FM)
WCOR (900 AM)
WDBL (94.3 FM)
WDKN (1260 AM)
WHIN (1010 AM)
WNNY (102.9 FM)
WSIX (97.9 FM)
WSM (650 AM)
WSM (95.5 FM)
WYXE (1130 AM)

TEXAS

Abilene
KBCY (99.7 FM)
KCWS (102.7 FM)
KEAN (1280 AM)
KEAN (105.1 FM)
KVRP (1400 AM)
KVRP (95.5 FM)

Amarillo
KATP (101.9 FM)
KBUY (94.1 FM)
KDJW (1360 AM)
KGNC (97.9 FM)
KMML (96.9 FM)

Austin
KASE (100.7 FM)
KIKY (92.1 FM)
KTAE (1260 AM)
KVET (98.1 FM)

Beaumont/Port Arthur
KAYD (1450 AM)
KAYD (97.5 FM)
KOGT (1600 AM)

KYKR (95.1 FM)
KYKZ (96.1 FM)

Bryan/College Station
KAGG (96.1 FM)
KORA (98.3 FM)
KTTX (106.1 FM)

Corpus Christi
KFTX (97.5 FM)
KKBA (92.7 FM)
KOUL (103.7 FM)
KRYS (1360 AM)
KRYS (99.1 FM)

Dallas/Fort Worth
KBEC (1390 AM)
KPLX (99.5 FM)
KSCS (96.3 FM)
KYNG (105.3 FM)

El Paso
KHEY (96.3 FM)
KSET (94.7 FM)

Houston/Galveston
KCHC (1140 AM)
KIKK (650 AM)
KIKK (95.7 FM)
KILT (100.3 FM)
KKBQ (790 AM)
KKBQ (92.9 FM)
KVST (103.7 FM)

Killeen/Temple
KCKR (95.5 FM)
KKIK (104.3 FM)
KOOV (103.1 FM)
KRYL (98.3 FM)
WACO (99.9 FM)

Laredo
KOYE (94.9 FM)

Lubbock
KLLL (1590 AM)
KLLL (96.3 FM)
KONE (101.1 FM)
KRBL (105.7 FM)

**McAllen/Brownsville/
Harlingen**
KTEX (100.3 FM)
KZSP (95.3 FM)

Odessa/Midland
KCRS (103.3 FM)
KGEE (99.9 FM)
KJBC (1150 AM)
KNFM (92.3 FM)

KPET (690 AM)

San Angelo
KDCD (92.9 FM)
KGKL (960 AM)
KGKL (97.5 AM)

San Antonio
KAJA (97.3 FM)
KCYY (100.3 FM)
KKYX (680 AM)
KNBT (92.1 FM)
KRNH (95.1 FM)
KWED (1580 AM)

Texarkana
KARQ (92.1 FM)
KKYR (790 AM)
KKYR (102.5 FM)
KLLI (95.9 FM)
KZHE (100.5 FM)

Tyler/Longview
KKUS (104.1 FM)
KNUE (101.5 FM)
KPXI (100.7 FM)
KYKX (105.7 FMo

Waco
KCKR (95.5 FM)
WACO (99.9 FM)

Wichita Falls
KLUR (99.9 FM)
KWFS (103.3 FM)
KYYI (104.7 FM)

UTAH

Salt Lake City/Ogden/Provo
KBKK (106.5 FM)
KKAT (101.9 FM)
KSOP (1370 AM)
KSOP (104.3 FM)
KUBL (93.3 FM)

VERMONT

Burlington
WLFE (102.3 FM)
WOKO (98.9 FM)

VIRGINIA

Charlottesville
WCYK (810 AM)
WCYK (99.7 FM)
WLSA (105.5 FM)

Harrisburg
WKCY (104.3 FM)
WPKZ (98.5 FM)
WSIG (96.9 FM)
WSVG (790 AM)

Norfolk/Virginia Beach/Newport News
WCMS (1050 AM)
WCMS (100.5 FM)
WGH (97.3 FM)

Richmond
WGGM (820 AM)
WKHK (95.3 FM)
WXGI (950 AM)

Roanoke/Lynchburg
WJLM (93.5 FM)
WSLC (610 AM)
WYYD (107.9 FM)
WZZI (101.5 FM)

WASHINGTON

Seattle/Tacoma
KITZ (1400 AM)
KJUN (1450 AM)
KKBY (104.9 FM)
KMPS (1300 AM)
KMPS (94.1 FM)
KWYZ (1230 AM)
KYCW (96.5 FM)

Spokane
KCDA (103.1 FM)
KDRK (93.7 FM)
KNFR (96.1 FM)

Tri-Cities (Richland/Kennewick/Pasco)
KIOK (94.9 FM)
KORD (102.7 FM)

Yakima
KENE (1490 AM)
KXDD (104.1 FM)
KXXS (92.9 FM)

WEST VIRGINIA

Beckley
WJLS (99.5 FM)
WMTD (102.3 FM)
WTNJ (105.9 FM)

Charleston
WKWS (96.1 FM)
WQBE (97.5 FM)

Huntington/Ashland
WBVB (97.1 FM)
WDGG (93.7 FM)
WGOH (1370 AM)
WLGC (105.7 FM)
WPAY (104.1 FM)
WTCR (1420 AM)
WTCR (103.3 FM)

Morgantown/Clarksburg/Fairmont
WAJR (1440 AM)
WBUC (101.3 FM)
WFGM (97.9 FM)
WKMM (96.7 FM)
WTBZ (95.9 FM)
WTUS (102.7 FM)
WVUC (93.1 FM)

Parkersburg/Marietta
WHCM (99.1 FM)
WMOV (1360 AM)
WNUS (107.1 FM)
WXKX (103.1 FM)

Wheeling
WCDK (106.3 FM)
WOVK (98.7 FM)
WWVA (1170 AM)

WISCONSIN

Appleton/Oshkosh
WNCY (100.3 FM)
WPKR (99.5 FM)
WUSW (96.9 FM)

Eau Claire
WAXX (104.5 FM)
WMEQ (880 AM)
WQRB (95.1 FM)
WRDN (95.9 FM)

Green Bay
WGEE (99.7 FM)
WNCY (100.3 FM)

La Crosse
KQYB (98.3 FM)
WCOW (97.1 FM)
WQCC (106.3 FM)
WTRV (95.7 FM)

Madison
WIBU (1240 AM)
WWQM (106.3 FM)
WYZM (105.1 FM)

Milwaukee/Racine
WBWI (92.5 FM)
WMIL (106.1 FM)

Wausau/Stevens Point
WAXX (104.5 FM)
WDEZ (101.9 FM)
WYTE (96.7 FM)

WYOMING

Casper
KQLT (103.7 FM)
KTWO (1030 AM)
KVOC (1230 AM)

Cheyenne
KCGY (95.1 FM)
KKAZ (100.7 FM)
KMUS (101.9 FM)

CANADA

ALBERTA

Athabasca
CKBA (850 AM)

Brooks
CIBQ (1340 AM)

Calgary
CFAC (960 AM)
CKRY (105.1 FM)

Camrose
CFCW (790 AM)

Crowsnest Pass
CJPR (1490 AM)

Drumheller
CKDQ (910 AM)

Edmonton
CISN (103.9 FM)

Edson
CJYR (970 AM)

Fort McMurray
CJOK (1230 AM)

Grande Prairie
CJXX (840 AM)

High Prairie
CKVH (1020 AM)

High River
CHKB (1280 AM)

Lethbridge
CJOC (1220 AM)

Lloydminster
CKSA (1080 AM)

Medicine Hat
CHAT (1270 AM)

Red Deer
CKGY (1170 AM)

Saint Paul
CHLW (1310 AM)

Slave Lake
CKWA (1210 AM)

Stettler
CKSQ (1400 AM)

Taber
CKTA (1570 AM)

Wainwright
CKKY (830 AM)

Westlock
CFOK (1370 AM)

Wetaskiwin
CKJR (1440 AM)

BRITISH COLUMBIA

Fort Nelson
CFNL (590 AM)

Fort St. John
CKNL (560 AM)

Kamloops
CFJC (550 AM)

Nanaimo
CKEG (1570 AM)

One Hundred Mile House
CKBX (840 AM)

Penticton
CIGY (100.7 FM)

Port Alberni
CJAV (1240 AM)

Prince George
CJCI (630 AM)
CKNN (101.3 FM)

Quesnel
CKCQ (920 AM)

Terrace
CJFW (103.1 FM)

Vancouver
CJJR (93.7 FM)

Vanderhoof
CIVB (1340 AM)

Victoria
CKXM (1200 AM)

Williams Lake
CKWL (570 AM)

MANITOBA

Brandon
CKLQ (880 AM)
CKX (96.1 FM)

Dauphin
CKDM (730 AM)

Portage-la-Prairie
CFRY (920 AM)

Selkirk
CFQX (104.1 FM)

Winkler
CKMW (1570 AM)

NEW BRUNSWICK

Fredericton
CKBJ (105.3 FM)

Moncton
CFQM (103.9 FM)

Saint John
CHSJ (700 AM)

Sussex
CJCW (590 AM)

NEWFOUNDLAND

Carbonear
CHVO (560 AM)

Corner Brook
CKXX (1340 AM)

Gander
CKXD (1010 AM)

Grand Falls
CKCM (620 AM)
CKXG (680 AM)

Marystown
CHCM (740 AM)

St. John's
CKIX (99.1 FM)

NOVA SCOTIA

Bridgewater
CKBW (1000 AM)

Dartmouth
CFDR (780 AM)

Halifax
CHFX (101.9 FM)

Kentville
CKEN (1490 AM)

New Glasgow
CKEC (1320 AM)

Sydney
CKPE (94.9 FM)

Truro
CKCL (600 AM)

NORTHWEST TERRITORIES

Yellowknife
CKLD (101.9 FM)

ONTARIO

Ajax
CJKX (95.9 FM)

Bancroft
CJNH (1240 AM)

Belleville
CJBQ (800 AM)

Hamilton
CHAM (820 AM)

Kingston
CFMK (96.3 FM)

Kitchener
CKGL (570 AM)

Leamington
CHYR (96.7 FM)

London
CJBX (92.7 FM)

Midland
CICZ (104.1 FM)

New Liskeard
CJTT (1230 AM)

North Bay
CKAT (101.9 FM)

Orillia
CICX (105.9 FM)

Ottawa
CKBY (105.3 FM)

Peterborough
CKQM (105.1 FM)

Sarnia
CKTY (1110 AM)

Sault Sainte Marie
CJQM (104.3 FM)

Smiths Falls
CJET (630 AM)

Sudbury
CIGM (790 AM)

Thunder Bay
CJLB (1230 AM)

Timmins
CKGB (750 AM)

Toronto
CKYC (1430 AM)
CISS (92.3 FM)

Trenton
CJTN (1270 AM)

Welland
CHOW (1470 AM)

Wingham
CKNX (920 AM)

PRINCE EDWARD ISLAND

Charlottetown
CFCY (630 AM)

Summerside
CJRW (1240 AM)

QUEBEC

Alma
CFGT (1270 AM)

St.-Georges-de-Beauce
CIRO (99.7 FM)

SASKATCHEWAN

Estevan
CJSL (1280 AM)

Meadow Lake
CJNS (1240 AM)

Melfort
CIVR (750 AM)

Moose Jaw
CHAB (800 AM)

North Battleford
CJNB (1050 AM)

Regina
CKRM (980 AM)
CHMX (92.1 FM)

Saskatoon
CJWW (600 AM)
CFQC (92.9 FM)

Shaunavon
CJSN (1490 AM)

Swift Current
CKSW (570 AM)

Weyburn
CFSL (1190 AM)

Yorkton
CJGX (940 AM)

YUKON TERRITORY

Whitehorse
CHON (98.1 FM)

The following record labels are some of the bigger players in the country music field. You may want to contact them if you have questions regarding specific releases.

A&M Records
1416 N. LaBrea Ave.
Los Angeles, CA 90028
(213) 469-2411
Fax: (213) 856-2600

Aaron Records
PO Box 291234
Nashville, TN 37229-1234
(615) 889-1147
Fax: (615) 885-3259

Acoustic Disc
PO Box 4143
San Rafael, CA 94913
(800) 221-DISC
(415) 499-0365
Fax: (415) 492-9602

ALMO Sounds
1904 Adelicia Ave.
Nashville, TN 37212
(615) 321-0820
Fax: (615) 329-1018

American Recordings
3500 W. Olive Ave.
Ste. 1550
Burbank, CA 91505

(818) 973-4545
Fax: (818) 973-4571

Arhoolie Records
10341 San Pablo Ave.
El Cerrito, CA 94530
(510) 525-7471
Fax: (510) 525-1204

Arista Records
7 Music Circle N
Nashville, TN 37203
(615) 780-9100
Fax: (615) 780-9190

Arista/Texas
7447 Bee Caves Rd., Ste. 208
Austin, TX 78746
(512) 329-9910
Fax: (512) 329-0411

Asylum Records
1906 Acken Ave.
Nashville, TN 37212
(615) 292-7990
Fax: (615) 292-8219

Atlantic Records—Nashville
1812 Broadway
Nashville, TN 37203
(615) 327-9394
Fax: (615) 329-2008

Bar/None Records
1 Newark St., Ste. 9
Hoboken, NJ 07030
(201) 795-9424
Fax: (201) 795-5048
E-mail: barnonerec@aol.com

Bear Family Records
PO Box 1154
D-27729 Hambergen
Germany
(+49) 4797-9300-0
Fax: (+49) 4794-9300-20
E-mail: bear@bear-family.de

Benson Music
365 Great Circle Rd.
Nashville, TN 37228
(615) 742-6977
Fax: (615) 742-6915

Bellamy Brothers Records
13917 Restless Ln.
Dade City, FL 33525
(904) 588-3628
Fax: (904) 588-3322

Bloodshot Records
912 W. Addison, Ste. 1
Chicago, IL 60613
(773) 248-8709
Fax: (773) 248-8702
E-mail: bludshot@mcs.com

BNA Records
1 Music Circle N
Nashville, TN 37203
(615) 780-4400
Fax: (615) 780-4464

Capitol—Nashville
3322 W. End Ave.
11th Floor
Nashville, TN 37203
(615) 269-2000
Fax: (615) 269-2034

Career Records
7 Music Circle N
Nashville, TN 37203
(615) 313-2400
Fax: (615) 313-2401

CMH Records
PO Box 39439
Los Angeles, CA 90039
(213) 663-8073
Fax: (213) 669-1470

Columbia Records—Nashville
34 Music Square E
Nashville, TN 37203
(615) 742-4321
Fax: (615) 254-3879

Compass Records
117 30th Ave. S
Nashville, TN 37212
(615) 320-7672

Country Music Foundation Records
4 Music Square E
Nashville, TN 37203
(615) 256-1639
Fax: (615) 255-2245

County Records
PO Box 191
Floyd, VA 24091

Crystal Clear Sound
4902 Don Dr.
Dallas, TX 75247
(214) 630-2957
Fax: (214) 630-5936
E-mail: crstlclr@onramp.net

Curb Records/MCG Curb
47 Music Square E
Nashville, TN 37203
(615) 321-5080
Fax: (615) 327-1964

Dead Reckoning Records
PO Box 159178
Nashville, TN 37215
(615) 292-7773
Fax: (615) 383-9571

Decca Records
60 Music Square E
Nashville, TN 37203
(615) 244-8944
Fax: (615) 880-7475

Discovery Records
2034 Broadway
Santa Monica, CA 90404
(310) 828-1033
Fax: (310) 828-1584

Drive Archive
10351 Santa Monica Blvd.,
Ste. 404
Los Angeles, CA 90025

East Side Digital
530 N. 3rd St.
Minneapolis, MN 55401
(800) 468-4177
(612) 375-0233
Fax: (612) 3359-9580

Elektra Entertainment
75 Rockefeller Plaza
New York, NY 10019
(212) 275-4000
Fax: (212) 974-9314

Epic Records—Nashville
34 Music Square E
Nashville, TN 37203
(615) 742-4321
Fax: (615) 254-3879

Freedom Records
PO Box 650032
Austin, TX 78765
(512) 708-8672
E-mail: freedom@eden.com

Giant Records
1514 South St.
Nashville, TN 37212
(615) 256-3110
Fax: (615) 259-4011

Green Lineet Records
43 Beaver Brook Rd.
Danbury, CT 06810
(203) 730-0333

Heyday Records
2325 Third St., #339
San Francisco, CA 94107
(415) 252-5590
(415) 252-5599
E-mail: heyday@well.com

HighTone Records
220 Fourth St., Ste. 101
Oakland, CA 94607
(510) 763-8500

Honest Entertainment Group
33 Music Square W, Ste. 100
Nashville, TN 37203
(615) 242-4452
Fax: (615) 242-4453

Imprint Records
209 10th Ave. S, #500
Nashville, TN 37203
(615) 244-9585
Fax: (615) 244-9586

International Marketing Group
(Deluxe, Hollywood/IMG,
Richmond, Starday, King)
1900 Elm Hill Pike
Nashville, TN 37210
(615) 889-8000
(800) 251-4040

Intersound Entertainment
3200 W. End Ave. Ste. 500
Nashville, TN 37203
(615) 783-1639
Fax: (615) 783-1640

Island Records
825 8th Ave.
New York, NY 10019
(212) 333-8000

Justice Records
3100 Alabama Court
Houston, TX 77027
(713) 520-6669
Fax: (713) 525-4444

Koch International
2 Tri-Harbor Court
Port Washington, NY 11050-4617
(516) 484-1000

Fax: (516) 484-4746

K-Tel International Inc.
2605 Fernbrook Ln. N
Minneapolis, MN 55447
(612) 559-6800
(800) 328-6640
Fax: (612) 559-6848

LaserLight Records
2500 Broadway Ave.
Santa Monica, CA 90404
(310) 826-6151

Little Dog Records Entertainment
223 W. Alameda Ave., Ste. 201
Burbank, CA 91502
(818) 557-1595
Fax: (818) 567-1682

Magnatone Entertainment
1516 16th Ave. S
Nashville, TN 37212
(615) 383-3600
Fax: (615) 383-0020

Malaco Records
1012 18th Ave. S
Nashville, TN 37212
(615) 327-0440
Fax: (615) 329-3964

Mammoth Records
1290 Ave. of the Americas
New York, NY 10104
(212) 707-2600
Fax: (212) 405-5585
E-mail: mammothpr@aol.com

Margaritaville Records
66 Music Square W
Nashville, TN 37203
(615) 329-2899
Fax: (615) 726-2897

MCA—Nashville
60 Music Square E
Nashville, TN 37203
(615) 244-8944
Fax: (615) 880-7410

Mercury—Nashville
66 Music Square W
Nashville, TN 37203
(615) 320-0110
Fax: (615) 327-4856

Mobile Fidelity Sound Lab
105 Morris St.

Sebastopol, CA 95472-3857
(707) 829-0134
(800) 423-5759

MoodFood Records
1381 Kildaire Farms Rd., Ste. 246
Cary, NC 27511
(919) 557-8311
Fax: (919) 319-6785

Music of the World
PO Box 3620
Chapel Hill, NC 27515-3620
(919) 932-9600
Fax: (919) 932-9700

MusicMasters
1710 Highway 35
Oakhurst, NJ 07755
(908) 531-3375
Fax: (908) 531-1505

Oh Boy Records/Blue Plate Music/Red Pajamas Music
33 Music Square W, Ste. 102-B
Nashville, TN 37203
(615) 742-1250
Fax: (615) 742-1360

Pinecastle/Webco Records
5108 S. Orange Ave.
Orlando, FL 32809
(407) 856-0245
Fax: (407) 858-0007

Plantation Records/Sun Entertainment Corporation
3106 Belmont Boulevard
Nashville, TN 37212
(615) 385-1960
Fax: (615) 385-1964

Playback Records
2241 N.E. 201st St.
Miami, FL 33180
(305) 935-4880
(305) 933-4007

Private Music
8750 Wilshire Blvd.
Beverly Hills, CA 90211
(310) 358-4500
Fax: (310) 358-4520

Quarterstick Records
PO Box 25342
Chicago, IL 60625
(773) 388-8888

Razor & Tie Records
214 Sullivan St., 4A
New York, NY 10012
Fax: (212) 473-9173
(212) 473-9174
E-mail: razrntie@aol.com

RCA Records—Nashville
One Music Circle N
Nashville, TN 37203
(615) 664-1200
Fax: (615) 664-1226

Rebel Records
PO Box 3057
Roanoke, VA 24015
(540) 343-5355

Red House Records
PO Box 4044
St. Paul, MN 55104
(612) 379-1089

Relix Records
PO Box 92
Brooklyn, NY 11229
(718) 258-0009
E-mail: relixrec@aol.com

Restless Records
1616 Vista Del Mar
Hollywood, CA 90028-6420
(213) 957-4357
Fax: (213) 957-4355

Reunion Records
2908 Poston Ave.
Nashville, TN 37203
(615) 320-9200
Fax: (615) 320-1734

Rhino Records
10635 Santa Monica Blvd.
Los Angeles, CA 90025

(310) 474-4778
Fax: (310) 441-6575

Rising Tide Entertainment
48 Music Square E
Nashville, TN 37203
(615) 254-5050
Fax: (615) 313-3700

River North—Nashville
1222 16th Ave. S, 3rd Floor
Nashville, TN 37212
(615) 327-0770
Fax: (615) 327-0011

Rounder Records
1 Camp St.
Cambridge, MA 02140
(617) 354-0700
Fax: (617) 491-1970

Rykodisc
Shetland Park
27 Congress St.
Salem, MA 01970
(508) 744-7678
(800) 232-7385
Fax: (508) 741-4506
E-mail: rykodisc@aol.com

Shanachie Records Corp.
37 E. Clinton St.
Newton, NJ 07860
(201) 579-7763

Sierra Records
PO Box 5853
Pasadena, CA 91117-0853
(818) 355-0181

Signature Sounds Recording Company
PO Box 106
Whately, MA 01093

(800) 694-5354
Fax: (413) 665-9036
E-mail: ssrc2@aol.com

Smithsonian/Folkways
Office of Folklife Programs
955 l'Enfant Plaza, Ste. 2600
Washington, DC 20560
(202) 287-3657

Sparrow Records
PO Box 5010
Brentwood, TN 37024-5010
(615) 371-6800
Fax: (615) 371-6997

Star Song Communications
2325 Crestmoor Rd.
Nashville, TN 37215
(615) 269-0196
Fax: (615) 385-6920

Step One Records
1300 Division St.
Nashville, TN 37203
(615) 255-3009
Fax: (615) 255-6282

Sugar Hill Records
PO Box 55300
Durham, NC 27717-5300
(919) 489-4349
Fax: (919) 489-6080

Twin/Tone Records
2541 Nicollet Ave. S
Minneapolis, MN 55404
(612) 874-2400
Fax: (612) 872-0646

Vanguard Records/Welk Music Group/Ranwood
1299 Ocean Ave., Ste. 800
Santa Monica, CA 90401-1095

(310) 451-5727
Fax: (310) 394-4148

Varese Sarabande Records
11846 Ventura Blvd., Ste. 130
Studio City, CA 91604
(818) 753-4143

Virgin Records
1790 Broadway, 20th Floor
New York, NY 10019
(212) 332-0400

Warner/Reprise Nashville
20 Music Square E
Nashville, TN 37203
(615) 748-8000
Fax: (615) 214-1567

Windham Hill
8750 Wilshire Blvd.
Beverly Hills, CA 90211-2713
(310) 358-4800
Fax: (415) 329-1512

Word, Inc.
3319 W. End Ave., Ste. 200
Nashville, TN 37203
(615) 385-9673
Fax: (615) 385-9696

Warner/Alliance
20 Music Square E
Nashville, TN 37203
(615) 748-8000
Fax: (615) 214-1567

Watermelon Records
PO Box 49056
Austin, TX 78756
(512) 472-6192
Fax: (512) 472-6249

musicHound MOVIES

Looking for a movie with a country theme? The following films—rated on a scale of 1–4 bones—are available on video, so you can enjoy them at home. (For more information on these and other movies, consult MusicHound's *big brother,* VideoHound's Golden Movie Retriever.)*

Baja Oklahoma
(1987)
A made-for-cable-television film about a country barmaid with dreams of being a country singer. Songs by Willie Nelson, Emmylou Harris and Billy Vera.
🎵

Ballad of Billie Blue
(1972)
A top country singer, whose wife betrayed him, has his heart broken and dreams shattered. Fortunately, he finds that God's love eases the pain.
🎵

Bells of Rosarita
(1945)
Roy Rogers helps foil an evil plan to swindle Dale Evans out of the circus she inherited. All-star western cast under the big top.
🎵🎵🎵

The Best Little Whorehouse in Texas
(1982; R)
Dolly Parton is the buxom owner of The Chicken Ranch, a house of ill-repute that may be closed down unless sheriff-boyfriend Burt Reynolds can think of a way out. Strong performances don't quite make up for the erratically comic script. Based on the long-running Broadway musical, in turn based on a story by Larry McMurtry.
🎵🎵

Big Show
(1937)
A western adventure about the making of a western adventure. Gene Autry jangles spurs aplenty in dual role.
🎵🎵

The Buddy Holly Story
(1978; PG)
An acclaimed biography of the famed 1950s pop star, spanning the years from his meteoric career's beginnings in Lubbock, Texas, to his tragic early death in the now famous plane crash. Gary Busey performs Holly's hits himself.
🎵🎵🎵🎵

Cassie
(1987; R)
Follows the rise of Cassie, a successful country-western singer, and documents all her trials along the way.
🎵

Coal Miner's Daughter
(1980; PG)
A strong bio of country singer Loretta Lynn, who rose from Appalachian poverty to Nashville riches. Sissy Spacek is perfect in the lead, and she even provides acceptable rendering of Lynn's tunes. Band drummer Levon Helm shines as Lynn's father, and Tommy Lee Jones is strong as Lynn's downhome husband. Uneven melodrama toward the end, but the film is still a good one.
🎵🎵🎵

The Concrete Cowboys
(1979)
Two bumbling cowboys from Montana come to the metropolis of Nashville and promptly turn detective to foil a blackmail scheme and locate a missing singer. Barbara Mandrell and Roy Acuff play themselves. Silly made-for-TV pilot of short-lived series.
🎵🎵

Cowboy & the Senorita
(1944)
A cowboy solves the mystery of a missing girl and wins her lovely cousin. The first film that paired Roy Rogers and Dale Evans, who went on to become a winning team, on- and off-screen.
🎵🎵

Electric Horseman
(1979; PG)
A journalist (Jane Fonda) sets out to discover the reason behind the kidnapping of a prized horse by an ex-rodeo star (Robert Redford). The alcoholic cowboy has taken the horse to return it to its native environment, away from the clutches of corporate greed. As Fonda investigates the story she falls in love with rebel Redford. Excellent Las Vegas and remote western settings.
🎵🎵🎵

Elvis: The Movie
(1979)
A made-for-television biography of the legendary singer, from his high school days to his Las Vegas comeback. Kurt Russell gives a convincing performance and lip syncs effectively to the voice of the

King (provided by country singer Ronnie McDowell).
𝄞𝄞𝄞

Falling from Grace
(1992; PG-13)
Bud Parks (John Mellencamp) is a successful country singer who, accompanied by his wife and daughter, returns to his small Indiana hometown to celebrate his grandfather's 80th birthday. He's tired of both his career and his marriage and finds himself taking up once again with an old girlfriend (Kay Lenz), who is not only married to Bud's brother but is also having an affair with his father. Bud believes he's better off staying in his old hometown but the problems caused by his return may change his mind. Surprisingly sedate, although literate, family drama with good ensemble performances. Actor-director debut for Mellencamp.
𝄞𝄞𝄞

Great Balls of Fire
(1989; PG-13)
A florid, comic-book film of the glory days of Jerry Lee Lewis, from his first band to stardom. Most of the drama is derived from his marriage to his 13-year-old cousin. Somewhat overacted but full of energy. The soundtrack features many of the "Killer's" greatest hits re-recorded by Lewis for the film.
𝄞𝄞𝄞

**Hank Williams, Sr.:
The Show He Never Gave**
(1992)
An imaginary concert performance and portrayal of the country-western legend. On the night of December 31, 1952, the last night of Hank Williams' life, the singer is expected at a concert in Ohio. Traveling in his pale blue Cadillac he decides to stop at a roadside bar and winds up

giving an intimate concert for the bar patrons, as he recounts the triumphs and sorrows of his life and career.
𝄞𝄞𝄞

Hard Part Begins
(198?)
A naive country singer gets sucked into the pratfalls of show business.
𝄞

Headin' for the Rio Grande
(1936)
A cowboy and his sheriff brother drive off cattle-rustlers in this western saga. Tex Ritter's film debut. Songs include "Campfire Love Song," "Jailhouse Lament" and "Night Herding Song."
𝄞

Honeysuckle Rose
(1980; PG)
A road-touring country-western singer, whose life is a series of one night stands, falls in love with an adoring young guitar player who has just joined his band. This nearly costs him his marriage when his wife, while waiting patiently for him at home, decides she's had enough. Easygoing performance by Willie Nelson, essentially playing himself.
𝄞𝄞𝄞

Honkytonk Man
(1982; PG)
Unsuccessful change-of-pace Clint Eastwood vehicle set during the Depression. Aging alcoholic country singer tries one last time to make it to Nashville, hoping to perform at the Grand Ole Opry. This time he takes his nephew (played by Eastwoood's real-life son) with him.
𝄞𝄞

Honkytonk Nights
(197?; R)
A honky-tonkin' romp through an evening in a country-west-

ern bar, featuring legendary topless dancer Carol Doda, Georgina ("Devil in Mrs. Jones") Spelvin and the music of The Hot Licks (minus front man Dan Hicks).
𝄞

**Living Proof: The
Hank Williams Jr. Story**
(1983)
TV biopic focusing on the country singer's hell-raising ways as he seeks to get out from under the shadow of his famous father and into the spotlight on his own right. Based on Williams Jr.'s autobiography; includes 10 songs by Sr. and Jr.
𝄞𝄞𝄞

Murder in Coweta County
(1983)
Andy Griffith and Johnny Cash are strong in this true-crime drama based on the book by Margaret Anne Barnes. Griffith is a Georgia businessman who thinks he's gotten away with murder; Cash is the lawman who tenaciously pursues him. Based on an actual 1948 case. Made for television.
𝄞𝄞𝄞

Nashville
(1975; R)
Robert Altman's stunning, brilliant film tapestry that follows the lives of 24 people during a political campaign/music festival in Nashville. Seemingly extemporaneous vignettes, actors playing themselves (Elliott Gould and Julie Christie), funny, touching, poignant character studies concerning affairs of the heart and despairs of the mind. Repeatedly blurs reality and fantasy.
𝄞𝄞𝄞𝄞

**The Night the Lights
Went Out in Georgia**
(1981; PG)
Loosely based on the popular hit song, the film follows a

brother and sister as they try to cash in on the country music scene in Nashville. Kristy McNichol is engaging.
𝄞𝄞

Payday
(1972)
Rip Torn stars as a declining country music star on tour in this portrayal of the seamy side of show business, from groupies to grimy motels. Well-written script and fine performances make this an engaging, if rather draining, drama not easily found on the big screen.
𝄞𝄞𝄞

Pure Country
(1992; PG)
An easygoing movie about a familiar subject is held together by the charm of George Strait (in his movie debut) and the rest of the cast. Strait plays a country music superstar, tired of the career glitz, who decides to get out and go back to his home in Texas. He falls in love with the spunky Isabel Glasser and decides to run his career his own way. Lesley Ann Warren is effective as his tough manager and old-time cowboy Rory Calhoun is finely weathered as Glasser's gruff dad.
𝄞𝄞𝄞

Rhinestone
(1984; PG)
A country singer claims she can turn anyone, even a cabbie, into a singing sensation. Stuck with Sylvester Stallone, Dolly Parton prepares her protege to sing at New York City's roughest country-western club, The Rhinestone. Only die-hard Dolly and Rocky fans need bother with this bunk. Some may enjoy watching the thick, New York accented Stallone learn how to properly pronounce dog ("dawg") in country lingo.
𝄞

Riders of the Rockies
(1937)
An honest cowboy turns rustler in order to trap a border gang. One of Tex Ritter's very best cowboy outings; good fun, and a very long fistfight with Charles "Blackie" King.
♫♫♫

Road to Nashville
(1967; G)
An agent travels to Nashville to enlist talent for a new musical. Why do so many of these semi-musicals insist on having a plot? Good music.
♫♫

Saturday Night Special
(1992; R)
Country singer/songwriter Travis (played by Nashville stalwart Billy Burnette) gets a job fronting the house band of Tennessee tavern owner T.J. (Rick Dean). Travis also takes up with ambitious Darlene (Maria Ford), who happens to be T.J.'s wife. But it's Darlene who has the brains in this unpleasant trio; she decides to get rid of hubby and sets Travis up to take the fall. It's all been done before (and better).
♫♫

A Smoky Mountain Christmas
(1986)
Dolly Parton gets away from it all in a secluded cabin that has been appropriated by a gang of orphans, and sings a half dozen songs. Innocuous seasonal country fun. Henry Winkler's TV directing debut.
♫♫

Songwriter
(1984; R)
A high-falutin' look at the lives and music of two popular country singers with, aptly, plenty of country tunes written and performed by the stars. Singer-businessman Willie Nelson needs Kris Kristofferson's help keeping a greedy investor at bay. Never mind the plot; plenty of good music.
♫♫♫

Strawberry Roan
(1933)
Ken Maynard plays a stubborn rodeo cowboy, out to prove he ain't whipped yet. One of Maynard's most popular films. Gene Autry bought the story to help him out in later years; the 1948 Autry "remake" uses only the title.
♫♫

Sweet Country Road
(1981)
A rock singer journeys to Nashville to try to cross over into country music.
♫♫

Sweet Dreams
(1985; PG-13)
Biography of country singer Patsy Cline (Jessica Lange), focusing mostly on her turbulent marriage. Her quick rise to stardom ended in an early death. Fine performances throughout. Cline's original recordings are used.
♫♫♫

Tender Mercies
(1983; PG)
A down-and-out country-western singer finds his life redeemed by the love of a good woman. Aided by Horton Foote's script, Robert Duvall, Tess Harper and Ellen Barkin keep this from being simplistic and sentimental. Duvall wrote as well as performed the songs in his Oscar-winning performance. Wonderful, life-affirming flick.
♫♫♫

The Thing Called Love
(1993; PG-13)
Take 1992's surprise hit *Singles* and replace grunge rock and Seattle with country-western and Nashville for this unsentimental tale of four twentysomething singles trying to make their mark in the world of country music. The idea for the plot comes from the real-life Bluebird Cafe—the place where all aspiring singers and songwriters want to perform. River Phoenix, Samantha Mathis, Dermot Mulroney and Sandra Bullock did their own singing; look for K.T. Oslin as the cafe owner. Phoenix's last completed film role.
♫♫♫

Urban Cowboy
(1980; PG)
A young Texas farmer comes to Houston to work in a refinery. After work he hangs out at Gilley's, a roadhouse bar. Here he and his friends, dressed in their cowboy gear, drink, fight and prove their manhood by riding a mechanical bull. Film made Debra Winger a star, was an up in John Travolta's roller coaster career and began the craze for country-western apparel and dance and them there mechanical bulls. Ride 'em, cowboy!
♫♫♫

What Comes Around
(1985; PG)
A good-ole-boy drama about a doped-up country singer who is kidnapped by his brother for his own good. The singer's evil manager sends his stooges out to find him. Might have been funny, but isn't. Good Jerry Reed songs; mildly interesting plot.
♫♫

Wild West
(1993)
Three Pakistani brothers, living in London, dream of making it big in Nashville and decide to form an American-style country-western band they call the Honky Tonk Cowboys. A little romance and lots of energy, but too many gags leave the film unfocused.
♫♫

Awards for country music are presented annually by a number of awarding bodies. Some of the more prestigious awards are included in this section. (Note: Song titles are in quotation marks, album titles italicized.)

ACADEMY OF COUNTRY MUSIC AWARDS

Presented annually by the Academy of Country Music.

ENTERTAINER OF THE YEAR

1970	Merle Haggard
1971	Freddie Hart
1972	Roy Clark
1973	Roy Clark
1974	Mac Davis
1975	Loretta Lynn
1976	Mickey Gilley
1977	Dolly Parton
1978	Kenny Rogers
1979	Willie Nelson
1980	Barbara Mandrell
1981	Alabama
1982	Alabama
1983	Alabama
1984	Alabama
1985	Alabama
1986	Hank Williams Jr.
1987	Hank Williams Jr.
1988	Hank Williams Jr.
1989	George Strait
1990	Garth Brooks
1991	Garth Brooks
1992	Garth Brooks
1993	Garth Brooks
1994	Reba McEntire
1995	Brooks & Dunn
1996	Brooks & Dunn

TOP MALE VOCALIST

1965	Buck Owens
1966	Merle Haggard
1967	Glen Campbell
1968	Glen Campbell
1969	Merle Haggard
1970	Merle Haggard
1971	Freddie Hart
1972	Merle Haggard
1973	Charlie Rich
1974	Merle Haggard
1975	Conway Twitty
1976	Mickey Gilley
1977	Kenny Rogers
1978	Kenny Rogers
1979	Larry Gatlin
1980	George Jones
1981	Merle Haggard
1982	Ronnie Milsap
1983	Lee Greenwood
1984	George Strait
1985	George Strait
1986	Randy Travis
1987	Randy Travis
1988	George Strait
1989	Clint Black
1990	Garth Brooks
1991	Garth Brooks
1992	Vince Gill
1993	Vince Gill
1994	Alan Jackson
1995	Alan Jackson
1996	George Strait

TOP FEMALE VOCALIST

1965	Bonnie Owens
1966	Bonnie Guitar
1967	Lynn Anderson
1968	Cathie Taylor
1969	Tammy Wynette
1970	Lynn Anderson
1971	Loretta Lynn
1972	Donna Fargo
1973	Loretta Lynn
1974	Loretta Lynn
1975	Loretta Lynn
1976	Crystal Gayle
1977	Crystal Gayle
1978	Barbara Mandrell
1979	Crystal Gayle
1980	Dolly Parton
1981	Barbara Mandrell
1982	Sylvia
1983	Janie Fricke
1984	Reba McEntire
1985	Reba McEntire
1986	Reba McEntire
1987	Reba McEntire
1988	K.T. Oslin
1989	Kathy Mattea
1990	Reba McEntire
1991	Reba McEntire
1992	Mary Chapin Carpenter
1993	Wynonna
1994	Reba McEntire
1995	Patty Loveless
1996	Patty Loveless

TOP VOCAL DUET

1965	Merle Haggard/Bonnie Owens
1966	Merle Haggard/Bonnie Owens
1967	Merle Haggard/Bonnie Owens
1968	Merle Haggard/Bonnie Owens
	Johnny Mosby/Jonie Mosby
1971	Conway Twitty/Loretta Lynn
1974	Conway Twitty/Loretta Lynn
1976	Conway Twitty/Loretta Lynn
1979	Joe Stampley/Moe Bandy
1980	Shelly West/David Frizzell
1982	Shelly West/David Frizzell
1983	Dolly Parton/Kenny Rogers
1984	The Judds
1985	The Judds
1986	The Judds
1987	The Judds
1988	The Judds
1989	The Judds
1990	The Judds
1991	Brooks & Dunn
1992	Brooks & Dunn
1993	Brooks & Dunn
1994	Brooks & Dunn
1995	Brooks & Dunn
1996	Brooks & Dunn

TOP VOCAL GROUP

1967	Sons of the Pioneers
1969	Kimberlys
1970	Kimberlys
1972	Statler Brothers
1973	Brush Arbor
1977	Statler Brothers
1978	Oak Ridge Boys
1981	Alabama
1982	Alabama
1983	Alabama
1984	Alabama
1985	Alabama
1986	Forester Sisters
1987	Highway 101
1988	Highway 101
1989	Restless Heart
1990	Shenandoah
1991	Diamond Rio
1992	Diamond Rio
1993	Little Texas
1994	The Mavericks
1995	The Mavericks
1996	Sawyer Brown

TOP NEW MALE VOCALIST

1965	Merle Haggard
1966	Billy Mize
1967	Jerry Inman
1968	Ray Sanders
1969	Freddy Weller
1970	Buddy Alan
1971	Tony Booth
1972	Johnny Rodriguez
1973	Dorsey Burnette
1974	Mickey Gilley
1975	Freddy Fender
1967	Moe Bandy
1977	Eddie Rabbit
1978	John Conlee
1979	R.C. Bannon
1980	Johnny Lee
1981	Ricky Skaggs
1982	Michael Martin Murphy
1983	Jim Glaser
1984	Vince Gill
1985	Randy Travis
1986	Dwight Yoakam
1987	Ricky Van Shelton
1988	Rodney Crowell
1989	Clint Black
1990	Alan Jackson
1991	Billy Dean
1992	Tracy Lawrence
1993	John Michael Montgomery
1994	Tim McGraw
1995	Bryan White
1996	Trace Adkins

TOP NEW FEMALE VOCALIST

1965	Kaye Adams
1966	Cathie Taylor
1967	Bobbie Gentry
1968	Cheryl Poole
1969	Donna Fargo
1970	Sammi Smith
1971	Barbara Mandrell
1972	Tanya Tucker
1973	Olivia Newton-John
1974	Linda Ronstadt
1975	Crystal Gayle
1976	Billie Jo Spears
1977	Debbie Boone
1978	Christy Lane
1979	Lacy J. Dalton
1980	Teri Gibbs
1981	Juice Newton
1982	Karen Brooks
1983	Gus Hardin
1984	Nicolette Larson
1985	Judy Rodman
1986	Holly Dunn
1987	K.T. Oslin
1988	Suzy Bogguss
1989	Mary Chapin Carpenter
1990	Shelby Lynne
1991	Trisha Yearwood
1992	Michelle Wright
1993	Faith Hill
1994	Chely Wright
1995	Shania Twain
1996	LeAnn Rimes

TOP NEW VOCAL GROUP/DUET

1989	Kentucky HeadHunters
1990	Pirates of the Mississippi
1991	Brooks & Dunn
1992	Confederate Railroad
1993	Gibson Miller Band
1994	The Mavericks
1995	Lonestar
1996	Ricochet

SONG

1966	"Apartment #9," Tammy Wynette
	Writer: Bobby Austin
1967	"It's Such a Pretty World Today," Wynn Stewart
	Writer: Dale Noe
1968	"Wichita Lineman," Glen Campbell
	Writer: Jimmy Webb
1969	"Okie from Muskogee," Merle Haggard
	Writers: Merle Haggard, Roy Edward Burris
1970	"For the Good Times," Ray Price
	Writer: Kris Kristofferson
1971	"Easy Loving," Freddie Hart
	Writer: Freddie Hart
1972	"Happiest Girl," Donna Fargo
	Writer: Donna Fargo
1973	"Behind Closed Doors," Charlie Rich
	Writer: Kenny O'Dell
1974	"Country Bumpkin," Cal Smith
	Writer: Don Wayne
1975	"Rhinestone Cowboy," Glen Campbell
	Writer: Larry Weiss
1976	"Don't the Girls Get Prettier at Closing Time," Mickey Gilley
	Writer: Baker Knight
1977	"Lucille," Kenny Rogers
	Writers: Roger Bowling, Hal Bynum
1978	"You Needed Me," Anne Murray
	Writer: Randy Goodrum
1979	"It's a Cheatin' Situation," Moe Bandy
	Writers: Sonny Throckmorton, Curly Putnam
1980	"He Stopped Loving Her Today," George Jones

Writers: Bobby Braddock, Curly Putnam

1981 "You're the Reason God Made Oklahoma," David Frizzell/Shelly West
Writers: Sandy Pinkard, Larry Collins

1982 "Are the Good Times Really Over," Merle Haggard
Writer: Merle Haggard

1983 "The Wind Beneath My Wings," Gary Morris
Writers: Larry Henley, Jeff Silbar

1984 "Why Not Me," the Judds
Writers: Harlan Howard, Sonny Throckmorton, Brent Maher

1985 "Lost in the Fifties (in the Still of the Night)," Ronnie Milsap
Writers: Mike Reid, Troy Seals, Fred Parris

1986 "On the Other Hand," Randy Travis
Writers: Paul Schlitz, Paul Overstreet

1987 "Forever and Ever Amen," Randy Travis
Writers: Don Schlitz, Paul Overstreet

1988 "Eighteen Wheels and a Dozen Roses," Kathy Mattea
Writers: Paul Nelson, Gene Nelson

1989 "Where've You Been," Kathy Mattea
Writers: Jon Vezner, Don Henry

1990 "The Dance," Garth Brooks
Writer: Tony Arata

1991 "Somewhere in My Broken Heart," Billy Dean
Writers: Billy Dean, Richard Leigh

1992 "I Still Believe in You," Vince Gill
Writers: John Jarvis, Vince Gill

1993 "I Love the Way You Love Me," John Michael Montgomery
Writers: Victoria Shaw, Chuck Cannon

1994 "I Swear," John Michael Montgomery
Writers: Gary Baker, Frank J. Myers

1995 "The Keeper of the Stars," Tracy Byrd
Writers: Dicky Lee, Danny Mayo, Karen Staley

1996 "Blue," LeAnn Rimes
Writer: Bill Mack

SINGLE

1968 "Little Green Apples," Roger Miller
1969 "Okie from Muskogee," Merle Haggard
1970 "For the Good Times," Ray Price
1971 "Easy Loving," Freddie Hart
1972 "Happiest Girl," Donna Fargo
1973 "Behind Closed Doors," Charlie Rich
1974 "Country Bumpkin," Cal Smith
1975 "Rhinestone Cowboy," Glen Campbell
1976 "Bring It on Home," Mickey Gilley
1977 "Lucille," Kenny Rogers
1978 "Tulsa Time," Don Williams
1979 "All the Gold in California," Larry Gatlin
1980 "He Stopped Loving Her Today," George Jones
1981 "Elvira," Oak Ridge Boys
1982 "Always on My Mind," Willie Nelson
1983 "Islands in the Stream," Kenny Roger/Dolly Parton
1984 "To All the Girls I've Loved Before," Willie Nelson/Julio Iglesias
1985 "Highwayman," Willie Nelson/Waylon Jennings/Johnny Cash/Kris Kristofferson
1986 "On the Other Hand," Randy Travis
1987 "Forever and Ever Amen," Randy Travis
1988 "Eighteen Wheels and a Dozen Roses," Kathy Mattea
1989 "A Better Man," Clint Black
1990 "Friends in Low Places," Garth Brooks
1991 "Don't Rock the Jukebox," Alan Jackson
1992 "Boot Scootin' Boogie," Brooks & Dunn
1993 "Chattahoochee," Alan Jackson
1994 "I Swear," John Michael Montgomery
1995 "Check Yes or No," George Strait
1996 "Blue," LeAnn Rimes

ALBUM

1967 *Gentle on My Mind*, Glen Campbell
1968 *Glen Campbell & Bobbie Gentry*, Glen Campbell/Bobbie Gentry

1969 *Okie from Muskogee*, Merle Haggard
1970 *For the Good Times*, Ray Price
1971 *Easy Loving* Freddie Hart
1972 *Happiest Girl*, Donna Fargo
1973 *Behind Closed Doors*, Charlie Rich
1974 *Back Home Again*, John Denver
1975 *Feelings*, Loretta Lynn/Conway Twitty
1976 *Gilley's Smoking*, Mickey Gilley
1977 *Kenny Rogers*, Kenny Rogers
1978 *Y'all Come Back Saloon*, Oak Ridge Boys
1979 *Straight Ahead*, Larry Gatlin
1980 *Soundtrack*, Urban Cowboy
1981 *Feels So Right*, Alabama
1982 *Always on My Mind*, Willie Nelson
1983 *The Closer You Get*, Alabama
1984 *Roll On*, Alabama
1985 *Does Ft. Worth Ever Cross Your Mind*, George Strait
1986 *Storms of Life*, Randy Travis
1987 *Trio*, Dolly Parton, Emmylou Harris, Linda Ronstadt
1988 *This Woman*, K.T. Oslin
1989 *Killin' Time*, Clint Black
1990 *No Fences*, Garth Brooks
1991 *Don't Rock the Jukebox*, Alan Jackson
1992 *Brand New Man*, Brooks & Dunn
1993 *A Lot About Livin*, Alan Jackson
1994 *Not a Moment Too Soon*, Tim McGraw
1995 *The Woman in Me*, Shania Twain
1996 *Blue Clear Sky*, George Strait

VIDEO OF THE YEAR

1985 "All My Rowdy Friends Are Coming Over Tonight," Hank Williams Jr.
1986 "Whoever's in New England," Reba McEntire
1987 "80's Ladies," K.T. Oslin
1988 "Young Country," Hank Williams Jr.
1989 "There's a Tear in My Beer," Hank Williams Jr.
1990 "The Dance," Garth Brooks
1991 "Is There Life Out There," Reba McEntire
1992 "Two Sparrows in a Hurricane," Tanya Tucker
1993 "We Shall Be Free," Garth Brooks
1994 "The Red Strokes," Garth Brooks
1995 "The Car," Jeff Carson
1996 "I Think About You," Collin Raye

TOURING BAND OF THE YEAR

1965	Buckaroos/Buck Owens
1966	Buckaroos/Buck Owens
1967	Buckaroos/Buck Owens
1968	Buckaroos/Buck Owens
1969	The Strangers/Merle Haggard
1970	The Strangers/Merle Haggard
1971	The Strangers/Merle Haggard
1972	The Strangers/Merle Haggard
1973	Brush Arbor
1974	The Strangers/Merle Haggard
1975	The Strangers/Merle Haggard
1976	Red Rose Express/Mickey Gilley
1977	Sons of Pioneers/Asleep at the Wheel
1978	Original Texas Playboys
1979	Charlie Daniels Band
1980	Charlie Daniels Band
1981	The Strangers/Merle Haggard
1982	Ricky Skaggs Band
1983	Ricky Skaggs Band
1984	Ricky Skaggs Band
1985	Ricky Skaggs Band
1986	Ricky Skaggs Band
1987	The Strangers/Merle Haggard
1988	Desert Rose Band
1989	Desert Rose Band
1990	Desert Rose Band

NON-TOURING BAND OF THE YEAR

1972	Tony Booth Band
1973	Sound Company
1974	Palomino Riders
1975	Palomino Riders
1976	Possum Holler
1977	Palomino Riders
1978	Rebel Playboys
1979	Midnight Riders
1980	Palomino Riders
1981	Desperados
1982	Desperados
1983	The Tennesseans
1984	The Tennesseans
1985	Nashville Now Band
1986	Nashville Now Band
1987	Nashville Now Band
1988	Nashville Now Band
1989	Nashville Now Band
1990	Boy Howdy

GUITAR

1965	Phil Baugh
1966	Jim Bryant
1967	Jim Bryant
1968	Jim Bryant
1969	Al Bruno/Jerry Inman
1970	Al Bruno
1971	Al Bruno
1972	Al Bruno
1973	Al Bruno
1974	Al Bruno
1975	Jerry Inman/Russ Hanson
1976	Danny Michaels
1977	Roy Clark
1978	James Burton
1979	Al Bruno
1980	Al Bruno
1981	James Burton
1982	Al Bruno
1983	Reggie Young
1984	James Burton
1985	James Burton
1986	Chet Atkins
1987	Chet Atkins
1988	Al Bruno
1989	Brent Rowan
1990	John Jorgenson
1991	John Jorgenson
1992	John Jorgenson
1993	Brent Mason
1994	Brent Mason
1995	Brent Mason
1996	Brent Mason

FIDDLE

1965	Billy Armstrong
1966	Billy Armstrong
1967	Billy Armstrong
1968	Billy Armstrong
1969	Billy Armstrong
1970	Billy Armstrong
1971	Billy Armstrong
1972	Billy Armstrong
1973	Billy Armstrong
1974	Billy Armstrong
1975	Billy Armstrong
1976	Billy Armstrong
1977	Billy Armstrong
1978	Johnny Gimble
1979	Johnny Gimble
1980	Johnny Gimble
1981	Johnny Gimble
1982	Johnny Gimble
1983	Johnny Gimble
1984	Johnny Gimble
1985	Johnny Gimble
1986	Mark O'Connor
1987	Johnny Gimble
1988	Mark O'Connor
1989	Mark O'Connor
1990	Mark O'Connor
1991	Mark O'Connor
1992	Mark O'Connor
1993	Mark O'Connor
1994	Mark O'Connor
1995	Rob Hajacos
1996	Stuart Duncan

STEEL GUITAR

1965	Red Rhodes
1966	Ralph Monney/Tom Brumley
1967	Red Rhodes
1968	Red Rhodes
1969	Buddy Emmons
1970	Jay Dee Maness
1971	Jay Dee Maness
1972	Buddy Emmons
1973	Red Rhodes
1974	Jay Dee Maness
1975	Jay Dee Maness
1976	Jay Dee Maness
1977	Buddy Emmons
1978	Buddy Emmons
1979	Buddy Emmons
1980	Buddy Emmons/Jay Dee Maness
1981	Buddy Emmons
1982	Jay Dee Maness
1983	Jay Dee Maness
1984	Buddy Emmons
1985	Buddy Emmons
1986	Jay Dee Maness
1987	Jay Dee Maness
1988	Jay Dee Maness
1989	Jay Dee Maness
1990	Jay Dee Maness
1991	Paul Franklin
1992	Jay Dee Maness
1993	Jay Dee Maness
1994	Paul Franklin
1995	Paul Franklin
1996	Paul Franklin

DRUMS

1965	Muddy Berry
1966	Jerry Wiggins
1967	Pee Wee Adams
1968	Jerry Wiggins
1969	Jerry Wiggins
1970	Archie Francis
1971	Jerry Wiggins
1972	Jerry Wiggins
1973	Jerry Wiggins
1974	Jerry Wiggins
1975	Archie Francis
1976	Archie Francis
1977	Archie Francis/George Manz
1978	Archie Francis
1979	Archie Francis
1980	Archie Francis
1981	Buddy Harmon
1982	Archie Francis

AWARDS

1983	Archie Francis
1984	Larrie London
1985	Archie Francis
1986	Larrie London
1987	Archie Francis
1988	Steve Duncan
1989	Steve Duncan
1990	Steve Duncan
1991	Eddie Bayers
1992	Eddie Bayers
1993	Eddie Bayers
1994	Eddie Bayers
1995	Eddie Bayers
1996	Eddie Bayers

BASS

1965	Bob Morris
1966	Bob Morris
1967	Red Wooten
1969	Billy Graham
1970	Billy Graham/Doyle Holly
1971	Larry Booth
1972	Larry Booth
1973	Larry Booth
1974	Billy Graham
1975	Billy Graham
1976	Curtis Stone
1977	Larry Booth
1978	Rod Culpepper
1979	Billy Graham
1980	Curtis Stone
1981	Joe Osborn/Curtis Stone
1982	Red Wooten
1983	Joe Osborn
1984	Joe Osborn
1985	Joe Osborn
1986	Emory Gordy Jr.
1987	Emory Gordy Jr./David Hungate
1988	Curtis Stone
1989	Michael Rhodes
1990	Bill Bryson
1991	Roy Huskey Jr.
1992	Glenn Worf
1993	Glenn Worf
1994	Glenn Worf
1995	Glenn Worf
1996	Glenn Worf

KEYBOARD

1965	Billy Liebert
1966	Billy Liebert
1967	Earl Ball
1968	Earl Ball
1969	Floyd Cramer
1970	Floyd Cramer
1971	Floyd Cramer
1972	Floyd Cramer

1973	Floyd Cramer
1974	Floyd Cramer
1975	Jerry Lee Lewis
1976	Hargus"Pig" Robbins
1977	Hargus"Pig" Robbins
1978	Jimmy Pruett
1979	Hargus"Pig" Robbins
1980	Hargus"Pig" Robbins
1981	Hargus"Pig" Robbins
1982	Hargus"Pig" Robbins
1983	Floyd Cramer
1984	Hargus"Pig" Robbins
1985	Glen Hardin
1986	John Hobbs
1987	John Hobbs/Ronnie Milsap
1988	John Hobbs
1989	Skip Edwards
1990	John Hobbs
1991	Matt Rollings
1992	Matt Rollings
1993	Matt Rollings
1994	Matt Rollings
1995	Matt Rollings
1996	Matt Rollings

SPECIALTY INSTRUMENT

1969	John Hartford (Banjo)
1977	Charlie McCoy (Harmonica)
1978	Charlie McCoy (Harmonica)
1979	Charlie McCoy (Harmonica)
1980	Charlie McCoy (Harmonica)
1981	Charlie McCoy (Harmonica)
1982	James Burton (Dobro)
1983	Charlie McCoy (Harmonica)
1984	Ricky Skaggs (Mandolin)
1985	James Burton (Dobro)
1986	James Burton (Dobro)
1987	Jerry Douglas (Dobro)
	Ricky Skaggs (Mandolin)
1988	Charlie McCoy (Harmonica)
1989	Jerry Douglas (Dobro)
1990	Jerry Douglas (Dobro)
1991	Jerry Douglas (Dobro)
1992	Jerry Douglas (Dobro)
1993	Terry McMillan (Harmonica/Percussion)
1994	Terry McMillan (Harmonica/Percussion)
1995	Terry McMillan (Harmonica)
1996	Terry McMillan (Harmonica/Percussion)

ARTIST OF THE DECADE

1969	Marty Robbins (1960s)
1979	Loretta Lynn (1970s)
1989	Alabama (1980s)

PIONEER AWARD

1968	Uncle Art Satherley
1969	Bob Wills
1970	Tex Ritter
1970	Patsy Montana
1971	Tex Williams
1971	Bob Nolan
1971	Stuart Hamblen
1972	Gene Autry
1972	Cliffie Stone
1973	Hank Williams
1974	Johnny Bond
1974	Merle Travis
1974	Tennessee Ernie Ford
1975	Roy Rogers
1976	Owen Bradley
1977	Sons of the Pioneers
1978	Eddie Dean
1979	Patti Page
1980	Ernest Tubb
1981	Leo Fender
1982	Chet Atkins
1983	Eddy Arnold
1984	Roy Acuff
1985	Kitty Wells
1986	Minnie Pearl
1987	Roger Miller
1988	Buck Owens
1990	Johnny Cash
1991	Willie Nelson
1992	George Jones
1993	Charley Pride
1994	Loretta Lynn
1995	Merle Haggard
1996	Roy Clark

JIM REEVES MEMORIAL AWARD

1969	Joe Allison
1970	Bill Boyd
1971	Roy Rogers
1972	Thurston Moore
1973	Sam Luvullo
1974	Merv Griffin
1975	Dinah Shore
1976	Roy Clark
1977	Jim Halsey
1978	Joe Cates
1979	Bill Ward
1980	Ken Kragen
1981	Al Gallico
1982	Jo Walker-Meader
1994	Garth Brooks

MISC. INDIVIDUAL AWARDS

1965	Roger Miller (Man of the Year)
	Roger Miller (Songwriter)
	Billy Mize (TV Personality)

Ken Nelson (Producer/A&R Man)
Jack McFadden (Talent Manager)
Central Songs (Publisher)
Billboard (Publication)
1966 Dean Martin (Man of the Year)
Billy Mize (TV Personality)
Ken Nelson (Producer/A&R Man)
Jack McFadden (Talent Manager)
Central Songs (Publisher)
1967 Joey Bishop (Man of the Year)
Billy Mize (TV Personality)
Al Delory (Producer/A&R Man)
Freeway Music (Publisher)
1968 Tom Smothers (Man of the Year)
Glen Campbell (TV Personality)
Nudie (Director's Award)
1969 Frank Peppiatt/John Aylesworth
(Man of the Year)
Roy Clark (Comedy Act)
Johnny Cash (TV Personality)
1970 Hugh Cherry (Man of the Year)
Roy Clark (Comedy Act)
Johnny Cash (TV Personality)
Billboard (Publication)
1971 Walter Knott (Man of the Year)
Roy Clark (Comedy Act)
Glen Campbell (TV Personality)
1972 Lawrence Welk (Man of the Year)
Roy Clark (TV Personality)
1977 Johnny Paycheck (Career Achievement)
1980 George Burns (Special Achievement)
1986 Carl Perkins (Career Achievement)
1993 John Anderson (Career Achievement)
Mr. Bill Presents (Talent Buyer/Promoter)
1994 George Moffett (Talent Buyer/Promoter)
1995 Jeff Foxworthy (Special Achievement)
George Moffett (Talent Buyer/Promoter)
1996 Bob Romeo (Talent Buyer/Promoter)

RADIO STATION OF THE YEAR

1970 KLAC (Los Angeles, CA)
1971 KLAC (Los Angeles, CA)
1972 KLAC (Los Angeles, CA)
1973 KLAC (Los Angeles, CA)
1974 KLAC (Los Angeles, CA)
1975 KLAC (Los Angeles, CA)
1976 KLAC (Los Angeles, CA)
1977 KGBS (Los Angeles, CA)
1978 KVOO (Tulsa, OK)

1979 KFDI (Wichita, KS)
1980 KLAC (Los Angeles, CA)
1981 WPLO (Atlanta, GA)
1982 KIKK (Houston, TX)
1983 KRMD (Shreveport, LA)
1984 KVOO (Tulsa, OK)
1985 WAMZ (Louisville, KY)
1986 KNIX (Phoenix, AZ)
1987 KNIX (Phoenix, AZ)
1988 WSIX (Nashville, TN)
1989 WSIX (Nashville, TN)
1990 WSIX (Nashville, TN)
1991 WAMZ (Louisville, KY)
1992 KNIX (Phoenix, AZ)
1993 KNIX (Phoenix, AZ)
1994 WSIX (Nashville, TN)
1995 WSIX (Nashville, TN)
1996 WSIX (Nashville, TN)

TOP DISC JOCKEY OF THE YEAR

1965 Biff Collie
1966 Bob Kinglsey/Biff Collie
1968 Larry Scott/Tex Williams
1969 Dick Haynes
1970 Corky Mayberry
1971 Larry Scott
1972 Larry Scott
1973 Craig Scott
1974 Larry Scott
1975 Billy Parker
1976 Charlie Douglas
1977 Billy Parker
1978 Billy Parker
1979 King Edward IV
1980 Sammy Jackson
1981 Arch Yancey
1982 Lee Arnold
1983 Rhubarb Jones
1984 Coyote Calhoun/Don Hollander/Billy Parker
1985 Eddie Edwards
1986 Chris Taylor
1987 Jim Tabor
1988 Jon Conlon
1989 Jon Conlon, Dandalion
1990 Gerry House
1991 Gerry House
1993 Tim Hatrick & Willy D. Loon
1994 Gerry House
1995 Gerry House
1996 Gerry House

NIGHTCLUB OF THE YEAR

1965 Palomino
1966 Palomino
1967 Palomino
1968 Palomino, Golden Nugget

1969 Palomino
1970 Palomino
1971 Palomino
1972 Palomino
1973 Palomino
1974 Palomino
1975 Palomino
1976 Palomino
1977 Palomino
1978 Palomino
1979 Palomino
1980 Palomino, Gilley's
1981 Billy Bob's Texas
1982 Gilley's
1983 Gilley's
1984 Gilley's
1985 Billy Bob's Texas
1986 Crazy Horse Steak House and Saloon
1987 Crazy Horse Steak House and Saloon
1988 Crazy Horse Steak House and Saloon
1989 Crazy Horse Steak House and Saloon
1990 Crazy Horse Steak House and Saloon
1991 Crazy Horse Steak House and Saloon
1992 Billy Bob's Texas
1993 Toolie's Country
1994 Billy Bob's Texas
1995 Crazy Horse Steak House and Saloon
1996 Crazy Horse Steak House and Saloon

AMERICAN MUSIC AWARDS

Presented annually, based on votes cast by a cross-section of the American record-buying public. (Note: Only country music categories are listed.)

FAVORITE MALE COUNTRY ARTIST

1974 Charley Pride
1975 Charlie Rich
1976 John Denver
1977 Charley Pride
1978 Conway Twitty
1979 Kenny Rogers
1980 Kenny Rogers
1981 Kenny Rogers
1982 Willie Nelson
1983 Kenny Rogers
1984 Willie Nelson

1985	Kenny Rogers
1986	Willie Nelson
1987	Willie Nelson
1988	Randy Travis
1989	Randy Travis
1990	Randy Travis
1991	George Strait
1992	Garth Brooks
1993	Garth Brooks
1994	Garth Brooks
1995	Garth Brooks
1996	Garth Brooks
1997	Garth Brooks

FAVORITE FEMALE COUNTRY ARTIST

1974	Lynn Anderson
1975	Olivia Newton-John
1976	Olivia Newton-John
1977	Loretta Lynn
1978	Loretta Lynn
1979	Crystal Gayle
1980	Crystal Gayle
1981	Barbara Mandrell
1982	Barbara Mandrell
1983	Barbara Mandrell
1984	Barbara Mandrell
1985	Barbara Mandrell
1986	Crystal Gayle
1987	Barbara Mandrell
1988	Reba McEntire
1989	Reba McEntire
1990	Reba McEntire
1991	Reba McEntire
1992	Reba McEntire
1993	Reba McEntire
1994	Reba McEntire
1995	Reba McEntire
1996	Reba McEntire
1997	Shania Twain

FAVORITE COUNTRY BAND, DUO OR GROUP

1974	The Carter Family
1975	Conway Twitty & Loretta Lynn
1976	Donny & Marie Osmond
1977	Conway Twitty & Loretta Lynn
1978	Conway Twitty & Loretta Lynn
1979	The Statler Brothers
1980	The Statler Brothers
1981	The Statler Brothers
1982	The Oak Ridge Boys
1983	Alabama
1984	Alabama
1985	Alabama
1986	Alabama
1987	Alabama
1988	Alabama

1989	Alabama
1990	Alabama
1991	Alabama
1992	Alabama
1993	Alabama
1994	Alabama
1995	Alabama
1996	Alabama
1997	Brooks & Dunn

FAVORITE NEW COUNTRY ARTIST

1989	Patty Loveless
1990	Clint Black
1991	Kentucky HeadHunters
1992	Trisha Yearwood
1993	Billy Ray Cyrus
1994	John Michael Montgomery
1995	Tim McGraw
1996	Shania Twain
1997	LeAnn Rimes

FAVORITE COUNTRY SINGLE

1974	"Behind Closed Doors," Charlie Rich
1975	"The Most Beautiful Girl," Charlie Rich
1976	"Rhinestone Cowboy," Glen Campbell
1977	"Blue Eyes Cryin' in the Rain," Willie Nelson
1978	"Lucille," Kenny Rogers
1979	"Blue Bayou," Linda Ronstadt
1980	"Sleeping Single in a Double Bed," Barbara Mandrell
1981	"Coward of the County," Kenny Rogers
1982	"Could I Have this Dance," Anne Murray/"On the Road Again," Willie Nelson (tie)
1983	"Love Will Turn You Around," Kenny Rogers
1984	"Islands in the Stream," Kenny Rogers & Dolly Parton
1985	"Islands in the Stream," Kenny Rogers & Dolly Parton
1986	"Forgiving You Was Easy," Willie Nelson
1987	"Grandpa," the Judds
1988	"Forever and Ever, Amen," Randy Travis
1989	"I Told You So," Randy Travis
1990	"Deeper than the Holler," Randy Travis
1991	"If Tomorrow Never Comes," Garth Brooks
1992	"The Thunder Rolls," Garth Brooks

1993	"Achy Breaky Heart," Billy Ray Cyrus
1994	"Chattahoochee," Alan Jackson
1995	"Whenever You Come Around," Vince Gill

FAVORITE COUNTRY ALBUM

1974	*A Sun Shiny Day*, Charley Pride
1975	*Let Me Be There*, Olivia Newton-John
1976	*Back Home Again*, John Denver
1977	*Rhinestone Cowboy*, Glen Campbell
1978	*New Harvest, First Gathering*, Dolly Parton
1979	*Ten Years of Gold*, Kenny Rogers
1980	*The Gambler*, Kenny Rogers
1981	*The Gambler*, Kenny Rogers
1982	*Greatest Hits*, Kenny Rogers
1983	*Always on My Mind*, Willie Nelson
1984	*The Closer You Get*, Alabama
1985	*Eyes That See in the Dark*, Kenny Rogers
1986	*40 Hour Week*, Alabama
1987	*Greatest Hits*, Alabama
1988	*Always & Forever*, Randy Travis
1989	*Always & Forever*, Randy Travis
1990	*Old 8 x 10*, Randy Travis
1991	*Reba Live*, Reba McEntire
1992	*No Fences*, Garth Brooks
1993	*For My Broken Heart*, Reba McEntire
1994	*A Lot About Livin' (and a Little 'Bout Love)*, Alan Jackson
1995	*Read My Mind*, Reba McEntire
1996	*Hits*, Garth Brooks
1997	*Blue Clear Sky*, George Strait

FAVORITE COUNTRY VIDEO

1984	"Dixieland Delight," Alabama
1985	"A Little Good News," Anne Murray
1986	"Highwayman," Willie Nelson, Waylon Jennings, Kris Kristofferson, Johnny Cash
1987	"Grandpa," the Judds
1988	"Forever and Ever, Amen," Randy Travis

FAVORITE COUNTRY VIDEO ARTIST— MALE

1985	Willie Nelson
1986	Hank Williams Jr.
1987	George Jones

FAVORITE COUNTRY VIDEO ARTIST FEMALE

1985	Anne Murray
1986	Crystal Gayle
1987	Reba McEntire

FAVORITE COUNTRY VIDEO ARTIST— DUO OR GROUP

1985	The Oak Ridge Boys
1986	The Highwayman (Willie Nelson, Waylon Jennings, Kris Kristofferson, Johnny Cash)
1987	Alabama

CANADIAN COUNTRY MUSIC ASSOCIATION AWARDS

Presented annually by the Canadian Country Music Association.

ENTERTAINER OF THE YEAR

1982	Family Brown
1983	Family Brown
1984	Ronnie Prophet
1985	Dick Damron
1986	Family Brown
1987	k.d. lang
1988	k.d. lang
1989	k.d. lang
1990	k.d. lang
1991	Rita Macneil
1992	Rita Macneil
1993	Michelle Wright
1994	Prairie Oyster
1995	Michelle Wright
1996	Shania Twain

MALE VOCALIST OF THE YEAR

1982	Terry Carisse
1983	Dick Damron
1984	Terry Carisse
1985	Terry Carisse
1986	Terry Carisse
1987	Ian Tyson
1988	Ian Tyson
1989	Gary Fjellgaard
1990	George Fox
1991	George Fox
1992	Ian Tyson
1993	George Fox
1994	Charlie Major
1995	Charlie Major
1996	Charlie Major

FEMALE VOCALIST OF THE YEAR

1982	Carroll Baker
1983	Marie Bottrell
1984	Marie Bottrell
1985	Carroll Baker
1986	Anita Perras
1987	Anita Perras
1988	k.d. lang
1989	k.d. lang
1990	Michelle Wright
1991	Michelle Wright
1992	Michelle Wright
1993	Michelle Wright
1994	Patricia Conroy
1995	Shania Twain
1996	Shania Twain

DUO OF THE YEAR

1983	Donna & LeRoy Anderson
1984	Glory Anne Carriere/Ronnie Prophet
1985	Anita Perras/Tim Taylor
1986	Anita Perras/Tim Taylor
1987	Anita Perras/Tim Taylor
1988	Anita Perras/Tim Taylor
1989	Gary Fjellgaard/Linda Kidder
1990	Gary Fjellgaard/Linda Kidder
1991	The Johner Brothers

GROUP OF THE YEAR

1982	Family Brown
1983	Family Brown
1984	Family Brown
1985	The Mercey Brothers
1986	Family Brown
1987	Family Brown
1988	Family Brown
1989	Family Brown
1990	Prairie Oyster
1991	Prairie Oyster

VOCAL DUO OR GROUP OF THE YEAR

1992	Prairie Oyster
1993	The Rankin Family
1994	Prairie Oyster
1995	Prairie Oyster
1996	Prairie Oyster

VOCAL COLLABORATION OF THE YEAR

1992	Gary Fjellgaard/Linda Kidder
1993	Cassandra Vasik/Russell deCarle
1994	Quartette
1995	Jim Witter/Cassandra Vasik

VISTA (RISING STAR)

1982	Ruth Ann
1983	Kelita Haverland
1984	Roni Sommers
1985	Ginny Mitchell
1986	J.K. Gulley
1987	k.d. lang
1988	Blue Rodeo
1989	George Fox
1990	Patricia Conroy
1991	South Mountain
1992	Cassandra Vasik
1993	The Rankin Family
1994	Susan Aglukark
1995	Farmer's Daughter
1996	Terri Clark

SOCAN SONG OF THE YEAR

1982	"Some Never Stand a Chance" Writers: Family Brown
1983	"Raised on Country Music" Writers: Family Brown
1984	"Jesus It's Me Again" Writer: Dick Damron
1985	"Counting the I Love You's" Writers: Terry Carisse, Bruce Rawlins
1986	"Now and Forever" Writers: D. Fosterm, J. Vallance, C. Goodrum
1987	"Heroes" Writer: Gary Fjellgaard
1988	"One Smokey Rose" Writer: Tim Taylor
1989	"Town of Tears" Writers: Barry Brown, Randall Prescott, Bruce Campbell
1990	"Pioneers" Writer: Barry Brown
1991	"Lonely You, Lonely Me" Writer: Joan Besen
1992	"Did You Fall in Love with Me" Writer: Joan Besen
1993	"Backroads" Writer: Charlie Major
1994	"I'm Gonna Drive You Out of My Mind" Writers: Charlie Major, B. Brown
1995	"Whose Bed Have Your Boots Been Under?" Writers: Shania Twain, Robert John Lange
1996	"My Heart Has a History" Writers: Paul Brandt, Mark D. Sanders

SINGLE OF THE YEAR

1982	"Some Never Stand a Chance," Family Brown

1983	"Raised on Country Music," Family Brown
1984	"A Little Good News," Anne Murray
1985	"Riding on the Wind," Gary Fjellgaard
1986	"Now and Forever (You and Me)," Anne Murray
1987	"Navajo Rug," Ian Tyson
1988	"One Smokey Rose," Anita Perras
1989	"Town of Tears," Family Brown
1990	"Goodbye, So Long, Hello," Prairie Oyster
1991	"New Kind of Love," Michelle Wright
1992	"Take It Like a Man," Michelle Wright
1993	"He Would Be Sixteen," Michelle Wright
1994	"I'm Gonna Drive You Out of My Mind," Charlie Major
1995	"Any Man of Mine," Shania Twain
1996	"Better Things to Do," Terri Clark

ALBUM OF THE YEAR

1982	*Raised on Country Music*, Family Brown
1983	*Raised on Country Music*, Family Brown
1984	*Repeat After Me*, Family Brown
1985	*Closest Thing to You*, Terry Carisse
1986	*Feel the Fire*, Family Brown
1987	*Cowboyography*, Ian Tyson
1988	*Shadowland*, k.d. lang
1989	*Shadowland*, k.d. lang
1990	*Absolute Torch and Twang*, k.d. lang
1991	*Michelle Wright*, Michelle Wright
1992	*Everybody Knows*, Prairie Oyster
1993	*Bad Day for Trains*, Patricia Conroy
1994	*The Other Side*, Charlie Major
1995	*The Woman in Me*, Shania Twain
1996	*Terri Clark*, Terri Clark

TOP SELLING ALBUM (FOREIGN OR DOMESTIC)

1984	*Eyes that Could See in the Dark*, Kenny Rogers
1985	*Once Upon a Christmas*, Dolly Parton/Kenny Rogers
1986	*Hymns of Gold*, Carroll Baker
1987	*Storms of Life*, Randy Travis
1988	*Always & Forever*, Randy Travis
1989	*Old 8 x 10*, Randy Travis
1990	*Rita*, Rita MacNeil

1991	*Home I'll Be*, Rita MacNeil
1992	*Ropin' the Wind*, Garth Brooks
1993	*Some Gave All*, Billy Ray Cyrus
1994	*In Pieces*, Garth Brooks
1995	*The Hits*, Garth Brooks
1996	*Fresh Horses*, Garth Brooks

RECORD PRODUCER OF THE YEAR

1982	Jack Feeney
1983	Dallas Harms
1984	Dallas Harms/Mike Francis
1985	Terry Carisse
1986	Mike Francis
1987	Mike Francis
1988	Randall Prescott
1989	Randall Prescott
1990	Randall Prescott
1991	Randall Prescott
1992	Randall Prescott
1993	Randall Prescott
1994	Randall Prescott
1995	Randall Prescott
1996	Randall Prescott

ALBUM GRAPHICS OF THE YEAR

1990	*Absolute Torch and Twang*, Jeri Helden/k.d. lang
1991	*Michelle Wright*, Susan Mendola
1992	*Bad Day for Trains*, Rosamond Norbury
1993	*Feels Like Home*, Kathi Prosser
1994	*Already Restless*, Bill Johnson
1995	*This Child*, Patrick Duffy/Tom Chaggaris
1996	*Endless Seasons*, Patrick Duffy/Tom Chaggaris

VIDEO OF THE YEAR

1990	"Pioneers," Bob Holbrook
1991	"Springtime in Alberta," Michael Watt
1992	"Take It Like a Man," Steven Goldmann
1993	"He Would Be Sixteen," Steven Goldmann
1994	"Stolen Moments," Jim Witter
1995	"Any Man of Mine," Shania Twain
1996	"(If You're Not in it For Love) I'm Outta Here," Shania Twain

VIDEO DIRECTOR OF THE YEAR

1994	Keith Harrick, "Stolen Moments"
1995	Deborah Samuel, "Black-Eyed Susan"
1996	Steven Goldman, "(If You're Not in it for Love) I'm Outta Here"

COUNTRY MUSIC PERSON OF THE YEAR

1982	Ron Sparling
1983	Gordon Burnett
1984	Neville Wells
1986	Joe Brown
1987	Larry Delaney
1988	Larry Delaney
1989	Larry Delaney
1990	Larry Delaney
1991	Larry Delaney
1992	Michelle Wright
1993	Larry Delaney
1994	Tom Tompkins
1995	Leonard T. Rambeau
1996	Larry Delaney

HALL OF HONOUR INDUCTEES

1984	Will Carter
	Tommy Hunter
	William Harold Moon
	Orval Prophet
1985	Hank Snow
	Don Messer
1986	Papa Joe Brown
1987	Lucille Starr
1988	Jack Feeney
1989	Ian Tyson
	Don Grashey
1990	Gordie Tapp
	Ron Sperling
1991	The Rhythm Pals
	Hugh Joseph
1992	Carroll Baker
	Gordon Burnett
1993	Bob Nolan
	Hank Jones
1994	Hank Smith
	Dick Damron
1995	Gene MacLellan
	Stan Klees
1996	Myrna Lorrie
	Larry Delaney

OUTSTANDING INTERNATIONAL SUPPORT AWARD

1988	Jo Walker Meader
1989	George Hamilton IV
1990	Kees de Haan
1991	Bart Barton
	Tony Migliori
1992	Tim Dubois
1993	CTV Television Network
1995	Leonard T. Rambeau
1996	Paul Corbin

C. F. MARTIN LIFETIME ACHIEVEMENT AWARD

1981	Wilf Carter
1982	Dick Damron
1983	Barry Brown
1984	Papa Joe Brown
1985	Tommy Hunter
1987	The Mercey Brothers
1988	Ronnie Prophet
1989	Carroll Baker
1990	Jack Feeney

TMI FENDER GUITAR HUMANITARIAN AWARD

1989	Wayne Rostad
1990	Gary Fjellgaard

C. F. MARTIN HUMANITARIAN AWARD

1991	Carroll Baker
1992	John Allan Cameron
1993	"A Song For Brent"
1995	Joan Kennedy
1996	Tom Jackson

RADIO STATION OF THE YEAR (MAJOR MARKET)

1988	CHAM, Hamilton, ON
1989	CHAM, Hamilton, ON
1990	CHAM, Hamilton, ON
1991	CKRY, Calgary, AB
1992	CHAM, Hamilton, ON
1993	CKRY, Calgary, AB
1994	CKRY, Calgary, AB
1995	CKRY, Calgary, AB
1996	CKRY, Calgary, AB

RADIO STATION OF THE YEAR (SECONDARY MARKET)

1988	CJWW, Saskatoon, SK
1989	CFMK, Kingston, ON
1990	CHOO, Ajax, ON
1991	CJWW, Saskatoon, SK
1992	CJWW, Saskatoon, SK
1993	CKQM-FM, Peterborough, ON
1994	CKQM-FM, Peterborough, ON
1995	CKQM-FM, Peterborough, ON
1996	CJVR, Melfort, SK

ON-AIR PERSONALITY (MAJOR MARKET)

1988	Randy Owen, CKGL, Kitchener, ON
1989	Paul Kennedy, CHFX, Halifax, NS
1990	Cliff Dumas, CHAM, Hamilton, ON
1991	Cliff Dumas, CHAM, Hamilton, ON
1992	Cliff Dumas, CHAM, Hamilton, ON

1993	Ray & Robyn, CKRY-FM, Calgary, AB
1994	Ray & Robyn, CKRY-FM, Calgary, AB
1995	Robyn, Doug & Dan, CKRY-FM, Calgary, AB
1996	Robyn, Doug & Dan, CKRY-FM, Calgary, AB

ON-AIR PERSONALITY (SECONDARY MARKET)

1988	Fred King, CKRM, Regina, SK
1989	Fred King, CKRM, Regina, SK
1990	Fred King, CKRM, Regina, SK
1991	Ken Kilcullen, CKGY, Red Deer, AB
1992	Mark Cartland, CKTY, Sarnia, ON
1993	Mark Cartland, CKTY, Sarnia, ON
1994	Mark Cartland, CKTY, Sarnia, ON
1995	Mark Cartland, CKTY, Sarnia, ON
1996	John Cartwright, CHAT, Medicine Hat, AB

COUNTRY CLUB OF THE YEAR

1982	Golden Rall, Lafontaine Hotel, Ottawa
1983	Urban Corral, Moncton
1984	Urban Corral, Moncton
1985	Cook County Saloon, Edmonton
1986	Urban Corral, Moncton
1987	Rodeo Roadhouse, Kingston
1988	Rodeo Roadhouse, Kingston
1989	Rodeo Roadhouse, Kingston
1990	Cook County Saloon, Edmonton
1991	Cook County Saloon, Edmonton
1992	Cook County Saloon, Edmonton
1993	Cook County Saloon, Edmonton
1994	Cook County Saloon, Edmonton
1995	Ranchman's Restaurant, Calgary
1996	Ranchman's Restaurant, Calgary

COUNTRY MUSIC ASSOCIATION AWARDS

Presented annually by the Country Music Association.

ENTERTAINER OF YEAR

1967	Eddy Arnold
1968	Glen Campbell
1969	Johnny Cash
1970	Merle Haggard
1971	Charley Pride
1972	Loretta Lynn
1973	Roy Clark
1974	Charlie Rich
1975	John Denver

1976	Mel Tillis
1977	Ronnie Milsap
1978	Dolly Parton
1979	Willie Nelson
1980	Barbara Mandrell
1981	Barbara Mandrell
1982	Alabama
1983	Alabama
1984	Alabama
1985	Ricky Skaggs
1986	Reba McEntire
1987	Hank Williams Jr.
1988	Hank Williams Jr.
1989	George Strait
1990	George Strait
1991	Garth Brooks
1992	Garth Brooks
1993	Vince Gill
1994	Vince Gill
1995	Alan Jackson
1996	Brooks & Dunn

MALE VOCALIST OF THE YEAR

1967	Jack Greene
1968	Glen Campbell
1969	Johnny Cash
1970	Merle Haggard
1971	Charley Pride
1972	Charley Pride
1973	Charlie Rich
1974	Ronnie Milsap
1975	Waylon Jennings
1976	Ronnie Milsap
1977	Ronnie Milsap
1978	Don Williams
1979	Kenny Rogers
1980	George Jones
1981	George Jones
1982	Ricky Skaggs
1983	Lee Greenwood
1984	Lee Greenwood
1985	George Strait
1986	George Strait
1987	Randy Travis
1988	Randy Travis
1989	Ricky Van Shelton
1990	Clint Black
1991	Vince Gill
1992	Vince Gill
1993	Vince Gill
1994	Vince Gill
1995	Vince Gill
1996	George Strait

FEMALE VOCALIST OF THE YEAR

1967	Loretta Lynn
1968	Tammy Wynette

1969	Tammy Wynette
1970	Tammy Wynette
1971	Lynn Anderson
1972	Loretta Lynn
1973	Loretta Lynn
1974	Olivia Newton-John
1975	Dolly Parton
1976	Dolly Parton
1977	Crystal Gayle
1978	Crystal Gayle
1979	Barbara Mandrell
1980	Emmylou Harris
1981	Barbara Mandrell
1982	Janie Fricke
1983	Janie Fricke
1984	Reba McEntire
1985	Reba McEntire
1986	Reba McEntire
1987	Reba McEntire
1988	K.T. Oslin
1989	Kathy Mattea
1990	Kathy Mattea
1991	Tanya Tucker
1992	Mary Chapin Carpenter
1993	Mary Chapin Carpenter
1994	Pam Tillis
1995	Alison Krauss
1996	Patty Loveless

VOCAL DUO OF THE YEAR

1970	Porter Wagoner & Dolly Parton
1971	Porter Wagoner & Dolly Parton
1972	Conway Twitty & Loretta Lynn
1973	Conway Twitty & Loretta Lynn
1974	Conway Twitty & Loretta Lynn
1975	Conway Twitty & Loretta Lynn
1976	Waylon Jennings & Willie Nelson
1977	Jim Ed Brown & Helen Cornelius
1978	Kenny Rogers & Dottie West
1979	Kenny Rogers & Dottie West
1980	Moe Bandy & Joe Stampley
1981	David Frizzell & Shelly West
1982	David Frizzell & Shelly West
1983	Merle Haggard & Willie Nelson
1984	Willie Nelson & Julio Iglesias
1985	Anne Murray & Dave Loggins
1986	Dan Seals & Marie Osmond
1987	Ricky Skaggs & Sharon White
1988	The Judds
1989	The Judds
1990	The Judds
1991	The Judds
1992	Brooks & Dunn
1993	Brooks & Dunn
1994	Brooks & Dunn
1995	Brooks & Dunn
1996	Brooks & Dunn

VOCAL GROUP OF THE YEAR

1967	The Stoneman Family
1968	Porter Wagoner & Dolly Parton
1969	Johnny Cash & June Carter
1970	The Glaser Brothers
1971	The Osborne Brothers
1972	The Statler Brothers
1973	The Statler Brothers
1974	The Statler Brothers
1975	The Statler Brothers
1976	The Statler Brothers
1977	The Statler Brothers
1978	The Oak Ridge Boys
1979	The Statler Brothers
1980	The Statler Brothers
1981	Alabama
1982	Alabama
1983	Alabama
1984	The Statler Brothers
1985	The Judds
1986	The Judds
1987	The Judds
1988	Highway 101
1989	Highway 101
1990	Kentucky HeadHunters
1991	Kentucky HeadHunters
1992	Diamond Rio
1993	Diamond Rio
1994	Diamond Rio
1995	The Mavericks
1996	The Mavericks

SONG OF THE YEAR

1967	"There Goes My Everything" Writer: Dallas Frazier
1968	"Honey" Writer: Bobby Russell
1969	"Carroll County Accident" Writer: Bob Ferguson
1970	"Sunday Morning Coming Down" Writer: Kris Kristofferson
1971	"Easy Loving" Writer: Freddie Hart
1972	"Easy Loving" Writer: Freddie Hart
1973	"Behind Closed Doors" Writer: Kenny O'Dell
1974	"Country Bumpkin" Writer: Don Wayne
1975	"Back Home Again" Writer: John Denver
1976	"Rhinestone Cowboy" Writer: Larry Weiss
1977	"Lucille" Writers: Roger Bowling, Hal Bynum

1978	"Don't It Make My Brown Eyes Blue" Writer: Richard Leigh
1979	"The Gambler" Writer: Don Schlitz
1980	"He Stopped Loving Her Today" Writers: Bobby Braddock, Curly Putman
1981	"He Stopped Loving Her Today" Writers: Bobby Braddock, Curly Putman
1982	"Always On My Mind" Writers: Johnny Christopher, Wayne Carson, Mark James
1983	"Always On My Mind" Writers: Johnny Christopher, Wayne Carson, Mark James
1984	"Wind Beneath My Wings" Writers: Larry Henley, Jeff Silvar
1985	"God Bless the U.S.A." Writer: Lee Greenwood
1986	"On the Other Hand" Writers: Paul Overstreet, Don Schlitz
1987	"Forever and Ever, Amen" Writers: Paul Overstreet, Don Schlitz
1988	"80's Ladies" Writer: K.T. Oslin
1989	"Chiseled in Stone" Writers: Max D. Barnes, Vern Gosdin
1990	"Where've You Been" Writers: Jon Vezner, Don Henry
1991	"When I Call Your Name" Writers: Vince Gill, Tim DuBois
1992	"Look at Us" Writers: Vince Gill, Max D. Barnes
1993	"I Still Believe in You" Writers: Vince Gill, John Barlow Jarvis
1994	"Chattahoochee" Writers: Alan Jackson, Jim McBride
1995	"Independence Day" Writer: Gretchen Peters
1996	"Go Rest High on That Mountain" Writer: Vince Gill

SINGLE OF THE YEAR

1967	"There Goes My Everything," Jack Greene
1968	"Harper Valley P.T.A.," Jeannie C. Riley
1969	"A Boy Named Sue," Johnny Cash
1970	"Okie from Muskogee," Merle Haggard

1971   "Help Me Make It Through the Night," Sammi Smith

1972   "The Happiest Girl in the Whole U.S.A.," Donna Fargo

1973   "Behind Closed Doors," Charlie Rich

1974   "Country Bumpkin," Cal Smith

1975   "Before the Next Teardrop Falls," Freddy Fender

1976   "Good Hearted Woman," Waylon Jennings & Willie Nelson

1977   "Lucille," Kenny Rogers

1978   "Heaven's Just a Sin Away," the Kendalls

1979   "The Devil Went Down to Georgia," Charlie Daniels Band

1980   "He Stopped Loving Her Today," George Jones

1981   "Elvira," Oak Ridge Boys

1982   "Always on My Mind," Willie Nelson

1983   "Swingin'," John Anderson

1984   "A Little Good News," Anne Murray

1985   "Why Not Me," the Judds

1986   "Bop," Dan Seals

1987   "Forever and Ever Amen," Randy Travis

1988   "Eighteen Wheels and a Dozen Roses," Kathy Mattea

1989   "I'm No Stranger to the Rain," Keith Whitley

1990   "When I Call Your Name," Vince Gill

1991   "Friends in Low Places," Garth Brooks

1992   "Achy Breaky Heart," Billy Ray Cyrus

1993   "Chattahoochee," Alan Jackson

1994   "I Swear," John Michael Montgomery

1995   "When You Say Nothing at All," Alison Krauss & Union Station

1996   "Check Yes or No," George Strait

ALBUM OF THE YEAR

1967   *There Goes My Everything*, Jack Greene

1968   *Johnny Cash at Folsom Prison*, Johnny Cash

1969   *Johnny Cash at San Quentin Prison*, Johnny Cash

1970   *Okie from Muskogee*, Merle Haggard

1971   *I Won't Mention It Again*, Ray Price

1972   *Let Me Tell You About a Song*, Merle Haggard

1973   *Behind Closed Doors*, Charlie Rich

1974   *A Very Special Love Song*, Charlie Rich

1975   *A Legend in My Time*, Ronnie Milsap

1976   *Wanted—The Outlaws*, Waylon Jennings, Willie Nelson, Tompall Glaser, Jessi Colter

1977   *Ronnie Milsap Live*, Ronnie Milsap

1978   *It Was Almost Like a Song*, Ronnie Milsap

1979   *The Gambler*, Kenny Rogers

1980   *Coal Miner's Daughter*, Original Motion Picture Soundtrack

1981   *I Believe in You*, Don Williams

1982   *Always on My Mind*, Willie Nelson

1983   *The Closer You Get*, Alabama

1984   *A Little Good News*, Anne Murray

1985   *Does Fort Worth Ever Cross Your Mind*, George Strait

1986   *Lost in the Fifties Tonight*, Ronnie Milsap

1987   *Always and Forever*, Randy Travis

1988   *Born to Boogie*, Hank Williams Jr.

1989   *Will the Circle Be Unbroken Vol. II*, Nitty Gritty Dirt Band

1990   *Pickin' on Nashville*, Kentucky HeadHunters

1991   *No Fences*, Garth Brooks

1992   *Ropin' the Wind*, Garth Brooks

1993   *I Still Believe in You*, Vince Gill

1994   *Common Thread: The Songs of the Eagles*, Various Artists

1995   *When Fallen Angels Fly*, Patty Loveless

1996   *Blue Clear Sky*, George Strait

VOCAL EVENT OF THE YEAR

1988   *Trio*, Dolly Parton, Linda Ronstadt & Emmylou Harris

1989   Hank Williams Jr., Hank Williams, Sr.

1990   Lorrie Morgan, Keith Whitley

1991   Mark O'Connor & the New Nashville Cats (featuring Vince Gill, Ricky Skaggs and Steve Wariner)

1992   Marty Stuart, Travis Tritt

1993   "I Don't Need Your Rockin' Chair," George Jones with Vince Gill, Mark Chesnutt, Garth Brooks, Travis Tritt, Joe Diffie, Alan Jackson, Pam Tillis, T. Graham Brown, Patty Loveless, Clint Black

1994   "Does He Love You," Reba McEntire with Linda Davis,

1995   "Somewhere in the Vicinty of the Heart," Shenandoah with Alison Krauss,

1996   "I Will Always Love You," Dolly Parton with special guest Vince Gill

MUSICIAN OF THE YEAR

1967   Chet Atkins
1968   Chet Atkins
1969   Chet Atkins
1970   Jerry Reed
1971   Jerry Reed
1972   Charlie McCoy
1973   Charlie McCoy
1974   Don Rich
1975   Johnny Gimble
1976   Hargus "Pig" Robbins
1977   Roy Clark
1978   Roy Clark
1979   Charlie Daniels
1980   Roy Clark
1981   Chet Atkins
1982   Chet Atkins
1983   Chet Atkins
1984   Chet Atkins
1985   Chet Atkins
1986   Johnny Gimble
1987   Johnny Gimble
1988   Chet Atkins
1989   Johnny Gimble
1990   Johnny Gimble
1991   Mark O'Connor
1992   Mark O'Connor
1993   Mark O'Connor
1994   Mark O'Connor
1995   Mark O'Connor
1996   Mark O'Connor

INSTRUMENTAL GROUP OF THE YEAR

1967   The Buckaroos
1968   The Buckaroos
1969   Danny Davis & the Nashville Brass
1970   Danny Davis & the Nashville Brass
1971   Danny Davis & the Nashville Brass

1972	Danny Davis & the Nashville Brass
1973	Danny Davis & the Nashville Brass
1974	Danny Davis & the Nashville Brass
1975	Roy Clark and Buck Trent
1976	Roy Clark and Buck Trent
1977	Original Texas Playboys
1978	Oak Ridge Boys Band
1979	The Charlie Daniels Band
1980	The Charlie Daniels Band
1981	Alabama
1982	Alabama
1983	Ricky Skaggs Band
1984	Ricky Skaggs Band
1985	Ricky Skaggs Band
1986	Oak Ridge Boys Band

COMEDIAN OF THE YEAR

1967	Don Bowman
1968	Ben Colder
1969	Archie Campbell
1970	Roy Clark

MUSIC VIDEO OF THE YEAR

1985	"All My Rowdy Friends Are Comin' Over Tonight," Hank Williams Jr.
1986	"Who's Gonna Fill Their Shoes," George Jones
1987	"My Name Is Bocephus," Hank Williams Jr.
1989	"There's a Tear in My Beer," Hank Williams Jr., Hank Williams, Sr.
1990	"The Dance," Garth Brooks
1991	"The Thunder Rolls," Garth Brooks
1992	"Midnight in Montgomery," Alan Jackson
1993	"Chatahoochee," Alan Jackson
1994	"Independence Day," Martina McBride
1995	"Baby Likes to Rock It," the Tractors
1996	"My Wife Thinks You're Dead," Junior Brown

HORIZON AWARD

1981	Terri Gibbs
1982	Ricky Skaggs
1983	John Anderson
1984	The Judds
1985	Sawyer Brown
1986	Randy Travis
1987	Holly Dunn

1988	Ricky Van Shelton
1989	Clint Black
1990	Garth Brooks
1991	Travis Tritt
1992	Suzy Bogguss
1993	Mark Chesnutt
1994	John Michael Montgomery
1995	Alison Krauss
1996	Bryan White

COUNTRY MUSIC HALL OF FAME INDUCTEES

Artists are inducted by the Country Music Association

1961	Jimmie Rodgers
1961	Fred Rose
	Hank Williams
1962	Roy Acuff
1964	Tex Ritter
	Ernest Tubb
1966	Eddy Arnold
	James R. Denny
	George D. Hay
	Uncle Dave Macon
1967	Red Foley
	J.L. (Joe) Frank
	Jim Reeves
	Stephen H. Sholes
1968	Bob Wills
1969	Gene Autry
	Bill Monroe
1970	Original Carter Family (A.P. Carter, Maybelle Carter, Sara Carter)
1971	Arthur Edward Satherley
1972	Jimmie H. Davis
1973	Chet Atkins
	Patsy Cline
1974	Owen Bradley
	Frank "Pee Wee" King
1975	Minnie Pearl
1976	Paul Cohen
	Kitty Wells
1977	Merle Travis
1978	Grandpa Jones
1979	Hank Snow
	Hubert Long
1980	Johnny Cash
	Connie B. Gay
	Original Sons of the Pioneers (Hugh Farr, Karl Farr, Bob Nolan, Lloyd Perryman, Roy Rogers, Tim Spencer)
1981	Vernon Dalhart
	Grant Turner

1982	Lefty Frizzell
	Roy Horton
	Marty Robbins
1983	Little Jimmy Dickens
1984	Ralph Sylvester Peer
	Floyd Tillman
1985	Flatt & Scruggs
1986	Benjamin F. Ford
	Wesley H. Rose
1987	Rod Brasfield
1988	Loretta Lynn
	Roy Rogers
1989	Jack Stapp
	Cliffie Stone
	Hank Thompson
1990	Tennessee Ernie Ford
1991	Boudleaux & Felice Bryant
1992	George Jones
	Frances Williams Preston
1993	Willie Hugh Nelson
1994	Merle Haggard
1995	Roger Miller
	Jo Walker-Meador
1996	Patsy Montana
	Buck Owens
	Ray Price

GRAMMY AWARDS

Presented annually by the National Academy of Recording Arts and Sciences.
(Note: Only country music categories are listed.)

BEST COUNTRY AND WESTERN PERFORMANCE

1958	"Tom Dooley," the Kingston Trio
1959	"The Battle of New Orleans," Johnny Horton
1960	"El Paso," Marty Robbins
1961	"Big Bad John," Jimmy Dean
1962	"Funny Way of Laughin'," Burl Ives
1963	"Detroit City," Bobby Bare

BEST COUNTRY VOCAL PERFORMANCE, MALE

1964	"Dang Me," Roger Miller
1965	"King of the Road," Roger Miller
1966	"Almost Persuaded," David Houston
1967	"Gentle on My Mind," Glen Campbell
1968	"Folsom Prison Blues," Johnny Cash
1969	"A Boy Named Sue," Johnny Cash

1970 "For the Good Times," Ray Price

1971 "When You're Hot, You're Hot," Jerry Reed

1972 *Charley Pride Sings Heart Songs,* Charley Pride

1973 "Behind Closed Doors," Charlie Rich

1974 "Please Don't Tell Me How the Story Ends," Ronnie Milsap

1975 "Blue Eyes Crying in the Rain," Willie Nelson

1976 "(I'm a) Stand by My Woman Man," Ronnie Milsap

1977 "Lucille," Kenny Rogers

1978 "Georgia on My Mind," Willie Nelson

1979 "The Gambler," Kenny Rogers

1980 "He Stopped Loving Her Today," George Jones

1981 "(There's No) Gettin' Over Me," Ronnie Milsap

1982 "Always on My Mind," Willie Nelson

1983 "I.O.U.," Lee Greenwood

1984 "That's the Way Love Goes," Merle Haggard

1985 "Lost in the Fifties Tonight (in the Still of the Night)," Ronnie Milsap

1986 *Lost in the Fifties Tonight,* Ronnie Milsap

1987 *Always & Forever,* Randy Travis

1988 *Old 8 x 10,* Randy Travis

1989 *Lyle Lovett and His Large Band,* Lyle Lovett

1990 "When I Call Your Name," Vince Gill

1991 *Ropin' the Wind,* Garth Brooks

1992 *I Still Believe in You,* Vince Gill

1993 "Ain't that Lonely Yet," Dwight Yoakam

1994 *When Love Finds You,* Vince Gill

1995 "Go Rest High on that Mountain," Vince Gill

1996 "Worlds Apart," Vince Gill

BEST COUNTRY VOCAL PERFORMANCE, FEMALE

1964 "Here Comes My Baby," Dottie West

1965 "Queen of the House," Jody Miller

1966 "Don't Touch Me," Jeannie Seely

1967 "I Don't Wanna Play House," Tammy Wynette

1968 "Harper Valley P.T.A.," Jeannie C. Riley

1969 *Stand by Your Man,* Tammy Wynette

1970 "Rose Garden," Lynn Anderson

1971 "Help Me Make It Through the Night," Sammi Smith

1972 "Happiest Girl in the Whole U.S.A.," Donna Fargo

1973 "Let Me Be There," Olivia Newton-John

1974 "Love Song," Anne Murray

1975 "I Can't Help It (If I'm Still in Love with You)," Linda Ronstadt

1976 *Elite Hotel,* Emmylou Harris

1977 "Don't It Make My Brown Eyes Blue," Crystal Gayle

1978 *Here You Come Again,* Dolly Parton

1979 *Blue Kentucky Girl,* Emmylou Harris

1980 "Could I Have this Dance," Anne Murray

1981 "9 to 5," Dolly Parton

1982 "Break It to Me Gently," Juice Newton

1983 "A Little Good News," Anne Murray

1984 "In My Dreams," Emmylou Harris

1985 "I Don't Know Why You Don't Want Me," Rosanne Cash

1986 "Whoever's in New England," Reba McEntire

1987 "80's Ladies," K.T. Oslin

1988 "Hold Me," K.T. Oslin

1989 *Absolute Torch and Twang,* k.d. lang

1990 "Where've You Been," Kathy Mattea

1991 "Down at the Twist and Shout," Mary Chapin Carpenter

1992 "I Feel Lucky," Mary Chapin Carpenter

1993 "Passionate Kisses," Mary Chapin Carpenter

1994 "Shut Up and Kiss Me," Mary Chapin Carpenter

1995 "Baby, Now that I've Found You," Alison Krauss

1996 *Blue,* LeAnn Rimes

BEST COUNTRY PERFORMANCE BY A DUO OR GROUP WITH VOCAL

1967 "Jackson," Johnny Cash & June Carter

1969 "Macarthur Park," Waylon Jennings & the Kimberlys

1970 "If I Were a Carpenter," Johnny Cash & June Carter

1971 "After the Fire Is Gone," Conway Twitty & Loretta Lynn

1972 "Class of '57," the Statler Brothers

1973 "From the Bottle to the Bottom," Kris Kristofferson & Rita Coolidge

1974 "Fairytale," the Pointer Sisters

1975 "Lover Please," Kris Kristofferson & Rita Coolidge

1976 "The End Is Not in Sight (The Cowboy Tune)," Amazing Rhythm Aces

1977 "Heaven's Just a Sin Away," the Kendalls

1978 "Mamas Don't Let Your Babies Grow Up to Be Cowboys," Waylon Jennings & Willie Nelson

1979 "The Devil Went Down to Georgia," Charlie Daniels Band

1980 "That Lovin' You Feelin' Again," Roy Orbison & Emmylou Harris

1981 "Elvira," Oak Ridge Boys

1982 *Mountain Music,* Alabama

1983 *The Closer You Get,* Alabama

1984 "Mama He's Crazy," the Judds

1985 *Why Not Me,* the Judds

1986 "Grandpa (Tell Me 'Bout the Good Old Days), the Judds

1987 *Trio,* Dolly Parton, Linda Ronstadt & Emmylou Harris

1988 "Give a Little Love," the Judds

1989 *Will the Circle Be Unbroken Volume II,* the Nitty Gritty Dirt Band

1990 *Pickin' on Nashville,* the Kentucky HeadHunters

1991 "Love Can Build a Bridge," the Judds

1992 *Emmylou Harris & the Nash Ramblers at the Ryman,* Emmylou Harris & the Nash Ramblers

1993 "Hard Workin' Man," Brooks & Dunn

1994 "Blues for Dixie," Asleep at the Wheel with Lyle Lovett

1995 "Here Comes the Rain," the Mavericks

1996 "My Maria," Brooks & Dunn

BEST COUNTRY COLLABORATION WITH VOCALS

1987 "Make No Mistake, She's Mine," Ronnie Milsap & Kenny Rogers

1988 "Crying," Roy Orbison & k.d. lang

1989 "There's a Tear in My Beer," Hank Williams Jr. & Hank Williams, Sr.

1990	"Poor Boy Blues," Chet Atkins & Mark Knopfler
1991	"Restless," Steve Wariner, Ricky Skaggs & Vince Gill
1992	"The Whiskey Ain't Workin'," Travis Tritt & Mary Stuart
1993	"Does He Love You," Reba McEntire & Linda Davis
1994	"I Fall to Pieces," Aaron Neville & Trisha Yearwood
1995	"Somewhere in the Vicinity of the Heart," Shenandoah with Alison Krauss
1996	"High Lonesome Sound," Vince Gill featuring Alison Krauss and Union Station

BEST COUNTRY INSTRUMENTAL PERFORMANCE

1968	"Foggy Mountain Breakdown," Flatt & Scruggs
1969	*The Nashville Brass Featuring Danny Davis Play More Nashville Sounds,* Danny Davis and the Nashville Brass
1970	*Me & Jerry,* Chet Atkins & Jerry Reed
1971	"Snowbird," Chet Atkins
1972	*Charlie McCoy/the Real McCoy,* Charlie McCoy
1973	"Dueling Banjos," Eric Weissberg & Steve Mandell
1974	*The Atkins-Travis Traveling Show,* Chet Atkins & Merle Travis
1975	"The Entertainer," Chet Atkins
1976	*Chester & Lester,* Chet Atkins & Les Paul
1977	*Country Instrumentalist of the Year,* Hargus "Pig" Robbins
1978	"One O'Clock Jump," Asleep at the Wheel
1979	"Big Sandy/Leather Britches," Doc & Merle Watson
1980	"Orange Blossom Special/Hoedown," Gilley's Urban Cowboy Band
1981	*Country After All These Years,* Chet Atkins
1982	"Alabama Jubilee," Roy Clark
1983	"Fireball," the New South (Ricky Skaggs, Jerry Douglas, Tony Rice, J.D. Crowe, Todd Phillips)
1984	"Wheel Hoss," Ricky Skaggs
1985	"Cosmic Square Dance," Chet Atkins & Mark Knopfler
1986	"Raisin' the Dickens," Ricky Skaggs

1987	"String of Pars," Asleep at the Wheel
1988	"Sugarfoot Rag," Asleep at the Wheel
1989	"Amazing Grace," Randy Scruggs
1990	"So Soft, Your Goodbye," Chet Atkins, Mark Knopfler
1991	*The New Nashville Cats,* Mark O'Connor
1992	*Sneakin' Around,* Chet Atkins & Jerry Reed
1993	"Red Wing," Asleep at the Wheel featuring Eldon Shamblin, Johnny Gimble, Chet Atkins, Vince Gill, Marty Stuart & Reuben "Lucky Oceans" Gosfield
1994	"Young Thing," Chet Atkins
1995	"Hightower," Asleep at the Wheel featuring Bela Fleck and Johnny Gimble
1996	"Jam Man," Chet Atkins

BEST COUNTRY SONG

1964	"Dang Me" Writer: Roger Miller
1965	"King of the Road" Writer: Roger Miller
1966	"Almost Persuaded" Writers: Billy Sherrill, Glen Sutton
1967	"Gentle on My Mind" Writer: John Hartford
1968	"Little Green Apples" Writer: Bobby Russell
1969	"A Boy Named Sue" Writer: Shel Silverstein
1970	"My Woman, My Woman, My Wife" Writer: Marty Robbins
1971	"Help Me Make It Through the Night" Writers: Kris Kristofferson, Fred Foster
1972	"Kiss an Angel Good Mornin'" Writer: Ben Peters
1973	"Behind Closed Doors" Writer: Kenny O'Dell
1974	"A Very Special Love Song" Writers: Norris Wilson, Billy Sherrill
1975	"(Hey Won't You Play) Another Somebody Done Somebody Wrong Song" Writers: Chips Moman, Larry Butler
1976	"Broken Lady" Writer: Larry Gatlin

1977	"Don't It Make My Brown Eyes Blue" Writer: Richard Leigh
1978	"The Gambler" Writer: Don Schlitz
1979	"You Decorated My Life" Writers: Bob Morrison, Debbie Hupp
1980	"On the Road Again" Writer: Willie Nelson
1981	"9 to 5" Writer: Dolly Parton
1982	"Always on My Mind" Writers: Johnny Christopher, Mark James, Wayne Carson
1983	"Stranger in My House" Writer: Mike Reid
1984	"City of New Orleans" Writer: Steve Goodman
1985	"Highwayman" Writer: Jimmy L. Webb
1986	"Grandpa (Tell Me 'Bout the Good Old Days)" Writer: Jamie O'Hara
1987	"Forever and Ever, Amen" Writers: Paul Overstreet, Don Schlitz
1988	"Hold Me" Writer: K.T. Oslin
1989	"After All This Time" Writer: Rodney Crowell
1990	"Where've You Been" Writers: Jon Vezner, Don Henry
1991	"Love Can Build a Bridge" Writers: Naomi Judd, John Jarvis, Paul Overstreet
1992	"I Still Believe in You" Writers: Vince Gill, John Barlow Jarvis
1993	"Passionate Kisses" Writer: Lucinda Williams
1994	"I Swear" Writers: Gary Baker, Frank J. Myers
1995	"Go Rest High on That Mountain" Writer: Vince Gill

BEST COUNTRY ALBUM

1994	*Stones in the Road,* Mary Chapin Carpenter
1995	*The Woman in Me,* Shania Twain
1996	*The Road to Ensenada,* Lyle Lovett

BEST BLUEGRASS RECORDING

| 1988 | *Southern Flavor,* Bill Monroe |
| 1989 | "The Valley Road," Bruce Hornsby & the Nitty Gritty Dirt Band |

1990   *I've Got that Old Feeling,* Alison Krauss

1991   *Spring Training,* Carl Jackson & John Starling (& the Nash Ramblers)

1992   *Every Time You Say Goodbye,* Alison Krauss & Union Station

1993   *Waitin' for the Hard Times to Go,* the Nashville Bluegrass Band

1994   *The Great Dobro Sessions,* Jerry Douglas & Tut Taylor, Producers (Various Artists)

1995   *Unleashed,* the Nashville Bluegrass Band

1996   *True Life Blues: The Songs of Bill Monroe,* Various Artists

OTHER COUNTRY AWARDS

1964   *Dang Me/Chug-a-Lug,* Roger Miller (Best Country Album)

1964   "Dang Me," Roger Miller (Best Country Single)

1964   Roger Miller, (Best Country Artist)

1965   *The Return of Roger Miller,* Roger Miller (Best Country Album)

1965   "King of the Road," Roger Miller (Best Country Single)

1965   Statler Brothers, (Best Country Artist)

1966   "Almost Persuaded," David Houston (Best Country Recording)

1967   "Gentle on My Mind," Glen Campbell (Best Country Recording)

INTERNATIONAL BLUEGRASS MUSIC AWARDS

Presented annually by the International Bluegrass Music Association.

ENTERTAINER OF THE YEAR

1990   Hot Rize
1991   Alison Krauss & Union Station
1992   The Nashville Bluegrass Band
1993   The Nashville Bluegrass Band
1994   The Del McCoury Band
1995   Alison Krauss & Union Station
1996   Del McCoury

MALE VOCALIST OF THE YEAR

1990   Del McCoury
1991   Del McCoury
1992   Del McCoury
1993   Tim O'Brien
1994   Russell Moore
1995   Ronnie Bowman

1996   Del McCoury

FEMALE VOCALIST OF THE YEAR

1990   Alison Krauss
1991   Alison Krauss
1992   Laurie Lewis
1993   Alison Krauss
1994   Laurie Lewis
1995   Alison Krauss
1996   Lynn Morris

VOCAL GROUP OF THE YEAR

1990   The Nashville Bluegrass Band
1991   The Nashville Bluegrass Band
1992   The Nashville Bluegrass Band
1993   The Nashville Bluegrass Band
1994   IIIrd Tyme Out
1995   IIIrd Tyme Out
1996   IIIrd Tyme Out

INSTRUMENTAL GROUP OF THE YEAR

1990   The Bluegrass Album Band
1991   The Tony Rice Unit
1992   California
1993   California
1994   California
1995   The Tony Rice Unit
1996   Del McCoury Band

EMERGING ARTIST OF THE YEAR

1994   Lou Reid, Terry Baucom & Carolina
1995   David Parmley, Scott Vestal & Continental Divide
1996   Blue Highway

SONG OF THE YEAR

1990   "Little Mountain Church," Doyle Lawson & Quicksilver
Writers: Jim Rushing, Carl Jackson
1991   "Colleen Malone," Hot Rize
Writers: Pete Goble, Leroy Drumm
1992   "Blue Train," the Nashville Bluegrass Band
Writer: Dave Allen
1993   "Lonesome Standard Time," Lonesome Standard Time
Writers: Larry Cordle, Jim Rushing
1994   "Who Will Watch the Home Place," Laurie Lewis
Writer: Kate Long
1995   "Cold Virginia Night," Ronnie Bowman
Writer: Timmy Massey
1996   "Mama's Hand," Lynn Morris
Writer: Hazel Dickens

ALBUM OF THE YEAR

1990   *At the Old Schoolhouse,* the Johnson Mountain Boys

1991   *I've Got That Old Feeling,* Alison Krauss & Union Station

1992   *Carrying the Tradition,* the Lonesome River Band

1993   *Every Time You Say Goodbye,* Alison Kruass & Union Station

1994   *A Deeper Shade of Blue,* Del McCoury

1995   *Cold Virginia Night,* Ronnie Bowman

1996   *It's a Long, Long Road,* Blue Highway

INSTRUMENTAL RECORDING OF THE YEAR

1990   *The Masters,* Adcock, Baker, Graves & McReynolds

1991   *Norman Blake & Tony Rice—2,* Norman Blake & Tony Rice

1992   *Slide Rule,* Jerry Douglas

1993   *Stuart Duncan,* Stuart Duncan

1994   *Skip, Hop & Wobble,* Douglas, Barenberg & Meyer

1995   *The Great Dobro Sessions,* Various Artists

1996   *Ronnie and Rob McCoury,* Ronnie & Rob McCoury

RECORDED EVENT OF THE YEAR

1990   *Classic Country Gents Reunion,* Duffey, Waller, Adcock & Gray

1991   *Families Of Tradition,* Parmley & McCoury

1992   *Slide Rule,* Jerry Douglas

1993   *Saturday Night and Sunday Morning,* Ralph Stanley & Special Guests

1994   *A Touch of the Past,* Larry Perkins & Friends

1995   *The Great Dobro Sessions,* Various Artists

1996   *Bluegrass '95,* Various Artists

INSTRUMENTAL PERFORMERS OF THE YEAR

Banjo
1990   Bela Fleck
1991   Alison Brown
1992   Tom Adams
1993   Tom Adams
1994   J.D. Crowe
1995   Samm Shelor
1996   Scott Vestal, Sammy Shelor (tie)

Guitar

1990	Tony Rice
1991	Tony Rice
1992	David Grier
1993	David Grier
1994	Tony Rice
1995	David Grier
1996	Tony Rice

Fiddle

1990	Stuart Duncan
1991	Stuart Duncan
1992	Stuart Duncan
1993	Stuart Duncan
1994	Stuart Duncan
1995	Stuart Duncan
1996	Stuart Duncan

Bass

1990	Roy Huskey Jr.
1991	Roy Huskey Jr.
1992	Roy Huskey Jr.
1993	Roy Huskey Jr.
1994	Mark Schatz
1995	Mark Schatz
1996	Mike Bub

Dobro

1990	Jerry Douglas
1991	Jerry Douglas
1992	Jerry Douglas
1993	Jerry Douglas
1994	Jerry Douglas
1995	Jerry Douglas
1996	Rob Ickes

Mandolin

1990	Sam Bush
1991	Sam Bush
1992	Sam Bush
1993	Ronnie McCoury
1994	Ronnie McCoury
1995	Ronnie McCoury
1996	Ronnie McCoury

BEST GRAPHIC DESIGN—RECORDED PROJECT

1994	*I Got a Bullfrog: Folksongs for the Fun of It*, David Holt
1995	*Old Time, New Times*, Benton Flippen
1996	*Lonesome and Then Some*, James King

BEST LINER NOTES—RECORDED PROJECT

1994	*Don Reno & Red Smiley, 1951-1959*, Don Reno & Red Smiley

1995	*Hazel & Alice*, Hazel Dickens & Alice Gerrard
1996	*Lonesome and Then Some*, James King

AWARD OF MERIT RECIPIENTS

1986	Albert Brumley
	Ray Davis
	Bill Monroe
	Ruby Baker Moody
	Cuzin' Isaac Page
	Dr. Neil V. Roseberg
1987	Dewitt "Snuffy" Jenkins
	Bill Jones
	Don Owens
	Ralph Rinzler
	Charlie Waller
1988	John Duffey
	Tom Henderson
	Peter V. Kuykendall
	Ola Belle Reed
	Earl Scruggs
	Bill Vernon
1989	Lester Flatt
	David Freeman
	Kathy Kaplan
	Robert Larkin
	Dr. Bill C. Malone
1990	Carlton Haney
	Wade Mainer
	Joe Stuart
	Dr. Charles Wolfe
1991	Ralph Epperson
	The Blue Sky Boys (Bill & Earl Bolick)
	Dono Stover
1992	The Louvin Brothers (Charlie & Ira)
	Bill Clifton
	Burkette "Uncle Josh" Graves
	Lloyd Loar
1993	Curly Ray Cline
	Hazel Dickens
	Jim Eanes
	Charles Richard Freeland
1994	Wilma Lee Cooper
	Lance LeRoy
	Ken Irwin
	Johnnie Wright & Jack Anglin
1995	Rose Maddox
	Mike Seeger
	Joe Val
	Toshio & Saburo Watanabe
1996	G.B. Grayson
	Curly Seckler
	George Shuffler
	Martha White Foods

HALL OF HONOR INDUCTEES

1991	Bill Monroe
1991	Earl Scruggs
1991	Lester Flatt
1992	The Stanley Brothers, Carter & Ralph
1992	Don Reno & Arthur Lee "Red" Smiley
1993	Mac Wiseman
1993	Jim & Jesse McReynolds
1994	The Osborne Brothers
1995	Jimmy Martin
1996	Peter V. ("Pete") Kuykendall

GRAND OLE OPRY CAST

Artists are invited to become cast members by the Grand Ole Opry.

1947	Grandpa Jones
1948	Little Jimmy Dickens
1950	Hank Snow
1953	Bill Carlisle
	Teddy Wilburn
1955	Charlie Louvin
	Justin Tubb
	Jean Shepard
1956	Jimmy C. Newman
1957	Wilma Lee Cooper
	Porter Wagoner
1958	Roy Drusky
	Don Gibson
1959	Skeeter Davis
	Billy Grammer
1960	George Hamilton IV
	Hank Locklin
	Billy Walker
1961	Bill Anderson
1962	Loretta Lynn
1963	Jim Ed Brown
1964	Jim & Jesse
	Ernie Ashworth
1964	The Osborne Brothers
1966	Ray Pillow
	Del Reeves
1967	Jack Greene
	The 4 Guys
	Stu Phillips
	Jeannie Seely
	Charlie Walker
1969	Stonewall Jackson
	George Jones
	Dolly Parton
1971	Jan Howard
	Connie Smith
1972	Barbara Mandrell
1973	Jeanne Pruett

1978 Larry, Steve & Rudy— The Gatlins
Ronnie Milsap
1980 Tom T. Hall
1981 John Conlee
Boxcar Willie
1982 Ricky Skaggs
Riders in the Sky
(Ranger Doug, Too Slim, Woody
Paul)
1984 Lorrie Morgan
The Whites
1985 Johnny Russell
1986 Mel McDaniel
Reba McEntire
Randy Travis
1988 Patty Loveless
Ricky Van Shelton
1989 Holly Dunn
1990 Garth Brooks
Mike Snider
1991 Clint Black
Vince Gill
Alan Jackson
1992 Emmylou Harris
Marty Stuart
Travis Tritt
1993 Joe Diffie
Alison Krauss
Charley Pride
1994 Hal Ketchum
1995 Bashful Brother Oswald
Martina McBride
1996 Steve Wariner

JUNO AWARDS

Presented annually by the Canadian Academy of Recording Arts and Sciences. (Note: Only country music categories are listed.)

TOP COUNTRY MALE SINGER

1970 Stompin' Tom Connors
1971 Stompin' Tom Connors
1972 Stompin' Tom Connors
1973 Stompin' Tom Connors
1974 Stompin' Tom Connors
1975 Murray McLauchlan
1976 Murray McLauchlan
1977 Ronnie Prophet
1978 Ronnie Prophet
1979 Murray McLauchlan
1980 Eddie Eastman
1981 Ronnie Hawkins
1982 Eddie Eastman
1983 Murray McLauchlan

1984 Murray McLauchlan
1985 Murray McLauchlan
1986 Ian Tyson
1987 Murray McLauchlan
1989 George Fox
1990 George Fox
1991 George Fox
1992 Gary Fjellgaard
1993 Charlie Major
1994 Charlie Major
1995 Charlie Major
1996 Paul Brandt

TOP COUNTRY FEMALE SINGER

1970 Myrna Lorrie
1971 Myrna Lorrie
1972 Shirley Eikhard
1973 Shirley Eikhard
1974 Anne Murray
1975 Anne Murray
1976 Carroll Baker
1977 Carroll Baker
1978 Carroll Baker
1979 Anne Murray
1980 Anne Murray
1981 Anne Murray
1982 Anne Murray
1983 Anne Murray
1984 Anne Murray
1985 Anne Murray
1986 k.d. lang
1988 k.d. lang
1989 k.d. lang
1990 Rita MacNeil
1991 Cassandra Vasik
1992 Michelle Wright
1993 Cassandra Vasik
1994 Michelle Wright
1995 Shania Twain
1996 Shania Twain

COUNTRY GROUP OR DUO OF THE YEAR

1970 The Mercey Brothers
1971 The Mercey Brothers
1972 The Mercey Brothers
1973 The Mercey Brothers
1974 Carlton Showband
1975 The Mercey Brothers
1976 Good Brothers
1977 Good Brothers
1978 Good Brothers
1979 Good Brothers
1980 Good Brothers
1981 Good Brothers
1982 Good Brothers
1983 Good Brothers
1984 Family Brown

1985 Prairie Oyster
1986 Prairie Oyster
1987 Family Brown
1989 Family Brown
1990 Prairie Oyster
1991 Prairie Oyster
1992 Tracey Prescott & Lonesome
Daddy
1993 The Rankin Family
1994 Prairie Oyster
1995 Prairie Oyster
1996 The Rankin Family

NASHVILLE MUSIC AWARDS

Presented annually by Leadership Music, Nashville. (Note: Only country music categories are listed.)

ARTIST/SONGWRITER

1994 Rodney Crowell
1995 Alan Jackson
1996 Vince Gill

MALE VOCALIST

1994 Vince Gill
1995 Vince Gill
1996 Vince Gill

FEMALE VOCALIST

1994 Trisha Yearwood
1995 Alison Krauss
1996 Patty Loveless

GROUP/DUO

1994 The Mavericks
1995 BR5-49
1996 Jars of Clay

SONGWRITER

1994 Keith Thomas
1995 Gretchen Peters
1996 Matraca Berg

SONG OF THE YEAR

1994 "He Thinks He'll Keep Her"
Writers: Don Schlitz, Mary Chapin
Carpenter
1995 "Go Rest High on That Mountain"
Writer: Vince Gill
1996 "Change the World"
Writers: Tommy Sims, Wayne Kirkpatrick, Gordon Kennedy

BEST COUNTRY ALBUM

1994 *When Fallen Angels Fly*, Patty
Loveless
1995 *Wild Angels*, Martina McBride
1996 *BR5-49*, BR5-49

BEST BLUEGRASS/OLD-TIME MUSIC ALBUM

1994　*I Know Who Holds Tomorrow,* Alison Kruass & the Cox Family

1995　*Now That I've Found You: A Collection,* Alison Krauss

1996　*The Cold Hard Facts,* Del McCoury Band

BEST RE-ISSUE ALBUM

1994　*Only Daddy That'll Walk the Line: The RCA Years,* Waylon Jennings

1995　*King of the Road: The Genius of Roger Miller,* Roger Miller

1996　*Storyteller, Poet, Philosopher,* Tom T. Hall

PRODUCER

1994　Tony Brown

1995　Emory Gordy Jr.

1996　Tony Brown

AUDIO ENGINEER

1994　Lynn Peterzell

1995　John Van Etten

1996　Chuck Ainlay

ALBUM ARTWORK

1994　Bill Johnson for *When Angels Fly,* Patty Loveless

1995　Fun Girls from Mt. Pilot for *Fun Girls from Mt. Pilot*

1996　Maude Gilman for *BR5-49,* BR5-49

BACKGROUND VOCALIST

1994　Kathy Chiavola

1995　Jonell Mosser

1996　Harry Stinson

GUITARIST

1994　Brent Mason

1995　Kenny Greenberg

1996　Kenny Greenberg

BASSIST

1994　Michael Rhodes

1995　Victor Wooten

1996　David Pomeroy

PIANIST/KEYBOARDS

1994　Matt Rollings

1995　Matt Rollings

1996　Matt Rollings

DRUMMER/PERCUSSIONIST

1994　Eddie Bayers

1995　Eddie Bayers

1996　Chester Thompson

MISCELLANEOUS INSTRUMENTALIST

1994　Mark O'Connor (fiddle)

1995　Bela Fleck (banjo)

1996　Bela Fleck (banjo)

UNSIGNED ARTIST/ACT

1994　Kevin Welch

1995　Stone Deep

1996　Joe, Marc's Brother

VIDEO OF THE YEAR

1994　"Independence Day," Robert Deaton, George Flanigen, performed by Martina McBride

1995　"Safe in the Arms of Love," Steven Goldman/High Five, performed by Martina McBride

1996　"My Wife Thinks You're Dead," Director: Michael McNamara, performed by Junior Brown

BRIDGE AWARDS

1994　Dale Fanklin
　　　Mayor Phil Bredesen

1995　Jim Ed Norman, president Warner/Reprise

1996　E.W. (Bud) Wendell

HERITAGE AWARDS

1994　Fairfield Four

1995　Hoss Allen

1996　Owen Bradley

MUSIC VENUE (LARGE)

1994　The Ryman Auditorium

1995　The Ryman Auditorium

1996　The Ryman Auditorium

MUSIC VENUE (SMALL)

1994　Bluebird Cafe

1995　328 Performance Hall

1996　Caffe Milano

RADIO STATION

1994　WSIX-FM (97.9)

1995　WRLT-FM (100.1)

1996　WRLT-FM (100.1)

TNN/MUSIC CITY NEWS COUNTRY AWARDS

Presented annually by The Nashville Network and Music City News.

ENTERTAINER

1985　The Statler Brothers

1986　The Statler Brothers

1987　The Statler Brothers

1988　Randy Travis

1989　Randy Travis

1990　Ricky Van Shelton

1991　Ricky Van Shelton

1992　Garth Brooks

1993　Alan Jackson

1994　Alan Jackson

1995　Alan Jackson

MALE ARTIST

1967　Merle Haggard

1968　Merle Haggard

1969　Charley Pride

1970　Charley Pride

1971　Charley Pride

1972　Charley Pride

1973　Charley Pride

1974　Conway Twitty

1975　Conway Twitty

1976　Conway Twitty

1977　Conway Twitty

1978　Larry Gatlin

1979　Kenny Rogers

1980　Marty Robbins

1981　George Jones

1982　Marty Robbins

1983　Marty Robbins

1984　Lee Greenwood

1985　Lee Greenwood

1986　George Strait

1987　Randy Travis

1988　Randy Travis

1989　Ricky Van Shelton

1990　Ricky Van Shelton

1991　Ricky Van Shelton

1992　Alan Jackson

1993　Alan Jackson

1994　Alan Jackson

1995　Alan Jackson

FEMALE ARTIST

1967　Loretta Lynn

1968　Loretta Lynn

1969　Loretta Lynn

1970　Loretta Lynn

1971　Loretta Lynn

1972　Loretta Lynn

1973　Loretta Lynn

1974	Loretta Lynn
1975	Loretta Lynn
1976	Loretta Lynn
1977	Loretta Lynn
1978	Loretta Lynn
1979	Barbara Mandrell
1980	Loretta Lynn
1981	Barbara Mandrell
1982	Barbara Mandrell
1983	Janie Fricke
1984	Janie Fricke
1985	Reba McEntire
1986	Reba McEntire
1987	Reba McEntire
1988	Reba McEntire
1989	Reba McEntire
1990	Patty Loveless
1991	Reba McEntire
1992	Reba McEntire
1993	Reba McEntire
1994	Lorrie Morgan
1995	Reba McEntire

VOCAL DUET

1967	Wilburn Brothers
1968	Porter Wagoner & Dolly Parton
1969	Porter Wagoner & Dolly Parton
1970	Porter Wagoner & Dolly Parton
1971	Conway Twitty & Loretta Lynn
1972	Conway Twitty & Loretta Lynn
1973	Conway Twitty & Loretta Lynn
1974	Conway Twitty & Loretta Lynn
1975	Conway Twitty & Loretta Lynn
1976	Conway Twitty & Loretta Lynn
1977	Conway Twitty & Loretta Lynn
1978	Conway Twitty & Loretta Lynn
1979	Kenny Rogers & Dottie West
1980	Conway Twitty & Loretta Lynn
1981	Conway Twitty & Loretta Lynn
1982	David Frizzell & Shelly West
1983	David Frizzell & Shelly West
1984	Kenny Rogers & Dolly Parton
1985	The Judds
1986	The Judds
1987	The Judds

VOCAL DUO

1988	The Judds
1989	The Judds
1990	The Judds
1991	The Judds
1992	The Judds
1993	Brooks & Dunn
1994	Brooks & Dunn

VOCAL GROUP

1967	Tompall & the Glaser Brothers

1968	Tompall & the Glaser Brothers
1969	Tompall & the Glaser Brothers
1970	Tompall & the Glaser Brothers
1971	Statler Brothers
1972	Statler Brothers
1973	Statler Brothers
1974	Statler Brothers
1975	Statler Brothers
1976	Statler Brothers
1977	Statler Brothers
1978	Statler Brothers
1978	Statler Brothers
1979	Statler Brothers
1980	Statler Brothers
1981	Statler Brothers
1982	Statler Brothers
1983	Alabama
1984	Statler Brothers
1985	Statler Brothers
1986	Statler Brothers
1987	Statler Brothers
1988	Statler Brothers (MCN)
	Oak Ridge Boys (TNN)
1989	Statler Brothers (MCN)
	Oak Ridge Boys (TNN)
1990	Statler Brothers
1991	Statler Brothers
1992	Statler Brothers
1993	Statler Brothers
1994	Statler Brothers

VOCAL GROUP OR DUO

1995	Brooks & Dunn

VOCAL COLLABORATION

1988	Emmylou Harris, Dolly Parton & Linda Ronstadt
1989	Dwight Yoakam & Buck Owens
1990	Hank Williams & Hank Williams Jr.
1991	Lorrie Morgan & Keith Whitley
1992	Dolly Parton & Ricky Van Shelton
1993	Marty Stuart & Travis Tritt
1994	Reba McEntire & Linda Davis
1995	George Jones & Alan Jackson

MOST PROMISING MALE ARTIST

1967	Tom T. Hall
1968	Cal Smith
1969	Johnny Bush
1970	Tommy Cash
1971	Tommy Overstreet
1972	Billy "Crash" Craddock
1973	Johnny Rodriguez
1974	Johnny Rodriguez
1975	Ronnie Milsap
1976	Mickey Gilley
1977	Larry Gatlin

1978	Don Williams
1979	Rex Allen Jr.
1980	Hank Williams Jr.
1981	Boxcar Willie
1982	T.G. Sheppard

MOST PROMISING FEMALE ARTIST

1967	Tammy Wynette
1968	Dolly Parton
1969	Peggy Sue
1970	Susan Raye
1971	Susan Raye
1972	Donna Forgo
1973	Tonya Tucker
1974	Olivia Newton-John
1975	Crystal Gayle
1976	Barbara Mandrell
1977	Helen Cornelius
1978	Debby Boone
1979	Janie Fricke
1980	Charly McClain
1981	Louise Mandrell
1982	Shelly West

STAR OF TOMORROW AWARD

1983	Ricky Skaggs
1984	Ronny Robbins
1985	The Judds
1986	John Schneider
1987	Randy Travis
1988	Ricky Van Shelton
1989	Patty Loveless (MCN)
	Shenandoah (TNN)
1990	Clint Black
1991	Alan Jackson
1992	Travis Tritt
1993	Doug Stone
1994	John Michael Montgomery

STAR OF TOMORROW—MALE

1995	Tim McGraw

STAR OF TOMORROW—FEMALE

1995	Faith Hill

STAR OF TOMORROW—VOCAL GROUP OR DUO

1995	BlackHawk

SONG

1967	"There Goes My Everything" Writer: Dallas Frazier
1969	"All I Have to Offer You Is Me" Writers: Dallas Frazier, Doodle Owen
1970	"Hello Darlin'" Writer: Conway Twitty

1971	"Help Me Make It Through the Night"
	Writer: Kris Kristofferson
1972	"Kiss an Angel Good Morning"
	Writer: Ben Peters
1973	"Why Me Lord"
	Writer: Kris Kristofferson
1974	"You've Never Been this Far Before"
	Writer: Conway Twitty
1975	"Country Bumpkin"
	Writer: Don Wayne
1976	"Blue Eyes Crying in the Rain"
	Writer: Fred Rose
1977	"I Don't Want to Have to Marry You"
	Writers: Fred Imus, Phil Sweet
1981	"He Stopped Lovin' Her Today,"
	Writers: Bobby Braddock, Curly Putnam
1982	"Elvira"
	Writer: Dallas Frazier
1983	"I'm Gonna Hire a Wino to Decorate Our Home"
	Writer: Dewayne Blackwell
1984	"Swingin'"
	Writers: John Anderson, Lionel Delmore
1985	"Elizabeth"
	Writer: Jimmy Fortune
1986	"My Only Love"
	Writer: Jimmy Fortune
1987	"Too Much on My Heart"
	Writer: Jimmy Fortune
1988	"Forever and Ever, Amen"
	Writers: Don Schlitz, Paul Overstreet
1989	"I'll Leave this World Loving You"
	Writer: Mack Vickery
1990	"Here in the Real World"
	Writers: Alan Jackson, Mark Irwin
1991	"Here's a Quarter (Call Someone Who Cares)"
	Writer: Travis Tritt
1992	"I Still Believe in You"
	Writers: Vince Gill, John Jarvis
1993	"Chattahoochee"
	Writers: Alan Jackson, Jim McBride
1995	"Your Love Amazes Me"
	Writers: Amanda Hunt-Taylor, Chuck Jones

SINGLE

1978	"Heaven's Just a Sin Away," the Kendalls
1979	"The Gambler," Kenny Rogers
1980	"Coward of the County," Kenny Rogers
1981	"He Stopped Lovin' Her Today," George Jones
1982	"Elvira," the Oak Ridge Boys
1983	"Some Memories Just Won't Die," Marty Robbins
1984	"Elizabeth," the Statler Brothers
1985	"God Bless the U.S.A.," Lee Greenwood
1986	"My Only Love," the Statler Brothers
1987	"On the Other Hand," Randy Travis
1988	"Forever and Ever, Amen," Randy Travis
1989	"I'll Leave this World Loving You," Ricky Van Shelton
1990	"More than a Name on a Wall," the Statler Brothers
1991	"When I Call Your Name," Vince Gill
1992	"Don't Rock the Jukebox," Alan Jackson
1993	"I Still Believe in You," Vince Gill
1994	"Chattahoochee," Alan Jackson
1995	"Livin' on Love," Alan Jackson

ALBUM

1976	*When a Tingle Becomes a Chill,* Loretta Lynn
1977	*I Don't Want to Have to Marry You,* Jim Ed Brown & Helen Cornelius
1978	*Moody Blue,* Elvis Presley
1979	*Entertainers On & Off the Record,* the Statler Brothers
1980	*The Originals,* the Statler Brothers
1981	*Tenth Anniversary,* the Statler Brothers
1982	*Feels So Right,* Alabama
1983	*Come Back to Me,* Marty Robbins
1984	*The Closer You Get,* Alabama
1985	*Atlanta Blue,* the Statler Brothers
1986	*Pardners in Rhyme,* the Statler Brothers
1987	*Storms of Life,* Randy Travis
1988	*Always & Forever,* Randy Travis
1989	*Loving Proof,* Ricky Van Shelton (MCN)
	Old 8 x 10, Randy Travis (TNN)
1990	*Killin' Time,* Clint Black
1991	*Here in the Real World,* Alan Jackson
1992	*Don't Rock the Jukebox,* Alan Jackson
1993	*I Still Believe in You,* Vince Gill
1994	*A Lot About Livin' (And a Little 'Bout Love),* Alan Jackson
1995	*Who I Am,* Alan Jackson

SONGWRITER

1967	Bill Anderson
1968	Bill Anderson
1969	Bill Anderson
1970	Merle Haggard
1972	Kris Kristofferson
1973	Kris Kristofferson
1974	Bill Anderson
1975	Bill Anderson
1976	Bill Anderson
1977	Larry Gatlin
1978	Larry Gatlin
1979	Eddie Rabbitt
1980	Marty Robbins

BAND

1967	The Buckaroos
1968	The Buckaroos
1969	The Buckaroos
1970	The Buckaroos
1971	The Strangers
1972	The Strangers
1973	The Po' Boys
1974	The Buckaroos
1975	The Coalminers
1976	The Coalminers
1977	The Coalminers
1978	Larry Gatlin, Family & Friends
1979	The Oak Ridge Boys Band
1980	Charlie Daniels Band
1981	Marty Robbins Band
1982	Alabama
1983	Alabama

INSTRUMENTALIST

1969	Roy Clark
1970	Roy Clark
1971	Roy Clark
1972	Roy Clark
1973	Charlie McCoy
1974	Roy Clark
1975	Buck Owens
1976	Buck Owens
1977	Johnny Gimble
1978	Roy Clark
1979	Roy Clark
1980	Roy Clark
1981	Barbara Mandrell
1982	Barbara Mandrell
1988	Ricky Skaggs
1989	Ricky Skaggs
1990	Ricky Skaggs
1991	Vince Gill

1992	Vince Gill
1993	Vince Gill
1994	Vince Gill

INSTRUMENTAL ENTERTAINER

1974	Charlie McCoy
1975	Roy Clark
1976	Roy Clark
1977	Roy Clark

BLUEGRASS ACT

1971	Osborne Brothers
1972	Osborne Brothers
1973	Osborne Brothers
1974	Osborne Brothers
1975	Osborne Brothers
1976	Osborne Brothers
1977	Osborne Brothers
1978	Osborne Brothers
1979	Osborne Brothers
1980	Bill Monroe & His Blue Grass Boys
1981	Bill Monroe & His Blue Grass Boys
1982	Ricky Skaggs
1983	Ricky Skaggs
1984	Ricky Skaggs

GOSPEL GROUP/ACT

1979	Connie Smith
1980	Carter Family
1981	Hee Haw Gospel Quartet
1982	Hee Haw Gospel Quartet
1983	Hee Haw Gospel Quartet
1984	Hee Haw Gospel Quartet
1985	Hee Haw Gospel Quartet
1986	Hee Haw Gospel Quartet
1987	Hee Haw Gospel Quartet
1988	Chuck Wagon Gang
1989	The Whites
1990	Chuck Wagon Gang
1991	Chuck Wagon Gang
1992	Chuck Wagon Gang
1993	Chuck Wagon Gang

CHRISTIAN COUNTRY ARTIST

1994	Paul Overstreet
1995	Ricky Van Shelton

COMEDIAN

1972	Archie Campbell
1973	Mel Tillis
1974	Mel Tillis
1975	Mel Tillis
1976	Mel Tillis
1977	Mel Tillis
1978	Mel Tillis
1979	Jerry Clower

1980	Statler Brothers
1981	Mandrell Sisters
1982	Statler Brothers
1983	Statler Brothers
1984	Statler Brothers
1985	Statler Brothers
1986	Ray Stevens
1987	Ray Stevens
1988	Ray Stevens
1989	Ray Stevens
1990	Ray Stevens
1991	Ray Stevens
1992	Ray Stevens
1993	Ray Stevens
1994	Ray Stevens
1995	Jeff Foxworthy

MINNIE PEARL AWARD

1988	Minnie Pearl
1989	Roy Acuff
1990	Tennessee Ernie Ford
1991	Barbara Mandrell
1992	Emmylou Harris
1993	Vince Gill
1994	Dolly Parton
1995	Willie Nelson

FOUNDERS AWARD

1976	Faron Young
1977	Ralph Emery
1978	Ernest Tubb
1979	Pee Wee King
1980	Buck Owens
1981	Betty Cox Adler

LIVING LEGEND

1983	Roy Acuff
1984	Ernest Tubb
1985	Barbara Mandrell
1986	Loretta Lynn
1987	George Jones
1988	Conway Twitty
1989	Johnny Cash
1990	Merle Haggard
1991	Tammy Wynette
1992	Roy Rogers
1993	Kitty Wells
1994	Dolly Parton
1995	Waylon Jennings

COUNTRY MUSIC TV SHOW

1969	*Johnny Cash Show/Hee Haw* (tie)
1970	*Hee Haw*
1971	*Hee Haw*
1972	*Hee Haw*
1973	*Hee Haw*

1974	*Hee Haw*
1975	*Hee Haw*
1976	*Hee Haw*
1977	*Hee Haw*
1978	*50 Years of Country Music*
1979	*PBS Live from the Grand Ole Opry*
1980	*PBS Live from the Grand Ole Opry*
1981	*Barbara Mandrell & the Mandrell Sisters*
1982	*Barbara Mandrell & the Mandrell Sisters*
1983	*Hee Haw*
1984	*Hee Haw*
1985	*Nashville Now*
1986	*Nashville Now*
1987	*Nashville Now*
1988	*Nashville Now*
1989	*Nashville Now*

COUNTRY MUSIC TV SPECIAL

1983	*Conway Twitty on the Mississippi*
1984	*Another Evening with the Statler Brothers: Heroes, Legends & Friends*
1985	*Another Evening with the Statler Brothers: Heroes, Legends & Friends*
1986	*FarmAid*
1987	*Statler Brothers' Christmas Present*
1988	*Grand Ole Opry Live*
1989	*A Country Music Celebration*

VIDEO

1985	"Elizabeth," the Statler Brothers
1986	"My Only Love," the Statler Brothers
1987	"Whoever's in New England," Reba McEntire
1988	"Maple Street Memories," the Statler Brothers (MCN)
	"Forever and Ever, Amen," Randy Travis (TNN)
1989	"I'll Leave This World Loving You," Ricky Van Shelton
1990	"There's a Tear in My Beer," Hank Williams/Hank Williams Jr.
1991	"The Dance," Garth Brooks
1992	"Rockin' Years," Dolly Parton & Ricky Van Shelton
1993	"Midnight in Montgomery," Alan Jackson
1994	"Chattahoochee," Alan Jackson
1995	"Independence Day," Martina McBride

The following albums by individual artists or groups achieved the highest rating possible—5 bones—from our discriminating MusicHound Country writers. You can't miss with any of these recordings.

Eddy Arnold
The Essential Eddy Arnold (RCA)

Kenny Baker
Master Fiddler (County)

Dewey Balfa
The Balfa Brothers Play Traditional Cajun Music (Swallow)

Clint Black
Killin' Time (RCA)

Jimmy Buffett
All the Greatest Hits (Prism Leisure)
Songs You Know by Heart: Jimmy Buffett's Greatest Hit(s) (MCA)

The Byrds
The Byrds (Columbia)
Mr. Tambourine Man (Columbia/Legacy)
Sweetheart of the Rodeo (Columbia/Legacy)

The Carter Family
Anchored in Love: Their Complete Victor Recordings, 1927–1928 (Rounder)
Country Music Hall of Fame Series (MCA)
My Clinch Mountain Home: Their Compete Victor Recordings, 1928–1929 (Rounder)
Sunshine in the Shadows: Their Complete Victor Recordings, 1931–1932 (Rounder)

20 of the Best of the Carter Family (RCA International)
When the Roses Bloom in Dixieland: Their Complete Victor Recordings, 1929–1930 (Rounder)
Worried Man Blues: Their Complete Victor Recordings, 1930 (Rounder)

Johnny Cash
American Recordings (American)
Columbia Records, 1958–1986 (Columbia)
The Essential Johnny Cash, 1955–1983 (Columbia/Legacy)
The Sun Years (Sun/Rhino)

Rosanne Cash
King's Record Shop (Columbia)

Ray Charles
Greatest Country & Western Hits (DCC Compact Classics)
Modern Sounds in Country and Western Music (Rhino)

The Chuck Wagon Gang
The Chuck Wagon Gang Columbia Historic Edition (Columbia)

Patsy Cline
The Patsy Cline Collection (MCA)

Stompin' Tom Connors
Bud the Spud (Capitol/EMI Canada)
A Proud Canadian (Capitol/EMI Canada)

The Country Gentlemen
Country Songs Old and New (Smithsonian/Folkways)
Folk Songs and Bluegrass (Smithsonian/Folkways)

J.D. Crowe
J.D. Crowe & the New South (Rounder)

The Delmore Brothers
Brown's Ferry Blues (County)
Freight Train Boogie (Ace)
Sand Mountain Blues (County)
When They Let the Hammer Down (Bear Family)

Iris DeMent
Infamous Angel (Warner Bros.)
My Life (Warner Bros.)

Bob Dylan
Blonde on Blonde (Columbia)
Highway 61 Revisited (Columbia)

The Eagles
Hotel California (Asylum)
Their Greatest Hits, 1971–1975 (Asylum)

Duane Eddy
Have Twangy Guitar Will Travel (Jamie)
Twang Thing: The Duane Eddy Anthology (Rhino)

Dave Edmunds/Rockpile
Get It (Swan Song)
Repeat When Necessary (Swan Song)
Tracks on Wax 4 (Swan Song)

The Everly Brothers
Cadence Classics: Their 20 Greatest Hits (Rhino)

Flatt & Scruggs
The Mercury Sessions, Volume 1 (Rounder)

The Mercury Sessions, Volume 2 (Rounder)

John Fogerty (with Creedence Clearwater Revival)
Cosmo's Factory (Fantasy)

Red Foley
Country Music Hall of Fame Series (MCA)

Tennessee Ernie Ford
Sixteen Tons (Capitol)

Don Gibson
A Legend in His Time (Bear Family)

Vince Gill
I Still Believe in You (MCA)
Souvenirs (MCA)
When I Call Your Name (MCA)

Jimmie Dale Gilmore
After Awhile (Elektra Nonesuch)

Steve Goodman
No Big Surprise (Red Pajamas)

Vern Gosdin
Chiseled in Stone (Columbia)

The Grateful Dead
American Beauty (Warner Bros.)
Two from the Vault (Grateful Dead Records)
Workingman's Dead (Warner Bros.)

Nanci Griffith
Last of the True Believers (Rounder/Philo)
One Fair Summer Evening (MCA)
Other Voices, Other Rooms (Elektra)

Woody Guthrie
Bound for Glory (Smithsonian/Folkways)
Dust Bowl Ballads (Rounder)
Library of Congress Recordings (Rounder)

Merle Haggard
Down Every Road (Capitol)
The Lonesome Fugitive: The Merle Haggard Anthology (1963–1977) (Razor & Tie)
A Tribute to the Best Damn Fiddle Player in the World (or, My Salute to Bob Wills) (Koch)
Untamed Hawk (Bear Family)

Emmylou Harris
At the Ryman (Reprise)
Last Date (Warner Bros.)
Roses in the Snow (Warner Bros.)
Wrecking Ball (Asylum)

John Hartford
Mark Twang (Flying Fish)
Me Oh My, How the Time Does Fly (Flying Fish)

Ronnie Hawkins
The Best of Ronnie Hawkins & the Hawks (Rhino)

Hazel & Alice
Hazel & Alice (Rounder)

Joe Henry
Short Man's Room (Mammoth)

Chris Hillman (with Herb Pedersen)
Bakersfield Bound (Sugar Hill)

Buddy Holly
The Buddy Holly Collection (MCA)

The Holy Modal Rounders
Have Moicy! (Rounder)

The Hoosier Hot Shots
Rural Rhythm, 1935–1942 (Columbia/Legacy)

Alan Jackson
The Greatest Hits Collection (Arista)

Stonewall Jackson
Stonewall Jackson's Greatest Hits (Columbia)

Wanda Jackson
Vintage Collections Series (Capitol)

The Kingston Trio
At Large (Capitol)
The Capitol Years (Capitol)
The Kingston Trio (Capitol)
Live at the Hungry I (Capitol)
Live at Newport (Vanguard)

Alison Krauss
Now That I've Found You: A Collection (Rounder)

Doyle Lawson
Rock My Soul (Sugar Hill)

Jerry Lee Lewis
Milestones (Rhino)
Original Sun Greatest Hits (Rhino)
Rare Tracks: Wild One (Rhino)

Louvin Brothers
Tragic Songs of Life (Capitol)
When I Stop Dreaming: The Best of the Louvin Brothers (Razor & Tie)

Loretta Lynn
Honky-Tonk Girl: The Loretta Lynn Collection (MCA)

Lynyrd Skynyrd
Lynyrd Skynyrd (MCA)
Street Survivors (MCA)

Jimmy Martin
Jimmy Martin & the Sunny Mountain Boys (Bear Family)
You Don't Know My Mind (Rounder)

The Del McCoury Band
Classic Bluegrass (Rebel)
A Deeper Shade of Blue (Rounder)

Kate & Anna McGarrigle
French Record (Hannibal)
Kate & Anna McGarrigle (Hannibal)

Roger Miller
King of the Road: The Genius of Roger Miller (Mercury)

Bill Monroe & His Blue Grass Boys
Bill Monroe: Bluegrass, 1950–1958 (Bear Family)
The Essential Bill Monroe & His Blue Grass Boys, 1945–1949 (Columbia/Legacy)
Feast Here Tonight (RCA/Bluebird)
The Music of Bill Monroe from 1936 to 1994 (MCA)
16 Gems (Columbia)

The Morells
Shake and Push (East Side Digital)

The Nashville Bluegrass Band
To Be His Child (Rounder)
Unleashed (Sugar Hill)
Waitin' for the Hard Times to Go (Sugar Hill)

Willie Nelson
Nite Life: Greatest Hits and Rare Tracks, 1959–1971 (Rhino)
Phases and Stages (Atlantic)
Red Headed Stranger (Columbia)
Revolutions of Time . . . the Journey (Columbia/Legacy)
Shotgun Willie (Atlantic)
Shotgun Willie/Phases and Stages (Mobile Fidelity Sound Lab)
Who'll Buy My Memories? (The IRS Tapes) (Sony)

The New Lost City Ramblers
The New Lost City Ramblers, the Early Years, 1958–1962 (Smithsonian/Folkways)

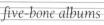

The New Lost City Ramblers Volume 2, 1963–1973: Out Standing in Their Field (Smithsonian/Folkways)

The Nitty Gritty Dirt Band
Will the Circle Be Unbroken (Liberty)

Mark O'Connor (with Yo Yo Ma)
Appalachia Waltz (Sony Classical)

Roy Orbison
The All-Time Greatest Hits of Roy Orbison, Volume 1 (Monument)
For the Lonely: A Roy Orbison Anthology, 1956–1964 (Rhino)
The Legendary Roy Orbison (CBS Special Products)

Gram Parsons
G.P./Grievous Angel (Reprise)

Dolly Parton
The RCA Years (1967–1986) (RCA)

Dolly Parton, Linda Ronstadt & Emmylou Harris
Trio (Columbia)

Les Paul
Les Paul: The Legend and the Legacy (Capitol)

Webb Pierce
King of the Honky-Tonk: From the Original Decca Masters, 1952–1959 (Country Music Foundation/MCA)

Elvis Presley
The Complete Sun Sessions (RCA)
Elvis' Golden Records, Volume I (RCA)
Elvis' Golden Records, Volume 3 (RCA)
50,000,000 Elvis Fans Can't Be Wrong: Elvis' Golden Records, Volume 2 (RCA)
From Nashville to Memphis: The Essential '60's Masters I (RCA)
The King of Rock 'n' Roll: The Complete 1950's Masters (RCA)
The Million Dollar Quartet (RCA)

Ray Price
The Essential Ray Price: 1951–1962 (Columbia)
Ray Price and the Cherokee Cowboys (Bear Family)

John Prine
John Prine (Atlantic)

The Missing Years (Oh Boy)

Rank & File
Long Gone Dead (Slash)

Don Reno & Red Smiley
Reno & Smiley & the Tennessee Cut-ups, 1951–1959 (King)

Jimmie Rodgers
First Sessions, 1927–1928 (Rounder)

Linda Ronstadt
Heart Like a Wheel (Capitol)
Prisoner in Disguise (Asylum)

Jean Shepard
The Melody Ranch Girl (Bear Family)

Ricky Skaggs
Highways and Heartaches (Epic)

Carl Smith
The Essential Carl Smith, 1950–1956 (Columbia/Legacy)

Hank Snow
I'm Movin' On and Other Great Country Hits (RCA)
The Singing Ranger, 1949–1953 (Bear Family)

Sons of the Pioneers
Country Music Hall of Fame (MCA)

The Stanley Brothers
Angel Band: The Classic Mercury Recordings (Mercury)
The Complete Columbia Stanley Brothers (Columbia/Legacy)

The Statler Brothers
Best of the Statler Brothers (Mercury)

John Stewart
California Bloodlines/Willard (Bear Family)
The Complete Phoenix Concerts (Bear Family)

Wynn Stewart
California Country: The Best of the Challenge Masters (AVI)

Jerry & Tammy Sullivan
A Joyful Noise (Country Music Foundation)

Russ Taff
Under Their Influence Volume 1 (Word)

James Talley
Got No Bread/Tryin' Like the Devil (Bear Family)

Pam Tillis
Sweetheart's Dance (Arista)

Ernest Tubb
Country Music Hall of Fame (MCA)

Townes Van Zandt
The Late Great Townes Van Zandt (Poppy)
Live at the Old Quarter, Houston, Texas (Tomato)

Don Walser
Rolling Stone from Texas (Watermelon)

Doc Watson/The Watson Family
Live Duet Recordings, 1963–1980: Off the Record, Volume 2 (Smithsonian/Folkways)
Doc Watson and Clarence Ashley: The Original Folkways Recordings, 1960–1962 (Smithsonian/Folkways)
The Doc Watson Family (Sugar Hill)
Doc Watson: The Vanguard Years (Vanguard)
The Watson Family (Smithsonian/Folkways)

Kitty Wells
Country Music Hall of Fame (MCA)

Hank Williams
The Collectors' Edition (Mercury)
40 Greatest Hits (Polydor)
The Hits Volume 1 (Mercury)
The Hits Volume 2 (Mercury)

Hank Williams Jr.
Hank Williams Jr. & Friends (MGM)

Lucinda Williams
Lucinda Williams (Rough Trade)

Bob Wills
Anthology, 1935–1973 (Rhino)

Tammy Wynette
Anniversary: 20 Years Of Hits (Epic)

Neil Young
Deja Vu (Atlantic)
Tonight's the Night (Reprise)

If you're looking for some good country music by a variety of performers, these compilation albums would be a good place to start. (We've broken the list down by type of music to make your life a little easier.)

AMERICANA

Hell-Bent: Insurgent Country, Vol. 2 (Bloodshot) ♪♪

HighTone Records: The First 10 Years (HighTone) ♪♪♪♪

Nashville—The Other Side of the Alley: Insurgent Country, Vol. 3 (Bloodshot) ♪♪♪

Points West: New Horizons in Country Music (HighTone) ♪♪♪♪

Revival: Brunswick Stew & Pig Pickin' (Yep Roc) ♪♪♪

Rig Rock Deluxe (Upstart) ♪♪♪♪

Rig Rock Jukebox (Diesel Only Records/Fruit of the Tune Music) ♪♪♪♪

Rig Rock Truck Stop (Diesel Only Records/Fruit of the Tune Music) ♪♪♪♪

Songs from Chippy (Hollywood) ♪♪♪♪

Straight Outta Boone County (Bloodshot) ♪♪♪

A Town South of Bakersfield, Vols. 1 & 2 (Restless) ♪♪♪♪♪

A Town South of Bakersfield, Vol. 3 (Restless) ♪♪♪♪

True Sounds of the New West (Freedom) ♪♪♪

White Mansions (A&M) ♪♪

BLUEGRASS

Acoustic Disc: 100% Handmade Music (Acoustic Disc) ♪♪♪

Acoustic Disc: 100% Handmade Music, Vol. II (Acoustic Disc) ♪♪♪

Appalachian Stomp: Bluegrass Classics (Rhino) ♪♪♪♪

The Best of Bluegrass: Preachin', Prayin' and Singin' (Mercury) ♪♪♪♪

The Best of Bluegrass, Vol. 1: Standards (Mercury) ♪♪♪♪

Blue Ribbon Bluegrass (Rounder) ♪♪♪♪

Bluegrass Class of 1990 (Rounder) ♪♪♪♪

Bluegrass from Heaven: The Essential Gospel Collection (CMH) ♪♪♪

Bluegrass Super Hits (Columbia) ♪♪♪♪

Fifty Years of Bluegrass Hits (CMH) ♪♪♪

Hand-Picked: Twenty-Five Years of Rounder Bluegrass (Rounder) ♪♪♪♪♪

Son of Rounder Banjo (Rounder) ♪♪♪♪

Top of the Hill Bluegrass: The Sugar Hill Collection (Sugar Hill) ♪♪♪♪

True Life Blues: The Songs of Bill Monroe (Sugar Hill) ♪♪♪♪

20 Bluegrass Originals: Hymns (Deluxe) ♪♪♪

BOX SETS

Fifty Years of Bluegrass Hits (CMH) ♪♪♪

Fifty Years of Country Music from Mercury, 1945–1995 (Mercury) ♪♪♪♪

From the Vaults: Decca Country Classics, 1934–1973 (MCA) ♪♪♪♪

The Sun Records Collection (Rhino) ♪♪♪♪

CAJUN/LOUISIANA

The Best of Louisiana Music (Rounder) ♪♪♪♪

Cajun Dance Hall Special (Rounder) ♪♪♪♪

Cajun Dance Party: Fais Do-Do (Columbia/Legacy) ♪♪♪♪

Cajun Music and Zydeco (Rounder) ♪♪♪♪

Cajun Spice: Dance Music from South Louisiana (Rounder) ♪♪♪♪

Cajun: Vol. 1, Abbeville Breakdown, 1929–1939 (Columbia) ♪♪♪♪

Le Gran Mamou, Vol. 1 (Country Music Foundation) ♪♪♪♪♪

Gran Prairie, Vol. 3 (Country Music Foundation) ♪♪♪♪♪

Louisiana Cajun from the Southwest Prairies, Vol. 1 (Rounder) ♪♪♪♪

Louisiana Cajun from the Southwest Prairies, Vol. 2 (Rounder) ♪♪♪♪

Louisiana Live from Mountain Stage (Blue Plate Music) ♪♪♪♪

Louisiana Spice: 25 Years of Louisiana Music on Rounder Records (Rounder) ♪♪♪♪

More Cajun Music and Zydeco (Rounder) ♪♪♪♪

Raise Your Window, Vol. 2 (Country Music Foundation) ♪♪♪♪♪

CHILDREN'S

The Best of Country Sing the Best of Disney (Walt Disney) ♪♪♪

Country Music for Kids (Walt Disney) ♪♪♪♪

Daddies Sing Good Night (Sugar Hill) ♪♪♪♪

'Til Their Eyes Shine . . . The Lullaby Album (Columbia) ♪♪♪

CHRISTMAS

Alligator Stomp, Vol. 4: Cajun Christmas (Rhino) ♪♪♪

An Americana Christmas (Winter Harvest) ♪♪♪♪

Billboard Greatest Country Christmas Hits (Rhino) ♪♪♪♪♪

Christmas at Mountain Stage (Blue Plate Music) ♪♪♪

Christmas for the '90s, Vol. 3 (Capitol) ♪♪♪

Christmas on the Range (Capitol) ♪♪♪♪

Christmas Time Back Home (Rebel) ♪♪♪

A Country Christmas Vol. V (RCA) ♪♪♪♪

A Giant Country Christmas (Giant) ♪♪♪

Heart of Christmas: 12 Favorites by Today's Country Stars (Sparrow) ♪♪♪

Hillbilly Holiday (Rhino) ♪♪♪♪♪

Must Be Santa: The Rounder Christmas Album (Rounder) ♪♪♪♪

Precious Child (Warner Bros.) ♪♪

Star of Wonder (Arista) ♪♪♪

Sugar Plums: Holiday Treats from Sugar Hill (Sugar Hill) ♪♪♪♪

A Tejano Country Christmas (Arista/Texas) ♪♪♪♪

Tinsel Tunes: More Holiday Treats from Sugar Hill (Sugar Hill) ♪♪♪

COWBOY

Back in the Saddle Again (New World) ♪♪♪♪♪

Cattle Call: Early Cowboy Music and Its Roots (Rounder) ♪♪♪♪

Cowboy Songs on Folkways (Smithsonian/Folkways) ♪♪♪♪

Cowboy Super Hits (Columbia) ♪♪♪

Don't Fence Me In: Western Music's Early Golden Era (Rounder) ♪♪♪♪

Saddle Up! The Cowboy Renaissance (Rounder) ♪♪♪♪

Songs of the West (four-CD box) *(Rhino)* ♪♪♪♪

Songs of the West: Cowboy Classics (Rhino) ♪♪♪♪

Songs of the West: Gene Autry and Roy Rogers (Rhino) ♪♪♪♪

Songs of the West: Movie and Television Themes (Rhino) ♪♪♪♪

Songs of the West: Silver Screen Cowboys (Rhino) ♪♪♪

Stampede! Western Music's Late Golden Era (Rounder) ♪♪♪♪

FOLK

The Acoustic Edge (Rhino) ♪♪♪

Christine Lavin Presents: Big Times in a Small Town — The Vineyard Tapes (Philo/Rounder) ♪♪♪

Christine Lavin Presents: Laugh Tracks, Vol. 1 (Shanachie) ♪♪♪

Christine Lavin Presents: Laugh Tracks, Vol. 2 (Shanachie) ♪♪♪

Christine Lavin Presents: On a Winter's Night (Philo/Rounder) ♪♪♪♪

Hills of Home: 25 Years of Folk Music on Rounder Records (Rounder) ♪♪♪♪

House on Fire: An Urban Folk Collection (Red House) ♪♪♪

Legacy: New Folk Music (Windham Hill) ♪♪♪♪

Legacy II: A Collection of Singer Songwriters (High Street) ♪♪♪♪

Philo So Far: The 20th Anniversary Folk Sampler (Philo) ♪♪♪♪

When October Goes (Philo/Rounder) ♪♪♪♪

GENERAL COUNTRY COLLECTIONS

All-Time Legends of Country Music (Columbia/Legacy) ♪♪♪

American Country Jukebox Classics, Vol. 1–5 (Sterling Gold) ♪♪♪

The Best of Country Sing the Best of Disney (Walt Disney) ♪♪♪

Billboard Top Country Hits: 1959 (Rhino) ♪♪♪

Billboard Top Country Hits: 1960 (Rhino) ♪♪♪

Billboard Top Country Hits: 1961 (Rhino) ♪♪♪♪

Billboard Top Country Hits: 1962 (Rhino) ♪♪♪

Billboard Top Country Hits: 1963 (Rhino) ♪♪♪♪

Billboard Top Country Hits: 1964 (Rhino) ♪♪♪♪

Billboard Top Country Hits: 1965 (Rhino) ♪♪♪

Billboard Top Country Hits: 1966 (Rhino) ♪♪♪♪

Billboard Top Country Hits: 1967 (Rhino) ♪♪♪♪

Billboard Top Country Hits: 1968 (Rhino) ♪♪♪♪

Billboard Top Country Hits: 1986 (Rhino) ♪♪

Billboard Top Country Hits: 1987 (Rhino) ♪♪♪

Billboard Top Country Hits: 1988 (Rhino) ♪♪♪♪

Billboard Top Country Hits: 1989 (Rhino) ♪♪♪

Billboard Top Country Hits: 1990 (Rhino) ♪♪♪

Classic Country Music (Smithsonian) ♪♪♪♪

Country Shots, Vol. 1: God Bless America (Rhino) ♪♪

Country Shots, Vol. 2: Heartbreak-ups (Rhino) ♪♪♪♪

Country Shots, Vol. 3: Two-Timing Tunes (Rhino) ♪♪♪♪

Deep in the Heart of Country (Drive) ♪♪

Dr. Demento's Country Corn (Rhino) ♪♪♪

Dynamic Duets Super Hits (Columbia) ♪♪♪

Golden Throats 3: Sweethearts of Rodeo Drive (Rhino) ♪♪

Hank Williams Songbook: 20 Songs by 11 Artists (Columbia/Legacy) ♪♪♪♪♪

Hillbilly Boogie (Columbia/Legacy) ♪♪♪

Hillbilly Fever! Vol. 1: Legends of Western Swing (Rhino) ♪♪♪♪

Hillbilly Fever! Vol. 2: Legends of Honky Tonk (Rhino) ♪♪♪♪

Hillbilly Fever! Vol. 3: Legends of Nashville (Rhino) ♪♪♪♪

Hillbilly Fever! Vol. 4: Legends of the West Coast (Rhino) ♪♪♪♪

Hillbilly Fever! Vol. 5: Legends of Country Rock (Rhino) ♪♪♪♪

Hillbilly Music, Thank God! (Capitol) ♪♪♪♪

Honky Tonk Super Hits (Columbia) ♪♪♪

Memphis Ramble (Rhino) ♪♪♪♪

NASCAR: Hotter Than Asphalt (Columbia) ♪♪♪

NASCAR: Runnin' Wide Open (Columbia) ♪♪♪

The Nashville Sound: Owen Bradley (Decca) ♪♪♪

One Voice (MCA) ♪♪♪

Outlaws Super Hits (Columbia) ♪♪♪

Red Hot + Country (Mercury) ♪♪♪♪

Rhythm, Country and Blues (MCA) ♪♪♪

When You're Hot You're Country (Drive) ♪♪

GOSPEL/RELIGIOUS

Amazing Grace: A Country Salute to Gospel (Sparrow) ♪♪♪

The Best of Bluegrass: Preachin', Prayin' and Singin' (Mercury) ♪♪♪

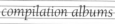

Bluegrass from Heaven: The Essential Gospel Collection (CMH) 🎵🎵🎵

Common Ground: Country Songs of Faith, Love & Inspiration (Epic) 🎵🎵🎵

Favorite Sacred Song (King) 🎵🎵🎵

The Gospel Tradition: The Roots and Branches, Vol. 1 (Columbia/Legacy) 🎵🎵🎵🎵

Jubilation! Vol. 3, Country Gospel (Rhino) 🎵🎵

Peace in the Valley (Arista) 🎵🎵🎵

Silent Witness (New Haven) 🎵🎵🎵

Something Got a Hold of Me: A Treasury of Sacred Music (RCA) 🎵🎵🎵🎵🎵

20 Bluegrass Originals: Hymns (Deluxe) 🎵🎵🎵

INSTRUMENTAL

The Banjos That Destroyed the World (CMH) 🎵🎵

The Great Dobro Sessions (Sugar Hill) 🎵🎵🎵🎵

Guitar Player Presents Legends of Country Guitar, Vols. 1 & 2 (Rhino) 🎵🎵🎵🎵🎵

Hats Off! A Tribute to Garth Brooks by Country Music's Hottest Pickers (CMH) 🎵🎵

The World's Greatest Country Fiddlers (CMH) 🎵🎵

LIVE RECORDINGS

The Best of Mountain Stage, Vol. 1 Live (Blue Plate Music) 🎵🎵🎵🎵

The Best of Mountain Stage, Vol. 2 Live (Blue Plate Music) 🎵🎵🎵🎵

The Best of Mountain Stage, Vol. 3 Live (Blue Plate Music) 🎵🎵🎵🎵

The Best of Mountain Stage, Vol. 4 Live (Blue Plate Music) 🎵🎵🎵🎵

The Best of Mountain Stage, Vol. 5 Live (Blue Plate Music) 🎵🎵🎵🎵

The Best of Mountain Stage, Vol. 6 Live (Blue Plate Music) 🎵🎵🎵🎵

The Best of Mountain Stage, Vol. 7 Live (Blue Plate Music) 🎵🎵🎵

Christmas at Mountain Stage (Blue Plate Music) 🎵🎵🎵

Folk Music at Newport, Vol. 1 (Vanguard) 🎵🎵🎵🎵

Live from Mountain Stage Rock (Blue Plate Music) 🎵🎵🎵🎵

Live from Mountain Stage, Vol. 8 (Blue Plate Music) 🎵🎵🎵

Louisiana Live from Mountain Stage (Blue Plate Music) 🎵🎵🎵🎵

Nashville at Newport (Vanguard) 🎵🎵🎵🎵

The Sullivan Years: Country Classics (TVT) 🎵🎵

Sunday Morning Sessions (Munich) 🎵🎵🎵

Texans Live from Mountain Stage (Blue Plate Music) 🎵🎵🎵🎵

Threadgill's Supper Session (Watermelon) 🎵🎵🎵🎵

OLD-TIME

Altamont: Black Stringband Music from the Library of Congress (Rounder) 🎵🎵🎵🎵🎵

Are You from Dixie? Great Country Brother Teams of the 1930s (RCA Heritage Series) 🎵🎵🎵🎵🎵

The Bristol Sessions (Country Music Foundation) 🎵🎵🎵🎵🎵

Fair and Tender Ladies: Mountain Music Collection, Vol. 2 (CMH) 🎵🎵🎵

Mountain Music of Kentucky (Smithsonian/Folkways) 🎵🎵🎵

The Music of Kentucky: Early American Rural Classics, 1927–1937, Vol. 1 (Yazoo) 🎵🎵🎵

The Music of Kentucky: Early American Rural Classics, 1927–1937, Vol. 2 (Yazoo) 🎵🎵🎵

Old Time Music on the Air, Vol. 1 (Rounder) 🎵🎵🎵🎵

Ragged but Right: Great Country String Bands of the 1930s (RCA) 🎵🎵🎵

Songs of the Civil War (Columbia) 🎵🎵🎵

White Country Blues, 1926–1938: A Lighter Shade of Blue (Columbia/Legacy) 🎵🎵🎵🎵

Wild and Reckless Men: Mountain Music Collection, Vol. 1 (CMH) 🎵🎵🎵🎵

The Young Fogies (Rounder) 🎵🎵🎵🎵

The Young Fogies, Vol. II (Rounder) 🎵🎵🎵🎵

RECORD LABEL COMPILATIONS

Columbia Country Classics, Vol. 1: The Golden Age (Columbia) 🎵🎵🎵🎵🎵

Columbia Country Classics, Vol. 2: Honky Tonk Heroes (Columbia) 🎵🎵🎵🎵🎵

Columbia Country Classics, Vol. 3: Americana (Columbia) 🎵🎵🎵🎵

Columbia Country Classics, Vol. 4: The Nashville Sound (Columbia) 🎵🎵🎵🎵

Columbia Country Classics, Vol. 5: A New Tradition (Columbia) 🎵🎵🎵

Defrost Your Heart: Sun Country, Vol. 1 (AVI) 🎵🎵🎵

The Essential Series (RCA) 🎵🎵🎵🎵

The Essential Series, Vol. II (RCA) 🎵🎵🎵🎵

Fifty Years of Country Music from Mercury, 1945–1995 (Mercury) 🎵🎵🎵🎵

From the Vaults: Decca Country Classics, 1934–1973 (MCA) 🎵🎵🎵🎵

Hand-Picked: Twenty-Five Years of Rounder Bluegrass (Rounder) 🎵🎵🎵🎵🎵

HighTone Records: The First 10 Years (HighTone) 🎵🎵🎵🎵

Hills of Home: Twenty-Five Years of Folk Music on Rounder Records (Rounder) 🎵🎵🎵🎵

Louisiana Spice: 25 Years of Louisiana Music on Rounder Records (Rounder) 🎵🎵🎵🎵🎵

Philo So Far: The 20th Anniversary Folk Sampler (Philo) 🎵🎵🎵🎵

The Sun Records Collection (Rhino) 🎵🎵🎵🎵🎵

Time Is on Our Side: The DejaDisc Sampler (DejaDisc) 🎵🎵🎵

Top of the Hill Bluegrass: The Sugar Hill Collection (Sugar Hill) 🎵🎵🎵🎵

The Watermelon Sampler (Watermelon) 🎵🎵🎵🎵

ROCKABILLY

Get Hot or Go Home (Country Music Foundation) 🎵🎵🎵🎵

Get with the Beat: The Mar-Vel Masters (Rykodisc) 🎵🎵🎵

Legends (Garland/DCC Compact Classics) 🎵🎵🎵🎵

Let's Bop: Sun Rockabilly, Vol. 1 (AVI) 🎵🎵🎵🎵

Rock Baby Rock It: Sun Rockabilly, Vol. 2 (AVI) 🎵🎵🎵

Rock Boppin' Baby: Sun Rockabilly, Vol. 3 (AVI) 🎵🎵🎵🎵

Rock This Town: Rockabilly Hits, Vol. 1 (Rhino) 🎵🎵🎵🎵

Rock This Town: Rockabilly Hits, Vol. 2 (Rhino) 🎵🎵🎵🎵

The Sun Story (Rhino) 🎵🎵🎵🎵🎵

Sun's Greatest Hits (RCA) 🎵🎵🎵🎵

SONGWRITERS

In Their Own Words, Vol. 1 (Razor & Tie) 🎵🎵🎵🎵

The Names Behind the Artists, Vol. 1 (Silver Eagle) 🎵🎵🎵🎵

The Names Behind the Artists, Vol. 2 (Silver Eagle) 🎵🎵🎵🎝

SOUNDTRACKS

The Beverly Hillbillies (television) (Columbia/Legacy) 🎵🎵
The Beverly Hillbillies (film) (Fox) 🎵🎵🎝
Chasers (Morgan Creek) 🎵🎵🎝
The Cowboy Way (Epic Soundtrax) 🎵🎵🎵
Dead Man Walking (Columbia) 🎵🎵🎵🎵
Eight Seconds (MCA) 🎵🎵🎵
Falling from Grace (Mercury) 🎵🎵🎝
High Lonesome (CMH) 🎵🎵🎵🎵
Honeymoon in Vegas (Epic Soundtrax) 🎵🎵🎵
Love & a .45 (Immortal/Epic Soundtrax) 🎵🎵
Maverick (Atlantic) 🎵🎵🎵🎵
My Heroes Have Always Been Cowboys (RCA) 🎵🎵🎵
Next of Kin (Columbia) 🎵🎵🎝
Pink Cadillac (Warner Bros.) 🎵🎵
Texas (Legacy) 🎵🎵🎵
The Thing Called Love (Giant) 🎵🎵🎝
Urban Cowboy (Elektra) 🎵🎵🎵🎝

TEJANO/TEX-MEX

Conjunto! Texas-Mexican Border Music, Vol. V: Polkas de Oro (Rounder) 🎵🎵🎵
A Tejano Country Christmas (Arista/Texas) 🎵🎵🎵

TEXAS MUSIC

Austin Country Nights (Watermelon) 🎵🎵🎵🎵
Texans Live from Mountain Stage (Blue Plate Music) 🎵🎵🎵🎵
Texas Music, Vol. 1: Postwar Blues Combos (Rhino) 🎵🎵🎵🎝
Texas Music, Vol. 2: Western Swing & Honky Tonk (Rhino) 🎵🎵🎵🎵
Texas Music, Vol. 3: Garage Bands & Psychedelia (Rhino) 🎵🎵🎵🎵
Texas Super Hits (Columbia) 🎵🎵🎝
Threadgill's Supper Session (Watermelon) 🎵🎵🎵🎝

TRIBUTE ALBUMS

Across the Great Divide: Songs of Jo Carol Pierce (DejaDisc) 🎵🎵🎵
Beat the Retreat: Songs by Richard Thompson (Capitol) 🎵🎵🎵
Brace Yourself! A Tribute to Otis Blackwell (Shanachie) 🎵🎵🎵
Come Together: America Salutes the Beatles (Capitol) 🎵🎵
Commemorativo: A Tribute to Gram Parsons (Rhino) 🎵🎵🎵
Common Thread: The Songs of the Eagles (Giant) 🎵🎵
Do Me Baby: Austin Does Prince (Fume) 🎵🎵🎵
For the Love of Harry: Everybody Sings Nilsson (Musicmasters) 🎵🎵🎵🎵

It's Now or Never: A Tribute to Elvis (Mercury) 🎵🎵🎝
Keith Whitley: A Tribute Album (BNA) 🎵🎵🎝
Love Gets Strange: The Songs of John Hiatt (Rhino) 🎵🎵🎵🎵
Mama's Hungry Eyes: A Tribute to Merle Haggard (Arista) 🎵🎵🎵
Minneapolis Does Denver (October) 🎵🎵🎝
Not Fade Away: Remembering Buddy Holly (MCA) 🎵🎵🎵
Pastures of Plenty: An Austin Celebration of Woody Guthrie (DejaDisc) 🎵🎵🎵
A Picture of Hank: The New Bluegrass Way (Mercury) 🎵🎵🎵
Skynyrd Frynds (MCA) 🎵🎵🎵
Tapestry Revisited: A Tribute to Carole King (Lava/Atlantic) 🎵🎵🎵
Till the Night Is Gone: A Tribute to Doc Pomus (Forward) 🎵🎵🎵🎵
Tower of Song: The Songs of Leonard Cohen (A&M) 🎵🎵🎵🎝
True Life Blues: The Songs of Bill Monroe (Sugar Hill) 🎵🎵🎵🎵
Twisted Willie (Justice) 🎵🎵🎵🎝
Working Class Hero: A Tribute to John Lennon (Hollywood) 🎵🎵🎵

WESTERN SWING

Honed on the Range, Vol. II: Contemporary Texas Swing (Texas Monthly) 🎵🎵🎵🎵
Okeh Western Swing (CBS Special Products) 🎵🎵🎵🎵🎵

INDEXES

Band Member Index

Producer Index

Roots Index

Category Index

Wondering what bands a certain musician or vocalist has been in? The Band Member Index will guide you to the appropriate entry (or entries).

Abernathy, Barry *See* IIIrd Tyme Out

Adair, Chuck *See* Frazier River

Adams, Ryan *See* Whiskeytown

Adams, Tom *See* Johnson Mountain Boys; The Lynn Morris Band

Adcock, Eddie *See* The Country Gentlemen

Adkins, Sammy *See* Ralph Stanley & the Clinch Mountain Boys

Alesi, Tommy *See* Beausoleil

Allen, Duane *See* The Oak Ridge Boys

Allen, John P. *See* Prairie Oyster

Allen, Lincoln *See* Tarnation

Allred, Rick *See* The Country Gentlemen

Alves, Rich *See* Pirates of the Mississippi

Alvin, Dave *See* The Blasters

Alvin, Phil *See* The Blasters

Amburgy, Greg *See* Frazier River

Amos, Bob *See* Front Range

Anderson, Cleave *See* Blue Rodeo

Andes, Mark *See* Firefall

Anger, Darol *See* Psychograss

Anglin, Jack *See* Johnnie & Jack

Anglin, Mike *See* David Parmley, Scott Vestal & Continental Divide/David Parmley

Anton, Alan *See* Cowboy Junkies

Antonakos, Stephen B. *See* Five Chinese Brothers

Applin, Herb *See* Joe Val & the New England Bluegrass Boys

Arbo, Rani *See* Salamander Crossing

Archer, Randy *See* Archer/Park

Armstrong, Billy *See* Sons of the Pioneers

Arnold, Harvey *See* The Outlaws

Arnson, Josh *See* Asylum Street Spankers

Arrant, Randy *See* The Vidalias

Auldridge, Mike *See* Chesapeake; The Seldom Scene

Austin, Tim *See* Lonesome River Band/Ronnie Bowman

Baggs, Perry *See* Jason & the Scorchers

Bailey, Anthony *See* The Warrior River Boys

Baillie, Kathie *See* Baillie & the Boys

Baker, Gary *See* Baker & Myers

Baker, John Lee *See* Dry Branch Fire Squad

Baldassari, Butch *See* Lonesome Standard Time/Larry Cordle

Balsley, Philip *See* The Statler Brothers

Barlow, Bruce *See* Commander Cody & His Lost Planet Airmen

Barnes, Danny *See* Bad Livers

Barnes, Randy *See* Lou Reid/Lou Reid & Carolina

Barnette, Wanda *See* The New Coon Creek Girls

Barr, Ralph *See* The Nitty Gritty Dirt Band

Bartley, Jock *See* Firefall

Bateman, Bill *See* The Blasters

Battin, Skip *See* The Byrds; Flying Burrito Brothers; New Riders of the Purple Sage

Baucom, Terry *See* Boone Creek; Lou Reid/Lou Reid & Carolina; IIIrd Tyme Out

Baverman, Brian "Gigs" *See* Frazier River

Baxter, Dorothy *See* Good Ol' Persons

Bayless, Pops *See* Asylum Street Spankers

Bazz, John *See* The Blasters

Bean, Janet Beveridge *See* Freakwater

Beck, Don *See* Flying Burrito Brothers

Beland, John *See* Flying Burrito Brothers

Bell, Derek *See* The Chieftains

Bell, Kelly *See* The Shivers

Bellamy, David *See* The Bellamy Brothers

Bellamy, Howard *See* The Bellamy Brothers

Belzer, Bill *See* Uncle Tupelo/Wilco/Son Volt

Benford, Mac *See* Mac Benford & the Woodshed All-Stars

Bennett, Gary *See* BR5-49

Benson, Ray *See* Asleep at the Wheel

Benson, Wayne *See* IIIrd Tyme Out

Bergen, Paul *See* Molly & the Heymakers

Berger, Rick *See* Molly & the Heymakers

Berline, Byron *See* Flying Burrito Brothers

Besen, Joan *See* Prairie Oyster

Bethea, Ken *See* The Old 97'S

Bibey, Alan *See* Lou Reid/Lou Reid & Carolina; IIIrd Tyme Out

Big Sandy *See* Big Sandy & His Fly-Rite Boys

Bills, Jeff *See* The V-Roys

Birkby, Michelle *See* The New Coon Creek Girls

Black, Bobby *See* Commander Cody & His Lost Planet Airmen

Blackwell, Kenny *See* The Laurel Canyon Ramblers

Blair, Warren *See* The Bluegrass Cardinals

Blizard, Ralph *See* Ralph Blizard & the New Southern Ramblers

Block, Billy *See* The Bum Steers

Blue, Buddy *See* The Beat Farmers

Blythe, Lance *See* Twister Alley

Bolick, Bill *See* The Blue Sky Boys

Bolick, Earl *See* The Blue Sky Boys

Bolin, Patrick *See* Pure Prairie League

Bonagura, Michael *See* Baillie & the Boys

Bonsall, Joe *See* The Oak Ridge Boys

Borden, Barry *See* The Outlaws

Borschied, Tommy *See* The Honeydogs

Botts, Mike *See* David Gates/Bread

Bowden, Richard *See* Austin Lounge Lizards; Pinkard & Bowden

Bowen, Jimmy *See* David Parmley, Scott Vestal & Continental Divide/David Parmley

Bowman, Ronnie *See* The Bluegrass Cardinals; Lonesome River Band/Ronnie Bowman

Bradley, Dale Ann *See* The New Coon Creek Girls

Brady, Pat *See* Sons of the Pioneers

Bramlett, Bekka *See* Bekka & Billy/Billy Burnette

Brayfield, Buddy *See* The Ozark Mountain Daredevils

Breaux, Jimmy *See* Beausoleil

Brigante, Merle *See* The Nitty Gritty Dirt Band

Britt, Bob *See* McBride & the Ride/Terry McBride & the Ride

Britt, Gena *See* New Vintage; Lou Reid/Lou Reid & Carolina

Britt, Michael *See* Lonestar

Brody, Bruce *See* Lone Justice/Maria McKee

Brokenbourgh, Will *See* Big Sandy & His Fly-Rite Boys

Brooks, Dan *See* The Rarely Herd

Brooks, Kix *See* Brooks & Dunn

Brown, Bonnie *See* The Browns/Jim Ed Brown

Brown, Bruce Ray *See* Charlie Daniels Band

Brown, Jim Ed *See* The Browns/Jim Ed Brown

Brown, Kelly *See* The Skeletons/The Morells

Brown, Maxine *See* The Browns/Jim Ed Brown

Browne, Jackson *See* The Nitty Gritty Dirt Band

Browning, Lex *See* Great Plains

Bruns, Henry *See* The Vidalias

Bryant, Jeff *See* Ricochet

Bryant, Jimmy *See* Speedy West & Jimmy Bryant

Bryant, Junior *See* Ricochet

Bryant, Steve *See* Boone Creek

Bryson, Bill *See* The Bluegrass Cardinals; The Laurel Canyon Ramblers

Bub, Mike *See* Lonesome Standard Time/Larry Cordle; The Del McCoury Band/Ronnie & Rob McCoury; The Sidemen

Buchanan, Jim *See* The Greenbriar Boys; Joe Val & the New England Bluegrass Boys

Buck, Mike *See* The LeRoi Brothers

Buckey, Jay *See* The Marty Warburton Band

Buckner, Clay *See* The Red Clay Ramblers

Bulla, Jenny Anne *See* Luke & Jenny Anne Bulla

Bulla, Luke *See* Luke & Jenny Anne Bulla

Bullard, Kim *See* Poco

Buono, Michael *See* The Nitty Gritty Dirt Band; Ranch Romance

Burch, Curtis *See* The New Grass Revival

Burleson, Jason *See* Blue Highway

Burnett, Larry *See* Firefall

Burnette, Billy *See* Bekka & Billy/Billy Burnette

Burns , Annie *See* Burns Sisters

Burns, Bob *See* Lynyrd Skynyrd

Burns, Jeannie *See* Burns Sisters

Burns, Kenneth "Jethro" *See* Homer & Jethro

Burns, Marie *See* Mac Benford & the Woodshed All-Stars; Burns Sisters

Burr, Gary *See* Pure Prairie League

Burris, Dave *See* Jolene

Burton, Barry "Byrd" *See* The Amazing Rhythm Aces

Burton, James *See* James Burton & Ralph Mooney

Bush, Roger *See* Flying Burrito Brothers; The Kentucky Colonels

Bush, Sam *See* The New Grass Revival; Strength in Numbers

Butler, Carl *See* Carl & Pearl Butler

Butler, Pearl *See* Carl & Pearl Butler

Byrom, Monty *See* Big House

Byrom, Tanner *See* Big House

Cable, John *See* The Nitty Gritty Dirt Band

Cage, Buddy *See* New Riders of the Purple Sage

Cake, Timothy *See* The Outlaws

Caldwell, Carl *See* New Vintage

Caldwell, Tommy *See* The Marshall Tucker Band

Caldwell, Toy *See* The Marshall Tucker Band

California, Sonny *See* Big House

Call, John David *See* Pure Prairie League

Callahan, Ken *See* The Jayhawks

Cameron, Duncan *See* The Amazing Rhythm Aces; Sawyer Brown

Campbell, Jimmy *See* The Sidemen

Canaday, Steve *See* The Ozark Mountain Daredevils

Carbone, Pat *See* Front Range

Card, Hank *See* Austin Lounge Lizards

Cardwell, Ray *See* The New Tradition

Carlson, Paulette *See* Highway 101

Carpenter, Bob *See* The Nitty Gritty Dirt Band

Carr, Brad *See* Brush Arbor

Carr, Teddy *See* Ricochet

Carroll, Lee *See* Exile/Les Taylor/J.P. Pennington

Carson, Ken *See* Sons of the Pioneers

Carter, A.P. *See* The Carter Family/The Carter Sisters & Mother Maybelle

Carter, Anita *See* The Carter Family/The Carter Sisters & Mother Maybelle

Carter, Anna *See* The Chuck Wagon Gang

Carter, David "Dad" *See* The Chuck Wagon Gang

Carter, Eddie *See* The Chuck Wagon Gang

Carter, Helen *See* The Carter Family/The Carter Sisters & Mother Maybelle

Carter, Jason *See* The Del McCoury Band/Ronnie & Rob McCoury

Carter, Jim *See* The Chuck Wagon Gang

Carter , June *See* The Carter Family/The Carter Sisters & Mother Maybelle

Carter, Maybelle *See* The Carter Family/The Carter Sisters & Mother Maybelle

Carter, Rose *See* The Chuck Wagon Gang

Carter, Roy *See* The Chuck Wagon Gang

Carter, Ruth Ellen *See* The Chuck Wagon Gang

Carter, Sara *See* The Carter Family/The Carter Sisters & Mother Maybelle

Cary, Caitlin *See* Whiskeytown

Cash, Johnny *See* The Highwaymen

Cash, Steve *See* The Ozark Mountain Daredevils

Casida, Aaron *See* The Smokin' Armadillos

Caughlan, Jim *See* Pure Prairie League

Centers, Roy Lee *See* Ralph Stanley & the Clinch Mountain Boys

Cernuto, Michelle *See* Tarnation

Chapman, Curt *See* J.D. Crowe/J.D. Crowe & the New South

Chapman, Jim *See* 4 Runner

Chapman, Steve *See* Poco

Chapman, Tommy *See* The Warrior River Boys

Chappell, Ruell *See* The Ozark Mountain Daredevils

Charles, Steve *See* Western Flyer

Chowning, Randle *See* The Ozark Mountain Daredevils; The Skeletons/The Morells

Chrisma, Paul *See* Riders in the Sky

Church, Ramona *See* The New Coon Creek Girls

Clark, Gene *See* The Byrds

Clark, Jackie *See* The Nitty Gritty Dirt Band

Clark, Roy *See* The Hee Haw Gospel Quartet

Clarke, Michael *See* The Byrds; Firefall; Flying Burrito Brothers

Clawson, Dan *See* Firefall

Clevenger, Mike *See* The Traditional Grass

Cline, Charlie *See* The Warrior River Boys

Cline, Curly Ray *See* Ralph Stanley & the Clinch Mountain Boys

Cohen, John *See* The New Lost City Ramblers

Coleman, T. Michael *See* Chesapeake; The Seldom Scene

Collins, Allen *See* Lynyrd Skynyrd

Collins, Larry *See* The Collins Kids

Collins, Lawrencine *See* The Collins Kids

Comeaux, Tommy *See* Beausoleil

Commander Cody *See* Commander Cody & His Lost Planet Airmen

Compton, Mike *See* The Nashville Bluegrass Band

Condo, Ray *See* Ray Condo & His Ricochets

Conley, Cabe *See* The Boys from Indiana

Conneff, Kevin *See* The Chieftains

Connell, Dudley *See* Johnson Mountain Boys; The Seldom Scene

Connor, Michael *See* Pure Prairie League

Cook, Greg *See* Ricochet

Cook, Jeff *See* Alabama

Cook, Stu *See* Southern Pacific

Cooley, Steve *See* The Dillards

Coomer, Ken *See* Uncle Tupelo/Wilco/Son Volt

Cooper, Dale *See* Brush Arbor

Cooper, Dale T. "Stoney" *See* Wilma Lee & Stoney Cooper

Cooper, Wilma Lee *See* Wilma Lee & Stoney Cooper

Copley, Rich *See* The Carpetbaggers

Cordle, Larry *See* Lonesome Standard Time/Larry Cordle

Cornelison, Buzz *See* Exile/Les Taylor/J.P. Pennington

Cotton, Paul *See* Poco

Couch, Frank *See* Blue Mountain

Cowan, John *See* The New Grass Revival

Cowsill, Billy *See* Blue Shadows

Cox, Evelyn *See* The Cox Family

Cox, Jim *See* The Country Gentlemen

Cox, Sidney *See* The Cox Family

Cox, Suzanne *See* The Cox Family

Cox, Willard *See* The Cox Family

Crabtree, Mike *See* The Carpetbaggers

Crase, Noah *See* The Boys from Indiana

Craven, Joe *See* Psychograss

Craver, Mike *See* The Red Clay Ramblers

Crittenden, Billy *See* 4 Runner

Croker, Brendan *See* The Notting Hillbillies

Crooke, John *See* Jolene

Crosby, David *See* The Byrds

Crouch, Dennis *See* Wylie & the Wild West Show

Crowe, Josh *See* Crowe & McLaughlin

Cua, Rick *See* The Outlaws

Cuddy, Jim *See* Blue Rodeo

Cummins, Jan *See* The New Coon Creek Girls

Cummins, Kelly *See* The New Coon Creek Girls

Cummins, Lance *See* One Riot One Ranger

Curtis, Ken *See* Sons of the Pioneers

Custer *See* Lynyrd Skynyrd

Dadisman, Bruce *See* One Riot One Ranger

Dadmun-Bixby, Denny *See* Great Plains

Dalton, Erlk *See* Flying Burrito Brothers

Daniels, Charlie *See* Charlie Daniels Band

Daniels, Jack *See* Highway 101

Darrow, Chris *See* The Nitty Gritty Dirt Band

Davis, Ben *See* Wagon

Davis, David *See* The Warrior River Boys

Davis, Jeff *See* The Amazing Rhythm Aces

Davis, John *See* The Bluegrass Cardinals

Dawson, John "Marmaduke" *See* New Riders of the Purple Sage

DeCastro, Dave *See* The Health & Happiness Show

Deakin, Paul *See* The Mavericks

Dean, Jimmie *See* Asylum Street Spankers

Dear, Tracy *See* The Waco Brothers

Deaton, Lester *See* The Bluegrass Cardinals

Deaton, Ray *See* IIIrd Tyme Out

Decarle, Russell *See* Prairie Oyster

Dee, Andy *See* Molly & the Heymakers

Delevante, Bob *See* The Delevantes

Delevante, Mike *See* The Delevantes

Della Penna, Erik *See* The Health & Happiness Show

Delmore, Alton *See* The Delmore Brothers

Delmore, Rabon *See* The Delmore Brothers

Delorme, Dennis *See* Prairie Oyster

Demeo, Pete *See* Five Chinese Brothers

Dennis, Jeff *See* The Backsliders

Denunzio, Vincent *See* The Health & Happiness Show

Desaulniers, Stephen *See* The Scud Mountain Boys

Deschamps, Kim *See* Blue Rodeo

Devonie, Nova Karina *See* Ranch Romance

Dewitt, Lew *See* The Statler Brothers

Dexter, Rolle *See* The Beat Farmers

Dick, Bob *See* Front Range

Dick, Dave *See* Southern Rail

Dickens, Hazel *See* Hazel & Alice/Hazel Dickens/Alice Gerrard

Dickerson, Deke *See* Dave & Deke Combo

Dickerson, Lance *See* Commander Cody & His Lost Planet Airmen

Deisler, Conrad *See* Austin Lounge Lizards

Digregorio, Joel "Taz" *See* Charlie Daniels Band

Dillard, Doug *See* The Dillards

Dillard, Rodney *See* The Dillards

Dilling, Steve *See* IIIrd Tyme Out

Dillon, John *See* The Ozark Mountain Daredevils

Dittrich, John *See* Restless Heart/Larry Stewart

Dix, David *See* The Outlaws

Dixon, Gabe *See* Six Shooter

Doerr, Joey *See* The LeRoi Brothers

Doerr, Steve *See* The LeRoi Brothers

Donahue, Jerry *See* The Hellecasters

Donovan, Bazil *See* Blue Rodeo

Dormire, Jimmy *See* Confederate Railroad

Doss, Tommy *See* Sons of the Pioneers

Dotson, Riche *See* The New Tradition

Doucet, David *See* Beausoleil

Doucet, Michael *See* Beausoleil; The Savoy-Doucet Cajun Band

Doughty, Alan *See* The Waco Brothers

Douglas, Jerry *See* Boone Creek; J.D. Crowe/J.D. Crowe & the New South; Strength in Numbers

Doyle, Ray *See* Wylie & the Wild West Show

Dryden, Spencer *See* New Riders of the Purple Sage

Duffey, John *See* The Country Gentlemen; The Seldom Scene

Dufresne, Mark *See* Confederate Railroad

Duggin, Fred *See* The New Tradition

Duncan, Glen *See* Lonesome Standard Time/Larry Cordle

Duncan, Stuart *See* The Nashville Bluegrass Band

Dunn, Ronnie *See* Brooks & Dunn

Durante, Mark *See* The Waco Brothers

Dye, Ed *See* The Sidemen

Earhart, Billy III *See* The Amazing Rhythm Aces

Edwards, Keith *See* McBride & the Ride/Terry McBride & the Ride

Egan, Bob *See* Freakwater

Egan, David *See* Filé

Egly, Jason *See* Six Shooter

Eldredge, Terry *See* The Sidemen

Eldridge, Ben *See* The Seldom Scene

Ely, Joe *See* The Flatlanders

Emerson, Bill *See* The Country Gentlemen

Enright, Pat *See* The Nashville Bluegrass Band

Ervin, Dick *See* Dry Branch Fire Squad

Erwin, Emily *See* The Dixie Chicks

Escovedo, Alejandro *See* Rank & File

Etheridge, Chris *See* Flying Burrito Brothers

Etzioni, Marvin *See* Lone Justice/Maria McKee

Eubanks, Jerry *See* The Marshall Tucker Band

Evans, Bill *See* Dry Branch Fire Squad

Evans, Gerald *See* The Traditional Grass

Evans, Slim *See* Rank & File

Everly, Don *See* The Everly Brothers

Everly, Phil *See* The Everly Brothers

Ewing, Tom *See* The Warrior River Boys

Ezell, Ralph *See* Shenandoah

Fadden, Jimmie *See* The Nitty Gritty Dirt Band

Famiglietta, Christian *See* The Shivers

Farlow, Billy C. *See* Commander Cody & His Lost Planet Airmen

Farnham, Tim *See* Salamander Crossing

Farr, Hugh *See* Sons of the Pioneers

Farr, Karl *See* Sons of the Pioneers

Farrar, Jay *See* Uncle Tupelo/Wilco/Son Volt

Farrell, Skip *See* The Hoosier Hot Shots

Fay, Martin *See* The Chieftains

Feinberg, Ron *See* The Fox Family

Felder, Don *See* The Eagles

Fender, Freddy *See* The Texas Tornados

Ferris, Ed *See* Johnson Mountain Boys

Ficca, Sandy *See* Firefall

Field, Jim *See* The Charles River Valley Boys

Fisher, Shug *See* Sons of the Pioneers

Flatt, Lester *See* Flatt & Scruggs; Bill Monroe & His Blue Grass Boys/Charlie Monroe/The Monroe Brothers

Fleck, Bela *See* Bela Fleck/Bela Fleck & the Flecktones; The New Grass Revival; Strength in Numbers

Fletcher, Guy *See* The Notting Hillbillies

Flynn, Pat *See* The New Grass Revival

Foglino, Paul *See* Five Chinese Brothers

Fontayne, Shayne *See* Lone Justice/Maria McKee

Forbes, Homer *See* The Forbes Family

Forbes, Jay *See* The Forbes Family

Forester, Christy *See* The Forester Sisters

Forester, June *See* The Forester Sisters

Forester, Kathy *See* The Forester Sisters

Forester, Kim *See* The Forester Sisters

Forster, Nick *See* Hot Rize/Red Knuckles & the Trailblazers

Forsyth, Guy *See* Asylum Street Spankers

Fortune, Jimmy *See* The Statler Brothers

Fosson, Mark *See* The Bum Steers

Foster, Radney *See* Foster & Lloyd

Fox, Barb *See* The Fox Family

Fox, Joel *See* The Fox Family

Fox, Ken *See* Jason & the Scorchers

Fox, Kim *See* The Fox Family

Fraley, Annadeene *See* J.P. & Annadeene Fraley

Fraley, J.P. *See* J.P. & Annadeene Fraley

Frank, Chris *See* The Red Clay Ramblers

Frayne, George *See* Commander Cody & His Lost Planet Airmen

Frazer, Paula *See* Tarnation

Frazier, Danny *See* Frazier River

Frazier, Randy *See* McBride & the Ride/Terry McBride & the Ride

Fredrickson, Mike *See* The Spanic Boys

Freese, Teddy *See* The Spanic Boys

French, Bob *See* Joe Val & the New England Bluegrass Boys

French, Mark *See* Blue Rodeo

Frey, Glenn *See* The Eagles

Fried, Mike *See* Wylie & the Wild West Show

Frizzell, David *See* David Frizzell & Shelly West

Fuller, Craig *See* Pure Prairie League

Fungaroli, Jim *See* The Cactus Brothers

Furay, Richie *See* Poco

Gabbard, Harley *See* The Boys from Indiana

Gadd, Pam *See* The New Coon Creek Girls

Gaines, Steve *See* Lynyrd Skynyrd

Garcia, Jerry *See* The Grateful Dead; New Riders of the Purple Sage

Gardner, Michael *See* The Nitty Gritty Dirt Band

Garnier, D'Jalma *See* Filé

Garth, Al *See* The Nitty Gritty Dirt Band

Gaskill, Mark *See* One Riot One Ranger

Gates, David *See* David Gates/Bread

Gatlin, Steve *See* Larry Gatlin & the Gatlin Brothers

Gatlin, Larry *See* Larry Gatlin & the Gatlin Brothers

Gatlin, Rudy *See* Larry Gatlin & the Gatlin Brothers

Gaudreau, Jimmy *See* Chesapeake; The Country Gentlemen

Gauthier, Rusty *See* New Riders of the Purple Sage
Gavin, Jack *See* Charlie Daniels Band
Gay, Dave *See* Freakwater
Gentry, Teddy *See* Alabama
Gerard, Vic *See* The Derailers
Gerrard, Alice *See* Hazel & Alice/Hazel Dickens/Alice Gerrard
Getman, Ron *See* The Tractors
Gibson, Dave *See* The Gibson/Miller Band
Gilbeau, Floyd "Gib" *See* Flying Burrito Brothers
Gill, Janis *See* Sweethearts of the Rodeo
Gill, Vince *See* Pure Prairie League
Gilmore, Jimmie Dale *See* The Flatlanders
Gilmore, Skillet *See* Whiskeytown
Ginn, Andy *See* Perfect Stranger
Giraud, Olivier *See* Asylum Street Spankers
Glass, Keith *See* Prairie Oyster
Godchaux, Donna *See* The Grateful Dead
Godchaux, Keith *See* The Grateful Dead
Goetzman, Steve *See* Exile/Les Taylor/J.P. Pennington
Goins, Melvin *See* The Goins Brothers; Ralph Stanley & the Clinch Mountain Boys
Goins, Ray *See* The Goins Brothers
Goins, Steve *See* Twister Alley
Golden, William Lee *See* The Oak Ridge Boys
Golding, Wes *See* Boone Creek
Golemon, John *See* The Cactus Brothers
Golemon, Will *See* The Cactus Brothers
Goodall, Jim *See* Flying Burrito Brothers
Goodman, Tim *See* Southern Pacific
Gordon, Jim *See* David Gates/Bread
Gosdin, Rex *See* The Hillmen
Gosdin, Vern *See* The Hillmen
Goshorn, Larry *See* Pure Prairie League
Goshorn, Timmy *See* Pure Prairie League
Goulding, Steve *See* The Waco Brothers
Graham, Josh *See* The Smokin' Armadillos
Graham, Randy *See* The Bluegrass Cardinals
Granda, Michael "Supe" *See* The Ozark Mountain Daredevils
Grandpa Jones *See* The Hee Haw Gospel Quartet
Grant, Bob *See* Bad Livers
Grantham, George *See* Poco
Gray, Del *See* Little Texas/Brady Seals
Gray, Doug *See* The Marshall Tucker Band

Gray, James *See* Blue Rodeo
Gray, Tom *See* The Seldom Scene
Green, Douglas B. *See* Riders in the Sky
Greene, Richard *See* Muleskinner
Gregg, Paul *See* Restless Heart/Larry Stewart
Gremp, Ron *See* The Skeletons/The Morells
Grier, David *See* Psychograss
Griffin, James *See* David Gates/Bread
Griffin, Kenny *See* Wylie & the Wild West Show
Grisman, David *See* Muleskinner
Grissom, Sean *See* The Health & Happiness Show
Grotberg, Karen *See* The Jayhawks
Grothman, Steve *See* Whiskeytown
Guard, Dave *See* The Kingston Trio
Guerin, John *See* The Byrds
Gust, Bruce *See* Western Flyer
Gustafson, Wylie *See* Wylie & the Wild West Show
Hale, Owen *See* Lynyrd Skynyrd
Hall, Randall *See* Lynyrd Skynyrd
Hammond, Murry *See* The Old 97'S
Hancock, Butch *See* The Flatlanders
Hancock, Tommy *See* The Flatlanders
Haney, Barry *See* The Shivers
Haney, Dave *See* Joe Val & the New England Bluegrass Boys
Hanna, Jeff *See* The Nitty Gritty Dirt Band
Hannah, Jack *See* Sons of the San Joaquin
Hannah, Joe *See* Sons of the San Joaquin
Hannah, Lon *See* Sons of the San Joaquin
Hardin, Glenn D. *See* Southern Pacific
Hargis, Marlon *See* Exile/Les Taylor/J.P. Pennington
Harrah, James *See* Brush Arbor
Harris, Joey *See* The Beat Farmers
Harrison, Charlie *See* Poco
Harrison, Mike *See* The V-Roys
Harrison, Nate *See* The Hoosier Hot Shots
Hart, Mickey *See* The Grateful Dead; New Riders of the Purple Sage
Hartgrove, Mike *See* IIIrd Tyme Out
Hatcher, Jeffrey *See* Blue Shadows
Hathaway, Richard *See* The Nitty Gritty Dirt Band
Haynes, Henry D. "Homer" *See* Homer & Jethro
Haynie, Aubrey *See* David Parmley, Scott Vestal & Continental Divide/David Parmley

Hays, Marty *See* The Warrior River Boys
Haywood, Charlie *See* Charlie Daniels Band
Hedgecock, Ryan *See* Lone Justice/Maria McKee
Heffington, Don *See* Lone Justice/Maria McKee
Heidorn, Mike *See* Uncle Tupelo/Wilco/Son Volt
Helberg, Dave *See* Five Chinese Brothers
Helton, Roger *See* Western Flyer
Henley, Don *See* The Eagles
Henneman, Brian *See* The Bottle Rockets
Henrie, Doug *See* Mac Benford & the Woodshed All-Stars
Herald, John *See* The Greenbriar Boys
Herndon, Mark *See* Alabama
Herndon, Ray *See* McBride & the Ride/Terry McBride & the Ride
Herrick, Jack *See* The Red Clay Ramblers
Herrman, John *See* Ralph Blizard & the New Southern Ramblers
Herron, Don *See* BR5-49
Hersom, Wally *See* Big Sandy & His Fly-Rite Boys
Hicks, Bill *See* The Red Clay Ramblers
Hicks, Bobby Lloyd *See* The Skeletons/The Morells
Hicks, Chris *See* The Outlaws
Hill, Joe Scott *See* Flying Burrito Brothers
Hilliard, Lee *See* 4 Runner
Hillman, Chris *See* The Byrds; The Hillmen
Hinds, Billy *See* Pure Prairie League
Hinners, Gordy *See* Ralph Blizard & the New Southern Ramblers
Hisey, John *See* Dry Branch Fire Squad
Hitt, Amy *See* Twister Alley
Hluszko, Bohdan *See* Prairie Oyster
Hobbs, Evelyn Cox *See* The Cox Family
Hodges, Warner *See* Jason & the Scorchers
Hofeldt, Brian *See* The Derailers
Holt, Aubrey *See* The Boys from Indiana
Holt, David Lee *See* The Mavericks
Holt, Jerry *See* The Boys from Indiana
Holt, Tom *See* The Boys from Indiana
Holt, Tony *See* The Boys from Indiana
Holtzer, Mike *See* Brush Arbor
Hooven, Herb *See* Joe Val & the New England Bluegrass Boys
Hopkins, Bil *See* Firefall
Horovitch, Sharon *See* Southern Rail
Howell, Jeff *See* The Outlaws

Howell, Kurt *See* Southern Pacific

Howell, Porter *See* Little Texas/Brady Seals

Howell, Steve *See* The Backsliders

Hubbard, Gregg "Hobie" *See* Sawyer Brown

Hudson, Cary *See* Blue Mountain

Hunter, Richard *See* Killbilly

Hurd, Cornell *See* The Cornell Hurd Band

Huskins, Jeff *See* Little Texas/Brady Seals

Ibbotson, Jimmy *See* The Nitty Gritty Dirt Band

Ickes, Rob *See* Blue Highway

Innis, Dave *See* Restless Heart/Larry Stewart

Irwin, Catherine *See* Freakwater

Jackson, Clive *See* Ray Condo & His Ricochets

Jamison, Phil *See* Ralph Blizard & the New Southern Ramblers

Jayne, Mitch *See* The Dillards

Jeffries, Sam *See* The Boys from Indiana

Jeffriess, Lee *See* Big Sandy & His Fly-Rite Boys

Jenewein, Gordon *See* Brush Arbor

Jenkins, David *See* Southern Pacific

Jennings, Greg *See* Restless Heart/Larry Stewart

Jennings , Waylon *See* The Highwaymen

Jimenez, Flaco *See* The Texas Tornados

Johansson, Jan *See* New Vintage

Johns, Evan *See* The LeRoi Brothers

Johnson, Courtney *See* The New Grass Revival

Johnson, Gene *See* Diamond Rio

Johnson, J.B. *See* Blue Shadows

Johnson, Jamie *See* The Boys from Indiana

Johnson, Jeff *See* Jason & the Scorchers

Johnson, Jim *See* The Vidalias

Johnson, Kraig *See* Golden Smog

Johnson, Rome *See* Sons of the Pioneers

Johnson, Russell *See* New Vintage

Johnston, Max *See* Uncle Tupelo/Wilco/Son Volt

Jones, Billy *See* The Outlaws

Jones, Clay *See* Lou Reid/Lou Reid & Carolina

Jones, Mark *See* Exile/Les Taylor/J.P. Pennington

Jones, Phylliss *See* The New Coon Creek Girls

Jorgenson, John *See* The Hellecasters

Judd, Naomi *See* The Judds

Judd, Wynonna *See* The Judds

Julian, Ivan *See* The Health & Happiness Show

Kahr, R. *See* Rank & File

Kallick, Kathy *See* Good Ol' Persons

Kane, Nick *See* The Mavericks

Kaser, Annie *See* The New Coon Creek Girls

Kathriner, Danny *See* Wagon

Katz, Nancy *See* Ranch Romance

Keane, Sean *See* The Chieftains

Keelor, Greg *See* Blue Rodeo

Keenan, David *See* Ranch Romance

Keith, Bill *See* Muleskinner

Kelley, Kevin *See* The Byrds

Kelliher, Jeff *See* Salamander Crossing

Kemp, Allen *See* New Riders of the Purple Sage

Kemper, Carey *See* The Shivers

Kendall, Jeannie *See* The Kendalls

Kendall, Royce *See* The Kendalls

Kenerly, Mike *See* Jolene

Kennedy, Anthony *See* The Kentucky HeadHunters/Brother Phelps

Kettering, Frank *See* The Hoosier Hot Shots

Kilgallon, Eddie *See* Ricochet

King, Billy *See* Sid King & the Five Strings

King, Ed *See* Lynyrd Skynyrd

King, J.P. *See* Six Shooter

King, Kevin *See* Twister Alley

King, Sid *See* Sid King & the Five Strings

Kingman, Ashley *See* Big Sandy & His Fly-Rite Boys

Kinman, Chip *See* Rank & File

Kinman, Tony *See* Rank & File

Kinsey, Andrew *See* Salamander Crossing

Kirby, Harris *See* Killbilly

Kirby, Paul *See* The Cactus Brothers

Kirchen, Bill *See* Commander Cody & His Lost Planet Airmen

Kirk, John *See* Mac Benford & the Woodshed All-Stars

Kirkendall, Terry *See* The Derailers

Kirkindoll, Darrin *See* The Smokin' Armadillos

Klay, T.J. *See* Western Flyer

Klein, Moondi *See* Chesapeake; The Seldom Scene

Kleinow, "Sneaky" Pete *See* Flying Burrito Brothers

Knechtel, Larry *See* David Gates/Bread

Knight, Cheri *See* Blood Oranges/Wooden Leg/Beacon Hillbillies

Knopfler, Mark *See* The Notting Hillbillies

Knudsen, Keith *See* Southern Pacific

Kreutzmann, Bill *See* The Grateful Dead

Kristofferson, Kris *See* The Highwaymen

Kuhn, Kathy *See* The New Coon Creek Girls

Kunkel, Bruce *See* The Nitty Gritty Dirt Band

Kurtz, Danny *See* The Backsliders

Kuykendall, Pete *See* The Country Gentlemen

LaBour, Fred *See* Riders in the Sky

Ladd, Bill *See* Jolene

Lamb, Barbara *See* Ranch Romance

Lamb, Michael *See* Confederate Railroad

Lane, Shawn *See* Blue Highway

Langford, Jon *See* The Waco Brothers

Lanham, Jim *See* Pure Prairie League

Lanham, Roy *See* Sons of the Pioneers

Lantz, Mike *See* Front Range

Lathum, Billy Ray *See* The Dillards; The Kentucky Colonels; The Laurel Canyon Ramblers

Lauber, Karl *See* Joe Val & the New England Bluegrass Boys

Lavendar, Cathy *See* The New Coon Creek Girls

Lawson, Doyle *See* The Country Gentlemen; J.D. Crowe/J.D. Crowe & the New South

Lawter, Tim *See* The Marshall Tucker Band

Layne, Berty *See* The Skillet Lickers

Leadbetter, Phil *See* J.D. Crowe/J.D. Crowe & the New South

Leadon, Bernie *See* The Eagles; Flying Burrito Brothers; The Nitty Gritty Dirt Band

Leady, Don *See* The LeRoi Brothers

Leahy, Larry *See* The Country Gentlemen

Lebouef, Allan *See* Baillie & the Boys

Lee, Larry *See* The Ozark Mountain Daredevils

Leet, Charlie *See* Dry Branch Fire Squad

Leet, Mary Jo *See* Dry Branch Fire Squad

Lefevre, Curt *See* The Spanic Boys

Leigh, Regina *See* Regina Regina

Lemaire, Sonny *See* Exile/Les Taylor/J.P. Pennington

Leport, Calvin *See* The Rarely Herd

Lesh, Phil *See* The Grateful Dead; New Riders of the Purple Sage

Lester, Al *See* The Warrior River Boys

Levenson, Eric *See* Joe Val & the New England Bluegrass Boys

Levy, Adam *See* The Honeydogs

Levy, Howard *See* Bela Fleck/Bela Fleck & the Flecktones

Levy, Noah *See* Golden Smog; The Honeydogs

Lewellyn, Earl *See* New Vintage

Lewis, Elizabeth *See* One Riot One Ranger

Lewis, James Roy "Pop" *See* The Lewis Family

Lewis, Roy Jr. "Little Roy" *See* The Lewis Family

Lewis, Laurie *See* Good Ol' Persons

Lewis, Miggie *See* The Lewis Family

Lewis, Pauline "Mom" *See* The Lewis Family

Lewis, Travis *See* The Lewis Family

Lewis, Wallace *See* The Lewis Family

Libbea, Gene *See* The Nashville Bluegrass Band

Liebert, Billy *See* Sons of the Pioneers

Lilly, Everett *See* The Lilly Brothers/Don Stover

Lilly, Everett A. *See* The Charles River Valley Boys

Lilly, John *See* Ralph Blizard & the New Southern Ramblers

Lilly, Michell Burt "Bea" *See* The Lilly Brothers/Don Stover

Lindley, Randy *See* The Warrior River Boys

Linn, Betty *See* The New Coon Creek Girls

Little, Keith *See* Lonesome Standard Time/Larry Cordle

Lloyd, Bill *See* Foster & Lloyd

Lloyd, Richard *See* The Health & Happiness Show

Lormand, Ward *See* Filé

Louris, Gary *See* Golden Smog; The Jayhawks

Louvin, Charlie *See* Louvin Brothers/Charlie Louvin

Louvin, Lonnie *See* Louvin Brothers/Charlie Louvin

Love, Stephen *See* New Riders of the Purple Sage

Lowe, Jimmy *See* Pirates of the Mississippi

Loyd, Randy *See* Twister Alley

Luck, Greg *See* The Bluegrass Cardinals; J.D. Crowe/J.D. Crowe & the New South

Lutke, Steve *See* Killbilly

Lynam, Ron *See* Front Range

Lynch, Laura *See* The Dixie Chicks

Lynch, Stan *See* Rank & File

Maby, Graham *See* The Health & Happiness Show

Mack, Leroy *See* The Kentucky Colonels

Macy, Robin *See* The Dixie Chicks

Maddox, Cal *See* The Maddox Brothers & Rose/Rose Maddox

Maddox, Cliff *See* The Maddox Brothers & Rose/Rose Maddox

Maddox, Don *See* The Maddox Brothers & Rose/Rose Maddox

Maddox, Fred *See* The Maddox Brothers & Rose/Rose Maddox

Maddox, Henry *See* The Maddox Brothers & Rose/Rose Maddox

Maddox, Rose *See* The Maddox Brothers & Rose/Rose Maddox

Magnuson, John *See* The Carpetbaggers

Maines, Natalie *See* The Dixie Chicks

Malo, Raul *See* The Mavericks

Maness, Jeff *See* The Bass Mountain Boys

Maness, Joel *See* The Bass Mountain Boys

Maness, John *See* The Bass Mountain Boys

Manshel, Stephen Thomas *See* Firefall

Maralie *See* The Skeletons/The Morells

Marion, Chris *See* Western Flyer

Marrs, Christina *See* Asylum Street Spankers

Mars, Chris *See* Golden Smog

Marshall, Mike *See* Psychograss

Martin, Greg *See* The Kentucky HeadHunters/Brother Phelps

Martin, Paul *See* Exile/Les Taylor/J.P. Pennington

Massey, Ken *See* Sid King & the Five Strings

Mastriani, Vic *See* The Nitty Gritty Dirt Band

Mastro, James *See* The Health & Happiness Show

McBride, Terry *See* McBride & the Ride/Terry McBride & the Ride

McCorkle, George *See* The Marshall Tucker Band

McCorvey, Bill *See* Pirates of the Mississippi

McCoury, Del *See* The Del McCoury Band/Ronnie & Rob McCoury

McCoury, Rob *See* The Del McCoury Band/Ronnie & Rob McCoury

McCoury, Ronnie *See* The Del McCoury Band/Ronnie & Rob McCoury; The Sidemen

McCoy, Hank *See* One Riot One Ranger

McCade, Butch *See* The Amazing Rhythm Aces

McDaniel, Chris *See* Confederate Railroad

McDonald, Richie *See* Lonestar

McDorman, Joe *See* The Statler Brothers

McDowell, Chris *See* Six Shooter

McDowell, Ronnie Dean *See* Six Shooter

McDowell, Smilin' Jay *See* BR5-49

McEuen, John *See* The Nitty Gritty Dirt Band

McFee, John *See* Southern Pacific

McGarrigle, Anna *See* Kate & Anna McGarrigle

McGarrigle, Kate *See* Kate & Anna McGarrigle

McGuinn, Roger *See* The Byrds

McGuire, Mike *See* Shenandoah

McKee, Maria *See* Lone Justice/Maria McKee

McKernan, Ron "Pig Pen" *See* The Grateful Dead

McLaughlin, David *See* Crowe & McLaughlin; Johnson Mountain Boys; The Lynn Morris Band

McMichen, Clayton *See* The Skillet Lickers

McReynolds, Jesse *See* Jim & Jesse

McReynolds, Jim *See* Jim & Jesse

McVay, Roger *See* Baillie & the Boys

McWilson, Christy *See* The Picketts

Mead, Chuck *See* BR5-49

Medlocke, Rick *See* Lynyrd Skynyrd

Meeks, Scott *See* The Smokin' Armadillos

Meisner, Randy *See* The Eagles; Poco

Meltzer, Tom *See* Five Chinese Brothers

Mencher, Sean *See* High Noon

Mendelsohn, Barbara *See* Good Ol' Persons

Mensor, Bob *See* Sons of the Pioneers

Messina, Jim *See* Poco

Meyer, Edgar *See* Strength in Numbers

Meyers, Augie *See* The Texas Tornados

Michaelson, David *See* The Vidalias

Milchem, Glenn *See* Blue Rodeo

Milheim, Keith *See* The Hoosier Hot Shots

Miller, Blue *See* The Gibson/Miller Band

Miller, Jeff *See* The Bass Mountain Boys

Miller, Jo *See* Ranch Romance

Miller, Mark *See* Sawyer Brown

Miller, Rhett *See* The Old 97'S

Miller, Scott *See* The V-Roys

Mills, Jerry *See* The Ozark Mountain Daredevils

Mills, Jim *See* The Bass Mountain Boys

Milner, Rusty *See* The Marshall Tucker Band

Mitchell, Larry *See* Wylie & the Wild West Show

Mitchell, Ron *See* Big House

Mitschele, Mike *See* Jolene

Moffatt, Bob *See* The Moffatts

Moffatt, Clint *See* The Moffatts

Moffatt , Dave *See* The Moffatts

Moffatt, Scott *See* The Moffatts

Moffet, Bruce *See* Prairie Oyster

Molloy, Matt *See* The Chieftains

Moloney, Paddy *See* The Chieftains

Monroe, Bill *See* Bill Monroe & His Blue Grass Boys/Charlie Monroe/The Monroe Brothers

Monroe, Charlie *See* Bill Monroe & His Blue Grass Boys/Charlie Monroe/The Monroe Brothers

Montana, Country Dick *See* The Beat Farmers

Montana Slim, *See* Wilf Carter/Montana Slim

Mooney, Ralph *See* James Burton & Ralph Mooney

Moore, Russell *See* IIIrd Tyme Out

Morgan, Evan *See* New Riders of the Purple Sage

Morgan, Tom *See* The Country Gentlemen

Morris, Craig *See* 4 Runner

Morris, Dale *See* Sons of the Pioneers

Morris, Jim *See* Frazier River

Morris, Lynn *See* The Lynn Morris Band

Morris, Shellee *See* Twister Alley

Morrison, Shayne *See* Perfect Stranger

Morse, Gary *See* McBride & the Ride/Terry McBride & the Ride

Moser, Cactus *See* Highway 101

Mosley, Daryl *See* The New Tradition

Muir, Barry *See* Blue Shadows

Muller, Jim *See* Southern Rail

Muller, Paul *See* Southern Rail

Mullins, Joe *See* The Traditional Grass

Mullins, Paul *See* The Boys from Indiana; The Traditional Grass

Munde, Al *See* Flying Burrito Brothers

Murphy, Dan *See* Golden Smog

Murray, Steve *See* Perfect Stranger

Muse, David *See* Firefall

Mydland, Brent *See* The Grateful Dead

Myers, Frank *See* Baker & Myers

Myrick, Danny *See* Western Flyer

Mysterious John *See* Asylum Street Spankers

Nallie, Luther *See* Sons of the Pioneers

Nelson, David *See* New Riders of the Purple Sage

Nelson, Nikki *See* Highway 101

Nelson, Willie *See* The Highwaymen

Neuhauser, David *See* Big House

Newhouse, Jackie *See* The LeRoi Brothers

Nichols, Gates *See* Confederate Railroad

Nicks, Regina *See* Regina Regina

Nicolas, Cody *See* The Cornell Hurd Band

Nikleva, Stephen *See* Ray Condo & His Ricochets

Nolan, Bob *See* Sons of the Pioneers

Norris, Fate *See* The Skillet Lickers

Norton, Trent *See* The Honeydogs

O'Brien, Dwayne *See* Little Texas/Brady Seals

O'Brien, Mollie *See* Tim O'Brien/Tim & Mollie O'Brien

O'Brien, Tim *See* Hot Rize/Red Knuckles & the Trailblazers

O'Bryant, Alan *See* The Nashville Bluegrass Band

Oceans, Lucky *See* Asleep at the Wheel

O'Connor, Mark *See* Strength in Numbers

O'Hara, Jamie *See* Kieran Kane/The O'Kanes/Jamie O'Hara

O'Keefe, Frank *See* The Outlaws

Olander, Jimmy *See* Diamond Rio

Oldaker, Jamie *See* The Tractors

Oliver, Kristine *See* Sweethearts of the Rodeo

Olson, Mark *See* The Jayhawks

Olufs, John *See* The Picketts

O'Regan, Tim *See* The Jayhawks

Orr, Mark *See* The Kentucky HeadHunters/Brother Phelps

Orrall, Robert Ellis *See* Orrall & Wright/Robert Ellis Orrall/Curtis Wright

Ortmann, Mark *See* The Bottle Rockets

Osborne, Bobby *See* The Osborne Brothers

Osborne, Sonny *See* The Osborne Brothers

Owen, Jackie *See* Alabama

Owen, Randy *See* Alabama

Owens, Buck *See* The Hee Haw Gospel Quartet

Pahl, Russ *See* Great Plains

Paley, Tom *See* The New Lost City Ramblers

Park, Cary *See* Boy Howdy

Park, Johnny *See* Archer/Park

Park, Larry *See* Boy Howdy

Parks, Danny *See* The Amazing Rhythm Aces

Parmley, David *See* The Bluegrass Cardinals; David Parmley, Scott Vestal & Continental Divide/David Parmley

Parmley, Don *See* The Bluegrass Cardinals; The Hillmen

Parr, Tom *See* The Bottle Rockets

Parsons, Gene *See* The Byrds; Flying Burrito Brothers

Parsons, Gram *See* The Byrds; Flying Burrito Brothers

Paul, Henry *See* BlackHawk; The Outlaws

Pearson, Tony *See* The Flatlanders

Pedersen, Herb *See* The Dillards; The Laurel Canyon Ramblers

Peeler, Ben *See* The Mavericks

Peeples, Philip *See* The Old 97'S

Pennington, J.P. *See* Exile/Les Taylor/J.P. Pennington

Perkins, Al *See* Flying Burrito Brothers

Perkins, Larry *See* Lonesome Standard Time/Larry Cordle; The Sidemen

Perlman, Marc *See* Golden Smog; The Jayhawks

Pernice, Joe *See* The Scud Mountain Boys

Perry, Greg *See* Lonesome Strangers

Perry, Pam *See* The New Coon Creek Girls

Perryman, Lloyd *See* Sons of the Pioneers

Peterson, Chris *See* Wagon

Phelps, Doug *See* The Kentucky HeadHunters/Brother Phelps

Phelps, Ricky Lee *See* The Kentucky HeadHunters/Brother Phelps

Phillips, Janis Lewis *See* The Lewis Family

Phillips, Lewis *See* The Lewis Family

Phillips, Steve *See* The Notting Hillbillies

Seidel, Martie *See* The Dixie Chicks

Sellers, Paxton *See* The V-Roys

Severs, Pat *See* Pirates of the Mississippi

Shanahan, Tony *See* The Health & Happiness Show

Shane, Bob *See* The Kingston Trio

Shaw, Charlie *See* Five Chinese Brothers

Shaw, Ethan *See* The Derailers

Shea, Tom *See* The Scud Mountain Boys

Shearin, Kevin *See* Filé

Shelasky, Paul *See* Good Ol' Persons

Shelasky, Sue *See* Good Ol' Persons

Shelley, John *See* Wylie & the Wild West Show

Shelor, Sammy *See* Lonesome River Band/Ronnie Bowman

Shirley, Danny *See* Confederate Railroad

Shiver, Kelly *See* Thrasher Shiver

Shortlidge, Jack *See* One Riot One Ranger

Shuffler, George *See* Ralph Stanley & the Clinch Mountain Boys

Sibley, Nick *See* The Skeletons/The Morells

Siggins, Bob *See* The Charles River Valley Boys

Signer, Ethan *See* The Charles River Valley Boys

Silvius, Paul *See* Joe Val & the New England Bluegrass Boys

Simmons, Vicki *See* The New Coon Creek Girls

Simpkins, Rickie *See* David Parmley, Scott Vestal & Continental Divide/David Parmley

Simpkins, Ronnie *See* The Seldom Scene

Simpson, Bland *See* The Red Clay Ramblers

Singleman, Walt *See* The Picketts

Sizemore, Charlie *See* Ralph Stanley & the Clinch Mountain Boys

Sizemore, Herschel *See* The Bluegrass Cardinals

Skaggs, Ricky *See* Boone Creek; J.D. Crowe/J.D. Crowe & the New South; Ralph Stanley & the Clinch Mountain Boys

Skelton, Paul *See* The Cornell Hurd Band

Slate, Lori Forbes *See* The Forbes Family

Sleep, Leroy *See* The Picketts

Sloane, Bobby *See* The Kentucky Colonels

Slye, Leonard *See* Sons of the Pioneers

Small, Len *See* Wagon

Smiley, Red *See* Don Reno & Red Smiley

Smith, Billy *See* 4 Runner; Billy & Terry Smith

Smith, Kenny *See* Lonesome River Band/Ronnie Bowman

Smith, Kevin *See* Asylum Street Spankers; High Noon

Smith, Marcus *See* Lou Reid/Lou Reid & Carolina

Smith, Robin *See* Lonesome Standard Time/Larry Cordle

Smith, Russell *See* The Amazing Rhythm Aces

Smith, Stanley *See* Asylum Street Spankers

Smith, T.K. *See* Big Sandy & His Fly-Rite Boys

Smith, Terry *See* Billy & Terry Smith

Smith, Tim *See* The Bluegrass Cardinals

Smyth, Joe *See* Sawyer Brown

Snell, Bobby *See* The Cornell Hurd Band

Snodderly, Ed *See* The Brother Boys

Soliday, Lance Ray *See* Dave & Deke Combo

Southards, Wayne *See* Lonesome Standard Time/Larry Cordle

Spanic, Ian *See* The Spanic Boys

Spanic, Tom *See* The Spanic Boys

Sparks, Larry *See* Ralph Stanley & the Clinch Mountain Boys

Sparks, Speedy *See* The LeRoi Brothers

Spencer, Mark *See* Blood Oranges/Wooden Leg/Beacon Hillbillies

Spencer, Thad *See* The Jayhawks

Spencer, Tim *See* Sons of the Pioneers

Spinks, Doug *See* The Shivers

Spriggins, Deuce *See* Sons of the Pioneers

Stack, Alan *See* The Rarely Herd

Stack, Jim *See* The Rarely Herd

Stafford, Tim *See* Blue Highway

Stampfel, Peter *See* The Holy Modal Rounders

Stanley, Carter *See* The Stanley Brothers

Stanley, Ralph *See* Ralph Stanley & the Clinch Mountain Boys; The Stanley Brothers

Stanley, Ralph II *See* Ralph Stanley & the Clinch Mountain Boys

Starling, John *See* The Seldom Scene

Steele, Jeffrey *See* Boy Howdy

Steffey, Adam *See* Lonesome River Band/Ronnie Bowman

Stein, Andy *See* Commander Cody & His Lost Planet Airmen

Stephenson, Larry *See* The Bluegrass Cardinals

Stephenson, Van *See* BlackHawk

Sterban, Richard *See* The Oak Ridge Boys

Stevens, Michael *See* Austin Lounge Lizards

Stevens, Peter *See* Filé

Stewart, John *See* The Kingston Trio

Stewart, Larry *See* Restless Heart/Larry Stewart

Stirratt, John *See* Uncle Tupelo/Wilco/Son Volt

Stirratt, Laurie *See* Blue Mountain

Stokely, Jimmy *See* Exile/Les Taylor/J.P. Pennington

Stokes, Lowe *See* The Skillet Lickers

Stone, Curtis *See* Highway 101

Stoneman, Scott *See* The Kentucky Colonels; Ernest Stoneman/The Stoneman Family

Stover, Don *See* The Lilly Brothers/Don Stover

Street, Mike *See* The Bass Mountain Boys

Stubbs, Eddie *See* Johnson Mountain Boys

Stuckley, Dave *See* Dave & Deke Combo

Sullivan, Jerry *See* Jerry & Tammy Sullivan/The Sullivan Family

Sullivan, Matt Wendell *See* Tarnation

Sullivan, Tammy *See* Jerry & Tammy Sullivan/The Sullivan Family

Sundrud, Jack *See* Great Plains

Sutherland, Pete *See* Mac Benford & the Woodshed All-Stars

Sutton, Gregg *See* Lone Justice/Maria McKee

Sweeney, Paul *See* Austin Lounge Lizards

Sykes, Ernie *See* The Bluegrass Cardinals

Tanner, James Gideon "Gid" *See* The Skillet Lickers

Tate, Scott *See* Molly & the Heymakers

Taylor, Craig "Niteman" *See* Killbilly

Taylor, Gene *See* The Blasters

Taylor, Gil *See* The Hoosier Hot Shots

Taylor, Les *See* Exile/Les Taylor/J.P. Pennington

Taylor, Steve *See* Ray Condo & His Ricochets

Taylor, Wayne *See* Blue Highway

Terry, Joe *See* The Skeletons/The Morells

Thacker, Ernie *See* Ralph Stanley & the Clinch Mountain Boys

Tharp, Al *See* Beausoleil

Theiste, Jason *See* The Smokin' Armadillos

Theo, Lisa *See* Ranch Romance

Thomas, Billy *See* McBride & the Ride/Terry McBride & the Ride

Thomas, Neil *See* Five Chinese Brothers

Thomas, Suzanne *See* Dry Branch Fire Squad

Thomason, Ron *See* Dry Branch Fire Squad; Ralph Stanley & the Clinch Mountain Boys

Thomasson, Hughie *See* Lynyrd Skynyrd; The Outlaws

Thompson, Andy *See* The Thompson Brothers Band

Thompson, D. Clinton *See* The Skeletons/The Morells

Thompson, Les *See* The Nitty Gritty Dirt Band

Thompson, Matt *See* The Thompson Brothers Band

Thompson, Tommy *See* The Red Clay Ramblers

Thorn, Stan *See* Shenandoah

Thornton, Mark *See* Wylie & the Wild West Show

Thrasher, Neil *See* Thrasher Shiver

Thurman, Lynn Cox *See* The Cox Family

Tichy, John *See* Commander Cody & His Lost Planet Airmen

Tidwell, Bob *See* Joe Val & the New England Bluegrass Boys

Timmins, Margo *See* Cowboy Junkies

Timmins, Michael *See* Cowboy Junkies

Timmins, Peter *See* Cowboy Junkies

Tolhurst, Kerryn *See* The Health & Happiness Show

Too Slim *See* Riders in the Sky

Torbert, David *See* New Riders of the Purple Sage

Townson, Dean *See* Pirates of the Mississippi

Trainor, Kevin *See* Five Chinese Brothers

Tramp *See* The Cactus Brothers

Travers, Fred *See* The Seldom Scene

Tree, Edward *See* The Bum Steers

Trianosky, Paul *See* Southern Rail

Trietsch, Ken "Rudy" *See* The Hoosier Hot Shots

Trietsch, Paul "Hezzie" *See* The Hoosier Hot Shots

Trimble, Bobby *See* Big Sandy & His Fly-Rite Boys

Trischka, Tony *See* Psychograss

Trued, Stephen *See* Killbilly

Truman, Dan *See* Diamond Rio

Tucker, Diesel *See* The Shivers

Tull, Bruce *See* The Scud Mountain Boys

Tulucci, Johnny *See* The Cactus Brothers

Tweedy, Jeff *See* Golden Smog; Uncle Tupelo/Wilco/Son Volt

Tyminski, Dan *See* Lonesome River Band/Ronnie Bowman

Underwood, Richard *See* Johnson Mountain Boys

Val, Joe *See* The Charles River Valley Boys; Joe Val & the New England Bluegrass Boys

Van Beek, Casey *See* The Tractors

Van Meter, Sally *See* Good Ol' Persons

Van Zant, Johnny *See* Lynyrd Skynyrd

Van Zant, Ronnie *See* Lynyrd Skynyrd

Vartanian, Bennett *See* Alabama

Vaughn, Kenny *See* McBride & the Ride/Terry McBride & the Ride

Verret, Errol *See* Beausoleil

Vestal, Scott *See* David Parmley, Scott Vestal & Continental Divide/David Parmley

Vignaud, Robert *See* Beausoleil

Villanueva, Tony *See* The Derailers

Vogensen, Gary *See* New Riders of the Purple Sage

Wagner, Kurt *See* Lambchop

Wakefield, Frank *See* The Greenbriar Boys

Waldrep, Gary *See* The Warrior River Boys

Waldrop, Page *See* The Vidalias

Walker, Ebo *See* The New Grass Revival

Walle, Rune *See* The Ozark Mountain Daredevils

Waller, Charlie *See* The Country Gentlemen

Walsh, Joe *See* The Eagles

Walston, Charles *See* The Vidalias

Wammo *See* Asylum Street Spankers

Wandscher, Phil *See* Whiskeytown

Warburton, Kelly *See* The Marty Warburton Band

Warburton, Marty *See* The Marty Warburton Band

Warburton-Wilkey, April *See* The Marty Warburton Band

Ward, Otto "Gabe" *See* The Hoosier Hot Shots

Ware, Billy *See* Beausoleil

Warren, Dale *See* Sons of the Pioneers

Watkins, Kevin *See* Brush Arbor

Watson, Jim *See* The Red Clay Ramblers

Weaver, Jeff *See* The Rarely Herd

Webb, Darrell *See* J.D. Crowe/J.D. Crowe & the New South

Webb, Dean *See* The Dillards

Weber, Steve *See* The Holy Modal Rounders

Webster, Duane *See* Front Range

Weeks, Randy *See* Lonesome Strangers

Weil, Beth *See* Good Ol' Persons

Weinmeister, Steven *See* Firefall

Weir, Bob *See* The Grateful Dead

Weissberg, Eric *See* The Greenbriar Boys

Wernick, Pete *See* Hot Rize/Red Knuckles & the Trailblazers

Wertz, Kenny *See* Flying Burrito Brothers

Wesson, Steve *See* The Flatlanders

West, Shelly *See* David Frizzell & Shelly West

West, Speedy *See* Speedy West & Jimmy Bryant

West Virginia Creeper *See* Commander Cody & His Lost Planet Airmen

Whitaker, Gabe *See* The Laurel Canyon Ramblers

White, Buck *See* The Whites

White, Cheryl *See* The Whites

White, Clarence *See* The Byrds; The Kentucky Colonels; Muleskinner

White, Dave *See* Sid King & the Five Strings

White, Eric *See* The Kentucky Colonels

White, Ken *See* The New Tradition

White, Ralph *See* Bad Livers

White, Roland *See* The Kentucky Colonels; The Nashville Bluegrass Band

White, Sharon *See* The Whites

Whitley, Keith *See* J.D. Crowe/J.D. Crowe & the New South; Ralph Stanley & the Clinch Mountain Boys

Whitney, Lou *See* The Skeletons/The Morells

Whitstein, Charles *See* The Whitstein Brothers

Whitstein, Robert *See* The Whitstein Brothers

Whitty, Michael *See* The Thompson Brothers Band

Wiggins, Audrey *See* John & Audrey Wiggins

Wiggins, John *See* John & Audrey Wiggins

Wilborn, Marshall *See* The Lynn Morris Band

Wilburn, Doyle *See* The Wilburn Brothers

Wilburn, Teddy *See* The Wilburn Brothers

Wilemon, Stan *See* The Warrior River Boys

Wilkeson, Leon *See* Lynyrd Skynyrd

Wilkie, Frank *See* The Marshall Tucker Band

Wilkinson, Steve *See* Brush Arbor

Willborn, Marshall *See* Johnson Mountain Boys

Williams, Chas *See* One Riot One Ranger

Williams, Dana *See* Diamond Rio

Williams, Kirk *See* Austin Lounge Lizards

Williams, Linda *See* Robin & Linda Williams

Williams, Polly Lewis *See* The Lewis Family

Williams, Robin *See* Robin & Linda Williams

Williams, Roger *See* Joe Val & the New England Bluegrass Boys

Willis, Charles "Skeeter" *See* The Willis Brothers

Willis, James "Guy" *See* The Willis Brothers

Willis, Richard "Vic" *See* The Willis Brothers

Wilson, "Hawk" Shaw *See* BR5-49

Wilson, Bob *See* Frazier River

Wilson, Jeff *See* Pure Prairie League

Wilson, Mike *See* The Bass Mountain Boys

Wilson, Tim *See* Austin Lounge Lizards

Wimmer, Kevin *See* Good Ol' Persons

Wise, Chubby *See* Bill Monroe & His Blue Grass Boys/Charlie Monroe/The Monroe Brothers

Wiseman, Bob *See* Blue Rodeo

Wolf, Chris *See* The Shivers

Wolf, Eugene *See* The Brother Boys

Woody Paul *See* Riders in the Sky

Wooley, Alan *See* Killbilly

Wooten, Gene *See* The Sidemen

Wooten, Roy "Future Man" *See* Bela Fleck/Bela Fleck & the Flecktones

Wooten, Victor Lemonte *See* Bela Fleck/Bela Fleck & the Flecktones

Wormer, Chris *See* Charlie Daniels Band

Wright, Curtis *See* Orrall & Wright/Robert Ellis Orrall/Curtis Wright

Wright, Heath *See* Ricochet

Wright, Hugh *See* Boy Howdy

Wright, Johnnie *See* Johnnie & Jack

Wright, Norman *See* The Bluegrass Cardinals

Wrinkle, Jennifer *See* The New Coon Creek Girls

Wyatt, Mark *See* One Riot One Ranger

Yaffey, Carl *See* One Riot One Ranger

Yager, Earl *See* Johnson Mountain Boys

Yellin, Bob *See* The Greenbriar Boys

Yoho, Monte *See* The Outlaws

York, Andy *See* Jason & the Scorchers

York, John *See* The Byrds

Young, Danny Roy *See* The Cornell Hurd Band

Young, Fred *See* The Kentucky HeadHunters/Brother Phelps

Young, Michael *See* Great Plains

Young, Richard *See* The Kentucky HeadHunters/Brother Phelps

Young, Rusty *See* Poco

Young, Shaun *See* High Noon

Zonn, Brian *See* Six Shooter

The Producer Index compiles the albums in MusicHound Country that have a producer noted for them. (These are usually recommended discs, but we like to credit the producer for albums in the "What to Avoid" section, too, so a few of these could be downright dogs!) Under each producer's name is the name of the artist or group's entry (or entries) in which the album can be found, followed by the album title. If an album is produced by more than one individual/group, the album name will be listed separately under the names of each of the individuals/groups who had a hand in producing it.

Alan Abrahams
Pure Prairie League, *Dance*

William Ackerman
John Gorka, *Jack's Crows*

Ed Ackerson
The Carpetbaggers, *Sin Now . . . Pray Later*

Joe Adams
Ray Charles, *Modern Sounds in Country and Western Music*

Peter Afterman
Elvis Presley, *Honeymoon in Vegas*

Brian Ahern
Rodney Crowell, *Ain't Living Long Like This*
Emmylou Harris, *Cimarron*
Emmylou Harris, *Last Date*
Emmylou Harris, *Roses in the Snow*
George Jones, *The Bradley Barn Sessions*
Anne Murray, *Anne Murray's Greatest Hits*

Chuck Ainlay
Jason & the Scorchers, *Fervor*

Alabama
Alabama, *American Pride*
Alabama, *Cheap Seats*
Alabama, *40 Hour Week*
Alabama, *Greatest Hits*
Alabama, *In Pictures*
Alabama, *My Home's in Alabama*
Alabama, *Pass It On Down*

Howard Albert
Chris Hillman/The Desert Rose Band, *Slippin' Away*

Ron Albert
Chris Hillman/The Desert Rose Band, *Slippin' Away*

Richie Albright
Jessi Colter, *The Jesse Colter Collection*

Mary Katherine Aldin
The Kentucky Colonels, *Long Journey Home*
The Kingston Trio, *Live at Newport*
The New Lost City Ramblers, *The New Lost City Ramblers & Friends*
Doc Watson/The Watson Family/Doc & Merle Watson, *Doc Watson: The Vanguard Years*

Greg Alexander
Stella Parton, *A Woman's Touch*

Pat Alger
Pat Alger, *True Love & Other Short Stories*

Bob Allen
Faron Young, *Golden Hits*

Curtis Allen
Marty Stuart, *Marty Stuart*

John Allen
Tanya Tucker, *Tanya Tucker*

Terry Allen
Terry Allen, *Amerasia*

Terry Allen, *Bloodlines*
Terry Allen, *Human Remains*
Terry Allen, *Lubbock (on Everything)*
Terry Allen, *Songs from Chippy*

Joe Allison
Hank Thompson, *The Best of Hank Thompson 1966-1978*

Billy Altman
Bill Monroe & His Blue Grass Boys, *Are You from Dixie? Great Country Brother Teams of the 1930s*
Bill Monroe & His Blue Grass Boys, *Bill Monroe & His Blue Grass Boys: Muleskinner Blues*

Richard Alves
Pirates of the Mississippi, *Best of the Pirates of the Mississippi*
Pirates of the Mississippi, *Pirates of the Mississippi*

Dave Alvin
Dave Alvin, *Blue Blvd*
Dave Alvin, *Museum of Heart*
Big Sandy & His Fly-Rite Boys, *Swingin' West*
The Derailers, *Jackpot*
Rosie Flores, *Tulare Dust*
Chris Gaffney, *Loser's Paradise*

Phil Alvin
Phil Alvin, *Un "Sung Stories"*

Eric "Roscoe" Ambel
Blood Oranges/Wooden
Leg/Beacon Hillbillies, *The
Crying Tree*
Blood Oranges/Wooden
Leg/Beacon Hillbillies, *The
Knitter*
Blue Mountain, *Dog Days*
The Bottle Rockets, *The
Brooklyn Side*

David Anderle
Rita Coolidge, *Greatest Hits*
Rita Coolidge, *Out of the
Blues*
The Ozark Mountain Daredev-
ils, *The Best*
The Ozark Mountain Daredev-
ils, *The Car over the Lake
Album*
The Ozark Mountain Daredev-
ils, *It'll Shine When It Shines*
The Ozark Mountain Daredev-
ils, *Men from Earth*

John Anderson
John Anderson, *Blue Skies
Again*
John Anderson, *Seminole
Wind*

Pete Anderson
Pete Anderson, *Working Class*
The Backsliders, *Throwin'
Rocks at the Moon*
Blue Rodeo, *Casino*
Scott Joss, *Souvenirs*
Dwight Yoakam, *Dwight Live*
Dwight Yoakam, *Gone*
Dwight Yoakam, *Guitars,
Cadillacs, Etc., Etc.*
Dwight Yoakam, *Just Lookin'
for a Hit*
Dwight Yoakam, *This Time*

Angelo
Kim Richey, *Bitter Sweet*

Darol Anger
Psychograss, *Like Minds*
Psychograss, *Psychograss*

Ira Antelis
S. Alan Taylor, *Forever Dance*

Scott Ardoin
The Savoy-Doucet Cajun
Band, *Now & Then*

Rod Argent
Nanci Griffith, *Late Night
Grande Hotel*

Gary Arnold
Kate Jacobs, *What about Regret*

Moses Asch
The New Lost City Ramblers,
*The New Lost City Ramblers,
the Early Years, 1958–1962*

Peter Asher
Linda Ronstadt, *Hasten Down
the Wind*
Linda Ronstadt, *Heart Like a
Wheel*
Linda Ronstadt, *Mad Love*
Linda Ronstadt, *Prisoner in
Disguise*
James Taylor, *J.T.*
James Taylor, *James Taylor*
James Taylor, *Sweet Baby
James*

Chet Atkins
Floyd Cramer, *The Essential
Series: Floyd Cramer*
Don Gibson, *A Legend in His
Time*
Johnnie & Jack, *Johnnie & Jack*
Roy Orbison, *Little
Richard/Roy Orbison*
Roy Orbison, *The RCA Days*
Les Paul, *Chester & Lester*
Elvis Presley, *Elvis Presley*
Jerry Reed, *Me and Chet*
Jerry Reed, *Me and Jerry*
Jerry Reed, *Sneakin' Around*
Jim Reeves, *The Essential Se-
ries: Jim Reeves*

Dawn Atkinson
John Gorka, *Jack's Crows*

James Austin
Lefty Frizzell, *The Best of Lefty
Frizzell*
Buck Owens, *The Buck Owens
Collection, 1959–1990*
Merle Travis, *Best of Merle
Travis*
Bob Wills, *Anthology,
1935–1973*

Bad Livers
Bad Livers, *The Golden Years*

Ross Bagdasarian
The Chipmunks/Alvin & the
Chipmunks, *Urban Chip-
munk*
The Chipmunks/Alvin & the
Chipmunks, *A Very Merry
Chipmunk*

Scott Baggett
Al Anderson, *Pay Before You
Pump*

Ray Baker
Moe Bandy, *Greatest Hits*
Moe Bandy, *Honky Tonk Am-
nesia—The Hard Country
Sound of Moe Bandy*
Joe Stampley, *The Best of Joe
Stampley*
George Strait, *Greatest Hits
Volume Two*

Butch Baldassari
The Bass Mountain Boys,
Love of a Woman
The Bass Mountain Boys, *My
God Made It All*
New Vintage, *No Time for the
Blues*
The Rarely Herd, *Heartbreak
City*
The Rarely Herd, *Midnight
Loneliness*
The Rarely Herd, *Pure Home-
made Love*

Earl Ball
Stoney Edwards, *Mississippi
You're on My Mind*
Merle Haggard, *A Tribute to
the Best Damn Fiddle Player
in the World (or, My Salute
to Bob Wills)*
Jo-El Sonnier, *Cajun Life*

Brown Bannister
Bruce Carroll, *Sometimes Mir-
acles Hide*
Kim Hill, *Talk about Life*
Paul Overstreet, *Best of Paul
Overstreet*
Paul Overstreet, *Heroes*

Bobby Bare
Harlan Howard, *All-Time Favorite Country Songwriter*

Russ Barenberg
Russ Barenberg, *Moving Pic-
tures*
Russ Barenberg, *Skip, Hop, &
Wobble*
Jerry Douglas/Douglas,
Barenberg & Meyer, *Skip,
Hop & Wobble*

Craig Barker
Tish Hinojosa, *Taos to Tennessee*

Danny Barnes
Bad Livers, *Horses in the
Mines*

Max D. Barnes
Keith Whitley, *Wherever You
Are Tonight*

Fred Bartenstein
Mac Wiseman, *Classic Bluegrass*

Jock Bartley
Firefall, *Messenger*

Peter Bartok
The New Lost City Ramblers,
*The New Lost City Ramblers,
the Early Years, 1958–1962*

Terry Baucom
Lou Reid/Lou Reid & Carolina,
Carolina Blue

Kevin Beamish
Curtis Day, *Curtis Day*

The Beat Farmers
The Beat Farmers, *Manifold*

Beausoleil
Beausoleil, *La Danse de la Vie*

Roger Bechirian
Carlene Carter, *Blue Nun*
Carlene Carter, *C'est C Bon*
Carlene Carter, *Special Pain*
Orrall & Wright/Robert Ellis
Orrall/Curtis Wright, *Special
Pain*

Jim Beck
Ray Price, *Ray Price and the
Cherokee Cowboys*

Barry Beckett
T. Graham Brown, *Bumper to
Bumper*

Kenny Chesney, *All I Need to Know*
Kenny Chesney, *In My Wildest Dreams*
Kenny Chesney, *Me and You*
Confederate Railroad, *Confederate Railroad*
Confederate Railroad, *Notorious*
Bobbie Cryner, *Girl of Your Dreams*
Emilio, *Life Is Good*
Neal McCoy, *No Doubt about It*
Neal McCoy, *You Gotta Love That!*
Lorrie Morgan, *Leave the Light On*
Lee Roy Parnell, *Lee Roy Parnell*
John Prine, *Storm Windows*
Hank Williams Jr., *America (The Way I See It)*
Hank Williams Jr., *Lone Wolf*
Chely Wright, *Woman in the Moon*
Tammy Wynette, *Without Walls*

Richard Bennett
Marty Brown, *Wild Kentucky Skies*
George Ducas, *George Ducas*
George Ducas, *Where I Stand*
Steve Earle, *I Feel Alright*
Emmylou Harris, *At the Ryman*
Emmylou Harris, *Cowgirl's Prayer*
Becky Hobbs, *All Keyed Up*
The Mavericks, *From Hell to Paradise*
Bill Miller, *Raven in the Snow*
Bill Miller, *The Red Road*
Prairie Oyster, *Everybody Knows*
Jo-El Sonnier, *Come on Joe*
Jo-El Sonnier, *Have a Little Faith*
Marty Stuart, *Tempted*
Jerry & Tammy Sullivan/The Sullivan Family, *A Joyful Noise*

Ray Benson
Asleep at the Wheel, *Asleep at the Wheel: Tribute to the Music of Bob Wills and the Texas Playboys*
Asleep at the Wheel, *Collison Course*
Asleep at the Wheel, *Greatest Hits (Live & Kickin')*
Don Walser, *Rolling Stone from Texas*
Don Walser, *Texas Top Hand*
Wylie & the Wild West Show, *Way Out West*

Tony Berg
Ted Hawkins, *The Next Hundred Years*

Sam Berkow
Killbilly, *Foggy Mountain Anarchy*

Steve Berlin
Dave Alvin, *Romeo's Escape*
The Beat Farmers, *Tales of the New West*
Tish Hinojosa, *Homeland*
The Picketts, *Euphonium*

Byron Berline
Byron Berline, *Fiddle & a Song*
Byron Berline, *Jumpin' the Strings*

John Berry
John Berry, *O Holy Night*

Scott Billington
Sleepy LaBeef, *Nothin' but the Truth*
Charlie Rich, *Pictures and Paintings*
The Spanic Boys, *Spanic Boys*

Bitchin' Babes
Christine Lavin, *Buy Me Bring Me Take Me: Don't Mess My Hair!!! Volume 2*

Clint Black
Clint Black, *The Hard Way*
Clint Black, *Looking for Christmas*

Norman Blake
Norman Blake/Norman & Nancy Blake/Norman Blake & Tony Rice, *Blake & Rice*
Norman Blake/Norman & Nancy Blake/Norman Blake & Tony Rice, *The Norman and Nancy Blake Compact Disc*
Norman Blake/Norman & Nancy Blake/Norman Blake & Tony Rice, *Whiskey before Breakfast*

The Blasters
The Blasters, *American Music*
The Blasters, *The Blasters Collection*
The Blasters, *Over There: Live at the Venue, London*

Archie Bleyer
The Everly Brothers, *All They Had to Do Was Dream*
The Everly Brothers, *Cadence Classics: Their 20 Greatest Hits*
Johnny Tillotson, *Poetry in Motion: The Best of Johnny Tillotson*

Adam Block
Jason & the Scorchers, *Essential Jason & the Scorchers, Volume 1: Are You Ready for the Country?*

Ron Block
The Forbes Family, *In the Shadow of Your Wings*

Blood Oranges
Blood Oranges/Wooden Leg/Beacon Hillbillies, *Corn River*

Blue Highway
Blue Highway, *It's a Long, Long Road*
Blue Highway, *Wind to the West*

Blue Mountain
Blue Mountain, *Blue Mountain*

Blue Rodeo
Blue Rodeo, *Diamond Mine*
Blue Rodeo, *Nowhere to Here*

Richard Bock
The Kentucky Colonels, *Appalachian Swing!*

Steve Bogard
Brett James, *Brett James*

Bill Bolick
The Blue Sky Boys, *In Concert, 1964*

Michael Bonagura
Baillie & the Boys, *Lovin' Every Minute*

Boone Creek
Boone Creek, *Boone Creek*

Boz Boorer
Ronnie Dawson, *Rockinitis*

Dixie Bowen
Pam Tillis, *Above and Beyond the Doll of Cutey*

Jimmy Bowen
John Anderson, *Blue Skies Again*
John Berry, *John Berry*
John Berry, *Standing on the Edge*
Jimmy Buffett, *Last Mango in Paris*
Deana Carter, *Did I Shave My Legs for This?*
Lacy J. Dalton, *Survivor*
Linda Davis, *In a Different Light*
Linda Davis, *Linda Davis*
Chris LeDoux, *Best of Chris LeDoux*
Reba McEntire, *Whoever's in New England*
The Oak Ridge Boys, *Monongahela*
The Oak Ridge Boys, *The Oak Ridge Boys Have Arrived*
Pirates of the Mississippi, *Best of the Pirates of the Mississippi*
John Schneider, *Greatest Hits*
George Strait, *Chill of an Early Fall*
George Strait, *Greatest Hits*
George Strait, *Holding My Own*
George Strait, *Livin' It Up*
George Strait, *Merry Christmas Strait to You*
Mel Tillis, *The Very Best of Mel Tillis*
Pam Tillis, *Above and Beyond the Doll of Cutey*
Steve Wariner, *Greatest Hits*
Hank Williams Jr., *America (The Way I See It)*
Hank Williams Jr., *Family Tradition*

Hank Williams Jr., *Hank Williams Jr.'s Greatest Hits*

Boxcar Willie
Boxcar Willie, *Rocky Box*

Joe Boyd
Richard Greene/The Grass Is Greener, *Muleskinner: A Potpourri of Bluegrass Jam*
Kate & Anna McGarrigle, *Dancer with Bruised Knees*
Kate & Anna McGarrigle, *Kate & Anna McGarrigle*
Muleskinner, *Muleskinner: A Potpourri of Bluegrass Jam*

John Boylan
Baillie & the Boys, *The Best of Baillie & the Boys*
Charlie Daniels Band, *Full Moon*
Charlie Daniels Band, *Million Mile Reflections*
Pure Prairie League, *Two Lane Highway*

Owen Bradley
Patsy Cline, *The Patsy Cline Collection*
Patsy Cline, *The Patsy Cline Story*
Johnnie & Jack, *Johnnie & Jack*
Brenda Lee, *Greatest Country Hits*
Brenda Lee, *Merry Christmas from Brenda Lee*
Jimmy Martin, *Jimmy Martin & the Sunny Mountain Boys*
Bill Monroe & His Blue Grass Boys, *Bill Monroe: Bluegrass, 1950–1958*
Bill Monroe & His Blue Grass Boys, *Bill Monroe: Bluegrass, 1959–1969*
Conway Twitty, *Greatest Hits Volume 1*
Conway Twitty, *Greatest Hits Volume 2*

Gary Brewer
Gary Brewer, *Guitar*

Gary Brewer & the Kentucky Ramblers
Gary Brewer, *Money to Ride the Train*

David Briggs
Marty Haggard, *Borders & Boundaries*
Neil Young, *Old Ways*
Neil Young, *Rust Never Sleeps*
Neil Young, *Tonight's the Night*
Neil Young, *Unplugged*

Mark Bright
BlackHawk, *BlackHawk*
BlackHawk, *Strong Enough*
Jeff Wood, *Between the Earth and the Stars*

Gary Bristol
The Red Clay Ramblers, *A Lie of the Mind*

Brodsky Quartet
Elvis Costello, *The Juliet Letters*

Bruce Brody
Lone Justice/Maria McKee, *Life Is Sweet*

Dave Brogren
Fred Eaglesmith, *From the Paradise Motel*

Bruce Bromberg
Dave Alvin, *Blue Blvd*
Dave Alvin, *Museum of Heart*
Marty Brown, *Here's to the Honky Tonks*
Ted Hawkins, *Happy Hour*
Ted Hawkins, *Watch Your Step*
Lonesome Strangers, *The Lonesome Strangers*
Heather Myles, *Just Like Old Times*
Billy Lee Riley, *Blue Collar Blues*
Dale Watson, *Blessed or Damned*
Dale Watson, *Cheatin' Heart Attack*
Reverend Billy C. Wirtz, *Songs of Faith and Inflammation*

David Bromberg
David Bromberg, *David Bromberg*
David Bromberg, *How Late'll Ya Play 'Til*
John Hartford, *Aereo-Plain*

Clyde Brooks
Perfect Stranger, *You Have the Right to Remain Silent*
Ronna Reeves, *What Comes Naturally*

Alex Broussard
Jo-El Sonnier, *Cajun Life*

Michael Brovsky
Joe Ely, *Hi-Res*
Joe Ely, *Musta Notta Gotta Lotta*
Jerry Jeff Walker, *A Man Must Carry On, Volume 1*
Jerry Jeff Walker, *A Man Must Carry On, Volume 2*
Jerry Jeff Walker, *The Best of Jerry Jeff Walker*

Greg Brown
Greg Brown, *Songs of Innocence and Experience*

Gregg Brown
Chris LeDoux, *Stampede*
Molly & the Heymakers, *Molly & the Heymakers*
Travis Tritt, *It's All about to Change*
Travis Tritt, *T-R-O-U-B-L-E*
Gene Watson, *At Last*

Junior Brown
Junior Brown, *Guit with It*
Junior Brown, *Junior High*
Junior Brown, *Semi Crazy*

Marty Brown
Marty Brown, *Here's to the Honky Tonks*

Roger Brown
Roger Brown & Swing City, *Roger Brown & Swing City*

T. Graham Brown
T. Graham Brown, *Bumper to Bumper*

Terry Brown
Blue Rodeo, *Outskirts*

Tony Brown
Marty Brown, *Wild Kentucky Skies*
Tracy Byrd, *Big Love*
Lionel Cartwright, *I Watched It on the Radio*

Lionel Cartwright, *Lionel Cartwright*
Mark Collie, *Born and Raised in Black & White*
Mark Collie, *Hardin County Line*
Rodney Crowell, *Diamonds and Dirt*
Rodney Crowell, *Keys to the Highway*
Rodney Crowell, *Life Is Messy*
Bobbie Cryner, *Girl of Your Dreams*
Steve Earle, *Guitar Town*
Joe Ely, *Love and Danger*
Vince Gill, *High Lonesome Sound*
Vince Gill, *I Still Believe in You*
Vince Gill, *Souvenirs*
Vince Gill, *When I Call Your Name*
Vince Gill, *When Love Finds You*
Nanci Griffith, *Lone Star State of Mind*
Nanci Griffith, *One Fair Summer Evening*
James House, *Hard Times for an Honest Man*
James House, *James House*
Robert Earl Keen Jr., *Love and Danger*
Patty Loveless, *Patty Loveless Sings Songs of Love*
Patty Loveless, *Up against My Heart*
Patty Loveless, *When I Call Your Name*
Lyle Lovett, *Lyle Lovett*
Lyle Lovett, *Lyle Lovett and His Large Band*
Lyle Lovett, *Pontiac*
Mac McAnally, *Knots*
McBride & the Ride/Terry McBride & the Ride, *Burnin' Up the Road*
McBride & the Ride/Terry McBride & the Ride, *Hurry Sundown*
McBride & the Ride/Terry McBride & the Ride, *Sacred Ground*
Reba McEntire, *For My Broken Heart*
Reba McEntire, *Read My Mind*
David Lee Murphy, *Out with a Bang*

Todd Snider, *Songs for the Daily Planet*
George Strait, *Blue Clear Sky*
Marty Stuart, *Honky Tonkin's What I Do Best*
Marty Stuart, *Love and Luck*
Marty Stuart, *Tempted*
Steve Wariner, *Greatest Hits*
Steve Wariner, *Laredo*
Kelly Willis, *Bang Bang*
Kelly Willis, *Kelly Willis*
Kelly Willis, *Well-Travelled Love*
Wynonna, *Tell Me Why*

Denny Bruce
The Beat Farmers, *Loud and Plowed and . . . LIVE!!*
The LeRoi Brothers, *Forget about the Danger . . . Think of the Fun*

Trey Bruce
Suzy Bogguss, *Give Me Some Wheels*

Glen Brunman
Elvis Presley, *Honeymoon in Vegas*

Stephen Bruton
Alejandro Escovedo, *Gravity*
Alejandro Escovedo, *Thirteen Years*
Jimmie Dale Gilmore, *After Awhile*
Chris Smither, *Up on the Lowdown*

Bryndle
Karla Bonoff/Bryndle, *Bryndle*

Peter Buck
Uncle Tupelo/Wilco/Son Volt, *March 16–20, 1992*

Steve Buckingham
David Ball, *Starlite Lounge*
Ricky Van Shelton, *Super Hits, Volume 2*
Ricky Van Shelton, *Wild-Eyed Dream/Loving Proof/RVS III*
Rick Trevino, *Dos Mundos*
Rick Trevino, *Rick Trevino*

Jimmy Buffett
Jimmy Buffett, *Songs You Know by Heart: Jimmy Buffett's Greatest Hit(s)*

Bum Steers
The Bum Steers, *The Bum Steers*

Al Bunetta
Steve Goodman, *Tribute to Steve Goodman*

Peter Bunetta
Big House, *Big House*

Steve Burgh
David Bromberg, *How Late'll Ya Play 'Til*

Malcolm Burn
Amy Allison/Parlor James, *Dreadful Sorry*
Blue Rodeo, *Diamond Mine*

Pat Burnett
Phil Alvin, *Un "Sung Stories"*

T-Bone Burnett
T-Bone Burnett, *Trap Door*
Elvis Costello, *King of America*
Jimmie Dale Gilmore, *Braver Newer World*
Delbert McClinton, *Delbert & Glen*
Roy Orbison, *In Dreams: The Greatest Hits*
Roy Orbison, *Roy Orbison and Friends: A Black and White Night Live*
Gillian Welch, *Revival*

Gary Burr
Faith Hill, *Take Me As I Am*

Barry "Byrd" Burton
The Amazing Rhythm Aces, *Stacked Deck*

Sam Bush
Sam Bush, *Glamour & Grits*
Jon Randall, *What You Don't Know*

Kim Butler
The Cornell Hurd Band, *Cool and Unusual Punishment*

Larry Butler
Highway 101, *Highway 101 & Paulette Carlson Reunited*
Don McLean, *Chain Lightning*
Kenny Rogers, *20 Greatest Hits*
Kenny Rogers, *Kenny Rogers' Greatest Hits*

Kenny Rogers, *Ten Years of Gold*
Hank Thompson, *The Best of Hank Thompson 1966–1978*

Andy Byrd
Victoria Shaw, *In Full View*

Robert Byrne
The Forester Sisters, *I Got a Date*
Shenandoah, *The Road Not Taken*

Monty Byrom
Big House, *Big House*

Charles Caldarola
Tom Russell, *Poor Man's Dream*

California
Byron Berline, *Traveler*

Troy Campbell
Jo Carol Pierce, *Bad Girls Upset by the Truth*

Ray Campi
Ray Campi, *Hollywood Cats*
Ray Campi, *A Little Bit of Heartache*
Ray Campi, *Rockabilly Rocket*
Ray Campi, *Taylor, Texas 1988*

Donnie Canada
Jeff Copley, *Evergreen*

Tom Canning
Stephen Bruton, *Right on Time*
Stephen Bruton, *What It Is*

Buddy Cannon
4 Runner, *4 Runner*
Sammy Kershaw, *Haunted Heart*
Sammy Kershaw, *The Hits, Chapter 1*
Steve Kolander, *Pieces of a Puzzle*

Bob Carlin
Bob Carlin, *Banging and Sawing*
Bob Carlin, *The Fun of Open Discussion*
Bob Carlin, *Melodic Clawhammer Banjo*
Marvin Gaster, *Uncle Henry's Favorites*

John Hartford, *Wild Hog in the Red Brush and a Bunch of Others You Might Not Have Heard*

Mary Chapin Carpenter
Mary Chapin Carpenter, *Come On Come On*
Mary Chapin Carpenter, *Shootin' Straight in the Dark*
Mary Chapin Carpenter, *Stones in the Road*

The Carpetbaggers
The Carpetbaggers, *Country Miles Apart*

Pat Carter
Steve Earle, *Early Tracks*

Joe Casey
T. Graham Brown, *Super Hits*

Johnny Cash
Johnny Cash, *Classic Cash*

Rosanne Cash
Rosanne Cash, *Interiors*
Rosanne Cash, *Ten Song Demo*

Peter Casperson
Jonathan Edwards, *Jonathan Edwards*

Bill Caswell
Keith Whitley, *Wherever You Are Tonight*

Carson Chamberlain
Harley Allen, *Another River*
Keith Stegall, *Passages*
Mark Wills, *Mark Wills*

Blake Chancey
David Ball, *Thinkin' Problem*
Stacy Dean Campbell, *Hurt City*
Deryl Dodd, *One Ride in Vegas*

Don Chancey
Brenda Lee, *Greatest Country Hits*
Ricochet, *Ricochet*

Gary Chapman
Michael James, *Closer to the Fire*
Michael James, *Shoulder to the Wind*

Marshall Chapman
Marshall Chapman, *Dirty Linen*
Marshall Chapman, *Inside Job*
Marshall Chapman, *It's about Time . . .*

Don Charles
Connie Francis, *Souvenirs*

Jordan Chassan
Amy Allison/Parlor James, *The Maudlin Years*

Chinga Chavin
Kinky Friedman, *Old Testaments & New Revelations*

Chesapeake
Chesapeake, *Full Sail*

Charlie Chesterman
Charlie Chesterman, *Studebakersfield*

Kathy Chiavola
Kathy Chiavola, *Kathy Chiavola*

Adrian Chornowal
Ian Tyson, *Cowboyography*

Cindy Church
Cindy Church, *Just a Little Rain*

Guy Clark
Guy Clark, *Boats to Build*
Guy Clark, *Dublin Blues*
Guy Clark, *Old Friends*

Royce Clark
The Flatlanders, *More a Legend Than a Band*
Butch Hancock, *Two Roads: Live in Australia*

Terri Clark
Terri Clark, *Just the Same*

Jack Clement
Eddie Bond, *Walking Tall—The Legend of Buford Pusser*
Sonny Burgess, *Hittin' That Jug! The Best of Sonny Burgess*
The Carter Family/The Carter Sisters & Mother Maybelle, *Wildwood Flower*
Johnny Cash, *The Sun Years*

Johnny Cash, *Water from the Wells of Home*
Waylon Jennings, *Dreaming My Dreams*
Townes Van Zandt, *At My Window*
Townes Van Zandt, *The Late Great Townes Van Zandt*
Onie Wheeler, *Onie's Bop*

Vassar Clements
Vassar Clements, *Crossing the Catskills*
Vassar Clements, *Vassar's Jazz*

Doug Clifford
Doug Sahm, *Daydreaming at Midnight*

Bill Clifton
Bill Clifton, *The Early Years, 1957–1958*

Charlie Cline
Charlie Cline, *Return of a Legend*

Michael Clute
The Delevantes, *Long about That Time*
Diamond Rio, *IV*
Faith Hill, *Take Me As I Am*
Brett James, *Brett James*
Royal Wade Kimes, *Royal Wade Kimes*

Anita Cochran
Anita Cochran, *Back to You*

Barry Coffing
Maureen McCormick, *When You Get a Little Lonely*

Paul Cohen
Johnny Burnette, *Rockabilly Boogie*
Johnnie & Jack, *Johnnie & Jack*
Jimmy Martin, *Jimmy Martin & the Sunny Mountain Boys*
Bill Monroe & His Blue Grass Boys, *Bill Monroe: Bluegrass, 1950–1958*

Lawrence Cohn
Gene Autry, *Blues Singer 1929–1931: "Booger Rooger Saturday Night"*
Bill Monroe & His Blue Grass Boys, *16 Gems*

Bill Monroe & His Blue Grass Boys, *The Essential Bill Monroe & His Blue Grass Boys 1945–1949*

David Cole
Poco, *Legacy*

Jim Colegrove
Sid King & the Five Strings, *Let's Get Loose*

T. Michael Coleman
Chesapeake, *Docabilly*
The Seldom Scene, *Scene 20: 20th Anniversary Concert*
Doc Watson/The Watson Family/Doc & Merle Watson, *Docabilly*
Doc Watson/The Watson Family/Doc & Merle Watson, *Remembering Merle*

Pat Colgan
Chris Wall, *Cowboy Nation*
Chris Wall, *Honky Tonk Heart*

Biff Collie
Stoney Edwards, *Mississippi You're on My Mind*

Tom Collins
Barbara Mandrell, *The Best of Barbara Mandrell*
Barbara Mandrell, *Greatest Hits*
Ronnie Milsap, *Greatest Hits*
Ronnie Milsap, *Greatest Hits, Volume 2*
Ronnie Milsap, *Ronnie Milsap Live*

Mike Compton
David Grier, *Climbing The Walls*

Wade Conklin
Marty Haggard, *Borders & Boundaries*

Earl Thomas Conley
Earl Thomas Conley, *Too Many Times*

Stompin' Tom Connors
Stompin' Tom Connors, *Believe in Your Country*
Stompin' Tom Connors, *Bud the Spud*

Stompin' Tom Connors, *Dr. Stompin' Tom—Eh?*
Stompin' Tom Connors, *Fiddle and Song*
Stompin' Tom Connors, *Long Gone to the Yukon*
Stompin' Tom Connors, *More of the Stompin' Tom Phenomenon*
Stompin' Tom Connors, *My Stompin' Grounds*
Stompin' Tom Connors, *On Tragedy Trail*
Stompin' Tom Connors, *A Proud Canadian*
Stompin' Tom Connors, *Stompin' Tom and the Hockey Song*
Stompin' Tom Connors, *Stompin' Tom Connors Meets Big Joe Mufferaw*
Stompin' Tom Connors, *To It and At It*

Ry Cooder
Ry Cooder, *Chicken Skin Music*
Ry Cooder, *Live & Let Live*
Ry Cooder, *The Slide Area*

Don Cook
Brooks & Dunn, *Brand New Man*
Brooks & Dunn, *Hard Workin' Man*
Mark Collie, *Mark Collie*
Neil Diamond, *Tennessee Moon*
Wade Hayes, *Old Enough to Know Better*
Wade Hayes, *On a Good Night*
James House, *Days Gone By*
Lonestar, *Lonestar*
The Mavericks, *Music for All Occasions*
The Mavericks, *What a Crying Shame*
Shenandoah, *The Best of Shenandoah*
Shenandoah, *Shenandoah Christmas*
Keith Whitley, *Wherever You Are Tonight*

Denny Cordell
Willis Alan Ramsey, *Willis Alan Ramsey*
Leon Russell, *Carney*

Leon Russell, *Leon Russell & the Shelter People*

Larry Cordle
Lonesome Standard Time/Larry Cordle, *Larry Cordle, Glen Duncan & Lonesome Standard Time*
Lonesome Standard Time/Larry Cordle, *Lonesome As It Gets*

Stan Cornelius
Jimmy C. Newman, *Jimmy C. Newman & Cajun Country*
Jimmy C. Newman, *More Cajun Music*

Elvis Costello
Elvis Costello, *The Juliet Letters*

Jim Cotton
Billy Ray Cyrus, *Some Gave All*
Billy Ray Cyrus, *Storm in the Heartland*
John & Audrey Wiggins, *John and Audrey Wiggins*

Country Music Foundation
Patsy Cline, *Live at the Opry*
Patsy Cline, *The Patsy Cline Collection*
Jimmie Davis, *Country Music Hall of Fame Series*
Red Foley, *Country Music Hall of Fame Series*
Grandpa Jones, *Country Music Hall of Fame*
Loretta Lynn, *Country Music Hall of Fame*
Uncle Dave Macon, *Country Music Hall of Fame Series*
Webb Pierce, *King of the Honky-Tonk: From the Original Decca Masters 1952–1959*
Roy Rogers, *Country Music Hall of Fame*
Jean Shepard, *Honky-Tonk Heroine: Classic Capitol Recordings (1952–1964)*
Floyd Tillman, *The Country Music Hall of Fame*
Ernest Tubb, *Country Music Hall of Fame*
Faron Young, *Faron Young: Live Fast, Love Hard: Original Capitol Recordings, 1952–1962*

Billy Cowsill
Blue Shadows, *Lucky to Me*
Blue Shadows, *On the Floor of Heaven*

Mark Craig
Brush Arbor, *Brush Arbor*

Anthony Crawford
Pete Anderson, *Working Class*

Steve Cropper
John Prine, *Common Sense*

David Crosby
The Byrds, *The Byrds*

J.D. Crowe
J.D. Crowe/J.D. Crowe & the New South, *Flashback*

Rodney Crowell
Rosanne Cash, *King's Record Shop*
Rosanne Cash, *Right or Wrong*
Rosanne Cash, *Seven Year Ache*
Rodney Crowell, *Diamonds and Dirt*
Rodney Crowell, *Keys to the Highway*
Rodney Crowell, *Life Is Messy*
Jim Lauderdale, *Planet of Love*

Jerry Crutchfield
Lisa Brokop, *Every Little Girl's Dream*
Lisa Brokop, *Lisa Brokop*
Tracy Byrd, *No Ordinary Man*
Philip Claypool, *A Circus Leaving Town*
Rob Crosby, *Starting Now*
Lee Greenwood, *Greatest Hits*
Lee Greenwood, *Somebody's Gonna Love You*
Chris LeDoux, *Best of Chris LeDoux*
Marie Osmond, *Steppin' Stone*
Tanya Tucker, *Can't Run from Yourself*
Tanya Tucker, *Tanya Tucker*
Tanya Tucker, *What Do I Do with Me*

J.D. Cunningham
Michael James, *Closer to the Fire*
Michael James, *Shoulder to the Wind*

Jerry Cupit
Ken Mellons, *Ken Mellons*
Ken Mellons, *When Forever Begins*

Mike Curb
Marie Osmond, *Donny & Marie Osmond: Greatest Hits*

Lou Curtiss
Roy Acuff, *Roy Acuff & the Smoky Mountain Boys 1939–41*
Roy Acuff, *Roy Acuff: 1936–1939 "Steamboat Whistle Blues"*

Michael Cuscuna
Chris Smither, *Don't It Drag On*
Chris Smither, *I'm a Stranger Too*

Billy Ray Cyrus
Billy Ray Cyrus, *Trail of Tears*

Pappy Daily
George Jones, *George Jones Sings Bob Wills*
George Jones, *Homecoming in Heaven*
Melba Montgomery, *Vintage Collections*

Lacy J. Dalton
Lacy J. Dalton, *Survivor*

Green Daniel
Gretchen Peters, *Secret of Life*

Jeff Daniel
Jason & the Scorchers, *Essential Jason & the Scorchers, Volume 1: Are You Ready for the Country?*

Gail Davies
Gail Davies, *Best of Gail Davies*
Gail Davies, *Wild Choir*

Bob Dawson
John Jennings, *buddy*

Roy Dea
Steve Earle, *Early Tracks*
Johnny Rodriguez, *You Can Say That Again*
Gary Stewart, *Gary's Greatest*
Gary Stewart, *Out of Hand*
Jason D. Williams, *Tore Up*
Jason D. Williams, *Wild*

Andy Dee
Molly & the Heymakers, *B-Sides from the Milkhouse*
Molly & the Heymakers, *Big Things*

Warren Defever
Tarnation, *Gentle Creatures*

Conrad Deisler
Austin Lounge Lizards, *The Highway Cafe of the Damned*
Austin Lounge Lizards, *Live Bait*

John Delgatto
Doc Watson/The Watson Family/Doc & Merle Watson, *The Doc Watson Family*

Gary Delorme
k.d. lang, *a truly western experience*

Al DeLory
Glen Campbell, *By the Time I Get to Phoenix*
Glen Campbell, *Gentle on My Mind*
Glen Campbell, *Wichita Lineman*

Mike Deming
The Scud Mountain Boys, *Massachusetts*

Peter Dempsey
Carson Robison, *Home, Sweet Home on the Prairie*

David Dennard
Ronnie Dawson, *Rockin' Bones: The Legendary Masters 1957–1962*

B. Denny
Carl Perkins, *Carl Perkins On Top*

Rich DePaolo
Burns Sisters, *Close to Home*

Guy DeVito
Salamander Crossing, *Salamander Crossing*

Brian Dewan
Amy Allison/Parlor James, *The Maudlin Years*

Tom Diamant
Good Ol' Persons, *Anywhere the Wind Blows*
Good Ol' Persons, *I Can't Stand to Ramble*

Diamond Rio
Diamond Rio, *IV*

Neil Diamond
Neil Diamond, *Tennessee Moon*

Bob Dick
Southern Rail, *Glory Train*

Hazel Dickens
Jimmy Martin, *You Don't Know My Mind*

Jim Dickinson
Jason & the Scorchers, *Fervor*
Jason & the Scorchers, *Reckless Country Soul*

Jim Dickson
The Greenbriar Boys, *Di'an & the Greenbriar Boys*
Chris Hillman/The Desert Rose Band, *The Hillmen*
Chris Hillman/The Desert Rose Band, *Morning Sky*
The Hillmen, *The Hillmen*

Joe Diffie
Joe Diffie, *Third Rock from the Sun*

Stuart Dill
Emilio, *Quedate*
Emilio, *SoundLife*

Rodney Dillard
The Dillards, *There Is a Time: The Best of the Dillards 1963–1970*

Christy DiNapoli
Little Texas/Brady Seals, *Kick a Little*
Caryl Mack Parker, *Caryl Mack Parker*

Ron Diulio
Joe Stampley, *Joe Stampley & the Uniques—Golden Hits*

The Dixie Chicks
The Dixie Chicks, *Thank Heavens for Dale Evans*

Don Dixon
The Red Clay Ramblers, *King Mackerel & the Blues Are Running*
The Red Clay Ramblers, *Unsophisticated Time*
Robert Shafer, *Hillbilly Fever*

Richard Dodd
Steve Earle, *I Feel Alright*

Gerard Dole
Dewey Balfa/The Balfa Brothers, *J'ai Vu Le Loup, Le Renard et La Belette*

Steve Dorff
David Frizzell & Shelly West, *Greatest Hits—Alone & Together*

Michael Doucet
Beausoleil, *Cajun Conja*
Beausoleil, *La Danse de la Vie*
Jo-El Sonnier, *Cajun Roots*

Jerry Douglas
Russ Barenberg, *Skip, Hop, & Wobble*
The Brother Boys, *Plow*
Alison Brown, *I've Got That Old Feeling*
Jerry Douglas/Douglas, Barenberg & Meyer, *Everything Is Gonna Work Out Fine*
Jerry Douglas/Douglas, Barenberg & Meyer, *The Great Dobro Sessions*
Jerry Douglas/Douglas, Barenberg & Meyer, *Skip, Hop & Wobble*
Jerry Douglas/Douglas, Barenberg & Meyer, *Slide Rule*
Jerry Douglas/Douglas, Barenberg & Meyer, *Under the Wire*
Robbie Fulks, *Within Reach*

The Del McCoury Band/Ronnie & Rob McCoury, *Cold Hard Facts*
The Nashville Bluegrass Band, *Unleashed*
The Nashville Bluegrass Band, *Waitin' for the Hard Times to Go*
Tim O'Brien/Tim & Mollie O'Brien, *Oh boy! O'Boy*
Maura O'Connell, *Blue Is the Colour of Hope*
Maura O'Connell, *Stories*
Sally Van Meter, *All in Good Time*
Sally Van Meter, *The Great Dobro Sessions*

Tom Dowd
Chris Hillman/The Desert Rose Band, *Trouble in Paradise*
Lynyrd Skynyrd, *Gimme Back My Bullets*
Lynyrd Skynyrd, *Lynyrd Skynyrd 1991*
Lynyrd Skynyrd, *One More from the Road*

Pete Drake
Pete Drake, *Amazing and Incredible Pete Drake*
Pete Drake, *Hits I Played On*
B.J. Thomas, *New Looks*

George Drakoulias
The Jayhawks, *Hollywood Town Hall*
The Jayhawks, *Tomorrow the Green Grass*
Lone Justice/Maria McKee, *You Gotta Sin to Get Saved*

Frank Driggs
Woody Guthrie, *Dust Bowl Ballads*
Bill Monroe & His Blue Grass Boys, *Feast Here Tonight*

Dry Branch Fire Squad
Dry Branch Fire Squad, *Live! At Last*

Tim DuBois
BlackHawk, *BlackHawk*
Diamond Rio, *Diamond Rio*
Diamond Rio, *IV*
Diamond Rio, *Greatest Hits: Nine Well-Cut Gems*

Steve Wariner, *I Am Ready*

John Duffey
The Country Gentlemen, *Folk Songs and Bluegrass*

Glen Duncan
Lonesome Standard Time/Larry Cordle, *Larry Cordle, Glen Duncan & Lonesome Standard Time*
Lonesome Standard Time/Larry Cordle, *Lonesome As It Gets*

Stuart Duncan
Robbie Fulks, *Full Circle*
David Grier, *Lone Soldier*

Holly Dunn
Holly Dunn, *Getting It Dunn*

Bill Dwyer
Libbi Bosworth, *Outskirts of You*

Fred Eaglesmith
Fred Eaglesmith, *Drive-In Movie*

Steve Earle
Steve Earle, *The Hard Way*
Jack Ingram, *Livin' or Dyin'*
The V-Roys, *Just Add Ice*

Reed Easterwood
Jack Ingram, *Lonesome Questions*

Elliot Easton
Amy Rigby/The Last Roundup, *Diary of a Mod Housewife*

Dave Edmunds
Dave Edmunds/Rockpile, *The Best of Dave Edmunds*
Dave Edmunds/Rockpile, *D-E7*
Dave Edmunds/Rockpile, *Get It*
Dave Edmunds/Rockpile, *Repeat When Necessary*
Dave Edmunds/Rockpile, *Tracks on Wax 4*
k.d. lang, *Angel with a Lariat*

Jonathan Edwards
Cheryl Wheeler, *Cheryl Wheeler*
Cheryl Wheeler, *Mrs. Pinocci's Guitar*

Kenny Edwards
Karla Bonoff/Bryndle, *Karla Bonoff*
Karla Bonoff/Bryndle, *Restless Nights*

Randy Edwards
Joe Nichols, *Joe Nichols*

Dan Einstein
Steve Goodman, *Affordable Art*
John Prine, *John Prine Live*

Dino Elefante
Lisa Daggs, *Love Is the Bottom Line*

John Elefante
Lisa Daggs, *Love Is the Bottom Line*

Joe Ely
Terry Allen, *Songs from Chippy*
Joe Ely, *Hi-Res*
Joe Ely, *Love and Danger*
Joe Ely, *Musta Notta Gotta Lotta*

Jack Emerson
Jason & the Scorchers, *Fervor*
Jason & the Scorchers, *Reckless Country Soul*

Buddy Emmons
Darrell McCall, *A Way to Survive*

Jim Emrich
Byron Berline, *Traveler*
Kate Campbell, *Songs from the Levee*

Howie Epstein
Carlene Carter, *I Fell in Love*
Carlene Carter, *Little Love Letters*
John Prine, *The Missing Years*

Colin Escott
The Stanley Brothers, *Angel Band: The Classic Mercury Recordings*
Leroy Van Dyke, *Walk on By*

Todd Everett
Hoyt Axton, *American Originals*

Skip Ewing
Skip Ewing, *Following Yonder Star*

Exile
Exile/Les Taylor/J.P. Pennington, *Latest & Greatest*

Jeff Eyrich
The Blasters, *The Blasters Collection*
The Blasters, *Hard Line*
The Blasters, *Non Fiction*
T-Bone Burnett, *Proof through the Night*
Rank & File, *Long Gone Dead*

John Farrar
Olivia Newton-John, *Olivia's Greatest Hits, Volume 2*

Chris Farren
Boy Howdy, *Born That Way*
Boy Howdy, *She'd Give Anything*
Boy Howdy, *Welcome to Howdywood*
Deana Carter, *Did I Shave My Legs for This?*
Kevin Sharp, *Measure of a Man*

Rob Feaster
Molly & the Heymakers, *Big Things*

Charlie Feathers
Charlie Feathers, *Charlie Feathers, Volume I*
Charlie Feathers, *Charlie Feathers, Volume II*

Bob Feldman
Greg Brown, *Songs of Innocence and Experience*

Sid Feller
Ray Charles, *Greatest Country & Western Hits*
Ray Charles, *Modern Sounds in Country and Western Music*

Bob Ferguson
Connie Smith, *Connie Smith*

Christine Ferreira
Roy Drusky, *Songs of Love and Life*

R.S. Field
Mark Germino, *Radartown*
Mark Germino, *Rex Bob Lowenstein*
Billy Joe Shaver/Shaver, *Tramp on Your Street*
Webb Wilder, *It Came from Nashville*
Webb Wilder, *Town & Country*

John Strawberry Fields
John Denver, *Minneapolis Does Denver*
The Honeydogs, *The Honeydogs*

Filé
Filé, *La Vie Marron (The Runaway Life)*

Cathy Fink
Patsy Montana, *The Cowboy's Sweetheart*

Steve Fishell
Jann Browne, *It Only Hurts When I Laugh*
Jann Browne, *Tell Me Why*
Radney Foster, *Del Rio, TX 1959*
Radney Foster, *Labor of Love*
Charlie Major, *Here and Now*
Charlie Major, *The Other Side*
The Mavericks, *From Hell to Paradise*
McBride & the Ride/Terry McBride & the Ride, *Burnin' Up the Road*
The Thompson Brothers Band, *Cows on Main Street*
Pam Tillis, *Sweetheart's Dance*
Bob Woodruff, *Dreams & Saturday Nights*

Bob Fisher
Bob Wills, *Anthology, 1935–1973*

Reggie Fisher
T-Bone Burnett, *Trap Door*
T-Bone Burnett, *Truth Decay*
T-Bone Burnett, *When the Night Falls*

Five Chinese Brothers
Five Chinese Brothers, *Let's Kill Saturday Night*

Five Chinese Brothers, *Singer Songwriter Beggerman Thief*

Jonas Fjeld
Tom Russell, *Poor Man's Dream*

Bela Fleck
Stuart Duncan, *Stuart Duncan*
Maura O'Connell, *Helpless Heart*
Maura O'Connell, *Just in Time*

Guy Fletcher
The Notting Hillbillies, *Missing . . . Presumed Having a Good Time*

David Flint
Billy Montana, *No Yesterday*

Kira Florita
George Burns, *Young at Heart*
Reba McEntire, *Oklahoma Girl*

Flying Burrito Brothers
Flying Burrito Brothers, *The Gilded Palace of Sin*

Dan Fogelberg
Dan Fogelberg, *High Country Snows*
Dan Fogelberg, *Windows and Walls*

Jim Fogelsong
Roy Clark, *Banjo Bandits*

John Fogerty
John Fogerty, *The Blue Ridge Rangers*
John Fogerty, *Chronicle*
John Fogerty, *Mardi Gras*

The Forbes Family
The Forbes Family, *In the Shadow of Your Wings*

Homer Forbes
The Forbes Family, *Best of the Early Forbes Family*

The Forester Sisters
The Forester Sisters, *More Than I Am*

Nick Forster
Kate MacKenzie, *Age of Innocence*

Kate MacKenzie, *Let Them Talk*

David Foster
Kenny Rogers, *Timepiece: Orchestral Sessions with David Foster*
Kenny Rogers, *20 Greatest Hits*

Fred Foster
Harlan Howard, *All-Time Favorite Country Songwriter*
Kris Kristofferson, *Me and Bobby McGee*
Roy Orbison, *The All-Time Greatest Hits of Roy Orbison*
Roy Orbison, *For the Lonely: A Roy Orbison Anthology, 1956–1964*
Ray Stevens, *Greatest Hits*

Radney Foster
Foster & Lloyd, *Foster & Lloyd*
Radney Foster, *Del Rio, TX 1959*
Radney Foster, *Labor of Love*

Kim Fowley
Ben Vaughn, *Kings of Saturday Night*

The Fox Family
The Fox Family, *When It Comes to Blues*

Jeff Foxworthy
Jeff Foxworthy, *Crank It Up: The Music Album*
Jeff Foxworthy, *Live 1990*
Jeff Foxworthy, *You Might Be a Redneck If . . .*

Rob Fraboni
Pure Prairie League, *Something in the Night*

Michael Fracasso
Michael Fracasso, *Love & Trust*

Ronald Frangipane
Chris Smither, *I'm a Stranger Too*

Freakwater
Freakwater, *Feels Like the Third Time*
Freakwater, *Old Paint*

Carl B. Freedom
Libbi Bosworth, *Outskirts of You*

Mark Freegard
Lone Justice/Maria McKee, *Life Is Sweet*

Charles Freeland
The Country Gentlemen, *Calling My Children Home*

Ronnie Freeland
Johnson Mountain Boys, *Blue Diamond*

Dave Freeman
The Country Gentlemen, *25 Years*
The Delmore Brothers, *Sand Mountain Blues*
The Lilly Brothers/Don Stover, *Early Recordings*

Ed Freeman
Don McLean, *American Pie*

Janie Fricke
Janie Fricke, *Crossroads: Hymns of Faith*

Kinky Friedman
Kinky Friedman, *Kinky Friedman*
Kinky Friedman, *Lasso from El Paso*
Kinky Friedman, *Old Testaments & New Revelations*

Front Range
Front Range, *Back to Red River*
Front Range, *The New Frontier*
Front Range, *One Beautiful Day*

Garth Fundis
Bekka & Billy/Billy Burnette, *Bekka & Billy*
Ty England, *Ty England*
Paul Jefferson, *Paul Jefferson*
Kieran Kane/The O'Kanes/Jamie O'Hara, *Rise above It*
The New Grass Revival, *Hold to a Dream*
Jon Randall, *What You Don't Know*
Collin Raye, *In This Life*
Steve Wariner, *Laredo*

Lari White, *Wishes*
Keith Whitley, *Don't Close Your Eyes*
Trisha Yearwood, *Everybody Knows*
Trisha Yearwood, *The Song Remembers When*
Trisha Yearwood, *Thinkin' about You*
Trisha Yearwood, *Trisha Yearwood*

Tony Furtado
Robbie Fulks, *Within Reach*

Rob Galbraith
Ronnie Milsap, *Greatest Hits, Volume 2*
Ronnie Milsap, *Sings His Best Hits for Capitol Records*
Ronnie Milsap, *True Believer*

Jack Gale
Melba Montgomery, *Do You Know Where Your Man Is*
Del Reeves, *The Silver Anniversary Album*
Jeannie C. Riley, *Here's Jeannie*

Byron Gallimore
Ty England, *Two Ways to Fall*
Tim McGraw, *All I Want*
Tim McGraw, *Not a Moment Too Soon*
Tim McGraw, *Tim McGraw*
Jo Dee Messina, *Jo Dee Messina*

Don Gant
Jimmy Buffett, *Living and Dying in 3/4 Time*

Snuff Garrett
David Frizzell & Shelly West, *Greatest Hits—Alone & Together*

David Gates
David Gates/Bread, *Goodbye Girl*

Steve Gatlin
Larry Gatlin & the Gatlin Brothers, *Greatest Hits*

Heinz Geissler
Steve Young, *Solo/Live*

Gregg Geller
Ray Price, *The Essential Ray Price: 1951–1962*

Lowell George
The Grateful Dead, *Shakedown Street*

Phil Gernhard
Jim Stafford, *Greatest Hits*
Jim Stafford, *Jim Stafford*
Hank Williams Jr., *Family Tradition*

Alice Gerrard
The Red Clay Ramblers, *Twisted Laurel*

Joe Gibson
Billy Parker, *Billy Parker & Friends*

Steve Gibson
Freddy Fender, *The Freddy Fender Collection*
McBride & the Ride/Terry McBride & the Ride, *Hurry Sundown*
McBride & the Ride/Terry McBride & the Ride, *Sacred Ground*
Michael Martin Murphey, *Cowboy Songs*
MC Potts, *Straight to You*
Red Steagall, *Born to This Land*
Aaron Tippin, *Lookin' Back at Myself*

Janis Gill
Sweethearts of the Rodeo, *Beautiful Lies*
Sweethearts of the Rodeo, *Rodeo Waltz*

Lee Gillette
Tennessee Ernie Ford, *Sixteen Tons*
Tennessee Ernie Ford, *Songs of the Civil War*
Jack Guthrie, *Oklahoma Hills*
Merle Travis, *Folk Songs of the Hills*
Jimmy Wakely, *Vintage Collections Series*

Mickey Gilley
Mickey Gilley, *Mickey Gilley at His Best*

Jimmie Dale Gilmore
Jimmie Dale Gilmore, *Two Roads: Live in Australia*

Voyle Gilmore
The Kingston Trio, *At Large*
The Kingston Trio, *The Capitol Years*
The Kingston Trio, *The Kingston Trio*
The Kingston Trio, *Live at the Hungry I*
The Kingston Trio, *New Frontier*
The Kingston Trio, *String Along*

Tompall Glaser
Waylon Jennings, *Honky-Tonk Heroes*

Keith Glass
Jimmie Dale Gilmore, *Two Roads: Live in Australia*

Dick Glasser
Hank Williams Jr., *Hank Williams Jr. & Friends*

The Goins Brothers
The Goins Brothers, *Still Goin' Strong*

Andrew Gold
Nicolette Larson, *Sleep, Baby, Sleep*

Golden Smog
Golden Smog, *Down by the Old Mainstream*

Mark Goldenberg
Karla Bonoff/Bryndle, *New World*

Matt Goldman
Speedy West & Jimmy Bryant, *Stratosphere Boogie: The Flaming Guitars of Speedy West & Jimmy Bryant*

Steve Goodman
Steve Goodman, *Affordable Art*
Steve Goodman, *Santa Ana Winds*
John Prine, *Bruised Orange*

Randy Goodrum
Michael Johnson, *Departure*

Robert Gordon
Robert Gordon, *All for the Love of Rock 'n' Roll*

Emory Gordy Jr.
Alabama, *In Pictures*
Earl Thomas Conley, *The Heart of It All*
Steve Earle, *Guitar Town*
Jimmie Dale Gilmore, *Spinning around the Sun*
Patty Loveless, *Only What I Feel*
Patty Loveless, *Patty Loveless Sings Songs of Love*
Patty Loveless, *The Trouble with the Truth*
Patty Loveless, *Up against My Heart*
Patty Loveless, *When Fallen Angels Fly*
Steve Wariner, *Greatest Hits*

Skip Gorman
Skip Gorman, *Greener Prairie*
Skip Gorman, *Lonesome Prairie Love*

Vern Gosdin
Vern Gosdin, *The Gospel Album*
Vern Gosdin, *Warning: Contains Country Music (The Great Ballads of Vern Gosdin)*

Richard Gottehrer
Darden Smith, *Little Victories*

Joe Gracey
Butch Hancock, *Diamond Hill*
Butch Hancock, *Firewater Seeks Its Own Level*
Butch Hancock, *West Texas Waltzes & Dust Blown Tractor Tunes*
Kimmie Rhodes, *West Texas Heaven*

Royce Gracey
Butch Hancock, *Yella Rose*

Wayne Gracey
Butch Hancock, *Cause of the Cactus*

The Grateful Dead
The Grateful Dead, *American Beauty*

The Grateful Dead, *Workingman's Dead*

Doug Grau
Jeff Foxworthy, *Games Rednecks Play*
Little Texas/Brady Seals, *Kick a Little*

Great Plains
Great Plains, *Homeland*

Rick Grech
Gram Parsons, *G.P./Grievous Angel*

Richard Greene
Richard Greene/The Grass Is Greener, *The Greene Fiddler*
Richard Greene/The Grass Is Greener, *Muleskinner: A Potpourri of Bluegrass Jam*
Richard Greene/The Grass Is Greener, *Wolves A' Howlin'*
Muleskinner, *Muleskinner: A Potpourri of Bluegrass Jam*

Manny Greenhill
Doc Watson/The Watson Family/Doc & Merle Watson, *Old Timey Concert: Doc Watson, Clint Howard and Fred Price*

Mitch Greenhill
Doc Watson/The Watson Family/Doc & Merle Watson, *Watson Country: Doc & Merle Watson*

Bob Greenlee
Reverend Billy C. Wirtz, *Deep Fried and Sanctified*

Ricky Lynn Gregg
Ricky Lynn Gregg, *Get a Little Closer*

Clive Gregson
Alison Brown, *I Love This Town*

David Grier
David Grier, *Climbing The Walls*
David Grier, *Freewheeling*

Nanci Griffith
Nanci Griffith, *Last of the True Believers*
Nanci Griffith, *Lone Star State of Mind*

Nanci Griffith, *One Fair Summer Evening*

David Grisman
Red Allen, *Bluegrass Reunion*
Red Allen, *The Kitchen Tapes*
David Grisman, *David Grisman Quintet*
David Grisman, *DGQ-20*
Homer & Jethro, *Swing Low, Sweet Mandolin*
Peter Rowan, *High Lonesome Sound*

Pieter Groenveld
Good Ol' Persons, *Good n' Live*

Don Grolnick
James Taylor, *(Best Live)*
James Taylor, *(Live)*
James Taylor, *Never Die Young*
James Taylor, *New Moon Shine*

John Guess
Deana Carter, *Did I Shave My Legs for This?*
Linda Davis, *Some Things Are Meant to Be*
Kelly Willis, *Well-Travelled Love*

Jake Guralnick
Dick Curless, *Traveling Through*
Sleepy LaBeef, *I'll Never Lay My Guitar Down*
Sleepy LaBeef, *Strange Things Happening*

Peter Guralnick
Sleepy LaBeef, *Strange Things Happening*

Jaane Haavisto
High Noon, *Stranger Things*

Edward Haber
Kenny Kosek, *Angelwood*

Bob Haddad
Beausoleil, *Vintage Beausoleil*

Ron Haffkine
Shel Silverstein, *Songs and Stories*

Merle Haggard
Merle Haggard, *1996*

Pete Hakonen
High Noon, *Stranger Things*

Roy Halee
Shel Silverstein, *Freakin' at the Freakers Ball*

Rick Hall
Terri Gibbs, *The Best of Terri Gibbs*
Shenandoah, *The Road Not Taken*

Bill Halverson
Flaco Jimenez, *Flaco Jimenez*
Flaco Jimenez, *Partners*
Jo-El Sonnier, *Come on Joe*
Jo-El Sonnier, *Have a Little Faith*
The Texas Tornados, *The Best of Texas Tornados*
The Texas Tornados, *Los Texas Tornados*
The Texas Tornados, *Texas Tornados*

Dave Hamilton
Cindy Church, *Love on the Range*

Butch Hancock
Jimmie Dale Gilmore, *Two Roads: Live in Australia*
Butch Hancock, *Cause of the Cactus*
Butch Hancock, *Diamond Hill*
Butch Hancock, *Firewater Seeks Its Own Level*
Butch Hancock, *No Two Alike Tape of the Month Club*
Butch Hancock, *West Texas Waltzes & Dust Blown Tractor Tunes*
Butch Hancock, *Yella Rose*

Andrew Hardin
Katy Moffatt, *Walkin' on the Moon*
Tom Russell, *Hurricane Season*
Tom Russell, *Poor Man's Dream*

Brian Hardin
Ray Wylie Hubbard, *Loco Gringo's Lament*

Mike Hardwick
Michael Fracasso, *Love & Trust*

Joe Hardy
Steve Earle, *The Hard Way*

Mark Harman
Poco, *Rose of Cimarron*

Emmylou Harris
Emmylou Harris, *The Ballad of Sally Rose*

John Harrod
Roger Cooper, *Going Back to Old Kentucky*
J.P. & Annadeene Fraley, *Traditional Fiddle Music Of Kentucky, Volumes One and Two*

John Hartford
Bob Carlin, *The Fun of Open Discussion*
John Hartford, *Wild Hog in the Red Brush and a Bunch of Others You Might Not Have Heard*

Geoffrey Haslam
Delbert McClinton, *Subject to Change*

Harley Hatcher
Jack Scott, *Greatest Hits*

Jeffrey Hatcher
Blue Shadows, *Lucky to Me*
Blue Shadows, *On the Floor of Heaven*

Kerry Hay
Charlie Cline, *Return of a Legend*
The Goins Brothers, *We'll Carry On*
The Lilly Brothers/Don Stover, *Live at Hillbilly Ranch*

Walter Haynes
Bill Monroe & His Blue Grass Boys, *Bill Monroe: Bluegrass, 1970–1979*

Hazel & Alice
Hazel & Alice/Hazel Dickens/Alice Gerrard, *Hazel & Alice*

Lee Hazlewood
Duane Eddy, *Have Twangy Guitar Will Travel*

Dan Healy
The Grateful Dead, *Shakedown Street*

Michael Hearne
Tish Hinojosa, *Taos to Tennessee*

Don Heffington
Tammy Rogers, *In the Red*

The Hellcasters
The Hellcasters, *Escape from Hollywood*
The Hellcasters, *The Return of the Hellcasters*

Joshua Heller
Tarnation, *Gentle Creatures*

Tom Hemby
Bruce Carroll, *Sometimes Miracles Hide*

Scott Hendricks
Trace Adkins, *Dreamin' Out Loud*
Suzy Bogguss, *Give Me Some Wheels*
Brooks & Dunn, *Brand New Man*
Brooks & Dunn, *Hard Workin' Man*
Rob Crosby, *Another Time and Place*
Rob Crosby, *Solid Ground*
Faith Hill, *Take Me As I Am*
Alan Jackson, *The Greatest Hits Collection*
Alan Jackson, *A Lot about Livin' (And a Little 'bout Love)*
John Michael Montgomery, *John Michael Montgomery*
John Michael Montgomery, *Kickin' It Up*
Lee Roy Parnell, *We All Get Lucky Sometimes*
Aaron Tippin, *Call of the Wild*
Steve Wariner, *I Am Ready*

Joe Henry
Joe Henry, *Kindness of the World*
Joe Henry, *Short Man's Room*
Joe Henry, *Talk of Heaven*
Joe Henry, *Trampoline*

Billy Henson
Curly Seckler, *60 Years of Bluegrass with My Friends*

Tom Herbers
The Carpetbaggers, *Country Miles Apart*
The Shivers, *The Buried Life*
The Shivers, *The Shivers*

Jack Herrick
The Red Clay Ramblers, *A Lie of the Mind*
The Red Clay Ramblers, *Rambler*

Brother Wally Hersom
Dave & Deke Combo, *Hollywood Barn Dance*

Fraser Hill
Anne Murray, *Now & Forever*

Tommy Hill
Johnny Bush, *Greatest Hits 1968–1972*
Bill Carlisle/The Carlisles, *No Help Wanted*
David Houston, *At His Best*
David Houston, *David Houston*

Hilltops
Blue Mountain, *The Hilltops*

Gordy Hinners
Ralph Blizard & the New Southern Ramblers, *Southern Ramble*

Tish Hinojosa
Tish Hinojosa, *Culture Swing*
Tish Hinojosa, *Frontejas*
Tish Hinojosa, *Taos to Tennessee*

John Hobbs
Collin Raye, *Extremes*
Collin Raye, *I Think about You*
Collin Raye, *In This Life*

Mike Hoffman
The Spanic Boys, *Dream Your Life*
The Spanic Boys, *Early Spanic Boys*
The Spanic Boys, *Strange World*

John Hoke
John Stewart, *Bullets in the Hourglass*

Lee Holdridge
John Denver, *Earth Songs*

Michael Hollandsworth
Baker & Myers, *Baker & Myers*

James Hollihan Jr.
Marshall Chapman, *Inside Job*
Russ Taff, *Under Their Influence Volume 1*
Russ Taff, *The Way Home*
Russ Taff, *Winds of Change*

Peter Holsapple
Robin Holcomb, *Robin Holcomb*

Aubrey Holt
The Boys from Indiana, *Touchin Home'*

The Honeydogs
The Honeydogs, *The Honeydogs*

Jim Horn
Delbert McClinton, *Never Been Rocked Enough*

Paul Hornsby
The Marshall Tucker Band, *Greatest Hits*
The Marshall Tucker Band, *Searchin' for a Rainbow*

Wayne Horvitz
Robin Holcomb, *Robin Holcomb*
Robin Holcomb, *Rockabye*

Hot Rize
Hot Rize/Red Knuckles & the Trailblazers, *Take It Home*
Hot Rize/Red Knuckles & the Trailblazers, *Untold Stories*

Chuck Howard
John Berry, *John Berry*
John Berry, *O Holy Night*
John Berry, *Standing on the Edge*
Jeff Carson, *Jeff Carson*
Billy Dean, *Young Man*
Ricky Lynn Gregg, *Get a Little Closer*
Ricky Lynn Gregg, *Ricky Lynn Gregg*

LeAnn Rimes, *Blue*
The Smokin' Armadillos, *Smokin' Armadillos*

Dann Huff
Chris Ward, *One Step Beyond*
John & Audrey Wiggins, *The Dream*

Marvin Hughes
Jean Shepard, *The Melody Ranch Girl*

Bill Inglot
Al Anderson, *Peek-a-Boo: The Best of NRBQ 1969–1989*
George Jones, *The Best of George Jones*

Jimmy Iovine
Lone Justice/Maria McKee, *Lone Justice*

Bob Irwin
Gene Clark, *Mr. Tambourine Man*
Gene Clark, *Turn! Turn! Turn!*
John Denver, *The Wildlife Concert*

Ken Irwin
The Blue Sky Boys, *The Blue Sky Boys*
The Blue Sky Boys, *In Concert, 1964*
Charlie Cline, *New Beginnings—The Warrior River Boys*
Dry Branch Fire Squad, *Live! At Last*
Dry Branch Fire Squad, *Long Journey*
Johnson Mountain Boys, *Blue Diamond*
James King, *Lonesome & Then Some*
James King, *These Old Pictures*
Jimmy Martin, *You Don't Know My Mind*
D.L. Menard, *Cajun Saturday Night*
D.L. Menard, *D.L. Menard & the Louisiana Aces*
D.L. Menard, *No Matter Where You At, There You Are*
Jimmy C. Newman, *The Alligator Man*

Clayton Ivey
Mac McAnally, *Mac McAnally*

Carl Jackson
Bobbie Cryner, *Bobbie Cryner*
Carl Jackson, *Spring Training*
Jim & Jesse, *Music among Friends*

Kate Jacobs
Kate Jacobs, *What about Regret*

Randall Jamail
Jesse Dayton, *Raising Cain*
Jesse Dayton, *Right for the Time*
Billy Joe Shaver/Shaver, *Highway of Life*

Michael James
Michael James, *Where Love Runs Deep*

Phil Jamison
Ralph Blizard & the New Southern Ramblers, *Southern Ramble*

Mike Janas
Webb Wilder, *Town & Country*

Duane Jarvis
Duane Jarvis, *D.J.'s Front Porch*

Felton Jarvis
John Hartford, *Earthwords and Music*

S. Jarvis
Commander Cody & His Lost Planet Airmen, *Sleazy Roadside Stories*

Jason & the Scorchers
Jason & the Scorchers, *A-Blazing Grace*
Jason & the Scorchers, *Reckless Country Soul*

John Jennings
Beausoleil, *La Danse de la Vie*
Mary Chapin Carpenter, *Come On Come On*
Mary Chapin Carpenter, *Shootin' Straight in the Dark*
Mary Chapin Carpenter, *Stones in the Road*
John Jennings, *buddy*

Bill Morrissey, *Inside*

Waylon Jennings
Jessi Colter, *I'm Jessi Colter*
Jessi Colter, *The Jessi Colter Collection*
Waylon Jennings, *Dreaming My Dreams*
Waylon Jennings, *Honky-Tonk Heroes*
Waylon Jennings, *WW II*

Peter Jesperson
Duane Jarvis, *D.J.'s Front Porch*

Jack Jezzro
The New Tradition, *Love Here Today*

Jim & Jesse
Jim & Jesse, *In the Tradition*

Flaco Jimenez
Flaco Jimenez, *Buena Suerte, Senorita*

Glyn Johns
The Eagles, *Desperado*
The Eagles, *Their Greatest Hits, 1971–1975*
The Ozark Mountain Daredevils, *The Best*
The Ozark Mountain Daredevils, *It'll Shine When It Shines*

Dirk Johnson
Harley Allen, *Another River*

Doug Johnson
James Bonamy, *What I Live to Do*
Mark Collie, *Born and Raised in Black & White*
Mark Collie, *Hardin County Line*
Bobbie Cryner, *Bobbie Cryner*
The Gibson/Miller Band, *Red, White and Blue Collar*
The Gibson/Miller Band, *Where There's Smoke*
Ty Herndon, *Living in a Moment*
Ty Herndon, *What Mattered Most*
Doug Stone, *The First Christmas*
Doug Stone, *From the Heart*
Doug Stone, *Greatest Hits, Volume One*

Jack D. Johnson
Ronnie Milsap, *Greatest Hits*

Jimmy Johnson
Lynyrd Skynyrd, *Street Survivors*

Joe E. Johnson
Jerry Wallace, *Greatest Hits*

John Johnson
Tex Williams, *Vintage Collections Series*

Matt Johnson
Hank Williams, *Hanky Panky*

Michael Johnson
Michael Johnson, *Departure*

Johnson Mountain Boys
Johnson Mountain Boys, *Blue Diamond*

Bob Johnston
Johnny Cash, *At Folsom Prison/At San Quentin*
Leonard Cohen, *Songs from a Room*
Leonard Cohen, *Songs of Love and Hate*
Bob Dylan, *Blonde on Blonde*
Bob Dylan, *John Wesley Harding*
Bob Dylan, *Nashville Skyline*
Dan Hicks, *Dan Hicks & His Hot Licks*
Michael Martin Murphey, *Geronimo's Cadillac*

Booker T. Jones
Rita Coolidge, *Rita Coolidge*
Willie Nelson, *Pretty Paper*

Donal Jones
The Vidalias, *Melodyland*
The Vidalias, *Staying in the Doghouse*

Frank Jones
Stonewall Jackson, *Stonewall Jackson Recorded Live at the Grand Ole Opry*
Stonewall Jackson, *Stonewall Jackson's Greatest Hits*
Jim & Jesse, *Jim & Jesse: Bluegrass and More*
Ray Price, *Night Life*
Ray Price, *Ray Price and the Cherokee Cowboys*

Ray Price, *San Antonio Rose. Ray Price Sings a Tribute to the Great Bob Wills*

Gareth Jones
Simon Bonney, *Everyman*
Simon Bonney, *Forever*

Monroe Jones
Marcus Hummon, *All in Good Time*

Rex Jones
The Cornell Hurd Band, *Cool and Unusual Punishment*

Robert John Jones
Vern Gosdin, *The Gospel Album*
Vern Gosdin, *Warning: Contains Country Music (The Great Ballads of Vern Gosdin)*

Ernst Mikael Jorgensen
Elvis Presley, *Command Performances: The Essential '60s Masters II*
Elvis Presley, *From Nashville to Memphis: The Essential '60's Masters I*
Elvis Presley, *The King of Rock 'n' Roll: The Complete 1950's Masters*
Elvis Presley, *Walk a Mile in My Shoes: The Essential '70s Masters*

Cledus "T." Judd
Cledus "T." Judd, *Cledus "T." Judd (No Relation)*
Cledus "T." Judd, *I Stoled This Record*

Ralph Jungheim
Lynn Anderson, *Cowboy's Sweetheart*
Roy Clark, *Live in Branson, MO*

Bill Justis
Onie Wheeler, *Onie's Bop*

David Kahne
Alejandro Escovedo, *Sundown*
Rank & File, *Sundown*

Kathy Kallick
Kathy Kallick, *Use a Napkin (Not Your Mom)*

Kieran Kane
Kieran Kane/The O'Kanes/Jamie O'Hara, *Dead Reckoning*

Kieran Kane/The O'Kanes/Jamie O'Hara, *The O'Kanes*
Tammy Rogers, *In the Red*

Bruce Kaplan
The Red Clay Ramblers, *Twisted Laurel*

Ellen Karas
Greg Brown, *Friend of Mine*
Bill Morrissey, *Bill Morrissey*
Bill Morrissey, *Friend of Mine*
Bill Morrissey, *Night Train*

Janice Karman
The Chipmunks/Alvin & the Chipmunks, *A Very Merry Chipmunk*

Thomas Jefferson Kaye
Gene Clark, *No Other*

John Keane
Vic Chesnutt, *Is the Actor Happy?*
Cowboy Junkies, *Lay It Down*

Glenn Keener
Reba McEntire, *Reba McEntire*

Ben Keith
Neil Young, *Harvest Moon*
Neil Young, *Old Ways*

Toby Keith
Toby Keith, *Blue Moon*

John Kelton
Wesley Dennis, *Wesley Dennis*
Keith Stegall, *Passages*

Jerry Kennedy
Roy Drusky, *Songs of Love and Life*
Jim & Jesse, *Jim & Jesse: Bluegrass and More*
Jerry Lee Lewis, *Another Place, Another Time*
Jerry Lee Lewis, *Killer Country*
Linda Gail Lewis, *Together*
Mel McDaniel, *Baby's Got Her Blue Jeans On*
Mel McDaniel, *Greatest Hits*
Reba McEntire, *Reba McEntire*
Roger Miller, *The Return of Roger Miller*
Roger Miller, *Roger and Out*
Roger Miller, *Words and Music by Roger Miller*

Johnny Rodriguez, *You Can Say That Again*
The Statler Brothers, *Best of the Statler Brothers*
The Statler Brothers, *The Complete Lester "Roadhog" Moran & the Cadillac Cowboys*
The Statler Brothers, *Holy Bible: New Testament*
The Statler Brothers, *Holy Bible: Old & New Testament*
The Statler Brothers, *Holy Bible: Old Testament*
The Statler Brothers, *The Statler Brothers Sing Country Symphonies (in E Major)*
The Statler Brothers, *A 30th Anniversary Celebration*

Ray Kennedy
Moe Bandy, *Greatest Hits*
Steve Earle, *I Feel Alright*
Jack Ingram, *Livin' or Dyin'*
The V-Roys, *Just Add Ice*
Bob Woodruff, *Desire Road*

Paul Kennerley
Emmylou Harris, *The Ballad of Sally Rose*

The Kentucky HeadHunters
The Kentucky HeadHunters/Brother Phelps, *The Best of the Kentucky HeadHunters: Still Pickin'*
The Kentucky HeadHunters/Brother Phelps, *Pickin' on Nashville*

David Kershenbaum
Joan Baez, *Diamonds and Rust*
The Ozark Mountain Daredevils, *The Best*

Jamie Kidd
k.d. lang, *a truly western experience*

Rich Kienzle
Tennessee Ernie Ford, *16 Tons of Boogie: The Best of Tennessee Ernie Ford*
Tex Williams, *Vintage Collections Series*

Killbilly
Killbilly, *Foggy Mountain Anarchy*

Buddy Killen
Vassar Clements, *Superbow*
T.G. Sheppard, *All-Time Greatest Hits*
Six Shooter, *Six Shooter*

Kevin Killen
Elvis Costello, *The Juliet Letters*

Eddie Kilroy
Mickey Gilley, *Biggest Hits*
Mickey Gilley, *Greatest Hits, Volume 1*
Mickey Gilley, *Greatest Hits Volume 2*
Mickey Gilley, *Ten Years of Hits*
Jeannie C. Riley, *The Best of Jeannie C. Riley*
Gary Stewart, *Gary's Greatest*

Darrin Kirkindoll
The Smokin' Armadillos, *Out of the Burrow*

Wayne Kirkpatrick
Kim Hill, *So Far So Good*

Mark Knopfler
Chet Atkins, *Neck and Neck*
The Notting Hillbillies, *Missing . . . Presumed Having a Good Time*
The Notting Hillbillies, *Neck and Neck*

Walt Koken
Walt Koken, *Banjonique*
Walt Koken, *Hei-wa Hoedown*

Paul Kolderie
Blood Oranges/Wooden Leg/Beacon Hillbillies, *Corn River*
Uncle Tupelo/Wilco/Son Volt, *No Depression*
Uncle Tupelo/Wilco/Son Volt, *Still Feel Gone*

Bill Kollar
John Gorka, *Land of the Bottom Line*
Christine Lavin, *Good Thing He Can't Read My Mind*

Fred Koller
Fred Koller, *Songs from the Night Before*
Fred Koller, *Where the Fast Lane Ends*

Al Kooper
Lynyrd Skynyrd, *Pronounced Leh-nerd Skin-nerd*
Lynyrd Skynyrd, *Second Helping*

Danny Kortchmar
James Taylor, *New Moon Shine*

Kenny Kosek
Kenny Kosek, *Angelwood*

Barney Koumis
Ronnie Dawson, *Rockinitis*

Alison Krauss
The Cox Family, *Just When You're Thinking It's Over*
Alison Krauss, *I Know Who Holds Tomorrow*

Alison Krauss & Union Station
Alison Krauss, *Every Time You Say Goodbye*

Russ Kunkel
Jimmy Buffett, *Banana Wind*

Pete Kuykendall
The Country Gentlemen, *Folk Session Inside*
The Country Gentlemen, *Folk Songs and Bluegrass*

Marc L'Esperance
Ray Condo & His Ricochets, *Swing Brother Swing!*

Jimmy LaFave
Jimmy LaFave, *Buffalo Return to the Plains*
Jimmy LaFave, *Highway Trance*

Bruce Lampcov
Hank Williams, *Hanky Panky*

Richard Landis
Neil Diamond, *Tennessee Moon*
Lorrie Morgan, *War Paint*
Roy Rogers, *Tribute*

Doug Supernaw, *Deep Thoughts from a Shallow Mind*
Doug Supernaw, *Red and the Rio Grande*
Doug Supernaw, *You Still Got Me*

James Bunchberry Lane
Golden Smog, *Down by the Old Mainstream*

k.d. lang
k.d. lang, *Absolute Torch and Twang*
k.d. lang, *Ingenue*
k.d. lang, *a truly western experience*

Robert John "Mutt" Lange
Shania Twain, *The Woman in Me*

Jon Langford
Rico Bell, *The Return of Rico Bell*

Daniel Lanois
Emmylou Harris, *Wrecking Ball*

Nelson Larkin
Baker & Myers, *Baker & Myers*
Earl Thomas Conley, *Too Many Times*
Toby Keith, *Blue Moon*
Toby Keith, *Boomtown*
Billy Joe Royal, *The Best of Billy Joe Royal*

Nicolette Larson
Nicolette Larson, *Sleep, Baby, Sleep*

Christine Lavin
Christine Lavin, *Another Woman's Man*
Christine Lavin, *Attainable Love*
Cheryl Wheeler, *Christine Lavin Presents: Laugh Tracks, Volume 1*

Kent Lavoie
Jim Stafford, *Greatest Hits*

Don Law
Jimmy Dean, *Big Bad John*
Jimmy Dean, *Greatest Hits*

Little Jimmy Dickens, *I'm Little but I'm Loud: The Jimmy Dickens Collection*
Stonewall Jackson, *Stonewall Jackson's Greatest Hits*
Jim & Jesse, *Jim & Jesse: Bluegrass and More*
Ray Price, *Night Life*
Ray Price, *Ray Price and the Cherokee Cowboys*
Ray Price, *San Antonio Rose: Ray Price Sings a Tribute to the Great Bob Wills*
Marty Robbins, *Gunfighter Ballads and Trail Songs*
Marty Robbins, *More Gunfighter Ballads and Trail Songs*
Onie Wheeler, *Onie's Bop*

Mike Lawler
Twister Alley, *Twister Alley*

Doyle Lawson
Doyle Lawson/Quicksilver, *Heaven's Joy Awaits (A Cappella Quartets)*
Doyle Lawson/Quicksilver, *I'll Wonder Back Someday*
Doyle Lawson/Quicksilver, *Never Walk Away*
Doyle Lawson/Quicksilver, *Rock My Soul*
Doyle Lawson/Quicksilver, *There's a Light Guiding Me*

Al LeDoux
Chris LeDoux, *Melodies and Memories*

Larry Michael Lee
Alabama, *American Pride*
Alabama, *Cheap Seats*
Alabama, *Pass It On Down*

Kyle Lehning
Baillie & the Boys, *The Best of Baillie & the Boys*
Mandy Barnett, *Mandy Barnett*
Curtis Day, *Curtis Day*
Marie Osmond, *There's No Stopping Your Heart*
Dan Seals, *Rage On*
Keith Stegall, *Keith Stegall*
Randy Travis, *Always and Forever*
Randy Travis, *Full Circle*
Randy Travis, *Storms of Life*

Cheryl Wheeler, *Circles and Arrows*
Bryan White, *Between Now and Forever*
Bryan White, *Bryan White*

Jerry Leiber
Elvis Presley, *King Creole*

Greg Leisz
Dave Alvin, *King of California*

Josh Leo
Alabama, *American Pride*
Alabama, *Cheap Seats*
Alabama, *Pass It On Down*
Karla Bonoff/Bryndle, *Bryndle*
Paul Brandt, *Calm before the Storm*
Lisa Brokop, *Lisa Brokop*
McBride & the Ride/Terry McBride & the Ride, *Terry McBride & the Ride*
Orrall & Wright/Robert Ellis Orrall/Curtis Wright, *Flying Colors*
Prairie Oyster, *Everybody Knows*
Jo-El Sonnier, *Have a Little Faith*
Ray Vega, *Remember When*

Craig Leon
The LeRoi Brothers, *Forget about the Danger . . . Think of the Fun*

Stewart Lerman
Darden Smith, *Deep Fantastic Blue*

Jeffrey Lesser
Darden Smith, *Little Victories*

Bill Levenson
Connie Francis, *Souvenirs*

John Leventhal
Rosanne Cash, *Ten Song Demo*
Jim Lauderdale, *Planet of Love*
Kimmie Rhodes, *West Texas Heaven*
Kim Richey, *Bitter Sweet*
Kelly Willis, *Kelly Willis*

Stewart Levine
Matraca Berg, *The Speed of Grace*

Laurie Lewis
Laurie Lewis, *The Oak & the Laurel*
Laurie Lewis, *True Stories*
Scott Nygaard, *No Hurry*

Marty Lewis
Dan Fogelberg, *High Country Snows*

Henry Lewy
The Dillards, *The Fantastic Expedition of Dillard and Clark*
Flying Burrito Brothers, *The Gilded Palace of Sin*
Neil Young, *Harvest*

Ronny Light
Waylon Jennings, *Honky-Tonk Heroes*

Sonny Limbo
Alabama, *My Home's in Alabama*

Steve Lindsey
The Chipmunks/Alvin & the Chipmunks, *A Very Merry Chipmunk*
Aaron Neville/The Neville Brothers, *The Grand Tour*
Connie Smith, *The Essential Connie Smith*
Keith Whitley, *The Essential Keith Whitley*
Keith Whitley, *Wherever You Are Tonight*

Mark Linett
Dave Alvin, *The Pleasure Barons Live in Las Vegas*
Dave Alvin, *Romeo's Escape*
The Beat Farmers, *Live in Las Vegas*
The Beat Farmers, *Tales of the New West*

Tommy LiPuma
Dan Hicks, *Striking It Rich*
Dan Hicks, *Where's the Money*

Little Texas
Little Texas/Brady Seals, *Kick a Little*

Bill Lloyd
Foster & Lloyd, *Foster & Lloyd*
Kim Richey, *Feeling the Elephant*

Michael Lloyd
Pat Boone, *In a Metal Mood: No More Mr. Nice Guy*
George Burns, *As Time Goes By*

Lobo
Jim Stafford, *Jim Stafford*

Lou Lofredo
Sandy Posey, *I Take It Back*

Bud Logan
John Conlee, *20 Greatest Hits*
John Conlee, *Greatest Hits, Volume 2*
John Conlee, *Harmony*

Alan Lomax
Woody Guthrie, *Library of Congress Recordings*

John Lomax III
The Cactus Brothers, *The Cactus Brothers*

Lonesome River Band
Lonesome River Band/Ronnie Bowman, *Carrying the Tradition*
Lonesome River Band/Ronnie Bowman, *Old Country Town*

Lonesome Standard Time
Lonesome Standard Time/Larry Cordle, *Mighty Lonesome*

Jim Long
Charley Pride, *My Six Latest & Six Greatest*

Michael Lord
Ranch Romance, *Blue Blazes*
Ranch Romance, *Western Dream*

Jack Lothrop
Doc Watson/The Watson Family/Doc & Merle Watson, *Good Deal! Doc Watson in Nashville*

Lyle Lovett
Walter Hyatt/Uncle Walt's Band, *King Tears*
Lyle Lovett, *I Love Everybody*
Lyle Lovett, *Joshua Judges Ruth*
Lyle Lovett, *Lyle Lovett*
Lyle Lovett, *Lyle Lovett and His Large Band*

Lyle Lovett, *Pontiac*
Lyle Lovett, *The Road to Ensenada*

Nick Lowe
Carlene Carter, *Blue Nun*
Carlene Carter, *Musical Shapes*

Bill Lloyd
Kim Richey, *Feeling the Elephant*

Jeff Lynne
Olivia Newton-John, *Olivia's Greatest Hits, Volume 2*

Lynyrd Skynyrd
Lynyrd Skynyrd, *Street Survivors*

Gary Lyons
The Grateful Dead, *Go to Heaven*

Moe Lytle
David Houston, *At His Best*
David Houston, *David Houston*

Cousin Tim Maag
Dave & Deke Combo, *Hollywood Barn Dance*

Brent Maher
Stacy Dean Campbell, *Lonesome Wins Again*
Great Plains, *Homeland*
Michael Johnson, *Wings*
The Judds, *Greatest Hits*
The Judds, *Greatest Hits Volume Two*
The Judds, *Judd Music*
The Judds, *The Judds Collection 1983–1990*
The Judds, *Love Can Build a Bridge*
The Judds, *River of Time*
Shelby Lynne, *Restless*
Shelby Lynne, *Temptation*

Brian Maher
Rich McCready, *Rich McCready*

Lloyd Maines
Terry Allen, *Bloodlines*
Terry Allen, *Human Remains*
Richard Buckner, *Bloomed*
Wayne Hancock, *Thunderstorms and Neon Signs*

Ray Wylie Hubbard, *Loco Gringo's Lament*
Robert Earl Keen Jr., *No. 2 Live Dinner*
Wagon, *No Kinder Room*
Jerry Jeff Walker, *Christmas Gonzo Style*
Chris Wall, *Cowboy Nation*

David Malloy
Amie Comeaux, *Moving Out*
Mindy McCready, *Ten Thousand Angels*
Eddie Rabbitt, *All-Time Greatest Hits*
Eddie Rabbitt, *The Best of Eddie Rabbit/Greatest Hits, Volume II*
Eddie Rabbitt, *Greatest Country Hits*
Kenny Rogers, *20 Greatest Hits*
Daryle Singletary, *Daryle Singletary*

Jim Malloy
Ray Stevens, *Greatest Hits*

Raul Malo
The Mavericks, *From Hell to Paradise*
The Mavericks, *The Mavericks*
The Mavericks, *Music for All Occasions*

Owsley Manier
Mark Germino, *Rank and File*

Terry Manning
Jason & the Scorchers, *Fervor*
Jason & the Scorchers, *Lost & Found*

Cary Mansfield
Terri Gibbs, *The Best of Terri Gibbs*

Ken Mansfield
Jessi Colter, *The Jessi Colter Collection*
Waylon Jennings, *Honky-Tonk Heroes*

Abe Manuel Jr.
Merle Haggard, *1996*

Steve Marcantonio
Orrall & Wright/Robert Ellis Orrall/Curtis Wright, *Flying Colors*

Arif Mardin
Steve Goodman, *Somebody Else's Troubles*
John Prine, *John Prine*

Larry Marks
Flying Burrito Brothers, *The Gilded Palace of Sin*

Mike Marshall
Robbie Fulks, *Within Reach*
Laurie Lewis, *True Stories*
Psychograss, *Like Minds*
Psychograss, *Psychograss*

George Martin
Richard Greene/The Grass Is Greener, *Seatrain*

Grady Martin
Kimmie Rhodes, *Just One Love*

Jim Mason
Firefall, *Firefall*
Firefall, *Messenger*

George Massenburg
Lyle Lovett, *Joshua Judges Ruth*
Linda Ronstadt, *Trio*
James Taylor, *(Best Live)*
James Taylor, *(Live)*

James Mastro
The Health & Happiness Show, *Instant Living*
The Health & Happiness Show, *Tonic*

The Mavericks
The Mavericks, *The Mavericks*

Aubrey Mayhew
Johnny Paycheck, *The Real Mr. Heartache: The Little Darlin' Years*

Elliot Mazer
Neil Young, *Everybody's Rockin'*
Neil Young, *Harvest*
Neil Young, *Old Ways*

Mac McAnally
Mac McAnally, *Knots*
Sawyer Brown, *Greatest Hits 1990–1995*
Sawyer Brown, *This Thing Called Wantin' and Havin' It All*

Larry McBride
Alabama, *My Home's in Alabama*

Martina McBride
Martina McBride, *The Way That I Am*
Martina McBride, *Wild Angels*

Darrell McCall
Darrell McCall, *A Way to Survive*

Patrick McCarthy
Joe Henry, *Trampoline*

Jim McCaskill
The Cornell Hurd Band, *Cool and Unusual Punishment*

Mary McCaslin
Mary McCaslin, *Way Out West*

Delbert McClinton
Delbert McClinton, *Live from Austin*
Delbert McClinton, *Never Been Rocked Enough*

Ronnie McCoury
The Del McCoury Band/Ronnie & Rob McCoury, *Cold Hard Facts*
The Del McCoury Band/Ronnie & Rob McCoury, *A Deeper Shade of Blue*
The Del McCoury Band/Ronnie & Rob McCoury, *Ronnie & Rob McCoury*

Ronnie McDowell
Six Shooter, *Six Shooter*

Bill McElroy
The Red Clay Ramblers, *Merchants Lunch*
The Red Clay Ramblers, *Twisted Laurel*

Reba McEntire
Reba McEntire, *For My Broken Heart*
Reba McEntire, *Read My Mind*
Reba McEntire, *Whoever's in New England*

John McEuen
John McEuen, *Acoustic Traveller*
John McEuen, *String Wizards II*

William E. McEuen
The Nitty Gritty Dirt Band, *Uncle Charlie and His Dog Teddy*
The Nitty Gritty Dirt Band, *Will the Circle Be Unbroken*

Eleanor McEvoy
Eleanor McEvoy, *What's Following Me?*

T.J. McFarland
Don Walser, *Rolling Stone from Texas*
Don Walser, *Texas Top Hand*

Vince McGarry
The LeRoi Brothers, *Big Guitars from Texas*
The LeRoi Brothers, *Check This Action!*
The LeRoi Brothers, *Lucky Lucky Me*

Tim McGraw
Tim McGraw, *All I Want*
Jo Dee Messina, *Jo Dee Messina*

Andy McKaie
Brenda Lee, *The Brenda Lee Anthology, Volume II 1962–1980*
Lynyrd Skynyrd, *Lynyrd Skynyrd*

Maria McKee
Lone Justice/Maria McKee, *Life Is Sweet*

Jim McKell
Billy Montana, *No Yesterday*

Nancy McLaughlin
Crowe & McLaughlin, *Going Back*

Pat McMakin
David Kersh, *Goodnight Sweetheart*

DeClan McManus
Elvis Costello, *King of America*

Dave McNair
Monte Warden, *Monte Warden*

Guthrie T. Meade
J.P. & Annadeene Fraley, *Wild Rose of the Mountain*

Joe Meador
Six Shooter, *Six Shooter*

Huey P. Meaux
Freddy Fender, *Best of Freddy Fender*
Mickey Gilley, *Mickey Gilley*

Terry Melcher
Gene Clark, *Mr. Tambourine Man*
Gene Clark, *Turn! Turn! Turn!*

Mike Melford
Vassar Clements, *Crossing the Catskills*
John Hartford, *Mark Twang*
John Hartford, *Nobody Knows What You Do*

D.L. Menard
D.L. Menard, *No Matter Where You At, There You Are*

Steve Mendell
James Talley, *Got No Bread/Tryin' Like the Devil*

Scott Merritt
Fred Eaglesmith, *Drive-In Movie*
Fred Eaglesmith, *Things Is Changin'*

Jim Messina
Poco, *Deliverin'*
Poco, *Poco*

Blake Mevis
Vern Gosdin, *Warning: Contains Country Music (The Great Ballads of Vern Gosdin)*
Mila Mason, *That's Enough of That*
George Strait, *Greatest Hits Volume Two*
Keith Whitley, *A Hard Act to Follow*

Edgar Meyer
Russ Barenberg, *Skip, Hop, & Wobble*
Jerry Douglas/Douglas, Barenberg & Meyer, *Skip, Hop & Wobble*
Mark O'Connor, *Appalachia Waltz*

Liz Meyer
Liz Meyer, *Once a Day*

Liz Meyer, *Womanly Arts*

Glen Middleworth
Gary Stewart, *Gary's Greatest*

Blue Miller
The Gibson/Miller Band, *Red, White and Blue Collar*

Jo Miller
Ranch Romance, *Blue Blazes*

Mark Miller
The Cactus Brothers, *The Cactus Brothers*
Sawyer Brown, *Cafe on the Corner*
Sawyer Brown, *Greatest Hits 1990–1995*
Sawyer Brown, *Outskirts of Town*
Sawyer Brown, *This Thing Called Wantin' and Havin' It All*

Ronnie Milsap
Ronnie Milsap, *Greatest Hits*
Ronnie Milsap, *Greatest Hits, Volume 2*
Ronnie Milsap, *Ronnie Milsap Live*
Ronnie Milsap, *Sings His Best Hits for Capitol Records*
Ronnie Milsap, *True Believer*

David Miner
T-Bone Burnett, *T-Bone Burnett*

Ben Mink
k.d. lang, *Absolute Torch and Twang*
k.d. lang, *Ingenue*

Joey Miskulin
Don Edwards, *Songs of the Trail*
Waddie Mitchell, *Buckaroo Poet*
Waddie Mitchell, *Lone Driftin' Rider*
Michael Martin Murphey, *Cowboy Songs III: Rhymes of the Renegades*
Sons of the San Joaquin, *Songs of the Silver Screen*

Hugh Moffatt
Katy Moffatt, *Dance Me Outside*

Katy Moffatt
Katy Moffatt, *Dance Me Outside*
Katy Moffatt, *Evangeline Motel*
Katy Moffatt, *Walkin' on the Moon*

Kevin Moloney
Eleanor McEvoy, *What's Following Me?*

Paddy Moloney
The Chieftains, *Another Country*
The Chieftains, *The Long Black Veil*

Chips Moman
The Highwaymen, *Highwayman*
The Highwaymen, *Highwayman 2*
Waylon Jennings, *WW II*
Sandy Posey, *The Best of Sandy Posey*

Thom Monahan
The Scud Mountain Boys, *Massachusetts*

Billy Montana
Billy Montana, *No Yesterday*

Country Dick Montana
Dave Alvin, *The Pleasure Barons Live in Las Vegas*
The Beat Farmers, *Live in Las Vegas*

Bob Montgomery
Janie Fricke, *The Very Best of Janie Frickie*
Vern Gosdin, *Chiseled in Stone*
Shelby Lynne, *Sunrise*

Daniel J. Moore
Delbert McClinton, *Delbert & Glen*

Peter Moore
Cowboy Junkies, *The Caution Horses*
Cowboy Junkies, *The Trinity Session*

Michael Morales
Emilio, *Quedate*
Joel Nava, *Joel Nava*

Ron Morales
Emilio, *Quedate*
Joel Nava, *Joel Nava*

The Morells
The Skeletons/The Morells, *Shake and Push*

Gurf Morlix
Butch Hancock, *Eats Away the Night*
Lucinda Williams, *Lucinda Williams*
Lucinda Williams, *Sweet Old World*

Gary Morris
Gary Morris, *Plain Brown Wrapper*

John Morris
Larry Sparks, *Thank You Lord*

Lynn Morris
The Lynn Morris Band, *Mama's Hand*

The Lynn Morris Band
The Lynn Morris Band, *The Lynn Morris Band*

Bill Morrissey
Bill Morrissey, *Bill Morrissey*

Mickey Mulcahy
The Outlaws, *Hittin' the Road—Live!*

Johnny Mulhair
LeAnn Rimes, *All That*
LeAnn Rimes, *Blue*

Tim Mulligan
Neil Young, *Rust Never Sleeps*

Alan Munde
Alan Munde, *Blue Ridge Express*

Don Mundo
Earl Thomas Conley, *Too Many Times*

Michael Martin Murphey
Don Edwards, *Songs of the Trail*
Waddie Mitchell, *Lone Driftin' Rider*
Michael Martin Murphey, *Cowboy Songs*

Michael Martin Murphey, *Cowboy Songs III: Rhymes of the Renegades*

Anne Murray
Anne Murray, *Croonin'*

Laila Nabulsi
Todd Snider, *Fear and Loathing in Las Vegas*

John Nagy
The Holy Modal Rounders, *Have Moicy!*
Chris Smither, *Another Way to Find You*

Syd Nathan
Johnnie & Jack, *Johnnie & Jack*

Emilio Navaira
Emilio, *Quedate*
Emilio, *SoundLife*

Raul Navaira
Emilio, *Quedate*
Emilio, *SoundLife*

Ken Nelson
Hylo Brown, *Hylo Brown & the Timberliners*
James Burton & Ralph Mooney, *Corn Pickin' and Slick Slidin'*
Merle Haggard, *Same Train, a Different Time: Merle Haggard Sings the Great Songs of Jimmie Rodgers*
Ferlin Husky, *The Heart and Soul of Ferlin Husky*
Jim & Jesse, *Jim & Jesse*
Buck Owens, *The Instrumental Hits of Buck Owens & His Buckaroos*
Buck Owens, *Live at Carnegie Hall*
Jean Shepard, *The Melody Ranch Girl*
Gene Vincent, *Capitol Collectors Series*
Gene Vincent, *The Screaming End: The Best of Gene Vincent & His Blue Caps*
Jimmy Wakely, *Vintage Collections Series*

Rick Nelson
Rick Nelson, *Rick Nelson in Concert*

Michael Nesmith
Michael Nesmith, *The Newer Stuff*
Michael Nesmith, *The Older Stuff; The Best of the Early Years*

David Neuhauser
Big House, *Big House*

Bob Neuwirth
Vince Bell, *Phoenix*

The New Coon Creek Girls
The New Coon Creek Girls, *The L&N Don't Stop Here Anymore*

The New Grass Revival
The New Grass Revival, *Live*

Jimmy C. Newman
Jimmy C. Newman, *The Alligator Man*
Jimmy C. Newman, *Whatever Boils Your Crawfish*

Gary Nicholson
Keith Whitley, *Wherever You Are Tonight*

Justin Niebank
Patricia Conroy, *You Can't Resist*
Marty Stuart, *Honky Tonkin's What I Do Best*
Thrasher Shiver, *Thrasher Shiver*

Patrick Niglio
Connie Francis, *Souvenirs*

Stephen Nikleva
Ray Condo & His Ricochets, *Swing Brother Swing!*

Jack Nitzsche
Neil Young, *Harvest*

Gene Norman
Billy Lee Riley, *Billy Lee Riley in Action*

Jim Ed Norman
Anita Cochran, *Back to You*
The Forester Sisters, *The Christmas Card*
Janie Fricke, *Greatest Hits*
Mickey Gilley, *Biggest Hits*
Mickey Gilley, *Ten Years of Hits*

Herb Jeffries, *The Bronze Buckaroo (Rides Again)*
Michael Martin Murphey, *The Best of Michael Martin Murphey*
Anne Murray, *Anne Murray's Greatest Hits*
Mark O'Connor, *The New Nashville Cats*
Pinkard & Bowden, *Live in Front of a Bunch of D**kh**ds*
Victoria Shaw, *In Full View*
T.G. Sheppard, *All-Time Greatest Hits*
Southern Pacific, *Greatest Hits*
Southern Pacific, *Southern Pacific*
Hank Williams Jr., *America (The Way I See It)*
Hank Williams Jr., *Lone Wolf*

Frank Novicki
Legendary Stardust Cowboy, *Retro Rocket Back to Earth*

Scott Nygaard
Scott Nygaard, *Dreamer's Waltz*
Scott Nygaard, *No Hurry*

Ron Oates
Vern Gosdin, *Warning: Contains Country Music (The Great Ballads of Vern Gosdin)*

Derek O'Brien
Toni Price, *Hey*
Doug Sahm, *The Last Real Texas Blues Band*

Obie O'Brien
Liz Meyer, *Once a Day*

Ron O'Brien
Lynyrd Skynyrd, *Lynyrd Skynyrd*

Steve O'Brien
Fred Koller, *Songs from the Night Before*
Fred Koller, *Where the Fast Lane Ends*

Tim O'Brien
Tim O'Brien/Tim & Mollie O'Brien, *Away Out on the Mountain*
Ranch Romance, *Flip City*

Mark O'Connor
Mark O'Connor, *Appalachia Waltz*
Mark O'Connor, *The Fiddle Concerto*
Mark O'Connor, *Heroes*
Mark O'Connor, *The New Nashville Cats*

Lee Ogle
Joe Nichols, *Joe Nichols*

Jamie O'Hara
Kieran Kane/The O'Kanes/Jamie O'Hara, *The O'Kanes*

Milton Okun
John Denver, *An Evening with John Denver*
John Denver, *Rocky Mountain High*

Keith Olsen
The Grateful Dead, *Terrapin Station*

Michael Omartian
Gary Chapman, *The Light Inside*
Helen Darling, *Helen Darling*

Maury O'Rourk
Linda Gail Lewis, *International Affair*

Robert Ellis Orrall
Orrall & Wright/Robert Ellis Orrall/Curtis Wright, *Flying Colors*
Orrall & Wright/Robert Ellis Orrall/Curtis Wright, *Orrall & Wright*

Sonny Osborne
The Osborne Brothers, *Once More Volumes I & II*
Chubby Wise, *An American Original*

Wynn Osborne
The Nashville Superpickers/The Nashville Super Guitars, *Pickin' on the '50s*

K.T. Oslin
K.T. Oslin, *My Roots Are Showing*

Marge Friedrich Ostroushko
Peter Ostroushko, *Peter Ostroushko Presents the Mando Boys*

Peter Ostroushko
Peter Ostroushko, *Buddies of Swing*
Peter Ostroushko, *Peter Ostroushko Presents the Mando Boys*

Paul Overstreet
Paul Overstreet, *Best of Paul Overstreet*
Paul Overstreet, *Heroes*

Mas Palermo
Monte Warden, *Monte Warden*

Caryl Mack Parker
Caryl Mack Parker, *Caryl Mack Parker*

Scott Parker
Caryl Mack Parker, *Caryl Mack Parker*

Parlor James
Amy Allison/Parlor James, *Dreadful Sorry*

David Parmley
David Parmley, Scott Vestal & Continental Divide/David Parmley, *David Parmley, Scott Vestal & Continental Divide*
David Parmley, Scott Vestal & Continental Divide/David Parmley, *On The Divide*

Lee Roy Parnell
Lee Roy Parnell, *We All Get Lucky Sometimes*

Gene Parsons
Gene Parsons, *Birds of a Feather*
Gene Parsons, *Melodies*

Gram Parsons
Gram Parsons, *G.P./Grievous Angel*

Stella Parton
Stella Parton, *A Woman's Touch*

Rob Patterson
Libbi Bosworth, *Austin Country Nights*
The Derailers, *Austin Country Nights*

Les Paul
Les Paul, *Les Paul: The Legend and the Legacy*

Brian Paulson
Uncle Tupelo/Wilco/Son Volt, *Anodyne*
Uncle Tupelo/Wilco/Son Volt, *Trace*
Kelly Willis, *Fading Fast*

Gary S. Paxton
Vern Gosdin, *Warning: Contains Country Music (The Great Ballads of Vern Gosdin)*

Ed Pearl
The Kentucky Colonels, *Appalachian Swing!*

Herb Pedersen
The Dillards, *Homecoming and Family Reunion*
The Dillards, *There Is a Time: The Best of the Dillards 1963–1970*
Chris Hillman/The Desert Rose Band, *Bakersfield Bound*
The Laurel Canyon Ramblers, *Blue Rambler 2*
The Laurel Canyon Ramblers, *Rambler's Blues*
Herb Pedersen, *Lonesome Feeling*

Ralph Peer
Jimmie Rodgers, *First Sessions, 1927–1928*
Jimmie Rodgers, *Jimmie Rodgers*

Ed Penney
Terri Gibbs, *The Best of Terri Gibbs*

Ray Pennington
Grandpa Jones, *Grandpa Jones Live*
Clinton Gregory, *(If It Weren't for Country Music) I'd Go Crazy*
Clinton Gregory, *Freeborn Man*

Western Flyer, *Back in America*
Western Flyer, *Western Flyer*
The Whites, *Give a Little Back*
Faron Young, *Greatest Hits Volume 1*
Faron Young, *Greatest Hits Volume 2*
Faron Young, *Greatest Hits Volume 3*

Greg Penny
k.d. lang, *Absolute Torch and Twang*
k.d. lang, *Ingenue*
Maura O'Connell, *A Real Life Story*

Al Perkins
Chris Hillman/The Desert Rose Band, *Desert Rose*

Lynn Peterzell
Orrall & Wright/Robert Ellis Orrall/Curtis Wright, *Curtis Wright*
Orrall & Wright/Robert Ellis Orrall/Curtis Wright, *Orrall & Wright*

Norman Petty
Buddy Holly, *Buddy Holly*
Buddy Holly, *The Chirping Crickets*

Doug Phelps
The Kentucky HeadHunters/Brother Phelps, *Let Go*

Ricky Lee Phelps
The Kentucky HeadHunters/Brother Phelps, *Let Go*

Jerry Phillips
John Prine, *Pink Cadillac*

Knox Phillips
John Prine, *Pink Cadillac*

Sam Phillips
Sonny Burgess, *Hittin' That Jug! The Best of Sonny Burgess*
Roy Orbison, *For the Lonely: A Roy Orbison Anthology, 1956–1964*
Elvis Presley, *The Complete Sun Sessions*

Elvis Presley, *The Million Dollar Quartet*

Todd Phillips
Kathy Kallick, *Matters of the Heart*

Cary Pierce
Jack Ingram, *Jack Ingram*

Jim Pierce
Jeannie C. Riley, *Here's Jeannie*

Johnny Pierce
Kate Campbell, *Moonpie Dreams*
Kate Campbell, *Songs from the Levee*

John Pilla
Arlo Guthrie, *All over the World*
Arlo Guthrie, *Amigo*
Arlo Guthrie, *Outlasting the Blues*
Arlo Guthrie, *Together in Concert*

Pinkard & Bowden
Pinkard & Bowden, *Live in Front of a Bunch of D**kh**ds*

Poco
Poco, *Rose of Cimarron*

Mike Poole
Libbi Bosworth, *Outskirts of You*
Prairie Oyster, *Blue Plate Special*

Mike Porter
The Delevantes, *Long about That Time*

Barry Poss
Chris Thile, *Tinsel Tunes*
Doc Watson/The Watson Family/Doc & Merle Watson, *Riding the Midnight Train*

Mike Post
Herb Pedersen, *Southwest*

Jeff Powell
Jolene, *Hell's Half Acre*

Monty Powell
Diamond Rio, *Diamond Rio*

Diamond Rio, *Greatest Hits: Nine Well-Cut Gems*

Prairie Oyster
Prairie Oyster, *Blue Plate Special*

Elvis Presley
Elvis Presley, *Elvis*
Elvis Presley, *Elvis Is Back!*
Elvis Presley, *Elvis' Christmas Album*
Elvis Presley, *His Hand in Mine*
Elvis Presley, *Loving You*

Eric Prestidge
Herb Jeffries, *The Bronze Buckaroo (Rides Again)*

Greg Prestopino
Kate & Anna McGarrigle, *Kate & Anna McGarrigle*

Toni Price
Toni Price, *Hey*

John Prine
John Prine, *Aimless Love*
John Prine, *John Prine Live*

Sidney Prosen
Johnnie & Jack, *Johnnie & Jack*

Jack Joseph Puig
Russ Taff, *Russ Taff*

Norbert Putnam
Jimmy Buffett, *Changes in Latitudes, Changes in Attitudes*
Dan Fogelberg, *Home Free*

Benny Quinn
Keith Whitley, *Wherever You Are Tonight*

Frank Quintini
Jo Carol Pierce, *Bad Girls Upset by the Truth*

David Rachou
Filé, *La Vie Marron (The Runaway Life)*

Mike Ragogna
Patsy Cline, *The Birth of a Star*

Chick Rains
Wade Hayes, *Old Enough to Know Better*
Wade Hayes, *On a Good Night*

Bonnie Raitt
Delbert McClinton, *Never Been Rocked Enough*

Bo Ramsey
Greg Brown, *Down in There*

Willis Alan Ramsey
Willis Alan Ramsey, *Willis Alan Ramsey*

Ranch Romance
Ranch Romance, *Western Dream*

Steve Rathe
The New Lost City Ramblers, *New Lost City Ramblers' 20th Anniversary Concert*

Scott Rause
Jeff Foxworthy, *Games Rednecks Play*

Will Ray
Wylie & the Wild West Show, *Wylie & the Wild West Show*

The Red Clay Ramblers
The Red Clay Ramblers, *Merchants Lunch*
The Red Clay Ramblers, *Twisted Laurel*

Ross Reeder
Gene Watson, *Greatest Hits*

Wyman Reese
Chris Gaffney, *Chris Gaffney & the Cold Hard Facts*
Chris Gaffney, *Mi Vida Loca*
Chris Gaffney, *Road to Indio*
Lonesome Strangers, *The Lonesome Strangers*

Gary B. Reid
Kenny Baker/Kenny Baker & Josh Graves, *Master Fiddler*
The Delmore Brothers, *Brown's Ferry Blues*
Jim Eanes, *Classic Bluegrass*
Uncle Dave Macon, *Travelin' Down the Road*
Bill Monroe & His Blue Grass Boys, *In the Pines*
Don Reno & Red Smiley, *Reno & Smiley & the Tennessee Cut-ups, 1951–1959*
Larry Sparks, *Classic Bluegrass*

Ernest Stoneman/The Stoneman Family, *Edison Recordings—1928*
Mac Wiseman, *Early Dot Recordings, Volume 3*

Lou Reid
Lou Reid/Lou Reid & Carolina, *Carolina Blue*
Lou Reid/Lou Reid & Carolina, *Carolina Moon*

Joe Reisman
Ronnie Hawkins, *Folk Ballads of Ronnie Hawkins*
Ronnie Hawkins, *Mr. Dynamo/Ronnie Hawkins Sings the Songs of Hank Williams*

Allen Reynolds
Asleep at The Wheel, *Asleep at the Wheel: Tribute to the Music of Bob Wills and the Texas Playboys*
Garth Brooks, *Fresh Horses*
Garth Brooks, *Garth Brooks*
Garth Brooks, *The Garth Brooks Collection*
Garth Brooks, *The Hits*
Garth Brooks, *No Fences*
Garth Brooks, *Ropin' the Wind*
The Cactus Brothers, *The Cactus Brothers*
Crystal Gayle, *Classic Crystal*
Emmylou Harris, *At the Ryman*
Emmylou Harris, *Cowgirl's Prayer*
Hal Ketchum, *Every Little Word*
Hal Ketchum, *The Hits*
Hal Ketchum, *Past the Point of Rescue*
Hal Ketchum, *Sure Love*
Chris LeDoux, *Best of Chris LeDoux*
Ruby Lovett, *Ruby Lovett*
Kathy Mattea, *A Collection of Hits*
Kathy Mattea, *Walk the Way the Wind Blows*

Ron Rhoads Jr.
The Forbes Family, *I'll Look to Him*

Kimmie Rhodes
Kimmie Rhodes, *West Texas Heaven*

David Rhyne
Crystal Bernard, *The Girl Next Door*

Gary Rice
The LeRoi Brothers, *Check This Action!*

Tony Rice
Tony Rice, *Mar West*
Tony Rice, *Tony Rice Sings and Plays Bluegrass*

Zachary Richard
Zachary Richard, *Live in Montreal*
Zachary Richard, *Mardi Gras Mambo*
Zachary Richard, *Migration*

Jeff Richardson
Jimmie Rivers, *Brisbane Bop, Western Swing, 1961–1964*

George Richey
Tammy Wynette, *Anniversary: 20 Years Of Hits*

Lionel Richie
Kenny Rogers, *Kenny Rogers' Greatest Hits*
Kenny Rogers, *20 Greatest Hits*

Walt Richmond
The Tractors, *The Tractors*

Cameron Riddle
Flaco Jimenez, *Buena Suerte, Senorita*

J.P. Riedie
Monte Warden, *Do Me Baby: Austin Does Prince*

Billy Lee Riley
Billy Lee Riley, *Vintage*

Tim Riley
Alan Jackson, *A Lot about Livin' (And a Little 'bout Love: Music Row Theater World Premier*

Wilbur C. Rimes
LeAnn Rimes, *All That*
LeAnn Rimes, *Blue*

Robert Alan Ringe
Pure Prairie League, *Bustin' Out*

Ralph Rinzler
Bill Monroe & His Blue Grass Boys, *Live Duet Recordings, 1963–1980: Off the Record, Volume 2*
Bill Monroe & His Blue Grass Boys, *Live Recordings, 1965–69: Off the Record, Volume 1*
Doc Watson/The Watson Family/Doc & Merle Watson, *Live Duet Recordings, 1963–1980: Off the Record, Volume 2*
Doc Watson/The Watson Family/Doc & Merle Watson, *Doc Watson and Clarence Ashley: The Original Folkways Recordings: 1960–1962*
Doc Watson/The Watson Family/Doc & Merle Watson, *The Watson Family*

Steve Ripley
The Tractors, *The Tractors*

Steve Roberts
Mark Germino, *Rank and File*

Robbie Robertson
Jesse Winchester, *Jesse Winchester*

Kenny Rogers
Kenny Rogers, *Kenny Rogers' Greatest Hits*
Kenny Rogers, *Ten Years of Gold*
Kenny Rogers, *20 Greatest Hits*

Tammy Rogers
Tammy Rogers, *In the Red*
Tammy Rogers, *Tammy Rogers*

Tim Rogers
Connie Francis, *The Very Best of Connie Francis*

Jim Rooney
Pat Alger, *Seeds*
Pat Alger, *True Love & Other Short Stories*
Iris DeMent, *Infamous Angel*
Iris DeMent, *My Life*
David Grier, *Freewheeling*
Nanci Griffith, *Last of the True Believers*

Nanci Griffith, *Other Voices, Other Rooms*
Robert Earl Keen Jr., *West Textures*
Hal Ketchum, *Every Little Word*
Hal Ketchum, *The Hits*
Hal Ketchum, *Past the Point of Rescue*
Hal Ketchum, *Sure Love*
John Prine, *Aimless Love*
John Prine, *John Prine Live*
Peter Rowan, *Bluegrass Boy*
Barry & Holly Tashian, *Ready for Love*
Townes Van Zandt, *At My Window*
Jerry Jeff Walker, *Live at Gruene Hall*

Fred Rose
Hank Williams, *40 Greatest Hits*

Jeff Rosen
The Skeletons/The Morells, *Christmas Party with Eddie G.*

Steve Rosenthal
Christine Lavin, *Buy Me Bring Me Take Me: Don't Mess My Hair!!! Volume 2*
Christine Lavin, *Please Don't Make Me Too Happy*
Cheryl Wheeler, *Christine Lavin Presents: Laugh Tracks, Volume 1*

John Rotch
Ken Holloway, *He Who Made the Rain*
Ken Holloway, *Ken Holloway*

Paul Rothchild
The Charles River Valley Boys, *Beatle Country*
The Charles River Valley Boys, *Charles River Valley Boys*
The Outlaws, *Outlaws*

Brent Rowan
Kate Wallace, *Kate Wallace*

Peter Rowan
Peter Rowan, *Bluegrass Boy*

Jimmy Roy
Ray Condo & His Ricochets, *Swing Brother Swing!*

Tom Rozum
Laurie Lewis, *The Oak & the Laurel*

Mark Rubin
Asylum Street Spankers, *Spanks for the Memories*

Rick Rubin
Johnny Cash, *American Recordings*

Ray Ruff
Billy Parker, *Billy Parker & Friends*
Hank Williams Jr., *Family Tradition*

Tom Russell
Rosie Flores, *Tulare Dust*
Katy Moffatt, *Evangeline Motel*
Tom Russell, *Cowboy Real*
Tom Russell, *Hillbilly Voodoo*
Tom Russell, *Hurricane Season*
Tom Russell, *Poor Man's Dream*

Doug Sahm
Doug Sahm, *Daydreaming at Midnight*
Doug Sahm, *Juke Box Music*
Doug Sahm, *The Last Real Texas Blues Band*

Dave Samuelson
Kenny Baker/Kenny Baker & Josh Graves, *The Puritan*

Paul Samwell-Smith
Mark Germino, *London Town & Barnyard Remedies*

Jim Sangster
The Picketts, *Paper Doll*

Art Satherly
Molly O'Day, *Molly O'Day & the Cumberland Mountain Folks*
Sons of the Pioneers, *Columbia Historic Edition*

The Savoy-Doucet Cajun Band
The Savoy-Doucet Cajun Band, *Two-Step d' Amede*

Charles Sawtelle
Front Range, *Back to Red River*
Front Range, *The New Frontier*

Joe Scaife
Billy Ray Cyrus, *Some Gave All*
Billy Ray Cyrus, *Storm in the Heartland*
John & Audrey Wiggins, *John and Audrey Wiggins*

Molly Scheer
Molly & the Heymakers, *B-Sides from the Milkhouse*
Molly & the Heymakers, *Big Things*

Elliot Scheiner
Jimmy Buffett, *Feeding Frenzy*
Jimmy Buffett, *Off to See the Lizard*

Rocky Schnaars
Kate Wallace, *Kate Wallace*

Bill Schnee
Mandy Barnett, *Mandy Barnett*

John Schneider
John Schneider, *Greatest Hits*

Bill Schubart
Mary McCaslin, *Way Out West*

Alan Schulman
The Forester Sisters, *I Got a Date*

Randy Scruggs
Archer/Park, *We Got a Lot in Common*
The Cactus Brothers, *24 Hrs., 7 Days a Week*
Earl Thomas Conley, *The Heart of It All*
Iris DeMent, *The Way I Should*
Skip Ewing, *Following Yonder Star*
Sawyer Brown, *Cafe on the Corner*
Sawyer Brown, *Greatest Hits 1990–1995*
Russ Taff, *Winds of Change*
Steve Wariner, *Laredo*

The Scud Mountain Boys
The Scud Mountain Boys, *Massachusetts*

Dan Seals
Dan Seals, *In a Quiet Room*

Ed Seay
David Ball, *Starlite Lounge*
Davis Daniel, *I Know a Place*
Holly Dunn, *Getting It Dunn*
Ty Herndon, *What Mattered Most*
Highway 101, *Highway 101 & Paulette Carlson Reunited*
Martina McBride, *The Time Has Come*
Martina McBride, *The Way That I Am*
Martina McBride, *Wild Angels*
Molly & the Heymakers, *Molly & the Heymakers*
Marie Osmond, *All in Love*
Collin Raye, *Extremes*
Collin Raye, *I Think about You*
Ricochet, *Ricochet*
Pam Tillis, *Put Yourself in My Place*

Mike Seeger
The Country Gentlemen, *Country Songs Old and New*
Hazel & Alice/Hazel Dickens/Alice Gerrard, *The Strange Creek Singers*
The Lilly Brothers/Don Stover, *Folk Songs from the Southern Mountains*
The New Lost City Ramblers, *The New Lost City Ramblers, the Early Years, 1958–1962*
Earl Taylor/The Stoney Mountain Boys, *Mountain Music Bluegrass Style*

Barry Seidel
Bekka & Billy/Billy Burnette, *Billy Burnette*

Roger Semon
Elvis Presley, *Command Performances: The Essential '60s Masters II*
Elvis Presley, *From Nashville to Memphis: The Essential '60's Masters I*
Elvis Presley, *The King of Rock 'n' Roll: The Complete 1950's Masters*
Elvis Presley, *Walk a Mile in My Shoes: The Essential '70s Masters*

Alan Senauke
Kathy Kallick, *Use a Napkin (Not Your Mom)*

Tony Shanahan
The Health & Happiness Show, *Instant Living*
The Health & Happiness Show, *Tonic*

Tom Shapiro
Billy Dean, *It's What I Do*
Billy Dean, *Young Man*

Harold Shedd
Alabama, *40 Hour Week*
Alabama, *Greatest Hits*
Alabama, *My Home's in Alabama*
Amie Comeaux, *Moving Out*
Davis Daniel, *I Know a Place*
Toby Keith, *Boomtown*
Reba McEntire, *My Kind of Country*
K.T. Oslin, *Love in a Small Town*
K.T. Oslin, *This Woman*
Ronna Reeves, *What Comes Naturally*
Twister Alley, *Twister Alley*
Chely Wright, *Woman in the Moon*

Larry Shell
4 Runner, *4 Runner*

Terry Shelton
Billy Ray Cyrus, *Trail of Tears*

Billy Sherill
Tammy Wynette, *Best Loved Hits*

John Sherman
One Riot One Ranger, *Faces Made for Radio*

Judith Sherman
Robin Holcomb, *Little Three*

Billy Sherrill
David Allan Coe, *Just Divorced*
Elvis Costello, *Almost Blue*
Lacy J. Dalton, *Greatest Hits*
Janie Fricke, *Greatest Hits*
David Houston, *American Originals*
Jim & Jesse, *Jim & Jesse: Bluegrass and More*
George Jones, *Ladies' Choice*

Shelby Lynne, *Sunrise*
Johnny Paycheck, *Biggest Hits*
Johnny Paycheck, *Double Trouble*
Charlie Rich, *Behind Closed Doors*
Charlie Rich, *The Fabulous Charlie Rich*
Marty Robbins, *El Paso City*
Tanya Tucker, *Greatest Hits*
Tammy Wynette, *Anniversary: 20 Years Of Hits*
Tammy Wynette, *D-I-V-O-R-C-E*
Tammy Wynette, *Super Hits*

Kelly Shiver
Thrasher Shiver, *Thrasher Shiver*

The Shivers
The Shivers, *The Buried Life*
The Shivers, *The Shivers*

Michelle Shocked
Alison Brown, *Arkansas Traveler*
The Red Clay Ramblers, *Arkansas Traveler*

Jarvis Sholes
Elvis Presley, *Elvis Country*

Steve Sholes
Johnnie & Jack, *Johnnie & Jack*
Jimmy Martin, *Jimmy Martin & the Sunny Mountain Boys*
Elvis Presley, *Elvis*
Elvis Presley, *Elvis Country*
Elvis Presley, *Elvis Presley*
Elvis Presley, *Elvis' Christmas Album*

Kevin Short
The Fox Family, *Follow My Lead*
The Fox Family, *When It Comes to Blues*

The Sidemen
The Sidemen, *Almost Live at the Station Inn*

Peter K. Siegel
Red Allen, *The Kitchen Tapes*
The Charles River Valley Boys, *Beatle Country*
Hazel & Alice/Hazel Dickens/Alice Gerrard, *Pioneering Women of Bluegrass*

Peter Rowan, *The Great American Eagle Tragedy*

Chris Silagyi
Dave Alvin, *Blue Blvd*
Dave Alvin, *Museum of Heart*

Stan Silver
Donna Fargo, *The Best of Donna Fargo*

Harry Silverstein
Little Jimmy Dickens, *I'm Little but I'm Loud: The Jimmy Dickens Collection*
Jimmy Martin, *Jimmy Martin & the Sunny Mountain Boys*
Bill Monroe & His Blue Grass Boys, *Bill Monroe: Bluegrass, 1959–1969*
Bill Monroe & His Blue Grass Boys, *Bill Monroe: Bluegrass, 1970–1979*

Harry Simmons
Reverend Billy C. Wirtz, *Pianist Envy*

Russell Sims
Billy Parker, *Swingin' with Bob*

Shelby S. Singleton Jr.
David Allan Coe, *Texas Moon*
Dave Dudley, *Trucker Classics*
The Flatlanders, *Unplugged*
Jeannie C. Riley, *The Best of Jeannie C. Riley*
Jeannie C. Riley, *Country Girl*
Jeannie C. Riley, *Greatest Hits Volume Two*
Jeannie C. Riley, *Harper Valley P.T.A.*
Jeannie C. Riley, *Jeannie*
Jeannie C. Riley, *Yearbooks and Yesterdays*
Jason D. Williams, *Wild*

Ricky Skaggs
Ricky Skaggs, *Highways and Heartaches*
Ricky Skaggs, *Waitin' for the Sun to Shine*

The Skeletons
Boxcar Willie, *Rocky Box*
The Skeletons/The Morells, *In the Flesh!*

Sean Slade
Uncle Tupelo/Wilco/Son Volt, *No Depression*
Uncle Tupelo/Wilco/Son Volt, *Still Feel Gone*

Johnny Slate
Joe Diffie, *Honky Tonk Attitude*
Joe Diffie, *Third Rock from the Sun*

Terence Slemmons
Jack Ingram, *Jack Ingram*
Jack Ingram, *Lonesome Questions*

Arthur Smith
Mac Wiseman, *The Mac Wiseman Story*

Billy Smith
Billy & Terry Smith, *Long Live the Dead: A Tribute to the Grateful Dead*

Bubba Smith
Bruce Carroll, *The Great Exchange*

Gary Smith
The Forester Sisters, *More Than I Am*

Hazel Smith
Reba McEntire, *Oklahoma Girl*

Russell Smith
The Amazing Rhythm Aces, *Ride Again*

Steuart Smith
Lionel Cartwright, *I Watched It on the Radio*
Lionel Cartwright, *Lionel Cartwright*

Terry Smith
Billy & Terry Smith, *Long Live the Dead: A Tribute to the Grateful Dead*

Tim Smith
Lynyrd Skynyrd, *Street Survivors*

Ed Snodderly
The Brother Boys, *Presley's Grocery*

Floyd Soileau
Dewey Balfa/The Balfa Brothers, *The Balfa Brothers Play Traditional Cajun Music*
Dewey Balfa/The Balfa Brothers, *The Good Times Are Killing Me*
D.L. Menard, *The Back Door*

J. Steven Soles
Steve Young, *Switchblades of Love*

Maynard Solomon
Al Anderson, *Wildweeds*
Joan Baez, *The First Ten Years*

Son Volt
Uncle Tupelo/Wilco/Son Volt, *Trace*

Wally Sound
Tarnation, *Gentle Creatures*

Southern Pacific
Southern Pacific, *Greatest Hits*

Southern Rail
Southern Rail, *Glory Train*

Ian Spanic
The Spanic Boys, *Dream Your Life*
The Spanic Boys, *Strange World*

Larry Sparks
Larry Sparks, *The Rock I Stand On*
Larry Sparks, *Silver Reflections*
Larry Sparks, *Sings Hank Williams*

Buddy Spicher
The Boys from Indiana, *Touchin' Home'*

Dick Spottswood
D.L. Menard, *D.L. Menard & the Louisiana Aces*

Peter Stampfel
The Holy Modal Rounders, *The Holy Modal Rounders*

Joe Stampley
Joe Stampley, *Joe Stampley & the Uniques—Golden Hits*

John Starling
Carl Jackson, *Spring Training*

Jody Stecher
Katy Moffatt, *Kate Brislin & Katy Moffatt*

Keith Stegall
Terri Clark, *Just the Same*
Terri Clark, *Terri Clark*
Wesley Dennis, *Wesley Dennis*
Alan Jackson, *Everything I Love*
Alan Jackson, *The Greatest Hits Collection*
Alan Jackson, *A Lot about Livin' (And a Little 'bout Love)*
Keith Stegall, *Passages*
Randy Travis, *Storms of Life*
Mark Wills, *Mark Wills*

Tom Stern
Don Reno & Red Smiley, *Family & Friends*

Ray Stevens
Ray Stevens, *All-Time Hits*
Ray Stevens, *The Best of Ray Stevens*
Ray Stevens, *Great Gospel Songs*
Ray Stevens, *Greatest Hits*
Ray Stevens, *1,837 Seconds of Ray Stevens Humor*

John Stewart
John Stewart, *Airdream Believer*
John Stewart, *Bullets in the Hourglass*
John Stewart, *The Last Campaign*

Mike Stewart
Libbi Bosworth, *Austin Country Nights*
The Derailers, *Austin Country Nights*

Don Stiernberg
Homer & Jethro, *Swing Low, Sweet Mandolin*

Gary Stillens
Legendary Stardust Cowboy, *Retro Rocket Back to Earth*

Stephen Stills
Chris Hillman/The Desert Rose Band, *Manassas*

Harry Stinson
Kieran Kane/The O'Kanes/Jamie O'Hara, *Dead Reckoning*
Tammy Rogers, *Tammy Rogers*
Kevin Welch, *Life Down Here on Earth*
Trisha Yearwood, *Thinkin' about You*

Michael Stipe
Vic Chesnutt, *West of Rome*

Mike Stoller
Elvis Presley, *King Creole*

Steve Stone
Tennessee Ernie Ford, *Ernie Sings & Glen Picks*

Chris Strachwitz
Hazel & Alice/Hazel Dickens/Alice Gerrard, *The Strange Creek Singers*
The Maddox Brothers & Rose/Rose Maddox, *America's Most Colorful Hillbilly Band—Their Original Recordings 1946–1951*
The Maddox Brothers & Rose/Rose Maddox, *Maddox Brothers & Rose, Volume Two*
The Maddox Brothers & Rose/Rose Maddox, *On the Air: The 1940s*
D.L. Menard, *Louisiana Cajun Music—Underneath the Green Oak Tree*
The Savoy-Doucet Cajun Band, *Cajun Jam Session*
The Savoy-Doucet Cajun Band, *Home Music with Spirits*
The Savoy-Doucet Cajun Band, *Live! At the Dance*
The Savoy-Doucet Cajun Band, *Two-Step d'Amede*

George Strait
George Strait, *Blue Clear Sky*
George Strait, *Chill of an Early Fall*
George Strait, *Greatest Hits*
George Strait, *Holding My Own*

George Strait, *Livin' It Up*
George Strait, *Merry Christmas Strait to You*

Billy Strange
Jeannie C. Riley, *The Best of Jeannie C. Riley*

Strength in Numbers
Strength in Numbers, *The Telluride Sessions*

Stretchgrass Productions
Gary Brewer, *Guitar*

James Stroud
John Anderson, *Seminole Wind*
Clint Black, *The Hard Way*
Clint Black, *Killin' Time*
Clint Black, *Looking for Christmas*
Lacy J. Dalton, *Survivor*
Neil Diamond, *Tennessee Moon*
Ty England, *Two Ways to Fall*
Tracy Lawrence, *Alibis*
Tracy Lawrence, *Sticks and Stones*
Tim McGraw, *All I Want*
Tim McGraw, *Not a Moment Too Soon*
Tim McGraw, *Tim McGraw*
Lorrie Morgan, *Greater Need*
Orrall & Wright/Robert Ellis Orrall/Curtis Wright, *Curtis Wright*
Paul Overstreet, *Best of Paul Overstreet*
Pirates of the Mississippi, *Best of the Pirates of the Mississippi*
Pirates of the Mississippi, *Pirates of the Mississippi*
Regina Regina, *Regina Regina*
Daryle Singletary, *Daryle Singletary*
Doug Stone, *Greatest Hits, Volume One*
Clay Walker, *Clay Walker*

Marty Stuart
Marty Stuart, *Love and Luck*
Jerry & Tammy Sullivan/The Sullivan Family, *At the Feet of God*
Jerry & Tammy Sullivan/The Sullivan Family, *A Joyful Noise*

Glenn Sutton
Lynn Anderson, *Greatest Hits*
Jim & Jesse, *Jim & Jesse: Bluegrass and More*

J. Sutton
Rick Nelson, *Rick Nelson in Concert*

Billy Swan
Tony Joe White, *Black and White*
Tony Joe White, *Continued*
Tony Joe White, *Tony Joe*

Mike Swinson
Jim Eanes, *Heart of the South*

Michael Sykes
Brush Arbor, *Brush Arbor*
Barbara Fairchild, *Hymns That Last Forever*
Barbara Fairchild, *Stories*

Bill Szymczyk
The Eagles, *One of These Nights*
The Eagles, *Their Greatest Hits, 1971–1975*

Russ Taff
Russ Taff, *Under Their Influence Volume 1*
Russ Taff, *The Way Home*
Russ Taff, *Winds of Change*

Garry Tallent
Burns Sisters, *In This World*
The Delevantes, *Long about That Time*

James Talley
James Talley, *Blackjack Choir/Ain't It Somethin'*
James Talley, *Got No Bread/Tryin' Like the Devil*
James Talley, *"The Road to Torreon: Photographs of New Mexico Villages" by Cavalliere Ketchum; Songs by James Talley*

Brian Tankersley
Roger Brown & Swing City, *Roger Brown & Swing City*

Paul Tannen
Johnny Tillotson, *Poetry in Motion: The Best of Johnny Tillotson*

Johnny Tillotson, *Talk Back Trembling Lips/The Tillotson Touch*

Tarnation
Tarnation, *Gentle Creatures*

Chip Taylor
Stoney Edwards, *Blackbird*

Tut Taylor
Bashful Brother Oswald, *Brother Oswald*
Jerry Douglas/Douglas, Barenberg & Meyer, *The Great Dobro Sessions*
Sally Van Meter, *The Great Dobro Sessions*

The Texas Tornados
The Texas Tornados, *The Best of Texas Tornados*
The Texas Tornados, *Los Texas Tornados*
The Texas Tornados, *Texas Tornados*

Al Tharp
Beausoleil, *Cajun Conja*

Bob Thiele
Johnny Burnette, *Rockabilly Boogie*

IIIrd Tyme Out
IIIrd Tyme Out, *Letter to Home*
IIIrd Tyme Out, *Puttin' New Roots Down*

Joe Thomas
Steve Azar, *Heartbreak Town*
Steve Kolander, *Steve Kolander*
Ronna Reeves, *After the Dance*
S. Alan Taylor, *Forever Dance*

Hughie Thomasson
The Outlaws, *Hittin' the Road—Live!*

Bobby Thompson
Jim & Jesse, *The Jim & Jesse Story*

Peter Thompson
Good Ol' Persons, *Good n' Live*

Neil Thrasher
Thrasher Shiver, *Thrasher Shiver*

Pam Tillis
Pam Tillis, *Sweetheart's Dance*

Steve Tillisch
Mandy Barnett, *Always . . . Patsy Cline*

Michael Timmins
Cowboy Junkies, *Black Eyed Man*
Cowboy Junkies, *The Caution Horses*
Cowboy Junkies, *Lay It Down*

Nathan Tinkham
Cindy Church, *Just a Little Rain*
Cindy Church, *Love on the Range*

Russ Titelman
Ry Cooder, *Paradise & Lunch*
James Taylor, *Gorilla*

TK
Crystal Gayle, *Greatest Hits*
Willie Nelson, *Phases and Stages*
Willie Nelson, *Red Headed Stranger*
Willie Nelson, *Shotgun Willie*
Willie Nelson, *Stardust*
Willie Nelson, *Who'll Buy My Memories? (The IRS Tapes)*

Jack Tottle
Jim Eanes, *The Early Days Of Bluegrass, Volume 4*

The Traditional Grass
The Traditional Grass, *10th Anniversary Collection*
The Traditional Grass, *I Believe in the Old Time Way*

Dave Travis
Eddie Bond, *Rockin' Daddy from Memphis, Tennessee*

Randy Travis
Daryle Singletary, *Daryle Singletary*

Edward Tree
The Bum Steers, *The Bum Steers*

$\frac{6}{18}$ *jim yanaway*

Mark Chesnutt, *Wings*
Helen Darling, *Helen Darling*
Frazier River, *Frazier River*
Greg Holland, *Let Me Drive*
Pirates of the Mississippi, *Best of the Pirates of the Mississippi*
Jason D. Williams, *Tore Up*

Jim Yanaway
Legendary Stardust Cowboy, *Rock-It to Stardom*

Chip Young
Deryl Dodd, *One Ride in Vegas*

Joe Ely, *Honky Tonk Masquerade*

Neil Young
Neil Young, *Everybody's Rockin'*
Neil Young, *Harvest*
Neil Young, *Harvest Moon*
Neil Young, *Old Ways*

Neil Young, *Rust Never Sleeps*
Neil Young, *Tonight's the Night*

Russ Zavitson
Jeff Copley, *Evergreen*

Which artists or groups have had the most influence on the acts included in MusicHound *Country? The Roots Index will help you find out. Under each artist or group's name — not necessarily a country act — are listed the acts found in* MusicHound *Country that were influenced by that artist or group. By the way, Hank Williams is the influence champ: he appears in the* ◄◄ *section of a whopping 66 artists or groups.*

Nathan Abshire
Savoy-Doucet Cajun Band

Roy Acuff
Bill Anderson
Boxcar Willie
Patsy Cline
Wilma Lee & Stoney Cooper
J.P. & Annadeene Fraley
George Jones
Jimmy Martin
Conway Twitty
Ian Tyson
Porter Wagoner
Onie Wheeler
Hank Williams

Bryan Adams
Shania Twain

Doc Addington
Ralph Blizard & the New
    Southern Ramblers

Alabama
Diamond Rio
Exile
Foster & Lloyd
Kentucky HeadHunters
Pirates of the Mississippi
Prairie Oyster
Restless Heart
Sawyer Brown
Shenandoah
Southern Pacific
Western Flyer

Deborah Allen
Holly Dunn

Red Allen
Harley Allen

Rex Allen
Rex Allen Jr.
Don Edwards
Red Steagall

Terry Allen
Jo Carol Pierce

Mose Allison
Charlie Rich

Allman Brothers Band
Charlie Daniels Band
Lynyrd Skynyrd

Marshall Tucker Band
Travis Tritt
Outlaws
Ozark Mountain Daredevils

Herb Alpert
Legendary Stardust Cowboy

Dave Alvin
Mike Henderson

America
Scud Mountain Boys

Bill Anderson
Roy Drusky
Del Reeves

John Anderson
Scott Joss
Ken Mellons
Randy Travis

Liz Anderson
Lynn Anderson

Lynn Anderson
Janie Fricke
Barbara Mandrell
Connie Smith

Andrews Sisters
Dan Hicks

Anglin Brothers
Johnnie & Jack

Amedé Ardoin
Beausoleil
Zachary Richard
Savoy-Doucet Cajun Band

Jo-El Sonnier

Eddy Arnold
Garth Brooks
Ray Charles
Patsy Cline
Don Gibson
Mickey Gilley
Sonny James
Hank Locklin
George Morgan
Gary Morris
Elvis Presley
Jim Reeves
Carl Smith
Billy Walker
Don Walser
Willis Brothers

Asleep at the Wheel
Big Sandy & His Fly-Rite Boys
BR5-49
Brooks & Dunn
Roger Brown & Swing City
Cornell Hurd Band

Chet Atkins
Russ Barenberg
James Burton & Ralph
    Mooney
Gary Chapman
Anita Cochran
Floyd Cramer
Duane Eddy
Dave Edmunds
David Gates
Sonny James
Nashville Superpickers
Notting Hillbillies

Jerry Reed
Spanic Boys
Steve Wariner

Atlanta Rhythm Section
Alabama

Mike Auldridge
Jerry Douglas
Sally Van Meter

Gene Autry
Rex Allen
Johnny Bond
Ray Charles
Jimmy Dean
Herb Jeffries
Patsy Montana
Willie Nelson
Les Paul
Riders in the Sky
Tex Ritter
Marty Robbins
Roy Rogers
Sons of the San Joaquin
Red Steagall
Ian Tyson
Jimmy Wakely

Bad Company
Big House

Joan Baez
Tish Hinojosa
Kate & Anna McGarrigle

Bailes Brothers
Carl & Pearl Butler

**Dewey Balfa & the Balfa
Brothers**
Beausoleil
Jimmy C. Newman
Savoy-Doucet Cajun Band

Hank Ballard
Buddy Holly

The Band
Blue Rodeo
Joe Henry
Robin Holcomb
Prairie Oyster
Red Clay Ramblers
Jesse Winchester

Moe Bandy
Mel McDaniel

Bobby Bare
Jerry Jeff Walker

Russ Barenberg
Scott Nygaard

Lou Ann Barton
Toni Price

Count Basie
Asleep at the Wheel

Beat Farmers
Backsliders
Old 97's

Beatles
Blue Rodeo
Blue Shadows
Mary Chapin Carpenter
Gene Clark
Eagles
Foster & Lloyd
Walter Hyatt
Duane Jarvis
Peter Rowan
V-Roys

Beausoleil
Filé

Bee Gees
Scud Mountain Boys

Lola Beltran
Linda Ronstadt

Brook Benton
Conway Twitty

Matraca Berg
Gretchen Peters

Byron Berline
Stuart Duncan

Chuck Berry
Dave Alvin
Al Anderson
Blasters
Dave Edmunds
Buck Owens
Elvis Presley
John Prine
Ben Vaughn

**Big Sandy & His Fly-Rite
Boys**
Ray Condo & His Ricochets

Big Star
Foster & Lloyd

Conrad Birdie
Orion

Baxter Black
Jeff Foxworthy

Clint Black
Perfect Stranger

Mary Black
Eleanor McEvoy

Black Flag
Uncle Tupelo

Blackwood Brothers
Hee Haw Gospel Quartet
Statler Brothers

Bobby "Blue" Bland
Delbert McClinton
Doug Sahm

Blasters
Alejandro Escovedo
LeRoi Brothers
Rank & File
Dwight Yoakam

Blue Rodeo
Blue Mountain
Prairie Oyster

Blue Rose
Laurie Lewis

Blue Sky Boys
Delmore Brothers
Vern Gosdin
Lilly Brothers
Louvin Brothers
Whitstein Brothers
Mac Wiseman

Bluegrass Cardinals
David Parmley, Scott Vestal &
    Continental Divide

Sonny Bono
Skeletons
Ben Vaughn

Karla Bonoff
Caryl Mack Parker

Booker T. & the MGs
John Fogerty
Tony Joe White

Boone Creek
Lonesome River Band

Pat Boone
Johnny Tillotson
Jerry Wallace

Earl Bostic
Boots Randolph

Boston
Garth Brooks

Boxtops
Amazing Rhythm Aces

Boys from Indiana
Rarely Herd
Traditional Grass

Bradley Kincaid
Mac Wiseman

Bread
John Denver

Jacques Brel
Leonard Cohen

Brewer & Shipley
Bellamy Brothers

Elton Britt
Kenny Roberts

Brooks & Dunn
Archer/Park

Garth Brooks
Rhett Akins
Jeff Carson
Rob Crosby
Helen Darling
Ty England
Greg Holland
Brett James
David Kersh
Lonestar
Rich McCready
Tim McGraw
Smokin' Armadillos
Chris Ward
Jeff Wood

Big Bill Broonzy
Steve Goodman

Junior Brown
BR5-49

Milton Brown
Roger Brown & Swing City
Sid King & the Five Strings
Bob Wills

Milton Brown & His Brownies
Moon Mullican

Charlie Christian
Jimmie Rivers
Arthur "Guitar" Smith

Chuck Wagon Gang
Cox Family

Ceoltori Chuolann
Chieftains

Cimarron
Orrall & Wright

Clancy Brothers
Chieftains

Gene Clark
New Riders of the Purple Sage

Guy Clark
Rodney Crowell
Lyle Lovett
Darden Smith
Jerry Jeff Walker
Chris Wall
Kevin Welch

Petula Clark
Marie Osmond

Clash
Blood Oranges
Uncle Tupelo

Vassar Clements
Mark O'Connor

Patsy Cline
Mandy Barnett
Blood Oranges
Libbi Bosworth
Cowboy Junkies
Rosie Flores
Butch Hancock
k.d. lang
Patty Loveless
Heather Myles
K.T. Oslin
Ranch Romance
LeAnn Rimes
Linda Ronstadt
Jeannie Seely
Connie Smith
Tarnation
Wynonna

Rosemary Clooney
Anne Murray

Dorothy Love Coats
Jerry & Tammy Sullivan

Hank Cochran
Jeannie Seely

Jackie Lee Cochran
Ray Campi

Bruce Cockburn
Dan Fogelberg

Fred Cockerham
Bob Carlin

David Allan Coe
Confederate Railroad
Cornell Hurd Band

Mark Collie
David Lee Murphy

Judy Collins
Nanci Griffith

Tommy Collins
Wynn Stewart

Shawn Colvin
Judith Edelman

Amie Comeaux
Moffatts

Perry Como
Anne Murray

Confederate Railroad
Big House
Gibson/Miller Band

Arthur Conlee
Skeletons

John Conlee
Toby Keith

Continental Drifters
Amy Rigby

Sam Cooke
Ted Hawkins

Spade Cooley
Tex Williams

Coon Creek Girls
New Coon Creek Girls

Wilma Lee Cooper
Hazel & Alice
Jerry & Tammy Sullivan

Wilma Lee & Stoney Cooper
Carl & Pearl Butler
Johnnie & Jack

Elvis Costello
Blue Rodeo

Elizabeth Cotten
Woody Guthrie

Country Cooking
Tony Trischka

Country Gazette
Byron Berline
Laurel Canyon Ramblers
Nashville Bluegrass Band
New Grass Revival

Country Gentlemen
Boone Creek
J.D. Crowe
Hillmen
Doyle Lawson
Rarely Herd
Seldom Scene

Cousin Jody
Bashful Brother Oswald

Cowboy Junkies
Simon Bonney
Richard Buckner
Shivers

Cox Family
Fox Family
Marty Warburton Band

Billy "Crash" Craddock
Narvel Felts

Cream
Lynyrd Skynyrd

Creedence Clearwater Revival
Blue Mountain
Pure Prairie League
Rank & File
Southern Pacific
V-Roys
Bob Woodruff

Marshall Crenshaw
Jim Lauderdale

Bing Crosby
Eddy Arnold

J.D. Crowe & the New South
Boone Creek
Lonesome River Band

Rodney Crowell
Rosanne Cash
Hal Ketchum

Arthur "Big Boy" Crudup
Elvis Presley

Cumberland Three
John Stewart

Mac Curtis
Ray Campi
Ronnie Dawson

Billy Ray Cyrus
Jeff Copley
Ricky Lynn Gregg

Ted Daffan
Dave Dudley
Lefty Frizzell

Vernon Dalhart
Carson Robison

Charlie Daniels
Confederate Railroad
Chris LeDoux
Smokin' Armadillos
Hank Williams Jr.

Dave Clark Five
Texas Tornados

Joel Davidson
Uncle Dave Macon

Gail Davies
Pam Tillis

Rev. Gary Davis
David Bromberg

Linda Davis
Regina Regina

Skeeter Davis
Becky Hobbs
Sue Thompson

Davis Sisters
Brenda Lee

Ronnie Dawson
High Noon

Billy Dean
Steve Azar
Crystal Bernard
Ty Herndon

Delaney & Bonnie
Bekka & Billy
Rita Coolidge

Delmore Brothers
Crowe & McLaughlin

Rosie Flores
Kelly Willis

Flying Burrito Brothers
Backsliders
Beat Farmers
Firefall
Golden Smog
Lone Justice
New Riders of the Purple Sage
Poco
Pure Prairie League
Vidalias

Dan Fogelberg
Garth Brooks
Bruce Carroll
Bill Miller

Red Foley
Bill Anderson
Hawkshaw Hawkins
George Morgan
Charley Pride
Leroy Van Dyke

Canray Fontenot
Beausoleil
Savoy-Doucet Cajun Band

Steve Forbert
Michael Fracasso
Joe Henry

Tennessee Ernie Ford
Oak Ridge Boys

Forester Sisters
Dixie Chicks

Howdy Forrester
Chubby Wise

Foster & Lloyd
Blue Shadows
Delevantes
Kieran Kane
Lonesome Strangers
Thompson Brothers Band

Radney Foster
Deryl Dodd

Stephen Foster
Robin Holcomb

Connie Francis
Marie Osmond

Aretha Franklin
Lone Justice

Toni Price
Keith Stegall

Stan Freberg
Ray Stevens

David Frizzell
Marty Haggard

Lefty Frizzell
Moe Bandy
Marty Brown
Patsy Cline
Dick Curless
Davis Daniel
Jesse Dayton
Stoney Edwards
David Frizzell & Shelly West
Merle Haggard
Freddie Hart
George Jones
Willie Nelson
Gary Stewart
George Strait
James Talley
Randy Travis
Keith Whitley

Lowell Fulson
Elvis Presley

Jerry Garcia
Peter Rowan

David Gates
Steve Azar
Billy Dean

Gateway Singers
Kingston Trio

Danny Gatton
Robert Shafer

Crystal Gayle
Janie Fricke
Reba McEntire
Stella Parton
MC Potts
Ronna Reeves
Sylvia

Gear Daddies
Honeydogs

Bobbie Gentry
Matraca Berg
Crystal Bernard
Kate Campbell
Bobbie Cryner
Terri Gibbs

Reba McEntire
Kimmie Rhodes

Georgia Satellites
Vidalias

Bob Gibson
Steve Goodman

Don Gibson
Kenny Baker

Vince Gill
Paul Jefferson
Billy Montana
Jon Randall
Collin Raye
Lee Ann Womack

Mickey Gilley
T.G. Sheppard
Johnny Lee
Jason D. Williams

Jimmie Dale Gilmore
Alejandro Escovedo
Wayne Hancock

Johnny Gimble
Mark O'Connor

Gin Blossoms
Jolene

Golden Gate Quartet
Ry Cooder

Bobby Goldsboro
Rex Allen Jr.

Good Ol' Persons
Kathy Kallick
Laurie Lewis

Dickie Goodman
Ray Stevens

Lesley Gore
Sandy Posey

Gosdin Brothers
Chris Hillman

Vern Gosdin
Wesley Dennis
Ken Holloway
Ken Mellons

Grand Ole Opry
Ray Charles

Grandpa Jones
Boxcar Willie

Holy Modal Rounders
Willis Brothers

Stephane Grappelli
Kenny Kosek
Mark O'Connor

Grateful Dead
Walter Hyatt
Marshall Tucker Band
New Riders of the Purple Sage

Josh Graves
Jerry Douglas
Sally Van Meter

Dobie Gray
Aaron Neville

Great Plains
S. Alan Taylor

Jack Greene
Jeannie Seely
Ricky Van Shelton

Lee Greenwood
Billy Ray Cyrus
Collin Raye

Nanci Griffith
Suzy Bogguss
Kate Campbell
Iris DeMent
John Gorka
Kate Jacobs
Kathy Mattea
Darden Smith

David Grisman
Alison Brown
Peter Ostroushko
Psychograss
Strength in Numbers

Dave Guard
John Stewart

Woody Guthrie
Bob Dylan
Ramblin' Jack Elliott
Steve Goodman
John Gorka
Arlo Guthrie
Merle Haggard
Butch Hancock
Cisco Houston
Bill Morrissey
Fred Neil
Willis Alan Ramsey
James Talley

Wagon

Waylon Jennings
Hoyt Axton
Bobby Bare
Ed Bruce
Jessi Colter
Rodney Crowell
Charlie Daniels Band
Steve Earle
Radney Foster
Wade Hayes
Robert Earl Keen Jr.
Chris LeDoux
Marshall Tucker Band
Dale Watson

Jim & Jesse
Carl Jackson

Santiago Jimenez
Flaco Jimenez
Doug Sahm
Texas Tornados

Johnnie & Jack
Kitty Wells
Wilburn Brothers

Blind Willie Johnson
Ry Cooder

Johnson Mountain Boys
Bass Mountain Boys
Lynn Morris Band

Robert Johnson
Lucinda Williams

Freedy Johnston
Whiskeytown

Spike Jones & His City Slickers
Hoosier Hot Shots

George Jones
John Anderson
David Ball
Tracy Byrd
Mark Chesnutt
Philip Claypool
Earl Thomas Conley
Dick Curless
Davis Daniel
Joe Diffie
Five Chinese Brothers
Keith Gattis
Ken Holloway
Alan Jackson

Stonewall Jackson
Sammy Kershaw
Tracy Lawrence
Gene Pitney
Rank & File
Redneck Greece
Johnny Rodriguez
Shenandoah
Doug Stone
Mel Street
Randy Travis
Travis Tritt
Tanya Tucker
Monte Warden
Gene Watson
Mark Wills
Tammy Wynette

Tom Jones
Billy "Crash" Craddock
Legendary Stardust Cowboy

Janis Joplin
Lacy J. Dalton
Lone Justice

Louis Jordan
Bill Haley

Naomi Judd
Wynonna

Bill Keith
Tony Trischka

Kentucky Colonels
Laurel Canyon Ramblers
Nashville Bluegrass Band
New Grass Revival

Kentucky HeadHunters
Cactus Brothers
Billy Ray Cyrus
Ricky Lynn Gregg
Pirates of the Mississippi

Hal Ketchum
Marcus Hummon

Killbilly
Bad Livers

Bradley Kincaid
Blue Sky Boys
Hylo Brown
Red Foley

Albert King
Kentucky HeadHunters

Carole King
Victoria Shaw
James Taylor

Pee Wee King
Cowboy Copas

King Curtis
Boots Randolph

Kingsmen
Statler Brothers
Ben Vaughn

Kingston Trio
Kenny Rogers
John Stewart

Kinks
Duane Jarvis

Kiss
Garth Brooks

Knitters
Shivers

Buddy Knox
Jimmy Bowen

Ernie Kovacs
Michael Nesmith

Alison Krauss
Blue Highway
Alison Brown
Luke & Jenny Anne Bulla
Tammy Rogers
Chris Thile
Jeff White

Alison Krauss & Union Station
David Parmley, Scott Vestal & Continental Divide

Kris Kristofferson
Pat Alger
Stephen Bruton
T-Bone Burnett
Billy Joe Shaver
Keith Stegall

Jim Kweskin Jug Band
Nitty Gritty Dirt Band

Frankie Laine
Ferlin Husky

Ronnie Lane
Rico Bell

k.d. lang
Mandy Barnett
Shelby Lynne
Molly & the Heymakers
Twister Alley
Michelle Wright

Jim Lauderdale
Mandy Barnett
Buddy Miller

Christine Lavin
Cheryl Wheeler

Doyle Lawson & Quicksilver
Bass Mountain Boys
New Tradition
Lou Reid
IIIrd Tyme Out

Doyle Lawson
Blue Highway

Leadbelly
Leonard Cohen
Bill Morrissey

Led Zeppelin
Lynyrd Skynyrd

Lilly May Ledford
Molly O'Day

Albert Lee
Vince Gill
Hellecasters
Robert Shafer

Brenda Lee
Amie Comeaux
Holly Dunn
Barbara Fairchild
Rosie Flores
Forester Sisters
Wanda Jackson
Anne Murray
Marie Osmond
Sue Thompson

Freddie "Fingers" Lee
Jason D. Williams

Johnny Lee
T.G. Sheppard

Tom Lehrer
Shel Silverstein

Iry LeJeune
Doug Kershaw
Savoy-Doucet Cajun Band

Townes Van Zandt
Gene Vincent
Jerry Wallace
Wynonna
Dwight Yoakam

Ryder Preston
Orion

Ray Price
BR5-49
Johnny Bush
Patsy Cline
Radney Foster
Darrell McCall
Mel Tillis
Dale Watson
Faron Young

Charley Pride
Neal McCoy
Gary Morris
Aaron Tippin

John Prine
Vince Bell
Greg Brown
T-Bone Burnett
Cowboy Junkies
Joe Henry
Kieran Kane
Mac McAnally

Riley Puckett
Jimmie Rodgers

Roberto Pulido
Emilio

Pure Prairie League
Southern Pacific

R.E.M.
Vic Chesnutt
Jolene
Eleanor McEvoy
Vidalias

Eddie Rabbitt
T.G. Sheppard

Bonnie Raitt
Matraca Berg
Stephen Bruton
Marshall Chapman
Judds
Katy Moffatt
Juice Newton
Toni Price
Lucinda Williams

Wynonna

Ramones
Jason & the Scorchers

Raney Family
Wayne Raney

Rank & File
Blood Oranges

Johnny Ray
Gene Pitney

Collin Raye
Ty Herndon

Red
Southern Rail

Otis Redding
T. Graham Brown
Chris Gaffney
Ted Hawkins
Jim Lauderdale
Tony Joe White

Jimmy Reed
Grateful Dead
Delbert McClinton
Billy Lee Riley
Doug Sahm

Lou Reed
Cowboy Junkies

Del Reeves
Lee Greenwood

Jim Reeves
Browns
Roy Drusky
Don Gibson
Vince Gill
David Houston
Lambchop
Ned Miller

Django Reinhardt
Glen Campbell
Walter Hyatt
Les Paul

Herbie Remington
Pete Drake

Replacements
Honeydogs
V-Roys
Whiskeytown

Restless Heart
BlackHawk
Boy Howdy
Rob Crosby
Frazier River
Great Plains
Little Texas
McBride & the Ride
Billy Montana
Orrall & Wright
Ricochet
S. Alan Taylor

Tony Rice
David Grier
Robert Shafer

Tony Rice Unit
Chesapeake

Charlie Rich
Joe Henry
Ronnie Milsap

Don Rich
Vince Gill

Zachary Richard
Filé

Kim Richey
Kate Wallace

Tex Ritter
Rex Allen

Johnny Rivers
Billy Lee Riley

Marty Robbins
Stacy Dean Campbell
Merle Haggard
James House
Mary McCaslin
Ricochet
Ian Tyson

Kenny Roberts
Slim Whitman

Eck Robertson
Skip Gorman
New Lost City Ramblers

**Carson Robison & the
Pioneers**
Roy Rogers
Sons of the Pioneers

Rockpile
Picketts

Jimmie Rodgers
Gene Autry
Marty Brown
Wilf Carter
Johnny Cash
Jimmie Davis
Delmore Brothers
Flatlanders
Lefty Frizzell
Jimmie Dale Gilmore
Grandpa Jones
Merle Haggard
Butch Hancock
Wayne Hancock
Bill Monroe & His Blue Grass
     Boys
Webb Pierce
Elvis Presley
Redneck Greece
Marty Robbins
Hank Snow
Sons of the Pioneers
James Talley
Johnny Tillotson
Ernest Tubb
Don Walser

Johnny Rodriguez
Joel Nava
Rick Trevino

Tommy Roe
Billy Joe Royal

Aldus Roger
D.L. Menard

Gamble Rogers
Jimmy Buffett

Kenny Rogers
Lee Greenwood

Roy Rogers
Rex Allen
Michael Martin Murphey
Tex Ritter
Dan Seals
Sons of the San Joaquin

Stan Rogers
John Gorka

Rolling Stones
Beat Farmers
Five Chinese Brothers
Grateful Dead
Duane Jarvis
Lynyrd Skynyrd
Webb Wilder

Killbilly
Ricky Skaggs
Keith Whitley

**Ralph Stanley & the Clinch
Mountain Boys**
Warrior River Boys

Kay Starr
Patsy Cline
Connie Francis
Patti Page

Statesmen
Hee Haw Gospel Quartet
Statler Brothers

Statler Brothers
George Burns
Larry Gatlin & the Gatlin
    Brothers
Oak Ridge Boys

Red Steagall
Don Edwards
Waddie Mitchell

Ray Stevens
Cledus "T." Judd
Pinkard & Bowden
Billy Joe Royal
Jim Stafford

Gary Stewart
David Ball

Stone Poneys
Karla Bonoff

Doug Stone
Billy Dean

Scotty Stoneman
Richard Greene

Stoney Lonesome
Kate Mackenzie

Stooges
Killbilly

George Strait
Rhett Akins
Gary Allan
Garth Brooks
Tracy Byrd
Mark Chesnutt
Deryl Dodd
Emilio
Ty England
Alan Jackson

David Kersh
Tracy Lawrence
John Michael Montgomery
Rick Trevino

Syd Straw
Amy Allison
Amy Rigby

Mel Street
Wesley Dennis
Sammy Kershaw

Stringbean
John Hartford

Styx
Garth Brooks

Sugarbeat
Tony Furtado

J.B. Sullivan
Jerry & Tammy Sullivan

Sweethearts of the Rodeo
Burns Sisters

Swingin' Medallions
Skeletons

Tater Tate
John Hartford

James Taylor
Clint Black
Garth Brooks
Bruce Carroll
Jeff Carson
John Denver
Dan Fogelberg
David Gates
Michael Johnson
Mac McAnally
Dan Seals

Television
Health & Happiness Show

Tenneva Ramblers
Jimmie Rodgers

Sonny Terry
Les Paul

Sister Rosetta Tharpe
Sleepy LaBeef

Buddy Thomas
Roger Cooper

Irma Thomas
Jimmy Buffett

Benny Thomasson
Mark O'Connor

Hank Thompson
Derailers
Ferlin Husky
George Strait
Ernest Tubb
Charlie Walker

Big Mama Thornton
Elvis Presley

Mel Tillis
Pam Tillis

Pam Tillis
Ruby Lovett
Lari White

Floyd Tillman
Willie Nelson
Jimmy Wakely

Aaron Tippin
Kenny Chesney
Royal Wade Kimes

Merle Travis
Chet Atkins
Johnny Bond
Dave & Deke Combo
Tennessee Ernie Ford
Michael Nesmith
Jerry Reed
Tom Russell
Arthur "Guitar" Smith
Doc Watson

Randy Travis
Garth Brooks
Wesley Dennis
Alan Jackson
Paul Overstreet
Ricky Van Shelton
Daryle Singletary

Tony Trischka
Alison Brown
Bela Fleck

Travis Tritt
Keith Gattis
Gibson/Miller Band

True Believers
Backsliders

Ernest Tubb
Junior Brown
Cowboy Copas
Lefty Frizzell
Jack Greene
Jack Guthrie
Hawkshaw Hawkins
Harlan Howard
Billy Parker
Carl Perkins
Webb Pierce
Hank Snow
Marty Stuart
Justin Tubb
T. Texas Tyler
Charlie Walker
Onie Wheeler
Tony Joe White

Tanya Tucker
Deana Carter
Amie Comeaux
Mila Mason
Amy Rigby

Big Joe Turner
Dave Alvin
Phil Alvin
Blasters
Bill Haley
Moon Mullican
Billy Lee Riley

Turtle Island String Quartet
Psychograss

Shania Twain
Mindy McCready
Regina Regina

Conway Twitty
Earl Thomas Conley
Narvel Felts
Ronnie Hawkins
Ronnie McDowell
Ronnie Milsap
Johnny Russell
Joe Stampley
Doug Stone

Conway Twitty & Loretta Lynn
Kendalls

Uncle Tupelo
Blue Mountain
Jolene
Old 97's
Scud Mountain Boys
Wagon

Red Sovine
Joe Stampley
Marty Stuart
James Talley
Tarnation
B.J. Thomas
Aaron Tippin
Townes Van Zandt
Waco Brothers
Don Williams
Hank Williams Jr.
Dwight Yoakam
Steve Young

Hank Williams Jr.
Rhett Akins
Charlie Daniels Band
Toby Keith
Travis Tritt

Tex Williams
Big Sandy & His Fly-Rite Boys

Sonny Boy Williamson
Delbert McClinton

Kelly Willis
Libbi Bosworth

Bob Wills
Asleep at the Wheel
Big Sandy & His Fly-Rite Boys
Clint Black
Roger Brown & Swing City
Johnny Bush
Patsy Cline
Commander Cody & His Lost
   Planet Airmen
Jeff Foxworthy

Steve Goodman
Bill Haley
Wayne Hancock
Cornell Hurd Band
Walter Hyatt
Pee Wee King
Roger Miller
Buck Owens
Billy Parker
Prairie Oyster
Ricochet
George Strait
Hank Thompson
Mel Tillis

Bob Wills & the Texas Playboys
Kinky Friedman
Merle Haggard
James Talley
Don Walser

Jackie Wilson
B.J. Thomas

Chubby Wise
Stuart Duncan

Mac Wiseman
Cox Family
Flatt & Scruggs

Bob Woodruff
Jolene

Sheb Wooley
Roger Miller

Link Wray
Gene Vincent

Wrays
Collin Raye

Michelle Wright
Lisa Brokop
Patricia Conroy

Tammy Wynette
Donna Fargo
Lorrie Morgan
K.T. Oslin
MC Potts

Wynonna
Anita Cochran
Lisa Daggs
LeAnn Rimes

X
Alejandro Escovedo
Spanic Boys

XIT
Bill Miller

"Weird" Al Yankovic
Cledus "T." Judd

Yardbirds
Lynyrd Skynyrd

Trisha Yearwood
Stephanie Bentley
Lisa Brokop
Patricia Conroy
Lisa Daggs
Helen Darling
Caryl Mack Parker
Lari White

Yo La Tengo
Lambchop

Dwight Yoakam
Gary Allan
Richard Buckner
Bum Steers
George Ducas
Robbie Fulks
Scott Joss
Mavericks
Thompson Brothers Band
V-Roys
Rick Vincent

Dennis Yost
Billy Joe Royal

Faron Young
Patsy Cline
Darrell McCall
Johnny Paycheck
Mel Tillis

Neil Young
Backsliders
Beat Farmers
Bottle Rockets
Fred Eaglesmith
Jayhawks
Bill Miller
Uncle Tupelo

Frank Zappa
Austin Lounge Lizards

ZZ Top
Bottle Rockets
Webb Wilder

musicHound CATEGORY INDEX

**6
3
5**

The Category Index represents an array of categories put together to suggest just some of the many groupings under which country music and country acts can be classified. The Hound welcomes your additions to the existing categories in this index and also invites you to send in your own funny, sarcastic, prolific, poignant or exciting ideas for brand new categories.

All in the Family
Bekka & Billy
The Browns
The Burns Sisters
The Carter Family
The Cox Family
The Dillards
The Forbes Family
The Fox Family
The Judds
The Kendalls
The Lewis Family
The Maddox Brothers & Rose
Kate & Anna McGarrigle
The Moffats
Tim & Mollie O'Brien
The Spanic Boys
The Stoneman Family
The Sullivan Family

Sweethearts of the Rodeo
The Marty Warburton Band
The Watson Family
The Whites
John & Audrey Wiggins

Alt.Country
Amy Allison
Backsliders
Bad Livers
The Beacon Hillbillies
Blood Oranges
Blue Mountain
Bottle Rockets
Richard Buckner
The Carpetbaggers
Vic Chesnutt
Charlie Chesterman
Cigar Store Indians
Alejandro Escovedo
Freakwater
Robbie Fulks
The Honeydogs
Duane Jarvis
Jason & the Scorchers
Jolene
Cheri Knight
Lambchop
Last Roundup
Old 97's
One Riot One Ranger
Parlor James
The Picketts
Rank & File
Amy Rigby
The Shivers
Slobberbone
Tarnation

Uncle Tupelo/Son Volt/Wilco
Vidalias
The Waco Brothers
Wagon
Whiskeytown

Alternabilly
Pete Anderson
BR5-49
Junior Brown
Delevantes
The Derailers
Rosie Flores
Robbie Fulks
Wayne Hancock
Jack Ingram
Scott Joss
Steve Kolander
Dale Watson

Americana
Terry Allen
Dave Alvin
Al Anderson
Asylum Street Spankers
Backsliders
Bad Livers
Libbi Bosworth
Bottle Rockets
Richard Buckner
Burns Sisters
Kate Campbell
Sarah Elizabeth Campbell
Johnny Cash
Guy Clark
Slaid Cleaves
Ry Cooder
Dead Reckoners
Bob Dylan

Fred Eaglesmith
Nanci Griffith
Woody Guthrie
Mike Henderson
Tish Hinojosa
Robin Holcomb
John Jennings
Kris Kristofferson
Jimmy LaFave
Jim Lauderdale
Lynn Miles
Kimmie Rhodes
Kim Richey
Tammy Rogers
Chris Smither
Vidalias
Kate Wallace
Lucinda Williams
Townes Van Zandt

Appalachian Tremolo
The Cox Family
Iris DeMent
Nanci Griffith
Emmylou Harris
Alison Krauss
Dolly Parton
Gillian Welch
Kelly Willis

Austin City Limits
Asleep at the Wheel
Asylum Street Spankers
Austin Lounge Lizards
Bad Livers
David Ball
Marcia Ball
Ray Benson

Big Sandy & His Fly-Rite Boys
Libbi Bosworth
Junior Brown
Ray Campi
Cornell Hurd Band
The Derailers
Alejandro Escovedo
Rosie Flores
Michael Fracasso
Jimmie Dale Gilmore
The Gourds
Nanci Griffith
Butch Hancock
High Noon
Walter Hyatt
Robert Earl Keen Jr.
Steve Kolander
Jimmy LaFave
LeRoi Brothers
Delbert McClinton
Michael Martin Murphey
Jo Carol Pierce
Toni Price
Rank & File
Tom Russell
Charlie Sexton
The Shivers
Darden Smith
Jerry Jeff Walker
Chris Wall
Don Walser
Monte Warden
Dale Watson
Lucinda Williams
Kelly Willis

Bakersfield Boys
Gary Allan
Tommy Collins
Merle Haggard
Buck Owens
Wynn Stewart
Rick Vincent

Banjo Players
Alison Brown
Bill Emerson
Bela Fleck
Tony Furtado
Marvin Gaster
Grandpa Jones
John Hartford
Carl Jackson
Bill Keith
Walt Koken
Uncle Dave Macon
Alan Munde
Charlie Poole

Earl Scruggs
Ralph Stanley
Stringbean
Tony Trischka
Peter Wernick

Birdland
Bluegrass Cardinals
Tracy Byrd
The Byrds
J.D. Crowe
Robin Holcomb
Robin Lee
Marty Robbins

Bluegrass Acts
Eddie Adcock
Harley Allen
Red Allen
Mike Auldridge
Bad Livers
Bass Mountain Boys
Ralph Blizard & the New
   Southern Ramblers
Blue Highway
Blue Sky Boys
Bluegrass Cardinals
Boone Creek
The Boys from Indiana
Gary Brewer & the Kentucky
   Ramblers
Charles River Valley Boys
Chesapeake
Kathy Chiavola
Bill Clifton
Charlie Cline
The Cluster Pluckers
Country Gazette
The Country Gentlemen
The Cox Family
J.D. Crowe & the New South
The Cumberland Boys
The Dillards
Jerry Douglas
Dry Branch Fire Squad
Stuart Duncan
Bill Emerson
Dave Evans & River Bend
Gary Ferguson
Bela Fleck
The Forbes Family
The Fox Family
Front Range
Tony Furtado
Richard Greene/The Grass Is
   Greener
The Hillmen
Hot Rize

Jim & Jesse
The Johnson Mountain Boys
Bill Keith
The Kentucky Colonels
James King
Alison Krauss & Union Station
Laurel Canyon Ramblers
Doyle Lawson & Quicksilver
Laurie Lewis
The Lilly Brothers
Lonesome River Band
Lonesome Standard Time
Lost & Found
Claire Lynch
Jimmy Martin
Del McCoury
Bill Monroe & His Blue Grass
   Boys
Lynn Morris
Alan Munde
The Nashville Bluegrass Band
New Coon Creek Girls
New Grass Revival
New Vintage
Tim & Mollie O'Brien
Old & In the Way
The Osborne Brothers
David Parmley, Scott Vestal &
   Continental Divide
Psychograss
The Rarely Herd
Red Clay Ramblers
Lou Reid & Carolina
The Reno Brothers
Don Reno & Red Smiley
The Rice Brothers
Tony Rice
Peter Rowan
Salamander Crossing
The Sauceman Brothers
The Seldom Scene
The Sidemen
Charlie Sizemore
Ricky Skaggs
Southern Rail
Larry Sparks
The Stanley Brothers
Strength in Numbers
Chris Thile
IIIrd Tyme Out
Tony Trischka
Joe Val & the New England
   Bluegrass Boys
Rhonda Vincent
The Marty Warburton Band
The Warrior River Boys
Doc Watson

Jeff White
The Whitstein Brothers
Chubby Wise
Mac Wiseman

Bluegrass State Natives
Red Allen
Kenny Baker
Hylo Brown
Marty Brown
Sam Bush
Bill Carlisle
John Conlee
Billy Ray Cyrus
Skeeter Davis
The Everly Brothers
Red Foley
Crystal Gayle
Grandpa Jones
Tom T. Hall
Harlan Howard
Wynonna Judd
Patty Loveless
Loretta Lynn
Mila Mason
Bill Monroe
Molly O'Day
Ray Pennington
Boots Randolph
Ricky Skaggs
Gary Stewart
Stringbean
Merle Travis
Steve Wariner
Dwight Whitley
Keith Whitley
Dwight Yoakam

Born in 'Bama
Ernest Ashworth
The Delmore Brothers
Wesley Dennis
Vern Gosdin
Emmylou Harris
Ty Herndon
Tommy Jackson
Sonny James
The Louvin Brothers
Mac McAnally
Sandy Posey
Willis Alan Ramsey
Jerry & Tammy Sullivan
Dale Watson
Hank Williams

The Bottle Let Them Down
(died from alcohol/drug over-
   doses & related circumstances)

6
3
8

cowboy singers

Jimmy Buffett
T-Bone Burnett
The Byrds
Commander Cody & His Lost
   Planet Airmen
Cowboy Junkies
Charlie Daniels
The Eagles
Joe Ely
Firefall
Flying Burrito Brothers
John Fogerty
Lone Justice
Lynyrd Skynyrd
Marshall Tucker Band
Rick Nelson
Michael Nesmith
New Riders of the Purple Sage
The Outlaws
Ozark Mountain Daredevils
Gram Parsons
Poco
Pure Prairie League
Leon Russell
Doug Sahm
Southern Pacific
Neil Young

Cowboy Singers
Rex Allen
Gene Autry
Wilf Carter/Montana Slim
Don Edwards
Skip Gorman
Herb Jeffries
Waddie Mitchell
Patsy Montana
Michael Martin Murphey
Riders in the Sky
Tex Ritter
Carson Robison
Roy Rogers
Sons of the Pioneers
Sons of the San Joaquin
Red Steagall
Jimmy Wakely

Cowpunk
Bad Livers
Beat Farmers
Blood Oranges
Jason & the Scorchers
Killbilly
Lone Justice
Rank & File
Slobberbone
The Waco Brothers

Demo Singers
Stephanie Bentley
Garth Brooks
Joe Diffie
Paul Jefferson
Mindy McCready
Trisha Yearwood

Dobro Delights
Mike Auldridge
Bashful Brother Oswald
Anita Cochran
Jerry Douglas
Josh Graves
Sally Van Meter

Dynamic Duos
Archer/Park
Baker & Myers
Bekka & Billy
Bell & Shore
The Bellamy Brothers
Brooks & Dunn
Carl & Pearl Butler
Delevantes
The Delmore Brothers
Jeff & Sheri Easter
The Everly Brothers
Cathy Fink & Marcy Marxer
Flatt & Scruggs
Foster & Lloyd
J.P. & Annadeene Fraley
David Frizzell & Shelly West
Homer & Jethro
Jim & Jesse
Johnnie & Jack
The Judds
The Kendalls
The Louvin Brothers
Joe Maphis & Rose Lee
Bill & Charlie Monroe
Orrall & Wright
Les Paul & Mary Ford
Pinkard & Bowden
Reno & Smiley
Billy & Terry Smith
The Spanic Boys
Ralph & Carter Stanley
Jerry & Tammy Sullivan
Sweethearts of the Rodeo
Barry & Holly Tashian
Thrasher Shiver
The Whitstein Brothers
John & Audrey Wiggins
The Wilburn Brothers
Robin & Linda Williams
The Willis Brothers

Famous Floridians
John Anderson
The Bellamy Brothers
Vic Chesnutt
Billy Dean
Hank Locklin
Mindy McCready
Dude Mowrey
Fred Neil
Pam Tillis
Aaron Tippin
Lari White
Slim Whitman

Fiddlin' Fiends
Kenny Baker
Byron Berline
Luke & Jenny Anne Bulla
Vassar Clements
Roger Cooper
Stuart Duncan
Johnny Gimble
Richard Greene
Clinton Gregory
Kenny Kosek
Alison Krauss
Barbara Lamb
Mark O'Connor
Peter Ostroushko

Folk Folks
Clarence Ashley
Joan Baez
Norman & Nancy Blake
Greg Brown
Jimmy Buffett
Sara Elizabeth Campbell
Iris DeMent
Bob Dylan
Judith Edelman
Jonathan Edwards
Ramblin' Jack Elliot
Cathy Fink & Marcy Marxer
Jimmie Dale Gilmore
Steve Goodman
John Gorka
Nanci Griffith
Arlo Guthrie
Jack Guthrie
Woody Guthrie
Hazel & Alice
Cisco Houston
Dakota Dave Hull
Ian & Sylvia
Kathy Kallick
Lucy Kaplansky
The Kingston Trio
Christine Lavin

Kate MacKenzie
Mary McCaslin
Bill Morrissey
John Prine
Shel Silverstein
Chris Smither
James Talley
Ian Tyson
Gillian Welch
Cheryl Wheeler
Jesse Winchester

Generation Next
Rex Allen Jr. (son of Rex Allen)
Hoyt Axton (son of songwriter
   Mae Boren Axton)
Matraca Berg (daughter of
   session singer/songwriter
   Icee Berg)
Debby Boone (daughter of Pat
   Boone)
Bekka Bramlett (daughter of
   Delaney and Bonnie Bram-
   lett)
Billy Burnette (son of Dorsey
   Burnette)
Anita Carter (daughter of May-
   belle Carter)
Carlene Carter (daughter of
   June Carter)
Deana Carter (daughter of
   session guitarist Fred Carter
   Jr.)
June Carter (daughter of May-
   belle Carter)
Rosanne Cash (daughter of
   Johnny Cash)
Terry McBride (son of Dale
   McBride)
Dean Miller (son of Roger
   Miller)
Lorrie Morgan (daughter of
   George Morgan)
Marty Haggard (son of Merle
   Haggard)
Noel Haggard (son of Merle
   Haggard)
Wynonna Judd (daughter of
   Naomi Judd)
Ronnie & Rob McCoury (sons
   of Del McCoury)
Pam Tillis (daughter of Mel
   Tillis)
Justin Tubb (son of Ernest
   Tubb)
Merle Watson (son of Doc
   Watson)

Shelly West (daughter of Dottie West)
John and Audrey Wiggins (son and daughter of Ernest Tubb's "Singing Bus Driver," Johnny Wiggins)
Hank Williams Jr. (son of Hank Williams)

Geography 101
Alabama
The Bass Mountain Boys
California
Charles River Valley Boys
Chesapeake
Kentucky Colonels
Kentucky HeadHunters
Little Texas
Lou Reid & Carolina
Texas Tornados

Georgia On Their Minds
Rhett Akins
Stephanie Bentley
T. Graham Brown
Bruce Carroll
Ray Charles
J.D. Crowe
Pete Drake
Roy Drusky
Jeff Foxworthy
Terri Gibbs
Robin Holcomb
Greg Holland
Alan Jackson
Cledus "T." Judd
Brenda Lee
Emmett Miller
Riley Puckett
Jerry Reed
Daryle Singletary
Ray Stevens
Doug Stone
Travis Tritt
Trisha Yearwood
Steve Young

Hat Acts
Trace Adkins
Clint Black
Garth Brooks
Tracy Byrd
Mark Chesnutt
Terri Clark
Ty England
Alan Jackson
Ken Mellons
Daryle Singletary
Rick Trevino

Clay Walker
Dwight Yoakam

Honky-Tonkers
Gary Allan
The Backsliders
David Ball
Moe Bandy
Junior Brown
Marty Brown
Tracy Byrd
Mark Chesnutt
Mark Collie
The Cornell Hurd Band
Joe Ely
Rosie Flores
Keith Gattis
Jack Guthrie
Merle Haggard
Johnny Horton
Jason & the Scorchers
Robert Earl Keen Jr.
Darrell McCall
Delbert McClinton
Buck Owens
Johnny Paycheck
Webb Pierce
Red Knuckles & the Trailblazers
Redneck Greece
Joe Stampley
Jean Shepard
Marty Stuart
Dale Watson
Hank Williams

Jailbirds
Johnny Cash
Spade Cooley
Freddy Fender
Merle Haggard
Johnny Paycheck
Johnny Rodriguez
Randy Travis

Jersey Girls & Guys
Clint Black
Mary Chapin Carpenter
Delevantes
Don Edwards
Connie Francis
John Gorka
Ricky Nelson
Juice Newton

Land of Lincoln
Rex Allen Jr.
Suzy Bogguss

Kathy Chiavola
Davis Daniel
Dan Fogelberg
Steve Goodman
Kathy Kallick
Alison Krauss
David Lee Murphy
Scott Nygaard
John Prine
Shel Silverstein
Tex Williams

Louisiana
Trace Adkins
Dewey Balfa
James Burton
Kate Campbell
Amie Comeaux
Helen Darling
Jimmie Davis
Mickey Gilley
Ken Holloway
David Houston
Doug Kershaw
Sammy Kershaw
Claude King
Jerry Lee Lewis
Tim McGraw
D.L. Menard
Aaron Neville
Jimmy C. Newman
Webb Pierce
Eddy Raven
Chris Smither
Jo-El Sonnier
Joe Stampley
Hank Williams Jr.
Lucinda Williams
Jesse Winchester
Faron Young

Lubbock Legends
Terry Allen
Joe Ely
The Flatlanders
Jimmie Dale Gilmore
Butch Hancock
Legendary Stardust Cowboy
Delbert McClinton
Jo Carol Pierce

Mandolin Masters
Butch Baldassari
Sam Bush
David Grisman
Bill Monroe
Nashville Mandolin Ensemble
Peter Ostroushko

Peter Rowan
Chris Thile

Mississippi
Steve Azar
Moe Bandy
Charlie Feathers
Ted Hawkins
Mike Henderson
Faith Hill
Kim Hill
Chris LeDoux
Paul Overstreet
Elvis Presley
Charley Pride
LeAnn Rimes
Jimmie Rodgers
Conway Twitty
Jerry Wallace
Tammy Wynette

Missouri
T-Bone Burnett
Gene Clark
Ferlin Husky
The Kendalls
Wynn Stewart
Billy Swan
Leroy Van Dyke
Rhonda Vincent
Porter Wagoner
Onie Wheeler
Chely Wright

Movie Stars
Roy Acuff
Rex Allen
Bill Anderson
Eddy Arnold
Gene Autry
Hoyt Axton
Johnny Bond
Glen Campbell
Johnny Cash
Spade Cooley
Gail Davies
Jimmie Davis
Tennessee Ernie Ford
Mickey Gilley
Naomi Judd
Jerry Lee Lewis
Loretta Lynn
Reba McEntire
Rick Nelson
Willie Nelson
K.T. Oslin
Dolly Parton
Carl Perkins

6/4/0 *nashville cats*

Elvis Presley
Jerry Reed
Tex Ritter
Marty Robbins
Roy Rogers
Sons of the Pioneers
George Strait
Randy Travis
Jimmy Wakely
Dwight Yoakam
Faron Young

Nashville Cats
Matraca Berg
Deana Carter
Ken Mellons
Lorrie Morgan
Pam Tillis
Kitty Wells

Native American Themes
Johnny Cash
Stoney Edwards
Bill Miller
Jimmie Rivers
Todd Snider

Native New Yorkers
Pat Alger
Amy Allison
Joan Baez
Bob Carlin
Judith Edelman
Bela Fleck
Arlo Guthrie
John Hartford
Kieran Kane
Hal Ketchum
Kenny Kosek
Claire Lynch
Don McLean
Billy Montana
Eddie Rabbitt
Victoria Shaw
Tony Trischka
Jerry Jeff Walker
Chris Ward
Jeff White

New Acoustic
Alison Brown
Jerry Douglas
Judith Edelman
Bela Fleck
David Grisman
Kenny Kosek
Scott Nygaard
Mark O'Connor
Peter Ostroushko

Psychograss
Tony Rice
Sweethearts of the Rodeo
Tony Trischka
Rhonda Vincent

New Traditionalists
Gary Allan
Clint Black
Blue Shadows
Suzy Bogguss
Garth Brooks
Tracy Byrd
Deana Carter
Mark Chesnutt
Terri Clark
Joe Diffie
Vince Gill
Alan Jackson
Toby Keith
Patty Loveless
Lyle Lovett
Shelby Lynne
Kathy Mattea
Lorrie Morgan
Daryle Singletary
Ricky Skaggs
George Strait
Marty Stuart
Pam Tillis
Randy Travis
Dwight Yoakam

North Carolinians
Billy "Crash" Craddock
Charlie Daniels
Donna Fargo
Benton Flippen
Marvin Gaster
Mark Germino
Don Gibson
Joe Henry
Stonewall Jackson
Jim Lauderdale
John D. Loudermilk
Bascom Lamar Lunsford
Del McCoury
Ronnie Milsap
Charlie Poole
Del Reeves
Lou Reid
Earl Scruggs
Red Smiley
Randy Travis
Doc Watson

Occasional Español
Emilio
Freddy Fender

Tish Hinojosa
Flaco Jimenez
Johnny Rodriguez
The Texas Tornados
Rick Trevino

Oh, Canada
Blue Rodeo
Blue Shadows
Paul Brandt
Lisa Brokop
Wilf Carter/Montana Slim
Cindy Church
Terri Clark
Leonard Cohen
Ray Condo and His Ricochets
Stompin' Tom Connors
Patricia Conroy
Cowboy Junkies
Fred Eaglesmith
k.d. lang
Charlie Major
The Moffatts
Anne Murray
Prairie Oyster
The Rankin Family
Jack Scott
Hank Snow
Shania Twain
Ian Tyson
Jamie Warren
Michelle Wright

Okies (from Muskogee and Elsewhere)
Hoyt Axton
Johnny Bond
Garth Brooks
Jeff Carson
Spade Cooley
Cowboy Copas
Gail Davies
Joe Diffie
Ty England
David Gates
Vince Gill
Jack Guthrie
Woody Guthrie
Wade Hayes
Becky Hobbs
Wanda Jackson
Brett James
Toby Keith
Mel McDaniel
Reba McEntire
Patti Page
Billy Parker
Jimmie Rivers

Leon Russell
Jean Shepard
James Talley
Floyd Tillman
Bryan White
Buck White
Kelly Willis
Jeff Wood

The Pride of Pennsylvania
David Bromberg
Lacy J. Dalton
Robbie Fulks
MC Potts
Toni Price
Amy Rigby
Jeannie Seely
Curtis Wright

Pickers
Eddie Adcock
Pete Anderson
Chet Atkins
Russ Barenberg
David Bromberg
Junior Brown
James Burton
Roy Clark
Anita Cochran
Ry Cooder
Dan Crary
Duane Eddy
Gary Ferguson
Tony Furtado
David Grier
The Hellecasters
Mike Henderson
Bill Kirchen
Duke Levine
Jimmy Martin
John McEuen
Scott Nygaard
David Parmley
Les Paul
Herb Pedersen
Tony Rice
Larry Sparks
Doc Watson
Jeff White

Pop/Rock Country Charters
Andrews Sisters
Bee Gees
Debby Boone
Pat Boone
Jimmy Buffett

The Burrito Brothers (offshoot of the Flying Burrito Brothers)
The Captain & Tennille
Eric Carmen (with Louise Mandrell)
Kim Carnes
The Carpenters
Ray Charles
Cher
Eric Clapton
Petula Clark
Judy Collins
Perry Como
Creedence Clearwater Revival
Bing Crosby
Crosby, Stills & Nash
Burton Cummings
Bobby Darin
Paul Davis
Sammy Davis Jr.
John Denver
Neil Diamond
The Diamonds
Dr. Hook
The Eagles
Sheena Easton
Duane Eddy
Dave Edmunds (with Carlene Carter)
Fairground Attraction
5 Red Caps
Ella Fitzgerald
Dan Fogelberg
John Fogerty
Connie Francis
Jerry Fuller
Robert Gordon
Eydie Gorme
Dobie Gray
Erskine Hawkins
Don Henley (with Trisha Yearwood)
John Hiatt (with the Nitty Gritty Dirt Band)
Bertie Higgins
Bruce Hornsby and the Range
Englebert Humperdinck
Julio Iglesias (with Willie Nelson)
Tom Jones
Louis Jordan
The King Cole Trio (featuring Nat "King" Cole)
Kiss (backed Garth Brooks on "Hard Luck Woman")
Nicolette Larson

Lobo
Loggins & Messina
Los Lobos
Aaron Neville
Stevie Nicks
Gene Pitney
Linda Ronstadt
Jack Scott
Jo Stafford
Barbra Streisand (with Neil Diamond)

Ragin' Cajuns
Dewey Balfa
Beausoleil
Michael Doucet
Filé
The Hackberry Ramblers
Doug Kershaw
D.L. Menard
Jimmy C. Newman
Eddy Raven
Zachary Richard
Steve Riley & the Mamou Playboys
The Savoy-Doucet Cajun Band
Jo-El Sonnier
Wayne Toups

Razorbacks
Jim Ed Brown
Ed Bruce
Sonny Burgess
Shawn Camp
Glen Campbell
Johnny Cash
Roger Clinton
Barbara Fairchild
Narvel Felts
Ronnie Hawkins
Royal Wade Kimes
Sleepy LaBeef
Patsy Montana
Joe Nichols
Wayne Raney
Collin Raye
Charlie Rich
Russ Taff
T. Texas Tyler
Jimmy Wakely
Joy White

Rockabilly Cats
Dave Alvin
Bekka & Billy
Big Sandy & His Fly-Rite Boys
The Blasters
Sonny Burgess

Dorsey Burnette
Johnny Burnette
Ray Campi
The Carpetbaggers
Ray Condo & His Ricochets
Ronnie Dawson
Dave Edmunds
Charlie Feathers
Rosie Flores
Robert Gordon
Bill Haley
Ronnie Hawkins
High Noon
Buddy Holly
Johnny Horton
James House
Wanda Jackson
Sleepy LaBeef
Jerry Lee Lewis
Carl Mann
Janis Martin
Ricky Nelson
Roy Orbison
Carl Perkins
Elvis Presley
Billy Lee Riley
Jack Scott
Billy Swan
Gene Vincent

Roots Rock
The Blasters
Blue Rodeo
The Bottle Rockets
T. Bone Burnett
Cowboy Junkies
Bob Dylan
Steve Earle
The Everly Brothers
John Fogerty
The Hellecasters
Jason & the Scorchers
Jayhawks
Lone Justice/Maria McKee
John Prine
The Skeletons/The Morells
Spanic Boys
Uncle Tupelo/Son Volt/Wilco
Lucinda Williams

Silver Wings
(died in airplane crashes)
Patsy Cline
Cowboy Copas
Cassie Gaines (Lynyrd Skynyrd)
Steve Gaines (Lynyrd Skynyrd)
Hawkshaw Hawkins

Buddy Holly
Walter Hyatt
Rick Nelson
Jim Reeves
Ronnie Van Zant (Lynyrd Skynyrd)

Sister Acts
The Burns Sisters
The Carter Sisters
The Forester Sisters
Kate & Anna McGarrigle
Beth and April Stevens
Sweethearts of the Rodeo

Soulful Country
Donna B
DeFord Bailey
Ray Charles
Mary Cutrufello
Big Al Downing
Cleve Francis
Ted Hawkins
O.B. McClinton
Aaron Neville
Charley Pride

South Carolinians
Bill Anderson
David Ball
John Berry
Marshall Chapman
Rob Crosby
Hank Garland
Walter Hyatt
Don Reno
Arthur "Guitar" Smith
S. Alan Taylor
Rev. Billy C. Wirtz

Substance Abusers
Johnny Cash
Steve Earle
Freddy Fender
Ty Herndon
Waylon Jennings
Elvis Presley
Keith Whitley

Teen Wonders
Luke & Jenny Anne Bulla
The Collins Kids
Brenda Lee
The Moffatts
Rick Nelson
LeAnn Rimes
Chris Thile
Tanya Tucker

Television Tunesmiths
Crystal Bernard
Jimmy Dean
Maureen McCormick
Michael Nesmith
John Schneider

Tennesseans
Roy Acuff
Deborah Allen
Eddy Arnold
Chet Atkins
Mandy Barnett
Bashful Brother Oswald
Matraca Berg
Eddie Bond
Dorsey Burnette
Johnny Burnette
Carl Butler
Carlene Carter
Deana Carter
Rosanne Cash
Kenny Chesney
Philip Claypool
Mark Collie
Rita Coolidge
Lester Flatt
Tennessee Ernie Ford
Jack Greene
Uncle Dave Macon
Carl Mann
Jimmy Martin
Charly McClain
Ken Mellons
George Morgan
Lorrie Morgan
Dolly Parton
Carl Perkins
Kenny Roberts
Tammy Rogers
T.G. Sheppard
Carl Smith
Kitty Wells
John & Audrey Wiggins

Texans
Gene Autry
Vince Bell
Crystal Bernard
Boxcar Willie
Milton Brown
Roger Brown
Stephen Bruton

Tracy Byrd
Mark Chesnutt
Guy Clark
Rodney Crowell
Linda Davis
Mac Davis
Ronnie Dawson
Curtis Day
Jesse Dayton
Jimmy Dean
Deryl Dodd
George Ducas
Holly Dunn
Emilio
Alejandro Escovedo
Freddy Fender
Rosie Flores
Radney Foster
Kinky Friedman
Lefty Frizzell
Larry Gatlin
Keith Gattis
Jimmie Dale Gilmore
Ricky Lynn Gregg
Nanci Griffith
Wayne Hancock
Buddy Holly
Johnny Horton
Michael James
Waylon Jennings
George Jones
Robert Earl Keen Jr.
Kris Kristofferson
Tracy Lawrence
Johnny Lee
The Legendary Stardust Cowboy
Lyle Lovett
Barbara Mandrell
Terry McBride
Delbert McClinton
Neal McCoy
Roger Miller
Hugh Moffatt
Gary Morris
Moon Mullican
Joel Nava
Willie Nelson
Michael Nesmith
Mickey Newbury
Roy Orbison
Buck Owens

Caryl Mack Parker
Lee Roy Parnell
Ray Price
Jon Randall
Jim Reeves
Ronna Reeves
Jeannie C. Riley
Tex Ritter
Johnny Rodriguez
Kenny Rogers
Doug Sahm
Billy Joe Shaver
Darden Smith
Billie Jo Spears
Red Steagall
Keith Stegall
George Strait
Doug Supernaw
B.J. Thomas
Tony Toliver
Rick Trevino
Ernest Tubb
Justin Tubb
Tanya Tucker
Ray Vega
Billy Walker
Clay Walker
Monte Warden
Gene Watson
Don Williams

Truck Drivin' Sons of Guns
Dick Curless
Vernon Dalhart
Dave Dudley
C.W. McCall
Red Sovine
The Willis Brothers

The Virginians
Ralph Blizard
A.P. & Sara Carter
Maybelle Carter
Roy Clark
Patsy Cline
Steve Earle
Clinton Gregory
Kate Jacobs
John Jennings
James King
Shelby Lynne
Kathy Mattea
Tony Rice

Ricky Van Shelton
Ralph & Carter Stanley
Gene Vincent
Mac Wiseman

The West Virginians
Charlie Cline
Stoney & Wilma Lee Cooper
Jeff Copley
Hazel Dickens
Little Jimmy Dickens
Hawkshaw Hawkins
Robert Shafer
Red Sovine
Mel Street

Western Swingers
Asleep at the Wheel
Big Sandy & His Fly-Rite Boys
Milton Brown
Roger Brown & Swing City
Spade Cooley
Hank Thompson
Tex Williams
Bob Wills

Wreck on the Highway
(died in automobile or bus accidents)
Jack Anglin (Johnnie & Jack)
Tommy Caldwell (Marshall Tucker Band)
Eddie Cochran
Allen Collins (Lynyrd Skynyrd)
Betty Jack Davis (The Davis Sisters)
Johnny Horton
Ira Louvin (The Louvin Brothers)
Red Sovine
Dottie West
Clarence White (The Byrds)

Yodelers
Wilf Carter/Montana Slim
Patsy Montana
LeAnn Rimes
Kenny Roberts
Jimmie Rodgers
Roy Rogers
Jean Shepard
Don Walser
Slim Whitman
Wylie & the Wild West Show

FREE COUNTRY

from MusicHound and Mercury Nashville

The enclosed CD sampler from Mercury Nashville includes these hot artists:

Other Titles Available

Kim Richey

Kim Richey

Kathy Mattea

Now and Then

Good News

Lonesome Standard Time

A Collection of Hits

Walking Away a Winner

Ready for the Storm

Special Collection

John & Audrey Wiggins

John & Audrey Wiggins

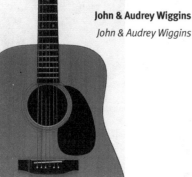

Kim Richey

Anyone who's listened to Kim Richey's emotionally powerful brand of singer/songwriter artistry knows that there is something special about her. Kim's sweet, angelic voice is so distinctive that her songs are instantly recognizable and even appearances as a backing vocalist are impossible to miss. And then there is her songwriting, including Radney Foster's "Nobody Wins" and Trisha Yearwood's "Believe Me Baby (I Lied)" (which received two Grammy nominations). Kim Richey's second release, *Bitter Sweet*, features 12 new tracks showcasing her songwriting skills. If you are a Mary Chapin Carpenter or Rosanne Cash fan, this is an album you won't want to miss.

Bitter Sweet Mercury Records #314-534255-2/4

Kathy Mattea

Kathy is one of country music's premiere female vocalists. With numerous awards, hit singles and albums, Kathy's music has continually been evolving. Now with this latest release, *Love Travels,* Kathy has again reached deep inside herself to create an album that transcends the traditional boundaries of country music and makes itself appealing to a broad audience. Produced by Ben Wisch (Mark Cohn), *Love Travels* is vibrant, fresh and full of energy.

Love Travels Mercury Records #314-532899-2/4

John & Audrey Wiggins

With crystal clear harmonies, enchanting performances and their genuine warmth and sincerity, brother and sister duo John & Audrey Wiggins are what country music is all about. *The Dream,* produced by famed guitarist Dann Huff, is their second release. Far from being cookie cutter country, their sound is fresh and draws upon a variety of musical influences, while showcasing their pure rich harmonies that are reminiscent of the early Judds.

The Dream Mercury Records #314-534286-2/4

Harley Allen

Harley Allen, son of famed bluegrass singer Red Allen, grew up with music in his blood. Since coming to Nashville in 1989, Harley has concentrated on honing his songwriting skills and has had his material covered by Garth Brooks, Alison Krauss, Alan Jackson and Linda Ronstadt, to name just a few. He also co-wrote all 12 songs on *Another River,* his major label debut. The project is solid country, with an acoustic feel that showcases Harley's haunting vocals.

Another River Mercury Records #314-528908-2/4

AVAILABLE WHEREVER MUSIC IS SOLD